FINANCIAL THEORY AND CORPORATE POLICY

FINANCIAL THEORY AND CORPORATE POLICY

SECOND EDITION

THOMAS E. COPELAND/J. FRED WESTON

University of California at Los Angeles

ADDISON-WESLEY PUBLISHING COMPANY
Reading, Massachusetts
Menlo Park, California · London
Amsterdam · Don Mills, Ontario
Sydney

Sponsoring Editor: *William Hamilton*
Production Editor: *Herb Merritt*

Text Designer: *Margaret Ong Tsao*
Illustrator and Art Coordinator: *Textbook Art Associates*
Cover Designer and Illustrator: *Hannus Design Associates*

Production Manager: *Sherry Berg*

The text of this book was composed in Times Roman by Kingsport Press

Library of Congress Cataloging in Publication Data

Copeland, Thomas E., 1946–
  Financial theory and corporate policy.

  Includes bibliographies and indexes.
  1. Corporations—Finance. 2. Finance. I. Weston J. Fred
(John Fred), 1916–   II. Title.
HG4011.C833 1983   658.1'5   82–11662
ISBN 0–201–10291–9

ISBN 0–201–10291–9
ABCDEFGHIJ-DO-89876543

This book is dedicated to our wives, Casey and June, who have provided their loving support; and to the pioneers in the development of the modern theory of finance: Hirshleifer, Arrow, Debreu, Miller, Modigliani, Markowitz, Sharpe, Lintner, Jensen, Fama, Roll, Black, Scholes, Merton, Ross and others cited in the pages which follow. Without their intellectual leadership this text could not exist.

Preface

In this second edition we will seek to build on our experiences and the inputs of other users of the first edition. The feedback that we have received from all sources confirms our original judgment that there was a need for a book like *Financial Theory and Corporate Policy*. Therefore we shall continue to emphasize our original objectives for the book. Primarily, our aim was to provide a bridge to the more theoretical articles and treatises on finance theory. Our hope was that for doctoral students the book would provide a framework of conceptual knowledge. This would enable them to understand what the literature on financial theory was trying to do and how it all fit together. For MBA's we sought to provide an in-depth experience with the subject of finance. Our aim here is to equip the MBA for his or her future development as a practicing executive. We seek to prepare the MBA for reading the new literature of the past, present, and future. This will help the practicing financial executive keep up to date with future developments in finance theory, particularly as they affect the financial executive's own thinking processes in making financial decisions.

    As before, our emphasis is on setting forth clearly

and succinctly the most important concepts in finance theory. We have given particular attention to testable propositions and to the literature which has developed empirical tests of important elements of finance theory. In addition, we have emphasized applications so that the nature and uses of finance theory can be better understood.

A. PURPOSE AND ORGANIZATION

Over the past 20 years a branch of applied microeconomics has been developed and specialized into what is known as modern finance theory. The historical demarcation point was roughly 1958, when Markowitz and Tobin were working on the theory of portfolio selection and Modigliani and Miller were working on capital structure and valuation. Prior to 1958, finance was largely a descriptive field of endeavor. Since then major theoretical thrusts have transformed the field into a positive science. As evidence of the changes which have taken place we need only look at the types of people who teach in the schools of business. Forty years ago the faculty were drawn from the ranks of business and government. They were respected and experienced statesmen within their fields. Today, finance faculty are predominantly academicians in the traditional sense of the word. The majority of them have no business experience whatsoever except for consulting. Their interest and training is in developing theories to explain economic behavior, then testing them with the tools provided by statistics and econometrics. Anecdotal evidence and individual business experience have been superseded by the analytic approach of modern finance theory.

   The rapid changes in the field of finance have profound implications for management education. As usual, the best students (and the best managers) possess rare intuition, initiative, common sense, strong reading and writing skills, and the ability to work well with others. But those with the greatest competitive advantage also have strong technical training in the analytical and quantitative skills of management. Modern finance theory emphasizes these skills. It is to the students and faculty who seek to employ them that this textbook is addressed.

   The six seminal and internally consistent theories upon which modern finance is founded are: (1) utility theory, (2) state-preference theory, (3) mean-variance theory and the capital asset pricing model, (4) arbitrage pricing theory, (5) option pricing theory, and (6) the Modigliani-Miller theorems. They are discussed in Chapters 4 through 8 and in Chapter 12. Their common theme is, "How do individuals and society allocate scarce resources through a price system based on the valuation of risky assets?" Utility theory establishes the basis of rational decision making in the face of risky alternatives. It focuses on the question "How do people make choices?" On the other hand, the objects of choice are described by state-preference theory, mean-variance portfolio theory, arbitrage pricing, and option pricing theory. When we combine the theory of choice with the objects of choice, we are able to determine how risky alternatives are valued in equilibrium. When correctly assigned, the asset prices provide useful signals to the economy for the necessary task of resource allocation. Finally, the Modigliani-Miller theory asks the question: "Does the method of financing have any effect on the value of assets (the firm in particular)?" The answer to this question has important implications for the firm's choice of capital structure (debt-to-equity mix) and dividend policy.

It is important to keep in mind that what counts for a positive science is the development of theories which yield valid and meaningful predictions about observed phenomena. The critical first test is whether or not the hypothesis is consistent with the evidence at hand. Further testing involves deducing new facts capable of being observed but not previously known, then checking those deduced facts against additional empirical evidence. As students of finance, we must not only understand the theory, but also review the empirical evidence in order to determine which hypotheses have been validated. Consequently, every effort has been made to summarize the empirical evidence related to the theory of finance. Chapter 7 discusses empirical evidence on the capital asset pricing model and the arbitrage pricing theory. Chapter 8 includes studies of how alternative option pricing models perform. Chapter 10 covers evidence on the efficient markets hypothesis. Chapter 13 reviews evidence on capital structure; Chapter 15 on dividend policy; Chapter 18 on mergers and acquisitions; and Chapter 20 on international finance.

Finally, in addition to the theory and empirical evidence there is always the practical question of how to apply the concepts to difficult and complex real-world problems. Toward this end, Chapters 2 and 3 are devoted to capital budgeting, Chapter 13 shows how to estimate the cost of capital for a large, publicly held corporation, and Chapter 15 determines the value of the same company. Throughout the text we attempt, wherever feasible, to give examples of how to apply the theory. Among other things we show how the reader can: estimate his or her own utility function, calculate porfolio means and variances, value a call option, determine the terms of a merger or acquisition, use international exchange rate relationships.

In sum, we believe that a sound foundation in finance theory requires not only a complete presentation of the theoretical concepts, but also a review of the empirical evidence which either supports or refutes the theory as well as enough examples to allow the practitioner to apply the validated theory.

B. CHANGES IN THE SECOND EDITION

We have tried to move all the central paradigms of finance theory into the first half of the book. This motivated our shifting the option pricing material into Chapter 8. Another reason for moving the option pricing material forward is that option-pricing concepts are being applied to almost all of the other areas of finance. The new literature on binomial option pricing has been added to the option pricing chapter.

In the materials on market equilibrium in Chapter 7, we have added a presentation on arbitrage pricing theory (APT). We demonstrate that the Capital Asset Pricing Model is a special case of the more general APT approach to asset pricing.

We have added a chapter on leasing in response to suggestions from users to do so. In addition, the leasing chapter utilizes a number of other important areas of finance such as capital structure, cost of capital, and option pricing.

We made numerous other minor changes. In general, we sought to reflect all of the new important literature of finance theory—published articles and treatises as well as working papers. Our aim was to keep the book as close as possible to the frontiers of the "state-of-the-art" in the literature of finance theory.

C. SUGGESTED USE IN CURRICULUM

The basic building blocks which will lead to the most advantageous use of this text include algebra and elementary calculus; basic finance skills such as discounting, cash flows, and pro-forma income statements and balance sheets; elementary statistics; and an intermediate-level microeconomics course. Consequently, the book would be applicable as a second semester (or quarter) in finance. This could occur at the junior or senior undergraduate year, for MBA's during the end of their first year or beginning of their second year, or as an introductory course for Ph.D students.

At UCLA we use the text as a second course in finance for MBA students and as the first finance course for doctoral students. We found that requiring all finance majors to take a theory-of-finance course before proceeding on to upper-level courses eliminated a great deal of redundancy. For example, a portfolio theory course which uses the theory of finance as a prerequisite does not have to waste time with the fundamentals. Instead, after a brief review, most of the course can be devoted to more recent developments and applications.

Because finance theory has developed into a cohesive body of knowledge, it underlies almost all of what had formerly been thought of as disparate topics. The theory of finance, as presented in this text, is prerequisite to security analysis, portfolio theory, money and capital markets, commercial banking, speculative markets, investment banking, international finance, insurance, case courses in corporation finance, and quantitative methods of finance. The theory of finance can, and is, applied in all of these courses. That is why, at UCLA at least, we have made it a prerequisite to all the aforementioned course offerings.

D. USE OF THE SOLUTIONS MANUAL

The end-of-chapter problems and questions ask the students not only to feed back what they have just learned, but also to take the concepts and extend them beyond the material covered directly in the body of the text. Consequently, we hope that the solutions manual will be employed almost as if it were a supplementary text. It should not be locked up in the faculty member's office, as so many instructor's manuals are. It is not an instructor's manual in a narrow sense. Rather, it is a solutions manual, intended for use by the students. (We place multiple copies on reserve in the library.)

Understanding of the theory is increased by efforts to apply it. Consequently, most of the end-of-chapter problems are oriented toward applications of the theory. They require analytical thinking as well as a thorough understanding of the theory. If the solutions manual is used as we hope it will be, then students who learn how to apply their understanding of the theory to the end-of-chapter problems will at the same time be learning how to apply the theory to real-world tasks.

E. ACKNOWLEDGMENTS

We have received help from many persons on both editions of the book. We especially benefitted from the insightful corrections, clarifications and suggestions of Eugene Fama. We are also indebted to the following individuals: Ed Altman, Enrique Arzac, Gerry Bierwag, Diran Bodenhorn, William Carleton, Don Chance, Nai-fu Chen, Kwang S. Chung, Halimah Clark, S. Kerry Cooper, Larry Dann, Harry and Linda E. DeAngelo, Dirk Davidson, David Eiteman, Chapman Findlay, Kenneth French, Dan Galai, Robert Geske, Mark Grinblatt, W. Haley, Ronald Hanoian, Iraj Heravi, Tom Ho, Chi-Cheng Hsia, William C. Hunter, Herb Johnson, Ashok Korwar, Clement Krouse, Steven Lippman, Stephen Magee, Charles Martin, Ronald Masulis, David Mayers, Guy Mercier, Timothy J. Nantell, Ron Necoechea, Jørgen Nielson, R. Richardson Pettit, Richard Pettway, Richard Roll, Shigeki Sakakibara, Jim Scott, Jandhyala Sharma, Kuldeep Shastri, Kilman Shin, Keith Smith, Dennis Soter, Joel Stern, Sheridan Titman, Brett Trueman, Marty Weingartner, Richard West, Randy Westerfield, Stuart Wood, and Bill Ziemba. Nai-fu Chen and Ronald Bibb wrote Appendixes B and D, respectively. For their patient help in preparation of the text we thank Susan Hoag, Kathy Masulis, and Marilyn McElroy. Finally, we are indebted to the Addison-Wesley staff: Bill Hamilton and Herb Merritt.

There are undoubtedly errors in the final product, both typographical and conceptual as well as differences of opinion. We invite leaders to send suggestions, comments, criticisms, and corrections to the authors at the Graduate School of Management, University of California, Los Angeles, CA 90024. Any form of communication will be welcome.

Los Angeles, California T. E. C.
October 1982 J. F. W.

Contents

THE
THEORY
OF
FINANCE

PART **I**

Part I of this text covers what has come to be the accepted theory of financial decision making. Its theme is an understanding of how individuals and their agents make choices among alternatives which have uncertain payoffs over multiple time periods. The theory which explains how and why these decisions are made has many applications in the various topic areas which traditionally make up the study of finance. The topics include security analysis, portfolio management, financial accounting, corporate financial policy, public finance, commercial banking, and international finance.

Chapter 1 shows why the existence of financial marketplaces is so important for economic development. Chapters 2 and 3 describe the appropriate investment criterion in the simplest of all possible worlds—a world where all outcomes are known with certainty. For many readers they will represent a summary and extension of material covered in traditional texts on corporate finance. Chapter 4 covers utility theory. It provides a model of how individuals make choices among risky alternatives. An understanding of individual behavior in the face of uncertainty is fundamental to understanding how financial markets operate. Chapter 5 introduces the objects of investor choice under uncertainty in the most general theoretical framework—state-preference theory. Chapter 6 describes the objects of choice in a mean-variance partial equilibrium framework. In a world of uncertainty each combination of assets provides risky outcomes which are assumed to be described in terms of two parameters: mean and variance. Once the opportunity set of all possible choices has been described, we are able to combine Chapter 4, "The Theory of Choice," with Chapter 6, "The Objects of Choice," in order to predict exactly what combination of assets an individual will choose. Chapter 7 extends the study of choice into a market equilibrium framework, thereby closing the cycle of logic. Chapter 1 shows why capital markets exist and assumes that all outcomes are known with certainty. Chapter 7 extends the theory of capital markets to include equilibrium with uncertain outcomes and, even more important, describes the appropriate concept of risk and shows how it will be priced in equilibrium, including the very general arbitrage pricing theory. Chapter 8 on the option pricing models includes a treatment of the equilibrium prices of assets which cannot be completely described by their mean and variance. Therefore, these materials provide a framework for decision making under uncertainty which can be applied by financial managers throughout the economy. Chapter 9, the last chapter in Part I, discusses the concept of efficient capital markets. It serves as a bridge between theory and reality. Most of the theory assumes that markets are perfectly frictionless, that is, free of transactions costs and other "market imperfections" which cannot be easily modeled. The questions arise: What assumptions are needed to have efficient (but not necessarily frictionless) capital markets? How well does the theory fit reality?

The empirical evidence on these and other questions is left to Part II of the text. It focuses on applications of financial theory to corporate policy issues such as capital budgeting, the cost of capital, capital structure, dividend policy, leasing, mergers and acquisitions, and international finance. For almost every topic there is material which covers the implications of theory for policy and the empirical evidence relevant to the theory, and which provides detailed examples of applications.

Introduction: Capital Markets, Consumption, and Investment

Through the alterations in the income streams provided by loans or sales, the marginal degrees of impatience for all individuals in the market are brought into equality with each other and with the market rate of interest.

IRVING FISHER, *THE THEORY OF INTEREST*
MACMILLAN, NEW YORK, 1930, P. 122

A. INTRODUCTION

The objective of this chapter is to study consumption and investment decisions made by individuals and firms. Logical development is facilitated if we begin with the simplest of all worlds, a one-person one-good economy. The decision maker, Robinson Crusoe, must choose between consumption now and consumption in the future. Of course, the decision not to consume now is the same as investment. Thus Robinson Crusoe's decision is simultaneously one of consumption and investment. In order to decide, he needs two types of information. First, he needs to understand his own subjective tradeoffs between consumption now and consumption in the future. This information is embodied in the utility and indifference curves depicted in Figs. 1.1 through 1.3. Second, he must know the feasible tradeoffs between present and future consumption which are technologically possible. These are given in the investment and production opportunity sets of Figs. 1.4 and 1.5.

From the analysis of a Robinson Crusoe economy we will find that the optimal consumption/investment decision establishes an interest rate for Robinson Crusoe. Shown in Fig. 1.5, it represents his optimal rate of exchange between consumption now and in the future. Thus interest rates are an integral part of consumption/investment decisions. One can think of the interest rate as the price of (or rate of return on) investment. After the Robinson Crusoe economy we will introduce opportunities to exchange consumption across time by borrowing or lending in a multiperson economy (shown in Fig. 1.7). It will be demonstrated that the introduction of exchange opportunities results in a single market interest rate which everyone can use as a signal for making optimal consumption/investment decisions (Fig. 1.8). Furthermore, no one is worse off in an exchange economy when compared to a Robinson Crusoe economy and almost everyone is better off (Fig. 1.9). Thus an exchange economy which uses market prices (interest rates) to allocate resources across time will be seen to be superior to an economy without the price mechanism.

The obvious extension to the introductory material in this chapter is for the investment decision to be made by firms in a multiperiod context. Managers need optimal decision rules to help in selecting those projects which maximize the wealth of shareholders. This material will be discussed in depth in Chapters 2 and 3.

B. CONSUMPTION AND INVESTMENT WITHOUT CAPITAL MARKETS

The answer to the question "Do capital markets benefit society?" requires that we compare a world without capital markets to one with them and show that no one is worse off and at least one individual is better off in a world with capital markets. In order to make things as simple as possible, we assume that all outcomes from investment are known with certainty, that there are no transactions costs or taxes, and that decisions are made in a one-period context. Individuals are endowed with income (manna from heaven) at the beginning of the period, y_0, and at the end of the period, y_1. They must decide how much to actually consume now, C_0, and how much to invest in productive opportunities in order to provide end-of-period consumption, C_1. Every individual is assumed to prefer more consumption to less. In other words, the marginal utility of consumption is always positive. Also, we assume that the marginal utility of consumption is decreasing. The total utility curve (Fig. 1.1) shows the utility of consumption at the beginning of the period, assuming that the second-period consumption is held constant. Changes in consumption have been marked off in equal increments along the horizontal axis. Note that each increase in consumption causes total utility to increase (marginal utility is positive), but that the increments in utility become smaller and smaller (marginal utility is decreasing). We can easily construct a similar graph to represent the utility of end-of-period

Total Utility = $U(C_0)$

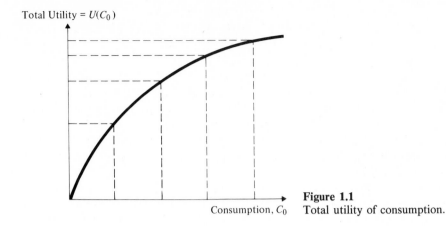

Consumption, C_0

Figure 1.1
Total utility of consumption.

consumption, $U(C_1)$. When combined with Fig. 1.1, the result (shown in Fig. 1.2) provides a description of trade-offs between consumption at the beginning of the period, C_0, and consumption at the end of the period, C_1. The dashed lines represent contours along the utility surface where various combinations of C_0 and C_1 provide the same total utility (measured along the vertical axis). Since all points along the same contour (for example, points A and B) have equal total utility, the individual will be indifferent with respect to them. Therefore, the contours are called *indifference curves*. Looking at Fig. 1.2 from above, we can project the indifference curves onto the consumption argument plane (i.e., the plane formed by the C_0, C_1 axes in Fig. 1.3). To reiterate, all combinations of consumption today and consumption tomorrow which lie on the same indifference curve have the same total utility. The decision maker whose indifference curves are depicted in Fig. 1.3 would be indifferent as to point A with consumption (C_{0a}, C_{1a}) and point B with consumption (C_{0b}, C_{1b}).

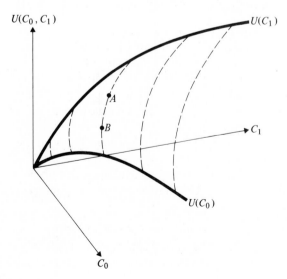

$U(C_0, C_1)$

$U(C_1)$

A

B

C_1

$U(C_0)$

C_0

Figure 1.2
Trade-offs between beginning and end-of-period consumption.

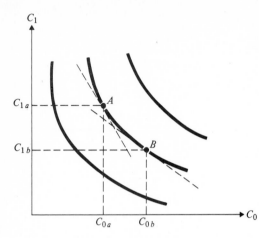

Figure 1.3
Indifference curves representing the time preference of consumption.

Point A has more consumption at the end of the period but less consumption at the beginning than point B does.

The slope of the straight line just tangent to the indifference curve at point B measures the rate of trade-off between C_0 and C_1 at point B. This trade-off is called the *marginal rate of substitution* (MRS) between consumption today and consumption tomorrow. It also reveals the decision maker's subjective rate of time preference, r_i, at point B. We can think of the subjective rate of time preference as an interest rate because it measures the rate of substitution between consumption bundles over time. It reveals how many extra units of consumption tomorrow must be received in order to give up one unit of consumption today and still have the same total utility. Mathematically, it is expressed as[1]

$$\text{MRS}^{C_0}_{C_1} = \left.\frac{\partial C_1}{\partial C_0}\right|_{U=\text{const.}} = -(1 + r_i). \tag{1.1}$$

Note that the subjective rate of time preference is greater at point A than at point B. The individual has less consumption today at point A and will therefore demand relatively more future consumption in order to have the same total utility.

Thus far we have described preference functions which tell us how individuals will make choices among consumption bundles over time. What happens if we introduce productive opportunities which allow a unit of current savings/investment to be turned into more than one unit of future consumption? We assume that each individual in the economy has a schedule of productive investment opportunities which can be arranged from the highest rate of return down to the lowest (Fig. 1.4). Although we have chosen to graph the investment opportunities schedule as a straight line, any decreasing function would do. This implies diminishing marginal

---

[1] Equation (1.1) can be read as follows: The marginal rate of substitution between consumption today and end-of-period consumption, $\text{MRS}^{C_0}_{C_1}$, is equal to the slope of a line tangent to an indifference curve given constant total utility $[\partial C_1/\partial C_0]|_{U=\text{const.}}$. This in turn is equal to the individual's subjective rate of time preference, $-(1 + r_i)$.

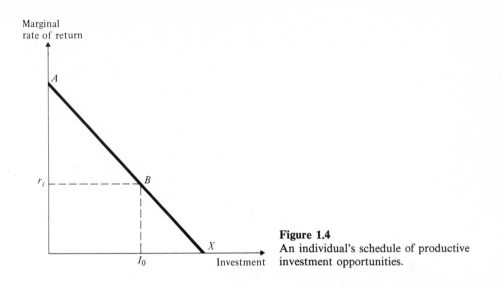

Figure 1.4
An individual's schedule of productive investment opportunities.

returns to investment because the more an individual invests, the lower the rate of return on the marginal investment. Also, all investments are assumed independent of one another and perfectly divisible.

An individual will make all investments in productive opportunities which have rates of return higher than his or her subjective rate of time preference, r_i. This can be demonstrated if we transform the schedule of production investment opportunities into the consumption argument plane (Fig. 1.5).[2] The slope of a line tangent to curve ABX in Fig. 1.5 is the rate at which a dollar of consumption foregone today is transformed into a dollar of consumption tomorrow. It is the *marginal rate of*

Figure 1.5
The production opportunity set.

---

[2] See problem 1.6 at the end of the chapter for an example of how to make the transition between the schedule of productive investment opportunities and the consumption argument plane.

transformation (MRT) offered by the production/investment opportunity set. The line tangent to point A has the highest slope in Fig. 1.5 and represents the highest rate of return at point A in Fig. 1.4. An individual endowed with a resource bundle (y_0, y_1) which has utility U_1 can move along the production opportunity set to point B, where the indifference curve is tangent to it and he or she receives the maximum attainable utility, U_2. Because current consumption, C_0, is less than the beginning-of-period endowment, y_0, the individual has chosen to invest. The amount of investment is $y_0 - C_0$. Of course, if $C_0 > y_0$, he or she will disinvest.

Note that the marginal rate of return on the last investment made (i.e., MRT, the slope of a line tangent to the investment opportunity set at point B) is exactly equal to the investor's subjective time preference (i.e., MRS, the slope of a line tangent to his or her indifference curve, also at point B). In other words, the investor's subjective marginal rate of substitution is equal to the marginal rate of transformation offered by the production opportunity set.

$$MRS = MRT$$

This will always be true in a Robinson Crusoe world where there are no capital markets, i.e. no opportunities to exchange. The individual decision maker starts with an initial endowment (y_0, y_1) and compares the marginal rate of return on a dollar of productive investment (or disinvestment) with his or her subjective time preference. If the rate on investment is greater (as it is in Fig. 1.5), he or she will gain utility by making the investment. This process continues until the rate of return on the last dollar of productive investment just equals the rate of subjective time preference (at point B). Note that at point B the individual's consumption in each time period is exactly equal to the output from production, i.e. $P_0 = C_0$ and $P_1 = C_1$.

Without the existence of capital markets individuals with the same endowment and the same investment opportunity set may choose completely different investments because they have different indifference curves. This is shown in Fig. 1.6. Individual 2, who has a lower rate of time preference (why?), will choose to invest more than individual 1.

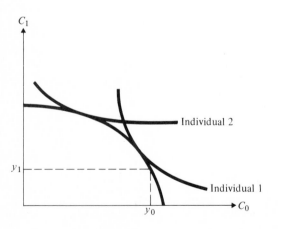

Figure 1.6
Individuals with different indifference curves choose different production/consumption patterns.

C. CONSUMPTION AND INVESTMENT WITH CAPITAL MARKETS

A Robinson Crusoe economy is characterized by the fact that there are no opportunities to exchange intertemporal consumption among individuals. What happens if instead of one person, many individuals are said to exist in the economy? Intertemporal exchange of consumption bundles will be represented by the opportunity to borrow or lend unlimited amounts at r, a market-determined rate of interest.[3]

Financial markets facilitate the transfer of funds between lenders and borrowers. Assuming that interest rates are positive, any amount of funds lent today will return interest plus principal at the end of the period. Ignoring production for the time being, we can graph borrowing and lending opportunities along the *capital market line* in Fig. 1.7 (line W_0ABW_1). With an initial endowment of (y_0, y_1) with utility U_1 we can reach any point along the market line by borrowing or lending at the market interest rate plus repaying the principal amount, X_0. If we designate the future value as X_1, we can write

$$X_1 = X_0 + rX_0, \qquad X_1 = (1 + r)X_0.$$

Similarly, the present value, W_0, of our initial endowment, (y_0, y_1), is the sum of current income, y_0, and the present value of our end-of-period income, $y_1 (1 + r)^{-1}$.

$$W_0 = y_0 + \frac{y_1}{(1 + r)}. \tag{1.2}$$

Referring to Fig. 1.7, we see that with endowment (y_0, y_1) we will maximize utility by moving along the market line to the point where our subjective time preference

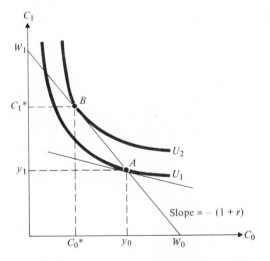

Figure 1.7
The capital market line.

---

[3] The market rate of interest is provided by the solution to a general equilibrium problem. For simplicity, we assume that the market rate of interest is a given.

equals the market interest rate (at point B). At the initial endowment (point A) our subjective time preference, represented by the slope of a line tangent to the indifference curve at point A, is less than the market rate of return. Therefore, we will desire to lend because the capital market offers a rate of return higher than what we subjectively require. Ultimately we reach a consumption decision (C_0^*, C_1^*) where we maximize utility. The utility, U_2, at point B is greater than the utility, U_1, at our initial endowment, point A. The present value of this consumption bundle is also equal to our wealth, W_0:

$$W_0 = C_0^* + \frac{C_1^*}{1+r}. \tag{1.3}$$

This can be rearranged to give the equation for the capital market line:

$$C_1^* = W_0(1+r) - (1+r)C_0^*, \tag{1.4}$$

and since $W_0(1+r) = W_1$, we have

$$C_1^* = W_1 - (1+r)C_0^*. \tag{1.5}$$

Thus, the market line in Fig. 1.7 has an intercept at W_1 and a slope of $-(1+r)$. Also note that by equating (1.2) and (1.3) we see that the present value of our endowment equals the present value of our consumption, and both are equal to our wealth, W_0. Moving along the capital market line does not change one's wealth, but it does offer a pattern of consumption which has higher utility.

What happens if the consumption/production decision takes place in a world where capital markets facilitate the exchange of funds at the market rate of interest? Figure 1.8 combines production possibilities with market exchange possibilities. With

Figure 1.8
Consumption and production with capital markets.

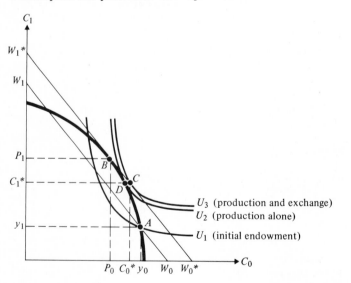

the family of indifference curves U_1, U_2, and U_3 and endowment (y_0, y_1) at point A, what actions will we take in order to maximize our utility? Starting at point A, we can move either along the production opportunity set or along the capital market line. Both alternatives offer a higher rate of return than our subjective time preference, but production offers the higher return, i.e., a steeper slope. Therefore, we choose to invest and move along the production opportunity frontier. Without the opportunity to borrow or lend along the market line we would stop investing at point D, where the marginal return on productive investment equals our subjective time preference. This was the result shown for consumption and investment without capital markets in Fig. 1.5. At this point, our level of utility has increased from U_1 to U_2. However, with the opportunity to borrow, we can actually do better. Note that at point D the borrowing rate, represented by the slope of the market line, is less than the rate of return on the marginal investment, which is the slope of the production opportunity set at point D. Since further investment returns more than the cost of borrowed funds, we will continue to invest until the marginal return on investment is equal to the borrowing rate at point B. At point B we receive the output from production (P_0, P_1) and the present value of our wealth is W_0^* instead of W_0. Furthermore, we can now reach any point on the market line. Since our time preference at point B is greater than the market rate of return, we will consume more than P_0, which is the current payoff from production. By borrowing, we can reach point C on the market line. Our optimal consumption is found, as before, where our subjective time preference just equals the market rate of return. Our utility has increased from U_1 at point A (our initial endowment), to U_2 at point D (the Robinson Crusoe solution), to U_3 at point C (the exchange economy solution). We are clearly better off when capital markets exist since $U_3 > U_2$.

The decision process which takes place with production opportunities and capital market exchange opportunities occurs in two separate and distinct steps: (1) First choose the optimal production decision by taking on projects until the marginal rate of return on investment equals the objective market rate, and (2) choose the optimal consumption pattern by borrowing or lending along the market line to equate your subjective time preference with the market rate of return. The separation of the investment (step 1) and consumption (step 2) decisions is known as the Fisher separation theorem.

Fisher separation theorem.   Given perfect and complete capital markets, the production decision is governed solely by an objective market criterion (represented by maximizing attained wealth) without regard to individuals' subjective preferences which enter into their consumption decisions.

An important implication for corporate policy is that the investment decision can be delegated to managers. Given the same opportunity set, every investor will make the same production decision (P_0, P_1) regardless of the shape of his or her indifference curves. This is shown in Fig. 1.9. Investor 1 and investor 2 both will direct the manager of their firm to choose production combination (P_0, P_1). They can then take the output of the firm and adapt it to their own subjective time preferences by borrowing or lending in the capital market. Either way they are both better

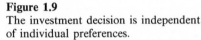

Figure 1.9
The investment decision is independent of individual preferences.

off with a capital market. Without capital market opportunities, investor 1 would choose to produce at point Y, which has lower utility. Similarly, investor 2 would be worse off at point X.

In equilibrium, the marginal rate of substitution for all investors is equal to the market rate of interest, and this in turn is equal to the marginal rate of transformation for productive investment. Mathematically, the marginal rates of substitution for investors i and j are:

$$\text{MRS}_i = \text{MRS}_j = -(1 + r) = \text{MRT}.$$

Thus, all individuals use the same time value of money in making their production/ investment decisions.

The importance of capital markets cannot be overstated. They allow the efficient transfer of funds between borrowers and lenders. Individuals who have insufficient wealth to take advantage of all their investment opportunities which yield rates of return higher than the market rate are able to borrow funds and invest more than they would without capital markets. In this way, funds can be efficiently allocated from individuals with few productive opportunities and great wealth to individuals with many opportunities and insufficient wealth. As a result, all (borrowers and lenders) are better off than they would have been without capital markets.

D. MARKETPLACES AND TRANSACTIONS COSTS

The foregoing discussion has demonstrated the advantages of capital markets for funds allocation in a world without transactions costs. In such a world there is no need for a central location for exchange; that is, there is no need for a marketplace

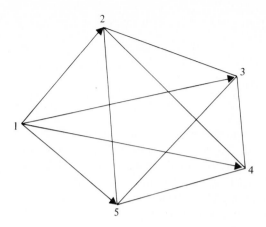

Figure 1.10
A primitive exchange economy with no central marketplace.

per se. But let us assume that we have a primitive economy with N producers, each making a specialized product and consuming a bundle of all N consumption goods. Given no marketplace, bilateral exchange is necessary. During a given time period each visits the other in order to exchange goods. The cost of each leg of a trip is T dollars. If there are 5 individuals and 5 consumption goods in this economy, then individual 1 makes four trips, one to each of the other four producers. Individual 2 makes three trips, and so on. Altogether there are $[N(N - 1)]/2 = 10$ trips, at a total cost of $10T$ dollars. This is shown in Fig. 1.10. If an entrepreneur establishes a central marketplace and carries an inventory of each of the N products, as shown in Fig. 1.11, the total number of trips can be reduced to five with a total cost of $5T$ dollars. Therefore, if the entrepreneur has a total cost (including the cost of living) of less than $10T - 5T$ dollars, he or she can profitably establish a marketplace and everyone will be better off.[4]

This example provides a simple explanation for the productivity of marketplaces. Among other things, they serve to efficiently reduce transactions costs. Later on, we shall refer to this fact as the *operational efficiency* of capital markets. The lower

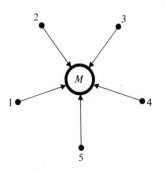

Figure 1.11
The productivity of a central marketplace.

---

[4] In general, for N individuals making two-way exchanges there are $\binom{N}{2} = N(N - 1)/2$ trips. With a marketplace the number of trips is reduced to N. Therefore the savings is $[N(N - 1)/2 - N]T$.

the transactions costs are, the more operationally efficient a market will be said to be.

E. TRANSACTIONS COSTS AND THE BREAKDOWN OF SEPARATION

If transactions costs are nontrivial, financial intermediaries and marketplaces will provide a useful service. In such a world, the borrowing rate will be greater than the lending rate. Financial institutions will pay the lending rate for money deposited with them and then issue funds at a higher rate to borrowers. This will have the effect of invalidating the Fisher separation principle. As shown in Fig. 1.12, individuals with different indifference curves will now choose different levels of investment. Without a single market rate they will not be able to delegate the investment decision to the manager of their firm. Individual 1 would direct the manager to use the lending rate and invest at point B. Individual 2 would use the borrowing rate and choose point A. A third individual might choose investments between points A and B, where the indifference curve is directly tangent to the production opportunity set.

The theory of finance is greatly simplified if we assume that capital markets are perfect. Obviously they are not. The relevant question then is whether the theories which assume frictionless markets fit reality well enough to be useful or whether they need to be refined in order to provide greater insights into reality. This is an empirical question which will be addressed later on in the text.

Through most of this text we shall adopt the convenient and simplifying assumption that capital markets are perfect. The only major imperfection to be considered in detail is the impact of corporate and personal taxes. The effects of taxes are certainly nontrivial and, as we shall see, they do change the predictions of many models of financial policy.

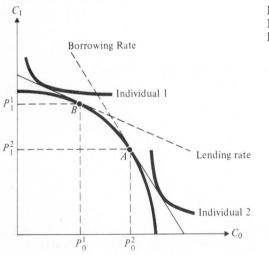

Figure 1.12
Markets with different borrowing and lending rates.

SUMMARY _____

The rest of the text follows almost exactly the same logic as this chapter, except that from Chapter 4 onward it focuses on decision making under uncertainty. The first step is to develop indifference curves to model individual decision making in a world with uncertainty. Chapter 4 is analogous to Fig. 1.3. It will describe a theory of choice under uncertainty. Next, the opportunity set, which represents choices among combinations of risky assets, is developed. Chapters 5 and 6 are similar to Fig. 1.5. They describe the objects of choice—the opportunity set. The tangency between the indifference curves of a risk-averse investor and his or her opportunity set provides a theory of individual choice in a world without capital markets (this is discussed in Chapter 6). Finally in Chapter 7, we introduce the opportunity to borrow and lend at a riskless rate and develop a model of capital market equilibrium. Chapter 7 follows logic similar to Fig. 1.8. In fact, we show that a type of separation principle (two-fund separation) obtains, given uncertainty and perfect capital markets. Chapters 9 and 10 take a careful look at the meaning of efficient capital markets and at empirical evidence which relates to the question of how well the perfect capital market assumption fits reality.

PROBLEM SET

1.1 Graphically demonstrate the Fisher separation theorem for the case where an individual ends up lending in financial markets. Label the following points on the graph: initial endowment, W_0; optimal production/investment (P_0, P_1); optimal consumption (C_0^*, C_1^*); present value of final wealth, W_0^*.

1.2 Graphically analyze the effect of an exogenous decrease in the interest rate on (a) the utility of borrowers and lenders, (b) the present wealth of borrowers and lenders, and (c) the investment in real assets.

1.3 The interest rate cannot fall below the net rate from storage. True or False. Why?

1.4 Graphically illustrate the decision-making process faced by an individual in a Robinson Crusoe economy where (a) storage is the only investment opportunity and (b) there are no capital markets.

1.5 Suppose that the investment opportunity set has N projects all of which have the same rate of return, R^*. Graph the investment set.

1.6 Suppose your production opportunity set in a world with perfect certainty consists of the following possibilities:

Project	Investment Outlay	Rate of Return
A	$1,000,000	8%
B	1,000,000	20%
C	2,000,000	4%
D	3,000,000	30%

a) Graph the production opportunity set in a C_0, C_1 framework.

b) If the market rate of return is 10%, draw in the capital market line for the optimal investment decision.

REFERENCES

Alderson, W., "Factors Governing the Development of Marketing Channels," reprinted in Richard M. Clewett, *Marketing Channels for Manufactured Products.* Irwin, Homewood, Ill., 1954.

Fama, E. F., and M. H. Miller, *The Theory of Finance.* Holt, Rinehart and Winston, New York, 1972.

Fisher, I., *The Theory of Interest.* Macmillan, New York, 1930.

Hirshleifer, J., *Investment, Interest, and Capital.* Prentice-Hall, Englewood Cliffs, N.J., 1970.

Investment Decisions: The Certainty Case

When the first primitive man decided to use a bone for a club instead of eating its marrow, that was investment.

ANONYMOUS

A. INTRODUCTION

The investment decision is essentially how much not to consume in the present in order that more can be consumed in the future. The optimal investment decision maximizes the expected satisfaction (expected utility) gained from consumption over the planning horizon of the decision maker. We assume that all economic decisions ultimately reduce to questions about consumption. Even more fundamentally, consumption is related to survival.

The consumption-investment decision is important to all sectors of the economy. An individual who saves does so because the expected benefit of future consumption provided by an extra dollar of saving exceeds the benefit of using it for consumption today. Managers of corporations, who act as agents for the owners (sharehold-

17

ers) of the firm, must decide between paying out earnings in the form of dividends, which may be used for present consumption, and retaining the earnings to invest in productive opportunities which are expected to yield future consumption. Managers of not-for-profit organizations try to maximize the expected utility of contributors—those individuals who provide external funds. And public sector managers attempt to maximize the expected utility of their constituencies.

The examples of investment decisions in this chapter are taken from the corporate sector of the economy, but the decision criterion, which is to maximize the present value of lifetime consumption, can be applied to any sector of the economy. For the time being, we assume that intertemporal decisions are based on knowledge of the market-determined time value of money—the interest rate. Furthermore, the interest rate is assumed to be known with certainty in all time periods. It is nonstochastic. That is, it may change over time, but each change is known with certainty. The interest rate is assumed not to be a random variable. In addition, all future payoffs from current investment decisions are known with certainty. And finally, there are no imperfections (e.g. transactions costs or taxes) in capital markets. These assumptions are obviously an oversimplification, but they are a good place to start. Most of the remainder of the text after this chapter is devoted to decision making under uncertainty. But for the time being it is useful to establish the fundamental criterion of economic decision making—the maximization of the net present value of wealth, assuming perfect certainty.

The most important theme of this chapter is that the objective of the firm is to maximize the wealth of its shareholders. This will be seen to be the same as maximizing the present value of shareholders' lifetime consumption and no different than maximizing the price per share of stock. Alternative issues such as agency costs are also discussed. Then the maximization of shareholder wealth is more carefully defined as the discounted value of future expected cash flows. Finally, techniques for project selection are reviewed and the net present value criterion is shown to be consistent with shareholder wealth maximization.

B. FISHER SEPARATION: THE SEPARATION OF INDIVIDUAL UTILITY PREFERENCES FROM THE INVESTMENT DECISION

To say that the goal of the firm is the maximization of its shareholders' wealth is one thing, but the problem of how to do it is another. We know that interpersonal comparison of individuals' utility functions is not possible. For example, if we give individuals A and B one hundred dollars each, they will both be happy. However, no one, not even the two individuals, will be able to discern which person is happier. How then can a manager maximize shareholders' utility when individual utility functions cannot be compared or combined?

The answer to the question is provided if we turn to our understanding of the role of capital markets. If capital markets are perfect in the sense that they have no frictions which cause the borrowing rate to be different from the lending rate, then (as we saw in Chapter 1) Fisher separation obtains. This means that individuals can delegate investment decisions to the manager of the firm in which they are owners. Regardless of the shape of the shareholders' individual utility functions, the managers maximize the owners' individual (and collective) wealth positions by choosing to invest until the rate of return on the least favorable project is exactly equal to the market-determined rate of return. This result is shown in Fig. 2.1. The optimal production/investment decision, (P_0, P_1), is the one which maximizes the present value of the shareholders' wealth, W_0. The appropriate decision rule is the same, independent of the shareholders' time preferences for consumption. The manager will be directed, by all shareholders, to undertake all projects which earn more than the market rate of return.

If the marginal return on investment equals the market-determined opportunity cost of capital, then the shareholders' wealth, W_0, is maximized. Individual shareholders can then borrow or lend along the capital market line in order to satisfy their time pattern for consumption. In other words, they can take the cash payouts from the firm and use them for current consumption or save them for future consumption according to their individual desires.

The separation principle implies that the maximization of the shareholders' wealth is identical to maximizing the present value of their lifetime consumption. Mathematically, this was demonstrated in Eq. (1.3),

$$W_0 = C_0 + \frac{C_1}{1+r}.$$

Even though the two individuals in Fig. 2.1 choose different levels of current and future consumption, they have the same current wealth, W_0. This follows from the fact that they receive the same income from productive investments (P_0, P_1).

Figure 2.1
Separation of shareholder preferences from the production/investment decision.

Because exchange opportunities permit borrowing and lending at the same rate of interest, an individual's productive optimum is independent of his or her resources and tastes. Therefore, if asked to vote on their preferred production decisions at a shareholders' meeting, different shareholders of the same firm will be unanimous in their preference. This is known as the *unanimity principle*. It implies that the managers of the firm, in their capacity as agents of the shareholders, need not worry about making decisions which reconcile differences of opinion among shareholders. All shareholders will have identical interests. In effect, the price system by which wealth is measured conveys the shareholders' unanimously preferred productive decisions to the firm.

C. THE AGENCY PROBLEM. DO MANAGERS HAVE THE CORRECT INCENTIVE TO MAXIMIZE SHAREHOLDERS' WEALTH?

So far, we have shown that in perfect markets all shareholders will agree that managers should follow a simple investment decision rule: Take projects until the marginal rate of return equals the market-determined discount rate. Therefore, the shareholders' wealth is seen to be the present value of cash flows discounted at the opportunity cost of capital (the market-determined rate).

Shareholders can agree on the decision rule which they should give to managers. But they must be able to costlessly monitor management decisions if they are to be sure that management really does make every decision in a way which maximizes their wealth. There is obviously a difference between ownership and control, and there is no reason to believe that the manager, who serves as an agent for the owners, will always act in the best interest of the shareholders. In most agency relationships the owner will incur nontrivial monitoring costs in order to keep the agent in line. Consequently, the owner faces a trade-off between monitoring costs and forms of compensation which will cause the agent to always act in the owner's interest. At one extreme, if the agent's compensation were all in the form of shares in the firm, then monitoring costs would be zero. Unfortunately, this type of scheme is practically impossible because the agent will always be able to receive some compensation in the form of nonpecuniary benefits such as larger office space, expensive lunches, an executive jet, etc. At the opposite extreme, the owner would have to incur inordinate monitoring costs in order to guarantee that the agent always makes the decision the owner would prefer. Somewhere between these two extremes lies an optimal solution. The reader who wishes to explore this classic problem in greater depth is referred to books by Williamson [1964], Marschak and Radner [1972], or Cyert and March [1963], and to articles by Jensen and Meckling [1976], Machlup [1967], Coase [1937], and Alchian and Demsetz [1972] as good references to an immense literature in this area. The issue is also explored in greater depth in Chapter 13 of this text.

In spite of the above discussion, we shall assume that managers always make decisions which maximize the wealth of the firm's shareholders. In order to do so, they must find and select the best set of investment projects to accomplish their objective.

D. MAXIMIZATION OF
SHAREHOLDERS' WEALTH

1. Dividends vs. Capital Gains

Assuming that managers behave as though they were maximizing the wealth of the shareholders, we need to establish a usable definition of what is meant by shareholders' wealth. We can say that shareholders' wealth is the discounted value of after-tax cash flows paid out by the firm.[1] After-tax cash flows available for consumption can be shown to be the same as the stream of dividends, D_t, paid to shareholders. The discounted value of the stream of dividends is

$$S_0 = \sum_{t=0}^{\infty} \frac{D_t}{(1 + k)^t},$$ (2.1)

where S_0 is the present value of shareholders' wealth (in Fig. 2.1 it is W_0) and k is the market-determined rate of interest.

Equation (2.1) is a multiperiod formula which assumes that future cash flows paid to shareholders are known with certainty and that the market-determined discount rate is nonstochastic and constant over all time periods. These assumptions are maintained throughout this chapter because our main objective is to understand how the investment decision, shown graphically in Fig. 2.1 in a one-period context, can be extended to the more practical setting of many time periods in a manner consistent with the maximization of the shareholders' wealth. For the time being, we shall ignore the effect of personal taxes on dividends, and we shall assume that the discount rate, k, is the market-determined opportunity cost of capital for equivalent income streams. It is determined by the slope of the market line in Fig. 2.1.

One question that often arises is: What about capital gains? Surely shareholders receive both capital gains and dividends; why then do capital gains not appear in Eq. (2.1)? The answer to this question is that capital gains *do* appear in Eq. (2.1). This can be shown by use of a simple example. Suppose a firm pays a dividend, D_1, of \$1.00 at the end of this year and \$1.00 $(1 + g)^t$ at the end of each year thereafter, where g is the growth rate of the dividend stream. If the growth rate in dividends, g, is 5% and the opportunity cost of investment, k, is 10% how much will an investor pay today for the stock? Using the formula for the present value of a growing annuity stream, we get[2]

$$S_0 = \frac{D_1}{k - g} = \frac{\$1.00}{.10 - .05} = \$20.00.$$

---

[1] Since much of the rest of this chapter assumes familiarity with discounting, the reader is referred to Appendix A for a review.

[2] The formula used here, sometimes called the Gordon growth model, is derived in Appendix A. It assumes that the dividend grows forever at a constant rate, g, which is less than the discount rate, $g < k$.

Next, suppose that an investor bought the stock today for $20 and held it for five years. What would it be worth at the end of the fifth year?

$$S_5 = \frac{D_6}{k - g}.$$

The dividend, D_6, at the end of the sixth year is

$$D_6 = \$1.00(1 + g)^5, \qquad D_6 = \$1.00(1.05)^5 = \$1.2763.$$

Therefore, the value of the stock at the end of the fifth year would be

$$S_5 = \frac{\$1.2763}{.10 - .05} = \$25.5256.$$

The value of the stock at the end of the fifth year is the discounted value of all dividends from that time on. Now we can compute the present value of the stream of income of an investor who holds the stock only five years. He or she gets five dividend payments plus the market price of the stock in the fifth year. The discounted value of these payments is S_0.

$$S_0 = \frac{D_1}{1 + k} + \frac{D_1(1 + g)}{(1 + k)^2} + \frac{D_1(1 + g)^2}{(1 + k)^3} + \frac{D_1(1 + g)^3}{(1 + k)^4} + \frac{D_1(1 + g)^4}{(1 + k)^5} + \frac{S_5}{(1 + k)^5}$$

$$= \frac{1.00}{1.1} + \frac{1.05}{1.21} + \frac{1.10}{1.33} + \frac{1.16}{1.46} + \frac{1.22}{1.61} + \frac{25.52}{1.61}$$

$$= .91 + .87 + .83 + .79 + .76 + 15.85$$

$$= 20.01.$$

Except for a one-cent rounding difference, the present value of the stock is the same whether an investor holds it forever, or for only, say, five years. Since the value of the stock in the fifth year is equal to the future dividends from that time on, the value of dividends for five years plus a capital gain is exactly the same as the value of an infinite stream of dividends. Therefore, equation (2.1) is the discounted value of the stream of cash payments to shareholders and is equivalent to the shareholders' wealth. Because we are ignoring the different tax rates between dividends and capital gains (this will be discussed in Chapter 14, "Dividend Policy") we can say that Eq. (2.1) incorporates all cash payments, both dividends and capital gains.

2. The Economic Definition of Profit

Frequently there is a great deal of confusion over what is meant by profits. An economist uses the word "profits" to mean rates of return in excess of the opportunity cost for funds employed in projects of equal risk. In order to estimate economic profits one must know the exact time pattern of *cash flows* provided by a project and the opportunity cost of capital. As we shall see below, the pattern of cash flows is the same thing as the stream of dividends paid by the firm to its owners. Therefore, the appropriate profits for managers to use when making decisions are the discounted stream of cash flows to shareholders; in other words, dividends. Note, however, that "dividends" should be interpreted very broadly. Our definition of dividends includes *any* cash payout to shareholders. In addition to what we ordinarily think of as dividends the general definition includes capital gains, spinoffs to shareholders, payments in liquidation or bankruptcy, repurchase of shares, awards in shareholders' lawsuits, and payoffs resulting from merger or acquisition. Stock dividends, which involve no cash flow, are *not* included in our definition of dividends.

We can use a very simple model to show the difference between the economic definition of profit and the accounting definition. Assume that we have an all-equity firm and that there are no taxes.[3] Then sources of funds are revenues, R, and sale of new equity (on M shares at P dollars per share). Uses of funds are wages, salaries, materials, and services, W&S; investment, I; and dividends, D. For each time period, t, we can write the *equality between sources and uses of funds* as

$$R_t + M_t P_t = D_t + (W\&S)_t + I_t. \tag{2.2}$$

To simplify things even further, assume that the firm issues no new equity, that is, $M_t P_t = 0$. Now we can write dividends as

$$D_t = R_t - (W\&S)_t - I_t, \tag{2.3}$$

which is the *simple cash flow definition of profit.* Dividends are the cash flow left over after costs of operations and new investment are deducted from revenues. Using Eq. (2.3) and the definition of shareholders' wealth (Eq. 2.1), we can rewrite shareholders' wealth as

$$S_0 = \sum_{t=0}^{\infty} \frac{R_t - (W\&S)_t - I_t}{(1+k)^t}. \tag{2.4}$$

The accounting definition of profit does not deduct gross investment, I_t, as investment outlays are made. Instead the book value of new investment is capitalized on the balance sheet and written off at some depreciation rate, dep. The *accounting definition of profit* is

$$A_t = R_t - (W\&S)_t - \text{dep}_t. \tag{2.5}$$

Let N_t be the net change in the book value of assets during a year. The net change will equal gross new investment during the year, I_t, less the change in accumulated depreciation during the year, dep_t,

$$N_t = I_t - \text{dep}_t. \tag{2.6}$$

We already know that the accounting definition of profit, A_t, is different from the economic definition, D_t. However, it can be adjusted by subtracting net investment. This is done in Eq. (2.7):

---

[3] The conclusions to be drawn from the model do not change if we add debt and taxes, but the arithmetic becomes more complex.

$$S_0 = \sum_{t=0}^{\infty} \frac{R_t - (W\&S)_t - \mathrm{dep}_t - (I_t - \mathrm{dep}_t)}{(1+k)^t}$$

$$= \sum_{t=0}^{\infty} \frac{A_t - N_t}{(1+k)^t}. \tag{2.7}$$

The main difference between the accounting definition and the economic definition of profit is that the former does not focus on cash flows when they occur, while the latter does. The economic definition of profit, for example, correctly deducts the entire expenditures for investment in plant and equipment at the time the cash outflow occurs.

Financial managers are frequently misled when they focus on the accounting definition of profit, or earnings per share. The objective of the firm is *not* to maximize earnings per share. The correct objective is to maximize shareholders' wealth, which is the price per share which in turn is equivalent to the discounted cash flows of the firm. There are two good examples which point out the difference between maximizing earnings per share and maximizing discounted cash flow. The first example is the difference between FIFO and LIFO inventory accounting during a time period of inflation. Earnings per share are higher if the firm adopts first-in/first-out (FIFO) inventory accounting. The reason is that the cost of manufacturing the oldest items in inventory is less than the cost of producing the newest items. Consequently, if the cost of the oldest inventory (the inventory which was first in) is written off as expense against revenue, earnings per share will be higher than if the cost of the newest items (the inventory which was in last) is written off. A numerical example is given in Table 2.1. It's easy to see how managers might be tempted to use FIFO accounting techniques. Earnings per share are higher. However, FIFO is the wrong technique to use in an inflationary period because it minimizes cash flow by maximizing taxes. In our example, production has taken place during some previous time period, and we are trying to make the correct choice of inventory accounting in the present. The sale of an item from inventory in Table 2.1 provides $100 of cash inflow (revenue) regardless of which accounting system we are using. Cost of goods sold involves no current cash flow, but taxes do. Therefore, with FIFO, earnings per share are 45¢ but cash flow per share is ($100 − $30)/100 shares, which equals 70¢ per share. On the other hand, with last-in/first-out inventory accounting (LIFO), earnings per

Table 2.1   LIFO vs. FIFO

	LIFO	*FIFO*	*Inventory at Cost*
Revenue	100	100	4th item in 90 → LIFO
Cost of goods sold	−90	−25	3rd item in 60
Operating income	10	75	2nd item in 40
Taxes at 40%	−4	−30	1st item in 25 → FIFO
Net income	6	45	
Earnings per share (100 shs)	.06	.45	

share are only 6¢ but cash flow is ($100 − $4)/100 shares, which equals 96¢ per share. Since shareholders care only about discounted cash flow, they will assign a higher value to the shares of the company using LIFO accounting. The reason is that LIFO provides higher cash flow because it pays lower taxes to the government.[4] This is a good example of the difference between maximizing earnings per share and maximizing shareholders' wealth.[5]

A second example is the accounting treatment of goodwill in mergers. Since the accounting practices for merger are discussed in detail in Chapter 18, only the salient features will be mentioned here. There are two types of accounting treatment for merger: pooling and purchase. Pooling means that the income statements and balance sheets of the merging companies are simply added together. With purchase, the acquiring company adds two items to its balance sheet: (1) the book value of the assets of the acquired company and (2) the difference between the purchase price and the book value. This difference is an item called *goodwill*. Opinion 17 of the Accounting Principles Board (APB No. 17, effective October 31, 1970) of The American Institute of Certified Public Accountants requires that goodwill be written off as an expense against earnings *after* taxes over a period not to exceed 40 years. Obviously earnings per share will be lower if the same merger takes place by purchase rather than pooling. There is empirical evidence, collected in a paper by Jean-Marie Gagnon [1979], which indicates that managers choose to use pooling rather than purchase if the write-off of goodwill is substantial. Managers seem to behave as if they were trying to maximize earnings per share. The sad thing is that some mergers which are advantageous to the shareholders of acquiring firms may be rejected by management if substantial goodwill write-offs are required. This would be unfortunate because *there is no difference in the effect on cash flows between pooling and purchase.* The reason is that goodwill expense is not a cash flow and it has no effect on taxes because it is written off *after* taxes.[6]

It is often argued that maximization of earnings per share is appropriate if investors use earnings per share to value the stock. There is good empirical evidence to indicate that this is not the case. Shareholders do, in fact, value securities according to the present value of discounted cash flows. Evidence which substantiates this is presented in detail in Chapter 10.

E. TECHNIQUES FOR CAPITAL BUDGETING

Having argued that maximizing shareholders' wealth is equivalent to maximizing the discounted cash flows provided by investment projects, we now turn our attention to a discussion of investment decision rules. We assume, for the time being, that

---

[4] In 1979 the Internal Revenue Service estimated that if every firm which could have switched to LIFO had actually done so, approximately $18 billion less corporate taxes would have been paid.

[5] See Chapter 10 for a discussion of empirical research on this issue.

[6] See Chapter 10 for a discussion of empirical evidence relating to this issue.

the stream of cash flows provided by a project can be estimated without error, and that the opportunity cost of funds provided to the firm (this is usually referred to as *the cost of capital*) is also known. We also assume that capital markets are frictionless so that financial managers can separate investment decisions from individual shareholder preferences, and that monitoring costs are zero so that managers will maximize shareholders' wealth. All that they need to know is cash flows and the required market rate of return for projects of equivalent risk.

Three major problems face managers when they make investment decisions. First they have to search out new opportunities in the marketplace or new technologies. These are the basis of growth. Unfortunately, the Theory of Finance cannot help with this problem. Second, the expected cash flows from the projects have to be estimated, and finally the projects have to be evaluated according to sound decision rules. These latter two problems are central topics of this text. In the remainder of this chapter we look at project evaluation techniques assuming that cash flows are known with certainty, and in Chapter 11 we'll assume that cash flows are uncertain.

Investment decision rules are usually referred to as *capital budgeting techniques.* The best technique will possess the following essential property: it will maximize shareholders' wealth. This essential property can be broken down into separate criteria:

- All cash flows should be considered.
- The cash flows should be discounted at the opportunity cost of funds.
- The technique should select from a set of mutually exclusive projects the one which maximizes shareholders' wealth.
- Managers should be able to consider one project independently from all others (this is known as the *value-additivity principle*).

The last two criteria need some explanation. *Mutually exclusive projects* are a set from which only one project can be chosen. In other words, if a manager chooses to go ahead with one project from the set, he cannot choose to take on any of the others. For example, there may be three or four different types of bridges which could be constructed to cross a river at a given site. Choosing a wooden bridge excludes other types, e.g., steel. Projects are also categorized in other ways. *Independent projects* are those which permit the manager to choose to undertake any or all, and *contingent projects* are those which have to be carried out together or not at all. For example, if building a tunnel also requires a ventilation system, then the tunnel and ventilation system should be considered as a single, contingent project.

The fourth criterion, the *value-additivity principle,* implies that if we know the value of separate projects accepted by management, then simply adding their values, V_j, will give us the value of the firm, V. In mathematical terms, if there are N projects, then the value of the firm is

$$V = \sum_{j=1}^{N} V_j. \tag{2.8}$$

This is a particularly important point because it means that projects can be considered on their own merit without the necessity of looking at them in an infinite variety of combinations with other projects.

Table 2.2   Four Mutually Exclusive Projects

			Cash Flows		
Year	A	B	C	D	PV factor at 10%
0	−1000	−1000	−1000	−1000	1.000
1	100	0	100	200	.909
2	900	0	200	300	.826
3	100	300	300	500	.751
4	−100	700	400	500	.683
5	−400	1300	1250	600	.621

There are four widely used capital budgeting techniques: (1) the payback method, (2) the accounting rate of return, (3) the net present value, and (4) the internal rate of return. Our task is to choose the technique which best satisfies the four desirable properties discussed above. It will be demonstrated that only one technique—the net present value method—is correct. It is the only technique which is always consistent with shareholder wealth maximization.

In order to provide an example for discussion, Table 2.2 lists the estimates of cash flow for four projects, each of which has a five-year life. Since they are mutually exclusive, there is only one which will maximize the price of the firm's stock; in other words, there is only one which will maximize shareholders' wealth. We would normally assume at this point that all four projects are equally "risky." However, according to the assumption used throughout this chapter, their cash flows are known with certainty; therefore, their "risk" is zero. The appropriate discount rate in a world with no risk is the risk-free rate (for example, the Treasury Bill rate).

1. The Payback Method

The payback period for a project is simply the number of years it takes to recover the initial cash outlay on a project. The payback periods for the four projects in Table 2.2 are:

Project A,   2 years;
Project B,   4 years;
Project C,   4 years;
Project D,   3 years.

If management were adhering strictly to the payback method, it would choose project A, which has the shortest payback period.[7] A casual inspection of the cash flows shows that this is clearly wrong. The difficulty with the payback method is that it does not consider all cash flows and it fails to discount them. Failure to consider

---

[7] It isn't too hard to find real-world examples of projects which have negative future cash flows and cannot be abandoned. A good example is nuclear power plants. At the end of their useful life they must be decommissioned at considerable expense.

all cash flows results in ignoring the large negative cash flows which occur in the last two years of project *A*. Failure to discount them means that management would be indifferent in its choice between project *A* and a second project which paid $900 in the first year and $100 in the second. Both projects would have the same payback period. We reject the payback method because it violates (at least) the first two of the four properties which are desirable in capital budgeting techniques.[8]

2. The Accounting Rate of Return (ARR)

The *accounting rate of return* is the average after-tax profit divided by the initial cash outlay. It is very similar to (and in some uses exactly the same as) the return on assets (ROA) or the return on investment (ROI) and they suffer from the same deficiencies. Assuming, for the sake of convenience, that the numbers in Table 2.2 are accounting profits, the average after-tax profit for project *A* is

$$\frac{-1000 + 100 + 900 + 100 - 100 - 400}{5} = -80,$$

and the ARR is

$$ARR = \frac{\text{Average after-tax profit}}{\text{Initial Outlay}} = \frac{-80}{1000} = -8\%. \qquad (2.9)$$

The ARR's for the four projects are:

Project *A*,   ARR $= -8\%$;

Project *B*,   ARR $= 26\%$;

Project *C*,   ARR $= 25\%$;

Project *D*,   ARR $= 22\%$.

If we were using the ARR, we would choose project *B* as the best. The problem with the ARR is that it uses accounting profits instead of cash flows and it does not consider the time value of money. The difference between accounting profits and cash flows has been discussed at length, and it is therefore unnecessary to repeat here why it is incorrect to use the accounting definition of profits. Failure to use the time value of money (i.e., failure to discount) means that managers would be indifferent in their choice between project *B* and a project with after-tax profits which occur in the opposite chronological order because both projects would have the same accounting rate of return.

3. Net Present Value (NPV)

The *net present value* criterion will accept projects which have an NPV greater than zero. The NPV is computed by discounting the cash flows at the firm's opportunity

---

[8] See problem 2.10 at the end of the chapter. It demonstrates that the payback technique also violates the value additivity principle.

cost of capital. For the projects in Table 2.2 we assume that the cost of capital is 10%. Therefore, the present value of project A is[9]

(Cash Flow)	$\times$	*(PV Factor)*	$=$	*PV*
−1000		1.000		−1000.00
100		.909		90.90
900		.826		743.40
100		.751		75.10
−100		.683		−68.30
−400		.621		−248.40
			NPV =	−407.30

We have discounted each of the cash flows back to the present and summed them. Mathematically this can be written as

$$\text{NPV} = \sum_{t=1}^{N} \frac{\text{NCF}_t}{(1+k)^t} - I_0, \tag{2.10}$$

where NCF_t is the net cash flow in time period t, I_0 is the initial cash outlay, k is the firm's cost of capital, and N is the number of years in the project. The net present values of the four projects are:

Project A, NPV = −407.30;

Project B, NPV = 510.70;

Project C, NPV = 530.75;

Project D, NPV = 519.20.

If these projects were independent instead of mutually exclusive, we would reject A and accept B, C, and D. (Why?) Since they are mutually exclusive, we select the project with greatest NPV, project C. The NPV of a project is exactly the same as the increase in shareholders' wealth. This fact makes it the correct decision rule for capital budgeting purposes. More will be said about this when we compare the NPV rule with the internal rate of return.

4. Internal Rate of Return (IRR)

The *internal rate of return* on a project is defined as that rate which equates the present value of the cash outflows and inflows. In other words, it is the rate which makes the computed NPV exactly zero. Hence this is the rate of return on invested capital which the project is returning to the firm. Mathematically, we solve for the rate of return where the NPV equals zero:

---

[9] The reader who wishes to brush up on the algebra of discounting is referred to Appendix A.

Table 2.3   IRR for Project C

Year	Cash Flow	PV at 10%		PV at 20%		PV at 25%		PV at 22.8%	
0	−1000	1.000	−1000.00	1.000	−1000.00	1.000	−1000.00	1.000	−1000.00
1	100	.909	90.90	.833	83.33	.800	80.00	.814	81.40
2	200	.826	165.20	.694	138.80	.640	128.00	.663	132.60
3	300	.751	225.30	.579	173.70	.512	153.60	.540	162.00
4	400	.683	273.20	.482	192.80	.410	163.84	.440	176.00
5	1250	.621	776.15	.402	502.50	.328	410.00	.358	447.50
	1250		530.75		91.13		−64.56		−.50

$$\text{NPV} = 0 = \sum_{t=1}^{N} \frac{\text{NCF}_t}{(1 + \text{IRR})^t} - I_0. \tag{2.11}$$

We can solve for the IRR on project C by trial and error. (Most firms have computer programs which can quickly solve for the IRR by using similar iterative techniques.) This is done in Table 2.3, and graphed in Fig. 2.2.

Figure 2.2 shows that the NPV of the given set of cash flows decreases as the discount rate is increased. If the discount rate is zero, there is no time value of money and the NPV of a project is simply the sum of its cash flows. For project C, the NPV equals $1250 when the discount rate is zero. At the opposite extreme, if the discount rate is infinite, then future cash flows are valueless and the NPV of project C is its current cash flow, −$1000. Somewhere between these two extremes is a discount rate which makes the present value equal to zero. Called the IRR on the project, this rate equates the present value of cash inflows with the present value of cash outflows. The IRR's for the four projects are:

Project A, IRR = −200%;
Project B, IRR = 20.9%;
Project C, IRR = 22.8%;
Project D, IRR = 25.4%.

Figure 2.2
NPV of project C at different discount rates.

If we use the IRR criterion and the projects are independent, we accept any project which has an IRR greater than the opportunity cost of capital, which is 10%. Therefore, we would accept projects B, C, and D. However, since these projects are mutually exclusive, the IRR rule leads us to accept project D as the best.

F. COMPARISON OF NET PRESENT VALUE WITH INTERNAL RATE OF RETURN

As the example shows, the net present value and the internal rate of return can favor conflicting project choices. The net present value favors project C while the IRR favors project D. Both techniques consider all cash flows and both use the concept of the time value of money in order to discount cash flows. However, we must choose from among the four mutually exclusive projects the one project which maximizes shareholders' wealth. Consequently, only one of the two techniques can be correct. We shall see that the NPV criterion is the only one which is necessarily consistent with maximizing shareholders' wealth.

Figure 2.3 compares projects B, C, and D. For very low discount rates project B has the highest net present value, for intermediate discount rates project C is best, and for high discount rates, project D is best. The NPV rule compares the three projects at the same discount rate. Remember, 10% was not arbitrarily chosen. It is the market-determined opportunity cost of capital. We saw earlier in the chapter that this market-determined discount rate is the one managers should use if they desire to maximize the wealth of all shareholders. Consequently, no other discount rate is appropriate. Project C is the best project because it gives the greatest NPV when the opportunity cost of funds invested is 10%.

The IRR rule does not discount at the opportunity cost of capital. Instead, it

Figure 2.3
Comparison of three mutually exclusive projects.

implicitly assumes that the time value of money is the IRR, since all cash flows are discounted at that rate. This implicit assumption has come to be called the reinvestment rate assumption.

1. The Reinvestment Rate Assumption

The reinvestment rate is really the same thing as the opportunity cost of capital. Both the NPV rule and the IRR rule make implicit assumptions about the reinvestment rate. The NPV rule assumes that shareholders can reinvest their money at the opportunity cost of capital, which in our example was 10%. Because 10% is the market-determined opportunity cost of funds, the NPV rule is making the correct reinvestment rate assumption. On the other hand, the IRR rule assumes that investors can reinvest their money at the IRR for each project. Therefore, in our example, it assumes that shareholders can reinvest funds in project C at 22.8% and in project D at 25.4%. But we have been told that both projects have the same risk (namely, cash flows are known with certainty). Why should investors be able to reinvest at one rate for project C and at another rate for project D? Obviously, the implicit reinvestment rate assumption in the IRR rule defies logic. Although the IRR does discount cash flows, it does not discount them at the opportunity cost of capital. Therefore it violates the second of the four properties mentioned earlier.

2. The Value Additivity Principle

The fourth of the desirable properties of capital budgeting rules demands that managers be able to consider one project independently of all others. This is known as the value additivity principle and it implies that the value of the firm is equal to the sum of the values of each of its projects (Eq. 2.8). In order to demonstrate that the IRR rule can violate the value additivity principle, consider the three projects whose cash flows are given in Table 2.4. Projects 1 and 2 are mutually exclusive

Table 2.4   Example of Value Additivity

Year	Project 1	Project 2	Project 3	PV Factor at 10%	1 + 3	2 + 3
0	−100	−100	−100	1.000	−200	−200
1	0	225	450	.909	450	675
2	550	0	0	.826	550	0

Project	NPV at 10%	IRR
1	354.30	134.5%
2	104.53	125.0%
3	309.05	350.0%
1 + 3	663.35	212.8%
2 + 3	413.58	237.5%

and project 3 is independent of them. If the value additivity principle holds, we should be able to choose the better of the two mutually exclusive projects without having to consider the independent project. The NPV's of the three projects as well as their IRR's are also given in Table 2.4. If we use the IRR rule to choose between projects 1 and 2, we would select project 1. But if we consider combinations of projects, then the IRR rule would prefer projects 2 and 3 to projects 1 and 3. The IRR rule prefers project 1 in isolation but project 2 in combination with the independent project. In this example, the IRR rule does not obey the value additivity principle. The implication for management is that it would have to consider all possible combinations of projects and choose the combination which has the greatest internal rate of return. If, for example, a firm had only five projects, it would need to consider 32 different combinations.[10]

The NPV rule always obeys the value additivity principle. Given that the opportunity cost of capital is 10%, we would choose project 1 as being the best either by itself or in combination with project 3. Note that the combinations of 1 and 3 or 2 and 3 are simply the sums of the NPV's of the projects considered separately. Consequently, if we adopt the NPV rule, the value of the firm is the sum of the values of the separate projects. Later (in Chapter 7) we shall see that this result holds even in a world with uncertainty where the firm may be viewed as a portfolio of risky projects.

3. Multiple Rates of Return

Still another difficulty with the IRR rule is that it can result in multiple rates of return if the stream of estimated cash flows changes sign more than once. A classic example of this situation has come to be known as the oil-well pump problem. An oil company is trying to decide whether or not to install a high-speed pump on a well which is already in operation. The estimated incremental cash flows are given in Table 2.5. The pump will cost $1600 to install. During its first year of operation it will produce $10,000 more oil than the pump which is currently in place. But during the second year, the high-speed pump produces $10,000 less oil because the well has been depleted. The question is whether or not to accept the rapid pumping

Table 2.5 Oil-Well Pump Incremental Cash Flows

Year	Estimated Cash Flow
0	−1,600
1	10,000
2	−10,000

---

[10] The number of combinations for 5 projects is

$$\binom{5}{0} + \binom{5}{1} + \binom{5}{2} + \binom{5}{3} + \binom{5}{4} + \binom{5}{5} = 32.$$

Imagine the number of combinations which would have to be considered if there were 50 projects.

Figure 2.4
Multiple internal rates of return.

technique, which speeds up cash flows in the near term at the expense of cash flows in the long term. Figure 2.4 shows the NPV of the project for different discount rates. If the opportunity cost of capital is 10%, the NPV rule would reject the project because it has negative NPV at that rate. If we are using the IRR rule, the project has two IRR's, 25% and 400%. Since both exceed the opportunity cost of capital, the project would probably be accepted.

Mathematically, the multiple IRR's are a result of Descartes' rule of signs, which implies that every time the cash flows change signs there will be a new (positive, real) root to the problem solution. For the above example, the signs of cash flows change twice. The IRR is the rate which causes the discounted value of the cash flows to equal zero. Hence we solve the following equation for IRR.

$$NPV = 0 = \frac{-1600}{(1 + IRR)^0} + \frac{10,000}{(1 + IRR)^1} + \frac{-10,000}{(1 + IRR)^2}$$

$$0 = \frac{-1600(1 + IRR)^2 + 10,000(1 + IRR) - 10,000}{(1 + IRR)^2},$$

$$1600(1 + IRR)^2 - 10,000(1 + IRR) + 10,000 = 0.$$

This is clearly a quadratic equation and has two roots. It has the general form

$$ax^2 + bx + c = 0,$$

and can be solved using the quadratic formula

$$x = \frac{-b \pm \sqrt{b^2 - 4ac}}{2a}.$$

Therefore, for our example, the roots are

$$(1 + \text{IRR}) = x = \frac{10,000 \pm \sqrt{10,000^2 - 4(1600)10,000}}{2(1600)},$$

$$(1 + \text{IRR}) = \frac{10,000 \pm 6000}{3200},$$

$$\text{IRR} = 25\% \quad \text{or} \quad 400\%.$$

An economic interpretation to the multiple root problem can be found in a textbook by Teichroew [1964]. We can think of the project as an investment, with the firm putting money into it twice: -1600 at the time of the initial investment, and $-10,000$ in the second time period. The project can be thought of as lending $+10,000$ to the firm in the first time period. Let us assume that the positive cash flows provided by the project to the firm are lent at 10%, which is the opportunity cost of capital. This assumption makes sense because the $+10,000$ received by the firm cannot be invested in another oil-well pump (only one is available). Therefore, it is appropriate to assume that the $+10,000$ received by the firm in the first period is reinvested at the opportunity cost of capital, namely 10%. On the other hand, the firm expects to earn the IRR (whatever it is) on the cash flows which it puts into the project. Therefore, the firm invests -1600 now and expects to earn the IRR at the end of the first time period. Mathematically, the value at the end of the first period should be

$$1600(1 + \text{IRR}).$$

The difference between this result and the amount of money ($+10,000$) which the project lends to the firm at the opportunity cost of capital, 10%, in the second period is the amount borrowed at rate k. The net amount lent to the firm is given in brackets below. The future value of this amount in the second period is the net amount multiplied by $(1 + k)$,

$$[10,000 - 1600(1 + \text{IRR})](1 + k).$$

The firm then invests $-10,000$ at the end of the second period. This is set equal to the future value of the project which was given above. The result is:

$$10,000 = [10,000 - 1600(1 + \text{IRR})](1 + k).$$

Recalling that the opportunity cost of capital, k, is 10%, we can solve for the rate of return on investment:

$$\frac{10,000 - 11,000}{-1760} = 1 + \text{IRR},$$

$$-43.18\% = \text{IRR}.$$

This way of looking at the cash flows of the project solves the multiple root problem because positive cash flows lent to the firm are assumed to be provided at a known rate of return equal to the opportunity cost of capital. This makes it possible to isolate the rate of return on money invested in the project. This rate can be thought of as the IRR. For the example of the oil-well pump we see that when it is viewed properly, the IRR gives the same answer as the NPV. We should reject the project because the internal rate of return is less than the opportunity cost of capital.

4. Summary of Comparison of IRR and NPV

The IRR rule errs in several ways. First, it does not obey the value additivity principle, and consequently managers who use the IRR cannot consider projects independently of each other. Second, the IRR rule assumes that funds invested in projects have opportunity costs equal to the IRR for the project. This implicit reinvestment rate assumption violates the requirement that cash flows be discounted at the market-determined opportunity cost of capital. Finally, the IRR rule can lead to multiple rates of return whenever the sign of cash flows changes more than once. However, we saw that this problem can be avoided by the simple expedient of assuming that all cash inflows are loaned to the firm by the project at the market opportunity cost and that the rate of return on negative cash flows invested in the project is the IRR.

The NPV rule avoids all the problems which the IRR is heir to. It obeys the value additivity principle, it correctly discounts at the opportunity cost of funds, and most important, it is precisely the same thing as maximizing the shareholders' wealth.

G. CASH FLOWS FOR CAPITAL BUDGETING PURPOSES

Up to this point we have made the implicit assumptions that the firm has no debt and that there are no corporate taxes. This section adds a note of realism by providing a definition of cash flows for capital budgeting purposes given debt and taxes. In particular, we shall see that some cash flows, such as interest paid on debt and repayment of principal on debt, should not be considered cash flows *for capital budgeting purposes.* At the same time, we shall demonstrate, by using an example, that there is only one definition of cash flows which is consistent with shareholder wealth maximization.

In order to understand discounted cash flows it is also necessary to have a rudimentary understanding of the opportunity cost of capital of the firm. Chapter 12 discusses the cost of capital in great depth; however, the basics will be given here. The firm receives its investment funds from two classes of investors: creditors and shareholders. They provide debt and equity capital respectively. Both groups expect to receive a rate of return which compensates them for the level of risk which they accept.[11]

---

[11] The assumption that future cash flows are known with certainty must be relaxed at this point, in order to allow risk-free debt and risky equity. The reader who is interested in the related theoretical problems is referred to Chapters 12 and 13.

Table 2.6   Pro Forma Income Statement

R	Revenue	1300
$-VC$	Variable costs	-600
$-FCC$	Fixed cash costs	0
$-$dep.	Noncash charges (depreciation)	-300
EBIT	Earnings before interest and taxes	400
$-rD$	Interest expenses	-50
EBT	Earnings before taxes	350
$-T$	Taxes @ 50%	-175
NI	Net income	175

Debt holders receive a stream of fixed payments and can force the firm into receivership or bankruptcy if they do not receive payment. On the other hand, shareholders receive the firm's residual cash flows which remain after all other payments are made. Consequently, the interest rate paid to debt holders is less than the required rate of return on equity because it is less risky.

It is important to understand that projects undertaken by the firm must earn enough cash flow to provide the required rate of return to creditors, repayment of the face amount of debt, and payment of expected dividends to shareholders. Only when cash flows exceed these amounts will there be any gain in shareholders' wealth. When we discount cash flows at the weighted average cost of capital this is exactly what we are saying. A positive NPV is achieved only after creditors and shareholders receive their expected risk-adjusted rates of return.

In order to provide an example of this very important concept, consider the following (somewhat artificial) situation. A firm is going to be created from scratch. It will require an initial investment, I, of \$1000 for equipment which will depreciate at the rate of \$300 per year. Owners have decided to borrow \$500 at 10% interest. In other words, the before-tax cost of debt capital, k_d, is 10%. The expected annual cash flows for the project are implicit in the pro forma income statement given in Table 2.6. We shall assume that shareholders require a rate of return of 23.33% in order to compensate them for the riskiness of their position. Thus, the cost of equity, k_e, is 23.33%.

In order to provide the simplest possible example, assume that all the cash flows are perpetual, i.e. the firm has no growth. This assumption has the effect of keeping the firm's market value debt-to-equity ratio constant through time.[12] Perpetual cash flows are obtained first by writing a consol bond which never matures and pays a coupon of \$50 each year; and second by investing \$300 annually to replace the depreciation on the equipment.

Table 2.7 details the exact cash flows assuming that the project is held for five

---

[12] Without a constant debt-to-equity ratio, the weighted average cost of capital would change through time and the problem would become much more complex.

Table 2.7 Total Cash Flows for the Project

Year	Inflow	Outflow	Depre- ciation	Replacement Investment	Interest	Tax	Net Income	Residual Cash Flow
0	1000	−1000						
1	700		300	−300	−50	−175	175	175
2	700		300	−300	−50	−175	175	175
3	700		300	−300	−50	−175	175	175
4	700		300	−300	−50	−175	175	175
5	700	−500	300	−300	−50	−175	175	175 + 1250

years. At the end of five years the firm will be sold for its market value. Shareholders will receive the cash, use some of it ($500) to pay off bondholders, and keep the remainder.

Current cash flows are $500 provided by creditors and $500 from equity holders; outflows are $1000 paid for the equipment. In years 1 through 5 the project returns $700 in cash after the cash costs of production ($600) are subtracted from revenues ($1300). Then depreciation, a noncash charge ($300), is deducted, leaving $400 in earnings before interest and taxes. The deduction of $50 of interest expenses leaves taxable income of $350. After taxes there is $175 in net income. In order to compute free cash flows available for payment to shareholders, depreciation ($300), a noncash charge, must be added back and replacement investment ($300), a cash outflow, must be subtracted. Thus residual cash flow available to shareholders is $175 per year.

Shareholders' wealth, S, is the present value of their stream of residual cash flows, discounted at the cost of equity capital, $k_e = 23.33\%$. Recalling that their stream of residual cash flows continues forever, we can compute their wealth as shown below.[13]

$$S = \frac{\text{residual cash flow}}{k_e} = \frac{\$175}{.2333} = \$750.$$

The present value of bondholders' wealth, B, is the discounted value of their perpetual stream of coupon payments,

$$B = \frac{\text{interest payments}}{k_d} = \frac{\$50}{.10} = \$500.$$

Thus we see that the market value of the firm, V, is expected to be

$$V = B + S = \$500 + \$750 = \$1250.$$

Note that the present value of debt and equity are not affected by the fact that they will be sold at the end of year 5. The new bondholders and shareholders simply

---

[13] This formula is exact for perpetual cash flows. See Appendix A.

take over ownership of their streams of cash, paying $500 and $750 respectively. As shown in the last row of Table 2.7, the shareholders receive $1250 in year 5 for the firm, but must pay $500 to bondholders. Note also that the present value of shareholders' wealth is $750, but they had put up $500 of the initial investment. Therefore, their change in wealth, ΔS, is $750 minus $500, which equals $250. We shall see that this is exactly the same thing as the NPV of the project.

Instead of working through the complicated procedure given above, it will be easier to analyze capital budgeting projects by defining *cash flows for capital budgeting purposes* and discounting them at the firm's weighted average cost of capital. First, what is the weighted average cost of capital (WACC)? As shown in Eq. 2.12 below, it is the after-tax cost of debt capital, $k_d(1 - \tau_c)$, multiplied by the percent of the market value of the firm owned by creditors $[B/(B + S)]$ plus the cost of equity, k_e, multiplied by the percent of the firm's value owned by shareholders, $[S/(B + S)]$. Note that τ_c is the firm's marginal tax rate.

$$\text{WACC} = k_d(1 - \tau_c)\frac{B}{B + S} + k_e\frac{S}{B + S} \tag{2.12}$$

$$= .10(1 - .5)(.4) + .2333(.6) = 16\%$$

In a world without any taxes, the cost of capital would simply be a weighted average of the costs of debt and equity. However, in the real world, the government allows corporations to deduct the interest paid on debt as an expense before paying taxes. This tax shield on debt payments makes the cost of debt even less expensive from the firm's point of view. The weighted average cost of capital is the same as the after-tax market-determined opportunity cost of funds provided to the firm.

After determining the after-tax weighted average cost of capital, we need to find a definition of cash flow for use in standard capital budgeting procedures which is consistent with maximizing shareholders' wealth. The appropriate definition of cash flow for capital budgeting purposes is after-tax cash flows from operations, assuming that the firm has no debt and net of gross investment, ΔI. Marginal operating cash flows are the change in revenues, R, minus the change in direct costs which include variable costs of operations, VC, and the change in fixed cash costs, FCC, such as property taxes and administrative salaries and wages:

Marginal operating cash flows $= \Delta R - \Delta VC - \Delta FCC.$

Operating cash flows net of investment, ΔI, are called free operating cash flows.

Free operating cash flows $= \Delta R - \Delta VC - \Delta FCC - \Delta I.$

Taxes on operating cash flows are the tax rate, τ_c, times the change in revenues minus the change in direct cash costs and depreciation (dep).[14]

Taxes on operating cash flows $= \tau_c(\Delta R - \Delta VC - \Delta dep - \Delta FCC).$

---

[14] Depreciation is a noncash charge against revenues. If there are other noncash charges, they should also be included here.

Table 2.8   Cash Flows for Capital Budgeting

Year	Operating Cash Flow	Depre- ciation	Tax*	Cash Flow
0	−1000			−1000
1	700	300	175	200
2	700	300	175	200
3	700	300	175	200
4	700	300	175	200
5	700	300	175	200 + 1250

* The tax is the tax on operating income.

Therefore, the correct definition of cash flows for capital budgeting purposes is[15]

$$\text{CF for cap. budgeting} = (\Delta R - \Delta VC - \Delta FCC) - \tau_c(\Delta R - \Delta VC - \Delta FCC - \Delta dep) - \Delta I$$

$$= (\Delta R - \Delta VC - \Delta FCC)(1 - \tau_c) + \tau_c(\Delta dep) - \Delta I. \quad (2.13)$$

This definition is very different from the accounting definition of net income. Cash flows for capital budgeting purposes can be thought of as the after-tax cash flows which the firm would have if it had no debt. Interest expenses and their tax shield are not included in the definition of cash flow for capital budgeting purposes. The reason is that when we discount at the weighted average cost of capital we are implicitly assuming that the project will return the expected interest payments to creditors and the expected dividends to shareholders. Hence, inclusion of interest payments (or dividends) as a cash flow to be discounted would be double counting. Furthermore, the tax shield provided by depreciation, $\tau_c(\Delta dep)$, is treated as if it were a cash inflow. Table 2.8 shows the appropriate cash flows for capital budgeting purposes using the numbers from the example we have been using. To demonstrate that these are the correct cash flows, we can discount them at the weighted average cost of capital. The resulting number should exactly equal the increment to the shareholders' wealth, that is, $250 (see Table 2.9). It is no coincidence that this works out correctly. We are discounting the after-tax cash flows from operations at the weighted average cost of capital. Thus, the NPV of the project is exactly the same thing as the increase in shareholders' wealth.

One of the advantages of discounting the firm's free cash flows at the after-tax weighted average cost of capital is that this technique separates the investment decisions

---

[15] An equivalent definition is

$$\text{CF for cap. budgeting} = \Delta NI + \Delta dep + (1 - \tau_c)\Delta rD - \Delta I. \quad (2.13a)$$

where ΔNI stands for the change in net income, the accounting definition of profit, and ΔrD is the change in the coupon rate on debt times the change in the face value of debt. Although sometimes easier to use, it obscures the difference between cash flows for capital budgeting purposes and the accounting definition of profit.

Table 2.9   NPV of Cash Flows*

Year	Cash Flow	PV Factor at 16%	PV
0	−1000	1.000	−1,000.00
1	200	.862	172.41
2	200	.743	148.63
3	200	.641	128.13
4	200	.552	110.46
5	200	.476	95.22
5	1250	.476	595.14
			250.00

* Recall that in year 5 the firm was sold for a market value of $1250. This amount is the present value of cash flows from year 5 on, i.e. 200 ÷ .16 = 1250.

of the firm from its financing decisions. The definition of free cash flows shows what the firm will earn after taxes assuming that it has no debt capital. Thus, changes in the firm's debt to equity ratio have no effect on the definition of cash flows for capital budgeting purposes. The effect of financial decisions (e.g., changes in the ratio of debt to equity) is reflected in the firm's weighted average cost of capital.

The theory of the firm's cost of capital is discussed in greater detail in Chapter 12. In most applications it is assumed that the firm has an optimal ratio of debt to equity which is called the target capital structure. For the firm as a whole, the ratio of debt to equity is assumed to remain constant across time even though the financing for individual projects may require that debt be paid off over the life of the project. Without this assumption, the cost of capital would have to change each time period.

Another relevant issue, worth pointing out, is that the definition of cash flows for capital budgeting purposes includes all incremental cash flows attributable to a project. Too often, analysts forget that the total investment in a project includes working capital requirements as well as the cash outlays for buildings and equipment. Working capital includes any changes in short-term balance sheet items such as increases in inventories, accounts receivable, and accounts payable which are expected to result from undertaking a project. Net working capital requirements are the difference between changes in short-term assets and short-term liabilities.

SUMMARY AND CONCLUSION

The objective of the firm is assumed to be the maximization of shareholders' wealth. Toward this end managers should take projects with positive NPV's down to the point where the NPV of the last acceptable project is zero. When cash flows are properly defined for capital budgeting purposes and are discounted at the weighted average cost of capital, the NPV of a project is exactly the same as the increase in shareholders' wealth. Given perfect capital markets, the owners of the firm will unanimously support the acceptance of all projects with positive NPV. Other decision criteria, such as the payback method, the accounting rate of return, and the IRR, do not necessarily guarantee undertaking projects which maximize shareholders' wealth.

PROBLEM SET

2.1 *Basic capital budgeting problem with straight-line depreciation.* The Roberts Company has cash inflows of $140,000 per year on project A and cash outflows of $100,000 per year. The investment outlay on the project is $100,000; its life is 10 years; the tax rate τ_c is 40%. The opportunity cost of capital is 12%.

a) Present two alternative formulations of the net cash flows adjusted for the depreciation tax shelter.

b) Calculate the net present value for project A, using straight-line depreciation for tax purposes.

2.2 *Basic capital budgeting problem with accelerated depreciation.* Assume the same facts as in Problem 2.1, except that the earnings before depreciation, interest, and taxes are $22,000 per year.

a) Calculate the net present value, using straight-line depreciation for tax purposes.

b) Calculate the net present value, using the sum-of-the-years digits method of accelerated depreciation, for tax purposes.

2.3 *Basic replacement problem.* The Virginia Company is considering replacing a riveting machine with a new design that will increase the earnings before depreciation from $20,000 per year to $51,000 per year. The new machine will cost $100,000 and have an estimated life of eight years, with no salvage value. The applicable corporate tax rate is 40% and the firm's cost of capital is 12%. The old machine has been fully depreciated and has no salvage value. Should it be replaced by the new machine?

2.4 *Replacement problem when old machine has a positive book value.* Assume the same facts as in Problem 2.3 except that the Virginia Company will be able to realize an investment tax credit of 7% on the purchase of the new machine which will have a salvage value of $12,000. Assume further that the old machine has a book value of $40,000 with a remaining life of eight years. If replaced, the old machine can, at present, be sold for $15,000. Should the machine replacement be made?

2.5 *Cash flows.* The Cary Company is considering a new investment which costs $10,000. It will last five years and have no salvage value. The project would save $3000 in salaries and wages each year and would be financed with a loan with interest costs of 15% per year and amortization costs (repayment of principal on the loan) of $2000 per year. If the firm's tax rate is 40% and its after-tax cost of capital is 20%, what is the present value of the project? [*Note:* The annuity factor for five years at 20% is 2.991.]

2.6 Calculate the internal rate of return for the following set of cash flows.

$$
\begin{array}{ll}
t_1: & 400 \\
t_2: & 400 \\
t_3: & -1000
\end{array}
$$

If the opportunity cost of capital is 10%, should the project be accepted?

2.7 Calculate the internal rate of return on the following set of cash flows:

$$
\begin{array}{rl}
t_0: & -1000 \\
t_1: & 100 \\
t_2: & 900 \\
t_3: & 100 \\
t_4: & -100 \\
t_5: & -400
\end{array}
$$

2.8 The Ambergast Corporation is considering a project which has a three-year life and costs $1200. It would save $360 per year in operating costs and increase revenue by $200 per year. It would be financed with a three-year loan with the following payment schedule (the annual rate of interest is 5%).

Payment	Interest	Repayment of principal	Balance
440.65	60.00	380.65	819.35
440.65	40.97	399.68	419.67
440.65	20.98	419.67	0
	121.95	1200.00	

If the company has a 10% after-tax weighted average cost of capital, a 40% tax rate, and uses straight-line depreciation, what is the net present value of the project?

2.9 The treasurer of United Southern Capital Co. has submitted a proposal to the board of directors which, he argues, will increase profits for the all-equity company by a whopping 55%. It costs $900 and saves $290 in labor costs, providing a 3.1 year payback even though the equipment has an expected five-year life (with no salvage value). If the firm has a 50% tax rate, uses straight-line depreciation, and has a 10% weighted average after-tax cost of capital, should the project be accepted? Income statements before and after the project are given in Tables Q2.9A and Q2.9B, respectively.

Table Q2.9A

Before	Year 1	Year 2	Year 3	Year 4	Year 5
Revenue	1000	1000	1000	1000	1000
Variable cost	500	500	500	500	500
Fixed cost	300	300	300	300	300
Net operating income	200	200	200	200	200
Interest expense	0	0	0	0	0
Earnings before taxes	200	200	200	200	200
Taxes	-100	-100	-100	-100	-100
Net income	100	100	100	100	100

Table Q2.9B

After	Year 1	Year 2	Year 3	Year 4	Year 5
Revenue	1000	1000	1000	1000	1000
Variable cost	210	210	210	210	210
Fixed cost	480	480	480	480	480
Net operating income	310	310	310	310	310
Interest expense	0	0	0	0	0
Earnings before taxes	310	310	310	310	310
Taxes	−155	−155	−155	−155	−155
Net income	155	155	155	155	155

2.10 The cash flow for projects A, B, and C are given below. Calculate the payback period and net present value for each project (assume a 10% discount rate). If A and B are mutually exclusive and C is independent, which project, or combination of projects, is preferred using (a) the payback method or (b) the net present value method? What do the results tell you about the value additivity properties of the payback method?

		Project	
Year	A	B	C
0	−1	−1	−1
1	0	1	0
2	2	0	0
3	−1	1	3

2.11 Calculate the internal rate of return on the following set of cash flows, according to Teichroew's economic interpretation of internal rate of return. Assume that the opportunity cost of capital is 10%.

Year	Cash Flow
0	−5,000
1	10,000
2	−3,000

REFERENCES

Alchian, A. and H. Demsetz, "Production, Information Costs, and Economic Organization," *American Economic Review,* 1972, 777–795.

Bierman, H. Jr., and S. Smidt, *The Capital Budgeting Decision,* 4th ed. Macmillan, New York, 1975.

Bodenhorn, D., "A Cash-Flow Concept of Profit," *The Journal of Finance,* March 1964, 16–31.

Coase, R. H., "The Nature of the Firm," *Economica,* 1937, 386–405.

Cyert, R. M., and J. G. March, *A Behavioral Theory of the Firm.* Prentice-Hall, Englewood Cliffs, N.J., 1963.

Gagnon, J.-M., "The Purchase-Pooling Choice: Some Empirical Evidence," *The Journal of Accounting Research,* Spring 1971, 52–72.

Hirshleifer, J., *Investment, Interest and Capital.* Prentice-Hall, Englewood Cliffs, N.J., 1970.

Hong, J., R. S. Kaplan, and G. Mandelker, "Pooling vs. Purchase: The Effects of Accounting Mergers on Stock Prices," *The Accounting Review,* January 1978, 31–47.

Jensen, J., and W. Meckling, "Theory of the Firm: Managerial Behavior, Agency Costs and Ownership Structure," *Journal of Financial Economics,* October 1976, 305–360.

Machlup, F., "Theories of the Firm: Marginalist, Behavior, Managerial," *The American Economic Review,* March 1967, 1–33.

Marschak, J., and R. Radner, *Economic Theory of Teams* (Cowles Foundation Monograph 22), Yale University Press, New Haven, 1972.

Stern, J., "Earnings Per Share Doesn't Count," *Financial Analysts Journal,* July/August 1974, 39–43.

Sunder, S., "Stock Price and Risk Related to Accounting Changes in Inventory Valuation," *Accounting Review,* April 1975, 305–315.

————, "Relationship between Accounting Changes and Stock Prices: Problems of Measurement and Some Empirical Evidence," *Empirical Research in Accounting: Selected Studies,* 1973, 1–45.

Teichroew, D., *An Introduction to Management Science: Deterministic Models.* Wiley, New York, 1964, 78–82.

Williamson, O. E., *The Economics of Discretionary Behavior: Managerial Objectives in a Theory of the Firm.* Prentice-Hall, Englewood Cliffs, N.J., 1964.

More Advanced Capital Budgeting Topics

The basic problem of time valuation which Nature sets us is always that of translating the future into the present, that is, the problem of ascertaining the capital value of future income.

IRVING FISHER, *THE THEORY OF INTEREST,*
MACMILLAN, NEW YORK, 1930, P. 14

A. INTRODUCTION

Although Chapter 2 introduced the net present value (NPV) criterion, there were several implied assumptions which require further investigation. For example, all of the illustrations in Chapter 2 assumed that mutually exclusive projects had the same life and scale. What happens when these assumptions are relaxed? This question is dealt with in the first part of this chapter.

Next, we will turn the usual capital budgeting problem around and attempt to determine the optimal life for a project with growing cash flows. For example, when should growing trees be harvested or aging wine be bottled? Finally, let us suppose that the firm is operating under a fixed budget. How will this affect the project selection process?

The above topics are not usually covered in introductory finance texts. One reason is that they require more than an introductory level of mathematical sophistication. For example, the optimal harvest problem requires calculus optimization techniques (see Appendix D), and multiperiod constrained capital budgeting requires linear programming. The reader who is not interested in the mathematics need read only the introduction and conclusion to Sections C.2 and D.2 of this chapter.

Section E discusses the problem of capital budgeting in an inflationary environment. Needless to say, there has been growing interest over the last decade in this important applied problem. The reader should be cautioned, however, that solution techniques assume that future rates of inflation are known with certainty. Therefore an important element of realism, namely uncertainty, is lacking. Capital budgeting under uncertainty is covered in Chapter 11.

The last topic covered is the term structure of interest rates. All of the discounting procedures up to this point have assumed that the market interest rate is constant in every time period. What if it is expected to change to different levels each period? How does this problem affect capital budgeting analysis? How is the term structure of interest rates determined?

B. CAPITAL BUDGETING TECHNIQUES IN PRACTICE

Chapter 2 argued that the NPV and the internal rate of return (IRR) techniques of capital budgeting were the most sophisticated of the four commonly used criteria. They both consider cash flows (not earnings per share) and discount them in order to take into account the time value of money. Yet the question often arises: Do corporations actually employ these techniques?

A survey of large corporations conducted by Klammer [1972] and reported in the *Journal of Business* has provided an estimate of the actual usage of different capital budgeting techniques. His results are duplicated in Table 3.1.

Approximately 180 firms responded in 1970, 150 in 1964, and 145 in 1959. For our purposes the most interesting statistic is the most sophisticated primary evaluation standard. Note the increased usage of discounted cash flow techniques such as the IRR or NPV and the simultaneous decrease in payback. With the advent of computer technology and pocket calculators it is very easy to use the more sophisticated, and more correct, discounted cash flow techniques. A more recent study by Schall, Sundem, and Geijsbeek [1978] sampled 424 large firms (with a 46.4% response rate) and found that 86% use discounted cash flow methods, most of them combined with a payback or ARR analysis.

C. PROJECTS WITH DIFFERENT LIVES

All examples used in Chapter 2 compared projects with the same life. Now we turn our attention toward methods of choosing among mutually exclusive projects with

Table 3.1   Project Evaluation Techniques

	Percentage Using in*		
Technique	1970	1964	1959
Profit contribution analysis required:			
For over 75% of projects	53	53	50
For 25%–75% of projects	41	40	34
For less than 25% of projects	6	7	16
Total	100	100	100
Minimum profitability standards required:			
For most projects	77	65	58
For some projects	13	23	20
For few projects	10	12	22
Total	100	100	100
Most sophisticated primary evaluation standard:			
Discounting (rate of return or present worth)	57	38	19
Accounting rate of return	26	30	34
Payback or payback reciprocal	12	24	34
Urgency	5	8	13
Total	100	100	100

* Percentages shown are yes divided by yes + no multiplied by 100.

Klammer, T., "Empirical Evidence of the Adoption of Sophisticated Capital Budgeting Techniques," reprinted from *The Journal of Business*, July 1972, 393.

different lives. We begin by demonstrating the correct technique. It uses the NPV rule assuming that projects are replicated indefinitely at constant scale. A good example of a replicable project is the harvesting of trees. After the harvest the identical acreage is replanted and the project is started anew at the same scale. Next we will borrow from Hirshleifer [1970] to show why the NPV criterion (when correctly formulated) is superior to the IRR criterion given that projects have different lives and are replicable.

1. An NPV Technique for Evaluating Projects with Different Lives

Consider the cash flows estimated for the two projects in Table 3.2. If the opportunity cost of capital is 10%, the (simple) NPV's of the projects are

$$\text{NPV (project } A) = 41\cent, \qquad \text{NPV (project } B) = 50\cent.$$

However, if it makes sense that if the projects can be replicated at constant scale, project A should be superior to project B because it recovers cash flow faster. In

Table 3.2   **Projects with Different Lives**

Year	Project A	Project B
0	−10	−10
1	6	4
2	6	4
3		4.75

order to compare projects with different lives we compute the NPV of an infinite stream of constant scale replications. Let NPV (N, ∞) be the NPV of an N-year project with NPV(N), replicated forever. This is exactly the same as an annuity paid at the beginning of the first period and at the end of every N years from that time on. The NPV of the annuity is

$$\text{NPV}(N, \infty) = \text{NPV}(N) + \frac{\text{NPV}(N)}{(1+k)^N} + \frac{\text{NPV}(N)}{(1+k)^{2N}} + \cdots \qquad (3.1)$$

In order to obtain a closed-form formula, let

$$\frac{1}{(1+k)^N} = U.$$

Then we have

$$\text{NPV}(N, \infty) = \text{NPV}(N)(1 + U + U^2 + \cdots + U^n). \qquad (3.2)$$

Multiplying both sides by U, this becomes

$$U[\text{NPV}(N, \infty)] = \text{NPV}(N)(U + U^2 + \cdots + U^n + U^{n+1}). \qquad (3.3)$$

Subtracting Eq. (3.3) from (3.2) gives

$$\text{NPV}(N, \infty) - U\text{NPV}(N, \infty) = \text{NPV}(N)(1 - U^{n+1}),$$

$$\text{NPV}(N, \infty) = \frac{\text{NPV}(N)(1 - U^{n+1})}{1 - U}.$$

And taking the limit as the number of replications, n, approaches infinity gives

$$\operatorname*{Lim}_{n \to \infty} \text{NPV}(N, \infty) = \frac{\text{NPV}(N)}{1 - U} = \text{NPV}(N)\left[\frac{1}{1 - [1/(1+k)^N]}\right],$$

$$\text{NPV}(N, \infty) = \text{NPV}(N)\left[\frac{(1+k)^N}{(1+k)^N - 1}\right]. \qquad (3.4)$$

Equation (3.4) is the NPV of an N-year project replicated at constant scale an infinite number of times. We can use it to compare projects with different lives because when their cash flow streams are replicated forever it is as if they had the same (infinite) life.

In our example, the value of the two-year project, A, replicated at constant scale forever, is

$$\text{NPV}(2, \infty) = \text{NPV}(2) \left[\frac{(1 + .10)^2}{(1 + .10)^2 - 1} \right]$$

$$= (\$.41) \left[\frac{1.21}{.21} \right]$$

$$= \$2.36,$$

and for project B, the three-year project, we have

$$\text{NPV}(3, \infty) = \text{NPV}(3) \left[\frac{(1 + .10)^3}{(1.10)^3 - 1} \right]$$

$$= (\$.50) \left[\frac{1.33}{.33} \right]$$

$$= \$2.02.$$

Consequently, we would choose to accept project A over project B, because when the cash flows are adjusted for different project lives, A provides the greater wealth. Another way of comparing the projects is to multiply the NPV's of the infinitely replicated projects by the opportunity cost of capital to obtain what is called the annual equivalent value which is given in Eq. (3.5).[1]

$$k\text{NPV}(N, \infty) = \text{NPV}(N) \left[\frac{k(1 + k)^N}{(1 + k)^N - 1} \right]. \tag{3.5}$$

This decision rule is equivalent to that provided by Eq. (3.4) as long as the projects being compared have equal risk. If they have different risk the annual equivalent should not be used. For example, suppose we were considering two projects just like project A in the previous example, but that they have different risk. The computation of $\text{NPV}(N, \infty)$ tells us that they will provide the same increment to the present value of the firm. Yet if one has a risk-adjusted opportunity cost of $k = 10\%$ and the other $k = 20\%$, the annual equivalent method, $k\text{NPV}(N, \infty)$, will incorrectly lead us to prefer the riskier project.

2. The Duration Problem

We have just seen that when projects have different lives the simple NPV rule, when misused, can lead to incorrect decisions. Correct use of the simple NPV rule depends on whether or not one can reasonably assume a project is replicable. If it

---

[1] Note that Eq. (3.5) is equivalent to

$$k\text{NPV}(N, \infty) = \frac{\text{NPV}(N)}{\text{annuity factor}},$$

where the annuity factor $= [1 - (1 + k)^{-N}]/k$.

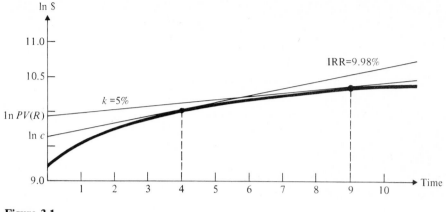

Figure 3.1
Tree-harvesting problem.

is unique and cannot be repeated, then the simple NPV computes the increment to shareholders' wealth from a single replication. If it is replicable (and many projects are) then NPV(N, ∞) gives the change in the value of the firm from a strategy of replicating at constant scale every N years. But why is constant scale replication the correct decision criterion for replicable projects? Why does it maximize the NPV of the shareholders' wealth when a simple comparison of NPV's or use of the IRR rule does not?

An interesting type of problem which highlights the differences between simple NPV, NPV with infinite replication at constant scale, and IRR is the determination of the optimal life, or duration, of a project. For example, when should growing trees be harvested or when should aging wine be bottled?

A. USING THE SIMPLE NPV RULE TO SOLVE THE DURATION PROBLEM   Assume that we own a growing stand of trees. Let the revenue, R_t, which can be obtained from harvesting them at time t be represented by the expression

$$R_t = 10,000\sqrt{1 + t}\,.$$

Also, let the initial cost, c, be \$15,000 and the opportunity cost of capital be 5% compounded continuously.[2] Figure 3.1 is a graph of the revenues as a function of time. Note that the vertical axis is a logarithmic scale so that geometrically increasing functions, for example continuously compounded interest, appear as straight lines.

First, we shall determine the harvesting time which maximizes the simple NPV of the project. For a project with a life of t years,

$$NPV = R_t e^{-kt} - c.$$

In order to find the harvesting time, t, which maximizes the NPV, we take the first derivative of NPV with respect to t and set it equal to zero:

---

[2] Appendix A contains a complete reference to the mathematics of continuous compounding.

$$\frac{d\text{NPV}}{dt} = -kR_t e^{-kt} + \frac{dR_t}{dt} e^{-kt} = 0.$$

Solving for k, we have

$$k = \frac{dR_t/dt}{R_t},$$

which says that the NPV is maximized when the marginal rate of return, $(dR_t/dt)/R_t$, is equal to the opportunity cost of capital, k. Graphically, this is the point of tangency between the straight line whose slope is 5% and the revenue function. As shown in Fig. 3.1, tangency occurs at $t = 9$ years. The same result can be shown mathematically by using the revenue function to solve for marginal revenue per unit time and setting the result equal to $k = 5\%$. The revenue function is

$$R_t = 10,000(1 + t)^{1/2}.$$

Its derivative with respect to t is the marginal revenue

$$\frac{dR_t}{dt} = \frac{1}{2}(10,000)(1 + t)^{-1/2},$$

and the marginal rate of return is

$$\frac{dR_t/dt}{R_t} = \frac{5,000(1 + t)^{-1/2}}{10,000(1 + t)^{1/2}} = \frac{1}{2(1 + t)}.$$

Setting this equal to the opportunity cost of capital, k, we get

$$\frac{1}{2(1 + t)} = .05, \qquad t = 9 \text{ years.}$$

B. USING THE IRR RULE TO SOLVE THE DURATION PROBLEM   Next, we would like to compare the simple NPV result with the harvest time which maximizes the IRR of the project. The IRR is the rate which sets the NPV of the project equal to zero. Mathematically, this is

$$\text{NPV} = 0 = R_t e^{-(\text{IRR})t} - c.$$

Adding c to both sides and taking the natural logarithm, we have

$$\ln R_t - (\text{IRR})t = \ln c,$$

and solving for IRR, we have

$$\text{IRR} = \frac{1}{t} \ln\left(\frac{R_t}{c}\right).$$

Substituting in the revenue function, we obtain

$$\text{IRR} = \frac{1}{t} \ln\left[\frac{10,000(1 + t)^{1/2}}{15,000}\right].$$

If we try different values of t, the project life which maximizes the IRR at a value of 9.98% is four years.

We can find this result graphically in Fig. 3.1 by rotating a line which passes through an intercept of $\ln c$ (at $t = 0$, if the natural logarithm of the present value of revenue is equal to $\ln c$, then the NPV of the project is zero) until it is just tangent to the revenue curve. The point of tangency gives the optimal harvest time, four years, and the slope of the line is the maximum IRR, 9.98%.

It is frequently argued that the IRR rule gives the best solution to the simple duration problem. However, this is incorrect because the IRR rule implicitly assumes that the funds provided by the project can continuously be reinvested in projects with proportional expansion of scale. In other words, we started out in our example with an investment of $15,000. After four years we would reinvest

$$\$15,000e^{\mathrm{IRR}(t)} = \$22,359,$$

and so on, in ever increasing amounts. So long as the IRR is greater than the opportunity cost of capital (5% in our example) the present value of an infinite replication of a proportionately growing stream of projects is infinite. This is patently absurd.

C. USING THE NPV RULE WITH CONSTANT SCALE REPLICATION   The correct formulation of the optimal duration problem is to assume that the project can be replicated indefinitely at constant scale. In the tree-harvesting problem this is equivalent to assuming that once the trees are harvested, the same acreage is replanted so that the project begins again at constant scale.

If the project is reformulated with constant scale replication, the NPV of an infinite stream of projects would be

$$\mathrm{NPV} = -c + (R_t - c)e^{-kt} + (R_t - c)e^{-2kt} + \cdots.$$

The second term is the present value of the revenue received at the time of harvest less the cash outlay for replanting at constant scale. The third term is the present value of the cash flows at the time of the second harvest, and so on. The NPV of this stream is

$$\mathrm{NPV} = -c + \frac{R_t - c}{e^{kt} - 1}.$$

In order to maximize, we set the derivative of the NPV with respect to project life, t, equal to zero.[3]

---

[3]

$$\frac{d\mathrm{NPV}}{dt} = \frac{d}{dt}[-c + (R_t - c)(e^{kt} - 1)^{-1}] = 0,$$

$$= \frac{dR_t}{dt}(e^{kt} - 1)^{-1} + [(R_t - c)](-1)(e^{kt} - 1)^{-2}ke^{kt} = 0,$$

$$= \frac{dR_t}{dt}(e^{kt} - 1) - (R_t - c)ke^{kt} = 0,$$

$$= \frac{dR_t}{dt} = \frac{k(R_t - c)}{1 - e^{-kt}}.$$

Table 3.3   Solution to the Duration Problem with Constant Scale Replication

t	Left-hand Side	Right-hand Side	Difference
4	2236.07	2033.31	202.76
4.5	2132.20	2097.76	34.44
4.6	2112.89	2108.81	4.08
5	2041.24	2146.38	−105.14

$$\frac{dNPV}{dt} = \frac{dR_t}{dt} - \frac{(R_t - c)k}{1 - e^{-kt}} = 0, \qquad \frac{dR_t}{dt} = \frac{(R_t - c)k}{1 - e^{-kt}}.$$

Using the numbers from our example, we get

$$\frac{5000}{(1+t)^{1/2}} = \frac{(10,000(1+t)^{1/2} - 15,000).05}{1 - e^{-.05t}}.$$

Table 3.3 shows the values at the left- and right-hand sides of the solution for various values of t. The optimal duration is approximately 4.6 years. This answer lies between the solution for simple duration with the NPV rule (nine years) and replication with proportionately increasing scale using the IRR rule (four years).

D. A COMPARISON OF THE THREE TECHNIQUES FOR SOLVING THE DURATION PROBLEM   Table 3.4 compares the three project evaluation techniques (simple NPV, IRR, and NPV with constant scale replication) for projects of different lives. Given the data from the tree harvesting problem, recall that all three projects have the same scale because each requires an outlay of $15,000. However, their lives vary between four and nine years. An important question is: How much would you pay to purchase the forestry operation assuming that you harvest after t years, then replant, and that the time value of money to you is 5%? The answer is $18,505. It is the current value of the forestry operation because it represents the present value of the cash stream provided by the operation into the indefinite future. It is the present value of a strategy of harvesting every 4.6 years.

Table 3.4   Comparison of Three Techniques

		A	B	C
Initial outlay		−15,000	−15,000	−15,000
Cash inflow at t years	4.0 years	22,361	0	0
	4.6 years	0	23,664	0
	9.0 years	0	0	31,623
IRR		9.98%	9.91%	8.29%
Simple NPV		3,308	3,802	5,164
NPV with constant scale replication		18,246	18,505	14,249

The above example demonstrates that the correct procedure for comparing projects with different lives is the same as the correct solution to the optimal duration problem. Both require that NPV maximization be formulated as the maximization of the NPV of a stream of projects replicated at constant scale.

D. CONSTRAINED CAPITAL BUDGETING PROBLEMS

A capital budgeting constraint implies that the firm can obtain only N dollars of funding at a fixed cost of capital. Implicitly the cost of capital in excess of N dollars is infinite. Therefore the firm is limited to a fixed budget. Most economists would agree that strict capital constraints simply do not exist in the real world. For example, consider a small firm with a "budget" of only a few thousand dollars of capital which suddenly acquires a new patent for economically converting garbage into gasoline. Certainly the firm would not find it very difficult to raise large amounts of money even though its initial budget was quite limited. As long as capital markets are reasonably efficient, it will always be possible for a firm to raise an indefinite amount of money so long as the projects are expected to have a positive net present value.

Weingartner [1977] discusses capital rationing in terms of situations imposed from within the firm and those imposed by the capital market. Self-imposed expenditure limits may arise to preserve corporate control or reflect the view of owners of closely held firms that the sale of the firm as a whole at a future date will provide a greater present value of wealth than the piecemeal sale that may permit faster growth. Externally imposed capital rationing could result from an attitude of the capital markets that providing funds beyond a specific amount would lead to increased risks of high bankruptcy costs—so high that feasible interest rates would not be adequate compensation. An aspect of this is the "Penrose effect" which holds that the organizational problems of obtaining and training additional personnel are large. Hence growth that involves increasing the organization's size by more than some percentage, for example 50%, in one year is fraught with high risks of organizational inefficiencies which increase risks of bankruptcy and give rise to high costs due to the loss of efficiency of a previously effectively functioning organization system or firm.

Although it is hard to justify the assumption of limited capital, nevertheless we shall review various decision-making techniques, assuming that capital constraints do, in fact, exist.

1. Projects with Different Scale. The Present Value Index (PVI)

Suppose we are comparing two mutually exclusive projects which have the same life. Furthermore, they are the only projects available. Project A costs $1,000,000 and has a net present value of $1,000, while project B costs $10 and has a net present value of $500. It is very tempting to argue that project B is better because it returns more net present value per dollar of cost. However, the NPV rule is very clear. If these are mutually exclusive projects, the correct decision is to take the one that has the highest NPV, project A.

But let us assume that there is a meaningful capital constraint imposed on our firm. How should the NPV rule be modified to consider projects of different scale? Table 3.5 shows the present value of the cash inflows and outflows of four independent projects which have identical lives. If there were no capital constraint we would accept all four projects because they all have positive NPV's. Project 1 has the highest NPV, followed by project 3, then 2, and finally 4. Suppose that there is a capital constraint which limits our spending to $300,000 or less. Now we would accept only projects 2 and 3 because they have the greatest NPV among those combinations of projects which use no more than $300,000. The logic leading to this decision is formalized by what is known as the *present value index* (PVI).

The PVI is defined as the present value of cash inflows divided by the present value of cash outflows:

$$PVI = \frac{\text{Present value of inflows}}{\text{Present value of outflows}}. \tag{3.6}$$

When used correctly, it is equivalent to maximizing the NPV of a set of projects subject to the constraint that project outlays be less than or equal to the firm's budget. The PVI for each project is given in Table 3.5. The PVI of excess funds, not invested in any of the projects, is always assumed to be equal to 1.0. (Why?)

The objective is to compare all sets of projects which meet the budget and find the one which maximizes the weighted average PVI. For example, if projects 2 and 3 are selected, the weighted average PVI is

$$PVI = \frac{125,000}{300,000}(1.13) + \frac{175,000}{300,000}(1.11) = 1.1183.$$

It is computed by multiplying the PVI of each project by the percentage of the total budget allocated to it. If project 1 is selected, no additional project can be undertaken; therefore the PVI for project 1 is

$$PVI = \frac{200,000}{300,000}(1.15) + \frac{100,000}{300,000}(1.00) = 1.1000.$$

Project 1 is not preferred to projects 2 and 3 because $100,000 must be invested in marketable securities which have a PVI of 1.0 (i.e., their cost is always equal to the present value of their cash inflows).

Table 3.5   Present Value Index

Project	PV of Inflows	Current Outflows	PVI	NPV
1	230,000	200,000	1.15	30,000
2	141,250	125,000	1.13	16,250
3	194,250	175,000	1.11	19,250
4	162,000	150,000	1.08	12,000

The PVI can be used to solve simple problems where there is a one-period capital constraint. It can also be used to compare mutually exclusive projects of different scale although a simple comparison of NPV's provides the same result. For example, refer to projects A and B (Section D.1). The first project cost $1,000,000 and had an NPV of $1,000 while the second cost only $10 and had an NPV of $500. If these are the only two projects available to the firm and if they are mutually exclusive, we can evaluate them by comparing their PVI's with the assumption that the firm has a $1,000,000 budget.[4]

The PVI of project A is

$$\frac{1,000,000}{1,000,000}\left(\frac{1,001,000}{1,000,000}\right) = 1.001,$$

and the PVI of project B is

$$\frac{10}{1,000,000}\left(\frac{510}{10}\right) + \frac{999,990}{1,000,000}(1.00) = 1.0005.$$

Because project A has a higher PVI it is superior. The PVI solution is exactly the same as the NPV solution; that is, we take the project with the highest NPV. The PVI merely helps to highlight the assumption that if the projects really are mutually exclusive, then the extra $999,990 which is not invested in project B must be invested in marketable securities with a PVI of 1.0.

Usually, the projects to be compared are not so exaggerated as the above example; however, it does help to illustrate the meaning of a capital constraint. If a strict budget exists, then the PVI should be used. Otherwise the firm should accept all projects with a positive NPV.

2. Multiperiod Capital Constraints.
Programming Solutions

The capital constraint problem can be extended to consider budget constraints $(C_0, C_1, \ldots, C_t)$ in many future time periods. If we assume that it is possible to undertake fractions of projects, then the problem may be formulated using linear programming. If projects are indivisible, then integer programming may be used. With binding capital constraints it is conceivable that a project with negative NPV may be accepted in the optimal solution if it supplies the funds needed during the later time period to undertake very profitable projects.

A great deal has been written on the topic of constrained capital budgeting.[5] However, because of space limitations, only the simplest model is presented here. Lorie and Savage [1955] posed the two-period problem given in Table 3.6.

Let us assume that cash flows cannot be transferred between time periods, that projects are infinitely divisible, and that the cash budget in period 1 is $50 while in

---

[4] We could also assume any budget whatsoever as long as it is greater than $1,000,000 without changing the results. (Why?)

[5] The interested reader is referred to Lorie and Savage [1955], Weingartner [1963], Baumol and Quandt [1965], Carleton [1969], Bernhard [1969], and Myers [1972] as an excellent set of references.

Table 3.6   Two-period Capital Constraint

Project	Period-1 Outlay	Period-2 Outlay	NPV
1	12	3	14
2	54	7	17
3	6	6	17
4	6	2	15
5	30	35	40
6	6	6	12
7	48	4	14
8	36	3	10
9	18	3	12

period 2 it is $22. The problem is to find the set of projects which maximizes NPV and satisfies the cash constraints. Weingartner [1963] solved the problem by using linear programming. If we designate b_j as the NPV of each project, X_j as the fraction of each project which is accepted, c_{tj} as the cash outlay used by the jth project in the tth time period, and C_t as the cash budget, the linear programming problem is written as

$$\text{MAX} \sum_j b_j X_j, \quad \text{(Primal problem)} \tag{3.7}$$

$$\text{subject to } \sum_j c_{tj} X_j \leq C_t,$$

$$X_j \leq 1.$$

If S_t and q_j are designated as slack variables, the primal problem can be rewritten as

$$\text{MAX} \sum_j b_j X_j, \tag{3.8}$$

$$\text{subject to } \sum_j c_{tj} X_j + S_t = C_t,$$

$$X_j + q_j = 1.$$

The objective is to choose the set of weights, X_j, which maximize the combined NPV of all projects. The constraints require (1) that the set of projects undertaken use less cash than is budgeted and (2) that no more than 100% of any project be undertaken.

Every linear programming problem has a counterpart called the *dual problem* where the primal constraints appear in the dual objective function and the primal decision variables become dual constraints. The dual for this problem can be written as

$$\text{MIN} \sum_t \rho_t C_t + \mu_j \cdot 1, \qquad (\textit{Dual problem}) \qquad (3.9)$$

$$\text{subject to} \sum_t \rho_t c_{tj} + \mu_j - \gamma_j = b_j,$$

$$\rho_t, \mu_j \geq 0.$$

The dual introduces three new variables, ρ_t, μ_j, and γ_j. The last, γ_j, is a slack variable. We can define μ_j by using the notion of complementary slackness. When one of the projects enters into the primal solution (that is, $X_j > 0$), then the corresponding constraint in the dual is binding and therefore $\gamma_j = 0$. Thus the dual constraint can be written as an equality

$$\sum_t \rho_t c_{tj} + \mu_j = b_j,$$

or, solving for μ_j, we have

$$\mu_j = b_j - \sum_t \rho_t c_{tj}. \qquad (3.10)$$

Therefore, μ_j may be thought of as the difference between the NPV of a project's cash flows, b_j, and the imputed value of the outlays needed to undertake the project, $\sum \rho_t c_{tj}$. Conceptually, it is similar to the PVI in the single-period problem because it is a measure of the benefit (NPV) minus the imputed cash cost of a project. Finally, ρ_t may be thought of as the implicit one-period discount rate caused by the cash constraints in the linear programming problem. It is the value of relaxing the cash constraint by one dollar, the shadow price. This can be demonstrated by using (3.10) and noting that for fractionally accepted projects, where the constraint is binding, $\mu_j = 0$. Therefore, (3.10) becomes

$$\sum_t \rho_t c_{tj} = b_j.$$

This says that the NPV of a project, b_j, equals the discounted value of its cash flows. Consequently ρ_t is the one-period discount rate

$$\rho_t = \frac{1}{1 + {}_0 r_{t+1}}. \qquad (3.11)$$

Table 3.7 shows the linear programming problem and solution to the Lorie-Savage problem. Projects 1, 3, 4, and 9 are accepted, and projects 6 and 7 are fractionally accepted into the optimal solution which has an NPV of $70.27. Cash constraints in both time periods are binding since the primal slacks, S_1 and S_2 are zero. The project with the greatest net "benefit" is project 4 with $\mu_4 = 10.45$. Although it has a smaller NPV than several of the other projects, it also uses less cash than the others. Finally, a comparison of the dual variables, ρ_1 and ρ_2, tells us that the value of relaxing the second-period constraint is greater. In other words, providing extra cash in the second period would increase the firm's NPV more than providing

Table 3.7   Linear Programming Model and Solution

Maximize:

$$14x_1 + 17x_2 + 17x_3 + 15x_4 + 40x_5 + 12x_6 + 14x_7 + 10x_8 + 12x_9$$

Subject to:

$$12x_1 + 54x_2 + 6x_3 + 6x_4 + 30x_5 + 6x_6 + 48x_7 + 36x_8 + 18x_9 + s_1 = 50$$
$$3x_1 + 7x_2 + 6x_3 + 2x_4 + 35x_5 + 6x_6 + 4x_7 + 3x_8 + 3x_9 + s_2 = 20$$

$x_1 + q_1 = 1$	$x_4 + q_4 = 1$	$x_7 + q_7 = 1$
$x_2 + q_2 = 1$	$x_5 + q_5 = 1$	$x_8 + q_8 = 1$
$x_3 + q_3 = 1$	$x_6 + q_6 = 1$	$x_9 + q_9 = 1$

Solution	Primal Slack	Dual variable	Dual Slacks
$x_1^* = 1.0$	$q_1^* = 0$	$\mu_1^* = 6.77$	$\gamma_1^* = 0$
$x_2^* = 0$	$q_2^* = 1.0$	$\mu_2^* = 0$	$\gamma_2^* = 3.41$
$x_3^* = 1.0$	$q_3^* = 0$	$\mu_3^* = 5.0$	$\gamma_3^* = 0$
$x_4^* = 1.0$	$q_4^* = 0$	$\mu_4^* = 10.45$	$\gamma_4^* = 0$
$x_5^* = 0$	$q_5^* = 1.0$	$\mu_5^* = 0$	$\gamma_5^* = 29.32$
$x_6^* = 0.970$	$q_6^* = 0.030$	$\mu_6^* = 0$	$\gamma_6^* = 0$
$x_7^* = 0.045$	$q_7^* = 0.955$	$\mu_7^* = 0$	$\gamma_7^* = 0$
$x_8^* = 0$	$q_8^* = 1.0$	$\mu_8^* = 0$	$\gamma_8^* = 0.5$
$x_9^* = 1.0$	$q_9^* = 0$	$\mu_9^* = 3.95$	$\gamma_9^* = 0$

$s_1^* = 0$ —primal slacks— $s_2^* = 0$
$\rho_1^* = 0.136$ —dual variables— $\rho_2^* = 1.864$

Total present value: $70.27

Weingartner, H. M., reprinted from *Mathematical Programming and the Analysis of Capital Budgeting Problems,* Prentice-Hall, Englewood Cliffs, N.J., 1963 (reissued by Kershaw Publishing Co., London, 1974).

extra cash in the first time period. We can also use the values of ρ_t to calculate the one-period implicit interest rates:

$$_1r_2 = \frac{1 - \rho_1}{\rho_1} = 635\%,$$

$$_2r_3 = \frac{1 - \rho_2}{\rho_2} = -46.4\%.$$

Linear programming solutions to capital budgeting have great versatility and have been applied to many types of problems. However, it is difficult to justify the existence of capital constraints in the first place. Also, once uncertainty is introduced as a major consideration, linear programming models fail to adequately handle it. For these and other reasons, linear programming models have become less popular in recent years.

E. CAPITAL BUDGETING PROCEDURES UNDER INFLATION[6]

The United States has experienced persistent inflation since 1966 at levels exceeding the moderate price level changes of previous peacetime periods. What effects does this have on the results of capital budgeting analysis? We can analyze the impacts of inflation by using an illustrative example to clarify the new influences introduced.

Let us begin with the standard capital budgeting case in which inflation is absent. The expression for calculating the NPV of the investment is shown in Eq. 3.12.

$$\text{NPV} = \sum_{t=1}^{N} \frac{\text{NCF}_t}{(1+k)^t} - I_0. \tag{3.12}$$

The symbols used have the following meanings and values:

NPV = net present value of the project,

NCF_t = net cash flows per year from the project = \$26,500,

k = cost of capital applicable to the project = 9%,

N = number of years the net cash flows are received = 5,

I_0 = required investment outlay for the project = \$100,000,

τ_c = applicable tax rate of 50%.

With the data provided, we can utilize (3.12) as follows:

$$\text{NPV}_0 = \sum_{t=1}^{N} \frac{\$26,500}{(1.09)^t} - \$100,000$$

$$= 26,500(3.8896) - 100,000$$

$$= 103,074 - 100,000$$

$$= \$3,074.$$

We find that the project has an expected NPV of \$3,074 and under the simple conditions assumed, we would accept the project. Now let us consider the effects of inflation. Suppose that inflation at an annual rate of 6% will take place during the five years of the project. Note that we assume that the future inflation rate is known with certainty.

Since investment and security returns are based on expected future returns, the anticipated inflation rate will be reflected in the required rate of return on the project or the applicable cost of capital for the project. This relationship has long been recognized in financial economics and is known as the *Fisher effect*. In formal terms we have:

$$(1 + k_j)(1 + \eta) = (1 + K_j), \tag{3.13}$$

---

[6] For articles on this subject see Van Horne [1971] and Cooley, Roenfeldt, and Chew [1975]; also see their exchange with Findlay and Frankle [1976].

where K_j is the required rate of return in nominal terms and η is the anticipated annual inflation rate over the life of the project. For our example, Eq. (3.13) would be:

$$(1 + .09)(1 + .06) = (1 + .09 + .06 + .0054).$$

If the cross-product term, .0054, is included in the addition, we would have .1554 as the required rate of return in nominal terms. However, since the cross-product term is generally small and since both k_j, the required rate of return in real terms, and the anticipated inflation rate are estimates, it is customary to make a simple addition of the real rate and the inflation rate. The required nominal rate of return that would be used in the calculation would therefore be 15%. Note, then, that the applicable discount rate reflects the summation of the 6% anticipated inflation rate to the 9% rate of return in real terms to obtain the total of 15%.

It is at this point that some biases in capital budgeting under inflationary conditions may be introduced. The market data utilized in the estimated current capital costs will include a premium for anticipated inflation. But while the market remembers to include an adjustment for inflation in the capitalization factor, the cash-flow estimates used by the firm in the capital budgeting analysis may fail to include an element to reflect future inflation. Given that the cost of capital (observed using market rates of return) already includes expected inflation, the decision-maker can correct for inflation either by (a) adding an estimate of inflation to the cash flows in the numerator or (b) expressing the numerator without including an adjustment for inflation and subtracting an inflationary factor from the market rate in the denominator.

It is more natural to utilize market data and to explicitly incorporate estimates of the anticipated inflation rate in the cash flows in the numerator. But either way, the difficult problem is how to estimate the expected future inflation rate. Some ideas on how to do this will be discussed in the next section of this chapter.

Without an adjustment for inflation in the cash flows the analysis would appear as follows for NPV_1:

$$NPV_1 = \sum_{t=1}^{N} \frac{\$26,500}{(1.09)^t (1.06)^t} - \$100,000 = \sum_{t=1}^{N} \frac{\$26,500}{(1.15)^t} - \$100,000$$

$$= 26,500(3.3522) - 100,000$$

$$= 88,833 - 100,000 = -\$11,167.$$

It now appears that the project will have a negative NPV over $11,000. With a negative NPV of substantial magnitude, the project would be rejected. However, a sound analysis requires that the anticipated inflation rate also be taken into account in the cash flow estimates. Initially, for simplicity, let us assume that the same inflation rate of 6% is applicable to the net cash flows. We take this step in setting forth the expression for NPV_2 as follows:

$$NPV_2 = \sum_{t=1}^{N} \frac{\$26,500(1.06)^t}{(1.09)^t(1.06)^t} - 100,000 = \sum_{t=1}^{N} \frac{\$26,500}{(1.09)^t} - \$100,000.$$

Since inflation factors are now in both the numerator and the denominator and are the same, they can be canceled. The result for the calculation of NPV_2 will therefore be the same as for NPV_0, which was a positive $3,074. Thus when anticipated inflation is properly reflected in both the cash flow estimates in the numerator and the required rate of return from market data in the denominator, the resulting NPV calculation will be in both real and nominal terms. This was noted by Findlay [1976] as follows: "Any properly measured, market-determined wealth concept is, simultaneously, *both nominal and real.* NPV, or any other wealth measure, gives the amount for which one can 'cash out' now (nominal) and also the amount of today's goods that can be consumed at today's prices (real)." Thus if inflation is reflected in both the cash flow estimates and in the required rate of return, the resulting NPV estimate will be free of inflation bias.

To this point we have purposely kept the analysis simple to focus on the basic principles, since controversy has erupted over the issues involved. We may expect that the effect of the anticipated inflation on the required rate of return will differ from that on the cash flow estimates. Indeed, the components of the net cash flows, the cash outflows and the cash inflows, may themselves be influenced to different degrees by the anticipated inflation. These complications will not, however, change the basic method of analysis, only the specifics of the calculations. The nature of the more complex case is illustrated by Eq. (3.14):

$$NPV_0 = \sum_{t=1}^{N} \frac{[(inflows)_t(1+\eta_i)^t - (outflows)_t(1+\eta_0)^t](1-\tau_c) + (dep.)_t(\tau_c)}{(1+K)^t} - I_0.$$

(3.14)

The cash inflows may be subject to a rate of inflation η_i that is different from the rate of inflation in the cash outflows η_0. Both may differ from the anticipated rate of inflation reflected in the required rate of return in the denominator. Also, depreciation (dep.) may be constant in nominal dollars, but the value of the depreciation tax shield will fall in real terms. Some illustrative data will demonstrate the application of (3.14).

Table 3.8 sets forth data for expected cash flows without inflation effects. The pattern is a constant $26,500 per year for five years as in the original example. In

Table 3.8   Expected Net Cash Flows Without Inflation Effects

	Year 1	Year 2	Year 3	Year 4	Year 5
Expected cash inflows	$53,000	$53,000	$53,000	$53,000	$53,000
Expected cash outflows	20,000	20,000	20,000	20,000	20,000
Earnings before taxes	$33,000	$33,000	$33,000	$33,000	$33,000
Multiplied by $(1-\tau_c)$	16,500	16,500	16,500	16,500	16,500
Earnings after taxes	$16,500	$16,500	$16,500	$16,500	$16,500
Depreciation tax shelter	10,000	10,000	10,000	10,000	10,000
Expected net cash flows	$26,500	$26,500	$26,500	$26,500	$26,500

Table 3.9   Expected Net Cash Flows Including Inflation Effects

	1	2	3	4	5
Expected cash inflows ($\eta_i = 6\%$)	$56,180	$59,551	$63,124	$66,912	$70,927
Expected cash outflows ($\eta_o = 7\%$)	21,400	22,898	24,501	26,216	28,051
Earnings before taxes	$34,780	$36,653	$38,623	$40,696	$42,876
Multiplied by ($1 - \tau_c$)	17,390	18,327	19,312	20,348	21,438
Earnings after taxes	$17,390	$18,327	$19,312	$20,348	$21,438
Depreciation tax shelter	10,000	10,000	10,000	10,000	10,000
Expected net cash flows	$27,390	$28,327	$29,312	$30,348	$31,438

Table 3.9 the estimates of expected net cash flows include inflation effects. The cash inflows are subject to a 6% inflation rate while the cash outflows are subject to a 7% inflation rate. The resulting expected net cash flows are shown in the bottom line of the table. The required rate of return of 15% is assumed to reflect a 6% inflation rate as before.

The calculation of the expected NPV ($\overline{NPV}_3$) is shown in Table 3.10. Taking all the inflation influences into account, we find that $\overline{NPV}_3$ is a negative $2,507. The project would be rejected. In this example, the inflationary forces on the cash outflows were greater than on the cash inflows. Some have suggested that this influence has been sufficiently widespread and that it accounts for the sluggish rate of capital investment in the United States since the early 1970's.

The situation we illustrated initially was that failure to take inflation into account in the expected cash flows resulted in an erroneous capital budgeting analysis. A project was accepted which, when measured correctly, produced a return below the required rate of return. The allocation of capital would be unsound if the bias in the analysis due to inflation had not been taken into account. In our second and more complex example, inflation caused the cash outflows to grow at a higher rate than the cash inflows. As a consequence, the expected NPV of the project was negative. Making the inflation adjustment does not always necessarily result in a positive NPV

Table 3.10   Calculation of $\overline{NPV}_3$

Year	Cash Flow (1)	Discount Factor 15% (2)	PV (1 × 2)
1	$27,390	.8696	$23,818
2	28,327	.7561	21,418
3	29,312	.6575	19,273
4	30,348	.5718	17,353
5	31,438	.4972	15,631
			$\overline{NPV}_3 = \$97,493 - \$100,000 = -\$2,507$

for the project—it simply results in a more accurate estimate of the net benefits from the project, positive or negative.

F. THE TERM STRUCTURE OF INTEREST RATES

Throughout Chapters 2 and 3 there has been the implicit assumption that interest rates are nonstochastic and constant in a multiperiod setting. This has been a convenient but misleading assumption. Interest rates are not constant through time. The yield on a particular financial instrument (a bond, for example) depends on the length of time to maturity. The yield also depends on the risk of the security, but we shall continue to assume, for the time being, that there is no risk.

Figure 3.2 shows the term structure of interest rates for United States Treasury securities at two points in time, March 1976, and August 1981. Each point on the graph gives the yield to maturity, $_0R_T$, on a bond which is bought today (at time zero) and which matures T years hence. The bond is assumed to be default free. Default free means that there is no uncertainty about the nominal payments promised by the bond. There are, however, other kinds of risk. For example, unexpected changes in future interest rates will induce risk because the market value of the bond will change when interest rate expectations do.

1. The Yield to Maturity

The yield to maturity, $_0R_T$, is computed in exactly the same way one would solve for the internal rate of return on a security. Consider the following hypothetical example: A bond promises to pay a 15% coupon at the end of each year for three years, then pay a face value of $1000. We observe the current market price, B_0, of

Figure 3.2
The yield to maturity on U.S. Treasury securities.

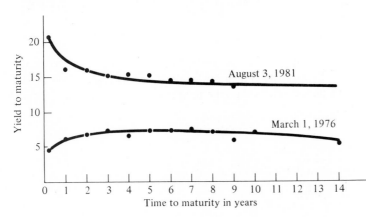

the bond to be $977.54. The yield to maturity on the bond may be computed by solving for $_0R_T$ in the following present value formula:

$$B_0 = \sum_{t=1}^{T} \frac{\text{coupon}_t}{(1 + {_0R_T})^t} + \frac{\text{face value}}{(1 + {_0R_T})^T}, \tag{3.15}$$

$$977.54 = \sum_{t=1}^{T} \frac{150}{(1 + {_0R_T})^t} + \frac{1000}{(1 + {_0R_T})^T}.$$

Solving iteratively, we find that the yield to maturity, $_0R_T$, is 16%.

The term structure shows the yield to maturity for all bonds of all maturities. In March of 1976 the term structure was upward sloping. Long-term bonds paid higher yields than short-term bonds. In August of 1981 the opposite pattern existed. The term structure was downward sloping. One thing that both term structure patterns have in common is that the interest rate is not constant. The yield on securities clearly depends on when they mature.

The yield to maturity on a bond, as calculated in the hypothetical example used to illustrate Eq. 3.15, is really nothing more than a geometric average of the one-period forward rates. This brings us to the first of three theories which have been put forth to explain the term structure. The *unbiased expectations hypothesis* was first postulated by Irving Fisher [1896] then further developed by Friedrich Lutz [1940].

2. Forward Rates, Future Rates, and Unbiased Expectations

The term structure is said to be unbiased if the expected *future interest rates* are equivalent to the *forward rates* computed from observed bond prices. An example will help to clarify the meaning of forward rates and expected future rates.[7] Suppose we have three bonds, each paying $150 per year (at the end of each year) and a face value of $1000 at maturity. They mature one, two, and three years hence and are observed to have current market prices of $950.41, $953.03, and $977.54 respectively. The observed yield to maturity, $_0R_T$, is assumed to be the product of the one-period forward rates, $_tf_{t+1}$, as shown in Eq. 3.16.

$$[(1 + {_0R_T})]^T = (1 + {_0R_1})(1 + {_1f_2}) \cdots (1 + {_{T-1}f_T}). \tag{3.16}$$

The forward rate, $_1f_2$, is the one-period rate computed for a bond bought at the end of the first period and held to the end of the second period. Hence, it is a one-period rate for the second period. Note that the forward rate for the first year can be observed directly. It is $_0R_1$.

In order to compute the implied forward rates, one would first compute the

---

[7] In order to keep things simple, we assume that forward rates are one-period rates and that all prices and yields are observed at the present time. One could also discuss N-period forward rates observed at any time, t. For an excellent discussion of the term structure, the reader is referred to *Financial Rates and Flows* by James C. Van Horne [1978].

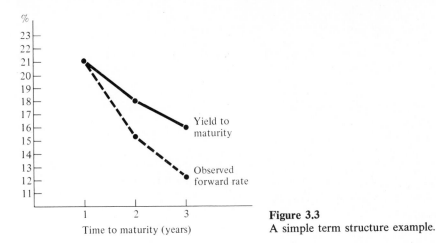

Figure 3.3
A simple term structure example.

yields to maturity using Eq. 3.15.[8] For the three bonds in our example, the yields to maturity are 21%, 18%, and 16% respectively. The term structure for this example is shown in Fig. 3.3. Suppose we want to know the forward rate implied for the third time period. It can be computed by taking the ratio of the (geometric product of the) yields to maturity on the three- and two-period bonds as shown below.

$$1 + {}_2f_3 = \frac{(1 + {}_0R_3)^3}{(1 + {}_0R_2)^2},$$

$$1 + {}_2f_3 = \frac{(1 + {}_0R_1)(1 + {}_1f_2)(1 + {}_2f_3)}{(1 + {}_0R_1)(1 + {}_1f_2)},$$

$$1 + {}_2f_3 = \frac{(1.16)^3}{(1.18)^2} = \frac{1.560895}{1.3924} = 1.121,$$

$${}_2f_3 = 12.10\%.$$

Similarly, one can compute the second-period forward rate as 15.07%, and of course the one-period rate is observed directly to be 21%. The pattern of forward rates in this example would be consistent with expectations that future inflation will be less than current inflation.

By itself, the forward rate is merely an algebraic computation from observed bond data. The unbiased expectations theory attempts to explain observed forward rates by saying that expected future rates, ${}_tr_{t+1}$, will on average, be equal to the implied forward rates if (1) investors' expectations of future one-period rates are unbiased and (2) if bonds of different maturity are perfect substitutes for each other.

---

[8] Note that like the internal rate of return, the yield to maturity implicitly assumes that funds are reinvested at the implied yield. This contrasts with the assumption of discounting at the market-determined rate to get a net present value.

Table 3.11   An Investor's Expectations

Time to Maturity	Bond Price	Yield	Observed Forward Rate	Investor's Forward Rate
1 year	$950	21%	21.0%	21.0%
2 years	953	18	15.1	17.0
3 years	978	16	12.1	12.1

Among other things this second condition requires that the risk and transactions costs for a strategy of rolling over a one-period bond three times is the same as holding a three-period bond. If the two strategies are in fact perfect substitutes, then investors will keep the rates in line with expectations by forming arbitrage positions whenever interest rates (and bond prices) are "out of line."

To show how arbitrage might work, suppose that we believe that the pattern of future rates in our example is out of line. Table 3.11 shows the actual prices and rates along with our expectations. We believe that the implied forward rate in the second year is too low, that it should be 17% instead of 15.1%. What should we do? The logical action would be to sell short the two-year bonds for $953.03. If we are right, interest rates in the second year will be higher than the market expects and we will make a capital gain. If enough people believe the observed forward rate is too low, the decreased demand for two-year bonds will lower their prices until the implied forward rate rises to 17%. Then interest rates will be in line with revised expectations.

If there were no transactions costs and if there were no uncertainty, then there is every reason to believe that the unbiased expectations theory of the term structure would hold. Implied forward rates would be exact forecasts of expected future rates.

3. Liquidity Premia in the Term Structure

Future interest rates become more uncertain the further into the future one tries to predict. Attempts to deal with this fact have lead to theories of *liquidity premia* in the term structure of interest rates.[9] Hicks argues that liquidity premia exist because a given change in interest rates will have a greater effect on the price of long-term bonds than on short-term bonds. Hence there is greater risk of loss (and, one should add, a greater probability of gain) with long-term bonds.[10] Consequently, risk averse investors will require a higher yield in order to hold longer-term bonds. This extra yield is called a *liquidity premium.*

In order to illustrate the sensitivity of bond prices to changes in the interest rate, consider two bonds. They both pay $100 per year in coupons and have a $1000

---

[9] For example see Hicks [1946], Keynes [1936], Kessel [1965], Hirshleifer [1972], and Woodward [1979].

[10] A more lengthy discussion of bond risk, including default risk and duration, can be found in the Appendix to Chapter 12.

face value, but one has five years to maturity and the other has ten. If current interest rates are 10% the present value of the five-year bond B_5, is

$$B_5 = \sum_{t=1}^{5} \frac{\$120}{(1+.10)^t} + \frac{\$1000}{(1+.10)^5} = \$1075.82,$$

and the present value of the ten-year bond is

$$B_{10} = \sum_{t=1}^{10} \frac{\$120}{(1+.10)^t} + \frac{\$1000}{(1+.10)^{10}} = \$1122.89.$$

What happens to the market prices of the bonds if the interest rate increases from 10% to 15%, a 50% increase? By similar calculations, we find that

$$B_5 = \$899.44 \quad \text{and} \quad B_{10} = \$849.44.$$

The market value of the 5-year bond has decreased 16.4% while the 10-year bond has fallen by 24.4%. Clearly, the 10-year bond is more sensitive to the increase in interest rates. This is the risk which Hicks had in mind when he described the liquidity premium.

Figure 3.4 shows how the liquidity premium is posited to change with the time to maturity on bonds. Note that the liquidity premium increases for bonds of longer maturity, but that it increases at a decreasing rate. Figure 3.5 shows how the liquidity premium is added to unbiased expectations in order to arrive at the observed term structure.

4. The Market Segmentation Hypothesis

A third theory of the term structure, attributable to Culbertson [1957], Walker [1954] and Modigliani and Sutch [1966], is called the *market segmentation hypothesis.* It is argued that there is relatively little substitution between assets of different maturity because investors have preferred "habitats." For example, a firm which borrows to undertake an investment program will try to tailor its debt payments to the expected cash flows from the project. Capital intensive firms which construct long-term plant and equipment will prefer to issue long-term debt rather than rolling over short-term debt. Insurance companies with long-term liabilities (their life insurance policies)

% Liquidity premium

Time to maturity

Figure 3.4
The liquidity premium.

Figure 3.5   The liquidity premium added to a decreasing term structure (a) and to an increasing term structure (b).

prefer to lend long-term. Thus the market segmentation hypothesis argues that suppliers and users of funds have preferred habitats. Interest rates for a given maturity are explained mainly by the supply and demand for funds of that specific maturity.

While the market segmentation hypothesis can explain why implied forward and expected future rates may differ, the direction and magnitudes are not systematic. Recall that the Hicksian liquidity premium causes forward and future rates to differ systematically depending on the maturity of the bonds.

5. Implications for Capital Budgeting

Regardless of which theory of the term structure is correct, the fact that one-year forward rates are not constant is relevant for the capital budgeting decision. The cash flows estimated for each year should be discounted to the present using the information revealed in the term structure of interest rates. Let's use the hypothetical term structure example which was given earlier in the chapter in order to illustrate the relationship between the term structure and capital budgeting. Table 3.12 gives the yields to maturity, the implied forward rates, and cash flows for two projects. It is not uncommon for corporate treasurers to compute the NPV of these projects by discounting at the cost of capital for "three-year money," namely 16%. After

Table 3.12   The Term Structure and Capital Budgeting

Year	Yield to Maturity	Forward Rate	CF for A	CF for B	Discount Factor
0	—	—	$−100	$−100	1.0000
1	21%	21.00%	62	48	.8265
2	18	15.07	50	52	.7182
3	16	12.10	28	44	.6407

all, both projects have a three-year life. When the cash flows are discounted at 16%, project A has a NPV of $8.55 while B has a lower NPV of $8.21. Project A appears to be superior. Unfortunately, this procedure does not account for the fact that the real opportunity cost of funds is 21% for cash flows received in the first year, 15.07% for second-year cash flows, and 12.1% for third-year cash flows. The correct discount rate for cash flows in each year is the yield to maturity for that year. Note that this is also equal to the product of the implied forward rates from year 1 up to the year of the cash flows. For example, the three-year discount factor is

$$(1.16)^{-3} = [(1.21)(1.1507)(1.1210)]^{-1} = .6407.$$

The correct discount factors are given in the last column of Table 3.12. When the cash flows are appropriately discounted, the NPV's of projects A and B are $5.08 and $5.21 respectively. Now project B is preferred over A.

When the term structure is downward sloping, as in our simple example, a firm which uses the long-term rate (the three-year rate) to discount all cash flows will tend to overestimate the NPV's of projects. Of course, when the term structure is upward sloping, the opposite bias exists. In addition, as the example has shown, it is possible for the wrong project to be selected if the information given in the term structure is ignored.

It has been suggested that the term structure provides the best estimate of expected inflation.[11] If so, a downward-sloping term structure implies that investors expect near-term inflation to be higher than long-term. An upward-sloping term structure (removing the liquidity premium) implies the opposite. If the firm's capital budgeting procedure discounts nominal cash flows (cum inflation) at market rates, then the cash flow estimates should reflect inflationary estimates on a year-by-year basis.

SUMMARY AND CONCLUSIONS

Perhaps the single most important decision faced by management is the selection of investment projects which maximize the present value of shareholders' wealth. Therefore, it is hardly surprising that much of the literature in finance focuses on the capital budgeting problem. Both this chapter and its predecessor have emphasized capital budgeting techniques. However, the story is far from complete. Throughout we have maintained the assumption that future cash flows are known with certainty and can be estimated without error. In addition, we assumed that the opportunity cost of capital (the discount rate) was given.

Chapters 4 through 7 introduce the reader to a world where decisions must be made under the assumption of uncertainty. It is not until Chapter 11 that we return, for a second time, to the important capital budgeting decision. However, at that time we will be able to discuss the problem of project selection under uncertainty. Fortunately, the inclusion of uncertainty does not change the material presented in

---

[11] For empirical evidence consistent with this point of view see Fama [1975].

Chapters 2 and 3. However, some important extensions to project selection techniques will be introduced. Finally, the logical cycle is completed in Chapter 12, when we discuss the determination of the appropriate opportunity cost of capital in a world of uncertainty. At that time all the necessary elements will have been covered under the assumption of uncertainty. They include: the correct definition of cash flows for capital budgeting purposes; determination of the appropriate cost of capital; and a proof of why the NPV criterion is consistent with shareholder wealth maximization.

PROBLEM SET

3.1 The Johnson Company is considering the following mutually exclusive projects:

	Project J	Project K	Project L	Project M
Investment	$48,000	$60,000	$60,000	$36,000
CF	20,000	12,000	16,000	10,000
N	5	15	10	15

The cost of capital used by the Johnson Company is 16%.

a) How should the fact that the projects have differences in scale be taken into consideration?

b) Rank the projects, assuming that they can be repeated with constant scale replication, and that the differences in scale are invested at the cost of capital.

3.2 If the opportunity cost of capital is 10%, which of the following three projects has the highest PVI? Which will increase shareholders' wealth the most?

Year	Project A	Project B	Project C
0	−1,000	−2,000	−3,000
1	1,000	1,000	4,000
2	1,000	1,000	
3		1,000	

3.3 The Hansen Company is considering four mutually exclusive projects as follows:

	Project A	Project B	Project C	Project D
Investment	$40,000	$25,000	$40,000	$30,000
CF	12,000	8,000	8,000	6,500
N	5	5	10	10
k	12%	12%	12%	12%

a) Compute the NPV and IRR of each project, and rank the investments from best to worst under each method. What factors are responsible for the differences in rankings between the two approaches?

b) Compute the PVI for each project and rank the alternatives. What are the implicit assumptions of the PVI method with respect to scale and duration of projects? When is it appropriate to use the PVI method?

c) If the projects are mutually exclusive, which should be accepted if they are independent? Why?

3.4 The Dandy Candy Company is considering two mutually exclusive projects. They are the only projects available. The risk-free rate is 5%. The cash flows from the projects are known with certainty and are given below.

Year	Project 1	Project 2
0	−10,000	−1,000
1	4,000	2,700
2	4,000	2,700
3	4,000	
4	4,000	

a) Which project has the higher net present value?

b) If the firm has no capital constraints, which project would you select?

c) If the firm has a capital constraint of $12,000, which project would you select? Why?

3.5 *Optimal duration.* Plaid Scotch Ltd. has just kegged its latest Scotch whiskey at a cost of $50,000. The whiskey's value will increase over the years according to the following formula:

$$V_t = \$100,000 \ln t.$$

What is the optimal time of bottling for the Scotch if the firm's cost of capital is 15% compounded continuously?

3.6 You are given the following information: the Dorkin Company has made an investment of $40,000 which is expected to yield benefits over a five-year period. Annual cash inflows of $90,000 and annual cash outflows of $75,000 are expected, excluding taxes and the depreciation tax shelter. The tax rate is 40% and the cost of capital is 8%. Dorkin Company uses straight-line depreciation.

a) Compute the NPV of the investment.

b) On investigation, you discover that no adjustments have been made for inflation or price-level changes. The data for the first year are correct but after that inflows are expected to increase at 4% per year, outflows at 6% per year, and the annual rate of inflation is expected to be about 6%. Reevaluate the NPV of the project in light of this information.

3.7 The Baldwin Company is considering investing in a machine that produces bowling balls. The cost of the machine is $100,000. Production by year during the five-year life of the machine is expected to be as follows: 5,000 units, 8,000 units, 12,000 units, 10,000 units, and 6,000 units.

The interest in bowling is declining, and hence management believes that the price of bowling balls will increase at only 2% per year, compared to the general rate of inflation of 5%. The price of bowling balls in the first year will be $20.

On the other hand, plastic used to produce bowling balls is rapidly becoming more expensive. Because of this, production cash outflows are expected to grow at 10% per year. First-year production cost will be $10 per unit.

Depreciation of the machine will be straight-line for five years, after which time the salvage value will be zero. The company's tax rate is 40% and its cost of capital is 15% based on the existing rate of inflation. Should the project be undertaken?

3.8 The yields to maturity on five bonds are given below:

Years to Maturity	Yield
1	12.0%
2	14.0
3	15.0
4	15.5
5	15.7

a) What is the implied forward rate of interest for the third year?

b) What rate of interest would you receive if you bought a bond at the beginning of the second year and sold it at the beginning of the fourth year?

REFERENCES

Baumol, W. S., and R. E. Quandt, "Investment and Discount Rates Under Capital Rationing," *The Economic Journal,* June 1965.

Bernhard, R. H., "Mathematical Programming Models for Capital Budgeting—A Survey, Generalization and Critique," *Journal of Financial and Quantitative Analysis,* June 1969, 111–158.

Bierman, H., Jr., and S. Smidt, *The Capital Budgeting Decision,* 4th ed., Macmillan, New York, 1975.

Carleton, W., "Linear Programming and Capital Budgeting Models: A New Interpretation," *Journal of Finance,* December 1969, 825–833.

Cooley, P. L., R. L. Roenfeldt, and I. K. Chew, "Capital Budgeting Procedures Under Inflation," *Financial Management,* Winter 1975, 18–27.

Cox, J. C., J. Ingersoll Jr., and S. A. Ross, "A Theory of the Term Structure of Interest Rates," unpublished working paper, Stanford University, 1980.

Culbertson, J. M., "The Term Structure of Interest Rates," *Quarterly Journal of Economics,* November 1957, 489–504.

Fama, E. F., "Short-term Interest Rates as Predictors of Inflation," *American Economic Review,* June 1975, 269–282.

_____, and G. W. Schwert, "Asset Returns and Inflation," *Journal of Financial Economics,* November 1977, 113–146.

Findlay, M. C., and A. W. Frankle, "Capital Budgeting Procedures under Inflation: Cooley, Roenfeldt and Chew vs. Findlay and Frankle," *Financial Management,* Autumn 1976, 83–90.

Fisher, I., "Appreciation and Interest," *Publications of the American Economic Association,* August 1896, 23–29, 91–92.

Hicks, J. R., *Value and Capital,* 2nd edition, Oxford University Press, London, 1946.

Hirshleifer, J., *Investment, Interest and Capital,* Prentice-Hall, Englewood Cliffs, N.J., 1970.

_____, "Liquidity, Uncertainty, and the Accumulation of Information," in Carter and Ford, eds., *Essays in Honor of G. L. S. Shackle,* Basil Blackwell, Oxford, 1972.

Kessel, R. A., *The Cyclical Behavior of the Term Structure of Interest Rates,* National Bureau of Economic Research, New York, 1965.

Keynes, J. M., *The General Theory of Employment, Interest and Money,* Harcourt, Brace and World Inc., 1936.

Klammer, T., "Empirical Evidence of the Adoption of Sophisticated Capital Budgeting Techniques," *The Journal of Business,* July 1972, 387–397.

Lorie, J. H., and L. J. Savage, "Three Problems in Capital Rationing," *Journal of Business,* October 1955, 229–239.

Lutz, F. A., "The Structure of Interest Rates," *Quarterly Journal of Economics,* November 1940, 36–63.

Malkiel, B. G., "Expectations, Bond Prices, and the Term Structure of Interest Rates," *Quarterly Journal of Economics,* May 1962, 197–218.

McCulloch, J. H., "An Estimate of the Liquidity Premium," *Journal of Political Economy,* January–February 1975, 95–119.

Meiselman, D., *The Term Structure of Interest Rates,* Princeton University Press, Princeton, N.J., 1966.

Modigliani, F., and R. Sutch, "Innovation and Interest Rate Policy," *American Economic Review,* May 1966, 178–197.

Myers, S. C., "A Note on Linear Programming and Capital Budgeting," *Journal of Finance,* March 1972, 89–92.

Nelson, C., *The Term Structure of Interest Rates,* Basic Books, New York, 1972.

Roll, R., *The Behavior of Interest Rates: An Application of the Efficient Market Model to U.S. Treasury Bills,* Basic Books, New York, 1970.

Sargent, T., "Rational Expectations and the Term Structure of Interest Rates," *Journal of Money, Credit and Banking,* February 1972, 74–97.

Schall, L., G. Sundem, and W. Geijsbeek, Jr., "Survey and Analysis of Capital Budgeting References," *Journal of Finance,* March 1978, 281–287.

Van Horne, J. C., "A Note on Biases on Capital Budgeting Introduced by Inflation," *Journal of Financial and Quantitative Analysis,* January 1971, 653–658.

_____, *Financial Markets and Flows,* Prentice Hall, Englewood Cliffs, N.J., 1978.

Walker, C. E., "Federal Reserve Policy and the Structure of Interest Rates on Government Securities," *Quarterly Journal of Economics,* February 1954, 22–23.

Weingartner, H. M., *Mathematical Programming and the Analysis of Capital Budgeting Problems,* Prentice-Hall, Englewood Cliffs, N.J., 1963.

————, "Capital Rationing: *N* Authors in Search of a Plot," *The Journal of Finance,* December 1977, 1403–1432.

Wood, J. H., "Expectations, Error and the Term Structure of Interest Rates," *Journal of Political Economy,* April 1963, 160–171.

Woodward, S., "The Liquidity Premium," (working paper, The University of California at Santa Barbara, 1979).

The Theory of Choice: Utility Theory Given Uncertainty

We wish to find the mathematically complete principles which define "rational behavior" for the participants in a social economy, and derive from them the general characteristics of that behavior.

J. VON NEUMANN AND O. MORGENSTERN,
THEORY OF GAMES AND ECONOMIC BEHAVIOR,
PRINCETON UNIV. PRESS, PRINCETON, 1947,
P. 31

Economics is the study of how people and societies choose to allocate scarce resources and distribute wealth among one another and over time. Therefore, one must understand the objects of choice and the method of choice. The following two chapters (Chapters 5 and 6) are devoted to the objects of choice faced by an investor. Here, we focus on the theory of how people make choices when faced with uncertainty. Later on, once the theory of choice and the objects of choice are understood, we shall combine the two in order to produce a theory of optimal decision making under uncertainty. In particular, we shall study the allocation of resources in an economic system where prices provide a system of signals for optimal allocation. There are, however, other means of allocation. Instead

77

Figure 4.1
Indifference curves for various types of choices: (a) Choice between consumption
goods under certainty; (b) choice between consumption and investment under
certainty; (c) choice between risk and return.

of using prices, we might allow an individual or committee to make all the allocation
decisions, or we might program allocational rules into an algorithm run by machine.

We shall begin with a discussion of the axioms of behavior used by economists.
However, before rushing into them, we must recognize that there are other theories
of behavior. Social sciences such as anthropology, psychology, political science, socio-
biology, and sociology also provide great insight into the theory of choice. And very
early in this chapter we shall be forced to recognize that individuals have different
tastes for the time preference of consumption and different degrees of risk aversion.
Economic theory recognizes these differences but has little to say about why they
exist or what causes them.[1] The other social sciences study these problems. However,
as we shall see, there is much one can say about the theory of choice under uncertainty
without, for example, understanding why a 70-year-old person is more or less risk
averse than the same person at age 20, or why some people prefer meat while others
prefer vegetables.

The theory of investor choice is only one corner of what has come to be known
as utility theory. Most students are already familiar with the microeconomic price
theory treatment of choices among various bundles of perishable commodities such
as apples and oranges at an instant in time. The indifference curves which result
are shown in Fig. 4.1(a). Another type of choice available to individuals is whether
to consume now or to save (invest) and consume more at a later date. This is the
utility theory of choices over time which is fundamental for understanding interest
rates. This type of one-period consumption/investment decision was discussed in
Chapter 1 and is illustrated in Fig. 4.1(b). Our main concern here is the choice
between timeless risky alternatives which we call the theory of investor choice. The
theory begins with nothing more than five assumptions about the behavior of individuals when confronted with the task of ranking risky alternatives and the assumption

---

[1] An interesting exception is an article by Rubin and Paul [1979] which suggests a theory of why people
exhibit different attitudes toward risk at different stages in their lives.

of nonsatiation (i.e., greed). The theory ends by parameterizing the objects of choice as the mean and variance of return and by mapping trade-offs between them which provide equal utility to investors. These mappings are indifference curves for timeless (or one-period) choices under uncertainty. They are shown in Fig. 4.1(c), and are used extensively in Chapters 6 and 7.

A. FIVE AXIOMS OF CHOICE UNDER UNCERTAINTY

In order to develop a theory of rational decision making in the face of uncertainty, it is necessary to make some very precise assumptions about an individual's behavior. Known as the axioms of cardinal utility, these assumptions provide the minimum set of necessary conditions for consistent and rational behavior. Once they are established, all the remaining theory must follow.[2]

Axiom 1   Comparability (sometimes called completeness).   For the entire set, S, of uncertain alternatives, an individual can say either that outcome x is preferred to outcome y (we write this $x \succ y$) or y is preferred to x ($y \succ x$) or the individual is indifferent as to x and y ($x \sim y$).[3]

Axiom 2   Transitivity (sometimes called consistency).   If an individual prefers x to y and y to z, then x is preferred to z. (If $x \succ y$ and $y \succ z$, then $x \succ z$.) If an individual is indifferent as to x and y and is also indifferent as to y and z, then he is indifferent as to x and z. (If $x \sim y$ and $y \sim z$, then $x \sim z$.)

Axiom 3   Strong independence.   Suppose we construct a gamble where an individual has a probability α of receiving outcome x and a probability $(1 - \alpha)$ of receiving outcome z. We shall write this gamble as $G(x, z{:}\alpha)$. Strong independence says that if the individual is indifferent as to x and y, then he will also be indifferent as to a first gamble, set up between x with probability α and a mutually exclusive outcome z, and a second gamble, set up between y with probability α and the same mutually exclusive outcome, z.

$$\text{If } x \sim y, \text{ then } G(x, z{:}\alpha) \sim G(y, z{:}\alpha).$$

Axiom 4   Measurability.   If outcome y is preferred less than x but more than z, then there is a *unique* α (a probability) such that the individual will be indifferent between y and a gamble between x with probability α and z with probability $1 - \alpha$.[4]

If $x \succ y \geq z$ or $x \geq y \succ z$ then there exists a unique α, such that $y \sim G(x, z{:}\alpha)$.

---

[2] The notation and much of the conceptual outline follow the development found in Fama and Miller [1972].

[3] The symbol used to indicate preference ($\succ$) is not a mathematical inequality. It can rank only preferences. For example, an individual may prefer one Picasso to two Rembrandts or vice versa.

[4] The reason for bounding y on only one side or the other is to eliminate the possibility of $x \sim y \sim z$, in which case any α would satisfy the indifference condition required by the gamble.

Axiom 5   Ranking.   If alternatives y and u both lie somewhere between x and z and we can establish gambles such that an individual is indifferent between y and a gamble between x (with probability α_1) and z, while he is also indifferent between u and a second gamble, this time between x (with probability α_2) and z, then if α_1 is greater than α_2, y is preferred to u.

If $x \succeq y \succeq z$ and $x \succeq u \succeq z$, then if $y \sim G(x, z:\alpha_1)$ and $u \sim G(x, z:\alpha_2)$, it follows that if $\alpha_1 > \alpha_2$, then $y \succ u$, or if $\alpha_1 = \alpha_2$, then $y \sim u$.

These are known as the axioms of cardinal utility. They boil down to the following assumptions about behavior. First, all individuals are assumed to always make completely rational decisions. A statement that "I like Chevrolets more than Fords and Fords more than Toyotas, but Toyotas more than Chevrolets" is not rational. Second, people are assumed to be able to make these rational choices among thousands of alternatives—not a very simple task.

The axiom of strong independence is usually the hardest to accept. In order to illustrate it, consider the following example. Let outcome x be winning a left shoe, let y be a right shoe, and let z also be a right shoe. Imagine two gambles. The first is a fifty-fifty chance of winning x or z, i.e., a left shoe or a right shoe. The second gamble is a fifty-fifty chance of winning y or z, i.e., a right shoe or a right shoe. If we were originally indifferent between the choice of a left shoe (by itself) or a right shoe (by itself), then strong independence implies that we will also be indifferent between the two gambles which we constructed. Of course, left shoes and right shoes are complementary goods and we would naturally prefer to have both if possible. The point of strong independence is that outcome z in the above examples is always mutually exclusive. In the first gamble the payoffs are a left shoe *or* a right shoe but never both. And in the second gamble the payoffs are a right shoe *or* a right shoe, but never both. The mutual exclusiveness of the third alternative z is critical to the axiom of strong independence.

Having established the five axioms, we add to them the assumption that individuals always prefer more wealth to less. In other words, people are greedy. The marginal utility of wealth is always positive. This assumption, in conjunction with the other five, is all that is needed to provide a complete development of utility theory.

Next, we need to answer the question, How do individuals rank various combinations of risky alternatives? We can use the axioms of preference to show how preferences can be mapped into measurable utility. How do we establish a utility function which allows the assignment of a unit of measure (a number) to various alternatives so that we can look at the number and know that, if, for example, the utility of x is 35 and the utility of y is 27, then x is preferred to y? In order to do this we need to discuss two properties of utility functions.

B. DEVELOPING UTILITY FUNCTIONS

The utility function will have two properties: (1) It will be order preserving. In other words if we measure the utility of x as greater than the utility of y, $U(x) > U(y)$,

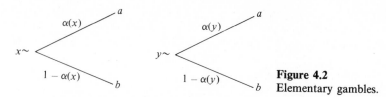

Figure 4.2
Elementary gambles.

it means that x is actually prefered to y, $x \succ y$. (2) Expected utility can be used to rank combinations of risky alternatives. Mathematically, this means that

$$U(G(x, y{:}\alpha)) = \alpha U(x) + (1 - \alpha) U(y).$$

In order to prove that utility functions are order preserving, consider the set of risky outcomes, S, which is assumed to be bounded above by outcome a and below by outcome b. Next consider two intermediate outcomes x and y such that

$$a \succ x \succeq b \quad \text{or} \quad a \succeq x \succ b$$

and

$$a \succ y \succeq b \quad \text{or} \quad a \succeq y \succ b.$$

By using Axiom 4 (measurability) we can choose unique probabilities for x and y in order to construct the following gambles:

$$x \sim G(a, b{:}\alpha(x)), \qquad y \sim G(a, b{:}\alpha(y)).$$

Then we can use Axiom 5 (ranking) so that the probabilities $\alpha(x)$ and $\alpha(y)$ can be interpreted as numerical utilities which uniquely rank x and y. By Axiom 5,

$$\text{If} \quad \alpha(x) > \alpha(y), \quad \text{then} \quad x \succ y.$$

$$\text{If} \quad \alpha(x) = \alpha(y), \quad \text{then} \quad x \sim y.$$

$$\text{If} \quad \alpha(x) < \alpha(y), \quad \text{then} \quad x \prec y.$$

In this way we have developed an order-preserving utility function. The maximum and minimum outcomes, a and b, may be assigned any number at all (for example, let $a = 100$ and $b = 0$). Then by forming simple gambles we can assign cardinal utility numbers to the intermediate outcomes x and y.

Next it is important to show that expected utility can be used to rank risky alternatives. This is the second property of utility functions. Let us begin by establishing the elementary gambles in exactly the same way as before. This is illustrated in Fig. 4.2. Next, consider a third alternative, z. Note that we can rely on Axiom 3 (strong independence) to say that the choice of z will not affect the relationship between x and y. Next, by Axiom 4 there must exist a unique probability, $\beta(z)$, which would make us indifferent as to outcome z and a gamble between x and y. (See Fig. 4.3). Now we can relate z to the elemental prospects a and b. If we can trace the branches in the decision tree represented by Fig. 4.3, we will be indifferent between z and outcome a with probability $\gamma = \beta(z)\alpha(x) + (1 - \beta(z))\alpha(y)$ and outcome b with probability $1 - \gamma$. This is shown in Fig. 4.4. We can write the gamble as follows:

$$z \sim G[a, b{:}\beta(z)\alpha(x) + (1 - \beta(z))\alpha(y)].$$

Figure 4.3
Outcome z compared with a gamble between outcomes x and y.

Figure 4.4
Outcome z related to elementary prospects a and b.

Now we have already established, by Axioms 4 and 5, that the utilities of x and y can be represented by their probabilities, namely $U(x) = \alpha(x)$ and $U(y) = \alpha(y)$. Therefore, the above gamble can be rewritten as

$$z \sim G[a, b : \beta(z)U(x) + (1 - \beta(z))U(y)].$$

Finally, by using Axioms 4 and 5 a second time, it must be true that the unique probability of outcome z can be used as a cardinal measure of its utility relative to the elemental prospects of a and b. Therefore, we have

$$U(z) = \beta(z)U(x) + (1 - \beta(z))U(y). \tag{4.1}$$

In this way we have shown that the correct ranking function for risky alternatives is expected utility. Equation (4.1) says that the utility of z is equal to the probability of x times its utility plus the probability of y times its utility. This is an expected utility which represents a linear combination of the utilities of outcomes.

In general, we can write the expected utility of wealth as follows:

$$E[U(W)] = \sum_i p_i U(W_i).$$

Given the five axioms of rational investor behavior and the additional assumption that all investors always prefer more wealth to less, we can say that investors will always seek to maximize their expected utility of wealth. In fact, the above equation is exactly what we mean by the theory of choice. All investors will use it as their objective function. In other words, they will seem to calculate the expected utility of wealth for all possible alternative choices and then choose the outcome which maximizes their expected utility of wealth.

Now, we can use the properties of utility functions to demonstrate how our utility function might be constructed. Suppose we arbitrarily assign a utility of -10

utiles to a loss of $1000 and ask the following question: When we are faced with a gamble with probability α of winning $1000 and probability $(1 - \alpha)$ of losing $1000, what probability would make us indifferent between the gamble and $0.0 with certainty? Mathematically, this problem can be expressed as

$$0 \sim G(1000, -1000: \alpha)$$

or

$$U(0) = \alpha U(1000) + (1 - \alpha) U(-1000).$$

Suppose that the probability of winning $1000 must be .6 in order for us to be indifferent between the gamble and a sure $0.0. By assuming that the utility of $0.0 with certainty is zero and substituting $U(-1000) = -10$ and $\alpha = .6$ into the above equation, we can solve for the utility of $1000:

$$U(1000) = \frac{(1 - \alpha) U(-1000)}{\alpha}$$

$$= -\frac{(1 - .6)(-10)}{.6} = 6.7 \text{ utiles.}$$

By repeating this procedure for different payoffs it is possible to develop a utility function. Table 4.1 shows various gambles, their probabilities, and the utility of payoffs for a risk-averse investor. The cardinal utility function which obtains for the set of preferences indicated in Table 4.1 is given in Fig. 4.5.[5]

Table 4.1   Payoffs, Probabilities, and Utilities

Loss	Gain	Probability of Gain	Utility of Gain	Utility of Loss
-1000	1000	.60	6.7	-10.0
-1000	2000	.55	8.2	-10.0
-1000	3000	.50	10.0	-10.0
-1000	4000	.45	12.2	-10.0
-1000	5000	.40	15.0	-10.0
-1000	6000	.35	18.6	-10.0
-1000	7000	.30	23.3	-10.0
-2000	2000	.75	8.2	-24.6
-3000	3000	.80	10.0	-40.0
-4000	4000	.85	12.2	-69.2
-5000	5000	.90	15.0	-135.0

From *Dividend Policy and Enterprise Evaluation*, by James E. Walter. © 1967 by Wadsworth Publishing Company, Inc., Belmont, Calif. Reprinted by permission of the publisher.

---

[5] This example can be found in Walter [1967].

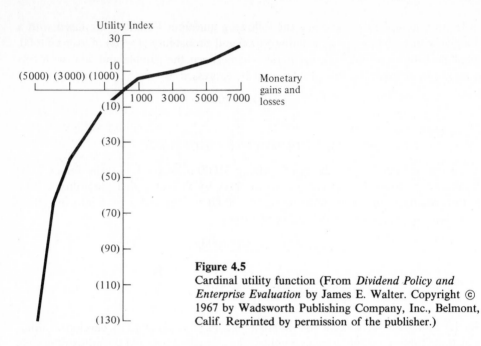

Figure 4.5
Cardinal utility function (From *Dividend Policy and Enterprise Evaluation* by James E. Walter. Copyright © 1967 by Wadsworth Publishing Company, Inc., Belmont, Calif. Reprinted by permission of the publisher.)

An important thing to keep in mind is that utility functions are specific to individuals. There is no way to compare one individual's utility function to another's. For example, we could perform an experiment by giving two people $1000. We would see that they are both happy, having just experienced an increase in utility. But whose utility increased more? It is impossible to say! Interpersonal comparison of utility functions is impossible. If it were not, we could establish a social welfare function which would combine everyone's utility, and could then use it to solve such problems as the optimal distribution of wealth. We could maximize society's utility by taking wealth from individual i and giving it to individual j. However, it is not possible to know how real-world utility functions for different individuals should be aggregated. It follows that group utility functions such as the utility function of a firm have no meaning.

Another important property of cardinal utility functions is that we can sensibly talk about increasing or decreasing marginal utility. This can best be illustrated with an example taken from the centigrade and Fahrenheit temperature scales. Consider two outcomes: the freezing point of water and its boiling point. Call them x and y, respectively. Each scale may be likened to a function which maps various degrees of heat into numbers. Utility functions do the same thing for risky alternatives. The difference between two outcomes is marginal utility. On the centigrade scale the difference between freezing and boiling is 100°C. On the Fahrenheit scale the difference is 180°F. The ratio of the "changes" is

$$\frac{212° - 32°}{100° - 0°} = 1.8.$$

If the two scales really do provide the same ranking for all prospects, then the ratio of changes should be the same for all prospects. Mathematically,

$$\frac{U(x) - U(y)}{\psi(x) - \psi(y)} = \text{constant},$$

where $U(\cdot)$ and $\psi(\cdot)$ are the two utility functions. Compare any two points on the two temperature scales and you will see the ratio of changes between them is a constant, that is, 1.8. Hence, changes in utility between any two wealth levels have exactly the same meaning on the two utility functions, i.e., one utility function is just a "transformation" of the other.

C. ESTABLISHING A DEFINITION OF RISK AVERSION

Having established a way of converting the axioms of preference into a utility function, we can make use of the concept to establish definitions of risk premia and also precisely what is meant by risk aversion. A useful way to begin is to compare three simple utility functions (Fig. 4.6) which assume that more wealth is preferred to less—in other words, the marginal utility of wealth is positive $(MU(W) > 0)$. Suppose that we establish a gamble between two prospects, a and b. Let the probability of receiving prospect a be α and the probability of b be $(1 - \alpha)$. The gamble can be written as before: $G(a, b:\alpha)$. Now the question is this: Will we prefer the actuarial value of the gamble (i.e., its expected or average outcome) with certainty—or the gamble itself? In other words, would we like to receive \$10 for sure or would we prefer to "roll the dice" in a gamble which pays off \$100 with a 10% probability and \$0 with a 90% probability? A person who prefers the gamble is a risk lover; one who is indifferent is risk neutral; and one who prefers the actuarial value with certainty is a risk averter. In Fig. 4.7, we have graphed a logarithmic utility function: $U(W) = \ln(W)$. The gamble is an 80% chance of winning \$5 or a 20% chance of winning

Figure 4.6
Three utility functions with positive marginal utility: (a) Risk lover;
(b) risk neutral; (c) risk averter.

W	U(W)
1	0
5	1.61
10	2.30
20	3.00
30	3.40

Figure 4.7
Logarithmic utility function.

$30. The *actuarial value of the gamble* is its expected outcome. In other words, the expected wealth is

$$E(W) = .8(\$5) + .2(\$30) = \$10.$$

The utility of the expected wealth can be read directly from the utility function: $U[E(W)] = 2.3$. That is, if an individual with a logarithmic utility function could receive $10 with certainty, it would provide him or her with 2.3 utiles. The other possibility is the utility of the gamble. We know from Eq. (4.1) that it is equal to the expected utility of wealth provided by the gamble.

$$E[U(W)] = .8\,U(\$5) + .2\,U(\$30),$$

$$= .8(1.61) + .2(3.40) = 1.97.$$

Because we receive more utility from the actuarial value of the gamble obtained with certainty than from taking the gamble itself, we are risk averse. In general, if the utility of expected wealth is greater than the expected utility of wealth, the individual will be risk averse. The three definitions are:[6]

> If $U[E(W)] > E[U(W)]$, then we have risk aversion. (4.2a)

> If $U[E(W)] = E[U(W)]$, then we have risk neutrality. (4.2b)

> If $U[E(W)] < E[U(W)]$, then we have risk loving. (4.2c)

Note (see Fig. 4.6) that if our utility function is strictly concave, we will be risk averse; if it is linear, we will be risk neutral; and if it is convex, we will be risk lovers.

It is even possible to compute the maximum amount of wealth an individual would be willing to give up in order to avoid the gamble. This is called a *risk premium*. Suppose that Mr. Smith is faced with the gamble illustrated in Fig. 4.7, has a current

---

[6] These definitions can be found in Markowitz [1959].

level of wealth of $10, and has a logarithmic utility function. How much will he pay to avoid the gamble? If he does nothing, he has an 80% chance of ending up with $5 (a decline of $5) and a 20% chance of ending up with $30 (an increase of $20). The expected utility of the gamble has already been determined to be 1.97 utiles. From the logarithmic utility function in Fig. 4.7 we see that the level of wealth which provides 1.97 utiles is $7.17. On the other hand, Smith receives an expected level of wealth of $10 (equal to his current wealth) if he accepts the gamble. Therefore, given a logarithmic utility function, he will be willing to pay up to $2.83 in order to avoid the gamble. We shall call this the *Markowitz risk premium*. If Smith is offered insurance against the gamble which costs less than $2.83, he will buy it.

We shall adopt the convention of measuring the *risk premium* as the difference between an individual's expected wealth, given the gamble, and the level of wealth that individual would accept with certainty if the gamble were removed, i.e., his or her *certainty equivalent wealth*. There is another convention which might be called the *cost of the gamble*. It is defined as the difference between an individual's current wealth and the certainty equivalent wealth. Note that in the first example, given above, expected wealth and current wealth were identical because the expected change in wealth was zero. Thus, there was no difference between the risk premium and the cost of the gamble. In order to illustrate the difference between the two definitions, consider the following example. A risk-averse individual has the same logarithmic utility function as in Fig. 4.7 but the gamble is a 10% chance of winning $10 and a 90% chance of winning $100. We can compute the following numbers:

$$\text{current wealth} = \$10,$$

$$\text{expected wealth} = \$101,$$

$$\text{certainty equivalent wealth} = \$92.76.$$

Our convention will be to define the risk premium as the difference between expected wealth and certainty equivalent wealth, i.e.:

$$\text{risk premium} = \text{expected wealth} - \text{certainty equivalent wealth}$$

$$= \$101 - \$92.76 = \$8.24.$$

This measures, in dollars, the risk premium associated with the gamble. Note, however, that since the gamble is favorable we would be willing to pay a positive amount to take the gamble. The cost of the gamble is

$$\text{cost of the gamble} = \text{current wealth} - \text{certainty equivalent}$$
$$= \$10 - \$92.76 = \$-82.76.$$

In other words, we would be willing to pay up to $82.76 in order to take the gamble. We would pay even more if we were less risk averse. Note that for a risk averter the risk premium as defined above is always positive while the cost of the gamble can be positive, negative, or zero, depending on the risk of the gamble and on how much it is expected to change one's current wealth.

Throughout the remainder of this text we shall assume that all individuals are risk averse. Their utility functions are assumed to be strictly concave and increasing. Mathematically, this implies two things: (1) they always prefer more wealth to less (the marginal utility of wealth is positive, $MU(W) > 0$), and (2) their marginal utility of wealth decreases as they have more and more wealth ($dMU(W)/dW < 0$).

Now we know how to characterize a risk-averse utility function and how to measure a risk premium for a given gamble, but it is even more interesting to provide a specific definition of risk aversion. This was done by Pratt [1964] and Arrow [1971]. Take an individual, say Ms. Torres, with a current amount of wealth, W, and present her with an actuarially neutral gamble of $\tilde{Z}$ dollars (by actuarially neutral we mean that $E(\tilde{Z}) = 0$). What risk premium, $\pi(W, \tilde{Z})$, must be added to the gamble to make her indifferent between it and the actuarial value of the gamble? In Fig. 4.7, which illustrates our first example, the risk premium is analogous to the difference between $U[E(W)]$ and $E[U(W)]$ if it is measured in utiles, or the difference between \$10 and \$7.17 if measured in dollars. Presumably, the risk premium will be a function of the level of wealth, W, and the gamble $\tilde{Z}$. Mathematically, the risk premium, π, can be defined as the value which satisfies the following equality:

$$E[U(W + \tilde{Z})] = U[W + E(\tilde{Z}) - \pi(W, \tilde{Z})]. \tag{4.3}$$

The left-hand side is the expected utility of the current level of wealth given the gamble. Its utility must equal the utility of the right-hand side, namely current level of wealth, W, plus the utility of the actuarial value of the gamble, $E(\tilde{Z})$, minus the risk premium, $\pi(W, \tilde{Z})$. We can use a Taylor's series approximation to expand the utility function of wealth (whatever it might be) around both sides of Eq. (4.3).[7] Working with the right-hand side of (4.3) we have

$$U[W + E(\tilde{Z}) - \pi(W, \tilde{Z})] = U[W - \pi(W, \tilde{Z})].$$

Since $E(\tilde{Z}) \equiv 0$, an actuarially neutral risk, the Taylor's series expansion is[8]

$$U(W - \pi) = U(W) - \pi U'(W) + \text{terms of order at most } (\pi^2). \tag{4.4}$$

The Taylor's series expansion of the left-hand side of (4.3) is

$$E[U(W + \tilde{Z})] = E[U(W) + \tilde{Z}U'(W) + \tfrac{1}{2}\tilde{Z}^2 U''(W)$$

$$+ \text{terms of order at most } (\tilde{Z}^3)]$$

$$= U(W) + \tfrac{1}{2}\sigma_Z^2 U''(W)$$

$$+ \text{terms of smaller order than } \sigma_Z^2. \tag{4.5}$$

The above result may require a little explanation. It is true because

---

[7] Students not familiar with Taylor's series approximations are referred to Appendix D.

[8] We assume that the third absolute central moment of $\tilde{Z}$ is of smaller order than σ_Z^2 (normally it is of the order of σ_Z^3).

$$E[U(W)] = U(W), \qquad \text{wealth is not random;}$$

$$E[\tilde{Z}] \equiv 0, \qquad \text{the risk is actuarially neutral;}$$

$$E[\tilde{Z}^2] = \sigma_Z^2, \qquad \text{because } \sigma_Z^2 \equiv E[\tilde{Z} - E(\tilde{Z})]^2.$$

Next we can equate (4.4) and (4.5),

$$U(W) - \pi U'(W) + \cdots = U(W) + \tfrac{1}{2}\sigma_Z^2 U''(W) + \cdots. \qquad (4.6a)$$

Solving (4.6a) for the risk premium, we obtain

$$\pi = \tfrac{1}{2}\sigma_Z^2 \left(-\frac{U''(W)}{U'(W)} \right). \qquad (4.6b)$$

This is the *Pratt-Arrow measure* of a local risk premium. Since $\tfrac{1}{2}\sigma_Z^2$ is always positive, the sign of the risk premium is always determined by the sign of the term in parentheses. We shall define the measure of absolute risk aversion (ARA) as

$$\text{ARA} = -\frac{U''(W)}{U'(W)}. \qquad (4.7)$$

It is called *absolute risk aversion* because it measures risk aversion for a given level of wealth. The Pratt-Arrow definition of risk aversion is useful because it provides much more insight into people's behavior in the face of risk. For example, how does ARA change with one's wealth level? Casual empiricism tells us that ARA will probably decrease as wealth increases. A $1000 gamble may seem trivial to a billionaire, but a pauper would probably be very risk averse toward it. On the other hand we can multiply the measure of absolute risk aversion by the level of wealth to obtain what is known as *relative risk aversion* (RRA):

$$\text{RRA} = -W\frac{U''(W)}{U'(W)}. \qquad (4.8)$$

Constant relative risk aversion implies that an individual will have constant risk aversion to a proportional loss of wealth even though the absolute loss increases as wealth does.

We can use these definitions of risk aversion to provide a more detailed examination of various types of utility functions to see whether or not they have decreasing ARA and constant RRA. The quadratic utility function has been used widely in academic literature. It can be written (for $W \leq a/2b$)

quadratic utility function $\qquad\qquad U(W) = aW - bW^2; \qquad (4.9)$

first derivative, marginal utility, $\qquad\qquad U'(W) = a - 2bW;$

second derivative, change in MU with $\qquad U''(W) = -2b.$
respect to changes in wealth

For the quadratic utility function ARA and RRA are:

$$\text{ARA} = -\frac{2b}{a - 2bW}, \qquad \frac{d(\text{ARA})}{dW} > 0,$$

$$\text{RRA} = \frac{2b}{(a/W) - 2b}, \qquad \frac{d(\text{RRA})}{dW} > 0.$$

Unfortunately, the quadratic utility function exhibits increasing ARA and increasing RRA. Neither of these properties makes sense intuitively.

Friend and Blume [1975] have used Internal Revenue Service data to replicate, from reported dividends, the portfolios held by individual investors. Sophisticated econometric techniques were used to estimate changes in ARA and RRA as a function of the wealth of investors. The results were consistent with decreasing ARA and constant RRA equal to 2.0. These properties are consistent with a power utility function with $a = -1$ (for $W > 0$). It can be written as:

$$U(W) = -W^{-1}, \qquad U'(W) = W^{-2} > 0, \qquad U''(W) = -2W^{-3} < 0. \quad (4.10)$$

For this power utility function, ARA and RRA are:

$$\text{ARA} = -\frac{-2W^{-3}}{W^{-2}} = \frac{2}{W}, \qquad \frac{d(\text{ARA})}{dW} < 0,$$

$$\text{RRA} = W\frac{2}{W} = 2, \qquad \frac{d(\text{RRA})}{dW} = 0.$$

The power function given by Eq. (4.10) is consistent with the empirical results of Friend and Blume and exhibits all the intuitively plausible properties: the marginal utility of wealth is positive, it decreases with increasing wealth, the measure of ARA decreases with increasing wealth, and RRA is constant.

D. COMPARISON OF RISK AVERSION IN THE SMALL AND IN THE LARGE

The Pratt-Arrow definition of risk aversion provides useful insights into the properties of ARA and RRA, but it assumes that risks are small and actuarially neutral. The Markowitz concept, which simply compares $E[U(W)]$ with $U[E(W)]$, is not limited by these assumptions.

An interesting comparison of the two measures of risk premiums is offered in the following example. An individual with a logarithmic utility function and a level of wealth of $20,000 is exposed to two different risks: (1) a 50/50 chance of gaining or losing $10, and (2) an 80% chance of losing $1000 and a 20% chance of losing $10,000. What is the risk premium required by the individual faced with each of these risks? Note that the first risk is small and actuarially neutral, so that it approximates the assumptions which were used to derive the Pratt-Arrow risk premium. The second risk, however, is large and very asymmetric.

The first risk is a small, actuarially neutral gamble, so the Pratt-Arrow measure of the risk premium (Eq. 4.6b) should yield a result almost identical to the Markowitz measure. The Pratt-Arrow measure is

$$\pi = -\frac{1}{2}\sigma_Z^2 \frac{U''(W)}{U'(W)}.$$

The variance of the first risk is

$$\sigma_Z^2 = \sum p_i(X_i - E(X))^2$$

$$= \tfrac{1}{2}(20{,}010 - 20{,}000)^2 + \tfrac{1}{2}(19{,}990 - 20{,}000)^2$$

$$= 100.$$

The ratio of the second and the first derivatives of a logarithmic utility function evaluated at a level of wealth of $20,000 is

$$U'(W) = \frac{1}{W}, \qquad U''(W) = -\frac{1}{W^2}, \qquad \frac{U''(W)}{U'(W)} = -\frac{1}{W} = -\frac{1}{20{,}000}.$$

Combining these results, we obtain an estimate of the Pratt-Arrow risk premium:

$$\pi = -\frac{100}{2}\left(-\frac{1}{20{,}000}\right) = \$.0025.$$

The Markowitz approach requires computation of the expected utility of the gamble as follows:

$$E[U(W)] = \sum_i p_i U(W_i),$$

$$= \tfrac{1}{2}U(20{,}010) + \tfrac{1}{2}U(19{,}990)$$

$$= \tfrac{1}{2}\ln(20{,}010) + \tfrac{1}{2}\ln(19{,}990) = 9.903487428.$$

The certainty equivalent wealth level which would make us indifferent to our current level of wealth given the gamble and a lower but certain level of wealth is the level of wealth which has a utility of 9.903487428. This is

$$W = e^{\ln(W)} = \$19{,}999.9974998.$$

Therefore we would pay a risk premium as large as $.0025002. The difference between the Pratt-Arrow risk premium and that of Markowitz is negligible in this case.

If we repeat similar computations for the second risk in the above example, the Pratt-Arrow assumptions of a small, actuarially neutral risk are not closely approximated. Nevertheless, if we apply the Pratt-Arrow definition, the risk premium is calculated to be $324. The Markowitz risk premium for the same risk is the difference between expected wealth, $17,200, and the certainty equivalent wealth, $16,711, or $489. Now the dollar difference between the two risk premia is much larger.[9]

---

[9] Had we calculated the cost of the gamble instead of the risk premium we would have subtracted the certainty equivalent wealth, $16,711, from the individual's current wealth, $20,000, to find that the individual would have paid up to $3289 to avoid the gamble.

The above example illustrates the difference between risk aversion for small, actuarially neutral risks, where the Pratt-Arrow assumptions are closely approximated, and risk aversion in the large, where the magnitude of the gamble is large or where it is not actuarially neutral. In general, the Markowitz measure of a risk premium is superior for large or asymmetric risks. This does not mean that the Pratt-Arrow definition of risk aversion is not useful. As we have seen, the intuition provided by the definition of risk aversion was useful for distinguishing between various types of concave utility functions.

E. STOCHASTIC DOMINANCE

So far we have discussed the axioms of investor preference, then used them to develop cardinal utility functions, and finally employed the utility functions to measure risk premia and derive measures of risk aversion. Clearly, any investor, whether risk averse or not, will seek to maximize the expected utility of his or her wealth. The expected utility rule can be used to introduce the economics of choice under uncertainty. An asset (or portfolio) is said to be stochastically dominant over another if an individual receives greater wealth from it in every (ordered) state of nature. This definition is known as *first order stochastic dominance*. Mathematically, asset x, with cumulative probability distribution $F_x(W)$, will be stochastically dominant over asset y, with cumulative probability distribution $G_y(W)$, for the set of all nondecreasing utility functions if

$$F_x(W) \le G_y(W) \quad \text{for all } W,$$

First-order stochastic dominance   (4.11)

$$F_x(W_i) < G_y(W_i) \quad \text{for some } W_i,$$

In other words, the cumulative probability distribution (defined on wealth, W) for asset y always lies to the left of the cumulative distribution for x. If true, then x is said to dominate y. Figure 4.8 shows an example of first-order stochastic dominance

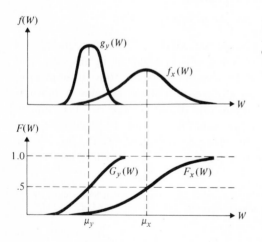

Figure 4.8
An example of first-order stochastic dominance.

assuming that the distribution of wealth provided by both assets is a (truncated) normal distribution. It is obvious from the figure that x dominates y because the cumulative distribution of y always lies to the left of x.

First-order stochastic dominance applies to all increasing utility functions. This means that individuals with any of the three utility functions in Fig. 4.6 would prefer asset x to asset y, because first-order stochastic dominance guarantees that the expected utility of wealth offered by x will be greater than that offered by y for all increasing utility functions. This fact can be illustrated by using Fig. 4.9 and the definition of expected utility:

$$E[U(W)] \equiv \int_{-\infty}^{\infty} U(W)f(W)dW, \qquad (4.12)$$

where

$U(W) =$ the utility function,

$W =$ the level of wealth,

$f(W) =$ the frequency distribution of wealth.

The utility functions in Fig. 4.9 are linear, but they could just as easily be any of the set of increasing functions which we are comparing with any set of nonincreasing functions. Expected utility is the sum of the utilities of all possible levels of wealth weighted by their probability. For a given frequency of wealth, $f_i(W)$, in the top half of Fig. 4.9, the increasing utility function assigns higher utility to the level of wealth offered by asset x than by asset y. This is true for every frequency. Consequently, the expected utility of wealth from asset x is greater than that from asset y for the set of increasing utility functions (that is, all utility functions which have a positive marginal utility of wealth). Of course, the opposite would be true for utility functions nonincreasing in wealth.

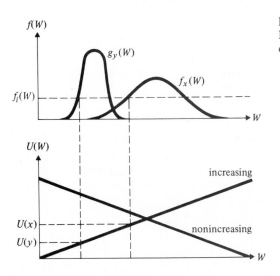

Figure 4.9
First-order stochastic dominance and expected utility.

Second-order stochastic dominance not only assumes utility functions where marginal utility of wealth is positive, but also that total utility must increase at a decreasing rate. In other words, utility functions are nondecreasing and strictly concave. Thus individuals are assumed to be risk averse. Asset x will be stochastically dominant over asset y for all risk averse investors if

$$\int_{-\infty}^{W_i} [G_y(W) - F_x(W)]dW \geq 0 \quad \text{for all } W,$$

Second-order stochastic dominance

$$G_y(W_i) \neq F_x(W_i) \quad \text{for some } W_i, \tag{4.13}$$

This means that in order for asset x to dominate asset y for all risk-averse investors, the accumulated area under the cumulative probability distribution of y must be greater than the accumulated area for x, below any given level of wealth. This implies that, unlike first-order stochastic dominance, the cumulative density functions can cross. Figure 4.10 provides a graphic example, this time assuming normal distributions. Obviously asset x will dominate asset y if an investor is risk averse because they both offer the same expected level of wealth ($\mu_x = \mu_y$), and because y is riskier. It has greater variance. The second-order stochastic dominance criterion requires that the difference in areas under the cumulative density functions be positive below any level of wealth, W_i. Up to the mean, $G_y(W)$ is strictly greater than $F_x(W)$. Beyond the mean, the opposite is true. Figure 4.11 shows the difference between the two cumulative density functions is always greater than or equal to zero, therefore x dominates y.

Figure 4.10
An example of second-order stochastic dominance.

(a)   (b)

$\int [G_y(W) - F_x(W)] \, dW$

$\mu_x = \mu_y$ W

Figure 4.11
Graphical representation of
the sum of the differences in
cumulative probabilities.

Figure 4.10(b) ties the concept of second-order stochastic dominance back to the notion of maximizing expected utility.[10] The concave utility function has the property that the increase in utility for constant changes in wealth declines as a function of wealth. Therefore, if we select a given frequency of wealth such as $f_i(W)$, it maps out equal changes in wealth ΔW_1 and ΔW_2. The difference in utility between x and y below the mean is much greater than the difference in utility for the same change in wealth above the mean. Consequently, if we take the expected utility by pairing all such differences with equal probability, the expected utility of x is seen to be greater than the expected utility of y. If the individual were risk neutral, with a linear utility function, the differences in utility above and below the mean would always be equal. Hence a risk-neutral investor would be indifferent relative to x and y.

Stochastic dominance is an extremely important and powerful result. It is properly founded on the basis of expected utility maximization, and even more important, it applies to any probability distribution whatsoever. This is because it takes into account every point in the probability distribution. Furthermore, we can be sure that if an asset demonstrates second-order stochastic dominance, it will be preferred by all risk-averse investors, regardless of the specific shape of their utility functions. We could use stochastic dominance as the basis of a complete theory of how risk-averse investors choose among various risky alternatives. All we need to do is find the set of portfolios which is stochastically dominant and then select a portfolio from among those in the set.[11]

F. USING MEAN AND VARIANCE AS CHOICE CRITERIA

If the distribution of returns offered by assets is jointly normal, then we can maximize expected utility simply by selecting the best combinations of mean and variance.[12]

---

[10] The graphical presentation given here is intuitive and not meant to be a proof of the fact that second-order stochastic dominance maximizes expected utility for risk-averse investors. For proof, the reader is referred to Hanoch and Levy [1969].

[11] There is a growing body of literature which uses this concept. The interested reader is referred to Bawa [1975, 1976], Whitmore [1970], Porter, Wart, and Ferguson [1973], Levy and Kroll [1976], Vickson and Altman [1977], Jean [1975], and Kira and Ziemba [1977].

[12] By *jointly* normal we mean that all assets are individually normally distributed and, in addition, their interrelationships (covariances) obey the normal probability laws. This is developed further in Chapter 6.

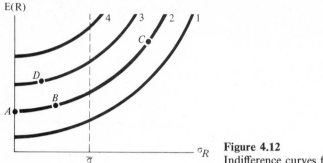

Figure 4.12
Indifference curves for a risk-averse investor.

This is computationally much simpler than stochastic dominance, but requires that we restrict ourselves to normal distributions. Every normal distribution can be completely described by two parameters: its mean and variance—return and risk. If we adopt utility functions which maximize expected utility of end-of-period wealth (assuming a single-period model), it is easy to show the relationship between wealth and return:

$$R_j = \frac{\tilde{W}_j - W_0}{W_0}.$$

If the end-of-period wealth from investing in asset j is normally distributed with mean $\bar{W}$ and variance σ_W^2, then the return on asset j will also be normally distributed with mean $E(R_j) = [(E(W_j)/W_0) - 1]$ and variance $\sigma_R^2 = (\sigma_W^2/W_0^2)$.

Assuming that the return on an asset is normally distributed with mean E and variance σ^2, we can write our utility functions as[13]

$$U = U(R_j; E, \sigma).$$

Our expected utility is

$$E(U) = \int_{-\infty}^{\infty} U(R)f(R; E, \sigma)dR. \tag{4.14}$$

We would like to express the indifference curve of a risk-averse investor as a function of the mean and standard deviation of a distribution of returns. The indifference curve is a mapping of all combinations of risk and return (standard deviation or variance) which yield the same expected utility of wealth. Obviously, if the combinations offer identical expected utility, the investor will be indifferent between them. Figure 4.12 shows the end result of the following proofs, i.e., the indifference curves of a risk-averse investor.

We want to show that the marginal rate of substitution between return and

---

[13] This proof can be found in Tobin [1958]. Also note that the proof applies equally well to any continuous, symmetric two-parameter distribution.

risk is positive and that the indifference curves are convex. This can be done, first by converting the random return into a unit normal variable, Z, which has a mean of zero and a variance of one.

$$\tilde{Z} = \frac{\tilde{R} - E}{\sigma}. \tag{4.15}$$

From this we see that

$$\tilde{R} = E + \sigma\tilde{Z}, \qquad \frac{dR}{dZ} = \sigma, \qquad dR = \sigma dZ,$$

and when $R = -\infty$, then $Z = -\infty$, and when $R = \infty$, then $Z = \infty$. Now, by using the change of variables technique from integral calculus, we can rewrite (4.14) as[14]

$$E(U) = \int_{-\infty}^{\infty} U(E + \sigma\tilde{Z})f(Z;0,1)dZ. \tag{4.16}$$

Next, we take the derivative of the expected utility with respect to a change in the standard deviation of return:[15]

$$\frac{dE(U)}{d\sigma} = \int_{-\infty}^{\infty} U'(E + \sigma\tilde{Z})\left(\frac{dE}{d\sigma} + \tilde{Z}\right)f(Z;0,1)dZ = 0. \tag{4.17}$$

An indifference curve is defined as the locus of points where the change in the expected utility is equal to zero. Therefore (4.17) has been set equal to zero and the solution of the equation represents an indifference curve. Separating terms, we have

$$0 = \frac{dE}{d\sigma} \int_{-\infty}^{\infty} U'(E + \sigma\tilde{Z})f(Z;0,1)dZ + \int_{-\infty}^{\infty} U'(E + \sigma\tilde{Z})Zf(Z;0,1)dZ.$$

Therefore, the slope of the indifference curve is

$$\frac{dE}{d\sigma} = -\frac{\int U'(E + \sigma\tilde{Z})Zf(Z;0,1)dZ}{\int U'(E + \sigma\tilde{Z})f(Z;0,1)dZ} > 0. \tag{4.18}$$

The denominator must be positive because of the assumption that marginal utility, $U'(E + \sigma\tilde{Z})$, must always be positive. People always prefer more return to less. The numerator will be positive only if we have a risk-averse investor with a strictly concave utility function. The marginal utility of every negative value of Z in Fig. 4.13 is greater than the marginal utility of an equally likely positive value of Z. Because this is true for every pair of outcomes $\pm$ Z, the integral in the numerator of (4.18) is negative and the (entire) numerator is positive. Consequently, the slope of a risk averter's indifference curve in Fig. 4.12, that is, his or her marginal rate

---

[14] Since $f(R; E, \sigma) = (1/\sigma)f(Z;0,1)$, it follows that

$$E(U) = \int_{-\infty}^{\infty} U(E + \sigma\tilde{Z})f(Z;0,1)\frac{\sigma}{\sigma} dZ.$$

[15] $\partial f(Z)/\partial\sigma = 0$.

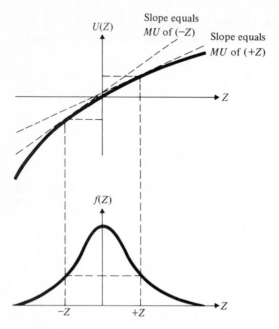

Slope equals MU of $(-Z)$

Slope equals MU of $(+Z)$

$U(Z)$

Z

$f(Z)$

$-Z$ $+Z$ Z

Figure 4.13
Graphic representation for $\int U'(E + \sigma Z)Zf(Z;0,1)dZ < 0$.

of substitution between mean and variance, is everywhere positive, excepting when $\sigma = 0$ where the slope is also zero.[16]

The indifference curves in Fig. 4.12 will be used throughout the remainder of the text to represent the theory of choice for risk-averse investors. Any points along a given indifference curve provide us with equal total utility. For example, we would not care whether we were at point A in Fig. 4.12, which has no risk, at point B with higher risk and return, or at point C. They all lie on the same indifference curve. Moving from right to left across the family of indifference curves provides us with increasing levels of expected utility. We would prefer point D on indifference curve 3 to point C on indifference curve 2, even though D has a lower return. The reason, of course, is that it has a much lower risk, which more than makes up for the lower return. The easiest way to see that expected utility increases from right

---

[16] The convexity of the utility function can be shown as follows. Let (E_1, σ_1) and (E_2, σ_2) be two points on the same indifference curve so that they have the same expected utility. If a third point is constructed to be a weighted average of the first two, $(E_1 + E_2)/2$, $(\sigma_1 + \sigma_2)/2$, the indifference curve is convex, if for every Z,

$$\tfrac{1}{2}U(E_1 + \sigma_1 Z) + \tfrac{1}{2}U(E_2 + \sigma_2 Z) < U\left(\frac{E_1 + E_2}{2} + \frac{\sigma_1 + \sigma_2}{2}Z\right).$$

In the case of declining marginal utilities this is obviously true because the utility of the second point, (E_2, σ_2), will be less than twice the utility of the first. Consequently,

$$E\left[U\left(\frac{E_1 + E_2}{2}, \frac{\sigma_1 + \sigma_2}{2}\right)\right] > E[U(E_1, \sigma_1)] = E[U(E_2, \sigma_2)],$$

and the third point, which is a weighted average of the first two, lies above the indifference curve. This is shown graphically in Fig. 4.A (see next page).

to left is to fix the level of risk at $\bar{\sigma}$ and then note that the expected return increases as we move from curve 1 to curve 4. Although the indifference curves in Fig. 4.12 appear to be parallel, they need not be. The only requirement is that they never touch or cross.

G. A MEAN-VARIANCE PARADOX

Although it is convenient to characterize return and risk by the mean and variance of distributions of return offered by assets, it is not always correct. In fact, it is correct only when the returns have a normal distribution. Consider the following example. Two companies with equal total assets and exactly the same distribution of net operating income differ only with regard to their financial leverage. Table 4.2 shows their respective income statements in different, equally likely, states of nature.

The mean and standard deviation of earnings per share for firm A are \$5 and \$1.41 respectively. For firm B, they are \$7 and \$2.82. These alternatives are plotted in Fig. 4.14. According to the mean-variance criterion, individual I would be indifferent between the risk-return combinations offered by A and B. Individual II, who is less risk averse, would prefer alternative B, which has a greater return. Finally, individual III would prefer alternative A, which has lower risk. The paradox arises when we reexamine the earnings per share offered by the two firms. The earnings per share for firm B are equal to or greater than the earnings per share for firm A in every state of nature. Obviously, the mean-variance criterion provides misleading results. No investor with positive marginal utility would prefer firm A.

The trouble with trying to apply the mean-variance criterion to the above problem is that the distribution of outcomes is not normal. Instead it is a rectangular distribution with equal probabilities for each state of nature. However, we can use second-order stochastic dominance regardless of the shape of the probability distribution.[17] This

Figure 4A
Convexity of the risk-averters' indifference curve.

---

[17] First-order stochastic dominance also obtains in this example. We have used second-order dominance because we assume a risk-averse decision maker.

Table 4.2   Mean-variance Paradox

	Economic State of Nature				
	Horrid	Bad	Average	Good	Great
Net operating income	$1200	$1600	$2000	$2400	$2800
Probability	.2	.2	.2	.2	.2
Firm A					
Interest expense	0	0	0	0	0
Earnings before tax	1200	1600	2000	2400	2800
Tax at 50%	−600	−800	−1000	−1200	−1400
Net income	600	800	1000	1200	1400
Earnings per share (200 shares)	$3.00	$4.00	$5.00	$6.00	$7.00
Firm B					
Interest expense	−600	−600	−600	−600	−600
Earnings before tax	600	1000	1400	1800	2200
Tax at 50%	−300	−500	−700	−900	−1100
Net income	300	500	700	900	1100
Earnings per share (100 shares)	$3.00	$5.00	$7.00	$9.00	$11.00

	Firm A			Firm B	
Assets	Liabilities		Assets	Liabilities	
	Debt	0		Debt	10,000
	Equity	20,000		Equity	10,000
$20,000		$20,000	$20,000		$20,000

is done in Table 4.3. Because the accumulated area under the distribution of earnings per share offered by firm *B* is always less than or equal to the accumulated distribution for firm *A*, we can say that *B* clearly dominates *A*. The density functions and cumulative density functions are shown in Fig. 4.15.

This mean-variance paradox example demonstrates very clearly the short-comings

E(eps)

Figure 4.14
A mean-variance paradox.

Table 4.3   Using Second-order Stochastic Dominance

Eps	Prob. (B)	Prob. (A)	F(B)	G(A)	F − G	Σ (F − G)
3.00	.2	.2	.2	.2	0	0
4.00	0	.2	.2	.4	−.2	−.2
5.00	.2	.2	.4	.6	−.2	−.4
6.00	0	.2	.4	.8	−.4	−.8
7.00	.2	.2	.6	1.0	−.4	−1.2
8.00	0	0	.6	1.0	−.4	−1.6
9.00	.2	0	.8	1.0	−.2	−1.8
10.00	0	0	.8	1.0	−.2	−2.0
11.00	.2	0	1.0	1.0	0	−2.0
	1.0	1.0				

Figure 4.15
Stochastic dominance applied to the mean-variance paradox.

of a theory of choice which relies on the (somewhat heroic) assumption that returns are normally distributed. Nevertheless, much of the remainder of this text will assume that returns are, in fact, normally distributed.

SUMMARY

The logic of the theory of investor choice can best be summarized by listing the series of logical steps and assumptions necessary to derive the indifference curves of Fig. 4.12.

- First the five axioms of rational behavior were described.
- The expected utility rule was derived from the axioms.

- Cardinal utility functions were derived from the axioms.
- We assumed positive marginal utility. This and the expected utility rule were used to argue that individuals will always maximize the expected utility of wealth.
- Risk premia were defined and a Pratt-Arrow measure of local risk aversion was developed.
- Stochastic dominance was shown to be a general theory of choice which maximizes expected utility for various classes of utility functions.
- Mean-variance indifference curves (which exhibit second-order stochastic dominance for normally distributed returns) were developed as a parametric theory of choice.

In Chapter 6 we shall use the mean-variance theory of choice as embodied in the mean-variance indifference curves to describe the manner in which investors actually choose optimal portfolios.

PROBLEM SET

4.1 State in your own words the minimum set of necessary conditions needed to obtain mean-variance indifference curves like those graphed in Fig. Q4.1.

4.2 Figure 4.6 shows the utility curve of a risk lover. What does the indifference curve of a risk lover look like?

4.3 You have a logarithmic utility function, $U(W) = \ln W$, and your current level of wealth is $5000.

a) Suppose you are exposed to a situation which results in a 50/50 chance of winning or losing $1000. If you can buy insurance which completely removes the risk for a fee of $125, will you buy it or take the gamble?

b) Suppose you accept the gamble outlined in (a) and lose, so that your wealth is reduced to $4000. If you are faced with the same gamble and have the same offer of insurance as before, will you buy the insurance the second time around?

4.4 Assume that you have a logarithmic utility function for wealth $U(W) = \ln (W)$ and that you are faced with a 50/50 chance of winning or losing $1000. How much will you pay to avoid this risk if your current level of wealth is $10,000? How much would you pay if your level of wealth were $1,000,000?

Mean

Variance

Figure Q4.1
Mean-variance indifference curves.

4.5 Given the exponential utility function $U(w) = -e^{-aw}$.

a) Graph the function, assuming $a > 0$.

b) Does the function exhibit positive marginal utility and risk aversion?

c) Does the function have decreasing absolute risk aversion?

d) Does the function have constant relative risk aversion?

4.6 What kind of utility function of wealth might be consistent with an individual gambling and paying insurance at the same time?

4.7 Suppose that $A > B > C > D$ and that the utilities of these alternatives satisfy $U(A) + U(D) = U(B) + U(C)$. Is it true that $U(\frac{1}{2}B + \frac{1}{2}C)$ is greater than $U(\frac{1}{2}A + \frac{1}{2}D)$ because the former has a smaller variance? Why or why not?

4.8 A small businesswoman faces a 10% chance of having a fire which will reduce her net worth to $1.00, a 10% chance that fire will reduce it to $50,000, and an 80% chance that nothing detrimental will happen, so that her business will retain its worth of $100,000. What is the maximum amount she will pay for insurance if she has a logarithmic utility function? In other words, if $U(W) = \ln W$, compute the cost of the gamble. [*Note:* The insurance pays $99,999 in the first case, $50,000 in the second, and nothing in the third.]

4.9 If you are exposed to a 50/50 chance of gaining or losing $1000 and insurance which removes the risk costs $500, at what level of wealth will you be indifferent relative to taking the gamble or paying the insurance? That is, what is your certainty equivalent wealth? Assume your utility function is $U(W) = -W^{-1}$.

4.10 Consider a lottery which pays $2 if n consecutive heads turn up in $n + 1$ tosses of a fair coin (i.e., the sequence of coin flips ends with the first tail). If you have a logarithmic utility function, $U(W) = \ln W$, what is the utility of the expected payoff? What is the expected utility of the payoff?

4.11 (Our thanks to David Pyle, University of California, Berkeley, for providing this problem.) Mr. Casadesus's current wealth consists of his home, which is worth $50,000, and $20,000 in savings, which are earning 7% in a savings and loan account. His (one-year) homeowner's insurance is up for renewal and he has the following estimates of the potential losses on his house due to fire, storm, etc., during the period covered by the renewal:

Value of Loss, $	Probability, %
0	.98
5,000	.01
10,000	.005
50,000	.005

His insurance agent has quoted the following premiums:

Amount of Insurance, $	Premium, $
30,000	$30 + AVL_1$*
40,000	$27 + AVL_2$
50,000	$24 + AVL_3$

* Actuarial value of loss = expected value of the *insurer's* loss.

Mr. Casadesus expects neither to save nor dissave during the coming year, and he does not expect his home to change appreciably in value over this period. His utility for wealth at the end of the period covered by the renewal is logarithmic, that is, $U(W) = \ln(W)$.

a) Given that the insurance company agrees with Mr. Casadesus's estimate of his losses, should he renew his policy for the full value of his house, for $40,000, for $30,000, or should he cancel it?

b) Suppose that Mr. Casadesus had $320,000 in a savings account. Would this change his insurance decision?

c) If Mr. Casadesus has $20,000 in savings, and if his utility function is

$$U(W) = -200,000\, W^{-1},$$

should he renew his home insurance, and if so, for what amount of coverage?

[*Note:* Insurance covers the first x dollars of loss. For simplicity, assume all losses occur at the end of the year, and the premium is paid at the beginning of the year.]

4.12 Assume that security returns are normally distributed. Compare portfolios A and B, using both first and second-order stochastic dominance

Case 1	Case 2	Case 3
$\sigma_A > \sigma_B$	$\sigma_A = \sigma_B$	$\sigma_A < \sigma_B$
$E_A = E_B$	$E_A > E_B$	$E_A < E_B$

4.13 Given the following probability distributions for risky assets X and Y.

Probability X_i	X_i	Probability Y_i	Y_i
.1	−10	.2	2
.4	5	.5	3
.3	10	.2	4
.2	12	.1	30

a) If the only available choice is 100% of your wealth in X or 100% in Y and you choose on the basis of mean and variance, which asset is preferred?

b) According to the second-order stochastic dominance criterion, how would you compare them?

4.14 You have estimated the following probabilities for earnings per share of companies A and B:

Probability	A	B
.1	0	−.50
.2	.50	−.25
.4	1.00	1.50
.2	2.00	3.00
.1	3.00	4.00

a) Calculate the mean and variance of the earnings per share for each company.

b) Explain how some investors might choose A and others might choose B if preferences are based on mean and variance.

c) Compare A and B using the second-order stochastic dominance criterion.

4.15 Answer the following questions either true or false:

a) T____ F____ If asset A is stochastically dominant over asset B according to the second-order criterion, it is also dominant according to the first-order criterion.

b) T____ F____ If asset A has a higher mean and higher variance than asset B, it is stochastically dominant according to the first-order criterion.

c) T____ F____ A risk-neutral investor will use second-order stochastic dominance as a decision criterion only if the returns of the underlying assets are normally distributed.

d) T____ F____ A second-order stochastic dominance criterion is consistent with utility functions which have positive marginal utility and risk aversion.

4.16 Consider the following two risky scenarios for future cash flows for a firm:

Project 1		Project 2	
Probability	Cash flow, $	Probability	Cash flow, $
.2	4,000	.4	0
.6	5,000	.2	5,000
.2	6,000	.4	10,000

Given that the firm has fixed debt payments of $8000, and limited liability, which scenario will shareholders choose and why? How would your answer change if there were not limited liability?

4.17 (Our thanks to Nils Hakansson, University of California, Berkeley, for providing this problem.) Two widows, each with $10,000 to invest, have been advised by a trusted friend to put their money into a one-year real estate trust which requires a minimum investment of $10,000. They have been offered a choice of six trusts with the following estimated yields:

								Probability That Yield Will Be								
Trust	−2	−1	0	1	2	3	4	5	6	7	8	9	10	11	12	13	14
A							.4	.2	.2	.2							
B	.1		.1	.1		.1	.1			.1			.1	.1	.1	.1	
C					.2	.2	.2	.2	.2								
D		.2		.2			.1	.1		.1	.1						.2
E							.4		.6								
F		.2		.2			.1	.1		.1	.1					.1	.1

Before making up their minds, they have called on you for advice.

a) The first widow leaves you unsure as to whether she is risk averse. What advice can you give her?

b) The second widow shows definite risk aversion. What is your advice to her?

4.18

a) Reorder the six real estate trusts in Problem 4.17, using the mean-variance criterion.

b) Is the mean-variance ranking the same as that achieved by second-order stochastic dominance?

REFERENCES

Arrow, K. J., *Essays in the Theory of Risk-Bearing.* North-Holland, Amsterdam, 1971.

Bawa, V. J., "Optimal Rules for Ordering Uncertain Prospects," *Journal of Financial Economics,* March 1975, 95–121.

Fama, E. F., and M. H. Miller, *The Theory of Finance,* Chapter 5, Holt, Rinehart and Winston, New York, 1972.

Friedman, M., and L. J. Savage, "The Utility Analysis of Choices Involving Risk," *The Journal of Political Economy,* August 1948, 279–304.

Friend, I., and M. Blume, "The Demand for Risky Assets," *The American Economic Review,* December 1975, 900–922.

Hanoch, G., and H. Levy, "The Efficiency Analysis of Choices Involving Risk," *Review of Economic Studies,* 1969, 335–346.

Herstein, I. N., and J. Milnor, "An Axiomatic Approach to Expected Utility," *Econometrica,* April 1953, 291–297.

Jean, W., "Comparison of Moment and Stochastic Dominance Ranking Methods," *Journal of Financial and Quantitative Analysis,* March 1975, 151–162.

Keeney, R. L., and H. Raiffa, *Decisions with Multiple Objectives: Preferences and Value Tradeoffs,* John Wiley and Sons, New York, 1976.

Kira D., and W. T. Ziemba, "Equivalence Among Alternative Portfolio Selection Criteria," in H. Levy and M. Sarnat, *Financial Decision Making Under Uncertainty,* Academic Press, New York, 1977, 151–161.

Levy, H., and Y. Kroll, "Stochastic Dominance with Riskless Assets," *Journal of Financial and Quantitative Analysis,* December 1976, 743–778.

Markowitz, H., *Portfolio Selection.* Yale University Press, New Haven, 1959.

Porter, R. B., J. R. Wart, and D. L. Ferguson, "Efficient Algorithms for Conducting Stochastic Dominance Tests of Large Numbers of Portfolios," *Journal of Financial and Quantitative Analysis,* January 1973, 71–82.

Pratt, J. W., "Risk Aversion in the Small and in the Large," *Econometrica,* January–April, 1964, 122–136.

Rubin, P. H., and C. W. Paul II, "An Evolutionary Model of Taste for Risk," *Economic Inquiry,* October 1979, 585–596.

Tobin, J., "Liquidity Preference as a Behavior Toward Risk," *The Review of Economic Studies,* February 1958, 65–86.

Vickson, R. G., "Stochastic Dominance for Decreasing Absolute Risk Aversion," *Journal of Financial and Quantitative Analysis,* December 1975, 799–812.

————, and M. Altman, "On the Relative Effectiveness of Stochastic Dominance Rules: Extension to Decreasingly Risk-Averse Utility Functions," *Journal of Financial and Quantitative Analysis,* March 1977, 73–84.

Von Neumann, J., and O. Morgenstern, *Theory of Games and Economic Behavior,* Princeton University Press, Princeton, N.J., 1947.

Walter, J. E., *Dividend Policy and Enterprise Valuation,* Wadsworth, Belmont, Cal., 1967.

Whitmore, G. A., "Third Degree Stochastic Dominance," *American Economic Review,* June 1970, 457–459.

————, and M. C. Findlay, *Stochastic Dominance,* Lexington Books, D.C. Heath and Co., Lexington, Mass., 1975.

Ziemba, W. T. and R. G. Vickson (eds.), *Stochastic Optimization Models in Finance,* Academic Press, New York, 1975.

State-Preference Theory*

In this formulation the objects of choice are not derivative statistical measures of the probability distribution of consumption opportunities but rather the contingent consumption claims themselves set out in extensive form.

J. HIRSHLEIFER, "EFFICIENT ALLOCATION OF CAPITAL IN AN UNCERTAIN WORLD," *THE AMERICAN ECONOMIC REVIEW,* MAY 1964, P. 80.

Finance deals with investment decisions of individuals and firms which are linked through the supply and demand for securities in the capital market. Firms borrow capital for investment in real assets by *selling* securities; individuals obtain claims to firms' real assets by *investing* in securities. Thus securities present opportunities for intertemporal shifts of consumption through the financing of productive activities. Both individual consumption-investment decisions which determine aggregate security demand and firm investment decisions which determine aggregate security supply are affected by security prices.

---

* Ronald W. Masulis was the primary author of the chapter text, and has benefited from lecture notes on this topic by Herbert Johnson.

By equating security supply and demand, these security prices yield a consistent set of firm and individual investment decisions. In this chapter we will analyze how optimal individual investment decisions and optimal firm investment decisions are determined under uncertainty for a given set of security prices.

In chapter four we found that, under certain conditions, individual decision making under uncertainty is accomplished by maximizing *expected* utility of end-of-period wealth. This decision criterion was shown to be valid when individuals are rational, prefer more wealth to less, and follow the five axioms of choice under uncertainty. Implicitly, it was also assumed that individuals can assess a security's probability distribution of end-of-period payoffs. It was shown that the expected utility criterion is a very simple way of choosing among mutually exclusive investments having different probability distributions of end-of-period payoffs. By choosing the investment with the highest expected utility, the optimal investment is immediately determined, thus condensing a choice across N probability distributions of end-of-period payoffs into a comparison among N expected utility values.

In this and following chapters, we wish to move beyond the individual's choice problem of mutually exclusive investments to the more general problem of portfolio decision making; that is, the optimal choice of investing in more than one risky security. This is equivalent to the problem of choosing an individual's probability distribution of end-of-period wealth which is consistent with the set of available risky securities and the individual's initial wealth. The individual's choice problem is to find that portfolio or linear combination of risky security quantities that is optimal given his or her initial wealth and tastes. We assume a perfect capital market to ensure that there are no costs of portfolio construction.

A. UNCERTAINTY AND ALTERNATIVE FUTURE STATES

Securities inherently have a time dimension. The securities investment decisions of individuals are determined by their desired consumption over future time intervals. The passage of time involves uncertainty about the future and hence about the future value of a security investment. From the standpoint of both the issuing firm and the individual investors the uncertain future value of a security can be represented as a vector of possible payoffs at some future date, and an individual's portfolio of investments is a matrix of possible payoffs on the different securities that compose the portfolio.

In the state-preference model, uncertainty takes the form of not knowing what the state of nature will be at some future date. To the investor, a security is a set of possible payoffs, each one associated with a mutually exclusive state of nature. Once the uncertain state of the world is revealed, the payoff on the security is determined exactly. Thus a security represents a claim to a vector (or bundle) of state-contingent payoffs.

In the simplest case, there are two possible outcomes with probabilities π_1 and π_2 and therefore two mutually exclusive states of nature with probabilities π_1 and

Figure 5.1
Elementary state contingent claim.

π_2. Take as an example an investment in a lottery ticket with outcomes ($10,000, $0). With probability π_1, state 1 is realized and the lottery ticket pays off $10,000; with probability $\pi_2 = 1 - \pi_1$, state 2 is realized and the lottery ticket pays off nothing (Fig. 5.1).

The probability of a state of nature occurring is thus equal to the probability of the associated end-of-period security payoff. The states of nature are assumed to capture the fundamental causes of economic uncertainty in the economy, e.g., state 1 could represent peace and state 2 could represent war or state 1 could represent prosperity and state 2 could represent depression. Once the state of nature is known, the end-of-period payoff of each risky security is also known. By summing over individual security holdings and then over individuals it follows that once the state of nature is known, individual and aggregate end-of-period wealth are also known.

In principle, there can be an infinite number of states of nature and thus an infinite number of end-of-period payoffs for a risky asset. This set of states must meet the critical properties of being mutually exclusive and exhaustive. That is to say, one and only one state of nature will be realized at the end of period and the sum of the probabilities of the individual states of nature occurring equals one. It is also assumed that (1) individuals can associate an outcome from each security's probability distribution of its end-of-period payoff with each state of nature that could occur, and (2) individuals are only concerned about the amount of wealth they will have if a given state occurs; once their wealth is known they are otherwise indifferent as to which state of nature occurs (i.e., individuals have state-independent utility functions).[1]

B. DEFINITION OF PURE SECURITIES

Analytically, the generalization of the standard, timeless, microeconomic analysis under certainty to a multiperiod economy under uncertainty with securities markets is facilitated by the concept of a pure security. A pure or primitive security is defined as a security which pays one dollar at the end of the period if a given state occurs and nothing if any other state occurs. The concept of the pure security allows the logical decomposition of market securities into portfolios of pure securities.[2] Thus

---

[1] For example, if an individual's utility was a function of other individuals' wealth positions as well as one's own, then the utility function would generally be state dependent.

[2] Pure or primitive securities are often called Arrow-Debreu securities, since Arrow [1964] and Debreu [1959] set forth their original specification.

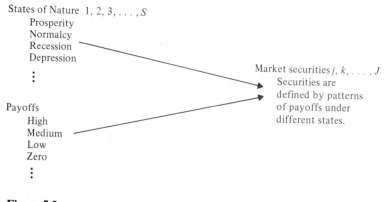

States of Nature 1, 2, 3, . . . , S
    Prosperity
    Normalcy
    Recession
    Depression
    ⋮

Market securities $j, k, . . . , J$
Securities are
defined by patterns
of payoffs under
different states.

Payoffs
    High
    Medium
    Low
    Zero
    ⋮

Figure 5.2
States, payoffs, and securities.

every market security may be considered a combination of various pure securities.

In terms of state-preference theory, a security represents a position with regard to each possible future state of nature. In Fig. 5.2, market securities are defined with respect to the characteristics of their payoffs under each alternative future state. A market security thus consists of a set of payoff characteristics distributed over states of nature. The complexity of the security may range from numerous payoff characteristics in many states to no payoff at all in all but one state.

C. COMPLETE CAPITAL MARKET

In the state preference framework, uncertainty about securities' future values is represented by a set of possible state-contingent payoffs. Linear combinations of this set of state-contingent *security* payoffs represent an individual's opportunity set of state-contingent *portfolio* payoffs. An important property of this opportunity set is determined by whether or not the capital market is complete. When the number of unique linearly independent securities is equal to the total number of alternative future states of nature, the market is said to be complete. For the case of three states of nature, suppose that a risk-free asset with payoff $(1, 1, 1)$, an unemployment insurance contract with payoff $(1, 0, 0)$, and risky debt with payoff $(0, 1, 1)$ all exist, but no other securities can be traded. In this case we have three securities and three states of nature, but we do not have a complete market since the payoff on the risk-free asset is just the sum of the payoffs on the other two market securities, i.e., the three securities are not linearly independent. If, as in this example, the market is incomplete, then not every possible security payoff can be constructed from a portfolio of the existing securities. For example, the security payoff $(0, 1, 0)$ cannot be obtained from $(1, 1, 1)$, $(1, 0, 0)$, and $(0, 1, 1)$. The existing securities will, of course, have well-defined prices, but any possible new security that is not *spanned* by these securities (i.e., cannot be created from the existing securities) will not have a unique price.[3]

Suppose now that in addition to the security payoffs (1, 1, 1), (1, 0, 0), and (0, 1, 1), a stock with payoff (0, 1, 3) also exists. Then among these four securities there are three that are linearly independent state contingent payoffs, and with three states the market is complete. Assuming the market is perfect, any pattern of returns can be created in a complete market. In particular, a complete set of pure securities with payoffs (1, 0, 0), (0, 1, 0), (0, 0, 1) can be created as linear combinations of existing securities. It takes some linear algebra to figure out how to obtain the pure securities from any arbitrary complete set of market securities, but once we know how to form them, it is easy to replicate any other security from a linear combination of the pure securities. For example: a security with payoff (a, b, c) can be replicated by buying (or short selling if a, b, or c is negative) a of (1, 0, 0), b of (0, 1, 0) and c of (0, 0, 1).[4]

Given a complete securities market, we could theoretically reduce the uncertainty about the value of our future wealth to zero. It does not make any difference which uncertain future state of nature will actually occur. That is, by dividing our wealth in a particular way among the available securities, we could, if we chose, construct a portfolio that was equivalent to holding equal amounts of all the pure securities. This portfolio would have the same payoff in every state even though the payoffs of individual securities varied over states.[5]

Without going through a complex solution process to attain the general equilibrium results which the concept of a pure security facilitates, we shall convey the role of the concept of a pure security in a more limited setting. We shall demonstrate how in a perfect and complete capital market the implicit price of a pure security can be derived from the prices of existing market securities and how the prices of other securities can then be developed from the implicit prices of pure securities.

D. DERIVATION OF PURE
SECURITY PRICES

Given that we know the state-contingent payoff vectors of both the market securities and the pure securities, we wish to develop the relationship between the *prices* of the market securities and pure securities in a perfect and complete capital market.

The following notation will be used throughout this chapter:

---

[3] One person might think the security with payoff (0, 1, 0) is worth more than someone else does, but if the security cannot be formed from a portfolio of existing market securities, then these virtual prices that different people would assign to this hypothetical security need not be the same.

[4] See Appendix A to this chapter for a general method of determining whether a complete market exists.

[5] While a complete market may appear to require an unreasonably large number of independent securities, Ross [1976] showed that in general if option contracts can be written on market securities and market securities have sufficiently variable payoffs across states, an infinite number of linearly independent security and option payoffs can be formed from a small number of securities.

Table 5.1 Payoffs in Relation to Prices of Baskets of Fruit

	Bananas	Apples	Prices*
Basket 1	10	20	$8
Basket 2	30	10	$9

* The probabilities of the states are implicit in the prices.

p_s = prices of pure securities,

p_j = prices of market securities,

π_s = state probabilities—individuals' beliefs about the relative likelihoods of states occurring,

Q_s = number of pure securities.

Let us begin with an analogy. The Mistinback Company sells baskets of fruit, limiting its sales to only two types of baskets. Basket 1 is composed of 10 bananas and 20 apples and sells for $8. Basket 2 is composed of 30 bananas and 10 apples and sells for $9. The situation may be summarized by the payoffs set forth in Table 5.1.

Using the relationships in Table 5.1 we can solve for the prices of apples and bananas separately. Let us denote apples by A, bananas by B, the baskets of fruit by 1 and 2, and the quantity of apples and bananas in a basket by Q_{jA} and Q_{jB} respectively. Using this notation we can express the prices of the two baskets as follows:

$$p_1 = p_A Q_{1A} + p_B Q_{1B}, \qquad p_2 = p_A Q_{2A} + p_B Q_{2B}.$$

Only p_A and p_B are unknown. Thus there are two equations and two unknowns, and the system is solvable as follows (substitute the known values in each equation):

$$(1) \quad \$8 = p_A 20 + p_B 10, \qquad (2) \quad \$9 = p_A 10 + p_B 30.$$

Subtract three times Eq. (1) from Eq. (2) to obtain p_A:

$$\begin{aligned}
\$9 &= p_A 10 + p_B 30 \\
-\$24 &= -p_A 60 - p_B 30 \\
\hline
-\$15 &= -p_A 50 \\
p_A &= \$.30.
\end{aligned}$$

Then substituting the value of p_A into Eq. (1), we have

$$\$8 = (\$.30)20 + p_B 10 = \$6 + p_B 10,$$

$$\$2 = p_B 10,$$

$$p_B = \$.20.$$

Table 5.2   Payoff Table for Securities j and k

Security	State 1	State 2	
j	$10	$20	$p_j = \$8$
k	$30	$10	$p_k = \$9$

Given that we know the prices of the market securities, we may now apply this same analysis to the problem of determining the implicit prices of the pure securities. Consider security j, which pays $10 if state 1 occurs and $20 if state 2 occurs. The price of security j is $8. Security k pays $30 if state 1 occurs and $10 if state 2 occurs; its price is $9. Note that state 1 might be a GNP growth rate of 8% in real terms during the year while state 2 might represent a GNP growth rate of only 1% in real terms. This information is summarized in Table 5.2.

Any individual security is similar to a mixed basket of goods with regard to alternative future states of nature. Recall that a pure security pays $1 if a specified state occurs and nothing if any other state occurs. We may proceed to determine the price of a pure security in a manner analogous to that employed for the fruit baskets. The equations for determining the price for two pure securities related to the situation described are

$$p_1 Q_{j1} + p_2 Q_{j2} = p_j,$$

$$p_1 Q_{k1} + p_2 Q_{k2} = p_k,$$

where Q_{j1} represents the quantity of pure securities paying $1 in state 1 included in security j. Proceeding analogously to the situation for the fruit baskets, we insert values into the two equations. Substituting the respective payoffs for securities j and k, we obtain $.20 as the price of pure security 1 and $.30 as the price of pure security 2:

$$p_1 10 + p_2 20 = \$8$$

$$p_1 30 + p_2 10 = \$9$$

$$p_1 = \$.20, \qquad p_2 = \$.30$$

It should be emphasized that the p_1 of $.20 and the p_2 of $.30 are the prices of the two pure securities and not the prices of the market securities j and k. Securities j and k represent portfolios of pure securities. Any actual security provides different payoffs for different future states. But under appropriately defined conditions, the prices of market securities permit us to determine the prices of pure securities. Thus our results indicate that for pure security 1, a $.20 payment is required for a promise of a payoff of $1 if state 1 occurs and nothing if any other states occur. The concept of pure security is useful for analytical purposes as well as for providing a simple description of uncertainty for financial analysis.

E. NO ARBITRAGE PROFIT CONDITION

Capital market equilibrium requires that market prices be set so that supply equals demand for each individual security. In the context of the state preference framework, one condition necessary for market equilibrium requires that any two securities or portfolios with the same state-contingent payoff vectors must be priced identically.[6] Otherwise, everyone would want to buy the security or portfolio with the lower price and to sell the security or portfolio with the higher price. If both securities or portfolios are in positive supply, such prices cannot represent an equilibrium. This condition is often called the single price law of markets.

If short selling is allowed in the capital market, we can obtain a second related necessary condition for market equilibrium, namely, the absence of any riskless arbitrage profit opportunity. To short sell a security, an individual borrows the security from a current owner and then immediately sells the security in the capital market at the current price. Then at a later date, the individual goes back to the capital market and repurchases the security at the then current market price and immediately returns the security to the lender. If the security price fell over the period of the short sale, the individual makes a profit; if the security price rose, he or she takes a loss. In either case the short seller's gain or loss is always the negative of the owner's gain or loss over this same period.

When two portfolios A and B sell at different prices, where $p_A > p_B$, but have identical state-contingent payoff vectors, we could short sell the more expensive portfolio and realize a cash flow of p_A and then buy the less expensive portfolio for a negative cash flow of p_B. We would realize a positive net cash flow of $p_A - p_B$ and at the end of the period we could at no risk take our payoff from owning portfolio B to *exactly* repay our short position in portfolio A. Thus the positive net cash flow at the beginning of the period represents a riskless arbitrage profit opportunity. Since all investors are assumed to prefer more wealth to less, this arbitrage opportunity is inconsistent with market equilibrium.

In a perfect and complete capital market, any market security's payoff vector can be exactly replicated by a portfolio of pure securities. Thus it follows that when short selling is allowed, the no arbitrage profit condition requires that the price of the market security must be equal to the price of any linear combination of pure securities which replicates the market security's payoff vector.

F. ECONOMIC DETERMINANTS OF SECURITY PRICES

To gain an understanding of what determines the price of a market security, we will first consider what determines the price of individual pure securities. Since a

---

[6] This condition implies the absence of any first order stochastically dominated market securities. Otherwise the former payoff per dollar of investment would exceed the latter payoff per dollar of investment in every state. The latter security would be first order stochastically dominated by the former security.

market security can always be constructed from the set of pure securities in a complete market, we can then answer the first question as well.

The prices of the pure securities will be determined by trading among individuals. Even if these pure securities themselves are not directly traded, we can still infer prices for them in a complete market from the prices of the market securities which *are* traded. The prices of pure securities will be shown to depend on

1. time preferences for consumption and the productivity of capital,
2. expectations as to the probability that a particular state will occur,
3. individuals' attitudes toward risk given the variability across states of aggregate end of period wealth.

To understand how (1) affects security prices, we need to recognize that a riskless security can always be constructed in a complete capital market simply by forming a portfolio composed of one pure security for each state. Hence, the payoff on this portfolio is riskless since a dollar will be paid regardless of what state is realized. In the case of three states, the price of this riskless portfolio is the sum of the prices of the three individual pure securities $p_1 + p_2 + p_3 = .8$, for example. The price of a riskless claim to one dollar at the end of the period is just the present value of a dollar discounted at the risk-free rate r, that is to say $1/(1 + r) = p_1 + p_2 + p_3$, so for the above example $r = 25\%$. In general, the risk-free interest rate is found from $1/(1 + r) = \Sigma_s p_s$. If there is positive time value of money, the riskless interest rate will be positive. The actual size of this interest rate will reflect individual time preferences for consumption and the productivity of capital just as is the case in a simple world of certainty.[7] Thus one determinant of the price of a pure security paying a dollar if state s occurs is the market discounted rate on a certain end-of-period dollar payoff.

The second determinant of a pure security's price and a cause for differences in security prices are individuals' beliefs concerning the relative likelihood of different states occurring. These beliefs are often termed "state probabilities," π_s. Individuals' subjective beliefs concerning state probabilities can differ in principle. However, the simplest case is one in which individuals agree on the relative likelihoods of states. This assumption is termed *homogeneous expectations* and implies that there is a well-defined set of state probabilities known to all individuals in the capital market. Under the assumption of homogeneous expectations, the price of a pure (state-contingent) security, p_s, can be decomposed into the probability of the state, π_s, and the price, θ_s, of an expected dollar payoff contingent on state s occurring, $p_s = \pi_s \cdot \theta_s$. This follows from the fact that pure security s pays a dollar only when s is realized. Thus the expected end of period payoff on pure security s is a dollar multiplied by the probability of state s occurring. This implies that we can decompose the end-

---

[7] The property that individuals prefer to consume a dollar of resources today, rather than consume the same dollar of resources tomorrow, is called time preference for consumption. As discussed in Chapter 1, an individual's marginal rate of time preference for consumption is equal to his or her marginal rate of substitution of current consumption and *certain* end-of-period consumption. In a perfect capital market, it was also shown that the marginal rates of time preference for all individuals are equal to the market interest rate.

of-period expected payoff into an expected payoff of a dollar and the probability of state s. Even when prices of expected dollar payoffs contingent on a particular state s occurring are the same across states ($\theta_s = \theta_t$ for all s and t), the prices of pure securities will differ as long as the probabilities of states occurring are not all identical ($\pi_s \neq \pi_t$; for all s and t).

A useful alternative way to see this point is to recognize that the price of a pure security is equal to its *expected* end-of-period payoff discounted to the present at its expected rate of return

$$p_s = \frac{\$1 \cdot \pi_s}{1 + E(R_s)}$$

where $0 < p_s < 1$. Thus, the pure security's expected rate of return is

$$E(R_s) = \frac{\$1 \cdot \pi_s}{p_s} - 1 = \frac{\$1}{\theta_s} - 1 \quad \text{where} \quad 0 < \theta_s < 1,$$

since $p_s = \pi_s \theta_s$ under the assumption of homogeneous expectations. So if the θ_s's were identical across states, the expected rates of return would be equal for all pure securities. But given that the probabilities across states differ, the expected payoffs across pure securities must also differ. If expected payoffs vary, expected rates of return can be the same only when the prices of the pure securities vary proportionally with the state probabilities.

The third determinant of security prices and a second cause for differences in these prices are individuals' attitudes toward risk when there is variability in aggregate wealth across states. Assuming that individuals are risk averse, they will diversify by investing in some of each pure security to ensure that they are not penniless regardless of what state is realized.[8] In fact, if the prices, θ_s's, of expected payoffs of a dollar contingent on a particular state occurring were the same for all states (and thus the expected rates of return of pure securities were all equal), then each risk averse individual would want to invest in an equal number of each pure security so as to eliminate all uncertainty about his or her future wealth. Not everyone can do this, however, since aggregate wealth is not the same in every state; that is, there is *nondiversifiable risk* in the economy and it must be borne by someone. Consider the following example. End-of-the-period aggregate wealth can be one, two, or three trillion dollars, depending on whether the depressed, normal, or prosperous state occurs; then the average investor must hold a portfolio with a payoff vector of the form $(X, 2X, 3X)$. Because individuals are risk averse, dollar payoffs are more valuable in states where they have relatively low wealth, which in this example is state 1. In order for people to be induced to bear the risk associated with a payoff vector of form $(X, 2X, 3X)$, pure security prices must be adjusted to make the state 1 security relatively expensive and the state 3 security relatively cheap. In other words, to increase demand for the relatively abundant state 3 securities, prices must adjust to lower the expected rate of return on state 1 securities and to raise the expected rates of return on state 3 securities.

---

[8] This also requires the utility function to exhibit infinite *marginal* utility at a zero wealth level.

If aggregate wealth were the same in some states, then risk-averse investors would want to hold the same number of pure securities for these states and there would be no reason for prices of expected dollar payoffs to be different in these states. Investors would not want to hold unequal numbers of claims to the states with the same aggregate wealth because this would mean bearing risk that could be diversified away, and there is no reason to expect a reward for bearing *diversifiable risk*. So it is the prospect of a higher portfolio expected return which induces the risk-averse investors to bear nondiversifiable risk. Thus, risk aversion combined with variability in end-of-period aggregate wealth causes variation in the prices (θ_s's) of dollar expected payoffs across states, negatively related to the aggregate end-of-period wealth or aggregate payoffs across states. This in turn causes like variations in the pure security prices.

There is a very important condition implicit in the previous discussion. We found that when investors are risk averse, securities which pay off relatively more in states with low aggregate wealth have relatively low expected rates of return, while securities which pay off relatively more in states with high aggregate wealth have relatively high expected rates of return. Since aggregate wealth is equal to the sum of the payoffs on all market securities, it is also termed the payoff on the *market portfolio*. Securities with state-contingent payoffs positively related to the state-contingent payoffs on the market portfolio, and which therefore involve significant nondiversifiable risk bearing, have higher expected rates of return than securities that have payoffs negatively or less positively related to the payoffs on the market portfolio and which therefore involve little nondiversifiable risk bearing. We will return to this important condition in Chapter 7.

It follows from this analysis that a pure security price can be decomposed into three factors:

$$p_s = \pi_s \theta_s = \frac{\$1 \pi_s}{1 + E(R_s)} = \frac{\$1}{1 + r} \pi_s \left(\frac{1 + r}{1 + E(R_s)} \right)$$

$$= \frac{\$1}{1 + r} \pi_s \left[1 - \frac{E(R_s) - r}{1 + E(R_s)} \right] \quad \text{where} \quad E(R_s) \geq r.$$

The first factor is an end-of-period dollar payoff discounted to the present at the riskless rate. It is multiplied by the second factor, which is the probability of payoff. The third factor, in brackets, is a risk adjustment factor. Note that if investors are all risk neutral, the expected rate of return on all securities will be equal to the riskless interest rate, in which case the above risk adjustment factor (i.e., the factor in brackets) becomes one. In summary, security prices are affected by (1) the time value of money, (2) the probability beliefs about state-contingent payoffs, and (3) individual preferences toward risk and the level of variability in aggregate state-contingent payoffs or wealth (i.e., the level of nondiversifiable risk in the economy).

G. OPTIMAL PORTFOLIO DECISIONS

Now that we have developed the basic structure of state preference theory, we will return to the problem of optimal portfolio choice in a perfect and complete capital market. This will then be followed by an analysis of a firm's optimal investment problem, also in a perfect and complete capital market. Since any portfolio payoff pattern can be constructed from the existing market securities or from a full set of pure securities in a complete capital market, we can obtain the same optimal portfolio position whether we frame the analysis in terms of market securities or pure securities. Since pure securities are much simpler to analyze, we will phrase the optimal portfolio problem in terms of these securities. Thus we can write an individual's expected utility of end-of-period wealth as $\sum_s \pi_s U(Q_s)$, where Q_s = number of pure securities paying a dollar if state s occurs. In this context Q_s represents the number of state s pure securities the individual buys as well as his or her end-of-period wealth if state s occurs.

Now consider the problem we face when we must decide how much of our initial wealth, W_0, to spend for current consumption, C, and what portfolio of securities to hold for the future. We wish to solve the problem[9]

$$\text{Max}\left[u(C) + \sum_s \pi_s U(Q_s) \right] \qquad (5.1)$$

subject to

$$\sum_s p_s Q_s + \$1 C - W_0. \qquad (5.2)$$

That is, we are maximizing our expected utility of current and future consumption subject to our wealth constraint. Our portfolio decision consists of the choices we make for Q_s, the number of pure securities we buy for each state s. Note that there is no explicit discounting of future utility, but any such discounting could be absorbed in the functional form for $U(Q_s)$. In addition, the p_s's include an implicit market discount rate. There is no need to take an expectation over $u(C)$, our utility of current consumption, since there is no uncertainty concerning the present.

There are two ways to maximize expected utility subject to a wealth constraint. We could solve (5.2) for one of the Q_s, say Q_1, and then eliminate this variable from (5.1). Sometimes this is the easiest way, but more often it is easier to use the Lagrange multiplier method (see Appendix D at end of book),

$$L = u(C) + \sum_s \pi_s U(Q_s) - \lambda\left(\sum_s p_s Q_s + \$1 C - W_0 \right), \qquad (5.3)$$

where λ is called a Lagrange multiplier. The Lagrange multiplier λ is a measure of how much our utility would increase if our initial wealth were increased by one dollar. To obtain the investor's optimal choice of C and Q_s's, we take the partial derivatives with respect to each of these variables and set them equal to zero. Taking the partial derivative with respect to C yields

$$\frac{\partial L}{\partial C} = u'(C) - \$1\lambda = 0, \qquad (5.4)$$

---

[9] This formulation assumes that the utility function is separable into utility of current consumption and utility of end-of-period consumption. In principle, the utility functions, $u(C)$ and $U(Q_s)$, can be different functions.

where the prime denotes partial differentiation with respect to the argument of the function. Next, we take partial derivatives with respect to Q_1, Q_2, and so on. For each Q_t we will pick up one term from the expected utility and one from the wealth constraint (all other terms vanish):

$$\frac{\partial L}{\partial Q_t} = \pi_t U'(Q_t) - \lambda p_t = 0, \qquad (5.5)$$

where $\pi_t U'(Q_t)$ = expected marginal utility of an investment Q_t in pure security s. We also take the partial derivative with respect to λ:

$$\frac{\partial L}{\partial \lambda} = \left(\sum_s p_s Q_s + \$1C - W_0 \right) = 0. \qquad (5.6)$$

This just gives us back the wealth constraint. These first order conditions allow us to determine the individual's optimal consumption-investment choices.[10]

As an example, consider an investor with a logarithmic utility function of wealth and initial wealth of $10,000. Assume a two state world where the pure security prices are .4 and .6 and the state probabilities are $\frac{1}{3}$ and $\frac{2}{3}$ respectively. The Lagrangian function is

$$L = \ln C + \tfrac{1}{3} \ln Q_1 + \tfrac{2}{3} \ln Q_2 - \lambda(.4Q_1 + .6Q_2 + C - 10{,}000)$$

and the first order conditions are

(a) $\dfrac{\partial L}{\partial C} = \dfrac{1}{C} - \lambda = 0,$ which implies $C = \dfrac{1}{\lambda},$

(b) $\dfrac{\partial L}{\partial Q_1} = \dfrac{1}{3Q_1} - .4\lambda = 0,$ which implies $Q_1 = \dfrac{1}{1.2\lambda},$

(c) $\dfrac{\partial L}{\partial Q_2} = \dfrac{2}{3Q_2} - .6\lambda = 0,$ which implies $Q_2 = \dfrac{1}{.9\lambda},$

(d) $\dfrac{\partial L}{\partial \lambda} = 10{,}000 - C - .4Q_1 - .6Q_2 = 0.$

Substituting equations (a-c) into (d) yields

(d') $\dfrac{1}{\lambda} + \dfrac{.4}{1.2\lambda} + \dfrac{.6}{.9\lambda} = 10{,}000,$

and multiplying by λ yields

(d") $1 + \tfrac{1}{3} + \tfrac{2}{3} = 10{,}000\lambda,$ which yields $\lambda = \dfrac{1}{5{,}000}$

Now, substituting this value of λ back into equations (a-c) yields the optimal consumption and investment choices, $C = \$5{,}000$, $Q_1 = 4166.7$ and $Q_2 = 5555.5$. Substituting

---

[10] We also are assuming that the second order conditions for a maximum hold.

these quantities back into the wealth constraint verifies that this is indeed a feasible solution. The investor in this problem divides his or her wealth equally between current and future consumption, which is what we should expect since the risk-free interest rate is zero (i.e., $\Sigma p_s = 1 = 1/(1 + r)$) and there is no time preference for consumption in this logarithmic utility function. However, the investor does buy more of the state 2 pure security since the expected rate of return on the state 2 pure security is greater. Because the utility function exhibits risk aversion, the investor also invests some of his or her wealth in the state 1 pure security.

In this example we assumed that the investor is a price taker. In a general equilibrium framework, the prices of the pure securities would be determined as part of the problem, i.e., they would be *endogenous*. The prices would be determined as a result of individuals' constrained expected utility maximization, (which determines the aggregate demands for securities), and firms' optimal investment decisions (which determine the aggregate supplies of securities). The critical condition required for equilibrium is that the supply of each market security equal its aggregate demand. In a complete capital market this equilibrium condition can be restated by saying that aggregate supply of each pure security is equal to its aggregate demand.

H. PORTFOLIO OPTIMALITY CONDITIONS AND PORTFOLIO SEPARATION

In a complete capital market, we can obtain a number of important portfolio optimality conditions. These conditions hold for any risk averse expected utility maximizer. Rewriting equation (5.4) and equation (5.5) in terms of λ and eliminating λ yields two sets of portfolio optimality conditions:

$$\frac{\pi_t U'(Q_t)}{u'(C)} = \frac{p_t}{\$1} \quad \text{for any state } t \tag{5.7}$$

and

$$\frac{\pi_t U'(Q_t)}{\pi_s U'(Q_s)} = \frac{p_t}{p_s} \quad \text{for any two states } s \text{ and } t. \tag{5.8}$$

In both cases, the optimal allocation of wealth represents choosing C and the Q_s's so that the ratio of expected marginal utilities equals the ratio of market prices for the C and the Q_s's. That is, the optimal consumption and investment choices involve choosing points on the various indifference curves (curves of constant *expected* utility) which are tangent to the associated market lines. This is equivalent to choosing consumption and investment weights so that the slopes of the indifference curves (which are defined as the negative of the marginal rates of substitution) representing current consumption and future consumption contingent on state t (as in Fig. 5.3) or representing future consumption contingent on state s and state t (as in Fig. 5.4) are equal to the slopes of the respective market lines (representing the market exchange rates, e.g. $-p_t/p_s$).

Figure 5.3
Optimal consumption-investment decisions.

Figure 5.4
Optimal portfolio decisions.

An alternative way of stating the optimality conditions of the above portfolio is that the expected marginal utilities of wealth in state s, divided by the price of the state s pure security, should be equal across all states, and this ratio should also be equal to the marginal utility of current consumption. This is a reasonable result; if expected marginal utility per pure security price were high in one state and low in another, then we must not have maximized expected utility. We should increase investment in the high expected marginal utility security at the expense of the security which is yielding low expected marginal utility. But as we do that, we lower expected marginal utility where it is high and raise it where it is low, because a risk-averse investor's marginal utility decreases with wealth (his or her utility function has a positive but decreasing slope). Finally, when Eq. (5.8) is satisfied, there is no way left to increase expected utility.[11]

When investors' portfolio choices over risky securities are independent of their individual wealth positions, we have a condition known as *portfolio separation*. This condition requires that there are either additional restrictions on investor preferences or additional restrictions on security return distributions.[12] Under portfolio separation,

---

[11] This entire procedure will ordinarily not work if the investor is risk-neutral instead of risk-averse. A risk-neutral investor will plunge entirely in the security with the highest expected return. He or she would like to invest even more in this security, but, being already fully invested in it, cannot do so. Equation (5.8) will not hold for risk neutrality.

[12] Cass and Stiglitz [1970] proved that for arbitrary security return distributions, utility functions with the property of linear risk tolerance yield portfolio separation. The risk tolerance of the utility function is the reciprocal of the Pratt-Arrow measure of absolute risk aversion discussed in Chapter 4. Thus a linear risk-tolerance utility function can be expressed as a *linear* function of wealth:

$$-U'(W)/U''(W) = a + bW. \tag{5.9}$$

If investors also have homogeneous expectations about state probabilities and all investors have the same b, then there is *two-fund separation* where all investors hold combinations of two basic portfolios.

Utility functions exhibiting linear risk tolerance include the quadratic, logarithmic, power, and exponential functions. Ross [1976] proved that for arbitrary risk-averse utility functions, a number of classes investors choose among only a few basic portfolios of market securities. Thus the importance of having a complete market is greatly decreased. Recall that when capital markets are incomplete, individuals are limited in their choices of state-contingent payoff patterns to those payoff patterns which can be constructed as linear combinations of existing market securities. However, with portfolio separation, investors will often find that the infeasible payoff opportunities would not have been chosen even if they were available. Thus, under portfolio separation, investor portfolio decisions will often be unaffected by whether or not the capital market is complete.

Portfolio separation has been shown to depend on the form of the utility function of individuals and the form of the security return distributions. In the special case where investor utility functions of wealth are quadratic, or security returns are joint-normally distributed, portfolio separation obtains. With the addition of homogeneous expectations, portfolio separation provides sufficient conditions for a security pricing equation. This security-pricing relationship can be expressed in terms of means and variances and is called the *capital asset pricing model*.[13] The resulting form of the security-pricing equation is particularly convenient for formulating testable propositions and conducting empirical studies. As we shall discuss in the following chapters, many of the implications of portfolio separation in capital markets appear to be consistent with observed behavior and have been supported by empirical tests.

I. FIRM VALUATION, THE FISHER SEPARATION PRINCIPLE, AND OPTIMAL INVESTMENT DECISIONS[14]

In state-preference theory, individuals save by purchasing firm securities. Firms obtain resources for investment by issuing securities. Securities are precisely defined as conditional or unconditional payoffs in terms of alternative future states of nature. All individual and firm decisions are made and all trading occurs at the beginning of the period. Consumers maximize their expected utility of present and future consumption and are characterized by their initial endowments (wealth) and their preferences. Firms are characterized by production functions which define the ability to transform current resources into state-contingent future consumption goods; e.g., where I_j is initial investment, $Q_{sj} = \phi_j(I_j, s)$. Total state-contingent output produced by a firm must equal the sum of the payoffs from all securities issued by a firm.

Firms maximize an objective function which, in its most general form, is maximization of the expected utility of its current shareholders. To do this it may appear that firms would need to know the utility functions of all their current shareholders.

---

of security return distributions (including the normal distribution, some stable Paretian distributions, and some distributions which are not stable Paretian, e.g., fat-tailed distributions with relatively more extreme values) yield portfolio separation.

[13] The capital asset pricing model is discussed in detail in Chapter 7.

[14] Hirshleifer [1964, 1965, 1966] and Myers [1968] were among the first papers to apply state-preference theory to corporate finance problems.

However, in Chapter 1 it was shown that in a perfect capital market (a frictionless and perfectly competitive market) under certainty, actions which maximize the price of the firm's shares maximize both the wealth and the utility of each current shareholder. So managers need not be concerned with the specific preferences of their shareholders, but need only know the market discount rate and the cash flows of their investment projects to make optimal investment decisions. This separation of investment/operating decisions of firms from shareholder preferences or tastes is termed the *Fisher separation principle.*

In shifting from firm decision making under certainty to decision making under uncertainty, it is important to know under what conditions, if any, Fisher separation continues to hold. It can be shown that firms which are maximizing the price of current shares are also maximizing current shareholders' *expected* utility when the capital market is (1) perfectly competitive and frictionless and (2) complete. The first condition ensures that firm actions will not be perceived to affect other firms' market security prices, while the second ensures that the state-space "spanned" by the existing set of linearly independent market securities (i.e., the set of risk opportunities) is unaffected by the firm's actions. Thus firm actions affect shareholders' expected utility only by affecting their wealth through changes in the firm's current share price. This is analogous to the certainty case in Chapter 1.

The two conditions of a perfect and complete capital market ensure that the prices of a full set of pure securities can be obtained from the prices of the market securities and vice versa, given the state-contingent payoff vectors of the market securities. As a result, the firm's objective function of maximizing current share price can be phrased in terms of a portfolio of pure securities which replicates its shares. The firm's objective function then becomes $\Sigma \ Q_{js} p_s$, where Q_{js} is defined as the state s contingent end-of-period payoff on firm j's existing securities. In this formulation the price of a firm's current shares is determined by (1) the firm's state-contingent production function $Q_{js} = \phi_j(I_j, s)$, which transforms current resources into state-contingent future payoffs, and (2) the initial investment I_j, which represents the current cost to the firm of producing its state-contingent payoff. It follows that the price Y_j, for which the current owners could sell the firm prior to making the investment I_j is

$$Y_j = \sum_s p_s Q_{js} - I_j, \qquad (5.10)$$

where the firm's technological constraints are captured in its production function $Q_{js} = \phi_j(I_j, s)$.

For divisible investment projects, the production function is assumed to be a continuous differentiable function of I_j which exhibits diminishing returns to scale and has the property that zero investment yields zero output. The firm's optimal investment scale is determined by the first order condition

$$\frac{dY_j}{dI_j} = \sum_s p_s \phi_j'(I_j, s) - 1 = 0. \qquad (5.11)$$

For indivisible investment projects with finite scale, the optimal investment rule is to accept all projects with positive net present value. In this context, (5.10) represents the net present value of the project's state-contingent net cash flow.

Table 5.3 Firm A's Stock and Investment Project Payoffs

States of Nature	State-contingent Payoffs on Firm A's	
	Stock	Proposed investment project
State 1	100	10
State 2	30	12

Firm A's stock price = 62, initial investment cost of its project = 10.

It is important to note that acceptance of positive NPV investments increases the price of the firm's current stock and therefore the wealth and expected utility of all current shareholders in a perfect and complete capital market. Since all shareholders are made better off by these investment decisions, these firm investment decisions are unanimously supported by all the firm's current shareholders. However, if the capital market is incomplete or imperfect, this is not necessarily true, because the firm's investment decisions may affect the price of other firms' shares or the feasible set of state-contingent payoffs. As a result, increasing the price of a firm's shares may *not* increase the wealth of all current shareholders (since the prices of some of their other share holdings may fall) and may not maximize shareholder expected utility (since the opportunity set of feasible end-of-period payoffs may have changed).[15]

Let us now consider an example of a firm investment decision problem in a two-state world of uncertainty. Assume that all investors are expected utility maximizers and exhibit positive marginal utility of wealth (i.e., more wealth is preferred to less). Consider the following two firms and their proposed investment projects described in Tables 5.3 and 5.4.

To determine whether either firm should undertake its proposed project, we need to first determine whether the capital market is complete. Since the state-contin-

Table 5.4 Firm B's Stock and Investment Project Payoffs

States of Nature	State-contingent Payoffs on Firm B's	
	Stock	Proposed investment project
State 1	40	12
State 2	90	6

Firm B's stock price = 56, initial investment cost for its project = 8.

---

[15] See DeAngelo [1981] for a critical analysis of the unanimity literature and a careful formulation of the conditions under which it holds in incomplete and complete capital markets.

gent payoffs of the two firms' stocks are linearly independent, the capital market is complete. In a complete market, the Fisher separation principle holds, so that the firm need only maximize the price of current shares to maximize its current shareholders' expected utility. This requires that the firm invest only in positive net present value investment projects, which requires knowing the pure security prices in the two states. These two prices can be obtained from the market prices of the two firms' stocks and their state-contingent payoffs by solving the two simultaneous equations

$$100p_1 + 30p_2 = 62,$$

$$40p_1 + 90p_2 = 56,$$

to obtain the solution $p_1 = .5$ and $p_2 = .4$. To calculate the net present value of the two projects, we use the NPV definition in (5.10)

$$\text{NPV}_A = 10p_1 + 12p_2 - I_0^A = 10(.5) + 12(.4) - 10 = -.2$$

and

$$\text{NPV}_B = 12p_1 + 6p_2 - I_0^B = 12(.5) + 6(.4) - 8 = .4.$$

Since firm A's project has a negative NPV, it should be rejected, while firm B's project should be accepted since it has a positive NPV.

In examining this optimal investment rule, it should be clear that the prices of the pure securities affect the firm's investment decisions. It follows that since these security prices are affected by (1) time preference for consumption and the productivity of capital, (2) the probability of state-contingent payoffs, and (3) individual preferences toward risk and the level of nondiversifiable risk in the economy, firm investment decisions are also affected by these factors.

We have applied state-preference theory to the firm's optimal investment decision while assuming that the firm has a simple capital structure represented by shares of stock. However, it is also possible to allow the firm to have more complicated capital structures which include various debt, preferred stock, and warrant contracts. In doing this, state-preference theory can be used to address the important question of a firm's optimal financing decision.[16] For this purpose it has been found useful to order the payoffs under alternative states. One can think of the payoffs for future states as arranged in an ordered sequence from the lowest to the highest payoff. Keeping in mind the ordered payoffs for alternative future states, we can specify the conditions under which a security such as corporate debt will be risk free or risky.[17]

The state-preference model has also been very useful in developing option pricing theory. By combining securities with claims on various portions of the ordered payoffs and by combining long and short positions, portfolios with an infinite variety of

---

[16] There are many examples of the usefulness state-preference theory in the area of optimal capital structure or financing decisions, see for example Stiglitz [1969], Mossin [1977], and DeAngelo-Masulis [1980a and 1980b].

[17] For applications of this approach see Kraus and Litzenberger [1973] and DeAngelo-Masulis [1980b].

payoff characteristics can be created. From such portfolios various propositions with regard to option pricing relationships can be developed.[18]

SUMMARY _____

Wealth is held over periods of time, and the different future states of nature will change the value of a person's wealth position over time. Securities represent positions with regard to the relation between present and future wealth. Since securities involve taking a position over time, they inherently involve risk and uncertainty.

The states of nature capture a wide variety of factors that influence the future values of risky assets. Individuals must formulate judgments about payoffs under alternative future states of nature. From these state-contingent payoffs and market prices of securities, the prices of the underlying pure securities can be developed in a complete and perfect capital market. Given these pure security prices, the price of any other security can be determined from its state-contingent payoff vector. Conceptually, the equilibrium prices of the pure securities reflect the aggregate risk preferences of investors and investment opportunities of firms. Furthermore, the concept of a pure security facilitates analytical solutions to individuals' consumption/portfolio investment decisions under uncertainty.

The state-preference approach is a useful way of looking at firm investment decisions under uncertainty. In a perfect and complete capital market, the net present value rule was shown to be an optimal firm investment decision rule. The property that firm decisions can be made independently of shareholder utility functions is termed the Fisher separation principle. State-preference theory also provides a conceptual basis for developing models for analyzing firm capital structure decisions and the pricing of option contracts. Thus the state-preference approach provides a useful way of thinking about finance problems both for the individual investor and for the corporate manager.

In summary, the state-preference model has been shown to be very useful in a world of uncertainty. It can be used to develop optimal portfolio decisions for individuals and optimal investment rules for firms. We have found that in perfect and complete capital markets, a set of equilibrium prices of all outstanding market securities can be derived. Further, these prices have been shown to be determined by (1) individual time preferences for consumption and the investment opportunities of firms, (2) probability beliefs concerning state-contingent payoffs, and (3) individual preferences toward risk and the level of nondiversifiable risk in the economy.

A number of important concepts developed in this chapter will be found to be very useful in the analysis to follow. In Chapter 6 we develop the fundamental properties of the mean-variance model, where the concept of diversifiable and nondiversifiable risk takes on added importance. In Chapter 7, the mean-variance framework is used

---

[18] For some further applications of state-preference theory to option pricing theory see Merton [1973] and Ross [1976], and for application of both theories to investment and financing decision making see Appendices B and C or Banz-Miller [1978].

to develop market equilibrium relationships that provide an alternative basis for pricing securities. Known as the capital asset pricing model, this model, like the state preference model, has the property that securities having relatively high levels of nondiversifiable risk have relatively higher expected rates of return. The concept of arbitrage is fundamental to the development of Arbitrage Pricing Theory (APT) in Chapter 7 and the Option Pricing Model (OPM) in Chapter 8.

PROBLEM SET

5.1 Security A pays \$30 if state 1 occurs and \$10 if state 2 occurs. Security B pays \$20 if state 1 occurs and \$40 if state 2 occurs. The price of security A is \$5 and the price of security B is \$10.

a) Set up the payoff table for securities A and B.

b) Determine the prices of the two pure securities.

5.2 You are given the following information:

	Payoffs		Security Prices
	State 1	State 2	
Security j	\$12	\$20	$p_j = \$22$
Security k	\$24	\$10	$p_k = \$20$

a) What are the prices of pure security 1 and pure security 2?

b) What is the initial price of a third security i, for which the payoff in state 1 is \$6 and the payoff in state 2 is \$10?

5.3 Interplanetary starship captain José Ching has been pondering the investment of his recent pilot's bonus of 1000 stenglers. His choice is restricted to two securities: Galactic Steel, selling for 20 stenglers per share, and Nova Nutrients, at 10 stenglers per share. The future state of his solar system is uncertain. If there is a war with a nearby group of asteroids, Captain Ching expects Galactic Steel to be worth 36 stenglers per share. However, if peace prevails, Galactic Steel will be worth only 4 stenglers per share. Nova Nutrients should sell at a future price of 6 stenglers per share in either eventuality.

a) Construct the payoff table which summarizes the starship captain's assessment of future security prices, given the two possible future states of the solar system. What are the prices of the pure securities implicit in the payoff table?

b) If the captain buys only Nova Nutrients shares, how many can he buy? If he buys only Galactic Steel, how many shares can he buy? What would be his final wealth in both cases in peace? At war?

c) Suppose Captain Ching can issue (sell short) securities as well as buy them, but he must be able to meet all claims in the future. What is the maximum number of Nova Nutrients shares he could sell short to buy Galactic Steel? How many shares of Galactic Steel could he sell short to buy Nova Nutrients? What would be his final wealth in both cases and in each possible future state?

d) Suppose a third security, Astro Ammo, is available and should be worth 28 stenglers per share if peace continues, and 36 stenglers per share if war breaks out. What would be the current price of Astro Ammo?

e) Summarize the results of (a) through (d) on a graph with axes W_1 and W_2.

f) Suppose the captain's utility function can be written $U = W_1^{.8}W_2^{.2}$. If his investment is restricted to Galactic Steel and/or Nova Nutrients, what is his optimal portfolio, i.e., how many shares of each security should he buy or sell?

5.4 Ms Mary Kelley has initial wealth $W_0 = \$1200$ and faces an uncertain future which she partitions into two states, $s = 1$ and $s = 2$. She can invest in two securities, j and k, with initial prices of $p_j = \$10$ and $p_k = \$12$, and the following payoff table:

	Payoffs	
Security	$s = 1$	$s = 2$
j	$10	$12
k	$20	$ 8

a) If she buys only security j, how many shares can she buy? If she buys only security k, how many can she buy? What would her final wealth, W_s, be in both cases and each state?

b) Suppose Ms Kelley can issue as well as buy securities; however, she must be able to meet all claims under the occurrence of either state. What is the maximum number of shares of security j she could sell to buy security k? What is the maximum number of shares of security k she could sell to buy security j? What would her final wealth be in both cases and in each state?

c) What are the prices of the pure securities implicit in the payoff table?

d) What is the initial price of a third security i for which $Q_{i1} = \$5$ and $Q_{i2} = \$12$?

e) Summarize the results of (a) through (d) on a graph with axes W_1 and W_2.

f) Suppose Ms Kelley has a utility function of the form $U = W_1^{.6}W_2^{.4}$. Find the optimal portfolio, assuming the issuance of securities is possible, if she restricts herself to a portfolio consisting only of j and k. How do you interpret your results?

5.5 Two securities have the following payoffs in two equally likely states of nature at the end of one year:

	Payoffs	
Security	$s = 1$	$s = 2$
j	$10	$20
k	$30	$10

Security j costs \$8 today while k costs \$9, and your total wealth is currently \$720.

a) If you wanted to buy a completely risk-free portfolio (i.e., one which has the same payoff in both states of nature), how many shares of j and k would you buy? (You may buy fractions of shares.)

b) What is the one-period risk-free rate of interest?

c) If there were two securities and three states of nature, you would not be able to find a completely risk-free portfolio. Why not?

5.6 Suppose there are only two possible future states of the world, and the utility function is logarithmic. Let the probability of state 1, π_1, equal $\frac{2}{3}$, and the prices of the pure securities, p_1 and p_2, equal \$0.60 and \$0.40 respectively. An individual has an initial wealth or endowment, W_0, of \$50,000.

a) What amounts will the risk-averse individual invest in pure securities 1 and 2?

b) How will the individual divide his or her initial endowment between current and future consumption?

(Hint: Use the wealth constraint instead of the Lagrange multiplier technique.)†

REFERENCES

Arrow, K. J., *Theory of Risk-Bearing*. Markham, Chicago, 1971.

———, "The Role of Securities in the Optimal Allocation of Risk-Bearing," *Review of Economic Studies*, 1964, 91–96.

Banz, R. W., and M. Miller, "Prices for State-contingent Claims: Some Estimates and Applications," *Journal of Business*, October 1978, 653–672.

Breeden, D. T., and R. H. Litzenberger, "Prices of State-Contingent Claims Implicit in Option Prices," *Journal of Business*, October 1978, 621–651.

Brennan, M. J., and A. Kraus, "The Geometry of Separation and Myopia," *Journal of Financial and Quantitative Analysis*, June 1976, 171–193.

Cass, D., and J. E. Stiglitz, "The Structure of Investor Preferences and Asset Returns, and Separability in Portfolio Allocation: A Contribution to the Pure Theory of Mutual Funds," *Journal of Economic Theory*, June 1970, 122–160.

De Angelo, H. C., "Competition and Unanimity," *American Economic Review*, March 1981, 18–28.

———, and R. W. Masulis, "Optimal Capital Structure Under Corporate and Personal Taxation," *Journal of Financial Economics*, March 1980a, 3–29.

———, "Leverage and Dividend Irrelevance Under Corporate and Personal Taxation," *Journal of Finance*, May 1980b, 453–464.

Debreu, G., *The Theory of Value*. Wiley, New York, 1959.

Dreze, J. H., "Market Allocation Under Uncertainty," *European Economic Review*, Winter 1970–1971, 133–165.

---

† Problem 5.6 was suggested by Professor Herb Johnson of Louisiana State University, Baton Rouge.

Fama, E. F., and M. H. Miller, *The Theory of Finance,* New York, Holt, Rinehart and Winston, 1972.

Fisher, Irving, *The Theory of Interest,* Macmillan, London, 1930.

Garman, M., "The Pricing of Supershares," *The Journal of Financial Economics,* March 1978, 3–10.

Hirshleifer, J., *Investment, Interest and Capital,* Englewood Cliffs, Prentice-Hall, 1970, 215–210 and 231–276.

_____, "Efficient Allocation of Capital in an Uncertain World," *The American Economic Review,* May 1964, 77–85.

_____, "Investment Decision Under Uncertainty: Choice-Theoretic Approaches," *Quarterly Journal of Economics,* November 1965, 509–536.

_____, "Investment Decision Under Uncertainty: Application of the State-Preference Approach," *Quarterly Journal of Economics,* May 1966, 252–277.

Kraus, A., and R. Litzenberger, "A State-Preference Model of Optimal Financial Leverage," *Journal of Finance,* September 1973, 911–922.

Krouse, C. G., *Foundations of Financial Economics,* monograph manuscript, University of California at Santa Barbara, 1982.

Leland, H. E., "Production Theory and the Stock Market," *Bell Journal of Economics and Management Science,* 1974, 125–144.

Merton, R., "The Theory of Rational Option Pricing," *The Bell Journal of Economics and Management Science,* Spring 1973, 141–183.

Mossin, J., *The Economic Efficiency of Financial Markets,* D.C. Heath, Lexington, 1977, 21–40.

Myers, S. C., "A Time-State Preference Model of Security Valuation," *Journal of Financial and Quantitative Analysis,* March 1968, 1–33.

Ross, S. A., "Options and Efficiency," *Quarterly Journal of Economics,* February 1976, 75–86.

_____, "Return, Risk and Arbitrage," in *Risk and Return in Finance, Volume 1.* I. Friend and J. L. Bicksler, eds., Ballinger Publishing Company, Cambridge, Mass., 1977, 189–218.

_____, "Mutual Fund Separation in Financial Theory—The Separating Distributions," *Journal of Economic Theory,* December 1978, 254–286.

Sharpe, W. F., *Portfolio Theory and Capital Markets,* Chapter 10, "State-Preference Theory," McGraw-Hill, New York, 1970, 202–222.

Stiglitz, J. E., "A Re-Examination of the Modigliani-Miller Theorem," *American Economic Review,* December 1969, 784–793.

Appendix A to Chapter 5
Forming a Portfolio of Pure Securities

If we have n market securities and n states of the world, but we are not sure the n market securities are independent, we can find out by taking the determinant of the payoffs from the securities: a nonzero determinant implies independence. For example, the set of pure securities is independent since

$$\begin{vmatrix} 1 & 0 & 0 \\ 0 & 1 & 0 \\ 0 & 0 & 1 \end{vmatrix} = 1; \quad \text{but} \quad \begin{vmatrix} 1 & 0 & 0 \\ 0 & 1 & 1 \\ 1 & 1 & 1 \end{vmatrix} = \begin{vmatrix} 1 & 1 \\ 1 & 1 \end{vmatrix} = 0$$

implies that the security payoffs $(1, 0, 0)$, $(0, 1, 1)$, and $(1, 1, 1)$ are not linearly independent.

We can use Appendix B, Matrix Algebra, found at the end of the book, to form a portfolio of pure securities from an arbitrary complete set of market securities. This involves computing the inverse of the payoff matrix for the actual securities. For example, if $(1, 0, 0)$, $(0, 1, 1)$, and $(0, 1, 3)$ are available, then define

$$A = \begin{pmatrix} 1 & 0 & 0 \\ 0 & 1 & 1 \\ 0 & 1 & 3 \end{pmatrix}$$

as the payoff matrix. Thus the determinant of A is

$$|A| = \begin{vmatrix} 1 & 0 & 0 \\ 0 & 1 & 1 \\ 0 & 1 & 3 \end{vmatrix} = \begin{vmatrix} 1 & 1 \\ 1 & 3 \end{vmatrix} = 2 \neq 0.$$

Let X_{ij} be the amount of the jth security one buys in forming the ith pure security, and let X be the matrix formed from the X_{ij}. Then we require that

$$XA = I \text{ where } I = \begin{pmatrix} 1 & 0 & 0 \\ 0 & 1 & 0 \\ 0 & 0 & 1 \end{pmatrix}$$

is the identity matrix and also the matrix of payoffs from the pure securities. Hence, $X = A^{-1}$. In the present example

$$A^{-1} = \frac{1}{2} \begin{pmatrix} 2 & 0 & 0 \\ 0 & 3 & -1 \\ 0 & -1 & 1 \end{pmatrix} = \begin{pmatrix} 1 & 0 & 0 \\ 0 & \frac{3}{2} & -\frac{1}{2} \\ 0 & -\frac{1}{2} & \frac{1}{2} \end{pmatrix}$$

We then multiply X times A or equivalently $A^{-1}A$ to obtain a matrix of payoffs from the pure securities. We have:

$$\begin{pmatrix} 1 & 0 & 0 \\ 0 & \frac{3}{2} & -\frac{1}{2} \\ 0 & -\frac{1}{2} & \frac{1}{2} \end{pmatrix} \begin{pmatrix} 1 & 0 & 0 \\ 0 & 1 & 1 \\ 0 & 1 & 3 \end{pmatrix} = \begin{pmatrix} 1 & 0 & 0 \\ 0 & 1 & 0 \\ 0 & 0 & 1 \end{pmatrix}$$

We can now see that the purpose of finding the inverse of A is to obtain directions for forming a portfolio that will yield a matrix of payoffs from the pure securities—the identity matrix. Recall that the three securities available are: $(1, 0, 0)$, $(0, 1, 1)$, and $(0, 1, 3)$. To obtain the pure security payoff $(1, 0, 0)$, we buy the security with that pattern of payoffs under the three states. To obtain $(0, 1, 0)$, we buy $\frac{3}{2}$ of $(0, 1, 1)$ and sell short $\frac{1}{2}$ of $(0, 1, 3)$. To obtain $(0, 0, 1)$, we sell short $\frac{1}{2}$ of $(0, 1, 1)$ and buy $\frac{1}{2}$ of $(0, 1, 3)$.

Appendix B to Chapter 5
Use of Prices for State-Contingent Claims in Capital Budgeting

Banz and Miller [1978] develop estimates of prices for state-contingent claims that can be applied in capital budgeting problems of the kind discussed in Chapter 11. They employ option pricing concepts discussed later in this book in Chapter 8. Similar methodologies were developed about the same time by Garman [1978] and by Breeden and Litzenberger [1978].

Banz and Miller note that a fundamental breakthrough was provided in Ross [1976] who demonstrated that by selling or buying options on a portfolio of existing securities, investors could obtain any desired pattern of returns—"investors could span the return space to any degree of fineness desired." (Banz and Miller, 1978, p. 658.)

Banz and Miller present their estimates of state prices in a format similar to standard interest tables. Like other interest tables, the estimates of state prices can in principle be used by any firm in any industry or activity (subject to some important cautions and qualifications). Thus the reciprocals (minus one) of the state prices computed are analogous to single-period interest rates. Banz-Miller handle the multi-period case by assuming stability in the relations between initial states and outcome states. Thus the two-period matrix is simply the square of the one-period matrix, the three-period matrix is the product of the one-period matrix and the two-period matrix, the four-period matrix is the product of the one-period matrix and the three-period matrix, and so on. In equation form,

$$V^n = V \cdot V^{n-1} \tag{B.5.1}$$

The perpetuity matrix is the one-period matrix times the inverse of the identity matrix minus the one-period matrix, or $V(I - V)^{-1}$.

Their computations for a V matrix of real discount factors for three states of the world is provided in Table B5.1. In the definition of states in Table B5.1 the state boundaries are defined over returns on the market. The conditional means are expected market returns under alternative states. The elements of any matrix V may be interpreted by use of the first group of data. The .5251 represents the outcome for state 1 when the initial state was also state 1. The .2935 represents the outcome for state 2 when state 1 was the initial state. The .1735 represents the outcome for state 3 when state 1 was the initial state. By analogy the .1612 represents an outcome for state 3 when state 3 was the initial state.

For equal probabilities the current price of a claim to funds in a state in which funds are scarce (a depression) will be higher than in a boom state when returns are more favorable. Thus a project with most of its payoffs contingent on a boom will have a lower value per dollar of expected returns than a project whose payoffs are relatively more favorable during a depression.

Table B5.1   Three-state Matrix of State Prices and Matrix Powers

A. Definition of States		
State	State boundaries*	Conditional mean ($\overline{R}_{i,mr}$)
1	$-.8647 - +.0006$	$-.1352$
2	$+.0006 - +.2042$	$+.0972$
3	$+.2042 - +1.7183$†	$+.3854$

B. State Prices

State	1	2	3	Row sum	Implied annual real riskless rate
1 year (V):					
1	.5251	.2935	.1735	.9921	.0079
2	.5398	.2912	.1672	.9982	.0018
3	.5544	.2888	.1612	1.0044	$-.0044$
2 years (V^2):					
1	.5304	.2897	.1681	.9882	.0056
2	.5333	.2915	.1693	.9941	.0030
3	.5364	.2934	.1705	1.0003	$-.0001$
3 years (V^3):					
1	.5281	.2886	.1676	.9843	.0053
2	.5313	.2903	.1686	.9902	.0033
3	.5345	.2921	.1696	.9962	.0013
4 years (V^4):					
1	.5260	.2874	.1669	.9803	.0050
2	.5291	.2892	.1679	.9862	.0035
3	.5324	.2909	.1689	.9922	.0026
5 years (V^5):					
1	.5239	.2863	.1662	.9764	.0048
2	.5270	.2880	.1672	.9822	.0036
3	.5302	.2897	.1682	.9881	.0024
6 years (V^6):					
1	.5217	.2851	.1655	.9723	.0047
2	.5249	.2868	.1665	.9782	.0037
3	.5281	.2886	.1676	.9843	.0027
7 years (V^7):					
1	.5197	.2840	.1649	.9685	.0046
2	.5228	.2857	.1659	.9744	.0043
3	.5260	.2874	.1669	.9803	.0033
8 years (V^8):					
1	.5176	.2828	.1642	.9646	.0045
2	.5207	.2845	.1652	.9704	.0038
3	.5239	.2863	.1662	.9764	.0030

Table B5.1   *(Cont.)*

		B. State Prices			
State	1	2	3	Row sum	Implied annual real riskless rate
9 years (V^9):					
1	.5155	.2817	.1636	.9608	.0045
2	.5186	.2834	.1645	.9665	.0038
3	.5218	.2851	.1655	.9724	.0031
10 years (V^{10}):					
1	.5134	.2806	.1629	.9569	.0044
2	.5165	.2823	.1639	.9627	.0038
3	.5197	.2840	.1649	.9686	.0032
Perpetuity $[V(I - V)^{-1}]$:					
1	132.50	72.41	42.05	246.96	.0040
2	133.31	72.85	42.30	248.46	.0040
3	134.14	73.29	42.55	249.98	.0040

* Chosen to yield ranges of R_{mr} that are approximately equally probable.
† Arbitrary truncations.
Source: Banz and Miller (1978), p. 666.

The vector of gross present values of the project, G_k will be:

$$G_k = \sum_{t=1}^{p} V^t \overline{X}_k(t), \qquad (B5.2)$$

where $\overline{X}_k(t)$ is a vector whose elements represent the expected real cash flows of project k in year t assuming the economy is in state i. The summation is performed over time periods ending in p, the last period during which the project's cash flows are nonzero in any state.

An example of how the "interest factors" in Table B5.1 can be applied is based on the illustration presented by Banz and Miller. The Omega Corporation is analyzing an investment project whose cash flow pattern in constant 1980 dollars (ignoring taxes and tax shields), is presented in Table B5.2.

Table B5.2   Cash Flow Patterns for an Investment

State of the Economy	*Range of Rates of Return on the Market Portfolio*	*Cash Flow Before Competition Enters $\overline{X}_m$*	*Steady-state Cash Flow After Competition Enters X_c*
Depression	$-.8647 - +.0006$	300	-20
Normal	$+.0006 - +.2042$	400	20
Boom	$+.2042 - +1.7183$	500	40

Table B5.3 Calculation of Risk-adjusted Present Values

$$
\begin{bmatrix} g_D \\ g_N \\ g_B \end{bmatrix} = \begin{bmatrix} .5251 & .2935 & .1735 \\ .5398 & .2912 & .1672 \\ .5544 & .2888 & .1612 \end{bmatrix} \begin{bmatrix} 300 \\ 400 \\ 500 \end{bmatrix}
$$

$$
+ \begin{bmatrix} .5304 & .2897 & .1681 \\ .5333 & .2915 & .1693 \\ .5364 & .2934 & .1705 \end{bmatrix} \begin{bmatrix} 204 \\ 286 \\ 362 \end{bmatrix} + \begin{bmatrix} .5281 & .2886 & .1676 \\ .5313 & .2903 & .1686 \\ .5345 & .2921 & .1696 \end{bmatrix} \begin{bmatrix} 108 \\ 172 \\ 224 \end{bmatrix}
$$

$$
+ \begin{bmatrix} .5260 & .2874 & .1669 \\ .5291 & .2892 & .1679 \\ .5324 & .2909 & .1689 \end{bmatrix} \begin{bmatrix} 132.50 & 72.41 & 42.05 \\ 133.31 & 72.85 & 42.30 \\ 134.14 & 73.29 & 42.55 \end{bmatrix} \begin{bmatrix} -20 \\ 20 \\ 40 \end{bmatrix}
$$

$$
= \begin{bmatrix} 1{,}230.09 \\ 1{,}235.68 \\ 1{,}241.48 \end{bmatrix}
$$

The Banz-Miller example is sophisticated in illustrating that both the level and risk of the cash flows vary with the degree of competition. In our example we modify their estimates of the cumulative probabilities of competitive entry, estimated to be zero in the year of introduction, .3 one year later, .6 two years later, and 1 three years later. The risk-adjusted gross present value vector for the project was set forth in Eq. (B5.2). For the assumptions of our example, the particular gross present value vector is $G_k = V\overline{X}_m + V^2(0.7\overline{X}_m + 0.3\overline{X}_c) + V^3(0.4\overline{X}_m + 0.6\overline{X}_c) + V^4[V(I - V)^{-1}]\overline{X}_c$. We use the values of V and its powers as presented in Table B5.1 to obtain the results shown in Table B5.3.

If the initial investment was \$1,236 in every state of the economy, the project would not have a positive net present value if the economy were depressed or normal. However, the net present value would be positive if the economy were strong. If initial investment costs had cyclical behavior, particularly if supply bottlenecks developed during a boom, investment outlays might vary so strongly with states of the world that net present values could be positive for a depressed economy and negative for a booming economy.

The Banz-Miller use of state prices in capital budgeting is a promising application of the state-preference model. Further applications will provide additional tests of the feasibility of their approach. More work in comparing the results under alternative approaches will provide increased understanding of the advantages and possible limitations of the use of state prices as discount factors in capital budgeting analysis.

Appendix C to Chapter 5
Application of the SPM in Capital Structure Decisions

The State-Preference Model (SPM) can also be used to analyze financing decisions if estimates of state prices as provided in the Banz-Miller paper are available. While capital structure decisions are discussed in Chapters 12 and 13, the following explanation is self-contained and provides an overview of some key aspects of the subject. In addition to the formal framework an illustrative numerical example will be developed.

The symbols that will be employed are listed and explained in Table C5.1. In the capital structure analysis three broad categories of alternative outcomes may take place. The outcomes are defined by the amount of net operating income achieved in relation to the amount of the debt obligations incurred. These three alternative outcomes are specified by column (1) in Table C5.2. Under Outcome 1 the state dependent net operating income, X_s, is equal to or greater than the amount of the debt obligations, B. Debt holders will receive the total amount of promised payments, B. Equity holders will receive the after-tax income remaining after the debt payments. The amounts received by debt holders and equity holders are listed in columns (2) and (3) in Table C5.2.

Table C5.1   Symbols Used in the SPM Analysis of Capital Structure Decisions

p_s = Market price of the primitive security that represents a claim on one dollar in State s and zero dollars in all other states

X_s = Earnings before interest and taxes that the firm will achieve in State s (EBIT)

B = Nominal payment to debt, representing a promise to pay Fixed Amount B, irrespective of the state that occurs

$S(B)$ = Market value of the firm's equity as a function of the amount of debt issued by the firm

$V(B)$ = Market value of the firm as a function of the amount of debt issued

f_s = Costs of failure in State s; $0 < f_s \leq X_s$

τ = Corporate tax rate = 40%.

Table C5.2   Amounts Received Under Alternative Outcomes

Outcome	Amount of X_s in Relation to B	Debt Holders Receive	Equity Holders Receive
	(1)	(2)	(3)
1	$X_s \geq B$	B	$(X_s - B)(1 - \tau)$
2	$0 \leq X_s < B$	$(X_s - f_s)$	0
3	$X_s < 0$	0	0

138

Table C5.3 Formulas for the Value of the Firm Under Alternative Outcomes

	Amount of X_s in Relation to B	Debt Holders Receive	Value of Debt Holders' Receipts in State s	Equity Holders Receive	Value of Equity Holders' Receipts in State s	Value of the Firm in State s
	(1)	(2)	(3)	(4)	(5)	(6)
Outcomes						
1	$X_s \geq B$	B	Bp_s	$(X_s - B)(1 - \tau)$	$(X_s - B)(1 - \tau)p_s$	$Bp_s + (X_s - B)(1 - \tau)p_s$
2	$0 \leq X_s < B$	$(X_s - f_s)$	$(X_s - \tau_s)p_s$	0	0	$(X_s - f_s)p_s$
3	$X_s < 0$	0	0	0	0	0

Under Outcome 2, the state dependent net operating income is less than B but positive. Debt holders will receive the net operating income less bankruptcy costs that may be incurred. Equity holders will receive nothing. If the state dependent income is negative, neither the debt holders nor equity holders will receive anything.

In Table C5.3 the applicable state prices are multiplied times what the debt holders receive under alternative outcomes to determine the value of the debt holders' receipts in each state. Similarly, what the equity holders receive is multiplied by the state prices to give the value of equity. The value of the firm in each state is the sum of the market value of debt and the market value of equity.

This formal framework is next utilized in an illustrative numerical example. The basic data to be utilized are set forth in Table C5.4. In Table C5.5, the data are used to calculate the value of the firm under alternative debt levels. On the left-hand column labeled *Outcomes* we begin by specifying the amount of debt and the resulting relationships between X_s, the EBIT under alternative states, and the promised debt payment. The applicable formulas for calculating the state contingent value of the firm are specified for each level of debt. Utilizing the illustrative data from Table C5.4 we can then obtain the value of the firm's state payoff for alternative debt levels.

When the firm is unlevered ($B = 0$) its value is equal to the after-tax EBIT times the state price for each state, summed over all the states. The resulting value is $408.

When debt is $200 the value of the firm under State 1 is zero. For States 2, 3, and 4 both the debt and equity have value as shown in Table C5.5. When the value of debt is $500, again the firm has no value under State 1. Under States 2, 3, and 4 both debt and equity have value. The total value of the firm sums to $550.

Similarly, for a debt level of $800 the value of the firm is calculated as $386. For a value of debt of $2000 the value of the firm is $350.

The debt level which results in the highest indicated value of the firm as shown by Table C5.5 is $500. For alternative levels of debt the value of the firm is lower. This result follows from the numerical values chosen for the illustration. The example illustrates the tax advantage of debt. Also, substantial bankruptcy costs are postulated. In addition, the bankruptcy costs are assumed to have a substantial fixed element as well as to rise with the amount of resources that may become available under each of the alternative states. Further aspects of capital structure decisions will be developed in Chapters 12 and 13.

Table C5.4   Data for SPM
Analysis of Capital Structure
Decisions

s (1)	X_s (2)	p_s (3)	f_s (4)
1	$ 100	$0.30	$ 100
2	500	0.50	400
3	1000	0.20	500
4	2000	0.10	1200

**Table C5.5   Calculations of the Value of the Firm Under
Alternative Debt Levels**

Debt Levels	State	Value of Firm's State s Payoff
$B = 0,\ X_s > B$ for all s	1	$100(0.6)0.3 = \quad 18$
	2	$500(0.6)0.5 = \quad 150$
$V_s(0) = \sum\limits_{s=1}^{4} X_s(1-T)p_s$	3	$1000(0.6)0.2 = \quad 120$
	4	$2000(0.6)0.1 = \underline{\quad 120}$
$B = 200,\ X_s < B$ for $s = 1$		$V(0) = \$408$
$B = 200,\ X_s \geq B$ for $s = 2,3,4$		
$V_s(200) = (X_s - f_s)p_s$ for $s = 1$		
	1	$(100 - 100)(0.6)0.3 = \quad 0$
$V_s(200) = \sum\limits_{s=2}^{4} Bp_s + \sum\limits_{s=2}^{4}(X_s - B)(1-T)p_s$	2	$200(0.5) + (500 - 200)(0.6)0.5 = \quad 190$
	3	$200(0.2) + (1000 - 200)(0.6)0.2 = \quad 136$
$B = 500,\ X_s < B$ for $s = 1$	4	$200(0.1) + (2000 - 200)(0.6)0.1 = \underline{\quad 128}$
$B = 500,\ X_s \geq B$ for $s = 2,3,4$		$V(200) = \$454$
$V_s(500) = (X_s - f_s)p_s$ for $s = 1$		
	1	$(100 - 100)0.3 = \quad 0$
$V_s(500) = \sum\limits_{s=2}^{4} Bp_s + \sum\limits_{s=2}^{4}(X_s - B)(1-T)p_s$	2	$500(0.5) + (500 - 500)(0.6)0.5 = \quad 250$
	3	$500(0.2) + (1000 - 500)(0.6)0.2 = \quad 160$
$B = 800,\ X_s < B$ for $s = 1,2$	4	$500(0.1) + (2000 - 500)(0.6)0.1 = \underline{\quad 140}$
$B = 800,\ X_s \geq B$ for $s = 3,4$		$V(500) = \$550$
$V_s(1000) = \sum\limits_{s=1}^{2}(X_s - f_s)p_s$		
	1	$(100 - 100)0.3 = \quad 0$
$V_s(1000) = \sum\limits_{s=3}^{4} Bp_s + \sum\limits_{s=3}^{4}(X_s - B)(1-T)p_s$	2	$(500 - 400)0.5 = \quad 50$
	3	$800(0.2) + (1000 - 800)(0.6)0.2 = \quad 184$
$B = 2000,\ X_s < B$ for $s = 1,2,3$	4	$800(0.1) + (2000 - 800)(0.6)0.1 = \underline{\quad 152}$
$B = 2000,\ X_s \geq B$ for $s = 4$		$V(800) = \$386$
$V_s(2000) = \sum\limits_{s=1}^{3} (X_s - f_s)p_s$	1	$(100 - 100)0.3 = \quad 0$
	2	$(500 - 400)0.5 = \quad 50$
$V_s(2000) = Bp_s + (X_s - B)(1-T)p_s$	3	$(1000 - 500)0.2 = \quad 100$
for $s = 4$	4	$2000(0.1) + (2000 - 2000)(0.6)0.1 = \underline{\quad 200}$
		$V(2000) = \$350$

Objects of Choice: Mean-Variance Uncertainty

The results of a portfolio analysis are no more than the logical consequence of its information concerning securities.

HARRY MARKOWITZ, *PORTFOLIO SELECTION,*
YALE UNIVERSITY PRESS, NEW HAVEN, 1959,
P. 205

Chapter 4 introduced the theory of how risk-averse investors make choices in a world with uncertainty. Chapter 5 used a state-preference framework to show that the fundamental objects of choice are payoffs offered in different states of nature. While this is a very general approach, it lacks empirical content. It would be difficult, if not impossible, to list all payoffs offered in different states of nature. In order to provide a framework for analysis where objects of choice are readily measurable, this chapter develops mean-variance objects of choice. Investors' indifference curves are assumed to be defined in terms of the mean and variance of asset returns. While much less general than state-preference theory, the mean-variance portfolio theory introduced here is statistical in nature and therefore lends itself to empirical testing. Some of the empirical tests of a mean-variance equilibrium pricing model are discussed in Chapter 7.

142

One of the most important developments in finance theory in the last few decades is the ability to talk about risk in a quantifiable fashion. If we know how to correctly measure and price financial risk, we can properly value risky assets. This in turn leads to better allocation of resources in the economy. Investors can do a better job of allocating their savings to various types of risky securities, and managers can better allocate the funds provided by shareholders and creditors among scarce capital resources.

This chapter begins with simple measures of risk and return for a single asset and then complicates the discussion by moving to risk and return for a portfolio of many risky assets. Decision rules are then developed to show how individuals choose optimal portfolios which maximize their expected utility of wealth, first in a world without riskless borrowing and lending, then with such opportunities.

A. MEASURING RISK AND RETURN FOR A SINGLE ASSET

Suppose the task at hand is to describe the relevant features of a common stock to a friend who is an investor. What are the really crucial facts which you should communicate? You could start off by giving the company's name, say Bayside Cigar Co. Then you would discuss the financial ratios of the company: its earnings per share, its inventory turnover, its financial leverage, its interest coverage, and so on. All of this data are merely one way of getting at what is crucial—how will your friend's wealth position be affected if he or she invests in Bayside Cigar? Consequently, it is wise to talk about measures of effect on relative wealth at the end of an investment period. The terminology used is end-of-period wealth.

The link between end-of-period wealth and an initial dollar investment is the rate of return. For the time being, we will not specify what calendar interval we are working with except to say that it is a single time period. If the initial investment is $\$I$ and the final wealth is $\$W$, then the investor's rate of return, R is

$$R = \frac{W - I}{I} . \tag{6.1}$$

As you see, this is the same expression as that used for the present- or future-value formulas for one time period.

$$W = (1 + R)I, \qquad \text{future-value formulation;} \tag{6.1a}$$

$$I = (1 + R)^{-1}W, \qquad \text{present-value formulation.} \tag{6.1b}$$

If end-of-period wealth is known with certainty, then so is the present value of the investment and the rate of return. However, this is seldom the case in the real world. Even short-term default-free bonds such as United States Government Treasury Bills are not completely risk free (although later on we shall use them as a close approximation to a risk-free security).

For risky assets often the best that can be done is to assign probabilities to

Table 6.1   Hypothetical Prices for Bayside Cigar Co.

p_i = Probability	End-of-Period Price Per Share	R_i = Return
.1	$20.00	−20%
.2	22.50	−10%
.4	25.00	0%
.2	30.00	+20%
.1	40.00	+60%
1.0		

various possible outcomes. Suppose the current price (P_0) of Bayside Cigar is $25 per share and you tell your friend that after a careful analysis the best estimate of the price per share at the end of the time period is given in Table 6.1.

1. Measures of Location

It is desirable to develop some statistics which can summarize a wide set of possible outcomes. The most commonly used statistics are measures of location and dispersion. Measures of location are intended to describe the most likely outcome in a set of events. The most often used measure of location is the mean or expectation. It is defined as (the tilde, ~, is used to designate randomness):

$$E(\tilde{X}) = \sum_{i=1}^{N} p_i X_i, \tag{6.2}$$

where p_i is the probability of a random event, X_i, and N is the total number of possible events. Hence, the mean weights each event by its probability, then sums all events. For Bayside Cigar, the expected end-of-period price is

$$E(\tilde{P}) = .1(20) + .2(22.5) + .4(25) + .2(30) + .1(40) = \$26.50.$$

The expected or mean return is the expected price less the current price divided by the current price.

$$E(\tilde{R}) = \frac{E(\tilde{P}) - P_0}{P_0} = \frac{26.50 - 25}{25} = .06 \quad \text{or} \quad 6\%. \tag{6.3}$$

Implicitly, we have used two probability properties of the expected value operator to obtain Eq. (6.3).

Property 1.   The expected value of a random variable $\tilde{X}$ plus a constant a is equal to the expected value of the random variable plus the constant:

$$E(\tilde{X} + a) = E(\tilde{X}) + a. \tag{6.4}$$

Property 1 can be proved by using the definition of expected value. Since the random variable is $\tilde{X} + a$, we take its expectation by substituting $X_i + a$ for X_i in Eq. (6.2):

$$E(\tilde{X} + a) = \sum_{i=1}^{N} p_i(X_i + a).$$

Writing out all the terms in the sum, we have

$$E(\tilde{X} + a) = [(p_1(X_1 + a) + p_2(X_2 + a) + \cdots + p_n(X_n + a)].$$

By simply collecting terms, we get

$$E(\tilde{X} + a) = \sum_{i=1}^{N} p_i X_i + a \sum_{i=1}^{N} p_i.$$

And since we know that the sum of the probabilities of all events must add to 1 ($\sum p_i \equiv 1$), we have proved Property 1:

$$E(\tilde{X} + a) = \sum_{i=1}^{N} p_i(X_i) + a$$

$$E(\tilde{X} + a) = E(\tilde{X}) + a. \qquad \text{QED}$$

Property 2. The expected value of a random variable $\tilde{X}$ multiplied by a constant a is equal to the constant multiplied by the expected value of the random variable:

$$E(a\tilde{X}) = aE(\tilde{X}). \tag{6.5}$$

Property 2 can also be proved by using the definition of the expected-value operator. Substituting aX_i for X_i in Eq. (6.2), we get

$$E(a\tilde{X}) = \sum_{i=1}^{N} p_i[aX_i].$$

Then by expanding the sum, we have

$$E(a\tilde{X}) = p_1 a X_1 + p_2 a X_2 + \cdots + p_n a X_n.$$

Next, a can be factored out:

$$E(a\tilde{X}) = a \sum_{i=1}^{N} p_i X_i.$$

And finally recognizing that $\sum p_i X_i = E(\tilde{X})$, we have

$$E(a\breve{X}) = aE(\tilde{X}). \qquad \text{QED}$$

When we used the definition of return and the expected end-of-period price to derive the expected return, we were using both properties of the expected-value operator described above. In the numerator of (6.3) the price of Bayside Cigar today, P_0, is known and is a constant. The end-of-period price is a random variable. Therefore, the right-hand side of Eq. (6.3) uses Property 1 in the numerator and Property 2 when the numerator is multiplied by ($1/P_0$), a constant.

The expected outcome, or *the average,* is the most frequently used statistical measure of location, but it is not the only one. Before moving on to measures of dispersion, we should also mention *the median* and *the mode,* which are also measures

Table 6.2   Set of Numbers With Equal Probability

17	0	7	10	13	3
15	−4	6	−1	17	13
13	25	13	150	−1	6
−8	2	54	32	202	16
13	21	120	24	29	37

of location. The median is defined as the outcome in the middle, often referred to as the 50th percentile. Consider the set of numbers (which are equally likely, that is $p_i = 1/N$) given in Table 6.2.

Figure 6.1 is a histogram for the set of numbers. Note that most of the probability (in fact 53.3%) lies between −1 and 20. However, the mean, which assigns equal weight to all observations in this case, gives 28.13 as the best measure of location. The median is 13. Clearly, in this case, where we have a distribution of outcomes which is skewed to the right, the median is a better measure of location than the mean is. Later on, when we actually look at empirical distributions of security returns, the choice of mean return as the best measure of central tendency will depend a great deal on whether or not the actual distributions are skewed.

The last measure of location to be considered is the mode. It is defined as the most frequent outcome. In the above example it is the number 13, which occurs five times, or the interval between 6 and 13, which contains 23.3% of the probability. The mode is not often used as a measure of location for empirical distributions of security returns because security returns are real numbers (that is, they can take on any decimal value) and consequently do not repeat themselves frequently.

2. Measures of Dispersion

So far we have looked at statistical measures which can be used to best describe the most likely outcome when our friend invests in Bayside Cigar. An investment of $1000 can be expected to bring an end-of-period wealth of $1060. (Why?) But the question still remains—what risk is being taken? There are five measures of dispersion which we could use: the range, the semi-interquartile range, the variance, the semivariance, and the mean absolute deviation. Each of these has slightly different implications for risk.

The *range* is the simplest statistic and is defined as the difference between the

Figure 6.1
Histogram.

highest and lowest outcomes. For an investment in one share of Bayside Cigar (see Table 6.1) the worst outcome is $20 and the best outcome is $40. Therefore, the range is $20. However, the range is a very poor descriptive statistic because it becomes larger as sample size increases. Whenever the underlying probability distribution of investment outcomes is being estimated, for example, by looking at observations of past performance, the estimated range will increase as more observations are included in the sample.

The *semi-interquartile range* is the difference between the observation of the 75th percentile, $X_{.75}$, and the 25th percentile, $X_{.25}$, divided by 2

$$\text{Semi-interquartile range} = \frac{X_{.75} - X_{.25}}{2}. \tag{6.6}$$

Unlike the range, this statistic does not increase with sample size and is therefore much more reliable than the range.[1] For the set of 30 numbers which we were using earlier (in Table 6.2) the semi-interquartile range is

$$\text{Semi-interquartile range} = \frac{27.0 - 4.5}{2} = 11.25.$$

This statistic is frequently used as a measure of dispersion when the variance of a distribution does not exist.

The variance is the statistic most frequently used to measure the dispersion of a distribution, and later on in this chapter it will be used as a measure of investment risk. It is defined as the expectation of the squared differences from the mean.

$$\text{VAR}(\tilde{X}) = E[(X_i - E(\tilde{X}))^2]. \tag{6.7a}$$

Recalling the definition of the mean as the sum of the probabilities of events times the value of the events, the definition of variance can be rewritten as

$$\text{VAR}(\tilde{X}) = \sum_{i=1}^{N} p_i (X_i - E(\tilde{X}))^2. \tag{6.7b}$$

Therefore, for Bayside Cigar the variance of end-of-period prices is

$$\text{VAR}(\tilde{P}) = .1(20 - 26.5)^2 + .2(22.5 - 26.5)^2 + .4(25 - 26.5)^2$$

$$+ .2(30 - 26.5)^2 + .1(40 - 26.5)^2$$

$$= .1(42.25) + .2(16) + .4(2.25) + .2(12.25) + .1(182.25)$$

$$= 29.00, \quad \text{which represents dollars squared.}$$

Note that the variance is expressed in dollars squared. Since people do not usually think in these terms, the standard deviation, which is the positive square root of the variance, is often used to express dispersion:

$$\sigma(\tilde{P}) = \sqrt{\text{VAR}(\tilde{P})} = \$5.39.$$

---

[1] The interested reader is referred to Crámer [1961, pp. 367–370] for proof that sample quantiles converge to consistent estimates as sample sizes increase.

The variance of the return from investing in Bayside Cigar is

$$\text{VAR}(\tilde{R}) = \frac{\text{VAR}(\tilde{P})}{P_0^2} = \frac{29}{(25)^2} = 4.64\%,$$

and the standard deviation is

$$\sigma(\tilde{R}) = \sqrt{\text{VAR}(\tilde{R})} = 21.54\%.$$

This result is derived by using two properties of the variance in much the same way as properties of the mean were used earlier.

Property 3.   The variance of a random variable plus a constant is equal to the variance of the random variable.

It makes sense that adding a constant to a random variable would have no effect on the variance because the constant by itself has zero variance. This is demonstrated by using the definition of variance (Eq. 6.7) and substituting $(X_i + a)$ for X_i as follows:

$$\text{VAR}(\tilde{X} + a) = E[((X_i + a) - E(\tilde{X} + a))^2].$$

From Property 1 of the expected-value operator, we know that

$$E(\tilde{X} + a) = E(\tilde{X}) + a;$$

therefore

$$\text{VAR}(\tilde{X} + a) = E[((X_i) + a - E(\tilde{X}) - a)^2].$$

Because the constant terms cancel out, we have

$$\text{VAR}(\tilde{X} + a) = E[(X_i - E(\tilde{X}))^2] = \text{VAR}(\tilde{X}). \qquad \text{QED} \qquad (6.8)$$

Property 4.   The variance of a random variable multiplied by a constant is equal to the constant squared times the variance of the random variable.

For proof we again refer to the definitions of variance and substitute aX_i for X_i in Eq. (6.7):

$$\text{VAR}(a\tilde{X}) = E[(aX_i - aE(\tilde{X}))^2].$$

The constant term can be factored out as follows:

$$\text{VAR}(a\tilde{X}) = E[(a(X_i - E(\tilde{X})))^2]$$
$$= E[a^2(X_i - E(\tilde{X}))^2]$$
$$= a^2 E[(X_i - E(\tilde{X}))^2] = a^2\text{VAR}(\tilde{X}). \qquad \text{QED} \qquad (6.9)$$

Going back to the example where we computed the variance of return on Bayside Cigar directly from the variance of its price, we can readily see how Properties 3 and 4 were used. Let us recall that the definition of return is

$$R_i = \frac{P_i - P_0}{P_0},$$

and that the expected return is

$$E(\tilde{R}) = \frac{E(\tilde{P}) - P_0}{P_0}.$$

Therefore the variance of return is

$$VAR(\tilde{R}) = E[(R_i - E(\tilde{R}))^2]$$

$$= E\left[\left(\frac{P_i - P_0}{P_0} - \frac{E(\tilde{P}) - P_0}{P_0}\right)^2\right].$$

Because P_0 is a constant, we can use Property 4 to write

$$VAR(\tilde{R}) = \frac{1}{P_0^2} E[(P_i - E(\tilde{P}))^2]$$

$$= \frac{VAR(\tilde{P})}{P_0^2}.$$

And, of course, this is exactly the formula used earlier to compute the variance of return from our knowledge of the variance of prices.

The next section of this chapter uses the properties of the mean and variance which we have developed here in order to discuss the mean and variance of a portfolio of assets. At this point we could summarize the investment opportunity offered by Bayside Cigar by saying that the expected price is $26.50 with a standard deviation of $5.39. Or else we could say that the expected return on this investment is 6% with a standard deviation of 21.54%. However, before moving on, it will be useful to contrast the variance as a measure of risk with the *semivariance* and the *mean absolute deviation.*

One problem with the variance is that it gives equal weight to possibilities above as well as below the average. However, suppose that risk-averse investors are more concerned with downside risk. The semivariance is a statistic which relates to just that risk. It is defined as the expectation of the mean differences *below* the mean, squared. Mathematically, the definition is as follows. Let

$$X_i = \begin{cases} X_i - E(\tilde{X}) & \text{if} \quad X_i < E(\tilde{X}) \\ 0 & \text{if} \quad X_i \geq E(\tilde{X}) \end{cases},$$

then

$$SEMIVAR = E[(X_i)^2]. \tag{6.10}$$

If the semivariance is used as a measure of risk, an increase in the probability of events above the mean will change risk only slightly because the only effect would be to increase the mean slightly. For example, the semivariance of return for Bayside Cigar is

$$SEMIVAR = .1(-.20 - .06)^2 + .2(-.10 - .06)^2 + .4(0 - .06)^2$$

$$= 1.332\%.$$

But if the probability of a 60% return (in Table 6.1) were to increase to .2 while the probability of a 20% return fell to .1, the impact on semivariance would be slight. The new expected return would be 10% and the semivariance would increase to 2.1%. Given the same change in probabilities, the variance would increase from 4.64% to 7.824%.

Both the variance and the semivariance are sensitive to observations distant from the mean because the mean differences are squared. Squaring gives them greater weight. A statistic that avoids this difficulty is the *mean absolute deviation* (MAD), which is defined as the expectation of the absolute value of the differences from the mean:

$$MAD = E[|X_i - E(\tilde{X})|]. \tag{6.11}$$

For the Bayside Cigar example, the mean absolute deviation is

$$MAD = .1|(-.2 - .06)| + .2|(-.1 - .06)| + .4|(0 - .06)|$$
$$+ .2(.2 - .06) + .1(.6 - .06)$$
$$= 16.4\%.$$

Although for the most part we shall measure risk and return by using the variance (or standard deviation) and the mean return, it is useful to keep in mind that there are other statistics which, in some situations, may be more appropriate. An understanding of these statistics helps to put the mean and variance into proper perspective.

B. MEASURING PORTFOLIO RISK AND RETURN

From this point we assume that investors measure the expected utility of choices among risky assets by looking at the mean and variance provided by combinations of those assets. For a financial manager, the operating risk of the firm may be measured by estimating the mean and variance of returns provided by the portfolio of assets which the firm holds: its inventory, cash, accounts receivable, marketable securities, and physical plant. For a portfolio manager, the risk and return are the mean and variance of the weighted average of the assets in his or her portfolio. Therefore, in order to understand how to manage risk it becomes necessary to explore the risk and return provided by combinations of risky assets.

1. The Normal Distribution

By looking only at mean and variance, we are necessarily assuming that no other statistics are necessary to describe the distribution of end-of-period wealth. Unless investors have a special type of utility function (quadratic utility function), it is necessary to assume that returns have a normal distribution, which can be completely described by mean and variance. This is the bell-shaped probability distribution which many natural phenomena obey. For example, measures of IQs follow this distribution. An example is given in Fig. 6.2. The frequency of a return is measured

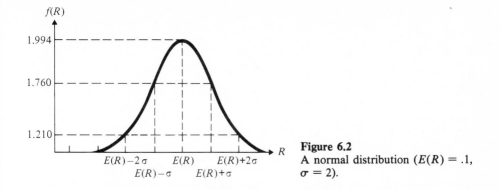

Figure 6.2
A normal distribution ($E(R) = .1$, $\sigma = 2$).

along the vertical axis, and the returns are measured along the horizontal axis. The normal distribution is perfectly symmetric and 50% of the probability lies above the mean, 15.9% above a point one standard deviation above the mean, and 2.3% above a point two standard deviations above the mean. Because of its symmetry, the variance and semivariance are equivalent measures of risk for the normal distribution. Furthermore, if you know the mean and standard deviation (or semivariance) of a normal distribution, you know the likelihood of every point in the distribution. This would not be true if the distribution were not symmetric. If it were skewed to the right, for example, one would also need to know a measure of skewness in addition to the mean and standard deviation, and the variance and semivariance would not be equivalent.

The equation for the frequency of returns, R, which are normally distributed is given below:

$$f(R) = \frac{1}{\sigma\sqrt{2\pi}} e^{-\frac{1}{2}\left(\frac{R - E(R)}{\sigma}\right)^2} \tag{6.12}$$

If we know the mean, $E(R)$, and the standard deviation, σ, of the distribution, then we can plot the frequency of any return. For example, if $E(R) = 10\%$ and $\sigma = 20\%$, then the frequency of a 13% rate of return is

$$f(.13) = \frac{1}{.2\sqrt{2\pi}} e^{-\frac{1}{2}\left(\frac{.13 - .10}{.2}\right)^2},$$

$$f(.13) = 1.972.$$

Often a normal distribution is converted into a unit normal distribution which always has a mean of zero and a standard deviation of one. Most normal probability tables (like that given at the end of Chapter 8) are based on a unit normal distribution. In order to convert a return, R, into a unit normal variable, z, we subtract the mean, $E(R)$, and divide by the standard deviation, σ, as shown below

$$z = \frac{R - E(R)}{\sigma}. \tag{6.13}$$

The frequency function for a unit normal variable is

$$f(z) = \frac{1}{\sqrt{2\pi}} \, e^{-\frac{1}{2}z^2}. \tag{6.14}$$

This could be plotted in Figure 6.2. Of course the scales would change.

2. Calculating the Mean and Variance of a Two-Asset Portfolio

Consider a portfolio of two risky assets which are both normally distributed. How can we measure the mean and standard deviation of a portfolio with $a\%$ of our wealth invested in asset X and $b\% = (1 - a\%)$ invested in asset Y? Mathematically, the portfolio return can be expressed as the sum of two random variables.

$$\tilde{R}_p = a\tilde{X} + b\tilde{Y}.$$

By using the properties of mean and variance derived earlier we can derive the mean and variance of the portfolio. The mean return is the expected outcome

$$E(\tilde{R}_p) = E[a\tilde{X} + b\tilde{Y}].$$

Separating terms, we have

$$E(\tilde{R}_p) = E(a\tilde{X}) + E(b\tilde{Y}).$$

Using Property 2 [i.e., that $E(a\tilde{X}) = aE(\tilde{X})$], we have

$$E(\tilde{R}_p) = aE(\tilde{X}) + bE(\tilde{Y}). \tag{6.15}$$

Thus the portfolio mean return is seen to be simply the weighted average of returns on individual securities, where the weights are the percentage invested in those securities.

The variance of a portfolio return is expressed as

$$\text{VAR}(\tilde{R}_p) = E[\tilde{R}_p - E(\tilde{R}_p)]^2$$
$$= E[(a\tilde{X} + b\tilde{Y}) - E(a\tilde{X} + b\tilde{Y})]^2.$$

Again, using Property 2 and rearranging terms, we have

$$\text{VAR}(\tilde{R}_p) = E[(a\tilde{X} - aE(\tilde{X})) + (b\tilde{Y} - bE(\tilde{Y}))]^2.$$

By squaring the term in brackets and using Property 4, we have

$$\text{VAR}(\tilde{R}_p) = E[a^2(\tilde{X} - E(\tilde{X}))^2 + b^2(\tilde{Y} - E(\tilde{Y}))^2 + 2ab(\tilde{X} - E(\tilde{X}))(\tilde{Y} - E(\tilde{Y}))].$$

You will recall that from the definition of variance and by Property 4,

$$\text{VAR}(a\tilde{X}) = a^2 E[(\tilde{X} - E(\tilde{X}))^2] = a^2\text{VAR}(\tilde{X}).$$

Also,

$$\text{VAR}(b\tilde{Y}) = b^2 E[(\tilde{Y} - E(\tilde{Y}))^2] = b^2\text{VAR}(\tilde{Y}).$$

Therefore the portfolio variance is the sum of the variances of the individual securities multiplied by the square of their weights plus a third term, which is called the *covariance*, $COV(\tilde{X}, \tilde{Y})$:

$$VAR(\tilde{R}_p) = a^2 VAR(\tilde{X}) + b^2\ VAR(\tilde{Y}) + 2ab E[(\tilde{X} - E(\tilde{X}))(\tilde{Y} - E(\tilde{Y}))],$$

$$COV(\tilde{X}, \tilde{Y}) \equiv E[(\tilde{X} - E(\tilde{X}))(\tilde{Y} - E(\tilde{Y}))].$$

The covariance is a measure of the way in which the two random variables move in relation to each other. If the covariance is positive, the variables move in the same direction. If it is negative, they move in opposite directions. The covariance is an extremely important concept because it is the appropriate measure of the contribution of a single asset to portfolio risk. The variance of a random variable is really the same thing as its covariance with itself:[2]

$$COV(aX, aX) = a \cdot aE[(X - E(X))(X - E(X))]$$

$$= a^2 E[(X - E(X))^2] = a^2 VAR\ X.$$

We now see that the variance for a portfolio of two assets is

$$VAR(R_p) = a^2 VAR(X) + b^2 VAR(Y) + 2ab COV(X, Y). \qquad (6.16)$$

In order to provide a better intuitive feel for portfolio variance and for the meaning of covariance, consider the following set of returns for assets X and Y.

Probability	X_i	Y_i
.2	11%	−3%
.2	9%	15%
.2	25%	2%
.2	7%	20%
.2	−2%	6%

In order to simplify matters we have assumed that each pair of returns $[X_i, Y_i]$ has equal probability (Prob = .2). The expected value of X is 10%, and the expected value of Y is 8%. The variances are computed below.

$$VAR(X) = .2(.11 - .10)^2 + .2(.09 - .10)^2 + .2(.25 - .10)^2$$

$$+ .2(.07 - .10)^2 + .2(-.02 - .10)^2$$

$$= .0076.$$

$$VAR(Y) = .2(-.03 - .08)^2 + .2(.15 - .08)^2 + .2(.02 - .08)^2$$

$$+ .2(.20 - .08)^2 + .2(.06 - .08)^2$$

$$= .00708.$$

---

[2] From this point on, the tilde, ˜, will be used to designate a random variable only when it is needed to prevent ambiguity.

The covariance between X and Y is

$$
\begin{aligned}
\text{COV}(X, Y) &= E[(X - E(X))(Y - E(Y))] \\
&= .2(.11 - .10)(-.03 - .08) + .2(.09 - .10)(.15 - .08) \\
&\quad + .2(.25 - .10)(.02 - .08) + .2(.07 - .10)(.20 - .08) \\
&\quad + .2(-.02 - .10)(.06 - .08) \\
&= -.0024.
\end{aligned}
$$

Negative covariance implies that the returns on asset X and asset Y tend to move in opposite directions. If we invest in both securities at once, the result is a portfolio which is less risky than holding either asset separately: while we are losing with asset X we win with asset Y. Therefore our investment position is partially hedged, and risk is reduced.

As an illustration of the effect of diversification, suppose we invest half our assets in X and half in Y. By using Eqs. (6.15) and (6.16) we can compute portfolio return and risk directly.

$$
E(R_p) = aE(X) + bE(Y) \tag{6.15}
$$

$$
= .5(.10) + .5(.08) = 9\%.
$$

$$
\text{VAR}(R_p) = a^2\text{VAR}(X) + b^2\text{VAR}(Y) + 2ab\text{COV}(X, Y) \tag{6.16}
$$

$$
= (.5)^2(.0076) + (.5)^2(.00708) + 2(.5)(.5)(-.0024)
$$

$$
= .00247 \quad \text{or} \quad \sigma(R_p) = 4.97\%.
$$

The advantage of portfolio diversification becomes clear in this example. With half our assets in X and half in Y, the expected return is halfway between that offered by X and by Y, but the portfolio risk is considerably less than either VAR(X) or VAR(Y).

Of course, we may choose any combination of X and Y. Table 6.3 gives the mean and standard deviation of returns for some of the possibilities. Figure 6.3 graphs them.

If we can sell an asset short without restriction, then the dashed portions of the lines in Fig. 6.3 are also feasible. Selling short means that you sell an asset which you don't already have. For example, it might be possible to sell short 50%

Table 6.3 Mean and Standard Deviation of Returns

Percent in X	Percent in Y	$E(\tilde{R}_p)$	$\sigma(\tilde{R}_p)$
100	0	10.0%	8.72%
75	25	9.5%	6.18%
50	50	9.0%	4.97%
25	75	8.5%	5.96%
0	100	8.0%	8.41%

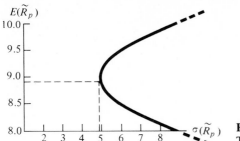

Figure 6.3
Trade-off between mean and standard deviation.

of your wealth in asset X (even though you don't already own shares of asset X) and buy 150% of asset Y. If you sell X short, you should receive the proceeds which you can then use to buy an extra 50% of Y. This is not possible in the real world because investors do not receive funds equal to the value of securities which they sell short. Nevertheless, for expositional purposes, we assume that short sales are not constrained. The mean and variance of the above short position are calculated below.

$$E(R_p) = -.5E(X) + 1.5E(Y)$$

$$= -.5(.10) + 1.5(.08) = 7.0\%.$$

$$\text{VAR}(R_p) = (-.5)^2\text{VAR}(X) + (1.5)^2\text{VAR}(Y) + 2(-.5)(1.5)\text{COV}(X, Y)$$

$$= .25(.0076) + (2.25)(.00708) + 2(-.75)(-.0024) = .02143.$$

$$\sigma(R_p) = \sqrt{\text{VAR}(R_p)} = 14.64\%.$$

Now that we have developed ways of measuring the risk (variance) and return (mean) of returns for a portfolio of assets, there are several interesting questions to explore. For example, what happens if the covariance between X and Y is zero, that is, what happens if the two securities are independent? On the other hand, what happens if they are perfectly correlated? How do we find the combination of X and Y which gives minimum variance?

3. The Correlation Coefficient

In order to answer some of these questions, it is useful to explain the concept of correlation, which is similar to covariance. The *correlation, r_{xy},* between two random variables is defined as the covariance divided by the product of the standard deviations:

$$r_{xy} \equiv \frac{\text{COV}(X, Y)}{\sigma_x \sigma_y} . \tag{6.17}$$

Obviously, if returns on the two assets are independent, that is, if the covariance between them is zero, then the correlation between them will be zero. Such a situation is shown in Fig. 6.4, which is a scatter diagram of two independent returns.

The opposite situation occurs when the returns are perfectly correlated, as in

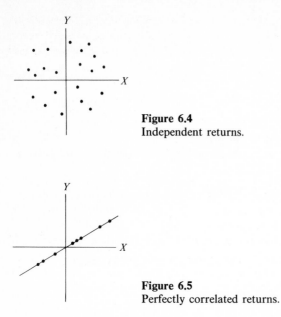

Figure 6.4
Independent returns.

Figure 6.5
Perfectly correlated returns.

Fig. 6.5, in which the returns all fall on a straight line. Perfect correlation will result in a correlation coefficient which is equal to 1. To see that this is true we can use the fact that Y is a linear function of X. In other words, if we are given the value of X, we know for sure what the corresponding value of Y will be. This is expressed as a linear function:

$$Y = a + bX$$

We also use the definition of the correlation coefficient. First, we derive the expected value and standard deviation of Y by using Properties 1 through 4:

$$E(Y) = a + bE(X),$$

$$\text{VAR}(Y) = b^2\text{VAR}(X),$$

$$\sigma_y = b\sigma_x.$$

The definition of the correlation coefficient is

$$r_{xy} = \frac{\text{COV}(X, Y)}{\sigma_x \sigma_y} = \frac{E[(X - E(X))(Y - E(Y))]}{\sigma_x \sigma_y}.$$

By substituting the mean and variance of Y, we obtain

$$r_{xy} = \frac{E[(X - E(X))(a + bX - a - bE(X))]}{\sigma_x b \sigma_x}$$

$$= \frac{E[(X - E(X))b(X - E(X))]}{b\sigma_x^2} = \frac{b\sigma_x^2}{b\sigma_x^2} = 1.$$

Therefore, the correlation coefficient equals $+1$ if the returns are perfectly correlated, and equals -1 if the returns are perfectly inversely correlated.[3] It is left as an exercise for the student to prove that the latter is true. The correlation coefficient ranges between $+1$ and -1:

$$-1 \le r_{xy} \le 1. \tag{6.18}$$

For the example we have been working with, the correlation between X and Y is

$$r_{xy} = \frac{\text{COV}(X, Y)}{\sigma_x \sigma_y} = \frac{-.0024}{(.0872)(.0841)} = -.33$$

By rearranging the definition of the correlation coefficient (Eq. 6.17) we get another definition of covariance whereby it is seen to be equal to the correlation coefficient times the product of the standard deviations.

$$\text{COV}(X, Y) = r_{xy} \sigma_x \sigma_y. \tag{6.19}$$

This in turn can be substituted into the definition of the variance of a portfolio of two assets. Substituting (6.19) into (6.16), we have

$$\text{VAR}(R_p) = a^2 \text{VAR}(X) + b^2 \text{VAR}(Y) + 2ab r_{xy} \sigma_x \sigma_y. \tag{6.20}$$

4. The Minimum Variance Portfolio

This reformulation of the variance definition is useful in a number of ways. First, it can be used to find the combination of random variables, X and Y, which provides the portfolio with minimum variance. This portfolio is the one where changes in variance (or standard deviation) with respect to changes in the percentage invested in X are zero.[4] First, recall that since the sum of weights must add to 1, $b = 1 - a$. Therefore the variance can be rewritten:

$$\text{VAR}(R_p) = a^2 \sigma_x^2 + (1 - a)^2 \sigma_y^2 + 2a(1 - a) r_{xy} \sigma_x \sigma_y.$$

We can minimize portfolio variance by setting the first derivative equal to zero:

$$\frac{d\,\text{VAR}(R_p)}{da} = 2a\sigma_x^2 - 2\sigma_y^2 + 2a\sigma_y^2 + 2r_{xy}\sigma_x\sigma_y - 4ar_{xy}\ \sigma_x\sigma_y = 0$$

$$a(\sigma_x^2 + \sigma_y^2 - 2r_{xy}\sigma_x\sigma_y) + r_{xy}\ \sigma_x\sigma_y - \sigma_y^2 = 0.$$

Solving for the optimal percentage to invest in X in order to obtain the minimum variance portfolio, we get

$$a^* = \frac{\sigma_y^2 - r_{xy}\sigma_x\sigma_y}{\sigma_x^2 + \sigma_y^2 - 2r_{xy}\sigma_x\sigma_y}. \tag{6.21}$$

Continuing with the example used throughout this section, we see that the minimum variance portfolio is the one where

---

[3] The linear relationship between Y and X for perfect inverse correlation is $Y = a - bX$.

[4] The student who wishes to review the mathematics of maximization is referred to Appendix D.

$$a* = \frac{.00708 - (-.33)(.0872)(.0841)}{.0076 + .00708 - 2(-.33)(.0872)(.0841)} = .487.$$

The portfolio return and variance for the minimum variance portfolio are:

$$E(R_p) = aE(X) + (1 - a)E(Y)$$

$$= .487(.10) + (.513)(.08) = 8.974\%$$

$$VAR(R_p) = a^2VAR(X) + (1 - a)^2VAR(Y) + 2(a)(1 - a)r_{xy}\sigma_x\sigma_y$$

$$= (.487)^2(.0076) + (.513)^2(.00708) + 2(.487)(.513)(-.33)(.0872)(.0841)$$

$$= .0018025 + .0018632 - .0012092 = .0024565.$$

$$\sigma_p = 4.956\%.$$

The minimum variance portfolio is represented by the intersection of the dashed lines in Fig. 6.3.

5. Perfectly Correlated Assets

Up to this point we have considered an example where the returns of the two risky assets had a negative correlation. What happens if they are perfectly correlated? Suppose $r_{xy} = 1$. Table 6.4 gives an example of security returns where $X = 1.037Y + 1.703$. All combinations of X and Y lie along a straight line and hence are perfectly correlated.

Since we have used the same numbers for the returns on asset Y as were used in the previous example, its standard deviation is 8.41%. We can derive the standard deviation of X by using Property 4 and the covariance between X and Y by using the definition of covariance (Eq. 6.19). It is also interesting to look at the graph of mean versus variance (Fig. 6.6). Point A represents the risk and return for a portfolio consisting of 100% of our investment in X and B represents 100% in Y. The dashed line represents the risk and return provided for all combinations of X

Table 6.4   Perfectly Correlated Security Returns

Probability	X	Y
.2	−1.408%	−3%
.2	17.258%	15%
.2	3.777%	2%
.2	22.443%	20%
.2	7.925%	6%

$$\sigma_x = 1.037\sigma_y = 8.72\%,$$

$$\sigma_y = 8.41\%,$$

$$COV(X, Y) = r_{xy}\sigma_x\sigma_y = .007334.$$

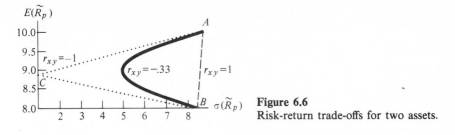

Figure 6.6
Risk-return trade-offs for two assets.

and Y when they are perfectly correlated. To see that this trade-off is a straight line, in the mean variance argument plane, we take a look at the definitions of mean and variance when $r_{xy} = 1$:

$$E(R_p) = aE(X) + (1 - a)E(Y),$$

$$VAR(R_p) = a^2\sigma_x^2 + (1 - a)^2\sigma_y^2 + 2a(1 - a)\sigma_x\sigma_y. \qquad (6.22)$$

Note that the variance can be factored:

$$VAR(R_p) = [a\sigma_x + (1 - a)\sigma_y]^2,$$

therefore the standard deviation is

$$\sigma(R_p) = a\sigma_x + (1 - a)\sigma_y. \qquad (6.23)$$

The easiest way to prove that the line between A and B is a straight line is to show that its slope does not change as, a, the proportion of the portfolio invested in X changes. The slope of the line will be the derivative of expected value with respect to the weight in X divided by the derivative of standard deviation with respect to the weight in X.

$$\text{Slope} = \frac{dE(R_p)}{d\sigma(R_p)} = \frac{dE(R_p)/da}{d\sigma(R_p)/da}.$$

The derivative of the expected portfolio return with respect to a change in a is

$$\frac{dE(R_p)}{da} = E(X) - E(Y),$$

and the derivative of the standard deviation with respect to a is

$$\frac{d\sigma(R_p)}{da} = \sigma_x - \sigma_y.$$

Therefore, the slope is

$$\frac{dE(R_p)}{d\sigma(R_p)} = \frac{E(X) - E(Y)}{\sigma_x - \sigma_y} = \frac{.10 - .08}{.0872 - .0841} = 6.45.$$

This proves that AB is a straight line because no matter what percentage of wealth, a, we choose to invest in X, the trade-off between expected value and standard deviation is constant.

Finally, suppose the returns on X and Y are perfectly inversely correlated; in other words $r_{xy} = -1$. In this case, the graph of the relationship between mean and standard deviation is the dotted line ACB in Fig. 6.6. We should expect that if the assets have perfect inverse correlation it would be possible to construct a perfect hedge. That is, the appropriate choice of a will result in a portfolio with zero variance. The mean and variance for a portfolio with two perfectly inversely correlated assets are

$$E(R_p) = aE(X) + (1-a)E(Y),$$

$$\text{VAR}(R_p) = a\sigma_x^2 + (1-a)^2\sigma_y^2 - 2a(1-a)\sigma_x\sigma_y, \quad \text{since} \quad r_{xy} = -1. \quad (6.24)$$

The variance can be factored as follows:

$$\text{VAR}(R_p) = (a\sigma_x - (1-a)\sigma_y)^2,$$

$$\sigma(R_p) = \pm(a\sigma_x - (1-a)\sigma_y). \quad (6.25)$$

Note that Eq. (6.25) has both a positive and a negative root. The dotted line in Fig. 6.6 is really two segments, one with a positive slope and the other with a negative slope. The following proofs show that the signs of the slopes of the line segments are determined by Eq. (6.25) and that they will always intersect the vertical axis in Fig. 6.6 at a point where the minimum variance portfolio has zero variance.

In order to show this result, we can use Eq. (6.21) to find the minimum variance portfolio:

$$a^* = \frac{\sigma_y^2 - r_{xy}\sigma_x\sigma_y}{\sigma_x^2 + \sigma_y^2 - 2r_{xy}\sigma_x\sigma_y}.$$

Because $r_{xy} = -1$, we have

$$a^* = \frac{\sigma_y^2 + \sigma_x\sigma_y}{\sigma_x^2 + \sigma_y^2 + 2\sigma_x\sigma_y} = \frac{\sigma_y}{\sigma_x + \sigma_y} = \frac{.0841}{.0872 + .0841} = 49.095\%.$$

By substituting this weight into the equations for mean and standard deviation we can demonstrate that the portfolio has zero variance.

$$E(R_p) = .49095(.10) + (1-.49095)(.08) = 8.982\%,$$

$$\sigma(R_p) = .49095(.0872) - (1-.49095)(.0841) = 0\%.$$

This result is represented by point C in Fig. 6.6.

Next, let's examine the properties of the line segments AC and CB in Fig. 6.6. In order to do so it is important to realize that the expression for the standard deviation (Eq. 6.25) for a portfolio with two perfectly inversely correlated assets has both positive and negative roots. In our example, suppose that none of the portfolio is invested in X. Then $a = 0$, and the standard deviation is a negative number,

$$\sigma(R_p) = -(1-0)\sigma_y < 0.$$

Because standard deviations cannot be negative, the two roots of Eq. (6.25) need to be interpreted as follows. So long as the percentage invested in X is greater than or equal to 49.095% (which is a^*, the minimum variance portfolio), the standard deviation of the portfolio is

$$\sigma(R_p) = a\sigma_x - (1-a)\sigma_y \quad \text{if} \quad a \geq \frac{\sigma_y}{\sigma_x + \sigma_y} . \tag{6.25a}$$

On the other hand, if less than 49.095% of the portfolio is invested in X, the standard deviation is

$$\sigma(R_p) = (1-a)\sigma_y - a\sigma_x \quad \text{if} \quad a < \frac{\sigma_y}{\sigma_x + \sigma_y} . \tag{6.25b}$$

We can use these results to show that the line segments AC and CB are linear. The proof proceeds in precisely the same way that we were able to show that AB is linear if $r_{xy} = 1$. For the positively sloped line segment, AC, using Eq. (6.24), we have

$$\frac{dE(R_p)}{da} = E(X) - E(Y),$$

and using Eq. (6.25a), we have

$$\frac{d\sigma(R_p)}{da} = \sigma_x + \sigma_y \quad \text{if} \quad a \geq \frac{\sigma_y}{\sigma_x + \sigma_y} .$$

Therefore the slope of the line is

$$\frac{dE(R_p)}{d\sigma(R_p)} = \frac{dE(R_p)/da}{d\sigma(R_p)/da} = \frac{E(X) - E(Y)}{\sigma_x + \sigma_y} = \frac{.10 - .08}{.0872 + .0841} = .117 > 0.$$

The slope of AC is positive and AC is linear because the slope is invariant to changes in the percentage of an investor's portfolio invested in X.

For the negatively sloped line segment, CB, using Eq. (6.24), we have

$$\frac{dE(R_p)}{da} = E(X) - E(Y),$$

and using Eq. (6.25b), we have

$$\frac{d\sigma(R_p)}{da} = -\sigma_y - \sigma_x \quad \text{if} \quad a < \frac{\sigma_y}{\sigma_x + \sigma_y} .$$

Therefore the slope of the line is

$$\frac{dE(R_p)}{d\sigma(R_p)} = \frac{dE(R_p)/da}{d\sigma(R_p)/da} = \frac{E(X) - E(Y)}{-(\sigma_y + \sigma_x)} = \frac{.10 - .08}{-(.0872 + .0841)} = -.117 < 0.$$

The slope of CB is negative and CB is linear.

6. The Minimum Variance Opportunity Set

Line AB in Fig. 6.6 shows the risk-return trade-offs available to the investor if the two assets are perfectly correlated, and line segments AC and CB represent the trade-offs if the assets are perfectly inversely correlated. However, these are the two extreme cases. Usually assets are less than perfectly correlated, that is $-1 < r_{xy} < 1$. The general slope of the mean-variance opportunity set is the solid line in Fig. 6.6 The opportunity set can be defined as follows:

> *Minimum variance opportunity set.*   The minimum variance opportunity set is the locus of risk and return combinations offered by portfolios of risky assets which yield the minimum variance for a given rate of return.

In general, the minimum variance opportunity set will be convex (as represented by the solid line in Fig. 6.6). This property is rather obvious because the opportunity set is bounded by the triangle ACB. Intuitively, any set of portfolio combinations formed by two risky assets which are less than perfectly correlated must lie inside the triangle ACB and will be convex.

The concepts developed in this section can now be used to discuss the way we, as investors, are able to select portfolios which maximize our expected utility. The portfolio mean return and variance are the measures of return and risk. We choose the percentages of our wealth which we want to invest in each security in order to obtain the required risk and return. We have shown the choices which are possible if two risky assets are perfectly correlated, perfectly inversely correlated, and where their correlation lies between -1 and $+1$. We have also seen how we can find the minimum variance portfolio. Later in this chapter these results will be extended from the two-asset case to portfolios of many assets.

C. OPTIMAL PORTFOLIO CHOICE: THE
EFFICIENT SET WITH TWO RISKY ASSETS
(AND NO RISK-FREE ASSET)

The assumption of no risk-free asset is the same as saying that there are no borrowing or lending opportunities. In other words, this section shows how a single individual (Robinson Crusoe) will choose his optimal portfolio of risky assets in a world where there is no opportunity for exchange. As we shall see, the following discussion is analogous to the Robinson Crusoe economy described in Chapter 1, except that the objects of choice are risk and return rather than consumption and investment. The results are also similar. Robinson Crusoe's optimal portfolio will be that where his subjective marginal rate of substitution between risk and return is exactly equal to the objectively determined marginal rate of transformation (along his mean-variance opportunity set) between risk and return. At his optimal portfolio the equality between MRS and MRT determines his subjective price of risk. Later on, in section E.4, we shall introduce a marketplace with opportunities to exchange by borrowing and lending unlimited amounts of money at the risk-free rate. This exchange economy setting will show the existence of a single market-determined price of risk. All individuals and their agents (firms for example) will use the market price of risk for optimal decisions in the face of uncertainty.

In the chapter on utility theory we saw that indifference curves for the risk-

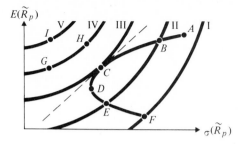

Figure 6.7
Optimal portfolio choice for a risk-averse
investor and two risky assets.

averse investor were convex in the mean-variance plane. Figure 6.7 shows a family of indifference curves as well as the convex set of portfolio choices offered by various percentages of investment in two risky assets. If we know our risk-return trade-off and also know the possibilities offered by combinations of risky assets, we will maximize our expected utility at point C in Fig. 6.7. This is where our indifference curve is tangent to the opportunity set offered by combinations of X and Y. Each indifference curve maps out all combinations of risk and return which provide us with the same total utility. Moving from right to left in Fig. 6.7, we know (from Chapter 4) that indifference curve I has less total utility than indifference curve II, and so on. We could put all of our money in one asset and receive the risk and return at point F, which is on indifference curve I, but of course we can do better at points B and E, and best at point C (on indifference curve III). Points G, H, and I have higher total utility than point C, but they are not feasible because the opportunity set offered by the risky assets does not extend that far.

An important feature of the optimal portfolio we chose to maximize our utility is that the marginal rate of substitution between our preference for risk and return represented by our indifference curves must equal the marginal rate of transformation offered by the minimum variance opportunity set. The slope of the dashed line drawn tangent to our indifference curve at point C is our marginal rate of substitution between risk and return. This line is also tangent to the opportunity set at point C. Hence its slope also represents the trade-off between risk and return offered by the opportunity set. Therefore, the way we can find a utility-maximizing portfolio is to try different portfolios along the opportunity set until we find the one where the marginal rate of transformation between risk and return along the minimum variance opportunity set just equals the marginal rate of substitution along our indifference curve.

$$\text{MRS}^{E(R_p)}_{\sigma(R_p)} = \text{MRT}^{E(R_p)}_{\sigma(R_p)}$$

The fact that this point is unique is guaranteed by the convexity of our indifference curve and the convexity of the upper half of the minimum variance opportunity set.

Let's take a look at Fig. 6.8. Suppose we find ourselves endowed with a portfolio which has the mean-variance opportunities at point A. By changing the percentage of our wealth in each of the risky assets, we can reach any point along the minimum variance opportunity set. At point A, the marginal rate of transformation between

Figure 6.8
The utility maximizing choice equates the marginal rates of substitution and transformation.

return and risk along the minimum variance opportunity set is equal to the slope of the line *DAF*. The low slope indicates that we will get rid of a lot of risk in exchange for giving up only a little return. On the other hand, the slope of our indifference curve, U_1, the slope of the line *CAB* at point *A*, indicates our subjective trade-off between return and risk, i.e., our marginal rate of substitution. At point *A*, where we already have a relatively high level of risk, we are willing to give up a lot of return in order to get rid of a little risk. If we can move along the opportunity set toward point *E* without incurring any cost, we will clearly do so because the opportunity set at point *A* allows us to trade off return and risk at a more favorable rate than we require (according to our indifference curve). We will continue to move along the opportunity set until we reach point *E*. At this point we attain the highest possible expected utility on indifference curve U_2. Furthermore, the marginal rate of transformation between return and risk along the opportunity set is exactly equal to the marginal rate of substitution along the indifference curve. Thus we have shown that a necessary condition for expected utility maximization is that the marginal rate of substitution must equal the marginal rate of transformation. This also implies that at the optimum portfolio choice, we have a linear trade-off between return, $E(R_p)$, and risk, $\sigma(R_p)$.[5]

Even though different investors may have the same assessment of the return and risk offered by risky assets, they may hold different portfolios. Later we shall discover that when a riskless asset is introduced into the opportunity set, investors will hold identical combinations of risky assets even though they have different attitudes toward risk. However, in the current framework for analysis, we assume that investors have homogeneous beliefs about the opportunity set, that no risk-free asset exists, and that investors have different indifference curves which reflect their differing attitudes toward risk.[6] Figure 6.9 shows three different indifference curves and the invest-

---

[5] For an excellent mathematical development of this fact, see Fama and Miller [1972], Chapter 6.

[6] Homogeneous beliefs mean simply that everyone has exactly the same information so that they all perceive exactly the same opportunity set.

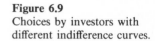

Figure 6.9
Choices by investors with
different indifference curves.

ment opportunity set. Investor III is more risk averse than investor II, who, in turn, is more risk averse than investor I. (Why is this true?) Consequently, they each will choose to invest a different percentage of their portfolio in the risky assets which make up the opportunity set.

Note that rational investors will never choose a portfolio below the minimum variance point. They can always attain higher expected utility along the positively sloped portion of the opportunity set represented by the line segment *EDCBA*. This concept leads to the definition of the efficient set.

> *Efficient set.* The efficient set is the set of mean-variance choices from the invest-
> ment opportunity set where for a given variance (or standard deviation) no other
> investment opportunity offers a higher mean return.

The notion of an efficient set considerably narrows the number of portfolios from which an investor might choose. In Fig. 6.9, for example, the portfolios at points *B* and *F* offer the same standard deviation, but *B* is on the efficient set because it offers a higher return for the same risk. Hence no rational investor would ever choose point *F* over point *B* and we can ignore point *F*. Point *B* is stochastically dominant over point *F*.

Interesting special cases of the efficient set for two risky assets occur when their returns are perfectly correlated. Figure 6.10 shows perfect correlation, and Fig. 6.11

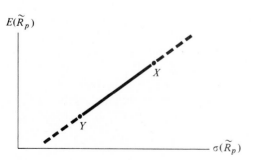

Figure 6.10
Two perfectly correlated assets.

Figure 6.11
Two assets with perfect inverse correlation.

shows perfect inverse correlation. In both cases, the efficient set is linear. In Fig. 6.10 it is line XY and in Fig. 6.11 it is line XZ.

In general, the locus of feasible mean-variance opportunities can be found by solving either of the following two mathematical programming problems. The first defines the minimum variance opportunity set and the second defines the efficient set.

Programming Problem 1:

$$\text{Min } \sigma^2(R_p) \quad \text{subject to} \quad E(R_p) = K. \tag{6.26a}$$

Programming Problem 2:

$$\text{Max } E(R_p) \quad \text{subject to} \quad \sigma^2(R_p) = K. \tag{6.26b}$$

Note that the minimum variance opportunity set is found by finding all combinations which give the lowest risk for a given return. The efficient set is the locus of highest returns for a given risk. If we write out the first problem at greater length,

$$Min\{\sigma^2(R_p) = [a^2\sigma_x^2 + (1-a)^2\sigma_y^2 + 2abr_{xy}\sigma_x\sigma_y]\},$$

subject to

$$E(R_p) = aE(X) + (1-a)E(Y) = K,$$

we see that it is a quadratic programming problem because the objective function contains squared terms in the choice variable, a. The decision variable in either problem, of course, is to choose the percentage, a, to invest in asset X which minimizes variance subject to the expected return constraint. Markowitz [1959] was the first to define the investor's portfolio decision problem in this way and to show that it is equivalent to maximizing the investor's expected utility. The interested student is referred to his book for an excellent exposition. However, it is beyond the scope of the present text to explore the details of a quadratic programming solution to the efficient set. Furthermore, the problem can be simplified greatly by introducing a risk-free asset into the analysis.

D. THE EFFICIENT SET WITH ONE RISKY AND ONE RISK-FREE ASSET

If one of the two assets, R_f, has zero variance, then the mean and variance of the portfolio become

$$E(R_p) = aE(X) + (1 - a)R_f,$$

$$\mathrm{VAR}(R_p) = a^2\mathrm{VAR}(X)$$

We have assumed that the risk-free asset is R_f. Its variance and its covariance with the risky asset are zero, therefore the second and third terms in the general expression for variance, Eq. (6.20), are equal to zero, and portfolio variance is simply the variance of the risky asset.

Knowledge of the mean and variance of a portfolio with one risk-free and one risky asset allows us to plot the opportunity set in Fig. 6.12. It is linear. Proof of linearity proceeds in the same way as earlier proofs. All we need to do is show that the slope is independent of a, the percentage of the portfolio invested in the risky asset. The change in expected return with respect to the percentage invested in X is

$$\frac{dE(R_p)}{da} = E(X) - R_f,$$

and the change in standard deviation with respect to a is

$$\frac{d\sigma(R_p)}{da} = \sigma_x.$$

Therefore the slope of the line is

$$\frac{dE(R_p)}{d\sigma(R_p)} = \frac{dE(R_p)/da}{d\sigma(R_p)/da} = \frac{E(X) - R_f}{\sigma_x}.$$

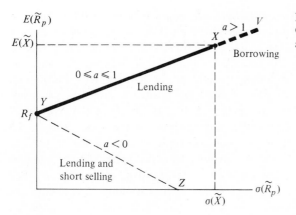

Figure 6.12
Opportunity set with one risky and one risk-free asset.

Consequently, the line VXY must be linear because its slope does not change with the percentage invested in X.

It is usually assumed that the rate of return on the risk-free asset is equal to the borrowing and lending rate in the economy. In the real world, of course, the borrowing and lending rates are not equal. One possible cause is transactions costs, i.e., frictions in the marketplace. However, like physicists who assume that friction does not exist in order to derive the laws of mechanics, economists assume that asset markets are frictionless in order to develop price theory. A frictionless world to an economist is one where all assets are infinitely divisible and where there are no transaction costs. In such a world, the borrowing rate would equal the lending rate for risk-free assets. We shall use this assumption to develop a theory for the price of risk, then provide empirical evidence which indicates that in spite of several unrealistic assumptions, the theory describes reality surprisingly well.

Given the assumption that the borrowing rate equals the lending rate, YXV is a straight line. To reach portfolios along the line segment XV it is necessary to borrow in order to invest more than 100% of the portfolio in the risky asset. Note that borrowing is analogous to selling short the risk-free asset. Therefore, along the line segment XV, the percentage invested in X is greater than 1; in other words $a > 1$. The mean and standard deviation of the portfolio along this portion of the line are

$$E(R_p) = aE(X) + (1 - a)R_f,$$

$$\sigma(R_p) = a\sigma_x.$$

On the other hand, when we decide to invest more than 100% of our portfolio in the risk-free asset, we must sell short the risky asset. Assuming no restrictions on short sales (another assumption necessary for frictionless markets) the mean and variance of the portfolio for $a < 0$ are

$$E(R_p) = (1 - a)R_f + aE(X),$$

$$\sigma(R_p) = |a|\sigma_x.$$

Note that because negative standard deviations are impossible, the absolute value of a is used to measure the standard deviation of the portfolio when the risky asset is sold short. The line segment YZ represents portfolio mean and variance in this case.

What about the efficient set for portfolios composed of one risk-free and one risky asset? Clearly no risk-averse investor would prefer line segment YZ in Fig. 6.12 because he or she can always do better along the positively sloped line segment YXV. Therefore, the efficient set is composed of long positions in the risky asset combined with borrowing or lending. Why then do we observe short sales in the real world? The answer, of course, is that not all people hold the same probability beliefs about the distributions of returns provided by risky assets. Some investors may believe that the expected return on asset X is negative, in which case they would sell short. In equilibrium, however, we know that so long as investors are risk averse, the final price of the risky asset X must be adjusted so that its expected rate of return is greater than the risk-free rate. In equilibrium, assets of higher risk must have higher expected return.

E. OPTIMAL PORTFOLIO CHOICE: MANY ASSETS

Until now it has been convenient to discuss portfolios of only two assets. By generalizing the argument to many assets we can discuss several important properties such as portfolio diversification, the separation principle, and the capital market line. We begin by developing the mean and variance for portfolios of many assets.

1. Portfolio Mean, Variance, and Covariance with N Risky Assets

Suppose we wish to talk about the mean and variance of portfolios of three assets instead of just two. Let w_1, w_2, and w_3 be the percentages of a portfolio invested in the three assets; let $E(R_1)$, $E(R_2)$, and $E(R_3)$ be the expected returns; let σ_1^2, σ_2^2, and σ_3^2 be the variances; and let σ_{12}, σ_{23}, and σ_{13} be the covariances. Finally, let R_1, R_2, R_3 be the random returns. The definition of the portfolio mean is

$$E(R_p) = E[w_1R_1 + w_2R_2 + w_3R_3],$$

and using Property 1, we have

$$E(R_p) = w_1E(R_1) + w_2E(R_2) + w_3E(R_3).$$

As was the case for a portfolio with two assets, the expected portfolio return is simply a weighted average of the expected return on individual assets. This can be rewritten as

$$E(R_p) = \sum_{i=1}^{3} w_iE(R_i). \tag{6.27}$$

The definition of portfolio variance for three assets is the expectation of the sum of the mean differences squared.

$$
\begin{aligned}
\text{VAR}(R_p) &= E\{[(w_1R_1 + w_2R_2 + w_3R_3) - (w_1E(R_1) + w_2E(R_2) + w_3E(R_3))]^2\} \\
&= E\{[w_1(R_1 - E(R_1)) + w_2(R_2 - E(R_2)) + w_3(R_3 - E(R_3))]^2\} \\
&= E\{w_1^2(R_1 - E(R_1))^2 + w_2^2(R_2 - E(R_2))^2 + w_3^2(R_3 - E(R_3))^2 \\
&\quad + 2w_1w_2(R_1 - E(R_1))(R_2 - E(R_2)) + 2w_1w_3(R_1 - E(R_1))(R_3 - E(R_3)) \\
&\quad + 2w_2w_3(R_2 - E(R_2))(R_3 - E(R_3))\} \\
&= w_1^2\text{VAR}(R_1) + w_2^2\text{VAR}(R_2) + w_3^2\text{VAR}(R_3) + 2w_1w_2\text{COV}(R_1,R_2) \\
&\quad + 2w_1w_3\text{COV}(R_1,R_3) + 2w_2w_3\text{COV}(R_2,R_3).
\end{aligned}
$$

The portfolio variance is a weighted sum of variance and covariance terms. It can be rewritten as

$$VAR(R_p) = \sum_{i=1}^{3} \sum_{j=1}^{3} w_i w_j \sigma_{ij}, \tag{6.28}$$

where w_i and w_j are the percentages invested in each asset and σ_{ij} is the covariance of asset i with asset j. You will recall from the discussion of covariance earlier in the text that the variance is really a special case of covariance. The variance is the covariance of an asset with itself. For example when $i = 2$ and $j = 2$, then we have $w_2 w_2 \sigma_{22}$, which is the same thing as $w_2^2 VAR(R_2)$. Therefore, Eq. (6.28) contains three variance and six covariance terms.

If we replace the three assets with N, Eqs. (6.27) and (6.28) can be used as general representations of the mean and variance of a portfolio of N assets. We can also write Eqs. (6.27) and (6.28) in matrix form,[7] which for two assets looks like this

$$E(R_p) = [E(R_1)\ E(R_2)] \begin{bmatrix} w_1 \\ w_2 \end{bmatrix} = \mathbf{R'W}$$

$$VAR(R_p) = [w_1\ w_2] \begin{bmatrix} \sigma_{11} & \sigma_{12} \\ \sigma_{21} & \sigma_{22} \end{bmatrix} \begin{bmatrix} w_1 \\ w_2 \end{bmatrix} = \mathbf{W'} \sum \mathbf{W}$$

The expected portfolio return is the $(1XN)$ row vector of expected returns, $[E(R_1),\ E(R_2)] = \mathbf{R'}$, postmultiplied by the $(NX1)$ column vector of weights held in each asset, $[w_1 w_2] = \mathbf{W}$. The variance is the (NXN) variance-covariance matrix, $\sum$, premultiplied and postmultiplied by the vector of weights, $\mathbf{W}$. To see that the matrix definition of the variance is identical to Eq. (6.28) first postmultiply the variance-covariance matrix by the column vector of weights to get:

$$VAR(R_p) = [w_1 w_2] \begin{bmatrix} w_1\sigma_{11} + w_2\sigma_{12} \\ w_1\sigma_{21} + w_2\sigma_{22} \end{bmatrix}.$$

Postmultiplying the second vector times the first, we have

$$VAR(R_p) = w_1^2\sigma_{11} + w_1 w_2 \sigma_{12} + w_2 w_1 \sigma_{21} + w_2^2 \sigma_{22}.$$

Finally, collecting terms, we see that this is equal to

$$VAR(R_p) = \sum_{i=1}^{N} \sum_{j=1}^{N} w_i w_j \sigma_{ij}, \quad \text{where } N = 2.$$

This shows that the matrix definition of variance is equivalent to Eq. (6.28).

Suppose we want to express the covariance between two portfolios, A and B, using matrix notation. This will prove to be an extremely powerful and useful tool later on. Let $\mathbf{W'_1}$ be the $(1XN)$ row vector of weights held in portfolio A. For example, we might construct portfolio A by holding 50% of our wealth in asset X and the remaining 50% in asset Y. Next, let $\mathbf{W_2}$ be the $(NX1)$ column vector of weights

---

[7] The reader is referred to Appendix B for a review of matrix algebra.

used to construct portfolio B. For example we might have 25% in X and 75% in Y. If Σ is the ($N X N$) variance-covariance matrix, then the covariance between the two portfolios is defined as

$$\text{COV}(R_A, R_B) \equiv \mathbf{W}_1' \sum \mathbf{W}_2 \qquad (6.29)$$

$$= [w_{1a} \quad w_{2a}] \begin{bmatrix} \sigma_{11} & \sigma_{12} \\ \sigma_{21} & \sigma_{22} \end{bmatrix} \begin{bmatrix} w_{1b} \\ w_{2b} \end{bmatrix}$$

Postmultiplying the variance-covariance matrix, Σ, by the column vector, $\mathbf{W}_2$, we have

$$\text{COV}(R_A, R_B) = [w_{1a} \quad w_{2a}] \begin{bmatrix} w_{1b}\sigma_{11} + w_{2b}\sigma_{12} \\ w_{1b}\sigma_{21} + w_{2b}\sigma_{22} \end{bmatrix},$$

and postmultiplying the row vector, $\mathbf{W}_1'$, by the column vector above, we obtain

$$\text{COV}(R_A, R_B) = w_{1a}w_{1b}\sigma_{11} + w_{1a}w_{2b}\sigma_{12} + w_{2a}w_{1b}\sigma_{21} + w_{2a}w_{2b}\sigma_{22}.$$

In order to show that this matrix result is indeed the same as the traditional definition, we begin with the usual covariance equation

$$\text{COV}(R_A, R_B) = E[(R_A - E(R_A))(R_B - E(R_B))].$$

We know that

$$R_A = w_{1a}R_x + w_{2a}R_y,$$

$$R_B = w_{1b}R_x + w_{2b}R_y.$$

Substituting these expressions as well as their expected values into the covariance definition, we have

$$\text{COV}(R_A, R_B) = E[(w_{1a}R_x + w_{2a}R_y - w_{1a}E(R_x) - w_{2a}E(R_y))$$

$$\times (w_{1b}R_x + w_{2b}R_y - w_{1b}E(R_x) - w_{2b}E(R_y))]$$

$$= E\{[w_{1a}(R_x - E(R_x)) + w_{2a}(R_y - E(R_y))]$$

$$\times [w_{1b}(R_x - E(R_x)) + w_{2b}(R_y - E(R_y))]\}$$

$$= w_{1a}w_{1b}\sigma_{11} + w_{1a}w_{2b}\sigma_{12} + w_{2a}w_{1b}\sigma_{21} + w_{2a}w_{2b}\sigma_{22}.$$

Note that this is exactly the same as the expanded covariance expression obtained from the matrix definition, Eq. (6.29).

The matrix definitions of portfolio mean, variance, and covariance are particularly powerful and useful because the size of the vectors and matrices can easily be expanded to handle any number of assets. The matrix form also lends itself naturally to computer programs.

2. The Opportunity Set with N Risky Assets

When considering portfolios with many assets, we can discover the opportunity set and efficient set if we know the expected returns and the variances of individual

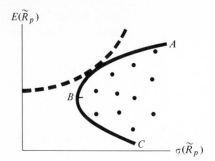

Figure 6.13
The investment opportunity set with many risky assets.

assets as well as the covariances between each pair of assets. This requires a great deal of information. The New York Stock Exchange alone lists at least 2000 securities. In order to determine the opportunity set it would be necessary to estimate 2000 mean returns, 2000 variances, and 1,999,000 covariances.[8] Fortunately, we shall soon see that there are ways around this computational nightmare.

The investment opportunity set has the same shape with many risky assets as it did with two.[9] The only difference is that with many assets to be considered, some will fall in the interior of the opportunity set (Fig. 6.13). The opportunity set will be composed of various portfolios and of some individual assets which are mean-variance efficient by themselves. As long as there is no riskless asset, a risk-averse investor would maximize his or her expected utility in the same way as before—by finding the point of tangency between the efficient set and the highest indifference curve. But in order to do so, he or she would have to estimate all the means, variances, and covariances mentioned earlier.

3. The Efficient Set with N Risky Assets and One Risk-Free Asset

Once the risk-free asset is introduced into the analysis, the problem of portfolio selection is simplified. If, as before, we assume that the borrowing rate equals the lending rate, we can draw a straight line between any risky asset and the risk-free asset. Points along the line represent portfolios consisting of combinations of the risk-free and risky assets. Several possibilities are graphed in Fig. 6.14. Portfolios along any of the lines shown are possible, but only one line dominates. All investors will prefer combinations of the risk-free asset and portfolio M on the efficient set. (Why?) These combinations lie along the positively sloped portion of line NMR_fO. Therefore, the efficient set (which is represented by line segment R_fMN) in the presence of a risk-free asset is linear. All an investor needs to know is the combination of assets which makes up portfolio M in Fig. 6.14 as well as the risk-free asset. This is true for any investor, regardless of his or her degree of risk aversion. Figure 6.15

---

[8] In general, if N securities are analyzed, the variance-covariance matrix will have $\frac{1}{2}(N-1)N$ *different* covariance elements and N variance elements.

[9] For proof, see Merton [1972].

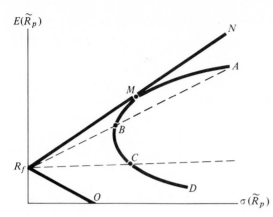

Figure 6.14
The efficient set with one risk-free and many risky assets.

clarifies this point. Investor III is the most risk averse of the three pictured in Fig. 6.15, and will choose to invest nearly all of his or her portfolio in the risk-free asset. Investor I, who is the least risk averse, will borrow (at the risk-free rate) to invest more than 100% of his or her portfolio in the risky portfolio M. However, no investor will choose to invest in any other risky portfolio except portfolio M. For example, all three could attain the minimum variance portfolio at point B, but none will choose this alternative because all can do better with some combination of the risk-free asset and portfolio M. Next we shall see that portfolio M can be identified as the market portfolio of all risky assets.

4. A Description of Equilibrium

In section C we analyzed a Robinson Crusoe economy where there was no opportunity for exchange. Robinson Crusoe's optimal portfolio resulted from maximizing his expected utility, given his risk preferences, subject to the feasible set of mean variance tradeoffs offered by a combination of two risky assets. In section D we

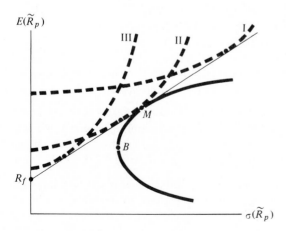

Figure 6.15
Dominance of the linear efficient set.

saw how a linear efficient set could be formed from one risky and one risk-free asset. So far in section E, we have first described the opportunity set with risky assets, then with one risk-free asset and many risky assets.

The introduction of a risk-free asset may be thought of as creating an exchange or market economy where there are many individuals. Each of them may borrow or lend unlimited amounts at the risk-free rate. With the introduction of an exchange economy we shall be able to describe a fundamental principle called two-fund separation. Analogous to Fisher separation found in Chapter 1, two-fund separation implies that there is a single market-determined equilibrium price of risk. This concept will prove extremely useful later on in the text when, for example, we want to conceptualize the opportunity cost of capital for projects of different risk.

If, in addition to the earlier assumption of equality between the borrowing and lending rate which follows given frictionless capital markets, we add the assumption that all investors have homogeneous (i.e., identical) beliefs about the expected distributions of returns offered by all assets, then all investors will perceive the same efficient set. Therefore, they will all try to hold some combination of the risk-free asset, R_f, and portfolio M.

For the market to be in equilibrium, we require a set of market-clearing prices. All assets must be held. In other words, the existence of an equilibrium requires that all prices be adjusted so that the excess demand for any asset will be zero. This market-clearing condition implies that an equilibrium is not attained until the single-tangency portfolio, M, which all investors (with homogeneous expectations) try to combine with risk-free borrowing or lending, is a portfolio in which all assets are held according to their market value weights. If V_i is the market value of the ith asset, then the percent of wealth held in each asset is equal to the ratio of the market value of the asset to the market value of all assets. Mathematically,

$$w_i = \frac{V_i}{\sum\limits_{i=1}^{N} V_i},$$

where w_i is the weight of the ith asset in the market portfolio and ΣV_i is the total market value of all assets. Market equilibrium is not reached until the tangency portfolio, M, is the market portfolio. Also, the value of the risk-free rate must be such that aggregate borrowing and lending are equal.

The fact that the portfolios of all risk-averse investors will consist of different combinations of only two portfolios is an extremely powerful result. It has come to be known as the two-fund separation principle. Its definition is given below.

Two-fund separation.   Each investor will have a utility maximizing portfolio which is a combination of the risk-free asset and a portfolio (or fund) of risky assets which is determined by the line drawn from the risk-free rate of return tangent to the investor's efficient set of risky assets.

The straight line in Fig. 6.15 will be the efficient set for all investors. This line has come to known as the capital market line. It represents a linear relationship between portfolio risk and return.

Capital market line (CML). If investors have homogeneous beliefs, then they all have the same linear efficient set called the capital market line.

Figure 6.16 is a graph of the capital market line. The intercept is the risk-free rate, R_f, and its slope is $[E(R_m) - R_f]/\sigma(R_m)$. Therefore, the equation for the capital market line is

$$E(R_p) = R_f + \frac{E(R_m) - R_f}{\sigma(R_m)} \sigma(R_p). \tag{6.30}$$

It provides a simple linear relationship between the risk and return for *efficient portfolios* of assets. Having established the principle of two-fund separation and defined the capital market line, we find it useful to describe the importance of capital market equilibrium from an individual's point of view.

We wish to compare expected utility-maximizing choices in a world without capital markets (as depicted in Fig. 6.8) with those in a world with capital markets (seen in Fig. 6.17). As in Chapter 1, a capital market is nothing more than the opportunity to borrow and lend at the risk-free rate. Chapter 1 emphasized that in

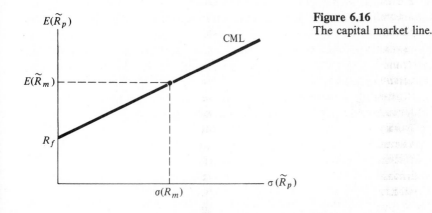

Figure 6.16
The capital market line.

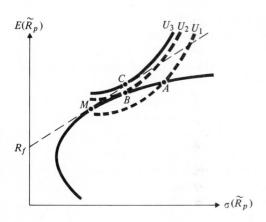

Figure 6.17
Individual expected utility maximization in a world with capital markets.

a world with certainty, everyone was better off given that capital markets existed and Fisher separation obtained. Now we have extended this result to a world with mean variance uncertainty. Everyone is better off with capital markets where two-fund separation obtains.

Figure 6.17 shows us endowed with the mean-variance combination at point A. With a capital market, we always have two choices available. We can move along the mean-variance opportunity set (by changing our portfolio of risky assets) or we can move along the capital market line by borrowing or lending. Initially, at point A, the trade-off between return and risk is more favorable along the opportunity set than along the market line. Therefore, we will move along the opportunity set toward point B where the marginal rate of transformation between return and risk on the opportunity set is equal to our subjective marginal rate of substitution along our indifference curve. In the absence of capital markets we would have maximized our expected utility at point B. This would be the Robinson Crusoe solution and our level of utility would have increased from U_1 to U_2. However, if we have the opportunity to move along the capital market line, we can be even better off. By moving to point M, then borrowing to reach point C, we can increase our expected utility from U_2 to U_3. Therefore we have three important results. First, nearly everyone is better off in a world with capital markets (and no one is worse off). Second, two-fund separation obtains. This means that everyone, regardless of the shape of his or her indifference curve, will decide to hold various combinations of two funds: the market portfolio and the risk-free asset. And third, in equilibrium, the marginal rate of substitution (MRS) between return and risk is the same for all individuals, regardless of their subjective attitudes toward risk.

If the marginal rate of substitution between risk and return is the same for every individual in equilibrium, then the slope of the capital market line is the equilibrium price of risk (EPR):

$$\text{EPR} = \text{MRS}_{\sigma(R_p)}^{E(R_p)} = \frac{E(R_m) - R_f}{\sigma(R_m)}. \tag{6.31}$$

The implication is that decision makers, for example managers of firms, can use the market-determined equilibrium price of risk to evaluate investment projects regardless of the tastes of shareholders. Every shareholder will unanimously agree on the price of risk, even though different shareholders have different degrees of risk aversion. Also the marginal rates of substitution between risk and return for the ith and jth individuals in equilibrium will equal the marginal rate of transformation and both will be equal to the equilibrium price of risk.

$$\text{MRS}_i = \text{MRS}_j = \frac{E(R_m) - R_f}{\sigma(R_m)} = \text{MRT}.$$

Next, and in Chapter 7, we turn our attention to the problem of measuring risk. We have already established that variance is an adequate measure of risk for portfolios of assets; however, it is not particularly useful when we wish to evaluate the risk of individual assets which do not lie on the efficient set. Nor is it possible, given our current development of the theory, to compare a single risky asset with a well-diversified portfolio. Therefore it is necessary to distinguish between portfolio risk and the contribution of a single asset to the riskiness of a well-diversified portfolio (such as the market portfolio).

In order to set the framework for the difference between portfolio risk and individual asset risk, we observe the average return and variance of return calculated for a single asset, Bayside Cigar, and for a 100-stock portfolio of randomly selected common stocks. Return on the assets was defined as total return, i.e., dividends, D_t, plus capital gains $P_t - P_{t-1}$. The equation for a monthly return is given below:

$$R_t = \frac{P_t - P_{t-1} + D_t}{P_{t-1}}.$$

Data were collected for the 306 months between January 1945 and June 1970.[10] The average monthly return on Bayside Cigar was .45%, which is approximately 5.4% per year, and the standard deviation was 7.26%. By comparison, the 100-stock portfolio had an average return of .91% per month or 10.9% per year. Its standard deviation was 4.45%. Normally, one would expect the standard deviation of a well-diversified portfolio to be lower than for a single asset, and the empirical results bear this out. But we also know that riskier assets should have higher returns. Therefore, if standard deviation is the appropriate measure of risk for an individual asset, then Bayside Cigar should have a higher return. But it doesn't! We shall see in the next chapter that the resolution to this apparent paradox is that although the standard deviation is appropriate for measuring the risk of an efficient portfolio, it is not the appropriate measure of risk for individual assets, or for comparing the riskiness of portfolios with the riskiness of assets.

F. PORTFOLIO DIVERSIFICATION AND INDIVIDUAL ASSET RISK

We begin by taking a look at what happens to portfolio variance as we increase the number of assets in a portfolio. Equation (6.28),

$$\text{VAR}(R_p) = \sum_{i=1}^{N} \sum_{j=1}^{N} w_i w_j \sigma_{ij},$$

provided an expression for the variance of a portfolio of many assets.

We shall see that as the number of assets in the portfolio increases, the portfolio variance decreases and approaches the average covariance. There are several ways to prove this. The easiest is simply to note that a two-asset portfolio has two variance and two covariance terms. A three-asset portfolio has three variance but six covariance terms. A four-asset portfolio has four variance terms and 12 covariance terms. In general, the number of variance terms equals the number of assets in the portfolio,

---

[10] See Modigliani and Pogue [1974].

N, while the number of covariance terms equals $N^2 - N$ or $N(N - 1)$. Suppose that we have an equally weighted portfolio so that $w_i = w_j = 1/N$. Then the portfolio variance can be written from Eq. (6.28) as

$$\text{VAR}(R_p) = \sum_{i=1}^{N} \sum_{j=1}^{N} \frac{1}{N} \frac{1}{N} \sigma_{ij} = \frac{1}{N^2} \sum_{i=1}^{N} \sum_{j=1}^{N} \sigma_{ij}.$$

This expression can be separated into variance and covariance terms as follows:

$$\text{VAR}(R_p) = \frac{1}{N^2} \sum_{i=1}^{N} \sigma_{ii} + \frac{1}{N^2} \sum_{i=1}^{N} \sum_{\substack{j=1 \\ i \neq j}}^{N} \sigma_{ij}. \tag{6.32}$$

Suppose that the largest individual asset variance is V. Then the first term, the variance term, is always less than or equal to

$$\frac{1}{N^2} \sum_{i=1}^{N} V = \frac{VN}{N^2} = \frac{V}{N},$$

and as the number of assets in the portfolio becomes large, this term approaches zero.

$$\lim_{N \to \infty} \frac{V}{N} = 0.$$

On the other hand, the covariance terms do not vanish. Let $\bar{\sigma}_{ij}$ be the average covariance. Then in the right-hand term in Eq. (6.32), there are $(N^2 - N)$ covariance terms, all equal to $\bar{\sigma}_{ij}$: therefore the right-hand term can be rewritten as

$$\frac{1}{N^2} (N^2 - N) \bar{\sigma}_{ij} = \frac{N^2}{N^2} \bar{\sigma}_{ij} - \frac{N}{N^2} \bar{\sigma}_{ij}$$

and the limit as N approaches infinity is

$$\lim_{N \to \infty} \left(\frac{N^2}{N^2} \bar{\sigma}_{ij} - \frac{N}{N^2} \bar{\sigma}_{ij} \right) = \bar{\sigma}_{ij}. \tag{6.33}$$

Consequently, as we form portfolios which have large numbers of assets and which are better diversified, the covariance terms become relatively more important.

Fama [1976] has illustrated this result empirically.[11] His results are shown in Fig. 6.18. He randomly selected 50 securities listed on the New York Stock Exchange and calculated their standard deviations using monthly data from July 1963 to June 1968. Then a single security was selected randomly. Its standard deviation of return was around 11%. Next, this security was combined with another (also randomly selected) to form an equally weighted portfolio of two securities. The standard deviation fell to around 7.2%. Step by step more securities were randomly added to the portfolio until all 50 securities were included. Almost all of the diversification was obtained after the first 10–15 securities were randomly selected. In addition the portfolio stan-

---

[11] See Fama [1976], *Foundations of Finance,* pp. 253–254.

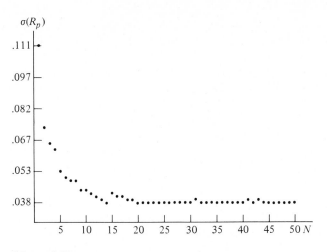

Figure 6.18
The standard deviation of portfolio return as a function
of the number of securities in the portfolio. (From Fama,
E. F., *Foundations of Finance,* reprinted with permission
of the author.)

dard deviation quickly approached a limit which is roughly equal to the average
covariance of all securities. One of the practical implications is that most of the
benefits of diversification (given a random portfolio selection strategy) can be achieved
with fewer than 15 stocks.

Still another way of looking at the risk of a single asset is to evaluate its contribution
to total portfolio risk. This can be done by taking the partial derivative of the expression
for portfolio variance (Eq. 6.28) with respect to w_i, the percentage invested in the
ith risky asset:

$$\frac{\delta \, \text{VAR}(R_p)}{\delta w_i} = 2 w_i \sigma_i^2 + 2 \sum_{j=1}^{N} w_j \sigma_{ij}. \tag{6.34}$$

Again, consider a portfolio where an equal percentage is invested in each asset, $w_i =$
$1/N$. As the number of assets in the portfolio increases, w_i approaches zero and
Σw_j approaches one. Therefore, for well-diversified portfolios, the appropriate measure
of the contribution of an asset to portfolio risk is its covariance with the other assets
in the portfolio. In the marketplace for assets (the stock market for example), the
number of risky assets is extremely large. We shall see (in Chapter 7) that the contribution of a single asset to market risk is its covariance with the market portfolio. Hence
this is the measure appropriate to risk for a single asset, even though individual
investors may not, in reality, hold well-diversified portfolios. Relationships (6.33)
and (6.34) help provide an intuitive appeal for covariance as the appropriate measure
of risk for individual assets, but they are not proofs. For proof, we need to consider
market equilibrium. In the next chapter we shall show that the covariance risk of
an asset is the only portion of an asset's risk which an investor will pay to avoid.

This important idea is embodied in what has come to be known as the *capital asset pricing model.* It is an equilibrium theory of risk and return which is the main topic of Chapter 7.

But why can't variance be used as a measure of risk? After all, we know that expected utility-maximizing investors choose their optimal portfolios on the basis of mean and variance. The answer lies in Fig. 6.19. Asset *I* is inefficient because it does not lie on the capital market line. Consequently, even though we know the mean and variance of asset *I,* we cannot be sure what rate of return the market will require to hold the asset because it is not on the efficient frontier. Investors have available to them other opportunities which have the same expected return but lower variance. Therefore, we cannot use our knowledge of the mean and variance of asset *I* to determine the rate of return which the market will require from asset *I* in order to hold it in equilibrium. In Chapter 7, given a market equilibrium setting, we shall see that only the portion of total variance which is correlated with the economy is relevant. Any portion of total risk which is not correlated with the economy is irrelevant and can be avoided at zero cost through diversification. Assets *I, J,* and *K* have the same expected return, $\bar{R}$, yet they all have different variances. If variance is the correct measure of the riskiness of an individual asset, then the implication is that these three assets, each with different "risk," all have the same expected return. This is nonsense. It would violate what has come to be known as the single price law of securities.

> *The single price law of securities.* All securities or combinations of securities which have the same joint distributions of return will have the same price in equilibrium.

Since the three securities clearly have different distributions of return, they also have different prices. Even though we know the mean and variance of return offered by assets *I, J,* and *K,* we cannot be sure what prices they will have in equilibrium. The reason is that we do not know their joint distribution with all other assets. The missing information is the variance-covariance matrix of all assets. In Chapter 7 we shall see that variance is not the appropriate measure of risk for an individual asset. This was the point of Eqs. (6.33) and (6.34). As the number of assets in a portfolio increases, the risk which an asset contributes to a portfolio reduces to be exclusively the covariance risk. Therefore, the portion of an asset's risk which is uncorrelated with the economy can be avoided at no cost. No rational investor will

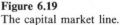

Figure 6.19
The capital market line.

pay a premium to avoid diversifiable risk. On the other hand, because covariance risk cannot be diversified away, investors will pay a premium to escape it. Therefore covariance is the relevant measure of risk for an asset because it measures the contribution of an individual asset to the variance of a well-diversified portfolio.

SUMMARY

This chapter has combined our knowledge of the theory of investor choice (utility theory) with the objects of investor choice (the portfolio opportunity set) to show how risk-averse investors wishing to maximize expected utility will choose their optimal portfolios. We began with simple measures of risk and return, (and simple probability theory) and ended with portfolio theory. Finally, we saw that when a risk-free asset exists, the opportunity set can be reduced to the simple, linear capital market line. Given frictionless capital markets and homogeneous investor expectations, all individuals will choose to hold some combination of the risk-free asset and the market portfolio.

PROBLEM SET

6.1 Historically, the empirical distributions of stock prices on the NYSE have been skewed right. Why?

6.2 Given the following relationship between x and y,

$$y = a + bx, \qquad b < 0,$$

prove that x and y are perfectly negatively correlated.

6.3 Given the following hypothetical end-of-period prices for shares of the Drill-On Corporation,

Probability	.15	.10	.30	.20	.25
End-of-period price per share	35.00	42.00	50.00	55.00	60.00

and assuming a current price of $50/share:

a) Calculate the rate of return for each probability. What is the expected return? the variance of end-of-period returns? the range? the semi-interquartile range?

b) Suppose forecasting is refined such that probabilities of end-of-period prices can be broken down further, resulting in the following distribution:

Probability	.01	.05	.07	.02	.10	.30	.20	.15	.05	.05
End-of-period price per share	0	35.00	38.57	40.00	42.00	50.00	55.00	57.00	60.00	69.00

Calculate and explain the change in

a) the expected return;

b) the range of returns;

c) the semi-interquartile range of returns.

Calculate the semivariance of end-of-period returns. Why might some investors be concerned with semivariance as a measure of risk?

6.4 Derive an expression for the expectation of the product of two random variables:

$$E(\tilde{x}\tilde{y}) = ?$$

6.5 Using the definition of portfolio variance, prove that a perfectly hedged stock portfolio that is 100 shares long and 100 shares short is perfectly risk free.

6.6 Given the variance-covariance matrix

$$\begin{bmatrix} 24 & -10 & 25 \\ -10 & 75 & 32 \\ 25 & 32 & 12 \end{bmatrix}$$

a) Calculate the variance of an equally weighted portfolio.

b) Calculate the covariance of a portfolio which has 10% in asset 1, 80% in asset 2, and 10% in asset 3 with a second portfolio which has 125% in asset 1, −10% in asset 1, and −15% in asset 3.

6.7 Given two random variables, x and y.

Probability of State of Nature	State of Nature	Variable x	Variable y
.2	I	18	0
.2	II	5	−3
.2	III	12	15
.2	IV	4	12
.2	V	6	1

a) Calculate the mean and variance of each of these variables, and the covariance between them.

b) Suppose x and y represent the returns from two assets. Calculate the mean and variance for the following portfolios:

% in x	125	100	75	50	25	0	−25
% in y	−25	0	25	50	75	100	125

c) Find the portfolio which has the minimum variance.

d) Let portfolio A have 75% in x and portfolio B have 25% in x. Calculate the covariance between the two portfolios.

e) Calculate the covariance between the minimum variance portfolio and portfolio A, and the covariance between the minimum variance portfolio and portfolio B.

f) What is the covariance between the minimum variance portfolio and any other portfolio along the efficient set?

g) What is the relationship between the covariance of the minimum variance portfolio with other efficient portfolios, and the variance of the minimum variance portfolio?

6.8 Prove that for any securities, $\tilde{X}$ and $\tilde{Y}$:

a) $E(a\tilde{X} + b\tilde{Y}) = aE(\tilde{X}) + bE(\tilde{Y})$.

b) $\text{VAR}(a\tilde{X} + b\tilde{Y}) = a^2\text{VAR}(\tilde{X}) + b^2\text{VAR}(\tilde{Y}) + 2ab\ \text{COV}(\tilde{X},\ \tilde{Y})$.

c) $\text{COV}[(a\tilde{X} + b\tilde{Z}),\ \tilde{Y}] = a\ \text{COV}(\tilde{X},\ \tilde{Y}) + b\ \text{COV}(\tilde{Z},\ \tilde{Y})$.

d) $E(\tilde{X}^2) = (E(\tilde{X}))^2 + \text{VAR}(\tilde{X})$.

e) If $r_{xy} = 1$, then $\sigma(\tilde{X} + \tilde{Y}) = \sigma_x + \sigma_y$. If $r_{xy} = -1$, then $\sigma(\tilde{X} + \tilde{Y}) = \sigma_x - \sigma_y$.

6.9 Let R_1 and R_2 be the returns from two securities with $E(R_1) = .03$ and $E(R_2) = .08$, $\text{VAR}(R_1) = .02$, $\text{VAR}(R_2) = .05$, and $\text{COV}(R_1,R_2) = -.01$.

a) Plot the set of feasible mean-variance combinations of return, assuming that the two securities above are the only investment vehicles available.

b) If we want to minimize risk, how much of our portfolio will we invest in security 1?

c) Find the mean and standard deviation of a portfolio which is 50% in security 1.

6.10 (Our thanks to Nils Hakansson, University of California, Berkeley, for providing this problem.) Two securities have the following joint distribution of returns, r_1 and r_2:

$$P\{r_1 = -1.0 \text{ and } r_2 = .15\} = .1,$$
$$P\{r_1 = .5 \text{ and } r_2 = .15\} = .8,$$
$$P\{r_1 = .5 \text{ and } r_2 = 1.65\} = .1.$$

a) Compute the means, variances, and covariance of returns for the two securities.

b) Plot the feasible mean-standard deviation $(E(R),\sigma)$ combinations, assuming that the two securities are the only investment vehicles available.

c) Which portfolios belong to the mean-variance efficient set?

d) Show that security 2 is mean-variance dominated by security 1, yet enters all efficient portfolios but one. How do you explain this?

e) Suppose that the possibility of lending, but not borrowing at 5% (without risk) is added to the previous opportunities. Draw the new set of $(E(R),\sigma)$ combinations. Which portfolios are now efficient?

6.11 Suppose a risk-averse investor can choose a portfolio from among N assets with independently distributed returns, all of which have identical means $(E(R_i) = E(R_j))$ and identical variances $(\sigma_i^2 = \sigma_j^2)$. What will be the composition of his optimal portfolio?

6.12 Given decreasing marginal utility, it is possible to prove that in a mean-variance framework no individual will hold 100% of his or her wealth in the risk-free asset. Why? [*Hint:* The answer requires an understanding of the shape of investors' indifference curves as well as the capital market line.]

6.13 Given that assets X and Y are perfectly correlated such that $Y = 6 + .2X$ and the probability distribution for X is

Probability	X
.1	30%
.2	20
.4	15
.2	10
.1	−50

What is the percent of your wealth to put into asset X to achieve zero variance? Graph the opportunity set and the zero variance point.

REFERENCES

Crámer, H., *Mathematical Methods in Statistics.* Princeton University Press, Princeton, N.J., 1961.

Fama, E. F., *Foundations of Finance,* Basic Books, New York, 1976.

Fama, E., and M. Miller, *The Theory of Finance.* Holt, Rinehart and Winston, New York, 1972.

Markowitz, H. M., *Portfolio Selection: Efficient Diversification of Investment* (Cowles Foundation Monograph 16). Yale University Press, New Haven, 1959.

Merton, R., "An Analytic Derivation of the Efficient Set," *Journal of Financial and Quantitative Analysis,* September 1972, 1851–1872.

Modigliani, F., and G. Pogue, "An Introduction to Risk and Return: Concepts and Evidence," *Financial Analysts Journal,* March/April and May/June, 1974, 68–80 and 69–85.

Sharpe, W., "A Simplified Model for Portfolio Analysis," *Management Science,* January 1963, 277–293.

―――, *Portfolio Theory and Capital Markets.* McGraw-Hill, New York, 1970.

Tobin, J., "Liquidity Preference as Behavior Towards Risk," *Review of Economic Studies,* February 1958, 65–86.

Market Equilibrium: CAPM and APT

Lucy: "I've just come up with the perfect theory. It's my theory that Beethoven would have written even better music if he had been married."
Schroeder: "What's so perfect about that theory?"
Lucy: "It can't be proved one way or the other!"

CHARLES SCHULZ, *PEANUTS,* 1976

A. INTRODUCTION

The greater portion of this chapter is devoted to extending the concept of market equilibrium in order to determine the market price for risk and the appropriate measure of risk for a single asset. One economic model used to solve this problem was developed almost simultaneously by Sharpe [1963, 1964], and Treynor [1961], while Mossin [1966], Lintner [1965a, 1969], and Black [1972] developed it further. The first model which we will discuss is usually referred to as the *Capital Asset Pricing Model* (CAPM). It will show that the equilibrium rates of return on all risky assets are a function of their covariance with the market portfolio. A second important equilibrium pricing model, called the *Arbitrage Pricing Theory* (APT), was developed by Ross [1976]. It is similar to the CAPM in that it is also an equilibrium asset pricing model. The return on any risky asset is seen to be a linear combination of various factors. It is more general than the CAPM because it allows numerous factors to explain the equilibrium return on a risky asset. However, it is in the same spirit as the CAPM. In fact, the CAPM can be shown to be a special case of the APT.

The organization of the chapter is to first develop the CAPM and its extensions, then to summarize the empirical evidence relating to its validity. Thereafter, the APT will be developed and empirical evidence on it will be described. We begin with a list of the assumptions which were first used to derive the CAPM.

The CAPM is developed in a hypothetical world where the following assumptions are made about investors and the opportunity set:

1. Investors are risk-averse individuals who maximize the expected utility of their end-of-period wealth.

2. Investors are price takers and have homogeneous expectations about asset returns which have a joint normal distribution.

3. There exists a risk-free asset such that investors may borrow or lend unlimited amounts at the risk-free rate.

4. The quantities of assets are fixed. Also, all assets are marketable and perfectly divisible.

5. Asset markets are frictionless and information is costless and simultaneously available to all investors.

6. There are no market imperfections such as taxes, regulations, or restrictions on short selling.

Many of these assumptions have been discussed earlier. However, it is worthwhile to discuss some of their implications. For example, if markets are frictionless, the borrowing rate equals the lending rate, and we are able to develop a linear efficient set called the capital market line (Fig. 6.16 and Eq. 6.30). If all assets are divisible and marketable, we exclude the possibility of human capital as we usually think of it. In other words, slavery is allowed in the model. We are all able to sell (not rent for wages) various portions of our human capital (e.g., typing ability, or reading ability) to other investors at market prices. Another important assumption is that investors have homogeneous beliefs. They all make decisions based on an identical opportunity set. In other words, no one can be fooled because everyone has the same information at the same time. Also, since all investors maximize the expected utility of their end-of-period wealth, the model is implicitly a one-period model.

Although not all these assumptions conform to reality, they are simplifications which permit the development of the CAPM, which is extremely useful for financial decision making because it quantifies and prices risk. Most of the restrictive assumptions will be relaxed later on.

B. THE EFFICIENCY OF THE MARKET PORTFOLIO

Proof of the CAPM requires that in equilibrium, the market portfolio must be an efficient portfolio. It must lie on the upper half of the minimum-variance opportunity set graphed in Fig. 7.1. One way to establish its efficiency is to argue that so long as investors have homogeneous expectations, they will all perceive the same minimum variance opportunity set.[1] Even without a risk-free asset, they will all select efficient portfolios regardless of their individual risk tolerances. As shown in Fig. 7.1, individual I chooses efficient portfolio B while individual II, who is less risk averse, chooses efficient portfolio C. Given that all individuals hold positive proportions of their wealth in efficient portfolios, then the market portfolio must be efficient because (1) the market is simply the sum of all individual holdings and (2) all individual holdings are efficient.

Thus, in theory, when all individuals have homogeneous expectations, the market portfolio must be efficient. Without homogeneous expectations, the market portfolio is not necessarily efficient and the equilibrium model of capital markets which is derived in the next section does not necessarily hold. Thus the efficiency of the market portfolio and the capital asset pricing model are inseparable, joint hypotheses. It is not possible to test the validity of one without the other. We shall return to this important point when we discuss Roll's critique later in the chapter.

C. DERIVATION OF THE CAPM

Figure 7.2 shows the expected return and standard deviation of the market portfolio, M, the risk-free asset, R_f, and a risky asset, I. The straight line connecting the risk-free asset and the market portfolio is the capital market line. For example, see

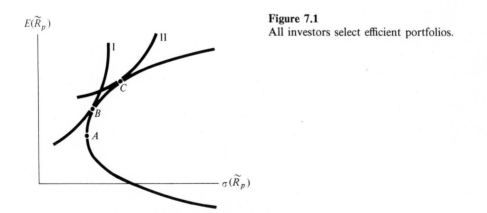

Figure 7.1
All investors select efficient portfolios.

---

[1] For a more rigorous proof of the efficiency of the market portfolio see Fama [1976], Chapter 8.

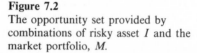

Figure 7.2
The opportunity set provided by combinations of risky asset I and the market portfolio, M.

Fig. 6.16, in Chapter 6. We know that if a market equilibrium is to exist, the prices of all assets must adjust until all are held by investors. There can be no excess demand. In other words, prices must be established so that the supply of all assets equals the demand for holding them. Consequently, in equilibrium the market portfolio will consist of all marketable assets held in proportion to their value weights. The equilibrium proportion of each asset in the market portfolio must be

$$w_i = \frac{\text{market value of individual asset}}{\text{market value of all assets}}. \tag{7.1}$$

A portfolio consisting of $a\%$ invested in risky asset I and $(1 - a)\%$ in the market portfolio will have the following mean and standard deviation:

$$E(\tilde{R}_p) = aE(\tilde{R}_i) + (1 - a)E(\tilde{R}_m), \tag{7.2}$$

$$\sigma(\tilde{R}_p) = [a^2\sigma_i^2 + (1 - a)^2\sigma_m^2 + 2a(1 - a)\sigma_{im}]^{1/2}. \tag{7.3}$$

where

$\sigma_i^2 =$ the variance of risky asset I,

$\sigma_m^2 =$ the variance of the market portfolio,

$\sigma_{im} =$ the covariance between asset I and the market portfolio.

We shall see shortly that it is important to note that the market portfolio already contains asset I held according to its market value weight. The opportunity set provided by various combinations of the risky asset and the market portfolio is the line IMI' in Fig. 7.2. The change in the mean and standard deviation with respect to the percent of the portfolio, a, invested in asset I is determined as follows:

$$\frac{\delta E(\tilde{R}_p)}{\delta a} = E(\tilde{R}_i) - E(\tilde{R}_m), \tag{7.4}$$

$$\frac{\delta \sigma(\tilde{R}_p)}{\delta a} = \tfrac{1}{2}[a^2\sigma_i^2 + (1 - a)^2\sigma_m^2 + 2a(1 - a)\sigma_{im}]^{-1/2}$$

$$\times [2a\sigma_i^2 - 2\sigma_m^2 + 2a\sigma_m^2 + 2\sigma_{im} - 4a\sigma_{im}]. \tag{7.5}$$

Sharpe and Treynor's insight, which allowed them to use the above facts to determine a market equilibrium price for risk, was that in equilibrium, the market portfolio already has the value weight, w_i percent, invested in the risky asset I. Therefore, the percent a in the above equations is the excess demand for an individual risky asset. But we know that in equilibrium the excess demand for any asset must be zero. Prices will adjust until all assets are held. Therefore, if Eqs. (7.4) and (7.5) are evaluated where excess demand, a, equals zero, then we can determine the equilibrium price relationships at point M in Fig. 7.2. This will provide the equilibrium price of risk. Evaluating Eqs. (7.4) and (7.5), where $a = 0$, we obtain

$$\left. \frac{\delta E(\tilde{R}_p)}{\delta a} \right|_{a=0} = E(\tilde{R}_i) - E(\tilde{R}_m), \tag{7.6}$$

$$\left. \frac{\delta \sigma(\tilde{R}_p)}{\delta a} \right|_{a=0} = \tfrac{1}{2}[\sigma_m^2]^{-1/2}[-2\sigma_m^2 + 2\sigma_{im}] = \frac{\sigma_{im} - \sigma_m^2}{\sigma_m}. \tag{7.7}$$

The slope of the risk-return trade-off evaluated at point M, in market equilibrium, is

$$\left. \frac{\delta E(\tilde{R}_p)/\delta a}{\delta \sigma(\tilde{R}_p)/\delta a} \right|_{a=0} = \frac{E(\tilde{R}_i) - E(\tilde{R}_m)}{(\sigma_{im} - \sigma_m^2)/\sigma_m}. \tag{7.8}$$

The final insight is to realize that the slope of the opportunity set IMI' provided by the relationship between the risky asset and the market portfolio at point M must also be equal to the slope of the capital market line, $R_f M$.

As established in Chapter 6, the capital market line is also an equilibrium relationship. Given market efficiency, the tangency portfolio, M, must be the market portfolio where all assets are held according to their market value weights. Recall that the slope of the capital market line in Eq. (6.30) is

$$\frac{E(\tilde{R}_m) - R_f}{\sigma_m},$$

where σ_m is the standard deviation of the market portfolio. Equating this with the slope of the opportunity set at point M, we have

$$\frac{E(\tilde{R}_m) - R_f}{\sigma_m} = \frac{E(\tilde{R}_i) - E(\tilde{R}_m)}{(\sigma_{im} - \sigma_m^2)/\sigma_m}.$$

This relationship can be arranged to solve for $E(\tilde{R}_i)$ as follows:

$$E(\tilde{R}_i) = R_f + [E(\tilde{R}_m) - R_f] \frac{\sigma_{im}}{\sigma_m^2}. \tag{7.9}$$

Equation (7.9) is known as the *Capital Asset Pricing Model*, CAPM. It is shown graphically in Fig. 7.3 where it is also called the *Security Market Line*. The required rate of return on *any* asset, $E(R_i)$ in Eq. (7.9), is equal to the risk-free rate of return plus a risk premium. The risk premium is the price of risk multiplied by the quantity of risk. In the terminology of the CAPM, the price of risk is the slope of

Figure 7.3
The capital-asset pricing model.

the line, the difference between the expected rate of return on the market portfolio and the risk-free rate of return.[2] The quantity of risk is often called beta, β_i. It is the covariance

$$\beta_i = \frac{\sigma_{im}}{\sigma_m^2} = \frac{COV(R_i, R_m)}{VAR(R_m)} \qquad (7.10)$$

between returns on the risky asset, I, and market portfolio, M, divided by the variance of the market portfolio. The risk-free asset has a beta of zero because its covariance with the market portfolio is zero. The market portfolio has a beta of one because the covariance of the market portfolio with itself is identical to the variance of the market portfolio:

$$\beta_m = \frac{COV(R_m, R_m)}{VAR(R_m)} = \frac{VAR(R_m)}{VAR(R_m)} = 1.$$

D. PROPERTIES OF THE CAPM

There are several properties of the CAPM which are important. First, in equilibrium, every asset must be priced so that its risk-adjusted required rate of return falls exactly on the straight line in Fig. 7.3, which is called the *security market line*. This means, for example, that assets such as I and J in Fig. 6.19, which do not lie on the mean-variance efficient set, will lie exactly on the security market line in Fig. 7.3. This is true because not all of the variance of an asset's return is of concern to risk-averse

---

[2] Note that the CAPM terminology is somewhat different from that used in Chapter 6. Earlier, the equilibrium price of risk was seen to be the marginal rate of substitution between return and risk and was defined as

$$\frac{E(R_m) - R_f}{\sigma_m}.$$

Using this definition for the price of risk, the quantity of risk is

$$\frac{COV(R_i, R_m)}{\sigma_m}.$$

Because σ_m, the standard deviation of the market, is assumed to be constant it doesn't make much difference which terminology we adopt. Hereafter, risk will be β and the price of risk will be $[E(R_m) - R_f]$.

investors. As we saw in the previous chapter, investors can always diversify away all risk except the covariance of an asset with the market portfolio. In other words, they can diversify away all risk except the risk of the economy as a whole, which is inescapable (undiversifiable). Consequently, the only risk which investors will pay a premium to avoid is covariance risk. The total risk of any individual asset can be partitioned into two parts—systematic risk, which is a measure of how the asset covaries with the economy, and unsystematic risk, which is independent of the economy. Mathematical precision,

$$\text{Total risk} = \text{systematic risk} + \text{unsystematic risk}, \tag{7.11}$$

can be attached to this concept by noting that empirically the return on any asset is a linear function of market return plus a random error term $\tilde{\epsilon}_j$, which is independent of the market:

$$\tilde{R}_j = a_j + b_j \tilde{R}_m + \tilde{\epsilon}_j.$$

This equation contains three terms: a constant, a_j, which has no variance; a constant times a random variable, $b_j \tilde{R}_m$; and a second random variable, $\tilde{\epsilon}_j$, which has zero covariance with $\tilde{R}_m$. Using properties 3 and 4 of random variables (given in Chapter 6) we can immediately write the variance of this relationship as

$$\sigma_j^2 = b_j^2 \sigma_m^2 + \sigma_\epsilon^2. \tag{7.12}$$

The variance is total risk; it can be partitioned into systematic risk, $b_j^2 \sigma_m^2$, and unsystematic risk, σ_ϵ^2. It turns out that b_j in the simple linear relationship between individual asset return and market return is exactly the same as β_j in the CAPM.[3]

If systematic risk is the only type of risk which investors will pay to avoid, and if the required rate of return for every asset in equilibrium must fall on the security market line, we should be able to go back to the example of Bayside Cigar Company and resolve the paradox which was introduced in Chapter 6. Table 7.1 summarizes the empirical findings. We know that if investors are risk averse, there should be a positive trade-off between risk and return. When we tried to use the standard deviation as a measure of risk for an individual asset, Bayside Cigar, we were forced to make the inappropriate observation that the asset with higher risk has a lower return. The difficulty was that we were using the wrong measure of

Table 7.1   Risk and Return for Bayside Cigar and a 100 Stock Portfolio

	Annual Return	*Standard Deviation*	*Beta*
100-stock portfolio	10.9%	4.45%	1.11
Bayside Cigar	5.4%	7.25%	.71

[3] The interested reader is referred to Appendix C on linear regression for proof that the slope coefficient, b_j, equals

$$b_j = COV(R_j, R_m)/VAR(R_m).$$

risk. One cannot compare the variance of return on a single asset with the variance for a well-diversified portfolio. The variance of the portfolio will almost always be smaller. The appropriate measure of risk for a single asset is beta, its covariance with the market divided by the variance of the market. This risk is nondiversifiable and is linearly related to the rate of return [$E(R_i)$ in Eq. (7.9)] required in equilibrium. When we look at the appropriate measure of risk, we see that Bayside Cigar is *less risky* than the 100-stock portfolio, and we have the sensible result that lower risk is accompanied by lower return.

Table 7.2 shows the realized rates of return and the betas of many different assets between January 1945 and June 1970. The calculations are taken from an article by Modigliani and Pogue [1974] which used monthly observations. In most cases the risk-return relationships make sense. Consumer product companies like Swift and Co., Bayside Cigar, American Snuff are all less risky than the market portfolio (represented here by the NYSE index). On the other hand, steel, electronics, and automobiles are riskier. Figure 7.4 plots the empirical relationship between risk (measured by beta) and return for the companies listed in Table 7.2. The linearity of the relationship appears to be reasonable, and the trade-off between risk and return is positive. A more thorough discussion of empirical tests of the CAPM will be given later in this chapter.

A second important property of the CAPM is that the measure of risk for individual assets is linearly additive when the assets are combined into portfolios. For example, if we put $a\%$ of our wealth into asset X, with systematic risk of β_x, and $b\%$ of our wealth into asset Y, with systematic risk of β_y, then the beta of the resulting portfolio β_p, is simply the weighted average of the betas of the individual securities.

$$\beta_p = a\beta_x + b\beta_y. \tag{7.13}$$

Table 7.2   Rates of Return and Betas for Selected Companies (1945–1970)

	Average Annual Return	Standard Deviation	Beta
City Investing Co.	17.4%	11.09%	1.67
Radio Corporation of America	11.4%	8.30%	1.35
Chrysler Corporation	7.0%	7.73%	1.21
Continental Steel Co.	11.9%	7.50%	1.12
100-stock portfolio	10.9%	4.45%	1.11
NYSE index	8.3%	3.73%	1.00
Swift and Co.	5.7%	5.89%	.81
Bayside Cigar	5.4%	7.26%	.71
American Snuff	6.5%	4.77%	.54
Homestake Mining Co.	4.0%	6.55%	.24

Modigliani, F., and G. Pogue, "An Introduction to Risk and Return," reprinted from *The Financial Analysts Journal,* March/April 1974, 71.

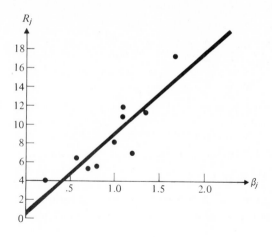

Figure 7.4
An empirical security market line.

Proof of this follows from the definition of covariance and the properties of the mean and variance. The definition of the portfolio beta is

$$\beta_p = \frac{E\{[aX + bY - aE(X) - bE(Y)][R_m - E(R_m)]\}}{VAR(R_m)}.$$

Rearranging terms, we have

$$\beta_p = \frac{E\{[a[X - E(X)] + b[Y - E(Y)]][R_m - E(R_m)]\}}{VAR(R_m)}.$$

Next, we factor out a and b:

$$\beta_p = a\frac{E[(X - E(X))(R_m - E(R_m))]}{VAR(R_m)} + b\frac{E[(Y - E(Y))(R_m - E(R_m))]}{VAR(R_m)}.$$

Finally, using the definition of β,

$$\beta_p = a\beta_x + b\beta_y. \qquad \text{QED}$$

The fact that portfolio betas are linearly weighted combinations of individual asset betas is an extremely useful tool. All that is needed to measure the systematic risk of portfolios is the betas of the individual assets. It is not necessary to solve a quadratic programming problem (see Eqs. 6.26a and 6.26b) to find the efficient set.

It is worth reiterating the relationship between individual asset risk and portfolio risk. The correct definition of an individual asset's risk is its contribution to portfolio risk. Referring to Eq. (6.28), we see that the variance of returns for a portfolio of assets is

$$VAR(\tilde{R}_p) = \sigma^2(\tilde{R}_p) = \sum_{i=1}^{N} \sum_{j=1}^{N} w_i w_j \sigma_{ij}, \qquad (6.28)$$

which can be rewritten as[4]

$$\sigma^2(\tilde{R}_p) = \sum_{i=1}^{N} w_i \left(\sum_{j=1}^{N} w_j \sigma_{ij} \right) = \sum_{i=1}^{N} w_i \, \text{COV}(R_i, R_p). \tag{7.14}$$

One could interpret

$$w_i \, \text{COV}(R_i, R_p) \tag{7.15}$$

as the risk of security i in portfolio p. However, at the margin, the change in the contribution of asset i to portfolio risk is simply

$$\text{COV}(R_i, R_p). \tag{7.16}$$

Therefore covariance risk is the appropriate definition of risk since it measures the change in portfolio risk as we change the weighting of an individual asset in the portfolio.

Although the use of systematic risk and undiversifiable risk have arisen in the literature as synonyms for covariance risk, they are somewhat misleading. They rely on the existence of costless diversification opportunities and on the existence of a large market portfolio. The definition of covariance risk given above does not. It continues to be relevant, even when the market portfolio under consideration has few assets.

E. USE OF THE CAPM FOR VALUATION: SINGLE-PERIOD MODELS, UNCERTAINTY

Because it provides a quantifiable measure of risk for individual assets, the CAPM is an extremely useful tool for valuing risky assets. For the time being, let us assume that we are dealing with a single time period. This assumption was built into the derivation of the CAPM. We want to value an asset which has a risky payoff at

---

[4] In order to see that $\Sigma \, w_i(\Sigma \, w_j \sigma_{ij}) = \Sigma \, w_i \text{COV}(R_i, R_p)$, consider a simple three-asset example. Rewriting the left-hand side, we have

$$\sum w_i \left(\sum w_j \sigma_{ij} \right) = w_1(w_1 \sigma_{11} + w_2 \sigma_{12} + w_3 \sigma_{13})$$
$$+ w_2(w_1 \sigma_{21} + w_2 \sigma_{22} + w_3 \sigma_{23})$$
$$+ w_3(w_1 \sigma_{31} + w_2 \sigma_{32} + w_3 \sigma_{33}).$$

From the definition of covariance, we have

$$\text{COV}(R_1, R_p) = \begin{bmatrix} 1 & 0 & 0 \end{bmatrix} \begin{bmatrix} \sigma_{11} & \sigma_{12} & \sigma_{13} \\ \sigma_{21} & \sigma_{22} & \sigma_{23} \\ \sigma_{31} & \sigma_{32} & \sigma_{33} \end{bmatrix} \begin{bmatrix} w_1 \\ w_2 \\ w_3 \end{bmatrix}$$
$$= w_1 \sigma_{11} + w_2 \sigma_{12} + w_3 \sigma_{13}.$$

Then by multiplying by the weight in the first asset, we obtain

$$w_1 \, \text{COV}(R_1, R_p) = w_1(w_1 \sigma_{11} + w_2 \sigma_{12} + w_3 \sigma_{13}).$$

Finally, by repeating this procedure for each of the three assets we can demonstrate the equality in Eq. (7.14).

the end of the period. Call this $\tilde{P}_e$. It could represent the capital gain on a common stock or the capital gain plus a dividend. If the risky asset is a bond, it is the repayment of the principal plus the interest on the bond. The expected return on an investment in the risky asset is determined by the price we are willing to pay at the beginning of the time period for the right to the risky end-of-period payoff. If P_0 is the price we pay today, our risky return, R_j, is

$$\tilde{R}_j = \frac{\tilde{P}_e - P_0}{P_0}. \tag{7.17}$$

The CAPM can be used to determine what the current value of the asset, P_0, should be. The CAPM is

$$E(R_j) = R_f + [E(R_m) - R_f]\frac{\text{COV}(R_j, R_m)}{\text{VAR}(R_m)},$$

which can be rewritten as

$$E(R_j) = R_f + \lambda\,\text{COV}(R_j, R_m), \quad \text{where } \lambda = \frac{E(R_m) - R_f}{\text{VAR}(R_m)}. \tag{7.18}$$

Note that λ can be described as the market price per unit risk. From Eq. (7.17) and the properties of the mean, we can equate the expected return from Eq. (7.17) with the expected return in Eq. (7.18):

$$\frac{E(\tilde{P}_e) - P_0}{P_0} = R_f + \lambda\,\text{COV}(R_j, R_m).$$

We can now interpret P_0 as the equilibrium price of the risky asset. Rearranging the above expression, we get

$$P_0 = \frac{E(\tilde{P}_e)}{1 + R_f + \lambda\,\text{COV}(\tilde{R}_j, \tilde{R}_m)}, \tag{7.19}$$

which is often referred to as the *risk-adjusted rate of return valuation formula*. The numerator is the expected end-of-period price for the risky asset and the denominator can be thought of as a discount rate. If the asset has no risk, then its covariance with the market will be zero and the appropriate one-period discount rate is $1 + R_f$, that is $1 +$ the risk-free rate. For assets with positive systematic risk, a risk premium, $\lambda\,\text{COV}(\tilde{R}_j, \tilde{R}_m)$, is added to the risk-free rate so that the discount rate is risk-adjusted.

An equivalent approach to valuation is to deduct a risk premium from $E(\tilde{P}_e)$ in the numerator, then discount at $1 + R_f$. The covariance between the risky asset and the market can be rewritten as

$$\text{COV}(\tilde{R}_j, \tilde{R}_m) = \text{COV}\left[\frac{\tilde{P}_e - P_0}{P_0}, \tilde{R}_m\right]$$

$$= E\left[\left(\frac{\tilde{P}_e - P_0}{P_0} - \frac{E(\tilde{P}_e) - P_0}{P_0}\right)(\tilde{R}_m - E(\tilde{R}_m))\right]$$

$$= \frac{1}{P_0}\,\text{COV}(\tilde{P}_e, \tilde{R}_m).$$

By substituting this into the risk-adjusted rate-of-return equation (Eq. (7.19)),

$$P_0 = \frac{E(\tilde{P}_e)}{1 + R_f + \lambda\,(1/P_0)\mathrm{COV}(\tilde{P}_e,\tilde{R}_m)},$$

we can derive the *certainty-equivalent valuation formula:*

$$P_0 = \frac{E(\tilde{P}_e) - \lambda\,\mathrm{COV}(\tilde{P}_e,\tilde{R}_m)}{1 + R_f}. \tag{7.20}$$

The risk-adjusted rate of return and the certainty-equivalent approaches are equivalent for one-period valuation models. It is important to realize that in both cases value does not depend on the utility preferences of individuals. All one needs to know in order to determine value is the expected end-of-period cash payoff, the quantity of risk provided by the asset, the risk-free rate, and the price of risk (which are market-determined variables). Consequently, individuals who perceive the same distribution of payoffs for a risky asset will price it in exactly the same way regardless of their individual utility functions. The separation of valuation from attitudes toward risk is a consequence of two-fund separation. This was discussed in Chapter 6, section E.4.

F. APPLICATIONS OF THE CAPM FOR CORPORATE POLICY

In Chapter 12 these one-period valuation models will be used to develop decision-making rules for the selection of investment projects by the firm, for measuring the firm's cost of capital, and for capital structure (optimal debt/equity ratio) decisions. However, for the sake of curiosity, we shall take a quick look at the implications of the CAPM for some corporate policy decisions, assuming that our firm has no debt and that there are no corporate or personal taxes. The more complex results in a world with debt and taxes are left to Chapter 12.

The cost of equity capital for a firm is given directly by the CAPM. After all, the company's beta is measured by calculating the covariance between the return on its common stock and the market index. Consequently the beta measures the systematic risk of the common stock and if we know the systematic risk we can use the CAPM to determine the required rate of return on equity. Equation (7.21) is the capital asset pricing model.

$$E(R_j) = R_f + [E(R_m) - R_f]\beta_j. \tag{7.21}$$

If it is possible to estimate the systematic risk of a company's equity as well as the market rate of return, then $E(R_j)$ is the required rate of return on equity, i.e., the cost of equity for the firm. If we designate the cost of equity as k_e, then

$$E(R_j) = k_e.$$

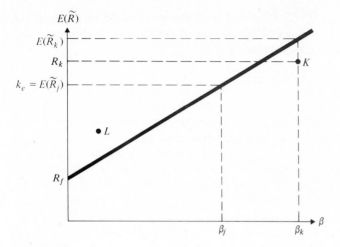

Figure 7.5
The cost of equity using the CAPM.

This is shown in Fig. 7.5. As long as all projects have the same risk as the firm, then k_e may also be interpreted as the minimum required rate of return on new capital projects.

But what if the project has a different risk from the firm as a whole? Then all that is necessary is to estimate the systematic risk of the project and use the CAPM to determine the appropriate required rate of return. For example, in Fig. 7.5, the expected rate of return on project K is higher than the cost of equity for the firm. But the project also is riskier than the firm because it has greater systematic risk. If the managers of the firm were to demand that it earn the same rate as the firm (k_e), the project would be accepted since its anticipated rate of return, R_k, is greater than the firm's cost of equity. However, this would be incorrect. The market requires a rate of return, $E(\tilde{R}_k)$, for a project with systematic risk of β_k, but the project will earn less. Therefore, since $R_k < E(\tilde{R}_k)$, the project is clearly unacceptable. (Is project L acceptable? Why?)

Because the CAPM allows decision makers to estimate the required rate of return for projects of different risk, it is an extremely useful concept. Although we have assumed no debt or taxes in the above simple introduction, Chapter 12 will show how the model can be extended to properly conceptualize more realistic capital budgeting and cost of capital decisions.

G. EXTENSIONS OF THE CAPM

Virtually every one of the assumptions under which the CAPM is derived is violated in the real world. If so, then how good is the model? There are two parts to this question: (1) Is it possible to extend the model to relax the unrealistic assumptions without drastically changing it? (2) How well does the model stand up to empirical testing? The first part is the subject of this section of the chapter. Surprisingly, the model is fairly resilient to various extensions of it.

1. No Riskless Asset

First, how will the model change if investors cannot borrow and lend at the risk-free rate? In other words, how is the CAPM affected if there is no risk-free asset which has constant returns in every state of nature? This problem was solved by Black [1972]. His argument is illustrated in Fig. 7.6. Portfolio M is identified by the investors as the market portfolio which lies on the efficient set.[5] Now, suppose that we can identify all portfolios which are uncorrelated with the true market portfolio.[6] This means that their returns have zero covariance with the market portfolio, and they have the same systematic risk (i.e., they have zero beta). Because they have the same systematic risk each must have the same expected return. Portfolios A and B in Fig. 7.6 are both uncorrelated with the market portfolio M and have the same expected return, $E(R_z)$. However, only one of them, portfolio B, lies on the opportunity set. It is the minimum-variance zero-beta portfolio and it is unique. Portfolio A also has zero beta, but it has a higher variance and therefore does not lie on the minimum variance opportunity set.

We can derive the slope of the line $E(R_z)M$ by forming a portfolio with $a\%$ in the market portfolio and $(1 - a)\%$ in the minimum variance zero beta portfolio. The mean and standard deviation of such a portfolio can be written as follows:

$$E(R_p) = aE(R_m) + (1 - a)E(R_z)$$

$$\sigma(R_p) = [a^2\sigma_m^2 + (1 - a)^2\sigma_z^2 + 2a(1 - a)r_{zm}\sigma_z\sigma_m]^{1/2}.$$

---

[5] Note, however, that the extension of the CAPM which follows can be applied to *any* efficient portfolio, not just the market portfolio.

[6] As an example of how to calculate the vector of weights in a world with only two assets, see Problem 7.13. For portfolios with many assets, we are interested in identifying the portfolio which (a) has zero covariance with the market portfolio and (b) has the minimum variance. The solution will be the vector of weights which satisfies the following quadratic programming problem.

$$\text{Min}\quad \sigma_p^2 = W_1' \Sigma W_1$$

$$\text{Subject to}\quad W_1' \Sigma W_m = \sigma_{1m} = 0,$$
$$W_1'e = 1,$$

where

$\sigma_p^2 =$ the variance of the zero-beta portfolio,

$W_1' =$ the row vector of weights in the minimum-variance zero-beta portfolio (W_1 is a column vector with the same weights),

$\Sigma =$ the variance/covariance matrix for all N assets in the market,

$W_m =$ the vector of weights in the market portfolio,

$\sigma_{1m} =$ the covariance between the zero-beta portfolio and the market—which must equal zero,

$e =$ a column vector of ones.

Figure 7.6
The capital market line with no risk-free rate.

But since the correlation, r_{zm}, between the zero-beta portfolio and the market portfolio is zero, the last term drops out. The slope of a line tangent to the efficient set at point M, where 100% of the investor's wealth is invested in the market portfolio, can be found by taking the partial derivatives of the above equations and evaluating them where $a = 1$. The partial derivative of the mean portfolio return is

$$\frac{\delta E(R_p)}{\delta a} = E(R_m) - E(R_z),$$

and the partial derivative of the standard deviation is

$$\frac{\delta \sigma(R_p)}{\delta a} = \tfrac{1}{2}[a^2\sigma_m^2 + (1-a)^2\sigma_z^2]^{-1/2}\,[2a\sigma_m^2 - 2\sigma_z^2 + 2a\sigma_z^2].$$

Taking the ratio of these partials and evaluating where $a = 1$, we obtain the slope of the line $E(R_z)M$ in Fig. 7.6:

$$\frac{\delta E(R_p)/\delta a}{\delta \sigma(R_p)/\delta a} = \frac{E(R_m) - E(R_z)}{\sigma_m}. \tag{7.22}$$

Furthermore, since the line must pass through the point $[E(R_m), \sigma(R_m)]$, the intercept of the tangent line must be $E(R_z)$. Consequently, the equation of the line must be

$$E(R_p) = E(R_z) + \frac{E(R_m) - E(R_z)}{\sigma_m}\,\sigma_p. \tag{7.23}$$

This is exactly the same as the capital market line (Eq. 6.30), except that the expected rate of return on the zero-beta portfolio, $E(R_z)$, has replaced the risk-free rate.

Given the above result, it is not hard to prove that the expected rate of return on *any* risky asset, whether or not it lies on the efficient set, must be a linear combination of the rate of return on the zero-beta portfolio and the market portfolio. To show this, recall that in equilibrium the slope of a line tangent to a portfolio composed of the market portfolio and any other asset at the point represented by the market portfolio must be equal to Eq. (7.8):

$$\left.\frac{\delta E(R_p)/\delta a}{\delta \sigma (R_p)/\delta a}\right|_{a=0} = \frac{E(R_i) - E(R_m)}{(\sigma_{im} - \sigma_m^2)/\sigma_m} . \tag{7.8}$$

If we equate the two definitions of the slope of a line tangent to point M (that is, if we equate 7.8 and 7.22), we have

$$\frac{E(R_m) - E(R_z)}{\sigma_m} = \frac{[E(R_i) - E(R_m)]\sigma_m}{\sigma_{im} - \sigma_m^2} .$$

Solving for the required rate of return on asset i, we have

$$E(R_i) = (1 - \beta_i)E(R_z) + \beta_i E(R_m), \tag{7.24}$$

where

$$\beta_i = \sigma_{im}/\sigma_m^2 = \mathrm{COV}(R_i, R_m)/\sigma_m^2 .$$

Equation (7.24) shows that the expected rate of return on any asset can be written as a linear combination of the expected rate of return of two assets—the market portfolio and the unique minimum-variance, zero-beta portfolio (which is chosen to be uncorrelated with the market portfolio). Interestingly, the weight to be invested in the market portfolio is the beta of the ith asset. If we rearrange (7.24), we see that it is exactly equal to the CAPM (Eqs. 7.9 and 7.21) except that the expected rate of return on the zero-beta portfolio has replaced the rate of return on the risk-free asset:

$$E(R_i) = E(R_z) + [E(R_m) - E(R_z)]\beta_i . \tag{7.25}$$

The upshot of this proof is that the major results of the CAPM do not require the existence of a pure riskless asset. Beta is still the appropriate measure of systematic risk for an asset and the linearity of the model still obtains. The version of the model given by Eq. (7.25) is usually called the *two-factor model.*

One limitation of the two-factor model is that it relies rather heavily on the assumption that there are no short sales constraints. In other words, investors are assumed to be able to sell shares which they don't already own, then use the proceeds to purchase other shares. Empirically, almost all asset returns have positive correlations. This makes it virtually impossible to construct a zero-beta portfolio composed of only long positions in securities. Therefore, the unconstrained use of short sales is a practical necessity to obtain zero-beta portfolios. With short positions the correlation between asset returns is reversed. For example, if you have sold IBM short, you make positive returns when the asset price falls. In general, zero-beta portfolios would have to be composed of both long and short positions of risky assets. Ross [1977] has shown that in a world with short sales restrictions and no riskless asset the linear CAPM is invalid. Thus, in order to obtain the CAPM in a linear form (Eqs. 7.9 and 7.25) we require either (1) a risk-free asset which can be freely short sold or (2) no constraints on short sales.

2. Returns not Jointly Normal

Obviously, returns on assets cannot be normally distributed because the largest negative return possible, given limited liability of the investor, is minus 100%. Unfortunately, the assumption of normally distributed returns implies that there is a finite possibility that returns will be less than minus 100% and that asset prices will be negative. However, as a practical matter, the probability of observing returns as low as minus 100% may be so small that it has no impact on the empirical validity of the CAPM.

Another implication of the normality assumption is that only two parameters are needed to completely describe the distribution: its mean and its variance. Fama [1965a] has investigated the empirical distribution of daily returns on New York Stock Exchange securities and discovered that they are distributed symmetrically but that the empirical distribution has "fat tails" and no finite variance.[7] In Fig. 7.7 the dashed line represents the empirical distribution of stock prices. The important question which arises is how can investors make choices based on mean and variance if the actual distribution of security prices is such that a variance does not exist? Fama [1965b] has shown that as long as the distribution is symmetric (and stable), investors can use measures of dispersion other than the variance (for example, the semi-interquartile range) and the theory of portfolio choice is still valid.[8]

If security returns are measured over longer periods of time, their distribution is better approximated by a lognormal distribution which has positive skewness.[9] Figure 7.8 compares a normal with a lognormal distribution. There is no limit to the positive returns which may be realized on a successful investment but the maximum negative return is minus 100%. This explains why the distribution of annual returns, for example, tends to be lognormal. The CAPM makes no provision for investor preference for skewness; it is therefore an empirical question whether or not the model fits reality well enough to permit us to ignore the fact that the empirical distribution of returns is not normal. The empirical evidence is reviewed in the next section of this chapter.

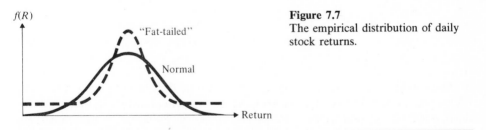

Figure 7.7
The empirical distribution of daily stock returns.

---

[7] There are various theories which explain the empirical distribution of daily returns. The interested reader is referred to Fama [1965a] for the stable Paretian hypothesis, and to Clark [1973] for the subordinated stochastic process hypothesis.

[8] Usually we refer to distributions which are stable under addition. This means that the addition of two distributions (for example, two normal distributions) will result in the same type of distribution.

[9] The natural logarithm of a lognormal distribution is normally distributed. See Eq. 6.12 for the equation of a normal distribution.

Figure 7.8
Over long intervals of time, security returns are lognormal.

3. The Existence of Nonmarketable Assets

Suppose the cost of transactions in an asset is infinite or that by law or regulation the asset is not marketable. Perhaps the most important example of such an asset is human capital. You can rent your skills in return for wages, but you cannot sell yourself or buy anyone else. Slavery is forbidden. This has the effect of introducing a nondiversifiable asset into your portfolio—your human capital. Because you cannot divide up your skills and sell them to different investors, you are forced into making portfolio decisions where you are constrained to hold a large risky component of your wealth in the form of your own human capital. What impact does this have on portfolio decisions and the CAPM?

We saw earlier that if there are no transaction costs and if all assets are perfectly divisible, two-fund separation obtains (see Chapter 6). Every investor, regardless of the shape of his or her indifference curve, will hold one of two assets: the risk-free asset or the market portfolio. Of course, casual empiricism tells us that this is not what actually happens. People do hold different portfolios of risky assets. There are many reasons why this may be true and the existence of nonmarketable assets is a good possibility.

Mayers [1972] shows that when investors are constrained to hold nonmarketable assets which have risky rates of return, $\tilde{R}_H$, the CAPM takes the following form:

$$E(R_j) = R_f + \lambda[V_m \text{COV}(R_j, R_m) + \text{COV}(R_j, R_H)], \qquad (7.26)$$

where

$$\lambda = \frac{E(R_m) - R_f}{V_m \sigma_m^2 + \text{COV}(R_m, R_H)},$$

V_m = the current market value of all marketable assets,

R_H = the total dollar return on all nonmarketable assets.

In this version of the model, λ may be interpreted as the market price per unit risk where risk contains not only the market variance, σ_m^2, but also the covariance between the rate of return on marketable assets and the aggregate dollar return on nonmarketable assets. This result is obtained by first deriving an individual's demand curves for holding marketable assets, then aggregating them to obtain Eq. (7.26), which is the return on a marketable asset required by the market equilibrium. There are three important implications: First, individuals will hold different portfolios of risky assets because their human capital has differing amounts of risk. Second, the market equilibrium price of a risky asset may still be determined independently of the shape of the individual's indifference curves. This implies that the separation principle still holds. There is still an objectively-determined market price of risk which is independent of individual attitudes toward risk. No variable in Eq. (7.26) is subscripted for the preferences of the ith individual. Both the price of risk and the amount of risk depend only on properties of the jth asset, the portfolio of all marketable assets, and the portfolio of aggregated nonmarketable assets. Third, the appropriate measure of risk is still the covariance, but we must now consider the covariance between the jth risky asset and two portfolios, one composed of marketable and a second of nonmarketable assets.[10]

4. The Model in Continuous Time

Merton [1973] has derived a version of the CAPM which assumes (among other things) that trading takes place continuously over time, and that asset returns are distributed lognormally. If the risk-free rate of interest is nonstochastic over time, then (regardless of individual preferences, the distribution of individuals' wealth, or their time horizon), the equilibrium returns must satisfy

$$E(R_i) = r_f + [E(R_m) - r_f]\beta_i. \tag{7.27}$$

Equation (7.27) is the continuous-time analogy to the CAPM. In fact, it is exactly the same as the CAPM except that instantaneous rates of return have replaced rates of return over discrete intervals of time, and the distribution of returns is lognormal instead of normal.

If the risk-free rate is stochastic, investors are exposed to another kind of risk, namely the risk of unfavorable shifts in the investment opportunity set. Merton shows that investors will hold portfolios chosen from three funds: the riskless asset, the market portfolio, and a portfolio chosen so that its returns are perfectly negatively correlated with the riskless asset. This model exhibits three-fund separation. The third fund is necessary to hedge against unforeseen changes in the future risk-free rate. The required rate of return on the jth asset is

$$E(R_j) = r_f + \gamma_1[E(R_m) - r_f] + \gamma_2[E(R_N) - r_f], \tag{7.28}$$

where

R_N = the instantaneous rate of return on a portfolio which has perfect negative correlation with the riskless asset,

$$\gamma_1 = \frac{\beta_{jm} - \beta_{jN}\beta_{Nm}}{1 - \rho_{Nm}^2}, \quad \gamma_2 = \frac{\beta_{jN} - \beta_{jm}\beta_{Nm}}{1 - \rho_{Nm}^2},$$

ρ_{Nm} = the correlation between portfolio N and the market portfolio, M,

$$\beta_{ik} = \frac{\text{COV}(R_i, R_k)}{\sigma_k^2}.$$

---

[10] See Fama and Schwert [1977] for an empirical test of the model set forth by Mayers.

Merton argues that the sign of γ_2 will be negative for high beta assets and positive for low beta assets. As we shall see, in the next section, which discusses the empirical tests of the CAPM, Merton's argument is consistent with the empirical evidence.

5. The Existence of Heterogeneous Expectations and Taxes

If investors do not have the same information about the distribution of future returns, they will perceive different opportunity sets and will obviously choose different portfolios. Lintner [1969] has shown that the existence of heterogeneous expectations does not critically alter the CAPM except that expected returns and covariances are expressed as complex weighted averages of investor expectations. However, if investors have heterogeneous expectations, then the market portfolio is not necessarily efficient. This makes the CAPM nontestable. In fact, as we shall see when we discuss Roll's critique later in this chapter, the only legitimate test of the CAPM is a joint test to determine whether or not the market portfolio is efficient.

No one has investigated the equilibrium model in a world with personal as well as corporate taxes. However, Brennan [1970] has investigated the effect of differential tax rates on capital gains and dividends. Although he concludes that beta is the appropriate measure of risk, his model includes an extra term which causes the expected return on an asset to depend on dividend yield as well as systematic risk:

$$E(R_j) = \gamma_1 R_f + \gamma_2 \beta_j + \gamma_3 D_j, \tag{7.29}$$

where

$$D_j = \text{the dividend yield on asset } j.$$

We shall leave a complete discussion on the Brennan model to Chapters 14 and 15, which cover the theory and empirical evidence related to the corporate dividend policy decision. For now it is sufficient to note that Brennan's model predicts that higher rates of return will be required on assets with higher dividend yields. In other words, investors don't like dividends because they must pay ordinary income tax rates on dividends but only capital gains rates on stock price increases.

H. EMPIRICAL TESTS OF THE CAPM

The CAPM is a simple linear model which is expressed in terms of expected returns and expected risk. In its *ex ante* form, we have

$$E(R_j) = R_f + [E(R_m) - R_f]\beta_j. \tag{7.30}$$

Although many of the aforementioned extensions of the model support this simple linear form, others suggest that it may not be linear, that factors other than beta are needed to explain $E(R_j)$, or that R_f is not the appropriate riskless rate. Therefore, with so many alternative possibilities, a great deal of energy has been devoted to the empirical question: How well does the model fit the data?

There have been numerous empirical tests of the CAPM, so many in fact that it would be fruitless to mention all of them. Also, the literature is interwoven with many serious and difficult econometric problems which must be confronted in order to provide the best empirical tests of the model.[11] Most of the econometric subtleties are beyond the scope of this text and are therefore ignored. However, in the opinion of the authors, the tests of the CAPM which are summarized below represent the best of the work which has been done to date.

The first step necessary to empirically test the theoretical CAPM is to transform it from expectations or *ex ante* form (expectations cannot be measured) into a form which uses observed data. This can be done by assuming that the rate of return on any asset is a fair game.[12] In other words, on average, the expected rate of return on an asset is equal to the realized rate of return. We can write the fair game as follows:

$$R_{jt} = E(R_{jt}) + \beta_j \delta_{mt} + \epsilon_{jt}, \tag{7.31}$$

where

$$\delta_{mt} = R_{mt} - E(R_{mt}),$$
$$E(\delta_{mt}) = 0,$$
$$\epsilon_{jt} = \text{a random-error term},$$
$$E(\epsilon_{jt}) = 0,$$
$$\text{COV}(\epsilon_{jt}, \delta_{mt}) = 0,$$
$$\text{COV}(\epsilon_{jt}, \epsilon_{j,t-1}) = 0,$$
$$\beta_{jt} = \text{COV}(R_{jt}, R_{mt})/\text{VAR}(R_{mt}).$$

Equation (7.31) is seen to be a fair game because if we take the expectation of both sides, the average realized return is equal to the expected return. In other words, on average, you get the return which you expected:

$$E(R_{jt}) = E(R_{jt}).$$

If we use the CAPM assumption that asset returns are jointly normal, then β_j in the fair-game model is defined in exactly the same way as β_j in the CAPM. By substituting $E(R_j)$ from the CAPM into Eq. (7.31), we obtain

$$R_{jt} = R_{ft} + [E(R_{mt}) - R_{ft}]\beta_j + \beta_j[R_{mt} - E(R_{mt})] + \epsilon_{jt}$$
$$= R_{ft} + (R_{mt} - R_{ft})\beta_j + \epsilon_{jt}.$$

Finally, by subtracting R_{ft} from both sides, we have

$$R_{jt} - R_{ft} = (R_{mt} - R_{ft})\beta_j + \epsilon_{jt}, \tag{7.32}$$

---

[11] For papers which discuss some of the econometric problems involved in testing the CAPM, the reader is referred to Miller and Scholes [1972], Roll [1977, 1981], Scholes and Williams [1977], and Dimson [1979].

[12] Chapter 9 explains the theory of efficient capital markets which describes a fair game at length. Also, empirical evidence is presented which suggests that the market is, in fact, a fair game.

Figure 7.9
(a) Ex post CAPM, (b) Ex ante CAPM.

which is the *ex post* form of the CAPM. We derived it by simply assuming that returns are normally distributed and that capital markets are efficient in a fair-game sense. Now we have an empirical version of the CAPM which is expressed in terms of *ex post* observations of return data instead of *ex ante* expectations.

One important difference between the *ex post* empirical model and the *ex ante* theoretical model is that the former can have a negative slope while the latter cannot. After the fact we may have experienced a state of nature where the market rate of return was negative. When this happens the empirical security market line will slope downward as in Fig. 7.9(a). On the other hand, the theoretical CAPM always requires the expected return on the market to be higher than the risk-free rate of return, as shown in Fig. 7.9(b). This is because prices must be established in such a way that riskier assets have higher expected rates of return. Of course, it may turn out that after the fact their return was low or negative, but that is what is meant by risk. If a risky asset has a beta of 2.0, it will lose 20% when the market goes down by 10%.

When the CAPM is empirically tested, it is usually written in the following form:

$$R'_{pt} = \gamma_0 + \gamma_1\beta_p + \epsilon_{pt}, \qquad (7.33)$$

where

$\gamma_1 = R_{mt} - R_{ft}$,
R'_{pt} = the excess return on portfolio p, $R_{pt} - R_{ft}$.

This is the same as Eq. (7.32) except that a constant term, γ_0, has been added. Exactly what predictions made by the CAPM are tested in Eq. (7.33)? The predictions should meet the following criteria:

a) The intercept term, γ_0, should not be significantly different from zero. If it is different from zero, then there may be something "left out" of the CAPM which is captured in the empirically estimated intercept term.

b) Beta should be the only factor which explains the rate of return on a risky asset. If other terms such as residual variance, dividend yield, price-earnings ratios, firm size, or beta squared are included in an attempt to explain return, they should have no explanatory power.

c) The relationship should be linear in beta.

d) The coefficient of beta, γ_1, should be equal to $R_{mt} - R_{ft}$.

e) When the equation is estimated over very long periods of time, the rate of return on the market portfolio should be greater than the risk-free rate. Because the market portfolio is riskier, on average it should have a higher rate of return.

The major empirical tests of the CAPM were published by Blume and Friend [1970, 1973], Black, Jensen, and Scholes [1972], Miller and Scholes [1972], Blume and Husick [1973], Fama and Macbeth [1973], Basu [1977], Reinganum [1981a], Litzenberger and Ramaswamy [1979], and Banz [1981]. Most of the studies use monthly total returns (dividends are reinvested) on listed common stocks as their data base. A frequently used technique is to estimate the betas of every security during a five-year holding period, by computing the covariance between return on the security and a market index which is usually an equally weighted index of all listed common stocks. The securities are then ranked by beta and placed into N portfolios (where N is usually 10, 12, or 20). By grouping the individual securities into large portfolios chosen to provide the maximum dispersion in systematic risk, it is possible to avoid a good part of the measurement error in estimating betas of individual stocks. Next, the portfolio betas and returns are calculated over a second five-year period and a regression similar to Eq. (7.33) is run.

With few exceptions, the empirical studies agree on the following conclusions:

a) The intercept term, γ_0, *is* significantly different from zero, and the slope, γ_1, is less than the difference between the return on the market portfolio minus the risk-free rate.[13] The implication is that low beta securities earn more than the CAPM would predict and high beta securities earn less.

b) Versions of the model which include a squared beta term or unsystematic risk find that at best these explanatory factors are useful only in a small number of the time-periods sampled. Beta dominates them as a measure of risk.

c) The simple linear empirical model (Eq. 7.33) fits the data best. It is linear in beta. Also, over long periods of time, the rate of return on the market portfolio is greater than the risk-free rate (that is, $\gamma_1 > 0$).

d) Factors other than beta are successful in explaining that portion of security returns not captured by beta. Basu [1977] found that low price/earnings portfolios have

---

[13] Empirical studies have used a 90-day Treasury bill as a proxy for the risk-free rate and they have also laboriously calculated the return on the zero-beta portfolio. Either approach results in an intercept term significantly different from zero.

rates of return higher than could be explained by the CAPM. Banz [1981] and Reinganum [1981a] found that the size of a firm is important. Smaller firms tend to have high abnormal rates of return. Litzenberger and Ramaswamy [1979] found that the market requires higher rates of return on equities with high dividend yields.

Figure 7.10 shows the average monthly returns on 10 portfolios vs. their systematic risk for the 35-year period 1931–1965 (taken from the Black-Jensen-Scholes study [1971]). The results shown here are typical. The empirical market line is linear with a positive trade-off between return and risk, but the intercept term is significantly different from zero. In fact, it is 9.79 standard deviations away. This forces us to reject the CAPM, given the empirical techniques of the previously mentioned studies. In addition, the ability of other variables such as price/earnings ratios to explain the portion of returns which are unexplained by the CAPM suggests either (1) that the CAPM is misspecified and requires the addition of factors other than beta to explain security returns or (2) that the problems in measuring beta are systematically related to variables such as firm size. Work which is consistant with this second point of view has been published by Rosenberg and Marathe [1977] who find that beta can be predicted much better if variables such as dividend yield, trading volume, and firm size are added to the predictive model. Roll [1981] suggests that infrequent trading of shares in small firms may explain much of the measurement error in estimating betas.

The empirical evidence has led scholars to conclude that the pure theoretical form of the CAPM does not agree well with reality. However, the empirical form of the model, which has come to be known as the *empirical market line,*

$$R_{it} = \hat{\gamma}_{0t} + \hat{\gamma}_{1t}\beta_{it} + \epsilon_{it}, \tag{7.34}$$

Intercept	= .00519
Standard error	= .00053
Slope	= .01081
Standard error	= .00050

Figure 7.10
Average monthly returns versus systematic risk for ten portfolios 1931–1965. (From *Studies in the Theory of Capital Markets,* edited by Michael C. Jensen. Copyright © 1972 by Praeger Publishers, Inc. Reprinted by permission of Holt, Rinehart and Winston.)

does provide an excellent model of security returns. The practitioner who wishes to have unbiased estimates of the empirical market-line parameters, $\hat{\gamma}_{0t}$ and $\hat{\gamma}_{1t}$, estimated each month from January 1935 through June 1968, is referred to Fama [1976]. Obviously, if one can estimate a security's beta for a given period, then by knowing the empirical market-line parameters he can estimate the security's required rate of return from Eq. (7.34).

1. THE PROBLEM OF MEASURING PERFORMANCE: ROLL'S CRITIQUE

One of the potentially most useful applications of the securities market line in its *ex post* form (Eq. 7.32) or the empirical market line (Eq. 7.34) is that they might be used as benchmarks for security performance. The residual term, ϵ_{jt}, has been interpreted as abnormal because, as shown in Fig. 7.11, it represents return in excess of what is predicted by the securities market line.

Roll [1977] takes exception to this interpretation of cross-section abnormal performance measures and to empirical texts of the CAPM in general. In brief, his major conclusions are:

1. The only legitimate test of the CAPM is whether or not the market portfolio (which includes *all* assets) is mean-variance efficient.

2. If performance is measured relative to an index which is *ex post* efficient, then from the mathematics of the efficient set, no security will have abnormal performance when measured as a departure from the security market line.[14]

3. If performance is measured relative to an *ex post* inefficient index, then any ranking of portfolio performance is possible depending on which inefficient index has been chosen.

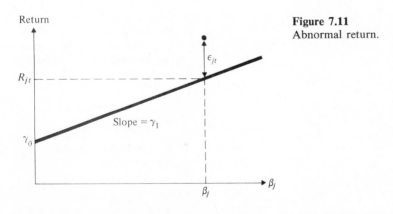

Figure 7.11
Abnormal return.

---

[14] It is important to note that Roll does not take exception to time series measures of abnormal performance such as those described by the market model in Chapter 10.

This is a startling statement. It implies that even if markets are efficient and the CAPM is valid, then the cross-section securities market line cannot be used as a means of measuring the *ex post* performance of portfolio selection techniques. Furthermore, the efficiency of the market portfolio and the validity of the CAPM are joint hypotheses which are almost impossible to test because of the difficulty of measuring the true market portfolio.

To understand Roll's critique, we must go back to the derivation of the zero-beta portfolio. Recall that if there is no risk-free asset, it is still possible to write the securities market line as a combination of the market portfolio and a zero-beta portfolio which is uncorrelated with the market index. Therefore, the expected return on any asset could be written as

$$E(R_i) = E(R_z) + [E(R_m) - E(R_z)]\beta_i. \tag{7.35}$$

Roll points out that there is nothing unique about the market portfolio. It is always possible to choose any efficient portfolio as an index, then find the minimum variance portfolio which is uncorrelated with the selected efficient index. This is shown in Fig. 7.12. Once this has been done, then Eq. (7.35) can be derived and written as

$$E(R_i) = E(R_{z,I}) + [E(R_I) - E(R_{z,I})]\beta_{i,I}. \tag{7.36}$$

Note that the market portfolio, R_m, has been replaced by any efficient index, R_I, and the beta is measured relative to the selected efficient index, $\beta_{i,I}$. Also, the zero beta portfolio is measured relative to the index, $R_{z,I}$. Because the expected return on any asset can be written as a linear function of its beta measured relative to any efficient index, it is not necessary to know the market index. One only need know the composition of an efficient index in order to write Eq. (7.36). Furthermore, if the index turns out to be *ex post* efficient, then every asset will fall exactly on the securities market line. There will be no abnormal returns. If there are systematic abnormal returns, it simply means that the index which has been chosen is not *ex post* efficient.

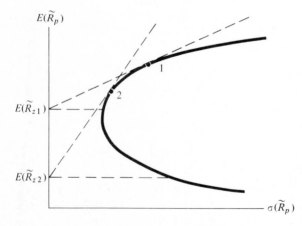

Figure 7.12
Two index portfolios with their respective orthogonal portfolios.

The Roll critique does not imply that the CAPM is an invalid theory. However, it does mean that tests of the CAPM must be interpreted with great caution. The fact that portfolio residuals exhibited no significant departures from linearity merely implies that the market index which was selected (usually an equally weighted index of all listed shares of common stock) was *ex post* efficient. In fact, the only way to test the CAPM directly is to see whether or not the true market portfolio is *ex post* efficient. Unfortunately, because the market portfolio contains all assets (marketable and nonmarketable, e.g., human capital, coins, houses, bonds, stocks, options, land, etc.) it is impossible to observe.

J. THE ARBITRAGE PRICING THEORY (APT)

Formulated by Ross [1976], the arbitrage pricing theory offers a testable alternative to the capital asset pricing model. The CAPM predicts that security rates of return will be linearly related to a single common factor—the rate of return on the market portfolio. The APT is based on similar intuition, but is much more general. It assumes that the rate of return on any security is a linear function of k factors as shown below:

$$\tilde{R}_i = E(\tilde{R}_i) + b_{i1}\tilde{F}_1 + \cdots + b_{ik}\tilde{F}_k + \tilde{\epsilon}_i, \qquad (7.37)$$

where

$\tilde{R}_i$ = the random rate of return on the ith asset,

$E(\tilde{R}_i)$ = the expected rate of return on the ith asset,

b_{ik} = the sensitivity of the ith asset's returns to the kth factor,

$\tilde{F}_k$ = the mean zero kth factor common to the returns of all assets under consideration,

$\tilde{\epsilon}_i$ = a random zero mean noise term for the ith asset.

As we shall see later on, the CAPM may be viewed as a special case of the APT when the market rate of return is assumed to be the single relevant factor.

The APT is derived under the usual assumptions of perfectly competitive and frictionless capital markets. Furthermore, individuals are assumed to have homogeneous beliefs that the random returns for the set of assets being considered are governed by the linear k-factor model given in Eq. (7.37). The theory requires that the number of assets under consideration, n, be much larger than the number of factors, k, and that the noise term, $\tilde{\epsilon}_i$, be the unsystematic risk component for the ith asset. It must be independent of all factors and all error terms for other assets.

The most important feature of the APT is reasonable and straightforward. In equilibrium all portfolios which can be selected from among the set of assets under consideration and which satisfy the conditions of (a) using no wealth and (b) having no risk, must earn no return on average. These portfolios are called arbitrage portfolios.

To see how they can be constructed, let w_i be the *change* in the dollar amount invested in the ith asset as a percentage of an individual's total invested wealth. In order to form an arbitrage portfolio which requires no change in wealth, the usual course of action would be to sell some assets and use the proceeds to buy others. Mathematically, the zero change in wealth is written as

$$\sum_{i=1}^{n} w_i = 0. \tag{7.38}$$

If there are n assets in the arbitrage portfolio, then the additional portfolio return gained is

$$\tilde{R}_p = \sum_{i=1}^{n} w_i \tilde{R}_i$$

$$= \sum_i w_i E(\tilde{R}_i) + \sum_i w_i b_{i1} \tilde{F}_1 + \cdots + \sum_i w_i b_{ik} \tilde{F}_k + \sum_i w_i \tilde{\epsilon}_i. \tag{7.39}$$

In order to obtain a riskless arbitrage portfolio, it is necessary to eliminate both diversifiable (i.e., unsystematic) and undiversifiable (i.e., systematic) risk. This can be done by meeting three conditions: (1) selecting percentage changes in investment ratios, w_i, which are small, (2) diversifying across a large number of assets, and (3) choosing changes, w_i, so that for each factor, k, the weighted sum of the systematic risk components, b_k, is zero. Mathematically, these conditions are:

$$w_i \approx 1/n, \tag{7.40a}$$

$$n \text{ chosen to be a large number,} \tag{7.40b}$$

$$\sum_i w_i b_{ik} = 0 \quad \text{for each factor.} \tag{7.40c}$$

Because the error terms, $\tilde{\epsilon}_i$, are independent the law of large numbers guarantees that a weighted average of many of them will approach zero in the limit as n becomes large. In other words, costless diversification eliminates the last term (the unsystematic risk) in Eq. (7.39) above. Thus we are left with

$$\tilde{R}_p = \sum_i w_i E(\tilde{R}_i) + \sum_i w_i b_{i1} \tilde{F}_1 + \cdots + \sum_i w_i b_{ik} \tilde{F}_k. \tag{7.41}$$

At first glance the return on our portfolio appears to be a random variable, but we have chosen the weighted average of the systematic risk components for each factor to be equal to zero ($\Sigma \, w_i b_{ik} = 0$). This eliminates all systematic risk. One might say that we have selected an arbitrage portfolio with zero beta in each factor. Consequently, the return on our arbitrage portfolio becomes a constant. Correct choice of the weights has eliminated all uncertainty, so that R_p is not a random variable. Therefore, Eq. (7.41) becomes

$$R_p = \sum_i w_i E(\tilde{R}_i). \tag{7.41a}$$

Recall that the arbitrage portfolio, so constructed, has no risk (of any kind) and requires no new wealth. If the return on the arbitrage portfolio were not zero, then it would be possible to achieve an infinite rate of return with no capital requirements and no risk. Such an opportunity is clearly impossible if the market is to be in equilibrium. In fact, if the individual arbitrageur is in equilibrium (hence content with his or her current portfolio) then the return on any and all arbitrage portfolios must be zero. In other words,

$$R_p = \sum_i w_i E(\tilde{R}_i) = 0. \tag{7.42}$$

Eqs. (7.38), (7.40c), and (7.42) are really statements in linear algebra. Any vector which is orthogonal to the constant vector, i.e.,

$$\left(\sum_i w_i \right) \cdot 1 = 0, \tag{7.38}$$

and to each of the coefficient vectors, i.e.,

$$\sum_i w_i b_{ik} = 0 \quad \text{for each } k \tag{7.40c}$$

must also be orthogonal to the vector of expected returns, i.e.,

$$\sum_i w_i E(\tilde{R}_i) = 0. \tag{7.42}$$

An algebraic consequence of this statement is that the expected return vector must be a linear combination of the constant vector and the coefficient vectors. Algebraically, there must exist a set of $k + 1$ coefficients, $\lambda_0, \lambda_1, \ldots, \lambda_k$ such that

$$E(\tilde{R}_i) = \lambda_0 + \lambda_1 b_{i1} + \cdots + \lambda_k b_{ik}. \tag{7.43}$$

Recall that the b_{ik} are the "sensitivities" of the returns on the ith security to the kth factor. If there is a riskless asset with a riskless rate of return, R_f, then $b_{0k} = 0$ and

$$R_f = \lambda_0.$$

Hence, Eq. (7.43) can be rewritten in "excess returns form" as

$$E(R_i) - R_f = \lambda_1 b_{i1} + \cdots + \lambda_k b_{ik}. \tag{7.44}$$

Figure 7.13 illustrates the arbitrage pricing relationship (7.44) assuming that there is only a single stochastic factor, k. In equilibrium, all assets must fall on the *arbitrage pricing line*. A natural interpretation for λ is that it represents the risk premium (i.e., the price of risk), in equilibrium, for the kth factor. Because the arbitrage pricing relationship is linear we can use the slope-intercept definition of a straight line to rewrite Eq. (7.44) as

$$E(R_i) = R_f + [\bar{\delta}_k - R_f] b_{ik},$$

where $\bar{\delta}_k$ is the expected return on a portfolio with unit sensitivity to the kth factor and zero sensitivity to all other factors. Therefore, the risk premium, λ_k, is equal

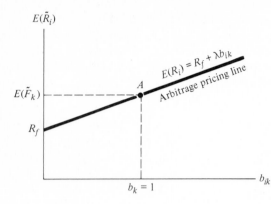

Figure 7.13
The arbitrage pricing line.

to the difference between (1) the expectation of a portfolio which has unit response to the kth factor and zero response to the other factors and (2) the risk-free rate, R_f.

$$\lambda_k = \bar{\delta}_k - R_f.$$

In general, the arbitrage pricing theory can be rewritten as

$$E(R_i) - R_f = [\bar{\delta}_1 - R_f]b_{i1} + \cdots + [\bar{\delta}_k - R_f]b_{ik}. \qquad (7.45)$$

If Eq. (7.45) is interpreted as a linear regression equation (assuming that the vectors of returns have a joint normal distribution and that the factors have been linearly transformed so that their transformed vectors are orthonormal) then the coefficients, b_{ik}, are defined in exactly the same way as beta in the capital asset pricing model, i.e.,

$$b_{ik} = \frac{\mathrm{COV}(\tilde{R}_i, \tilde{\delta}_k)}{\mathrm{VAR}(\tilde{\delta}_k)}, \qquad (7.45a)$$

where

$\mathrm{COV}(R_i, \tilde{\delta}_k) =$ the covariance between the ith asset's returns and the linear transformation of the kth factor,

$\mathrm{VAR}(\tilde{\delta}_k) =$ the variance of the linear transformation of the kth factor.

Hence, the CAPM is seen to be a special case of the APT (where asset returns are assumed to be joint normal).

The arbitrage pricing theory is much more robust than the capital asset pricing model for several reasons:

1. The APT makes no assumptions about the empirical distribution of asset returns.
2. The APT makes no strong assumptions about individuals' utility functions (at least nothing stronger than greed and risk aversion).
3. The APT allows the equilibrium returns of assets to be dependent on many factors, not just one (e.g., beta).

4. The APT yields a statement about the relative pricing of any subset of assets, hence one need not measure the entire universe of assets in order to test the theory.

5. There is no special role for the market portfolio in the APT, whereas the CAPM requires that the market portfolio be efficient.

6. The APT is easily extended to a multiperiod framework (see Ross [1976]).

Suppose that asset returns are determined by two underlying factors such as unanticipated changes in real output and unanticipated inflation. The arbitrage pricing theory can easily account for the effect of changes in both factors on asset returns. Because the capital asset pricing model relies on a single factor (the market index) it cannot do as well. Using the CAPM is a little like being lost while piloting a private plane. You call the air controller and ask "Where am I?" If the controller is using a unidimensional model like the CAPM, he or she is likely to respond "Two hundred miles from New York City." Obviously, this is not a very helpful answer. A multidimensional model like the APT would be more useful. It would be nice to know latitude, longitude, and altitude.

Figure 7.14 illustrates the same point. The factor loadings (or factor sensitivities), b_{i1} and b_{i2}, for our two hypothetical factors—changes in unanticipated real output and changes in unanticipated inflation—are plotted on the axes. The origin represents the risk-free rate which is the rate of return received when an asset has zero beta in both factors. Points along the diagonal dashed lines have equal expected return but not the same risk. For example, all points along the line OJ have an expected rate of return equal to the risk-free rate but are not riskless portfolios. If the risk-free rate is 10%, one can obtain that rate either with a truly riskless portfolio which pays 10% in every state of nature or with a second portfolio which has positive sensitivity to one factor and negative sensitivity to the other factor.

Figure 7.14
A graph of the CAPM and the APT.

Suppose the arbitrage pricing model, Eq. (7.45),

$$E(R_i) - R_f = [\bar{\delta}_1 - R_f]b_{i1} + [\bar{\delta}_2 - R_f]b_{i2}$$

is estimated to have the following numerical values: $R_f = 10\%$, $\bar{\delta}_1 = 20\%$, and $\bar{\delta}_2 = 15\%$. If b_{i1} is plotted on the vertical axis, then the vertical intercept for a given return $E(R_i)$ is

$$\alpha = \text{vertical intercept} = \frac{E(R_i) - R_f}{\bar{\delta}_1 - R_f}$$

and the slope of the equal return line is

$$m = \text{slope} = -\frac{\bar{\delta}_2 - R_f}{\bar{\delta}_1 - R_f}$$

where the equation for the equal return line is $b_{i1} = \alpha + mb_{i2}$.

Next, suppose that we know that a CAPM efficient index portfolio has been chosen, that its expected return is 30%, and that its sensitivities to changes in unanticipated real output and changes in unanticipated inflation are $b_{I1} = 1.5$ and $b_{I2} = 1.0$. The CAPM index portfolio is plotted at point I in Figure 7.14. We know from the CAPM (Eq. 7.9) that the security market line is represented by all linear combinations of the risk-free asset and the market index portfolio. Therefore, the security market line is represented by the ray OI from the origin (which is the risk-free asset) to the efficient index portfolio (point I).

The CAPM measures risk only in one dimension, rather than two. If we are told that a portfolio's CAPM β is .5, then it will plot at point P in Fig. 7.14, halfway between the riskless asset and the index portfolio. However, according to the APT there are an infinite number of portfolios, all with the same expected return as portfolio P and each having a different sensitivity to the APT risk parameters b_{i1} and b_{i2}. If people are, in fact, sensitive to more than one type of risk when choosing among portfolios of equal return, then the APT is superior to the CAPM because the CAPM is unidimensional in risk. It is perfectly reasonable that portfolio P' might be preferred to portfolio P by some investors because it has the same return as portfolio P but a preferable combination of sensitivities to the underlying factors. Later on we shall discuss some empirical work which provides evidence that more than one factor is significant in explaining security returns.

In order to illustrate how arbitrage pricing might be employed in practice, suppose that empirical work reveals that the expected returns on assets can be explained by two factors, F_1 and F_2. Table 7.3 shows the subjectively estimated returns on three assets ($X, Y,$ and Z) and the changes in (orthogonal transformations of) the two factors for five equally likely states of nature. To make the problem tractable, assume that all factors and returns are normally distributed. In addition, suppose we know that the expected return on the risk-free asset, R_f, is 10%.

One of the requirements of the factor analysis program usually used to test the arbitrage pricing model is that we are working with linear transformations of the underlying factors. The transformations must be orthogonal, i.e., the product of their

Table 7.3   Data for an APT Example

State of nature	Prob.	Asset Returns (%)			Transformed Factor Changes (%)	
		$\tilde{X}$	$\tilde{Y}$	$\tilde{Z}$	$\tilde{\delta}_1$	$\tilde{\delta}_2$
Horrid	.2	−55.23	468.17	53.00	−10.00	−5.00
Bad	.2	70.70	10.00	413.37	−5.00	38.48
Average	.2	−9.00	25.00	−1493.12	25.00	8.00
Good	.2	−12.47	−140.59	1058.75	40.00	−1.44
Great	.2	61.00	−237.58	83.00	50.00	0.00

row and column vectors must equal zero. This is shown below for the transformed factors in Table 7.3

$$[-10 \quad -5 \quad 25 \quad 40 \quad 50] \begin{bmatrix} -5.00 \\ 38.48 \\ 8.00 \\ -1.44 \\ 0 \end{bmatrix} = 0.$$

How can we tell from the bewildering set of numbers in Table 7.3 whether or not there are any arbitrage opportunities? And, if there are, how can we take advantage of them by forming an arbitrage portfolio?

If there are only two factors which govern all returns then the APT becomes

$$E(R_i) = R_f + [\bar{\delta}_1 - R_f]b_{i1} + [\bar{\delta}_2 - R_f]b_{i2}.$$

The data from Table 7.3 can be used to compute all of the terms on the right-hand side of this equation.[15] The expectations of each asset and transformed factor, and the factor loadings, are given in Table 7.4. By substituting this data into the APT equation, we can determine the market equilibrium rate of return, $E(R_i)$, for each of the three assets. This is done below:

Table 7.4   Statistics Computed from Table 7.3

Asset	$\bar{R}_i$	Factor Loadings		Transformed Factor Expectations
		b_{i1}	b_{i2}	
X	11%	.5	2.0	$\bar{\delta}_1 = 20\%$
Y	25	1.0	1.5	$\bar{\delta}_2 = 8\%$
Z	23	1.5	1.0	

[15] Given the assumption of normally distributed returns and orthogonal transformations of the factors, the factor loadings are the same as beta. See Eq. (7.45a).

$$E(R_x) = .10 + [.20 - .10].5 + [.08 - .10]2.0 = 11\%,$$

$$E(R_y) = .10 + [.20 - .10]1.0 + [.08 - .10]1.5 = 17\%,$$

$$E(R_z) = .10 + [.20 - .10]1.5 + [.08 - .10]1.0 = 23\%.$$

Note that the equilibrium return, $E(R_i)$, on assets X and Z is the same as the expected return, $\bar{R}_i$, computed from the data. Hence, no arbitrage opportunities exist for trading in these two assets. On the other hand, the expected return on asset Y, $\bar{R}_y$, is 25% when computed from the data and the market equilibrium return, $E(R_y)$, is only 17%. Therefore, by selling the correct proportions of assets X and Z and buying asset Y, we can form an arbitrage portfolio which requires no new capital, has no change in risk, and earns a positive rate of return.

Suppose that we currently have one-third of our wealth in each of the three assets. How should we change our portfolio to form a riskless arbitrage position? It turns out that, so long as there are more assets than factors, there are virtually an infinite number of ways of forming arbitrage portfolios. But let's suppose that we desire to put the maximum investment into asset Y without actually selling short either X or Z. Our investment proportion in Y would go from one-third to one, thus the *change* in holdings of asset Y would be $w_y = \frac{2}{3}$. We also require that the change portfolio have zero beta in each factor and that it need no net wealth. These conditions are stated in Eqs. (7.38) and (7.40c), which are repeated below:

$$\left(\sum_{i=1}^{3} w_i \right) \cdot 1 = 0. \tag{7.38}$$

$$\sum_{i=1}^{3} w_i b_{ik} = 0 \quad \text{for each } k. \tag{7.40c}$$

Expanding these equations, we have

$$w_x + w_y + w_z = 0,$$

$$w_x b_{x1} + w_y b_{y1} + w_z b_{z1} = 0 \quad \text{for factor 1,}$$

$$w_x b_{x2} + w_y b_{y2} + w_z b_{z2} = 0 \quad \text{for factor 2.}$$

And, substituting in the numbers of our problem, we get

$$w_x + \tfrac{2}{3} + w_z = 0,$$

$$w_x(.5) + \tfrac{2}{3}(1.0) + w_z(1.5) = 0,$$

$$w_x(2.0) + \tfrac{2}{3}(1.5) + w_z(1.0) = 0.$$

Solving, we find that

$$w_x = -\tfrac{1}{3}, \qquad w_y = \tfrac{2}{3}, \qquad w_z = -\tfrac{1}{3}.$$

Thus we would sell all of our holdings in assets X and Z and invest the proceeds in asset Y. This strategy would require no new wealth and would have no change in risk. Note that our risk position before making the change was

$$\tfrac{1}{3}(.5) + \tfrac{1}{3}(1.0) + \tfrac{1}{3}(1.5) = 1.0 \text{ for factor 1,}$$

$$\tfrac{1}{3}(2) + \tfrac{1}{3}(1.5) + \tfrac{1}{3}(1.0) = 1.5 \text{ for factor 2.}$$

After undertaking the new investment strategy our risk will be

$$0(.5) + 1(1.0) + 0(1.5) = 1.0 \text{ for factor 1,}$$

$$0(2) + 1(1.5) + 0(1.0) = 1.5 \text{ for factor 2.}$$

Since our total risk has not changed, the extra risk created by the arbitrage portfolio is zero. Our original portfolio return was

$$\tfrac{1}{3}(11\%) + \tfrac{1}{3}(25\%) + \tfrac{1}{3}(23\%) = 19.67\%.$$

But after investing in the arbitrage portfolio we will have a rate of return of

$$0(11\%) + 1(25\%) + 0(23\%) = 25\%.$$

Thus the arbitrage portfolio increases our return by 5.33% without changing our risk.

Figure 7.15 provides a visual description of the example problem. Expected rates of return are plotted on the vertical axis and asset betas in each of the two factors are plotted along the horizontal axes. Note that the expected returns for assets X and Z plot exactly on the arbitrage pricing plane. They are in equilibrium. But asset Y plots above the plane. Its return lies considerably above what the market

Figure 7.15
Arbitrage pricing plane for two factors.

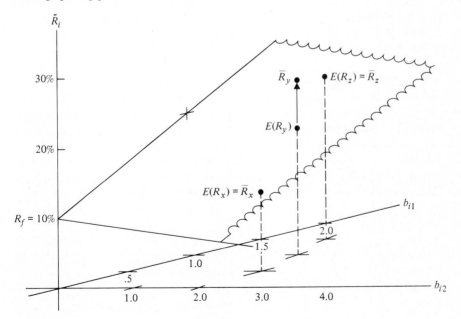

requires for its factor loadings, b_{y1} and b_{y2}. Hence an arbitrage opportunity exists. If enough people take advantage of it the price of asset Y will rise, thereby forcing its rate of return down and back into equilibrium.

K. EMPIRICAL TESTS OF THE ARBITRAGE PRICING THEORY

Papers by Gehr [1975], Roll and Ross [1980], Reinganum [1981b] and Chen [1981] have tested the APT using data on equity daily rates of return for New York and American Stock Exchange listed stocks. The usual empirical procedure has the following steps:

1. Collect a time series of daily stock returns data for a group of stocks.
2. Compute the empirical variance-covariance matrix from the returns data.
3. Use a (maximum-likelihood) factor analysis procedure to identify the number of factors and their factor loadings, b_{ik}.
4. Use the estimated factor loadings, b_{ik}, to explain the cross-sectional variation of individual estimated expected returns, and to measure the size and statistical significance of the estimated risk premia associated with each factor.

The Roll and Ross [1980] study used daily returns data for NYSE and AMEX companies listed on the exchanges on both July 3, 1962 and December 31, 1972. There were a maximum of 2619 daily returns for each stock. The 1260 securities selected were divided alphabetically into groups of 30. For each group of 30, the procedure described above was carried out. The analysis showed that there are at least three and probably four "priced" factors. There may be other zero-priced factors but this procedure cannot identify them because their regression coefficients in step 4 would be zero.

One of the frustrating things about using factor analysis to test the APT is that this procedure cannot tell us what the factors are. However, we can reject the APT if a specified alternative variable such as the total variance of individual returns, firm size, or the asset's last period return were to be significant in explaining the expected returns. Roll and Ross [1980], after correcting for the problem that positive skewness in lognormal returns can create dependence between the sample mean and the sample standard deviation, found that the total variance of security returns does not add any explanatory power for estimated expected returns. Therefore, the APT could not be rejected on this basis. Although a different procedure was employed by Chen [1981], he was able to confirm this result. He also finds that the asset's last period return adds no explanatory power.

Currently there is a question whether or not firm size can be used to refute the APT because it adds explanatory power to the factor loadings. Reinganum [1981b] finds that it does. His test consisted of estimating the factor loadings in year $t - 1$ for all securities, then combining securities with similar loadings into control portfolios. In year t, excess security returns are computed by subtracting the daily control portfolio returns from the daily security returns. Finally, with excess returns in hand, the securities are ranked on the basis of the market value of all of the firm's outstanding common stock at period $t - 1$. The APT predicts (if factor loadings are stationary across time) that all deciles of the market-value ranked excess returns should have the same mean. Reinganum finds that there are significant differences between the mean excess returns and rejects the APT. Chen [1981] on the other hand, finds that firm size adds no explanatory power. His procedure uses Reinganum's data for the market value of each firm's equity. He divides the sample of firms into two groups—those with greater than the median market value and those with less. Then portfolios are formed from the high- and low-value firms so that the following conditions are satisfied: (1) each security in the portfolio has nonnegative weight and the weight should not be too far from $1/n$, where n is the number of securities in the portfolio, and (2) the resultant two portfolios have exactly the same factor loadings (arbitrage risk factors) in each factor. The factor loadings are determined by using returns data from odd days during each test period; the even-days returns from the same test period are used for measuring the average portfolio returns of the high- and low-valued portfolios. If the APT is correct, the returns of the two portfolios should not be statistically different, because they are selected to have the same "risk" as determined by the factor loadings. In only one of the four periods tested is the difference in returns statistically different at the 95% confidence level. Therefore, Chen argues that firm size effects have insufficient explanatory power to reject the APT.

There is one parameter in the APT, namely the intercept term $\lambda_0 = R_f$, which should be identical across groups of securities when the model is estimated separately for each group during a time period. Other factors need not be the same because the factor loadings are not unique from group to group. For example, factor one in group A might correspond to factor three in group B. The intercept term, λ_0, however, has the same meaning in each group because it is the return on an asset which has no sensitivity to the common factors. Roll and Ross [1980] tested for the equivalence of the λ_0 terms across 38 groups and found absolutely no evidence that the intercept terms were different. Again, the APT could not be rejected.

A direct comparison of the APT and the CAPM was performed by Chen [1981]. First the APT model was fit to the data as in the following equation:

$$\tilde{R}_i = \hat{\lambda}_0 + \hat{\lambda}_1 b_{i1} + \cdots + \hat{\lambda}_n b_{in} + \tilde{\epsilon}_i. \qquad \text{(APT)}$$

Then the CAPM was fit to the same data

$$\tilde{R}_i = \hat{\lambda}_0 + \hat{\lambda}_1 \hat{\beta}_i + \tilde{\eta}_i. \qquad \text{(CAPM)}$$

Next the CAPM residuals, η_i, were regressed on the arbitrage factor loadings, $\hat{\lambda}_k$, and the APT residuals, ϵ_i, were regressed on the CAPM coefficients. The results showed that the APT could explain a statistically significant portion of the CAPM residual variance but the CAPM could not explain the APT residuals. This is strong evidence that the APT is a more reasonable model for explaining the cross-sectional variation in asset returns.

SUMMARY _____

This chapter has derived two theoretical models, the CAPM and the APT, which enable us to price risky assets in equilibrium. Within the CAPM framework the appropriate measure of risk is the covariance of returns between the risky asset in question and the market portfolio of all assets. The APT model is more general. Many factors (not just the market portfolio) may explain asset returns. For each factor the appropriate measure of risk is the sensitivity of asset returns to changes in the factor. For normally distributed returns the sensitivity is analogous to the beta (or systematic risk) of the CAPM.

The CAPM was shown to provide a useful conceptual framework for capital budgeting and the cost of capital. It is also reasonably unchanged by the relaxation of many of the unrealistic assumptions which made its derivation simpler. Finally, although the model is not perfectly validated by empirical tests, its main implications are upheld, namely that systematic risk (beta) is a valid measure of risk, that the model is linear, and that the trade-off between return and risk is positive.

The APT can also be applied to cost of capital and capital budgeting problems. Chapter 11 will show how the APT can be used for capital budgeting in a multiperiod framework. The earliest empirical tests of the APT have shown that asset returns are explained by three or possibly four factors, and have ruled out the variance of an asset's own returns as one of the factors.

PROBLEM SET

7.1 Let us assume a normal distribution of returns and risk-averse utility functions. Under what conditions will all investors demand the same portfolio of risky assets?

7.2 The following data have been developed for the Donovan Company, the manufacturer of an advanced line of adhesives:

State	Probability	Market Return, R_m	Return for the Firm, R_j
1	.1	−.15	−.30
2	.3	.05	.00
3	.4	.15	.20
4	.2	.20	.50

The risk-free rate is 6%. Calculate the following:

a) The expected market return.

b) The variance of the market return.

c) The expected return for the Donovan Company.

d) The covariance of the return for the Donovan Company with the market return.

e) Write the equation of the security market line.

f) What is the required return for the Donovan Company? How does this compare with its expected return?

7.3 The following data have been developed for the Milliken Company:

Year	Market Return	Company Returns
1978	.27	.25
1977	.12	.05
1976	−.03	−.05
1975	.12	.15
1974	−.03	−.10
1973	.27	.30

The yield to maturity on Treasury bills is .066 and is expected to remain at this point for the foreseeable future. Calculate the following:

a) The expected market return.

b) The variance of the market return.

c) The expected return for the Milliken Company.

d) The covariance of the return for the Milliken Company with the return on the market.

e) Write the equation of the security market line.

f) What is the required return for the Milliken Company?

7.4 For the data in Table Q7.4, perform the indicated calculations.

7.5 For the data in Table Q7.5, calculate the items indicated.

7.6 What are the assumptions sufficient to guarantee that the market portfolio is an efficient portfolio?

7.7 In the CAPM, is there any way to identify the investors who are more risk averse? Explain. How would your answer change if there were not a riskless asset?

7.8 Given risk-free borrowing and lending, efficient portfolios have no unsystematic risk. True or False? Explain.

7.9 What is the beta of an efficient portfolio with $E(R_j) = 20\%$ if $R_f = 5\%$, $E(R_m) = 15\%$, and $\sigma_m = 20\%$? What is its σ_j? What is its correlation with the market?

7.10 Given the facts of Problem 7.9, and that the common stock of the Rapid Rolling Corporation has $E(R_k) = 25\%$ and $\sigma_k^2 = 52\%$, what is the systematic risk of the common stock? What is its unsystematic risk?

7.11

a) If the expected rate of return on the market portfolio is 14% and the risk-free rate is 6%, find the beta for a portfolio which has an expected rate of return of 10%. What assumptions concerning this portfolio and/or market conditions do you need to make to calculate the portfolio's beta?

Table Q7.4   Estimates of Market Parameters

Year	S&P 500 Price Index	Percent Change in Price	Dividend Yield	Percent Return	Return Deviation	Market Variance	
	P_t	$\dfrac{P_t}{P_{t-1}} - 1$	$\dfrac{D_t}{P_t}$	R_{mt} $(3+4)$	$(R_{mt} - \bar{R}_m)$ $(5 - \bar{R}_m)$	$(R_{mt} - \bar{R}_m)^2$ (6^2)	R_f
(1)	(2)	(3)	(4)	(5)	(6)	(7)	(8)
1960	55.85						
1961	66.27		.0298				.03
1962	62.38		.0337				.03
1963	69.87		.0317				.03
1964	81.37		.0301				.04
1965	88.17		.0300				.04
1966	85.26		.0340				.04
1967	91.93		.0320				.05
1968	98.70		.0307				.05
1969	97.84		.0324				.07
1970	83.22		.0383				.06

a) $\bar{R}_m = ?$ b) $\text{VAR}(R_m) = ?$ c) $\sigma(R_m) = ?$

Table Q7.5   Calculation of Beta for General Motors

Year	GM Price	Percent Change in Price	Dividend Yield	Percent Return	Deviation of Returns	Variance of Returns	Covariance with Market
	P_t	$\dfrac{P_t}{P_{t-1}} - 1$	$\dfrac{D_t}{P_t}$	R_{jt} $(3+4)$	$(R_{jt} - \bar{R}_j)$ $(5 - \bar{R}_m)$	$(R_{jt} - \bar{R}_j)^2$ (6^2)	$(R_{jt} - \bar{R}_j)(R_{mt} - \bar{R}_m)$ (Col. 6 × Q7.4 Col. 6)
(1)	(2)	(3)	(4)	(5)	(6)	(7)	(8)
1960	48						
1961	49		.05				
1962	52		.06				
1963	74		.05				
1964	90		.05				
1965	102		.05				
1966	87		.05				
1967	78		.05				
1968	81		.05				
1969	74		.06				
1970	70		.05				

a) $\bar{R}_j = ?$ b) $\text{VAR}(R_j) = ?$ c) $\text{COV}(R_j, R_m) = ?$ d) $\beta_j = ?$

b) What percentage of this portfolio must an individual put into the market portfolio in order to achieve an expected return of 10%?

7.12 You believe that the Beta Alpha Watch Company will be worth $100 per share one year from now. How much are you willing to pay for one share today if the risk-free rate is 8%, the expected rate of return on the market is 18%, and the company's beta is 2.0?

7.13 Given the following variance-covariance matrix and expected returns vector (for assets X and Y respectively) for a two asset world:

$$\Sigma = \begin{bmatrix} .01 & 0 \\ 0 & .0064 \end{bmatrix}, \qquad \bar{R}'_i = [.2 \quad .1]$$

a) What is the expected return of a zero-beta portfolio given that 50% of the index portfolio is invested in asset X and in asset Y?

b) What is the vector of weights in the global minimum-variance portfolio?

c) What is the covariance between the global minimum-variance portfolio and the zero-beta portfolio?

d) What is the equation of the market line?

7.14 Given the following variance-covariance matrix, calculate the covariance between portfolio A, which has 10% in asset 1 and 90% in asset 2, and portfolio B, which has 60% in asset 1 and 40% in asset 2:

$$\Sigma = \begin{bmatrix} .01 & -.02 \\ -.02 & .04 \end{bmatrix}.$$

7.15 Suppose that securities are priced as if they are traded in a two-parameter economy. You have forecast the correlation coefficient between the rate of return on Knowlode Mutual Fund and the market portfolio at .8. Your forecast of the standard deviations of the rates of return are .25 for Knowlode, and .20 for the market portfolio. How would you combine the Knowlode Fund and a riskless security to obtain a portfolio with a volatility (beta) of 1.6?

7.16 You currently have 50% of your wealth in a risk-free asset, and 50% in the four assets below:

Asset	Expected Return on Asset i	β_i	Percent Invested in Asset i
$i = 1$	7.6%	.2	10%
$i = 2$	12.4%	.8	10%
$i = 3$	15.6%	1.2	10%
$i = 4$	18.8%	1.6	20%

If you want an expected rate of return of 12%, you can obtain it by selling some of your holdings of the risk-free asset and using the proceeds to buy the market portfolio. If this is the way you decide to revise your portfolio, what will the set of weights in your revised portfolio be? If you hold only the risk-free asset and the market portfolio, what set of weights would give you an expected 12% return?

7.17 The market price of a security is $40, the security's expected rate of return is 13%, the riskless rate of interest is 7%, and the market risk premium, $[E(R_m) - R_f]$, is 8%. What will be the security's current price if its expected future payoff remains the same but the covariance of its rate of return with the market portfolio doubles?

7.18 Suppose you are the manager of an investment fund in a two-parameter economy. Given the following forecast:

$$E(R_m) = .16, \qquad \sigma(R_m) = .20, \qquad R_f = .08.$$

a) Would you recommend investment in a security with $E(R_j) = .12$ and $COV(R_j, R_m) = .01$? [*Note:* Assume that this price change has no significant effect on the position of the security market line.]

b) Suppose that in the next period, security R_j has earned only 5% over the preceding period. How would you explain this *ex post* return?

7.19 Why is the separation principle still valid in a world with

a) nonmarketable assets?

b) a nonstochastic risk-free rate?

7.20 Assume that the mean-variance opportunity set is constructed from only two risky assets, A and B. Their variance-covariance matrix is given below.

$$\sum = \begin{bmatrix} .0081 & 0 \\ 0 & .0025 \end{bmatrix}$$

Asset A has an expected return of 30% and asset B has an expected return of 20%. Answer the following questions:

a) Suppose investor I chooses his "market portfolio" to consist of 75% in asset A and 25% in asset B, while investor J chooses a different "market portfolio" with 50% in asset A and 50% in asset B.

> Weights chosen by I are: [.75 .25]
> Weights chosen by J are: [.50 .50]

Given these facts, what β will each investor calculate for asset A?

b) Given your answer to part (a) above, which of the following is true and why?
  1. Investor I will require a higher rate of return on asset A than will investor J.
  2. They will both require the same return on asset A.
  3. Investor J will require a higher rate of return on asset A than will investor I.

c) Compute the zero-beta portfolios and the equations for the security market lines for each investor.

REFERENCES

Banz, R. W., "The Relationship Between Return and Market Value of Common Stocks," *Journal of Financial Economics,* March 1981, 3–18.

Basu, S., "Investment Performance of Common Stocks in Relation to Their Price-Earnings Ratios: A Test of the Efficient Markets Hypothesis," *Journal of Finance,* June 1977, 663–682.

Black, F., "Capital Market Equilibrium with Restricted Borrowing," *Journal of Business,* July 1972, 444–455.

————, M. C. Jensen, and M. Scholes, "The Capital Asset Pricing Model: Some Empirical Tests," reprinted in M. C. Jensen, ed., *Studies in the Theory of Capital Markets.* Praeger, New York, 1972, 79–124.

Blume, M., "Portfolio Theory: A Step Toward Its Practical Application," *Journal of Business,* April 1970, 152–173.

————, "On the Assessment of Risk," *Journal of Finance,* March 1971, 1–10.

————, and I. Friend, "A New Look at the Capital Asset Pricing Model," *Journal of Finance,* March 1973, 19–34.

Blume, M., and F. Husick, "Price, Beta and Exchange Listing," *The Journal of Finance,* May 1973, 283–299.

Breeden, D. T., "An Intertemporal Asset Pricing Model with Stochastic Consumption and Investment Opportunities," *Journal of Financial Economics,* September 1979, 265–296.

Brennan, M. J., "Taxes, Market Valuation and Corporation Financial Policy," *National Tax Journal,* December 1970, 417–427.

Chen, N. F., "Arbitrage Asset Pricing: Theory and Evidence." Unpublished PhD. thesis, UCLA, Graduate School of Management, 1981.

Clark, P. K., "A Subordinated Stochastic Process Model with Finite Variance for Speculative Prices," *Econometrica,* January 1973, 135–155.

Copeland, T. E., and D. Mayers, "The Value Line Enigma (1965–1978): A Case Study of Performance Evaluation Issues," forthcoming, *Journal of Financial Economics.*

Cornell, B., "Asymmetric Information and Portfolio Performance Measurement," *Journal Financial Economics,* December 1979, 381–390.

Dimson, E., "Risk Measurement When Shares are Subject to Infrequent Trading," *Journal of Financial Economics,* June 1979, 197–226.

Fama, E. F., "The Behavior of Stock Market Prices," *Journal of Business,* January 1965a, 34–105.

————, "Portfolio Analysis in a Stable Paretian Market," *Management Science,* January 1965b, 404–419.

————, "Risk, Return and Equilibrium: Some Clarifying Comments," *The Journal of Finance,* March 1968, 29–40.

————, "Risk, Return and Equilibrium," *Journal of Political Economy,* January/February 1971, 30–55.

————, *Foundations of Finance.* Basic Books, New York, 1976.

————, and J. MacBeth, "Risk, Return and Equilibrium: Empirical Test," *Journal of Political Economy,* May/June 1973, 607–636.

Fama, E. F., and G. W. Schwert, "Human Capital and Capital Market Equilibrium," *The Journal of Financial Economics,* January 1977, 95–125.

Friend, I., and M. Blume, "Measurement of Portfolio Performance under Uncertainty," *American Economic Review,* September 1970, 561–575.

Gehr, A., Jr., "Some Tests of the Arbitrage Pricing Theory," *Journal of the Midwest Finance Association*, 1975, 91–105.

Hamada, R. S., "The Effect of the Firm's Capital Structure on the Systematic Risk of Common Stocks," *The Journal of Finance*, May 1972, 435–452.

Ibbotson, R., and R. Sinquefield, "Stocks, Bonds, Bills and Inflation: Year-by-year Historical Returns (1926–1974)," *Journal of Business*, January 1976, 11–47.

Jensen, M. C., "Capital Markets: Theory and Evidence," *The Bell Journal of Economics and Management Science*, Autumn 1972, 357–398.

Lawley, D. N., and A. E. Maxwell, *Factor Analysis as a Statistical Method*. Butterworths, London, 1963.

Lintner, J., "The Valuation of Risk Assets and the Selection of Risky Investments in Stock Portfolios and Capital Budgets," *The Review of Economics and Statistics*, February 1965a, 13–37.

————, "Security Prices and Maximal Gains from Diversification," *Journal of Finance*, December 1965b, 587–616.

————, "The Aggregation of Investor's Diverse Judgments and Preferences in Purely Competitive Security Markets," *Journal of Financial and Quantitiative Analysis*, December 1969, 347–400.

Litzenberger, R., and K. Ramaswamy, "The Effect of Personal Taxes and Dividends and Capital Asset Prices: Theory and Empirical Evidence," *Journal of Financial Economics*, June 1979, 163–195.

Mayers, D., "Non-Marketable Assets and the Capital Market Equilibrium under Uncertainty," reprinted in M. C. Jensen, ed., *Studies in the Theory of Capital Markets*. Praeger, New York, 1972, 223–248.

————, and E. Rice, "Measuring Portfolio Performance and the Empirical Content of Asset Pricing Models," *The Journal of Financial Economics*, March 1979, 3–28.

Merton, R., "An Intertemporal Capital Asset Pricing Model," *Econometrica*, September 1973, 867–888.

————, "On Estimating the Expected Return on the Market: An Exploratory Investigation," *Journal of Financial Economics*, December 1980, 323–361.

Miller, M., and M. Scholes, "Rates of Return in Relation to Risk: A Re-examination of Some Recent Findings," in M. C. Jensen, ed., *Studies in the Theory of Capital Markets*. Praeger, New York, 1972, 47–78.

Modigliani, F., and G. Pogue, "An Introduction to Risk and Return," *Financial Analysts Journal*, March/April 1974 and May/June 1974, 68–80 and 69–85.

Mossin, J., "Equilibrium in a Capital Asset Market," *Econometrica*, October 1966, 768–783.

Oldfield, G., Jr., and R. Rogalski, "Treasury Bill Factors and Common Stock Returns," *The Journal of Finance*, May 1981, 337–350.

Pettit, R. R., and R. Westerfield, "Using the Capital Asset Pricing Model and the Market Model to Predict Security Returns," *Journal of Financial and Quantitative Analysis*, September 1974, 579–605.

Reinganum, M. R., "Misspecification of Capital Asset Pricing: Empirical Anomolies Based on Earnings Yields and Market Values," *Journal of Financial Economics*, March 1981a, 19–46.

————, "The Arbitrage Pricing Theory: Some Empirical Results," *The Journal of Finance,* May 1981b, 313–321.

Roll, R., "A Critique of the Asset Pricing Theory's Tests," *Journal of Financial Economics,* March 1977, 129–176.

————, "A Possible Explanation of the Small Firm Effect," *Journal of Finance,* September 1981, 879–888.

————, and S. Ross, "An Empirical Investigation of the Arbitrage Pricing Theory," *The Journal of Finance,* December 1980, 1073–1103.

Rosenberg, B., and V. Marathe, "Tests of Capital Asset Pricing Hypotheses." Unpublished manuscript, University of California at Berkeley, 1977.

Ross, S. A., "Return, Risk and Arbitrage," in Friend and Bicksler, eds., *Risk and Return in Finance,* Heath Lexington: New York, 1974.

————, "The Arbitrage Theory of Capital Asset Pricing," *Journal of Economic Theory,* December 1976, 343–362.

————, "The Capital Asset Pricing Model (CAPM), Short Sales Restrictions and Related Issues," *The Journal of Finance,* March 1977, 177–184.

————, "A Simple Approach to the Valuation of Risky Streams," *The Journal of Business,* July 1978, 453–475.

Rubinstein, M. E., "A Mean-Variance Synthesis of Corporate Financial Theory," *Journal of Finance,* March 1973, 167–182.

Scholes, M., and J. Williams, "Estimating Betas From Non-synchronous Data," *Journal of Financial Economics,* December 1977, 309–327.

Sharpe, W. F., "A Simplified Model for Portfolio Analysis," *Management Science,* January 1963, 277–293.

————, "Capital Asset Prices: A Theory of Market Equilibrium Under Conditions of Risk," *Journal of Finance,* September 1964, 425–442.

Treynor, J., "Toward a Theory of the Market Value of Risky Assets." Unpublished manuscript, 1961.

Vasicek, O. A., "Capital Market Equilibrium with No Riskless Borrowing," March 1971. Mimeograph available from the Wells Fargo Bank.

Verrecchia, R. E., "The Mayers-Rice Conjecture—A Counterexample," *Journal of Financial Economics,* March 1980, 87–100.

Pricing Contingent Claims: Option Pricing Theory and Evidence

. . . option pricing theory is relevant to almost every area of finance. For example, virtually all corporate securities can be interpreted as portfolios of puts and calls on the firm.

J. C. COX, S. A. ROSS, AND M. RUBINSTEIN,
"OPTION PRICING: A SIMPLIFIED APPROACH,"
JOURNAL OF FINANCIAL ECONOMICS,
SEPTEMBER 1979, P. 230.

A. INTRODUCTION

The theory of option pricing has undergone rapid advances in recent years. Simultaneously, organized option markets have developed in the United States. On April 26, 1973, the Chicago Board of Options Exchange (CBOE) became the first organized exchange for trading standardized options contracts. By the end of 1974, in terms of share equivalents, volume on the CBOE was larger than that on the American Stock Exchange. By the end of 1976 there were 1337 registered CBOE exchange members and the bid-ask price for a seat was

Table 8.1 CBOE Option Price Listing

Chicago Board

Listed Options
Quotations

Tuesday, October 4, 1977

Closing prices of all options. Sales unit usually is 100 shares. Security description includes exercise price. Stock close is New York Stock Exchange final price. p-Put option. o-Old shares.

Option & price	Oct Vol.	Oct Last	Jan Vol.	Jan Last	Apr Vol.	Apr Last	N.Y. Close
Alcoa 40	66	b	13	4¾	41	2¾	43¾
Alcoa 45	5	½	27	2	101	½	43¾
Alcoa 50		1-16			38	1	43¾
Am Exp 35	25	2¾	26	3¾	18	4½	37⅜
Am Exp 40	166	1-16	6	¾	76	1½	37⅜
Am Tel 60	197	2	70	2⅞	76	2⅞	62
Am Tel 65	53	1-16	210	⅜	86	⅜	62
Atl R 50	276	1-16	70	4¼	154	5⅞	52½
Atl R 55	32	1-16	62	1½	33	1¼	52½
Avon 45	226	2½	105	3	216	3¾	47
Avon 45 p	257	⅜	234	1-16	223	2 1-16	47
Avon 50	444	1-16	247	11-16	283	1 5-16	47
Avon 50 p	44	3¾	48	4⅜	186	5	47
BankAm 25	84	¼	32	¾	30	1¼	24¼
BankAm 25	25	1-16				b	24¼
BankAm 30	191	1-16	108	1 5-16	129	2⅛	24¼
Beth S 20	3	1-16	161	¼	198	9-16	19⅞
Beth S 25	a	a	5	1-16	25	3-16	19⅞
Beth S 25	a	a	17	2¾	142	11-16	12⅝
Bruns 10	4	1-16	93	3-16	69	7-16	12⅝
Bruns 15	a	3½	a	4⅜	a	4½	43½
Burl N 40	57	¼	62	1¾	41	1⅞	43½
Burl N 45	35	a	5	5-16	25	11-16	69
Burrgh 50	306	19	194	b	a	b	69
Burrgh 60	420	⅞	384	10¾	27	11½	69
Burrgh 70	109	3½	59	1¼	219	4⅞	69
Citicp 25	2	1-16	109	¼	220	1¾	24¼
Citicp 30	55	3¾	a	4¾	16	7-16	24¼
Delta 30	88	¼	53	1¾	a	a	33¾
Delta 35	186	11⅞	32	12⅞	a	b	46¾
Dig Eq 35	231	6⅞	70	4⅛	a	b	46¾
Dig Eq 40	479	2 5-16	251	4¼	65	6	46¾
Dig Eq 45	210	¼	175	1¾	a	4¾	46¾
Disney 35	60	3⅜	14	4⅜	6	5⅞	38⅝
Disney 40	177	¼	81	1⅞	54	2⅜	38⅝
Disney 45	183	⅞	115	5-16	247	2⅞	30½
Dow Ch 35	64	1-16	323	⅜	63	⅞	30½
Du Pnt 110	644	1¾	199	4¾	100	6⅝	110
Du Pnt 120	108	1-16	241	1 5-16	100	2¾	110
Du Pnt 130	13	1-16	110	b	a	b	110
Eas Kd 50	252	10¾	148	11⅜	154	11⅜	60¾
Eas Kd 60	30	1-16			48	9-16	60¾
Eas Kd 70 p	2006	1 9-?			71	3½	60¾
Eas Kd ? p	1086	?				1½	60¾

Option & price	Oct Vol.	Oct Last	Jan Vol.	Jan Last	Apr Vol.	Apr Last	N.Y. Close
Xerox 45	268	8¾	282	8⅞	271	9⅝	53¾
Xerox 50	1306	3¾	411	4⅞	203	5⅞	53¾
Xerox 60	130	1-16	545	¾	578	1½	53¾
A E P 24⅞	67	3-16	15	5-16		b	24¼
A E P 25	¼	4	5	b	10	b	24¼
Am Hos 20	20	3⅜	18	20	a	a	24
Am Hos 25	4	b	3⅜	a	1¼	a	24
A M P 25	306	7-16	7-16	a	a	a	28⅝
A M P 30	260	b	164 1 15-16	3	1⅞	28⅝
Bally 20	187	10	269	b	211	7	20⅛
Bally 25	58	1-16	a	1-16	232	⅞	20⅛
Baxter 30	58	5⅞	10	a	a	7	35⅜
Baxter 35	88	1½	31	2 5-16	7	3½	35⅜
Baxter 40	5	¼	b	b	229	a	46¾
Blk Dk 15	122	1¾	78	1¾	16	1¾	16
Blk Dk 20	23	1-16	11	¼	13	2 1-16	16
Boeing o 20	29	4	4	¼	32	½	23⅞
Boeing o 22½	87	2	2	b	b	b	23⅞
Boeing o 25	323	⅜	455	⅜	178	1¾	23⅜
Bois C 25	110	1¾	9	1⅜	a	¾	25¼
Bois C 30	168	1½	7	2¼	16	a	25¼
Bois C 30 p	63	b	⅞	7-16	16	a	25¼
C B S 35	2	a	a	a	a	15	25¼
Co? 45	47	⅞				½	51⅞

Option & price	Oct Vol.	Oct Last	Jan Vol.	Jan Last	Apr Vol.	Apr Last	N.Y. Close
Pfizer 25	11	1⅞	18	2⅜	a	a	26½
Pfizer 30	a	a	5	3-16	9	7-16	26½
Phelps 25	a	b	a	⅜	7	3¾	23¾
Phelps 30	a	a	7	1-16	33	1¼	23¾
Phelps 35	a	a			a	a	23¾
Ph Mor 50	21	13¾	77	14⅛	2	14⅞	63¾
Ph Mor 60	482	3⅞	75	4⅜	459	5½	63¾
Pitney 15	1	1⅞	a	a	50	a	16¾
Pitney 20		1-16	20	¼	a	½	16¾
Proc G 70	15	13⅞	88	13⅞	a	b	83⅜
Proc G 80	74	3⅜	88	4⅞	10	6¼	83⅜
Proc G 90	41	1-16	80	11-16	79	1½	83⅜
Rite A 15	29	3⅜	21	3⅜	23	4	18⅝
Rite A 20	47	⅛	21	1⅜	20	11-16	18⅝
St Cal 40	a	a	41	2¼	24	7⅞	41½
St Cal 45	15	1-16	15	7-16	16	1¾	41½
T R W 35		7-16	15	1 3-16		7-16	34¼
T R W 40	a	a	8	¾	2	1¾	34¼
Tandy 20	a	a	8	9⅞	a	a	29¼
Tandy 25	41	4½	35	5½	2	6¼	29¼
Tandy 30	201	7-16	160	2⅛	52	3	29¼
Tedy 35	13	1-16	268	½	3	b	29¼
Texaco 25	15	3⅜	9	3½	7	a	28⅜
Texaco 30	384	1-16	275	⅜	56	9-16	28⅜
U Carb 45	83	3⅜	67	1½	34	2⅜	43⅞
U Carb 50	4	1-16	73	5-16	84	¾	43⅞
U Carb 60	a	b	3	b	17	b	29⅜
U S St 25	a	a	73	4⅞	5	b	29⅜
U S St 30	456	5-16	804	1½	200	2 3-16	29⅜
U S St 35	a	a	183	5-16	103	2 3-16	29⅜
U S St 40	a	a	50	⅛	a	b	29⅜
Wrn Lm 25	20	11-16	105	1½	10	a	25⅜
Wrn Lm 30	a	a	20	1-16	10	2⅛	25⅜
Westng 15	249	2½	109	2⅜	36	3⅛	17⅜
Westng 20	320	1-16	274	½	204	⅞	17⅜
Westng 25		a	32	1-16	22	a	17¾
A M F 15	6 2 13-16	a	a	8	a	17½
A M F 20	28	1-16	a	8	9-16	17½
A S A 15	a	a	10	7¼	a	22
A S A 20	327	2⅜	183	3⅜	59	22
A S A 25	144	¼	278	15-16	3½	22
Avnet 15	55	2 3-16	13	2¾	2	22
Avnet 20	26	½	83	7-16	15	3½	17¼
Bally 15			911 15-16	73		
Bally 20			63	½		

$55,000 to $62,000.[1] This phenomenal growth in option trading has been catalyzed, at least in part, by the standardization of contracts which has had the effect of lowering the transaction costs of option trading.

There are many types of options, and at first the terminology is confusing with calls, puts, straps, strips, straddles, spreads, in-the-money options, out-of-the-money options, and so forth. This nomenclature can be greatly simplified if we recognize that all contracts are made up of four basic securities: puts, calls, stocks (the underlying asset), and default-free bonds. A *call option* is a contract which is contingent on the value of an underlying asset. For example, a call option on the CBOE allows its holder to purchase a share of stock in the underlying company at a fixed price, usually called the *exercise price* or the *striking price,* for a fixed length of time. Table 8.1 is a clipping from *The Wall Street Journal* of October 4, 1977. We see, for example, that three Bethlehem Steel call options were being traded based on the value of its common stock, which closed that day at $19\frac{7}{8}$ per share. The first option had an exercise price of $20 and three maturity dates, the third Friday in October 1977, January 1978, and April 1978.

Should the price of the common stock have climbed above $20 per share, a trader who held the call option with an exercise price of $20 could have exercised his or her option and kept the difference between the exercise price and the stock price. A *put* is exactly the opposite of a call option. The holder of a put has the right to sell the stock at the exercise price any time up to and including the maturity date of the put. For example, the holder of a January put option on Avon with the exercise price of $45 could have made a profit if the stock, which was then selling for $47 per share, fell below $45 before the third Friday in January.

B. A DESCRIPTION OF THE FACTORS
WHICH AFFECT PRICES OF
EUROPEAN OPTIONS

In order to keep the theory simple for the time being, we assume that all options can be exercised only on their maturity date and that there are no cash payments (such as dividends) made by the underlying asset. Options of this type are called *European* options. They are considerably easier to price than their *American* option counterparts, which can be exercised at any date up to maturity.

A quick look at the option prices in Table 8.1 shows that at least three factors are important for the market value of an option. Since most of the options on the CBOE are call options, we shall, for the moment, confine our discussion to the determination of their value. Obviously, the higher the value of the underlying asset, S, the greater the value of an option written on it, *ceteris paribus.* Alcoa, American Express, Burlington Northern, Digital Equipment, and Walt Disney all have call options with an exercise price of $40 and a maturity date on the third Friday in

---

[1] By comparison, during December 1976, nine seats on the New York Stock Exchange exchanged hands at prices ranging from $58,000 to $80,000.

Figure 8.1
The relationship between the call price and the stock price.

January. Figure 8.1 clearly shows that the value of the call increases as a function of the value of the stock for a given exercise price and maturity date. Note also that the option still has a positive value even though the stock price is less than the exercise price. As long as investors believe that there is a chance that the stock price will exceed the exercise price before the option matures, the option will be valuable. Three of these companies, American Express, Digital Equipment, and Disney, have a second option with a lower exercise price of $35. Note that the relationship between the call price and the stock price has shifted upward. The lower the exercise price, the greater the value of a call option. The third obvious factor which affects call prices is the length of time to maturity. A quick look at any option in Table 8.1 shows that the longer the time to maturity, the higher the value of the option. The reason is that with more time to maturity, there is a greater chance that the stock price will climb higher above the exercise price. Hence options with longer maturity have higher prices. In fact, a call option which has an infinite maturity date will have the same value as the stock, regardless of its exercise price. This is because the option will never be exercised. (Why not?)

In addition to the stock price, the exercise price, and the time to maturity, there are two other important (but less obvious) factors which affect the option's value: the instantaneous variance rate of the price of the underlying asset (the common stock), and the risk-free rate of return. The holder of a call option will prefer more variance in the price of the stock to less. The greater the variance, the greater the probability that the stock price will exceed the exercise price, and this is of value to the call holder. A call option is a type of contingent claim. In other words, the option holder gains only under the condition that the stock price exceeds the exercise price at the maturity date. Suppose we hold options and are faced with the two

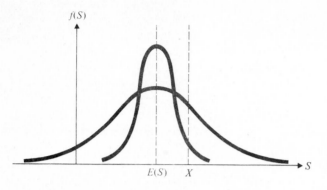

Figure 8.2
Hypothetical distributions of
stock prices.

hypothetical stock price distributions shown in Fig. 8.2. Both distributions have identical means but one has a larger variance. Which would we prefer if both have an identical exercise price, X? Recalling that option holders gain only when the stock price is greater than the exercise price, it becomes clear that we will prefer the option on the security which has the higher variance because the cumulative probability of receiving a gain is greater for a security of this sort.[2] This points out an important difference between the value of options and the value of the underlying asset. If we hold the asset, we receive payoffs offered by the entire probability distribution of outcomes. If we are risk averse, we will dislike higher variance, which means that we must accept low returns along with high returns. On the other hand, if we hold an option, we receive payoffs only from the tail of the distribution. The contingent claim feature of options makes higher variance desirable.

The value of higher variance is also illustrated in the following example. Suppose that a company has borrowed long-term debt with fixed interest payments of $8000 per year and that it finds itself with one of the two investment projects below:

	Project 1		Project 2
Probability	Cash flow	Probability	Cash flow
.2	4,000	.4	0
.6	5,000	.2	5,000
.2	6,000	.4	10,000

Both projects have identical expected cash flows of $5000. However, if the shareholders accept Project 1, the firm will surely go bankrupt because all possible cash flows are less than the debt commitment of $8000. On the other hand, if they accept Project 2, which has higher variance, there is a 40% chance that they will be able to pay off their debt obligation and have $2000 left over. Obviously they will choose the riskier project because it offers them a 40% chance of a positive value. This

[2] This example is given merely as an illustration, and the result holds only if $X > E(S)$. The example which follows is more accurate and more general.

example further illustrates the fact that holders of contingent claims, that is holders of options, will prefer more variance to less. It also introduces the notion that the shareholders of a firm are really holders of call options on the market value of the firm. If the value of the firm is less than the required debt payoff (the exercise price on the option), shareholders will allow their option to expire unexercised and turn over the assets of the firm to bondholders. If the value of the firm exceeds the debt payoff, they will exercise their option by paying off the debt holders and keeping any excess for themselves. In many of the chapters which follow we shall utilize option-pricing theory for applications in corporate financial policy.

The final factor in determining the value of an option is the risk-free rate of interest. Of all the factors it is the least intuitive. Black and Scholes [1973] have shown that it is possible to create a risk-free hedged position consisting of a long position in the stock and a short position (where the investor writes a call) in the option. This insight allows them to argue that the rate of return on the equity in the hedged position is nonstochastic. Therefore the appropriate rate is the risk-free rate, and as it increases so does the rate of return on the hedged position. This implies that the value of the call option will increase as a function of the risk-free rate of return. The mechanics of forming the risk-free hedge, as well as a more precise exposition of the logic, will be given later in the chapter.

The preceding intuitive description shows that five factors are important in determining the value of a European option: the price of the underlying asset, S; the exercise price of the option, X; the instantaneous variance of the returns of the underlying asset, σ^2; the time to maturity of the option, T; and the risk-free rate, r_f. This may be written in functional form as

$$c = f(S, X, \sigma^2, T, r_f), \tag{8.1}$$

and the partial derivatives of the call price, c, with respect to its various arguments are:

$$\frac{\delta c}{\delta S} > 0, \frac{\delta c}{\delta X} < 0, \frac{\delta c}{\delta \sigma^2} > 0, \frac{\delta c}{\delta T} > 0, \frac{\delta c}{\delta r_f} > 0. \tag{8.2}$$

C. COMBINING OPTIONS, A GRAPHIC PRESENTATION

One of the most fascinating features of options is that they can be combined in many different ways to provide almost any desired pattern of payoffs. For the sake of simplicity, assume that European put and call options have the same maturity date, the same underlying asset, and that the exercise price is set equal to the asset price.[3] A graphic representation of the value of buying or selling a call option as a function of changes in the stock price is given in Fig. 8.3. When selling a call, we receive the call price now. If the stock price stays the same or falls, the option will

---

[3] We also assume that capital markets are frictionless and there are no taxes. This implies, among other things, that the risk-free borrowing rate equals the risk-free lending rate.

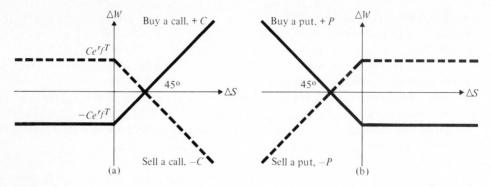

Figure 8.3
Payoffs from put and call options where $S = X$.

mature unexpired and we keep the future value of the sale price, $+e^{r_f T}C$. This is the horizontal portion of the dashed line in Fig. 8.3(a) with an intercept at $+e^{r_f T}C$. If the stock price rises, we lose one dollar for each dollar that it rises. This is the portion of the dashed line with an intercept at $+e^{r_f T}C$ and a slope of -1. Buying a call is the opposite of selling a call. If we sell a put, we receive $+P$ dollars now and lose a dollar for every dollar that the stock price falls below the exercise price. This is represented by the dashed line in Fig. 8.3(b). The solid line, which represents buying a put, is just the opposite.

The payoffs for long and short positions for stocks and risk-free pure discount bonds are shown in Fig. 8.4. If we hold a long position in a stock we gain or lose one dollar for every dollar that the stock price changes. If we hold a bond, we receive the same payoff regardless of changes in the stock price because a risk-free bond is presumed to have identical payoffs irrespective of which state of the world obtains.

Figure 8.4
Payoffs from stock or bond.

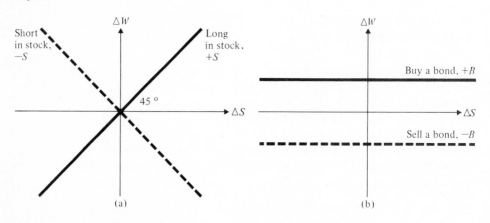

These elemental securities may be combined in various ways according to the following relationship:

$$S + P = B + C. \tag{8.3}$$

Buying a share of stock and buying a put written on that share yield the same payoff as holding a bond and buying a call. Alternatively, holding a portfolio made up of long positions in the stock and the put and a short position in the call is equivalent to the perfectly risk-free payoff offered by holding the bond. This can be seen by simply rearranging Eq. (8.3) as follows:

$$S + P - C = B. \tag{8.4}$$

Figure 8.5 shows how the payoffs can be combined graphically by adding the payoffs. The dashed line is the payoff from holding a put and a share of stock. On the graph it is the vertical sum of the payoffs of the two securities. Note that there is no risk if the stock price falls, because the put gains a dollar in value for every dollar that the stock loses. In the terminology of Wall Street we say that the put insures against downside losses. If we also sell a call, any upside variability is eliminated too, and the result is a perfectly risk-free payoff. Thus a portfolio composed of a long position in a stock, a put on the stock, and a short position in a call on the stock is completely risk free.

The reader may use the above graphic analysis to investigate the payoff patterns of many different securities. One often hears of straddles, spreads, straps, and strips. They are defined as follows:

- *Spread.* A combination of put and call options in a single contract, with the exercise price of the put usually less than the exercise price of the call. Because of the put-call parity relationship (discussed in the next section) the value of a spread is less than for a straddle.

- *Straddle.* A combination of put and call options in the same contract where the exercise price and maturity date are identical for both options. A straddle is graphed in Fig. 8.6.

Figure 8.5
Graphical representation of
$S + P - C = B.$

Figure 8.6
Payoff on a straddle.

- *Straps and strips.* Combinations of two calls and one put, and two puts and one call, respectively.

A straddle loses money for small changes in the stock price and gains money for large changes. This may seem to be "a good deal," but let us keep in mind that the market values of the put and call options are determined in a way which already incorporates the market's best estimate of the instantaneous variance in the price of the underlying security. The greater the variance, the more we have to pay for the put and call options. Therefore greater price fluctuations will be needed to make a profit. In the final analysis the securities will always be priced to yield a fair return for their riskiness.

D. PUT-CALL PARITY

Table 8.1 shows some securities with both put and call options written against them. For example, Avon has puts and calls with exercise prices of $45 and $50. We show below that, for European options, there is a fixed relationship between the price of put and call options with the same maturity date which are written on a single underlying security. This relationship, derived by Stoll [1969], is called *put-call parity.*
 Suppose we have a portfolio where we purchase one share of stock, one put option, and sell (write) one call option. Both options are written on the share of stock. Also, they have the same maturity date, T, and the same exercise price, X. At maturity all states of the world can be divided into those where the stock price is less than the exercise price, $S < X$, and those where it is greater than or equal to the exercise price, $S \geq X$. The payoffs from the portfolio in either state are listed below.

 If $S < X$:
a) you hold the stock S
b) the call option is worthless   0
c) the put option is worth $X - S$
d) therefore, your net position is X

If $S \geq X$:
  a) you hold the stock S
  b) the call option is worth $-(S - X)$
  c) and the put option is worthless 0
  d) therefore, your net position is X

No matter what state of the world obtains at maturity, the portfolio will be worth $X. Consequently, the payoff from the portfolio is completely risk free, and we can discount its value at the risk-free rate, r_f. Using discrete discounting, this is

$$S_0 + P_0 - c_0 = \frac{X}{1 + r_f} \, .$$

This can be rearranged to give the put-call parity formula

$$(c_0 - P_0) = \frac{(1 + r_f)S_0 - X}{1 + r_f} \, . \tag{8.5}$$

Note that the interest rate, r, is a one-period rate but that the time period need not equal a calendar year. For example, if the option expires in six months and r is an annual rate, then we can replace $(1 + r)$ in Eq. (8.5) with $(1 + r)^{1/2}$. Equation (8.5) is referred to as the *put-call parity* relationship for European options. A special case occurs when the exercise price, X, is set equal to the current stock price, S. When $S = X$, we have

$$c_0 - P_0 = \frac{r_f S_0}{1 + r_f} > 0. \tag{8.6}$$

This shows that when all the valuation parameters are identical (the same stock price, instantaneous variance, exercise price, time to expiration, and risk-free rate) and the exercise price equals the stock price, the call option will have greater present value than the put option.

An equivalent continuous compounding formula for put-call parity is

$$c_0 - P_0 = S_0 - X e^{-r_f T} \tag{8.7}$$

where r_f is the annual risk-free rate and T is the time to maturity (in years) of the put and call options. The put-call parity relationship is extremely useful for the valuation of European options because if we know the value of a European call, the put-call parity relationship also gives the value of a corresponding put.

E. SOME DOMINANCE THEOREMS WHICH BOUND THE VALUE OF A CALL OPTION

The value of a call option has been described as a function of five parameters: the price of the underlying asset, S; the instantaneous variance of the asset returns, σ^2; the exercise price, X; the time to expiration, T; and the risk-free rate, r_f:

$$c = f(S, \sigma^2, X, T, r_f).\qquad(8.1)$$

Perhaps even more interesting are some factors which do not affect the value of an option. For example, the option price does not depend on investor attitudes toward risk nor does it depend on the expected rate of return of the underlying security. This section of the chapter provides a logical, rather than descriptive or intuitive, framework for understanding why the above five parameters affect option value and why investor attitudes toward risk and the rate of return on the underlying security do not.

All the following discussion is based on the notion of stochastic dominance, which was introduced in Chapter 4. We shall use first-order stochastic dominance which says that one asset will be preferred by all investors (be they risk averse, risk neutral, or risk loving) if the return which it offers is superior in every state of nature to the return offered by a second asset. If this is true, we say that the first asset is stochastically dominant over the second. Clearly, if all the following analysis is based on this simple notion, the value of a call option will not depend on individual risk preferences.

Before developing the analysis and some related theorems it is useful to spell out in detail the assumptions which have been used in developing valuation models for options:

- Frictionless capital markets with no transactions costs or taxes and with information simultaneously and costlessly available to all individuals.
- No restrictions on short sales.
- Asset trading is continuous, with all asset prices following continuous and stationary stochastic processes.[4]
- The risk-free rate is nonstochastic (constant over time).[5]
- No dividends.[6]

Most of these assumptions are self-explanatory and are consistent with efficient capital markets. By continuous stochastic processes we mean that the price of the underlying asset can vary over time but does not have any discontinuities or jumps. In other words, we could graph the price movement over time without lifting our pen from the paper. A stationary stochastic process is one which is determined in the same way for all time periods of equal length. In particular, the instantaneous price variance does not change over time. If the underlying asset is a common stock, we assume no dividend payments so that there are no jumps in the stock price. It is well known that the stock price falls by approximately the amount of the dividend on the ex-dividend date.

Our objectives are (1) to show the boundary conditions which limit the values

---

[4] Cox and Ross [1975] have relaxed this assumption.
[5] Merton [1976] has relaxed this assumption.
[6] Geske [1977] has relaxed this assumption.

a call option can take and (2) to prove that American calls on nondividend-paying stocks will optimally not be exercised prior to maturity. The reader who wishes to carefully study the theorems of option pricing is referred to the seminal work of Merton [1973a]. We shall adopt the convention that European calls which can be exercised only at maturity will be written with a lowercase c, while American calls which can be exercised any time will be written with an uppercase C.

The payoff to a call option at maturity is the maximum of zero, if the stock price is less than the exercise price, or the difference between the stock price and the exercise price if the stock price exceeds the exercise price, i.e.,

$$c \geq C = \text{MAX}[0, S - X] \geq 0. \tag{8.8}$$

Clearly the call price must be nonnegative. Also, because the American call, C, can be exercised prior to maturity, its value must be greater than or equal to the European call value, c.

Equation 8.8 also tells us that the call price can never fall below $S - X$. Additionally, the option price will never exceed the price of the stock on which it is written. Even if the exercise price, X, is zero and the option never matures, it can be worth at most S. Even in this extreme case the option may be worth less than the stock because shareholders have voting rights while option holders do not.

The preceding discussion serves to limit the possible values which option prices may take relative to the stock price. The results are illustrated in Fig. 8.7. The call option is a function of the stock price, S, the time to maturity, T, and the exercise price, $C(S, T, X)$. Its value is nonnegative, less than S, and greater than $S - X$. Note that the boundaries $C \leq S$ and $C \geq S - X$ are 45° lines.

Next, we shall prove that an American call option written on a nondividend-paying stock will not be exercised before the expiration date of the option. Along the way we will further bound the value which call options can take and we will see why the call value will increase when the risk-free rate does. The result we wish to prove is stated as Theorem 8.1.

Theorem 8.1. An American call on a nondividend paying stock will not be exercised before the call expiration date.

Figure 8.7
Boundaries for the value of a call option.

Table 8.2   Relationship Between the Value of a Share of Stock and a Portfolio Made up of a European Call and X Risk-free Bonds

Portfolio	Current Value	Portfolio Value, Given Stock Price at T	
		$S < X$	$S \geq X$
A	$c(S, T, X) + XB(T)$	$0 + X$	$S - X + X$
B	S_0	S	S
Relationship between terminal values of A and B		$V_a > V_b$	$V_a = V_b$

In order to prove this, we first assume that $B(T)$ is the current price of a risk-free pure discount bond. A pure discount bond pays no coupons. Given positive interest rates and assuming that the bond pays one dollar upon maturity, we have[7]

$$B(T) = (\$1)e^{-r_f T}, \tag{8.9}$$

where r_f is the one-year risk-free rate and T is the number of years (or fraction of a year) to maturity. We shall adopt the convention that $T_1 > T_2 > \cdots > T_n$; therefore

$$0 = B(\infty) < B(T_1) < B(T_2) < \cdots < B(0) = \$1.$$

Now let us consider two portfolios. Portfolio A represents the purchase of one European call for $c(S, T, X)$ dollars and X bonds for $XB(\tau)$ dollars.[8] Portfolio B is the purchase of one share of stock for S dollars. Table 8.2 demonstrates the relationship between the terminal values for the two portfolios. If the stock price is less than the exercise price at the expiration date, the option will expire unexercised, with no value, and portfolio A will be worth X dollars. But since $X > S$, portfolio A will be worth more than portfolio B, which is one share of stock. On the other hand, when the stock price is greater than the exercise price, portfolios A and B have the same payoff. In any state of nature portfolio A pays an amount greater than or equal to portfolio B. Therefore, in order to prevent dominance, portfolio A must have a higher price than portfolio B:

$$c(S, T, X) + XB(T) \geq S.$$

This restriction may be rearranged to obtain

$$c(S, T, X) \geq \text{MAX}[0, S - XB(T)].$$

Finally, from (8.9), we have

$$c(S, T, X) \geq \text{MAX}[0, S - e^{-r_f T}X]. \tag{8.11}$$

---

[7] This is the continuous discounting version of the more familiar discrete discounting formula

$$B(T) = \frac{\$1}{(1 + r_f)^T} = (\$1)(1 + r_f)^{-T}.$$

[8] In this proof we have defined T as the time to maturity for the call option.

Equation (8.11) applies to a European call, but we have already discussed the fact that an American call is always at least as valuable as an equivalent European call; therefore

$$C(S,\ T,\ X) \geq c(S,\ T,\ X) \geq \text{MAX}[0,\ S - e^{-r_f T}X]. \qquad (8.12)$$

Furthermore, if exercised, the value of an American call is $\text{MAX}[0,\ S - X]$, which is less than $\text{MAX}[0,\ S - XB(T)]$, since $B(T) = e^{-r_f T}$, which is less than one, for positive r_f. Consequently, the holder of an American option can always do better by selling it in the marketplace rather than exercising it prior to expiration. This is an important result because European options are much simpler than American options.

Theorem 8.1 further limits the set of feasible prices for call options because the requirement that

$$c(S,\ T,\ X) \geq \text{MAX}[0,\ S - XB(T)]$$

is more restrictive than

$$c(S,\ T,\ X) \geq \text{MAX}[0,\ S - X].$$

This is shown in Fig. 8.8. Also, it is now possible to demonstrate, in a plausible fashion, that the call price will increase when the risk-free rate increases. Suppose the stock price is $50, the exercise price is $30, and the option expires in one year. If the risk-free rate is 5%, the lower bound on the option price will be $21.46. If the risk-free rate changes to 10%, the lower bound increases to $22.85. Intuitively, the call option is worth more because an investor has to pay less today to acquire the risk-free discount bond which guarantees one dollar at the end of the year. This makes portfolio A in Table 8.3 more valuable relative to portfolio B.

Theorem 8.2 introduces more realism into the analysis by showing what happens to the value of an American call option when the underlying stock pays a dividend. Since most firms pay dividends, investors who hold CBOE call options must be careful; the options are not protected against a drop in value when the underlying stock falls in price because it goes ex-dividend.

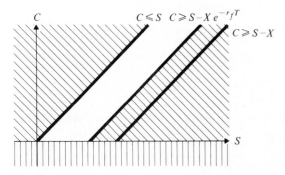

C $C \leqslant S$ $C \geqslant S - X e^{-r_f T}$
$C \geqslant S - X$
S

Figure 8.8
Further limitation of the feasible set of call prices.

Table 8.3   Options on Dividend-paying Stocks may be Exercised Prematurely

Portfolio	Current Value	Portfolio Value Given Stock Price at T	
		S < X	S ≥ X
A	$c(S, T, X) + (X + D)B(T)$	$0 + X + D$	$S - X + X + D$
B	S	$S + D$	$S + D$
Relationship between terminal values of A and B		$V_a > V_b$	$V_a = V_b$

Theorem 8.2.   Premature exercise of an American call may occur if the underlying security (common stock) pays dividends (and if the option is inadequately protected against the dividend payment).

In December of 1976, General Motors stock was selling at around $75 per share. Call options were outstanding with an exercise price of $60. On the next day the company was scheduled to go ex-dividend with a dividend of $3 per share. This implied that the stock price would fall to approximately $72 per share. CBOE call options provide no protection against dividend payments, and hence option holders found themselves with the following dilemma. Before the ex-dividend date the option price could not fall below $S - X$, or $15. (Why?) On the following day everyone knew the stock price would fall to around $72 per share, and that the option price would also fall (it fell to around $12\frac{5}{8}$). On one day their option was worth $15 and on the next they knew it would have a lower price. Obviously, the rational thing to do was to exercise the option just before the stock went ex-dividend.

The rationality of the above example can be demonstrated by assuming that a security makes a certain dividend payment, D, on the expiration date of an option. Consider two portfolios. Portfolio A is one European call and $X + D$ bonds. Portfolio B is one share of stock. Table 8.3 shows the terminal values of the two portfolios. The value of A is greater than that of B when the stock price is less than the exercise price and equal to it otherwise. Therefore

$$c(S, T, X) + (X + D)B(T) \geq S.$$

By rearranging this and using Eq. (8.9), we obtain

$$c(S, T, X) \geq \text{MAX}[0, S - (X + D)e^{-r_f T}]. \qquad (8.13)$$

Depending on the size of the dividend payment and the risk-free rate, it is possible to have the following situation,

$$(X + D)e^{-r_f T} > S,$$

in which case the value of the call in (8.13) is zero, at best. Therefore, in some cases it may be advantageous to exercise an American option prematurely.[9]

---

[9] The reader who is interested in the valuation of call options written on dividend-paying stocks is referred to Roll [1977].

The preceding discussion has served to bound the possible values of call prices as shown in Fig. 8.8. This is done without any mention whatsoever of the risk preferences of different individuals. The dominance arguments used in the analysis are very robust. They require only that arbitrage opportunities in efficient capital markets do not result in dominated securities. Further, the theorems provide considerable insight into the relationship between option prices, the price of the underlying asset, S; the exercise price, X; the time to maturity, T; and the risk-free rate, r_f. In the next section, we demonstrate the call valuation formula which can be used to determine the price of a European call, given that we know the above four parameters and the instantaneous variance of the price of the underlying asset.

F. DERIVATION OF THE OPTION PRICING FORMULA—THE BINOMIAL APPROACH

We shall discuss two derivations of the (Black-Scholes) option pricing model, OPM. The first, a closed-form solution, was provided by Black and Scholes [1973]. They recognized that given the assumption of frictionless markets and continuous trading opportunities, it is possible to form a riskless hedge portfolio consisting of a long position in a stock and a short position in a European call written on that stock. As we shall see, this insight is critical for solving the option pricing problem. However, because their derivation requires the use of advanced mathematical tools such as stochastic differential equations it is relegated to the appendix of this chapter. A somewhat more intuitive approach, which uses binomial distributions, was independently derived by Cox, Ross and Rubinstein [1979] and Rendelman and Bartter [1979]. Besides being easier to understand, the binomial approach provides solutions, not only for a closed-form European option pricing model but also for the more difficult American option problem where numerical simulations must be employed.

1. The Simple Binomial Model for Pricing Call Options

In addition to the usual assumption of frictionless and competitive capital markets where no riskless arbitrage opportunities can exist, assume that the stock price, S, obeys a binomial generating process as shown in Fig. 8.9 where

$S = \$20.00 =$ the stock price,

$q = .5 =$ the probability the stock price will move upward,

$r_f = 1.1 =$ one plus the risk-free rate of interest,

$u = 1.2 =$ the multiplicative upward movement in the stock price $(u > r_f > 1)$,

$d = .67 =$ the multiplicative downward movement in the stock price $(d < r_f)$.

At the end of one time period the stock price may increase to uS with probability q or decrease to dS with probability $1 - q$. Figure 8.9 provides a simple example where the current stock price is $20. There is a 50–50 chance (i.e., $q = .5$) it will increase to $24 or fall to $13.40 by the end of the period. Note that the downward

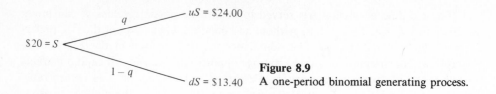

Figure 8.9
A one-period binomial generating process.

multiplier for the stock price, *d*, must be less than one. This assumption ensures that the stock price will not fall below a value of $0, no matter how many time periods are eventually added. If there are *n* periods, then

$$\underset{n \to \infty}{Lim} \; d^n = 0 \quad \text{iff} \quad 0 \le d < 1.$$

Of course, there is no upper bound on the value which the stock price may take.

Next, denote r_f as one plus the riskless rate of interest over the single time period ($r_f = 1.1$ in our example). The derivation requires that $u > r_f > d$. If these inequalities did not hold, then riskless arbitrage opportunities would exist. Also, for convenience, we assume that $r_f > 1$.

Now, imagine a call option *c*, with an exercise price of $X = \$21$ which is written on the stock. The payoffs for the call are shown in Fig. 8.10. Given our numerical example, there is a 50–50 chance of ending up with $MAX[0, uS - X] = \$3$, or $MAX[0, dS - X] = \$0$. The question is how much would we pay for the call right now?

In order to answer this question, we begin by constructing a risk-free hedge portfolio composed of one share of stock, *S*, and *m* shares of a call option written against the stock. Figure 8.11 shows the payoffs for the hedge portfolio. If the end-of-period payoffs are equal, the portfolio will be risk free. Equating the payoffs, we have

$$uS - mc_u = dS - mc_d,$$

and solving for *m*, the number of call options to be written against the share of stock, we have

$$m = \frac{S(u - d)}{c_u - c_d}. \tag{8.14}$$

Substituting the numbers from our example problem, we see that the hedge ratio is

$$m = \frac{\$20(1.2 - .67)}{\$3 - \$0} = 3.53.$$

Figure 8.10
Payoffs for a one-period call option.

Figure 8.11
The payoffs for a risk-free hedge portfolio.

Thus the riskless hedge portfolio consists of buying one share of stock and writing 3.53 call options against it. The payoffs in the two states of nature are identical as shown below.

State of Nature	Portfolio	Payoff
favorable	$uS - mc_u$	1.2($20) − 3.53($3) = $13.40
unfavorable	$dS - mc_d$	.67($20) − 3.53(0) = $13.40

Before we can determine what rate of return this payoff represents, we must figure out the call price, c, in order to know exactly what our original investment was.

We also know that because the hedge portfolio is constructed to be riskless, the current value of the portfolio multiplied by one plus the risk-free rate must equal the end-of-period payoff. Mathematically, this is

$$r_f(S - mc) = uS - mc_u,$$

$$c = \frac{S(r_f - u) + mc_u}{mr_f}. \tag{8.15}$$

Substituting the hedge ratio, m, into this equation, and rearranging terms, we can solve for the value of the call option

$$c = \left[c_u \left(\frac{r_f - d}{u - d} \right) + c_d \left(\frac{u - r_f}{u - d} \right) \right] \div r_f. \tag{8.16}$$

It can be simplified by letting

$$p = \frac{r_f - d}{u - d} \quad \text{and} \quad 1 - p = \frac{u - r_f}{u - d}.$$

Thus we have

$$c = [pc_u + (1 - p)c_d] \div r_f. \tag{8.17}$$

We shall call p the *hedging probability*. It is always greater than zero and less than one, so it has all the properties of a probability. In fact p is the value q would have in equilibrium if investors were risk neutral. Referring back to Fig. 8.9, a risk-neutral investor would require only the risk-free rate on an investment in the common stock, hence

$$r_f S = quS + (1 - q)dS,$$

and solving for q, we have

$$q = \frac{r_f - d}{u - d}.$$

Thus $p = q$ for a risk-neutral investor, and Eq. (8.16), which gives the value of a call, can be interpreted as the expectation of its discounted future value in a risk neutral world. Of course, this does not imply that in equilibrium the required rate of return on a call is the risk-free rate. A call option has risk similar to that of buying the stock on margin.[10]

Continuing with our numerical example, we can use Eq. (8.17) to solve for the value of the call option:

$$c = [pc_u + (1 - p)c_d] \div r_f$$

$$= \left[\left(\frac{1.1 - .67}{1.2 - .67}\right) \$3 + \left(\frac{1.2 - 1.1}{1.2 - .67}\right) \$0\right] \div 1.1$$

$$= [(.8113)\$3 + (.1887)\$0] \div 1.1 = \$2.2126.$$

Referring back to Fig. 8.11, we can now compute the dollar investment required for our hedge portfolio and confirm that the payoff of $13.40 at the end of the period yields the risk-free rate of return. The hedge portfolio consists of one share of stock and 3.53 call options written against it, therefore the dollar investment is

$$S - mc = \$20.00 - 3.53(\$2.2126) = \$12.19$$

and the rate of return on investment is

$$\frac{\$13.40}{\$12.19} = 1.1 = r_f.$$

The preceding derivation of the value of a call option depends critically on the existence of a hedge portfolio and on the fact that the call option must be priced so that the risk-free hedge earns exactly the risk-free rate of return. If the call had a higher (or lower) price the hedge portfolio would earn more (or less) than the riskless rate and opportunities to earn risk-free arbitrage profits would exist.

There are three interesting features of the call pricing formula:

- It does not depend on q, the probability of an upward movement in the stock price. Consequently, even though investors might have heterogeneous expectations about q, they will still agree on the call value relative to its other parameters, namely u, S, X, and r_f (in the one-period model).

- Individuals' attitudes toward risk are irrelevant in deriving the call option formula. All that is required for our results is that people prefer more wealth to less so that arbitrage profits are eliminated.

---

[10] Buying on margin means that part of the investment in the stock is borrowed. In fact the exact payoffs of the call option can be duplicated by buying $(c_u - c_d)/[(u - d)S]$ shares of stock and $[uc_d - dc_u]/(u - d)r_f$ units of the risk-free bond. See Cox, Ross, and Rubinstein [1979].

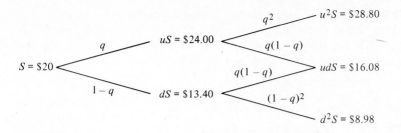

Figure 8.12
Stock prices with a two-period binomial process, $S = \$20$, $u = 1.2$,
$d = .833$.

- The only random variable on which the call value depends is the stock itself. It does not depend, for example, on the market portfolio of all securities.

The next logical step is to extend the one-period model to many time periods in order to show how an option's time to maturity affects its value. First consider the two-period graphs of the stock prices and the call option payoffs as shown in Figs. 8.12 and 8.13. We assume that the two-period risk-free rate is simply r_f^2. Next, we can employ the one-period option-pricing model, Eq. (8.16), to solve for c_u and c_d, the values of the one-period options which started the end of the first period.

$$c_u = [pc_{uu} + (1-p)c_{ud}] \div r_f,$$
$$c_d = [pc_{du} + (1-p)c_{dd}] \div r_f. \qquad (8.18)$$

As before, we can construct a riskless hedge during the first period to prevent riskless arbitrage opportunities. The result gives the following equation for the present value of the call,

$$c = [pc_u + (1-p)c_d] \div r_f.$$

Substituting the values of c_u and c_d from Eq. (8.18), we have

$$c = [p^2 c_{uu} + p(1-p)c_{ud} + (1-p)pc_{du} + (1-p)^2 c_{dd}] \div r_f^2. \qquad (8.19)$$

Figure 8.13
Two-period binomial call payoffs, $S = \$20$, $u = 1.2$, $d = .67$, $X = \$21$.

$q^2 \qquad c_{uu} = \text{MAX}[0, u^2 S - X] = \$7.80$

c_u

$q \qquad q(1-q)$

$c \qquad q(1-q) \qquad c_{ud} = c_{du} = \text{MAX}[0, udS - X] = \$0$

$1-q \qquad c_d$

$(1-q)^2$

$c_{dd} = \text{MAX}[0, d^2 S - X] = \$0$

Equation (8.19) is the result of applying the one-period model twice.[11] The terms within the brackets of Eq. (8.19) are a binomial expansion of the terms within the brackets in Eq. (8.17), the one-period model. The terms c_{uu}, c_{ud}, and c_{dd} are the three possible values which the call can have after two time periods:

$$c_{uu} = \text{MAX}[0, \ u^2S - X],$$

$$c_{ud} = c_{du} = \text{MAX}[0, \ udS - X],$$

$$c_{dd} = \text{MAX}[0, \ d^2S - X].$$

Another way of looking at Eq. (8.19) is to say that the call value is equal to the expected two-period payoffs (where the expectation uses the hedging probabilities, p and $1 - p$) discounted at the risk-free rate.

2. A Digression on the Binomial Distribution

The reader who is already familiar with the binomial distribution can skip to part 3 of this Section, otherwise a digression is in order. Binomial trials, as the name suggests, can take only two values, for example heads, h, or tails, t, in the flip of a coin. The coin flip need not be fair, so let p be the probability of a head and $1 - p$ the probability of a tail. A binomial distribution tells us the probability of observing n heads given T flips of a coin. Designate this probability as $\Pr\{n|T\}$. A typical question might be, what is the probability, $\Pr\{2|3\}$, of observing two heads out of three coin flips? Useful for answering this question is Pascal's triangle, which is shown below. Each row is constructed from the sum of the numbers in the adjacent two columns in the row immediately above it.

Number of Trials	Pascal's Triangle
$T = 0$	1
$T = 1$	1 1
$T = 2$	1 2 1
$T = 3$	1 3 3 1
$T = 4$	1 4 6 4 1
Number of heads, $n =$	$T, \ T - 1, \dots, \ T - T$

The numbers in the rows of Pascal's triangle are the coefficients for a binomial expansion, say $[p + (1 - p)]^T$. For example, if T is three and we want to know the coefficients in $[p + (1 - p)]^3$, they are 1, 3, 3, and 1 as in $1 \cdot p^3 + 3 \cdot p^2(1 - p) + 3 \cdot p(1 - p)^2 + 1 \cdot (1 - p)^3$. In general the probability of observing n heads in T trials is

$$\Pr\{n|Y\} = (\text{coef.}) \ p^n \ (1 - p)^{T-n}$$

where (coef.) is the correct coefficient taken from Pascal's triangle. Thus the probability of observing two heads in three flips of a fair (i.e., $p = .5$) coin is

$$\Pr\{n = 2|T = 3\} = 3(.5)^2(.5) = .375, \quad \text{where coef.} = 3.$$

---

[11] One can easily imagine how this iterative technique lends itself easily to a computer program.

For large numbers, Pascal's triangle is cumbersome. Another way of figuring out the coefficient is to use combinatorial notation as shown below:

$$\text{coef.} = \binom{T}{n} = \frac{T!}{(T-n)!n!}.$$

The term in parentheses can be read "The number of combinations of T things chosen n at a time." For example, what are all of the possible ways of getting two heads out of three coin flips? There should be three different ways of doing it, and they are: *hht, hth, thh*. The right-hand term uses factorial notation to compute the number of combinations. The term $T!$ (read T factorial) is the product of all of the numbers from T down to 1. Thus if we want to compute the number of combinations of two heads in three coin flips, we have

$$\frac{T!}{(T-n)!n!} = \frac{3!}{(3-2)!2!} = \frac{3 \cdot 2 \cdot 1}{(1)2 \cdot 1} = 3.$$

By the way, 0! is always defined as being equal to one.

The binomial probability of observing n heads out of T trials, given that the probability of a head is p, can be written

$$B(n|T,p) = \frac{T!}{(T-n)!n!} p^n(1-p)^{T-n} = \binom{T}{n} p^n(1-p)^{T-n}.$$

The mean, $E(n)$, of a binomial distribution is the expected number of heads in T trials. It is written

$$E(n) = Tp$$

and the variance is $\text{VAR}(n) = Tp(1-p)$.[12]

3. The Complete Binomial Model for Pricing Call Options

The T-period generalization of the binomial call pricing formula is simply the probability of each final outcome multiplied by the value of that outcome and discounted at the risk-free rate for T time periods. Then the general form of the payoff is

$$\text{MAX}[0, u^n d^{T-n}S - X],$$

where T is the total number of time periods and n is the number of upward movements in the stock price ($n = 0, 1, 2 \ldots T$). The general form of the probabilities of each payoff is given by the binomial distribution

$$B(n|T,p) = \frac{T!}{(T-n)!n!} p^n(1-p)^{T-n}.$$

---

[12] The reader who wants to read more on binomial trials is referred to Feller [1968], Chapter 6.

Multiplying the payoffs by the probabilities and summing across all possible payoffs, we have

$$c = \left\{ \sum_{n=0}^{T} \frac{T!}{(T-n)!n!} p^n (1-p)^{T-n} \text{MAX}[0, u^n d^{T-n} S - X] \right\} \div r_f^T. \quad (8.20)$$

Equation (8.20) is a complete expression for binomial option pricing. However, one of our objectives is to compare the binomial model, which is derived in discrete time, with the Black-Scholes model, which is a continuous time model. Therefore, the following paragraphs show how to rewrite the binomial model so that it may be easily compared with the Black-Scholes model, which is given in the next section of this chapter.

First, let's make use of the fact that many of the final payoffs for a call option will be zero because the option finishes out-of-the-money. Denote a as the positive integer which bounds those states of nature where the option has a nonnegative value. Then Eq. (8.20) can be rewritten as

$$C = \left\{ \sum_{n=a}^{T} \frac{T!}{(T-n)!n!} p^n (1-p)^{T-n} [u^n d^{T-n} S - X] \right\} \div r_f^T. \quad (8.21)$$

The summation in Eq. (8.20) was $n = 0 \ldots T$ and now it is $n = a \ldots T$. Also we are able to drop the notation $\text{MAX}[0, u^n d^{T-n} S - X]$ because we are dealing only with nonnegative payoffs.

Next, separate Eq. (8.21) into two parts as follows:

$$c = S \left[\sum_{n=a}^{T} \frac{T!}{(T-n)!n!} p^n (1-p)^{T-n} \frac{u^n d^{T-n}}{r_f^T} \right]$$

$$- X r_f^{-T} \left[\sum_{n=a}^{T} \frac{T!}{(T-n)!n!} p^n (1-p)^{T-n} \right]. \quad (8.22)$$

The second bracketed expression is the discounted value of the exercise price, $X r_f^{-n}$ multiplied by a complementary binomial distribution $B(n \geq a \,|\, T, p)$. The complementary binomial probability is the cumulative probability of having in-the-money options (i.e., where $n \geq a$) where the probabilities are the hedging probabilities determined by the risk-free hedge portfolio. The first bracketed expression is the stock price, S, multiplied by a complementary binomial probability. It may be interpreted in the same way if we let

$$p' \equiv (u/r_f)p \qquad \text{and} \qquad 1 - p' = (d/r_f)(1-p).$$

We then have

$$p^n (1-p)^{T-n} \frac{u^n d^{T-n}}{r_f^T} = \left[\frac{u}{r_f} p \right]^n \left[\frac{d}{r_f} (1-p) \right]^{T-n} = (p')^n (1-p')^{T-n}.$$

The binomial model for the pricing of a European call option can be summarized as follows:

$$c = S B(n \geq a \,|\, T, p') - X r_f^{-T} B(n \geq a \,|\, T, p), \quad (8.23)$$

where

$$p \equiv \frac{r_f - d}{u - d} \quad \text{and} \quad p' \equiv \left(\frac{u}{r_f}\right) p,$$

$a \equiv$ the smallest nonnegative integer greater than $\ln(X/Sd^n)/\ln(u/d)$, and if $a > T$ then $c = 0$,

$B(n \geq a | T, p) =$ the complementary binomial probability that $n \geq a$.

The complementary binomial distribution function is the probability that the sum of n random variables, each of which can take on the value 1 with probability p and 0 with probability $1 - p$, will be greater than or equal to a. Mathematically it is

$$B(n \geq a | T, p') = \sum_{n=a}^{T} \frac{T!}{(T-n)!n!} (p')^n (1-p')^{T-n},$$

$T =$ the total number of time periods.

It is obvious from (8.23) that the call option increases in value when the stock price, S, rises, and decreases when the exercise price, X, rises. In addition, the risk-free rate, r_f, the number of time periods before the option matures, T, and the variance of the binomial distribution, $\sigma^2 = Tp(1-p)$, affect the call value. When the risk-free rate increases, its main effect is to decrease the discounted value of the exercise price, Xr_f^{-n}, and this increases the call value (although there are secondary effects causing p and p' to decrease as r_f increases). An increase in the number of time periods to maturity clearly increases the call price. Recall that the call value is equivalent to the discounted value of the final payoffs multiplied by their hedging probabilities. The number of time periods does not change the hedging probabilities, p. However, it does increase the number of positive payoffs, because in Eq. (8.21) the integer, a, which bounds the positive payoffs will decrease as T increases. Also, the expected value of the binomial payoffs, $E(n) = pT$, increases with T. Finally, the call value will increase with increases in the binomial variance, $\text{VAR}(n) = Tp (1 - p)$. This happens because when the size of the stock price change, u, goes up, so does the variance of the binomial distribution. A greater variance increases the chances that the stock price will exceed the exercise price in the final payoffs, and therefore the call price goes up.

4. Extending the Binomial Model to Continuous Time—The Black-Scholes Option Pricing Model

The binomial pricing model can be extended to derive a continuous time equivalent if we hold the amount of calendar time (say one year) constant and divide it into more and more binomial trials. We will define T as the life of the option expressed as a fraction of a year and will divide T into n smaller time intervals. As n becomes larger, the calendar interval between binomial trials becomes shorter and shorter until, in the limit, we have a continuous stochastic process.[13] Note that, in this section of the chapter, we are interpreting T as one time interval—e.g., 1.6 years—where previously we used T as the number of periods until maturity. A continuous stochastic process has the stock price constantly changing, so its path can be drawn without ever lifting pen from paper.

Of particular concern is the way that the annual risk-free rate, r_f, the up and down movements, u and d, and the binomial process are to be handled as the number of time intervals, n, becomes infinite. If we define r_f as one plus the rate of return for one year, and let j be the rate which when compounded n times in interval T (a fraction of a year, e.g., six months) then in the limit we have[14]

$$\lim_{n \to \infty} \left(1 + \frac{j}{n/T}\right)^{n/T} = e^j = r_f. \tag{8.24}$$

Equation (8.24) shows how an annual rate of interest can be converted into the rate of interest for a binomial model with n binomial trials per year. Next, we need to know how the up and down movements, u and d, in a single binomial trial relate to the annual standard deviation of a stock's rate of return. Cox, Ross, and Rubinstein [1979] prove the following relationships:

$$u = e^{\sigma\sqrt{T/n}}$$

and

$$d = e^{-\sigma\sqrt{T/n}}. \tag{8.25}$$

The relationships given in Eq. (8.25) are extremely useful for translating continuous time variables such as the annualized standard deviation, σ, into discrete variables such as u and d for use in the binomial option pricing model.

The continuous time option pricing formula, derived by Black and Scholes [1973] is given below[15]

$$c = SN(d_1) - Xe^{-r_f T} N(d_2), \tag{8.26}$$

where

$$d_1 = \frac{\ln(S/X) + r_f T}{\sigma\sqrt{T}} + \frac{1}{2}\sigma\sqrt{T}, \tag{8.26a}$$

$$d_2 = d_1 - \sigma\sqrt{T}. \tag{8.26b}$$

The terms $N(d_1)$ and $N(d_2)$ are the cumulative probabilities for a unit normal variable z where, for example, $N(-\infty) = 0$, $N(0) = .5$, and $N(\infty) = 1.0$. Mathematically,

---

[13] The binomial formula can also be used to model a jump stochastic process as a limiting case. See Cox, Ross, and Rubinstein [1979, pp. 254–255] for the derivation. With a jump process the stock price will usually move in a smooth deterministic way but will occasionally experience sudden discontinuous jumps.

[14] For proof, see Appendix A at the end of the book.

[15] The appendix to this chapter gives the stochastic calculus derivation.

this is

$$N(d_1) = \int_{-\infty}^{d_1} f(z)dz,$$

where $f(z)$ is distributed normally with mean zero and standard deviation one.

The binomial model is rewritten below so that it can be readily compared with the Black-Scholes model.

$$c = SB(n \geq a \mid T,p') - Xr_f^{-n} B(n \geq a \mid T,p). \qquad (8.23)$$

The two equations look very similar. The variables S and X are exactly the same and Eq. (8.24) shows the relationship between r_f^{-n} and $e^{-r_f T}$. Cox, Ross, and Rubinstein [1979] have proven that as n, the number of binomial jumps per year, becomes large the two formulas converge, because

$$B(n \geq a \mid T,p') \rightarrow N(d_1) \quad \text{and} \quad B(n \geq a \mid T,p) \rightarrow N(d_2).$$

Thus the binomial option pricing formula contains the Black-Scholes formula as a limiting case.

Both formulae will be used throughout the remainder of the text, and the student should be familiar with how to use them. The next section gives a numerical example using both artificial data and data for Digital Equipment call options. Because Digital Equipment paid no dividends during the valuation period, the Black-Scholes and binomial pricing models can be used directly, without further modification.

G. VALUATION OF AN AMERICAN CALL WITH NO DIVIDEND PAYMENTS

1. An Example with Artificial Data

In order to understand the mechanics of using the OPM we can first use a simple example where all of the parameters are given. Then we can proceed to a problem which uses real-world data.

Suppose that the current stock price is $50, that the exercise price of an American call written on the stock is $45, that the annual risk-free rate is $r_f = 6\%$, that the option matures in three months, and that the instantaneous variance of the stock price is estimated to be 20%. Given these facts and the assumption that the stock will pay no dividends or undertake any other capital distributions, we can use the Black-Scholes OPM, Eq. (8.26), to value the call:

$$c = S N(d_1) - X e^{-r_f T} N(d_2), \qquad (8.26)$$

where

$$d_1 = \frac{\ln(S/X) + r_f T}{\sigma\sqrt{T}} + \frac{1}{2}\sigma\sqrt{T}, \qquad (8.26a)$$

$$d_2 = d_1 - \sigma\sqrt{T}. \qquad (8.26b)$$

To evaluate (8.26), we first calculate the value of d_1. The time to maturity, three months, must be expressed as a fraction of a year, that is one-fourth of a year. Setting $T = .25$, and substituting in the values of the other parameters, we get

$$d_1 = \frac{\ln(50/45) + .06(.25)}{\sqrt{.2}\sqrt{.25}} + \frac{1}{2}(\sqrt{.2})\sqrt{.25}$$

$$= \frac{.12036}{.2236} + .1118 = .65.$$

Using (8.26b), we can solve for d_2:

$$d_2 = d_1 - \sigma\sqrt{T} = .65 - \sqrt{.2}\sqrt{.25} = .4264.$$

Substituting these values back into (8.26), we have

$$c = SN(.65) - e^{-r_f T} XN(.4264).$$

Recall that $N(\cdot)$ are cumulative probabilities for a unit normal variable. Therefore $N(d_1)$ is the cumulative probability from minus infinity to $+.65$ standard deviations above the mean (which is defined to be zero for a unit normal distribution). The probability contained in the shaded area of Fig. 8.14 will give us the value of $N(d_1)$. Table 8.6, Areas Under the Normal Curve (on page 274), shows that if $d_1 = .65$, the cumulative probability from the mean ($\mu = 0$) to .65 is approximately .242. If we add this to the cumulative probability from minus infinity to zero (which equals .5), we get

$$N(d_1) = \int_{-\infty}^{0} f(z)dz + \int_{0}^{d_1} f(z)dz$$

$$= .5 + .242 = .742.$$

Repeating this procedure for $N(d_2)$, we get $N(d_2) = .6651$. Substituting these probabilities into the call valuation formula, we have

$$c = 50(.742) - e^{-.06(.25)}(45)(.6651)$$

$$= 37.10 - .9851(45)(.6651)$$

$$= 37.10 - 29.48 = \$7.62.$$

Figure 8.14
Illustration of $N(d_1)$.

Table 8.4 $c(S, T, \sigma^2, X, r_f)$ for **Different Stock Prices**

Stock Price	d_1	$N(d_1)$	d_2	$N(d_2)$	Call Price	Given
$30	−1.63	.052	−1.85	.032	$ .14	
40	− .35	.363	− .57	.284	$ 1.93	$T = 3$ months
50	.65	.742	.43	.665	$ 7.62	$r_f = .06$
60	1.47	.929	1.24	.893	$16.15	$\sigma^2 = 20\%$
70	2.15	.984	1.93	.973	$25.75	$X = \$45$

Table 8.4 gives the value of the call option for various stock prices and Fig. 8.15 plots the call price as a function of the stock price. Note that the call has little value until the stock price rises to the point where it is near the exercise price ($X = \$45$). When the stock price is well below the exercise price, the option is said to be "out-of-the-money," and the call will not be worth much. On the other hand, when the stock price is above the exercise price, the option is "in-the-money," and its value increases until in the limit it reaches $S - Xe^{-r_f T}$ for very high stock prices.

When pricing a real-world call it is important to keep in mind that (1) the Black-Scholes formula cannot be used if the common stock is expected to pay a dividend during the life of the option, (2) a CBOE call option is not really a simple option, but rather an option on an option, and (3) the instantaneous variance is not stationary over time. If the common stock of a firm is really an option on the assets of the firm, then a call option written against the common stock is really an option on an option. The Black-Scholes formula tends to misprice deep out-of-the-money options and deep in-the-money options. One possible reason is that the simple OPM does not accurately price compound options, and that the bias increases as the stock price moves away from the exercise price.

It is also of interest to contrast the call prices obtained from the binomial model with those given by the Black-Scholes model. Suppose we assume there are only two time periods in a year (each six weeks long). How closely does the binomial model with only two periods approximate the Black-Scholes continuous time call price of $7.62 given a $45 exercise price?

Figure 8.15
Call pricing example.

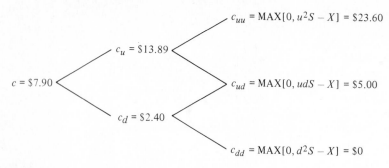

$c_{uu} = \text{MAX}[0, u^2 S - X] = \$23.60$

$c_u = \$13.89$

$c = \$7.90$

$c_{ud} = \text{MAX}[0, udS - X] = \$5.00$

$c_d = \$2.40$

$c_{dd} = \text{MAX}[0, d^2 S - X] = \$0$

Figure 8.16
Binomial call payoffs.

First, we need to convert the annual effective risk-free rate, 6%, into a semiannual rate, j. This is done below for $T = 3$ months, i.e., .25 years.[16]

$$\left(1 + \frac{j}{2/.25}\right)^{2/.25} = 1 + .06,$$

$$j/8 = .731\%.$$

Next, we need to convert the annualized standard deviation, $\sigma = \sqrt{.2} = .4472$, into the up and down variables of the option pricing formula. Using Eq. (8.25) we have

$$u = e^{\sigma\sqrt{T/n}} = e^{.4472\sqrt{.25/2}} = 1.1713,$$

$$d = e^{-\sigma\sqrt{T/n}} = e^{-.4472\sqrt{.25/2}} = .8538.$$

These numbers are needed to estimate the complimentary binomial probabilities in the binomial option pricing formula. The easiest way to solve for the value of a call option is to use the iterative approach illustrated in Figs. 8.12 and 8.13 and given algebraically in Eq. (8.18). For the particular example at hand, the call option payoffs are given in Fig. 8.16. First solve for c_u, the option value at the end of the first period, given that the stock price moved up. Using Eq. (8.18) we have

$$c_u = [p\, c_{uu} + (1 - p)c_{ud}] \div r_f,$$

where $p = (r_f - d)/(u - d)$

$$= (1.00731 - .8538)/(1.1713 - .8538) = .4835$$

and $1 - p = .5165.$

Therefore,

$$c_u = [.4835(23.60) + .5165(5.00)] \div 1.00731 = \$13.8916.$$

---

[16] See Eq. (8.24) or Appendix A at the back of the book.

A similar calculation reveals that

$$c_d = [p\, c_{du} + (1-p)c_{dd}] \div r = \$2.4000.$$

Now, the above results for c_u and c_d can be used to solve for the current call value, c

$$c = [p\, c_u + (1-p)c_d] \div r_f$$
$$= [.4835(13.8916) + .5165(2.4000)] \div 1.00731$$
$$= \$7.90.$$

From the same data the Black-Scholes call value was computed to be \$7.62. A two-period binomial approximation is reasonably accurate in this case. However, as the number of binomial trials is increased, the accuracy of the binomial approximation improves considerably. Figure 8.17 shows how the binomial approximation approaches the Black-Scholes answer as n increases. It is fairly easy to write a computer program to estimate the binomial pricing formula using either the iterative technique as illustrated above or Eq. (8.23).

2. An Example Using Real Data

Of the options listed in Table 8.1 only one, Digital Equipment, paid no dividend. For close-to-the-money calls on Digital Equipment, the assumptions of the Black-Scholes model are closely approximated. Therefore, we should be able to use it to give reasonable estimates of the price of the calls. Table 8.5 provides most of the information needed to value the call. The stock price, the exercise price, and the number of days to maturity are given for each option. The risk-free rate is estimated by using the average of the bid and ask quotes on U.S. Treasury bills of approximately the same maturity as the option. The only missing piece of information is the instanta-

Figure 8.17
The binomial option pricing closely approximates the Black-Scholes result.

Table 8.5 Data Needed to Price Digital Equipment Calls

Exercise price	Call Price, 4 Oct.			Closing stock price
	Oct.	Jan.	Apr.	
35	$11\frac{7}{8}$	$12\frac{7}{8}$	NA	$46\frac{3}{4}$
40	$6\frac{7}{8}$	8	NA	$46\frac{3}{4}$
45	$2\frac{5}{16}$	$4\frac{1}{4}$	6	$46\frac{3}{4}$
50	$\frac{1}{4}$	$1\frac{3}{4}$	3	$46\frac{3}{4}$
Maturity date	21 Oct.	20 Jan.	21 April	
Days to maturity	17	108	199	

Treasury Bill Rates on 4 Oct.				
Maturity date	Bid	Ask	Average	r_f
20 Oct., 1977	6.04	5.70	5.87	5.9
19 Jan., 1978	6.15	6.07	6.11	6.1
4 Apr., 1978	6.29	6.21	6.25⎫	6.2
2 May, 1978	6.20	6.12	6.16⎭	

neous variance of the stock price. Several different techniques have been suggested for estimating it (for example, see Latane and Rendleman [1976] or Parkinson [1977]). We shall use the implicit variance estimated from one call price in valuing the others. The implicit variance is calculated by simply using the actual call price and the four known exogenous parameters in the Black-Scholes formula, Eq. (8.26), to solve for an estimate of the instantaneous variance. We did this, using the January 45s on Digital Equipment, which were priced at $4\frac{1}{4}$ on October 4th. The estimate of instantaneous variance was approximately 7.84% (this is a standard deviation of 28%).

Substituting our estimates of the five parameters into the Black-Scholes valuation equation, we can estimate the price of the April 45s as follows:

$$c = SN(d_1) - e^{-r_f T} XN(d_2),$$

where

$$r_f = .062, \qquad T = 199/365, \qquad S = \$46.75, \qquad X = \$45, \qquad \sigma = .28,$$

$$d_1 = \frac{\ln(S/X) + r_f T}{\sigma\sqrt{T}} + \frac{1}{2}\sigma\sqrt{T}, \qquad d_2 = d_1 - \sigma\sqrt{T}.$$

The estimated call price turns out to be $5.58 while the actual call price is $6.00. If we repeat the procedure for the October 45s (now $r_f = .059$ and $T = 17/365$), the estimated call price is $2.28 while the actual price is $2.94. Since both of the estimated prices are lower than the actual prices, our estimate of the instantaneous variance is probably too low.

The above examples show how the Black-Scholes valuation model may be used to price call options on nondividend paying stocks. Roll [1977] and Geske [1979] have solved the problem of valuing American calls when the common stock is assumed to make known dividend payments before the option matures. However, the mathematics involved in the solution is beyond the level of this text.

3. Forming Hedge Portfolios

Suppose we wish to form a riskless hedge portfolio consisting of shares of Digital Equipment and call options written against them. If we own 100 shares, how many call options should be written? The answer is derived by noting that the Black-Scholes formula is

$$c = SN(d_1) - Xe^{-r_f T} N(d_2),$$

and its partial derivative with respect to a change in the stock price is[17]

$$\frac{\delta c}{\delta S} = N(d_1). \tag{8.27}$$

A riskless hedge portfolio will contain Q_S shares of stock and Q_c call options written against it. Its dollar return per unit time will be approximately

$$Q_S \left(\frac{dS}{dt}\right) - Q_c \left(\frac{dc}{dt}\right).$$

If we write $1/N(d_1)$, call options for each share of stock (i.e., $Q_S = 1$), the return on the hedge is approximately zero, as shown below

$$1 \cdot \left(\frac{dS}{dt}\right) - \frac{1}{dc/dS} \left(\frac{dc}{dt}\right) = 0.$$

If we use the Digital Equipment January 45s to hedge against 100 shares of Digital Equipment common stock, then we would have to write 100 times $1/N(d_1)$ options. Computing $N(d_1)$ we have

$$d_1 = \frac{\ln(S/X) + r_f T}{\sigma\sqrt{T}} + \frac{1}{2}\sigma\sqrt{T}$$

$$= \frac{\ln(46.75/45) + .062(199/365)}{.28\sqrt{199/365}} + \frac{1}{2}(.28)\sqrt{199/365}$$

$$= .451409.$$

And referring to Table 8.6 (p. 274), we see that

$$N(d_1) = .5 + .1741 = .6741.$$

Therefore we want to write 100 times $1/N(d_1)$, or 148.3 call options.

---

[17] Equation (8.27) is the exact solution even though the derivative is complicated by the fact that $N(d_1)$ is a function of S. The curious reader is referred to Galai and Masulis [1977] for the math.

It is important to bear in mind that this type of hedge is riskless only for small changes in the stock price. The hedge ratio must be adjusted whenever the stock price changes.

H. PRICING AMERICAN PUT OPTIONS

Knowledge of put-call parity, Eq. (8.5), and the call option pricing formula is sufficient to value a European put option. Unfortunately, American put options can be exercised before maturity. Therefore put-call parity doesn't hold for them and they must be evaluated directly.

All known solutions to the American put valuation problem involve computerized numerical methods. Solutions have been provided by Parkinson [1977], Brennan and Schwartz [1977], and Cox, Ross, and Rubinstein [1979]. Because we have already made use of the binomial approach to option pricing in Section F of this chapter, the easiest thing to do is show how it may be employed to value American puts on nondividend-paying common stock.

In order to provide a concrete example, suppose we know the following facts for a two-period American put:

$u = 1.2$ = the multiplicative upward movement in the stock price, $u > r_f > 1$,

$d = .6$ = the multiplicative downward movement in the stock price, $d < r_f$,

$r_f = 1.1$ = one plus the risk-free rate,

$X = \$50$ = the exercise price for the option,

$S = \$50$ = the current value of the stock,

P_0 = the present value of an American put.

Figure 8.18 shows the payoffs to the holder of an American put at the end of the first of two time periods. A hedge portfolio can be formed by purchasing a fraction, m, of the risky asset and simultaneously buying a put option written against it. The hedge portfolio and its payoffs are given in Fig. 8.19. By equating the end-of-period payoffs, we can solve for the hedging fraction, m, which gives a risk-free hedge.

$$muS + P_u = mdS + P_d,$$

$$m = \frac{P_d - P_u}{S(u - d)} = \frac{20 - 0}{50(1.2 - .6)} = .667. \tag{8.28}$$

MAX$[0, X - uS] = \$0$

q

P_0

$1 - q$

MAX$[0, X - dS] = \$20$

Figure 8.18
Payoffs to the American put after one period.

Figure 8.19
One-period hedge portfolio payoffs.

The numerical payoffs from using a hedge consisting of two-thirds of a share of stock, and one put option are given in Fig. 8.19. This risk-free hedge pays $40 regardless of whether the stock price moves up (to $60) or down (to $30). Also note, that the proper hedge does not depend on investors' subjective probabilities (q and $1 - q$ in Fig. 8.18) of an upward or downward movement in the stock price.

Next, we can solve for the hedging probabilities (p and $1 - p$) by multiplying the current price of the hedge portfolio by one plus the risk-free rate and equating this to the end-of-period payoff

$$r_f(mS + P_0) = muS + P_u.$$

Substituting the value of m (Eq. (8.28)) into this equation and solving for the current put price, P_0, gives

$$P_0 = \left[\left(\frac{u - r_f}{u - d}\right) P_d + \left(\frac{r_f - d}{u - d}\right) P_u\right] \div r_f,$$

or

$$P_0 = [pP_d + (1 - p)P_u] \div r_f, \tag{8.29}$$

where p and $(1 - p)$ are the hedging probabilities:

$$p = \frac{u - r_f}{u - d}, \qquad (1 - p) = \frac{r_f - d}{u - d}. \tag{8.30}$$

This one-period put valuation equation can easily be extended recursively into a multi-period framework to derive a binomial pricing equation for European puts similar to that for European calls (Eq. 8.23). However, our objective in this section is to price American puts which may be exercised before maturity. Figure 8.20 shows

Figure 8.20
Payoffs for a two-period American put.

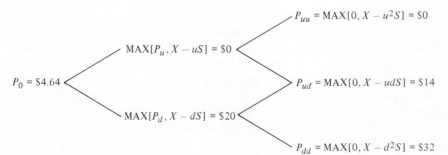

the payoffs for a two-period American put. Note that the problem is complicated by the fact that the put holder may decide to exercise his or her option at the end of the first period if the value from exercising, say $X - dS$, is greater than the market value of the put, P_d. Given the numbers chosen for our example, this is exactly what will happen. For example, use the one-period put formula to evaluate P_u and P_d, the put values at the end of the first period. First, we know that the hedging probability is

$$p = \frac{u - r_f}{u - d} = \frac{1.2 - 1.1}{1.2 - .6} = .167.$$

Substituting this into Eq. (8.29) we have

$$P_u = [p\,P_{ud} + (1 - p)P_{uu}] \div r_f$$
$$= [.167(14) + .833(0)] \div 1.1 = 2.12$$

and

$$P_d = [p\,P_{dd} + (1 - p)P_{ud}] \div r_f$$
$$= [.167(32) + .833(14)] \div 1.1 = 15.45.$$

Given that the stock price has fallen to $dS = \$30$ at the end of the first period, a rational investor can either exercise the option and receive $X - dS = \$50 - \$30 = \$20$ or hold it, in which case it is worth \$15.45. Obviously it is better to exercise early and not hold the option to the end of the second period. This fact makes it impossible to come up with a closed-form solution to the American put valuation problem. However, a computer program which uses an iterative technique starting with the set of possible final payoffs in periods and working backwards, as illustrated in Fig. 8.20, can solve for the present value of American puts.

The opportunity to exercise early makes an American put option have a value equal to or greater than its European counterpart. For the numerical example we have been using, the put option is worth \$4.64 if it is an American put and only \$3.95 if it is a European put.

I. EXTENSIONS OF THE OPTION PRICING MODEL

All of the models discussed so far have assumed that the stock price is generated by a continuous stochastic process with a constant variance. Changes in the assumptions about the distribution of stock prices which change the model are discussed in part 1 of this section. There are also various special circumstances (such as unusual types of contracts) which cause us to consider alterations in the model parameter definitions. For example, the exercise price might be a random variable or it may change in a predetermined fashion over the life of the option. Extensions of this type are discussed in part 2.

1. Changing the Distributional Assumptions

All changes in the distributional assumptions involve either the continuity assumption or the constant variance assumption. Black and Scholes assumed that stock prices are generated according to the following differential equation:

$$\frac{dS}{S} = \mu dt + \sigma dz, \tag{8.31}$$

where

μ = the instantaneous expected rate of return (measuring the drift on the random walk of the stock price through time),

σ = the instantaneous standard deviation of the rate of return, assumed constant,

dt = a small increment in time,

dz = a Wiener process.

If the stock price does not follow a continuous path through time, then it follows either a pure jump process or a mixed diffusion-jump model.

The *pure jump model* was introduced by Cox and Ross [1975]. The stock price path through time is described as a deterministic movement upon which are superimposed discrete jumps. It can be written as

$$\frac{dS}{S} = \mu dt + (k - 1)d\pi$$

$$\tag{8.32}$$

$$= \mu dt + \begin{array}{c} \nearrow^{\lambda dt} \quad k - 1 \\ \searrow_{1 - \lambda dt} \quad 0 \end{array}$$

where

π = a continuous-time Poisson process,

λ = the intensity of the process,

$k - 1$ = the jump amplitude.

Equation (8.32) says that the percentage jump on the stock price is composed of a drift term, μdt, and a term $d\pi$ which with probability λdt will jump the percentage stock change to $k - 1$ and with probability $1 - \lambda dt$ will do nothing.

The *mixed diffusion-jump model,* developed by Merton [1976], is something of a mixture of the continuous and pure jump models. Its plausibility comes from the intuition that stock prices seem to have small, almost continuous movements most of the time but sometimes experience large discrete jumps when important new information arrives.

The next three models relax the Black-Scholes assumption that the instantaneous standard deviation is constant through time.

The *constant elasticity of variance model* was derived by Cox [1975] and Cox and Ross [1976]. Its mathematical statement is

$$dS = \mu S dt + \sigma S^{\alpha/2} dz,$$ (8.33)

where

α = the elasticity factor ($0 \leq \alpha < 2$).

Note that if $\alpha = 2$, the constant elasticity of variance model reduces to the Black-Scholes model. For $\alpha < 2$ the standard deviation of the return distribution moves inversely with the level of the stock price. The intuitive appeal of such an argument is that every firm has fixed costs which have to be met regardless of the level of its income. A decrease in income will decrease the value of the firm and simultaneously increase its riskiness. Either operating or financial leverage may explain the inverse relationship between variance and stock price.

The *compound option model* of Geske [1977] shows how to price options on options. This may seem to be a complex abstraction until one considers that the equity in a levered firm is really an option on the assets of the firm. An example of this was given in Section B of this chapter. A CBOE listed call option is, therefore, an option on the firm's equity which in turn is an option on the firm's assets. Thus a CBOE call option is really an option on an option. In Geske's model a compound call option is a function of seven variables instead of the usual five variables found in the Black-Scholes model

$$c = f(S, X, r_f, T, \sigma, D/V, t_B)$$

The two new variables are D/V, the ratio of the face value of debt to the market value of the firm, and t_B, the time to maturity of the firm's debt. Under certain conditions the compound option model can be made equal to the constant elasticity of variance model.

The *displaced diffusion model* by Rubinstein [1981a] focuses on the assets side of a firm's balance sheet and divides it into a portfolio of riskless assets and risky assets. Like Geske's model it is a compound option formula and requires two parameters in addition to those of the Black-Scholes model. They are (1) the instantaneous volatility of the rate of return on the firm's risky assets and (2) the proportion of total assets invested in risky assets.

Section J of this chapter discusses the empirical evidence on option pricing formulae. Most of the research along these lines is very recent and, therefore, the conclusions are tentative. Yet the evidence seems to provide support for the extensions of the Black-Scholes model over the original model.

2. Options to Value Special Situations

What happens to the value of an option if the exercise price is stochastic, if the stock price changes in a deterministic fashion, if the risk-free rate is stochastic, or if the payouts are truncated in unusual ways?

Fisher [1978] and Margrabe [1978] solve the problem of valuing an option when the exercise price is uncertain. An example of this problem is the option to exchange one asset for another. One example of this type of problem is a stock exchange offer between two unlevered firms.[18] Firm A tenders for the shares of firm B (a much smaller firm) by offering one of its own shares currently priced at, let's say, $S_A = \$50$ for one of firm B's shares priced at $S_B = \$30$. The offer might be good for 30 days. The shareholders of firm B have received an option to exchange one asset for another. The exercise price on the call option is the value of firm B's stock, a random variable.

Margrabe [1978] and Fisher [1978] show that the value of an option to exchange one asset for another depends on the standard deviations of the two assets and the correlation between them. Their formula is given below:

$$C(S_A, S_B, T) = S_A N(d_1) - S_B N(d_2),$$

where

$$d_1 = \frac{\ln(S_A/S_B) + V^2 T}{V\sqrt{T}},$$

$$d_2 = d_1 - V\sqrt{T},$$

$$V^2 = V_A^2 - 2\rho_{AB} V_A V_B + V_B^2.$$

Note that V^2 is the instantaneous proportional variance of the change in the ratio of the asset prices, S_A/S_B, and ρ_{AB} is the instantaneous correlation between them. The option is less (more) valuable if the assets are positively (negatively) correlated.

Another interesting option is the *truncated option* discussed by Johnson [1981]. Examples of a truncated option are an option on a firm consisting of two divisions, an option entitling the owner to a choice between two risky assets, and competing tender offers. Consider the case of an option on a firm with two risky divisions. Rubinstein's [1981a] displaced diffusion model is a special case because it considers an option on a firm consisting of one riskless and one risky asset. Here we are examining the value of an option on a portfolio of two risky assets. If A_1 and A_2 are the lognormally distributed returns of the two divisions, the payoff to this type of truncated option at maturity is

$$C = \text{MAX}[0, A_1 + A_2 - X].$$

The actual solution is too complex for this text; however, the interested reader is referred to Johnson [1981] for the mathematics of this and three other truncated option cases. One of the implications is that an option on a portfolio of risky assets is less valuable than the corresponding portfolio of options.

Merton [1973a] solved the problem of pricing options when the value of the underlying asset and the risk-free rate are both stochastic. Option problems which as yet have no known solution are (1) options with stochastic variances and (2) options with random maturity dates.

---

[18] If the firms were levered the problem would be much the same except that we would have to deal with options on options.

J. EMPIRICAL EVIDENCE ON THE OPTION PRICING MODEL

Tests of the option pricing model (OPM), like those of the capital asset pricing model (CAPM), are faced with the problem that two hypotheses are being tested simultaneously: first that the model is valid, and second, that the market is efficient. A common procedure is to employ the pricing model to identify over- or underpriced securities, then to form trading rules designed to earn abnormally high risk-adjusted returns. If no profitable trading rule exists, the market is said to be efficient. If profitable trading rules are discovered, the market is presumed to be inefficient. Another procedure is to compare the ability of different option pricing models to explain market prices in an unbiased fashion.

1. The Black-Scholes Study

The earliest empirical test of the Black-Scholes OPM was done by Black and Scholes themselves [1973]. They used price data from the over-the-counter option market (OTCOM) for contracts written on 545 securities between 1966 and 1969. Options traded on the OTCOM did not have standardized exercise prices or maturity dates; however, they were "dividend protected."[19] Whenever the common stock went ex-dividend, the exercise price on outstanding options was lowered by the amount of the dividend.

The secondary market in nonstandardized OTCOM options was virtually nonexistent. Therefore, Black and Scholes adopted a test procedure which used the OPM to generate the expected prices of each option on each trading day. By comparing the model prices with actual prices at the issuing date they divided options into those "overvalued" and those "undervalued" by the market. For each option bought (if undervalued) or sold (if overvalued), a perfectly risk-free hedged portfolio was formed by selling or buying shares in the underlying stock. The excess dollar return on the hedged portfolio was defined as

$$\Delta V_H - V_H r_f \Delta t$$

$$\left(\Delta C - \frac{\delta C}{\delta S} \Delta S \right) - \left(C - \frac{\delta C}{\delta S} S \right) r_f \, \Delta t.$$

The first expression is the dollar return on the hedged portfolio, ΔV_H, where ΔC is the change in the value of a call option and where $\delta C / \delta S = N(d_1)$ is the number of shares which is multiplied by ΔS, the change in the price per share. The second expression, which is subtracted from the first in order to obtain *excess* returns, is the dollar return on a risk-free position. Theoretically, the difference between the

---

[19] Of course, there is no such thing as perfect dividend protection. For example, if shareholders were to issue a liquidating dividend equal to the value of the firm's assets, the value of common stock would fall to zero, and no amount of dividend protection could keep the value of a call option from falling to zero.

two terms should be equal to zero because the portfolio is chosen to be a risk-free hedge. Therefore, the portfolio should have zero beta and earn the risk-free rate.

The option position was maintained throughout the life of the option. The risk-free hedge was adjusted daily by buying or selling shares of stock in order to maintain the proportion $\delta C/\delta S = N(d_1)$. At the end of each day, the hedged position was assumed to be liquidated so that the daily dollar return could be calculated. The option position was then immediately reestablished and a new hedge position constructed.

Black and Scholes computed the systematic risk of the hedged portfolio by regressing its excess returns against a market index. The results verified that it has a beta which is not significantly different from zero (even though the hedge was not adjusted continuously).

Their results showed that (given *ex post* estimates of actual variances of the returns on the underlying stock over the holding period), in the absence of transaction costs, buying "undervalued" contracts and selling "overvalued" contracts at model prices produced insignificant average profits. However, when *ex ante* variances were estimated from past stock price histories, buying "undervalued" contracts and selling "overvalued" contracts at model prices resulted in significant negative excess portfolio returns. The same procedure, when repeated using market prices, yielded substantial positive excess returns. These results indicate that the market uses more than past price histories to estimate the *ex ante* instantaneous variance of stock returns. But when actual variances are used in the model, it matches actual option prices quite accurately.

When the transaction costs of trading in options were included, the implied profits vanished. Therefore, even though the option market does not appear to be efficient before transaction costs are taken into account, there is no opportunity for traders to take advantage of this inefficiency.

2. The Galai Study

Galai [1977] used data from the Chicago Board Options Exchange (CBOE) for each option traded between April 26, 1973 and November 30, 1973. Option contracts on the CBOE have standardized striking prices and expiration dates. Although the options are not "dividend protected," the standardization of contracts has resulted in a substantial volume of trading and lower transaction costs.

The fact that option prices are listed every day allowed Galai to extend the Black-Scholes procedure. Black and Scholes established an initial option position and then maintained a hedge position by buying or selling shares of stock. They could not adjust the option position because they did not have market prices for the options. They were unable to exploit all the information available in the daily deviation of the option's actual prices from the model prices.

Galai duplicated the Black-Scholes tests and extended them by adjusting the option position each day. Undervalued options were bought and overvalued options were sold at the end of each day, and, in addition, the hedged position was maintained by buying or selling the appropriate number of shares of common stock. Galai used two tests: (1) an *ex post* test which assumed that traders can use the closing price on day t to determine whether the option is over- or undervalued and that they could transact at the closing prices on day t, and (2) a more realistic *ex ante* test which assumed that the trading rule is determined from closing prices on day t but the transaction is not executed until the closing price at day $t + 1$. Both tests used various estimates of the variance of common stock rates of return which were based on data gathered *before* the trading rule was executed.

The main results of the test are:

1. Using *ex post* hedge returns, trading strategies (in the absence of transaction costs) which were based on the Black-Scholes model earned significant excess returns.

2. Given 1% transaction costs, the excess returns vanished.

3. The results were robust to changes in various parameters such as the risk-free rate or instantaneous variance.

4. The results are sensitive to dividend adjustment. Trading in options written on common stocks paying high dividends yielded lower profits than trading in options written on low-dividend stocks. This result, however, simply reflects the fact that the Black-Scholes formula assumes no dividend payments.

5. Deviations from the model's specifications led to worse performance.

6. Tests of spreading strategies yielded results similar to those produced by the hedging strategies described above.

Taken together, the two studies mentioned above seem to indicate that the Black-Scholes OPM predicts option prices very well indeed. So well in fact, that excess returns can be earned in the absence of transaction costs. However, once transaction costs are introduced into the trading strategies, excess profits vanish. This confirms the usual result that nonmember traders cannot beat the market. Prices are efficiently determined down to the level of transaction costs.

3. Klemkosky and Resnick on Put-Call Parity

Since June of 1977 standardized put options have been offered on the CBOE. Klemkosky and Resnick [1979] collected continuous transactions data for put and call options for each of 15 companies for 12 days (one each month) during the July 1977 to June 1978 interval. A total of 606 long and short hedge portfolios were constructed. The put, call, and underlying stock had to have traded within one minute of each other. The hedge portfolios were based on the following inequalities:

$$(C - P - S)(1 + r_f) + X + \sum_{j=1}^{n} D_j(1 + r_f)^{\delta j} \leq 0 \quad \text{long hedge,}$$

$$(S + P - C)(1 + r_f) - X - \sum_{j=1}^{n} D_j(1 + r_f)^{\delta j} \leq 0 \quad \text{short hedge.}$$

These hedges are based on the gross terminal profit from engaging in a long or short hedge constructed from American options and the stock. The terms are as defined in the put-call parity equation (Eq. 8.5) where r_f is the risk-free rate of return covering the life of the option. The last term in each equation is the terminal value of the dividends where D_j is assumed to be the known nonstochastic dividend paid during the life of the option and δ_j is the length of time between the dividend and the expiration date of the options. The strongest assumption, of course, is that dividends were nonstochastic. However, the virtue of a test based on put-call parity is that it is not necessary to make any assumptions about which version of the option pricing model is best. If put-call parity holds, then there are no arbitrage profits and the market is efficient, regardless of how options are valued.

Klemkosky and Resnick find their results to be consistent with put-call parity and with efficiency for the registered options markets. If $20 is the minimum transactions cost for a member firm to take a hedge position, then only 27% of the hedges were profitable. If $60 is the minimum transactions cost for a nonmember investor, then only 7% of the hedges were profitable.

4. The Bhattacharya Study

If one is empirically testing the null hypothesis that observed market prices and the Black-Scholes theoretical prices exhibit no systematic differences, the null hypothesis can be rejected for any of three reasons:

1. Inputs to the Black-Scholes model have been incorrectly measured, or

2. the options market is inefficient, or

3. the mathematical structure of the Black-Scholes model is correct.

Bhattacharya [1980] avoids difficulties (2) and (3) by creating hypothetical hedge portfolios based on simulated B-S option values. If a neutral hedge is adjusted daily (continuously would be even better) the excess return should be zero if the B-S formula is correct. The only observed data inputs are the stock price, the stock price variance estimated directly from stock data during the life of the hedge, and the risk-free rate. Bhattacharya's results show no operationally significant mispricing by the B-S formula except for at-the-money options very close to maturity where the B-S model overvalues options.

5. The MacBeth/Merville and Beckers Studies

Using CBOE daily closing prices between December 31, 1975, and December 31, 1976, for all call options listed for six major companies (AT&T, Avon, Kodak, Exxon, IBM, and Xerox), MacBeth and Merville [1979] tested the Black-Scholes model to see whether or not it over- or underpriced options. Also [1980], using the same data set, they tested the Black-Scholes model against an alternative constant elasticity of variance model (derived by Cox [1975] and Cox and Ross [1976]).

In their first paper [1979], MacBeth and Merville estimate the implied standard deviation of the rate of return for the underlying common stock by employing the Black-Scholes model Eq. (8.26). Then, by assuming that the B-S model correctly prices at-the-money options with at least ninety days to expiration they are able to estimate the percent deviation of observed call prices from B-S call prices. They conclude that:

1. The Black-Scholes model prices are on average less (greater) than market prices for in-the-money (out-of-the-money) options.

2. The extent to which the Black-Scholes model underprices (overprices) an in-the-money (out-of-the-money) option increases with the extent to which the option is in-the-money (out-of-the-money), and decreases as the time to expiration decreases.

3. The Black-Scholes model prices of out-of-the-money options with less than 90 days to expiration are, on the average, greater than market prices; but there does not appear to be any consistent relationship between the extent to which these options are overpriced by the B-S model and the degree to which these options are out-of-the-money or the time to expiration.

The second MacBeth and Merville paper [1980] compares the Black-Scholes model against the constant elasticity of variance (CEV) model. The primary difference between the two models is that the B-S model assumes the variance of returns on the underlying asset remains constant while the constant elasticity of variance model assumes the variance changes when the stock price does. Empirical evidence on the relationship between the level of stock prices and the rate of return variance is somewhat mixed. Blattberg and Gonedes [1974] suggest that the variance may change randomly through time. Rosenberg [1973] finds that it follows an autoregressive scheme. And Black [1976] observes that the variance of returns varies inversely with stock prices. For the six securities which MacBeth and Merville studied, the variance relative to the stock price seems to decrease as the stock price rises. Using their estimates of the constant elasticity of variance, they find that the Cox model fits the data better than the Black-Scholes model. Their empirical results are also consistent with the compound option model of Geske [1979].

Beckers [1980] also compares the constant elasticity of variance model with the Black-Scholes model. First, however, he uses 1253 daily observations (Sept. 18, 1972 to Sept. 7, 1977) for 47 different stocks to test the Black-Scholes assumption that the stock variance is not a function of the stock price. The data rejects this hypothesis. The variance was an inverse function of the stock price for 38 of the 47 stocks—a result consistent with the constant elasticity of variance model. When testing simulated Black-Scholes call prices against the constant elasticity of variance prices, Beckers found that the CEV model gives higher option prices than B-S for in-the-money options. This is consistent with the empirical work of MacBeth and Merville, who found that the B-S model undervalues in-the-money options.

6. Rubinstein-Nonparametric Tests of Alternative Option Pricing Models

The five extensions of the option pricing model, discussed in Section I, have been compared by Rubinstein [1981b]. He used the MDR (market data report) data-base of the Chicago Board of Options Exchange which has been consolidated into the Berkeley Options Data-base. The data is a time-stamped record, to the nearest second, including option trade prices, quotes, and volume, coupled with the stock price at the corresponding time during the day.

Rubinstein's experimental design was to select matched pairs of options, for example all options belonging to the same stock, observed on the same day during the same constant stock price interval, having the same exercise price, and falling within a predetermined range of out-of-the-money values (e.g., $S/X = .75$ to $.85$). Pairing in this case was on the basis of different times to maturity. For example, one option might fall within the 71 to 120 day range and another on the 171 to 220 day range. There were actually 373 of these particular matched pairs (overall there were 19,094 pairs based on differences on time to expiration and 12,239 pairs based on equal time to maturity but different exercise prices). If the Black-Scholes formula is unbiased there should be a 50–50 chance that the implied option variance for the shorter maturity option is higher than for the longer maturity option. In fact, 94.1% of the shorter maturity options had higher variance. Thus, in this case the Black-Scholes formula could be rejected.

Nonparametric tests of options paired either by differences in time to maturity or in exercise prices were performed for two time periods (1) August 21, 1976, to October 21, 1977, and (2) October 24, 1977, to August 31, 1978. Two interesting conclusions were found. First, if the time to maturity is held constant, then the Black-Scholes model is biased but the direction of the bias is different in the two time periods which were investigated. During the 76–77 interval in-the-money options were undervalued by the Black-Scholes formula. This confirms the work of MacBeth and Merville [1979]. The direction of the bias is reversed during the 77–78 period. No one knows why the bias should reverse. The second conclusion was that although some of the alternative option pricing models (e.g., the displaced diffusion model) were more compatible with the empirical results, none of them were superior in both time periods.

7. Summary of the Empirical Work

Studies which have used different versions of the option pricing model to try to find economically exploitable biases have been unsuccessful in doing so when transactions costs were deducted from trading rule profits. From this one can conclude that the option pricing models fit observed prices well in an economic sense. Also the results are consistent with market efficiency.

On the other hand, there are statistically significant biases in the Black-Scholes model. This suggests that some alternative (perhaps composite) model can do better.

Much work remains to be done in testing the OPM. Rubinstein's [1981b] study suggests that none of the alternative models (the jump model, the mixed diffusion-jump model, the constant elasticity of variance model, the compound option model, or the displaced diffusion model) can explain all of the biases all of the time.

Table 8.6   Areas Under the Normal Curve

Areas Under the Standard Normal Distribution Function $\int_0^z f(z)\,dz.$

z	.00	.01	.02	.03	.04	.05	.06	.07	.08	.09
0.0	.0000	.0040	.0080	.0120	.0160	.0199	.0239	.0279	.0319	.0359
0.1	.0398	.0438	.0478	.0517	.0557	.0596	.0636	.0675	.0714	.0753
0.2	.0793	.0832	.0871	.0910	.0948	.0987	.1026	.1064	.1103	.1141
0.3	.1179	.1217	.1255	.1293	.1331	.1368	.1406	.1443	.1480	.1517
0.4	.1554	.1591	.1628	.1664	.1700	.1736	.1772	.1808	.1844	.1879
0.5	.1915	.1950	.1985	.2019	.2054	.2088	.2123	.2157	.2190	.2224
0.6	.2257	.2291	.2324	.2357	.2389	.2422	.2454	.2486	.2517	.2549
0.7	.2580	.2611	.2642	.2673	.2704	.2734	.2764	.2794	.2823	.2852
0.8	.2881	.2910	.2939	.2967	.2995	.3023	.3051	.3078	.3106	.3133
0.9	.3159	.3186	.3212	.3238	.3264	.3289	.3315	.3340	.3365	.3389
1.0	.3413	.3438	.3461	.3485	.3508	.3531	.3554	.3577	.3599	.3621
1.1	.3643	.3665	.3686	.3708	.3729	.3749	.3770	.3790	.3810	.3830
1.2	.3849	.3869	.3888	.3907	.3925	.3944	.3962	.3980	.3997	.4015
1.3	.4032	.4049	.4066	.4082	.4099	.4115	.4131	.4147	.4162	.4177
1.4	.4192	.4207	.4222	.4236	.4251	.4265	.4279	.4292	.4306	.4319
1.5	.4332	.4345	.4357	.4370	.4382	.4394	.4406	.4418	.4429	.4441
1.6	.4452	.4463	.4474	.4484	.4495	.4505	.4515	.4525	.4535	.4545
1.7	.4554	.4564	.4573	.4582	.4591	.4599	.4608	.4616	.4625	.4633
1.8	.4641	.4649	.4656	.4664	.4671	.4678	.4686	.4693	.4699	.4706
1.9	.4713	.4719	.4726	.4732	.4738	.4744	.4750	.4756	.4761	.4767
2.0	.4772	.4778	.4783	.4788	.4793	.4798	.4803	.4808	.4812	.4817
2.1	.4821	.4826	.4830	.4834	.4838	.4842	.4846	.4850	.4854	.4857
2.2	.4861	.4864	.4868	.4871	.4875	.4878	.4881	.4884	.4887	.4890
2.3	.4893	.4896	.4898	.4901	.4904	.4906	.4909	.4911	.4913	.4916
2.4	.4918	.4920	.4922	.4925	.4927	.4929	.4931	.4932	.4934	.4936
2.5	.4938	.4940	.4941	.4943	.4945	.4946	.4948	.4949	.4951	.4952
2.6	.4953	.4955	.4956	.4957	.4959	.4960	.4961	.4962	.4963	.4964
2.7	.4965	.4966	.4967	.4968	.4969	.4970	.4971	.4972	.4973	.4974
2.8	.4974	.4975	.4976	.4977	.4977	.4978	.4979	.4979	.4980	.4981
2.9	.4981	.4982	.4982	.4982	.4984	.4984	.4985	.4985	.4986	.4986
3.0	.4987	.4987	.4987	.4988	.4988	.4989	.4989	.4989	.4990	.4990

SUMMARY _____

Closed form solutions to the option pricing problem have been developed relatively recently. Yet their potential for application to problems in finance is tremendous. Almost all financial assets are really contingent claims. For example, common stock is really a call option on the value of the assets of a levered firm. Similarly, risky debt, insurance, warrants, and convertible debt may all be thought of as options. Also, option pricing theory has implications for the capital structure of the firm, for investment policy, for mergers and acquisitions, for spinoffs, and for dividend policy. Much of the rest of this book is devoted to exploring applications of the theories discussed so far: state-preference theory, the capital asset pricing model, arbitrage pricing theory, and option pricing. As we shall see, option pricing plays a major role in shaping our thinking.

We have established that option prices are functions of five parameters: the price of the underlying security, its instantaneous variance, the exercise price on the option, the time to maturity, and the risk-free rate. Only one of these variables, the instantaneous variance, is not directly observable. Even more interesting is the fact that the option price does not depend on (1) individual risk preferences or (2) the expected rate of return on the underlying asset. Both results follow from the fact that option prices are determined from pure arbitrage conditions available to the investor who establishes perfectly hedged portfolios.

Much remains to be done to empirically test the validity of the options pricing model in general and of various versions of it such as the Black-Scholes model, the jump diffusion model, the constant elasticity of variance model, etc. The empirical results thus far tend to accept the options pricing model in the sense that differences between the prices it predicts and observed market prices are not economically significant. On the other hand, statistically significant departures from the Black-Scholes model have been discovered but as yet no single superior model has been found.

PROBLEM SET

8.1 What is the value of a European call option with an exercise price of $40 and a maturity date six months from now if the stock price is $28, the instantaneous variance of the stock price is .5, and the risk-free rate is 6%?

8.2 What is the price of a European put if the price of the underlying common stock is $20, the exercise price is $20, the risk-free rate is 8%, the variance of the price of the underlying stock is .36 (that is, $\sigma = .6$), and the option expires six months from now?

8.3

a) Graph changes in wealth, ΔW, vs. changes in the price of the underlying security, ΔS, for a portfolio where you sell one call option and sell one put option (both with the same X, T, σ, and r_f). Would this be a good strategy if you have inside information which leads you to expect the instantaneous variance of the underlying security will increase?

b) Graph ΔW against ΔS for a portfolio where you buy a call and sell a put. Would this be a good strategy if you expect an increase in the instantaneous variance?

8.4 Assume you are a senior financial analyst at Morgan Stanley. You are asked by a client to determine the maximum price he or she should be willing to pay to purchase Honeywell call options having an exercise price of $45 and expiring in 156 days. The current price of Honeywell stock is $44\frac{3}{8}$, the riskless interest rate is 7%, and the estimated rate of return variance of the stock is $\sigma^2 = .0961$. No dividends are expected to be declared over the next six months.

8.5 Given two European put options which are identical except that the exercise price of the first put, X_1, is greater than the exercise price of the second put, X_2, use first-order stochastic dominance and equilibrium in a perfect capital market to prove that one of the puts must have a higher price than the other. Which put option has the higher price? [*Hint:* Determine the relevant states of the world.]

8.6 Consider a firm with current value of $5,000,000 and outstanding debt of $4,000,000 which matures in 10 years. The firm's asset rate-of-return variance is .5. The interest on the debt is paid at maturity, and the firm has a policy of not paying cash dividends. Use the OPM to determine the change in the prices of the firm's debt and equity if there is an unanticipated rise in the rate of inflation of 5% which raises the riskless nominal interest rate from 5% to 10%. Which class of security holders benefits from the rise in R_f?

8.7 Figure 8.3 graphs the value of a call option as a function of the value of the underlying stock. Graph the value of a call option (vertical axis) against

a) σ, the instantaneous standard deviation of the returns on the underlying asset;

b) R_f, the risk-free rate;

c) T, the time to maturity.

8.8 What are the conditions under which an American put would be exercised early on a stock that pays no dividends?

8.9 Consider the case of a firm with secured debt, subordinated debentures, and common stock, where the secured debt and subordinated debentures mature at the same time. Find the equations for the values of the three classes of securities using the OPM framework. Assume no dividends or interest payments prior to the debt's maturity and a lognormal distribution of the future value of the firm's assets, $\tilde{V}_t$, as shown in Fig. Q8.9, where V = market value

Figure Q8.9

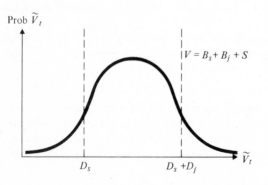

V = market value of the firm
S = market value of the stock
B_s = market value of the senior debt
B_j = market value of the junior debt
D_s = face value of the senior debt
D_j = face value of the junior debt

of the firm, S = market value of the stock, B_S = market value of the senior debt, B_j = market value of the junior debt, D_S = face value of the senior debt, D_j = face value of the junior debt.

8.10 Why will the value of an American put always be greater than or equal to the value of a corresponding European put?

8.11 Options listed for Digital Equipment were used in the text as an example of option price estimation using implicit variance. The implicit variance from the January 45 option resulted in estimated call prices lower than actual call prices for the April 45 and October 45 options. Assuming the Black-Scholes OPM is correct, and that all assumptions of the model are met in the marketplace: What hedge (i.e., riskless) portfolio can be formed to make arbitrage profits with Digital Equipment April 45 options?

8.12 The share price of Honeybear Inc. is \$44.75. Call options written on Honeybear have an exercise price of \$40 and mature in 71 days. The risk-free rate is $6\frac{1}{2}\%$, and the instantaneous price variance of Honeybear is 9.61% (that is, $\sigma = .31$). What actions must you take in order to create a perfect hedge in the following situations:

a) If you own 100 shares of Honeybear stock, how many call options must you buy (sell)?

b) If you own five put option contracts, how many shares of stock do you need?

c) If you own one call contract, how many put contracts do you need?

8.13 After a call contract is created, the outcome must be a zero-sum game; that is, the call writer may win or lose $\$N$, but the call buyer will experience an opposite return of exactly $\$N$ and consequently their aggregate payoff is zero. Given this fact, can you explain how they could both enter into the contract anticipating a positive return?

8.14 Suppose that the government passes a usury law which prohibits lending at more than 5% interest but normal market rates are much higher due to inflation. You have a customer, a Ms. Olsen, who wants to borrow at 20% and can put up her \$100,000 store as collateral. Rather than refusing her request you decide to create a 5-year contract with the following terms: You hold title to the store and receive the right to sell her the store for $\$X$ at the end of 5 years. If you decide to sell she *must* buy. In return you give her \$80,000 in cash (the amount she wants to borrow) and the right to buy the store from you for $\$X$ at the end of 5 years. How can this contract provide you with a 20% annual rate of return on the \$80,000?

REFERENCES

Beckers, S., "The Constant Elasticity of Variance Model and Its Implications for Option Pricing," *Journal of Finance,* June 1980, 661–673.

———, "A Note on Estimating the Parameters of the Diffusion-Jump Model of Stock Returns," *Journal of Financial and Quantitative Analysis,* March 1981, 127–139.

Bhattacharya, Mihir, "Empirical Properties of the Black-Scholes Formula Under Ideal Conditions," *Journal of Financial and Quantitative Analysis,* December 1980, 1081–1106.

Black, F., "Studies of Stock Price Volatility Changes." Proceedings of the Meetings of the American Statistical Association, Business and Economics Statistics Section, Chicago, 1976.

———, and M. Scholes, "The Valuation of Option Contracts and a Test of Market Efficiency," *The Journal of Finance,* May 1972, 399–418.

————, "The Pricing of Options and Corporate Liabilities," *Journal of Political Economy,* May/June 1973, 637–659.

Blattberg, R., and N. Gonedes, "A Comparison of the Stable and Student Distributions as Stochastic Models for Stock Prices," *Journal of Business,* 1974, 244–280.

Boyle, P., and D. Emmanuel, "Discretely Adjusted Option Hedges," *Journal of Financial Economics,* September 1980, 259–282.

Brennan, M., and E. Schwartz, "The Valuation of American Put Options," *The Journal of Finance,* May 1977, 449–462.

Chiras, D., and S. Manaster, "The Informational Content of Option Prices and a Test of Market Efficiency," *Journal of Financial Economics,* June/September 1978, 213–234.

Cox, J., "Notes on Option Pricing I: Constant Elasticity of Diffusions." Unpublished draft, Stanford University, September 1975.

————, and S. Ross, "The Pricing of Options for Jump Processes," working Paper No. 2-75, University of Pennsylvania, April 1975.

————, "The Valuation of Options for Alternative Stochastic Processes," *Journal of Financial Economics,* January/March 1976, 145–166.

————, and M. Rubinstein, "Option Pricing: A Simplified Approach," *Journal of Financial Economics,* September 1979, 229–263.

Cox, J., and M. Rubinstein, *Options Markets,* Prentice-Hall, Englewood Cliffs, N.J., forthcoming.

Feller, W., *An Introduction to Probability Theory and Its Applications,* Vol. 1, 3rd edition, John Wiley and Sons, New York, 1968.

Finnerty, J., "The Chicago Board Options Exchange and Market Efficiency," *Journal of Financial and Quantitative Analysis,* March 1978, 29–38.

Fisher, S., "Call Option Pricing When the Exercise Price is Uncertain and the Valuation of Index Bonds," *The Journal of Finance,* March 1978, 169–186.

Galai, D., "Tests of Market Efficiency of the Chicago Board Options Exchange," *Journal of Business,* April 1977, 167–197.

————, "On the Boness and Black-Scholes Models for the Valuation of Call Options," *Journal of Financial and Quantitative Analysis,* March 1978, 15–27.

————, and R. Masulis, "The Option Pricing Model and the Risk Factor of Stock," *Journal of Financial Economics,* January/March 1976, 53–82.

Garman, M., "An Algebra for Evaluating Hedge Portfolios," *Journal of Financial Economics,* October 1976, 403–428.

Geske, R., "The Valuation of Corporate Liabilities as Compound Options," *Journal of Financial and Quantitative Analysis,* November 1977, 541–552.

————, "The Pricing of Options with Stochastic Dividend Yield," *Journal of Finance,* May 1978, 617–625.

————, "The Valuation of Compound Options," *Journal of Financial Economics,* March 1979a, 63–81.

————, "A Note on an Analytical Valuation Formula for Unprotected American Call Options on Stocks with Known Dividends," *Journal of Financial Economics,* December 1979b, 375–380.

Gould, J., and D. Galai, "Transaction Costs and the Relationship Between Put and Call Prices," *Journal of Financial Economics,* July 1974.

Hsia, C., "Relationships Among the Theories of MM, CAPM, and OPM," Mimeograph, UCLA, 1978.

Johnson, H., "Three Topics in Option Pricing." Ph.D. thesis, UCLA Graduate School of Management, 1981.

Klemkosky, R., and B. Resnick, "Put-Call Parity and Market Efficiency," *The Journal of Finance,* December 1979, 1141–1155.

Kruizenga, R. J., "Introduction to the Option Contract," reprinted in P. Cootner, ed., *The Random Character of Stock Market Prices.* MIT Press, Cambridge, Mass., 1964, 377–391.

Latane, H., and R. J. Rendleman, Jr., "Standard Deviations of Stock Price Ratios Implied in Option Prices," *The Journal of Finance,* May 1976, 369–382.

MacBeth, J., and L. Merville, "An Empirical Examination of the Black-Scholes Call Option Pricing Model," *Journal of Finance,* December 1979, 1173–1186.

―――, "Tests of the Black-Scholes and Cox Call Option Valuation Models," *Journal of Finance,* May 1980, 285–300.

Margrabe, W., "The Value of an Option to Exchange One Asset for Another," *The Journal of Finance,* March 1978, 177–186.

Merton, R., "The Theory of Rational Option Pricing," *The Bell Journal of Economics and Management Science,* Spring 1973a, 141–183.

―――, "An Intertemporal Capital Asset Pricing Model," *Econometrica,* September 1973b, 867–887.

―――, "On the Pricing of Corporate Debt: The Risk Structure of Interest Rates," *Journal of Finance,* May 1974, 449–470.

―――, "Option Pricing When Underlying Stock Returns are Discontinuous," *Journal of Financial Economics,* January–March 1976, 125–144.

Parkinson, M., "Option Pricing: The American Put," *The Journal of Business,* January 1977, 21–36.

Rendleman, R., Jr., and B. Bartter, "Two-State Option Pricing," *Journal of Finance,* December 1979, 1093–1110.

Roll, R., "An Analytic Valuation Formula for Unprotected American Call Options on Stocks with Known Dividends," *Journal of Financial Economics,* November 1977, 251–258.

Rosenberg, B., "The Behavior of Random Variables with Nonstationary Variance and the Distribution of Security Prices," Manuscript, University of California, Berkeley, 1973.

Ross, S., "Options and Efficiency," *Quarterly Journal of Economics,* February 1976, 75–89.

Rubinstein, M., "The Valuation of Uncertain Income Streams and the Pricing of Options," *Bell Journal of Economics,* Autumn 1976, 407–425.

―――, "Displaced Diffusion Option Pricing," Working Paper No. 118, University of California, Berkeley, Research Program in Finance, 1981a.

―――, "Nonparametric Tests of Alternative Option Pricing Models," Working Paper No. 117, University of California, Berkeley, Research Program in Finance, 1981b.

Schmalensee, R., and R. Trippi, "Common Stock Volatility Expectations Implied by Option Premia," *The Journal of Finance,* March 1978, 129–147.

Smith, C., "Option Pricing Review," *Journal of Financial Economics,* January/March 1976, 1–51.

Stoll, H. R., "The Relationship Between Put and Call Option Prices," *The Journal of Finance,* December 1969, 802–824.

Appendix to Chapter 8
Derivation of the Black-Scholes Option Pricing Model

Black and Scholes [1973] were the first to provide a closed-form solution for the valuation of European calls. They recognized that given the assumption of frictionless markets and continuous trading opportunities, it is possible to form a risk-free hedge portfolio consisting of a long position in the stock and a short position in the European call written on that stock. If the stock price changes over time, the risk-free hedge can be maintained by continuously readjusting the proportions of stock and calls. The value of the hedge portfolio, V_H, can be expressed as the number of shares of stock, Q_S, times the price per share, S, plus the quantity of calls, Q_c, times their price:

$$V_H = SQ_S + cQ_c. \tag{A8.1}$$

The change in the value of the hedge portfolio is the total derivative of (A8.1).

$$dV_H = Q_S dS + Q_c dc. \tag{A8.2}$$

Of course, the stock price moves randomly over time. We assume that it follows a geometric Brownian motion process. Its rate of return can be described as

$$\frac{dS}{S} = \mu \, dt + \sigma \, dz, \tag{A8.3}$$

where

$\mu =$ the instantaneous expected rate of return (it measures the drift in the random walk through time, dt),
$\sigma =$ the instantaneous standard deviation of the rate of return,
$dt =$ a small increment of time,
$dz =$ a Wiener process.

Since the option's price is a function of the stock's price, its movement over time must be related to the stock's movement over time. Black and Scholes [1973] show that if the stock price follows a geometric Brownian motion process such as (A8.3), then using stochastic calculus (which is far beyond the mathematical capabilities assumed for this text) and employing a technique known as Ito's lemma, one can express the change in the option price by the following stochastic differential equation:

$$dc = \frac{\delta c}{\delta S} \, dS + \frac{\delta c}{\delta t} \, dt + \frac{1}{2} \frac{\delta^2 c}{\delta S^2} \, \sigma^2 S^2 \, dt. \tag{A8.4}$$

Note that the only stochastic term in the expression for dc is dS. The others are deterministic.

281

Figure A8.1
Forming a continually adjusted
riskless hedge portfolio.

Substituting (A8.4) into (A8.2), we obtain

$$dV_H = Q_s dS + Q_c \left[\frac{\delta c}{\delta S} dS + \frac{\delta c}{\delta t} dt + \frac{1}{2} \frac{\delta^2 c}{\delta S^2} \sigma^2 S^2 dt \right]. \qquad (A8.5)$$

As mentioned earlier, the insight which Black and Scholes provided was to notice that it is possible to continuously adjust the hedge portfolio, V_H, so that it becomes risk free. How this may be done is illustrated in Fig. A8.1. The curved line, labeled $c(S, T, X)$, represents the theoretical relationship between the call price and the stock price. If we buy one share of stock and sell a number of call options equal to the inverse of the slope of a line tangent to the curve $c(S, T, X)$, we can create a riskless hedge. For example, let us suppose that the current stock price is $15, and the option price is $5. We form a hedge portfolio by selling two calls (for which we receive $10) and by buying one share of stock for $15. Our net equity position would be $5. This is illustrated in Table A8.1. Next, for the sake of argument, let us assume that the stock price rises to $20 and the option price to 7\frac{7}{8}$. We gain $5 from the stock and lose 5\frac{3}{4}$ on the two call options. Our net equity has decreased by $.75. A similar small loss may be expected if the stock price falls by $5. Of course, for smaller changes in the stock price, our equity loss is even smaller. And if we continuously adjust our hedge portfolio to maintain a ratio of stock to call options of $1/(\delta c/\delta S)$, the hedge will be perfectly risk free. Therefore, the risk-free hedge portfolio will earn the risk-free rate in equilibrium if capital markets are efficient. This is really the main insight. It is possible, given continuous trading, to form risk-

Table A8.1   An Example of a Riskless Hedge

	$\Delta S = -5$	*Initial*	$\Delta S = +5$
Stock price X	$10	$15	$20
Call price c	$ 2$\frac{7}{8}$	$ 5	$ 7$\frac{7}{8}$
Short two calls	$ 5$\frac{3}{4}$	$10	15\frac{3}{4}$
Equity position	$ 4$\frac{1}{4}$	$ 5	$ 4$\frac{1}{4}$

free hedges with only two securities, the underlying asset and a call option. This equilibrium relationship is expressed as

$$\frac{dV_H}{V_H} = r_f \, dt. \tag{A8.6}$$

This fact and the fact that the riskless hedge is maintained by purchasing one share of stock and selling $1/(\delta c/\delta S)$ calls,

$$Q_S = 1, \quad Q_c = -\frac{1}{(\delta c/\delta S)}, \tag{A8.7}$$

allows us to substitute (A8.6) and (A8.7) into (A8.5) in order to simplify it. This is done below:

$$dV_H = r_f \, dt V_H = (1) \, dS - \frac{\delta S}{\delta c}\left[\frac{\delta c}{\delta S}\, dS + \frac{\delta c}{\delta t}\, dt + \frac{1}{2}\frac{\delta^2 c}{\delta S^2}\,\sigma^2 S^2 \, dt\right],$$

$$\frac{\delta c}{\delta t} = r_f V_H \left(-\frac{\delta c}{\delta S}\right) - \frac{1}{2}\frac{\delta^2 c}{\delta S^2}\,\sigma^2 S^2.$$

Substituting (A8.1) for V_H and using (A8.7) again, we have

$$\frac{\delta c}{\delta t} = r_f(SQ_S + cQ_c)\left(-\frac{\delta c}{\delta S}\right) - \frac{1}{2}\frac{\delta^2 c}{\delta S^2}\,\sigma^2 S^2$$

$$= r_f c - r_f S \frac{\delta c}{\delta S} - \frac{1}{2}\frac{\delta^2 c}{\delta S^2}\,\sigma^2 S^2. \tag{A8.8}$$

Equation (A8.8) is a nonstochastic differential equation for the value of the option. By using the notion of a riskless hedge, Black and Scholes eliminate the only stochastic term, dS. Now the nonstochastic differential equation may be solved subject to the boundary conditions that at the terminal date the option price must be

$$c = \text{MAX}[0, S - X]$$

and that, for any date,

$$c(S = 0, T, X) = 0.$$

Black and Scholes [1973] transform the equation into the heat exchange equation from physics to find the following solution:[1]

$$c = S \cdot N \left\{\frac{\ln(S/X) + [r_f + (\sigma^2/2)]T}{\sigma\sqrt{T}}\right\} - e^{-r_f T} X \cdot N \left\{\frac{\ln(S/X) + [r_f - (\sigma^2/2)]T}{\sigma\sqrt{T}}\right\}, \tag{A8.9}$$

---

[1] Note that once we are given the call pricing solution (Eq. A8.9), we see that the hedge ratio in terms of the number of calls per share is

$$Q_c = -1/(\delta c/\delta S) = -1/N(d_1),$$

where $N(d_1)$ is the first term in braces in Eq. (A8.9). This fact is needed in order to continuously construct risk-free hedges.

where all variables are as defined previously except that

$N(\cdot)$ = the cumulative normal probability of a unit normal variable; where, for example, $N(-\infty) = 0$, $N(0) = .5$, and $N(\infty) = 1.0$;

$N(\cdot) = \int_{-\infty}^{z} f(z)dz$, where $f(z)$ is distributed normally with mean zero and standard deviation one.

Efficient Capital Markets: Theory

In a world of uncertainty, information becomes a useful commodity—acquisition of information to eliminate uncertainty should then be considered as an alternative to productive investment subject to uncertainty.

J. HIRSHLEIFER, *INVESTMENT, INTEREST AND CAPITAL,*
PRENTICE HALL, ENGLEWOOD CLIFFS, N.J.,
1970, P. 311

A. DEFINING CAPITAL MARKET EFFICIENCY

The purpose of capital markets is to efficiently transfer funds between lenders (savers) and borrowers (producers). Individuals or firms may have an excess of productive investment opportunities with anticipated rates of return which exceed the market-determined borrowing rate but not enough funds to take advantage of all these opportunities. However, if capital markets exist, they can borrow the needed funds. Lenders, who have excess funds after exhausting all their productive opportunities with expected returns greater than the borrowing rate, will be willing to lend their excess funds because the borrowing/lending rate is higher than what they might otherwise earn. Therefore both borrowers and lenders are better off if efficient capital markets are used to facilitate fund transfers. The borrowing/ lending rate is used as an important piece of information by each producer, who will accept projects until the rate of return on the least profitable project just equals the opportunity cost of external funds (the borrowing/lending rate). Thus a market is said to be *allocationally efficient* when prices are determined in a way which equates the *marginal* rates of return (adjusted for risk) for all producers and savers. In an allocationally efficient market, scarce savings are optimally allocated to productive investments in a way which benefits everyone.

In order to describe *efficient capital markets* it is useful, first of all, to contrast them with *perfect capital markets.* The following conditions are necessary for perfect capital markets:

- Markets are frictionless, i.e., there are no transaction costs or taxes, all assets are perfectly divisible and marketable, and there are no constraining regulations.

- There is perfect competition in product and securities markets. In product markets this means that all producers supply goods and services at minimum average cost, and in securities markets it means that all participants are price takers.

- Markets are informationally efficient, i.e., information is costless, and it is received simultaneously by all individuals.

- All individuals are rational expected utility maximizers.

Given these conditions both product and securities markets will be both allocationally and operationally efficient. Allocational efficiency has already been defined, but what about operational efficiency? *Operational efficiency* deals with the cost of transferring funds. In the idealized world of perfect capital markets, transaction costs are assumed to be zero; therefore we have perfect operational efficiency.[1] However, we shall see later, when we focus on empirical studies of real-world phenomena, that operational efficiency is, indeed, an important consideration.

Capital market efficiency is much less restrictive than the notion of perfect capital markets outlined above. In an efficient capital market, prices fully and instantaneously reflect all available relevant information. This means that when assets are traded, prices are accurate signals for capital allocation.

To show the difference between perfect markets and efficient capital markets we can relax some of the perfect market assumptions. For example, we can still have efficient capital markets if markets are not frictionless. Prices will still fully reflect all available information if, for example, securities traders have to pay brokerage fees, or if an individual's human capital (which after all is an asset) cannot be divided into a thousand parts and auctioned off. More important, there can be imperfect competition in product markets and we still have efficient capital markets. Hence, if a firm can reap monopoly profits in the product market, the efficient capital market

---

[1] Note that even in perfect markets the minimum cost of transferring funds may not be zero if the transfer of funds also involves risk bearing.

will determine a security price which fully reflects the present value of the anticipated stream of monopoly profits. Hence we can have allocative inefficiencies in product markets but still have efficient capital markets. Finally, it is not necessary to have costless information in efficient capital markets. This point is discussed in greater detail in Section E of this chapter.

Still, in a somewhat limited sense, efficient capital markets imply operational efficiency as well as asset prices which are allocationally efficient. Asset prices are correct signals in the sense that they fully and instantaneously reflect all available relevant information and are useful for directing the flow of funds from savers to investment projects which yield the highest return (even though the return may reflect monopolistic practices in product markets). Capital markets are operationally efficient if intermediaries, who provide the service of channeling funds from savers to investors, do so at the minimum cost which provides them a fair return for their services.

Fama [1970, 1976] has done a great deal to operationalize the notion of capital market efficiency. He defines three types of efficiency each of which is based on a different notion of exactly what type of information is understood to be relevant in the phrase "all prices fully reflect all *relevant* information."

1. *Weak-form efficiency.* No investor can earn excess returns by developing trading rules based on historical price or return information. In other words, the information in past prices or returns is not useful or relevant in achieving excess returns.

2. *Semistrong-form efficiency.* No investor can earn excess returns from trading rules based on any publicly available information. Examples of publicly available information are: annual reports of companies, investment advisory data such as "Heard on the Street" in the *Wall Street Journal,* or ticker tape information.

3. *Strong-form efficiency.* No investor can earn excess returns using any information, whether publicly available or not.

Obviously, the last type of market efficiency is very strong indeed. If markets were efficient in their strong form, prices would fully reflect all information even though it might be held exclusively by a corporate insider. Suppose, for example, we know that our company has just discovered how to control nuclear fusion. Even before we have a chance to trade based on the news, the strong form of market efficiency predicts that prices will have adjusted so that we cannot profit.

B. A FORMAL DEFINITION OF THE VALUE OF INFORMATION

The notion of efficient capital markets depends on the precise definition of information and the value of information.[2] An information structure may be defined as a message about various events which may happen. For example, the message "there are no clouds in the sky" provides a probability distribution for the likelihood of rain within the next 24 hours. This message may have various values to different people depending

---

[2] For an excellent review of the economics of information, see Hirshleifer and Riley [1979].

on (1) whether or not they can take any actions based on the message and (2) what net benefits (gain in utility) will result from their actions. For example, a message related to rainfall can be of value to farmers, who can act on that information to increase their wealth. If there is to be no rain, the farmers might decide that it would be a good time to harvest hay. On the other hand, messages about rainfall have no value to deep-pit coal miners because they probably will not alter the miners' actions at all.

A formal expression of the above concept defines the value of an information structure, $V(\eta)$, as

$$V(\eta) \equiv \sum_m q(m) \underset{a}{\text{MAX}} \sum_e p(e|m) U(a,e), \qquad (9.1)$$

where

$q(m) =$ the marginal probability of receiving a message m,

$p(e|m) =$ the conditional probability of an event e given a message m,

$U(a,e) =$ the utility resulting from an action a if an event e occurs. We shall call this a *benefit function*.

According to Eq. (9.1), a decision maker will evaluate an information structure (which, for the sake of generality, is defined as a set of messages) by choosing an action which will maximize his or her expected utility given the arrival of a message. For example, if we receive a message (one of many that we could have received) that there is a 20% chance of rain, we may carry an umbrella because of the high "disutility" of getting drenched and the low cost of carrying it. For each possible message we can determine our optimal action. Mathematically, this is the solution to the problem

$$\underset{a}{\text{MAX}} \sum_e p(e|m) U(a,e).$$

Finally, by weighting the expected utility of each optimal action (in response to all possible messages) by the probability, $q(m)$ of receiving the message which gives rise to the action, the decision maker knows the expected utility of the entire set of messages, which we call the *expected utility* (or *utility value*) of an information set, $V(\eta)$.

The following example applies the value-of-information concept to the theory of portfolio choice. We will choose our optimal portfolio as a combination of two funds: either the risk-free asset which yields 6%, or the market portfolio which may yield 16%, or 10%, or −5%.[3] Assume that we know the standard deviation of the market portfolio, σ_m, with certainty. Figure 9.1 shows the linear efficient set (the capital market line) for each of the three possible states of the world. As risk-averse investors, in this case, we will maximize our expected utility by choosing the portfolio where our indifference curve is tangent to the efficient set.

---

[3] A more general, but also more complicated, example would assign a continuous probability distribution to the possible returns offered by the market portfolio.

Figure 9.1
Optimal choices for two states of the world.

In order to calculate the value of an information set we need to know the payoff function $U(a,e)$, which tells us the utility of having taken a course of action, a, when an event or state of the world, e, occurs. For the sake of convenience, we will label the three states of the world by their market returns: $e_3 = 16\%$, $e_2 = 10\%$, and $e_1 = -5\%$.

If the market return were 16%, we would choose portfolio 3 in Fig. 9.1, which is where indifference curve U_7 is tangent to the capital market line e_3. On the other hand, we would put all of our portfolio in the risk-free asset (portfolio 1) if the market return were known to be -5%. This occurs where indifference curve U_4 passes through R_f. If we choose portfolio 3, and if the market rate of return really is 16%, then our payoff is $U_7 = 40$. But if we make a mistake and choose portfolio 3 when the market rate of return turns out to be -5%, our portfolio is suboptimal. After the fact, we would have been much better off with portfolio 1, the risk-free asset. Our utility for holding portfolio 3 when state 1 obtains (point A in Fig. 9.1) is $U_1 = 10$ less our regret, which is the difference between where we actually are and where we would like to be.[4] In this case our regret is the difference between U_4 and U_1. Therefore, our net utility is $U_1 - (U_4 - U_1) = 2U_1 - U_4 = -6$. When we receive a message which provides estimates of the likelihood of future states of the world, we will choose an action (in our example this amounts to choosing a portfolio) which will maximize our expected utility given that message. The utility provided by each portfolio choice (i.e., each action) in each state of the world can be taken from Fig. 9.2, which is similar to Fig. 9.1 except that it gives all possible

---

[4] Needless to say, the computation of "regret" as suggested here is not necessarily accurate and is only for purposes of illustration. However, it is consistent with the fact that utilities may be state contingent. (See Chapter 5, state-preference theory.)

Figure 9.2
Optimal actions given various states of the world.

portfolios and states of the world. The corresponding benefit function, $U(a,e)$, is given in Table 9.1.

In addition to a benefit matrix it is also necessary to have an information structure (a Markov matrix) which gives the probability that an event will actually occur given that a particular message has been received. The two obvious polar cases are perfect information and no information. Their matrices are given in Table 9.2. If the information structure is perfect, receipt of a message implies that a given state of the world will occur with certainty. This makes it easy to select a course of action which results in the highest utility. If you receive m_1, then the state of the world e_1 will obtain with certainty; therefore the best action is a_1, with expected utility $U_4 = 26$. Thus for each message it is possible to find the optimal action. Implicitly this procedure amounts to solving Eq. (9.1), which tells us the utility value of information. Given perfect information, the optimal action (and its utility) for each message is seen to be:

Message	Optimal Action	Utility
m_1	a_1 (invest in portfolio 1)	26
m_2	a_1 (invest in portfolio 2)	30
m_3	a_1 (invest in portfolio 3)	40

These actions represent the solution to one part of the value of information, that is, Eq. (9.1)

$$\text{MAX}_{a} \sum_{e} p(e|m)U(a,e).$$

Table 9.1 Benefit Function $U(a,e)$

Action	$e_1(R_M = -5\%)$	$e_2(R_M = 10\%)$	$e_3(R_M = 16\%)$
Portfolio 1 (action a_1)	$U_4 = 26$	$2U_4 - U_5 = 22$	$2U_4 - U_7 = 12$
Portfolio 2 (action a_2)	$2U_2 - U_4 = 14$	$U_5 = 30$	$2U_6 - U_7 = 24$
Portfolio 3 (action a_3)	$2U_1 - U_4 = -6$	$2U_3 - U_5 = 20$	$U_7 = 40$

Finally, the utility of each action which results from a message is weighted by the probability of the message. In our example, each of the three messages is assumed to be equally likely; therefore, using the notation of Eq. (9.1), we have $q(m_1) = \frac{1}{3}$, $q(m_2) = \frac{1}{3}$, and $q(m_3) = \frac{1}{3}$. The utility value of perfect information is

$$V(\eta_2) = \tfrac{1}{3}(26) + \tfrac{1}{3}(30) + \tfrac{1}{3}(40) = 32.$$

It is also useful to compute the dollar value of this information set to the ith individual. Of course, different individuals will have different utility functions and therefore different demand curves for a given information set. But for now, we will focus only on the dollar value of information to one individual.[5] Suppose his utility function is

$$U(W) = 10\ln(W - \$100).$$

Then if the expected utility of perfect information is 32 utiles, the corresponding dollar value is

$$32 = 10\ln(W(\eta_2) - \$100)$$

$$3.2 = \ln(W(\eta_2) - \$100)$$

$$\$24.5325 = W(\eta_2) - \$100$$

$$\$124.53 = W(\eta_2)$$

This is the increment to wealth which the ith individual would receive were he or she to acquire the information (at no cost).

Table 9.2 Information Structures

	$\eta_2 = $ *perfect information*				$\eta_0 = $ *no information*				$\eta_1 = $ *noisy information*		
	m_1	m_2	m_3		m_1	m_2	m_3		m_1	m_2	m_3
e_1	1.0	0	0	e_1	$\frac{1}{3}$	$\frac{1}{3}$	$\frac{1}{3}$	e_1	.6	.3	.1
e_2	0	1.0	0	e_2	$\frac{1}{3}$	$\frac{1}{3}$	$\frac{1}{3}$	e_2	.2	.5	.3
e_3	0	0	1.0	e_3	$\frac{1}{3}$	$\frac{1}{3}$	$\frac{1}{3}$	e_3	.2	.2	.6

Next, consider the value of no information. In Table 9.2 we see that no information means that all messages are identical. Each says the same thing: "All events are equally likely." For example, suppose a friend asks whether or not a movie was

---

[5] For more on this topic see Huang, Vertinsky, and Ziemba [1977].

worth seeing. If we always reply "yes," whether or not the movie is good, then the message contains no information. If we always say "no," the result is the same—no information. In the example at hand, when asked about the probability of a state of the world, we always answer, "one-third." In order to compute the value of no information, we begin just as before, by selecting the optimal action for each message. For example, let us assume that we receive message 1:

If we take action	*the expected utility is*
a_1(invest in portfolio 1)	$\frac{1}{3}(26) + \frac{1}{3}(22) + \frac{1}{3}(12) = 20$
a_2(invest in portfolio 2)	$\frac{1}{3}(14) + \frac{1}{3}(30) + \frac{1}{3}(24) = 22.67$
a_3(invest in portfolio 3)	$\frac{1}{3}(-6) + \frac{1}{3}(20) + \frac{1}{3}(40) = 18$

Suppose we receive message 2:

If we take action	*the expected utility is*
a_1(invest in portfolio 1)	$\frac{1}{3}(26) + \frac{1}{3}(22) + \frac{1}{3}(12) = 20$
a_2(invest in portfolio 2)	$\frac{1}{3}(14) + \frac{1}{3}(30) + \frac{1}{3}(24) = 22.67$
a_3(invest in portfolio 3)	$\frac{1}{3}(-6) + \frac{1}{3}(20) + \frac{1}{3}(40) = 18$

And if we receive message 3, the expected utilities of our actions are the same (obviously, since the three messages are the same). Regardless of the message our optimal action is always the same—invest in portfolio 2; and our expected utility is 22.67. As with perfect information the selection of optimal actions, given various messages, is the first part of the problem. The second part is to weight the expected utility of an action, given a message, by the probability of the message. The result is the utility value of information. The utility value of no information is

$$V(\eta_0) = \frac{1}{3}(22.67) + \frac{1}{3}(22.67) + \frac{1}{3}(22.67) = 22.67.$$

Using the same utility function as above, the dollar value of information in this case is $W(\eta_0) = \$109.65$. The difference between the dollar value of perfect information and no information is the maximum gain from information for the ith individual.

$$W(\eta_2) - W(\eta_0) = \$14.88$$

Finally, consider the third information structure in Table 9.2. In this case the messages received are noisy. The first message says that there is a .6 probability that the first state of the world might obtain, but .4 of the time the message will err, with a .2 probability that e_2 will actually occur and a .2 probability that e_3 will obtain. In order to value the noisy information, we proceed as before. We choose the optimal action given a message. For example, let us assume that m_1 is received.

If we take action	*the expected utility is*
a_1(invest in portfolio 1)	$.6(26) + .2(22) + .2(12) = 22.4$
a_2(invest in portfolio 2)	$.6(14) + .2(30) + .2(24) = 19.2$
a_3(invest in portfolio 3)	$.6(-6) + .2(20) + .2(40) = 8.4$

Therefore the optimal action is to invest in portfolio 1 if message 1 is received. Similarly,

If we receive	the optimal action is	with expected utility
m_2	a_2	24.0
m_3	a_3	29.4

Finally, if we weight the utility of the optimal actions, given the three messages, by the probability of the messages, we have the utility value of the noisy information structure:

$$V(\eta_1) = \tfrac{1}{3}(22.4) + \tfrac{1}{3}(24) + \tfrac{1}{3}(29.4) = 25.27.$$

Its corresponding dollar value, for the ith individual, is $W(\eta_1) = \$112.52$.

C. THE RELATIONSHIP BETWEEN THE VALUE OF INFORMATION AND EFFICIENT CAPITAL MARKETS

Equation (9.1) can be used to evaluate any information structure. It also points out some ideas which are only implicit in the definition of efficient markets. Fama [1976] defines efficient capital markets as those where the joint distribution of security prices, $f_m(P_{1t}, P_{2t}, \ldots, P_{nt}|\eta_{t-1}^m)$, given the set of information that the *market uses* to determine security prices at $t + 1$, is identical to the joint distribution of prices which would exist if *all relevant information* available at $t - 1$ were used, $f(P_{1t}, P_{2t}, \ldots, P_{nt}|\eta_{t-1})$. Mathmetically, this is

$$f_m(P_{1t}, \ldots, P_{nt}|\eta_{t-1}^m) = f(P_{1t}, \ldots, P_{nt}|\eta_{t-1}). \tag{9.2}$$

If an information structure is to have value, it must accurately tell us something we do not already know. If the distribution of prices in time period t (which was predicted in the previous time period $t - 1$ and based on the information structure which the market uses) is not different from the prices predicted by using all relevant information from the previous time period, then there must be no difference between the information which the market uses and the set of all relevant information. This is the essence of an efficient capital market—it instantaneously and fully reflects all relevant information. Using information theory, this also means that *net of costs,* the utility value of the gain from information to the ith individual must be zero.

$$V(\eta_i) - V(\eta_0) \equiv 0. \tag{9.3}$$

For example, consider capital markets which are efficient in their weak form. The relevant information structure, η_i, is defined to be the set of historical prices on all assets. If capital markets are efficient, then Eq. (9.2) says that the distribution of security prices today has already incorporated past price histories. In other words, it is not possible to develop trading rules (courses of action) based on past prices which will allow anyone to beat the market. Equation (9.3) says that no one would pay anything for the information set of historical prices. The value of the information is zero. Empirical evidence on trading rules which use past price data is discussed in section F of this chapter.

It is important to emphasize that the value of information is determined net of costs. These include the cost of undertaking courses of action and the costs of transmitting and evaluating messages. Some of these costs in securities markets are transactions costs: for example, brokerage fees, bid-ask spreads, costs involved in searching for the best price (if more than one price is quoted), and taxes, as well as data costs and analysts' fees. The capital market is efficient relative to a given information set only after consideration of the costs of acquiring messages and taking actions pursuant to a particular information structure.

D. RATIONAL EXPECTATIONS AND MARKET EFFICIENCY

The utility value of information has three parts: (1) the utilities of the payoffs given an action; (2) the optimal actions given receipt of a message; and (3) the probabilities of states of nature provided by the messages. We are interested in understanding how the individual's decision-making process, given the receipt of information, is reflected in the market prices of assets. This is not easy because it is impossible to observe the quantity and quality of information or the timing of its receipt in the real world. There is even disagreement among theorists about what information will be used by investors. For example, Forsythe, Palfrey, and Plott [1982] identify four different hypotheses. Each hypothesis assumes that investors know with certainty what their own payoffs will be across time but they also know that different individuals may pay different prices because of differing preferences.

The first hypothesis is particularly nonsensical (call it the *naive hypothesis*) in that it asserts that asset prices are completely arbitrary and unrelated either to how much they will pay out in the future or the probabilities of various payouts. The second hypothesis, call it the *speculative equilibrium hypothesis,* is captured in a quote taken from Keynes' *General Theory* [1936, p. 156]

> ... *professional investment may be likened to those newspaper competitions in which the competitors have to pick out the six prettiest faces from a hundred photographs, the prize being awarded to the competitor whose choice most nearly corresponds to the average preferences of the competitors as a whole; so that each competitor has to pick, not those faces which he himself finds the prettiest, but those which he thinks likeliest to catch the fancy of the other competitors, all of whom are looking at the problem from the same point of view. It is not a case of choosing those which, to the best of one's judgement, are really the prettiest, nor even those which average opinion genuinely thinks the prettiest. We have reached the third degree where we devote our intelligences to anticipating what average opinion expects the average opinion to be. And there are some, I believe, who practice the fourth, fifth and higher degrees.*

Table 9.3 Parameters for an Experimental Double Auction Spot Market

Investor Type	Initial Working Capital	Initial Shares Held	Fixed Cost	Dividends (Francs)	
				Period A	Period B
I (3 people)	10,000 francs	2 shares	10,000 francs	300	50
II (3 people)	10,000 francs	2 shares	10,000 francs	50	300
III (3 people)	10,000 francs	2 shares	10,000 francs	150	250

We might debate about what Keynes really meant, but one interpretation is that all investors base their investment decisions entirely on their anticipation of other individuals' behavior without any necessary relationship to the actual payoffs which the assets are expected to provide. The third hypothesis is that asset prices are systematically related to their future payouts. Called the *intrinsic value hypothesis,* it says that prices will be determined by each individual's estimate of the payoffs of an asset without consideration of its resale value to other individuals. The fourth hypothesis may be called the *rational expectations hypothesis.* It predicts that prices are formed on the basis of the expected future payouts of the assets, including their resale value to third parties. Thus a rational expectations market is an efficient market because prices will reflect all information.

In order to make these hypotheses more concrete it is useful to review an experiment by Forsythe, Palfrey, and Plott [1982]. They set up an oral double auction market which had two time periods, one asset, and three "types" of individuals. An oral double auction market is one where individuals can call out both buying and selling prices for an asset. The largest market of this type is the New York Stock Exchange. All participants knew exactly how much the asset would pay them in each time period. They also knew that the asset would pay different amounts to the other market participants, but not how much. Thus, the asset had different values to different individuals. Table 9.3 shows the experimental parameters. If you held an asset at the end of the first time period you received 300, 50, or 150 "francs" depending on whether you were individual I, II, or III.[6] The differences in the franc payouts across individuals were designed to reflect differences among individual preferences and information sets at an instant in time. Each individual was endowed with 10,000 francs in working capital and two shares.[7] The 10,000 franc endowment was paid back at the end of the second time period (this is the fixed cost column in Table 9.3) but any dividends received and any trading profits were kept by the market participants.

The interesting question is what will the market equilibrium prices be at the end of each of the two time periods? If either of the intrinsic value or rational expectations hypotheses are true, the period *B* price should be 300 francs (or very close to it) because there are three people competing for that payoff. While the hypotheses

---

[6] Each "franc" was worth $.002.

[7] No short sales were allowed, thus the supply of assets was fixed.

agree about the second period price they make different predictions concerning the first period price. The intrinsic value hypothesis predicts that people will bid their own values. For example, if individual type III holds the asset for two periods, he can collect 400 francs in dividends (150 in period *A* and 250 in period *B*). This will also be the predicted first period equilibrium price because it represents the high bid. The rational expectations hypothesis predicts that the first period equilibrium price will be 600 francs because type I individuals can collect a 300 franc dividend in the first time period, then sell the asset for 300 francs to type II individuals in the second time period.

Figure 9.3 shows the results of eight replications of the experiment for two periods each. Note that the period *B* price quickly converges on the anticipated equilibrium value of 300 francs. This result alone repudiates the naive value and the speculative equilibrium hypotheses because the asset value is clearly based on its actual second period payout. The first period price starts out at 400 francs, seemingly verifying the intrinsic value hypothesis; but it then rises gradually until, by the eighth replication of the experiment ("year" 8), it closes in on the rational expectations value.

The experiment seems to confirm the rational expectations hypothesis, but why did it take so long to do so? The reason is that prices are determined in the first period before second period prices are known. In order for type I individuals to bid the full 600 franc value, they need to have the information that the second period value is really 300 francs. Obviously they don't know this during the first trial of the experiment, but they learn quickly.

Figure 9.3
Spot price equilibria in an experimental market. (From Forsythe, Palfrey, and Plott "Asset Valuation in an Experimental Market," reprinted from *Econometrica*, May 1982, 550.)

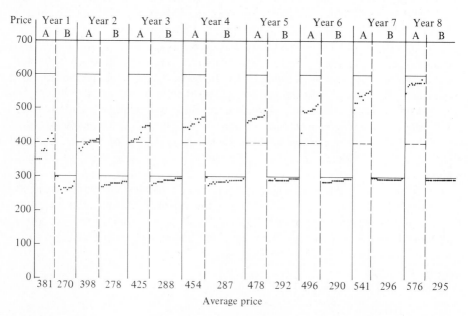

Table 9.4   Parameters for an Experimental Double Auction Futures Market

Investor Type	Initial Working Capital	Initial Shares Held	Fixed Cost	Dividends (Francs)	
				Period A	Period B
I	15,000 francs	2 shares	15,500 francs	403	146
II	15,000 francs	2 shares	15,500 francs	284	372
III	15,000 francs	2 shares	15,500 francs	110	442

If instead, bidding had taken place in both period *A* and *B* markets simultaneously, perhaps the speed of adjustment to a rational expectations equilibrium would have been faster. In another experiment, Forsythe, Palfrey, and Plott [1982] opened a *futures market*. Everything remained the same as before except bidding for period *B* holdings was held concurrently with the period *A* spot market, and the payoffs were as shown in Table 9.4.

The rational expectations hypothesis predicts that the period *A* price will be 845 francs, while the intrinsic value hypothesis predicts 403 francs. They both predict a period *B* price of 442 francs. The results are shown in Fig. 9.4. Even in the first trial, the period *A* spot price closed at 742 francs, much closer to the rational expectations prediction. In subsequent trials ("years") the closing prices were even closer to the results predicted by the rational expectations hypothesis. Perhaps the most valuable implication of the experiment is that it clearly demonstrates the usefulness of futures markets. By allowing simultaneous trading in both markets, the speed

Figure 9.4
Rational expectations with a futures market. (From Forsythe, Palfrey, and Plott, "Asset Valuation in an Experimental Market," reprinted from *Econometrica,* May 1982, 554.)

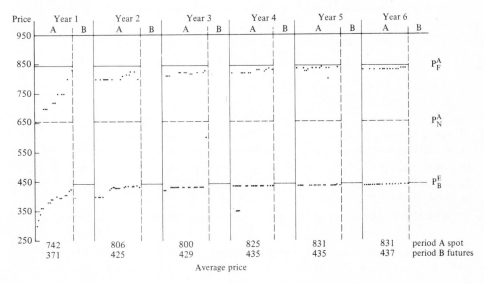

with which information is made public is increased through price transactions. Information about the future value of assets is revealed today.

In the rational expectations equilibria described above, all traders knew with certainty what their own payoffs would be in each time period but didn't know the asset clearing price because other individuals had different payoffs in the same state of nature. These different payoffs represent a form of heterogeneous expectations. In the above experiments all market participants were equally well informed. There is a different way of looking at heterogeneous expectations, however. Suppose that some traders are better informed about which states of nature will actually occur. Furthermore, suppose that different individuals have different information about which states will occur. For example, suppose investor I knows for sure that a Republican will be elected President but knows nothing else. Investor J, on the other hand, knows that both houses of Congress will be Democratic, but knows nothing else. The question is this: Will market prices reflect the full impact of both pieces of information as though the market were fully informed, or will prices reflect only some average of the impact of both pieces of information? If prices reflect all information, the market is said to be *fully aggregating;* otherwise it is only *averaging* prices.

Very little is known about whether real world capital markets fully aggregate information or merely average it. A fully aggregating market, however, would be consistent with Fama's [1970] definition of strong-form market efficiency. In a fully aggregating market even insiders who possess private information would not be able to profit by it. One mechanism for aggregation has been suggested by Grossman and Stiglitz [1976] and Grossman [1976].[8] In a market with two types of traders, "informed" and "uninformed," informed traders will acquire better estimates of future states of nature and take trading positions based on this information. When all informed traders do this, current prices are affected. Uninformed traders invest no resources in collecting information, but they can infer the information of informed traders by observing what happens to prices. Thus the market prices may aggregate information so that all traders (both informed and uninformed) become informed. In Chapter 10 we will suggest that capital markets do not instantaneously and fully aggregate information because empirical evidence on insider trading reveals that insiders can and do make abnormal returns.

E. MARKET EFFICIENCY WITH COSTLY INFORMATION

If capital markets are efficient, then no one can earn abnormal returns, but without abnormal returns there is no strong incentive to acquire information. Random selection of securities is just as effective. How, then, can prices reflect information if there is no incentive to search it out and use it for arbitrage? How can a securities analysis industry exist?

The above argument may have some merit in a world with costless information

---

[8] Actually, this idea can be traced back to Hayek's classic article, "The Use of Knowledge in Society" [1945].

Table 9.5 Net Payoffs Given Costly Information

		His Opponent Analyzes?	
		Yes	No
The Trader	Yes	$r - c_2 = -2\%$	$dr - c_2 = 4\%$
Analyzes?	No	$r/d - c_1 = -1\%$	$r - c_1 = 2\%$

r = normal return = 6%
d = competitive advantage = 2×
c_2 = cost of analysis = 8%
c_1 = cost with no analysis = 4%

because all investors would have zero abnormal returns.[9] However, it is probably premature to predict the demise of the security analysis industry or to argue that prices are uninformative. Grossman and Stiglitz [1976, 1980] and Cornell and Roll [1981] have shown that a sensible asset market equilibrium must leave some room for analysis. Their articles make the more reasonable assumption that information acquisition is a costly activity. Because of its simplicity, the Cornell and Roll model is discussed below.

We want to analyze the rational behavior of individuals when information is useful—in the sense that having it will improve one's decisions—but also where information is costly. Imagine two simple strategies. The first is to pay a fee, say $c_2 = 8\%$, for acquiring valuable information. This is called the analyst strategy. The opposing strategy is to pay a minimal fee, say $c_1 = 4\%$, for the right to trade. Call this the random selector's strategy. Table 9.5 shows the net payoffs for various two-way trades involving all combinations of analysts and random selectors. Note that the "normal" rate of return, r, is 6% ($c_1 < r < c_2$).

The example in Table 9.5 assumes that the costly information doubles the competitive advantage, d, of an analyst whenever he or she trades with a random selector. The analyst, being better informed, grosses 12% and nets 4% after paying 8% for the information. Conversely, the random selector finds his or her gross return halved when trading with an analyst. He or she grosses only 3% and nets −1% after paying 4% on transactions costs. When an analyst trades with another analyst there is no competitive advantage because they possess the same information. Thus their gross return is only 6% and they net −2%.

A stable equilibrium can exist if (1) all trading is anonymous and if (2) the expected payoff to the analysis strategy equals the expected payoff to the random selection strategy.[10] If p is the probability of utilizing an analyst's strategy and $1 - p$ is the probability of random selection, then the equilibrium condition is:

$$E(\text{Payoff to analysis strategy}) = E(\text{Payoff to random selection})$$

$$p(r - c_2) + (1 - p)(dr - c_2) = p(r/d - c_1) + (1 - p)(r - c_1). \qquad (9.4)$$

---

[9] Abnormal returns are returns in excess of what can be earned for a given level of risk.

[10] Anonymous trading is necessary so that uninformed random selectors will actually consummate a trade with an analyst with superior information. One service provided by brokers is to ensure the anonymity of their clients.

The expected payoff to analysis (the left-hand side of Eq. 9.4) is the probability that an analyst will confront another analyst multiplied by the net payoff given this event, plus the probability of confronting a random selector multiplied by the net payoff in that event. Similar logic produces the expected payoff for a random selector (the right-hand side of Eq. 9.4). Solving Eq. (9.4) for p, the probability of using analysis, we have

$$p = \frac{r(1-d) + c_2 - c_1}{2r - rd - r/d}.$$ (9.5)

A *mixed* stable strategy is one where $0 < p < 1$, that is, where analysts and random selectors will coexist in equilibrium. The necessary conditions for a mixed stable strategy are:

$$r(d-1) > c_2 - c_1$$ (9.6)

$$\text{and} \quad r(1 - 1/d) < c_2 - c_1$$

These conditions can be derived from the definition of the equilibrium probability, p, Eq. (9.5). We know that the "normal" rate of return, r, is greater than zero and the competitive advantage, d, is greater than one. Therefore, the denominator of Eq. (9.5), must be negative, as shown below.

$$2r - rd - r/d < 0$$

$$2d - d^2 - 1 < 0$$

$$(d-1)^2 > 0, \quad \text{since } d > 1 \quad \text{QED.}$$

It follows that the numerator of Eq. (9.5) must also be negative if the probability, p, is to be positive. Therefore,

$$r(1-d) + c_2 - c_1 < 0$$

$$r(d-1) > c_2 - c_1$$

and we have derived the first necessary condition in Eq. (9.6). Also, in order for $p < 1$ the numerator of Eq. (9.5) must be greater than the denominator (since both are negative numbers). This fact gives us the second necessary condition

$$r(1-d) + c_2 - c_1 > 2r - rd - r/d$$

$$c_2 - c_1 > r(1 - 1/d)$$

If there is no net economic profit when the mixed stable strategy evolves, then there will be no incentive for new entrants to disturb the equilibrium. This zero profit condition is equivalent to setting both sides of Eq. (9.4), the expected payoff equation, equal to zero. This results in two equations, which when equated and simplified give the further result that

$$d = c_2/c_1 \quad \text{and} \quad p = (rd - c_2)/(rd - r)$$

for a stable mixed strategy where all net profits are zero.

Using the numbers in Table 9.5, we see that a stable mixed strategy with $p = \frac{2}{3}$ will exist. Thus with costly information we will observe the analyst strategy being used $\frac{2}{3}$ and the random selection strategy $\frac{1}{3}$ of the time. No one will be tempted to change strategies because there is no incentive to do so. Also, we will observe that the gross return for analysis is higher than for random selection. But once the cost of obtaining information is subtracted the net rate of return to both strategies is the same.

The simple model of Cornell and Roll [1981] shows that there is nothing inconsistent about having efficient markets and security analysis at the same time. The average individual who utilizes costly information to perform security analysis will outperform other individuals who use less information, but only in terms of gross returns. The net return to both strategies will be identical. Some empirical evidence consistent with this point of view is presented in Chapter 10 where mutual fund performance is discussed.

F. STATISTICAL TESTS UNADJUSTED FOR RISK

Historically it was possible to test certain predictions of the efficient markets hypothesis even before a theory of risk-bearing allowed comparison of risk-adjusted returns. For example, if the riskiness of an asset does not change over time or if its risk changes randomly over time, then there should be no pattern in the time series of security returns. If there were a recurring pattern of any type, investors who recognize it could use it to predict future returns and make excess profits. However, in their very efforts to use the patterns, they would eliminate them.

Three theories of the time series behavior of prices can be found in the literature: (1) the fair-game model, (2) the martingale or submartingale, and (3) the random walk. The fair-game model is based on the behavior of average returns (not on the entire probability distribution). Its mathematical expression is

$$\epsilon_{j,t+1} = \frac{P_{j,t+1} - P_{jt}}{P_{jt}} - \frac{E(P_{j,t+1}|\eta_t) - P_{jt}}{P_{jt}} \qquad (9.7)$$

$$= \frac{P_{j,t+1} - E(P_{j,t+1}|\eta_t)}{P_{jt}},$$

where

$P_{j,t+1}$ = the actual price of security j next period,

$E(P_{j,t+1}|\eta_t)$ = the predicted end-of-period price of security j given the current information structure, η_t,

$\epsilon_{j,t+1}$ = the difference between actual and predicted returns.

Note that (9.7) is really written in returns form. If we let the one-period return be defined as

$$r_{j,t+1} = \frac{P_{j,t+1} - P_{jt}}{P_{jt}},$$

then (9.7) may be rewritten as

$$\epsilon_{j,t+1} = r_{j,t+1} - E(r_{j,t+1}|\eta_t)$$

and

$$E(\epsilon_{j,t+1}) = E(r_{j,t+1} - E(r_{j,t+1}|\eta_t)) = 0. \tag{9.8}$$

A fair game means that, on average, across a large number of samples, the expected return on an asset equals its actual return. An example of a fair game would be games of chance in Las Vegas. Because of the house percentage you should expect to lose, let's say 10%, and, sure enough, on the average that is what people actually lose. A fair game does not imply that you will earn a positive return, only that expectations are not biased.

Given the definition of a fair game in Eq. (9.7), a *submartingale* is a fair game where tomorrow's price is expected to be greater than today's price. Mathematically, a submartingale is

$$E(P_{j,t+1}|\eta_t) > P_{jt}.$$

In returns form this implies that expected returns are positive. This may be written as follows:

$$\frac{E(P_{j,t+1}|\eta_t) - P_{jt}}{P_{jt}} = E(r_{j,t+1}|\eta_t) > 0. \tag{9.9a}$$

A *martingale* is also a fair game. With a martingale, however, tomorrow's price is expected to be the same as today's price. Mathematically, this is

$$E(P_{j,t+1}|\eta_t) = P_{jt},$$

or in returns form, it is written as

$$\frac{E(P_{j,t+1}|\eta_t) - P_{jt}}{P_{jt}} = E(r_{j,t+1}|\eta_t) = 0. \tag{9.9b}$$

A submartingale has the following empirical implication: Because prices are expected to increase over time, any test of the abnormal return from an experimental portfolio must compare its return from a buy-and-hold strategy for a control portfolio of the same composition. If the market is an efficient submartingale, both portfolios will have a positive return, and the difference between their returns will be zero. In other words, we will observe a fair game with positive returns: a submartingale.

Finally, a random walk says that there is no difference between the distribution of returns conditional on a given information structure and the unconditional distribution of returns. Equation (9.2) is a random walk in prices. Equation (9.10) is a random walk in returns:

$$f(r_{1,t+1}, \ldots, r_{n,t+1}) = f(r_{1,t+1}, \ldots, r_{n,t+1}|\eta_t). \tag{9.10}$$

Random walks are much stronger conditions than fair games or martingales because they require all the parameters of a distribution (for example, mean, variance, skewness, and kurtosis) to be the same with or without an information structure. Furthermore, successive drawings over time must (1) be independent and (2) be taken from the same distribution. If returns follow a random walk, then the mean of the underlying distribution does not change over time, and a fair game will result.

Most empirical evidence indicates that security returns do not follow a process that has all the properties of a random walk. This makes sense because the condition that the entire underlying probability distribution of returns remain stationary through time is simply too strong. It is reasonable to believe that because of changes in the risk of a firm, the variance of stock returns will change over time. This, in fact, appears to be the case. The fair-game model makes no statement about the variance of the distribution of security returns, and consequently the nonstationarity of return variances is irrelevant to its validity.[11]

A statistical difference between fair games and random walks is that the latter hypothesis requires that all drawings be independently taken from the same distribution while the former does not. This means that the random walk requires that serial covariances between returns for any lag must be zero. However, significant serial covariances of one-period returns are not inconsistent with a fair game. To see this, suppose that the relevant information structure consists of past returns. In other words, assume weak-form market efficiency. When Eq. (9.7) is written in returns form, we have

$$\epsilon_{j,t+1} = r_{j,t+1} - E(r_{j,t+1}|r_{jt}, r_{j,t-1}, \ldots, r_{j,t-n}). \qquad (9.11)$$

and

$$E(\epsilon_{j,t+1}) = 0$$

Note that the fair-game variable, $\epsilon_{j,t+1}$, is the deviation of the return in period $t + 1$ from its conditional expectation, i.e., the residual. If the residual is a fair game, then it must have zero serial covariance for all lags. Yet even though the residual is a fair-game variable, the conditional expectation of returns for $t + 1$ can depend on the return observed for t. Therefore, the serial covariances of *returns* need not be zero. The serial covariance for one-period returns is[12]

$$E[(r_{j,t+1} - E(r_{j,t+1}))(r_{jt} - E(r_{jt}))] = \text{COV}(r_{j,t+1}, r_{jt})$$

$$= \int_{r_{jt}} [r_{jt} - E(r_{jt})][r_{j,t+1} - E(r_{j,t+1})] f(r_{jt}) dr_{jt}. \qquad (9.12)$$

---

[11] For example, consider a situation where random drawings are taken randomly from two normal distributions which have a mean return of zero but different return variances. The expected value of a large sample of alternative drawings would be zero, therefore we have a fair game. However, the experiment violates the random walk requirement that all drawings be taken from the same distribution.

[12] The reader who is unfamiliar with covariances is referred to Chapter 6. In general, the covariance between two random variables, x and y, is

$$\text{COV}(x,y) = E[(x - E(x))(y - E(y))].$$

From (9.11) we know that $E[r_{j,t+1}|r_{jt})] = r_{j,t+1}$. Therefore,

$$\text{COV}(r_{j,t+1},r_{jt}) = \int_{r_{jt}} [r_{jt} - E(r_{jt})][E(r_{j,t+1}|r_{jt}) - E(r_{j,t+1})]f(r_{jt})dr_{jt}.$$

But the fair game in residuals, Eq. (9.11), does not imply that $E(r_{j,t+1}|r_{jt}) = E(r_{j,t+1})$. We have the result that the *deviation* of return for $t + 1$ from its conditional expectation is a fair game but the conditional expectation of return itself can depend on the return observed for t. Therefore, serial covariances of one-period returns are not inconsistent with a fair-game model. However, they are inconsistent with a random walk because the latter requires that successive drawings be independent (a serial covariance of zero for all lags).

Fama [1965] has presented evidence to show that the serial correlations of one-day changes in the natural logarithm of price are significantly different from zero for 11 out of 30 of the Dow Jones Industrials.[13] Furthermore, 22 of the 30 estimated serial correlations are positive. This, as well as evidence collected by other authors, shows that security returns are not, strictly speaking, random walks. However, the evidence is not inconsistent with fair-games models or, in particular, the submartingale.

Direct tests of the fair-game model were provided by Alexander [1961] and Fama and Blume [1966]. They used a technical trading filter rule which states: Using price history, buy a stock if the price rises $x\%$, hold it until the security falls $x\%$, then sell and go short. Maintain the short position until the price rises $x\%$, then cover the short position and establish a long position. This process is repeated for a fixed time interval, and the performance according to the filter rule is then compared with a buy-and-hold strategy in the same security. Because each security is compared with itself, there is no need to adjust for risk.

Filter rules are designed to make the investor a profit if there are any systematic patterns in the movement of prices over time. It is only a matter of trying enough different filters so that one of them picks up any serial dependencies in prices and makes a profit which exceeds the simple buy-and-hold strategy.

The filter rule tests have three important results. First, they show that even before subtracting transactions costs, filters greater than 1.5% cannot beat a simple buy-and-hold strategy. Second, filters below 1.5%, on the average, make very small profits which, because of frequent trading, can beat the market. This is evidence of a very short-term serial dependence in price changes. However, it is not necessarily evidence of capital market inefficiency. First one must subtract from gross profits the cost of taking action based on the filter rule. Fama and Blume [1966] show that even a floor trader (the owner of a seat on the NYSE) must pay at least .1% per transaction. Once these costs are deducted from the profits of filters that are less than 1.5%, the profits vanish. Therefore, the capital market is allocationally

---

[13] To show that the logarithm of successive price changes is a good approximation of returns, assume one-period continuous compounding:

$$P_{t+1} = P_t e^{rt}, \quad \text{where } t = 1,$$

$$\ln P_{t+1} - \ln P_t = \frac{P_{t+1} - P_t}{P_t}, \quad \text{where } r = \frac{P_{t+1} - P_t}{P_t}.$$

efficient down to the level of transaction costs. The smaller the transactions costs are, the more operationally efficient the market is, and smaller price dependencies are eliminated by arbitrage trading. Capital markets are efficient in their weak form because the return on a portfolio managed with price-history information is the same as a buy-and-hold strategy which uses no information. Therefore, the value of messages provided by filter rules is zero. Technical trading doesn't work.

The third inference which can be drawn from filter tests is that the market appears to follow a submartingale. All the securities tested had average positive returns. This makes sense because risky assets are expected to yield positive returns to compensate investors for the risk they undertake.

G. THE JOINT HYPOTHESIS OF MARKET EFFICIENCY AND THE CAPM

Statistical tests and filter rules are interesting and present evidence of weak-form efficiency, but are limited by the fact that they cannot compare assets of different risk. The CAPM provides a theory which allows the expected return of a fair-game model to be conditional on a relevant costless measure of risk.[14] If the CAPM is written as a fair game, we have

$$\epsilon_{jt} = R_{jt} - E(R_{jt}|\hat{\beta}_{jt}),$$

$$E(R_{jt}|\hat{\beta}_{jt}) = R_{ft} + [E(R_{mt}|\hat{\beta}_{mt}) - R_{ft}]\hat{\beta}_{jt}, \tag{9.14}$$

$$E(\epsilon_{jt}) = 0, \tag{9.15}$$

where

$E(R_{jt}|\hat{\beta}_{jt}) =$ the expected rate of return on the jth asset during this time period, given a prediction of its systematic risk, $\hat{\beta}_{jt}$,

$R_{ft} =$ the risk-free rate of return during this time period,

$E(R_{mt}|\hat{\beta}_{mt}) =$ the expected market rate of return, given a prediction of its systematic risk, $\hat{\beta}_{mt}$,

$\hat{\beta}_{jt} =$ the estimated systematic risk of the jth security based on last time period's information structure η_{t-1}.

The CAPM is graphed in Fig. 9.5. According to the theory, the only relevant parameter necessary to evaluate the expected return for every security is its systematic risk.[15] Therefore, if the CAPM is true *and* if markets are efficient, the expected return of every asset should fall exactly on the security market line. Any deviation from the expected return is interpreted as an abnormal return, ϵ_{jt}, and can be taken as evidence of market inefficiency *if* the CAPM is correct.

---

[14] Note that the discussion which follows also applies the Arbitrage Pricing Theory if one allows the expected return to depend on multiple factor loadings (i.e., multiple betas).

[15] For a detailed explanation of the CAPM and empirical tests of it, see Chapter 7.

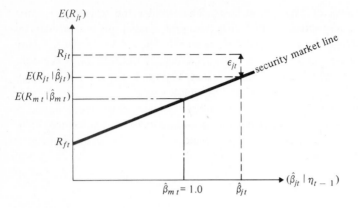

Figure 9.5
The CAPM as a fair game.

The CAPM is derived from a set of assumptions which are very similar to those of market efficiency. For example, the Sharpe-Lintner-Mossin derivation of the CAPM assumes:

- All investors are single-period expected-utility-of-wealth maximizers whose utility functions are based on the mean and variance of return.

- All investors can borrow or lend an indefinite amount at the risk-free rate, and there are no restrictions on short sales.

- All investors have homogeneous expectations of the end-of-period joint distributions of returns.

- Securities markets are frictionless and perfectly competitive.

In Chapter 10 we shall report the results of several empirical studies which use the CAPM as a tool for analyzing capital market efficiency. However, one should always keep in mind the fact that the CAPM and capital market efficiency are joint and inseparable hypotheses. If capital markets are inefficient, then the assumptions of the CAPM are invalid and a different model is required. And if the CAPM is inappropriate, even though capital markets are efficient, then the CAPM is the wrong tool to use in order to test for efficiency.

Various sophisticated empirical tests of the CAPM by Black, Jensen, and Scholes [1972], Black and Scholes [1974], and Fama and MacBeth [1973] show that the CAPM fits reality surprisingly well. However, because the theoretical CAPM assumes market efficiency, any empirical results which show that on the average there are no significant deviations from the model are merely consistent with market efficiency. They do not necessarily prove market efficiency because the model might be wrong. Therefore, any test of market efficiency which uses the CAPM to adjust for risk is, as mentioned before, a joint test of the CAPM which assumes market efficiency for its derivation and of market efficiency itself.

One may also ask the question: "If I can accurately predict systematic risk, $\hat{\beta}_{jt}$, I can also predict the expected rate of return on an asset; doesn't this mean that I can beat the market?" The answer, of course, is: "Probably not." If the information necessary to estimate $\hat{\beta}_{jt}$ is publicly available and if markets are efficient in their semistrong form, then prices will instantaneously and fully reflect all the information relevant for estimating $\hat{\beta}_{jt}$, the expected return of the security will fall exactly on the security line, and no abnormal returns will be observed.

Perhaps the most interesting use of the CAPM is to examine historical situations to see whether or not the market was efficient for a particular set of information. If the CAPM is valid (we shall assume it is, but keep in mind that it is a joint hypothesis with market efficiency), then any evidence of persistent deviations from the security market line can be interpreted as evidence of capital market inefficiency with regard to a particular information set. Chapter 10 is devoted to tests of market efficiency with regard to various information sets.

SUMMARY

The hypothesis of capital market efficiency has attracted a great deal of interest and critial comment. This is somewhat surprising because capital market efficiency is a fairly limited concept. It says that the prices of securities instantaneously and fully reflect all available relevant information. It does not imply that product markets are perfectly competitive or that information is costless.

Capital market efficiency relies on the ability of arbitrageurs to recognize that prices are out of line and to make a profit by driving them back to an equilibrium value which is consistent with available information. Given this type of behavioral paradigm, one often hears the following questions: "If capital market efficiency implies that no one can beat the market (i.e., make an abnormal profit), then how can analysts be expected to exist since they too cannot beat the market?" "If capital markets are efficient, how can we explain the existence of a multibillion dollar security analysis industry?" The answer, of course, is that neither of these questions is inconsistent with efficient capital markets. First, analysts can and do make profits. However, they compete with each other to do so. If the profit to analysis becomes abnormally large, then new individuals will enter the analysis business until, on average, the return from analysis equals the cost (which, by the way, includes a fair return to the resources which are employed). As shown by Cornell and Roll [1981] it is reasonable to have efficient markets where people earn different gross rates of return because they pay differing costs for information. However, net of costs their rates of return will be equal (to zero).

As we shall see in the next chapter, the concept of capital market efficiency is important in a wide range of applied topics, such as accounting information, new issues of securities, and portfolio performance measurement. By and large, the evidence seems to indicate that capital markets are efficient in the weak and semistrong forms, but not in the strong form.

PROBLEM SET

9.1 Suppose you know with certainty that the Clark Capital Corporation will pay a dividend of $10 per share on every January 1 forever. The continuously compounded risk-free rate is 5% (also forever).

a) Graph the price path of the Clark Capital common stock over time.

b) Is this (highly artificial) example a random walk? A martingale? A submartingale? (Why?)

9.2 Given the following situations, determine in each case whether or not the hypothesis of an efficient capital market (semistrong form) is contradicted.

a) Through the introduction of a complex computer program into the analysis of past stock price changes, a brokerage firm is able to predict price movements well enough to earn a consistent 3% profit, adjusted for risk, above normal market returns.

b) On the average, investors in the stock market this year are expected to earn a positive return (profit) on their investment. Some investors will earn considerably more than others.

c) You have discovered that the square root of any given stock price multiplied by the day of the month provides an indication of the direction in price movement of that particular stock with a probability of .7.

d) An SEC suit was filed against Texas Gulf Sulfur Company in 1965 because its corporate employees had made unusually high profits on company stock which they had purchased after exploratory drilling had started in Ontario (in 1959), and before stock prices rose dramatically (in 1964) with the announcement of the discovery of large mineral deposits in Ontario.

9.3 The First National Bank has been losing money on automobile consumer loans, and is considering the implementation of a new loan procedure which requires a credit check on loan applicants. Experience indicates that 82% of the loans were paid off while the remainder defaulted. However, if the credit check is run, the probabilities can be revised as follows:

	Favorable Credit Check	Unfavorable Credit Check
Loan is paid	.9	.5
Loan is defaulted	.1	.5

An estimated 80% of the loan applicants receive a favorable credit check. Assume that the bank earns 18% on successful loans, loses 100% on defaulted loans, suffers an opportunity cost of 18% when the loan is not granted but would have been successful, and an opportunity cost of 0% when the loan is not granted and would have defaulted. If the cost of a credit check is 5% of the value of the loan and the bank is risk neutral, should the bank go ahead with the new policy?

9.4 Hearty Western Foods, one of the nation's largest consumer products firms, is trying to decide whether it should spend $5 million to test market a new ready-to-eat product (called Kidwich), to proceed directly to a nationwide marketing effort, or to cancel the product. The expected payoffs (in millions of dollars) from cancellation versus nationwide marketing are given below:

	Action	
Market Conditions	*Cancel*	*Go Nationwide*
No acceptance	0	−10
Marginal	0	10
Success	0	80

Prior experience with nationwide marketing efforts has been:

Market Conditions	*Probability*
No acceptance	.6
Marginal	.3
Success	.1

If the firm decides to test market the product, the following information will become available:

		Probability		
		No acceptance	Marginal	Success
Outcome Pre-	No acceptance	.9	.1	0
dicted by the	Marginal	.1	.7	.2
Test Market	Success	.1	.3	.6

For example, if the test market results predict a success, there is a 60% chance that the nationwide marketing effort really will be a success but a 30% chance it will be marginal and a 10% chance it will have no acceptance.

1. If the firm is risk neutral, should it test market the product or not?
2. If the firm is risk averse with a utility function

$$U(W) = \ln(W + 11),$$

should it test market the product or not?

9.5 The efficient-market hypothesis implies that abnormal returns are expected to be zero. Yet in order for markets to be efficient, arbitrageurs must be able to force prices back into equilibrium. If they earn profits in doing so, is this fact inconsistent with market efficiency?

9.6

a) In a poker game with six players, you can expect to lose 83% of the time. How can this still be a martingale?

b) In the options market, call options expire unexercised over 80% of the time.[16] Thus the option holders frequently lose all their investment. Does this imply that the options market is not a fair game? Not a martingale? Not a submartingale?

---

[16] See Chapter 8 for a description of call options.

9.7 If securities markets are efficient, what is the NPV of any security, regardless of its risk?

9.8 From time to time the federal government considers passing into law an excess profits tax on U.S. corporations. Given what you know about efficient markets and the CAPM, how would you define excess profits? What would be the effect of an excess profits tax on the investor?

9.9 State the assumptions inherent in this statement: A condition for market efficiency is that there be no second-order stochastic dominance.

REFERENCES

Alexander, S. S., "Price Movements in Speculative Markets: Trends or Random Walks," *Industrial Management Review*, May 1961.

Black, F., M. Jensen, and M. Scholes, "The Capital Asset Pricing Model: Some Empirical Tests," in Jensen, ed., *Studies in the Theory of Capital Markets*. Praeger, New York, 1972, 79–124.

Black, F., and M. Scholes, "The Effects of Dividend Yield and Dividend Policy on Common Stock Prices and Returns," *Journal of Financial Economics*, May 1974, 1–22.

Cornell, B., and R. Roll, "Strategies for Pairwise Competitions in Markets and Organizations," *The Bell Journal of Economics*, Spring 1981, 201–213.

Fama, E. F., "The Behavior of Stock Market Prices," *The Journal of Business*, 1965, 34–105.

————, "Efficient Capital Markets: A Review of Theory and Empirical Work," *The Journal of Finance*, May 1970, 383–417.

————, *Foundations of Finance*. Basic Books, New York, 1976.

————, and M. Blume, "Filter Rules and Stock Market Trading Profits," *The Journal of Business*, January (spec. supp.), 1966, 226–241.

Fama, E. F., and J. MacBeth, "Risk, Return and Equilibrium: Empirical Test," *Journal of Political Economy*, May/June 1973, 607–636.

Finnerty, J. E., "Insiders and Market Efficiency," *Journal of Finance*, September 1976, 1141–1148.

Forsythe, R., T. Palfrey, and C. R. Plott, "Asset Valuation in an Experimental Market," *Econometrica*, May 1982, 537–567.

Green, J. R., "Information, Efficiency and Equilibrium," discussion paper No. 284, Harvard Institute of Economic Research, March 1974.

Grossman, S. J., "On the Efficiency of Competitive Stock Markets Where Trades Have Diverse Information," *The Journal of Finance*, May 1976, 573–586.

————, and J. Stiglitz, "Information and Competitive Price Systems," *The American Economic Review*, May 1976, 246–253.

————, "The Impossibility of Informationally Efficient Markets," *The American Economic Review*, June 1980, 393–408.

Harrison, J. M., and D. M. Kreps, "Speculative Investor Behavior in a Stock Market with Heterogeneous Expectations," *Quarterly Journal of Economics*, May 1978, 323–336.

Hayek, F. H., "The Use of Knowledge in Society," *American Economic Review*, September 1945.

Hirshleifer, J., and J. Riley, "The Analytics of Uncertainty and Information—An Expository Survey," *The Journal of Economic Literature,* December 1979, 1375–1421.

Huang, C. C., I. Vertinsky, and W. T. Ziemba, "Sharp Bounds on the Value of Perfect Information," *Operations Research,* January–February 1977, 128–139.

Jaffe, J., "The Effect of Regulation Changes on Insider Trading," *The Bell Journal of Economics and Management Science,* Spring, 1974, 93–121.

Keynes, J. M., *The General Theory of Employment, Interest and Money.* Harcourt Brace, New York, 1936.

Lucas, R. E., "Expectations and the Neutrality of Money," *Journal of Economic Theory,* April 1972, 103–124.

Marschak, J., *Economic Information, Decisions, and Predictions, Selected Essays,* vol II. Reidel, Boston, 1974.

Miller, R. M., C. R. Plott, and V. L. Smith, "Intertemporal Competitive Equilibrium: An Empirical Study of Speculation," *The American Economic Review,* June 1981, 448–459.

Plott, C. R., and S. Sunder, "Efficiency of Experimental Security Markets with Insider Information: An Application of Rational Expectations Models," *Journal of Political Economy,* forthcoming.

Samuelson, P. A., "Proof that Properly Anticipated Prices Fluctuate Randomly," *Industrial Management Review,* Spring 1965, 41–49.

Smith, V. L., "Experimental Economics: Induced Value Theory," *American Economic Review,* May 1976, 274–279.

CORPORATE POLICY: THEORY, EVIDENCE, AND APPLICATIONS

  The first part of the text covers most of what has come to be recognized as a unified theory of decision making under uncertainty as applied to the field of finance. The theory of finance, as presented in the first half of the text, is applicable to a wide range of finance topics. The theoretical foundations are prerequisite to almost any of the traditional subject areas in finance curricula; for example, portfolio management, corporation finance, commercial banking, money and capital markets, financial institutions, security analysis, international finance, investment banking, speculative markets, insurance, and case studies in finance. Since all these topics require a thorough understanding of decision making under uncertainty, all use the theory of finance.

The second half of this text focuses, for the most part, on applications of the theory of finance to a corporate setting. The fundamental issues are: Does financing matter? Does the type of financing (debt or equity) have any real effect on the value of the firm? Does the form of financial payment (dividends or capital gains) have any effect on the value of claims held by various classes of security holders?

313

Because these issues are usually discussed in the context of corporate finance they may seem to be narrow. This is not the case. First of all, the definition of a corporation is very broad. The class of corporations includes not only manufacturing firms, but also commercial banks, savings and loan associations, many brokerage houses, some investment banks, and even the major security exchanges. Second, the debt equity decision applies to all individuals as well as all corporations. Therefore, although the language is narrow, the issues are very broad indeed. They affect almost every economic entity in the private sector of the economy.

As we shall see, the theoretical answer to the question "Does financing matter?" is often a loud and resounding "Maybe." Often the answer depends on the assumptions of the model employed to study the problem. Under different sets of assumptions, different and even opposite answers are possible. This is extremely disquieting to the student of finance. Therefore, we have presented empirical evidence related to each of the theoretical hypotheses. Frequently, but not always, the preponderance of evidence supports a single conclusion.

It is important to keep in mind that hypotheses cannot be tested by the realism of the assumptions used to derive them. What counts for a positive science is the development of theories which yield valid and meaningful predictions about observed phenomena. On the first pass, what counts is whether or not the hypothesis is consistent with the evidence at hand. Further testing involves deducing new facts capable of being observed but not previously known, then checking those deduced facts against additional empirical evidence. As students of finance, which seeks to be a positive science, we must not only understand the theory, but also study the empirical evidence in order to determine which hypothesis is validated.

Chapter 10 is devoted to various empirical studies related to the efficient market hypothesis. Most of the evidence is consistent with the weak and semistrong forms of market efficiency, but inconsistent with the strong form. In certain situations, individuals with inside information appear to be able to earn abnormal returns. In particular, corporate insiders can beat the market when trading in the securities of their firm. Also, block traders can earn abnormal returns when they trade at the block price, as can purchasers of new equity issues. The last two situations will surely lead to further research because current theory cannot explain why, in the absence of barriers to entry, there appear to be inexplicable abnormal rates of return. Chapter 11 returns to the theoretical problem of how to evaluate multiperiod investments in a world with uncertainty. It shows the set of assumptions necessary in order to extend the simple one-period CAPM rules into a multiperiod world. It also discusses two interesting applied issues: the abandonment problem, and the technique for discounting uncertain costs.

Chapter 12 explores the theory of capital structure and the cost of capital. This is the first of the corporate policy questions which relate to whether or not the value of the firm is affected by the type of financing it chooses. Also, we define a cost of capital which is consistent with the objective of maximizing the wealth of the current shareholders of the firm. This helps to complete, in a consistent fashion, the theory of project selection. Capital-budgeting decisions which are consistent with shareholder wealth maximization require use of the correct technique (the NPV criterion), the correct definition of cash flows (operating cash flows after taxes), and the correct cost of capital definition.

Chapter 13 discusses empirical evidence on whether or not the debt-to-equity ratio (i.e., the type of financing) affects the value of the firm. This is one of the most difficult empirical issues in finance. Although not conclusive, the evidence is consistent with increases in the value of the firm resulting from increasing debt (up to some range) in the capital structure. However, much work remains to be done in this area. Chapter 13 also provides a short example of how to actually compute the cost of capital.

Chapter 14 looks at the relationship between dividend policy and the value of the firm. There are several competing theories. However, the dominant argument seems to be that the value of an all-equity firm depends on the expected returns from current and future investment and not on the form in which the returns are paid out. If investment is held constant, it makes no difference whether the firm pays out high or low dividends. On the other hand, a firm's announcement of increase in dividend payout may be interpreted as a signal by shareholders that the firm anticipates permanently higher levels of return from investment, and, of course, higher returns on investment will result in higher share prices.

Chapter 15 presents empirical evidence on the relationship between dividend policy and the value of the firm which, for the most part, seems to be consistent with the theory—namely, that dividend policy does not affect shareholder's wealth. The chapter also applies the valuation models (presented in Chapter 14) to an example.

Chapter 16 uses the subject of leasing to bring together a number of further applications of capital structure and cost of capital issues. We also illustrate how option pricing can help clarify the nature of an operating lease under which the lessee may exercise a contractual right to cancel (with some notice and with moderate penalties).

Chapters 17 and 18 consider the widespread phenomenon of mergers. They begin with the proposition that without synergy, value additivity holds in mergers as it does in other types of capital budgeting analysis. Mergers do not affect value unless the underlying determinants of value—the patterns of future cash flows or the applicable capitalization factors—are changed by combining firms. Empirical tests of mergers indicate that the shareholders of acquired firms benefit, on the average, but the shareholders of acquiring firms experience neither significant benefit nor harm.

Chapters 19 and 20 conclude the book by placing finance in its increasingly important international setting. A framework for analyzing the international financial decisions of business firms is developed by summarizing the applicable fundamental propositions. The Fisher effect which states that nominal interest rates reflect anticipated rates of inflation is carried over to its international implications. This leads to the Interest Rate Parity Theorem, which states that the current forward exchange rate for a country's currency in relation to the currency of another country will reflect the present interest rate differentials between the two countries. The Purchasing Power Parity Theorem states that the difference between the current spot exchange rate and the future spot exchange rate of a country's currency in relation to the currency of another country will reflect the ratio of the rates of price changes of their internationally traded goods. We point out that exchange risk is a "myth" in the sense that departures from fundamental parity theorems reflect changes in underlying demand and supply conditions that would cause business risks even if international markets were not involved. The fundamental relations provide the principles to guide firms in adjusting their policies to the fluctuations in the exchange rate values of the currencies in which their business is conducted.

Efficient Capital Markets: Evidence

The only valid statement is that the current price embodies all knowledge, all expectations and all discounts that infringe upon the market.

C. W. J. GRANGER AND O. MORGENSTERN,
PREDICTABILITY OF STOCK MARKET PRICES,
HEATH LEXINGTON BOOKS, LEXINGTON, MASS.,
1970, p. 20

Empirical evidence for or against the hypothesis that capital markets are efficient takes many forms. This chapter is arranged by topic rather than chronological order, degree of sophistication, or type of market efficiency being tested. Not all the articles mentioned completely support the efficient-market hypothesis. However, most agree that capital markets are efficient in the weak and semistrong forms, but not in the strong form. The majority of the studies are very recent, dating from the late 1960s and continuing up to the most recently published papers. Usually capital market efficiency has been tested in the large and sophisticated capital markets of developed countries. Therefore, one must be careful to limit any conclusions to the appropriate arena from which they are drawn.

317

Research into the efficiency of capital markets is an ongoing process, and the work is being extended to include assets other than common stock as well as to smaller and less sophisticated marketplaces.

A. EMPIRICAL MODELS USED FOR RESIDUAL ANALYSIS

Before discussing the empirical tests of market efficiency it is useful to review the three basic types of empirical models which are frequently employed. The differences between them are important. The simplest model, called the market model, simply argues that returns on security j are linearly related to returns on a "market" portfolio. Mathematically, the *market model* is described by

$$R_{jt} = a_j + b_j R_{mt} + \epsilon_{jt}. \tag{10.1}$$

The market model is not supported by any theory. It assumes that the slope and intercept terms are constant over the time period during which the model is fit to the available data. This is a strong assumption, particularly if the time series is long.

The second model uses the capital asset pricing theory. It requires the intercept term to be equal to the risk-free rate, or the rate of return on the minimum variance zero-beta portfolio, both of which change over time. The model, the CAPM, is written

$$R_{jt} = R_{ft} + [R_{mt} - R_{ft}] \beta_j + \epsilon_{jt}. \tag{7.32}$$

Note, however, that systematic risk is assumed to remain constant over the interval of estimation. The use of the CAPM for residual analysis was explained at the end of Chapter 9.

Finally, we sometimes see the *empirical market line,* which was explained in Chapter 7 and is written as

$$R_{jt} = \hat{\gamma}_{0t} + \hat{\gamma}_{1t} \beta_{jt} + \epsilon_{jt}. \tag{7.34}$$

Although related to the CAPM, it does not require the intercept term to equal the risk-free rate. Instead, both the intercept, $\hat{\gamma}_{0t}$, and the slope, $\hat{\gamma}_{1t}$, are the best linear estimates taken from cross-section data each time period (typically each month). Furthermore, it has the advantage that no parameters are assumed to be constant over time.

All three models use the residual term, ϵ_{jt}, as a measure of risk-adjusted abnormal performance. However, only one of the models, the second, relies exactly on the theoretical specification of the Sharpe-Lintner capital asset pricing model.

In each of the empirical studies which are discussed, we shall mention the empirical technique by name because the market model is not subject to Roll's critique (discussed in Chapter 7), while the CAPM and the empirical market line are. Thus, residual analysis which employs the CAPM or the empirical market line may be subject to criticism.

B. ACCOUNTING INFORMATION

Market efficiency requires that security prices instantaneously and fully reflect all available relevant information. But what information is *relevant?* And how *fast* do security prices really react to new information? The answers to these questions are of particular interest to corporate officers who report the performance of their firm to the public, to the accounting profession which audits these reports, and to the Securities and Exchange Commission which regulates securities information.

The market value of assets is the present value of their cash flows discounted at the appropriate risk-adjusted rate. Investors should care only about the cash-flow implications of various corporate decisions. However, corporations report accounting definitions of earnings, not cash flow, and frequently the two are not related. Does an efficient market look at the effect of managerial decisions on earnings per share (eps) or cash flow? This is not an unimportant question, because frequently managers are observed to maximize eps rather than cash flow because they believe that the market value of the company depends on reported eps, when in fact (as we shall see), it does not.

Inventory accounting provides a good example of a situation where managerial decisions have opposite effects on eps and cash flow. During an inflationary economy the cost of producing the most recent inventory continues to rise. On the books, inventory is recorded at cost so that in the example given in Table 10.1 the fourth item added to the inventory costs more to produce than the first. If management elects to use first-in-first-out (FIFO) accounting, it will record a cost of goods sold of $25 against a revenue of $100 when an item is sold from inventory. This results in eps of $.45. On the other hand, if LIFO (last-in-first-out) is used, eps is $.06. The impact of the two accounting treatments on cash flow is in exactly the opposite direction. Because the goods were manufactured in past time periods, the actual costs of production are sunk costs and irrelevant to current decision making. Therefore, current cash flows are revenues less taxes. The cost of goods sold is a noncash charge. Therefore, with FIFO, cash flow per share is $.70 while with LIFO it is $.96. LIFO provides more cash flow because taxes are lower.

Table 10.1 FIFO versus LIFO

	LIFO	FIFO	Inventory at Cost	
Revenue	100	100		
Cost of goods sold	90	25	Fourth item	90 → LIFO
Operating income	10	75	Third item	60
Taxes at 40%	4	30	Second item	40
Net income	6	45	First item	25 → FIFO
eps (100 shares)	.06	.45		
Cash flow per share	.96	.70		

If investors really value cash flow and not eps, we should expect to see stock prices rise when firms announce a switch from FIFO to LIFO accounting during inflationary periods. Sunder [1973, 1975] collected a sample of 110 firms which switched from FIFO to LIFO between 1946 and 1966 and 22 firms which switched from LIFO to FIFO. His procedure was to look at the pattern of cumulative average residuals from the market model. A residual return is the difference between the actual return and the return estimated by the model:

$$\epsilon_{jt} = R_{jt} - E(R_{jt}|\hat{\beta}_{jt}).$$

The usual technique is to estimate ϵ_{jt} over an interval surrounding the economic event of interest. Taking monthly data, Sunder used all observations of returns except for those occurring plus or minus 12 months around the announcement of the inventory-accounting change. He then used the estimated $\hat{\beta}_{jt}$, the actual risk-free rate, and the actual market return during the 24-month period around the announcement date to predict the expected return.[1] Differences between estimated and actual returns were then averaged across all companies for each month. The average abnormal return in a given month is

$$AR_t = \frac{1}{N} \sum_{j=1}^{N} \epsilon_{jt}, \quad \text{where } N = \text{the number of companies.}$$

The cumulative average return is the sum of average returns over all months from the start of the data up to and including the current month, T.

$$\text{CAR} = \sum_{t=1}^{T} AR_t,$$

where

$T =$ the number of months being summed ($T = 1, 2, \ldots, M$),

$M =$ the total number of months in the sample.

If there were no abnormal change in the value of the firm associated with the switch from FIFO to LIFO, we should observe no pattern in the residuals. They would fluctuate around zero and on the average would equal zero. In other words, we would have a fair game. Figure 10.1 shows Sunder's results. Assuming that risk does not change during the 24-month period, the cumulative average residuals for the firms switching to LIFO rise by 5.3% during the 12 months prior to the announcement of the accounting change. This is consistent with the fact that shareholders actually value cash flow, not eps. However, it does not necessarily mean that a switch to LIFO causes higher value. Almost all studies of this type, which focus on a particular phenomenon, suffer from what has come to be known as *post-selection bias*. In this case, firms may decide to switch to LIFO because they are already doing well and their value may have risen for that reason, not because of the switch in accounting method. Either way, Sunder's results are inconsistent with the fact that shareholders

---

[1] Sunder used a moving-average beta technique in his second study [1975]. However, it did not substantially change his results.

Figure 10.1
Cumulative average residuals for 24 months around the
accounting change. (From Sunder, S., "Relationship Between
Accounting Changes and Stock Prices: Problems of
Measurement and Some Empirical Evidence," reprinted from
Empirical Research in Accounting: Selected Studies, 1973, 18.)

look only at changes in eps in order to value common stock. There is no evidence
that the switch to LIFO lowered value even though it did lower eps.

Kaplan and Roll [1972] investigated two types of accounting changes which
have the effect of increasing reported eps but have no effect on cash flows. In 1964
companies were allowed to report to shareholders the entire amount of the investment
tax credit for an investment in the year it was made, instead of taking the tax saving
into income spread over the life of the asset as they were still required to do for
tax purposes. Three hundred and thirty-two companies elected this approach. It increased their eps but had no effect on their tax books or cash flows. Figure 10.2
shows the pattern of cumulative average residuals using weekly data. It's hard to
tell whether or not there are any statistically significant departures from a fair game.

Figure 10.2
Cumulative average residuals for 60 weeks around a change to the flow-through
method of reporting investment tax credits. (From Kaplan, R. S., and R.
Roll, "Investor Evaluation of Accounting Information: Some Empirical
Evidence," reprinted from *The Journal of Business,* April 1972, 237.)

Changes of ±2% are not large and are within the range of deviations which may be wiped out by transactions costs. But even if one considers the positive residuals following the reported accounting change of higher eps to be significant, it appears that people were only temporarily fooled because cumulative residuals return to zero approximately 25 weeks after the announcement.

The second type of accounting change was a switchback from reporting accelerated to straight-line depreciation which was permitted on the annual report but not on the tax books. Again, the effect is to increase reported eps while there is no change in cash flow. The pattern of cumulative average residuals for a sample of 71 firms is shown in Fig. 10.3. The residuals are negative because firms using the depreciation change were, in general, doing worse than the market. Furthermore, there is no evidence that the accounting change which increased reported eps had any positive effect on the value of the firm. Again, the evidence is consistent with the fact that investors actually discount cash flows and disregard changes in eps which do not reflect real economic events.

The two studies above indicate that investors in efficient markets attempt to evaluate news about the effect of managerial decisions on cash flows—not on eps. This fact has direct implications for the accounting treatment of mergers and acquisitions. Two types of accounting treatment are possible: pooling or purchase. In a pooling arrangement the income statements and balance sheets of the merging firms are simply added together. On the other hand, when one company purchases another, the assets of the acquired company are added to the acquiring company's balance sheet along with an item called *goodwill*. Goodwill is the difference between the purchase price and the book value of the acquired company's assets. Regulations require that goodwill be written off as a charge against earnings *after taxes* in a period not to exceed 40 years. Because the writeoff is after taxes, there is no effect on cash flows but reported eps decline. The fact that there is no difference in cash flows between pooling and purchase and the fact that cash flows, not eps, are the relevant information used by investors to value the firm should convey to management the message that the accounting treatment of mergers and acquisitions is a matter

Figure 10.3

Cumulative average residuals for 60 weeks around a switchback to reporting straight-line depreciation. (From Kaplan, R. S., and R. Roll, "Investor Evaluation of Accounting Information: Some Empirical Evidence," reprinted from *The Journal of Business,* April 1972, 239.)

of indifference.[2] Yet many managements prefer pooling, presumably because they don't like to see eps decline due to the writeoff of goodwill. No economically rational basis for this type of behavior can be cited.

In a recent empirical study Hong, Kaplan, and Mandelker [1978] tested the effect of pooling and purchase techniques on stock prices of acquiring firms. Using monthly data between 1954 and 1964, they compared a sample of 122 firms which used pooling and 37 which used purchase. The acquired firm had to be at least 3% of the net asset value of the acquiring firm. Mergers were excluded from the sample if another merger took place within 18 months, if the acquiring firm was not NYSE listed, or if the merger terms were not based on an exchange of shares. (This last criterion rules out taxable mergers.)

Using the simple time-series market model given below, they calculated cumulative abnormal residuals:

$$\ln R_{jt} = \alpha_j + \beta_j \ln R_{mt} + u_{jt},$$

where

R_{jt} = return on the jth security in time period t,

α_j = an intercept term assumed to be constant over the entire time period,

β_j = systematic risk assumed to be constant over the entire time period,

R_{mt} = market return in time period t,

u_{jt} = abnormal return for the jth security in time period t.

When the cumulative average residuals were centered around the month of the actual merger, the patterns revealed no evidence of abnormal performance for the sample of 122 poolings. This is shown in Fig. 10.4. Therefore there is no evidence that "dirty pooling" raises the stock prices of acquiring firms. Investors are not fooled by the accounting convention.

These results are just as important for acquiring firms which had to write off goodwill against their after-tax earnings because they used the purchase technique. As shown in Fig. 10.5, there is no evidence of negative abnormal returns, which is what we would expect if investors looked at eps. Instead, there is weak evidence that shareholders of acquiring firms experienced positive abnormal returns when the purchase technique was used. This is consistent with the hypothesis that investors value cash flows and that they disregard reported eps.

The empirical studies of Sunder [1973, 1975], Kaplan and Roll [1972], and Hong, Kaplan, and Mandelker [1978] provide evidence on what is meant by relevant accounting information. By relevant we mean any information about the *expected distribution*

---

[2] The IRS allows the book value of the assets of the acquired firm to be written up upon purchase. This reduces the amount of goodwill-created, but even more important, it creates a depreciation tax shield which would not exist in a pooling arrangement. Therefore, in many cases cash flows for purchase will be higher than pooling. In these cases purchase is actually preferable to pooling, at least from the point of view of the acquiring firm.

Figure 10.4
Cumulative abnormal residuals for 122 poolings with market value greater than
book value in the month relative to merger. (From Hong, H., R. S. Kaplan,
and G. Mandelker, "Pooling vs. Purchase: the Effects of Accounting for Mergers
on Stock Prices," reprinted with permission of *The Accounting Review*, January
1978, 42.)

of future cash flows. Next, a study by Ball and Brown [1968] provides some evidence
about the speed of adjustment of efficient markets to new information.

   Earnings data and cash flows are usually highly correlated. The examples discussed
above merely serve to point out some situations where they are not related and
therefore allow empiricists to distinguish between the two. Ball and Brown [1968]
used monthly data for a sample of 261 firms between 1946 and 1965 to evaluate
the usefulness of information in annual reports. First, they separated the sample
into companies which had earnings that were either higher or lower than those predicted by a naive time-series model. The model for change in earnings was

$$\Delta I_{jt} = \hat{a} + \hat{b}_j \, \Delta m_t + \epsilon_{jt},$$ (10.2)

where

$\Delta I_{jt} =$ the change in earnings per share for the jth firm,
$\Delta m_t =$ the change in the average eps for all firms (other than firm j) in the market.

Figure 10.5
Thirty-seven purchases with market value greater than book value in the month
relative to merger. (From Hong, H., R. S. Kaplan, and G. Mandelker, "Pooling
vs. Purchase: the Effects of Accounting for Mergers on Stock Prices," reprinted
with permission of *The Accounting Review*, January 1978, 42.)

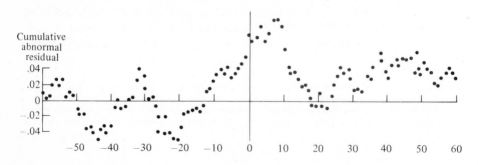

Next, this regression was used to predict next year's change in earnings, $\widehat{\Delta I}_{j,t+1}$:

$$\widehat{\Delta I}_{j,t+1} = \hat{a} + \hat{b}_j \, \Delta m_{t+1}, \tag{10.3}$$

where

$\hat{a}, \hat{b}$ = coefficients estimated from time-series fits of Eq. (10.3) to the data,

Δm_{t+1} = the actual change in market average eps during the $(t + 1)$th time period.

Finally, estimated earnings changes were compared with actual earnings changes. If the actual change was greater than estimated, the company was put into a portfolio where returns were expected to be positive, and vice versa.

Figure 10.6 plots an abnormal performance index (API) which represents the value of one dollar invested in a portfolio 12 months before an annual report and held for T months (where $T = 1, 2, \ldots, 12$). It is computed as follows:

$$\text{API} = \frac{1}{N} \sum_{j=1}^{N} \prod_{t=1}^{T} (1 + \epsilon_{jt}),$$

where

N = the number of companies in a portfolio,

$T = 1, 2, \ldots, 12$,

ϵ_{jt} = abnormal performance measured by deviations from the market model.

A quick look at Fig. 10.6 shows that when earnings are higher than predicted, returns are abnormally high. Furthermore, returns appear to adjust gradually until, by the time of the annual report, almost all the adjustment has occurred. Most of the information contained in the annual report is anticipated by the market *before* the annual report is released. In fact, anticipation is so accurate that the actual income number does not appear to cause any unusual jumps in the API in the announcement month. Most of the content of the annual report (about 85% to 90%) is captured by more timely sources of information. Apparently market prices adjust continuously to new information as it becomes publicly available throughout the year. The annual report has little new information to add.

These results suggest that prices in the marketplace continuously adjust in an unbiased manner to new information. Two implications for the corporate treasurers are: (1) Significant new information, which will affect the future cash flows of the firm, should be announced as soon as it becomes available so that shareholders can use it without the (presumably greater) expense of discovering it from alternative sources; and (2) it probably doesn't make any difference whether cash flow effects are reported in the balance sheet, the income statement, or footnotes—the market can evaluate the news as long as it is publicly available, whatever form it may take.

The Ball and Brown study raised the question of whether or not annual reports contain any new information. More recent studies by Aharony and Swary [1980], Joy, Litzenberger and McEnally [1977], and Watts [1978] have focused on quarterly earnings reports where information revealed to the market is (perhaps) more timely

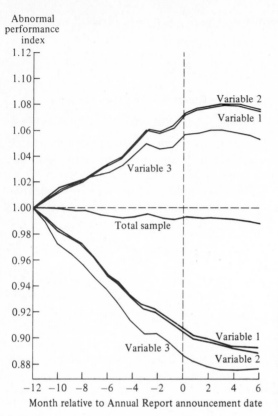

Figure 10.6
Abnormal performance index of portfolios chosen on the basis of differences between actual and predicted accounting income. (From Ball, R., and P. Brown, "An Empirical Evaluation of Accounting Income Numbers," reprinted with permission of *The Journal of Accounting Research,* Autumn 1968, 169.)

than annual reports.[3] They typically use a time series model to predict quarterly earnings, then form two portfolios of equal risk, one consisting of firms with earnings higher than predicted and the other of firms with lower than expected earnings. The combined portfolio, which is long in the higher than expected earnings firms and short in the lower than expected earnings firms, is a zero beta portfolio which (in perfect markets) requires no investment. It is an arbitrage portfolio and should have zero expected return. Watts [1978] finds a statistically significant return in the quarter of the announcement—a clear indication that quarterly earnings reports contain new information. However, he also finds a statistically significant return in the following quarter and concludes that "the existence of those abnormal returns is evidence that the market is inefficient."

Quarterly earnings reports are sometimes followed by announcements of dividend changes which also affect the stock price. To study this problem, Aharony and Swary [1980] examine all dividend and earnings announcements within the same quarter which are at least 11 trading days apart. They conclude that both quarterly earnings announcements and dividend change announcements have statistically significant effects on the stock price. But more important they find no evidence of market inefficiency when the two types of announcement effects are separated. They used daily data

---

[3] See also articles by Brown [1978], Griffin [1977] and Foster [1977].

and Watts [1978] used quarterly data, so we cannot be sure that the conclusions of the two studies regarding market inefficiency are inconsistent. All we can say is that unexpected changes in quarterly dividends and in quarterly earnings both have significant effects on the value of the firm and that more research needs to be done on possible market inefficiencies following the announcement of unexpected earnings changes.

C. BLOCK TRADES

During a typical day for an actively traded security on a major stock exchange, thousands of shares will be traded, usually in round lots ranging between one hundred and several hundred shares. However, occasionally a large block, say 10,000 shares or more, is brought to the floor for trading. The behavior of the marketplace during the time interval around the trading of a large block provides a "laboratory" where the following questions can be investigated: (1) Does the block trade disrupt the market? (2) If the stock price falls when the block is sold, is the fall a liquidity effect, an information effect, or both? (3) Can anyone earn abnormal returns from the fall in price? (4) How fast does the market adjust to the effects of a block trade?

In perfect (rather than efficient) capital markets all securities of equal risk are perfect substitutes for each other. Because all individuals are assumed to possess the same information and because markets are assumed to be frictionless, the number of shares traded in a given security should have no effect on its price. If markets are less than perfect, the sale of a large block may have two effects (see Fig. 10.7).

Figure 10.7
Competing hypotheses of price behavior around the sale of a large block.

Figure 10.8
Abnormal performance index on days around a secondary
distribution. (From Scholes, M., "The Market for
Securities: Substitution vs. Price Pressure and the Effects
of Information on Share Prices," reprinted with permission
of *The Journal of Business,* April 1972, 193.)

First, if it is believed to carry with it some new information about the security, the
price will change (permanently) to reflect the new information. As illustrated in parts
(c) and (d) of Fig. 10.7, the closing price is lower than the opening price and it
remains low permanently.[4] Second, if buyers must incur extra costs when they accept
the block, there may be a (temporary) decline in price to reflect what has been in
various articles described as a price pressure, or distribution effect, or liquidity premium, as shown in parts (a) and (c). Figure 10.7 depicts how hypothesized information
or price pressure effects can be expected to show up in continuous transactions data.
For example, if the sale of a large block has both effects (Fig. 10.7(c)) we may
expect the price to fall from the price before the trade $(-T)$ to the block price
(BP) at the time of the block trade (BT), then recover quickly from any price pressure
effect by the time of the next trade $(+T)$ but to remain at a permanently lower
level which reflects the impact of new information on the value of the security.

Scholes [1972] and Kraus and Stoll [1972] provided the first empirical evidence
about the price effects of block trading. Scholes used daily returns data to analyze
345 secondary distributions between July 1961 and December 1965. Secondary distributions, unlike primary distributions, are not initiated by the company but by shareholders who will receive the proceeds of the sale. The distributions are usually underwritten by an investment banking group which buys the entire block from the seller.
The shares are then sold on a subscription basis *after* normal trading hours. The
subscriber pays only the subscription price and not stock exchange or brokerage
commissions. Figure 10.8 shows an abnormal performance index based on the market
model and calculated for 40 trading days around the date of a secondary distribution.

---

[4] The permanent decline in price is also tested by looking at the pattern of day-to-day closing prices.
Evidence on this is reported in Fig. 10.8.

Table 10.2 Abnormal Performance Index for Secondary Distributions Partitioned by Vendor Category

No. of Observations in Sample	Category	API −10 to +10 days	API 0 to +10 days
192	Investment companies and mutual funds	−2.5%	−1.4%
31	Banks and insurance companies	−.3	−0.0
36	Individuals	−1.1	−.7
23	Corporations and officers	−2.9	−2.1
50	Estates and trusts	−.7	−.5

Scholes, M., "The Market for Securities: Substitution vs. Price Pressure and the Effects of Information on Share Prices," reprinted with permission of *The Journal of Business,* April 1972, 202.

The abnormal performance index falls from an initial level of 1.0 to a final value of .977 14 days after the sale, a decline of 2.2%. On the day of the secondary distribution, the average abnormal performance was −.5%. Because this study uses only close-to-close daily returns data, it focuses only on permanent price changes. We have characterized these as information effects (Fig. 10.7(c) and (d)). Further evidence that the permanent decline in price is an information effect is revealed when the API is partitioned by vendor classification. These results appear in Table 10.2.

On the day of the offering the vendor is not usually known, but we may presume that the news becomes available soon thereafter. One may expect that an estate liquidation or portfolio rebalancing by a bank or insurance company would not be motivated by information about the performance of the firm. On the other hand, corporate insiders as well as investment companies and mutual funds (with large research staffs) may be selling on the basis of adverse information. The data seem to support these suppositions. Greater price changes after the distribution are observed when the seller is presumed to have a knowledgeable reason for trading.[5]

The data available to Kraus and Stoll [1972] were a little more complete. They examined price effects for all block trades of 10,000 shares or more carried out on the NYSE between July 1, 1968, and September 30, 1969. They had prices for the close the day before the block trade, the price immediately prior to the transaction, the block price, and the closing price the day of the block trade. Abnormal performance indices based on daily data were consistent with Scholes' results. More interesting were intra-day price effects which are shown in Fig. 10.9. There is clear evidence of a price-pressure or distribution effect. The stock price recovers substantially from the block price by the end of the trading day. The recovery averages .713%. For example, a stock which sold for $50.00 before the block transaction would have a

---

[5] A second test performed by Scholes showed that there was no relationship between the size of the distribution (as a percentage of the firm) and changes in the API on the distribution date. This would lead us to reject the hypothesis that investment companies and mutual funds may have had an impact because they sold larger blocks.

Price (logarithmic)

Closing price (P_{-1})

1.8610% (E_1)

Price prior to block (PPB)

Closing price (P_0)

1.1380% (E_3)

.7130% (E_2)

Block Price (BP)

Time

End of day −1   End of day 0

Figure 10.9
Intra-day impacts of block trading. (From Kraus, A., and
H. R. Stoll, "Price Impacts of Block Trading on the New
York Stock Exchange," reprinted with permission of *The
Journal of Finance,* June 1972, 575.)

block price of $49.43, but by the end of the day the price would have recovered to
$49.79.

The Scholes and Kraus-Stoll studies find evidence of a permanent price decline
which is measured by price drops from the closing price the day before the block
trade to the closing price the day of the block transaction. These negative returns
seem to persist for at least a month after the block trade. In addition, Kraus and
Stoll found evidence of temporary intra-day price pressure effects. The implications
of these findings are discussed by Dann, Mayers, and Raab [1977], who collected
continuous transactions data during the day of a block trade for a sample of 298
blocks between July 1968 and December 1969. The open-to-block price decline was
at least 4.56% for each block in the sample. The reason for restricting the sample
to blocks with large price declines was to provide the strongest test of market efficiency.
If an individual or a group of investors can establish a trading rule which allows
them to buy a block whose open-to-block price change is at least 4.56%, then sell
at the end of the day, they may be able to earn abnormal profits. This would be
evidence of capital market inefficiency.

Testing a trading rule of this type takes great care. Normally, a block trade is
not made publicly available until the trade has already been consummated and the
transaction is recorded on the ticker. The semistrong form of market efficiency is
based on the set of publicly available information. Therefore, a critical issue is: Exactly
how fast must we react after we observe that our −4.56% trading rule has been
activated by the first publicly available announcement which occurs on the ticker

tape? Figure 10.10 shows annualized rates of return using the -4.56% rule with the purchase made x minutes after the block and the stock then sold at the close. Returns are net of actual commissions and New York State transfer taxes. For both time periods which are reported, we would have to react in less than five minutes in order to earn a positive return. Such a rapid reaction is, for all practical purposes, impossible. It seems that no abnormal returns are available to individuals who trade on publicly available information about block trades because prices react so quickly. Fifteen minutes after the block trade, transaction prices have completely adjusted to unbiased estimates of closing prices. This gives some idea of how fast the market adjusts to new, unexpected information like a block trade.

What about people who can transact at the block price? Who are they and don't they earn an abnormal return? Usually, the specialist, the floor trader (a member of the NYSE), brokerage houses, and favored customers of the brokerage houses can participate at the block price. Dann, Mayers, and Raab show that with a -4.56%

Figure 10.10
Annualized rates of return on the -4.56 rule. (From Dann, L., D. Mayers, and R. Raab, "Trading Rules, Large Blocks, and the Speed of Adjustment," reprinted from *The Journal of Financial Economics,* January 1977, 18.)

Annualized[a] rates of return on initial wealth, -4.56 percent rule; purchase at first price at least x minutes after block, sell at close[b] (using only first block per day). Gross returns less actual commissions and NY State transfer taxes (curves represent levels of initial wealth).

[a] Annualized rates of return are calculated by squaring the quantity one plus the respective six-month return.

[b] Blocks occurring within x minutes of the close were assumed not to have been acted upon.

trading rule, an individual participating in every block with purchases of $100,000 or more could have earned a net annualized rate of return of 203% for the 173 blocks which activated the filter rule. Of course, this represents the maximum realizable rate of return. Nevertheless, it is clear that even after adjusting for risk, transaction costs, and taxes, it is possible to earn rates of return in excess of what any existing theory would call "normal." This may be interpreted as evidence that capital markets are inefficient in their strong form. Individuals who are notified of the pending block trade and who can participate at the block price before the information becomes publicly available do, in fact, appear to earn excess profits.

However, Dann, Mayers, and Raab caution us that we may not properly understand all the costs which a buyer faces in a block trade. One possibility is that the specialist (or anyone else) normally holds an optimal utility-maximizing portfolio. In order to accept part of a block trade, which forces him away from that portfolio, he will charge a premium rate of return. In this way, what appear to be abnormal returns may actually be fair, competitively determined fees for a service rendered— the service of providing liquidity to a seller.

To date, the empirical research into the phenomenon of price changes around a block trade shows that block trades do not disrupt markets, that markets are efficient in the sense that they very quickly (less than 15 minutes) fully reflect all publicly available information. There is evidence of both a permanent effect and a (very) temporary liquidity or price pressure effect as illustrated in Fig. 10.7(c). The market is efficient in its semistrong form, but the fact that abnormal returns are earned by individuals who participate at the block price may indicate strong form inefficiency.

D. INSIDER TRADING

A direct test of strong-form efficiency is whether or not insiders with access to information which is not publicly available can outperform the market.[6] Jaffe [1974] collected data on insider trading from the *Official Summary of Security Transactions and Holdings* published by the Securities and Exchange Commission. He then defined an intensive trading month as one during which there were at least three more insiders selling than buying or vice versa. If a stock was intensively traded during a given month, it was included in an intensive-trading portfolio. Using the empirical market line, Jaffe then calculated cumulative average residuals. If the stock had intensive selling, its residual (which would presumably be negative) was multiplied by -1 and added to the portfolio returns, and conversely for intensive buying. For 861 observations during the 1960s, the residuals rose approximately 5% in eight months following the intensive trading event with 3% of the rise occurring in the last six months. These returns are statistically significant and are greater than transaction costs. A sample of insider trading during the 1950s produces similar results. These findings

---

[6] The Securities and Exchange Commission defines insiders as members of the Board of Directors, corporate officers, and any beneficial owner of more than 10% of any class of stock. They must disclose, on a monthly basis, any changes in their stock holdings.

suggest that insiders do earn abnormal returns and that the strong-form hypothesis of market efficiency does not hold.

Jaffe also investigated the effect of regulation changes on insider trading. Two of the most significant changes in security regulation resulted from (1) the Cady-Roberts decision in November 1961, when the SEC first exercised its power to punish insider trading and thus established the precedent that corporate officials trading on insider information were liable for civil prosecution, and (2) the Texas Gulf Sulphur case in August 1966, when the courts upheld the earlier (April 1965) SEC indictment of company officials who had suppressed and traded on news about a vast mineral strike. After examining abnormal returns from intensive insider-trading samples around dates of these historic decisions, Jaffe was forced to the following conclusion: the data could not reject the null hypothesis that the enforcement of SEC regulations in these two cases had no effect on insider trading in general. At best the regulations prohibit only the most flagrant examples of speculation based on inside information.

A study by Finnerty [1976] corroborates Jaffe's conclusions. The major difference is that the Finnerty data sample was not restricted to an intensive trading group. By testing the entire population of insiders, the empirical findings allow an evaluation of the "average" insider returns. The data include over 30,000 individual insider transactions between January 1969 and December 1972. Abnormal returns computed from the market model indicate that insiders are able to "beat the market" on a risk-adjusted basis, both when selling and when buying.

One of the interesting implications of the empirical work on insider trading is that it is consistent with the point of view that markets do *not* aggregate information. In Chapter 9, fully aggregating markets were described as those which reflect all available information even though it is not known to all market participants. In a fully aggregating market an insider should not be able to make abnormal returns because his trading activity would reveal his information to the market. The evidence on profitable insider trading shows that this is clearly not the case.

E. NEW ISSUES

There has been a long history of articles which have studied the pricing of the common stock of companies which is issued to the public for the first time. To mention a few, the list includes papers by the Securities and Exchange Commission [1963], Reilly and Hatfield [1969], Stickney [1970], McDonald and Fisher [1972], Logue [1973], Stigler [1964], and Shaw [1971]. They all faced a seemingly insoluble problem: How could returns on unseasoned issues be adjusted for risk if time-series data on pre-issue prices were nonexistent? Any estimate of systematic risk, for example, requires the computation of the covariance between time-series returns for a given security and returns on a market portfolio. But new issues are not priced until they become public. An ingenious way around this problem was employed by Ibbotson [1975]. Portfolios of new issues with identical seasoning (defined as the number of months since issue) were formed. The monthly return on the *XYZ* Company in March of 1964, say two months after its issue, was matched with the market return

Table 10.3   Gain and Loss Situations for a New Issue

	Situation	Investors	Investment Banker
I	Maximum offering price ≥ Market price ≥ Offering price	Gain	Parity
II	Maximum offering price ≥ Offering price ≥ Market price	Parity	Loss
III	Maximum offering price = Offering price ≥ Market price	Parity	Loss
IV	Market price ≥ Maximum offering price = Offering price	Gain	Parity

that month, resulting in one pair of returns for a portfolio of two months seasoning. By collecting a large number of return pairs for new issues which went public in different calendar months but which all had two months seasoning, it was possible to form a vector of returns of issues of two months seasoning for which Ibbotson could compute a covariance with the market. In this manner, he estimated the systematic risk of issues with various seasoning. Using the empirical market line, he was able to estimate abnormal performance indices in the month of initial issue (initial performance from the offering date price to the end of the first month) and in the aftermarket (months following the initial issue). From 2650 new issues between 1960 and 1969, Ibbotson randomly selected one new issue for each of the 120 calendar months.

The estimated systematic risk (beta) in the month of issue was 2.26 and the abnormal return was estimated to be 11.4%. Even after transaction costs, this represents a statistically significant positive abnormal return. Therefore, either the offering price is set too low or investors systematically overvalue new issues at the end of the first month of seasoning. Later evidence shows that the aftermarket is efficient; therefore Ibbotson focused his attention on the possibility that offering prices determined by the investment banking firm are systematically set below the fair market value of the security. Regulations of the SEC require a maximum offering price for a new issue which is usually filed two weeks in advance of the actual offering, although it can be adjusted in some cases.[7] The actual offering price is set immediately before the offering. The existence of a regulation which requires the actual offering price to be fixed creates the possibility of a "heads I lose, tails you win" situation for the underwriter. Table 10.3 shows the four possibilities which can occur in a firm commitment offering (the underwriting syndicate buys the issue from the firm for the offering price less an underwriting spread, then sells the issue to the public at the fixed offering price). The best the underwriter can do is achieve a parity situation with no gain or loss. This happens whenever the market price turns out to be above the offering price (situations I and IV). Obviously, the investment banker does not want the market price to equal or exceed the *maximum* offering price (situations III and IV). This would infuriate the issuing firm and lead to a loss of future underwriting business. Therefore, we usually observe situations I and II. But if the investment

---

[7] In most cases, the maximum offering price is set high enough to cause little concern that it may actually constrain the actual offering price.

banker receives adequate compensation from his underwriting spread for the risk he undertakes, and if he cannot gain by setting the offer price lower than the market price, then why don't we observe offer prices (which, after all, are established only moments before the issues are sold to the public) set equal to the market value? Why can investors systematically earn an abnormal return of 11.4% during the first month of issue? This conundrum, like the difference between the block price and the closing price on the day of the block, cannot easily be explained by existing finance theory.

What about new issue performance in the aftermarket, that is, for prices from the first market price onward? Figure 10.11 shows abnormal returns (based on the empirical market line) in the aftermarket for six-month holding periods and the significance tests (t-tests). The nine periods other than the initial offering period include only two periods with results which are statistically different from zero (and returns in these two periods are negative). Ibbotson concludes that the evidence cannot allow us to reject the null hypothesis that aftermarkets are efficient, although it is interesting to note that returns in seven out of ten periods show negative returns.

Figure 10.12 shows plots of changes in systematic risk in the aftermarket. Note the downward decline. The results show that the systematic risk of new issues is greater than the systematic risk of the market (which always has a beta equal to one) and that their systematic risk is not stable in that it drops as the new issues become seasoned.

Weinstein [1978] studied the price behavior of newly issued corporate bonds by measuring their excess holding period returns. Excess returns were defined as the

Figure 10.11
Abnormal returns for issues of different seasoning. (From Ibbotson, R., "Price Performance of Common Stock New Issues," reprinted from *The Journal of Financial Economics,* September 1975, 254.)

[a] Months of seasoning (n), $n = 1, 7, 13, 19, 25, 31, 37, 43, 49, 55$; $r = 6$; regressions 1-6, 7-12, ..., 55-60.

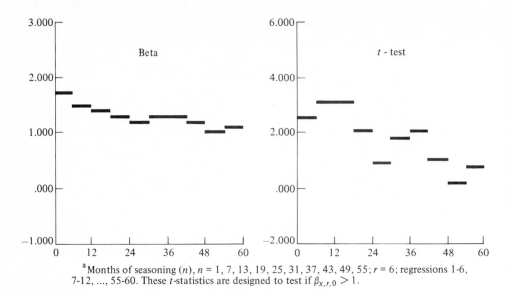

^aMonths of seasoning (n), n = 1, 7, 13, 19, 25, 31, 37, 43, 49, 55; r = 6; regressions 1-6, 7-12, ..., 55-60. These t-statistics are designed to test if $\beta_{x,r,0} > 1$.

Figure 10.12
Systematic risk of issues with different seasoning. (From Ibbotson, R., "Price Performance of Common Stock New Issues," reprinted from *The Journal of Financial Economics,* September 1975, 260.)

difference between the return on the ith newly issued bond and a portfolio of seasoned bonds with the same (Moody's) bond rating. Data were collected for 179 new issues between June 1962 and July 1974. Weinstein's conclusions for new issued bonds are similar to those of Ibbotson [1975] for newly issued stock, namely that the offering price is below the market equilibrium price but that the aftermarket is efficient. Weinstein found a .383% rate of return during the first month and only a .06% rate of return over the next six months.

F. STOCK SPLITS

Why do stocks split, and what effect, if any, do splits have on shareholder wealth? The best known study of stock splits was conducted by Fama, Fisher, Jensen, and Roll [1969]. Cumulative average residuals were calculated from the simple market model, using monthly data for an interval of 60 months around the split date for 940 splits between January 1927 and December 1959. Figure 10.13 shows the results. It plots the cumulative average return for the stock-split sample. Positive abnormal returns are observed before the split but not afterward. This would seem to indicate that splits are the cause of the abnormal returns. But such a conclusion has no economic logic to it. When the stock splits, there is no change whatsoever in the distribution of expected future cash flows which can be attributed to the split *per se.* Stock splits and stock dividends are merely paper transactions with no real economic meaning.

Cumulative average
   residual, U_m

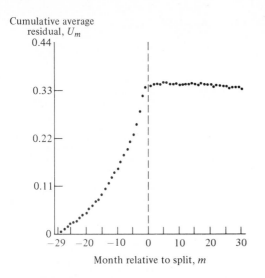

Month relative to split, m

Figure 10.13
Cumulative average residuals for 60 months
around stock splits. (From Fama, E., L. Fisher,
M. Jensen, and R. Roll, "The Adjustment of
Stock Prices to New Information," reprinted with
permission of *The International Economic
Review*, February 1969, 13. Copyright © *The
International Economic Review*.)

The run-up in the cumulative average returns prior to the stock split in Fig.
10.13 can be explained by selection bias. Stocks split because their price has increased
prior to the split date. Consequently, it should hardly be surprising that when we
select a sample of split-up stocks we observe that they have positive abnormal performance prior to the split date. Selection bias occurs because we are studying a selected
data set of stocks that have been observed to split.

Fama *et al* [1969] speculated that stock splits might be interpreted by investors
as a message about future changes in the firm's expected cash flows. They hypothesized
that stock splits might be interpreted as a message about dividend increases, which
in turn imply that the managers of the firm feel confident that it can maintain a
permanently higher level of cash flows. In order to test this hypothesis, the sample
was divided into those firms which increased their dividends beyond the average
for the market in the interval following the split, and those which paid out lower
dividends. The results, shown in Fig. 10.14, reveal that stocks in the dividend "increased" class have slightly positive returns following the split. This is consistent
with the hypothesis that splits are interpreted as messages about dividend increases.[8]
Of course, a dividend increase does not always follow a split. Hence the slightly

---

[8] This does not imply that higher dividend payout *per se* causes an increase in the value of the firm. In
Chapter 14 (Dividend Policy) we shall see that higher dividends are interpreted as signals that the future
cash flows from the firm will increase.

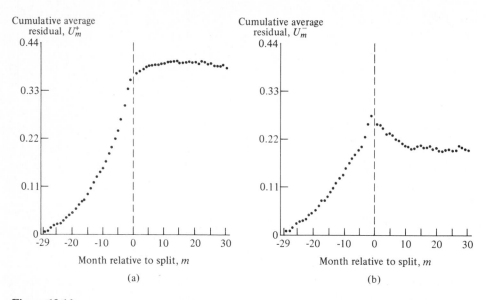

Figure 10.14
Cumulative average residuals for splits with (a) dividend increases and (b) decreases. (From Fama, E., L. Fisher, M. Jensen, and R. Roll, "The Adjustment of Stock Prices to New Information," reprinted with permission of *The International Economic Review*, February 1969, 15. Copyright © *The International Economic Review*.)

positive abnormal return for the dividend-increase group reflects small price adjustments which occur when the market is absolutely sure of the increase. On the other hand, the cumulative average residuals of split-up stocks with poor dividend performance decline until about a year after the split, by which time it must be very clear that the anticipated dividend increase is not forthcoming. When we combine the results for the dividend increases and decreases, these results are consistent with the hypothesis that on the average the market makes unbiased dividend forecasts for split-up securities and these forecasts are fully reflected in the price of the security by the end of the split month.

The results of Fama, Fisher, Jensen, and Roll [1969] are consistent with the semistrong form of market efficiency. Prices appear to fully reflect information about expected cash flows. The split *per se* has no effect on shareholder wealth. Rather it merely serves as a message about dividend changes. There seems to be no way to use a split to increase one's expected returns, unless, of course, inside information concerning the split or subsequent dividend behavior is available.

One often hears that stocks split because there is an "optimal" price range for common stocks. Moving the security price into this range makes the market for trading in the security "wider" or "deeper," hence there is more trading liquidity. Copeland [1979] reports that contrary to the above argument, market liquidity is actually lower following a stock split. Trading volume is proportionately lower than its presplit level, brokerage revenues (a major portion of transaction costs) are proportionately higher, and bid-ask spreads are higher as a percentage of the bid price.[9] Taken together, these empirical results point to lower post-split liquidity. Hence, we can say that the market for split-up securities has lower operational efficiency relative to its presplit level.

G. PERFORMANCE OF MANAGED PORTFOLIOS

1. Mutual Funds

Mutual funds allege that they can provide two types of service to their clients. First, they may minimize the amount of unsystematic risk an investor must face. This is done through efficient diversification in the face of transactions costs. Second, they may be able to use their professional expertise to earn abnormal returns through successful prediction of future security prices. This second claim is contradictory to the semistrong form of capital market efficiency unless, for some reason, mutual fund managers can consistently obtain information which is not publicly available.

A number of studies have focused their attention on the performance of mutual funds. A partial list includes Friend and Vickers [1965], Sharpe [1966], Treynor [1965], Farrar [1962], Friend, Blume, and Crockett [1970], Jensen [1968], and Mains [1977]. Various performance measures are used. Among them are:

$$\text{Reward to variability ratio} = \frac{R_{jt} - R_{ft}}{\sigma_j}, \tag{10.4}$$

$$\text{Treynor index} = \frac{R_{jt} - R_{ft}}{\hat{\beta}_j}, \tag{10.5}$$

$$\text{Abnormal performance} = \alpha_{jt} = (R_{jt} - R_{ft}) - [\hat{\beta}_j(R_{mt} - R_{ft})], \tag{10.6}$$

where

R_j = the return of the jth mutual fund,

R_f = the return on a risk-free asset (usually Treasury bills),

σ_j = the standard deviation of return on the jth mutual fund,

$\hat{\beta}_j$ = the estimated systematic risk of the jth mutual fund.

Of these, the abnormal performance measure Eq. (10.6) makes the best use of the CAPM. It was developed by Jensen [1968], who used it to test the abnormal performance of 115 mutual funds, using annual data between 1955 and 1964. If the performance index, α, is positive, then after adjusting for risk and for movements in the market index, the abnormal performance of a portfolio is also positive. The average α for returns measured "net of costs" (such as research costs, management fees, and brokerage commissions) was −1.1% per year over the 10-year period. This sug-

---

[9] The bid price is the price which a potential buyer offers, say $20, and the ask price is what the seller requires, suppose it's $20\frac{1}{2}$. The bid-ask spread is the difference, specifically $\frac{1}{2}$.

gests that, on the average, the funds were not able to forecast future security prices well enough to cover their expenses. When returns were measured "gross of expenses" (excepting brokerage commissions), the average α was $-.4\%$ per year. Apparently, the gross returns were not sufficient to recoup even brokerage commissions.

In sum, Jensen's study of mutual funds provides evidence that the 115 mutual funds, on the average, were not able to predict security prices well enough to outperform a buy-and-hold strategy. In addition, there was very little evidence that any individual fund was able to do better than what might be expected from mere random chance. These conclusions held even when fund returns were measured gross of management expenses and brokerage costs. Results obtained are consistent with the hypothesis of capital market efficiency in its semistrong form, because we may assume that, at the very least, mutual fund managers have access to publicly available information. However, they do not necessarily imply that mutual funds will not be held by rational investors. On the average, the funds do an excellent job of diversification. This may, by itself, be a socially desirable service to investors.

More recently, Mains [1977] has reexamined the issue of mutual fund performance. He criticizes Jensen's work on two accounts: (1) the rates of return were underestimated, (a) because dividends were assumed to be reinvested at year end rather than during the quarter they were received and (b) because when expenses were added back to obtain gross returns, they were added back at year end instead of continuously throughout the year. By using monthly data instead of annual data, Mains is able to better estimate both net and gross returns. (2) Jensen assumed that mutual fund betas were stationary over long periods of time (note that $\hat{\beta}_j$ has no time subscript in Eq. 10.6). Using monthly data, Mains obtains lower estimates of $\hat{\beta}_j$ and argues that Jensen's estimates of risk were too high.

The abnormal performance results calculated for a sample of 70 mutual funds indicate that as a group, the mutual funds had neutral risk-adjusted performance on a net return basis. On a gross-return basis (i.e., before operating expenses and transactions costs), 80% of the funds sampled performed positively. This suggests that mutual funds are able to outperform the market well enough to earn back their operating expenses. It is also consistent with the theory of efficient markets given costly information. Recall from Chapter 9 that the theoretical work of Cornell and Roll [1981] and Grossman [1980] predicts a market equilibrium where investors who utilize costly information will have higher gross rates of return than their uninformed competitors. But because information is costly, the equilibrium net rates of return for informed and uninformed investors will be the same. This is just what Mains' work shows. Mutual funds' gross rates of return are greater than the rate on a randomly selected portfolio of equivalent risk, but when costs (transactions costs and management fees) are subtracted, the net performance of mutual funds is the same as that for a naive investment strategy.

2. The Value Line Investor Survey

Hundreds of investment advisory services sell advice which predicts the performance of various types of assets. Perhaps the largest is the Value Line Investor Survey. Employing over 200 people, it ranks around 1700 securities each week. Securities are ranked 1 to 5 (with 1 being highest), based on their expected price performance relative to the other stocks covered in the Survey. Security rankings result from a complex filter rule which utilizes four criteria: (1) the earnings and price rank of each security relative to all others; (2) a price momentum factor; (3) year-to-year relative changes in quarterly earnings; and (4) an earnings "surprise" factor. Roughly 53% of the securities are ranked third, 18% are ranked second or fourth, and 6% are ranked first or fifth.

The Value Line predictions have been the subject of many academic studies because they represent a clear attempt to use historical data in a complex computerized filter rule to try to predict future performance.[10] Figure Q10.8 (problem 10.8 in the problem set at the end of this chapter) shows a ten-year price performance record assuming that all Value Line ranking changes had been followed between April 1965 and December 1974. Group 1 had price appreciation of +160% and Group 5 declined in price by 91%. However, this is only the realized *price* appreciation. The rates of return reported in Fig. Q10.8 are not total returns because they do not include dividends. Furthermore, they are not adjusted for risk. The problem is how to measure the performance of a portfolio of securities assuming that the Value Line recommendations are used for portfolio formation.

Black [1971] performed the first systematic study utilizing Jensen's abnormal performance measure as given in Eq. (10.6). Black's results indicate statistically significant abnormal performance for equally weighted portfolios formed from stocks ranked 1, 2, 4 and 5 by Value Line and rebalanced monthly. Before transactions costs, portfolios 1 and 5 had risk-adjusted rates of return of +10% and −10% respectively. Even with round-trip transactions costs of 2%, the net rate of return for a long position in portfolio 1 would still have been positive, thereby indicating economically significant performance. One problem with these results is the Jensen methodology for measuring portfolio performance. It has been criticized by Roll [1977, 1978] who argues that any methodology based on the Capital Asset Pricing Model will measure either (1) no abnormal performance if the market index portfolio is ex post efficient, or (2) a meaningless abnormal performance if the index portfolio is ex post inefficient.[11]

Copeland and Mayers [1982] measured Value Line portfolio performance by using a *future benchmark technique* which avoids selection bias problems associated with using historic benchmarks as well as the known difficulties of using Capital Asset Pricing Model benchmarks.[12] The future benchmark technique uses the market model (described in part A of this chapter) fit using data after the test period where portfolio performance is being measured. The steps in the procedure are:

1. Using a sample from after the test period, calculate the market model equation for the portfolio being evaluated.

---

[10] A partial list of Value Line related studies is: Shelton [1967], Hausman [1969], Black [1971], Kaplan and Weil [1973], Brown and Rozeff [1978], Holloway [1981], and Copeland and Mayers [1982].

[11] For a more complete discussion of Roll's critique, see Chapter 7.

[12] Using historic benchmarks creates a selection bias problem because Value Line uses a variant of the "relative strength" criterion to choose rankings. Portfolio 1 stocks tend to have abnormally high historic rates of return, thus subtracting these rates from test period returns would tend to bias the results against Value Line.

2. Use the parameters of the model as a benchmark for computing the portfolio's unexpected return during a test period.

3. Repeat the procedure and test to see whether the mean unexpected return is significantly different from zero.

In other words, rather than using a particular (perhaps suspect) model (such as the CAPM) of asset pricing as a benchmark, estimate the expected returns directly from the data. The future benchmark technique is not without its problems, however. It assumes that the portfolio characteristics (e.g., risk and dividend yield) remain essentially the same throughout the test and benchmark periods.

Copeland and Mayers find considerably less abnormal performance than Black, who used the Jensen methodology. Where Black reported (roughly) 20% per year for an investor who was long on portfolio 1 and short on portfolio 5, Copeland and Mayers find an annual rate of return of only 6.8%. Moreover, only portfolio 5 had statistically significant returns. Nevertheless, any significant performance is a potential violation of semistrong market efficiency. Thus Value Line remains an enigma.

3. Dual Purpose Funds

Dual purpose funds are companies whose only assets are the securities of other companies. However, unlike open-end mutual funds, closed-end dual purpose funds neither issue new shares nor redeem outstanding ones. Investors who wish to own shares in a closed-end fund must purchase fund shares on the open market. The shares are divided into two types, both of which have claim on the same underlying assets. The *capital shares* of a dual fund pay no dividends and are redeemable at net asset value at the (predetermined) maturity date of the fund.[13] The *income shares* receive any dividends or income which the fund may earn, subject to a stated minimum cumulative dividend, and are redeemed at a fixed price at the fund's maturity date. Dual funds were established on the premise that some investors may wish to own a security providing only income while other investors may desire only potential capital gains.

There are two very interesting issues which are raised when one observes the market price of closed-end shares. First, the market value of the fund's capital shares does not equal the *net asset value.*[14] Most often, the net asset value per share exceeds the actual price per share of the dual fund. In this case the dual fund is said to sell at a discount. Given that a speculator (especially a tax exempt institution) could buy all of a fund's outstanding shares and liquidate the fund for its net asset value, it is a mystery why a discount (or premium) can persist. The second issue has to do with whether or not risk-adjusted abnormal rates of return accrue to investors

---

[13] The net asset value received at maturity is the market value of the securities in the fund at that date less the promised repayment of capital to income shares.

[14] The net asset value is the value to shareholders measured as the market value of the securities held by the fund at a given point in time.

who buy a dual fund when it is selling at a discount, then hold it for a period of time, possibly to maturity.

There have been several theories put forth to explain why dual fund shares should sell at a discount from their net asset value. Malkiel [1977] suggests that two of the important possibilities are (1) unrealized capital gains and (2) holdings of letter stock. If a fund is holding a portfolio of securities which have had substantial capital gains, then an investor who purchases shares in the fund automatically incurs a built-in capital gains liability which must be paid when the securities are sold by the dual fund.[15] The same investor would incur no such tax liability by simply buying the same portfolio of securities on his or her own. One of the problems with this explanation, discussed by Thompson [1978] is that nontaxable institutions should be able to make a profit whenever a tax induced discount occurs. They simply buy up all of a fund's outstanding shares, then liquidate the fund at its net asset value. Why this hasn't happened is something of a mystery. In addition to capital gains tax liabilities, Malkiel finds that dual fund holdings of letter stock helps to explain discounts. In most cases letter stock sells at a discount from market value, presumably because it is not marketable. The fund that buys letter stock is required to sign an "investment letter" pledging that the stock has been bought for investment purposes, and indicating that the fund will hold the shares for a considerable period of time. Even though the stock is often purchased at discounts from the market price of the unrestricted shares of the company, the shares are recorded at market value on the dual fund's books. Hence, for accounting reasons, the net asset value may be overstated.

Ingersoll [1976] shows that the capital shares of a dual fund are analogous to call options written on the dividend-paying securities held by the fund. Holders of income shares are entitled to all income produced by the portfolio plus an amount equal to their initial investment payable when the fund matures. If S is the value of the fund at maturity and X is the promised payment to income shares, then capital shareowners receive the maximum of $S - X$ or zero, whichever is larger, at maturity. This payoff can be written as

$$\text{MAX}[S - X, 0]$$

and is exactly the same as the payoff to a call option.[16] We know, from option pricing theory, that the present value of a call option is bounded from below by $S - e^{-r_f T} X$. However, dual funds are characterized by the fact that cash disbursements in the form of dividends and management fees are made over the life of the fund. If these disbursements are assumed to be continuous, then the present value of the fund is $Se^{-\gamma T}$, where γ is the rate of payment. Ingersoll shows that given the cash disbursements, the lower bound on the value of the capital shares must be $e^{-\gamma T} S -$

---

[15] Tax treatment of capital gains is not symmetrical. Although realized capital losses may be carried forward to offset future capital gains, the losses may not be distributed to a fund's shareholders as a tax shield. The tax argument, if valid, can also be used to explain dual fund premia. If a fund has unrealized losses, a taxable investor would prefer the fund over the alternative of investing in the underlying securities because expected future capital gains taxes would be lower with the dual fund.

[16] See, for example, Eq. (8.8).

Figure 10.15
Capital share price as a function of asset value. (From Ingersoll, J., "A Theoretical and Empirical Investigation of Dual Purpose Funds," reprinted from the **Journal of Financial Economics**, Jan./March 1976, 87.)

$Xe^{-r_f T}$ as shown in Fig. 10.15. The dashed line, $S - X$, is the net asset value of the capital shares.[17] When the fund value is above a critical level, S_c, the capital shares will sell at a discount. Below S_c they sell at a premium.

When Ingersoll used the option pricing model to estimate the market value of capital shares, he found that it tracked actual prices very well in spite of the fact that no tax effects were taken into account. The data consisted of prices for seven funds on a weekly basis between May 1967 and December 1973. Furthermore, he simulated a trading rule which bought (sold) capital shares when the option model price was above (below) the market price and financed the investment by an opposite position in the securities of the fund and borrowing or lending at the riskless rate. Thus a hedged portfolio was created which required no investment and which had very low risk.[18] The returns on the hedge portfolio were (almost always) insignificantly different from zero. This suggests that even though capital shares may sell for a discount or premium, they are efficiently priced in a semistrong form sense.

Thompson [1978] measures the performance of closed-end dual funds by using all three versions of the empirical models described at the beginning of this chapter. He used monthly data for 23 closed-end funds. The longest-lived fund was in existence from 1940 until 1975 (when the data set ended). A trading rule purchased shares in each fund which was selling at a discount at the previous year's end, then held the fund and reinvested all distributions until the end of the year. The procedure was repeated for each year that data existed and abnormal returns were then calculated for a portfolio based on this trading strategy. Thompson found that discounted closed-end fund shares tend to outperform the market, adjusted for risk. By one performance measure the annual abnormal return (i.e., the return above that earned by NYSE stocks of equivalent risk) was in excess of 4%. It is interesting to note that a trading strategy which purchased shares of funds selling at a premium would have experienced

---

[17] Figure 10.15 is very similar to Fig. 8.15 in the option-pricing chapter. The valuation of dual fund capital shares is an application of option-pricing theory.

[18] Not all risk could be eliminated because of (1) weekly rather than continuous adjustment of the hedge position, (2) changes in the model deviation, and (3) improper hedge ratios if the option model of capital shares is incorrect.

a -7.9% per year abnormal return, although the results were not statistically significant.

There are several explanations for Thompson's [1978] results. First, the market may be inefficient, at least for tax exempt institutions which could seemingly be able to profit from the above-mentioned trading rule. Second, so long as taxable investors persist in holding closed-end shares the gross rates of return before taxes may have to exceed the market equilibrium rate of return in order to compensate for unrealized tax liabilities. Third, abnormal return measures based on the capital asset pricing model may be inappropriate for measuring the performance of closed-end fund capital shares which are call options.

The problem of analyzing dual funds is not yet completely resolved. The observed discounts (premia) on capital shares may be attributable to (1) unrealized capital gains tax liabilities, (2) fund holdings of letter stock, (3) management and brokerage costs or (4) the option nature of capital shares. The relative importance of these factors has not yet been completely resolved. In addition, there remains some question about whether or not abnormal returns can be earned by utilizing trading rules based on observed discounts (premia). Thompson's [1978] work suggests that abnormal returns are possible, while Ingersoll [1976] finds no evidence of abnormal returns.

H. WEEKEND AND YEAREND EFFECTS

Any predictable pattern in asset returns may be exploitable and, therefore, judged as evidence against semistrong market efficiency. Even if the pattern cannot be employed directly in a trading rule because of prohibitive transactions costs, it may enable people who were going to trade anyway to increase their portfolio returns over what they otherwise may have received without knowledge of the pattern. Two statistically significant patterns in stock market returns are the weekend effect and the turn-of-the-year effect.

French [1980] studied daily returns on the Standard and Poor's composite portfolio of the 500 largest firms on the New York Stock Exchange over the period 1953 to 1977. Table 10.4 shows the summary statistics for returns by day of the week. The negative returns on Monday were highly significant. They were also significantly negative in each of the five-year subperiods which were studied.

An immediate natural reaction to explain this phenomenon is that firms wait until after the close of the market on Fridays to announce bad news. The problem is that soon people would anticipate such behavior and discount Friday prices to account for it. In this way negative returns over the weekend would soon be eliminated. Another explanation is that negative returns are caused by a general "market closed" effect. French eliminated this possibility by showing that for days following holidays, only Tuesday returns were negative. All other days of the week which followed holidays had positive returns.

At present there is no satisfactory explanation for the weekend effect. It is not directly exploitable by a trading rule because transactions costs of even .25 percent eliminate all profits. However, it may be considered a form of market inefficiency

Table 10.4 Summary Statistics for Daily Returns on the S&P 500 Stock Index 1953–1977 (French, K., "Stock Returns and the Weekend Effect," Reprinted From the *Journal of Financial Economics,* March 1980, 58.)

Means, standard deviations, and t-statistics of the percent return from the close of the previous trading day to the close of the day indicated.[a]

		Monday	Tuesday	Wednesday	Thursday	Friday
1953–1977	Mean	−0.1681	0.0157	0.0967	0.0448	0.0873
	Standard deviation	0.8427	0.7267	0.7483	0.6857	0.6600
	t-statistic	−6.823[c]	0.746	4.534[c]	2.283[b]	4.599[c]
	observations	1170	1193	1231	1221	1209

[a] Returns for periods including a holiday are omitted. These returns are defined as $R_t = \ln(P_t/P_{t-1}) \cdot 100$.

[b] 5% significance level.

[c] 0.5% significance level.

because people who were going to trade anyway can delay purchases planned for Thursday or Friday until Monday and execute sales scheduled for Monday on the preceding Friday.

Another interesting pattern in stock prices is the so-called yearend effect which has been documented by Dyl [1973], Branch [1977], Keim [1981], Reinganum [1982], and Roll [1982]. Stock returns decline in December of each year, especially for small firms and for firms whose price had already declined during the year. Then the prices increase during the following January. Roll [1982] reported that for 18 consecutive years from 1963 to 1980, average returns of small firms have been larger than average returns of large firms on the first trading of the calendar year. That day's difference in returns between equally-weighted indices of AMEX and NYSE-listed stocks averaged 1.16 percent over the 18 years. The t-statistic of the difference was 8.18.

Again quoting Roll [1982] "To put the turn-of-the-year period into perspective, the average annual return differential between equally-weighted and value-weighted indices of NYSE and AMEX stocks was 9.31 percent for calendar years 1963–1980 inclusive. During those same years, the average return for the five days of the turn-of-the-year (last day of December and first five days of January) was 3.45%. Thus, about 37% of the annual differential is due to just five trading days, 67% of the annual differential is due to the first twenty trading days of January plus the last day of December."

The most likely cause of the yearend effect is tax selling. At least there is a significant correlation between the realized rates of return during the year and the size of the turn-of-the-year price recovery. Whether or not this phenomenon is exploitable with a trading rule remains to be seen. However, an individual who was going to transact anyway can benefit by altering his or her timing to buy in late December or sell in early January.

SUMMARY _____

Most evidence suggests that capital markets are efficient in their weak and semistrong forms, that security prices conform to a fair-game model but not precisely to a random walk because of small first-order dependencies in prices and nonstationarities in the underlying price distribution over time, and that the strong-form hypothesis does not hold. However, any conclusions about the strong form of market efficiency need to be qualified by the fact that capital-market efficiency must be considered jointly with competition and efficiency in markets for information. If insiders have monopolistic access to information, this fact may be considered an inefficiency in the market for information rather than in capital markets. Filter rules (described in Chapter 9) have shown that security prices exhibit no dependencies over time, at least down to the level of transaction costs. Thus capital markets are allocationally efficient up to the point of operational efficiency. If transaction costs amounted to a greater percentage of value traded, price dependencies for filter rules greater than 1.5% might have been found.

At least in two instances, special types of "abnormal" returns could not be explained. Block traders who can buy at the block price and sell at the market close could earn annual abnormal returns of over 200% per year even after transaction costs. Individuals who could buy new issues at the subscription price and sell at the end of the month could earn annual abnormal returns of 11.4% per month (this is over 350% per year). Although both of these results may be interpreted as strong-form inefficiencies, the authors were quick to point out that they may simply represent fair returns for services by the block positioner or the investment banker. It is best to say at this point that we do not know.

Most of the studies reviewed in this chapter have used data from the stock market. However, there is evidence that other markets are also efficient. Roll [1970] showed that prices in the Treasury bill market obey a fair-game model. Schwert [1977] concluded that the prices of New York Stock Exchange seats follow a multiplicative random walk. Stein [1977] examined the auction market for art and found it efficient. Larson [1960] looked at corn futures, and Mandelbrot [1964] investigated spot prices in cotton. In addition to these studies, we should mention in passing that there are many other topics related to the question of market efficiency which have not been discussed here.

PROBLEM SET

10.1 Roll's critique of tests of the CAPM shows that if the index portfolio is *ex post* efficient, it is mathematically impossible for abnormal returns, as measured by the empirical market line, to be statistically different from zero. Yet the Ibbotson study on new issues uses the cross-section empirical market line and finds significant abnormal returns in the month of issue and none in the following months. Given Roll's critique, this should have been impossible. How can the empirical results be reconciled with the theory?

10.2 In a recent study on corporate disclosure by a special committee of the Securities and Exchange Commission, we find the following statement (1977, p. D6):

The "efficient market hypothesis"—which asserts that the current price of a security reflects all publicly available information—even if valid, does not negate the necessity of a mandatory disclosure system. This theory is concerned with how the market reacts to disclosed information and is silent as to the optimum amount of information required or whether that optimum should be achieved on a mandatory or voluntary basis; market forces alone are insufficient to cause all material information to be disclosed, ...

Two questions that arise are:

a) What is the difference between efficient markets for securities and efficient markets for information?

b) What criteria define "material information"?

10.3 In your own words, what does the empirical evidence on block trading tell us about market efficiency?

10.4 Which of the following types of information provides a likely opportunity to earn abnormal returns on the market:

a) The latest copy of a company's annual report.

b) News coming across the NYSE ticker tape that 100,000 shares of Lukens Steel Company were just traded in a single block.

c) Advance notice that the *XYZ* Company is going to split its common stock three for one, but not increase dividend payout.

d) Advance notice that a large new issue of common stock in the *ABC* Company will be offered soon.

10.5 Mr. *A* has received, over the last three months, a solicitation to purchase a service which claims to be able to forecast movements in the Dow Jones Industrial Index. Normally, he doesn't believe in such things, but the service provides evidence of amazing accuracy. In each of the last three months, it was always right in predicting whether or not the index would move up more than 10 points, stay within a 10-point range, or go down by more than 10 points. Would you advise him to purchase the service? Why or why not?

10.6 The Ponzi Mutual Fund (which is not registered with the SEC) guarantees a 2% per month (24% per year) return on your money. You have looked into the matter and found that they have indeed been able to pay their shareholders the promised return for each of the 18 months they have been in operation. What implications does this have for capital markets? Should you invest?

10.7 Empirical evidence indicates that mutual funds which have abnormal returns in a given year are successful in attracting abnormally large numbers of new investors the following year. Is this inconsistent with capital market efficiency?

10.8 The Value Line Investment Survey publishes weekly stock performance forecasts. Stocks are grouped into five portfolios according to expected price performance, with Group 1 comprising the most highly recommended stocks. The chart of each portfolio's actual performance over a 10-year period (Fig. Q10.8) assumes that each of the five portfolios was adjusted on a weekly basis in accordance with Value Line's stock ratings. The chart shows that the portfolios' actual performances are consistent with Value Line's forecasts. Is this evidence against an efficient securities market?

	1965*	1966	1967	1968	1969	1970	1971	1972	1973	1974	1965–1974
Group 1	+28.8%	− 5.5%	+53.4%	+37.1%	−10.4%	+ 7.3%	+30.6%	+12.6%	−19.1%	−11.1%	+160%
Group 2	+18.5	− 6.2	+36.1	+26.9	−17.5	− 3.2	+13.7	+ 7.4	−28.9	−29.5	− 6
Group 3	+ 6.7	−13.9	+27.1	+24.0	−23.8	− 8.0	+ 9.3	+ 3.5	−33.6	−34.1	− 50
Group 4	− .4	−15.7	+23.8	+20.9	−33.3	−16.3	+ 8.4	− 7.1	−37.9	−40.6	− 74
Group 5	− 3.2	−18.2	+21.5	+11.8	−44.9	−23.3	− 5.5	−13.4	−43.8	−55.7	− 91

*April through December — all other years cover a 12-month period.

Figure Q10.8
Ten-year record of actual forecast assumes all rank changes have been followed.
(From Bernhard, A., "The Value Line Investment Survey," *Investing in Common Stock,* Arnold Bernhard and Company, Inc. Reprinted with permission of the author.)

10.9 In each of the following situations, explain the extent to which the empirical results offer reliable evidence for (or against) market efficiency.

a) A research study using data for firms continuously listed on the Compustat computer tapes from 1953–1973 finds no evidence of impending bankruptcy costs reflected in stock prices as a firm's debt/equity ratio increases.

b) One thousand stock brokers are surveyed via questionnaire, and their stated investment preferences are classified according to industry groupings. The results can be used to explain rate of return differences across industries.

c) A study of the relationships between size of type in the *New York Times* headline and size of price change (in either direction) in the subsequent day's stock index reveals a significant positive correlation. Further, when independent subjects are asked to qualify the headline news as good, neutral, or bad, the direction of the following day's price change (up or down) is discovered to vary with the quality of news (good or bad).

d) Using 25 years of data in exhaustive regression analysis, a *Barron's* writer develops a statistical model that explains the 25-year period of stock returns (using 31 variables) with minuscule error.

REFERENCES

Aharony, J., and I. Swary, "Quarterly Dividend and Earnings Announcements and Stockholders' Returns: An Empirical Analysis," *Journal of Finance,* March 1980, 1–12.

Alexander, S. S., "Price Movements in Speculative Markets: Trends or Random Walks," *Industrial Management Review,* May 1961, 7–26.

Ball, R., and P. Brown, "An Empirical Evaluation of Accounting Income Numbers," *Journal of Accounting Research,* Autumn, 1968, 159–178.

Barker, A., "Evaluation of Stock Dividends," *Harvard Business Review,* July/August 1958, 99–114.

Bernhard, A., *Investing in Common Stocks.* Arnold Bernhard & Co., Inc., New York, 1975.

————, *Value Line Methods of Evaluating Common Stocks,* Arnold Bernhard & Co., Inc., New York, 96 pp.

Black, F., "Yes, Virginia, There is Hope: Tests of the Value Line Ranking System." Graduate School of Business, University of Chicago, May 1971.

————, M. Jensen, and M. Scholes, "The Capital Asset Pricing Model: Some Empirical Tests," in M. Jensen, ed., *Studies in the Theory of Capital Markets,* Praeger, New York, 1972, 79–121.

Black, F., and M. Scholes, "The Effects of Dividend Yield and Dividend Policy on Common Stock Prices and Returns," *Journal of Financial Economics,* May 1974, 1–22.

Boudreaux, K., "Discounts and Premiums on Closed-End Funds: A Study on Valuation," *Journal of Finance,* May 1973, 515–522.

Branch, B., "A Tax Loss Trading Rule," *Journal of Business,* April 1977, 198–207.

Brimmer, A., "Credit Conditions and Price Determination in the Corporate Bond Market," *Journal of Finance,* September 1960, 353–370.

Brown, L., and M. Rozeff, "The Superiority of Analysts Forecasts as Measures of Expectations: Evidence From Earnings," *Journal of Finance,* March 1978, 1–16.

Brown, S., "Earnings Changes, Stock Prices and Market Efficiency," *Journal of Finance,* 1978, 17–28.

Chottiner, S., and A. Young, "A Test of the AICPA Differentiation Between Stock Dividends and Stock Splits," *Journal of Accounting Research,* Autumn 1971, 367–374.

Copeland, T. E., "Liquidity Changes Following Stock Splits," *The Journal of Finance,* March 1979.

————, and D. Mayers, "The Value Line Enigma (1965–1978): A Case Study of Performance Evaluation Issues," *Journal of Financial Economics,* forthcoming.

Cornell, B., and R. Roll, "Strategies for Pairwise Competitions in Markets and Organizations," *The Bell Journal of Economics,* Spring 1981, 201–213.

Dann, L., D. Mayers, and R. Raab, "Trading Rules, Large Blocks and the Speed of Adjustment," *The Journal of Financial Economics,* January 1977, 3–22.

Dyl, E., "The Effect of Capital Gains Taxation on the Stock Market." Unpublished Ph.D. thesis, Stanford University Graduate School of Business, August 1973.

Ederington, L., "The Yield Spread on New Issues of Corporate Bonds," *The Journal of Finance,* December 1974, 1531–1543.

Fama, E. F., "The Behavior of Stock Market Prices," *The Journal of Business,* January 1965, 34–105.

———, "Efficient Capital Markets: A Review of Theory and Empirical Work," *The Journal of Finance,* May 1970, 383–417.

———, *Foundations of Finance.* Basic Books, New York, 1976.

Fama, E. F., and M. Blume, "Filter Rules and Stock Market Trading Profits," *The Journal of Finance,* May 1970, 226–241.

Fama, E. F., L. Fisher, M. Jensen, and R. Roll, "The Adjustment of Stock Prices to New Information," *International Economic Review,* February 1969, 1–21.

Fama, E. F., and J. MacBeth, "Risk, Return and Equilibrium: Empirical Test," *Journal of Political Economy,* May/June 1973, 607–635.

Farrar, D. E., *The Investment Decision Under Uncertainty.* Prentice-Hall, Englewood Cliffs, N.J., 1962.

Finnerty, J. E., "Insiders and Market Efficiency," *Journal of Finance,* September 1976, 1141–1148.

Foster, G., "Quarterly Accounting Data: Time Series Properties and Predictive Ability Results," *Accounting Review,* 1977, 1–21.

Foster, T., III, and D. Vickrey, "The Information Content of Stock Dividend Announcements," *The Accounting Review,* April 1978, 360–370.

Friend, I., M. Blume, and J. Crockett, *Mutual Funds and Other Institutional Investors.* McGraw Hill, New York, 1970.

Friend, I., F. E. Brown, E. S. Herman, and D. Vickers, *A Study of Mutual Funds.* U.S. Government Printing Office, Washington, D.C., 1962.

Friend, I., and D. Vickers, "Portfolio Selection and Investment Performance," *Journal of Finance,* September 1965, 391–415.

French, K., "Stock Returns and the Weekend Effect," *Journal of Financial Economics,* March 1980, 55–69.

Griffin, P., "The Time-Series Behavior of Quarterly Earnings: Preliminary Evidence," *Journal of Accounting Research,* 1977, 71–83.

Grossman, S., "The Impossibility of Informationally Efficient Markets," *The American Economic Review,* June 1980, 393–408.

Hausman, W., "A Note on the Value Line Contest: A Test of the Predictability of Stock Price Changes," *Journal of Business,* July 1969, 317–320.

Holloway, C., "A Note on Testing in Aggressive Investment Strategy Using Value Line Ranks," *Journal of Finance,* June 1981, 711–719.

Hong, H., R. S. Kaplan, and G. Mandelker, "Pooling vs. Purchase: The Effects of Accounting for Mergers on Stock Prices," *The Accounting Review,* January 1978, 31–47.

Ibbotson, R., "Price Performance of Common Stock New Issues," *Journal of Financial Economics,* September 1975, 235–272.

Ingersoll, J., Jr., "A Theoretical and Empirical Investigation of the Dual Purpose Funds: An Application of Contingent Claims Analysis," *Journal of Financial Economics,* January/March 1976, 83–124.

Jaffe, J., "The Effect of Regulation Changes on Insider Trading," *The Bell Journal of Economics and Management Science,* Spring 1974, 93–121.

Jensen, M., "The Performance of Mutual Funds in the Period 1945–64," *The Journal of Finance*, May 1968, 389–416.

———, "Risk, the Pricing of Capital Assets, and the Evaluation of Investment Portfolios," *The Journal of Business*, April 1969, 167–247.

———, "Capital Markets: Theory and Evidence," *The Bell Journal of Economics and Management Science*, Autumn 1972, 357–398.

Joy, M., R. Litzenberger, and R. McEnally, "The Adjustment of Stock Prices to Announcements of Unanticipated Changes in Quarterly Earnings," *Journal of Accounting Research*, Autumn 1977.

Kaplan, R. S., and R. Roll, "Investor Evaluation of Accounting Information: Some Empirical Evidence," *Journal of Business*, April 1972, 225–257.

———, and R. Weil, "Risk and the Value Line Contest," *Financial Analysts Journal*, July/August 1973, 56–60.

Keim, D., "Size Related Anomalies and Stock Return Seasonality: Further Empirical Evidence." University of Chicago Graduate School of Business, October 1981.

Kraus, A., and H. R. Stoll, "Price Impacts of Block Trading on the New York Stock Exchange," *The Journal of Finance*, June 1972, 569–588.

Larson, A. B., "Measurement of a Random Process in Futures Prices," reprinted in P. Cootner, ed., *The Random Character of Stock Market Prices*. MIT Press, Cambridge, Mass., 1964, 219–230.

Lindvall, J., "New Issue Corporate Bonds, Seasoned Market Efficiency, and Yield Spreads," *The Journal of Finance*, September 1977, 1057–1067.

Lintner, J., "The Valuation of Risky Assets and the Selection of Risky Investments in Stock Portfolios and Capital Budgets," *Review of Economics and Statistics*, February 1965, 13–37.

Litzenberger, R., and H. Sosin, "The Structure and Management of Dual Purpose Funds," *Journal of Financial Economics*, March 1977, 203–230.

Logue, D. E., "On the Pricing of Unseasoned Equity Offerings: 1965–1969," *Journal of Financial and Quantitative Analysis*, January 1973, 91–104.

Mains, N. E., "Risk, the Pricing of Capital Assets, and the Evaluation of Investment Portfolios: Comment," *Journal of Business*, July 1977, 371–384.

Malkiel, B., "The Valuation of Closed-End Investment Company Shares," *Journal of Finance*, June 1977, 847–859.

Mandelbrot, B., "The Variation of Certain Speculative Prices," reprinted in P. Cootner, ed., *The Random Character of Stock Market Prices*. MIT Press, Cambridge, Mass., 1964, 307–332.

McDonald, J. G., and A. K. Fisher, "New Issue Stock Price Behavior," *The Journal of Finance*, March 1972, 97–102.

Mossin, J., "Security Pricing and Investment Criteria in Competitive Markets," *American Economic Review*, December 1969, 749–756.

Pratt, E., "Myths Associated with Closed-End Investment Company Discounts," *Financial Analysts Journal*, 1966, 79–82.

Reilly, F. K., and K. Hatfield, "Investor Experience with New Stock Issues," *Financial Analysts Journal*, September/October 1969, 73–80.

Reinganum, M., "The Anomalous Stock Behavior of Small Firms in January: Empirical Tests for Year-End Tax Effects." University of Southern California Graduate School of Business, January 1982.

Report of the Advisory Committee on Corporate Disclosure to the Securities and Exchange Commission. U.S. Government Printing Office, Washington, D.C., November 1977.

Roendfelt, R., and D. Tuttle, "An Examination of Discounts and Premiums of Closed-End Investment Companies," *Journal of Business Research,* 1973, 129–140.

Roll, R. *The Behavior of Interest Rates.* Basic Books, New York, 1970.

_____, "A Critique of the Asset Pricing Theory's Tests," *Journal of Financial Economics,* March 1977, 129–176.

_____, "Ambiguity When Performance is Measured by the Securities Market Line," *Journal of Finance,* September 1978, 1051–1069.

_____, "The Turn-of-the-Year Effect and the Return Premia of Small Firms," UCLA Graduate School of Management, Working Paper No. 2-82, January 1982.

Scholes, M., "The Market for Securities: Substitution versus Price Pressure and the Effects of Information on Share Prices," *Journal of Business,* April 1972, 179–211.

Schwert, W., "Stock Exchange Seats as Capital Assets," *Journal of Financial Economics,* January 1977, 51–78.

Securities and Exchange Commission, *Report of the Special Study on Securities Markets.* U.S. Government Printing Office, Washington, D.C., 1963.

Sharpe, W. F., "Mutual Fund Performance," *Journal of Business,* January 1966, 119–138.

Shaw, D., "The Performance of Primary Stock Offerings: A Canadian Comparison," *The Journal of Finance,* December 1971, 1103–1113.

Shelton, J., "The Value Line Contest: A Test of the Predictability of Stock Price Changes," *Journal of Business,* July 1967, 251–269.

Stein, J. P., "The Monetary Appreciation of Paintings," *Journal of Political Economy,* October 1977, 1021–1036.

Stickney, C. P., Jr., *A Study of the Relationships of Accounting Principles and Common Stock Prices of Firms Going Public.* Ph.D. Thesis, Florida State University, Tallahassee, 1970.

Stigler, G., "Public Regulation of Security Markets," *Journal of Business,* April 1964, 117–142.

Sunder, S., "Relationship between Accounting Changes and Stock Prices: Problems of Measurement and Some Empirical Evidence," *Empirical Research in Accounting: Selected Studies,* 1973, 1–45.

_____, "Stock Price and Risk Related Accounting Changes in Inventory Valuation," *Accounting Review,* April 1975, 305–315.

Thompson, R., "The Information Content of Discounts and Premiums on Closed-End Fund Shares," *Journal of Financial Economics,* June/September 1978, 151–186.

Treynor, J. L., "How to Rate Mutual Fund Performance," *Harvard Business Review,* January/February 1965, 63–75.

Watts, R., "Systematic 'Abnormal' Returns After Quarterly Earnings Announcements," *Journal of Financial Economics,* June/September 1978, 127–150.

Weinstein, M., "The Seasoning Process of New Corporate Bond Issues," *The Journal of Finance,* December 1978, 1343–1354.

Capital Budgeting Under Uncertainty: The Multiperiod Case

Former Student: Professor, this is the same examination that you gave to my class when I was a student twenty years ago. Don't you ever change the questions?

Professor: The questions don't change, just the answers.

A. INTRODUCTION

Chapters 2 and 3 discussed capital budgeting given the assumption that all future cash flows were known with certainty. The appropriate discount rate was assumed to be the risk-free rate, and the chapters focused on selection of discounting techniques consistent with the goal of maximizing the net present value of shareholders' wealth. Subsequent chapters introduced uncertainty in the context of a one-period equilibrium pricing model, the capital asset pricing model.

In this chapter we introduce some of the difficulties implicit in the use of the CAPM to determine the appropriate multiperiod risk-adjusted discount rate for capital budgeting purposes. Given multiperiod uncertainty, under what conditions can one use the following formula to determine the NPV of risky projects?

$$\mathrm{NPV}_j = \sum_{t=0}^{N} \frac{\mathrm{NCF}_{jt}}{[1 + E(R_j)]^t}, \tag{11.1}$$

where

NPV_j = the net present value of project j,

NCF_{jt} = the net cash flow of project j in time t,

$E(R_j)$ = the risk-adjusted required rate of return for project j.

In particular, we are interested in the conditions under which the required rate of return on the project, frequently called the *weighted average cost of capital,* can be determined by the CAPM as written below:

$$E(R_j) = r_f + [E(R_m) - r_f]\beta_j. \tag{11.2}$$

Presumably, one would use *current* estimates of the risk-free rate, r_f, the expected rate of return on the market, $E(R_m)$, and the systematic risk of the project, β_j, in order to determine the multiperiod discount rate, $E(R_j)$.

In the first half of this chapter, which deals mainly with theoretical issues, we review the results of three articles. First, Bogue and Roll [1974] show that the problem may not be as simple as suggested in Eq. (11.1). They show that a much more complex procedure becomes necessary if we consider a world where the risk-free rate in future time periods is not known with certainty. Later Fama [1977] shows the set of assumptions necessary to use the risk-adjusted discounting procedure of Eq. (11.1), and Constantinides [1980] shows the minimum set of assumptions necessary for the multiperiod CAPM to be valid.

Section D of the chapter shows how to use the Arbitrage Pricing Theory for capital budgeting purposes. While the technique is not easier to use in practice than the risk-adjusted discount rate, it has the advantage that it requires less stringent assumptions to be empirically valid.

Sections E and F deal with two applied issues. Both sections assume that the risk-adjusted discount rate may be used for multiperiod capital budgeting under uncertainty. The simpler of the two problems shows how to adjust the risk-adjusted discount rate when comparing cost (rather than total income) data for mutually exclusive projects. We demonstrate that the correct technique is to use a lower discount rate for more variable cost cash flows. The second issue has come to be known as the *abandonment problem.* How should one evaluate the residual value of investment assets?

B. MULTIPERIOD CAPITAL BUDGETING WITH "IMPERFECT" MARKETS FOR PHYSICAL CAPITAL

Bogue and Roll [1974] analyze capital budgeting of risky projects in a multiperiod framework and conclude that it may be incorrect to discount cash flows by using the single-period risk-adjusted discount rate. However, under specified conditions, the investment decision for a multiperiod project can be made with a one-period forecast. If appropriate secondary markets exist for the project, only a one-period analysis is required for a decision. The firm makes a comparison between the current investment outlay and the value of the forecast of cash flows during the first period plus the forecasted end-of-period secondary market price.

In addition, even with imperfect secondary markets for physical capital, some investment decisions can still be made with one-period forecasts. If the machine is acceptable on the basis of its one-period cash flow plus its net salvage value after the first period, the possibility of values in subsequent periods will only add to the acceptability of the project. Because the single-period analysis is important in its own right, and also because it will be used in a dynamic programming framework to solve the multiperiod problem, Bogue and Roll start the analysis with a single-period valuation model. They begin with the CAPM in value form. We derive their basic valuation expressed by starting with the CAPM in return form as shown in Eq. (11.3).

$$E(\tilde{R}_1) = r_{f0} + [E(\tilde{R}_{m1}) - r_{f0}]\frac{\text{COV}(\tilde{R}_1, \tilde{R}_{m1})}{\sigma^2(\tilde{R}_{m1})}. \tag{11.3}$$

By definition,

$$\tilde{R}_{m1} = \frac{\tilde{V}_{m1} - V_{m0}}{V_{m0}} = \frac{\tilde{V}_{m1}}{V_{m0}} - 1, \qquad \tilde{R}_1 = \frac{\tilde{V}_1 - V_0}{V_0} = \frac{\tilde{V}_1}{V_0} - 1,$$

$$\sigma^2(\tilde{R}_{m1}) = \sigma^2\left(\frac{\tilde{V}_{m1}}{V_{m0}} - 1\right) = \sigma^2\left(\frac{\tilde{V}_{m1}}{V_{m0}}\right) = \frac{1}{(V_{m0})^2}\sigma^2(\tilde{V}_{m1}),$$

$$\text{COV}(\tilde{R}_1, \tilde{R}_{m1}) = \text{COV}\left(\frac{\tilde{V}_1}{V_0} - 1, \frac{\tilde{V}_{m1}}{V_{m0}} - 1\right) = \frac{1}{V_0 V_{m0}}\text{COV}(\tilde{V}_1, \tilde{V}_{m1}),$$

where

V_0 = the certain current value of the firm,

$\tilde{V}_1$ = the uncertain end-of-period value of the firm (including any dividends paid over the period),

$\tilde{V}_{m1}$ = the uncertain end-of-period value of the market portfolio,

r_{f0} = the risk-free rate of interest over the period.

Then the security market line (SML) is

$$\frac{E(\tilde{V}_1)}{V_0} - 1 = r_{f0} + \left[\frac{E(\tilde{V}_{m1})}{V_{m0}} - 1 - r_{f0}\right]\left(\frac{V_{m0}}{V_0}\right)\frac{\text{COV}(\tilde{V}_1, \tilde{V}_{m1})}{\sigma^2(\tilde{V}_{m1})}. \tag{11.4}$$

Substituting and rearranging, we can obtain a certainty-equivalent value for the firm. First, we multiply both sides by V_0:

$$E(\tilde{V}_1) - V_0 = V_0 r_{f0} + [E(\tilde{V}_{m1}) - (1 + r_{f0})V_{m0}][\text{COV}(\tilde{V}_1, \tilde{V}_{m1})/\sigma^2(\tilde{V}_{m1})].$$

Next, we subtract $V_0 r_{f0}$ and $E(\tilde{V}_1)$ from both sides and change signs:

$$(1 + r_{f0})V_0 = E(\tilde{V}_1) - [E(\tilde{V}_{m1}) - (1 + r_{f0})V_{m0}][\text{COV}(\tilde{V}_1, \tilde{V}_{m1})/\sigma^2(\tilde{V}_{m1})].$$

Solving for V_0, we have

$$V_0 = \frac{E(\tilde{V}_1) - [E(\tilde{V}_{m1}) - (1 + r_{f0})V_{m0}][\text{COV}(\tilde{V}_1, \tilde{V}_{m1})/\sigma^2(\tilde{V}_{m1})]}{1 + r_{f0}}.$$

Using λ_0 (the market price per unit risk) to simplify, we obtain the certainty-equivalent value of the firm:

$$V_0 = \frac{E(\tilde{V}_1) - \lambda_0 \text{COV}(\tilde{V}_1, \tilde{V}_{m1})}{1 + r_{f0}}, \tag{11.5}$$

where

$$\lambda_0 \equiv \frac{E(\tilde{V}_{m1}) - (1 + r_{f0})V_{m0}}{\sigma^2(\tilde{V}_{m1})} = \text{the market price per unit of risk.}$$

Now let $\tilde{X}_1$ be an incremental end-of-period net cash inflow from a project requiring current cash outlay of X_0. With the addition of the project, the end-of-period value of the firm will be $\tilde{V}_1 + \tilde{X}_1$. The new value of the firm is expressed by

$$V_0 + \Delta V_0 = \frac{E(\tilde{V}_1 + \tilde{X}_1) - \lambda_0 \text{COV}(\tilde{V}_1 + \tilde{X}_1, \tilde{V}_{m1})}{1 + r_{f0}}. \tag{11.6}$$

When V_0 is subtracted from both sides of Eq. (11.6), we obtain

$$\Delta V_0 = \frac{E(\tilde{X}_1) - \lambda_0 \text{COV}(\tilde{X}_1, \tilde{V}_{m1})}{1 + r_{f0}}, \tag{11.7}$$

which is the certainty-equivalent value of a project. If the left-hand side of Eq. (11.7) exceeds the right-hand side, the project is acceptable and should be undertaken. The methodology is to begin with an uncertain cash flow from which a certainty-equivalent value is constructed. The end-of-period certainty-equivalent value should be discounted at the risk-free rate to obtain its current value. This one-period result is used as the basis of generalization to the multiperiod case, which is considered next.

The firm is considering a project lasting over n periods. The net uncertain cash flows from the project are $\tilde{X}_t$, leading to increments to the value of the firm for each time period t of $\Delta \tilde{V}_t$. To solve the problem we start at the end where for the last period of the project we have[1]

$$\Delta \tilde{V}_n = \tilde{X}_n.$$

The next-to-last period represents a one-period valuation problem. Assuming that the capital market for equities is in equilibrium, the one-period valuation model can be used to find the value of the final cash flow at the end of the next-to-last period.

---

[1] Note that there is the implicit assumption that the project returns cash only in the nth time period.

This will enable us to obtain the discounted certainty equivalent of $\tilde{X}_n$ for period $n - 1$ expressed by

$$\frac{E(\tilde{X}_n | \tilde{\epsilon}_{n-1}) - \tilde{\lambda}_{n-1} \, \tilde{\mathrm{COV}}(\tilde{X}_n, \, \tilde{V}_{mn} | \tilde{\epsilon}_n)}{1 + \tilde{r}_{f(n-1)}}, \qquad (11.8)$$

where

$\tilde{\epsilon}_{n-1} = $ state of the world at time $n - 1$,

$\tilde{\lambda}_{n-1} = $ market price of risk at $n - 1$,

$\tilde{r}_{f(n-1)} = $ risk-free rate at $n - 1$ (assumed to be stochastic),

$E(\tilde{X}_n | \tilde{\epsilon}_{n-1}) = $ conditional expectation at $n - 1$ of cash flows at n.

This enables us to obtain the incremental value at $n - 1$:

$$\Delta V_{n-1} = X_{n-1} + \frac{\tilde{E}(\tilde{X}_n | \tilde{\epsilon}_{n-1}) - \tilde{\lambda}_{n-1} \, \tilde{\mathrm{COV}}(\tilde{X}_n, \, \tilde{V}_{mn} | \tilde{\epsilon}_n)}{1 + \tilde{r}_{f(n-1)}}. \qquad (11.9)$$

The result in Eq. (11.9) can be generalized to the recursive relationship for the incremental value at any time k:

$$\Delta \tilde{V}_k = \tilde{X}_k + \frac{\tilde{E}(\Delta \tilde{V}_{k+1} | \tilde{\epsilon}_k) - \tilde{\lambda}_k \, \tilde{\mathrm{COV}}[\Delta \tilde{V}_{k+1}, \, \tilde{V}_{m(k+1)} | \tilde{\epsilon}_k]}{1 + \tilde{r}_{fk}}. \qquad (11.10)$$

From Eq. (11.10) we see that for an n-period project, an n-period infinite-state dynamic programming problem must be solved. Each step involves an application of the one-period valuation model with the parameters depending on the state of the world at the beginning of that particular period. Next, the nature of this solution is illustrated for the special case of a project with a single cash inflow two periods in the future. Using Eq. (11.10) with the risk-free interest-rate expression placed on the left-hand side, we can obtain the incremental value for period 1 and period 0 as shown below:

$$\Delta \tilde{V}_1 (1 + \tilde{r}_{f1}) = \tilde{E}(\tilde{X}_2 | \tilde{\epsilon}_1) - \tilde{\lambda}_1 \, \tilde{\mathrm{COV}}(\tilde{X}_2, \, \tilde{V}_{m2} | \tilde{\epsilon}_1), \qquad (11.11)$$

$$\Delta V_0 (1 + r_{f0}) = E(\Delta \tilde{V}_1) - \lambda_0 \, \mathrm{COV}(\Delta \tilde{V}_1, \, \tilde{V}_{m1}). \qquad (11.12)$$

Note that the second-period risk-free rate, $\tilde{r}_{f1}$, is currently uncertain and will not be revealed until the end of the first period. Next, we take expectations of Eq. (11.11) and, making use of the covariance identity,

$$COV(\tilde{X}, \, \tilde{Y}) = E(\tilde{X}, \, \tilde{Y}) - E(\tilde{X})E(\tilde{Y}),$$

we have[2]

---

[2] The covariance identity follows directly from the definition of covariance:

$$\begin{aligned} COV(X, Y) &= E[(X - E(X))(Y - E(Y))] \\ &= E[XY - E(X)Y - E(Y)X + E(X)E(Y)] \\ &= E(XY) - E(X)E(Y) - E(Y)E(X) + E(X)E(Y) \\ &= E(XY) - E(X)E(Y). \end{aligned}$$

This result is applied to the left-hand side of Eq. (11.11) because it is the expectation of the product of two random variables.

$$E(\Delta \tilde{V}_1)E(1 + \tilde{r}_{f1}) + \mathrm{COV}(\Delta \tilde{V}_1, \tilde{r}_{f1}) = E(\tilde{X}_2) - E[\tilde{\lambda}_1 \mathrm{C\tilde{O}V}(\tilde{X}_2, \tilde{V}_{m2}|\tilde{\epsilon}_1)].$$

We then solve Eq. (11.12) for $E(\Delta \tilde{V}_1)$ and substitute in the preceding expression and arrange terms. The result is

$$\Delta V_0(1 + r_{f0})E(1 + \tilde{r}_{f1}) = E(\tilde{X}_2) - E[\tilde{\lambda}_1 \mathrm{C\tilde{O}V}(\tilde{X}_2, \tilde{V}_{m2}|\tilde{\epsilon}_1)]$$
$$- \lambda_0 \mathrm{COV}(\Delta \tilde{V}_1, \tilde{V}_{m1})E(1 + \tilde{r}_{f1}) - \mathrm{COV}(\Delta \tilde{V}_1, \tilde{r}_{f1}). \quad (11.13)$$

Equation (11.13) can also be written in the following form: ΔV_0, the present value of the single uncertain cash flow two periods in the future is equal to

$$\Delta V_0 = \frac{E(\tilde{X}_2)}{(1 + r_{f0})E(1 + \tilde{r}_{f1})} - \frac{E[\tilde{\lambda}_1 \mathrm{C\tilde{O}V}(\tilde{X}_2, \tilde{V}_{m2}|\tilde{\epsilon}_1)]}{(1 + r_{f0})E(1 + \tilde{r}_{f1})} - \frac{\lambda_0 \mathrm{COV}(\Delta \tilde{V}_1, \tilde{V}_{m1})}{(1 + r_{f0})}$$
$$- \frac{\mathrm{COV}(\Delta \tilde{V}_1, \tilde{r}_{f1})}{(1 + r_{f0})E(1 + \tilde{r}_{f1})}. \quad (11.14)$$

The first of the four terms on the right-hand side of (11.14) is the two-period discounted current expectation of the uncertain cash flow two periods in the future. Subtracted from it are three risk premiums: (1) covariation risk within the second period—i.e., beta risk, (2) covariation risk of the intermediate value of the project which may be thought of as a reinvestment opportunity cost related to the sale of rights to the cash flow after one period has elapsed, and (3) the risk premium for interest rate fluctuations over the two time periods which could cause changes in the project's value at intermediate periods.

In its rearranged form, Eq. (11.13) is in the same form and spirit as the single-period pricing model (Eq. 11.7). However, it contains two additional risk premia that have to be deducted from the two-period discounted current expectation of the single uncertain cash flow two periods in the future. The first is the covariation risk of the intermediate value of the project, and the second is the risk premium charged for the risk of interest fluctuations over the two time periods.

Bogue and Roll conclude by observing that if the errors in probability assessments of the cash flows over the multiple time periods are not systematically biased, stockholders can diversify away most of the error as the number of projects becomes large. Thus unbiased misassessments can be diversified in the personal portfolios of stockholders, whereas the use of a wrong capital-budgeting criterion will result in aggregate errors that stockholders will not be able to reduce by diversification. In concept, the multiperiod capital budgeting problem must utilize a valuation expression which includes two additional risk measures over and above the discounted current expectation of cash flows and the usual covariation of those flows with total market values.

C. AN EXAMINATION OF ADMISSIBLE UNCERTAINTY IN A MULTIPERIOD CAPITAL ASSET PRICING WORLD

In the previous section we presented Bogue and Roll's suggestion that in a two-period context the present value of the firm (Eq. 11.14) cannot be calculated by simply discounting the certainty-equivalent cash flows at the end of the second time period back to the present. In addition, it is necessary to subtract two additional risk premia: (1) a term for the covariation risk of the intermediate value of the project and (2) a term for the risk of fluctuations in the risk-free rate over the two time periods.

Fama [1977] reexamines the multiperiod capital-budgeting problem under uncertainty and clarifies the Bogue and Roll analysis by showing that within a CAPM world, certain types of uncertainty which are allowed by Bogue and Roll are inadmissible. He then shows that given the CAPM assumptions, the last two terms of Eq. (11.14) vanish, and it is possible to use the discounted rate of return approach to capital budgeting as suggested in Eq. (11.1).

If we assume that the firm has net cash earnings, $\tilde{X}_t$, at time t and no cash flows at any other time, then the recursive relationship for the value of the firm at $t - 1$ can be written in a form similar to Eq. (11.5):

$$V_{t-1} = \frac{E(\tilde{X}_t) - \phi_t \, \text{COV}(\tilde{X}_t, \tilde{R}_{mt})}{1 + r_{ft}}, \tag{11.15}$$

where $\phi_t = [E(\tilde{R}_{mt}) - r_{ft}]/\sigma^2(\tilde{R}_{mt})$. This is a certainty-equivalent expression for the value of the firm at $t - 1$. The firm's value at $t - 1$ can also be expressed using the risk-adjusted discount rate to compute the present value of the expected end-of-period cash flows:

$$V_{t-1} = \frac{E(\tilde{X}_t)}{1 + E(\tilde{R}_t)}, \tag{11.16}$$

where $E(\tilde{R}_t) = r_{ft} + [E(\tilde{R}_{mt}) - r_{ft}]\beta_t$.

So far all we have is a one-period expression for the value of cash flows at t, evaluated at $t - 1$. The way we write the value of the firm in a two-period context, at $t - 2$, depends on where we admit uncertainty into expression (11.16). Bogue and Roll allow uncertainty in the parameters of the market opportunity set, namely (1) a stochastic risk-free rate, $\tilde{r}_{ft}$, and (2) uncertainty in the intermediate value of the firm, $\text{COV}(\Delta \tilde{V}_1, \tilde{V}_{m1})$. However, Fama points out that in a world where securities are priced according to the CAPM, relationships between uncertainty in the returns realized at $t - 1$ and the characteristics of the portfolio opportunity set are ruled out. Were such relationships to exist, they would provide initiative for investors to use their portfolio opportunities at $t - 2$ to hedge against uncertainty in portfolio opportunities at $t - 1$. The result is a pricing process different from the CAPM. The alternative pricing model which results has been discussed by Merton [1973] and Long [1974].[3] Therefore, if we assume that the CAPM is the appropriate model, then any variation through time in the market parameters r_{ft} and ϕ_t is nonstochastic.

Having ruled out uncertainty about r_{ft} and ϕ_t, we can see from (11.15) that any uncertainty about V_{t-1} must arise from uncertainty about the values of $E(\tilde{X}_t)$ and $\text{COV}(\tilde{X}_t, \tilde{R}_{mt})$ assessed as of $t - 1$. The strongest assumption is that there is no intermediate uncertainty about $E(\tilde{X}_t)$ and $\text{COV}(\tilde{X}_t, \tilde{R}_{mt})$. If so, then the value in period $t - 2$ becomes

---

[3] The Merton [1973] study is discussed briefly in Chapter 7.

$$V_{t-2} = \frac{V_{t-1}}{1 + r_{f,t-1}},$$

and at $t = 0$ it is

$$V_0 = \prod_{k=1}^{t-1} \left(\frac{1}{1 + r_{fk}} \right) V_{t-1}.$$

Finally, using (11.16), we obtain

$$V_0 = \prod_{k=1}^{t-1} \left(\frac{1}{1 + r_{fk}} \right) \left(\frac{E(\tilde{X}_t)}{1 + E(R_t)} \right). \tag{11.17}$$

In this case, the appropriate discount rates prior to period t are the risk-free rates because there is no uncertainty until period t. For period t, the risk-adjusted rate is given by the CAPM relationships.

Of course, the previous assumption is unreasonably strong. However, if V_{t-1} is to be uncertain prior to $t - 1$, the uncertainty must be introduced in a fashion consistent with the CAPM. Suppose that the cash flow in period t is estimated in an unbiased fashion in period $t - 1$ conditional on all information available at that time. This process can be expressed as

$$\tilde{X}_t = E_{t-1}(\tilde{X}_t)(1 + \tilde{\epsilon}_t) = E_{t-1}(\tilde{X}_t) + E_{t-1}(\tilde{X}_t)\tilde{\epsilon}_t, \tag{11.18}$$

where $E_{t-1}(\tilde{X}_t)$ is the expected value of $\tilde{X}_t$ and $\tilde{\epsilon}_t$ is a random variable with expected value equal to zero. Prior to $t - 1$ the expected value itself is a random variable. This process evolves in the following fashion:

$$\tilde{E}_\tau(\tilde{X}_t) = E_{\tau-1}(\tilde{X}_t)(1 + \tilde{\epsilon}_\tau) = E_{\tau-1}(\tilde{X}_t) + E_{\tau-1}(\tilde{X}_t)\tilde{\epsilon}_\tau. \tag{11.19}$$

Again, the expected value of $\tilde{\epsilon}_\tau$, conditional on the availability of information at $\tau - 1$, is equal to zero. Therefore, given rational expectations, the value of cash flow at time t, $\tilde{X}_t$, evolves as a martingale.[4] Note that $\tilde{\epsilon}_\tau$ is the change in the expected value of $\tilde{X}_t$ per unit of $E_{t-1}(\tilde{X}_t)$.

$$\tilde{\epsilon}_\tau = \frac{\tilde{E}_\tau(\tilde{X}_t) - E_{\tau-1}(\tilde{X}_t)}{E_{\tau-1}(\tilde{X}_t)} = \frac{\tilde{E}_\tau(\tilde{X}_t)}{E_{\tau-1}(\tilde{X}_t)} - 1. \tag{11.20}$$

Substituting (11.18) into (11.15), we have the value of the firm as of $t - 1$:

$$V_{t-1} = E_{t-1}(\tilde{X}_t) \left[\frac{1 - \phi_t \, \text{COV}(\tilde{\epsilon}_t, \tilde{R}_{mt})}{1 + r_{ft}} \right] = E_{t-1}(\tilde{X}_t) \left[\frac{1}{1 + E(\tilde{R}_t)} \right]. \tag{11.21}$$

Note that because $\tilde{V}_t = \tilde{X}_t$, we have the following:

$$\frac{\text{COV}(\tilde{V}_t, \tilde{R}_{mt})}{E_{t-1}(\tilde{V}_t)} = \frac{\text{COV}(\tilde{X}_t, \tilde{R}_{mt})}{E_{t-1}(\tilde{X}_t)} = \text{COV}(\tilde{\epsilon}_t, \tilde{R}_{mt}). \tag{11.22}$$

In (11.21) the return expected from the firm, $E(\tilde{R}_t)$, is part of the portfolio opportunity set perceived by investors at $t - 1$. Any stochastic change in this expected return between $t - 2$ and $t - 1$ is likely to affect the value of the firm at $t - 1$. If such a stochastic relationship were to exist, the return realized at $t - 1$, $\tilde{R}_{t-1}$, would

---

[4] See Chapter 9 for a discussion of martingales.

not be independent of the expected return, $E(\tilde{R}_t)$, from $t - 1$ to t, a result which would be inconsistent with the CAPM. Therefore uncertainty at $t - 2$ about the risk-adjusted discount rate, $E(\tilde{R}_t)$, in Eq. (11.21) is inadmissible in the multiperiod version of the CAPM. Since uncertainty about ϕ_t and r_{ft} have already been ruled out, the implication is that uncertainty about $COV(\tilde{\epsilon}_t, \tilde{R}_{mt})$ in Eq. (11.21) is also inadmissible. Consequently, the expected earnings, $E_{t-1}(\tilde{X}_t)$, are the only parameter whose value can be uncertain at $t - 2$. This fact will allow us to simplify things considerably.

If $E(\tilde{R}_t)$ is certain, then by substituting (11.19) into (11.21) we have

$$\tilde{V}_{t-1} = [E_{t-2}(\tilde{X}_t) + E_{t-2}(\tilde{X}_t)\tilde{\epsilon}_{t-1}]\left[\frac{1}{1 + E(\tilde{R}_t)}\right]. \tag{11.23}$$

The implication of (11.23) is that the value of the firm at $t - 1$ is perfectly correlated with $E_{t-1}(\tilde{X}_t)$, which is the assessment of the expected value of earnings turning up at $t - 1$.

Taking the expectation of (11.23), we see that the expected value of $\tilde{V}_{t-1}$ as of $t - 2$ is

$$E_{t-2}(\tilde{V}_{t-1}) = E_{t-2}(\tilde{X}_t)\left[\frac{1}{1 + E(\tilde{R}_t)}\right], \tag{11.24}$$

and using (11.22), we see that

$$COV(\tilde{V}_{t-1}, \tilde{R}_{m,t-1}) = E_{t-2}(\tilde{X}_t)\left[\frac{1}{1 + E(\tilde{R}_t)}\right]COV(\tilde{\epsilon}_{t-1}, \tilde{R}_{m,t-1}). \tag{11.25}$$

Finally, taking the ratio of (11.24) and (11.25), we have

$$\frac{COV(\tilde{V}_{t-1}, \tilde{R}_{m,t-1})}{E_{t-2}(\tilde{V}_{t-1})} = COV(\tilde{\epsilon}_{t-1}, \tilde{R}_{m,t-1}), \tag{11.26}$$

and from (11.20),

$$\frac{COV[\tilde{E}_{t-1}(\tilde{X}_t), \tilde{R}_{m,t-1}]}{E_{t-2}(\tilde{X}_t)} = COV(\tilde{\epsilon}_{t-1}, \tilde{R}_{m,t-1}). \tag{11.27}$$

Therefore the covariance between the value of the firm at $t - 1$ and the market portfolio per unit of $E_{t-2}(\tilde{V}_{t-1})$ is identical to the covariance between the expected value of earnings and the market portfolio per unit of $E_{t-2}(\tilde{X}_t)$. Now the value of the firm as of $t - 2$ may be written as

$$V_{t-2} = \frac{E_{t-2}(\tilde{V}_{t-1}) - \phi_{t-1}COV(\tilde{V}_{t-1}, \tilde{R}_{m,t-1})}{1 + r_{f,t-1}}$$

$$= E_{t-2}(\tilde{V}_{t-1})\left[\frac{1 - \phi_{t-1}COV(\tilde{V}_{t-1}, R_{m,t-1})/E_{t-2}(\tilde{V}_{t-2})}{1 + r_{f,t-1}}\right],$$

and using (11.26), we have

$$V_{t-2} = E_{t-2}(\tilde{V}_{t-1}) \left[\frac{1 - \phi_{t-1} \, \text{COV}(\tilde{\epsilon}_{t-1}, \tilde{R}_{m,t-1})}{1 + r_{f,t-1}} \right]$$

$$= E_{t-2}(\tilde{V}_{t-1}) \left[\frac{1}{1 + E(\tilde{R}_{t-1})} \right] \tag{11.28}$$

We can rewrite $E_{t-2}(\tilde{V}_{t-1})$ by using (11.24) to obtain

$$V_{t-2} = E_{t-2}(\tilde{X}_t) \left[\frac{1}{1 + E(\tilde{R}_t)} \right] \left[\frac{1}{1 + E(\tilde{R}_{t-1})} \right],$$

and, in general, we obtain the recursive relationship

$$V_\tau = E_\tau(\tilde{X}_t) \left[\frac{1}{1 + E(\tilde{R}_{\tau+1})} \right] \cdots \left[\frac{1}{1 + E(\tilde{R}_t)} \right]. \tag{11.29}$$

The market value of the firm at τ is the expected value at τ of the earnings to be realized at time t, discounted at the risk-adjusted discount rates for each of the periods between τ and t.

Fama points out that if the CAPM is assumed to hold, only uncertainty about $\tilde{E}_\tau(\tilde{X}_t)$ is admissible. Uncertainty about the risk-adjusted discount rates, $E(\tilde{R}_{\tau+1})$, ..., $E(\tilde{R}_t)$, is not admissible. The risk adjustments in the discount rates arise because of the uncertain evolution through time of the expected value of cash flow.

If we are to obtain the usual solution to the multiperiod capital-budgeting problem, we must also assume that the risk-free rate, r_{ft}, the covariance, $\text{COV}(\tilde{\epsilon}_t, \tilde{R}_{mt})$, and the risk-adjusted rate, $E(\tilde{R}_\tau)$, are constant through time. If so, we obtain

$$V_0 = \frac{E_0(\tilde{X}_t)}{[1 + E(\tilde{R})]^t},$$

which, of course, is equal to Eq. (11.1) for an example with cash flow only in the last time period.

Bogue and Roll [1974] show that if the expected risk-free rate and therefore the expected portfolio opportunity set are stochastic, then the multiperiod capital-budgeting problem is not easily solved. The investor must not only consider systematic risk in the usual CAPM sense, but must also take into account two additional factors: (1) the risk of fluctuations in the risk-free rate and (2) the covariation risk of the intermediate value of the project. These results are consistent with various multiperiod versions of the CAPM (e.g., Merton [1973] and Long [1974]) which assume a stochastic risk-free rate.

Fama [1977] carefully examines the types of variability admissible under a stationary CAPM which assumes that the portfolio opportunity set is nonstochastic. In general, the only admissible form of uncertainty is in the expected cash earnings in time t, assessed as of time $\tau < t$. The risk-adjusted discount rates in each future time period are known with certainty at time τ. Given the somewhat unpalatable assumptions of the stationary multiperiod CAPM, we have the result that the usual textbook treatment of multiperiod capital budgeting under uncertainty is reasonable.

Constantinides [1980] focuses on the minimum set of assumptions necessary for the CAPM to be valid in a multiperiod framework. In particular he utilizes the assumptions that (1) we have perfect markets, (2) investors all have homogeneous expectations, (3) investor utility functions are independent of the realized states of nature, and (4) there are competitive profit maximizing firms whose output in period t is a function of input in period $t - 1$ and a random shock which is not dependent on the state of the economy in period $t - 1$. If the distribution of returns is normal or stable Paretian, then the multiperiod CAPM is valid. The important implication is that the multiperiod CAPM is valid even if the portfolio investment opportunity set is stochastic. Therefore, Constantinides shows the CAPM to be valid under a less restrictive set of assumptions than Fama. Nonstationarity in the distribution of the market portfolio return, the return on the riskless asset, the security betas, and the market price of risk are all admissible in the context of the Sharpe, Lintner, Mossin CAPM. This is the good news. Unfortunately, the bad news, according to Constantinides, is that "the sequential application of the SLM model in the discounting of stochastic cash flows of multiperiod projects becomes computationally complex and of little practical use, unless one can produce convincing evidence to the effect that these nonstationarities are unimportant in practice."

Although the issues discussed in this chapter may seem exceedingly academic to the reader, they are no less important than the issue of whether to use the NPV or the IRR criterion as discussed in Chapter 2. Proper use of capital-budgeting techniques is not a trivial issue. Until the question was posed by Bogue and Roll, little formal consideration had been given to the problems involved in the complex issue of multiperiod capital budgeting under uncertainty. Although the Fama article does much to clarify matters, we see that the standard solution to the problem requires a set of fairly restrictive assumptions.

D. USING THE ARBITRAGE PRICING THEORY FOR MULTIPERIOD CAPITAL BUDGETING

Recall, from Chapter 7, that the assumptions of the Arbitrage Pricing Theory (APT) are less restrictive than those of the Capital Asset Pricing Model (CAPM), especially in its multiperiod form. The APT does not require that the market portfolio be observable nor does it require intertemporal stationarity in the investment opportunity set. Rather, it requires only that at any instant in time there be no available arbitrage opportunities.

Ross [1979] shows how the APT can be used to value risky income streams and Gehr [1981] shows how the idea can be applied specifically to the multiperiod capital budgeting problem. Gehr's example uses the APT to avoid the problems implicit in using a multiperiod risk-adjusted discount rate, but it is no panacea because it requires that we estimate a relationship between the future price of (some) publicly traded asset and future cash flows for a project.

We begin by studying a simple one-period, two-state problem. Table 11.1 contains the data necessary to determine the net present value of a project which costs $8,000

Table 11.1 One Period APT Example

Period	Economic State	Subjective Probability	Project CF	r_f Risk-free Rate	S Comparison Stock
0	current	1.0	−8,000	NA	$ 9.00
1	bad	.3	8,000	10%	$ 8.00
1	good	.7	15,000	10%	$25.50

today and which will return cash flows of $8,000 if economic conditions are bad or $15,000 otherwise. If we can create a *cash-equivalent portfolio* from the risk-free asset and the comparison stock, then we can value the project. The cash equivalent portfolio will have exactly the same payoffs as the project in each state of nature. Because we know the prices of the risk-free asset and the comparison stock, the price of the cash equivalent portfolio will be the value of the project, otherwise arbitrage opportunities would exist.

How much should we invest in the risk-free asset and in the comparison stock to obtain exactly the same payoffs as the project? Let Q_r be the dollars invested in the risk-free asset and Q_s be the number of shares of the comparison stock (which costs $9.00 per share). The two equations below show the payoffs of the cash equivalent portfolio in each state of nature.[5]

$$\text{Bad economic conditions} \quad 8.00 \ Q_s + 1.10 \ Q_r = 8,000,$$

$$\text{Good economic conditions} \quad 25.50 \ Q_s + 1.10 \ Q_r = 15,000.$$

With two equations and two unknowns we can solve to find that $Q_s = 400$ shares and $Q_r = \$4,363.64$. Therefore, the current value of the cash equivalent portfolio, PV, is

$$\text{PV} = (400 \text{ shares})(\$9.00/\text{share}) + \$4,363.64,$$

$$\text{PV} = \$3,600 + \$4,363.64 = \$7,963.64.$$

This is also the present value of the project because the cash equivalent portfolio duplicates the project's payoffs in each state of nature. The NPV of the project is its present value minus the cash outlay needed to acquire it.

$$\text{NPV} = \text{PV} - I$$

$$= \$7,964 - \$8,000 = -\$36.$$

Because the NPV is negative the project should be rejected.

Note that it was never necessary to use the probability estimates of states of nature. The risk-adjusted discount rate was never computed, and nothing was known about the risk tolerances of the firm (or investors) which evaluated the project. All of this information is implicitly included in the relative prices (across time and across

---

[5] The price per share of the stock is $9 and implicitly the price per unit of the risk-free asset is $1.

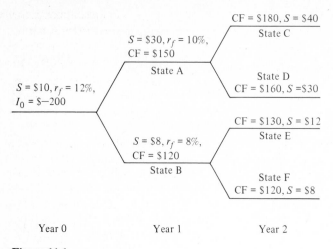

Figure 11.1
Two-period APT example, first stage.

states of nature) of the risk-free asset and the risky comparison stock. As long as their prices are true equilibrium prices, then the market information tells us all that we need to know.

The technique can readily be extended to a multiperiod economy, even one where the risk-free rate changes through time. Figure 11.1 gives data for a two-period example. The probabilities of states of nature are not given because they are not explicitly needed to solve the problem. Note that the risk-free rate is state contingent. If a favorable state of the economy prevails in year 1, then $r_f = 10\%$, otherwise it is 8%. Also, the correlation between the project and the comparison stock need not be stationary through time.

The project can be evaluated by finding the cash equivalent portfolios between years 1 and 2, then using this information to find the year 0 cash equivalent portfolio.[6] The two sets of simultaneous equations given below are used to determine the period 1 cash equivalent portfolios.

$$
\begin{array}{llll}
\text{State C} & 40Q_s + 1.10\,Q_r = 180 & \left.\vphantom{\begin{matrix}a\\b\end{matrix}}\right\} & Q_s = 2,\ Q_r = \$90.91 \\
\text{State D} & 30Q_s + 1.10\,Q_r = 160 & & V_A = \$150.91 \\
\text{State E} & 12Q_s + 1.08\,Q_r = 130 & \left.\vphantom{\begin{matrix}a\\b\end{matrix}}\right\} & Q_s = 2.5,\ Q_r = \$92.59 \\
\text{State F} & 8Q_s + 1.08\,Q_r = 120 & & V_B = \$112.59.
\end{array}
$$

As shown in Fig. 11.2, the values of the cash equivalent portfolios in States A and B are $150.91 and $112.59, respectively. The value of the project, in State A for example, is the cash flow which it provides in that state of nature plus the cash

---

[6] If this procedure sounds similar to the Cox, Ross, Rubinstein binomial model, derived in Chapter 8, it is. The arbitrage pricing theory, the option pricing model and state preference theory (even the CAPM) are all consistent with each other.

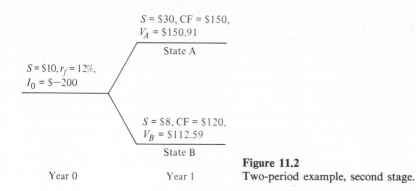

$S = \$30, CF = \$150,$
$V_A = \$150.91$

State A

$S = \$10, r_f = 12\%,$
$I_0 = \$-200$

$S = \$8, CF = \$120,$
$V_B = \$112.59$

State B

Figure 11.2

Year 0   Year 1   Two-period example, second stage.

equivalent value, V_A. This information can be used to write the appropriate set of payoffs for the period 1 cash equivalent portfolio as shown below.

State A $30Q_s + 1.12\ Q_r = 150 + 150.91$

State B $8Q_s + 1.12\ Q_r = 120 + 112.59.$

Solving, we find that $Q_s = 3.11$ shares and $Q_r = \$185.49$. Thus the value of the cash equivalent portfolio for the two-year project is

$$PV = (3.11\ shares)(\$10.00/share) + \$185.49$$

$$= \$216.59,$$

and the net present value of the project is

$$NPV = PV - I = \$216.59 - \$200 = \$16.59.$$

Therefore, the project should be accepted.

Despite the obvious theoretical advantages of using the arbitrage pricing theory for capital budgeting, there remains the practical problem of estimating the state contingent prices of the comparison stock and the risk-free asset. Obviously this is no easy task. Whether or not decision makers will find this new technique of practical value remains to be seen. Who knows, maybe a decade from now, questionnaires on capital budgeting techniques will ask sophisticated firms whether or not they employ the APT capital budgeting technique. Only time can tell.

E. COMPARING RISKY COST STRUCTURES

Applied capital budgeting problems are almost always multiperiod, and frequently it is reasonable to assume that the revenues from two mutually exclusive projects will be identical. For example, this is the usual assumption in machine replacement problems. The revenues of the firm will be invariant to the choice of equipment. Therefore the usual capital-budgeting process simply discounts the various incremental costs associated with the mutually exclusive alternatives and chooses the project with the lowest discounted cost.

Assuming that the multiperiod risk-adjusted rate of return is the appropriate technique for capital budgeting, how should it be used to compare cash outflows on a risk-adjusted basis? As we shall see, the correct approach discounts the expected costs at a lower rate when the cash outflows have greater variance. As long as the absolute value of the cash outflows is positively correlated with the market portfolio, greater variance in the outflows will imply lower overall project risk, i.e., there will be a lower project beta. In order to develop this result let's look at a simple one-period case. At the end of the period, the after-tax cash flows from operations may be written as follows:

$$\tilde{CF} = (\tilde{R} - \tilde{VC})(1 - \tau_c) + \tau_c \, \text{dep},$$

where

$\tilde{CF}$ = after-tax cash flows for capital-budgeting purposes,

$\tilde{R}$ = end-of-period revenues,

$\tilde{VC}$ = end-of-period variable cash costs,

τ_c = the corporate tax rate,

dep = depreciation.

The rate of return, $\tilde{r}_j$, on the project is the return on investment (where investment is I_0):

$$\tilde{r}_j = \frac{(\tilde{R} - \tilde{VC})(1 - \tau_c) + \tau_c \, \text{dep} - I_0}{I_0}.$$

If we assume that the project is fully depreciated during the period, then $I_0 = \text{dep}$, and we have

$$\tilde{r}_j = \frac{(\tilde{R} - \tilde{VC})(1 - \tau_c) - I_0(1 - \tau_c)}{I_0}$$

$$= \frac{(1 - \tau_c)}{I_0} \tilde{R} - \frac{(1 - \tau_c)}{I_0} \tilde{VC} - (1 - \tau_c).$$

Using the properties of random variables derived in Chapter 6, we can write the covariance between the return on the project and the return on the market portfolio as

$$\text{COV}(\tilde{r}_j, \tilde{r}_m) = \frac{(1 - \tau_c)}{I_0} \text{COV}(\tilde{R}, \tilde{r}_m) - \frac{(1 - \tau_c)}{I_0} \text{COV}(\tilde{VC}, \tilde{r}_m). \quad (11.30)$$

Equation (11.30) shows that the covariance risk of a project can be partitioned into two parts: the covariance risk of its revenue stream, and the covariance risk of its cost stream. Note that if the costs have positive covariance with the market in the sense that they are high when the market return is high and vice versa, then their contribution to the project's covariance risk will be large and negative. This implies that the cost streams of riskier projects should be discounted at lower (and even negative) discount rates in order to properly adjust for risk. Note also that Eq. (11.30)

Table 11.2   Projects with Different Risky Costs

	Proba-bility	$\tilde{r}_m$	r_f	$\tilde{R}_1$	$\check{V}C_1$	$\check{C}F_1$	$\tilde{r}_1$	$\tilde{R}_2$	$\check{V}C_2$	$\check{C}F_2$	$\tilde{r}_2$
				Project 1				*Project 2*			
State 1	.33	.26	.04	610	500	105	.05	610	495	107.5	.075
State 2	.33	.14	.04	600	470	115	.15	600	500	100.0	0
State 3	.33	.20	.04	610	520	95	−.05	610	505	102.5	.025

can be rewritten in terms of systematic risk by dividing both sides by the variance of market return. This yields

$$\beta_j = \left(\frac{1 - \tau_c}{I_0}\right)\beta_{jR} - \left(\frac{1 - \tau_c}{I_0}\right)\beta_{jVC}, \tag{11.31}$$

where

β_j = the systematic risk of the project where $j = 1,2$,

β_{jR} = the systematic risk of the revenue stream,

β_{jVC} = the systematic risk of the variable cost stream.

As an illustration, consider the following example. The two mutually exclusive projects given in Table 11.2 have identical revenue streams but different costs. In addition to the project cash flows, the table also provides the rate of return on the market portfolio, $\tilde{r}_m$, and the risk-free rate, r_f, in each of the three equally likely states of the world. The cost of the project, I_0, is \$100 and the corporate tax rate is 50%. The rate of return, $\tilde{r}_j$, on each project (columns 7 and 11) is calculated as follows:

$$\tilde{r}_j = \frac{\check{C}F_j - I_0}{I_0}.$$

By inspecting the cash flows in Table 11.2, we see that the revenue streams are positively correlated with the market return, and so are the variable cost streams of the projects. However, the correlation between the variable cost stream of project 1 and the market return is such that it causes the project's net cash flow, CF, to be negatively correlated with the market. The higher variance and the positive correlation between (the absolute value of) the cash outflows of the first project and the market return requires that its cash costs be discounted at a lower rate. Project 1 has a lower β than project 2.

Table 11.3 shows the results of computations of various statistics necessary for the calculation of the risk-adjusted rate of return. By using the CAPM and the statistics in Table 11.3, we can calculate the appropriate discount rates for the projects' net cash flow streams, or their cost streams. Using project 1 as an example, we employ the CAPM

$$E(\tilde{r}_j) = r_f + [E(\tilde{r}_m) - r_f]\beta_j,$$

Table 11.3 A List of Relevant Statistics

	Mean			Covariance with r_m			β		
	r	R	VC	r	R	VC	j	R	VC
Project 1	.050	606.67	496.67	−.0020	.20	.60	−.833	83.33	250.00
Project 2	.033	606.67	500.00	.0015	.20	−.10	.625	83.33	−41.67
Market return	.200	—	—	.0024	—	—	1.000	—	—

and use Eq. (11.31) to compute the correct, *adjusted betas:* for the project, β_j, its revenues, β_{jR}, and its costs, β_{jVC}.

$$\beta_j = \left(\frac{1-\tau_c}{I_0}\right)\beta_{jR} - \left(\frac{1-\tau_c}{I_0}\right)\beta_{jVC}.$$

Substituting data from Table 11.3, we see that the systematic risk for the project is a weighted average of the betas for the revenue and cost streams.[7]

$$-.833 = \left(\frac{1-.5}{100}\right)(83.33) - \left(\frac{1-.5}{100}\right)(250)$$

$$= .4167 - 1.25.$$

Now we have $\beta_1 = -.833$, $\beta_{1R} = .4167$, and $\beta_{1VC} = -1.25$.

Figure 11.3 graphs the security market line given by the CAPM and shows the betas and required rates of return for the project's cash flows, its revenue stream, and its cost stream.[8] Table 11.4 gives the appropriate discount rates and betas for

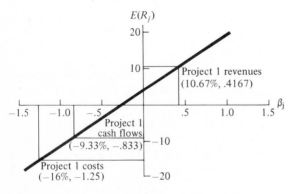

Figure 11.3
Systematic risk and required rate of return for Project 1.

---

[7] Note that the beta for the cost stream is negative because the costs are outflows. The absolute value of the cost stream is positively correlated with the market, but the signed cash costs are negatively correlated with the market.

[8] It may seem unusual to discount cash flows at negative rates of return. Normally, this would not be the case because real-world projects are almost always positively correlated with the market. However, in the artificially constructed example above, it is perfectly consistent with the CAPM to require negative rates on projects with negative betas.

Table 11.4   Discount Rates and Adjusted Betas

	Discount Rates			Adjusted β		
	CF	R	VC	CF	R	VC
Project 1	−9.33%	10.67%	−16.00%	−.833	.4167	−1.2500
Project 2	14.00%	10.67%	7.33%	.625	.4167	.2083

the overall project cash flows and for the revenues and costs. Note that the cost stream should be discounted at −16%. Similar calculations show that for project 2 the cost stream should be discounted at 7.33%. Thus we have demonstrated the result that when (the absolute value of) cash outflows are positively correlated with the market, then cash outflows with greater variability should be discounted at lower rates. They have the effect of lowering project betas.

A word of caution to the practitioner is appropriate at this point. It is never advisable to totally ignore revenues or the riskiness of the revenue stream (even though this is frequent practice). In the above example, the market required rate of return on project 2 is 14%, and the expected rate of return (the mean return in Table 10.3) is only 3.3%. Therefore, project 2 is unacceptable under any circumstances. This may have been true for both projects. The practitioner who ignores revenues and chooses the project with the lower discounted cost may easily accept a project with negative NPV. Costs tell only half the story. Decision making on the basis of cost comparisons alone is inappropriate unless the decision maker is absolutely sure that the mutually exclusive projects all have positive net present value.

Given the results of Fama [1977] and Constantinides [1980], which were discussed in the previous section, it is possible to extend the one-period cost comparison procedure into a multiperiod framework. So long as the market parameters are assumed *ex ante* to be stationary over time, we still have the result that cost streams with higher variance should be discounted at lower rates.

F. ABANDONMENT VALUE

A critical aspect of the capital-budgeting decision is the consideration of the residual value of the investment assets. The residual values will be known only at some future date, so they are necessarily uncertain at the time investments are being made. However, for investments such as land and buildings, values may actually increase with inflation in future years. For machinery and equipment, subject to a high rate of obsolescence, the residual value may drop to virtually nothing even before the end of the expected life of the machine used in the initial capital-budgeting analysis.

Clearly, the residual value of an investment asset may be substantial. Hence, to make a capital-budgeting decision without taking residual value into account may lead to serious errors. In addition, for a number of reasons, the sales value or *abandonment value* of an asset may be greater than the present value of the continued use of the asset by the firm which owns the asset.

Thus there are two aspects of the abandonment decision. One aspect is to take the resale value or abandonment value of the asset into account in the capital-budget analysis. The second is the requirement that the analysis consider the optimal period at which abandonment of the asset or its sale at its current market value should take place.

The first article emphasizing the importance of taking abandonment value into account was by Robichek and Van Horne [1967], who proposed that the project be abandoned in the first year that its abandonment value exceeds the present value of the remaining expected cash flows associated with the continued operation of the investment. They pointed out that considering abandonment before the end of the life of a project could increase the project's NPV so that an otherwise unacceptable project would become desirable.

In a comment on the Robichek-Van Horne analysis, Dyl and Long [1969] point out that there may be an even greater advantage to abandonment in a period subsequent to the first instance when abandonment value exceeds the present value of continued operations. They argue that it is necessary to consider future abandonment possibilities in addition to the year in which abandonment value first exceeds the present value of continued operations. Consideration of future abandonment values will provide a measure of maximum present value resulting from the selection of the optimum abandonment timing.

Robichek-Van Horne acknowledge that deferred abandonment may be preferred to present abandonment. However, they observe that future operating cash flows and abandonment values are not known with certainty. They suggest that a practical operational procedure does not require a forecast over the full estimated economic life of the investment, and go on to offer a revised formulation which requires only one period for which the present value of continued operation exceeds abandonment value. If such an instance exists, the project is held another year and then reevaluated. The reevaluation would be based on the new formulation of expectations made at that time. Thus it is not required that the decision maker provide a complete enumeration of all possible present values of continued operations and of abandonment values in future years. The benefits of a sequential decision process can be obtained.

Joy [1976] has formulated a clear statement of the revised Robichek-Van Horne abandonment value algorithm. Let

C_t = expected operating cash flow in year t,

k_0 = cost of capital,

n = maximum expected feasible life of project,

AV_a = expected abandonment value in period a.

Step 1. Set $a = 1$.

Step 2. Compute NPV_a, where

$$NPV_a = \sum_{t=0}^{a} \frac{C_t}{(1+k_0)^t} + \frac{AV_a}{(1+k_0)^a} - I_0$$

= NPV of project, given abandonment in period a.

Step 3. If $NPV_a > 0$, accept. If $NPV_a < 0$, go to step 4.

Step 4. Repeat steps 2 and 3 for $a = 2, 3, \ldots, n$ until

either $NPV_a > 0$ for some *a:* accept,

or $NPV_a < 0$ for all *a:* reject.

Joy points out that the basic decision is whether to relinquish the asset now or to hold it for one more period. A decision to keep the asset requires only one instance where the present value of continuing to hold the asset exceeds the abandonment value. The same analysis applies to currently owned assets. The decision to abandon leads to immediate abandonment. Otherwise the asset will be held for one additional year and a keep-vs.-abandon decision will then again be made. At that time revisions in estimates of expected future operating cash flows and abandonment values may be made.

Joy then points out that the foregoing analysis is applicable to accept-reject decisions for independent investments. However, if mutually exclusive projects are being compared, it is necessary to make the analysis over the full planning horizon for each to determine which of the projects dominates. Hence an exhaustive search for abandonment possibilities over a full planning horizon will be required utilizing the Dyl-Long approach. Joy formulates this abandonment algorithm as follows:

Step 1. Compute NPV_a for $a = 1, 2, \ldots, n$ for each project.

Step 2. Select the maximum value of NPV_a for each project, and select that project with the largest positive maximum value of NPV_a.

A comparison of the accept-reject decision approach with the mutually exclusive choice decision approach is illustrated utilizing the data presented in Table 11.5. The investment costs of the project are assumed to be $10,000. Present value estimates are made for two series of flows. Line 1 is the estimated present value of the project in period *a* if operated for its remaining years of life and then abandoned. Line 2 is the estimated present value of the project if abandoned in period *a*. A plausible real-world counterpart to such a pattern of flows could be an investment in a fruit or citrus orchard. With such an investment there is always the alternative of selling the annual product from the orchard or to sell the orchard at various time periods. The values from selling the product of the orchard may fluctuate with estimates of demand and supply conditions in those markets in particular years. In addition,

Table 11.5

	Period				
Series of flows	1	2	3	4	5
1. Estimated present values of project in period *a* if operated for remaining years of life and then abandoned	11,000	11,000	11,000	10,000	9,000
2. Estimated present value of abandonment in period *a*	4,000	6,000	12,000	10,000	8,000

there may be a demand for the trees for decorative or other purposes which will be sensitive to fluctuations in demand conditions in individual years, and over longer periods of time supply conditions may change as well. Thus a wide variety of patterns in gains from selling the product of the orchard, selling the orchard for future product yields, or selling the orchard for immediate decorative-tree purposes could create a wide variety of year-by-year present value estimates.

Let us first illustrate the accept-reject decision. The first column of figures in Table 11.5 provides a basis for undertaking the investment and deferring the abandonment decision for at least one year. The estimated present value of the project at the beginning of period 1 if operated for five additional periods and then abandoned is $11,000. Hence the net value of the project is positive. In addition, the NPV of the project with deferred abandonment is greater than the estimated present value of abandonment of the project in period 1. At the beginning of period 2, another assessment of future prospects could be made. If the estimates are as indicated in column 2, the decision would be to continue to operate the project another year.

At the beginning of the third year another analysis is made with the estimates as indicated in the column for period 3. Now the estimated present value of the project given abandonment in period 3 is $12,000. The estimated present value of the project in period 3 if operated for the remaining years of its life and then abandoned is seen to be only $11,000. According to the Robichek-Van Horne formulation as revised by Joy, the project would then be abandoned in the third year. However, in our judgment the Dyl-Long criticism is still valid. Before such a determination could be made, a complete enumeration would be required over the remaining years of the investment planning horizon. For example, if in the fourth year the estimated present value of abandonment in period 4 were $13,000, then it would have been even more favorable to defer the abandonment until the fourth year rather than to abandon the project in the third year. Thus the Dyl-Long comment remains valid even when the accept-reject decision is involved. Complete enumeration can be avoided for any individual year until the year in which a tentative decision to abandon the project is made. Then it is still necessary to make an analysis for the remaining years of the planning horizon to determine the year in which abandonment will yield the highest present value.

Thus far in the analysis the discussion has been in terms of best estimates of the cash flows over the time pattern of years. The analysis could be extended by an additional step which would consider estimates of probabilities of various levels of cash flow in each year and then show the calculations of expected values and their standard deviations. However, in terms of the central issues of the role of abandonment value and the optimal timing of abandonment covered in the literature, the discussion to this point covers both issues.

With the rise in replacement or market values of investments that has developed as a result of the high rate of inflation in the United States which began in 1966, the issue of abandonment value takes on increasingly greater significance for the planning and control of existing operations. Management is under increased pressure to improve revenue levels and more effectively control cost increases in order to justify not only new investments but also the continued operation of present investments instead of selling them in the open market where a greater NPV could be realized. Thus the issue is whether to continue operations or to abandon by selling at higher current present values. This issue is developed in the following illustrative example.

The Cincinnati Company operates a cement factory. The historical depreciated cost of the factory and equipment is $10,000,000. It has an expected life of another 10 years. The effective corporate tax rate is 40%, and the applicable cost of capital is 12%. The current market value of the plant is $20,000,000.

Over a 10-year planning horizon, it is estimated that revenues will be $10,000,000 per year and total costs (excluding depreciation) will be $6,600,000 per year. The Cincinnati Company will use the double-declining balance method of depreciation.

On the basis of the present estimates of revenues and costs, what is the NPV of the cement factory? The solution is given below,[9]

$$\text{NPV} = [3,400,000(1 - \tau_c) + \tau_c \text{ dep}] \text{ PVIF}_a$$

$$= 2,040,000(5.650) + .4(10,000,000)(.643)$$

$$= 11,526,000 + 2,572,000$$

$$= 14,098,000,$$

that is, Cincinnati Company should sell the plant for $20,000,000, which exceeds the present value of future net flows by $5,902,000.

Thus we see that the present value of the cement factory is positive. However, in relation to the plant's current market value (if sold) of $20 million, the investment in continued operation is simply not justifiable. In other words, the present value derived from continuing to operate the cement factory is $14.1 million. However, the plant could be sold in the open market at something like $20 million. Thus management would add more to present value by "abandoning" the plant than by continuing its operation.

This illustrates a general problem facing many business firms today. Inflation has pushed up the replacement costs of plant and equipment. Also, materials and wage costs continue to rise. As a consequence, there is a squeeze on profits even in nominal terms, and profits have to rise in nominal terms for profit ratios to be maintained. Market values of shares have not kept up with inflation.

On the average the market values of nonfinancial corporations are 70% to 80% of the current replacement values of their assets. Often firms can buy other companies below replacement values while new investments in their own line of business do not offer prospects of NPVs that would be positive. This is one of the reasons why new investments in the economy as a whole have lagged. Profit margins capitalized at applicable discount factors result in present values that are below current replacement values of the investment projects.

---

[9] *Note:* PVIF$_a$ is the present-value factor for an annuity with payments at the end of each year for a years. Also, when we multiply the book value of the assets, $10,000,000, by the factor .643, we are accounting for the present value assuming double-declining depreciation.

SUMMARY

By considering the relations between periods recursively, Bogue and Roll [1974] develop an equation for multiperiod capital budgeting. In addition to the usual beta risk, the resulting equation contains two additional risk premia: the covariation risk of the intermediate values of the project and the risk premium related to the risk of interest fluctuations. Fama [1977] points out that in a world in which securities are priced according to the CAPM, the only admissible form of uncertainty is the expected cash earnings in time t assessed one period earlier. The risk-free rate, the covariance, and the risk-adjusted rate are then constant through time and the traditional capital budgeting model can be employed.

Gehr [1981] shows how the arbitrage pricing model can be employed to solve multiperiod capital budgeting problems. The technique avoids all of the difficulties of the multiperiod CAPM but, unfortunately, requires estimates of state-contingent future security prices.

In most equipment replacement problems it is plausible that revenues from two mutually exclusive types of equipment will be identical. However, the riskiness of the cost streams may be different. We are accustomed to increasing the amount of risk-adjustment in the capitalization factor applied to riskier net cash flow streams. This has the effect of penalizing riskier investments. When the streams under comparison are costs alone, we need to have higher present values for riskier cost streams. This is accomplished by lowering the discount rate, rather than increasing it.

Another important aspect of the assessment of risky investments is to estimate residual values. In addition, the sales or abandonment value of an asset may be greater than the present value of the continued use of the asset. The initial criterion proposed abandonment in the first year that abandonment value exceeded the present value of continued use of the asset. Later studies pointed out the necessity of consideration of abandonment possibilities in future years to obtain the maximum present value from the selection of the optimal time for abandonment.

PROBLEM SET

11.1 Which of the following types of uncertainty are inadmissible in a multiperiod model if we are using the CAPM? Why?

a) $COV(\tilde{\epsilon}_t, \tilde{R}_{mt})$ d) $COV(\tilde{V}_{t-1}, \tilde{R}_{m,t-1})$

b) $\tilde{r}_{ft}$ e) $(E(\tilde{R}_{mt}) - r_{ft})/\sigma^2(\tilde{R}_{mt})$

c) $E_{t-1}(\tilde{X}_t)$

11.2 The Ramsden Company is installing 10 new forklift trucks. Electric trucks cost $8000 each, while gas-powered trucks cost $5000 each. The operating costs for the electric trucks would be $5200 per truck per year compared with $6000 per gas truck for the eight-year expected life of each vehicle. Expected salvage value is zero and straight-line depreciation is to be used. Ramsden will apply a 10% discount factor for analysis of the electric trucks and a 2% differential to the gas trucks due to their higher operating risks. The applicable tax rate is 40%. Should electric or gas forklift trucks be purchased by Ramsden?

11.3 You are asked to perform a capital budgeting analysis of two projects. Both will require an immediate cash outlay of $1000. Both projects last one year and they both produce revenues at the end of the year amounting to $1500 with certainty. Cash outflows at the end of the year, however, are risky. They are given below, along with the market rate of return, R_m.

| State of nature | Probability | End-of-period Outflows | | R_m |
		Project A	Project B	
Great	$\frac{1}{3}$	$500	$600	20%
Average	$\frac{1}{3}$	400	400	10%
Horrid	$\frac{1}{3}$	300	200	0%

Since you are given the cash flows, there is no need to worry about taxes, depreciation, or salvage value. Note that the cash outflows of Project B have higher variance than those of Project A. Which project has greater NPV? Show your work and explain your reasoning.

11.4 Your firm is trying to choose between two mutually exclusive projects. Both cost $10,000, have a five-year life and no salvage value. The company uses straight-line depreciation and the corporate tax rate is 40%. Over the life of the project the annual expected rate of return on the market portfolio is 15% and the risk-free rate is 5%. The first project has expected revenues of $5000 per year with an adjusted β_R of 1.5 and expected variable costs of $2333 per year with an adjusted β_{VC} of -1.4 (i.e., both the revenues and variable costs are positively correlated with the market). The second project has expected revenues of $6067 per year with an adjusted β_R of 1.3 and expected variable costs of $2400 with an adjusted β_{VC} of .3 (i.e., revenues are positively correlated with the market, and variable costs are negatively correlated with the market). Which project should the firm accept? [*Note:* Adjusted βs are discussed in Section E of Chapter 11.]

11.5 Figure Q11.5 gives the cash flows, CF, for a two-period project which requires a $300 initial outlay. Also shown are the state-contingent risk-free rates of return, r_f, and the state-contingent prices of a comparison risky asset. What is the NPV of the project?

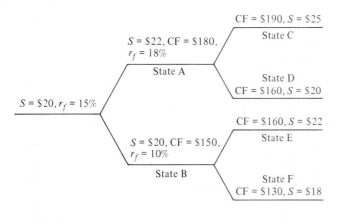

Year 0   Year 1   Year 2

Figure Q11.5

11.6 The following investment decision is being considered by Citrus Farms. For $7000 the company can acquire ownership of 10 acres of 15-year-old orange trees and a 15-year lease on the land. The productive life of an orange tree is divided into stages as follows:

State	Age of Trees, Years	Expected Annual Profit from 10 Acres, $
Peak	16–20	1000
Adult	21–25	900
Mature	26–30	800

There is a market for decorative orange trees. Suppliers will buy trees and remove them according to a schedule based on the age of the tree. Expected prices that can be obtained for the 10-acre harvest are: $9000 at end of age 20, $12,000 at age 25, and $8000 at age 30. Citrus Farms has a 10% cost of capital.

a) What is the present value of each alternative? Since the land and anything on it will belong to the lessor in 15 years, assume that once the trees are harvested the land will not be replanted by Citrus.

b) As an alternative to this investment, Citrus can use the $7000 to buy a new orange-sorting machine. The machine would reduce sorting expenses by $1300 a year for 15 years. Which investment would you make? Why? Assume that all other investment opportunities for the next 15 years will earn the cost of capital.

c) In the 10th year Citrus discovers that everyone else with 25-year-old trees has sold them. As a consequence, the price the firm can get for the trees is only $8000. Since so many trees have been sold for decoration, small orange crops are expected for the next five years. As a result, the price of oranges will be higher. Your acreage will yield $1200 a year. The selling price of your trees in another five years is expected to be still depressed to $6000. What should you do?

d) Given the situation in (c), what was the NPV of your actual investment over the 15-year period?

e) What would the NPV be if the trees had been sold in year 10 for $8000?

11.7 *Southern Electric Power Company*[10]
The State Public Service Commission (PSC) is charged with the responsibility of regulating the two large public utility companies in the state. The PSC is comprised of seven persons; four elected, one gubernatorial appointee, and one representative each from the two public utilities.

The PSC is currently considering a capacity expansion program submitted by Southern Electric Power (SE). SE operates three power plants as shown in Table Q11.7a. The population in the area served by SE has been growing 2% per year. This trend is expected to continue for at least the next 10 years. Industrial growth is even more rapid, about 4% per year. As a result, demand for electricity is growing at approximately 3% per year. Peak-load demand is very near SE's capacity, so it is necessary to begin some expansion within the year.

---
[10] This is really a short case, rather than a problem in the usual sense of the word. It does not necessarily have a simple, cut-and-dried solution.

Table Q11.7b

Type of Plant	Date Constructed	Percent of Current Power Needs Supplied	Remaining Life in Years
Coal	1946	25	30
Hydroelectric	1958	10	35
Natural gas generating	1963	65	45

Another problem the company is confronted with is the growing shortage of natural gas. Last year SE was unable to buy enough natural gas to meet the full electric power needs of the area. The company was able to buy electricity generated by a company in an adjoining state which has coal, but there is no assurance that this source of power can be relied on in the future.

Given the uncertainty of future natural gas supplies, and the fact that hydroelectric power is already being fully utilized, SE feels the only sensible course is to expand its own coal generating capacity. This would be especially desirable since it would use the large soft-coal deposits in the northern part of the state.

There are two ways to increase the capacity for coal generation. For $40,000,000 it would be possible to double the generating capacity of the existing plant. This would fully satisfy the growing demand for electricity for the next six to eight years, after which time additional capacity would be needed. The expansion would have a useful life of 30 years. The existing plant is located 20 miles from the center of the largest city in the state. In 1946, when the plant was originally built, the location was selected specifically to be at a considerable distance from any populated area so that the smoke produced by burning coal would not be an environmental nuisance.

In 30 years the city has grown considerably. Heavily populated suburbs are now located within four miles of the plant, and pollution created by SE is a growing political issue. The company believes it probable that within the next five years political pressure will require that smoke scrubbers be installed at the existing plant (Table Q11.7b). Scrubbers can be installed any time at the existing plant for $4,000,000. If plant capacity is doubled and scrubbers are installed at that time, the total cost would be $5,500,000. (This would be in addition to the base cost of the new plant discussed below.) If the installation of scrubbers is postponed, and carried out as a separate capital investment, the total cost is estimated to be $8,000,000 subject to the same probability that installation might never occur (see Table Q11.7b).

The alternative to expanding the capacity of the old plant is to build an entirely new plant. Such a plant would cost $110,000,000 and would have a maximum capacity of three

Table Q11.7b   Probability That Scrubbers Will Be Required

Time Frame	Probability
In year 2	0%
In year 3	10%
In year 4	50%
In year 5	40%

times the existing coal plant. With the new capacity in addition to the existing plant, energy needs could be met for the next 18 to 20 years. The useful life of the plant would be 40 years. If desired, the capacity of the new plant could be increased to the point that the old plant could be abandoned and capacity would still be adequate for the same period. The additional cost of the extra capacity would be $22,082,000, which would be depreciated over the full life of the plant. If the old plant is abandoned, equipment worth $7,000,000 could be used in the new plant, and sale of the land would provide additional capital of $3,000,000.

Annual operating costs of the old plant are $2,000,000. If its capacity is doubled, operating costs will rise by $1,500,000. Cost of operating the new plant will be $4,000,000 per year. If the old plant is abandoned, operating costs of the new plant will increase by $450,000 per year for the remaining life of the old plant. SE uses straight-line depreciation to zero salvage value on all capital investments discussed here. The cost of scrubbers is amortized over the remaining life of the plant in which they are installed. Book value of the existing coal plant is $10,000,000.

SE has an effective tax rate of 40%. SE's weighted average cost of capital is 10%. Revenues and other costs will be the same under either alternative. Excess capacity can be sold outside the state at the same rate as within the state.

1. As a representative of the utility company, you are concerned with maximizing the present value of the project. Analyze the alternatives and indicate your recommendation.

2. Keeping in mind that you are working only with costs, how would you adjust the discount rate to account for: (a) the extra uncertainty for any alternative which includes delayed installation of smoke scrubbers; (b) the pollution that would result from operating the old plant without smoke scrubbers?

3. How would these factors affect your recommendation? As an elected member of the PSC, what factors would you include in your analysis of the project? How would each of these factors bear on your decision?

REFERENCES

Beedles, W., "Evaluating Negative Benefits," *Journal of Financial and Quantitative Analysis,* March 1978, 173–176.

Bogue, M. C., and R. R. Roll, "Capital Budgeting of Risky Projects with 'Imperfect' Markets for Physical Capital," *Journal of Finance,* May 1974, 601–613.

Booth, L., "Correct Procedures for the Evaluation of Risky Cash Outflows," *Journal of Financial and Quantitative Analysis,* June 1982, 287–300.

Breeden, D., "An Intertemporal Asset Pricing Model with Stochastic Investment Opportunities," *Journal of Financial Economics,* September 1979, 265–296.

Brennan, M., "An Approach to the Valuation of Uncertain Income Streams," *Journal of Finance,* June 1973, 661–674.

Celec, S., and R. Pettway, "Some Observations on Risk-Adjusted Discount Rates: A Comment," *Journal of Finance,* September 1979, 1061–1063.

Constantinides, G., "Admissible Uncertainty in the Intertemporal Asset Pricing Model," *Journal of Financial Economics,* March 1980, 71–86.

Dyl, E. A., and H. W. Long, "Abandonment Value and Capital Budgeting: Comment," *Journal of Finance,* March 1969, 88–95.

Fama, E. F., "Multiperiod Consumption-Investment Decisions," *American Economic Review,* March 1970, 163–174.

_____, "Risk-Adjusted Discount Rates and Capital Budgeting Under Uncertainty," *Journal of Financial Economics,* August 1977, 3–24.

_____, and J. D. MacBeth, "Tests of the Multiperiod Two-Parameter Model," *Journal of Financial Economics,* May 1974, 43–66.

Gehr, A., "Risk-Adjusted Capital Budgeting Using Arbitrage," *Financial Management,* Winter 1981, 14–19.

Joy, O. M., "Abandonment Values and Abandonment Decisions: A Clarification," *Journal of Finance,* September 1976, 1225–1228.

Lewellen, W., "Some Observations on Risk-Adjusted Discount Rates," *Journal of Finance,* September 1977, 1331–1337.

_____, "Reply to Pettway and Celec," *Journal of Finance,* September 1979, 1065–1066.

Long, J. B., Jr., "Stock Prices, Inflation and the Term Structure of Interest Rates," *Journal of Financial Economics,* July 1974, 131–170.

Merton, R. C., "An Intertemporal Capital Asset Pricing Model," *Econometrica,* September 1973, 867–887.

Miles, J., and D. Choi, "Comment: Evaluating Negative Benefits," *Journal of Financial and Quantitative Analysis,* December 1979, 1095–1099.

Myers, S. C., "Procedures for Capital Budgeting Under Uncertainty," *Industrial Management Review,* Spring 1968, 1–20.

_____, and S. M. Turnbull, "Capital Budgeting and the Capital Asset Pricing Model: Good News and Bad News," *Journal of Finance,* May 1977, 321–332.

Robichek, A., and S. Myers, "Conceptual Problems in the Use of Risk-Adjusted Discount Rates," *Journal of Finance,* December 1966, 727–730.

Robichek, A., and J. C. Van Horne, "Abandonment Value and Capital Budgeting," *Journal of Finance,* December 1967, 577–590.

Ross, S., "A Simple Approach to the Valuation of Risky Streams," *Journal of Business,* July 1979, 254–286.

Stapleton, R., and M. Subrahmanyam, "A Multiperiod Equilibrium Asset Pricing Model," *Econometrica,* September 1978, 1077–1096.

_____, "Multiperiod Equilibrium: Some Implications for Capital Budgeting," *TIMS Studies in the Management Sciences,* Vol. 11, 1979, 233–248.

Capital Structure and the Cost of Capital: Theory

The average cost of capital to any firm is completely independent of its capital structure and is equal to the capitalization rate of a pure equity stream of its class.

F. MODIGLIANI AND M. MILLER, "THE COST OF CAPITAL, CORPORATION FINANCE, AND THE THEORY OF INVESTMENT," *THE AMERICAN ECONOMIC REVIEW*, JUNE 1958, P. 268.

Funds for investment are provided to the firm by investors who hold various types of claims on the firm's cash flows. Debt holders have contracts (bonds) which promise to pay them fixed schedules of interest in the future in exchange for their cash now. Equity holders provide retained earnings (internal equity provided by *existing* shareholders) or purchase new shares (external equity provided by *new* shareholders). They do so in return for claims on the residual earnings of the firm in the future. Also, shareholders retain control of the investment decision while bondholders have no direct control except for various types of indenture provisions in the bond which may constrain the decision-making of shareholders. In addition to these two basic categories of claimants, there are others such as holders of convertible debentures, leases, preferred stock, nonvoting stock, and warrants.

Each investor category is confronted with a different type of risk and therefore each requires a different expected rate of return in order to provide funds to the firm. The required rate of return is the opportunity cost to the investor of investing scarce resources elsewhere in projects of equivalent risk. As we shall see, the fact that shareholders are the ones who decide whether to accept or reject new projects is critical to understanding the cost of capital. They will accept only those projects which increase their expected utility of wealth. Each project must earn, on a risk-adjusted basis, enough net cash flow to pay investors (bondholders and shareholders) their expected rates of return, to repay the principal amount which they originally provided, and to have something left over which will increase the wealth of existing shareholders. The cost of capital is the minimum risk-adjusted rate of return which a project must earn in order to be acceptable to shareholders.

The investment decision cannot be made without knowledge of the cost of capital. Consequently many textbooks introduce the concept of the cost of capital before they discuss investment decisions. It probably does not matter which topic comes first. Both topics are important and they are interrelated. Figure 12.1 shows the investment decision as the intersection of the demand and supply of investment capital. All projects are assumed to have equivalent risk. Also, fund sources have equal risk (in other words in Fig. 12.1 we make no distinction between equity and debt). Chapters 2, 3, and 11 discussed the ranking of projects assuming that the appropriate cost of capital was known. The schedule of projects with their rates of return is sometimes called the marginal efficiency of investment schedule and is shown as the demand curve in Fig. 12.1. The supply of capital, represented as the marginal cost of capital curve, is assumed to be infinitely elastic. Implicitly, the projects are

Figure 12.1
Demand and supply of investment for projects of equal risk.

assumed to have equal risk. Therefore, the firm faces an infinite supply of capital at the rate $E(R_j)$ because it is assumed that the projects it offers are only a small portion of all investment in the economy. They affect neither the total risk of the economy nor the total supply of capital. The optimal amount of investment for the firm is I_j^*, and the marginally acceptable project must earn at least $E(R_j)$. All acceptable projects, of course, earn more than the marginal cost of capital.

Figure 12.1 is an oversimplified explanation of the relationship between the cost of capital and the amount of investment. However, it demonstrates the interrelatedness of the two concepts. For a given schedule of investments, a rise in the cost of capital will result in less investment. This chapter shows how the firm's mix of debt and equity financing affects the cost of capital, explains how the cost of capital is related to shareholders' wealth, and shows how to extend the cost-of-capital concept to the situation where projects do not all have the same risk. If the cost of capital can be minimized via some judicious mixture of debt and equity financing, then the financing decision can maximize the value of the firm. Whether or not an optimal capital structure exists is one of the most important issues in corporate finance. This chapter discusses the relevant theory. Chapter 13 discusses the empirical evidence regarding capital structure and provides some realistic applications.

A. THE COST OF CAPITAL WITH PROJECTS OF EQUAL RISK AND RISKLESS DEBT

1. The Value of the Levered Firm

Modigliani and Miller [1958, 1963] wrote the seminal paper on cost of capital, corporate valuation, and capital structure. They assumed that:

- Capital markets are frictionless.
- Individuals can borrow and lend at the risk-free rate.
- There are no costs to bankruptcy.
- Firms issue only two types of claims: risk-free debt and (risky) equity.
- All firms are assumed to be in the same risk class.
- Corporate taxes are the only form of government levy (i.e., there are no wealth taxes on corporations and no personal taxes).
- All cash flow streams are perpetuities (i.e., no growth).

It goes without saying that many of these assumptions are unrealistic, but later we can show that relaxing many of them does not really change the major conclusions of the model of firm behavior which Modigliani and Miller provide. Relaxing the assumption that corporate debt is risk free will not change the results (see Section D). However, the assumptions of no bankruptcy costs (discussed in Chapter 13) and no personal taxes (discussed in Section B of this chapter) are critical because they change the implications of the model.

One of the assumptions requires greater clarification. What is meant when we say that all firms have the same risk class? The implication is that the expected risky future net operating cash flows vary by, at most, a scale factor. Mathematically this is

$$\tilde{CF}_i = \lambda \tilde{CF}_j,$$

where

$\tilde{CF}$ = the risky net cash flow from operations (cash flow before interest and taxes),

λ = a constant scale factor.

This implies that the expected future cash flows from the two firms (or projects) are perfectly correlated.

If, instead of focusing on the level of cash flow, we focus on the returns, the perfect correlation becomes obvious because the returns are identical, as shown below:

$$\tilde{R}_{i,t} = \frac{\tilde{CF}_{i,t} - CF_{i,t-1}}{CF_{i,t-1}},$$

and because $\tilde{CF}_{i,t} = \lambda \tilde{CF}_{j,t}$, we have

$$\tilde{R}_{i,t} = \frac{\lambda \tilde{CF}_{j,t} - \lambda CF_{j,t-1}}{\lambda CF_{j,t-1}} = \tilde{R}_{j,t}.$$

Therefore, if two streams of cash flow differ by, at most, a scale factor, they will have the same distributions of returns, the same risk, and will require the same expected return.

Suppose the assets of a firm return the same distribution of net operating cash flows each time period for an infinite number of time periods. This is a no-growth situation because the average cash flow does not change over time. We can value this after-tax stream of cash flows by discounting its expected value at the appropriate risk-adjusted rate. The value of an unlevered firm, i.e., a firm with no debt, will be

$$V^U = \frac{E(\tilde{FCF})}{\rho} \tag{12.1}$$

where

V^U = the present value of an unlevered firm (i.e., all equity),

$E(\tilde{FCF})$ = the perpetual free cash flow after taxes (to be explained in detail below),

τ_c = the corporate income tax rate,

ρ = the discount rate for an all equity firm.

This is the value of an unlevered firm because it represents the discounted value of a perpetual, nongrowing stream of free cash flows after taxes which would accrue to shareholders if the firm had no debt. To clarify this point, let us look at the following *pro forma* income statement:

R	Revenues
$-VC$	Variable costs of operations
$-FCC$	Fixed cash costs (e.g., administrative costs and real estate taxes)
$-$dep	Noncash charges (e.g., depreciation and deferred taxes)
NOI	Net operating income
$-rD$	Interest on debt (interest rate, r, times principal, D)
EBT	Earnings before taxes
$-T$	Taxes $= \tau_c(\text{EBT})$, where τ_c is the corporate tax rate
NI	Net income

It is extremely important to distinguish between cash flows and the accounting definition of profit. After-tax cash flows from operations may be calculated as follows. Net operating income less taxes is

$$\tilde{\text{NOI}} - \tau_c(\tilde{\text{NOI}}).$$

Rewriting this using the fact that $\tilde{\text{NOI}} = \tilde{R} - \tilde{\text{VC}} - \text{FCC} - \text{dep}$, we have

$$(\tilde{R} - \tilde{\text{VC}} - \text{FCC} - \text{dep})(1 - \tau_c).$$

This is operating income after taxes, but it is not yet a cash flow definition because a portion of total fixed costs are noncash expenses such as depreciation and deferred taxes. Total fixed costs are partitioned in two parts: FCC is the cash-fixed costs and dep is the noncash-fixed costs.

In order to convert after-tax operating income into cash flows, we must add back depreciation and other noncash expenses. Doing this, we have

$$(\tilde{R} - \tilde{\text{VC}} - \text{FCC} - \text{dep})(1 - \tau_c) + \text{dep},$$

Finally, by assumption, we know that the firm has no growth, i.e., all cash flows are perpetuities. This implies that depreciation each year must be replaced by investment in order to keep the same amount of capital in place. Therefore, dep $= I$, and the after-tax free cash flow available for payment to creditors and shareholders is:

$$\tilde{\text{FCF}} = (\tilde{R} - \tilde{\text{VC}} - \text{FCC} - \text{dep})(1 - \tau_c) + \text{dep} - I,$$

$$\tilde{\text{FCF}} = (\tilde{R} - \tilde{\text{VC}} - \text{FCC} - \text{dep})(1 - \tau_c) \quad \text{since dep} = I.$$

The interesting result is that when all cash flows are assumed to be perpetuities, free cash flow ($\tilde{\text{FCF}}$) is the same thing as net operating income after taxes, i.e., the cash flow which the firm would have available if it had no debt at all. This is shown below.

$$\tilde{\text{NOI}}(1 - \tau_c) = \tilde{\text{FCF}} = (\tilde{R} - \tilde{\text{VC}} - \text{FCC} - \text{dep})(1 - \tau_c)$$

Note also that this approach to cash flows is exactly the same as that used to define cash flows for capital budgeting purposes in Chapter 2. The reader should keep in mind that in order to determine the value of the firm correctly, the definition of cash flows and the definition of the discount rate, i.e., the weighted average cost of capital, must be consistent. The material which follows will prove that they are.

Given perpetual cash flows, Eq. (12.1) can be written in either of two equivalent ways:

$$V^U = \frac{E(\tilde{FCF})}{\rho} \quad \text{or} \quad V^U = \frac{E(\tilde{NOI})(1 - \tau_c)}{\rho}.$$ (12.1)

From this point forward we shall use the net operating income definition of cash flows in order to be consistent with the language originally employed by Modigliani and Miller.

Next let us assume that the firm issues debt. The after-tax cash flows must be split up between debt holders and shareholders. Shareholders receive $\tilde{NI} + \text{dep} - I)$, net cash flows after interest, taxes, and replacement investment; and bondholders receive interest on debt, rD. Mathematically, this is equivalent to total cash flow available for payment to the private sector.[1]

$$\tilde{NI} + \text{dep} - I + rD = (\tilde{R} - \tilde{VC} - \text{FCC} - \text{dep} - rD)(1 - \tau_c) + \text{dep} - I + rD.$$

Given that dep $= I$, we can rearrange terms to obtain

$$\tilde{NI} + rD = (\tilde{R} - \tilde{VC} - \text{FCC} - \text{dep})(1 - \tau_c) - rD + rD\tau_c + rD$$
$$= \tilde{NOI}(1 - \tau_c) + rD\tau_c.$$ (12.2)

The first part of this stream, $\tilde{NOI}(1 - \tau_c)$, is exactly the same as the cash flows for the unlevered firm (the numerator of (12.1)), with exactly the same risk. Therefore, recalling that it is a perpetual stream, we can discount it at the rate appropriate for an unlevered firm, ρ. The second part of the stream, $rD\tau_c$, is assumed to be risk free. Therefore, we shall discount it at the before-tax cost of risk-free debt, k_d. Consequently, the value of the levered firm is the sum of the discounted value of the two types of cash flow which it provides:

$$V^L = \frac{E(\tilde{NOI})(1 - \tau_c)}{\rho} + \frac{rD\tau_c}{k_d}.$$ (12.3)

Note that rD is the perpetual stream of risk-free payments to bondholders and that k_d is the current before-tax market-required rate of return for the risk-free stream. Therefore, since the stream is perpetual, the market value of the bonds, B, is

$$B = rD/k_d.$$ (12.4)

Now we can rewrite Eq. (12.3) as

$$V^L = V^U + \tau_c B.$$ (12.5)

The value of the levered firm, V^L, is equal to the value of an unlevered firm, V^U, plus the present value of the tax shield provided by debt, $\tau_c B$. Later on we shall refer to the "extra" value created by the interest tax shield on debt as the *gain from leverage*. This is perhaps the single most important result in the theory of corporation finance obtained in the last 25 years. It says that in the absence of any

---

[1] The government receives all cash flows not included in Eq. (12.2), i.e., the government receives taxes (also a risky cash flow).

Table 12.1 Proposition I Arbitrage Example

	Company A	Company B
NOI	10,000	10,000
$-rD$	0	1,500
NI	10,000	8,500
k_e	10%	11%
S	100,000	77,272
B	0	30,000
$V = B + S$	100,000	107,272
WACC	10%	9.3%
B/S	0%	38.8%

market imperfections including corporate taxes, (i.e., if $\tau_c = 0$), the value of the firm is completely independent of the type of financing used for its projects. Without taxes, we have

$$V^L = V^U, \quad \text{if} \quad \tau_c = 0. \tag{12.5a}$$

Equation (12.5a) is known as *Modigliani-Miller Proposition* I. "The market value of any firm is independent of its capital structure and is given by capitalizing its expected return at the rate ρ appropriate to its risk class."[2] In other words, the method of financing is irrelevant. Modigliani and Miller went on to support their position by using one of the very first arbitrage pricing arguments in finance theory. Consider the income statements of the two firms given in Table 12.1. Both companies have exactly the same perpetual cash flows, NOI, but Company A has no debt while Company B has $30,000 of debt paying 5% interest. The example reflects greater risk in holding the levered equity of Company B because the cost of equity, $k_e = $ NI/S, for B is greater than that of Company A. The example has been constructed so that Company B has a greater market value than A and hence a lower weighted average cost of capital, WACC = NOI/V. The difference in values is a violation of Proposition I. However, the difference will not persist, because if we, for example, already own stock in B, we can earn a profit with no extra risk by borrowing (at 5%) and buying Company A. In effect, we create homemade leverage in the following way:

1. We sell our stock in B (say we own 1%, then we sell $772.72).

2. We borrow an amount equivalent to 1% of the debt in B, i.e., $300 at 5% interest.

3 We buy 1% of the shares in A.

Before arbitrage we held 1% of the equity of B and earned 11% on it, i.e., .11($772.72) = $85.00. After arbitrage we hold the following position:

---

[2] Modigliani, F. and M. Miller [1958], p. 268.

1% of A's equity and earn 10%, i.e., .10($1000.00) = $100.00
pay interest on $300 of debt, i.e., .05($300)   = −15.00
                                                         85.00

This gives us the same income as our levered position in Company B, but the amount of money we have available is $772.72 (from selling shares in B) plus $300 (from borrowing). So far, in the above calculation, we have used only $1000.00 to buy shares of A. Therefore, we can invest another $72.72 in shares of A and earn 10%. This brings our total income up to $85 + $7.27 = $92.27, and we own $772.72 of *net* worth of equity in A (the bank "owns" $300). Therefore, our return on equity is 11.94% (i.e., $92.27/$772.72). Furthermore, our personal leverage is the $300 in debt divided by the equity in A, $772.72. This is exactly the same leverage and therefore the same risk as we started with when we had an equity investment in B.

The upshot of the foregoing arbitrage argument is that we can use homemade leverage to invest in A. We earn a higher rate of return on equity without changing our risk at all. Consequently we will undertake the arbitrage operation by selling shares in B, borrowing, and buying shares in A. We will continue to do so until the market values of the two firms are identical. Therefore, Modigliani-Miller Proposition I is a simple arbitrage argument. In a world without taxes the market values of the levered and unlevered firms must be identical.

However, as shown by Eq. (12.5), when the government "subsidizes" interest payments to providers of debt capital by allowing the corporation to deduct interest payments on debt as an expense, the market value of the corporation can increase as it takes on more and more (risk-free) debt. Ideally (given the assumptions of the model) the firm should take on 100% debt.[3]

2. The Weighted Average Cost of Capital

Next, we can determine the cost of capital by using the fact that shareholders will require the rate of return on new projects to be greater than the opportunity cost of the funds supplied by them and bondholders. This condition is equivalent to requiring that original shareholders' wealth increase. From Eq. (12.3) we see that the change in the value of the levered firm, ΔV^L, with respect to a new investment, ΔI, is[4]

$$\frac{\Delta V^L}{\Delta I} = \frac{(1 - \tau_c)}{\rho} \frac{\Delta E(\tilde{NOI})}{\Delta I} + \tau_c \frac{\Delta B}{\Delta I}. \qquad (12.6)$$

If we take the new project, the change in the value of the firm, ΔV^L, will also be equal to the change in the value of original shareholder's wealth, ΔS^o, plus the

---

[3] We shall see later in this chapter that this result is modified when we consider a world with both corporate and personal taxes, or one where bankruptcy costs are nontrivial. Also, the Internal Revenue Service will disallow the tax deductability of interest charges on debt if, in its judgment, the firm is using excessive debt financing as a tax shield.

[4] Note that τ_c and ρ do not change with ΔI. The cost of equity for an all-equity firm doesn't change because new projects are assumed to have the same risk as the old ones.

new equity required for the project, ΔS^n, plus the change in the value of bonds outstanding, ΔB^o, plus new bonds issued, ΔB^n:

$$\Delta V^L = \Delta S^o + \Delta S^n + \Delta B^o + \Delta B^n. \tag{12.7a}$$

Alternatively, the changes with respect to the new investment are

$$\frac{\Delta V^L}{\Delta I} = \frac{\Delta S^o}{\Delta I} + \frac{\Delta S^n}{\Delta I} + \frac{\Delta B^o}{\Delta I} + \frac{\Delta B^n}{\Delta I}. \tag{12.7b}$$

Because the old bondholders hold a contract which promises fixed payments of interest and principal, because the new project is assumed to be no riskier than those already outstanding, and especially because both old and new debt are assumed to be risk free, the change in the value of outstanding debt is zero ($\Delta B^o = 0$). Furthermore, the new project must be financed with either new debt, new equity, or both. This implies that[5]

$$\Delta I = \Delta S^n + \Delta B^n. \tag{12.8}$$

Using this fact (12.7b) can be rewritten as

$$\frac{\Delta V^L}{\Delta I} = \frac{\Delta S^o}{\Delta I} + \frac{\Delta S^n + \Delta B^n}{\Delta I} = \frac{\Delta S^o}{\Delta I} + 1. \tag{12.9}$$

In order for a project to be acceptable to original shareholders, it must increase their wealth. Therefore, they will require that

$$\frac{\Delta S^o}{\Delta I} = \frac{\Delta V^L}{\Delta I} - 1 > 0, \tag{12.10}$$

which is equivalent to the requirement that $\Delta V^L/\Delta I > 1$.

When this condition is imposed on Eq. (12.6) we are able to determine the cost of capital[6]

$$\frac{\Delta V^L}{\Delta I} = \frac{(1 - \tau_c)}{\rho} \frac{\Delta E(\tilde{NOI})}{\Delta I} + \tau_c \frac{\Delta B^n}{\Delta I} > 1,$$

or, by rearranging terms, we have

$$\frac{(1 - \tau_c)\Delta E(\tilde{NOI})}{\Delta I} > \rho \left(1 - \tau_c \frac{\Delta B}{\Delta I}\right). \tag{12.11}$$

The left-hand side of (12.11) is the after-tax change in net operating cash flows brought about by the new investment, in other words, the after-tax return on the project.[7]

---

[5] Note that (12.8) does not require new issues of debt or equity to be positive. It is conceivable, for example, that the firm might issue $4000 in stock for a $1000 project and repurchase $3000 in debt.

[6] Note that $\Delta B = \Delta B^n$ because ΔB^o is assumed to be zero.

[7] Chapter 2, the investment decision, stressed the point that the correct cash flows for capital budgeting purposes were always defined as net cash flows from operations after taxes. Equation (12.11) reiterates this point and shows that it is the *only* definition of cash flows which is consistent with the opportunity cost of capital for the firm. The numerator on the left-hand side, namely $E(\tilde{NOI})(1 - \tau_c)$, is the after-tax cash flows from operations which the firm would have if it had no debt.

The right-hand side is the opportunity cost of capital applicable to the project. As long as the anticipated rate of return on investment is greater than the cost of capital, current shareholders' wealth will increase.

Note that if the corporate tax rate is zero, the cost of capital is independent of capital structure (the ratio of debt to total assets). This result is consistent with Eq. (12.5a), which says that the value of the firm is independent of capital structure. On the other hand, if corporate taxes are paid, the cost of capital declines steadily as the proportion of new investment financed with debt increases. The value of the levered firm reaches a maximum when there is 100% debt financing (so long as all of the debt is risk free).

3. Two Definitions of Market Value Weights

Equation (12.11) defines what has often been called the weighted average cost of capital, WACC, for the firm:

$$\text{WACC} = \rho \left(1 - \tau_c \frac{\Delta B}{\Delta I} \right). \qquad (12.12)$$

An often debated question is the correct interpretation of $\Delta B/\Delta I$. Modigliani and Miller [1963, p. 441] interpret it by saying that

If B^*/V^* denotes the firm's long run "target" debt ratio ... then the firm can assume, to a first approximation at least, that for any particular investment $dB/dI = B^*/V^*$.

Two questions arise in the interpretation of the leverage ratio, $\Delta B/\Delta I$. First, is the leverage ratio marginal or average? Modigliani and Miller, in the above quote, set the marginal ratio equal to the average by assuming the firm sets a long-run target ratio, which is constant. Even if this is the case, we still must consider a second issue, namely: Is the ratio to be measured as *book value leverage, replacement value leverage*, or *reproduction value leverage?* The last two definitions, as we shall see, are both market values. At least one of these three measures, book value leverage, can be ruled out immediately as being meaningless. In particular, there is no relationship whatsoever between book value concepts, (e.g., retained earnings) and the economic value of equity.

The remaining two interpretations, replacement and reproduction value, make sense because they are both market value definitions. By replacement value, we mean the economic cost of putting a project in place. For capital projects, a large part of this cost is usually the cost of purchasing plant, equipment, and working capital. In the Modigliani-Miller formulation, replacement cost is the market value of the investment in the project under consideration, ΔI. It is the denominator on both sides of the cost-of-capital inequality (12.11). On the other hand, reproduction value, ΔV, is the total present value of the stream of goods and services expected from the project. The two concepts can be compared by noting that the difference between them is the NPV of the project, that is,

$$\text{NPV} = \Delta V - \Delta I.$$

For a marginal project, where NPV = 0, replacement cost and reproduction value are equal.

Haley and Schall [1973, pp. 306–311] introduce an alternative cost of capital definition where the "target" leverage is the ratio of debt to reproduction value, as shown below:

$$\text{WACC} = \rho \left(1 - \tau_c \frac{\Delta B}{\Delta V} \right). \tag{12.13}$$

If the firm uses a reproduction value concept for its "target" leverage, it will seek to maintain a constant ratio of the market value of debt to the market value of the firm.

With the foregoing as background, we can now reconcile the apparent conflict in the measurement of leverage applicable to the determination of the relevant cost of capital for a new investment project. Modigliani and Miller define the target L^* as the average, in the long run, of the debt-to-value ratio or B^*/V^*. Then regardless of how a particular investment is financed, the relevant leverage ratio is dB/dV. For example, a particular investment may be financed entirely by debt. But the cost of that particular increment of debt is not the relevant cost of capital for that investment. The debt would require an equity base. How much equity? This is answered by the long run target B^*/V^*. So procedurally, we start with the actual amount of investment increment for the particular investment, dI. The L^* ratio then defines the amount of dB assigned to the investment. If the NPV from the investment is positive, then dV will be greater than dI. Hence, the debt capacity of the firm will have been increased by more than dB. However, the relevant leverage for estimating the WACC will still be dB/dV, which will be equal to B^*/V^*. We emphasize that the latter is a policy target decision by the firm, based on relevant financial economic considerations. The dV is an amount assigned to the analysis to be consistent with L^*.

The issue is whether to use dB/dV or dB/dI as the weight in the cost of capital formula. The following example highlights the difference between the two approaches. Suppose a firm can undertake a new project which costs $1000 and has expected cash flows with a present value of $9000 when discounted at the cost of equity for an all-equity project of equivalent risk. If the ratio of the firm's target debt to value is 50% and if its tax rate is 40%, how much debt should it undertake? If it uses replacement value leverage, then $dB/dI = .5$ and $dB = \$500$, i.e., half of the $1000 investment is financed with debt. Using equation (12.5), the value of the levered firm is

$$dV^L = dV^U + \tau_c dB$$

$$= 9000 + .4(500)$$

$$= 9200$$

The same formula can be used to compute the amount of debt if we use reproduction value leverage, i.e., $dB/dV^L = .5$, or $dV^L = 2dB$:

$$dV^L = 9000 + .4dB,$$

$$2dB = 9000 + .4dB \qquad \text{since} \quad dV^L = 2dB,$$

$$dB = 5625.$$

If our target is set by using reproduction values, then we should issue \$5625 of new debt for the \$1000 project, and repurchase \$4625 of equity. The change in the value of the firm will be

$$dV^L = dV^U + \tau_c dB$$

$$= 9000 + .4(5625)$$

$$= 11,250.$$

Clearly, the value of the firm is higher if we use the reproduction value definition of leverage. But as a practical matter, what bank would lend \$5625 on a project which has a \$1000 replacement value of assets? If the bank and the firm have homogeneous expectations this is possible. If they do not, then it is likely that the firm is more optimistic than the bank about the project. In case of heterogeneous expectations there is no clear solution to the problem. Hence we favor the original argument of Modigliani and Miller that the long-run target-debt-to-value ratio will be close to dB/dI, i.e., use the replacement value definition.

4. The Cost of Equity

If Eqs. (12.12) and (12.13) are the weighted average cost of capital, how do we determine the cost of the two components, debt and equity? The cost of debt is the risk-free rate, at least given the assumptions of this model. (We shall discuss risky debt in Section D.) The cost of equity capital is the change in the return to equity holders with respect to the change in their investment, $\Delta S^o + \Delta S^n$. The return to equity holders is the net cash flow after interest and taxes, NI. Therefore, their rate of return is $\Delta \text{NI}/(\Delta S^o + \Delta S^n)$. In order to solve for this, we begin with identity (12.2),

$$\text{NI} + rD = \text{NOI}(1 - \tau_c) + rD\tau_c.$$

Next we divide by ΔI, the new investment, and obtain

$$\frac{\Delta \text{NI}}{\Delta I} + \frac{\Delta(rD)}{\Delta I} - \frac{\tau_c \Delta(rD)}{\Delta I} = (1 - \tau_c)\frac{\Delta \text{NOI}}{\Delta I}. \qquad (12.14)$$

Substituting the left-hand side of (12.14) into (12.6), we get

$$\frac{\Delta V^L}{\Delta I} = \frac{\Delta \text{NI}/\Delta I + (1 - \tau_c)\Delta(rD)/\Delta I}{\rho} + \tau_c \frac{\Delta B}{\Delta I}. \qquad (12.15)$$

From (12.7), we know that

$$\frac{\Delta V^L}{\Delta I} = \frac{\Delta S^o + \Delta S^n}{\Delta I} + \frac{\Delta B^n}{\Delta I}, \qquad \text{since} \quad \Delta B^o \equiv 0. \qquad (12.16)$$

Consequently, by equating (12.15) and (12.16) we get

$$\frac{\Delta V^L}{\Delta I} = \frac{\Delta S^o + \Delta S^n}{\Delta I} + \frac{\Delta B}{\Delta I} = \frac{\Delta NI/\Delta I + (1 - \tau_c)\Delta(rD)/\Delta I}{\rho} + \tau_c \frac{\Delta B}{\Delta I}.$$

Then, multiplying both sides by ΔI, we have

$$\Delta S^o + \Delta S^n + \Delta B = \frac{\Delta NI + (1 - \tau_c)\Delta(rD) + \rho\tau_c\Delta B}{\rho}.$$

Subtracting ΔB from both sides gives

$$\Delta S^o + \Delta S^n = \frac{\Delta NI + (1 - \tau_c)\Delta(rD) + \rho\tau_c\Delta B - \rho\Delta B}{\rho},$$

$$\rho(\Delta S^o + \Delta S^n) = \Delta NI - (1 - \tau_c)(\rho - k_d)\Delta B, \qquad \text{since} \quad \Delta(rD) = k_d\Delta B.$$

And finally,

$$\frac{\Delta NI}{\Delta S^o + \Delta S^n} = \rho + (1 - \tau_c)(\rho - k_d)\frac{\Delta B}{\Delta S^o + \Delta S^n}. \tag{12.17}$$

The change in new equity plus old equity equals the change in the total equity of the firm ($\Delta S = \Delta S^o + \Delta S^n$). Therefore, the cost of equity, $k_e = \Delta NI/\Delta S$, is written

$$k_e = \rho + (1 - \tau_c)(\rho - k_d)\frac{\Delta B}{\Delta S}. \tag{12.18}$$

The implication of Eq. (12.18) is that the opportunity cost of capital to shareholders increases linearly with changes in the market value ratio of debt to equity. If the firm has no debt in its capital structure, the cost of equity capital, k_e, is equal to the cost of equity for an all equity firm, ρ.

5. A Graphical Presentation for the Cost of Capital

Figure 12.2 graphs the cost of capital and its components as a function of the ratio of debt to equity. The weighted average cost of capital is invariant to changes in capital structure in a world without corporate taxes; however, with taxes it declines as more and more debt is used in the firm's capital structure. In both cases, the cost of equity capital increases with higher proportions of debt. This makes sense because increasing financial leverage implies a riskier position for shareholders as their residual claim on the firm becomes more variable. They require a higher rate of return to compensate them for the extra risk they take.

The careful reader will have noticed that in Fig. 12.2, B/S is on the horizontal axis while Eqs. (12.13) and (12.18) are written in terms of $\Delta B/\Delta S$ or $\Delta B/\Delta V$, which are changes in debt with respect to changes in equity or value of the firm. The two are equal only when the firm's average debt-to-equity ratio is the same as its marginal

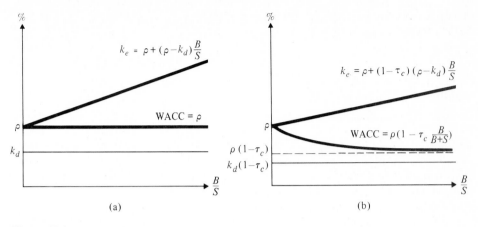

Figure 12.2
The cost of capital as a function of the ratio of debt to equity; (a) Assuming $\tau_c = 0$; (b) assuming $\tau_c > 0$.

debt-to-equity ratio. This will be true as long as the firm establishes a "target" debt-to-equity ratio equal to B/S and then finances all projects with the identical proportion of debt and equity so that $B/S = \Delta B/\Delta S$.

The usual definition of the weighted average cost of capital is to weight the after-tax cost of debt by the percentage of debt in the firm's capital structure and add the result to the cost of equity multiplied by the percentage of equity. The equation is

$$\text{WACC} = (1 - \tau_c)k_d \frac{B}{B+S} + k_e \frac{S}{B+S}. \tag{12.19}$$

We can see that this is the same as (12.13) by substituting (12.18) into (12.19) and assuming that $B/S = \Delta B/\Delta S$. This is done below:

$$\text{WACC} = (1 - \tau_c)k_d \frac{B}{B+S} + \left[\rho + (1 - \tau_c)(\rho - k_d)\frac{B}{S}\right]\frac{S}{B+S}$$

$$= (1 - \tau_c)k_d \frac{B}{B+S} + \rho\frac{S}{B+S} + (1 - \tau_c)\rho\frac{B}{S}\frac{S}{B+S} - (1 - \tau_c)k_d \frac{B}{S}\frac{S}{B+S}$$

$$= (1 - \tau_c)k_d \frac{B}{B+S} + \rho\left(\frac{S}{B+S} + \frac{B}{B+S}\right) - \rho\tau_c \frac{B}{B+S} - (1 - \tau_c)k_d \frac{B}{B+S}$$

$$= \rho\left(1 - \tau_c \frac{B}{B+S}\right) \qquad \text{QED.}$$

There is no inconsistency between the two definitions of the cost of capital (Eqs. (12.13) and (12.19)). They are identical.

B. THE VALUE OF THE FIRM IN A WORLD
WITH PERSONAL AND CORPORATE TAXES

In the original model, the *gain from leverage, G,* is the difference between the value of the levered and unlevered firms, which is the product of the corporate tax rate and the market value of debt:

$$G = V^L - V^U = \tau_c B. \tag{12.20}$$

Miller [1977] modifies this result by introducing personal as well as corporate taxes into the model. In addition to making the model more realistic, the revised approach adds considerable insight into the effect of leverage on value in the real world. We do not, after all, observe firms with 100% debt in their capital structure as the original Modigliani-Miller model suggests.

Assume for the moment that there are only two types of personal tax rates: the rate on income received from holding shares, τ_{ps}, and the rate on income from bonds, τ_{pB}. The expected after-tax stream of cash flows to shareholders of an all-equity firm would be $(NOI)(1 - \tau_c)(1 - \tau_{ps})$. By discounting this perpetual stream at the cost of equity for an all-equity firm we have the value of the unlevered firm:

$$V^U = \frac{E(NOI)(1 - \tau_c)(1 - \tau_{ps})}{\rho}. \tag{12.21}$$

Alternatively, if the firm has both bonds and shares outstanding, the earnings stream is partitioned into two parts. Cash flows to shareholders after corporate and personal taxes are:

$$\text{payments to shareholders} = (NOI - rD)(1 - \tau_c)(1 - \tau_{ps}),$$

and payments to bondholders, after personal taxes, are

$$\text{payments to bondholders} = rD(1 - \tau_{pB}).$$

Adding these together and rearranging terms, we have:

$$\begin{aligned}\text{total cash payments} \\ \text{to suppliers of capital} = NOI(1 - \tau_c)(1 - \tau_{ps}) - rD(1 - \tau_c)(1 - \tau_{ps}) \\ + rD(1 - \tau_{pB}). \end{aligned} \tag{12.22}$$

The first term on the right-hand side of (12.22) is the same as the stream of cash flows to owners of the unlevered firm, and its expected value can be discounted at the cost of equity for an all-equity firm. The second and third terms are risk free and can be discounted at the risk-free rate, k_d. The sum of the discounted streams of cash flow is the value of the levered firm:

$$\begin{aligned} V^L &= \frac{E(NOI)(1 - \tau_c)(1 - \tau_{ps})}{\rho} + \frac{rD[(1 - \tau_{pB}) - (1 - \tau_c)(1 - \tau_{ps})]}{k_d} \\ &= V^U + \left[1 - \frac{(1 - \tau_c)(1 - \tau_{ps})}{(1 - \tau_{pB})} \right] B, \end{aligned} \tag{12.23}$$

where $B = rD(1 - \tau_{pB})/k_d$, the market value of debt. Consequently, with the introduction of personal taxes, the gain from leverage is the second term in (12.23):

$$G = \left[1 - \frac{(1 - \tau_c)(1 - \tau_{ps})}{(1 - \tau_{pB})} \right] B. \qquad (12.24)$$

Note that when personal tax rates are set equal to zero, the gain from leverage in (12.24) equals the gain from leverage in (12.20), the earlier result. This finding also obtains when the personal tax rate on share income equals the rate on bond income. In the United States it is reasonable to assume that the effective tax rate on common stock is lower than that on bonds.[8] The implication is that the gain from leverage when personal taxes are considered (Eq. 12.24) is lower than $\tau_c B$ (Eq. 12.20).

If the personal income tax on stocks is less than the tax on income from bonds, then the before-tax return on bonds has to be high enough, other things being equal, to offset this disadvantage. Otherwise no investor would want to hold bonds. While it is true that owners of a levered corporation are subsidized by the interest deductibility of debt, this advantage is counterbalanced by the fact that the required interest payments have already been "grossed up" by any differential bondholders must pay on their interest income. In this way, the advantage of debt financing may be lost. In fact, whenever the following condition is met in Eq. (12.24),

$$(1 - \tau_{pB}) = (1 - \tau_c)(1 - \tau_{ps}), \qquad (12.25)$$

the advantage of debt vanishes completely.

Suppose that the personal tax rate on income from common stock is zero. We may justify this by arguing that (1) no one has to realize a capital gain until after death, (2) gains and losses in well-diversified portfolios can offset each other, thereby eliminating the payment of capital gains taxes, (3) the first several hundred dollars of dividend income received by individuals is not taxed, (4) 85% of dividends received by taxable corporations can be excluded from taxable income, or (5) many types of investment funds pay no taxes at all (nonprofit organizations, pension funds, trust funds, etc.).[9] Figure 12.3 portrays the supply and demand for corporate bonds. The rate paid on the debt of tax-free institutions (municipal bonds, for example) is r_0. If all bonds paid only r_0, no one would hold them with the exception of tax-free institutions which are not affected by the tax disadvantage of holding debt when $\tau_{pB} > \tau_{ps}$. An individual with a marginal tax rate on income from bonds equal to τ_{pB}^i will not hold corporate bonds until they pay $r_0/(1 - \tau_{pB}^i)$, that is, until their return is "grossed up." Since the personal income tax is progressive, the interest rate which is demanded has to keep rising to attract investors in higher and higher tax brackets.[10] The supply of corporate bonds is perfectly elastic, and bonds must

---

[8] The tax rate on stock is thought of as being lower than that on bonds because of the $100 dividend exclusion, and because of a relatively higher capital gains component of return.

[9] Also, as will be shown in Chapter 15, it is possible to shield up to $10,000 in dividend income from taxes.

[10] Keep in mind the fact that the tax rate on income from stock is assumed to be zero. Therefore, the higher an individual's tax bracket becomes, the higher the before-tax rate on bonds must be in order for the after-tax rate on bonds to equal the rate of return on stock (after adjusting for risk).

Figure 12.3
Aggregate supply and demand for corporate bonds (before tax rates).

pay a rate of $r_0/(1 - \tau_c)$ in equilibrium. To see that this is true, let us recall that the personal tax rate on stock is assumed to be zero ($\tau_{ps} = 0$) and rewrite the gain from leverage:

$$G = \left(1 - \frac{(1 - \tau_c)}{(1 - \tau_{pB})}\right) B. \qquad (12.26)$$

If the rate of return on bonds supplied by corporations is $r_s = r_0/(1 - \tau_c)$, then the gain from leverage, in Eq. (12.26), will be zero. The supply rate of return equals the demand rate of return in equilibrium:

$$r_s = \frac{r_0}{1 - \tau_c} = r_D = \frac{r_0}{1 - \tau_{pB}} .$$

Consequently,

$$(1 - \tau_c) = (1 - \tau_{pB}),$$

and the gain from leverage in (12.26) will equal zero. If the supply rate of return is less than $r_0/(1 - \tau_c)$, then the gain from leverage will be positive, and all corporations will try to have a capital structure containing 100% debt. On the other hand, if the supply rate of return is greater than $r_0/(1 - \tau_c)$, the gain from leverage will be negative and no debt will be issued. Thus we see that in equilibrium, taxable debt must be supplied to the point where the before-tax cost of corporate debt must equal the rate which would be paid by tax-free institutions "grossed up" by the corporate tax rate.

The implications of Miller's argument are that: (1) in equilibrium, under a set of fairly realistic assumptions, there is no optimal leverage from the point of view of the firm, and (2) there may be an equilibrium amount of aggregate debt outstanding in the economy which is determined by relative corporate and personal tax rates.

DeAngelo and Masulis [1980] extend Miller's work by analyzing the effect of tax shields other than interest payments on debt, for example noncash charges such as depreciation, oil depletion allowances, and investment tax credits. They are able to demonstrate the existence of an optimal (nonzero) corporate use of debt while still maintaining the assumption of zero bankruptcy (and zero agency) costs.

It is reasonable to expect depreciation expenses and investment tax credits to serve as tax shield substitutes for interest expenses. The DeAngelo and Masulis model predicts that firms will select a level of debt which is negatively related to the level of available tax shield substitutes such as depreciation, depletion, and investment tax credits. Also, as more and more debt is utilized, the probability of winding up with zero or negative earnings will increase, thereby causing the interest tax shield to decline in expected value. They further show that if there are positive bankruptcy costs, there will be an optimum tradeoff between the marginal expected benefit of interest tax shields and the marginal expected cost of bankruptcy. This issue will be further discussed in the next chapter.

In Chapter 13, we shall discuss several empirical studies which provide some evidence about the gain from leverage.

C. THE COST OF CAPITAL WHEN PROJECTS HAVE DIFFERENT RISKS

The CAPM discussed in Chapter 7 provides a natural theory for the pricing of risk. When combined with the cost of capital definitions derived by Modigliani and Miller [1958, 1963], it provides a unified approach to the cost of capital. The work which we shall describe was first published by Hamada [1969] and synthesized by Rubinstein [1973].

The CAPM may be written as

$$E(R_j) = R_f + [E(R_m) - R_f]\beta_j, \tag{12.27}$$

where

$E(R_j) =$ the expected rate of return on asset j,

$R_f =$ the (constant) risk-free rate,

$E(R_m) =$ the expected rate of return on the market portfolio,

$\beta_j =$ COV $(R_j, R_m)/$VAR(R_m).

Figure 12.4 illustrates the difference between the Modigliani-Miller cost of capital and the CAPM. Modigliani and Miller assumed that all projects within the firm had the same business or operating risk (mathematically, they assumed that $CF_i = \lambda CF_j$). This was expedient because in 1958, when the paper was written, there was no accepted theory which allowed adjustments for differences of this type. Consequently, the Modigliani-Miller theory is represented by the horizontal line in Fig. 12.4. The WACC for the firm (implicitly) does not change as a function of systematic risk, β. The systematic risk of a firm is a weighted average of the systematic risk of its projects.[11] As long as a new project has exactly the same systematic risk as the entire firm, the appropriate required rate of return is the WACC for the firm as a whole. However, only rarely will new projects have exactly the same risk as

---

[11] For proof, see Chapter 7.

the firm. Consider project A in Fig. 12.4. Its estimated rate of return $\hat{R}_A$, is less than the firm's weighted average cost of capital $[\text{WACC(firm)} = E(R_{\text{firm}})]$. Does this mean that the project should be rejected? The answer is no. The project may earn a rate of return which is less than for investment in the firm as a whole, but it is also less risky than the firm. It has lower systematic risk (that is, $\beta_A < \beta_{\text{firm}}$). Therefore, it is inappropriate to use the weighted average cost of capital for the firm when we evaluate a project whose risk differs from that of the firm as a whole. Instead, we should use the CAPM. It provides an estimate of the required rate of return for any project. In the case of project A the required rate of return, $E(R_A)$, given the estimated systematic risk of the project, β_A, is less than the anticipated rate of return, $\hat{R}_A$. If the anticipated rate is higher than the rate required by investors in the securities market, the project should be accepted. (Should project B be accepted or rejected?) Thus, we see that it is important to combine the CAPM with the Modigliani-Miller concept of the cost of capital in order to correctly evaluate new projects.

By using the fact that the correlation between two random variables is the covariance between them divided by the product of their standard deviations (see Chapter 6), we have

$$r_{jm} = \frac{\text{COV}(R_j, R_m)}{\sigma(R_j)\sigma(R_m)},$$ (12.28)

where

r_{jm} = the correlation between asset j and the market portfolio,

$\text{COV}(R_j, R_m)$ = the covariance between asset j and the market portfolio,

$\sigma(\cdot)$ = the standard deviation.

Therefore, the CAPM may be rewritten as

$$E(R_j) = R_f + [E(R_m) - R_f]\frac{r_{jm}\,\sigma(R_j)\sigma(R_m)}{\sigma^2(R_m)}$$

$$= R_f + \lambda^* r_{jm}\,\sigma(R_j),$$ (12.29)

where $\lambda^* \equiv [E(R_m) - R_f]/\sigma(R_m)$.

Figure 12.4
CAPM, the cost of capital, and capital budgeting.

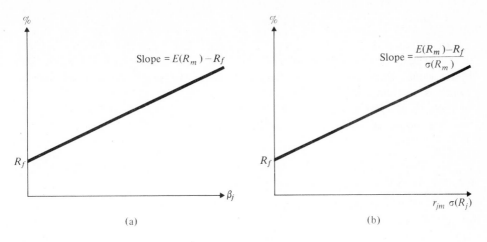

Figure 12.5
Two equivalent versions of the CAPM; (a) Eq. (12.27) and (b) Eq. (12.29).

Figure 12.5 shows both definitions of the security market line. Recall that if capital markets are efficient and if the CAPM is valid, then in equilibrium every risky asset must be priced so that it falls exactly on the securities market line. Consequently, if we know an asset's risk, we also know exactly what its required rate of return must be. This notion can be used directly to estimate the cost of capital for a firm with a given business risk and financial leverage.

The systematic risk of equity for a levered firm is the beta coefficient, β_e^L, which is estimated from the covariance between returns on the firm's common stock and the market index divided by the variance of the market. Therefore, the cost of equity capital for a levered firm is

$$k_e = R_f + [E(R_m) - R_f]\beta_e^L, \tag{12.30}$$

where β_e^L = the systematic risk of the equity of a levered firm.

If we still maintain the assumption that the corporation issues risk-free debt (that is, $k_d = R_f$), the after-tax weighted average cost of capital is[12]

$$\text{WACC} = (1 - \tau_c)k_d \frac{B}{B + S} + k_e \frac{S}{B + S}. \tag{12.31}$$

This result is useful in estimating the cost of capital for a firm as it actually is, but it doesn't shed any light on the relationship between the CAPM and the Modigliani-Miller cost of capital definitions. Nor is it useful as a means of telling us how to evaluate the cost of capital if the firm decides to change its capital structure. Answers to these questions require a more detailed look at the cost of capital.

---

[12] We also return to the assumption that there are corporate taxes but not personal taxes.

1. The Value of the Levered Firm

In order to see that the value of the levered firm is greater than the value of the unlevered firm (Eq. 12.5) when the CAPM is combined with the Modigliani-Miller valuation model, we note that the value of the shares of an unlevered firm (which is also the value of the firm) is

$$V^U = \frac{E(\tilde{N}OI)(1 - \tau_c)}{\rho} \tag{12.32}$$

and the value of the shares of a levered firm, S^L, is their expected stream of after-tax cash flows discounted at the cost of equity, k_e:

$$S^L = \frac{(E(\tilde{N}OI) - rD)(1 - \tau_c)}{k_e}$$

$$= \frac{(E(\tilde{N}OI) - R_f B)(1 - \tau_c)}{k_e}, \qquad \text{because} \quad rD = R_f B, \tag{12.33}$$

where

k_e = the cost of equity capital for a levered firm,

ρ = the cost of equity capital for an unlevered firm,

D = book value of debt,

B = market value of debt.

From the CAPM we know that all assets are priced so that they lie on the security market line. Therefore they all have the same slope, λ^*, in common. From (12.29) we can solve for λ^*:

$$\lambda^* = \frac{E(R_j) - R_f}{r_{jm}\,\sigma(R_j)}. \tag{12.34}$$

The levered and unlevered firms must both have the same λ^*; therefore

$$\frac{k_e - R_f}{r_{L,M}\,\sigma_L} = \frac{\rho - R_f}{r_{U,M}\,\sigma_U} = \lambda^*, \tag{12.35}$$

where

$r_{L,M}$ = correlation between the levered firm and the market,

$r_{U,M}$ = correlation between the unlevered firm and the market,

σ_L = standard deviation of the return on equity of the levered firm,

σ_U = standard deviation of the return on equity of the unlevered firm,

k_e = the expected rate of return on the equity of the levered firm, its cost of equity capital,

ρ = the expected rate of return on the unlevered firm (which is the cost of equity for an all-equity firm).

From the properties of random variables (see Chapter 6) we can solve for the standard deviation of k_e and ρ. However, first we note that

$$\rho = \frac{(E(\widetilde{NOI})(1 - \tau_c)}{V^U} \qquad \text{(from Eq. 12.32)}, \qquad (12.36)$$

and that

$$E(\widetilde{NOI}) = \frac{V^U \rho}{1 - \tau_c} \, .$$

The standard deviation of the 100% equity rate of return, ρ, is denoted as σ_U; therefore

$$\sigma(\widetilde{NOI}) = \frac{V^U}{1 - \tau_c} \sigma_U \qquad \text{(from property 4, Chapter 6).} \qquad (12.36a)$$

Also, from Eq. (12.33) we have the return on levered equity

$$k_e = \frac{(E(\widetilde{NOI}) - rD)(1 - \tau_c)}{S^L} \, . \qquad (12.37)$$

The standard deviation of the return on levered equity is designated as σ_L:

$$\sigma_L = \frac{1 - \tau_c}{S^L} \sigma(\widetilde{NOI}) \qquad \text{(from property 4, Chapter 6)} \qquad (12.37a)$$

$$= \frac{1 - \tau_c}{S^L} \frac{V^U}{1 - \tau_c} \sigma_U \qquad \text{(from Eq. (12.36a))} \qquad (12.28)$$

$$\sigma_L = \frac{V^U}{V^L - B} \sigma_U \qquad \text{because } V^L = S^L + B. \qquad (12.39)$$

Substituting (12.36), (12.37), and (12.38) into Eq. (12.35), we have

$$\frac{[(E(\widetilde{NOI}) - rD)(1 - \tau_c)/S^L] - R_f}{r_{L,M}(V^U/S^L)\sigma_U} = \frac{[E(\widetilde{NOI})(1 - \tau_c)/V^U] - R_f}{r_{U,M}\sigma_U} \, .$$

We note that $S^L = V^L - B$, that $rD = R_f B$, and that $r_{L,M} = r_{U,M}$;[13] therefore we

---

[13] Proof that $r_{LM} = r_{UM}$ follows from the definition of correlation and the definitions of k_e and ρ:

$$r_{L,M} = \frac{\text{COV}(k_e, R_M)}{\sigma_L \sigma_M} = r_{U,M} = \frac{\text{COV}(\rho, R_M)}{\sigma_U \sigma_M} \, , \qquad (a)$$

$$\text{COV}(k_e, R_M) = E\left\{ \left[\frac{(\widetilde{NOI} - R_f B)(1 - \tau_c)}{S^L} - E\left[\frac{(\widetilde{NOI} - R_f B)(1 - \tau_c)}{S^L} \right] \right] [\widetilde{R}_M - E(\widetilde{R}_M)] \right\}$$

$$= \frac{(1 - \tau_c)}{S^L} \text{COV}(\widetilde{NOI}, \widetilde{R}_M),$$

$$\text{COV}(\rho, R_M) = E\left\{ \left[\frac{\widetilde{NOI}(1 - \tau_c)}{V^U} - E\left[\frac{\widetilde{NOI}(1 - \tau_c)}{V^U} \right] \right] [\widetilde{R}_M - E(\widetilde{R}_M)] \right\}$$

$$= \frac{(1 - \tau_c)}{V^U} \text{COV}(\widetilde{NOI}, \widetilde{R}_M).$$

Therefore, substituting back into (a), and using Eqs. (12.36a) and (12.37a), we get

$$\frac{[(1 - \tau_c)/S^L] \text{COV}(\widetilde{NOI}, \widetilde{R}_M)}{[(1 - \tau_c)/S^L]\sigma(\widetilde{NOI})\sigma_M} = \frac{[(1 - \tau_c)/V^U] \text{COV}(\widetilde{NOI}, \widetilde{R}_M)}{[(1 - \tau_c)/V^U]\sigma(\widetilde{NOI})\sigma_M} \, , \qquad \text{QED.}$$

obtain

$$\frac{(E(\tilde{\text{NOI}}) - R_f B)(1 - \tau_c) - R_f(V^L - B)}{V^U} = \frac{E(\tilde{\text{NOI}})(1 - \tau_c) - R_f V^U}{V^U},$$

$$E(\tilde{\text{NOI}})(1 - \tau_c) - R_f B + R_f B \tau_c - R_f V^L + R_f B = E(\tilde{\text{NOI}})(1 - \tau_c) - R_f V^U,$$

$$V^L = V^U + \tau_c B. \tag{12.40}$$

This result is exactly the same as Eq. (12.5). The value of the levered firm is equal to the value of the unlevered firm plus the gain from leverage. Therefore, we see that the Modigliani-Miller results hold equally well in a world where assets are allowed to have different risk classes. If the marginal tax rate, τ_c, is zero, the value of the levered firm equals the value of the unlevered firm.

2. The Cost of Equity

Next we derive an expression for the cost of equity capital which combines the Modigliani-Miller result, Eq. (12.18), with the CAPM, Eq. (12.27). Substituting (12.40) into (12.39), we have

$$\sigma_L = \frac{V^L - \tau_c B}{V^L - B}\sigma_U = \frac{S^L + B - \tau_c B}{S^L}\sigma_U$$

$$= \left[1 + \frac{B}{S^L}(1 - \tau_c)\right]\sigma_U. \tag{12.41}$$

Substituting (12.41) into the market line equation (Eq. 12.29), we get

$$E(R_j) = R_f + \frac{E(R_M) - R_f}{\sigma_M}r_{L,M}\left[1 + \frac{B}{S^L}(1 - \tau_c)\right]\sigma_U,$$

$$k_e = E(R_j) = R_f + \frac{E(R_M) - R_f}{\sigma_M}r_{L,M}\sigma_U + \frac{E(R_m) - R_f}{\sigma_M}r_{L,M}\sigma_U(1 - \tau_c)\frac{B}{S^L}. \tag{12.42}$$

This is exactly the same as the Modigliani-Miller cost of equity capital, Eq. (12.18). To see the relationship, we observe that the required rate of return on an unlevered firm is given by the security market line as

$$\rho = E(R_j) = R_f + \frac{E(R_M) - R_f}{\sigma_M}r_{U,M}\sigma_U. \tag{12.43}$$

But we already know that $r_{L,M} = r_{U,M}$; thus the first two terms in (12.42) are the cost of equity capital for an unlevered firm. Consequently (12.42) can be rewritten as

$$k_e = \rho + (\rho - k_d)(1 - \tau_c)(B/S),$$

which is exactly the same as Eq. (12.18). Therefore, what we have done in Eq. (12.42) amounts to adding an adjustment for business risk to the original Modigliani-Miller cost of equity capital which assumed that all projects had equal business risk. Furthermore, the adjustment for risk follows naturally from the CAPM.

3. The Weighted Average Cost of Capital

Finally, in order to complete the task of combining the Modigliani-Miller results with the CAPM, we can derive an expression for the weighted average cost of capital. To do so, we begin with the traditional definition, Eq. (12.19):

$$\text{WACC} = (1 - \tau_c)R_f \frac{B}{B + S} + k_e \frac{S}{B + S} .$$

We then substitute the definition of k_e from Eq. (12.42):

$$\text{WACC} = R_f \frac{B}{B + S} - R_f \tau_c \frac{B}{B + S}$$

$$+ \left[R_f + \frac{E(R_M) - R_f}{\sigma_M} r_{U,M} \sigma_U + \frac{E(R_M) - R_f}{\sigma_M} r_{U,M} \sigma_U (1 - \tau_c) \frac{B}{S} \right] \frac{S}{B + S} ,$$

and obtain

$$\text{WACC} = R_f + \frac{E(R_M) - R_f}{\sigma_M} r_{U,M} \sigma_U - \tau_c \left[R_f + \frac{E(R_M) - R_f}{\sigma_M} r_{U,M} \sigma_U \right] \frac{B}{B + S} .$$

$$(12.44)$$

Once again, if we observe that the cost of equity capital for an all-equity firm is given by Eq. (12.43), then

$$\text{WACC} = \rho - \rho \tau_c \frac{B}{B + S} = \rho \left(1 - \tau_c \frac{B}{B + S} \right) .$$

Not surprisingly, this is exactly the same as the Modigliani-Miller definition of the weighted average cost of capital, i.e., Eq. (12.12). Once again we have demonstrated the consistency between the Modigliani-Miller results and the CAPM.

Before turning to a sample problem which will help to pull together the theory, it will be useful to compare the systematic risk of a levered firm with an unlevered firm. Equation (12.42) gives the cost of equity capital for a levered firm:

$$k_e = R_f + \frac{E(R_M) - R_f}{\sigma_M} r_{U,M} \sigma_U + \frac{E(R_M) - R_f}{\sigma_M} r_{U,M} \sigma_U (1 - \tau_c) \frac{B}{S} .$$

The definition of systematic risk for an unlevered firm is

$$\beta_U = \frac{\text{COV}(\rho, R_M)}{\sigma_M^2} .$$

If we recall that $r_{U,M} = \text{COV}(\rho, R_M)/\sigma_U \sigma_M$, then we can rewrite (12.42) as

$$k_e = R_f + [E(R_M) - R_f]\beta_U + [E(R_M) - R_f]\beta_U (1 - \tau_c) \frac{B}{S}$$

$$= R_f + [E(R_M) - R_f]\beta_U \left[1 + (1 - \tau_c) \frac{B}{S} \right] .$$

But we know from the CAPM that the cost of equity capital for a levered firm can be observed directly if we can estimate β_L, the systematic risk of the levered firm. This was defined as β_e^L in Eq. (12.30):

$$k_e = R_f + [E(R_M) - R_f]\beta_L.$$

Comparing the two equations above makes it clear that the relationship between the betas of the levered and unlevered firms is

$$\beta_L = \beta_U \left[1 + (1 - \tau_c)\frac{B}{S} \right]. \tag{12.45}$$

4. A Simple Example

The usefulness of the theoretical results can be demonstrated by considering the following problem. The United Southern Construction Company currently has a market value capital structure of 20% debt to total assets. The company's treasurer believes that more debt can be taken on, up to a limit of 35% debt, without losing the firm's ability to borrow at 7%, the prime rate (also assumed to be the risk-free rate). The firm has a marginal tax rate of 50%. The expected return on the market next year is estimated to be 17% and the systematic risk of the company's equity, β_L, is estimated to be .5.

- What is the company's current weighted average cost of capital, and its current cost of equity?
- What will the new weighted average cost of capital be if the "target" capital structure is changed to 35% debt?
- Should a project with a 9.25% expected rate of return be accepted if its systematic risk, β_L, is the same as that of the firm?

In order to calculate the company's current cost of equity capital we can use the CAPM:

$$k_e = R_f + [E(R_M) - R_f]\beta_L$$

$$= .07 + [.17 - .07].5 = .12.$$

Therefore, the weighted average cost of capital is

$$\text{WACC} = (1 - \tau_c)R_f \frac{B}{B + S} + k_e \frac{S}{B + S}$$

$$= (1 - .5).07(.2) + .12(.8) = 10.3\%.$$

The weighted average cost of capital with the new capital structure is shown in Fig. 12.6.[14] Note that the cost of equity increases with increasing leverage. This simply reflects the fact that shareholders face more risk with higher financial leverage

---

[14] Note that if debt to total assets is 20%, then debt to equity is 25%. Also, 35% converts to 53.85% in Fig. 12.6.

$$k_e = \rho + (1 - \tau_c)(\rho - k_d)\frac{B}{S}$$

$$\text{WACC} = \rho\left(1 - \tau_c \frac{B}{B+S}\right)$$

Figure 12.6
Changes in the cost of capital as leverage increases.

and that they require a higher return to compensate them for it. Therefore, in order to calculate the new weighted average cost of capital we have to use the Modigliani-Miller definition to estimate the cost of equity for an all equity firm:

$$\text{WACC} = \rho\left(1 - \tau_c \frac{B}{B+S}\right),$$

$$\rho = \frac{\text{WACC}}{1 - \tau_c[B/(B+S)]} = \frac{.103}{1 - .5(.2)} = 11.44\%.$$

As long as the firm does not change its business risk, its unlevered cost of equity capital, ρ, will not change. Therefore, we can use ρ to estimate the weighted average cost of capital with the new capital structure:

$$\text{WACC} = .1144(1 - .5(.35)) = 9.438\%.$$

Therefore, the new project with its 9.25% rate of return will not be acceptable even if the firm increases its ratio of debt to total assets from 20% to 35%.

A common error made in this type of problem is to forget that the cost of equity capital will increase with higher leverage. Had we estimated the weighted average cost of capital, using 12% for the old cost of equity and 35% debt as the target capital structure, we would have obtained 9.03% as the estimated weighted average cost of capital and we would have accepted the project.

A more difficult problem is to decide what to do if the project's risk is different from that of the firm. Suppose the new project would increase the replacement market value of the assets of the firm by 50% and that the systematic risk of the operating cash flows it provides is estimated to be 1.2. What rate of return must it earn in order to be profitable if the firm has (a) 20% or (b) 35% debt in its capital structure?

Figure 12.7 shows that the CAPM may be used to find the required rate of return given the beta of the project without leverage, $\beta_{U,p}$, which has been estimated to be 1.2. This is the beta for the *unlevered* project, because the beta is defined as the systematic risk of the operating cash flows. By definition this is the covariance between the cash flows *before* leverage and taxes and the market index. The required

Figure 12.7
Using the CAPM to estimate the required rate of return on a project.

rate of return on the project, if it is an all-equity project, will be computed as shown below:

$$E(R_j) = R_f + [E(R_M) - R_f]\beta_{U,P}$$
$$= .07 + [.17 - .07]1.2 = 19\%.$$

Next, we must "add in" the effect of the firm's leverage. If we recognize that 19% is the required rate if the project were all equity, we can find the required rate with 20% leverage by using the Modigliani-Miller weighted average cost of capital, Eq. (12.12):

$$\text{WACC} = \rho\left(1 - \tau_c \frac{B}{B+S}\right)$$
$$= .19[1 - .5(.2)] = 17.1\%.$$

And if the leverage is increased to 35%, the required return falls to 15.675%:

$$\text{WACC} = .19(1 - .5(.35)) = 15.675\%.$$

The examples above serve to illustrate the usefulness of the risk-adjusted cost of capital for capital-budgeting purposes. Each project must be evaluated at a cost of capital which reflects the systematic risk of its operating cash flows as well as the financial leverage of the firm as a whole. Estimates of the correct opportunity cost of capital are derived from a thorough understanding of the Modigliani-Miller cost of capital and the CAPM.

5. The Separability of Investment and Financing Decisions

The preceding example shows that the required rate of return on a new project is dependent on the firm's weighted average cost of capital, which in turn may or may not be a function of the capital structure of the firm. What implications does this have for the relationship between investment and financing decisions; that is, how independent is one of the other? The simplest possibility is that, after adjusting for project specific risk, we can use the same capital structure—the capital structure of the entire firm—to estimate the cost of capital for all projects. However, this may not be the case. In order to clarify the issue we shall investigate two different suppositions.

1. If the weighted average cost of capital is invariant to changes in the firm's capital structure (i.e., if WACC $= \rho$ in Eq. 12.12 because $\tau_c = 0$), then the investment and financing decisions are completely separable. This might actually be the case if Miller's [1977] paper is empirically valid. The implication is that we can use Eq. (12.44) and set $\tau_c = 0$ when estimating the appropriate cutoff rate for capital-budgeting decisions. In other words, it is unnecessary to consider the financial leverage of the firm. Under the above assumptions, it is irrelevant.

2. If there really is gain from leverage, as would be suggested by the Modigliani-Miller theory if $\tau_c > 0$, or if the DeAngelo-Masulis [1980] extension of Miller's [1977] paper is empirically valid, then the value of a project is not independent of the capital structure assumed for it. In the preceding simple example we saw that the required rate of return on the project was 19% if the firm had no debt, 17.1% if it had 20% debt, and 15.675% if it had 35% debt in its capital structure. Therefore the project has greater value as the financial leverage of the firm increases. As a practical matter, this problem is usually "handled" by assuming that the firm has decided on an "optimal" capital structure and that all projects are financed, at the margin, with the optimal ratio of debt to equity. The relevant factors which may be used to determine the optimal capital structure are discussed in the following chapter. However, assuming that an optimum does exist, and assuming that all projects are financed at the optimum, we may treat the investment decision *as if* it were separable from the financing decision. First the firm decides what optimal capital structure to use, then it applies the same capital structure to all projects. Under this set of assumptions the decision to accept or reject a particular project does not change the "optimal" capital structure. We could use Eq. (12.44) with $B/(B + S)$ set equal to the optimal capital structure in order to determine the appropriate cost of capital for a project. This is precisely what we did in the example.

But suppose projects carry with them the ability to change the optimal capital structure of the firm as a whole.[15] Suppose that some projects have more debt capacity than others. Then the investment and financing decisions cannot even be "handled" as if they were independent. There is very little in the accepted theory of finance which admits of this possibility, but it cannot be disregarded. One reason that projects may have separate debt capacities is the simple fact that they have different collateral values in bankruptcy. However, since the theory in this chapter has proceeded on the assumption that bankruptcy costs are zero, we shall refrain from further discussion of this point until the next chapter.

---

[15] This may be particularly relevant when a firm is considering a conglomerate merger with another firm in a completely different line of business with a completely different optimal capital structure.

D. THE COST OF CAPITAL WITH RISKY DEBT

So far it has been convenient to assume that corporate debt is risk free. Obviously it is not. Consideration of risky debt raises several interesting questions. First, if debt is risky, how are the basic Modigliani-Miller propositions affected? We know that riskier debt will require higher rates of return. Does this reduce the tax gain from leverage? The answer is given in section D.1 below. The second question is how to estimate the required rate of return on risky debt. This is covered in section D.2.

1. The Effect of Risky Debt in the Absence of Bankruptcy Costs

The fundamental theorem set forth by Modigliani and Miller is that, given complete and perfect capital markets, it doesn't make any difference how one splits up the stream of operating cash flows. The percentage of debt or equity doesn't change the total value of the cash stream provided by the productive investments of the firm. Therefore, so long as there are no costs of bankruptcy (paid to third parties like trustees and law firms), it shouldn't make any difference whether debt is risk free or risky. The value of the firm should be equal to the value of the discounted cash flows from investment. A partition which divides these cash flows into risky debt and risky equity has no impact on value. Stiglitz [1969] first proved this result, using a state-preference framework, and Rubinstein [1973] provided a proof, using a mean-variance approach.

Risky debt, just like any other security, must be priced in equilibrium so that it falls on the security market line. Therefore, if we designate the return on risky debt as $\tilde{R}_{dj}$, its expected return is

$$E(\tilde{R}_{dj}) = R_f + [E(\tilde{R}_M) - R_f]\beta_{dj} \tag{12.46}$$

where $\beta_{dj} = \text{COV}(\tilde{R}_{dj}, \tilde{R}_M)/\sigma_M^2$. The return on the equity of a levered firm, k_e, is similar to Eq. (12.33) except that risky debt replaces risk-free debt:

$$k_e = \frac{(\text{N}\tilde{\text{O}}\text{I} - \tilde{R}_{dj}B)(1 - \tau_c)}{S^L}. \tag{12.47}$$

Using the CAPM, we find that the expected return on equity will be[16]

$$E(k_e) = R_f + \lambda^*\text{COV}(k_e, R_M). \tag{12.48}$$

---

[16] In this instance, $\lambda^* \equiv (E(R_M) - R_f)/\sigma_M^2$.

The covariance between the expected rate of return on equity and the market index is

$$\text{COV}(k_e, R_M) = E \left\{ \left[\frac{(\text{NOI} - R_{dj}B)(1 - \tau_c)}{S^L} - E \left(\frac{(\text{NOI} - R_{dj}B)(1 - \tau_c)}{S^L} \right) \right] \right.$$

$$\left. \times [R_M - E(R_M)] \right\}$$

$$= \frac{1 - \tau_c}{S^L} \text{COV}(\text{NOI}, R_M) - \frac{(1 - \tau_c)B}{S^L} \text{COV}(R_{dj}, R_M). \qquad (12.49)$$

Substituting this result into (12.48) and the combined result into (12.47), we have the following relationship for a levered firm:

$$R_f S^L + \lambda^*(1 - \tau_c)\text{COV}(\text{NOI}, R_M) - \lambda^*(1 - \tau_c)B \, \text{COV}(R_{dj}, R_M)$$

$$= E(\text{NOI})(1 - \tau_c) - E(R_{dj})B(1 - \tau_c). \quad (12.50)$$

By following a similar line of logic for the unlevered firm (where $B = 0$, and $S^L = V^U$) we have

$$R_f V^U + \lambda^*(1 - \tau_c)\text{COV}(\text{NOI}, R_M) = E(\text{NOI})(1 - \tau_c). \qquad (12.51)$$

Substituting (12.51) for $E(\text{NOI})(1 - \tau_c)$ in the right-hand side of (12.50) and using the fact that $V^L = S^L + B$, we have

$$R_f S^L + \lambda^*(1 - \tau_c)\text{COV}(\text{NOI}, R_M) - \lambda^*(1 - \tau_c)B \, \text{COV}(R_{dj}, R_M)$$

$$= R_f V^U + \lambda^*(1 - \tau_c)\text{COV}(\text{NOI}, R_M) - E(R_{dj})B(1 - \tau_c),$$

$$R_f(V^L - B) - \lambda^*(1 - \tau_c)B \, \text{COV}(R_{dj}, R_M)$$

$$= R_f V^U - [R_f + \lambda^*\text{COV}(R_{dj}, R_M)]B(1 - \tau_c),$$

$$V^L = V^U + \tau_c B.$$

This is exactly the same Modigliani-Miller result that we obtained when the firm was assumed to issue only risk-free debt. Therefore the introduction of risky debt cannot, by itself, be used to explain the existence of an optimal capital structure. In Chapter 13 we shall see that direct bankruptcy costs such as losses to third parties (lawyers or the courts) or indirect bankruptcy costs (disruption of services to customers or disruption of the supply of skilled labor) are necessary in conjunction with risky debt and taxes in order to explain an optimal capital structure.

2. The Cost of Risky Debt

Even though risky debt without bankruptcy costs does not alter the basic Modigliani-Miller results, we are still interested in knowing how the cost of risky debt is affected by changes in capital structure. The simple algebraic approach which follows was proved by Hsia [1978, 1981] and it combines the option pricing model (OPM), the capital asset pricing model (CAPM), and the Modigliani-Miller theorems. They are all consistent with one another.

In order to present the issue in its simplest form, assume that (1) the firm issues pure discount bonds[17] which prohibit any capital distributions (such as dividend payments) until after the bonds mature T time periods hence, (2) there are no transactions costs or taxes, so that the value of the firm is unaffected by its capital structure (in other words, Modigliani-Miller Proposition I is assumed to be valid), (3) there is a known nonstochastic risk-free rate of interest, and (4) there are homogeneous expectations about the stochastic process which describes the value of the firm's assets. Given these assumptions we can imagine a simple firm which issues only one class of bonds secured by the assets of the firm. From the shareholders' point of view, cash is received from the sale of the bonds. The value of the shareholders' position is equal to the discounted value of the bonds and a call option. If, on the maturity date, the value of the firm, V, exceeds the face value of the bonds, D, the shareholders will exercise their call option by paying off the bonds and keeping the excess. On the other hand, if the value of the firm is less than the face value of the bonds, the shareholders will default on the debt by failing to exercise their option. Therefore, at maturity, the shareholders' wealth, S, is

$$S = \text{MAX}[0, V - D]. \tag{12.52}$$

This is, of course, a European call option, and we can use the Black-Scholes formula to value it. Bondholders' wealth at maturity is $B = \text{MIN}[V, D]$. In return for the cash which they lend to the firm, the bondholders receive what amounts to writing a call option on the value of the firm. If, at maturity, the value of the firm, V, exceeds the face value of debt, D, the bondholders receive D, which is the exercise price of the call option held by shareholders. If the value of the firm is less than the face value of debt, they get to keep the firm's assets.

The realization that the equity and debt in a firm can be conceptualized as options allows us to use the insights of Chapter 8 on option pricing theory. For example, if the equity, S, in a levered firm is analogous to a call option, then its value will increase with (1) an increase in the value of the firm's assets, V, (2) an increase in the variance of the value of the firm's assets, (3) an increase in the time to maturity of a given amount of debt with face value, D, and (4) an increase in the risk-free rate. The value of levered equity will decrease with a greater amount of debt, D, which is analogous to the exercise price on a call option.

Next, we wish to show the relationship between the CAPM measure of risk, i.e., β, and the option pricing model. First, however, it is useful to show how the CAPM and the OPM are related. Merton [1973] has derived a continuous time version of the CAPM which is given below:

$$E(R_i) = R_f + [E(R_M) - R_f]\beta_i, \tag{12.53}$$

---

[17] All accumulated interest on pure discount bonds is paid at maturity, hence $B(T)$, the current market value of debt with maturity T, must be less than its face value, D, assuming a positive risk-free rate of discount.

where

$E(R_i) = $ the instantaneous expected rate of return on asset i,

$\beta_i = $ the instantaneous systematic risk of the ith asset, $\beta_i = \text{COV}(R_i, R_M)/ \text{VAR}(R_M)$,

$E(R_M) = $ the expected instantaneous rate of return on the market portfolio,

$R_f = $ the nonstochastic instantaneous rate of return on the risk-free asset.

There appears to be no difference between the continuous-time version of the CAPM and the traditional one-period model derived in Chapter 7. However, it is important to prove that the CAPM also exists in continuous time because the Black-Scholes OPM requires continuous trading, and the assumptions underlying the two models must be consistent.

In order to relate the OPM to the CAPM it is easiest (believe it or not) to begin with the differential equation (A8.4), and to recognize that the call option is now the value of the common stock, S, which is written on the value of the levered firm, V. Therefore, (A8.4) may be rewritten as

$$dS = \frac{\delta S}{\delta V} dV + \frac{\delta S}{\delta t} dt + \frac{1}{2} \frac{\delta^2 S}{\delta V^2} \sigma^2 V^2 dt. \qquad (12.54)$$

This equation says that the change in the stock price is related to the change in the value of the firm, dV, movement of the stock price across time, dt, and the instantaneous variance of the firm's value, σ^2. Dividing by S, we have, in the limit as dt approaches zero,

$$\underset{dt \to 0}{\text{Lim}} \frac{dS}{S} = \frac{\delta S}{\delta V} \frac{dV}{S} = \frac{\delta S}{\delta V} \frac{dV}{V} \frac{V}{S}. \qquad (12.55)$$

We recognize dS/S as the rate of return on the common stock, r_S, and dV/V as the rate of return on the firm's assets, r_V, therefore

$$r_S = \frac{\delta S}{\delta V} \frac{V}{S} r_V. \qquad (12.56)$$

If the instantaneous systematic risk of common stock, β_S, and that of the firm, β_V, are defined as

$$\beta_S \equiv \frac{\text{COV}(r_S, r_M)}{\text{VAR}(r_M)}, \quad \beta_V \equiv \frac{\text{COV}(r_V, r_M)}{\text{VAR}(r_M)}, \qquad (12.57)$$

then we can use (12.56) and (12.57) to rewrite the instantaneous covariance as

$$\beta_S = \frac{\delta S}{\delta V} \frac{V}{S} \frac{\text{COV}(r_V, r_M)}{\text{VAR}(r_M)} = \frac{\delta S}{\delta V} \frac{V}{S} \beta_V. \qquad (12.58)$$

Now write the Black-Scholes OPM where the call option is the equity of the firm:

$$S = VN(d_1) - e^{-r_f T} D N(d_2), \qquad (12.59)$$

where

S = the market value of equity,

V = the market value of the firm's assets,

r_f = the risk-free rate,

T = the time to maturity,

D = the face value of debt (book value),

$N(\cdot)$ = the cumulative normal probability of the unit normal variate, d_i,

$$d_1 = \frac{\ln(V/D) + r_f T}{\sigma\sqrt{T}} + \frac{1}{2}\sigma\sqrt{T}, \quad d_2 = d_1 - \sigma\sqrt{T}.$$

Finally, the partial derivative of the equity value, S, with respect to the value of the underlying asset is

$$\frac{\delta S}{\delta V} = N(d_1), \quad \text{where} \quad 0 \le N(d_1) \le 1. \tag{12.60}$$

Substituting this into (12.58) we obtain

$$\beta_S = N(d_1)\frac{V}{S}\beta_V. \tag{12.61}$$

This tells us the relationship between the systematic risk of the equity, β_S, and the systematic risk of the firm's assets, β_V. The value of S is given by the OPM, Eq. (12.59); therefore we have

$$\beta_S = \frac{VN(d_1)}{VN(d_1) - De^{-r_f T}N(d_2)}\beta_V$$

$$= \frac{1}{1 - (D/V)e^{-r_f T}[N(d_2)/N(d_1)]}\beta_V. \tag{12.62}$$

We know that $D/V \le 1$, that $e^{-r_f T} < 1$, that $N(d_2) \le N(d_1)$, and hence that $\beta_S \ge \beta_V > 0$. This shows that the systematic risk of the equity of a levered firm is greater than the systematic risk of an unlevered firm, a result which is consistent with the results found elsewhere in the theory of finance. Note also that the beta of the levered firm increases monotonically with leverage.

The OPM provides insight into the effect of its parameters on the systematic risk of equity. We may assume that the risk characteristics of the firm's assets, β_V, are constant over time. Therefore, it can be shown that the partial derivatives of (12.62) have the following signs:

$$\frac{\delta\beta_S}{\delta V} < 0, \quad \frac{\delta\beta_S}{\delta D} > 0, \quad \frac{\delta\beta_S}{\delta r_f} < 0, \quad \frac{\delta\beta_S}{\delta\sigma^2} < 0, \quad \frac{\delta\beta_S}{\delta T} < 0. \tag{12.63}$$

Most of these have readily intuitive explanations. The systematic risk of equity falls as the market value of the firm increases, and it rises as the amount of debt issued increases. When the risk-free rate of return increases, the value of the equity option increases and its systematic risk decreases. The fourth partial derivative says that as the variance of the value of the firm's assets increases, the systematic risk of equity decreases. This result follows from the contingent claim nature of equity. The equity holders will prefer more variance to less because they profit from the probability that the value of the firm will exceed the face value of the debt. Therefore their risk actually decreases as the variance of the value of the firm's assets increases.[18] Finally, the fifth partial says that the systematic risk of equity declines as the maturity date of the debt becomes longer and longer. From the shareholders' point of view the best situation would be to never have to repay the face value of the debt.

It is also possible to use Eq. (12.61) to view the cost of equity capital in an OPM framework and to compare it with the Modigliani-Miller results. Substituting β_S from (12.61) into the CAPM, we obtain from Eq. (12.53) an expression for k_e, the cost of equity capital:

$$k_e = R_f + (R_M - R_f)N(d_1)\frac{V}{S}\beta_V. \tag{12.64}$$

Note that from Eq. (12.61), $\beta_S = N(d_1)(V/S)\beta_V$. Substituting this into (12.64) yields the familiar CAPM relationship $k_e = R_f + (R_M - R_f)\beta_S$. Furthermore, the CAPM can be rearranged to show that

$$\beta_V = \frac{R_V - R_f}{R_M - R_f},$$

which we substitute into (12.64) to obtain

$$k_e = R_f + N(d_1)(R_V - R_f)\frac{V}{S}. \tag{12.65}$$

Equation (12.65) shows that the cost of equity capital is an increasing function of financial leverage.

If we assume that debt is risky and assume that bankruptcy costs (i.e., losses to third parties other than creditors or shareholders) are zero, then the OPM, the CAPM, and the Modigliani-Miller propositions can be shown to be consistent. The simple algebraic approach given below was proved by Hsia [1978, 1981].

First, note that the systematic risk, β_B, of risky debt capital in a world without taxes can be written as[19]

$$\beta_B = \beta_V \frac{\delta B}{\delta V}\frac{V}{B}. \tag{12.66}$$

We know that in a world without taxes, the value of the firm is invariant to changes in its capital structure. Also, from Eq. (12.60), we know that if the common stock

---

[18] Note that since the value of the firm, V, and the debt equity ratio D/V are held constant, any change in total variance, σ^2, must be nonsystematic risk.

[19] See Galai and Masulis [1976, footnote 15].

of a firm is thought of as a call option on the value of the firm, then

$$\frac{\delta S}{\delta V} = N(d_1).$$

These two facts imply that

$$\frac{\delta B}{\delta V} = N(-d_1) = 1 - N(d_1). \tag{12.67}$$

In other words, any change in the value of equity is offset by an equal and opposite change in the value of risky debt.

Next, the required rate of return on risky debt, k_d, can be expressed by using the CAPM, Eq. (12.53):

$$k_d = R_f + (R_M - R_f)\beta_B. \tag{12.68}$$

Substituting Eqs. (12.66) and (12.67) into (12.68), we have

$$k_d = R_f + (R_M - R_f)\beta_V N(-d_1)\frac{V}{B} \cdot$$

From the CAPM, we know that

$$R_V - R_f = (R_M - R_f)\beta_V.$$

Therefore

$$k_d = R_f + (R_V - R_f)N(-d)\frac{V}{B} \cdot$$

And since $R_V \equiv \rho$,

$$k_d = R_f + (\rho - R_f)N(-d_1)\frac{V}{B} \cdot \tag{12.69}$$

Note that Eq. (12.69) expresses the cost of risky debt in terms of the OPM. The required rate of return on risky debt is equal to the risk-free rate, R_f, plus a risk premium, θ, where

$$\theta = (\rho - R_f)N(-d_1)\frac{V}{B} \cdot$$

In order to arrive at a weighted average cost of capital, we multiply Eq. (12.69), the cost of debt, by the percent of debt in the capital structure, B/V, then add this result to the cost of equity, Eq. (12.65) multiplied by S/V, the percent of equity in the capital structure. The result is

$$k_d\frac{B}{V} + k_e\frac{S}{V} = \left[R_f + (\rho - R_f)N(-d)\frac{V}{B} \right]\frac{B}{V} + \left[R_f + N(d_1)(\rho - R_f)\frac{V}{S} \right]\frac{S}{V}$$

$$= R_f\left(\frac{B+S}{V} \right) + (\rho - R_f)[N(-d_1) + N(d_1)]$$

$$= R_f + (\rho - R_f)(1 - N(d_1) + N(d_1))$$

$$= \rho. \tag{12.70}$$

Equation (12.70) is exactly the same as the Modigliani-Miller proposition that in a world without taxes, the weighted average cost of capital is invariant to changes in the capital structure of the firm. Also, simply by rearranging terms, we have

$$k_e = \rho + (\rho - k_d)\frac{B}{S}.$$ (12.71)

This is exactly the same as Eq. (12.18), the Modigliani-Miller definition of the cost of equity capital in a world without taxes. Therefore, if we assume that debt is risky, the OPM, the CAPM, and the Modigliani-Miller definition are all consistent with one another.

This result is shown graphically in Fig. 12.8(a). This figure is very similar to Fig. 12.2 which showed the cost of capital as a function of the debt to equity ratio, B/S, assuming riskless debt. The only differences between the two figures are that Fig. 12.8 has the debt to value ratio, $B/(B + S)$, on the horizontal axis and it assumes risky debt. Note that (in Fig. 12.8a) the cost of debt increases as more debt is used in the firm's capital structure. Also, if the firm were to become 100% debt (not a realistic alternative) then the cost of debt would equal the cost of capital for an all equity firm, ρ. Figure 12.8(b) depicts the weighted average cost of capital in a world with corporate taxes only. The usual Modigliani-Miller result is shown, namely that the weighted average cost of capital declines monotonically as more debt is employed in the capital structure of the firm. The fact that debt is risky does not change any of our previous results.

E. THE EFFECT OF OTHER FINANCIAL INSTRUMENTS ON THE COST OF CAPITAL

Other than straight debt and equity, firms issue a variety of other securities. The number of different possibilities is limited only by your imagination. However, the

Figure 12.8
The cost of capital given risky debt.

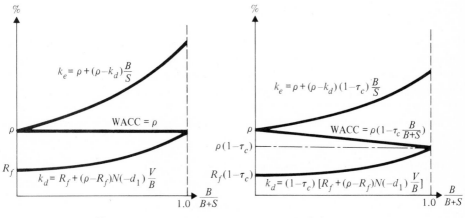

(a) No taxes   (b) Only corporate taxes

actual number of alternative financial instruments is fairly small and their use is limited. A possible explanation for why corporations tend to use only straight debt and equity has been offered by Fama and Jensen [1982]. They argue that it makes sense to separate the financial claims on the firm into only two parts: a relatively low risk component (i.e., debt capital), and a relatively high risk residual claim (i.e., equity capital). Specialized riskbearing by residual claimants is an optimal form of contracting which has survival value because (1) it reduces contracting costs (that is, the costs that would be incurred to monitor contract fulfillment)—and (2) it lowers the cost of riskbearing services. For example, shareholders and bondholders do not have to monitor each other. It is necessary only for bondholders to monitor shareholders. This form of one-way monitoring reduces the total cost of contracting over what it might otherwise be. Thus it makes sense that most firms keep their capital structure fairly simple by using only debt and equity. The theory of finance has no good explanation for why some firms use alternative financial instruments such as convertible debt, preferred stock, and warrants.

1. Warrants

A warrant is a security issued by the firm in return for cash. It promises to sell m shares (usually one share) of stock to an investor for a fixed exercise price at any time up to the maturity date. Therefore a warrant is very much like an American call option written by the firm. It is not exactly the same as a call because, when exercised, it increases the number of shares outstanding and thus dilutes the equity of the stockholders.

The problem of pricing warrants has been studied recently by Emanuel [1979], Schwartz [1977], Galai and Schneller [1978], and Constantinides [1981]. The simplest approach to the problem (Galai and Schneller [1978]) assumes a one-period model. The firm is assumed to be 100% equity financed, and its investment policy is not affected by its financing decisions. For example, the proceeds from issuing warrants are immediately distributed as dividends to the old shareholders. Also the firm pays no end-of-period dividends, and the warrants are assumed to be exercised as a block.[20] These somewhat restrictive assumptions facilitate the estimation of the warrant value and its equilibrium rate of return.

Galai and Schneller show, for the above-mentioned assumptions, that the returns on a warrant are perfectly correlated with those of a call option on the same firm *without* warrants. To obtain this result let V be the value of the firm's assets (without warrants) at the end of the time period, i.e., on the date when the warrants mature. Let n be the current number of shares outstanding and q be the ratio of warrants to shares outstanding.[21] Finally, let X be the exercise price of the warrant. If the

---

[20] Block exercise is, perhaps, the most restrictive assumption.

[21] The amount of potential dilution can be significant. For example, in July of 1977 there were around 118 warrants outstanding. Of them 41 had a dilution factor of less than 10%, 25 had a dilution factor between 10 and 19%, thirteen between 20 and 29%, and 21 a factor of over 50%.

firm had no warrants outstanding, the price per share at the end of the time period would be

$$S = \frac{V}{n}.$$

With warrants, the price per share, assuming that the warrants are exercised, will be

$$S = \frac{V + nqX}{n(1+q)} = \frac{S + qX}{(1+q)}.$$

Of course, nqX is the cash received and $n(1+q)$ is the total number of shares outstanding if the warrants are exercised. The warrants will be exercised if their value when converted is greater than the exercise price, i.e., if

$$S = \frac{S + qX}{1+q} > X.$$

This condition is exactly equivalent to $S > X$. In other words, the warrant will be exercised whenever the firm's end-of-period share price *without* warrants exceeds the warrant exercise price. Therefore, the warrant will be exercised in exactly the same states of nature as a call option with the same exercise price. Also, as shown in Table 12.2, the payoffs to the warrant are a constant fraction, $1/(1+q)$, of the payoffs to the call written on the assets of the firm (without warrants). Therefore, the returns on the warrant are perfectly correlated with the dollar returns on a call option written on the firm without warrants. In order to prevent arbitrage, the warrant price, W, will be a fraction of the call price, C, as shown below

$$W = \frac{1}{1+q} C. \tag{12.72}$$

Because the warrant and the call are perfectly correlated, they will have exactly the same systematic risk and therefore the same required rate of return.[22] This expected return is the before-tax cost of capital for issuing warrants and can easily be estimated for a company which is contemplating a new issue of warrants.

One problem with the above approach is that warrants are not constrained to be exercised simultaneously in one large block. Emanuel [1979] demonstrated that if all of the warrants were held by a single profit-maximizing monopolist, the warrants

---

[22] From Eq. (12.61) we know that the beta of an option is related to the beta of the underlying asset as follows:

$$\beta_c = N(d_1) \frac{S}{C} \beta_S.$$

From Eq. (12.72) we know that the warrant is perfectly correlated with a call option written on the shares of the company, *ex warrants,* therefore

$$\beta_w = \beta_c.$$

Consequently, it is not difficult to estimate the cost of capital for a warrant because we can estimate $\beta_c = \beta_w$ and then employ the CAPM.

Table 12.2   End-of-Period Payoffs for a Warrant and for a Call Option (Written on a Firm with no Warrants)

	End-of-Period Payoffs	
	If $S \leq X$	If $S > X$
Warrant on firm with warrants, W	0	$\dfrac{S + qX}{1 + q} - X = \dfrac{1}{1 + q}(S - X)$
Call on firm without warrants, C	0	$S - X$

would be exercised sequentially. Constantinides [1981] has solved the warrant valuation problem for competitive warrant holders and shown that the warrant price, given a competitive equilibrium, is less than or equal to the value it would have given block exercise.

2. Convertible Bonds

As the name implies, convertible debt is a hybrid bond which allows its bearer to exchange it for a given number of shares of stock anytime up to and including the maturity date of the bond. Preferred stock is also frequently issued with a convertible provision and may be thought of as a convertible security (a bond) with an infinite maturity date.

A convertible bond is equivalent to a portfolio of two securities: straight debt with the same coupon rate and maturity as the convertible bond, and a warrant written on the value of the firm. The coupon rate on convertible bonds is usually lower than comparable straight debt because the right to convert is worth something. For example, in February of 1982, the XYZ Company wanted to raise $50 million by using either straight debt or convertible bonds. An investment banking firm informed the company's treasurer that straight debt with a 25-year maturity would require a 17% coupon. Alternately, convertible debt with the same maturity would require only a 10% coupon. Both debt instruments would sell at par (i.e., $1000) and the convertible debt could be converted into 35.71 shares (i.e., an exercise price of $28 per share). The stock of the XYZ Company was selling for $25 per share at the time. Later on we will use these facts to compute the cost of capital for the convertible issue, but first, what do financial officers think of convertible debt?

Brigham [1966] received responses from the chief financial officers of 22 firms which had issued convertible debt. Of them, 68% said they used convertible debt because they believed their stock price would rise over time and that convertibles would provide a way of selling common stock at a price above the existing market. Another 27% said that their company wanted straight debt, but found conditions to be such that a straight bond issue could not be sold at a reasonable rate of interest. The problem is that neither reason makes much sense. Convertible bonds are not "cheap debt." Because convertible bonds are riskier, their true cost of capital is greater (on a before-tax basis) than the cost of straight debt. Also, convertible bonds are not a deferred sale of common stock at an attractive price.[23] The uncertain sale of shares for $28 each at some future date can hardly be compared directly with a current share price of $25.

Brennan and Schwartz [1977] and Ingersoll [1977b] have analyzed the valuation of convertible bonds, assuming that the entire outstanding issue, if converted, will be converted as a block. Constantinides [1981] has extended their work to study the value of convertible debt if conversion does not occur all at once. The reader is referred to these articles for the derivations which show that the market value of convertible debt, CV, is equal to the market value of straight debt, B, and a warrant, W.

$$CV = B + W.$$

Suppose you want to compute the cost of capital for the convertible debt being considered by the XYZ Company as mentioned above. You already know that the maturity date is 25 years, similar straight debt yields 17% to maturity, the convertible bond coupon rate is 10% (with semiannual coupons), the conversion price (exercise price) is $28 per share, the bond will sell at par value, i.e., $1000, and the current stock price is $25. In addition you need to know that: (1) if converted the issue would increase the firm's outstanding shares by 5%, i.e., the dilution factor, q, is 5%; (2) the standard deviation of the firm's equity rate of return is $\sigma = .3$; (3) the risk-free rate is 14.5% for 25-year Treasury Bonds; (4) the expected rate of return on the market portfolio is 20.6%; and (5) the firm's equity beta is 1.5. Given these facts it is possible to use the capital asset pricing model and the option pricing model to estimate the before-tax cost of capital, k_{CV}, on the firm's contemplated convertible bond issue as a weighted average of the cost of straight debt, k_d, and the cost of the warrant, k_w.[24]

$$k_{CV} = k_d \frac{B}{B + W} + k_w \frac{W}{B + W}.$$

The value of the straight debt, assuming semiannual coupons of $50, a principal payment of $1000 twenty-five years hence, and a 17% discount rate is $B = \$619.91$. Therefore, the remainder of the sale price, namely $1000 - 619.91 = \$380.09$, is the value of the warrant to purchase 35.71 shares at $28 each. The cost of straight debt was given to be $k_d = 17\%$ before taxes. All that remains is to find the cost of the warrant. From Section F.1 we know that the warrant implied in the convertible bond contract is perfectly correlated with a call option written on the firm (without warrants outstanding) and therefore has the same cost of capital. The cost of capital, k_c, for the call option can be estimated from the CAPM

$$k_c = R_f + [E(R_M) - R_f]\beta_c,$$

---

[23] From the theory of option pricing we know that $S + P = B + C$; i.e., a bond plus a call option is the same thing as owning the stock and a put option. Thus one could think of a convertible bond as equivalent to the stock plus a put.

[24] Throughout the analysis we assume that there is no tax gain to leverage. Therefore, the conversion of the bond will decrease the firm's debt-to-equity ratio but not change the value of the firm.

where

k_c = the cost of capital for a call option with 25 years to maturity,[25]

R_f = the risk-free rate for a 25-year Treasury Bond = 14.5%,

$E(R_M)$ = the expected rate of return on the market portfolio = 20.6%,

$\beta_c = N(d_1)(S/C)\beta_s$ = the systematic risk of the call option,

β_s = the systematic risk of the stock (without warrants) = 1.5,

$N(d_1)$ = the cumulative normal probability for option pricing in Chapter 8,

C = the value of a call option written on the stock, *ex warrants.*

$$d_1 = \frac{\ln(S/X) + R_f T}{\sigma\sqrt{T}} + \frac{1}{2}\sigma\sqrt{T}$$

Substituting in the appropriate numbers, we find that $d_1 = 3.09114$ and $N(d_1) = .999$. And using the Black-Scholes version of the option pricing model, we find that $C = \$24.74$. Therefore,

$$\beta_c = \frac{S}{C} N(d_1)\beta_s$$

$$= \frac{25.00}{24.74}(.999)(1.5) = 1.514,$$

and substituting into the CAPM we have

$$k_c = .145 + (.206 - .145)1.514$$

$$= 23.74\%.$$

The cost of capital for the warrant is slightly above the cost of equity for the firm. Actually, the warrant is not much riskier than the equity because its market value is almost equal to the market value of the firm's equity, given a 25-year life and only a $3 difference between the exercise price and the stock price.

Taken together, these facts imply that the before-tax cost of capital for the convertible issue will be

$$k_{CV} = .17\frac{619.91}{1000.00} + .2374\frac{380.09}{1000.00}$$

$$= 19.56\%.$$

This answer is almost double the 10% coupon rate which the convertible promises to pay, and it shows that the higher risk of convertible debt requires a higher expected rate of return.

The final point of discussion is why convertible debt is used if financial officers understand its true cost. It certainly is not a cheap form of either debt or equity.

---

[25] If the firm pays dividends which are large enough, then the convertible debentures may be exercised if the implied warrants are in-the-money. Exercise would occur just prior to the ex dividend date(s).

Another irrational explanation is that, until the accounting rules were changed to require reporting earnings per share on a fully diluted basis, it was possible for an aggressive firm to acquire another company via convertible debt financing. The lower interest charges of convertible debt meant that earnings of the merged company were often higher than the sum of premerger earnings of the separate entities. Also, the actual number of shares outstanding were lower than the number which would be reported if the conversion were to occur. Given all of the evidence in Chapter 10 on the efficiency of markets, it is hard to believe that the market was fooled by the accounting conventions. A possible reason for issuing convertibles is that they are better tailored to the cash flow patterns of rapidly growing firms. The lower coupon rate during the early years keeps the probability of bankruptcy lower than straight debt; then, if the firm is successful, more cash for growth will be supplied when conversion takes place. Also, convertible debt may be preferred to straight debt with warrants attached because convertible debt often has a call provision built in which allows a firm to force conversion. The call feature is discussed in the next section.

3. Call Provisions

Many securities have call provisions which allow the firm to force redemption. Frequently, ordinary bonds may be redeemed at a *call premium* roughly equal to one year's interest. For example, the call premium on a twenty-year $1000 face value bond with a 12% coupon might be $120 if the bond is called in the first year, $114 if called in the second year, and so on.

The call provision is equivalent to a call option written by the investors who buy the bonds from the firm. The bonds may be repurchased by the firm (at the exercise price, i.e., the call price) anytime during the life of the bond. If interest rates fall, the market price of the outstanding bonds may exceed the call price, thereby making it advantageous for the firm to exercise its option to call in the debt. Since the option is valuable to the firm, it must pay the bondholders by offering a higher interest rate on callable bonds than on similar ordinary bonds which do not have the call feature. New issues of callable bonds must often bear yields from one-quarter to one-half of one percent higher than the yields of noncallable bonds.

Brennan and Schwartz [1977b] show how to value callable bonds. If the objective of the firm is to maximize shareholders' wealth, then a call policy will be established to minimize the market value of callable debt. The value of the bonds will be minimized if they are called at the point where their uncalled value is equal to the call price. To call when the uncalled value is below the call price is to provide a needless gain to bondholders. To allow the uncalled bond value to rise above the call price is inconsistent with minimizing the bond value. Therefore, the firm should call the bond when the market price first rises to reach the call price. Furthermore, we would never expect the market value of a callable bond to exceed the call price plus a small premium for the flotation costs the firm must bear in calling the issue.

Almost all corporate bonds are callable and none are puttable. Why? A plausible answer has been put forth by Boyce and Kalotay [1979]. Whenever the tax rate of the borrower exceeds the tax rate of the lender, there is a tax incentive for issuing callable debt. Since corporations have marginal tax rates of around 50% while individuals have lower rates, corporations have an incentive to issue callable bonds.[26] From the firm's point of view the coupons paid and the call premium are both deductible as interest expenses. The investor pays ordinary income taxes on interest received and capital gains taxes on the call premium. If the stream of payments on debt is even across time, then low and high tax bracket lenders and borrowers will value it equally. However, if it is decreasing across time, as it is expected to be with a callable bond, then low tax bracket lenders will assign a higher value because they discount at a higher after-tax rate. Near term cash inflows are *relatively* more valuable to them. A high tax bracket borrower (i.e., the firm) will use a lower after-tax discount rate and will also prefer a decreasing cash flow pattern because the present value of the interest tax shield will be relatively higher. Even though the firm pays a higher gross rate, it prefers callable debt to ordinary debt because of the tax advantages for the net rate of return.

Brennan and Schwartz [1977b] and Ingersoll [1977b] both examined the effect of a call feature on convertible debt and preferred. Unlike simpler option securities, convertible bonds and preferred stocks contain dual options. The bondholder has the right to exchange a convertible for the company's common stock while the company retains the right to call the issue at the contracted call price. One interesting implication of the theory on call policies is that a convertible security should be called as soon as its conversion value (i.e., the value of the common stock which would be received in the conversion exchange) rises to equal the prevailing effective call price (i.e., the stated call price plus accrued interest). Ingersoll [1977a] collected data on 179 convertible issues which were called between 1968 and 1975. The calls on all but nine were delayed beyond the time when the theory predicted. The median company waited until the conversion value of its debentures was 43.9% in excess of the call price. As yet no research has provided a good explanation for this behavior.

4. Preferred Stock

Preferred stock is much like subordinated debt except that if the promised cash payments (i.e., the preferred coupons) are not paid on time, then preferred shareholders cannot force the firm into bankruptcy. All preferred stocks listed on the New York Stock Exchange must have voting rights in order to be listed. A high percentage of preferred stocks have no stated maturity date and also provide for cumulative dividend payments, i.e., all past preferred dividends must be paid before common stock dividends can be paid. Approximately 40% of new preferred stocks are convertible into common stock.

If preferred stock is not callable or convertible, and if its life is indefinite, then its market value is

$$P = \frac{\text{coupon}}{k_p}$$

---

[26] Interestingly, the opposite is true when the government is lending. The government has a zero tax rate and holders of government debt have positive rates. Consequently, the government has incentive to offer puttable debt and it does. Series E and H savings bonds are redeemable at the lender's option.

where k_p is the before-tax cost of preferred. Of course, the before- and after-tax costs are the same for preferred stock because preferred dividends are not deductible as an expense before taxes. The nondeductibility of preferred dividends has led many companies to buy back their preferred stock and use subordinated debt instead. It is a puzzle why preferred stock is issued at all, especially if there is a gain to leverage from using debt capital as a substitute.

SUMMARY

The cost of capital is seen to be a rate of return whose definition requires a project to improve the wealth position of the *current* shareholders of the firm. The original Modigliani-Miller work has been extended by using the CAPM so that a risk-adjusted cost of capital may be obtained for each project. When the expected cash flows of the project are discounted at the correct risk-adjusted rate, the result is the *NPV* of the project.

In a world without taxes, the value of the firm is independent of its capital structure. However, there are several important extensions of the basic model. With the introduction of corporate taxes, the optimal capital structure becomes 100% debt. Finally, when personal taxes are also introduced, the value of the firm is unaffected by the choice of financial leverage. Financing is irrelevant! The next chapter takes a more careful look at the question of optimal capital structure and summarizes some of the empirical work which has been done.

PROBLEM SET

12.1 The Modigliani-Miller theorem assumes that the firm has only two classes of securities, perpetual debt and equity. Suppose that the firm has issued a third class of securities—preferred stock—and that $X\%$ of preferred dividends may be written off as an expense ($0 \leq X \leq 1$).

a) What is the appropriate expression for the value of the levered firm?

b) What is the appropriate expression for the weighted average cost of capital?

12.2 The Acrosstown Company has an equity beta, β_L, of .5 and 50% debt in its capital structure. The company has risk-free debt which costs 6% before taxes, and the expected rate of return on the market is 18%. Acrosstown is considering the acquisition of a new project in the peanut-raising agribusiness which is expected to yield 25% on after-tax operating cash flows. The Carternut Company, which is the same product line (and risk class) as the project being considered, has an equity beta, β_L, of 2.0 and has 10% debt in its capital structure. If Acrosstown finances the new project with 50% debt, should it be accepted or rejected? Assume that the marginal tax rate, τ_c, for both companies is 50%.

12.3 The XYZ Company has a current market value of $1,000,000, half of which is debt. Its current weighted average cost of capital is 9%, and the corporate tax rate is 40%. The treasurer proposes to undertake a new project, which costs $500,000, and which can be financed completely with debt. The project is expected to have the same operating risk as the company and to earn 8.5% on its levered after-tax cash flows. The treasurer argues that the project is desirable because it earns more than 5%, which is the before-tax marginal cost of the debt used to finance it. What do you think?

12.4 Given a world with corporate taxes, τ_c, a personal tax rate paid on bonds, τ_{pB}, and a personal tax rate on income from equity, τ_{ps}, what would be the effect of a decrease in the corporate tax rate on

a) the aggregate amount of debt in the economy, and

b) the optimal capital structure of firms?

12.5 Congress has proposed to eliminate "double taxation" on dividends by reducing the personal tax on dividend income. At the same time, a compensating increase in taxes on capital gains (traditionally taxed at a much lower percentage than dividend income) has been proposed.

a) What effect would this joint proposal have on the optimal capital structure of a firm, according to the Miller model?

b) What effect would it have on the aggregate amount of corporate debt outstanding?

12.6 Consider firm B as an unlevered firm, and firm C as a levered firm with target debt-to-equity ratio $(B/S)^* = 1$. Both firms have exactly the same perpetual net operating income, NOI = 180, before taxes. The before-tax cost of debt, k_d, is the same as the risk-free rate. The corporate tax rate = .5. Given the following market parameters,

$$E(R_m) = .12, \qquad \sigma_m^2 = .0144, \qquad R_f = .06, \qquad \beta_B = 1, \qquad \beta_C = 1.5.$$

a) Find the cost of capital and value for each firm. (Ignore any effect from personal income taxes.)

b) Evaluate the following four projects to determine their acceptance (or rejection) by firms B and C. What do the results of this evaluation tell you about leverage in a world with corporate taxes but no personal taxes? (Note: r_{jm} is the correlation between the unlevered free cash flows of each project and the market.)

$Project_j$	$Cost_j$	$E(N\tilde{O}I_j)$ (After Tax)	σ_j	r_{jm} Correlation of j with the Market
1	100	9	.10	.6
2	120	11	.11	.7
3	80	9	.12	.8
4	150	18	.20	.9

12.7 A firm with $1,000,000 in assets and 50% debt in its capital structure is considering a $250,000 project. The firm's after-tax weighted average cost of capital is 10.4%, the marginal cost of debt is 8% (before taxes), and the marginal tax rate is 40%. If the project does not change the firm's operating risk and is financed exclusively with new equity, what rate of return must it earn to be acceptable?

12.8 The firm's cost of equity capital is 18%, the market value of the firm's equity is $8 million, the firm's cost of debt capital is 9%, and the market value of debt is $4 million. The firm is considering a new investment with an expected rate of return of 17%. This project is 30% riskier than the firm's average operations. The riskless rate of return is 5%; the variance of the market return is .08. Is the project profitable? [Assume a world without taxes.]

12.9 Susan Varhard, Treasurer of the Gammamax Company, has proposed that the company should sell equity and buy back debt in order to maximize its value. As evidence, she presents the financial statements given in Table Q12.9. The company currently has a price-earnings ratio of 50. Before the change in capital structure it has 10 shares outstanding; therefore its earnings per share are $1.00, and the price per share is $50. If 10 new shares are issued at $50 each, $500 is collected and used to retire $500 of debt (which pays a coupon rate of 8%). After the capital-structure change, earnings per share have increased to $1.50 (since there are now 20 shares outstanding); and with a price-earnings ratio of 50, presumably the price per share will increase from $50 before the capital-structure change to $75 afterward. Given your understanding of modern finance theory, discuss the above proposal.

Table Q12.9

Income Statement	Before	After
Net operating income	100	100
Interest expense	80	40
Earnings before taxes	20	60
Taxes at 50%	10	30
Net income	10	30

Balance Sheet

Before			After		
Asset	Liabilities		Assets	Liabilities	
	Debt	1000		Debt	500
	Equity	500		Equity	1000
Total = 1500	Total = 1500		Total = 1500	Total = 1500	

12.10 Community Bank must decide whether to open a new branch. The current market value of the bank is $2,500,000. According to company policy (and industry practice), the bank's capital structure is highly leveraged. The present (and optimal) ratio of debt to total assets is .9. Community Bank's debt is almost exclusively in the form of demand, savings, and time deposits. The average return on these deposits to the bank's clients has been 5% over the past five years. However, recently interest rates have climbed sharply, and as a result Community Bank presently pays an average annual rate of $6\frac{1}{4}$% on its accounts in order to remain competitive. In addition, the bank incurs a service cost of $2\frac{3}{4}$% per account. Because federal "Regulation Q" puts a ceiling on the amount of interest paid by banks on their accounts, the banking industry at large has been experiencing disintermediation—a loss of clients to the open money market (Treasury bills, etc.), where interest rates are higher. Largely because of the interest-rate situation (which shows no sign of improving), Community Bank's president has stipulated that for the branch project to be acceptable, its entire cost of $500,000 will have to be raised by 90% debt and 10% equity. The bank's cost of equity capital, k_e, is 11%. Community Bank's marginal tax rate is .48. Market analysis indicates that the new branch may be expected to return net cash flows according to the following schedule:

Year	0	1	2	3	4	5	6 to ∞
$	−500,000	25,000	35,000	45,000	45,000	50,000	50,000

Should Community Bank open the new branch?

12.11 A not-for-profit organization, such as a ballet company or a museum, usually carries no debt. Also, since there are no shareholders, there is no equity outstanding. How would you go about determining the appropriate weighted average cost of capital for not-for-profit organizations given that they have no debt or equity?

12.12 Firms A and B are each considering an unanticipated new investment opportunity which will marginally increase the value of the firm and will also increase the firm's level of diversification. Firm A is unlevered, and firm B has a capital structure of 50% debt. Assuming that the shareholders control the firm, will either firm make the investment?

12.13 In a world without taxes or transaction costs, the Modigliani-Miller model predicts shareholders' wealth invariant to changes in capital structure, while the OPM predicts increased shareholder wealth with increased leverage. Given what you know about option pricing, is a 20% increase in the variance of return on the firm's assets more likely to benefit shareholders in a low-leverage or in a high-leverage firm?

12.14 The Sharpe version of the CAPM results in the principle of two-fund separation. Every individual holds the same portfolio of risky assets, namely, the market portfolio. Therefore, individuals will be indifferent to redistribution effects caused by imperfect "me-first" rules. True or false? Why?

12.15 Consider a levered firm with $10 million face value of debt outstanding, maturing in one year. The riskless rate is 6% and the expected rate of return on the market is 12%. The systematic risk of the firm's assets is $\beta_V = 1.5$, the total risk of these assets is $\sigma_V = 1.3$, and their market value is $25 million.

a) Determine the market value of the firm's debt and equity.

b) Determine the cost of debt and equity capital (assuming a world without taxes).

12.16

a) True or false: The Modigliani-Miller model of cost of equity is equivalent to the OPM definition of cost of equity for an all-equity firm. Explain.

b) If we assume that $N(d_1) = 1$ in the OPM, what does this imply about $\delta S/\delta V$? About the firm's capital structure?

For Problems 12.17 and 12.18 assume the following:

a) We are dealing with a world where there are no taxes.

b) The changes in the parameters affecting value are unanticipated; therefore redistribution effects are possible.

c) Firms A and B initially have the following parameters:

$\sigma_A = \sigma_B = .2$	Instantaneous standard deviation
$T_A = T_B = 4$ years	Maturity of debt
$V_A = V_B = \$2,000$	Value of the firm, $V = B + S$
$R_f = .06$	Risk-free rate
$D_A = D_B = \$1,000$	Face value of debt

12.17 What is the initial market value of debt and equity for firms *A* and *B*?

12.18 Firm *A* decides to use some of its cash in order to purchase marketable securities. This has the effect of leaving its value, V_A, unchanged but increasing its instantaneous standard deviation from .2 to .3. What are the new values of debt and equity?

REFERENCES

Baxter, N. D., "Leverage, Risk of Ruin and the Cost of Capital," *Journal of Finance,* September 1967, 395–403.

Beranek, W., "The WACC Criterion and Shareholder Wealth Maximization," *Journal of Financial and Quantitative Analysis,* March 1977, 17–32.

Bierman, H., "The Cost of Warrants," *Journal of Financial and Quantitative Analysis,* June 1973, 499–503.

Black, F., and J. Cox, "Valuing Corporate Securities: Some Effects of Bond Indenture Provisions," *Journal of Finance,* 1976, 351–367.

Boyce, W. M., and Kalotay, A. J., "Tax Differentials and Callable Bonds," *Journal of Finance,* September 1979, 825–838.

Brennan, M. J., and E. S. Schwartz, "Savings Bonds, Retractable Bonds and Callable Bonds," *Journal of Financial Economics,* August 1977a, 67–88.

———, "Convertible Bonds: Valuation and Optimal Strategies for Call and Conversion," *Journal of Finance,* December 1977b, 1699–1715.

———, "Corporate Income Taxes, Valuation, and the Problem of Optimal Capital Structure," *Journal of Business,* January 1978, 103–114.

———, "Analyzing Convertible Bonds," *Journal of Financial and Quantitative Analysis,* November 1980, 907–929.

Brigham, E. F., "An Analysis of Convertible Debentures," *Journal of Finance,* March 1966, 35–54.

Chen, A. H. Y., "A Model of Warrant Pricing in a Dynamic Market," *Journal of Finance,* December 1970, 1041–1060.

———, and H. Kim, "Theories of Corporate Debt Policy: A Synthesis," *Journal of Finance,* May 1979, 371–384.

Constantinides, G., "Warrant Exercise and Bond Conversion in Competitive Markets," working paper, Graduate School of Business, University of Chicago, August 1981.

DeAngelo, H., and R. Masulis, "Optimal Capital Structure Under Corporate and Personal Taxation," *Journal of Financial Economics,* March 1980, 3–30.

Dyl, E., and M. Joehnk, "Sinking Funds and the Cost of Corporate Debt," *Journal of Finance,* September 1979, 887–893.

Emanuel, D. C., "Extensions and Developments of Option Pricing," Unpublished doctoral dissertation, Stanford University, 1979.

Fama, E. F., and M. C. Jensen, "Agency Problems and the Survival of Organizations," working paper, University of Rochester, February 1982.

Fama, E. F., and M. H. Miller, *The Theory of Finance.* Holt, Rinehart and Winston, New York, 1972.

Farrar, D. E., and L. Selwyn, "Taxes, Corporate Financial Policies and Returns to Investors," *National Tax Journal,* December 1967, 444–454.

Galai, D., and R. W. Masulis, "The Option Pricing Model and the Risk Factor of Stock," *Journal of Financial Economics,* January/March 1976, 53–82.

Galai, D., and M. Schneller, "The Pricing of Warrants and the Value of the Firm," *Journal of Finance,* December 1978, 1333–1342.

Haley, C. W., and L. D. Schall, *The Theory of Financial Decisions.* McGraw Hill, New York, 1973.

Hamada, R. S., "Portfolio Analysis, Market Equilibrium, and Corporation Finance," *Journal of Finance,* March 1969, 13–31.

———, "The Effect of the Firm's Capital Structure on the Systematic Risk of Common Stocks," *Journal of Finance,* May 1972, 435–452.

Hsia, C. C., "Coherence of the Modern Theories of Finance," Manuscript, University of California at Los Angeles, 1978.

———, "Coherence of the Modern Theories of Finance," *Financial Review,* Winter 1981, 27–42.

Ingersoll, J., "An Examination of Corporate Call Policies on Convertible Securities," *Journal of Finance,* May 1977a, 463–478.

———, "A Contingent-Claims Valuation of Convertible Securities," *Journal of Financial Economics,* May 1977b, 289–322.

Jen, F. C., and J. E. Wert, "The Effects of Sinking Fund Provisions on Corporate Bond Yields," *Financial Analysts Journal,* March/April 1967, 125–133.

Jennings, E. H., "An Estimate of Convertible Bond Premiums," *Journal of Financial and Quantitative Analysis,* January 1974, 33–56.

Kim, H., "A Mean-Variance Theory of Optimal Capital Structure and Corporate Debt Capacity," *Journal of Finance,* March 1978, 45–64.

Kraus, A., and R. Litzenberger, "A State-Preference Model of Optimal Financial Leverage," *Journal of Finance,* September 1973, 911–922.

Mason, S. P., and S. Bhattacharya, "Risky Debt, Jump Processes, and Safety Covenants," *Journal of Financial Economics,* September 1981, 281–307.

Merton, R. C., "An Intertemporal Capital Asset Pricing Model," *Econometrica,* September 1973, 867–887.

Mikkelson, W. H., "Convertible Calls and Security Returns," *Journal of Financial Economics,* September 1981, 237–264.

Miller, M. H., "Debt and Taxes," *Journal of Finance,* May 1977, 261–275.

———, and F. Modigliani, "Some Estimates on the Cost of Capital to the Electric Utility Industry 1954–57," *American Economic Review,* June 1966, 333–348.

Modigliani, F., and M. H. Miller, "The Cost of Capital, Corporation Finance, and the Theory of Investment," *American Economic Review,* June 1958, 261–297.

———, "Corporate Income Taxes and the Cost of Capital," *American Economic Review,* June 1963, 433–443.

Myers, S., "Determinants of Corporate Borrowing," *Journal of Financial Economics,* November 1977, 147–176.

Pye, G., "The Value of a Call Option on a Bond," *Journal of Political Economy,* April 1966, 200–205.

Robichek, A., and S. Myers, "Problems in the Theory of Optimal Capital Structure," *Journal of Financial and Quantitative Analysis,* June 1966, 1–35.

Rubinstein, M. E., "A Mean-Variance Synthesis of Corporate Financial Theory," *Journal of Finance,* March 1973, 167–181.

Samuelson, P. A., "Rational Theory of Warrant Pricing," *Industrial Management Review,* Spring 1965, 13–32.

Schneller, M., "Taxes and the Optimal Capital Structure of the Firm," *Journal of Finance,* March 1980, 119–127.

Schwartz, E. S., "The Valuation of Warrants: Implementing a New Approach," *Journal of Financial Economics,* January 1977, 79–93.

Stiglitz, J. E., "A Re-Examination of the Modigliani-Miller Theorem," *American Economic Review,* December 1969, 784–793.

————, "On the Irrelevance of Corporate Financial Policy," *American Economic Review,* December 1974, 851–866.

Stone, B. K., "Warrants Financing," *Journal of Financial and Quantitative Analysis,* March 1976, 143–153.

Walter, J. E., and A. V. Que, "The Valuation of Convertible Bonds," *Journal of Finance,* June 1973, 713–732.

Weil, R., J. E. Segall, and D. Green, Jr., "Premiums on Convertible Bonds," *Journal of Finance,* 1968, 445–463.

Appendix to Chapter 12
Duration and Optimal
Maturity Structure of the
Balance Sheet

In Chapter 12, we analyzed several aspects of the cost and value of financial instruments. Another aspect of the valuation of securities is the sensitivity of their present values to unexpected changes in interest rates. We can conceptualize this relationship as the elasticity of the price of securities (particularly bonds) to interest rates. For bonds, the elasticity is the ratio of percentage changes in prices to percentage changes in market rates of interest for a given coupon and face value.

A. DURATION

The "duration" of a payment stream is a measure of elasticity. Thus the duration of bond i can be expressed as follows:

$$D_i = - \frac{dB_i / B_i}{dr / r},$$ (A12.1)

where

B_i = price of bond i

r = market yield rate.

For measurement purposes, the expression in Eq. (A12.1) would provide only an approximation since it holds strictly for only infinitely small changes in the market yield rate. We can derive a more operational measurement expression. We start with the value of a bond, B_0, as in Eq. (A12.2):

$$B_0 = \frac{I_1}{1 + r} + \frac{I_2}{(1 + r)^2} + \cdots + \frac{I_T}{(1 + r)^T} + \frac{F}{(1 + r)^T},$$ (A12.2)

where

I_t = dollar value of coupon payment in period t,

F = dollar value of maturity payment,

T = maturity period.

Next we take the derivative of the bond price to the change in the market yield rate:

$$\frac{dB_0}{d(1+r)} = -I(1+r)^{-2} - 2I(1+r)^{-3} - \cdots - TI(1+r)^{-(T+1)} - TF(1+r)^{T-1}$$

$$= -\left[\frac{I}{(1+r)^2} + \frac{2I}{(1+r)^3} + \cdots + \frac{TI}{(1+r)^{T+1}} + \frac{TF}{(1+r)^{T+1}}\right].$$

Divide both sides by B_0 and $(1+r)$:

$$\frac{dB_0/B_0}{d(1+r)/(1+r)} = \frac{dB_0(1+r)}{d(1+r)B_0}$$

$$= -\frac{1}{B_0}\left[\frac{I}{1+r} + \frac{2I}{(1+r)^2} + \cdots + \frac{TI}{(1+r)^T} + \frac{TF}{(1+r)^T}\right].$$

Let C represent the appropriate cash flows, and express the result in summation form:

$$D_i = \frac{\displaystyle\sum_{t=1}^{T} \frac{tC_t}{(1+r)^t}}{B_0}. \tag{A12.3}$$

This result can also be expressed as in Eq. (A12.3a):

$$D_i = \frac{\displaystyle\sum_{t=1}^{T} \frac{tI_t}{(1+r)^t} + \frac{TF}{(1+r)^T}}{\displaystyle\sum_{t=1}^{T} \frac{I_t}{(1+r)^t} + \frac{F}{(1+r)^T}}. \tag{A12.3a}$$

From Eq. (A12.3a) we can see that duration is not the same as the time to maturity of the payment stream. Unlike maturity, duration considers all cash flows and gives some weight to their timing.

Thus duration is calculated as the weighted average of the lengths of time prior to the last cash flows, by using the ratios of the present values of each coupon payment to the present value of the bond as the weights. It identifies the "actual" weighted length of time needed to recover the current cost of the bond. For example, assume a five-year, $1000 bond has a coupon payment of $25 each six months (5% coupon rate), pays $1000 at the end of the fifth year, and has a yield rate of 12%. The duration of the bond can be calculated as shown in Table A12.1.

A short-cut method of calculating duration as originally formulated by Macaulay [1938] is the following:

$$D = \frac{R}{R-1} - \frac{QR + T(1+Q-QR)}{R^T - 1 - Q + QR}. \tag{A12.4}$$

The new terms in Eq. (A12.4) are

$R = (1+r) = 1.06,$

$Q = (F/I_t) = \$1000/\$25 = 40,$

$T = 10.$

Table A12.1 $1000 Bond Issue, 5-year, with 12% Yield Rate
and 5% Coupon Rate Paid Semiannually

(1) Period	(2) Cash Payments	(3) Discount Factor at 6% of Semiannual Yield Rate	(4) Present Value of Cash Payments (2) × (3)	(5) (4) × (1)
1	$ 25	.9434	$ 23.5850	$ 23.5850
2	25	.8900	22.2500	44.5000
3	25	.8396	20.9900	62.9700
4	25	.7921	19.8025	79.2100
5	25	.7473	18.6825	93.4125
6	25	.7050	17.6250	105.7500
7	25	.6651	16.6275	116.3925
8	25	.6274	15.6850	125.4800
9	25	.5919	14.7975	133.1775
10	1,025	.5584	572.3600	5,723.6000
		P.V. of bond =	$742.4050	$6,508.0775

$$D = \frac{\$6,508.0775}{\$742.4050} = 8.7662 \text{ (semiannual)}$$

$$= 4.3831 \text{ years}$$

Only for zero coupon bonds is duration the same as maturity. For other payment streams, duration is shorter than maturity. For a given par value of a bond, the higher the coupon payments and the higher the yield to maturity, the shorter is duration.

The relationship between the bond price and its duration is more complicated. For bonds selling at or above par, the duration increases with maturity, but at a decreasing rate, and is bounded by $(r + p)/rp$ years, where r is the yield to maturity and p is the number of times per year interest is paid and compounded. For discount bonds, duration increases with maturity to a maximum point before it matures, and then declines. For shorter-term bonds, the differences between duration and maturity are small. However, as maturity increases, the differences will be substantially larger.

B. IMMUNIZATION

Immunization is a technique designed to achieve a specified return target in the face of changes in interest rates. The problem arises because with changing interest rates the reinvestment income will change. However, a bond or a bond portfolio can be immunized against this risk by selecting a maturity or group of maturities whose duration will be equal to the planning horizon of the decision maker. An illustration based on an example by Leibowitz [1981] will convey the ideas involved. The initial facts are these. We have a 9% par bond with a maturity of 6.7 years resulting in a five-year duration related to the five-year horizon of the decision maker. With semiannual compounding the bond maturity is 13.4 periods. The simple sum of the coupon income, based on the 9% rate over five years (10 periods), is $450.

To verify the relation between the maturity of 6.7 years and the duration of five years, we employ the Macaulay formulation. The key inputs are

$$R = 1 + r = 1.045,$$

$$Q = 1000/45 = 22.22,$$

$$T = 13.4.$$

We can now calculate duration, D, as

$$D = \frac{1.045}{.045} - \frac{22.22(1.045) + 13.4[23.22 - 22.22(1.045)]}{(1.045)^{13.4} - 23.22 + 22.22(1.045)}$$

$$= \frac{10.35}{2} = 5.17 \approx 5.$$

Suppose the market yield rate now changes from 9% to 10%. There will be a capital loss because of the rise in the yield rate, but the reinvestment income will be higher. We shall demonstrate that if the investor's planning horizon is five years, the yield will remain 9% and the capital gain or loss will be exactly balanced by the present value of the changed reinvestment income. We can demonstrate this by looking at the situation at the end of the fifth year or taking those results and discounting them back to the present. The income at 10% will be

$$= \$45 \times \text{FVIF}_a(5\%, 10 \text{ pds})$$
$$= (\$45 \times 12.5779)$$
$$= \$566.$$

However, the interest that would have been earned at a 9% rate would be

$$= \$45 \times \text{FVIF}_a(4\tfrac{1}{2}\%, 10 \text{ pds})$$
$$= (\$45 \times 12.2882)$$
$$= \$553.$$

Thus the gain in interest income is $13 as of the end of the fifth year.

Next we calculate the price that would be received when the bond is sold at the end of the five-year planning horizon. At the end of five years or 10 periods the bond had 1.7 years, or 3.4 periods, remaining. Its value and the capital gain (loss) at 10% are shown below:

$$V_b = \$45(3.0572) + \$1000(.8471)$$
$$= \$137.57 + \$847.10$$
$$= \$984.67$$
$$\text{Capital Gain} = \$984.67 - \$1000 = -\$15.33.$$

Thus we see that the amount of the capital gain or loss is a negative $15. This is slightly different from the $13 gain on interest because we have used approximations for a duration of, for example, 5 years when the exact duration was 5.17 years.

Next we can verify that a 9% yield will actually be achieved and that the current market value of $1000 is immunized against the rise in the required market yield. In the analysis we use

$$\text{FVIF}_a(4\tfrac{1}{2}\%,\ 10\ \text{pds}) = 7.9127, \text{ and } \text{PVIF}(4\tfrac{1}{2}\%,\ 10\ \text{pds}) = .6439.$$

So we have

Coupon interest @ 9%	$\$\ 45 \times 7.9127 = \$356.07$
Interest @ 10%	$\$566 \times\ \ .6439 = \ \ 364.45$
Capital gain	$\$985 \times\ \ .6439 = \ \ 634.24$
Less*	$\$553 \times\ \ .6439 = (356.08)$
	$\$998.70$

* To adjust for the 9 percent interest rate implicit in the interest factor used to discount the present value of the coupon income.

The example illustrates that by choosing the duration of the payment stream to be equal to the length of the planning horizon, the present value of the payment stream is immunized against changes in the market rate of interest, and the initial yield on the stream is preserved.

Another example of immunization uses the total balance sheet position of a firm. Consider a bank portfolio manager with the following initial position:

	Initial Position	
	Assets	Liabilities
Portfolio value	$800,000	$800,000
Portfolio yield	12.0%	8.0%
Portfolio duration	8 yrs	3 yrs

With a 1% rise in yields, we can use Eq. (A12.1) to calculate the change in the equity position of the bank. For the assets side we have

$$dP_a = -D_a \left(\frac{dr}{r} \right) P_a$$

$$= -8 \frac{.01}{(1.12)} \$800,000$$

$$= -\$57,142.$$

For the liabilities (or claims on assets) side, we have

$$dP_c = -3 \frac{.01}{(1.08)} \$800,000$$

$$= -\$22,222.$$

So the decline in the value of assets exceeds the decline in the value of claims on assets by \$34,920. By changing the duration of the asset portfolio, the bank can be immunized against a change in the interest rate levels. The required duration for the asset portfolio is

$$dP_a = -D_a \frac{.01}{(1.12)} \$800,000 = -\$22,222.$$

Solving, we have D_a is 3.11, indicating the shorter duration required for immunization of the portfolio.

The examples above illustrate the mechanics of immunization procedures. In actual application immunization involves a wide range of assumptions in connection with its use in immunizing bond portfolios. One assumption is parallel shifts in the yield curve [Yawitz and Marshall, 1981]. The practical effects of this are small [Kolb and Gay, 1982, p. 83].

Also, there may be multiple rate changes during the planning horizon. This problem is dealt with by rebalancing the portfolio to maintain a duration matching the remaining life of the planning period. In addition, there are a wide variety of more aggressive approaches to managing the bond portfolio developed under the concept of contingent immunization [Leibowitz and Weinberger, 1981, 1982]. Contingent immunization is a form of active portfolio management. It generally involves some degree of rate anticipation reflecting the portfolio manager's judgments about the future direction of interest rates. The procedures are too detailed to be covered in this brief treatment.

C. APPLICATION OF DURATION TO DEBT MATURITY STRUCTURE

Redington [1952] applied the duration concept to the analysis of investment decisions made by insurance companies. He proposed an immunization rule under which the weighted duration of asset and liability streams are made equal so that the firm's net worth is hedged against interest rate movements. Redington noted that even for insurance companies the concept would be complex in its implementation. Grove [1974] analyzed immunization in a portfolio-choice model in a framework of uncertainty of income-stream patterns and of interest-rate changes.

Morris [1976a, 1976b] sought to apply the duration concept to the problem of corporate debt maturity strategies. Here the problem is even more complex than that faced by insurance companies. In theory insurance companies can formulate income and payment streams that are highly predictable by investing in fixed income securities, with payment streams related to the operation of life expectancy tables (which can be further hedged by combining death policies with annuity policies). For the industrial firm, the liability structure can be fixed by its corporate debt maturity pattern. However, the income stream varies with the impact of the economy and competition on the firm's revenues and costs.

Morris observes that when the covariance of interest costs with the firm's net operating income is high, a short-term borrowing policy will reduce the variation of net income, even though it increases the uncertainty of interest costs in future periods. Thus for a weighted asset life with long duration, immunization through the choice of the duration of the debt structure is not necessarily the least risky maturity policy because of the variability of the income streams from the assets. A shorter debt maturity policy may decrease the uncertainty of net income derived from the asset when there is a high covariance between net operating income and interest costs. If the duration of the asset structure is short, immunization calls for a weighted maturity of short-duration debt. But if long-term debt with a longer duration were employed, and if interest rates were negatively correlated with the firm's net operating income, a long-term borrowing policy could reduce the variance of net income. In addition, the level of interest costs would be fixed and certain over the life of the debt. Thus the concept of duration appears to have some potential for developing corporate debt maturity strategies. But the problem is more complex than that encountered in managing portfolios of financial assets and claims.

REFERENCES TO APPENDIX

Fisher, L., and R. L. Weil, "Coping with the Risk of Interest Rate Fluctuations: Returns to Bondholders from Naive and Optimal Strategies," *Journal of Business,* October 1971, 111–118.

Grove, M. A., "On 'Duration' and the Optimal Maturity Structure of the Balance Sheet," *Bell Journal,* Autumn 1974, 696–709.

Hicks, J. R., *Value and Capital.* Clarendon Press, Oxford, 1946.

Hopewell, J. R., and G. G. Kaufman, "Bond Price Volatility and Term to Maturity: A Generalized Respecification," *American Economic Review,* forthcoming.

Hsia, C. C., and J. F. Weston, "Price Behavior of Deep Discount Bonds," *Journal of Banking and Finance,* September 1981, 357–361.

Kolb, R. W., *Interest Rate Futures: A Comprehensive Introduction.* Dame, Richmond, Va., 1982.

————, and G. D. Gay, "Immunizing Bond Portfolios with Interest Rate Futures," *Financial Management,* Summer 1982, 81–89.

Leibowitz, M. L., "Specialized Fixed Income Security Strategies," in Edward I. Altman, ed., *Financial Handbook,* 5th ed. Wiley, New York, 1981, section 19.

————, and A. Weinberger, *Contingent Immunization: A New Procedure for Structured Active Management.* Salomon, New York, 1981.

————, *Risk Control Procedures Under Contingent Immunization.* Salomon, New York, 1982.

Macaulay, F. R., *Some Theoretical Problems Suggested by the Movements of Interest Rates, Bond Yields, and Stock Prices in the U.S. since 1856.* National Bureau of Economic Research, New York, 1938.

Morris, J. R., "On Corporate Debt Maturity Strategies," *Journal of Finance,* March 1976, 29–37.

————, "A Model for Corporate Debt Maturity Decisions," *Journal of Financial and Quantitative Analysis,* September 1976, 339–357.

Redington, F. M., "Review of the Principles of Life Office Valuations," *Journal of the Institute of Actuaries,* 1952 (vol. 78, part 3, no. 350), 286–340.

Samuelson, P. A., "The Effect of Interest Rate Increases on the Banking System," *American Economic Review,* March 1945, 16–27.

Weil, R. L., "Macaulay's Duration: An Appreciation," *Journal of Business,* October 1973, 589–592.

Yawitz, J. B., and W. J. Marshall, "The Shortcomings of Duration as a Risk Measure for Bonds," *The Journal of Financial Research,* Summer 1981, 91–101.

Capital Structure: Empirical Evidence and Applications

One kind of evidence in favor of the traditional position is that companies in various industry groups appear to use leverage as if there is some optimal range appropriate to each group. While significant intercompany differences in debt ratios exist within each industry, the average use of leverage by broad industrial groups tends to follow a consistent pattern over time.

E. SOLOMON, *THE THEORY OF FINANCIAL MANAGEMENT,*
COLUMBIA UNIVERSITY PRESS, NEW YORK,
1963, P. 98.

A. INTRODUCTION

The theories presented in the previous chapter provide some fairly unsettling conclusions about capital structure. On one hand it is argued that capital structure has no effect on the value of the firm (Modigliani and Miller [1958] or Miller [1977]), and on the other hand it is suggested that the firm carry 100% debt (Modigliani and Miller [1963]). Neither result is consistent with what seem to be cross-section regularities in the observed capital structures of U.S. firms. For example, the electric utility and steel industries have high financial leverage while service industries like accounting firms or brokerage houses have almost no long-term debt.

The first part of this chapter looks at some possible explanations for why there might be such a thing as an "optimal" capital structure which contains both debt and equity. Recall that in the previous chapter we examined the argument that risky debt (in a world without bankruptcy costs) may be the cause of an optimal capital structure and concluded that it has no effect. The first issue to be studied here is the effect of bankruptcy costs. It turns out that if they are nontrivial, then it is possible that an optimal capital structure can be obtained as the tax advantages of debt are traded off against the likelihood of incurring bankruptcy costs. Second, we discuss the implications of option-pricing theory for the capital structure of the firm and for the valuation of risky debt. Third, we discuss the effect of agency costs on optimal capital structure. Finally, we examine changes in capital structure as signals regarding the value of the firm. Agency costs and signaling theory are novel because they attempt to explain capital structure without taxes or bankruptcy costs.

Next, the discussion turns to the empirical evidence. The central issue is whether or not the value of the firm is affected by changes in its debt-equity ratio. Important related questions are: (1) Does the cost of equity increase as financial leverage does? (2) Are bankruptcy costs really nontrivial?

Finally, in an attempt to give a realistic example of how to calculate the cost of capital, we use a case study based on Bethlehem Steel. Also, we discuss the applied topics of debt refunding and the effect of flotation costs on the cost of capital.

B. POSSIBLE REASONS FOR AN "OPTIMAL" MIX OF DEBT AND EQUITY

1. The Effect of Bankruptcy Costs

In Chapter 12 we discussed the effect of risky debt on the value of the firm. In a world without transactions costs there was no effect. When we consider bankruptcy costs, the value of the firm in bankruptcy is reduced by the fact that payments must be made to third parties other than bond- or shareholders. Trustee fees, legal fees, and other costs of reorganization or bankruptcy are deducted from the net asset value of the bankrupt firm and from the proceeds which should go to bondholders. Consequently, the "dead-weight" losses associated with bankruptcy may cause the value of the firm in bankruptcy to be less than the discounted value of the expected cash flows from operations. This fact can be used to explain the existence of an optimal capital structure. Baxter [1967] was one of the first to suggest this possibility. Since then more sophisticated treatments have been offered by Stiglitz [1972], Kraus and Litzenberger [1973], and Kim [1978]. The interested reader is referred to these papers for explicit mathematical treatment of optimal capital structure. Figure 13.1 summarizes the results: Figure 13.1(a) shows the effects on various costs of capital. The dashed lines are the by now familiar Modigliani-Miller results, where the weighted average cost of capital (in a world with only corporate taxes) declines with leverage.

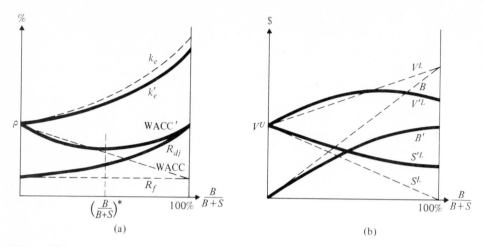

Figure 13.1
Optimal capital structure in the presence of bankruptcy costs: (a) the cost of capital; (b) the value of claims.

The solid lines show what might happen if nontrivial bankruptcy costs are introduced. As the proportion of debt in the firm's capital structure is increased, the probability of bankruptcy also increases. Consequently, the rate of return required by bondholders (the solid line, R_{dj}, in Fig. 13.1(a)) increases with leverage. This, in turn, results in a "U-shaped" weighted average cost of capital (solid line WACC') and an optimal capital structure, $[B/(B + S)]^*$. The optimal ratio of debt to equity is determined by taking on increasing amounts of debt until the marginal gain from leverage is equal to the marginal expected loss from bankruptcy costs. The optimal capital structure minimizes the weighted average cost of capital and maximizes the value of the firm.

An important question for the existence of optimal capital structure brought about by the dead-weight losses of bankruptcy is: Exactly how large are bankruptcy costs? If they are trivial, some other explanation for optimal capital structure is needed. Warner [1977a] collects data for 11 railroad bankruptcies which occurred between 1933 and 1955. He measures only direct costs, such as lawyers' and accountants' fees, other professional fees, and the value of managerial time spent in administering the bankruptcy. He does not estimate indirect costs to creditors, such as the opportunity cost of funds tied up during bankruptcy proceedings and losses in asset value due to forced capital structure changes, or indirect costs to shareholders, such as lost profits created by decreased sales in anticipation of bankruptcy or from disruptions in production during reorganization.[1] The evidence indicates that direct costs are trivial, averaging about 1% of the market value of the firm prior to bankruptcy. Furthermore, direct costs as a percent of value seem to decrease as a function of the size of the bankrupt firm. This would suggest that the direct costs of bankruptcy

---

[1] Some of the agency costs which are discussed in Section B.3 are closely related to bankruptcy and might also be considered indirect costs. For example, see Titman [1981].

are less important for the capital-structure decisions of large firms than of small firms. Although Warner's evidence is inconclusive because indirect costs are not measured, it does suggest that direct bankruptcy costs may not be sufficiently large to be important determinants of optimal leverage.

In a second paper, Warner [1977b] examines the effect of bankruptcy on the market returns of 73 defaulted bonds of 20 separate railroads, each of which was in bankruptcy at some time during the period from 1930 through 1955. None of the railroads was actually liquidated, although there were mergers, spinoffs, and abandonments of operations. The following effects were observed:

- The systematic risk of bonds increased prior to filing for bankruptcy. A reasonable explanation is that as the market value of equity, relative to bonds, falls prior to bankruptcy, the bondholders' claim becomes more like that of the shareholders of an all-equity firm, and hence their risk rises.

- After adjusting for risk, the performance of the bonds in the month of the bankruptcy petition was significantly negative.

- Investors who purchased a portfolio of bonds on the date of the bankruptcy petition appeared to earn significant risk-adjusted abnormal returns in the post-bankruptcy period. One possible explanation is that the courts approved capital structure simplifications which had been unanticipated and which benefited bondholders.

It is hard to argue that conclusions based on a study of the railroad industry can be generalized because federal regulations encourage the continued operation of railroad service even though the firm is in bankruptcy. Nevertheless, if one views the bondholders' position as being the residual claim at the time of bankruptcy, the significant negative return to bondholders on the date of the bankruptcy petition is evidence of nontrivial bankruptcy costs. Because the empirical evidence is mixed and somewhat limited, more research is necessary before the real importance of bankruptcy costs is fully understood.

2. Option Pricing Implications for Capital Structure

Black and Scholes [1973] suggest that the equity in a levered firm can be thought of as a call option. When shareholders issue bonds, it is equivalent to selling the assets of the firm (but not control over those assets) to the bondholders in return for cash (the proceeds of the bond issues) and a call option.

In order to reduce the analogy to its simplest form, assume that (1) the firm issues pure discount bonds[2] which prohibit any capital disbursements (such as interest payments) until after the bonds mature T time periods hence, (2) there are no transaction costs or taxes so that the value of the firm is unaffected by its capital structure

---

[2] All accumulated interest on pure discount bonds is paid at maturity, hence $B(T)$, the current market value of debt with maturity T, must be less than its face value, D, assuming a positive risk-free rate of discount.

(in other words, Modigliani-Miller Proposition I is assumed to be valid), (3) there is a known nonstochastic risk-free rate of interest, and (4) there are homogeneous expectations about the stochastic process which describes the value of the firm's assets. Given these assumptions, we can imagine a simple firm which issues only one class of bonds secured by the assets of the firm. From the shareholders' point of view, cash is received from the sale of the bonds. The value of the shareholders' position is equal to the discounted value of the bonds and a call option. If, on the maturity date, the value of the firm, V, exceeds the face value of the bonds, D, the shareholders will exercise their call option by paying off the bonds and keeping the excess. On the other hand, if the value of the firm is less than the face value of the bonds, the shareholders will default on the debt by deciding not to exercise their option. Therefore, at maturity, the shareholders' wealth, S, is

$$S = \text{MAX}[0, V - D].$$

This is a European call option. Bondholders' wealth is

$$B = \text{MIN}[V, D],$$

and this is the equivalent of writing a call option.

The option pricing model offers a great deal of insight into the way that capital structure changes may affect shareholders and bondholders. Although the arguments which follow are made intuitively, the reader who is interested in a mathematical presentation is referred to Galai and Masulis [1976].

In each of the following cases we rely on the Modigliani-Miller result that in the absence of transaction costs or taxes, the value of the firm remains constant regardless of the financial decisions made by management. Furthermore, we assume that any changes which affect the systematic risk of various securities, or their expected rate of return, are *unanticipated* changes. To the extent that changes in the value of securities are unanticipated, it is possible that there may be a redistribution of wealth from one class of security holders to another.

We also assume that two-fund separation does not apply. Two-fund separation implies, among other things, that all individuals hold the same portfolio of risky assets, namely, the market portfolio. For individuals holding both the equity and risky debt of a firm, any offsetting change in the market value of the debt and equity claims against the firm will not change their wealth position. Therefore, they would be indifferent to the redistribution effects which we are about to discuss. It is necessary, then, to rule out two-fund separation and discuss the wealth of shareholders and bondholders as if they were separate and distinct. If shareholders are not constrained by the indenture provisions of debt from issuing new debt with an equal claim on the assets of the firm, then current bondholders will experience a loss of wealth when new debt is issued. It is possible to increase the book value debt-to-equity ratio by issuing new debt and using the proceeds to repurchase equity. In this way the assets of the firm remain unchanged. If the new debt has equal claim on those assets, then the current bondholders end up with only a partial claim to the assets of the firm, whereas before the new debt was issued, they had complete claim on the assets. Clearly, this approach puts current bondholders in a riskier position, and they are unable to charge more for the extra risk because the discounted value of their bonds has already been paid (in other words, they cannot raise their coupon payments once the bonds have been issued). Consequently, the market value of their bonds will fall. At the same time, the value of the firm remains unchanged, and new bondholders pay a fair market price for their position. Therefore the value which is expropriated from current bondholders must accrue to shareholders, who are the residual claimants of the firm. Their wealth increases.

The theory of option pricing argues that in a world with no transaction costs or taxes the wealth of shareholders is increased by greater financial leverage. In Chapter 12, the Modigliani-Miller propositions argue that under the same set of assumptions the value of shareholders' wealth is unaffected by changes in capital structure. How can the seemingly contradictory conclusions of the two theories be explained? The crucial difference is that option pricing assumes that *unanticipated* redistributions of wealth are possible. To the extent that bondholders can appropriately assess the probability of shareholders' ability to expropriate their wealth, they can charge a rate of return which adequately compensates them for their risk or they can carefully write bond indenture provisions which restrict the actions of shareholders. Either way they can protect themselves against anticipated redistribution effects. Whether or not such protection is actually possible is an empirical question. Some of the empirical evidence will be discussed later on in this chapter.

3. The Effect of Agency Costs on Capital Structure

We saw, in Section B.1., that if there is a gain from leverage because of the tax deductibility of interest expenses, and if bankruptcy costs are nontrivial, then it is possible to construct a theory of optimal capital structure. One troublesome aspect of this approach is that even before income taxes existed in the United States, firms used debt in their capital structure. Furthermore, the same cross-sectional regularities in financial leverage which exist today can also be observed in data prior to the introduction of corporate taxes. This suggests that optimal leverage (if it exists) may be explained by causes other than debt tax shields and bankruptcy costs.

Jensen and Meckling [1976] use agency costs to argue that the probability distribution of cash flows provided by the firm is not independent of its ownership structure and that this fact may be used to explain optimal leverage. First, there is an incentive problem associated with the issuance of new debt. Consider an example where unbeknownst to lenders, the firm has two different investment projects (see Table 13.1), both having the same systematic risk but different variances. The first has a 50/50

Table 13.1 Two Investment Projects

Probability	Project 1	Project 2
.5	$ 9,000	$ 2,000
.5	11,000	18,000

chance of yielding an end-of-period cash flow of $9000 or $11,000. The second has a 50/50 chance of yielding $2000 or $18,000. Both cost $8000 and both have the same expected return. Suppose the firm shows only project 1 to lenders and asks to borrow $7000. From the lenders' point of view this request seems reasonable because project 1 will always earn enough to pay off the loan. Of course, if creditors lend $7000 and if the owners of the firm have the ability to switch to project 2, they will do so. (Why?) The result is the transfer of wealth from bondholders to shareholders. Hence bondholders may insist on various types of protective covenants and monitoring devices in order to protect their wealth from raids made on it by shareholders. However, the costs of writing and enforcing such covenants may well be nontrivial. Furthermore, these costs may increase with the percent of financing supplied by bondholders.

On the other hand, there are agency costs associated with external equity. Suppose we begin with a firm owned exclusively by a single individual, the owner-manager. The O-M will obviously take every action possible to increase his or her own wealth. However, if the O-M sells a portion of the ownership rights by selling external equity to new shareholders, there will arise conflicts in interest. Now the O-M is co-owner with the new shareholders. If the O-M can maximize his or her wealth at the expense of the new shareholders (e.g., by purchasing an executive jet and taking long vacations), then he or she will do so. Co-ownership of equity implies agency problems. The new shareholders will have to incur monitoring costs of one form or another in order to ensure that the original owner-manager acts in their interest. The agency costs of external equity may be reduced if the management and shareholders agree to hire an independent auditor. For an interesting exposition of this idea the reader is referred to an article by Watts and Zimmerman [1979].

Jensen and Meckling suggest that, given increasing agency costs with higher proportions of equity on the one hand and higher proportions of debt on the other, there is an optimum combination of outside debt and equity which will be chosen because it minimizes total agency costs. In this way it is possible to argue for the existence of an optimum capital structure even in a world without taxes or bankruptcy costs.

The discussion of agency costs need not be limited to costs associated with providing debt and equity capital. For example, Titman [1981] suggests that agency costs are important for contracts (whether implied or explicit) between the firm and its customers or between the firm and its employees. Consider the relationship between a firm and its customers. If the firm's product is durable and requires future services such as parts and repair, the customer is paying not only for ownership of the product but also for an expected future stream of services. If the firm goes bankrupt, its customers lose their anticipated services without any hope of being compensated. Consequently, they must assess the probability of bankruptcy and weigh it in their decision to purchase durable goods. Firms which produce durable goods will have lower demand for their products if they increase their probability of bankruptcy by carrying more debt. This is an example of an indirect cost of bankruptcy. *Ceteris paribus,* we would expect durable goods producers to carry less debt.[3] Agency costs

---

[3] An exception might be regulated firms. They can carry more debt because regulatory commissions are expected to "guarantee" a reasonable rate of return. Consequently, bankruptcy is very unlikely.

in labor contracts are also important. If a firm's labor force has acquired specialized skills which cannot easily be transferred to alternate employment, then laborers bear nontrivial costs if a firm goes bankrupt. They have to search for new jobs and learn new skills. There is no hope that the bankrupt firm will compensate them for their loss. Consequently, if labor markets are competitive, then laborers will charge lower wages to work for a firm which has a lower probability of bankruptcy. Thus we should expect to find firms which use a larger percentage of job-specific human capital will also tend to carry less debt, *ceteris paribus*.

Scott [1976] shows that the optimal leverage may be related to the collateral value of the tangible assets held by the firm. If a firm goes bankrupt, the losses of bondholders are limited by the salvage value of the property held in the firm. If the corporate tax rate is zero, the optimal amount of debt in the capital structure is the discounted value of the liquidation price of the firm's assets in bankruptcy. This approach fits in with that of Jensen and Meckling if the bondholders simply require that the loan be tied to the salvage value of specific assets. Such a scheme considerably reduces monitoring costs.

4. Bond Indenture Provisions and Bond Rating Agencies

In order to protect themselves from a wide variety of actions, it is necessary for bondholders to require protective covenants in their lending agreements with shareholders. Although no set of prearranged restrictions can cover every contingency, it is interesting to study the major types of covenants.

The riskiness of bonds, and therefore their required yield, is substantively affected by the bond covenants that are written into the bond contract. A good description of the multitude of specific provisions in debt contracts can be found in the American Bar Association compendium called *Commentaries on Model Debenture Indenture Provisions* [1971]. Bond covenants can be divided into four broad categories: (1) those restricting the issuance of new debt; (2) those with restrictions on dividend payments; (3) those with restrictions on merger activity; and (4) those with restrictions on the disposition of the firm's assets. Smith and Warner [1979] examined a random sample of 87 public issues of debt registered with the Securities and Exchange Commission between January 1974 and December 1975. They observed that fully 90.8% of the bonds restrict the issuance of additional debt, 23% restrict dividend payments, 39.1% restrict merger activity, and 35.6% constrain the firm's disposition of assets.

Bond covenants that restrict subsequent financing are by far the most common type. The covenant provisions are usually stated in terms of accounting numbers and consequently are easy to monitor. The issuance of debt may carry restrictions that require all new debt to be subordinate or prohibit the creation of new debt with a higher priority unless existing bonds are upgraded to have an equal priority. All these restrictions are designed to prevent the firm from increasing the riskiness of outstanding debt by issuing new debt with a superior or equal claim on the firm's assets. Alternate restrictions may prohibit the issuance of new debt unless the firm maintains minimum prescribed ratios between net tangible assets and funded (long-term) debt, capitalization and funded debt, tangible net worth and funded debt, income and interest charges, or current assets and current liabilities (working capital tests). There may also be "clean-up" provisions that require the company to be debt-free for limited periods.

If there is any advantage to the firm that holds debt in its capital structure, it is that bondholders can benefit by allowing new debt, but only under the condition that acquiring this obligation does not increase the riskiness of their position. Hence an outright prohibition of new debt under any condition is rare.

Other techniques that are used to protect bondholders against subsequent financing include restrictions on rentals, leases, and sale-leaseback agreements; sinking fund requirements (which roughly match the depreciation of the firm's tangible assets); required purchase of insurance; required financial reports and specification of accounting techniques; and required certifications of compliance by the officers of the firm.

Bond covenants that restrict dividend payments are necessary if for no other reason than to prohibit the extreme case of shareholders voting to pay themselves a liquidating dividend that would leave the bondholders holding an empty corporate shell. Kalay [1979] reported that in a random sample of 150 firms, every firm had a dividend restriction in at least one of its debt instruments. Restrictions on dividend policy are relatively easy to monitor, and they protect debtholders against the unwarranted payout of the assets that serve as collateral. Appropriately, most indentures refer not only to cash dividends, but to all distributions in respect to capital stock, whether they be dividends, redemptions, purchases, retirements, partial liquidations, or capital reductions, and whether in cash, in kind, or in the form of debt obligations to the company. Without such general provisions the firm could, for example, use cash to repurchase its own shares. From the bondholders' point of view, the effect would be the same as payment of cash dividends.[4] No matter what the procedure is called, once cash is paid out to shareholders, it is no longer available for collateral in the event of reorganization or bankruptcy.

Most restrictions on the payout of the firm's assets require that dividends increase only if the firm's earnings are positive, if the firm issues new equity capital, or if dividends paid out since the bonds were issued have been kept below a predefined minimum level. Mathematically, the "inventory" of funds allowable for dividend payment Div_T^* in quarter T, can be expressed as

$$\text{Div}_T^* = K \sum_{t=0}^{T} \text{NI}_t + \sum_{t=0}^{T} S_t + F - \sum_{t=0}^{T-1} \text{Div}_t,$$

where

NI_t = net earnings in quarter t,

K = predetermined constant, $0 \leq K \leq 1$,

S_t = net proceeds from issue of new equity,

F = number fixed over life of bonds, known as the "dip,"

Div_t = dividends paid out in quarter t.

---

[4] See Chapter 15 for empirical evidence regarding the effect of share repurchases on the wealth of bondholders and shareholders.

Thus the dividend covenant does not restrict dividends per se; rather, it restricts the financing of the payment of dividends with new debt or by sale of the firm's existing assets. This arrangement is in the interest of stockholders because it does not restrict the payment of earned income. It is also in the interest of bondholders because it prevents any dilution of their claim on the firm's assets.

Bond covenants that restrict merger activity prohibit many mergers. More often, though, they will allow mergers, provided certain conditions are met. The effect of a merger on bondholders can be beneficial if the cash flows of the merged firms are not perfectly correlated. Offsetting cash flow patterns can reduce the risk of default, thereby bettering the positions of the bondholders of both firms. Merger can also be detrimental to bondholders. For example, if firm A has much more debt in its capital structure than firm B, the bondholders of B will suffer increased risk after the merger.[5] Or if the maturity of debt in firm A is shorter than for firm B, the bondholders of B will (for all practical purposes) become subordinate to those of firm A after the merger.

To protect against the undesirable effects that can result from a merger, it is possible to require bond covenants that allow merger only if the net tangible assets of the firm, calculated on a postmerger basis, meet a certain dollar minimum or are at least a certain fraction of long-term debt. The merger can also be made contingent on the absence of default of any indenture provision after the transaction is completed.

Bond covenants that restrict production or investment policies are numerous. They are frequently difficult to enforce, however, given the impossibility of effectively monitoring the investment decisions that the managers of the firm decide not to undertake. Myers [1977] suggests that a substantial portion of the value of a firm is composed of intangible assets in the form of future investment opportunities. A firm with outstanding debt may have the incentive to reject projects that have a positive net present value if the benefit from accepting the project accrues to the bondholders without also increasing shareholders' wealth.

Direct restrictions on investment-disinvestment policy take the following forms: (1) restrictions on common stock investments, loans, extensions of credit, and advances that cause the firm to become a claimholder in another business enterprise, (2) restrictions on the disposition of assets, and (3) covenants requiring the maintenance of assets. Secured debt is an indirect restriction on investment policy. Assets that provide surety cannot be disposed of under the provisions of the indenture agreement. Collateralization also reduces foreclosure expenses because the lender already has established title via the bond covenant.

Even though covenants are designed to protect bondholders from various actions which can diminish the surety of their position, no set of covenants can eliminate all risk. Consequently there is considerable interest in accurate information about changes in the riskiness of corporate debt on a firm-by-firm basis.

The usual method for determining the default risk of corporate long-term debt is to refer to the bond ratings supplied by various agencies. Major bond rating agencies are Moody's Investors Service, Inc., Standard & Poor's Corp., and Fitch Investor

---

[5] For a more complete exposition, see Shastri [1981].

Service. Moody's bond rating has seven classifications, ranging from Aaa, which is the highest quality bond, down to Caa, the lowest quality. Weinstein [1977] collected data on 179 new bond issues between 1962 and 1964. Table 13.2 shows the distribution by risk class. About 40% of the new bonds qualified for the two highest quality ratings. Figure 13.2 shows the yields on bonds of different risk. Just as expected, the high-quality, low-risk bonds have lower yields than do the low-quality, high-risk bonds. A common-sense way of estimating the marginal cost of new debt for a firm (assuming that the new debt will not change the firm's bond rating) is to compute the yield to maturity on other bonds with maturities and bond ratings similar to the new issue.

Of the roughly 2000 major corporations that are evaluated by the agencies, approximately 500 are rerated quarterly because they issue commercial paper, another 500 are rerated annually (most of the utilities), and the remaining 1000 have no established review date but are usually reviewed annually.

From an investor's point of view, one might ask the following question: Do the agencies determine the prices and interest rates paid for bonds or do investors in the capital markets? The evidence collected by Wakeman [1978] and Weinstein [1978] shows that changes in bond ratings are not treated as new information by capital markets. In fact, changes in ratings usually occur several months after the capital markets have already reacted to the fundamental change in the bond's quality. Changes in agency ratings do not cause changes in required yields to maturity. It is the other way around. However, this does not imply that bond ratings are without value. On average, the ratings provide unbiased estimates of bond risk and are therefore a useful source of information.

5. Signaling Hypotheses

If we assume that financial markets are not fully aggregating in the sense that market prices do not reflect all information, especially that not publicly available, then it is possible that managers may elect to use financial policy decisions to convey information to the market. Changes in capital structure are an obvious candidate for a signaling device, and as we shall see in Chapter 15, so is dividend policy.

Table 13.2 Sample of New Issues by Moody's Rating of Issue

Rating	Industrials	% of Total	Utilities	% of Total
Aaa	29	26.1	14	20.6
Aa	18	16.2	14	20.6
A	38	34.3	18	26.5
Baa	20	18.0	20	29.4
Ba	1	0.9	2	2.9
B	5	4.5	0	0
	111	100.0	68	100.0

Adapted from Weinstein, Mark, "The Effect of a Rating Change Announcement on Bond Price," *Journal of Financial Economics,* December 1977.

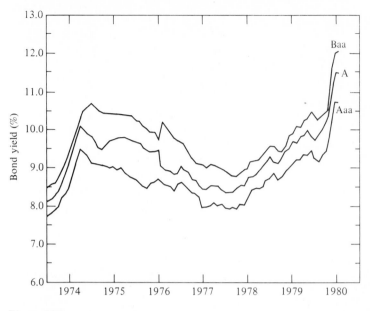

Figure 13.2
Comparison of bond yields for bonds of different risks. (From the *Federal Reserve Bulletin,* Board of Governors of the Federal Reserve System, various issues.)

The first application of signaling to finance theory has been put forth by Ross [1977]. He suggests that implicit in the Miller-Modigliani dividend irrelevancy proposition is the assumption that the market *knows* the (random) return stream of the firm and values this stream to set the value of the firm. What is valued in the marketplace, however, is the *perceived* stream of returns for the firm. Putting the issue this way raises the possibility that changes in the capital structure (or dividend payout) may alter the market's perception. In the terminology of Modigliani and Miller, by changing its financial structure (or dividend payout) the firm alters its perceived risk class, even though the actual risk class remains unchanged.

Managers, as insiders who have monopolistic access to information about the firm's expected cash flows, will choose to establish unambiguous signals about the firm's future if they have the proper incentive to do so. In order to show how this incentive-signaling process works, let us assume that managers are prohibited (perhaps by SEC regulations) from trading in the securities of their own firm. This keeps them from profiting by issuing false signals, such as announcing bad news and selling short even though they know the firm will do well.

In a simple one-period model the manager's compensation, M, paid at the end of the period may be expressed as

$$M = (1 + r)\gamma_0 V_0 + \gamma_1 \begin{cases} V_1 & \text{if} \quad V_1 \geq D, \\ V_1 - L & \text{if} \quad V_1 < D, \end{cases} \qquad (13.1)$$

where

$\gamma_0, \gamma_1 =$ positive weights,

$r =$ the one-period interest rate,

$V_0, V_1 =$ the current and future value of the firm,

$D =$ the face value of debt,

$L =$ a penalty paid if bankruptcy occurs, i.e., if $V_1 < D$.

This result can be used to establish a signaling equilibrium if we further assume that investors use D, the face value of debt, to tell them whether a firm is successful (type A) or unsuccessful (type B). Assume that D^* is the maximum amount of debt that an unsuccessful firm can carry without going bankrupt. If $D > D^*$, the market perceives the firm to be successful, and vice versa. For the signaling equilibrium to be established, (1) the signals must be unambiguous (that is, when investors observe $D > D^*$, the firm is always type A), and (2) managers must have incentive to always give the appropriate signal.

If the end-of-period value of a successful type-A firm is V_{1a} and is always greater than the value of an unsuccessful type-B firm, V_{1b}, then the compensation of the management of a type-A firm is

$$M_a = \begin{cases} \gamma_0(1+r)\dfrac{V_{1a}}{1+r} + \gamma_1 V_{1a} & \text{if} \quad D^* < D \le V_{1a} \qquad \text{(tell the truth)}, \\[2ex] \gamma_0(1+r)\dfrac{V_{1b}}{1+r} + \gamma_1 V_{1a} & \text{if} \quad D < D^* \qquad\qquad \text{(lie)}. \end{cases} \tag{13.2}$$

Clearly management of a type-A firm has incentive to establish a level of debt greater than D^* in order to earn maximum compensation. Therefore it will give the correct signal. But what about the management of a type-B firm? Doesn't it have incentive to lie by falsely signaling that its firm is type A? The answer is found by looking at the management-incentive scheme.

$$M_b = \begin{cases} \gamma_0(1+r)\dfrac{V_{1a}}{1+r} + \gamma_1(V_{1b} - L) & \text{if} \quad D^* \le D < V_{1a} \qquad \text{(lie)}, \\[2ex] \gamma_0(1+r)\dfrac{V_{1b}}{1+r} + \gamma_1 V_{1b} & \text{if} \quad D < D^* \qquad\qquad \text{(tell the truth)}. \end{cases} \tag{13.3}$$

In order for management of a type-B firm to have incentive to signal that the firm will be unsuccessful, the payoff from telling the truth must be greater than that produced by telling lies. Mathematically,

$$\gamma_0 V_{1a} + \gamma_1(V_{1b} - L) < \gamma_0 V_{1b} + \gamma_1 V_{1b},$$

which can be rewritten as

$$\gamma_0(V_{1a} - V_{1b}) < \gamma_1 L. \tag{13.4}$$

This condition says that management will give the correct signal if the marginal gain from a false signal, $V_{1a} - V_{1b}$, weighted by management's share, γ_0, is less than the bankruptcy costs incurred by management, L, weighted by its share, γ_1.

The incentive-signaling approach suggests that management might choose real financial variables such as financial leverage or dividend policy as the means of sending unambiguous signals to the public about the future performance of the firm. These signals cannot be mimicked by unsuccessful firms because such firms do not have sufficient cash flow to back them up and because managers have incentives to tell the truth.

The concept is easily applied to dividend policy as well as to financial structure. A firm which increases dividend payout is signaling that it has expected future cash flows which are sufficiently large to meet debt payments and dividend payments without increasing the probability of bankruptcy. Therefore we may expect to find empirical evidence that the value of the firm increases, because dividends are taken as signals that the firm is expected to have permanently higher future cash flows. Chapter 15 reviews the empirical evidence relevant to dividend policy.

Ross' paper suggests that greater financial leverage can be used by managers to signal an optimistic future for the firm. Another signaling paper, by Leland and Pyle [1977], focuses on owners instead of managers. They assume that entrepreneurs have better information about the expected value of their venture projects than do outsiders. The inside information held by an entrepreneur can be transferred to suppliers of capital because it is in the owner's interest to invest a greater fraction of his or her wealth in successful projects. Thus the owner's willingness to invest in his or her own projects can serve as a signal of project quality, and the value of the firm increases with the percent of the equity held by the entrepreneur relative to what he or she otherwise would have held given a lower quality project. An empirical implication of this signaling argument is that if the original founders of a company going public decide to keep a large fraction of the stock, then these firms should experience greater price-earnings multiples. A second implication is that if the firm's value is positively related to the fraction of the owner's wealth held as equity in the firm, then the firm will have greater debt capacity and will use greater amounts of debt. Although debt is not a signal in this model, its use will be positively correlated with the firm's value.

C. EMPIRICAL EVIDENCE ON OPTIMAL CAPITAL STRUCTURE

For the most part, the empirical literature on capital structure and the cost of capital has focused on the theory provided by Modigliani and Miller [1958, 1963]. The issue is whether or not the value of the firm can be changed by changing its capital structure. This may seem to be a relatively straightforward question, but the empirical testing is difficult and complex. For example, the Modigliani-Miller model assumes perpetual expected streams of cash flow which are not growing. How shall growth be included in the analysis? Even worse, the correct variable is anticipated *future* growth, which is impossible to measure directly. A second difficulty is that flotation costs for external debt and equity are higher for smaller firms. Therefore, size may be related to economies of scale in the cost of capital. This possibility must be considered. Third, the theory assumes that all companies have the same business risk.

But even for an industry as homogeneous as electric utilities, this may not be true (see Boness and Frankfurter [1977]). Also, firms do not choose a capital structure in isolation. Usually new financing simultaneously implies new investment with changes in the asset structure of the firm and (possibly) risk. Finally, much of the empirical work has used cross-section regressions which are likely to have highly correlated residuals across firms. This tends to exaggerate the significance of the regression coefficients, thereby weakening any conclusions which might be drawn. All of these problems make empirical tests troublesome to conduct and difficult to interpret.

There have been many empirical studies of the cost of capital. In order to keep our summary concise, we shall report on only a few. The empirical questions are whether the weighted average cost of capital: (1) does not change with changes in financial leverage, as would be predicted by the earliest Modigliani-Miller theory (Eq. 12.12 with zero corporate tax rate) or by the most recent Miller paper (Eq. 12.24 with condition 12.25) in a world with both corporate and personal taxes; (2) declines with increasing leverage, as would be predicted by the Modigliani-Miller theory where corporate taxes provide a gain to leverage (Eq. 12.12 with $\tau_c > 0$); or (3) is a "U-shaped" function of leverage which would indicate an optimal capital structure.

Modigliani and Miller [1958] use cross-section regression equations on data taken from 43 electric utility companies during 1947–1948 and 42 oil companies during 1953. They estimate the weighted average cost of capital as net operating cash flows after taxes divided by the market value of the firm.[6] When regressed against financial leverage (measured as the ratio of the market value of debt to the market value of the firm), the results were:[7]

$$\text{Electric utilities:} \quad \text{WACC} = 5.3 + .006d, \quad r = .12,$$
$$(\pm .008)$$

$$\text{Oil companies:} \quad \text{WACC} = 8.5 + .006d, \quad r = .04,$$
$$(\pm .024)$$

where

$$\text{WACC} = \frac{\text{NOI}(1 - \tau_c)}{V^L} = \frac{\text{NI} + k_d D}{V^L} = \text{weighted average cost of capital,}$$

$$r = \text{the correlation coefficient,}$$

$$d = \frac{B}{B + S} = \text{financial leverage.}$$

These results suggest that the cost of capital is not affected by capital structure because the t-statistics (the ratio of the slope coefficients to the standard errors, given in

---

[6] Net operating cash flows after taxes were actually estimated as net income after taxes plus interest payments on debt. This assumes that there is no growth in earnings and that replacement investment equals depreciation expense.

[7] Standard errors are given in parentheses.

parentheses) are too small to allow rejection of the null hypothesis that the weighted average cost of capital is unrelated to capital structure.

Weston [1963] criticizes the Modigliani-Miller results on two counts: First, the oil industry is not even approximately homogeneous in business risk; second, the valuation model from which the cost of capital is derived assumes that cash flows are perpetuities which do not grow. Mathematically,

$$V^L = \frac{E(\text{NOI})(1 - \tau_c)}{\text{WACC}}. \tag{13.5}$$

However, the stream of cash flows usually is expected to grow over time. Proper estimates of the cost of capital must attempt to measure anticipated future earnings, not earnings today. When growth is added to the cross-section regression the results are (for electric utilities):[8]

$$\text{WACC} = 5.91 \underset{(\pm .0079)}{- .0265d} \underset{(\pm .0001)}{+ .00A} \underset{(\pm .0024)}{- .0822E,} \qquad r = .5268,$$

where

A = total book value of assets (a proxy for firm size),

E = compound growth in earnings per share 1949–1959.

Weston's results are consistent with the Modigliani-Miller view of the cost of capital in a world where the tax shield provided by the deductibility of interest expenses causes the weighted average cost of capital to decline with leverage.

Miller and Modigliani [1966] also found results which appear to be consistent with a gain from leverage. The valuation model which they use (which is discussed in Chapter 14) assumes, among other things, that the firm grows more rapidly than the economy for a finite period of time, T, and that there are corporate taxes but no personal taxes. The valuation model is given below:

$$V^L = \frac{[E(\tilde{\text{NOI}}_1)](1 - \tau_c)}{\rho} + \tau_c B$$
$$+ K[E(\tilde{\text{NOI}})](1 - \tau_c)\left[\frac{r - \text{WACC}}{\text{WACC}(1 + \text{WACC})}\right] T, \tag{13.6}$$

where

K = the percent of earnings invested in new assets, $K \lesssim 1$,

r = the tax-adjusted rate of return on new assets, $r > \text{WACC}$,

T = the number of years where $r > \text{WACC}$.

The first term in (13.6) can be thought of as the capitalized value of the anticipated *level* of cash flows from operations. The second term is the gain from leverage. If

---

[8] Weston's sample was the same sample of 43 electric utilities that Modigliani and Miller used, but the cross-section was estimated in 1959 instead of 1947–1948. Standard errors are in parentheses.

it is greater than zero, the weighted average cost of capital falls with increasing leverage. The third term is a growth term. It is far from simple, and is represented by the product of three elements: the profitability of future growth opportunities (measured by the difference between r and WACC); the size of these opportunities $(K[E(\text{NOI})(1 - \tau_c)])$; and the length of duration of these opportunities, T.

Cross-section multiple regressions based on the above model were run on a sample of 63 electric utility firms in 1954, 1956, and 1957. Table 13.3 summarizes the contribution of the three above-mentioned variables as well as firm size to the value of the firm. For our purposes, the important result is that the empirical evidence indicates that the tax subsidy from debt does contribute a significant amount to the value of the firm. This is consistent with the notion that the WACC falls as leverage increases.

As was mentioned earlier, all the aforementioned empirical tests suffer from the impossibility of measuring future earnings and the fact that changes in the ratio of debt to assets usually are accompanied by changes in the asset structure of the firm, which in turn may imply changes in risk. None of the above papers attempts to adjust for risk directly. Instead, they rely on assumptions about the homogeneity of business risk across different firms within the electric utility industry. In a study which avoids most of these difficulties, Masulis [1980] uses a phenomenon known as corporate exchange offers to study the effects of capital-structure changes on security prices. This is a situation where one class of securities is exchanged in return for another. The most important feature is that with exchange offers there is no simultaneous change in the asset structure of the firm. Therefore, they represent a relatively pure type of financial event which allows the researcher to isolate the effects of changes in capital structure on value.

If protective covenants written into bond indenture provisions are incomplete because the cost of monitoring and enforcing them exceeds their likely benefit, then it may be possible for management to occasionally alter the firm's capital structure in such a way that a redistribution of wealth among the various classes of security holders may result. If, for example, debt is issued to retire equity, existing bondholders

Table 13.3   Sources Contributing to the Value of the Firm

	Absolute Contribution			Percentage Contribution		
	1957	1956	1954	1957	1956	1954
1. Capitalized earnings on assets currently held	.758	.808	.914	68.1	72.0	75.9
2. Tax subsidy on debt	.262	.254	.258	23.5	22.6	23.7
3. Growth potential	.112	.072	.028	10.0	6.4	2.3
4. Size of firm	−.019	−.008	−.021	−1.7	−.7	−1.7
$\dfrac{\text{Average market value}}{\text{book value}}$	1.113	1.123	1.204	100.0	100.0	100.0

Miller, M., and F. Modigliani, "Some Estimates of the Cost of Capital to the Electric Utility Industry, 1954–1957," *American Economic Review,* June 1966, 373. Reprinted by permission of the authors.

may suffer a wealth loss if the claim of the new debt on the assets of the firm is not subordinated. The effect is to make existing debt riskier without any compensation. Consequently, the market value of the debt claim will fall. Simultaneously, shareholders may benefit in two ways: (1) directly from the redistribution effect, and (2) from any tax shield provided by the new debt. It is also possible that an exchange offer which increases leverage is interpreted by the market as unanticipated favorable information about the firm's future prospects (i.e., a signal).

For a sample containing 163 exchanges between equity and debt during the period of 1962 through 1976, after removing general market movements and adjusting for risk, Masulis found abnormal two-day rates of return of 6.9% on common stock for both the day of the announcement of an exchange offering and the day following the announcement.[9] This was over 15 standard deviations from the mean and therefore statistically significant. For a subsample, where debt had incomplete protective covenants (27 events), the two-day abnormal loss to existing bondholders was .77%, which was over three standard deviations from the mean (again significant). These results are consistent with (1) a tax benefit from leverage, (2) a redistribution of wealth from debtholders to equityholders, and (3) an information effect.

In a cross-sectional study of 133 exchange offers made between 1963 and 1978 Masulis [1982] studies the change in the value of equity in the following regression equation:

$$\frac{\Delta S}{S} = R_j + d_1 \Delta B_1 + d_2 \Delta B_2 - e_1 B_1^* - e_2 B_2^* - e_3 B_3^* - e_4 B_4^* - e_p P^* + \epsilon. \quad (13.9)$$

The change in the value of equity is $\Delta S/S$. It is hypothesized to be a function of three major classes of variables. First, it will depend on the normal (nonannouncement) rate of return on the firm's equity, R_j. Second, it will depend on debt-level change variables ($d_1 \Delta B_1$ for debt decreases and $d_2 \Delta B_2$ for debt increases). The coefficients of the debt-level change variables, d_1 and d_2, capture the sum of three effects: (1) a debt tax shield effect, (2) an expected leverage cost effect predicted to be a negative value, and (3) an information effect concerning the changes in a firm's earnings prospects predicted to be positively related to changes in the firm's debt tax shield. The sum of these three effects is expected to be positive for leverage increases (d_1) and negative for leverage decreases (d_2). The third category of effects is wealth transfer effects, which will depend on the market values of senior security classes relative to common stock outstanding and the percent changes in leverage. The effects on debt outstanding are all expected to be negatively related to the equity return and are divided into (1) short-term debt, $e_1 B_1^*$, (2) nonconvertible protected debt, $e_2 B_2^*$, (3) nonconvertible unprotected debt, $e_3 B_3^*$, and (4) convertible debt, $e_4 B_4^*$. The preferred stock wealth transfer effect, $e_p P^*$, can be positive or negative because the sample contains both convertible preferred (which shouldn't be hurt because it can be ultimately exchanged for common) and nonconvertible preferred.

The actual cross-sectional regressions were able to explain around 55% of the

---

[9] For leverage-decreasing exchange offers, the rates of return were multiplied by minus one and added to the returns for leverage-increasing exchange offers.

variance in the announcement effects observed on changes in stock prices. The signs of the coefficients were as predicted, thereby supporting the following conclusions:

1. Changes in stock prices are positively related to leverage changes because of (1) a gain in value induced by tax shields on debt, and (2) a positive information effect from higher leverage.

2. Leverage increases induced wealth transfers across security classes with the greatest effect on unprotected nonconvertible debt.

An important part of the Modigliani-Miller theory is that the cost of equity capital increases with higher leverage. Hamada [1972] tests this proposition empirically by combining the Modigliani-Miller theory and the CAPM. He finds that on the average the systematic risk of the levered firm is greater than that for the unlevered firm:

$$\hat{\beta}^L = .91, \qquad \hat{\beta}^U = .70.$$

This, of course, is consistent with the increased risk associated with higher leverage. However, in order to construct the return on equity for an unlevered firm, Hamada had to assume that the Modigliani-Miller theory was correct. Suppose that it is not correct. Namely, what would happen if the return on equity (i.e., the cost of equity capital) did not increase with increasing leverage? We would expect that for a sample of firms with the same operating risk there would be no increase in systematic risk with higher financial leverage. Because it is almost impossible to find firms with identical operating risk, Hamada suggests that within an industry, if the β^U-values of individual firms are closer or less scattered than their β^L-values, then the Modigliani-Miller theory would be supported. Greater variability in the β^L-values implies that the cost of equity changes with financial leverage. In nine industries examined, β^L was greater than β^U in all cases, and the standard deviation of the β^L-values was greater than eight out of nine of the β^U-values. This may be taken as indirect evidence that the Modigliani-Miller proposition is valid.

D. REVIEW OF EMPIRICAL EVIDENCE ON CAPITAL STRUCTURE

Optimal capital structure, if it exists, will be explained by tradeoffs between the costs and benefits of utilizing debt versus equity in the firm's capital structure. The possible benefits of debt are (1) a tax shield provided by interest expenditures, (2) advantages of signaling, and (3) the capacity to collateralize loans. The costs of debt include (1) direct bankruptcy costs (e.g., payments to third parties such as law firms and the courts), (2) indirect costs such as the agency costs borne by specialized labor or customers who purchase goods requiring future services, and (3) agency costs such as writing and monitoring indenture provisions to avoid wealth transfers among classes of securityholders. Any or all of the variables mentioned above may be important.

The empirical evidence on capital structure and the cost of capital is inconclusive. Warner [1977a] argues that direct costs of bankruptcy are insignificant. However, his study is limited to the railroad industry. Other studies will surely expand in scope to examine other industries as well as indirect costs. Modigliani and Miller [1958], Weston [1963], Miller and Modigliani [1966], and Masulis [1980, 1982] all have looked at the relationship among the cost of capital, capital-structure changes, and the value of the firm's securities. Although the evidence partially supports the existence of a tax benefit from leverage, more work needs to be done. Hamada [1972] shows that the cost of equity increases with leverage, which is consistent with the Modigliani-Miller cost-of-capital propositions.

There are many other studies which are not reported here. Some of them find no leverage effect or even opposite effects. It is fair to say that the academic community is divided on the issue. A great deal of work needs to be done before a consensus about the effect of capital structure on the cost of capital will be reached.

E. COST OF CAPITAL: APPLICATIONS

Even when one is very familiar with the theoretical concept of the cost of capital, it is not a straightforward or easy task to apply the theory to practice. Too often one is confronted with questions not made explicit because theoretical expositions are deliberately oversimplified. For example, how do unusual liabilities such as accruals, preferred debt, convertibles, or accounts payable affect the cost of capital? How should the market value weights of various sources of capital be estimated? How can one tell whether or not the firm is at its long-run target capital structure?

This section further develops some of the cost-of-capital example calculations given in Chapter 12. First, however, a simple example shows how firms with high price-earnings ratios may choose to carry no debt—for the wrong reason. Second, a detailed cost of capital calculation is given for Bethlehem Steel. Third, the debt refunding decision is analyzed. And finally, the effect of flotation costs on the cost of capital is discussed.

1. The Wrong Reason for Carrying No Debt.
An Example

Companies with high price-earnings ratios can increase their earnings per share by issuing new equity and using the funds to buy back debt. Carried to the extreme, this process results in an optimal capital structure which contains zero debt. Much of the theory in Chapter 12 and the empirical evidence earlier in this chapter suggest that this idea is wrong. In fact, just the opposite is true. If there is a tax advantage to carrying debt, then shareholders' wealth will be increased if there is at least some debt. Nothing in the theory suggests that zero debt is optimal. Yet consider the following example, and see whether you can identify the error in its logic.

Betamax currently has a price-earnings ratio of 50. Before the change in capital structure it has 10 shares outstanding; therefore its earnings per share is $1.00, and the price per share is $50. If 10 new shares are issued at $50 each, $500 is collected and used to retire $500 of debt (which pays a coupon rate of 8%). After the capital-

Table 13.4   Higher Earnings per Share with Lower Leverage

Income statement	Before	After
Net operating income	100	100
Interest expense	− 80	− 40
Earnings before taxes	20	60
Taxes at 50%	− 10	− 30
Net income	10	30
Earnings per share	$1.00	$1.50

Balance Sheet

Before				After			
Assets		Liabilities		Assets		Liabilities	
Current	200	Debt	1,000	Current	200	Debt	500
Long-term	1,300	Equity	500	Long-term	1,300	Equity	1,000
	1,500		1,500		1,500		1,500

structure change, earnings per share have increased to $1.50 per share (since there are now 20 shares outstanding), and with a price-earnings ratio of 50, presumably the price per share will increase from $50 before the capital-structure change to $75 afterward. The pro-forma income statements and balance sheets are shown in Table 13.4.

The above example shows that if a firm with a high price-earnings ratio seeks to maximize earnings per share, it will carry little or no debt. The problem, of course, is that shareholders care about net cash flows (and the gain from leverage), not earnings per share. In the above example, the change in operating cash flows is zero. Before debt is retired, cash flow (neglecting depreciation, which is not given anyway) is equal to net income, $10, plus interest on debt after taxes $(1 − \tau_c)\Delta(rD)$, $40, or a total of $50.[10] After the swap of stock for bonds the cash flow is still $50. If there were no gain from leverage, the value of the firm would be unchanged. However, because there is a leverage effect in a world with corporate taxes, the value of the firm will actually fall, because leverage declines.

Using the Modigliani-Miller valuation model, Eq. (12.3), we can calculate the decrease in the value of the firm. The value of the firm before the change is

$$V^L = \frac{E(\text{NOI})(1 − \tau_c)}{\rho} + \left(\frac{rD}{k_d}\right)\tau_c, \qquad (12.3)$$

---

[10] This method for computing cash flows is covered in Chapter 2, footnote 15.

where

V^L = the market value of debt, B, plus the market value of equity, S,

$E(\text{NOI})$ = the expected operating income,

τ_c = the marginal corporate tax rate,

ρ = the cost of equity for an all-equity firm,

r = the coupon rate on bonds,

k_d = the market rate on new debt,

D = the book value of debt.

Using the numbers in the Betamax example, we have

$$500 + 1000 = \frac{100(1-.5)}{\rho} + \left(\frac{.08(1000)}{.08}\right).5.$$

Solving for ρ, the cost of equity for the unlevered firm, we have[11]

$$\rho = 5\%.$$

We can use the fact that ρ does not change when capital structure changes to determine the value of the firm after the repurchase of debt. Substituting the new, lower amount of debt into Eq. (12.3), we have

$$V^L = \frac{100(1-.5)}{.05} + \left(\frac{.08(500)}{.08}\right).5 = \$1250.$$

Therefore, the value of the firm has fallen from \$1500 to \$1250. Since $V^L = B + S$, the new value of equity is $\$1250 - 500 = \$750$.

We might also ask what the new price per share will be. It is common to assume that new shares can be issued at the preswap price of \$50. If this is the assumption, then 10 new shares are issued bringing the total number of shares outstanding to 20 and the implied price per share to \$37.50.

Another (better) approach requires that we compute the new equilibrium price per share in order to determine the number of shares which must be issued in order to supply the \$500 needed for the proposed exchange offer. We know that the value of equity *after* the exchange $S_0 + \Delta S$, is equal to the number of original shares, $n^0 = 10$, times the new price per share P^n plus the number of new shares n^n times the new price per share

$$S_0 + \Delta S = n^0 P^n + n^n P^n = \$750.$$

We also know that the number of new shares times the price per share, $n^n P^n$, must equal the dollar amount of bonds repurchased, $\Delta B^n < 0$. Therefore,

$$-\Delta B^n = n^n P^n = \$500.$$

---

[11] The astute reader will recognize that ρ, the cost of equity for the unlevered firm, is less than k_d, the before-tax cost of debt. This relationship is feasible in the presence of risky debt.

Combining these two expressions, we can solve for the price per share *after* the exchange offer

$$S_0 + \Delta S = n^0 P^n + \Delta B^n,$$

$$\frac{S_0 + \Delta S - \Delta B^n}{n^0} = P^n,$$

$$\frac{\$750 - \$500}{10} = \$25 \text{ per share.}$$

Hence the firm will need to issue 20 new shares at $25 each in order to raise the $500 needed for the exchange. The price per share will fall from $50 to $25 and the price-earnings ratio will decline from 50 to $16\frac{2}{3}$ if the proposed exchange offer is consummated.

2. The Cost of Capital: An Example Calculation (Bethlehem Steel)

From Chapter 12 we have two seemingly different, yet equivalent, definitions of the weighted average cost of capital. Equation (12.12), given below, is the Modigliani-Miller requirement that projects earn enough cash flow to increase the wealth of the original shareholders.

$$\text{WACC} = \rho \left(1 - \tau_c \frac{\Delta B}{\Delta I} \right), \tag{12.12}$$

where

ρ = the cost of equity for an all-equity firm,

τ_c = the marginal corporate tax rate,

ΔB = the market value of new debt,

ΔI = the replacement cost of new investment.

Given that the firm is at its long-run "optimal capital structure," we can say that an equivalent definition of the weighted average cost of capital is the weighted average of the marginal costs of various sources of capital, Eq. (12.19):

$$\text{WACC} = (1 - \tau_c)k_d \frac{B}{B + S} + k_e \frac{S}{B + S}. \tag{12.19}$$

In order to compute the weighted average cost of capital by means of Eq. (12.19), we must know (1) the marginal cost of debt and equity, k_d and k_e, and (2) the market-value capital structure used by the firm.

Although we use the term "weighted average cost of capital" to mean the cost of a mixture of sources of funds, it is important to emphasize that the costs of these funds must be measured as *marginal* costs. Hence the weighted average cost of capital is a weighted average of the marginal costs of the firm's various sources of capital.

Table 13.5 *Pro Forma* **Balance Sheet, Bethlehem Steel, December 1976 (in Thousands of Dollars)**

Assets		Liabilities	
Cash	45,600	Accounts payable	274,800
Marketable securities	355,600	Notes payable	—
Receivables	421,500	Accruals	948,600
Inventories	834,100	Long-term debt†	1,023,100
Other assets	274,700	Common stock at par‡	576,000
Long-term assets (net)	3,007,600	less Treasury stock	69,300
Total assets	4,939,100	Retained earnings	2,185,900
		Total liabilities	4,939,100

† Long-term debt is detailed in Table 13.6.

‡ 43,665,578 shares outstanding with a market price of $40⅝ per share on December 31, 1976.

In this context, the word "marginal" has two meanings. Foremost is that marginal cost means the cost of *new* financing at current market equilibrium rates of return—not historical cost. Second, and implied in the rate of return required by the market, is the impact of new financing on the perceived capital structure of the firm. For example, if the percentage of debt is perceived to be rising, the marginal cost of debt must include its impact on the weighted average cost of capital. We shall ignore this second possibility by adopting the convention that the firm establishes a target capital structure and sticks with it. Given this assumption, Eqs. (12.12) and (12.19) are identical. Consequently, there are no changes in leverage to complicate matters.

Some of the complexities which arise while we estimate the cost of capital are illustrated by the following example, the cost of capital for Bethlehem Steel Corporation during December 1976. Because market-equilibrium conditions change from day to day, so does the cost of capital. Therefore, the estimate which is given below is only an historical number, valid at the end of 1976.

Bethlehem Steel is the second-largest producer of steel in the United States. It manufactures steel products for markets in construction, transportation, service centers, and machinery. It also produces minerals and plastic products for industrial uses. Table 13.5 provides a simplified *pro forma* balance sheet.[12] In order to estimate a weighted average cost of capital we need the marginal cost of each capital source and the appropriate weighting scheme.

A. THE COST OF LONG-TERM DEBT   The first problem is estimating the current market rate of return which would be required if the firm issued new long-term debt. Almost all of Bethlehem Steel's long-term debt has had a maturity of 25 to 30 years when first issued. Therefore, we will assume that any new long-term debt will also be issued with a 30-year maturity and an Aa bond rating. What rate of

[12] Data taken from *Moody's Industrial Manual*.

Table 13.6   Composition of Long-term Debt (in Thousands of Dollars) in Table 13.5

Issue	Rating	Amount	Call Price	Recent Price	Yield	Year of Issue
Consol. Mtge. S.F. 3s, K, 1979	Aa	21,800	$100\frac{1}{8}$	NA	NA	1949
Debenture $3\frac{1}{4}$s, 1980	Aa	3,100	100	$89\frac{1}{2}$	3.6	1955
Debenture 5.40s, 1992	Aa	109,200	$102\frac{1}{2}$	$84\frac{3}{8}$	6.4	1967
Debenture $6\frac{7}{8}$s, 1999	Aa	85,800	$104\frac{1}{4}$	$94\frac{1}{4}$	6.6	1969
Debenture 9s, 2000	Aa	144,000	$105\frac{1}{2}$	$106\frac{1}{2}$	8.5	1970
Debenture 8.45s, 2005	Aa	250,000	107.45	$103\frac{1}{2}$	8.2	1975
Debenture $8\frac{3}{8}$s, 2001	Aa	200,000	106.63	$105\frac{1}{2}$	7.9	1976
Subord. Deb. $4\frac{1}{2}$s, 1990	A	94,500	102.40	$76\frac{1}{4}$	5.9	1965
Notes payable	—	30,000	—	NA	NA	NA
Subsidiary debt	—	3,200	—	NA	NA	NA
Revenue bonds $5\frac{1}{4}$s–6s, 2002	—	100,000	—	NA	NA	NA

return would the market require for a new issue with this risk? The "yield" provided by *The Wall Street Journal* is not useful because it assumes an infinite maturity for the debt. For example, take the $3\frac{1}{4}$% debentures which were due in 1980. The "yield" is the coupon divided by the market price:

$$\text{Yield} = \frac{32.50}{895.00} = 3.6\%.$$

This number is completely unrealistic. The required market rate of return is the rate which equates the discounted value of the expected future cash flows with the current market price of the security. We can find this rate by solving Eq. (13.8) for the before-tax cost of debt, k_d:

$$B_j = \sum_{t=1}^{T} \frac{E(\text{coupon})_t}{(1 + k_{dj})^t} + \frac{E(\text{face value})}{(1 + k_{dj})^T}, \tag{13.8}$$

where

$E(\text{coupon}) =$ the expected coupon payment in year t (assumed to be \$32.50),

$E(\text{face value}) =$ the expected face value (assumed to be \$1000),

$\qquad T =$ number of years to maturity,

$\qquad B_j =$ market value of the jth debt issue.

Note that we have assumed that the bond rated Aa will actually pay its full face value of \$1000 when it matures. This may not always be a valid assumption. If the bond is very risky, the expected payout may be less than \$1000. (Or if the bond is callable, the expected payout may be more than \$1000 and the time to maturity may be less than T if the bond is called early.) Given the above assumptions about the expected payout of the $3\frac{1}{4}$% debentures, the current required rate of return from

Table 13.7 Market Value Weights of Capital Sources

	Market Value (in Thousands of Dollars)	Percent	Cost
Accounts payable and Accruals	1,223,400	32.1	
Notes payable	0	0.0	4.9%
Long-term debt	815,945	21.4	8.3%
Equity	1,773,914	46.5	13.5%
		100.0	

them is approximately 8%. At the end of 1976, this was the appropriate interest rate for an Aa-rated debenture due to mature in around four years.[13] Bonds with the same rating but longer maturities are slightly riskier and therefore yield higher rates. For example, the 8.45s maturing in the year 2005 yield approximately 8.3%. In our judgment, if Bethlehem Steel had decided to issue new long-term debt in December of 1976 with an Aa bond rating and a maturity of between 25 and 30 years, the company would have had to pay approximately 8.3%. We shall use this as the before-tax cost, k_d, of long-term debt, because it is the best estimate of the marginal cost of *new* debt. Next, we need an estimate of the percent of long-term debt, $B/(B + S)$, used by Bethlehem in its target capital structure. Table 13.7 shows the market value weights of various capital sources.

B. MARKET VALUE WEIGHTS   The market value weights of long-term debt and equity are obvious. For long-term debt, we use the market values from Table 13.7, and when they are unavailable, we use book value. The market value of equity is simply the number of shares outstanding multiplied by the price per share. Short-term liabilities are calculated at book value. This is not an unreasonable assumption because, under normal circumstances, the market value of short-term debt rarely deviates much from its book value. We assume that the current market weights are a reasonable estimate of the firm's long-run "optimal" target capital structure. A quick, but somewhat unreliable, way of checking this assumption is to observe that the book value of long-term debt is currently 27.5% of total long-term debt plus equity. Its high between 1970 and 1976 was 27.5%, the average was 23.4%, and the low was 20.67%. Therefore the current capital structure is not too far from the normal pattern observed in recent years.

---

[13] Coupon payments of $16.25 per $1000 are made every May first and November first. The issue matured on May 1, 1980. Therefore, the actual computation is more complicated than Eq. (13.8). Students familiar with the actuarial complexities of discounting formulas will find the exact calculation to be

$$\frac{895.00}{(1 + k_{dj})^{1/6}} = \left\{ \frac{32.50}{2} \left[\frac{1 - (1 + k_{dj}/2)^{-6}}{k_{dj}/2} \right] + \frac{1016.25}{(1 + k_{dj}/2)^7} \right\},$$

where $k_{dj}/2$ is a semiannual nominal rate. The solution to this problem provides an annual effective rate of approximately 8%.

C.   THE COST OF SHORT-TERM LIABILITIES   The cost of short-term liabilities is an often-debated topic. One technique is to ignore it completely by arguing that payables and accruals may be thought of as "free" capital, because in the capital-budgeting process such spontaneously generated funds may be netted out against the required investment outlay. There are two alternatives. One is to include short-term liabilities as one of the components of the weighted average cost of capital and to use a short-term interest rate, such as the commercial paper rate (which was 4.91% in December 1976) to approximate their cost. The problem with this approach is that the costs of noninterest-bearing short-term liabilities such as accruals and accounts payable is already implicitly accounted for in the cash flows from operations. For example, industries with generous trade credit terms on accounts payable will charge higher prices than they otherwise might in order to compensate for the cost of extending trade credit. Consequently, trade credit is implicitly included in the cost of goods sold for firms purchasing the products of those industries. The opportunity cost of accruals is more difficult to justify, but the lender, whether it be the government or an unpaid worker, almost surely has an opportunity cost which is accounted for in tax or wage rates. If the cost of trade credit and accruals are already deducted from cash flows from operations, then there is no need to adjust the cost of capital. Therefore we recommend a second alternative, namely that one should include interest-bearing short-term liabilities (such as notes due) in the weighted average cost of capital but exclude noninterest-bearing items such as accounts payable and accruals.

Using the recommended approach, the market value weights—when expressed as a percentage of notes payable, long-term debt, and equity—are given in Table 13.8.

D.   THE COST OF EQUITY   The cost of equity capital, unfortunately, is still more an art than a science. We can use the CAPM to estimate the cost of equity, but two of the important parameters are judgmental. Equation (13.9) gives the CAPM equation for the cost of equity:

$$k_e = R_f + [E(R_m) - R_f]\beta_e^L. \tag{13.9}$$

The expected future rate of return on the market cannot be measured. However, a good way of guessing what it might be is to add three components: (1) the real rate of growth of the economy, 3%–4%, (2) an adjustment for inflation next year

Table 13.8   Market Value Weights Excluding Noninterest-bearing Liabilities

	Market Value (in Thousands)	Percent	Cost
Notes Due	0	0	4.9%
Long-Term Debt	$ 815,945	31.5	8.3%
Equity	$1,773,914	68.5	13.5%
		100.0	

(in December of 1976 a good guess might have been 6%–7%), and (3) a risk premium for the riskiness of the market portfolio (say 4%–5%). Using the mean of each of these components, we estimate the expected rate of return as 14.5%. The risk-free rate may be approximated by the 90-day rate on U.S. Government Treasury bills, which in December of 1976 was 4.67%. Finally, we need an estimate of the systematic risk of the common stock of the company, which was .9.[14] This is really an estimate of the future systematic risk of Bethlehem Steel, and it is as much a guess as is the future rate of return on the market index. Substituting these parameter estimates into Eq. (13.9), we estimate the cost of equity capital to be 13.52%.

E. THE WEIGHTED AVERAGE COST OF CAPITAL   Finally, by using the market-value weights and capital costs in Table 13.8 we can estimate the weighted average cost of capital for Bethlehem Steel as of December 1976 by using Eq. (12.19) and a marginal corporate tax rate assumed to be 48%. The weighted average cost of capital is 10.61%. The calculation is given below:

$$\text{WACC} = (1 - \tau_c) \, k_{dj} \frac{B_j}{\sum B_j + S} + k_e \frac{S}{\sum B_j + S},$$

where

k_{dj} = the before-tax cost of the jth nonequity liability (for example, k_{d1} is notes due and k_{d2} is long-term debt),

B_j = the market value of the jth nonequity liability,

k_e = the cost of equity,

S = the market value of equity.

Thus

$$\text{WACC} = (1 - .48)(0.0)(.049) + (1 - .48)(.083)(.315) + .135(.685) = 10.61\%.$$

3. The Debt Refunding Decision

In an era of falling interest rates a firm may find itself with bonds outstanding which pay a coupon rate higher than the prevailing market rate. A net present value analysis will reveal whether the outstanding bonds should be called or, if they are not callable, repurchased on the open market.[15] Almost all public bond issues have a call provision allowing the firm to force recall of the debt at a call premium.

---

[14] There are several companies which publish estimates of the systematic risk of individual firms. We used an estimate provided by Wilshire Associates, Santa Monica, California.

[15] The accounting treatment of bond repurchase when bonds are selling at a discount can cause extremely perverse behavior. Suppose that interest rates have risen, thereby causing fixed-rate outstanding debt to sell at a discount. Repurchase of this debt at market value has no economic gain or loss before taxes because the firm is paying the fair market price. However, the accounting treatment allows the firm to record the difference between the face value and the market value as profit. Therefore, firms that desire to increase their reported earnings per share may decide to repurchase discounted debt. Unfortunately, this is a negative present value decision because the firm has to pay (1) ordinary income taxes on its paper gain and (2) higher coupons on replacement debt.

To provide a focus for the analysis, consider the following facts. The L and S Company has a $10,000,000 bond issue outstanding with five years to maturity and a coupon rate of 16%, and with annual interest payments. The current market rate on debt of equivalent risk is 10%. The call price on the $1000 face value debt is $1050, and the firm has a 40% tax rate. What is the net present value of calling the outstanding bonds and replacing them with new bonds of equivalent maturity and risk? Assume no transactions costs.

This is a capital budgeting decision and the usual procedures apply. The changes in the after-tax cash flows should be discounted at the appropriate after-tax discount rate. In this case the appropriate rate is the after-tax rate on debt of equivalent risk, i.e., $(1 - \tau_c)k_d = (1 - .4) .10 = .06$. The after-tax cash flows have three components (in a world without transactions costs).

1. The *call premium* will cost $500,000. It is deductable as an expense, therefore its after-tax cost is $500,000(1 - .4) = $300,000.

2. The new debt issue will have to be $10,300,000 and it will pay a 10% coupon $(r_2 = 10\%)$, thus the new interest will be $1,030,000 per year. The old interest was 16% $(r_1 = 16\%)$ of $10,000,000 or $1,600,000 per year. Therefore the *after-tax interest saving* amounts to $(1 - \tau_c)(r_1 - r_2)B - (1 - \tau_c)r_2 \Delta B$ where B is the original book value and ΔB is the change in book value. Numerically the annual interest savings is

$$(1 - .4)(.16 - .10)(10,000,000) - (1 - .4)(.10)(300,000) = 342,000.$$

3. *Incremental principal* on the new debt, namely $300,000, must be paid off at maturity.

The net present value of these components is

$$NPV = \sum_{t=1}^{N} \frac{(1 - \tau_c)(r_1 - r_2)B}{[1 + (1 - \tau_c)k_d]^t} - \sum_{t=1}^{N} \frac{(1 - \tau_c)r_2 \Delta B}{[1 + (1 - \tau_c)k_d]^t} - \frac{\Delta B}{[1 + (1 - \tau_c)k_d]^N}$$

$$= \sum_{t=1}^{5} \frac{(1 - .4)(.16 - .10)10,000,000}{[1 + (1 - .4)(.10)]^t} - \sum_{t=1}^{5} \frac{(1 - .4).10(300,000)}{[1 + (1 - .4)(.10)]^t}$$

$$- \frac{300,000}{[1 + (1 - .4)(.10)]^5}$$

$$= 1,516,464 - 75,823 - 224,190$$

$$= 1,216,451.$$

Therefore, the debt should be refunded.

Two additional issues are pertinent. First, we should consider the fact that the debt refinancing will slightly alter the capital structure of the firm because the market value of the new debt issue exceeds the market value of the outstanding debt. This may create a tax gain from leverage. The second issue is that callable debt should never sell for more than the call price plus a small premium approximately equal to the flotation costs of exercising the call. No investor would rationally pay $1100 for a bond which might be called (any minute) at $1050.

4. The Effect of Flotation Costs on the Cost of Capital

The flotation costs of issuing new debt or equity include cash expenses such as legal, accounting, engineering, trustee and listing fees, printing and engraving expenses, Securities and Exchange Commission registration fees, Federal Revenue stamps, and State taxes. Also an important part of many new issues is the compensation paid to investment bankers for underwriting services.[16] The method used by many managerial finance textbooks to include flotation costs in the cost of capital is not generally consistent with value maximization. The normally followed procedure has been to adjust the required rate of return for flotation costs, F. For example, if one were using the Gordon growth model to estimate the cost of equity, the incorrect formulation would be:

$$k_e = \frac{D_1}{\left(1 - \frac{F}{S}\right) S} + g$$

where

$D_1 =$ the end-of-period expected dividends (aggregate dollar value),

$S =$ the current market value of equity,

$F =$ the dollar amount of flotation costs,

$g =$ the expected long-term growth in dividends.

The above approach is incorrect because it implicitly adjusts the opportunity cost of funds supplied to the firm. Yet the true market-determined opportunity cost is unaffected by the flotation costs of a particular firm.

The correct method is to begin with a definition of net present value that explicitly recognizes flotation costs. One approach, which uses reproduction cost leverage, has been provided by Ezzell and Porter [1976]. Another approach, which we prefer, uses replacement value leverage and is described below. Let F be the dollar amount of flotation costs for a project financed with ΔS dollars of equity and ΔB dollars of debt. Thus the firm's target leverage, L, is

$$L = \frac{\Delta B}{\Delta S + \Delta B}. \tag{13.10}$$

The total investment outlay for a project is ΔI dollars for capital invested and F dollars of flotation costs. Therefore, we have

$$\Delta I + F = \Delta S + \Delta B = \Delta S + L(\Delta I + F). \tag{13.11}$$

If the firm's equity flotation costs are $\alpha\%$ of the new equity issued and $\gamma\%$ of new debt, then

$$F = \alpha \Delta S + \gamma \Delta B \tag{13.12}$$

---

[16] For an excellent comparison of underwritten new issues versus rights issues, see Smith [1977].

and the weighted percentage flotation cost, ϵ, is

$$\epsilon = \alpha(1 - L) + \gamma L. \tag{13.13}$$

Substituting (13.10) and (13.11) into (13.12) yields

$$F = \alpha(\Delta I + F - L(\Delta I + F) + \gamma L(\Delta I + F)$$

$$= \frac{\epsilon \Delta I}{1 - \epsilon}. \tag{13.14}$$

The NPV of the project will be

$$\mathrm{NPV} = \sum_{t=1}^{N} \frac{\mathrm{NCF}_t}{(1 + \mathrm{WACC})^t} - \Delta I - F. \tag{13.15}$$

This definition explicitly recognizes that flotation costs are cash flows incurred at the present time, not stretched over the life of the project. Finally, substituting (13.14) into (13.15) we obtain

$$\mathrm{NPV} = \sum_{t=1}^{N} \frac{\mathrm{NCF}_t}{(1 + \mathrm{WACC})^t} - \frac{1}{1 - \epsilon} \Delta I.$$

Thus the correct procedure for the economic analysis of flotation costs does not alter the weighted average cost of capital, WACC. Rather, it grosses up the investment outlay by $[1/(1 - \epsilon)]$, a factor which considers the weighted average flotation costs of debt and equity.

SUMMARY

The cost of capital, the capital structure of the firm, and the capital-budgeting decision are all inextricably linked. The theory of finance provides equations which may be applied to the solution of the weighted average cost of capital under a variety of assumptions. Although no completely satisfactory theory has yet been found to explain the existence of optimal capital structure, casual empiricism suggests that firms behave as though it does exist. Therefore, for the time being, suggested techniques for estimating the weighted average cost of capital usually assume that each firm has a target capital structure. This target is then applied to the cost of capital formulas.

A major empirical issue is the impact of capital structure on the value of the firm and on the weighted average cost of capital. Although the evidence is mixed, the articles which were summarized seem to indicate that there is, in fact, a gain from leverage which seems to be between 10 and 20%. Of course, this is less than the marginal corporate tax rate (48%) and we could have used a tax rate of 10 to 20% in estimating the cost of capital for Bethlehem Steel. If we had done so, the weighted average cost of capital would have been 11.34%.

PROBLEM SET

13.1 The puzzle of optimal capital structure is that there appear to be cross-sectional regularities in the observed ratios of debt to equity of U.S. firms. For example, the steel industry appears to carry a higher percentage of debt than the public accounting industry does. These same regularities appeared even before the existence of corporate income taxes. How can optimal leverage be explained without relying on the tax shield of debt?

13.2 What are the empirical problems involved in testing for the effect of capital structure on the value of the firm?

13.3 Assume a world without taxes. How would the weighted average cost of capital vary with the ratio of debt to total assets, $B/(B + S)$, if the cost of equity remained constant, that is, $k_e = \rho > k_d$?

13.4 During recent years your company has made considerable use of debt financing, to the extent that it is generally agreed that the percent of debt in the firm's capital structure (either in book or market-value terms) is too high. Further use of debt will likely lead to a drop in the firm's bond rating. You would like to recommend that the next major capital investment be financed with a new equity issue. Unfortunately, the firm hasn't been doing very well recently (nor has the market). In fact, the rate of return on investment has been just equal to the cost of capital. As shown in the financial statement in Table Q13.4, the market value of the firm's equity is less than its book value. This means that even a profitable project will decrease earnings per share if it is financed with new equity. For example, the firm is considering a project which costs $400 but has a value of $500 (i.e., an NPV of $100), and which will increase total earnings by $60 per year. If it is financed with equity, the $400 will require approximately 200 shares, thus bringing the total shares outstanding to 1200. The new earnings will be $660, and earnings per share will fall to $.55. The president of the firm argues that the project should be delayed for three reasons.

a) It is too expensive for the firm to issue new debt.

b) Financing the project with new equity will reduce earnings per share because the market value of equity is less than book value.

c) Equity markets are currently depressed. If the firm waits until the market index improves, the market value of equity will exceed the book value and equity financing will no longer reduce earnings per share.

Critique the president's logic.

Table Q13.4   Balance Sheet as of December 31, 19xx

Assets		Liabilities	
Short-term assets	2,000	Debt	6,000
Plant and equipment	8,000	Equity	4,000
	10,000	Total	10,000
Total market value of equity = $2,000.00			
Number of shares outstanding =			1,000
Price per share =			2.00
Total earnings for the year 19xx =			600.00
Earnings per share =			.60

Table Q13.5

Year	Outflows	Inflows	Interest
1	250	10	7.5
2	250	20	15.0
3	250	25	22.5
4	250	60	30.0
5–30	0	110	30.0
31–40	0	80	30.0
41	0	40	0

13.5 *Southwestern Electric Company.* [17] John Hatteras, the financial analyst for Southwestern Electric Company, is responsible for preliminary analysis of the company's investment projects. He is currently trying to evaluate two large projects which management has decided to consider as a single joint project, because it is felt that the geographical diversification the joint project provides would be advantageous.

Southwestern Electric was founded in the early 1930s and has operated profitably ever since. Growing at about the same rate as the population in its service areas, the company has usually been able to forecast its revenues with a great deal of accuracy. The stable pattern in revenues and a favorable regulatory environment have caused most investors to view Southwestern as an investment of very low risk.

Hatteras is concerned because one of the two projects uses a new technology which will be very profitable, assuming that demand is high in a booming economy, but will do poorly in a recessionary economy. However, the expected cash flows of the two projects, supplied by the engineering department, are identical. The expected after-tax cash flows on operating income for the joint project are given in Table Q13.5. Both projects are exactly the same size, so the cash flow for one is simply half the joint cash flow. In order to better evaluate the project, Hatteras applies his knowledge of modern finance theory. He estimates that the beta of the riskier project is .75 while the beta for the less risky project is .4375. These betas, however, are based on the covariance between the return on after-tax operating income and the market. Hatteras vaguely recalls that any discount rate he decides to apply to the project should consider financial risk as well as operating (or business) risk. The beta for the equity of Southwestern is .5. The company has a ratio of debt to total assets of 50% and a marginal tax rate of 40%. Because the bonds of Southwestern are rated Aaa, Hatteras decides to assume that they are risk free. Finally, after consulting his investment banker, Hatteras believes that 18% is a reasonable estimate of the expected return on the market.

The joint project, if undertaken, will represent 10% of the corporation's assets. Southwestern intends to finance the joint project with 50% debt and 50% equity.

Hatteras wants to submit a report which answers the following questions:

a) What is the appropriate required rate of return for the new project?

b) What are the cost of equity capital and the weighted average cost of capital for Southwestern Electric before it takes the project?

---

[17] This problem is really a short case. It has a definite answer but requires knowledge of cash flows, discounting, the CAPM, and risky cost of capital.

c) Should the joint project be accepted?

d) What would the outcome be if the projects are considered separately?

e) If the joint project is accepted, what will the firm's new risk level be?

REFERENCES

American Bar Association, *Commentaries on Model Debenture Indenture Provisions*, Chicago, 1971.

Barges, A., *The Effect of Capital Structure on the Cost of Capital*. Prentice-Hall, Englewood Cliffs, N.J., 1963.

Baxter, N., "Leverage, Risk of Ruin and the Cost of Capital," *Journal of Finance*, September 1967, 395–403.

Beranek, W., *The Effect of Leverage on the Market Value of Common Stock*. Bureau of Business Research and Service, Madison, Wis., 1964.

Bhattacharya, S., "Imperfect Information, Dividend Policy, and 'The Bird in Hand' Fallacy," *Bell Journal of Economics*, Spring 1979, 259–270.

Black, F., and M. Scholes, "The Pricing of Options and Corporate Liabilities," *Journal of Political Economy*, May–June 1973, 637–654.

Boness, A. J., and G. M. Frankfurter, "Evidence of Non-Homogeneity of Capital Costs Within 'Risk-Classes,'" *Journal of Finance*, June 1977, 775–787.

Brennan, M., and E. Schwartz, "Savings Bonds, Retractable Bonds and Callable Bonds," *Journal of Financial Economics*, August 1977, 67–88.

Ezzell, J., and B. Porter, "Flotation Costs and the Weighted Average Cost of Capital," *Journal of Financial and Quantitative Analysis*, September 1976, 403–413.

Galai, D., and R. W. Masulis, "The Option Pricing Model and the Risk Factor of Stock," *Journal of Financial Economics*, January/March 1976, 53–82.

Haley, C., and L. Schall, *The Theory of Financial Decisions*. McGraw-Hill, New York, 1973.

Hamada, R. S., "The Effect of the Firm's Capital Structure on the Systematic Risk of Common Stocks," *Journal of Finance*, May 1972, 435–452.

Jensen, M., and W. Meckling, "Theory of the Firm: Managerial Behavior, Agency Costs, and Ownership Structure," *Journal of Financial Economics*, October 1976, 305–360.

Kalay, A., "Toward a Theory of Corporate Dividend Policy." Unpublished PhD. thesis, University of Rochester, Rochester, New York, 1979.

Kalotay, A., "On the Advanced Refunding of Discounted Debt," *Financial Management*, Summer 1978, 7–13.

Kim, E. H., "A Mean Variance Theory of Optimal Capital Structure and Corporate Debt Capacity," *Journal of Finance*, March 1978, 45–64.

———, W. Lewellen, and J. McConnell, "Financial Leverage and Clienteles: Theory and Evidence," *Journal of Financial Economics*, March 1979, 83–110.

Kraus, A., and R. Litzenberger, "A State-Preference Model of Optimal Financial Leverage," *Journal of Finance*, September 1973, 911–922.

Leland, H., and D. Pyle, "Informational Asymmetries, Financial Structure, and Financial Intermediation," *Journal of Finance*, May 1977, 371–388.

Livingston, M., "Bond Refunding Reconsidered: Comment," *Journal of Finance,* March 1980, 191–196.

Masulis, R., "The Effects of Capital Structure Change on Security Prices: A Study of Exchange Offers," *Journal of Financial Economics,* June 1980, 139–178.

———, "The Impact of Capital Structure Change on Firm Value, Some Estimates," working paper, UCLA Graduate School of Management, 1982, *Journal of Finance,* forthcoming.

Mayor, T., and K. McCorn, "Bond Refunding: One or Two Faces?" *Journal of Finance,* March 1978, 349–353.

Miller, M., "Debt and Taxes," *Journal of Finance,* May 1977, 261–275.

———, and F. Modigliani, "Some Estimates of the Cost of Capital to the Electric Utility Industry, 1954–57," *American Economic Review,* June 1966, 333–391.

———, "Some Estimates of the Cost of Capital to the Electric Utility Industry, 1954–57: Reply," *American Economic Review,* December 1967, 1288–1300.

Modigliani, F., and M. Miller, "The Cost of Capital, Corporation Finance and the Theory of Investment," *American Economic Review,* June 1958, 261–297.

———, "Taxes and the Cost of Capital: A Correction," *American Economic Review,* June 1963, 433–443.

Myers, S. C., "Determinants of Corporate Borrowing," *Journal of Financial Economics,* November 1977, 147–176.

Ofer, A., and R. Taggart, Jr., "Bond Refunding: A Clarifying Analysis," *Journal of Finance,* March 1977, 21–30.

———, "Bond Refunding Reconsidered: Reply," *Journal of Finance,* March 1980, 197–200.

Riley, J., "Competitive Signalling," *Journal of Economic Theory,* April 1975, 174–186.

Robichek, A., J. McDonald, and R. Higgins, "Some Estimates of the Cost of Capital to the Electric Utility Industry, 1954–57: Comment," *American Economic Review,* December 1967, 1278–1288.

Ross, S. A., "The Determination of Financial Structure: The Incentive Signalling Approach," *Bell Journal of Economics,* Spring 1977, 23–40.

Rothschild, M., and J. Stiglitz, "Equilibrium in Competitive Insurance Markets," *Quarterly Journal of Economics,* November 1976, 629–650.

Rubinstein, M., "A Mean-Variance Synthesis of Corporate Financial Theory," *Journal of Finance,* March 1973, 167–181.

Scott, J. H., Jr., "A Theory of Optimal Capital Structure," *Bell Journal of Economics,* Spring 1976, 33–54.

Shastri, K., "Two Essays Concerning the Effects of Firm Investment/Financing Decisions on Security Values: An Option Pricing Approach." Unpublished Ph.D. thesis, UCLA Graduate School of Management, 1981.

Smith, C., Jr., "Substitute Methods for Raising Additional Capital: Rights Offerings versus Underwritten Issues," *Journal of Financial Economics,* December 1977, 273–307.

———, and J. B. Warner, "On Financial Contracting: An Analysis of Bond Covenants," *Journal of Financial Economics,* June 1979, 117–161.

Spence, A. M., "Job Market Signaling," *Quarterly Journal of Economics,* August 1973, 355–379.

Stiglitz, J., "A Re-Examination of the Modigliani-Miller Theorem," *American Economic Review,* December 1969, 784–793.

———, "Some Aspects of the Pure Theory of Corporate Finance: Bankruptcies and Takeovers," *Bell Journal of Economics and Management Science,* Autumn 1972, 458–482.

———, "On the Irrelevance of Corporate Financial Policy," *American Economic Review,* December 1974, 851–866.

Titman, S., "The Effect of Capital Structure on a Firm's Liquidation Decision." Unpublished Ph.D. thesis, Graduate School of Industrial Administration, Carnegie-Mellon University, 1981.

———, "Determinants of Capital Structure: An Empirical Analysis," working paper, UCLA Graduate School of Management, 1982.

Wakeman, L. M., "Bond Rating Agencies and Capital Markets," working paper, Graduate School of Management, University of Rochester, Rochester, N.Y., 1978.

Warner, J., "Bankruptcy Costs: Some Evidence," *Journal of Finance,* May 1977a, 337–347.

———, "Bankruptcy, Absolute Priority, and the Pricing of Risky Debt Claims," *Journal of Financial Economics,* May 1977b, 239–276.

Watts, R., and J. Zimmerman, "Towards a Positive Theory of the Determination of Accounting Standards," *Accounting Review,* January 1978, 112–134.

———, "The Demand for and Supply of Accounting Theories: The Market for Excuses," *Accounting Review,* April 1979, 273–305.

Weinstein, M. I., "The Effect of a Rating Change Announcement on Bond Price," *Journal of Financial Economics,* December 1977, 329–350.

———, "The Seasoning Process of New Corporate Bond Issues," *Journal of Finance,* December 1978, 1343–1354.

Weston, J. F., "A Test of Capital Propositions," *Southern Economic Journal,* October 1963, 105–112.

Dividend Policy: Theory

The one thing that shareholders cannot do through their purchase and sale transactions is negate the consequences of investment decisions by management.

J. E. WALTER, "DIVIDEND POLICY: ITS INFLUENCE ON THE VALUE OF THE ENTERPRISE," *THE JOURNAL OF FINANCE,* MAY 1963, 284

Is the value of shareholders' wealth affected by the dividend policy of the firm? This is another variation on the basic question, Can any financing decision affect the value of the firm? The previous chapters looked at the relationship between capital structure and the value of the firm, using a fairly simple valuation model which assumed a nongrowing stream of cash flows from investment. Capital-structure theory shows that in a world without taxes, repackaging the firm's net operating cash flows into fixed cash flows for debt and residual cash flows for shareholders has no effect on the value of the firm in a world without taxes. This chapter develops valuation models which include growth opportunities, thereby adding a greater element of realism. Even so, we shall show that, in a world without taxes, it makes no difference whether shareholders receive their cash flows as dividends or as capital gains. Thus, in the absence of taxes, dividend policy is irrelevant. It does not affect shareholders' wealth. The argument is then extended to a valuation model which includes growth and corporate taxes, but the result does not change. Dividend payout does not affect the value of the firm. However, in a world with personal as well as corporate taxes the possibility arises that dividends may affect value.

Empirical tests of dividend policy and applications of corporate valuation are discussed in Chapter 15.

A. THE IRRELEVANCE OF DIVIDEND POLICY IN A WORLD WITHOUT TAXES

Miller and Modigliani [1961] present a cogent argument for the fact that the value of the firm is unaffected by dividend policy in a world without taxes or transactions costs. They begin by assuming that two firms are identical in every respect except for their dividend payout in the current time period. Their streams of future cash flows from operations are identical, their planned investment outlays are identical, and all future dividend payments from the second time period on are also identical. We can represent this mathematically as follows:

$$\tilde{\text{NOI}}_1(t) = \tilde{\text{NOI}}_2(t), \qquad t = 0, 1, \ldots, \infty,$$

$$\tilde{I}_1(t) = \tilde{I}_2(t), \qquad t = 0, 1, \ldots, \infty,$$

$$\tilde{D}_1(t) = \tilde{D}_2(t), \qquad t = 1, \ldots, \infty,$$

$$D_1(0) \neq D_2(0),$$

where

$\tilde{\text{NOI}}_i(t)$ = the random future cash flows from operations for the ith firm in time period, t,

$\tilde{I}_i(t)$ = the variable investment outlay for the ith firm in time period t,

$\tilde{D}_i(t)$ = the random dividend payout for firms in period t,

$D_i(0)$ = the dividend payout for the ith firm during the current time period.

1. A Recursive Valuation Formula

The important question is whether or not the two firms will have different value if their current dividend payouts are different. In order to supply an answer we first need a simple valuation model. Let us begin by assuming that the market-required rates of return for firms in the same risk class are identical.[1] The two firms above

---

[1] For the sake of simplicity, we assume that both firms are 100% equity. This avoids the problem of confusing capital-structure effects with possible dividend-policy effects.

obviously have the same risk because their streams of operating cash flows are identical. The rate of return is defined as dividends plus capital gains,

$$\rho(t+1) = \frac{d_i(t+1) + P_i(t+1) - P_i(t)}{P_i(t)}, \tag{14.1}$$

where

$\rho(t+1)$ = the market-required rate of return during the time period t,

$d_i(t+1)$ = dividends per share paid at the end of time period t,

$P_i(t+1)$ = price per share at the end of time period t,

$P_i(t)$ = price per share at the beginning of time period t.

If the numerator and denominator of (14.1) are multiplied by the current number of shares outstanding, $n_i(t)$, then by rearranging terms, we have

$$V_i(t) = \frac{D_i(t+1) + n_i(t)P_i(t+1)}{1 + \rho(t+1)}, \tag{14.2}$$

where

$D_i(t+1)$ = total dollar dividend payment = $n_i(t)d_i(t+1)$,

$V_i(t)$ = the market value of the firm = $n_i(t)P_i(t)$.

Hence the value of the firm is seen to be equal to the discounted sum of two cash flows: any dividends paid out, $D_i(t+1)$, and the end-of-period value of the firm. In order to show that the value of the firm is independent of dividend payout, we shall examine the sources and uses of funds for the two firms in order to rewrite (14.2) in a way that is independent of dividends.

2. Sources and Uses of Funds

There are two major sources of funds for an all-equity firm. First, it receives cash from operations, $\tilde{NOI}_i(t+1)$. Second, it may choose to issue new shares, $m_i(t+1)\tilde{P}_i(t+1)$, where $m_i(t+1)$ is the number of new shares. There are also two major uses of funds: dividends paid out, $\tilde{D}_i(t+1)$, and planned cash outlays for investment, $\tilde{I}_i(t+1)$.[2] By definition, sources and uses must be equal. Therefore, we have the following identity:

$$\tilde{NOI}_i(t+1) + m_i(t+1)\tilde{P}_i(t+1) \equiv \tilde{I}_i(t+1) + \tilde{D}_i(t+1). \tag{14.3}$$

We can use this fact to rewrite the numerator of the valuation equation (14.2). Calling the numerator of (14.2) the dollar return to shareholders, $\tilde{R}_i(t+1)$, we have

$$\tilde{R}_i(t+1) = \tilde{D}_i(t+1) + n_i(t)\tilde{P}_i(t+1). \tag{14.4}$$

---

[2] This argument assumes, for the sake of convenience, that sources and uses of funds from balance sheet items (e.g., changes in inventory or accounts receivable) are negligible.

We know that if new shares are issued, the total number of shares outstanding at the end of the period, $n(t + 1)$, will be the sum of current shares, $n(t)$, and new shares $m(t + 1)$:

$$n_i(t + 1) = n_i(t) + m_i(t + 1). \tag{14.5}$$

Using (14.5), we can rewrite (14.4) as

$$\tilde{R}_i(t + 1) = \tilde{D}_i(t + 1) + n_i(t + 1)\tilde{P}_i(t + 1) - m_i(t + 1)\tilde{P}_i(t + 1). \tag{14.6}$$

Finally, taking Eq. (14.3), which establishes the identity of the sources and uses of funds, to substitute for $m_i(t + 1)\tilde{P}_i(t + 1)$ in the above equation, we obtain

$$\tilde{R}_i(t + 1) = \tilde{D}_i(t + 1) + \tilde{V}_i(t + 1) - \tilde{I}_i(t + 1) + \text{N\~OI}_i(t + 1) - \tilde{D}_i(t + 1)$$

$$= \text{N\~OI}_i(t + 1) - \tilde{I}_i(t + 1) + \tilde{V}_i(t + 1), \tag{14.7}$$

where $\tilde{V}_i(t + 1) = n_i(t + 1)\tilde{P}_i(t + 1)$. Therefore, the valuation equation (14.2) may be rewritten

$$\tilde{V}_i(t) = \frac{\text{N\~OI}_i(t + 1) - \tilde{I}_i(t + 1) + \tilde{V}_i(t + 1)}{1 + \rho(t + 1)}. \tag{14.8}$$

3. Valuation and the Irrelevancy of Dividend Payout

It is no accident that dividends do not appear in the valuation equation (14.8). The firm can choose any dividend policy whatsoever without affecting the stream of cash flows received by shareholders. It could, for example, elect to pay dividends in excess of cash flows from operations and still be able to undertake any planned investment. The extra funds needed are supplied by issuing new equity. On the other hand, it could decide to pay dividends less than the amount of cash left over from operations after making investments. The excess cash would be used to repurchase shares. It is the availability of external financing in a world without transactions costs which makes the value of the firm independent of dividend policy.

We can use Eq. (14.8) to prove that two firms which are identical in every respect except for their current dividend payout must have the same value. The equation has four terms. First, the market required rate of return, ρ, must be the same because both firms have identical risk, $\text{N\~OI}_1(t) = \text{N\~OI}_2(t)$, for all t. Second, current cash flows from operations and current investment outlays for the two firms have been assumed to be identical:

$$\text{N\~OI}_1(1) = \text{N\~OI}_2(1), \qquad \tilde{I}_1(1) = \tilde{I}_2(1).$$

Finally, the end-of-period values of the two firms depend only on *future* investments, dividends, and cash flows from operations, which also have been assumed to be identical. Therefore, the end-of-period values of the two firms must be the same:

$$\tilde{V}_1(1) = \tilde{V}_2(1).$$

Consequently, the present values of the two firms must be identical regardless of their current dividend payout. Dividend policy is irrelevant because it has no effect on shareholders' wealth in a world without taxes or transactions costs.

Note that the proof of the irrelevancy of dividend policy was made using a multiperiod model whose returns were uncertain. Therefore it is an extremely general argument. In addition to providing insight into what does not affect the value of the firm, it provides considerable insight into what *does* affect value. The value of the firm depends only on the distribution of future cash flows provided by investment decisions. The key to the Miller-Modigliani argument is that investment decisions are completely independent of dividend policy. The firm can pay any level of dividends it wishes without affecting investment decisions. If dividends plus desired investment outlays use more cash flow than is provided from operations, the firm should seek external financing (e.g., equity). The desire to maintain a level of dividends should never affect the investment decision.

B. VALUATION, GROWTH, AND DIVIDEND POLICY

The Miller-Modigliani argument that the value of the firm is independent of dividend policy also extends into a world with corporate taxes but without personal taxes. In this section, the valuation model (Eq. 14.8) is extended to include corporate taxes and a growing stream of cash flows. The result is a valuation model which has realistic features and hence may be usefully applied to real-world valuation problems. Chapter 15 will expand on the usefulness of the valuation model by means of an example.

1. The Valuation of an All-Equity Firm with Growth

Figure 14.1 uses the time line as a graphic representation of the pattern of cash flows earned by a growing firm. Note that there is a current level of cash flow, NOI_1, which is assumed to be received at the end of each year forever. If the firm made no new investments and only maintained its current level of capital stock, it would receive cash flows each year equal to NOI_1, but it would not be growing. Growth comes from new investment, not replacement investment. The value of new investment depends on the amount of investment, I_t, and its rate of return, r_t.

Figure 14.1
Time pattern of cash flows for a growing firm.

$$V_0 \qquad NOI_1 - I_1 \quad \begin{array}{c} NOI_2 - I_2 = \\ NOI_1 + r_1 I_1 - I_2 \end{array} \quad \cdots \quad NOI_1 + \sum_{\tau=0}^{N-1} r_\tau I_\tau - I_N$$

$$t_0 \qquad\qquad t_1 \qquad\qquad t_2 \qquad\qquad \cdots \qquad\qquad t_N$$

We can extend the valuation equation (14.8) by assuming that the discount rate, ρ, does not change from time period to time period. This is reasonable if all new projects have the same risk as those currently held by the firm. Equation (14.8) is[3]

$$V_0 = \frac{NOI_1 - I_1}{1 + \rho} + \frac{V_1}{1 + \rho}.$$

(14.8)

Given a constant discount rate, ρ, it can be extended to an N-period model as follows:

$$V = \frac{NOI_1 - I_1}{1 + \rho} + \frac{NOI_2 - I_2}{(1 + \rho)^2} + \cdots + \frac{NOI_N - I_N}{(1 + \rho)^N} + \frac{V_N}{(1 + \rho)^N}.$$

(14.9)

A reasonable assumption is that in any time period the value of the firm, V_t, is finite.[4] Therefore, given a model with an infinite horizon, we have

$$V_0 = \lim_{N \to \infty} \sum_{t=1}^{N} \frac{NOI_t - I_t}{(1 + \rho)^t}.$$

(14.10)

Equation (14.10) is the same formula used in Chapter 2 on capital budgeting. The present value of the firm is the sum of the discounted cash flows from operations less the new investment outlays necessary to undertake them.

Referring to Fig. 14.1, we can see that the average return on investment, r_t, is assumed to continue forever at a constant rate. This is a perfectly reasonable assumption because if the capital budgeting decision is made correctly, each project will return enough cash to cover payments to suppliers of capital and to recover the initial investment. Thus the cash flows are sufficient to provide any needed replacement investment to sustain the project at a constant level forever. The stream of cash flows for the growing firm in Fig. 14.1 are given in Table 14.1 (also Eq. 14.11).

Table 14.1

Time Period	Cash Inflow	Cash Outflow	
1	NOI_1	$-I_1$	
2	$NOI_2 = NOI_1 + r_1 I_1$	$-I_2$	
3	$NOI_3 = NOI_1 + r_1 I_1 + r_2 I_2$	$-I_3$	(14.11)
$\vdots$	$\vdots$	$\vdots$	
N	$NOI_N = NOI_1 + \sum_{\tau=1}^{N-1} r_\tau I_\tau$	$-I_N$	

Substituting (14.11) into (14.10), we can express the present value of the growing

---

[3] The tildes (˜) are dropped for notational convenience. Also note that:

$$NOI_2 = NOI_1 + r_1 I_1.$$

[4] After all, no one has observed a firm with infinite value as yet.

firm as

$$V_0 = \frac{\text{NOI}_1 - I_1}{1 + \rho} + \frac{\text{NOI}_1 + r_1 I_1 - I_2}{(1 + \rho)^2} + \frac{\text{NOI}_1 + r_1 I_1 + r_2 I_2 - I_3}{(1 + \rho)^3}$$

$$+ \cdots + \frac{\text{NOI}_1 + \sum\limits_{\tau=1}^{N-1} r_\tau I_\tau - I_N}{(1 + \rho)^N} \, . \tag{14.12}$$

This extended equation can be simplified greatly. First, rewrite it by rearranging terms as follows.

$$V_0 = \frac{\text{NOI}_1}{1 + \rho} + \frac{\text{NOI}_1}{(1 + \rho)^2} + \cdots + \frac{\text{NOI}_1}{(1 + \rho)^N}$$

$$+ I_1 \left[\frac{r_1}{(1 + \rho)^2} + \frac{r_1}{(1 + \rho)^3} + \cdots + \frac{r_1}{(1 + \rho)^N} - \frac{1}{1 + \rho} \right]$$

$$+ I_2 \left[\frac{r_2}{(1 + \rho)^3} + \frac{r_2}{(1 + \rho)^4} + \cdots + \frac{r_2}{(1 + \rho)^N} - \frac{1}{(1 + \rho)^2} \right] + \cdots .$$

This result can be generalized as

$$V_0 = \sum_{t=1}^{N} \frac{\text{NOI}_1}{(1 + \rho)^t} + \sum_{t=1}^{N} I_t \left[\left(\sum_{\tau=t+1}^{N} \frac{r_t}{(1 + \rho)^\tau} \right) - \frac{1}{(1 + \rho)^t} \right] . \tag{14.13}$$

We can simplify Eq. (14.13) by recognizing that the first term is an infinite annuity with constant payments of NOI_1 per period. Therefore

$$\operatorname*{Lim}_{N \to \infty} \sum_{t=1}^{N} \frac{\text{NOI}_1}{(1 + \rho)^t} = \frac{\text{NOI}_1}{\rho} \, . \tag{14.14}$$

Next, the second term in (14.13) can be simplified as follows:

$$\sum_{\tau=t+1}^{N} \frac{r_t}{(1 + \rho)^\tau} = \frac{1}{(1 + \rho)^t} \sum_{\tau=1}^{N-t} \frac{r_t}{(1 + \rho)^\tau} ,$$

$$\frac{1}{(1 + \rho)^t} \operatorname*{Lim}_{N \to \infty} \sum_{\tau=1}^{N-t} \frac{r_t}{(1 + \rho)^\tau} = \frac{1}{(1 + \rho)^t} \frac{r_t}{\rho} \, . \tag{14.15}$$

Substituting (14.14) and (14.15) back into (14.13), we obtain a simplified expression for the present value of the firm:

$$V_0 = \operatorname*{Lim}_{N \to \infty} \left[\frac{\text{NOI}_1}{\rho} + \sum_{t=1}^{N} I_t \left[\left(\frac{r_t}{\rho(1 + \rho)^t} \right) - \frac{1}{(1 + \rho)^t} \right] \right]$$

$$= \frac{\text{NOI}_1}{\rho} + \sum_{t=1}^{\infty} \frac{I_t (r_t - \rho)}{\rho(1 + \rho)^t} \, . \tag{14.16}$$

2. Why Earnings per Share Growth Maximization is an Inappropriate Goal

This form of valuation equation provides important insights into the much abused term "growth stock." The first term in Eq. (14.16) is the present value of a firm which makes no new investments. It is the present value of an infinite stream of constant cash flows. In other words, it is the value of a firm which is not growing. But what about the firm which makes new investments? The present value of new investment is shown in the second term of Eq. (14.16). The *value* of new investment depends on two things: (1) the amount of investment made and (2) the difference between the average rate of return on the investment, r_t, and the market-required rate of return, ρ. The assets of a firm may grow, but they don't add anything to value unless they earn a rate of return greater than what the market requires for assets of equivalent risk. For example, supposing that the market requires a 10% rate of return (that is, $\rho = 10\%$) consider the three situations given in Table 14.2. Firm 3 has the greatest "growth" in earnings ($\Delta NOI = 5000$). But which firm has the greatest increase in value? Obviously, firm 1 does. The reason is that it is the only firm which has new investments which earn more than the required-market rate of return of 10%. Therefore, the objective of a firm should *never* be to simply maximize growth in earnings or cash flows. The objective should be to maximize the market value of the firm which is equivalent to maximizing wealth.

Another feature of Eq. (14.16) is that it is derived directly from Eq. (14.8), and in both we have the result that dividend policy is irrelevant in a world without taxes or transactions costs.

3. The Value of an All-Equity Firm which Grows at a Constant Rate Forever

Equation (14.16) is elegant, but somewhat cumbersome to use. It has two useful variations. The first, which is developed below, assumes that the firm experiences a constant rate of growth forever. We shall call it the infinite constant-growth model. The second, developed later on, assumes that the firm can maintain a supernormal rate of growth for a finite period of time, T, and realizes a normal rate of growth thereafter. It is called the finite super-growth model.

The constant-growth model can be derived from Eq. (14.16) if we assume that a constant fraction, K, of earnings is retained for investment and the average rate of return, r_t, on all projects is the same. The fraction of earnings to be retained for

Table 14.2

	$\Delta I, \$$	$r, \%$	$\Delta NOI, \$$	$\Delta V, \$$
Firm 1	10,000	20	2,000	9,090
Firm 2	30,000	10	3,000	0
Firm 3	100,000	5	5,000	−45,454

investment is usually called the retention ratio; however, there is no reason to restrict it to be less than 100% of cash flows from operations. Rather than calling K the retention rate, we shall call it the *investment rate*. As was mentioned in the first section of this chapter, the firm can invest more than cash flow from operations if it provides for the funds by issuing new equity. If investment is a constant proportion of cash flows, we have

$$I_t = K(\text{NOI}_t). \tag{14.17}$$

And if the rate of return on investment, r_t, is the same for every project, then

$$\text{NOI}_t = \text{NOI}_{t-1} + rI_{t-1},$$

$$= \text{NOI}_{t-1} + rK\,\text{NOI}_{t-1},$$

$$= \text{NOI}_{t-1}(1 + rK).$$

By successive substitution, we have

$$\text{NOI}_t = \text{NOI}_1(1 + rK)^{t-1}. \tag{14.18}$$

Note that rK is the same rate of growth, g, for cash flows. In other words, NOI in the tth time period is the future value of NOI in the first time period, assuming that cash flows grow at a constant rate, g:

$$\text{NOI}_t = \text{NOI}_1(1 + g)^{t-1}.$$

By substituting (14.17) into (14.16) and maintaining the assumption that $r_t = r$, we have

$$V_0 = \frac{\text{NOI}_1}{\rho} + \sum_{t=1}^{\infty} \frac{K\,\text{NOI}_t(r - \rho)}{\rho(1 + \rho)^t}. \tag{14.19}$$

Then by using (14.18) in (14.19) we obtain

$$V_0 = \frac{\text{NOI}_1}{\rho} + K\,\text{NOI}_1\left(\frac{r - \rho}{\rho}\right) \sum_{t=1}^{\infty} \frac{(1 + rK)^{t-1}}{(1 + \rho)^t}$$

$$= \frac{\text{NOI}_1}{\rho}\left[1 + \frac{K(r - \rho)}{1 + rK} \sum_{t=1}^{\infty} \left(\frac{1 + rK}{1 + \rho}\right)^t\right]. \tag{14.20}$$

If $rK < \rho$, then the last term in (14.20) will have a finite limit[5]

$$\lim_{N \to \infty} \sum_{t=1}^{N} \left(\frac{1 + rK}{1 + \rho}\right)^t = \frac{1 + rK}{\rho - rK} \quad \text{iff} \quad \rho > rK. \tag{14.20a}$$

---

[5] For proof let $(1 + rK)/(1 + \rho) = U$. This can be written as

$$S = U + U^2 + \cdots + U^N.$$

Multiplying this by U and subtracting the result from the above, we have

$$S = U/(1 - U) - U^{N+1}/(1 - U).$$

The second term approaches zero in the limit as N approaches infinity. By substituting back the definition of U, we get (14.20a).

Substituting (14.20a) into (14.20) and simplifying, we have an equation for the value of the firm, assuming infinite growth at a rate less than the market rate of return, ρ.

$$V_0 = \frac{\text{NOI}_1}{\rho}\left[1 + \frac{K(r-\rho)}{1+Kr}\frac{1+Kr}{\rho - rK}\right]$$

$$= \frac{\text{NOI}_1(1-K)}{\rho - Kr}. \tag{14.21}$$

Equation (14.21), rewritten in a somewhat different form, is frequently referred to as the *Gordon growth model*. Note that since K is the investment rate (although K need not be less than one), the numerator of (14.21) is the same as dividends paid at the end of the first time period:

$$\text{NOI}_1(1-K) = D_1.$$

Also, as was shown earlier, the product of the investment rate and the average rate of return on investment is the same as the growth rate, g, in cash flows; therefore

$$Kr = g.$$

Given these facts and the necessary condition that $g < \rho$, the infinite growth model, Eq. (14.21), can be rewritten as

$$V_0 = \frac{D_1}{\rho - g}, \tag{14.21a}$$

which is the *Gordon growth model*.

4. Independence Between Investment Plans and Dividend Payout

This form of the valuation model can be used to illustrate the relationship between the result that the value of the firm is independent of dividend policy and the assumption that investment decisions should never be affected by dividend payout. A commonly made error is to implicitly assume that there is some relationship between the amount of cash flow retained and the amount of investment which the firm undertakes. Suppose we take the partial derivative of Eq. (14.21) with respect to changes in the investment rate, K:

$$\frac{\delta V_0}{\delta K} = \frac{\text{NOI}_1(r - \rho)}{(\rho - rK)^2} > 0.$$

This suggests that if the rate of return on investments, r, is greater than the market-required rate of return, ρ, the value of the firm will increase as more cash flow is retained, and presumably the increased amount of retained cash flow implies lower dividend payout. This line of reasoning is incorrect for two reasons. First, the amount of cash flow retained has nothing to do with dividend payout. As was shown in the sources and uses of funds, identity (14.3), the firm can arbitrarily set dividend payout at any level whatsoever, and if the sum of funds used for dividends and investment is greater than cash flows from operations, the firm will issue new equity. Second, the investment decision which maximizes shareholder wealth depends only on the market-required rate of return. The amount of cash flow retained could exceed the amount of investment, which would imply that shares would be repurchased. Therefore there is no relationship between the value of the firm and either dividend payout or cash flow retention.

5. The Bird-in-Hand Fallacy

A more sophisticated argument for a relationship between the value of the firm and dividend payout is that although the dividend decision cannot change the present value of cash payments to shareholders, it can affect the temporal pattern of payouts. Suppose that investors view distant dividend payments as riskier than current payments, might they not prefer a bird in the hand to two in the bush? We can represent this argument mathematically by assuming that higher investment rates mean lower current dividend payout, more risk, and therefore an increase in the market rate of return, ρ, as a function of the investment rate, K. A simple example would be to specify the relationship as

$$\rho = \alpha + \beta K^2, \qquad \beta > 0.$$

Then we would have

$$\frac{\delta V_0}{\delta K} = \frac{\mathrm{NOI}_1(\beta K^2 - 2\beta K + r - \alpha)}{(\alpha + \beta K^2 - rK)^2}, \qquad \alpha + \beta K^2 - rK > 0.$$

This function will have a maximum where

$$\mathrm{NOI}_1(\beta K^2 - 2\beta K + r - \alpha) = 0.$$

In order to see the error in this line of reasoning, we need only to return to our understanding of valuation under uncertainty. The risk of the firm is determined by the riskiness of the cash flows from its projects. An increase in dividend payout today will result in an equivalent drop in the ex-dividend price of the stock. It will not increase the value of the firm by reducing the riskiness of future cash flows.

6. Finite Supernormal Growth Model for an All-Equity Firm

Perhaps the most useful variation of the valuation equation is one which assumes that the rate of return on investment is greater than the market-required rate of return for a finite number of years, T, and from then on is equal to the market-required rate of return. In other words, the firm experiences supernormal growth for a short period of time, then settles down, and grows at a rate which is equal to the rate of growth in the economy. Obviously a firm cannot grow faster than the economy forever or it would soon be larger than the economy.

In order to derive the finite growth model we start with Eq. (14.20). Note that the summation is no longer infinite:

$$V_0 = \frac{NOI_1}{\rho}\left[1 + \frac{K(r-\rho)}{1+rK}\sum_{t=1}^{T}\left(\frac{1+rK}{1+\rho}\right)^t\right]. \qquad (14.20)$$

Instead, growth lasts for only T years. After year T, we assume that $r = \rho$, which means that the second term adds nothing to the present value of the firm. The summation term in Eq. (14.20) can be evaluated as follows. Let

$$U = [(1 + rK)/(1+\rho)].$$

We can then expand the sum:

$$S = U + U^2 + \cdots + U^T.$$

By multiplying S by U and subtracting the result, we have

$$S - US = U - U^{T+1}.$$

Solving for S and substituting back for U, we obtain

$$S = \frac{U - U^{T+1}}{1 - U} = \frac{[(1 + Kr)/(1+\rho)] - [(1 + Kr)/(1+\rho)]^{T+1}}{1 - [(1 + Kr)/(1+\rho)]}$$

$$= \frac{(1 + Kr)[1 - [(1 + Kr)/(1+\rho)]^T]}{\rho - Kr}. \qquad (14.21b)$$

Substituting (14.21b) into (14.20) yields

$$V_0 = \frac{NOI_1}{\rho}\left\{1 + \frac{Kr - \rho K}{\rho - Kr}\left[1 - \left(\frac{1 + Kr}{1+\rho}\right)^T\right]\right\}. \qquad (14.22)$$

As long as Kr is approximately equal to ρ, and T is small, we can approximate the last term as[6]

$$\left(\frac{1 + Kr}{1+\rho}\right)^T \approx 1 - T\left(\frac{\rho - Kr}{1+\rho}\right). \qquad (14.23)$$

---

[6] The binomial expansion can be used to derive the approximation in the following way. Let $(1 + Kr)/(1 + \rho) = 1 + \Delta$. Then, recalling that $Kr = g$, we have:

$$\left(\frac{1+g}{1+\rho}\right)^T = (1 + \Delta) = \sum_{K=0}^{T}\binom{T}{K}(1)^{T-K}\Delta^K$$

$$= 1 + T\Delta + \sum_{K=2}^{T}\binom{T}{K}\Delta^K \approx 1 + T\Delta.$$

Solving for Δ, we have

$$\Delta = \frac{1 + Kr}{1+\rho} - 1 = \frac{Kr - \rho}{1+\rho}.$$

Therefore the correct approximation is

$$1 + T\Delta = 1 - T\left(\frac{\rho - Kr}{1+\rho}\right).$$

By substituting the approximation (14.23) into the valuation equation (14.22), we have an approximate valuation formula for finite supernormal growth:[7]

$$V_0 = \frac{\text{NOI}_1}{\rho} + \frac{K(r-\rho)}{\rho - Kr} T\left(\frac{\rho - Kr}{1+\rho}\right)\frac{\text{NOI}_1}{\rho}$$

$$= \frac{\text{NOI}_1}{\rho} + K(\text{NOI}_1)T\left[\frac{r-\rho}{\rho(1+\rho)}\right]. \qquad (14.24)$$

7. Finite Growth Model for a Firm with Debt and Taxes

Up to this point, we have maintained the assumption that we are dealing with an all-equity firm in a world without taxes. In order to extend the above valuation equation into a world where firms have debt as well as equity and where there are corporate taxes, we can rely on the results obtained in Chapter 12. The value of a levered firm with finite supernormal growth can be written as follows:

$$V = \frac{\text{NOI}_1(1-\tau_c)}{\rho} + \tau_c B + K(\text{NOI}_1(1-\tau_c))T\left[\frac{r-\text{WACC}}{\text{WACC}(1+\text{WACC})}\right], \qquad (14.25)$$

where

$\text{NOI}_1 =$ end-of-year net operating profits,

$\text{WACC} =$ weighted average cost of capital $= \rho[1 - \tau_c B/(B+S)]$,

$\quad B =$ market value of debt,

$\quad K =$ investment rate,

$\quad T =$ the number of years that $r > \text{WACC}$,

$\quad r =$ the average rate of return on investment,

$\quad \rho =$ the cost of equity capital for an all equity firm.

The first two terms in (14.25) are the value of a levered firm with no growth. They are the same as Eq. (12.3), the Modigliani-Miller result which assumes that firms

---

[7] To simulate the validity of the approximation, assume that the investment rate, K, is 50%, the rate of return on investment, r, is 20%, and the market-required rate of return is 15%. Figure 14.A is a plot of $[(1 + Kr)/(1 + \rho)]$. We can see visually that the linear approximation is reasonable.

$\left(\frac{1+Kr}{1+\rho}\right)^T$	T
.9545	1
.9112	2
.8696	3
.8300	4
.7925	5

Figure 14.A
The linear approximation of the growth term.

pay corporate taxes but are not growing. The third term in Eq. (14.25) is the effect of growth on the value of a levered firm. It depends on the amount of investment, $I_t = K(\text{NOI}_t)$, the difference between the expected average rate of return on investment and the weighted average cost of capital, $r - \text{WACC}$, and the length of time, T, that the new investment is expected to earn more than the weighted average cost of capital.

Equation (14.25) is used in Chapter 15 as the basis for the valuation of Bethlehem Steel. Note, however, that even in this model (which is the most realistic of those developed so far in this chapter), dividend payout is not relevant for determining the value of the firm.

C. DIVIDEND POLICY IN A WORLD WITH PERSONAL AND CORPORATE TAXES

Up to this point the models of firms which have been introduced assume a world with only corporate taxes. What happens when personal taxes are considered? In particular, how is dividend policy affected by the important fact that in the United States the capital gains tax is less than the personal income tax? An answer to this question is provided by Farrar and Selwyn [1967] and extended into a market equilibrium framework by Brennan [1970].[8]

Farrar and Selwyn [1967] use partial equilibrium analysis and assume that individuals attempt to maximize their after-tax income. Shareholders have two choices. They can own shares in an all-equity firm and borrow in order to provide personal leverage, or they can buy shares in a levered firm. Therefore, the first choice is the amount of personal versus corporate leverage which is desired. The second choice is the form of payment to be made by the firm. It can pay out earnings as dividends or it can retain earnings and allow shareholders to take their income in the form of capital gains. Shareholders must choose whether they want dividends or capital gains.

If the firm pays out all of its cash flows as dividends, the ith shareholder will receive the following after-tax income, $\tilde{Y}_i^d$.

$$\tilde{Y}_i^d = [(\text{N\tilde{O}I} - rD_c)(1 - \tau_c) - rD_{pi}](1 - \tau_{pi}),\tag{14.26}$$

where

$\tilde{Y}_i^d$ = the uncertain income to the ith individual if corporate income is received as dividends,

$\text{N\tilde{O}I}$ = the uncertain cash flows from operations provided by the firm,

r = the borrowing rate which is assumed to be equal for individuals and firms,

D_c = corporate debt,

D_{pi} = personal debt held by the ith individual,

τ_c = the corporate tax rate,

τ_{pi} = the personal income tax rate of the ith individual.

---

[8] More recently Miller and Scholes [1978] have also considered a world with dividends and taxes. The implications of this paper are discussed later in this chapter.

The first term within the brackets is the after-tax cash flow of the firm, which is $(\text{N\~OI} - rD)(1 - \tau_c)$. All of this is assumed to be paid out as dividends. The before-tax income to the shareholder is the dividends received minus the interest on debt used to buy shares. After subtracting income taxes on this income we are left with Eq. (14.26).

Alternatively, the firm can decide to pay no dividends, in which case we assume that all gains are realized *immediately* by investors and taxed at the capital gains rate.[9] In this event, the after-tax income of a shareholder is

$$\tilde{Y}_i^g = (\text{N\~OI} - rD_c)(1 - \tau_c)(1 - \tau_{gi}) - rD_{pi}(1 - \tau_{pi}), \qquad (14.27)$$

where

$\tilde{Y}_i^g$ = the uncertain income to the ith individual if corporate income is received as capital gains,

τ_{gi} = the capital gains rate for the ith individual.

Now the individual pays a capital gains tax rate on the income from the firm and deducts after-tax interest expenses on personal debt. The corporation can implement the policy of translating cash flows into capital gains by simply repurchasing its shares in the open market.

We can rewrite Eq. (14.27) as follows:

$$\tilde{Y}_i^g = [(\text{N\~OI} - rD_c)(1 - \tau_c) - rD_{pi}](1 - \tau_{gi}) + rD_{pi}(\tau_{pi} - \tau_{gi}). \qquad (14.28)$$

From Eqs. (14.26) and (14.28) the advantage to investors of receiving returns in the form of capital gains rather than dividends should be obvious. So long as the tax rate on capital gains is less than the personal tax rate ($\tau_{gi} < \tau_{pi}$), individuals will prefer capital gains to dividends for any positive operating cash flows, rate of interest, and level of debt (personal or corporate). The ratio of the two income streams,

$$\frac{\tilde{Y}_i^g}{\tilde{Y}_i^d} = \frac{[(\text{N\~OI} - rD_c)(1 - \tau_c) - rD_{pi}](1 - \tau_{gi}) + rD_{pi}(\tau_{pi} - \tau_{gi})}{[(\text{N\~OI} - rD_c)(1 - \tau_c) - rD_{pi}](1 - \tau_{pi})} > 1, \qquad (14.29)$$

is greater than one if $\tau_{gi} < \tau_{pi}$. In general, the best form of payment is the one which is subject to least taxation. The implication, of course, is that corporations should never pay dividends. If payments are to be made to shareholders, they should always be made via share repurchase. This allows shareholders to avoid paying income tax rates on dividends. Instead, they receive their payments in the form of capital gains which are taxed at a lower rate.

What about debt policy? Again the same principle holds. The debt should be held by the party who can obtain the greatest tax shield from the deductible interest payments. This is the party with the greatest marginal tax rate. If the firm pays out all its cash flow in the form of dividends, the favorable tax treatment of capital

---

[9] Obviously there is the third possibility that earnings are translated into capital gains and the capital gains taxes are deferred to a later date. This possibility is considered in Farrar and Selwyn [1967]; it does not change their conclusions.

gains is irrelevant. In this case, we have the familiar Modigliani-Miller [1963] result that the value of the firm is maximized by taking on the maximum amount of debt (see Chapter 12). Proof is obtained by taking the partial derivative of Eq. (14.26) with respect to personal and corporate debt and comparing the results.

Debt policy becomes more complex when the corporation repurchases shares instead of paying dividends. Taking the partial derivatives of the capital gains income equation, (14.27), we obtain

$$\text{Corporate debt: } \frac{\delta \tilde{Y}_i^g}{\delta D_c} = -r(1 - \tau_c)(1 - \tau_{gi}), \tag{14.30}$$

$$\text{Personal debt: } \frac{\delta \tilde{Y}_i^g}{\delta D_{pi}} = -r(1 - \tau_{pi}). \tag{14.31}$$

If the effective tax rate on capital gains is zero (as Miller [1977] suggests), then personal debt will be preferred to corporate debt by those individuals who are in marginal tax brackets higher than the marginal tax bracket of the firm. This result allows the possibility of clientele effects where low-income investors prefer corporate debt and high-income investors prefer personal debt. Miller [1977] takes this argument even further. He shows that if the borrowing rate on debt is "grossed up" so that the after-tax rate on debt equals the after-tax rate on other sources of capital, the marginal investor will be indifferent between personal and corporate debt.[10]

Kim, Lewellen, and McConnell [1979] tested for clientele effects. The hypothesis is that firms with low leverage tend to attract shareholders with high marginal tax rates who then use personal borrowing (such as buying shares on margin) to achieve their desired tax shield and risk level. Firms with similar characteristics, but high leverage, should be owned by shareholders with low marginal tax rates.[11] The data set for the empirical work consisted of the portfolios of 1140 companies whose stock was owned by at least three investors from among a group of 887. Questionnaires provided demographic and income data for the investors during a three-year period 1969–1971. From this data the marginal tax rates of the investors were imputed. Table 14.3 shows the results of a multiple regression which explains the corporate total debt to total capital ratio as a function of various shareholder characteristics. The coefficients of five of the seven independent variables are statistically significant as is the overall significance of the regression ($F = 7.51$). The coefficient of the investor tax rate is of the correct sign and is statistically significant, but its magnitude indicates that an increase in an investor's personal tax rate from zero to 70% is associated with an increase of only 5% in the corporate leverage ratio. As suggested by Kim, Lewellen, and McConnell, "A relationship that slight has to be interpreted as somewhat less than strongly supportive of the financial leverage clientele hypothesis."

Brennan [1970] extends the work of Farrar and Selwyn into a general equilibrium

---

[10] The reader is referred to Chapter 12 for a complete discussion of this point.

[11] Empirical evidence, discussed in Chapter 15, shows that there is a dividend clientele effect, i.e., firms with high dividend yield attract shareholders with low marginal tax rates and vice versa.

Table 14.3

Regression Results: Corporate Total Debt to Total Capital Ratios vs. Shareholder Characteristics. [a]

Independent variable	Estimated coefficient $(\times 10^{-2})$	Standard error $(\times 10^{-2})$	t-statistic
Constant term	45.69	2.72	16.82[c]
Shareholder characteristics			
Sex	2.38	0.72	3.31[c]
Educational level	−0.31	0.08	−3.74[c]
Employment status	1.30	0.64	2.00[b]
Marginal tax rate	−6.81	2.19	−3.11[c]
Age	−0.07	0.03	−2.28[b]
Family size	−0.13	0.24	−0.56
Marital status	0.14	0.76	0.18

[a] Variables listed in stepwise entry order: $R^2 = 0.008$, $N = 6217$, $F = 7.51$.
[b] Denotes significance at 0.05 level.
[c] Denotes significance at 0.01 level.

Source: Kim, E. H., W. Lewellen, and J. McConnell, "Financial Leverage Clienteles: Theory and Evidence," reprinted with permission of *The Journal of Financial Economics,* March 1979, 106.

framework where investors are assumed to maximize their expected utility of wealth. Although this framework is more robust, Brennan's conclusions are not much different from those of Farrar and Selwyn. With regard to dividend payout he concludes that "for a given level of risk, investors require a higher total return on a security the higher its prospective dividend yield is, because of the higher rate of tax levied on dividends than on capital gains." As we shall see in the next chapter, this statement has empirical implications for the CAPM. It suggests that dividend payout should be included as a second factor to explain the equilibrium rate of return on securities. If true, the empirical CAPM would become

$$\tilde{R}_{jt} - R_{ft} = \delta_0 + \delta_1 \beta_{jt} + \delta_2 (D_{jt} - R_{ft}) + \tilde{\epsilon}_{jt},$$

where

$\delta_0 = $ a constant,

$\delta_1 = $ influence of systematic risk on $\tilde{R}_{jt}$,

$\delta_2 = $ influence of dividend payout on $\tilde{R}_{jt}$,

$\beta_{jt} = $ the systematic risk of the jth security,

$D_{jt} = $ the dividend yield on the jth security,

$\tilde{\epsilon}_{jt} = $ a random error term,

$R_{ft} = $ the risk-free rate.

If the dividend yield factor turns out to be statistically significant, then we might conclude that dividend policy is not irrelevant.

A paper by Miller and Scholes [1977] shows that even with existing tax laws (where the tax on ordinary personal income is greater than the capital gains tax), many individuals need not pay more than the capital gains rate on dividends. The implication is that individuals will be indifferent between payments in the form of dividends or capital gains (if the firm decides to repurchase shares). Thus the firm's value may be unrelated to its dividend policy even in a world with taxes.

To clarify their argument, Miller and Scholes provide the following simple example. Let us suppose we have an initial net worth of $25,000, which is represented wholly by an investment of 2500 shares worth $10 each in a company which earns $1.00 per share. At the end of the year the company pays $.40 per share in dividends and retains $.60. Consequently its end-of-year price per share is $10.60. In order to neutralize our dividend income for tax purposes, we borrow $16,667 at 6% and invest the proceeds in a risk-free project (such as life insurance or a Keogh account) which pays 6% of tax-deferred interest. Our opening and closing balance sheets and our income statement are given in Table 14.4. Note that by investing in risk-free assets we have not increased the risk of our wealth position. The riskless cash inflows from insurance exactly match the required payments on debt. Our true economic income could be $1500 in *unrealized* capital gains plus the $1000 of tax-deferred interest from life insurance or our Keogh account.

Table 14.4

Opening Balance Sheet				*Closing Balance Sheet*			
Assets		Liabilities		Assets		Liabilities	
2,500 shares				2,500 shares			
at $10 = 25,000		Loan	16,667	at $10.60 = 26,500		Loan	16,667
Insurance	16,667	Net worth	25,000	Accrued		Accrued	
	41,667		41,667	dividends	1,000	interest	1,000
				Insurance	16,667	Net worth	26,500
					44,167		44,167

Ordinary income		Capital gains	
Dividends received	$1,000	Sale of 2,500 shares at $10.60 = $26,500	
Less interest expense	1,000	Less original basis	25,000
	0		1,500
Nontaxable income	1,000		
	1,000		

Of course, federal tax laws are complex and these transactions cannot be carried out without some transactions costs.[12] Nevertheless, the above argument is a clever way to demonstrate the fact that ordinary income taxes on dividends can be avoided.

D. TOWARD A THEORY OF OPTIMAL DIVIDEND POLICY

The Miller-Modigliani [1961] paper proved the irrelevance of dividend policy in a world where there were no taxes or transactions costs and where everyone was fully informed about the distribution of the firm's uncertain future cash flows. Once corporate and personal income taxes were introduced then the theory (e.g., Farrar and Selwyn [1967] and Brennan [1970]) suggested that perhaps it would be optimal to pay no dividends at all because of the tax disadvantage of ordinary income over capital gains. This point of view was modified somewhat by Miller and Scholes [1978] who showed how dividend income could, to a large extent, be sheltered from taxation. The papers mentioned below go one step further. They provide theories to explain benefits as well as costs of dividend payout in an effort to move toward a theory of optimal dividend policy.

1. Theories Based on the Informativeness of Dividend Payout

Ross [1977] suggests that implicit in the Miller-Modigliani dividend irrelevancy proposition is the assumption that the market *knows* the (random) return stream of the firm and values this stream to set the value of the firm. What is valued in the marketplace, however, is the *perceived* stream of returns for the firm. Putting the issue this way raises the possibility that changes in the capital structure (or dividend payout) may alter the market's perception. In the old terminology of Modigliani and Miller, by changing its financial structure (or dividend payout) the firm alters its perceived risk class, even though the actual risk class remains unchanged.

Managers, as insiders who have monopolistic access to information about the firm's expected cash flows, will choose to establish unambiguous signals about the firm's future if they have the proper incentive to do so. We saw, in Chapter 13, that changes in the capital structure of the firm may be used as signals. In particular, Ross [1977] proved that an increase in the use of debt will represent an unambiguous signal to the marketplace that the firm's prospects have improved.

The signaling concept is easily applied to dividend policy as well as to financial structure. We shall see that a possible benefit of dividends is that they provide valuable signals. This benefit can be balanced against the costs of paying dividends to establish a theory of optimal dividend policy.

A firm which increases dividend payout is signaling that it has expected future

---

[12] Also the maximum amount of dividends which can be sheltered in this way is $10,000. See Feenberg [1981].

cash flows which are sufficiently large to meet debt payments and dividend payments without increasing the probability of bankruptcy. Therefore we may expect to find empirical evidence which shows that the value of the firm increases because dividends are taken as signals that the firm is expected to have permanently higher future cash flows. Chapter 15 reviews the empirical evidence on dividends as signals.

Bhattacharya [1979] develops a model closely related to that of Ross [1977] which can be used to explain why firms may pay dividends despite the tax disadvantage of doing so. If investors believe that firms which pay greater dividends per share have higher values, then an unexpected dividend increase will be taken as a favorable signal. Presumably dividends convey information about the value of the firm which cannot be fully communicated by other means such as annual reports, earnings forecasts, or presentations before security analysts. It is expensive for less successful firms to mimic the signal because they must incur extra costs associated with raising external funds in order to pay the cash dividend.[13] Hence the signaling value of dividends is positive and can be traded off against the tax loss associated with dividend income (as opposed to capital gains). Even firms which are closely held would prefer to pay dividends because the value induced by the signal is received by current owners only when the dividend message is communicated to outsiders. One of the important implications of this signaling argument is that it suggests the possibility of optimal dividend policy. The signaling benefits from paying dividends may be traded off against the tax disadvantages in order to achieve an optimal payout.

Hakansson [1982] has expanded the understanding of informative signaling to show that in addition to being informative at least one of three sufficient conditions must be met. Either investors must have different probability assessments of dividend payouts, or they must have differing attitudes about how they wish to allocate consumption expenditures over time, or the financial markets must be incomplete. All three of these effects may operate in a complementary fashion, and all three are reasonable.

One problem which the above theories have in common is that although they explain how an optimal dividend policy may arise, none of them can succussfully explain cross-sectional differences in dividend payouts across firms. The next theory shows better promise in this regard.

2. Agency Costs, External Financing, and Optimal Dividend Payout

Rozeff [1981] suggests that optimal dividend policy may exist even though we ignore tax considerations. He suggests that cross-sectional regularities in corporate dividend payout ratios[14] may be explained by a trade-off between the flotation costs of raising external capital and the benefit of reduced agency costs when the firm increases its dividend payout. It is not hard to understand that owners prefer to avoid paying the transactions costs associated with external financing.

---

[13] This suggests that dividend payout and debt level increases are interrelated signals. A firm which simultaneously pays dividends and borrows may be giving a different signal than if it had made the same dividend payment without borrowing.

[14] The payout ratio is the ratio of dividends to net income.

As discussed earlier (Chapters 13, Section B.3), there are agency costs which arise when owner-managers sell portions of their stockholdings to so-called "outside" equity owners. The outsiders will charge, *ex ante,* for the potential problem that owner-managers may increase their personal wealth at the expense of outsiders by means of more perquisites or shirking. To decrease the *ex ante* charge, owner-managers will find it in their own interest to agree to incur monitoring or bonding costs if such costs are less than the *ex ante* charge which outsiders would be forced to request. Thus a wealth-maximizing firm will adopt an optimal monitoring/bonding policy which minimizes agency costs.

Dividend payments may well serve as a means of monitoring or bonding management performance. Although greater dividend payout implies costly external financing, the very fact that the firm must go to the capital markets implies that it will come under greater scrutiny. For example, banks will require a careful analysis of the creditworthiness of the firm and the Securities and Exchange Commission will require prospectus filings for new equity issues. Thus outside suppliers of capital help to monitor the owner-manager on behalf of outside equity owners. Of course, audited financial statements are a substitute means for supplying the same information, but they may not be a perfect substitute for the "adversary" relationship between the firm and suppliers of new capital.

Because of the transactions costs of external financing, Rozeff also argues that the variability of a firm's cash flows will affect its dividend payout. Consider two firms with the same average cash flows across time but different variability. The firm with greater volatility will borrow in bad years and repay in good. It will need to finance externally more often. Consequently, it will tend to have a lower dividend payout ratio.

Rozeff [1981] selected a sample of 1000 nonregulated firms in 64 different industries and examined their average dividend payout ratios during the 1974–1980 interval. Five proxy variables were chosen to test his theory. The results are shown in Table 14.5. The independent variables GROW1 and GROW2 are an attempt to measure the effect of costly external financing. Firms which grow faster can reduce their need to use external financing by paying lower dividends. GROW1 measures the growth rate in revenues between 1974 and 1979, while GROW2 is Value Line's forecast of the growth of sales revenue over the five-year period 1979–1984. Both variables are negatively related to dividend payout and are statistically significant. The variables INS and STOCK are proxies for the agency relationship. INS is the percent of the firm held by insiders. Dividend payout is negatively related to the percentage of insiders because given a lower percentage of outsiders there is less need to pay dividends to reduce agency costs.[15] On the other hand, if the distribution of outsider holdings is diffuse, then agency costs will be higher, hence one would expect STOCK, the number of stockholders, to be positively related to dividend payout. Both INS and STOCK are statistically significant and of the predicted sign. Finally, the variable BETA measures the riskiness of the firm. The prediction that riskier firms have lower dividend payout is verified by the regression.

---

[15] This relationship is also consistent with the tax argument which assumes that high tax bracket insiders prefer to take their return in the form of capital gains rather than dividends.

Table 14.5 Cross-Sectional Dividend Payout Regressions

	CONSTANT	INS	GROW1	GROW2	BETA	STOCK	R^2	D.W.	F-statistic
(1)	47.81 (12.83)	−0.090 (−4.10)	−0.321 (−6.38)	−0.526 (−6.43)	−26.543 (−17.05)	2.584 (7.73)	0.48	1.88	185.47
(2)	24.73 (6.27)	−0.068 (−2.75)	−0.474 (−8.44)	−0.758 (−8.28)	—	2.517 (6.63)	0.33	1.79	123.23
(3)	70.63 (40.35)	—	−0.402 (−7.58)	−0.603 (−6.94)	−25.409 (−15.35)	—	0.41	1.88	231.46
(4)	39.56 (10.02)	−0.116 (−4.92)	—	—	−33.506 (−21.28)	3.151 (8.82)	0.39	1.80	218.10
(5)	1.03 (0.24)	−0.102 (−3.60)	—	—	—	3.429 (7.97)	0.12	1.60	69.33

t-statistics are shown in parentheses under estimated values of the regression coefficients. R^2 is adjusted for degrees of freedom. D.W. is Durbin-Watson statistic.

Source: Rozeff, M., "Growth, Beta, and Agency Costs as Determinants of Dividend Payout Ratios," Working Paper series no. 81–11, University of Iowa, June 1981. Reprinted with permission of the author.

The best regression in Table 14.5 explains 48% of the cross-sectional variability in dividend payout across individual firms. Although the results cannot be used to distinguish among various theories of optimal dividend policy, they are consistent with Rozeff's predictions. Furthermore, the very existence of strong cross-sectional regularities suggests that there is an optimal dividend policy.

E. OTHER DIVIDEND POLICY ISSUES

1. Dividends and Shares Repurchase from a Bondholder's Point of View

Debt contracts, particularly when long-term debt is involved, frequently restrict a firm's ability to pay cash dividends. Such restrictions usually state that (1) future dividends can be paid only out of earnings generated after the signing of the loan agreement (i.e., future dividends cannot be paid out of past retained earnings), and (2) dividends cannot be paid when net working capital (current assets minus current liabilities) is below a prespecified amount.

One need not restrict the argument to only dividend payout. When any of the assets of a corporation are paid out to shareholders in any type of capital distribution, the effect is to "steal away" a portion of the bondholders' collateral. In effect, some of the assets which bondholders could claim, in the event that shareholders decide to default, are paid out to shareholders. This diminishes the value of debt and increases the wealth of shareholders.

Of course, the most common type of capital distribution is a dividend payment. A portion of the firm's assets is paid out in the form of cash dividends to shareholders. The most extreme example of defrauding bondholders would be to simply liquidate the assets of the firm and pay out a single, final dividend to shareholders, thereby leaving bondholders with a claim to nothing. For this very reason, most bond indentures explicitly restrict the dividend policy of shareholders. Usually dividends cannot exceed the current earnings of the firm, and they cannot be paid out of retained earnings.

Other types of capital distributions are share repurchase and spinoffs. Share repurchase has exactly the same effect as dividend payment except that the form of payment is capital gains instead of dividend income. The conventional procedure for a spinoff is to take a portion of a firm's assets, often a division relatively unrelated to the rest of the firm, and create an independent firm with these assets. The important fact is that the shares of the new entity are distributed solely to the *shareholders* of the parent corporation. Therefore, like dividend payment or share repurchase, this may be used as a technique for taking collateral from bondholders.

It is an interesting empirical question whether or not any dividend payment, no matter how large it is, will affect the market value of bonds. One would expect that the market price of bonds would reflect the risk that future dividend payments would lower the asset base which secures debt.[16] However, as changes in the dividend payments are actually realized, there may be changes in the expectations of the bond-holders which in turn would be reflected in the market price of bonds. All other things being equal, we may expect that higher dividend payments or share repurchases will be associated with a decline in the market value of debt. However, rarely do we have a situation where all other things are equal. For example, if announcements about dividend changes are interpreted as information about future cash flows, then a dividend increase means that current debt will be more secure because of the antici-pated higher cash flows, and we would observe dividend increases to be positively correlated with increases in the market value of debt.[17]

2. Stock Dividends and Share Repurchase

Stock dividends are often mentioned as part of the dividend policy of the firm. However, a stock dividend is nothing more than a small stock split. It simply increases the number of shares outstanding without changing any of the underlying risk or return characteristics of the firm. Therefore we might expect that it has little or no effect on shareholders' wealth except for the losses associated with the clerical and transactions costs which accompany the stock dividend. The reader who is interested in empirical studies of stock splits is referred to Chapter 9.

Another question which often arises is whether share repurchase is preferable to dividend payment as a means of distributing cash to shareholders. Share repurchase allows shareholders to receive the cash payment as a capital gain rather than as dividend income. Any shareholder who pays a higher tax rate on income than on capital gains would prefer share repurchase to dividend payment. But not all classes of shareholders have this preference. Some, like tax-free university endowment funds, are indifferent to income versus capital gains, while others, such as corporations with their dividend exclusions, would actually prefer dividends.

To see that share repurchase can result in the same benefit per share, consider the following example. The Universal Sourgum Company earns \$4.4 million in 1981 and decides to pay out 50%, or \$2.2 million, either as dividends or repurchase. The company has 1,100,000 shares outstanding with a market value of \$22 per share. It can pay dividends of \$2 per share or repurchase shares at \$22 each. We know that the market price for repurchase is \$22 rather than \$20 because \$22 will be the price per share after repurchase. To demonstrate this statement, we know that the current value of the (all equity) firm is \$24.2 million. For \$2.2 million in cash it can repurchase 100,000 shares. Therefore, after the repurchase the value of the firm falls to \$24.2 − 2.2 = \$22 million, and with 1,000,000 shares outstanding the price per share is \$22. Thus, in theory, there is no price effect from repurchase.

---

[16] Dividend payments do not necessarily change the assets side of the balance sheet. When cash balances are reduced in order to pay dividends, there is an asset effect. However, it is not necessary. Dividends can also be paid by issuing new debt or equity. In this case, assets remain unaffected, and the dividend decision is purely financial in nature.

[17] Empirical evidence on share repurchases via tender offer is reviewed in Chapter 15. Because share repurchases are a form of cash payment to shareholders, they are closely related to dividends.

A comparison of shareholders' wealth before taxes shows that it is the same with either payment technique. If dividends are paid, each shareholder receives a $2 dividend and the ex-dividend price per share is $20 ($22 million ÷ 1.1 million shares). Alternately, as shown above, each share is worth $22 under repurchase, and a shareholder who needs cash can sell off a portion of his or her shares. The preferred form of payment (dividends versus repurchase) will depend on shareholders' tax rates.

In the example shown above there is no price effect from share repurchase. However, recent empirical studies of repurchases via tender offers have found a positive announcement effect. These studies are discussed in detail in Chapter 15.

SUMMARY

Several valuation models with or without growth and with or without corporate taxes have been developed. Dividend policy is irrelevant in all instances. It has no effect on shareholders' wealth. Only when personal taxes are introduced do we have a result where dividends matter. For shareholders who pay higher taxes on dividends than on capital gains, the preferred dividend payout is zero; they would rather have the company distribute cash payments via the share repurchase mechanism. Yet corporations do pay dividends. Furthermore, as the Rozeff [1981] paper suggests, there appear to be strong cross-sectional regularities in dividend payout. Thus, there may be optimal dividend policies which result from a trade-off between the costs and benefits of paying dividends. The list of possible costs includes (1) tax disadvantages of receiving income in the form of dividends rather than capital gains and (2) the cost of raising external capital if dividends are paid out. The possible benefits of dividend payout are (1) higher perceived corporate value because of the signaling content of dividends, (2) lower agency costs of external equity, and (3) the ability of dividend payments to help complete the markets.

The next chapter presents empirical evidence which examines the relationship among the level of dividend payout, the value of the shares, and the amount of investment undertaken by the firm. Also changes in dividend payout are studied in relation to their effect on share value. These studies provide greater insight into the empirical validity of the theories discussed here.

PROBLEM SET

14.1 The chairman of the board of Alphanull Corporation has announced that the corporation will change its dividend policy from paying a fixed dollar dividend per share. Instead, dividends will be paid out as a residual. That is, any cash flows left over after the firm has undertaken all profitable investments will be paid out to shareholders. This new policy will obviously increase the variability of dividends paid. How do you think it will affect the value of the firm?

14.2 The XYZ Company (an all-equity firm) currently has after-tax operating cash flows of $3.00 per share and pays out 50% of its earnings in dividends. If it expects to keep the same payout ratio, and to earn 20% on future investments forever, what will its current price per share be? Assume that the cost of capital is 15%.

14.3 The Highrise Investment Co. (an all-equity firm) currently pays a dividend of $2.00 per share, which is 75% of its after-tax cash flows from operations. It is currently selling for $16 a share and earns 40% on invested capital. Its equity β is 2.0, the expected market rate of return is 12.5%, and the risk-free rate is 5%. How long will its supernormal rate of growth last before it levels off to equal the normal rate for a company with its risk?

14.4 The balance sheet of the Universal Sour Candy Company is given in Table Q14.4. Assume that all balance sheet items are expressed in terms of market values. The company has decided to pay a $2000 dividend to shareholders. There are four ways to do it:

1) Pay a cash dividend.
2) Issue $2000 of new debt and equity in equal proportions ($1000 each) and use the proceeds to pay the dividend.
3) Issue $2000 of new equity and use the proceeds to pay the dividend.
4) Use the $2000 of cash to repurchase equity.

What impact will each of the four policies above have on the following?

a) The systematic risk of the portfolio of assets held by the firm,
b) The market-value of original bondholders' wealth,
c) The market-value ratio of debt to equity,
d) The market value of the firm in a world without taxes.

Table Q14.4 Balance Sheet as of December 31, 19xx

Assets		Liabilities	
Cash	$ 2,000	Debt	$ 5,000
Inventory	2,000	Equity	5,000
Property, plant, and equipment	6,000		
Total assets	$10,000	Total liabilities	$10,000

14.5 According to the valuation model (14.25) with finite supernormal growth and corporate taxes, there are six variables which affect the value of the firm.

a) What are they?
b) Why can't the president of a firm cause the firm's market value to increase simply by reporting anticipated favorable changes in the six variables, for example, an increase in expected return on investment?

14.6 Prove the following for a firm with no supernormal growth (in a world with only corporate taxes):

$$V^L = \frac{E(NOI_1)(1 - \tau_c)}{WACC} = V^U + \tau_c B.$$

14.7 Calculate the value of a company that earned $50,000 this year, has a 40% investment rate, K, and a tax rate of 40%; has $200,000 in debt outstanding and a weighted average cost of capital of 12%; and is expected to earn 40% on invested capital for the next five years, then 25% for the following five years, before the rate of return declines to a normal rate of growth.

14.8 How does an increase in the investment (retention) rate affect the anticipated stream of investments that a company will undertake?

14.9 It was suggested that if a firm announces its intention to increase its dividends (paid from cash), the price of common stock increases—presumably because the higher dividend payout represents an unambiguous signal to shareholders that anticipated cash flows from investment are permanently higher. A higher level of cash flows is also beneficial to bondholders because it diminishes the probability of default. If dividends are paid from cash, what does the OPM suggest will happen to the market value of debt? How does this contrast with the prediction in the above paragraph?

REFERENCES

Bar-Yosef, S., and R. Kolodny, "Dividend Policy and Market Theory," *Review of Economics and Statistics,* May 1967, 181–190.

Bhattacharya, S., "Imperfect Information, Dividend Policy, and 'The Bird in the Hand' Fallacy," *Bell Journal of Economics,* Spring 1979, 259–270.

Black, F., "The Dividend Puzzle," *Journal of Portfolio Management,* Winter 1976, 5–8.

————, M. Jensen, and M. Scholes, "The Capital Asset Pricing Model: Some Empirical Tests," in M. Jensen, ed., *Studies in the Theory of Capital Markets.* Praeger, New York, 1972, 79–124.

Black, F., and M. Scholes, "The Effects of Dividend Yield and Dividend Policy on Common Stock Prices and Returns," *Journal of Financial Economics,* May 1974, 1–22.

Brennan, M., "Taxes, Market Valuation and Corporate Financial Policy," *National Tax Journal,* December 1970, 417–427.

Brittain, J. A., *Corporate Dividend Policy.* Brookings Institute, Washington, D.C. 1966.

Darling, P., "The Influence of Expectations and Liquidity on Dividend Policy," *Journal of Political Economy,* June 1957, 209–224.

Dobrovolsky, S., *The Economics of Corporation Finance.* McGraw-Hill, New York, 1971.

Fama, E., "The Empirical Relationships Between the Dividend and Investment Decisions of Firms," *American Economic Review,* June 1974, 304–318.

————, and H. Babiak, "Dividend Policy: An Empirical Analysis," *Journal of the American Statistical Association,* December 1968, 1132–1161.

Fama, E., and M. H. Miller, *The Theory of Finance.* McGraw-Hill, New York, 1971.

Farrar, D., and L. Selwyn, "Taxes, Corporate Financial Policy and Return to Investors," *National Tax Journal,* December 1967, 444–454.

Feenberg, D., "Does the Investment Interest Limitation Explain the Existence of Dividends?" *Journal of Financial Economics,* September 1981, 265–270.

Friend, I., and M. Puckett, "Dividends and Stock Prices," *American Economic Review,* September 1964, 656–682.

Gordon, M., "Dividends, Earnings, and Stock Prices," *Review of Economics and Statistics,* May 1959, 99–105.

———, "The Savings, Investment and Valuation of a Corporation," *Review of Economics and Statistics,* February 1962, 37–51.

Hakansson, N., "To Pay or Not to Pay Dividends," *Journal of Finance,* May 1982, 415–428.

Khoury, N., and K. Smith, "Dividend Policy and the Capital Gains Tax in Canada," *Journal of Business Administration,* Spring 1977.

Kim, E. H., W. Lewellen, and J. McConnell, "Financial Leverage Clienteles: Theory and Evidence," *Journal of Financial Economics,* March 1979, 83–110.

Lintner, J., "Distribution of Incomes of Corporations Among Dividends, Retained Earnings and Taxes," *American Economic Review,* May 1956, 97–113.

———, "Optimal Dividends and Corporate Growth Under Uncertainty," *The Quarterly Journal of Economics,* February 1964, pp. 49–95.

———, "The Valuation of Risky Assets and the Selection of Risky Investments in Stock Portfolios and Capital Budgets," *Review of Economics and Statistics,* February 1965, 13–37.

Long, J., Jr., "Efficient Portfolio Choice with Differential Taxation of Dividends and Capital Gains," *Journal of Financial Economics,* August 1977, 25–54.

Miller, M., "Debt and Taxes," *Journal of Finance,* May 1977, 261–275.

Miller, M., and F. Modigliani, "Dividend Policy, Growth and the Valuation of Shares," *Journal of Business,* October 1961, 411–433.

Miller, M., and K. Rock, "Dividend Policy Under Asymmetric Information: Part I," working paper, University of Chicago, March 1982.

Miller, M., and M. Scholes, "Dividends and Taxes," *Journal of Financial Economics,* December 1978, 333–364.

———, "Dividends and Taxes: Some Empirical Evidence," working paper, University of Chicago, March 1982, *The Journal of Political Economy,* forthcoming.

Modigliani, F., and M. Miller, "Corporate Income Taxes and the Cost of Capital: A Correction," *American Economic Review,* June 1963, 433–442.

Pettit, R. R., "Dividend Announcements, Security Performance, and Capital Market Efficiency," *Journal of Finance,* December 1972, 993–1007.

Ross, S. A., "The Determination of Financial Structure: The Incentive-Signalling Approach," *Bell Journal of Economics,* Spring 1977, 23–40.

———, "Some Notes on Financial Incentive—Signalling Models, Activity Choice and Risk Preferences," *Journal of Finance,* June 1978, 777–792.

Rozeff, M., "Growth, Beta and Agency Costs as Determinants of Dividend Payout Ratios," Working Paper series no. 81–11, University of Iowa, June 1981.

Walter, J. E., *Dividend Policy and Enterprise Valuation.* Wadsworth, Belmont, Calif., 1967.

Watts, R., "The Information Content of Dividends," *Journal of Business,* April 1973, 191–211.

Dividend Policy: Empirical Evidence and Applications

15

... in the real world a change in the dividend rate is often followed by a change in the market price (sometimes spectacularly so). Such a phenomenon would not be incompatible with irrelevance to the extent that it was merely a reflection of what might be called the "informational content" of dividends...

M. MILLER AND F. MODIGLIANI,
"DIVIDEND POLICY, GROWTH, AND THE
VALUATION OF SHARES,"
THE JOURNAL OF BUSINESS, OCTOBER 1961,
431.

Our discussion first deals with models which simply explain the behavior of corporate dividend policy over time. Evidence indicates that U.S. corporations behave as if they had some target dividend payout in mind and that they move toward it with a lag. They also show reluctance to lower dividends.

Second, we look at the possibility of clientele effects. Do people in high tax brackets avoid investing in high-dividend companies in order to escape higher income taxes on dividend income? On this question, the empirical evidence is mixed, although it does lean toward the existence of a clientele effect.

Third, the information content of dividend increases is tested. Although not conclusive, the evidence leans toward validation of the signaling hypothesis.

Fourth, we focus on the relationship between dividend yield and the market value of equity. The best empirical evidence indicates that dividend yield is not related to the value of the firm. Several explanations are given for why this result is plausible, even with our current tax system.

Fifth, the empirical literature relating to share repurchases via tender offer is reviewed. The announcement of share repurchases tends to be interpreted as unanticipated favorable news about the value of the company.

Finally, we apply the Miller-Modigliani valuation model to the case of Bethlehem Steel in order to demonstrate the relevance of the different factors which determine the value of a firm.

A. BEHAVIORAL MODELS OF DIVIDEND POLICY

Lintner [1956] conducted interviews with 28 carefully selected companies to investigate their thinking on the determination of dividend policy. His field work suggested that (1) managers focused on the change in the existing rate of dividend payout, not on the amount of the newly established payout as such; (2) most managements sought to avoid making changes in their dividend rates that might have to be reversed within a year or so; (3) major changes in earnings "out of line" with existing dividend rates were the most important determinants of the company's dividend decisions; and (4) investment requirements generally had little effect on modifying the pattern of dividend behavior. Taken together, these observations suggest that most companies had somewhat flexible but nevertheless reasonably well-defined standards regarding the speed with which they would try to move toward a full adjustment of dividend payout to earnings. Lintner suggests that corporate dividend behavior can be described on the basis of the following equation:

$$\Delta D_{it} = a_i + c_i(D_{it}^* - D_{i,t-1}) + U_{it}, \tag{15.1}$$

where

ΔD_{it} = the change in dividends per share,

c_i = the speed of adjustment to the difference between a target dividend payout and last year's payout,

D_{it}^* = the target dividend payout,

$D_{i,t-1}$ = last period's dividend payout,

a_i, U_{it} = a constant and a normally distributed random error term.

The target dividend payout, D_{it}^*, is a fraction, r_i, of this period's earnings, E_{it}. Upon fitting the equations to annual data from 1918 through 1941, Lintner found that the model explained 85% of the changes in dividends for his sample of companies.

The average speed of adjustment was approximately 30% per year, and the target payout was 50% of earnings.

Fama and Babiak [1968] investigated many different models for explaining dividend behavior. They used a sample of 201 firms with 17 years of data (1947–1964), then tested each explanatory model by using it to (1) explain dividend policy for a holdout sample of 191 firms and (2) predict dividend payments one year hence. Of the many models which they tried, the two best are Lintner's model (Eq. 15.1) and a similar model which suppresses the constant term and adds a term for the lagged level of earnings. The second model did slightly better than Lintner's.

One can conclude that U.S. corporations seem to increase dividends only after they are reasonably sure that they will be able to maintain them permanently at the new level. However, this does not help to answer the question of why corporations pay dividends in the first place.

B. CLIENTELE EFFECTS

The clientele effect was originally suggested by Miller and Modigliani [1961]:

> If for example the frequency distribution of corporate payout ratios happened to correspond exactly with the distribution of investor preferences for payout ratios, then the existence of these preferences would clearly lead ultimately to a situation whose implications were different, in no fundamental respect, from the perfect market case. Each corporation would tend to attract to itself a "clientele" consisting of those preferring its particular payout ratio, but one clientele would be as good as another in terms of the valuation it would imply for firms.

The clientele effect is a possible explanation for management reluctance to alter established payout ratios because such changes might cause current shareholders to incur unwanted transactions costs.

Elton and Gruber [1970] attempt to measure clientele effects by observing the average price decline when a stock goes ex-dividend. If we were current shareholders and sold our stock the instant before it went ex-dividend, we would receive its price, P_B, and pay the capital gains rate, t_g, on the difference between the selling price and the price at which it was purchased, P_c. Alternatively, we could sell the stock after it went ex-dividend. In this case we would receive the dividend, D, and pay the ordinary tax rate, t_0, on it. In addition, we would pay a capital gains tax on the difference between its ex-dividend price, P_A, and the original purchase price P_c. To prevent arbitrage profits, our gain from either course of action must be the same, namely

$$P_B - t_g(P_B - P_c) = P_A - t_g(P_A - P_c) + D(1 - t_0). \qquad (15.2)$$

Rearranging (15.2), we get

$$\frac{P_B - P_A}{D} = \frac{1 - t_0}{1 - t_g}. \qquad (15.3)$$

Therefore the ratio of the decline in stock price to the dividend paid becomes a means of estimating the marginal tax rate of the average investor, if we assume that the capital gains rate is half the ordinary tax rate.

Using 4148 observations between April 1, 1966 and March 31, 1967, Elton and Gruber discovered that the average price decline as a percent of dividend paid was 77.7%. This implied that the marginal tax bracket of the average investor was 36.4%. They continued by arguing

> ... the lower a firm's dividend yield the smaller the percentage of his total return that a stockholder expects to receive in the form of dividends and the larger the percentage he expects to receive in the form of capital gains. Therefore, investors who held stocks which have high dividend yields should be in low tax brackets relative to stockholders who hold stocks with low dividend yield.

Table 15.1 shows the dividend payout ranked from the lowest to highest deciles along with (1) the average drop in price as a percent of dividends and (2) the implied tax bracket. Note that the implied tax bracket decreases when dividend payout increases. Elton and Gruber conclude that the evidence suggests that Miller and Modigliani were right in hypothesizing a clientele effect.

A possible counterargument to this interpretation is that arbitrage may also be carried out by traders who do not own the stock initially. They would not receive

Table 15.1   Dividend Yield Statistics Ranked by Decile

		$\frac{P_B - P_A}{D}$ *				
Decile	D/P mean	Mean	Standard deviation	Z value	Probability true mean is one or more	Implied tax bracket
1	.0124	.6690	.8054	.411	.341	.4974
2	.0216	.4873	.2080	2.465	.007	.6145
3	.0276	.5447	.1550	2.937	.002	.5915
4	.0328	.6246	.1216	3.087	.001	.5315
5	.0376	.7953	.1064	1.924	.027	.3398
6	.0416	.8679	.0712	1.855	.031	.2334
7	.0452	.9209	.0761	1.210	.113	.1465
8	.0496	.9054	.0691	1.369	.085	.1747
9	.0552	1.0123	.0538	.229	.591	†
10	.0708	1.1755	.0555	3.162	.999	†

* Spearman's rank correlation coefficient between D/P and $(P_B - P_A)/D$ is .9152 which is significant at the 1% level.

† Indeterminate.

Source: Eldon, E. J., and M. J. Gruber, "Marginal Stockholders' Tax Rates and the Clientele Effect," reprinted from *The Review of Economics and Statistics*, February 1970, 72.

favored capital gains treatment but would have to pay ordinary income taxes on short-term gains. Their arbitrage profit, π, may be stated mathematically as

$$\pi = -P_B + D - t_0 D + P_A + t_0(P_B - P_A). \tag{15.4}$$

They spend P_B to acquire the stock before it goes ex-dividend, then receive the dividend and pay ordinary income taxes on it, and finally sell the stock after it goes ex-dividend (receiving P_A dollars) and receive a tax shield from their short-term loss. Rearranging (15.4), we see that their profit is

$$\pi = (1 - t_0)[P_A - P_B + D]. \tag{15.5}$$

In order to prevent arbitrage profits, the price decline must equal the amount of dividend payout, that is, $P_B - P_A = D$.

The above condition is completely different from Eq. (15.3) proposed by Elton and Gruber. Of course neither model has taken transactions costs into account. Nor have we considered other classes of investors, such as tax-free investors. Therefore no strong conclusion can be made regarding the existence of a clientele effect.

More recently, Pettit [1977] has tested for clientele effects by examining the portfolio positions of approximately 914 individual accounts handled by a large retail brokerage house between 1964 and 1970. He argues that stocks with low dividend yields will be preferred by investors with high income, by younger investors, by investors whose ordinary and capital gains tax rates differ substantially, and by investors whose portfolios have high systematic risk. His model is

$$DY_i = a_1 + a_2\beta_i + a_3\,\mathrm{AGE}_i + a_4\,\mathrm{INC}_i + a_5\,\mathrm{DTR}_i + \epsilon_i, \tag{15.6}$$

where

DY_i = dividend yield for the ith individual's portfolio in 1970,

β_i = the systematic risk of the ith individual's portfolio,

AGE_i = the age of the individual,

INC_i = the gross family income averaged over the last three years,

DTR_i = the difference between the income and capital gains tax rates for the ith individual,

ϵ_i = a normally distributed random error term.

He finds that[1]

$$DY_i = \underset{(11.01)}{.042} - \underset{(-16.03)}{.021\beta_i} + \underset{(6.15)}{.031\,\mathrm{AGE}_i} - \underset{(-2.25)}{.037\,\mathrm{INC}_i} + \underset{(1.57)}{.006\,\mathrm{DTR}_i}.$$

The evidence suggests that there is a clientele effect because a significant portion of the observed cross-sectional variation in individual portfolio dividend yields can be explained. However, the study in no way suggests that the market price of a security is determined by the dividend policy followed by the firm.

---

[1] The numbers in parentheses are t-statistics. The r^2 was .3 for 914 observations.

A second study by Lewellen, Stanley, Lease, and Schlarbaum [1978] was drawn from the same database as the Pettit study, but reached different conclusions. They ran a multiple regression to explain the dividend yields of investor portfolios as a function of various investor characteristics. Although the tax rate variable was negatively related to dividend yield and was statistically significant, it implied that a 10% increase in an investor's marginal (imputed) tax bracket was associated with only a .1% decline in the yield of securities held. This suggests only a very weak clientele effect.

C. DIVIDEND ANNOUNCEMENT EFFECTS ON THE VALUE OF THE FIRM: THE SIGNALING HYPOTHESIS

Most firms that pay dividends exhibit behavior which results in constant dividend payouts which are increased only when management is relatively certain that the higher dividend payout can be maintained indefinitely. Given this type of management behavior, it is likely that investors will interpret an increase in current dividend payout as a message that management anticipates permanently higher levels of cash flows from investment. We may, therefore, expect to observe an increase in share prices associated with public announcement of a dividend increase. The dividend *per se* does not affect the value of the firm. Instead it serves as a message from management that the firm is anticipated to do better. If dividend changes are to have an impact on share values, it is necessary that they convey information about future cash flows, but it is not sufficient. The same information may be provided to investors via other sources.[2] Therefore, it becomes an empirical question whether or not announcements of dividend changes actually affect share value.

The first study to look at this issue was the stock split study of Fama, Fisher, Jensen, and Roll [1969], which was discussed in Chapter 10. They found that when splits were accompanied by dividend announcements there was an increase in adjusted share prices for the group which announced dividend increases and a decline in share prices for the dividend decrease group. More recent studies of the effect of unexpected dividend changes on share prices have been made by Pettit [1972], Watts [1973], Kwan [1981], and Aharony and Swary [1980].

Watts finds a positive dividend announcement effect, but concludes that the information content is of no economic significance because it would not enable a trader with monopolistic access to the information to earn abnormal returns after transactions costs. On the other hand, Pettit finds clear support for the proposition that the market uses dividend announcements as information for assessing security values. Their methodologies are also different. Watts proceeds in two stages. First, he develops a model to predict dividend changes. It is the same model which Fama and Babiak [1968]

---

[2] Ross [1977] argues that an increase in dividend payout is an unambiguous message because (1) it cannot be mimicked by firms which do not anticipate higher earnings and (2) management has an incentive to "tell the truth."

found to provide the best prediction of next period's dividends. It may be written as follows:

$$\Delta D_t = \beta_1 D_{t-1} + \beta_2 E_t + \beta_3 E_{t-1} + Z_t, \tag{15.7}$$

where

ΔD_t = the change in dividends in period t,

D_{t-1} = the previous period's dividends,

E_t = this period's earnings,

E_{t-1} = last period's earnings,

Z_t = unanticipated dividend changes (the error term).

Using this equation, we are able to estimate unanticipated dividend changes, Z_t. Next, an abnormal performance index which measures departures from the risk-adjusted rate of return can be constructed from the market model,

$$R_{jt} = \alpha + \beta_j R_{mt} + \epsilon_{jt}, \tag{15.8}$$

where

R_{jt} = the total return (dividends and capital gains) on the common stock of the ith firm,

α = a constant term,

β_j = systematic risk,

R_{mt} = the rate of return on a market index,

ϵ_{jt} = the abnormal performance of the ith security.

The abnormal performance index for a security is computed as the product of its one-month abnormal returns.

$$\text{API} = \prod_{t=1}^{T} (1 + \epsilon_{jt}), \qquad T = 1, \ldots, N.$$

Watts looked at the abnormal performance index averaged across 310 firms. The abnormal performance index for 24 months around the dividend announcement for the subsamples of firms which had unanticipated dividend increases or decreases is given in Table 15.2. The performance of firms with dividend increases is better than that of firms with dividend decreases, but the greatest difference between the two samples in the six months around the dividend change is only .7% in the month of the dividend. This is a trivial difference.

Pettit used both monthly and daily data to investigate the abnormal performance index of firms which had dividend changes of −1% to −99%, 1% to 10%, 10% to 25%, and over 25%. Figure 15.1 shows the cumulative abnormal performance index using daily data for 135 firms. Most of the price adjustment takes place very quickly either on the dividend announcement date or the following day. Furthermore, the price changes appear to be significant. This leads Pettit to conclude that substantial information is conveyed by the announcement of dividend changes.

**Table 15.2   Abnormal Performance Indices for Subsamples of
Firms with Unanticipated Dividend Changes**

Month Relative to Last Month of Fiscal Year	API		χ^2 Statistic for Sign of Stock Return Residual for Month and Dividend Residual for Year	Total API
	$\hat{z}_{i,t} > 0$	$\hat{z}_{i,t} < 0$		
−11	0.996	0.995	0.2	0.995
−10	0.998	0.997	0.3	0.998
− 9	1.003	1.002	1.9	1.002
− 8	1.002	1.002	4.0	1.002
− 7	1.004	1.001	2.5	1.002
− 6	1.004	0.999	2.6	1.001
− 5	1.003	1.000	0.6	1.002
− 4	1.001	0.999	0.3	1.000
− 3	1.000	0.997	0.0	0.998
− 2	1.003	1.001	2.6	1.002
− 1	1.006	1.001	4.0	1.004
0	1.009	1.002	0.1	1.006
1	1.003	0.996	0.0	1.000
2	1.005	0.999	0.6	1.002
3	1.010	1.005	0.0	1.008
4	1.011	1.004	1.4	1.007
5	1.011	1.004	0.0	1.008
6	1.012	1.003	3.3	1.008
7	1.011	1.003	0.2	1.007
8	1.010	1.001	0.2	1.006
9	1.007	1.000	0.4	1.004
10	1.011	1.002	1.5	1.007
11	1.012	1.006	3.4	1.009
12	1.014	1.006	1.2	1.010

Note: Probability $(\chi^2 > 3.84 | x^2 = 0) = .05$ for 1 df; probability $(\chi^2 > 6.64 | x^2 = 0) = .01$ for 1 df.
Source: Watts, R., "The Information Content of Dividends," reprinted from *The Journal of Business,* April 1973, 206.

Pettit's results have been criticized because he used the observed dividend changes rather than the *unexpected* dividend changes. Kwan [1981] has improved on Pettit's design by forming portfolios based on unexpected dividend changes, and he finds statistically significant abnormal returns when firms announce unexpectedly large dividend changes. A study by Aharony and Swary [1980] separates the information content of quarterly earnings reports from that of unexpected quarterly dividend changes. They examine only those quarterly dividend and earnings announcements made public on different dates within any given quarter. Their findings strongly support the hypothesis that changes in quarterly cash dividends provide useful information

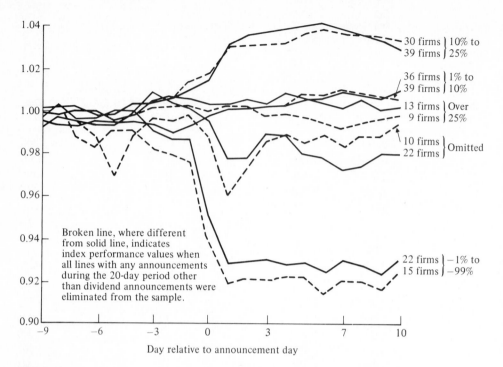

Figure 15.1
Abnormal performance index for dividend announcement effects, using daily data.
(From Pettit, R., "Dividend Announcements, Security Performance and Capital
Market Efficiency," reprinted with permission of *The Journal of Finance,* December
1972, 1004.)

beyond that provided by corresponding quarterly earnings numbers. The empirical
evidence (with the exception of Watts' study) seems to indicate that dividend changes
do convey some unanticipated information to the market.

D. THE RELATIONSHIP BETWEEN
DIVIDENDS AND VALUE

In Chapter 14 we saw that in a world with only corporate taxes, the Miller-Modigliani
proposition suggests that dividend policy is irrelevant to value. However, when personal taxes are introduced with a capital gains rate which is less than the rate on
ordinary income, the picture changes. Under this set of assumptions, the firm should
not pay any dividends. One way to test these theories is to look directly at the
relationship between dividend payout and the price per share of equity.

Friend and Puckett [1964] use cross-section data to test the effect of dividend
payout on share value. Prior to their work, most studies had related stock prices to
current dividends and retained earnings, and reported that higher dividend payout

was associated with higher price-earnings ratios. The "dividend multiplier" was found to be several times the "retained earnings multiplier." The usual cross-section equation was

$$P_{it} = a + bD_{it} + cR_{it} + \epsilon_{it},\tag{15.9}$$

where

P_{it} = the price per share,

D_{it} = aggregate dividends paid out,

R_{it} = retained earnings,

ϵ_{it} = the error term.

Friend and Puckett criticize the above approach on three major points. First, the equation is misspecified because it assumes that the riskiness of the firm is uncorrelated with dividend payout and price-earnings ratios. However, a look at the data suggests that riskier firms have both lower dividend payout and lower price-earnings ratios. Consequently, the omission of a risk variable may cause an upward bias in the dividend coefficient in Eq. (15.9). Second, there is almost no measurement error in dividends but there is considerable measurement error in retained earnings. It is well known that accounting measures of income often imprecisely reflect the real economic earnings of the firm. The measurement error in retained earnings will cause its coefficient to be biased downward. Third, Friend and Puckett argue that even if dividends and earnings *do* have different impacts on share prices, we should expect their coefficients in (15.9) to be equal. In equilibrium, firms would change their dividend payout until the marginal effect of dividends is equal to the marginal effect of retained earnings. This will provide the optimum effect on their price per share.

No theory had been developed to allow the pricing of risk when they wrote their paper, but Friend and Puckett were able to eliminate the measurement error on retained earnings by calculating a normalized earnings variable based on a time series fit of the following equation:

$$\frac{(E/P)_{it}}{(E/P)_{kt}} = a_i + b_i t + \epsilon_{it},\tag{15.10}$$

where

$(E/P)_{it}$ = the earnings-price ratio for the firm,

$(E/P)_{kt}$ = the average earnings price ratio for the industry,

t = a time index,

ϵ_{it} = the error term.

When normalized retained earnings were calculated by subtracting dividends from normalized earnings and then used in Eq. (15.9), the difference between the dividend and retained earnings coefficients was reduced. Unfortunately, no test was performed to see whether the differences between the impact of retained earnings and dividends were significant after Friend and Puckett had normalized earnings and controlled for firm effects.

A much more recent study by Black and Scholes [1974] uses capital-asset pricing theory to control for risk.[3] Their conclusion is quite strong. "It is not possible to demonstrate, using the best empirical methods, that the expected returns on high yield common stock differ from the expected returns on low yield common stocks either before or after taxes." They begin by pointing out that the assumption that capital gains tax rates are lower than income tax rates does not apply to all classes of investors. Some classes of investors might logically prefer high dividend yields. They include: (a) corporations, because they usually pay higher taxes on realized capital gains than on dividend income (because of the 85% exclusion of dividends); (b) certain trust funds in which one beneficiary receives the dividend income and the other receives capital gains; (c) endowment funds from which only the dividend income may be spent; and (d) investors who are spending from wealth and may find it cheaper and easier to receive dividends than to sell or borrow against their shares. Alternatively, investors who prefer low dividend yield will be those who pay higher taxes on dividend income than on capital gains. With all of these diverse investors, it is possible that there are clientele effects which imply that if a firm changes its dividend payout, it may lose some shareholders but they will be replaced by others who prefer the new policy. Thus dividend payout will have no effect on the value of an individual firm.[4]

The Black and Scholes [1974] study presents empirical evidence that the before-tax returns on common stock are unrelated to corporate dividend payout policy. They adjust for risk by using the CAPM.

The CAPM predicts that the expected return on any asset is a linear function of its systematic risk:

$$E(\tilde{R}_j) = R_f + [E(\tilde{R}_m) - R_f]\beta_j. \qquad (15.11)$$

However, it is derived by assuming, among other things, that there are no differential tax effects which would affect investors' demands for different securities. Brennan [1970] has shown that if effective capital gains tax rates are lower than effective rates on dividend income, then investors will demand a higher rate of return on securities with higher dividend payout. Using annual data, Black and Scholes test this hypothesis by adding a dividend payout term to an empirical version of the CAPM:

$$\tilde{R}_j = \gamma_0 + [\tilde{R}_m - \gamma_0]\beta_j + \gamma_1(\delta_j - \delta_m)/\delta_m + \epsilon_j, \qquad (15.12)$$

where

$\tilde{R}_j$ = the rate of return on the jth portfolio,

γ_0 = an intercept term which should be equal to the risk-free rate, R_f, according to the CAPM,

$\tilde{R}_m$ = the rate of return on the market portfolio,

---

[3] See Chapter 7 for a complete development of the capital asset pricing model.

[4] This does not rule out the possibility that in aggregate there is a desired equilibrium amount of dividend payout. For example, in the United States there are obviously a far greater number of companies with generous dividend payout than without.

β_j = the systematic risk of the ith portfolio,

γ_1 = the dividend impact coefficient,

δ_j = the dividend yield on the ith portfolio, measured as the sum of dividends paid during the previous year divided by the end-of-year stock price,

δ_m = the dividend yield on the market portfolio measured over the prior 12 months,

ϵ_j = the error term.

If the coefficient, γ_1, of the dividend yield is significantly different from zero, we would reject the null hypothesis that dividend payout has no impact on the required rate of return for securities. The results of Black and Scholes are summarized in Table 15.3. Note that the dividend impact coefficient, $\hat{\gamma}_1$, is not significantly different from zero (since the t-test is less than the level required to make it significant at the 95% confidence level) across the entire time period, 1936 through 1966, or in any subperiod. This means that the expected returns on high-yield securities are not significantly different from the expected returns on low-yield securities, other things being equal.[5]

The Black-Scholes study has been criticized because their test is not very powerful. Had the null hypothesis been that dividend yield does matter, it could not have been rejected either. Their test is inefficient because they grouped stocks into portfolios instead of using individual stock returns and, perhaps, because they used annual data.

Litzenberger and Ramaswamy [1979] also test the relationship between dividends and security returns. They use the Brennan [1970] model, Eq. (15.13) below, with monthly data for individual securities:

$$E(\tilde{R}_{jt}) - R_{ft} = a_1 + a_2\beta_j + a_3(d_{jt} - R_{ft}), \tag{15.13}$$

where

$E(\tilde{R}_{jt})$ = the expected before-tax return on the ith security,

R_{ft} = the before-tax return on the risk-free asset,

β_j = the systematic risk of the ith security,

a_1 = the constant term,

a_2 = the marginal effect of systematic risk,

a_3 = the marginal effective tax difference between ordinary income and capital gains rates,

d_{jt} = the dividend yield, i.e., dividend divided by price, for the ith security.

Litzenberger and Ramaswamy conclude that risk-adjusted returns are higher for securities with higher dividend yields. The implication is that dividends are undesir-

---

[5] The lower half of Table 15.3 shows that $\hat{\gamma}_0$ is significantly different from the risk-free rate. This is not important for the conclusions about dividend policy but is consistent with other empirical work (e.g., Black, Jensen, and Scholes [1972]) which shows that the intercept term in the CAPM is different from what theory would predict.

Table 15.3   Results of the Black-Scholes Test for Dividend Effects

	The Portfolio Estimators for γ_1 (Part A) and γ_0 (Part B)				
		Part A			
Period	$\alpha_1 = \hat{\gamma}_1$	t_α	$\hat{\beta}_1$	δ_1	δ_m
1936–66	0.0009	0.94	−0.01	0.044	0.048
1947–66	0.0009	0.90	0.08	0.047	0.049
1936–46	0.0011	0.54	−0.01	0.036	0.046
1947–56	0.0002	0.19	0.11	0.054	0.060
1957–66	0.0016	0.99	−0.14	0.040	0.038
1940–45	0.0018	0.34	0.15	0.051	0.052
		Part B			
Period	$\alpha_0 = \hat{\gamma}_0$	t_α	$\hat{\beta}_0$	δ_0	δ_m
1936–66	0.0060	3.02	0.02	0.048	0.048
1947–66	0.0073	3.93	0.03	0.049	0.049
1936–46	0.0033	0.72	−0.01	0.046	0.046
1947–56	0.0067	2.55	0.12	0.060	0.060
1957–66	0.0065	2.37	0.10	0.038	0.038

Source: Black, F., and M. Scholes, "The Effects of Dividend Yield and Dividend Policy on Common Stock Prices and Returns," reprinted from *The Journal of Financial Economics,* May 1974, 14.

able; hence higher returns are necessary to compensate investors in order to induce them to hold high dividend yield stocks.

There are (at least) three serious problems with testing for the dividend effect predicted by Eq. (15.13). The first is that investors use dividend announcements to estimate expected returns, $E(\tilde{R}_{jt})$, i.e., there is an information effect. The second is that measures of systematic risk, $\hat{\beta}_j$, are subject to a great deal of error. And the third is that individual security returns (rather than portfolio returns) are needed to obtain statistically powerful results. Litzenberger and Ramaswamy [1979] largely solved the second and third problems, but have been criticized by Miller and Scholes [1982] for their handling of the information effect of dividend announcements. When using monthly data, about two-thirds of the firms in the sample will have a zero yield because most firms pay dividends on a quarterly basis. Of the firms which pay their dividend (i.e., go ex-dividend) in month t, about 30% to 40% also announce the dividend in the same month. When the announcement date and the ex-dividend date occur in the same month, the monthly return will contain both the information effect and the tax effect (if any). In order to avoid confusing these effects, Litzenberger and Ramaswamy computed dividend yields in the following way:

- If a firm declared its dividend prior to month t and went ex-dividend in month t, then the dividend yield, d_{jt}, was computed using the actual dividend paid in t divided by the share price at the end of month t-1.

- If a firm both declared and went ex-dividend in month t, then the yield, d_{jt}, was computed using the last regular dividend, going back as far as one year.

Table 15.4 shows the results of regressions run by Miller and Scholes [1982] using Eq. (15.13). Regressions using the actual dividend yield in month t show that the dividend variable has a coefficient of .317 and it is highly significant, but recall that the actual yield confuses announcement effects with dividend tax effects. When the Litzenberger-Ramaswamy measure of dividend yield (called the level-revised yield) was duplicated by Miller and Scholes, the dividend coefficient dropped from .317 to .179 and also dropped in significance.

Table 15.4   Cross-sectional Estimates of the Dividend Yield Effect (Eq. 15.13) 1940–1978, t-statistics in Parentheses

Definition of Expected Dividend Yield	a_1	a_2	a_3
Actual dividend yield	.0059	.0024	.3173
	(4.5)	(1.6)	(10.2)
Level-revised monthly	.0065	.0022	.1794
dividend yield	(4.9)	(1.4)	(6.1)
Dividend yield of 12	.0038	.0019	.0376
months ago	(2.9)	(1.3)	(1.3)
Only firms with dividends	.0043	.0035	.0135
declared in advance	(2.5)	(2.2)	(0.1)

Source: Miller, M., and M. Scholes, "Dividends and Taxes: Some Empirical Evidence," forthcoming in *The Journal of Political Economy,* reprinted with permission of the authors.

The third regression in Table 15.4 corrects for a bias not contemplated in the two prior regressions. Namely, that some firms are expected to pay a dividend in month t but, for some reason, the Board of Directors suspends the dividend. Miller and Scholes call this the case of the "dog that didn't bark." Suppose that a $10 stock has a 50–50 chance of either announcing a $2 dividend (in which case the stock price doubles to $20) or suspending the dividend (thereby causing the stock price to fall to $5). The *ex ante* rate of return (and the average *ex post* return) is 35%, and the *ex ante* dividend yield is 10%.[6] However, if the level revised measure of dividend yield is used, then if the firm actually pays the $2 dividend the yield is 20% and the return is 120%. But if the dividend is passed, the yield is 0% and a −50% return is recorded. Thus the regressions with the level revised measure tend

---

[6] The *ex ante* return is computed as

$$.5 \left(\frac{20 - 10}{10} + \frac{2}{10} \right) + .5 \left(\frac{5 - 10}{10} \right) = .35$$

and the *ex ante* dividend yield is

$$.5 \left(\frac{2}{10} \right) + .5 \left(\frac{0}{10} \right) = .10.$$

to show what appears to be a positive association between returns and dividend yields. However, the correlation is spurious. A simple way to correct for the problem is to use the dividend yield of 12 months ago. Shown in the third regression in Table 15.4, the results indicate a small, statistically insignificant, relationship between dividend yields and returns.

Another approach, shown in the fourth regression in Table 15.4, is to drop from the sample all firms except those that both paid dividends in month t and announced them in advance. Again the dividend coefficient is insignificant.

The Friend and Puckett, Black and Scholes, and Miller and Scholes studies tend to support the conclusion that the value of the firm is independent of dividend yield. The Litzenberger and Ramaswamy study supports the conclusion that dividends are undesirable. The next study to be discussed concludes that dividends are desirable to shareholders, i.e., they will require a lower rate of return on shares which pay a high dividend yield.

Long [1978] provides a detailed analysis of two classes of shares issued by Citizens Utilities Company in 1956. They are virtually identical in all respects except for dividend payout. Series A shares pay only stock dividends which not taxable as ordinary income (due to a special Internal Revenue Service ruling granted to Citizens Utilities). Series B shares pay only cash dividends. Series A shares are freely convertible into Series B shares (on a one-for-one basis) at any time. However, the opposite is not true. Series B shares may not be converted into Series A shares. Historically, the directors of Citizens Utilities have semiannually declared stock dividends which (with a high degree of certainty) are 8–10% larger than the corresponding Series B cash dividends (paid on a quarterly basis).

Figure 15.2 shows the natural logarithm of the ratio of the prices of Series A to Series B shares on a monthly basis between 1956 and 1977. Note that the price of Series A shares, P_A, never falls significantly below the price of Series B shares, P_B. If it did, then Series A shareholders could immediately profit by converting to Series B. Figure 15.2 also shows, q, the ratio of Series A stock dividends to Series B cash dividends (illustrated by the circles). In a world without taxes the price per share of Series A "should" always equal q times the price per share of Series B stock, i.e., $P_{At} = qP_{Bt}$ ($t = 0,1, \ldots, N$). Figure 15.2 indicates that 80% of the dividend ratios, q, between 1962 and 1976 fall in the range 1.07 to 1.137. The ratio of stock prices, however, shows much more variability and is usually below the dividend ratio. How can this be explained?

In a world with taxes, cross-sectional heterogeneity in investor tax rates will cause the price ratio to differ from the dividend ratio. If very few investors face strictly higher taxes on stock dividends than on cash dividends, then the ratio of prices, P_A/P_B, should be greater than the dividend ratio, q. The equilibrium price ratio P_A/P_B will be less than q if there are sufficient numbers of investors who have a strict tax-induced preference for cash dividends over capital gains, and this is what is observed. Therefore, Long [1978] concludes that "claims to cash dividends have, if anything, commanded a slight premium in the market to claims to equal amounts (before taxes) of capital gains." The Citizens Utilities Case is anomolous

The natural log of $P_A/\hat{P}_B$ (the connected monthly observations) and the natural log of the semi-annual ratio of Series A to Series B dividends (the unconnected 0's) for the period 1956–1976. $\hat{P}_B$ is the price per share of Series B stock with dividends reinvested during each half-year prior to payment of the semi-annual Series A dividend. The unconnected points representing the log of the dividend ratio are placed in the figure at the end of the half-years to which they refer.

Figure 15.2
The natural log of $P_A/\hat{P}_B$ plotted monthly for the period April 1956 to December 1976. (From Long J., Jr., "The Market Valuation of Cash Dividends: A Case to Consider," reprinted from *The Journal of Financial Economics,* June/September 1978, 254.)

because it is the only major study which indicates an investor preference for cash dividends.

According to the Miller-Modigliani irrelevancy proposition, it is also important to know whether or not dividend policy can affect the investment decisions made by managers of the firm. This is a particularly difficult empirical question because the Miller-Modigliani theorem requires only that *dividend payout not affect investment decisions.* However, the opposite causality is not ruled out by Miller and Modigliani. That is, investment decisions can affect dividends. For example, the firm may simply choose to treat dividends as a residual payout after all profitable investment projects have been undertaken. This would not be inconsistent with the Miller-Modigliani proposition that the value of the firm is unaffected by dividend policy.

Fama [1974] uses a sophisticated two-stage least-squares econometric technique in order to determine the direction of causality, if any, between dividend and investment decisions. Because a description of two-stage least-squares is beyond the scope of this book, we refer the interested reader to Fama's article for a detailed exposition. His conclusion, however, is consistent with the Miller-Modigliani assumption that the period-by-period investment decisions of the firm are separable from its dividend decisions. There appears to be no causality in either direction. The data could not reject the hypothesis that investment and dividend decisions are completely independent from each other.

Although the foregoing studies appear to support the Miller-Modigliani irrelevancy proposition from the point of view of an individual firm, they do not necessarily rule out the possibility that there may exist an aggregate equilibrium supply of dividends which will increase if the difference between the ordinary income rate and the capital gains rate declines. This type of situation is implicit in Miller's [1977] paper "Debt and Taxes," which was discussed at length in Chapter 12.

Some empirical evidence which is consistent with the thesis that the aggregate supply of dividends is sensitive to the differential between the ordinary income and capital gains rates is contained in a study by Khoury and Smith [1977]. They observed that Canadian corporations significantly increased their dividend payout after a capital gains tax was introduced for the first time in 1972. A more recent paper by Morgan [1980] finds that the change in the Canadian tax code in 1972 affected the cross-sectional relationship between dividends and capital gains. Prior to 1972 they were imperfect substitutes, but afterward they became more or less perfect substitutes.

E. CORPORATE EQUITY REPURCHASES VIA TENDER OFFER

Corporations can repurchase their own shares in either of two ways: on the open market, or via tender offer. Open market repurchases usually (but not always) involve gradual programs to buy back shares over a period of time. In a tender offer, the company usually specifies the number of shares it is offering to repurchase, a tender price, and a period of time during which the offer is in effect. If the number of shares actually tendered by shareholders exceeds the maximum number specified by the company, then purchases are usually made on a *pro rata* basis. Alternatively, if the tender offer is undersubscribed the firm may decide to cancel the offer or extend the expiration date. Shares tendered during the extension may be purchased on either a *pro rata* or first-come, first-served basis.

Tender offers are usually significant corporate events. Dann [1981] reports that for a sample of 143 cash tender offers by 122 different firms between 1962 and 1976, the average cash distributions proposed by the tender represented almost 20% of the market value of the company's pre-tender equity value. The announcement effects of tender offers on the market values of corporate securities have been studied by Masulis [1980], Dann [1981] and Vermaelen [1981].[7] Share repurchases are not just a simple alternative to cash dividends. Tender offers for repurchase are related to (at least) five separate, but not mutually exclusive, hypotheses:

---

[7] The reader is also referred to studies by Woods and Brigham [1966], Bierman and West [1966], Young [1967], Elton and Gruber [1968], Stewart [1976], Coates and Fredman [1976], and Lane [1976].

1. *The information or signaling hypothesis.* The cash disbursed to shareholders in a tender offer may represent a signal that the firm is expected to have increased future cash flows but it may also imply that the firm has exhausted profitable investment opportunities. Therefore, the signal may be interpreted as either good or bad news by shareholders.

2. *The leverage hypothesis.* If the repurchase is financed by issuing debt rather than paying out cash, the leverage of the firm may increase—and if there is a gain to leverage as suggested by Modigliani and Miller [1963], then shareholders may benefit.

3. *The dividend tax avoidance hypothesis.* The tender for share repurchase will be taxed as a capital gain rather than a dividend if (according to Section 302 of the U.S. Internal Revenue Code) the redemption is "substantially disproportionate" to the extent that the individual shareholder must have sold more than 20% of his or her holdings in the tender.[8] This condition is rarely violated, consequently there may be a tax incentive for repurchases as opposed to large extraordinary dividends.

4. *The bondholder expropriation hypothesis.* If the repurchase unexpectedly reduces the asset base of the company, then bondholders are worse off because they have less collateral. Of course, bond indentures serve to protect against this form of expropriation. A direct test of this hypothesis is to look at bond price changes on the repurchase announcement date.

5. *Wealth transfers among shareholders.* Wealth transfers between tendering and nontendering stockholders may occur when there are differential constraints and/or costs across groups of owners. Even when the tender price is substantially above the pre-tender stock price, some shareholders may voluntarily decide not to tender their shares.

A great deal can be learned about these hypotheses if we focus on the price effects on shares, bonds, and preferred stock. Figure 15.3 shows the average pattern of share price changes around the tender announcement date and the expiration date. More or less the same results were reported by Masulis [1980], Dann [1981], and Vermaelen [1981]. The average tender price, P_T, is roughly 23% above the pre-announcement price, P_0. If all shares tendered were actually purchased by the firm, then the tender price, P_T, would equal the average post-announcement price, P_A. But because of *pro rata* repurchases given oversubscribed tenders we observe that on average $P_A < P_T$. The post-announcement price, P_A, averages 15% above the pre-announcement price, P_0. Finally, note that the average post-expiration price, P_E, is only 3% below the average post-announcement price, P_A, and is above the pre-announcement price, P_0. This suggests that the tender offer may have increased the market value of the firm's equity.

Unfortunately, the difference between the pre-announcement price and the post-expiration price does not measure the information effect of the tender offer. We have

---

[8] According to Vermaelen [1981] only three out of 105 tender offers which he studied actually were subject to ordinary income taxes.

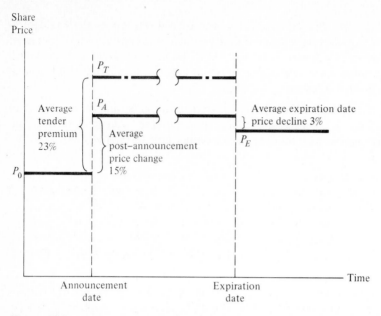

Figure 15.3
Schematic representation of average price changes surrounding tender offers for repurchase.

to look deeper. Begin by noting that the market value of the firm's equity after expiration, $P_E N_E$, is equal to the pre-announcement value, $P_0 N_0$, minus the cash paid out in the tender, $P_T(N_0 - N_E)$, plus the tender offer effect, ΔW.

$$P_E N_E = P_0 N_0 - P_T(N_0 - N_E) + \Delta W, \qquad (15.14)$$

where

$P_E = $ the post-expiration share price,

$N_E = $ the number of shares outstanding after repurchase,

$P_0 = $ the pre-announcement share price,

$N_0 = $ the pre-announcement number of shares outstanding,

$P_T = $ the tender price,

$\Delta W = $ the shareholder wealth effect attributable to the tender offer.

Note that the change in value attributable to the tender, ΔW, may be caused by (1) personal tax savings, (2) a leverage effect, (3) expropriation of bondholder wealth, or (4) the reassessment of the firm's earnings prospects.

If we define the fraction of shares repurchased, F_P, as

$$F_P = 1 - \frac{N_E}{N_0} \qquad (15.15)$$

and divide Eq. (15.14) by N_0, we have

$$P_E(1 - F_P) = P_0 - P_T F_P + \frac{\Delta W}{N_0}. \tag{15.16}$$

Solving for $\Delta W/N_0$ and dividing by P_0 gives

$$\frac{\Delta W}{N_0 P_0} = (1 - F_P)\frac{P_E - P_0}{P_0} + F_P\frac{P_T - P_0}{P_0} \tag{15.17}$$

Thus the rate of return created by the tender offer has two components. First is the rate of return received by nontendering shareholders weighted by the percent of untendered shares, $1 - F_P$; and second is the rate of return received by tendering shareholders weighted by the percent of shares purchased, F_P.

Vermaelen [1981] found that the average wealth effect, $\Delta W/N_0 P_0$, was 15.7% and that only 10.7% of the tender offers experienced a wealth decline. On average, both nontendered shares and tendered shares experienced a wealth increase, although not by equal amounts.

What causes the average 15.7% wealth gain from tender offers? Personal tax savings are a possibility but seem too small to explain the large wealth gain. For example, if 20% of the value of the firm is repurchased and if the marginal investor's tax rate is 40%, then the tax savings would imply a 4% rate of return. This is too small to explain the wealth gain.

The leverage hypothesis suggests that if the repurchase is financed with debt, and if there is a tax gain from leverage, then the shareholders will benefit. Both Masulis [1980] and Vermaelen [1981] find evidence consistent with a leverage effect. Masulis divided his sample into offers with more than 50% debt financing where the average announcement return was 21.9%, and offers with less than 50% debt where the average announcement return was only 17.1%. Vermaelen finds similar results and concludes that while it is not possible to reject the leverage hypothesis outright, it is possible to conclude that it is not the predominant explanation for the observed abnormal returns following the tender offer. Also, if leverage is a signal, then it is not possible to separate the leverage signaling effect from the leverage tax effect.

The best explanation for the shareholder wealth gain from the tender offer is that the offer represents a favorable signal. Vermaelen [1981] finds that the per-share earnings of tendering firms are above what would have been predicted by a time series model using preannouncement data. Thus the tender offer may be interpreted as an announcement of favorable earnings prospects. Also, the size of the tender premium, the fraction of shares repurchased, and the fraction of insider holdings are all positively related to the wealth gain, ΔW, and explain roughly 60% of its variance. These results are also consistent with interpreting the tender offer as a signal.

Evidence on the bondholder wealth expropriation hypothesis is provided by looking at bond price changes around the announcement date. Dann [1981] found 122 publicly traded debt and preferred stock issues for 51 tender offers. There were 41 issues of straight debt, 34 issues of convertible debt, 9 issues of straight preferred stock, and 38 issues of convertible preferred stock. An analysis of abnormal returns around the announcement date revealed significant positive rates of return for the convertible securities and rates which were insignificantly different from zero for straight debt and preferred. Furthermore, the correlation between common stock returns and straight debt (and preferred) returns was positive. Thus the evidence seems to contradict bondholder expropriation as the dominant effect.

Repurchases via tender offer represent an interesting and significant corporate event. The empirical evidence, although not rejecting leverage effects or dividend tax avoidance effects, seems to most strongly support the hypothesis that the tender offer for repurchase is interpreted by the marketplace as favorable information regarding future prospects of the firm.

F. OVERVIEW OF EMPIRICAL EVIDENCE

The theory of finance clearly demonstrates that in the absence of taxes dividend policy has no effect on the value of the corporation. However, if taxes are introduced, then the firm can maximize the value of shareholders' wealth by paying no dividends so long as the personal tax rate on dividend income is higher than that on capital gains. However, this is not true for all types of shareholders; hence there exists the possibility of clientele effects with shareholders choosing the firm with the payout they prefer. The evidence supporting dividend clientele effects is much stronger than the evidence for capital structure clientele effects. Another issue is the relationship between dividend yield and equity values. The preponderance of empirical evidence seems to favor the conclusion that dividend yield has no marked effect on the required rate of return on equity. The only two exceptions were the Litzenberger and Ramaswamy [1979] study which found that higher dividend yields required higher rates of return to compensate investors for the disadvantage of dividend payout and the Long [1978] study which found that dividends were desirable, at least in the Citizens Utilities case. On the other hand, changes in dividends paid out are interpreted as new information about the future cash flows of the firm. There is strong evidence to support a dividend signaling effect. There appears to be no causal relationship between investment and dividend policy. Finally, empirical evidence on share repurchase via tender offer indicates that the announcement effect is predominantly viewed as favorable news regarding the firm's future cash flows. Little or no expropriation of bondholders' wealth was observed.

G. VALUATION AND CORPORATE POLICY

The valuation models developed in Chapter 14 have many useful applications. For example, fundamental analysis techniques use them as a tool for estimating the impact of various types of new information on the value of the firm. Although the valuation models cannot aid in attempts to "beat" the market, they do provide a useful framework for concentrating on relevant information. When a corporate president asks

"How much should we pay to acquire Company X?" the valuation model is a useful tool. When a company is going public for the first time or when it becomes necessary to value a privately held company, again the valuation model provides a relevant framework for analysis.

In the next section we continue the Bethlehem Steel example which was started in Chapter 13. The object is to see how to apply the Miller-Modigliani finite-growth model. In so doing, it becomes possible to analyze six factors which affect corporate value.

1. Review of the Finite-Growth Valuation Formula

The most complicated, and the most realistic, valuation model discussed in Chapter 14 assumed that the firm grows at a rate, g, for a finite number of years, T, and at the same rate as the economy thereafter.

The model is written below:[9]

$$V^L = \frac{E(\text{NOI}_1)(1 - \tau_c)}{\rho} + \tau_c B$$
$$+ K[E(\text{NOI}_1)(1 - \tau_c)] T \left[\frac{r - \text{WACC}}{\text{WACC}(1 + \text{WACC})} \right], \quad (15.18)$$

where

V^L = the market value of the levered firm, i.e., the market value of equity, S, plus the market value of debt, B,

$E(\text{NOI}_1)$ = the expected net cash flows from operations during the current year, net of capitalized maintenance,

ρ = the cost of equity for the firm if it had no debt, i.e., the cost of equity for an all-equity firm,

τ_c = the marginal effective corporate tax rate,

B = the market value of debt,

r = the expected rate of return on new projects,

K = the firm's investment rate,

WACC = the firm's weighted average cost of capital,

T = the number of years that r, the rate of return, is expected to be different from WACC, the market-determined weighted average cost of capital.

The first term in (15.18) is the capitalized value of the expected level of after-tax cash flows from investment which is currently in place. The second term is the value added by tax-deductible financial leverage. And the third term is the present value of the growth in cash flows from new investment.

---

[9] Remember that we derive this version of the model by assuming, among other things, that corporate taxes are the only form of government levy. Personal taxes do not exist.

It is also useful to recall a few of the relationships between the parameters of Eq. (15.18). For example, the rate of growth, g, in the firm's cash flows is equal to Kr, the product of the investment rate, K, and the rate of return on new projects, r. Also, the anticipated amount of new investment, I, is equal to the investment rate times the firm's expected after-tax cash flow, $E(NOI_1)$. In other words, then, $I = K[E(NOI_1)]$.

Equation (15.18) is a useful construct which uses modern finance theory for valuation. However, realistically it is at best only a crude tool. No one should be advised that it is the only approach to valuation or that it provides perfect answers. Yet it does point out precisely which pieces of information are relevant. Interestingly, none of them is provided in the annual report of the corporation. The only relevant parameters are forward-looking. Although some can be estimated from historic accounting data, the most important information is hardly ever reported by corporate management to shareholders.

2. A Valuation Example: Bethlehem Steel

What are the six relevant valuation parameters? And how can they be estimated?

A. EXPECTED AFTER-TAX CASH FLOWS FROM CURRENT OPERATIONS   Perhaps the most important factor is the level of cash flows earned on the projects which the firm has already undertaken. It is assumed that this level of cash flows will be maintained into perpetuity. Furthermore, it is assumed that depreciation allowances are sufficient to allow the current level of equipment to be maintained indefinitely.

Table 15.5 is a *pro forma* income statement for Bethlehem Steel for the years

Table 15.5   *Pro forma* Income Statements, Bethlehem Steel
(in Thousands of Dollars)

	1976	1975	1974	1973
Net billings and other income	5,304,700	5,028,300	5,448,709	4,174,833
Cost of billings	4,082,100	3,854,300	4,052,478	3,138,048
Provisions for:				
depreciation	275,600	234,200	210,912	196,086
pensions	261,200	198,400	153,842	115,533
misc. taxes	179,400	175,000	169,616	150,982
Selling and administrative expenses	234,700	220,000	210,842	178,641
Earnings before interest and taxes	271,700	346,400	660,019	395,543
Interest expense	77,700	63,400	43,985	38,934
Income taxes*	26,000	41,000	274,000	150,000
Net income	168,000	242,000	342,034	206,609
Dividends paid to common	87,400	120,000	100,172	72,431

* During 1976 this includes current taxes (federal, foreign, and state) of −$9,000,000; and deferred taxes (federal and state) of $35,000,000. Note that deferred taxes are a noncash charge.

1973–1976. We are attempting to estimate the value of the company as of December 31, 1976. (That is the date of our estimate of the cost of capital in Chapter 13.) The expected after-tax cash flows from operations during 1977, $E(\text{NOI}_1)(1 - \tau_c)$, can be estimated by computing 1976 cash flows and assuming that they will grow during 1977.

Cash flows for 1976 from operations, NOI_0, can be calculated from the income statement in one of two equivalent ways. For example, consider the *pro forma* income statement in Table 15.6. The equation for net income can be rearranged as follows:

$$(R - \text{VC} - F - rD)(1 - \tau_c) = \text{NI},$$

$$(R - \text{VC} - F)(1 - \tau_c) = \text{NI} + rD(1 - \tau_c). \qquad (15.19)$$

By adding back noncash charges, such as depreciation expenses (and deferred income taxes), we have two definitions of cash flow from operations:[10]

$$(R - \text{VC})(1 - \tau_c) + \tau_c(\text{dep}) = \text{NI} + rD(1 - \tau_c) + \text{dep}. \qquad (15.20)$$

Table 15.6

$100	R	Revenues
−60	−VC	−Cash costs of operations
−20	−F	−Noncash costs (depreciation)
20	EBIT	Earnings before interest and taxes
−10	−rD	−Interest expense
10	EBT	Earnings before taxes
−5	−T	−Taxes at 50%
5	NI	Net income

The left-hand side starts at the top of the income statement in Table 15.6 and works down while the right-hand side starts at the bottom and works up. In order to obtain the correct definition of cash flows, one further adjustment must be made. Recall that the model assumes that depreciation is adequate to replace worn-out equipment. In other words, cash outflows used to replace equipment each year are exactly equivalent to depreciation. The two cancel each other. Therefore, because depreciation is used for replacement investment, it is not part of the *free cash flow* available to investors. Consequently, it is necessary to subtract depreciation from both sides of (15.20). The result is the correct definition of after-tax free cash flows from operations which can be maintained into perpetuity, $\text{NOI}_0(1 - \tau_c)$.

$$\text{NOI}_0(1 - \tau_c) = (R - \text{VC})(1 - \tau_c) - \text{dep}(1 - \tau_c) = \text{NI} + rD(1 - \tau_c). \quad (15.21)$$

For the simple example above (if $\tau_c = .5$),

$$\text{NOI}_0(1 - \tau_c) = (100 - 60)(1 - .5) - 20(1 - .5) = 5 + 10(1 - .5) = 10.$$

---

[10] Recall that we have assumed that $F = \text{dep}$.

For Bethlehem Steel the estimates are given in Table 15.7. Note that for 1976 estimates, we also have to add deferred taxes of $35 million, a noncash charge (discovered in the footnotes to the income statement). This makes our estimate of $NOI_0(1 - \tau_c)$ add up to be $243,404 instead of $208,404. Note that $\tau_c = .48$.

B. THE INVESTMENT RATE   The reason for estimating the investment rate, K, is that it is useful in estimating two more fundamental parameters: (1) the expected dollar amount of new investment $I = K(NOI_1)(1 - \tau_c)$, and (2) the expected rate of growth in the firm, $g = Kr$. There is no reason that the investment rate must be less than 100% of cash flows. A higher investment rate simply means that the firm will be issuing new equity in order to undertake new investment in excess of current cash flows. This is certainly feasible for a firm with $r > $ WACC.

From Table 15.6 we can estimate the investment rate by subtracting the dividend payout (dividends $\div NOI_0(1 - \tau_c)$) from 100%. Bethlehem did not issue new equity during the period 1973–1976. The average investment rate is 63.8%.

C. THE RATE OF RETURN ON NEW INVESTMENT   It is very difficult to come up with a reasonable projection of the rate of return on new investment. In Table 15.7 it has been estimated as the ratio of after-tax cash flows to the book value of assets. But the book value of assets is a number with little meaning, particularly during an inflationary economy. Also, what is really needed is not an historic estimate of return on capital in place, but rather an estimate of future return on investment. This information simply cannot be found in the accounting statements of the firm. The community of financial analysts make their living, at least in part, by trying to estimate the impact of future investment possibilities on the market value of the firm.

For lack of anything better to use, we have assumed that future growth is likely to be the same as that during the past four years. Estimated in Table 15.7, the average rate of return, r, on book value is 6.02%.

Table 15.7   Various Valuation Statistics for Bethlehem Steel ($ Given in Thousands)

	1976	1975	1974	1973
Net income	$168,000	$242,000	$342,034	$206,609
+ $rD(1 - \tau_c)$	40,404	32,968	22,872	20,246
$NOI_0(1 - \tau_c)$	$208,404	$274,968	$364,906	$226,855
Dividends	$ 87,400	$120,100	$100,172	$ 72,431
Dividends/$NOI_0(1 - \tau_c)$	.419	.437	.275	.319
(Investment rate) = K	58.1%	56.3%	72.5%	68.1%
Book value of assets	4,939,100	4,591,500	4,512,617	3,919,264
$(NOI_0(1 - \tau_c))/BV = r$	4.22%	5.99%	8.09%	5.79%
Growth = Kr	2.45%	3.37%	5.87%	3.94%

Once given the investment rate, $K = .638$, and the rate of return, $r = .0602$, we can estimate the rate of growth:

$$g = Kr = .0384.$$

D. THE TARGET CAPITAL STRUCTURE   The target capital structure is useful for two purposes. First, as we saw in Chapter 13, it is needed in order to estimate the weighted average cost of capital. And second, when used in combination with the investment rate, it determines the extent to which the company will issue new equity.

In Chapter 13 we saw that Bethlehem Steel has had a fairly stable ratio of long-term debt to total assets of around 31.5% (See Table 13.8). Also, the market value of long-term debt, B, was estimated to be $815,945.

E. THE WEIGHTED AVERAGE COST OF CAPITAL   Assuming that new projects undertaken by the firm will have the same risk as current projects, then the current estimate of the weighted average cost of capital represents the required rate of return on new investment. If the expected rate of return, r, is greater than the required rate, WACC, a quick glance at the third term in Eq. (15.18) reveals that new investment will add to the market value of the firm. If new investment does not meet this criterion, it cannot possibly increase value (although, as was shown in Chapter 14, if $0 < r < $ WACC it might cause growth in earnings per share).

We assume that Bethlehem Steel will take on new investments with approximately the same risk as its existing projects. Therefore, we can use the weighted average cost of capital, estimated in Chapter 13. It was WACC $= 10.61\%$. In addition, we need to know the cost of equity capital if Bethlehem Steel were an all-equity firm. This can be computed by using the Modigliani-Miller definition of cost of capital, Eq. (12.12):

$$\text{WACC} = \rho \left(1 - \tau_c \frac{B}{B+S} \right),$$

$$\rho = \frac{\text{WACC}}{\left(1 - \tau_c \dfrac{B}{B+S} \right)}, \qquad (12.12)$$

where

$\rho =$ the cost of equity for the all-equity firm,

$\tau_c =$ the corporate tax rate $= .48$,

$B/(B+S) =$ the percent of debt in the capital structure of the firm $= 31.5\%$ (using market value weights),

WACC $=$ the weighted average cost of capital $= 10.61\%$.

Solving for ρ, we have

$$\rho = \frac{.1061}{1 - .48(.315)} = 12.50\%.$$

F. THE DURATION OF ABNORMAL GROWTH   The final important question is how long the firm will be able to undertake new investment projects which earn abnormally high rates of return, that is, projects which earn more than the rate required for investments of equal risk. How long will r be greater than WACC? Usually, the period of supernormal growth can be conceptualized as the length of time required for competition to enter the market and eliminate the firm's economic advantage.

In the case of Bethlehem Steel the estimated future rate of return, 6.02%, is less than the rate which the market requires, 10.61%. This means that we need to estimate the length of time it will take them to get out of trouble. This is a matter of judgment, and we have assumed that the current "growth" pattern shall persist for three years ($T = 3$).

G. THE VALUE OF BETHLEHEM STEEL   All that remains is to use the estimates of the six valuation parameters in the valuation equation. For convenience it is rewritten below

$$V = \frac{E(\text{NOI}_1)(1 - \tau_c)}{\rho} + \tau_c B$$

$$+ K[E(\text{NOI}_1)(1 - \tau_c)]T \left[\frac{r - \text{WACC}}{\text{WACC}(1 + \text{WACC})}\right]. \quad (15.18)$$

Note that the expected 1977 after-tax cash flows from operations, $E(\text{NOI}_1)(1 - \tau_c)$, equal the estimated 1976 figure multiplied by the estimated growth rate ($g = Kr$):

$$E(\text{NOI}_1)(1 - \tau_c) = \text{NOI}_0(1 - \tau_c)(1 + Kr)$$

$$= 243{,}404(1 + .638(.0602))$$

$$= 243{,}404(1.0384076) = \$252{,}753.$$

Substituting the values of the remaining parameters into (15.18), we have

$$V = \frac{252{,}753}{.125} + .48(815{,}945) + .638(252{,}753)3 \left[\frac{.0602 - .1061}{.1061(1.1061)}\right]$$

$$= 2{,}022{,}024 + 391{,}653 - 189{,}209$$

$$= \$2{,}224{,}468 \quad \text{(thousands of dollars).}$$

The actual market value of Bethlehem Steel at the end of December 1976 was $2.590 billion.[11] Therefore, the estimate provided by the valuation model is around $.366 billion too low, an error of around 14.1%. The discrepancy may be due to

---

[11] The market value of equity was $40\frac{5}{8}$ per share and 43.665 million shares were outstanding. Thus the total value of equity was $1.774 billion. Adding this to the $.816 billion of long-term debt we obtain a market value of $2.590 billion.

any number of reasons. Most likely our estimates of the anticipated operating cash flows and the rate of return on future investment (which were based on historical accounting data) were too low.

The valuation model does serve to point out the contribution of the three major components. Most of the market value of Bethlehem Steel comes from the stream of cash flows provided by investments which are already in place. Some extra value is provided by the tax shield from debt. And almost no value—or more accurately, negative value—results from the profitability of anticipated growth opportunities.

3. Implications for Accounting Information

The valuation example given above is useful for two reasons. First, it shows an investor how to evaluate the effect of new information on the market value of the firm. Second, it provides a shopping list of relevant information.

Investors gain little benefit from historic accounting data because it contains no new information. Therefore, although the annual report may serve as a useful device for monitoring the performance of management, it has little value to the investment community. Relevant data is forward-looking. Investors seek out information about the six parameters mentioned in Section 2.

An interesting related issue is the behavior of the Securities and Exchange Commission. By charter, its chief function is to monitor the disclosure of information. Yet many of its rules are concerned with the quality of historic accounting data. For example, it supports the publication of segment-based revenue data. Companies are asked to break down their total sales by line of business. The justification is presumably that the line-of-business reporting improves the shareholder stewardship function and allows investors to better estimate future returns. As we have already argued, historic accounting data, whatever their form, are of little benefit to investors. Consequently, it is hard to understand why the SEC should ask companies to bear the added cost of meeting its requirement of reporting segmented sales revenue.

What investors would like to know is what the management estimates future performance to be. This kind of information can be supplied in the company president's letter in the annual report without legal liability in the event that things don't turn out as well as anticipated. In particular, investors would benefit from unbiased estimates of the rate of return on future investment, the dollar amount of new investment, the length of time supernormal growth is expected to persist, and the percent of new capital which will be provided from equity sources.

Once again, it is important to keep in mind that the valuation model used in the above example is only as good as the assumptions used in its derivation. Also, it is limited by the inevitable inaccuracies in estimating future cash flows. At best, it is only a framework for analysis which is useful for structuring the way we conceptualize corporate valuation.

Not only is it useful to understand which parameters determine value, but it is also important to understand those which do not. For example, accounting conventions which do not affect cash flows are irrelevant.

PROBLEM SET

15.1 Under what conditions might dividend policy affect the value of the firm?

15.2 According to federal tax law, corporations need not pay taxes on 85% of dividends received from shares held in other corporations. In other words, only 15% of the dividends received by a corporate holder are taxable. Given this fact, how much must the price of a stock fall on the ex-dividend date in order to prevent a corporate holder from making arbitrage profits? Assume that the capital gains rate equals the corporate tax rate, $\tau_c = .5$.

15.3 Empirical evidence supports the existence of a clientele effect. This implies that every time a company revises its dividend policy to pay out a greater (or smaller) percentage of earnings, the characteristics of its shareholders also change. For example, a firm with a higher payout ratio may expect to have more shareholders in lower tax brackets. Suppose that lower-income people are also more risk averse. Would this have an effect on the value of the firm?

15.4 Miller and Scholes [1978] suggest that it is possible to shelter income from taxes in such a way that capital gains rates are paid on dividend income. Furthermore, since capital gains need never be realized, the effective tax rate will become zero. Why wouldn't this scheme be used to shelter all income, instead of just dividend income? The implication would be that no one has to pay taxes—ever!

15.5 The Pettit study suggests an increase in the price per share of common stock commensurate with an increase in dividends. Can this be taken as evidence that the value of the firm is, in fact, affected by dividend policy?

15.6 Assume that the XYZ firm has the following parameters in a world with no taxes:

$\sigma = .2$	instantaneous standard deviation,
$T = 4$ years	maturity of debt,
$V = \$2000$	value of the firm; $V = B + S$,
$R_f = .06$	risk-free rate,
$D = \$1000$	face value of debt.

a) What will be the market value of equity cum dividend (i.e., before any dividend is paid)?

b) If the shareholders decide to pay themselves a $500 dividend out of cash, what will be ex-dividend wealth of shareholders? [*Note:* The dividend payment will have two effects. First, it will decrease the market value of the firm to $1500. Second, since cash has little or no risk, the instantaneous standard deviation of the firm's assets will increase to .25].

REFERENCES

Aharony, J., and I. Swary, "Quarterly Dividend and Earnings Announcements and Stockholders' Returns: An Empirical Analysis," *Journal of Finance,* March 1980, 1–12.

Austin, D., "Treasury Stock Reacquisition by American Corporations 1961–1967," *Financial Executive,* May 1969, 40–61.

Bar-Yosef, S., and R. Kolodny, "Dividend Policy and Market Theory," *Review of Economics and Statistics,* May 1976, 181–190.

Bierman, H., and R. West, "The Acquisition of Common Stock by the Corporate Issuer," *Journal of Finance,* December 1966, 687–696.

Black, F., M. Jensen, and M. Scholes, "The Capital Asset Pricing Model: Some Empirical Tests," in M. Jensen, ed., *Studies in the Theory of Capital Markets.* Praeger, New York, 1972, 79–124.

Black, F., and M. Scholes, "The Effects of Dividend Yield and Dividend Policy on Common Stock Prices and Returns," *Journal of Financial Economics,* May 1974, 1–22.

Blume, M., "Stock Returns and Dividend Yields: Some More Evidence," *Review of Economics and Statistics,* November 1980, 567–577.

Brennan, M., "Taxes, Market Valuation and Corporate Financial Policy," *National Tax Journal,* December 1970, 417–427.

Brittain, J. A., *Corporate Dividend Policy.* Brookings Institution, Washington, D.C., 1966.

Charest, G., "Dividend Information, Stock Returns and Market Efficiency," *Journal of Financial Economics,* June/September 1978, 297–330.

Coates, C., and A. Fredman, "Price Behavior Associated With Tender Offers to Repurchase Common Stock," *Financial Executive,* April 1976, 40–44.

Dann, L., "Common Stock Repurchases: An Analysis of Returns to Bondholders and Stockholders," *Journal of Financial Economics,* June 1981, 113–138.

Darling, P., "The Influence of Expectations and Liquidity on Dividend Policy," *Journal of Political Economy,* June 1957, 209–224.

Dielman, T., T. Nantell, and R. Wright, "Price Effects of Stock Repurchasing: A Random Coefficient Regression Approach," *Journal of Financial and Quantitative Analysis,* March 1980, 175–189.

Ellis, C., "Repurchase Stock to Revitalize Equity," *Harvard Business Review,* July/August 1965, 119–128.

Elton, E. J., and M. J. Gruber, "The Effect of Share Repurchase on the Value of the Firm," *Journal of Finance,* March 1968, 135–149.

———, "Marginal Stockholders' Tax Rates and the Clientele Effect," *Review of Economics and Statistics,* February 1970, 68–74.

Fama, E., "The Empirical Relationship Between the Dividend and Investment Decisions of Firms," *American Economic Review,* June 1974, 304–318.

———, and H. Babiak, "Dividend Policy: An Empirical Analysis," *Journal of the American Statistical Association,* December 1968, 1132–1161.

Fama, E., L. Fisher, M. Jensen, and R. Roll, "The Adjustment of Stock Prices to New Information," *International Economic Review,* February 1969, 1–21.

Farrar, D., and L. Selwyn, "Taxes, Corporate Financial Policy and Return to Investors," *National Tax Journal,* December 1967, 444–454.

Friend, I., and M. Puckett, "Dividends and Stock Prices," *American Economic Review,* September 1964, 656–682.

Gonedes, N., "Corporate Signaling, External Accounting, and Capital Market Equilibrium: Evidence on Dividends, Income, and Extraordinary Items," *Journal of Accounting Research,* Spring 1978, 26–79.

Gordon, M., "Dividends, Earnings, and Stock Prices," *Review of Economics and Statistics,* May 1959, 99–105.

———, "The Savings, Investment and Valuation of a Corporation," *Review of Economics and Statistics,* February 1962, 37–51.

Gordon, R., and D. Bradford, "Taxation and the Stock Market Valuation of Capital Gains and Dividends," *Journal of Public Economics,* October 1980, 103–136.

Griffin, P., "Competitive Information in the Stock Market: An Empirical Study of Earnings, Dividends and Analysts Forecasts," *Journal of Finance,* May 1976, 631–650.

Guthart, L., "Why Companies Are Buying Their Own Stock," *Financial Analysts Journal,* March/April 1967, 105–110.

Hess, P., "The Ex-Dividend Behavior of Stock Returns: Further Evidence on Tax Effects," *Journal of Finance,* May 1982.

Higgins, R., "The Corporate Dividend-Saving Decision," *Journal of Financial and Quantitative Analysis,* March 1972, 1527–1541.

Kalay, A., "Essays in Dividend Policy." Ph.D. thesis, University of Rochester, 1977.

_____, "Signaling, Information Content, and the Reluctance to Cut Dividends," *Journal of Financial and Quantitative Analysis,* November 1980, 855–870.

Khoury, N., and K. Smith, "Dividend Policy and the Capital Gains Tax in Canada," *Journal of Business Administration,* Spring 1977.

Kwan, C., "Efficient Market Tests of the Informational Content of Dividend Announcements: Critique and Extension," *Journal of Financial and Quantitative Analysis,* June 1981, 193–206.

Lane, W., "Repurchase of Common Stock and Managerial Discretion." Unpublished Ph.D. dissertation, University of North Carolina, Chapel Hill, N.C., 1976.

Laub, P. M., "On the Informational Content of Dividends," *Journal of Business,* January 1976, 73–80.

Lewellen, W., K. Stanley, R. Lease, and G. Schlarbaum, "Some Direct Evidence on the Dividend Clientele Phenomenon," *Journal of Finance,* December 1978, 1385–1399.

Lintner, J., "Distribution of Incomes of Corporations Among Dividends, Retained Earnings and Taxes," *American Economic Review,* May 1956, 97–113.

_____, "Optimal Dividends and Corporate Growth Under Uncertainty," *Quarterly Journal of Economics,* February 1964, 49–95.

_____, "The Valuation of Risk Assets and the Selection of Risky Investments in Stock Portfolios and Capital Budgets," *Review of Economics and Statistics,* February 1965, 13–37.

Litzenberger, R., and K. Ramaswamy, "The Effect of Personal Taxes and Dividends on Capital Asset Prices: Theory and Empirical Evidence," *Journal of Financial Economics,* June 1979, 163–196.

_____, "Dividends, Short-Selling Restrictions, Tax-Induced Investor Clienteles and Market Equilibrium," *Journal of Finance,* May 1980, 469–482.

Long, J., Jr., "Efficient Portfolio Choice with Differential Taxation of Dividends and Capital Gains," *Journal of Financial Economics,* August 1977, 25–54.

_____, "The Market Valuation of Cash Dividends: A Case to Consider," *Journal of Financial Economics,* June/September 1978, 235–264.

Masulis, R., "Stock Repurchase by Tender Offer: An Analysis of the Causes of Common Stock Price Changes," *Journal of Finance,* May 1980, 305–318.

McCabe, G., "The Empirical Relationship Between Investment and Financing: A New Look," *Journal of Financial and Quantitative Analysis,* March 1979, 119–135.

Miller, M., "Debt and Taxes," *Journal of Finance,* May 1977, 261–275.

———, and F. Modigliani, "Dividend Policy, Growth, and the Valuation of Shares," *Journal of Business,* October 1961, 411–433.

Miller, M., and M. Scholes, "Dividends and Taxes," *Journal of Financial Economics,* December 1978, 333–364.

———, "Dividends and Taxes: Some Empirical Evidence," working paper, University of Chicago Graduate School of Business, March 1982, forthcoming in *Journal of Political Economy.*

Modigliani, F., and M. Miller, "Taxes and the Cost of Capital: A Correction," *American Economic Review,* June 1963, 433–443.

Morgan, I. G., "Dividends and Stock Price Behaviour in Canada," *Journal of Business Administration,* Fall 1980, 91–106.

Pettit, R. R., "Dividend Announcements, Security Performance, and Capital Market Efficiency," *Journal of Finance,* December 1972, 993–1007.

———, "The Impact of Dividend and Earnings Announcements: A Reconciliation," *Journal of Business,* January 1976, 86–96.

———, "Taxes, Transactions Costs and Clientele Effects of Dividends," *Journal of Financial Economics,* December 1977, 419–436.

Rosenberg, B., and V. Marathe, "Tests of the Capital Asset Pricing Hypothesis," *Research in Finance,* January 1979, 115–223.

Ross, S. A., "The Determination of Financial Structure: The Incentive-Signalling Approach," *Bell Journal of Economics,* Spring 1977, 23–40.

Stewart, S., "Should a Corporation Repurchase Its Own Stock?" *Journal of Finance,* June 1976, 911–921.

Van Horne, J., and J. G. McDonald, "Dividend Policy and New Equity Financing," *Journal of Finance,* May 1971, 507–520.

Vermaelen, T., "Common Stock Repurchases and Market Signaling: An Empirical Study," *Journal of Financial Economics,* June 1981, 139–183.

Walter, J. E., *Dividend Policy and Enterprise Valuation.* Wadsworth, Belmont, Calif., 1967.

Watts, R., "The Information Content of Dividends," *Journal of Business,* April 1973, 191–211.

———, "Comments on the Informational Content of Dividends," *Journal of Business,* January 1976, 81–85.

———, "Comments on 'The Impact of Dividend and Earnings Announcements: a Reconciliation,'" *Journal of Business,* January 1976, 97–106.

Woods, D., and E. Brigham, "Stockholder Distribution Decisions: Share Repurchases or Dividends?" *Journal of Financial and Quantitative Analysis,* March 1966, 15–28.

Young, A., "The Performance of Common Stocks Subsequent to Repurchase," *Financial Analysts Journal,* September/October 1967, 117–121.

———, "Financial, Operating and Security Market Parameters of Repurchasing," *Financial Analysts Journal,* July/August 1969, 123–128.

The Economics of Leasing

It is estimated that from 15 to 20 percent of all new capital put in use by business each year is leased.

PETER VANDERWICKEN, "THE POWERFUL LOGIC OF THE LEASING BOOM," *FORTUNE*, NOVEMBER 1973, 136.

A. INTRODUCTION

Lease contracts have long been an important alternative to outright ownership of an asset. For example, one may choose to lease an automobile or rent a house, rather than owning them outright. For the student of finance, leasing is an important applied issue because the use of an asset and the methods of financing it are seemingly intertwined. However, this is an illusion. As we shall see, it is critical to keep the investment decision separate from the financing decision in the analysis. Failure to do so has led many decision makers to make the wrong comparisons between the lease/own decision and the lease/borrow decision.

For the purpose of consistency, we shall assume

536

throughout most of the chapter that there are no transactions costs or economies of scale in financial contracts. Among other things, this implies that there are no flotation costs in issuing financial securities. Thus it would make no difference at all in the percentage of transactions costs whether one issues a bond for $100 or $100,000,000. We shall also assume: (1) that firms possess optimal capital structures without specifying the reason; (2) that firms may have different effective tax rates; and (3) that the Miller-Modigliani [1966] valuation framework is applicable. First, we review a detailed description of the legal and accounting treatment of different types of lease contracts. Then we analyze the economics of the lease/buy decision for noncancellable long-term leases, for cancellable leases, for leveraged leases, and for short-term leases. Finally, the scant empirical literature on leasing is reviewed.

B. THE LEGAL AND ACCOUNTING TREATMENT OF LEASES

1. Types of Leases

Leases take several different forms, the most important of which are sale and leaseback, service or operating leases, and straight financial leases. These three major types of leases are described below.

Under a *sale and leaseback arrangement,* a firm owning land, buildings, or equipment sells the property to a financial institution and simultaneously executes an agreement to lease the property back for a certain period under specific terms.

Note that the seller, or *lessee,* immediately receives the purchase price put up by the buyer, or *lessor.* At the same time, the seller-lessee retains the use of the property. This parallel is carried over to the lease payment schedule. Under a mortgage loan arrangement, the financial institution receives a series of equal payments just sufficient to amortize the loan and to provide the lender with a specified rate of return on investment. Under a sale and leaseback arrangement, the lease payments are set up in the same manner. The payments are sufficient to return the full purchase price to the financial institution in addition to providing it with some return on its investment.

Operating (or *service*) *leases* include both financing and maintenance services. IBM is one of the pioneers of the service lease contract. Computers and office copying machines, together with automobiles and trucks, are the primary types of equipment covered by operating leases. The leases ordinarily call for the lessor to maintain and service the leased equipment, and the costs of this maintenance are either built into the lease payments or contracted for separately.

Another important characteristic of the service lease is that it is frequently not fully amortized. In other words, the payments required under the lease contract are *not* sufficient to recover the full cost of the equipment. Obviously, however, the lease contract is written for considerably less than the expected life of the leased equipment, and the lessor expects to recover the cost either in subsequent renewal payments or on disposal of the equipment.

A final feature of the service lease is that it frequently contains a cancellation clause giving the lessee the right to cancel the lease and return the equipment before the expiration of the basic agreement. This is an important consideration for the lessee, who can return the equipment if technological developments render it obsolete or if it simply is no longer needed.

A *strict financial lease* is one that does not provide for maintenance services, is not cancellable, and is fully amortized (that is, the lessor contracts for rental payments equal to the full price of the leased equipment). The typical arrangement involves the following steps:

1. The user firm selects the specific equipment it requires and negotiates the price and delivery terms with the manufacturer or distributor.

2. Next, the user firm arranges with a bank or leasing company for the latter to buy the equipment from the manufacturer or distributor, simultaneously executing an agreement to lease the equipment from the financial institution. The terms call for full amortization of the financial institution's cost, plus a rate of return on investment. The lessee generally has the option to renew the lease at a reduced rental on expiration of the basic lease, but does not have the right to cancel the basic lease without completely paying off the financial institution.

Financial leases are almost the same as sale and leaseback arrangements, the main difference being that the leased equipment is new and the lessor buys it from a manufacturer or a distributor instead of from the user-lessee. A sale and leaseback can thus be thought of as a special type of financial lease.

2. Tax Treatment

The full amount of the annual lease payments is deductible for income tax purposes—provided the Internal Revenue Service agrees that a particular contract is a genuine lease and not simply an installment loan called a lease. This makes it important that the lease contract be written in a form acceptable to the IRS. Following are the major requirements for bona fide lease transactions from the standpoint of the IRS:

1. The term must be less than 30 years; otherwise the lease is regarded as a form of sale.

2. The rent must represent a reasonable return to the lessor.

3. The renewal option must be bona fide, and this requirement can best be met by giving the lessee the first option to meet an equal bona fide outside offer.

4. There must be no repurchase option; if there is, the lessee should merely be given parity with an equal outside offer.

3. Accounting Treatment

In November 1976, the Financial Accounting Standards Board issued its Statement of Financial Accounting Standards No. 13, *Accounting for Leases.* Like other FASB statements, the standards set forth must be followed by business firms if their financial statements are to receive certification by auditors. FASB Statement No. 13 has implications both for the utilization of leases and for their accounting treatment. Those elements of FASB Statement No. 13 that are most relevant for financial analysis of leases are summarized below.

For some types of leases, this FASB statement requires that the obligation be capitalized on the asset side of the balance sheet with a related lease obligation on the liability side. The accounting treatment depends on the type of lease. The classification is more detailed than the two categories of operating and financial leases described above.

From the lessee's point of view, the two accounting categories are capital leases and operating leases. A lease is classified in Statement No. 13 as a *capital lease* if it meets one or more of four Paragraph 7 criteria:

1. The lease transfers ownership of the property to the lessee by the end of the lease term.
2. The lease gives the lessee the option to purchase the property at a price sufficiently below the expected fair value of the property that the exercise of the option is highly probable.
3. The lease term is equal to 75% or more of the estimated economic life of the property.
4. The present value of the minimum lease payments exceeds 90% of the fair value of the property at the inception of the lease. The discount factor to be used in calculating the present value is the implicit rate used by the lessor or the lessee's incremental borrowing rate, whichever is lower. (Note that the lower discount factor represents a higher present value factor and therefore a higher calculated present value for a given pattern of lease payments. It thus increases the likelihood that the 90% test will be met and that the lease will be classified as a capital lease.)

From the standpoint of the lessee, if a lease is not a capital lease, it is classified as an operating lease.

From the standpoint of the lessor, four types of leases are defined: (1) sales-type leases; (2) direct financing leases; (3) leveraged leases; and (4) operating leases representing all leases other than the first three types. *Sales-type leases* and *direct financing leases* meet one or more of the four Paragraph 7 criteria and both of the Paragraph 8 criteria, which are:

1. Collectibility of the minimum lease payments is reasonably predictable.
2. No important uncertainties surround the amount of unreimbursable costs yet be incurred by the lessor under the lease.

Sales-type leases give rise to profit (or loss) to the lessor—the fair value of the leased property at the inception of the lease is greater (or less) than its cost-of-carrying amount. Sales-type leases normally arise when manufacturers or dealers use leasing in marketing their products. Direct financing leases are leases other than leveraged leases for which the cost-of-carrying amount is equal to the fair value of the leased property at the inception of the lease. Leveraged leases are direct financing leases in which substantial financing is provided by a long-term creditor on a nonrecourse basis with respect to the general credit of the lessor.

The actual bookkeeping for lessees is set up in the following way. For operating leases, rentals must be charged to expense over the lease term, with disclosures of future rental obligations in total as well as by each of the following five years. For lessees, capital leases are to be capitalized and shown on the balance sheet both as a fixed asset and a noncurrent obligation. Capitalization represents the present value of the minimum lease payments minus that portion of lease payments representing executory costs such as insurance, maintenance, and taxes to be paid by the lessor (including any profit return in such charges). The discount factor is (as described in Paragraph 7(4)) the lower of the implicit rate used by the lessor or the incremental borrowing rate of the lessee.

The asset must be amortized in a manner consistent with the lessee's normal depreciation policy for owned assets. During the lease term, each lease payment is to be allocated between a reduction of the obligation and the interest expense to produce a constant rate of interest on the remaining balance of the obligation. Thus, for capital leases, the balance sheet includes the items in Table 16.1.

In addition to the balance sheet capitalization of capital leases, substantial additional footnote disclosures are required for both capital and operating leases. These include a description of leasing arrangements, an analysis of leased property under capital leases by major classes of property, a schedule by years of future minimum lease payments (with executory and interest costs broken out for capital leases), and contingent rentals for operating leases.

FASB Statement No. 13 sets forth requirements for capitalizing capital leases and for standardizing disclosures by lessees for both capital leases and operating leases. Lease commitments therefore do not represent "off-balance sheet" financing for capital assets, and standard disclosure requirements make general the footnote reporting of information on operating leases. Hence, the argument that leasing represents a form of financing that lenders may not take into account in their analysis of the financial position of firms seeking financing will be even less valid in the future than it is now.

It is unlikely that sophisticated lenders were ever fooled by off-balance sheet leasing obligations. However, the capitalization of capital leases and the standard disclosure requirements for operating leases will make it easier for general users of

Table 16.1   Balance Sheet for Capitalized Leases

Assets	*Liabilities*
	Current:
Leased property under capital	Obligations under capital leases
leases less accumulated	Noncurrent:
amortization	Obligations under capital leases

financial reports to obtain additional information on firms' leasing obligations. Hence, the requirements of FASB Statement No. 13 are useful. Probably the extent to which leasing is used will remain substantially unaltered, since the particular circumstances that have provided a basis for its use in the past are not likely to be greatly affected by the increased disclosure requirements.

C. THE THEORY OF LEASING

1. The Long-Term Lease from the Lessor's Point of View

The lessor is frequently a financial intermediary such as a commercial bank, an insurance company, or a leasing company. Also equipment manufacturers, for example GATX (railroad cars), IBM (computers and office equipment), and Xerox (copiers), are among the largest lessors. However, the institutional arrangements are largely arbitrary. Anyone who owns an asset also may decide to lease it. For example, suppose one owns a car or a house. There is always the choice between owning it and using it for one's own purposes, thereby gaining a direct (non-taxable) stream of consumption of transportation or housing services. Or alternatively, one can lease the asset to a second party. In return one then receives a (taxable) stream of income which can be used for the consumption of transportation and housing (among other things). The choice to own the asset in the first place was an investment decision. At the same time, there is a separate decision to make—namely the financing decision. Should use of the asset be financed with debt and equity or should it be leased? How much of the lease financing can be considered to be debt? How much is equity?

In the analysis which follows it is convenient to divide lease contracts into major categories: (1) strict financial leases and (2) operating leases. *Strict financial leases,* along with sale and leaseback arrangements, will be characterized as perfect substitutes for debt capital; in other words, they have exactly the same risk.[1] A lessee may not cancel a strict financial lease, the failure to meet lease payments can force the lessee into bankruptcy (or reorganization), and the lease is fully amortized (that is, the lessor receives lease payments which repay the full cost of the leased asset). *Operating leases* are riskier than financial leases. We assume that they may be cancelled at the option of the lessee, are usually not fully amortized, and require that the salvage value go to the lessor. Finally, either type of lease may involve a separable contract for various types of maintenance on the leased asset, for example automobile servicing. Because the maintenance contract is economically separable we shall not discuss it in this chapter.

Financial leases and operating leases involve very different risks to the lessor and must, therefore, be discussed separately. We shall defer a discussion of operating leases until later in the chapter and focus on the much simpler financial lease for

---

[1] This means that debt capital lent to the ith firm and leased to the same firm have the *same* risk. Of course, lending to different firms may have different risks.

the time being. Suppose that the lessor is a commercial bank. Recall that any commercial bank will hold a well-diversified portfolio of corporate debt as its major asset. Obviously, it requires that this portfolio earn (at least) the bank's after-tax weighted average cost of capital. On the other hand, what we call the rate of return to the bank is also the cost of debt to the borrowing firm. Therefore, if we designate the bank's *after-tax* weighted average cost of capital as $WACC_B$ and the firm's *before-tax* cost of debt as k_d, then

$$k_d = \frac{WACC_B}{(1 - \tau_c)},$$

where τ_c is the bank's marginal tax rate.

The Modigliani-Miller model may be employed to compute $WACC_B$, the lessor's after-tax weighted average cost of capital.[2] Designate ρ (lease) as the rate of return required on leasing projects, assuming that the lessor is 100% equity-financed. Then, given that B and S are the market values of debt and equity respectively, the MM cost of capital is

$$WACC_B = \rho(\text{lease}) \left[1 - \tau_c \frac{B}{B + S} \right].$$

If the required rate of return on the lease project is 9.375% and the leasing firm (the bank) uses 90% debt in its optimal capital structure, and has a 40% marginal tax rate, then

$$WACC_B = .09375[1 - .4(.9)] = .06.$$

Thus, from the lessor's point of view, the lease project will have a 6% after-tax weighted average cost of capital. From the lessee's point of view the before-tax cost of leasing will be

$$k_d = \frac{WACC_B}{1 - \tau_c} = \frac{.06}{1 - .4} = 10\%.$$

As mentioned before, each dollar in a pure financial lease is a perfect substitute for one dollar of debt in the capital structure of the lessee firm. Thus if a lessee is at its optimal capital structure prior to signing a lease contract, and wishes to maintain that structure, then it must displace one dollar of debt for each dollar in the lease contract.

What lease fee should the lessor charge for a pure financial lease? Assume the cost of the leased asset is $\$I$, the lessor's tax rate is τ_c, and the annual (straight-line) depreciation writeoff on the leased asset is dep_t.[3] Also, assume that there is

---

[2] See Chapter 12, p. 407.

[3] Although we have assumed straight-line depreciation for convenience, there is usually an optimal depreciation schedule which maximizes the present value of the depreciation tax shield. Our analysis will not change if, in practice, both the lessor and lessee use the same optimal depreciation schedule.

no salvage value and no investment tax credit. If the lessor charges an annual lease payment of L_t, then the net present value of the lease to the lessor is[4]

$$\text{NPV(to lessor)} = -I + \sum_{t=1}^{N} \frac{L_t(1 - \tau_c) + \tau_c \text{dep}_t}{(1 + \text{WACC}_B)^t} \tag{16.1}$$

The numerator of Eq. (16.1) is the standard definition of after-tax cash flows from an investment, including the depreciation tax shield.[5] In order to provide a numerical example, let $I = \$10,000$, $\tau_c = 40\%$, $\text{WACC}_B = 6\%$, and the life of the project, N, be 5 years. Given these facts and assuming that the lease fee is competitively determined so that NPV(to lessor) = 0, then the minimum lease fee, L_t is

$$0 = -10,000 + \sum_{t=1}^{5} \frac{L_t(1 - .4) + .4(2000)}{(1 + .06)^t},$$

$$0 = -10,000 + L_t(.6)(4.212) + .4(2000)(4.212),$$

$$\frac{10,000 - .4(2000)(4.212)}{.6(4.212)} = L_t = \$2624.$$

If the lessor charges \$2624, then it will earn a rate of return which just compensates it for taking a debt position in the lessee firm. A higher lease fee would result in a positive NPV.

2. The Investment Decision

Now suppose that, instead of leasing the asset, the *lessor* decides to own and operate it. What rate of return would be required? Clearly, owning the asset exposes the lessor to more risk than a lending position of an equivalent dollar amount. Owning the project involves the total risk of its cash flows, not merely the risk of a debt position. Suppose we define the required rate of return on the unlevered cash flows from the project as $\rho(\text{project})$. We know that $\rho(\text{project}) > k_d(\text{lease}) \geq \text{WACC}_B$. Furthermore, if one borrows to undertake the investment, the Modigliani-Miller definition of the cost of capital can be applied. Then if the project's optimal capital structure is $B/(B + S)$, the appropriate weighted average cost of capital is

$$\text{WACC(project)} = \rho(\text{project})\left(1 - \tau_c \frac{B}{B + S}\right). \tag{16.2}$$

Note that this weighted average cost of capital for owning the project is the same, no matter who owns it, so long as their marginal tax rates are the same. We assume that the optimal capital structure is project specific. For example, a commercial bank with 90–95% debt in its capital structure should not apply the same leverage to a wholly owned computer division. Presumably, the computer division has its own optimal leverage, different from (less than) the commercial bank's.

---

[4] For convenience, we have assumed that the stream of lease payments is an annuity with the first payment at the end of the first year. Most lease contracts require the first payment to be made immediately.

[5] If there is an investment tax credit it will also be counted as a cash inflow.

In order to continue with the numerical example, assume that the unlevered cost of capital, ρ(project), is 14% for the project and that its optimal capital structure is one-third debt to total assets; that is, $B/(B + S) = .33$. The required rate of return on the wholly-owned project is

$$\text{WACC(project)} = .14[1 - .4(.33)] = 12.152\%.$$

If the project has a positive net present value when its after-tax operating cash flows are discounted at the appropriate WACC, then it is a good investment.

In order to add realism to the investment decision, assume that the investment project has expected annual sales revenues of $S_t = \$20,000$, and expected annual cash costs of $C_t = \$16,711$. Then the NPV of the investment project is

$$\text{NPV(investment)} = -I + \sum_{t=1}^{N} \frac{(S_t - C_t)(1 - \tau_c) + \tau_c \text{dep}_t}{(1 + \text{WACC})^t}$$

$$= -10,000 + \sum_{t=1}^{5} \frac{.6(20,000 - 16,711) + .4(2000)}{(1.12152)^t}$$

$$= -10,000 + .6(20,000 - 16,711)(3.5912) + .4(2000)(3.5912)$$

$$= -10,000 + 7087 + 2873$$

$$= -40.$$

Under these assumptions, the project should be rejected.

3. The Long-Term Lease Contract from the Lessee's Point of View

As before, we assume that the lease is a perfect substitute for debt because it is assumed to be a strict financial lease. Operating leases are riskier for the lessor and will be discussed later on.

Failure to remember that strict financial leases are perfect substitutes for debt causes much confusion about how to evaluate a lease contract. For example, one often hears the mistaken phrase that leases are 100% debt financing. The advertising of leasing companies invariably points out that lease payments are deductible in full, whereas owners deduct only the machine's depreciation plus that part of the capital costs represented by interest payments. This is nonsense. If all of a project is provided by lease financing, then the lessee firm's debt capacity is reduced by an equivalent dollar amount. Other projects can carry less debt financing. Hence an opportunity cost of leasing is the displacement of the firm's debt capacity, and the associated loss of the tax shield provided by that debt.

The lessee firm must make two decisions. First, is the project acceptable as an investment? Does it have a positive net present value if financed at its optimal capital structure? This analysis was described in Part C.2 above. Second, should it be financed by leasing or borrowing? The user firm takes the lease-rental fee, L_t, as an input in making a comparison between the cost of leasing and the cost of borrowing. Myers, Dill, and Bautista [1976] have shown that the costs and benefits of leasing involve an analysis of the following cash flows:

1. A cash saving amounting to the dollar amount of the investment outlay, I, which the firm does not have to incur if it leases.

2. A cash outflow amounting to the present value of the after-tax lease payments, $PV[L_t(1 - \tau_c)]$.

3. The present value of the opportunity cost of the lost depreciation tax shield, $PV[\tau_c \text{dep}_t]$ (and lost investment tax credits, if relevant).

4. The present value of the *change* in the interest tax shield on debt, which is displaced by the lease financing, $PV[\tau_c \Delta(k_d D_t)]$, where D_t is the remaining book value of debt outstanding in period t.

These four terms are summarized in Eq. (16.3) below.

$$\text{NPV(to lessee)} = I - PV[(1 - \tau_c)L_t] - PV[\tau_c \text{dep}_t] - PV[\tau_c \Delta(k_d D_t)]. \quad (16.3)$$

We have assumed for strict financial leases that debt and lease financing are perfect substitutes. Therefore, the fourth term in Eq. (16.3) will reflect a dollar-for-dollar substitution of debt tax shield for leasing tax shield for the portion of the asset which would be debt-financed at the project's optimal capital structure. Furthermore, because leasing and debt are perfect substitutes, the cash inflows to the lessor and the cash outflows from the lessee have the same risk. Therefore, the appropriate before-tax discount rate for the cash flows in Eq. (16.3) is k_d, the borrowing rate. Eq. (16.3) may be rewritten as

$$\text{NPV(to lessee)} = I - \sum_{t=1}^{N} \frac{L_t(1 - \tau_c) + \tau_c \text{dep}_t + \tau_c \Delta(k_d D_t)}{(1 + k_d)^t}. \quad (16.4)$$

Table 16.2 illustrates how the cash flow definitions of Eq. (16.4) can be used to compute the present value of a lease contract. The example in Table 16.2 uses the same numbers as in sections B and C of this chapter. The annual lease fee (assumed to be paid at the end of each year) is \$2624. Except for a rounding error, the NPV of the lease is \$0. This is to be expected in a competitive market where the tax rates of the lessor and lessee are identical. There is no advantage to leasing over borrowing in these circumstances.

One problem in applying Eq. (16.4) is that the remaining debt balance, D_t, declines each year as the lease fees amortize the principal. This makes computations more cumbersome than they need be. A much simpler way of looking at the problem was derived by Levy and Sarnat [1979]. Eq. (16.4) puts the tax effect of displaced debt in the numerator and discounts at the before-tax rate, k_d. However, it has been our practice throughout the text to account for the tax effect of financing costs by discounting at the after-tax rate in the denominator and writing the numerator in terms of after-tax cash flows net of financing effects. If this is done, Eq. (16.4) is equivalent to Eq. (16.5) below

$$\text{NPV(to lessee)} = I - \sum_{t=1}^{N} \frac{L_t(1 - \tau_c) + \tau_c \text{dep}_t}{(1 + (1 - \tau_c)k_d)^t}. \quad (16.5)$$

Also, recall that $(1 - \tau_c)k_d = \text{WACC}_B$.

Table 16.2 NPV (to lessee) Using Eq. (16.4)

(1) Year	(2) dep_t	(3) $\tau_c dep_t$	(4) $(1-\tau_c)L_t$	(5) D_{t-1}	(6) $\Delta k_d D_t$	(7) $\tau_c \Delta k_d D_t$	(8) ΔD_t	(9) CF_t	(10) $(1+k_d)^{-t}$	(11) $PV(CF_t)$
1	2,000	800	1574.4	10,000	1,000	400.0	1,638	2774.4	.909	2,521.93
2	2,000	800	1574.4	8,362	836	334.4	1,802	2708.8	.826	2,237.47
3	2,000	800	1574.4	6,560	656	262.4	1,982	2636.8	.751	1,980.24
4	2,000	800	1574.4	4,578	458	183.2	2,180	2557.6	.683	1,746.84
5	2,000	800	1574.4	2,398	240	96.0	2,398	2470.4	.621	1,534.12
							10,000			10,020.60

L_t = the annual lease fee on a fully amortized lease, i.e., no salvage value,

dep_t = the annual (straight line) depreciation writeoff,

τ_c = the lessee's marginal tax rate,

D_{t-1} = the face value of debt displaced by the lease in the previous time period,

k_d = the before-tax cost of the displaced debt capital

$\Delta k_d D_t$ = the change in the interest payments on debt displaced by the lease,

$\tau_c \Delta k_d D_t$ = the change in the interest tax shield displaced by the lease,

ΔD_t = the repayment of principal on debt,

CF_t = the cash flow for the lease contract = columns 3 + 4 + 7,

$(1+k_d)^{-t}$ = the present value factor.

Substituting the numbers from our previous example in order to determine the NPV of the lease, and assuming that the tax rate of the lessee is the same as the lessor, namely 40%, we have

$$\text{NPV(to lessee)} = I - \sum_{t=1}^{N} \frac{L_t(1-\tau_c) + \tau_c\text{dep}_t}{(1+(1-\tau_c)k_d)^t}$$

$$= 10{,}000 - \sum_{t=1}^{5} \frac{2624(1-.4) + .4(2000)}{(1+.6(10))^t}$$

$$= 10{,}000 - 2624(.6)(4.212) - .4(2000)(4.212)$$

$$= 10{,}000 - 6631 - 3369$$

$$= 0.$$

The numerical result shows very clearly that the risk and cash flows to the lessor and lessee are identical if they have the same marginal tax rates. There is an equilibrium between the lessor market and the user market. Each term in Eq. (16.5) is identical to the corresponding term in Eq. (16.1) except that the signs are reversed. In other words, a cash outflow to the lessee is a cash inflow to the lessor and vice versa.

4. The Effect of Different Tax Rates on the Value of Leasing

Frequently the lessor and lessee have different marginal tax rates. If the lessor has a higher tax rate than the lessee, it may be possible to strike a bargain where the tax shield from owning the asset can be shared between the two. Suppose that we assume the lessor has a 40% marginal tax rate and charges a lease fee of $2624, as before, but that the marginal tax rate of the lessee is only 5%. What is the NPV of the lease contract to the lessee? Substituting into Eq. (16.5), we have

$$\text{NPV(to lessee)} = 10{,}000 - \sum_{t=1}^{5} \frac{2624(1-.05) + .05(2000)}{(1+(1-.05).10)^t}$$

$$= 10{,}000 - 2624(.95)(3.8397) - .05(2000)(3.8397)$$

$$= 10{,}000 - 9571.59 - 383.97$$

$$= 44.44.$$

Now the lease contract has a positive net present value for the lessee.

Actually, the positive net present value created by the difference in the marginal tax rates can be shared between the lessor and lessee. Also, note that any positive net present value from the lease contract which accrues to the lessee can be used to augment the net present value of the investment decision. It is conceivable that negative NPV projects might still be undertaken if the NPV of the lease contract is large enough. In our example, the NPV of the project, viewed as an investment, was −$40. But this can be offset by the positive value created by the lease financing, namely $44.44.

Although the above numerical example shows a benefit to the lessee given that the lessor's tax rate is higher, this may not always be true. The tax effect can go either way. As pointed out by Lewellen, Long, and McConnell [1976] the net tax benefit will depend on the specific asset life (lease period), depreciation schedule, capitalization rates, and leverage policies involved.

5. Leveraged Leasing

A leveraged lease is one where the lessor borrows a substantial portion of the purchase price of the asset. Figure 16.1 is a schematic representation of the parties to a leveraged lease. The lender typically holds a first mortgage on the asset. Also, the lessor assigns the lease payments to the lender (or a trustee). The debt interest and principal are deducted by the lender, who then returns the balance of the lease payment which is kept by the equity-holder. Equity may be supplied either directly by the lessor or indirectly by third parties. The loan arrangement is called a *nonrecourse loan* because its effect is to indemnify the lessor in the event of default. The lessor benefits from the investment tax credit created when the asset is purchased, the depreciation tax shield, the residual value of the equipment (if any), the interest tax deduction, and the equity payments (if not turned over to third party equity investors).

There is no real economic difference between the economics of leveraged lease contracts and strict financial lease contracts, which have already been discussed in detail.[6] In a strict financial lease, the lessor purchases the asset with a combination of debt and equity capital. The same is true in a leveraged lease with the possible exception that a different debt/equity mix may be used.

Leveraged leasing does, however, raise the issue of determining the opportunity cost of debt and equity funds employed in the lease. Suppose a lessor approaches your firm and asks that you lend funds or provide equity participation. What is your minimum acceptable rate of return?

In order to provide a concrete example we will use the same numerical example as employed earlier in the chapter. Also, as before, we will adopt the Modigliani-Miller valuation framework. Recall that the equipment cost $10,000, had a 5-year life with no salvage value, and there was no investment tax credit. The lease fee was determined to be $2,624. Both the lessor and lessee had marginal tax rates, τ_c, of 40%. The lessor earned 10% before taxes and had a 6% after-tax weighted average cost of capital.

The first question is, what is the cost of debt if it is lent by a third party? For straight financial leases the third party might be a depositor in a commercial bank or debtholders of an insurance company or a leasing company. For leveraged leases debt may be supplied, for example, by an insurance company. We can get an idea of the rate of return which will be required on debt by noting that the lease payments

---

[6] The existence of leveraged leases may be explained by various institutional considerations and agency costs. For example, for very large leveraged leases a single bank may be constrained from doing the deal because regulations prohibit it from lending more than a small percentage of its equity to a single firm. Also, leveraged leases match long-term borrowing against long-term lending (i.e., the lease) while most of a bank's other loans and deposits are short or intermediate term.

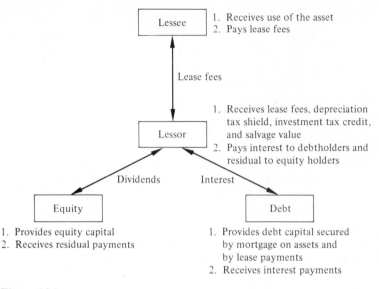

Figure 16.1
A schematic representation of a leveraged lease.

must be riskier than the debt. In the event of default on a leveraged lease the debtholders are somewhat protected because they own the mortgage on the leased assets. By way of contrast, the equity holders, being residual claimants, can lose everything. The lessor charges a 10% before-tax rate of return on the lease. Therefore, we assumed an 8% before-tax cost of borrowing, k_b, which is the rate at which the debtholders will supply capital to the leveraged lease.

The cost of equity depends on the amount of leverage used in the lease. For "blue-chip" leases the ratio of debt to total assets might be 90–95%. We assumed the ratio was 90%. Given these facts, we can employ the Modigliani-Miller cost of capital definitions (from Chapter 12) to compute the cost of equity in the leveraged lease. Recall that we assumed, earlier in the chapter, that the unlevered cost of equity, ρ, was 9.375%. The Modigliani-Miller definition of the cost of equity is

$$k_e = \rho + (\rho - k_b)(1 - \tau_c)\frac{B}{S},$$

where

ρ = the unlevered cost of equity = 9.375%,

k_b = the before-tax cost of borrowing = 8%,

τ_c = the marginal effective tax rate = 40%,

$\dfrac{B}{S}$ = the market value debt to equity ratio = 9.

Therefore, the required rate of return on equity in the leveraged lease is

$$k_e = .09375 + (.09375 - .08)(1 - .4)9,$$

$$k_e = 16.8\%.$$

This is more than double the borrowing rate on the same project and reflects the greater risk accepted by the equityholders in a leveraged lease.

6. Cancellable Operating Leases

Unlike straight financial leases, operating leases may be cancelled at the option of the lessee. From the point of view of the lessee, capital employed under operating lease contracts becomes a variable cost (rather than a fixed cost) because the lease contract may be terminated (sometimes requiring a penalty to be paid) and the leased asset returned whenever economic conditions become unfavorable. It is like having equipment which can be laid off. From the lessor's point of view, cancellable operating leases are riskier than straight financial leases. A straight lease, like a loan, is secured by all of the assets in the firm. A cancellable operating lease is not.

The risk that the lessor must bear depends on the economic depreciation of the asset. There is always uncertainty about the ability of an asset to physically withstand wear and tear. In addition there is obsolesence caused by technological advances which cause the economic value of an asset to decline vis-à-vis newer assets. And finally there is the risky end-of-period economic value of an asset which is usually called its salvage value. All of these concepts are different descriptions of economic depreciation which, henceforth, we shall call *replacement cost* uncertainty.

In order to focus on replacement cost risk by itself, assume that we know with certainty the future revenue stream which the leased asset will produce as well as other costs unassociated with the economic value of the leased asset. Figure 16.2 shows an example of how the economic value of the asset might change over time. The downward-sloping line illustrates the expected decline in the asset's value due to anticipated wear and tear and obsolesence. Note that the value is expected to decline from $\$I_0$ to $\$I_T$ over the life of the contract, T years. The expected salvage value is I_T.[7] It is reasonable to assume that the value of the asset never falls below zero. Given replacement cost uncertainty, the actual value of the asset at any time $t^* \leq T$ may be greater or less than expected. The particular situation which has been illustrated at t^* in Fig. 16.2 shows that if the value of the asset, V_t, falls far enough below the expected value, $E(V_t)$, it will pay the lessee to terminate the lease.

Thus the cancellation feature is really an option. In particular it is an American put held by the lessee. The present value of the relevant American put is derived by Copeland and Weston [1982], who utilize the binomial option pricing model. They use the following numerical example to illustrate the effect of the put option on leasing fees. Assume that a $10,000 asset is expected to have a three-year economic life and depreciate an equal amount each year (i.e., the replacement value declines

---

[7] For a paper on how to deal with uncertain salvage values the reader is referred to Lee, Martin, and Senchack [1980].

Figure 16.2
Changes in replacement value over time.

in a straight line at the rate of $1 - \theta$ each year, where $\theta = .667$). However, its value may be 50% higher or lower than expected at the end of a given year. Also, the lessor has a tax rate of 40% and will write a two-year lease. If the lease contract were a straight financial lease, it would require a 10% before-tax rate of return (i.e., $k_d = 10\%$). The salvage value is uncertain and requires a 16% risk-adjusted rate of return.[8] Using Eq. (16.1) we can write the competitive net present value of the lease, if it were noncancellable, as follows:

$$0 = -I + \sum_{t=1}^{2} \frac{(1 - \tau_c)L_t + \tau_c \text{dep}_t}{[1 + (1 - \tau_c)k_d]^t} + \frac{E(\text{MV})}{(1 + k_1)^2}, \qquad (16.6)$$

where

$E(\text{MV}) = $ the expected market value of the asset after two years,

$\quad k_1 = $ the risk-adjusted discount rate for the salvage value.

Substituting in the numbers, we have

$$0 = -10,000 + \sum_{t=1}^{2} \frac{(1 - .4)L_t + .4(3333)}{[1 + (1 - .4).10]^t} + \frac{3333}{(1.16)^2}.$$

Solving, we find that the competitive lease fee is \$4617.

Next, we want to determine the competitive lease payments assuming that the above contract is a cancellable operating lease. Equation (16.6) must be modified by subtracting out the present value of the American put option, P. The new valuation equation is

$$0 = -I + \sum_{t=1}^{2} \frac{(1 - \tau_c)L_t + \tau_c \text{dep}_t}{[1 + (1 - \tau_c)k_d]^t} + \frac{E(\text{MV})}{(1 + k_1)^2} - P.$$

---

[8] For simplicity we ignore capital gains taxation on the salvage value and investment tax credits.

The value of the put (see Copeland and Weston [1982]) is determined to be $850. Solving for the cancellable lease fee we find that it increases to $5392. The lease fee has increased substantially to reflect the extra risk of possible early cancellation of the operating lease.[9]

The example serves to illustrate that the replacement cost uncertainty borne by the lessor in a cancellable operating lease can have a profound impact on the competitive lease fee. In general the cancellation clause may be thought of as an American put purchased by the lessee. Its cost will increase with (1) greater uncertainty in the replacement value of the leased asset, and (2) decreases in the risk-free discount rate.

7. Short-term Leases

The distinction between long-term leases and short-term leases is not trivial. At one end of the continuum are very short-term leases such as hotel room, automobile, truck, and tool rentals. For these contracts the differences in transactions costs between leasing and owning are likely to be more important than tax considerations. It is much easier to rent a room for a night than to buy it in the afternoon then sell it back in the morning. On the other hand, for long-term leases, factors of this type are minimized and consideration of the differences in tax rates is the major consideration. Since we have already discussed tax considerations at some length, it is appropriate to focus on transactions costs and economies of scale from specialization. For a reference on this point of view see Flath [1980].

Transactions costs may include clerical costs, search costs, and costs of assessing, assuring, and maintaining quality. Leasing transaction costs are different from owning because the set of rights being exchanged differs. A lessee obtains the right to use an asset for a fixed period of time. When this time interval is less than the economic life of the asset, transactions costs become relevant.

Suppose that an individual wishes to use an asset for only a fraction of its economic life. For example, suppose that tuxedos go out of style in five-year cycles, whether they are used or not, and that you plan to wear the tuxedo only one day per year. Then you would be willing to pay anything up to 99.73% (= 364/365) of the value of the asset to rent it. Of course, if other people also plan to use tuxedos and if the timing of their use is independent of yours, then it will pay someone else to own the tuxedo and rent it out. Thus, if an individual wants to use an asset for an interval considerably shorter than the asset's economic life, then a demand for short-term leasing will arise. If enough people have uncorrelated demand, then the volume of business will be sufficient for someone to specialize in renting the asset, thereby creating a supply.

It is conceivable that even though you want to use a tuxedo for one day you could buy it at the beginning of the day and sell it at day's end. If so, why is leasing

---

[9] If a lessee takes the lease fee of $5392 as an input and tries to compute an internal rate of return on the contract using Eq. (16.6), the noncancellable lease formula, the IRR will be approximately 14%. However, the lessee would be mistaken to compare the 14% return on a cancellable lease with 10% on a straight financial lease (or comparable debt financing).

the preferred contract for obtaining short-term use of the asset? A supplier of short-term leases, for example a hotel owner, could arrange a one-day sale and buy-back of a room rather than renting it out. There are, of course, some obvious transaction cost savings from short-term leasing. For example, the transactions demand for money is much less if people only have to exchange currency worth one day's use of an asset rather than its full value. Also the need for the user to separately contract for insurance and financing is reduced.

Another consideration which favors short-term leasing over sale and buy-back is the cost of evaluating the quality of the leased asset. A lease is a contract for the use of asset, not its ownership. A potential owner of an asset, for example an automobile, will wish to have a detailed inspection of the car's quality. On the other hand, a lessee will only need to perform a less costly inspection because the potential loss from using a low quality asset for one day is less than the loss from owning it. Also, from the owner's point of view the gain from deceiving a customer about an asset's quality is not as great for a short-term lease as for long-term ownership. Thus the lower cost of quality evaluation favors lease contracts over ownership. However, this advantage must be weighed against higher average usage costs. For example, a lessee has less incentive to take proper care of an asset than an owner. Lessors know this and include a "moral hazard" cost as part of the lease fee. Still, leasing will be preferred if the moral hazard cost is less than the cost of the frequent detailed inspections which would be necessary if ownership were exchanged.

Thus, whenever the desired period of usage is less than the economic life of an asset, short-term leasing may be preferred to an ownership market such as a second-hand market.

D. EMPIRICAL EVIDENCE ON LEASING

The empirical evidence on leasing related issues is scant. There are (at least) four topics of interest. First is whether or not the theory of leasing is sufficiently rich to predict when a firm will use leasing instead of debt financing. Although debt and leasing are very similar, they are not necessarily perfect substitutes. Otherwise the form of financing being used would be randomly distributed across firms. Casual empiricism suggests that patterns of choice do exist. Factors such as tax shield utilization, economies of scale in service contracts, and comparative advantages in resale of equipment may explain the use of lease financing. Yet to date we know of no empirical studies on this issue.

A second issue is the extent to which lease financing is a substitute for debt financing *within* a given firm. The theory of leasing logically assumes that each dollar of leasing utilized by the firm will replace one dollar of debt capacity, i.e., they are perfect substitutes. Whether or not firms actually behave in this manner is an empirical issue. Bowman [1980] collected a 1973 sample of 92 firms in seven different industries (according to the two-digit SIC code) where both lease and debt financing were reported. A second sample of 158 firms which did not use leasing was also collected. Bowman then ran a cross-section regression to explain the systematic risk of the nonlease sample as a function of the accounting beta and the debt-to-equity ratio. The results are given below, with t-statistics in parentheses.

$$\beta_i = 1.223 + .088\,\beta_i^A + .104(D/S)_i, \qquad (\bar{R}^2 = .29),$$
$$(2.51) \qquad (4.19)$$

where

β_i = the systematic risk of the ith firm estimated using the last 60 months of data,

β_i^A = an estimate of the accounting beta for the ith firm. Two versions were tested without obtaining different results. One version used the first difference of net income before extraordinary items and the second used EBIT.

$(D/S)_i$ = the book value of debt over the market value of equity.

The association between systematic risk and lease utilization was then tested by first adjusting the beta of the ith firm by using the above estimated coefficients, then regressing the result against a lease utilization variable as shown below:

$$\beta_i - 1.223 - .088\,\beta_i^A - .104(D/S)_i = \lambda(L/S)_i + \epsilon_i,$$

where

$(L/S)_i$ = the book value of leasing over the market value of equity,

ϵ_i = the residual.

This research design controls for measurement error and multicollinearity. The relationship between systematic risk, β_i, and the use of leasing, $(L/S)_i$, was positive and statistically significant. This led Bowman to conclude that debt and lease financing both affected the market's estimate of the systematic risk of firms. Consequently, leasing and debt were recognized as close substitutes.

Other studies of leasing focus on whether or not the mandated disclosure of off-balance-sheet leasing had any measurable impact on the real decisions of firms. For example, in order to comply with the accounting disclosure changes, firms had to capitalize their lease obligations and report them on their balance sheets. When this was done, some firms found themselves in technical violation of their debt covenants. Ro [1978] tested whether the disclosure of lease information had an impact on security prices and concluded that it had an adverse impact. Abdel-Khalik, Thompson, and Taylor [1978] looked at the impact of lease disclosure on bond risk premia and found no impact on security prices. Thus the evidence is mixed. As more empirical research is reported we will obtain a better understanding of how the market reacts (if at all) to the initial disclosure of off-balance sheet financing.

Finally, studies by Sorensen and Johnson [1977], McGugan and Caves [1974], Gudikunst and Roberts [1975], and Crawford, Harper, and McConnell [1981] have empirically estimated the internal rates of return (i.e., the "yields") on commercial bank leases. They all report that the estimated yields were higher than debt of equivalent risk. If leases and debt are perfect substitutes in straight financial leases, this should not be so. So far there has been no adequate explanation for this empirical anomaly.

SUMMARY

We have examined the leasing problem from the point of view of the lessee and the lessor. If they have identical tax rates, then a competitive lease fee will have zero net present value to both parties. Yet if their lease fees are different—for example, the lessee may have a higher tax rate than the lessor—then it is possible that some negotiated lease fee can have a positive net present value to both parties. They can share the net present value of the tax shield from leasing (if any).

Strict financial leases are perfect substitutes for debt capital. There is no such thing as 100% lease financing, just as there is no such thing as 100% debt financing. For each dollar of leasing employed by a firm, one dollar of debt capacity is displaced.

Leveraged leasing is really no different from straight financial leasing. Both employ debt and equity which are used by the lessor to purchase the asset for leasing. If one knows the financing mix which will be used by the lessor, the rate of return on the lease payments and the (lower) rate of return received by debtholders in the contract, then it is possible to estimate the required rate of return on equity invested in leveraged leases.

Cancellable leases contain a put option sold to the lessee. Often valuable, this option may considerably raise the implied lease cost.

The character of short-term leases is quite different from that of long-term financial leases. In particular, the transactions costs and agency costs of short-term leases are important in explaining why we rent hotel rooms instead of buying them for one day and then selling them back the next.

The empirical evidence on leasing is scant. What little there is suggests that leasing is, indeed, viewed by the market as a close substitute for debt financing.

PROBLEM SET

16.1 Your firm is considering lease financing for a computer which is expected to have a five-year life and no salvage value (it is a strict financial lease). You have the following facts:

- Your firm's tax rate is 30%. There is no investment tax credit.
- If purchased, the project would require a capital outlay of $100,000.
- The project will be depreciated using the straight-line method.
- Debt of equivalent risk costs 10% before taxes.
- The annual lease fee is $32,000 paid at the beginning of each year for five years.
- The optimal capital structure for the project is 50% debt to total assets.

Should you use lease financing or not?

16.2 Giveaway State Teacher's College is trying to decide whether to buy a new computer or to lease it from Readi Roller Leasing. The computer costs $500,000. Giveaway has a zero tax rate while Readi Roller enjoys a 40% tax rate. There is no investment tax credit. The computer is expected to last five years and have no salvage value. It will be depreciated using the straight-line method. The college can borrow at a 15% interest rate. If the five annual lease fees are $147,577 paid at the end of each year,

a) What is the NPV of the lease for Readi Roller Leasing Co.?

b) What is the NPV of the lease for Giveaway State?

c) What do the results tell you about the lease-buy decision for tax-free institutions?

16.3 This question involves a more realistic set of facts and therefore requires a more detailed analysis of cash flows than contained in the chapter. Your company is going to negotiate a lease contract for manufacturing equipment. You have the following facts:

- The equipment cost $100,000, is expected to have a five-year life with an expected salvage value of $10,000; however, it can be fully depreciated in four years using the sum-of-years digits method of accelerated depreciation.

- Whether leased or owned, the equipment will be sold for one dollar at the end of the fifth year and the owner will pay a capital gains tax equal to one-half of the ordinary income tax rate on the difference between one dollar and the book value.

- Your firm will pay no taxes for the next two years and then will return to its normal 48% tax rate.

- The leasing firm will require equal annual lease payments paid at the beginning of each year. The leasing firm's tax rate is 48%.

- Your firm can borrow at the prime rate plus one percent, i.e., at 17%.

a) What is the maximum lease payment which your firm can afford to offer in the negotiations?

b) What is the minimum lease payment which you think the leasing company can accept in the negotiations?

16.4 Your firm has been approached to become an equity participant in a leveraged leasing deal. You need to estimate the minimum rate of return on equity which is acceptable. You have collected the following facts:

- The asset to be leased will cost $100,000,000. Ninety percent will be financed with debt and the remaining ten percent with equity.

- The debt portion of the financing is to receive a 14% rate of return before taxes.

- Your tax rate is 40%. The lessor's tax rate is 48%.

- The before-tax rate of return which the lessee will be paying is 18%.

Use the Modigliani-Miller cost of capital assumptions to make your analysis (i.e., assume a world with corporate taxes only).

16.5 The Mortar Bored Company was considering whether to buy a new $100,000 reduction machine or to lease it. It was estimated that the machine would reduce variable costs by $31,000 per year and have an eight-year life with no salvage value. The machine will be depreciated on a straight-line basis and there is no investment tax credit. The firm's optimal capital structure is 50% debt to total assets, its before-tax costs of debt and equity are 15%

and 25% respectively, and it has a 40% tax rate. If it were to lease, the fees would be $21,400 per year paid at the end of each year.

a) What is the NPV of the project if the firm owns the project?

b) What is the NPV of the lease to the company?

c) Should the company lease the project? Why or why not?

REFERENCES

Abdel-Khalik, A., R. Thompson, and R. Taylor, "The Impact of Reporting Leases Off the Balance Sheet on Bond Risk Premiums: Two Exploratory Studies," Accounting Research Center Working Paper #78-2, University of Florida, February 1978.

Athanosopoulos, P., and P. Bacon, "The Evaluation of Leveraged Leases," *Financial Management,* Spring 1980, 76–80.

Bower, R., "Issues in Lease Financing," *Financial Management,* Winter 1973, 25–33.

Bowman, R., "The Debt Equivalence of Leases: An Empirical Investigation," *Accounting Review,* April 1980, 237–253.

Copeland, T., and J. F. Weston, "A Note on the Evaluation of Cancellable Operating Leases," *Financial Management,* Summer 1982, 60–67.

Cox, J., S. Ross, and M. Rubinstein, "Option Pricing: A Simplified Approach," *Journal of Financial Economics,* September 1979, 229–264.

Crawford, P., C. Harper, and J. McConnell, "Further Evidence on the Terms of Financial Leases," *Financial Management,* Autumn 1981, 7–14.

Dyl, E., and S. Martin, Jr., "Setting Terms for Leveraged Leases," *Financial Management,* Winter 1977, 20–27.

Elam, R., "The Effect of Lease Data on the Predictive Ability of Financial Ratios," *Accounting Review,* January 1975, 25–43.

Flath, D., "The Economics of Short-Term Leasing," *Economic Inquiry,* April 1980, 247–259.

Franks, J., and S. Hodges, "Valuation of Financial Lease Contracts: A Note," *Journal of Finance,* May 1978, 647–669.

Gudikunst, A., and G. Roberts, "Leasing: Analysis of a Theoretic-Pragmatic Dilemma," paper presented at the annual meeting of the Financial Management Association, Kansas City, October 1975.

Johnson, R., and W. Lewellen, "Analysis of the Lease-or-Buy Decision," *Journal of Finance,* September 1972, 815–823.

Kim, E., W. Lewellen, and J. McConnell, "Sale-and-Leaseback Agreements and Enterprise Valuation," *Journal of Financial and Quantitative Analysis,* December 1978, 871–883.

Lee, W., J. Martin, and A. J. Senchack, "An Option Pricing Approach to the Evaluation of Salvage Values in Financial Lease Arrangements," working paper, University of Texas at Austin, September 1980.

Levy, H., and M. Sarnat, "Leasing, Borrowing and Financial Risk," *Financial Management,* Winter 1979, 47–54.

Lewellen, W., M. Long, and J. McConnell, "Asset Leasing in Competitive Capital Markets," *Journal of Finance*, June 1976, 787–798.

Long, M., "Leasing and the Cost of Capital," *Journal of Financial and Quantitative Analysis*, November 1977, 579–598.

McGugan, V., and R. Caves, "Integration and Competition in the Equipment Leasing Industry," *Journal of Business*, July 1974, 382–396.

Miller, M., and F. Modigliani, "Some Estimates of the Cost of Capital to the Electric Utility Industry, 1954–57," *American Economic Review*, June 1966, 333–391.

Miller, M., and C. Upton, "Leasing, Buying and the Cost of Capital Services," *Journal of Finance*, June 1976, 761–786.

Myers, S., "Interactions of Corporate Financing and Investment Decisions—Implications for Capital Budgeting," *Journal of Finance*, March 1974, 1–25.

_____, D. Dill, and A. Bautista, "Valuation of Financial Lease Contracts," *Journal of Finance*, June 1976, 799–819.

Ofer, A., "The Evaluation of the Lease Versus Purchase Alternatives," *Financial Management*, Summer 1976, 67–72.

Perg, W., "Leveraged Leasing: The Problem of Changing Leverage," *Financial Management*, Autumn 1978, 47–51.

Ro, B., "The Disclosure of Capitalized Lease Information and Stock Prices," *Journal of Accounting Research*, Autumn 1978, 315–340.

Roberts, G., and A. Gudikunst, "Equipment Financial Leasing Practices and Costs: Comment," *Financial Management*, Summer 1978, 79–81.

Schall, L., "Asset Valuation, Firm Investment, and Firm Diversification," *Journal of Business*, January 1972, 11–28.

_____, "The Lease-or-Buy and Asset Acquisition Decisions," *Journal of Finance*, September 1974, 1203–1214.

Snyder, N., "Financial Leases," *The Treasurer's Handbook*, J. Fred Weston and Maurice Goudzwaard, eds. Dow-Jones Irwin, Homewood, Ill., 1976, 783–822.

Sorensen, I., and R. Johnson, "Equipment Financial Leasing Practices and Costs: An Empirical Study," *Financial Management*, Spring 1977, 33–40.

Taylor, D., "Technological or Economic Obsolescence: Computer Purchase vs. Lease," *Management Accounting*, September 1968.

Vancil, R., "Lease or Borrow—New Method of Analysis," *Harvard Business Review*, September/October, 1961.

Vanderwicken, P., "Powerful Logic of the Leasing Boom," *Fortune*, November 1973.

Mergers and Tender Offers: Theory

Let me not to the marriage of true minds
Admit impediments....

SHAKESPEARE, SONNET 116

A. INTRODUCTION

Mergers and acquisitions have long played an important role in the growth of firms. Growth is generally viewed as vital to the well-being of a firm. Among other reasons, growth is needed for a firm to compete for the best managerial talent by offering rapid promotions and broadened responsibilities. Without a continued inflow of able executives, the firm is likely to decline in efficiency and value.

From a legal standpoint there are many distinctions between types of mergers and combinations. Most generally, merger means any transaction that forms one economic unit from two or more previous ones. A recent development is the increased use of tender offers. In a tender offer, the acquiring firm (the bidder) makes an offer to the stockholders of the firm it is seeking to control (the target) to submit or tender their shares in exchange for a specified price, expressed in cash or securities. Tender offers have been used for a number of years, but the pace greatly accelerated after 1965.

Another distinction, from an accounting standpoint, is between a purchase and a pooling of interest. A purchase generally refers to the acquisition of a much smaller entity which is absorbed into the acquiring firm. The excess of the purchase price of the equity obtained over its book value is recorded as goodwill on the balance sheet of the acquiring company. A pooling of interest represents the joining of two firms of not greatly unequal size followed by operations in which their identities are continued to a considerable degree. In pooling-of-interest accounting the total assets of the surviving firm is the sum of the total assets of the components. Any excess of market price paid over the book value of the equity acquired is reflected in adjustments to the net-worth accounts of the surviving firm.

1. Recent Developments

Merger activity has been dramatized in recent years by bidding wars in tender offers and mergers of very substantial size. Notable was duPont's November 1981 acquisition of Conoco for over $7.5 billion, in which duPont outbid Seagram and Mobil. Also dramatic was the action of U.S. Steel in outbidding Mobil to obtain Marathon Oil in March 1982 for about $6.5 billion.

Despite these and other large acquisitions, merger activity in constant dollars has not reached the levels of the late 1960s. Table 17.1 shows that the constant dollar consideration paid in mergers in 1968 exceeded the level of merger activity in 1981 by about $10 billion. Over the years, merger and acquisition activity has been highly correlated with plant and equipment expenditures, averaging about 16 to 20% of internal investments. In relation to total corporate assets, merger activity during an average year has represented somewhat less than one-half of one percent of total corporate assets. Expressed in relation to the total market value of equities, merger and acquisition activity, measured by the market value of acquired firms, has ranged from about 2–4% of the total market value of all equities. Beginning in the early 1970s, corporate divestitures or partial sales have represented about 40–50% of total merger and acquisition activity. This suggests that mergers perform a role in the reallocation of resources in the economy.

2. Forms of Mergers

Several alternative forms of merger activity have been distinguished. A horizontal merger involves two firms operating in the same kind of business activity. Thus a merger between two steel firms would represent a horizontal merger. Vertical mergers involve different stages of production operations. In the oil industry distinctions are made between exploration and production activity, refining operations, and marketing to the ultimate consumer. In the pharmaceutical industry one could distinguish between research and the development of new drugs, the production of drugs, and the marketing of drug products through retail drugstores. Conglomerate mergers involve firms engaged in unrelated types of business activity. Thus the merger between Mobil Oil and Montgomery Ward was generally regarded as a conglomerate merger.

Table 17.1 Merger Activity in Constant Dollars

Year	(1) Total Consideration*	(2) GNP Deflator (1972 = 100)	(3) 1972 Constant Dollar Consideration	(4) Index of Constant Dollar Consideration (1967–69 = 100)
1967	$18.0	79.0	$22.8	66.9
1968	43.0	82.5	52.1	152.8
1969	23.7	86.8	27.3	80.1
1970	16.4	91.4	17.9	52.5
1971	12.6	96.0	13.1	38.4
1972	16.7	100.0	16.7	49.0
1973	16.7	105.7	15.8	46.3
1974	12.5	114.9	10.9	32.0
1975	11.8	125.6	9.4	27.6
1976	20.0	132.1	15.1	44.3
1977	21.9	139.8	15.7	46.0
1978	34.2	150.1	22.8	66.9
1979	43.5	162.8	26.7	78.3
1980	44.3	177.4	25.0	73.3
1981	82.6	193.6	42.7	125.2

* $ billions

Source: Column (1)–W. T. Grimm and Co.
Column (2)–U.S. Department of Commerce.
Column (3)–Column (1) divided by Column (2) × 100.
Column (4)–Column (3) divided by average of 1967–69 in Column (3) × 100.

Among conglomerate mergers three types have been distinguished. Product extension mergers broaden the product lines of firms. For example, in the Mobil-Ward merger some might view the retailing operations of Ward as an extension of the retail petroleum product marketing experience of Mobil. A geographic market extension merger involves two firms whose operations had been conducted in nonoverlapping geographic areas. Finally, a pure conglomerate merger involves unrelated business activities that would not qualify as either product extension or market extension mergers.

These distinctions among types of mergers provide background for understanding the role of mergers. The different types of mergers have implications for alternative theories of mergers that have been formulated. These will be considered next.

B. THEORIES OF MERGERS

The following eight types of theories have been formulated:

1. Differential efficiency as a basis for mergers,
2. Tax considerations,

3. Inefficient management,
4. Agency problem—managerialism,
5. Undervalued company—asymmetric information,
6. Synergy,
7. Market power, or antitrust considerations
8. Strategic realignment to changing environments.

1. Differential Efficiency as a Basis for Mergers

The most general theory of mergers that can be formulated involves differential efficiency. In theory, if the management of firm A is more efficient than the management of firm B and if after firm A acquires firm B, the efficiency of firm B is brought up to the level of efficiency of firm A, efficiency is increased by merger. Note that this would be a social gain as well as a private gain. The level of efficiency in the economy would be raised by such mergers.

One difficulty in the differential efficiency theory is that if carried to its extreme, it would result in only one firm in the economy, indeed in the world—the firm with the greatest managerial efficiency. Clearly, problems of coordination in the firm would arise before that result was reached. Hence another formulation of the differential efficiency theory of mergers is that there are always many firms with below-average efficiency or that are not operating up to their potentials, however defined. It is further suggested that firms operating in similar kinds of business activity would be most likely to be the potential acquirers. They would have the background for detecting below-average or less-than-full-potential performance and have the managerial know-how for improving the performance of the acquired firm. The latter scenario is plausible, but in practice the acquiring firms may be over-optimistic in their judgments of their impact on the performance of the acquired firms. As a consequence, they may either pay too much for the acquired firm or fail to improve its performance to the degree reflected in the acquisition value placed upon it.

2. Tax Considerations

Tax considerations are also involved in mergers. One such tax consideration is to substitute capital gains taxes for ordinary income taxes by acquiring a growth firm with a small or no dividend payout and then selling it to realize capital gains. Also, when the growth of a firm has slowed so that earnings retention cannot be justified to the Internal Revenue Service, an incentive for sale to another firm is created. Rather than pay out future earnings as dividends subject to the ordinary personal income tax, an owner can capitalize future earnings in a sale to another firm. One often sees a small proprietor who develops an ongoing business (say, Company A) and begins to have a significant flow of net income. If he or she takes the net income as dividends, it is subject to a high personal income tax rate. Also, given potential competition from other firms, the ability of Company A to earn the income in the future is uncertain from the owner's standpoint. The certainty of that income flow would be increased if Company A were part of a larger firm which had the necessary full complement of management capabilities. The owner of Company A converts a nonmarketable ownership claim to a marketable one. These considerations are reinforced by tax considerations for Company A's owner to sell out. By selling out, the owner converts the uncertain future income into a capital gain. Usually the transaction is a tax-free exchange of securities. Company A's owner is not subject to taxes until he or she sells off the securities received; it will be a capital gain, and the owner can choose the time at which to recognize the gain.

Another tax factor is the sale of firms with accumulated tax losses. Although a business purpose must also be demonstrated, a firm with tax losses can shelter the positive earnings of another firm with which it is joined. The Economic Recovery Tax Act of 1981 provided for the sale of tax credits from the use of accelerated depreciation. These often involved sale and lease-back arrangements. This suggests that whether tax considerations induce mergers depends on whether there are alternative methods of achieving equivalent tax benefits.

Still other tax effects are associated with inheritance taxes. A closely held firm may be sold as the owners become older because of the uncertainty of the value placed on the firm in connection with estate taxes. Or a sale may be made to provide greater liquidity for the payment of estate taxes.

3. Inefficient Management

The inefficient-management theory may be difficult to distinguish from the differential-efficiency theory discussed above or the agency problem next treated. In one sense inefficient management is simply not performing up to its potential. Another control group might be able to manage the assets of this area of activity more effectively. Or inefficient management may simply represent management that is inept in some absolute sense. Almost anyone could do better. If so, this would provide a rationale for conglomerate mergers. The differential-efficiency theory is more likely to involve management that is superior because it has experience in a particular line of business activity. The differential-efficiency theory is more likely to be a basis for horizontal mergers. The inefficient-management theory could be a basis for unrelated mergers.

4. The Agency Problem and Managerialism

In their seminal paper, Jensen and Meckling [1976] formulated the implications of agency problems. An agency problem arises when managers own only a fraction of the ownership shares of the firm. This partial ownership may cause managers to work less vigorously than otherwise and/or to consume more perquisites (luxurious offices, company car, membership in clubs) because the majority owners bear most of the cost. Furthermore, the argument goes, in large corporations with widely dispersed ownership, there is not sufficient incentive for individual owners to expend the substantial resources required to monitor the behavior of managers.

A number of compensation arrangements and the market for managers may mitigate the agency problem [Fama, 1980]. Another market mechanism is the threat of takeovers. The threat of a takeover may substitute for the need for individual shareholders to monitor the managers. The agency theory extends the previous work by Manne [1965]. Manne emphasized the market for corporate control and viewed mergers as a threat of takeover if a firm's management lagged in performance either because of inefficiency or because of agency problems.

A variant of the agency problem is the managerialism theory of conglomerate mergers. The "managerialism" explanation for conglomerate mergers was set forth most fully by Mueller [1969]. Mueller hypothesizes that managers are motivated to increase the size of their firms further. He assumes that the compensation to managers is a function of the size of the firm, and he argues, therefore, that managers adopt a lower investment hurdle rate. But in a study critical of earlier evidence, Lewellen and Huntsman [1970] present findings that managers' compensation is significantly correlated with the firm's profit rate, not its level of sales. Thus the basic premise of the Mueller theory is doubtful.

5. Undervalued Company— Asymmetric Information

A company may be undervalued for a number of reasons. One is because management is not operating the company up to its potential. This is then one aspect of the inefficient-management theory. A second possibility is that the acquirers have inside information. How they acquired this special information may vary with circumstances, but if the bidders possess information which the general market does not have, they may place a higher value on the shares than currently prevails in the market.

Yet another aspect of the undervaluation theory is the difference in the position of a control group versus an individual investor. For example, in recent years the q-ratio has been running between .5 and .6. The q-ratio is the ratio of the market value of the firm's shares in relation to the replacement costs of the assets represented by these shares. Thus if a company wishes to obtain or add to capacity in producing a particular product, it can acquire the additional capacity more cheaply by buying a company that produces the product rather than building brick-and-mortar from scratch. If the q-ratio is .6 and if the average premium paid over market value is 50% (which is the average figure for recent years), the resulting purchase price is .6 times 1.5 which equals .9. This would mean that the average purchase price is still 10% below the current replacement costs of the assets acquired. This would provide a broad basis for the operation of the under-valued theory in recent years as the q-ratio has declined. Furthermore, for companies in natural resource industries, q-ratios have been as low as .2 because of the values of reserves in the ground. This provided a basis for even more substantial premiums where natural resource firms were involved in mergers. For example, although U.S. Steel paid a substantial premium over market value in the Marathon merger, Marathon shareholders threatened suit because they stated that independent appraisals had estimated the current value of Marathon assets at more than double the price paid by U.S. Steel. Of course, these appraisals were subject to considerable uncertainty.

6. Synergy

The business literature discusses various types of possible gains or economies from mergers. The theoretical literature of finance focuses on the issue of whether or not synergy is achieved by mergers. If synergy occurs, the value of the combined firm, V_{AB}, exceeds the value of the individual firms brought together by the mergers. With synergy,

$$V_{AB} > V_A + V_B.$$

Because much of the theoretical literature was stimulated in response to the dramatic conglomerate merger movement of the 1960s and because true social gains from conglomerate mergers were not readily perceived, much of the formal analysis in the scholarly literature assumed no synergy:

$$V_{AB} = V_A + V_B.$$

Myers [1968], Schall [1972], and Mossin [1973], in the spirit of the earlier Modigliani-Miller [1958] formulation, have all argued that value is conserved (value additivity obtains) under addition of income streams (mergers). Nielsen [1974] pointed out that they utilized a partial equilibrium approach in which prices and other parameters are assumed to be constant. Nielsen also called attention to the underlying assumption that the capital markets are complete and perfect, and to the further assumption that the equilibrium allocation of income (hence also the marginal utilities of all investors) is invariant with respect to a change in the number of trading instruments due to merger. The conditions for value additivity are identical to those required for the M-M propositions. Thus, at the theoretical level, the conditions under which value is conserved (even assuming the absence of synergy) are more restrictive than generally acknowledged.

Nevertheless, the dominant theme in the theoretical literature is that the value additivity principle holds in still another setting, the area of combining business entities through mergers or acquisitions. Much of the journal literature has sought to determine whether, in the absence of synergy, any theoretical justification for a merger could be found. However, the justification for mergers given by the executives engaging in mergers—and by some of the general literature as well—was that there were at least potential real gains from combining business firms. These arguments are stated in various forms but implicitly they all depend on one condition—that operating economies of scale may be achieved. This theory is based on a number of major assumptions. It assumes that economies of scale do exist in the industry and that prior to the merger, the firms are operating at levels of activity that fall short of achieving the potentials for economies of scale.

Basically, economies of scale involve "indivisibilities," such as people, equipment, and overhead, which provide increasing returns if spread over a larger number of units of output. Thus, in manufacturing operations, heavy investments in plant and equipment typically produce such economies. For example, costly machinery such as the large presses used to produce automobile bodies requires optimal utilization. Similarly, in the area of financing, data on flotation costs indicate that the cost of floating a larger issue amounts to a smaller percentage of the issue floated because the fixed costs of investigation and compliance with SEC regulations are spread over a larger dollar amount. And the same principle applies to the research and development departments of chemical and pharmaceutical companies which often have to have a large staff of highly competent scientists who, if given the opportunity, could develop and oversee a larger number of product areas. Finally, in marketing, having one organization cover the entire United States may yield economies of scale because of the increase in the ratio of calling-on-customer time to traveling time, which in turn is due to the higher density of customers who can be called on by the same number of salesmen.

One potential problem in merging firms with existing organizations is the question of how to combine and coordinate the good parts of the organizations and eliminate what is not required. Often the merger announcement will say that firm A is strong in research and development but weak in marketing, while firm B is strong in marketing but weak in R&D, and the two firms combined will complement each other. Analytically, this implies underutilization of some existing factors and inadequate investment in other factors of production. (Since the economies are jointly achieved, the assignment of the contributions of each firm to the merger is difficult both in theory and in practice.)

Economies in production, research, marketing, or finance are sometimes referred to as economies in the specific management functions. It has also been suggested that economies may be achieved in the generic management activity such as the planning and control functions of the firm. It is argued that firms of even moderate size need at least a minimum number of corporate officers. The corporate staff with capabilities for planning and control is therefore assumed to be underutilized to some degree. Acquisitions of firms just approaching the size where they need to add corporate staff would provide for fuller utilization of the corporate staff of the acquiring firm and avoid the necessity of adding such staff for the other firm.

A third area in which operating economies may be achieved is in vertical integration. Combining firms at different stages of an industry may achieve more efficient coordination of the different levels. The argument here is that costs of communication and various forms of bargaining can be avoided by vertical integration [Williamson, 1971; Arrow, 1975].

7. Market Power

One reason often given for a merger is that it will increase a firm's market share, but it is not clear how increasing the market share will achieve economies or synergies. If increasing the firm's market share simply means that the firm will be larger, then we are essentially talking about economies of scale, which we have already discussed. Increasing market share really means increasing the size of the firm *relative* to other firms in an industry. But it is not made clear why increasing the firm's relative size will provide economies or other social gains.

Indeed, this poses a challenge to the arguments for merger emphasizing economies of scale and vertical integration. These could also be achieved by the internal expansion of the firm. Why is the external acquisition of another firm necessary to achieve these economies if indeed they do exist? A number of possible explanations may be offered such as acquiring a larger volume of operations sooner. But it is not clear whether the price required by the selling firm (the firm to be acquired) will really make the acquisition route the more economical method of expanding a firm's capacity either horizontally or vertically.

An objection that is often raised against permitting a firm to increase its market share by merger is that the result will be "undue concentration" in the industry. Indeed, public policy in the United States holds that when four or fewer firms account for 40% or more of the sales in a given market or line of business, an undesirable market structure or "undue concentration" exists. The argument in brief is that if four or fewer firms account for a substantial percentage of an industry's sales, these firms will recognize the impact of their actions and policies upon one another. This recognized interdependence will lead to a consideration of actions and reactions to changes in policy that will tend toward "tacit collusion." As a result, the prices and profits of the firms will contain monopoly elements. Thus, if economies from mergers cannot be established, it is assumed that the resulting increases in concentration may lead to monopoly returns. If economies of scale can be demonstrated, then a comparison of efficiencies versus the effects of increased concentration must be made.

On June 14, 1982, the Department of Justice announced new merger guidelines to supersede those which had been issued in May 1968. The new merger guidelines adopt the Herfindahl index (H index) which takes into consideration the market shares of all of the firms in the industry. The theory behind the use of the Herfindahl index is that if one or more firms have relatively high market shares, this is of even greater concern than the share of the largest four firms. An example presented with the announcement of the new merger guidelines illustrates this point. In one market four firms each hold a 15% market share and the remaining 40% is held by 40 firms, each with a 1% market share. Its H index would be:

$$H = 4(15)^2 + 40(1)^2 = 940.$$

In another market one firm has a 57% market share and the remaining 43% is held by 43 firms, each with a 1% market share. Like the first market, the four-firm concentration ratio here would be the same 60%. However, the H index would be:

$$H = (57)^2 + 43(1)^2 = 3,292.$$

Thus the H index registers a concern about inequality as well as degree of concentration. The economic basis for either concern has not been well established.

While some economists hold that high concentration, however measured, causes some degree of monopoly, other economists hold that increased concentration is generally the *result* of active and intense competition. They argue further that the intense competition continues among large firms in concentrated industries because the dimensions of decision making over prices, outputs, types of product, quality of product, service, etc., are so numerous and of so many gradations that collusion simply is not feasible. This is an area where the issues continue to be unresolved.

8. Strategic Realignment to Changing Environments

The literature on long-range strategic planning has exploded in recent years. This literature is related to diversification through mergers. The emphasis of strategic planning is on areas related to firms' environments and constituencies, not just operating decisions [Summer 1980].

Earlier, the emphasis of long-range strategic planning was on doing something about the so-called gap. When it is necessary to take action to close a prospective gap between the firm's objectives and its potential based on its present capabilities, some difficult choices must be made. For example, shall the firm attempt to change its environment or capabilities? What will be the costs of such changes? What are the risks and unknowns? What are the rewards if successful? What are the penalties of failure? Because the stakes are large, the iterative process is employed. A tentative decision is made. The process is repeated, perhaps from a different management function orientation and at some point, the total-enterprise point of view is brought to bear on the problem. Ultimately, decisions are made and must involve entrepreneurial judgments.

Alternatively, the emphasis may be on broader orientations to the effective alignment of the firm with its environments and constituencies. Different approaches may be emphasized. One approach seeks to choose products related to the needs or missions of the customer that will provide large markets. A second approach focuses on technological bottlenecks or barriers, the solution of which may create new markets. A third strategy chooses to be at the frontiers of technological capabilities on the theory that some attractive product fallout will result from such competence. A fourth approach emphasizes economic criteria including attractive growth prospects and appropriate stability.

Other things being equal, a preferred strategy is to move into a diversification program from the base of some existing capabilities or organizational strengths. Guidance may be obtained by answers to the following questions: Is there strength in the general management functions? Can the company provide staff expertise in a wide range of areas? Does the firm's financial planning and control effectiveness have a broad carry-over? Are there specific capabilities such as research, marketing, and manufacturing that the firm is seeking to spread over a wider arena? [Chung and Weston, 1982].

It appears that the strategic planning approach to mergers implies either the possibilities of economies of scale or utilizing some unused capacity in the firm's present managerial capabilities. Another rationale is that by external diversification the firm acquires management skills for needed augmentation of its present capabilities.

This still leaves some questions unanswered. New capabilities and new markets could be developed internally. It may be less risky to buy established organizations but a competitive market for acquisitions implies that the net present value from such investments is likely to be zero. However, if these investments can be used as a base for still additional investments with positive net present values, the strategy may succeed.

C. CONGLOMERATE MERGERS

One reason for the study of conglomerate mergers is that after the tightening of the laws with respect to mergers that took place in 1950, most merger activity was conglomerate because major horizontal and vertical mergers were subject to legal challenge. In addition, the economic rationale for conglomerate mergers seemed to be the weakest. If by definition conglomerate mergers brought together unrelated activities, how could there be economic benefits? Some possible benefits of conglomerate mergers may be considered.

1. Financial Gains

Several financial gains from conglomerate mergers have been proposed. Arguments claiming financial gains from mergers other than the possible advantage of economies in financing are of dubious validity. As presented in most basic finance texts, it can readily be demonstrated that a differentially higher price-earnings ratio can achieve gains in earnings per share for acquiring firms. If merger terms represent a differentially higher price-earnings ratio for the acquiring firm, that firm's earnings per share after the acquisition will be higher and the earnings per share of the acquired firm will be lower. The acquiring firm achieves earnings accretion while the acquired firm suffers earnings dilution.

But it can be readily demonstrated that the higher price-earnings ratio must reflect differentially more favorable earnings growth prospects. The effect of acquiring firms with low price-earnings ratios and lower earnings growth prospects will be to depress the average rate of future growth in earnings of the combined firm. The new price-earnings ratio should reflect this change in the outlook for the growth in earnings of the merged firm so that there should be no gain in the value of the combined firm over the values of the two separate firms. Hence the differential price-earnings ratio theory and its immediate effects on earnings per share have no validity as a theory for measuring the potential gains of a merger, since it is valuation, not earnings per share, that is the relevant test.

2. Potential Sources of Synergy in Conglomerate Mergers

From the mid-1950s through 1968, economists and managers offered a number of reasons other than the ones discussed above to explain how economies might be achieved in conglomerate mergers. During this period, formal long-range enterprise planning developed, and computer technology began to be adapted to the management of the firm. Financial planning and control systems were extended with further improvements in the use of balanced, centralized-decentralized management-control systems. Further, World War II and the Korean conflict had stimulated new technologies, resulting in an uneven diffusion of and wide variations in advanced technological capabilities among firms.

The major conceptual point here is that the role of the general management functions (planning, control, organizing, information systems) and functions centralized at top management levels (research, finance, legal) increased in importance in the management of enterprises. As a consequence, the costs of managing large, diversified firms were substantially reduced relative to potential operating economies. This is the broader theoretical basis explaining the formation of conglomerates. However, there is considerable disagreement about whether synergy is achieved in conglomerate mergers from the sources just described. Most of the theoretical literature of finance has assumed no synergy in conglomerate mergers and has analyzed pure financial effects. For a theory of pure conglomerate mergers see Chung [1982].

3. Pure Financial Theories of Conglomerate Firms

The popular justification of conglomerate mergers was synergy—the $2 + 2 = 5$ effect. But other theories of conglomerate firms were set forth which did not require the assumption of synergy. Lewellen [1971], for example, offered a purely financial rationale for conglomerate mergers. His theory may be summarized initially in terms of the numerical examples he provides, concluding with his general statement of conditions.

Let us consider two firms, A and B, whose annual cash flows are independent (correlation coefficient is zero) and each distributed as shown in columns (1) through (3) of Table 17.2.

It is assumed that each firm has incurred borrowings to the point that its annual cash contractual obligation amounts to $240. The probability, $P(D)$, that one or

Table 17.2*

(1) State (s_1)	(2) $P(s_1)$	(3) Y_1
1	.1	100
2	.2	250
3	.7	500

* *Note:* s_1 = alternative future state of the world, $P(s_1)$ = probability of alternative states, Y_1 = annual cash flow outcomes under alternative states.

both firms will be unable to meet their debt service obligations of $240 each is shown below:

$$P(D) = P(Y_A < 240) + P(Y_B < 240) - P(Y_A < 240, Y_B < 240)$$

$$= .1 + .1 - (.1)(.1) = .19.$$

If the two firms merge, the distribution of their joint returns can be calculated as shown in the matrix in Table 17.3. The distribution of their joint returns would therefore become

Y_m	200	350	500	600	750	1,000
$P(Y_m)$	.01	.04	.04	.14	.28	.49

Since their aggregate debt burden would become $480 per annum, the probability of default now drops to .05 as compared with .19 before the merger.

The foregoing was based on the assumption of zero correlation between the two returns. If the correlation were -1, the gains from merger would be even greater. If the correlation were $+1$, reducing the probability of default would require other differences such as differences in the size of debt obligations. Thus if we assume the same distribution of returns for the two firms as before, but assume a correlation of $+1$ between the two and the debt obligations of A and B to be $255 and $240, respectively, the before-merger probability of default would be

$$P(D) = .3 + .1 - .1 = .3.$$

After merger, the total debt obligations would be $495, and they would be related to the following combined cash flow pattern:

Y_m	200	500	1,000
$P(Y_m)$	.1	.2	.7

The probability of default would therefore fall to only 0.1.

Levy and Sarnat [1970] set forth a similar argument. They state, "A somewhat stronger case can be made for conglomerate mergers when economies in capital costs are considered ... large firms have better access to the capital markets and also enjoy significant cost savings when securing their financing needs ... These cost

Table 17.3

		.1	.2	.7
.1	Joint probability	.01	.02	.07
	Amount	200	350	600
.2	Joint probability	.02	.04	.14
	Amount	350	500	750
.7	Joint probability	.07	.14	.49
	Amount	600	750	1,000

savings presumably reflect, at least in part, the reduction in lenders' risk achieved through diversification." (p. 801)

Galai and Masulis [1976] point out the confusion involved between the value of the merged firm and the positions of the debt and equity holders. They argue that the value of the merged firm is the simple sum of the constituent firms. "This can be seen once one recognizes that investors in the marketplace could have created an identical financial position by purchasing equal proportions of the debt and equity of the two firms." (p. 68) The OPM establishes that the relative position of the creditors and the equity holders of the firms will be changed. If the correlation between the returns of the merging firms is less than 1, the variance in the rate of return of the merged firm will be lower than the variance of the rates of return of the merging firms (assumed to be equal). (For numerical illustrations see problems 17.6 to 17.8.)

It follows from the OPM that the value of the equity of the merged firm will be less than the sum of the constituent equity values and the value of the debt will be higher. According to the OPM, increased variability increases the value of the option and conversely. Since the equity is an option on the face value of the debt outstanding, its value will fall with a decrease in volatility. "What is taking place, as Rubinstein points out, is that the bondholders receive more protection since the stockholders of each firm have to back the claims of the bondholders of both companies. The stockholders are hurt since their limited liability is weakened." [Galai and Masulis, 1976, p. 68]

Thus a pure diversification rationale for conglomerate mergers would not seem valid. Reducing the risk to bondholders represents a redistribution of value from shareholders, leaving the total value of the firm unchanged.

However, a number of alternatives could be used to return the wealth of different classes of security holders to the original position they held prior to the merger. One solution would be to increase the amount of the face value of debt and use the proceeds to retire equity. This process is continued until the original bondholders' holdings have a market value equal to their constituent sum prior to the merger. The debt-to-equity ratio of the merged firm can be increased to offset the decrease in the volatility of the merged firm's rate of return. The increased amount of debt implies that the total value of the firm is increased through merger due to the tax deductibility of interest payments. Galai and Masulis suggest that this may explain some conglomerate mergers.

4. Shastri's Extension of the Analysis of the Effects of Mergers on Corporate Security Values

Shastri [1982] extends the Galai-Masulis (G-M) study by allowing the two firms to have different variances, different debt ratios, and different debt maturities. Shastri's results for the effects of mergers on shareholder values versus bondholders' positions under these more general conditions are presented in Table 17.4. Because the correlation between the cash flow streams of the two firms can be either positive or negative, the resulting combined firm variance may be less than the variance of the individual

Table 17.4 The Effects of the Merger on Firm Security Values

				$S_c - (S_A + S_B)$
		Bond A	Bond B	Common Stock†
Variance Effect	$\sigma_A > \sigma_C > \sigma_B$	>0	<0	≧0
	$\sigma_A < \sigma_C < \sigma_B$	<0	>0	≧0
	$\sigma_{A,} \sigma_B > \sigma_C$	>0	>0	<0
Leverage Effect	$M_A/V_A > M_B/V_B$	>0	<0	<0
	$M_A/V_A < M_B/V_B$	<0	>0	<0
Maturity Effect		>0	≧0	<0

† The effect of the merger on each individual firm's stock would depend on the merger terms.

firms or greater than one of the firms and less than the other firm. However, the leverage effects and maturity effects are simply weighted average effects. The combined firm will simply have a weighted average of the leverage or maturity pattern of the combining firms.

The other relationship that stands out in the table is that the value of the common stock of the combined firm may under some conditions be larger than the addition of the pre-merger stock values of the two firms even in a pure conglomerate merger, assuming no synergy. The reasons for Shastri's conclusions are reviewed next.

There are three possibilities under the variance effect. The variance of the combined firm may be less than the variance of either of the individual firms before the merger. This is the G-M result where the variance effect is positive for the bonds of both firm A and firm B and negative for both stocks. However, the variance of the combined firm may be greater than one of the firms and lower than the other. For example, when $\sigma_A > \sigma_C > \sigma_B$, the securities of firm B become riskier with the merger, conversely with firm A. So there is a positive impact on the bonds of A and the stock of B, negative on the bonds of B and the stock of A. The effects on the value of the stock of the combined firm compared with the sum of the pre-merger stock values is ambiguous depending on the relative magnitudes of the pre-merger stock A and stock B values.

Shastri defines the leverage ratio as the ratio of the face value of debt to firm value. If the leverage ratio of firm A is greater than the ratio for B, the combined firm has a leverage ratio less than that of firm A and greater than that of firm B. The merger results in a decrease in the leverage-ratio related risk for bond A with the opposite result for bond B. This implies an increase in the value of bond A and a decrease in the value of bond B. When the leverage ratio of A is lower than that of B, the opposite results follow. Because of an unambiguous increase in the bankruptcy-related risk for the combined equity, the leverage effect is always negative for the combined common stock.

The maturity effect has two components. Assume that the maturity of bond A is shorter than the maturity of bond B. The effect of a merger from the point of view of bond B is equivalent to having the firm issue new debt with a shorter maturity. Thus bond A is paid in full ahead of bond B and in some sense becomes "senior" to bond B. This seniority effect would be positive for bond A and negative for bond B.

The second effect is a bankruptcy effect. If bankruptcy occurs at bond A's maturity date, debt B also shares in the proceeds of the bankruptcy and so gains from the merger. Hence the bankruptcy component of the maturity effect is negative for debt A and positive for debt B.

The size of these two effects depends both on the probability of bankruptcy and the bankruptcy sharing rules. Shastri argues that the first effect will dominate the second for bond A so that it always gains in a merger. But the net effect on debt B is ambiguous. From the point of view of debt B, the "new debt issue" is always accompanied by a change in firm value by an amount generally greater than the face value of the "new issue." So the maturity effect on debt B value is ambiguous. The effect on the combined stock value is always negative. This is essentially because with a merger the option a shareholder of B had of buying out the debt of B is no longer available directly because debt A has to be paid off first. This loss of an option leads to a decline in the combined stock price.

Thus Shastri's extension of previous work yields some different empirical predictions. The value of the stock of the combined firm may, under certain conditions, exceed the combined pre-merger stock values of the combined firms. In addition, all three of the effects under certain conditions can be negative on at least one of the bonds, leading to a decline in value. So bonds do not necessarily gain in a merger. This explains why bond indentures may include covenants restricting the freedom of the firm to engage in mergers. Thus, in general, the extension by Shastri results in a generalization of predictions of the effects of mergers.

5. Scott's Model of Conglomerate Mergers

Scott [1977] formulates a model of conglomerate mergers in a state-preference framework with two dates. He considers the effects of (1) noncontractual obligations such as damages awarded in lawsuits, etc., (2) bankruptcy costs, and (3) tax deductibility of debt and of losses.

The following notation is employed by Scott:

Q_{aj} = firm A, state j cash flows,

C_{aj} = noncontractual obligations such as sales taxes; these are junior to debt and fixed in amount,

R_a = debt obligations,

B_{aj} = bankruptcy costs.

For any firm A, then, the value of equity in state j is,

$$S_{aj} = (1 - t)\max[Q_{aj} - C_{aj} - R_a, 0].$$

The value of debt is,

$$Y_{daj} = \begin{cases} R_a & \text{if } Q_{aj} \geq (R_a + C_{aj}) \\ \min[R_a, Q_{aj} - B_{aj}] & \text{otherwise.} \end{cases}$$

This is using the fact that C is junior to debt.

Scott first analyzes the effects of merging all-equity firms. We have to assume that the merger does not affect the prices of the state-contingent claims, (primitive state security prices) i.e., the merger does not diminish the 'richness' of the market and cause spanning to break down. Scott obtains:

$$S_{abj} = (1 - t)\max[Q_{aj} - C_{aj} + Q_{bj} - C_{bj}, 0],$$

$$S_{abj} < (1 - t)\max[Q_{aj} - C_{aj}, 0] + (1 - t)\max[Q_{bj} - C_{bj}, 0].$$

Thus we obtain that:

$$S_{ab} < S_a + S_b.$$

This states that a conglomerate merger of all equity firms can never be profitable. The intuition is that the merger is unprofitable because the limited liability protection of a merged firm is weaker than that of two unmerged firms. This is a familiar result, but Scott's is the first paper to obtain this result so easily because of the state-preference approach he employs. Scott next analyzes the merger of levered firms. Evaluation relationships are as follows:

Mergers of Firms with Debt and Equity Outstanding

Y_{aj} represents the total value of A's outstanding securities in period 1:

$$Y_{aj} = \begin{cases} (1 - t)(Q_{aj} - C_{aj}) + tR_a, & \text{if } Q_{aj} \geq (R_a + C_{aj}), \\ \min[R_a, (Q_{aj} - B_{aj})], & \text{otherwise.} \end{cases}$$

Y_{abj} represents the period 1 value of debt plus equity of AB:

$$Y_{abj} = \begin{cases} [(1 - t)(Q_{aj} - C_{aj} + Q_{bj} - C_{bj}) + t(R_a + R_b)] = A, & \text{if } A > (R_a + R_b), \\ \min[(R_a + R_b), Q_{aj} + Q_{bj} - B_{abj}], & \text{otherwise.} \end{cases}$$

Using the valuation relationships above, Scott works out a table of the effects of pure conglomerate mergers. He explicitly considers all possible combinations of solvency and bankruptcy for the two merging firms and for the merged firm. He assumes economies of scale in bankruptcy costs. His table presents the incremental cash flows to security holders as a result of the conglomerate merger. His results are reproduced as our Table 17.5.

To aid in the interpretation of the table, consider the case where firm B would be bankrupt while firm A and the combined firm would remain solvent. The proof of his result is as follows:

Table 17.5 Incremental Cash Flows in Period 1 to Security Holders as a Result of Conglomerate Merger

$$Z_j = (Y_{abj} - Y_{aj} - Y_{bj})$$

	AB Solvent	*AB Bankrupt*
A, B Solvent*	0	
A Solvent B Bankrupt	$t(R_b + C_{bj} - Q_{bj}) - C_{bj}$ $+ \max[B_{bj}, Q_{bj} - R_b]$	$t(Q_{aj} - C_{aj} - R_a) + C_{aj}$ $+ \max[Q_{bj} - B_{abj}, R_a + R_b - Q_{aj}]$ $- \min[Q_{bj} - B_{bj}, R_b]$
A Bankrupt B Solvent	$t(R_a + C_{aj} - Q_{aj}) - C_{aj}$ $+ \max[B_{aj}, Q_{aj} - R_a]$	$t(Q_{bj} - C_{bj} - R_b) + C_{bj}$ $+ \max[Q_{aj} - B_{abj}, R_a + R_b - Q_{bj}]$ $- \min[Q_{aj} - B_{aj}, R_a]$
A, B Bankrupt		$\min[Q_{aj} + Q_{bj} - B_{abj}, R_a + R_b]$ $- \min[Q_{aj} - B_{aj}, R_a]$ $- \min[Q_{bj} - B_{bj}, R_b]$

* This should be interpreted as follows: If A and B had remained unmerged, these are the states in which neither would have gone bankrupt. The other entries are interpreted in a similar fashion.

From J. H. Scott, Jr., "On the Theory of Conglomerate Mergers," *Journal of Finance,* September 1977, 1244.

B Bankrupt, while A and AB Solvent

$$Z_j = Y_{abj} - Y_{aj} - Y_{bj}$$

$$Z_j = [(1 - t)(Q_{aj} + Q_{bj} - C_{aj} - C_{bj})] + t(R_a + R_b) - (1 - t)(Q_{aj} - C_{aj}) - tR_a$$
$$- \min[(Q_{bj} - B_{bj}), R_b]$$

$$Z_j = Q_{bj} - C_{bj} - tQ_{bj} + tC_{bj} + tR_b - \min[(Q_{bj} - B_{bj}), R_b]$$

$$Z_j = t(R_b + C_{bj} - Q_{bj}) - C_{bj} + Q_{bj} - \min[Q_{bj} - B_{bj}, R_b]$$

$$Z_j = t(R_b + C_{bj} - Q_{bj}) - C_{bj} + Q_{bj} + \max[B_{bj} - Q_{bj}, - R_b]$$

$$Z_j = t(R_b + C_{bj} - Q_{bj}) - C_{bj} + \max[B_{bj}, Q_{bj} - R_b] \lesseqgtr 0.$$

Some implications of his results may be noted. When one firm would have gone bankrupt by itself but the merged firm would not, the merged firm is able to use the loss of the component as a tax credit. Thus for Scott the corporate tax encourages mergers. Higgins and Schall [1975] assume that the bankrupt firm could have sold its tax credit to some other firm, so a merger is not needed to utilize the tax loss. Hence different assumptions about the use of tax credits give different results on the effects of a conglomerate merger.

Scott's introduction of noncontractual obligations (C) serves to decrease or increase the profitability of a conglomerate merger. A bankrupt firm could have defaulted on C because they are junior to debt. But the now-solvent merged firm cannot avoid paying C. On the other hand, if one firm by going bankrupt pulls the other one into bankruptcy when they are merged, the debt of the merged firm may be in a better position. In such states, payments which would have been made by the solvent (unmerged) firm to noncontractual creditors are diverted to pay the bondholders of the otherwise bankrupt (unmerged) firm. The practical importance of this case depends on the actual magnitudes of noncontractual obligations.

Bankruptcy costs play an important role in Scott's model. For some future states a merger may increase value by saving one of the firms from bankruptcy and its costs. But a merger may be unprofitable to the extent that there are future states in which the merger pulls an otherwise solvent firm into bankruptcy and its costs. Scott suggests that a merger between a large, stable firm and a small, profitable but unstable firm may reduce the present value of future bankruptcy costs and thus increase value. He suggests that a merger between a small, stable firm and a large, volatile one may reduce value by increasing the present value of future bankruptcy costs.

Finally, Scott illustrates the proposition that a merger may be unprofitable even though the cash flows are negatively correlated. He also illustrates how a profitable conglomerate merger need not increase debt capacity. His model is similar to that of Kraus and Litzenberger [1973], who demonstrated that the optimal level of debt is equal to one of the before-tax cash flows. Scott's numerical example assumes economies of scale in bankruptcy costs. The basic data for Scott's example are shown in Table 17.6.

Table 17.6 Data for Numerical Example

	Cash Flows of Solvent Firms			Bankruptcy Costs		
	Firm A	Firm B	Firm AB	Firm A	Firm B	Firm AB
State 1	$Q_{a1}=20$	$Q_{b1}=25$	$Q_{ab1}=45$	$B_{a1}=4$	$B_{b1}=10$	$B_{ab1}=13$
State 2	$Q_{a2}=30$	$Q_{b2}=20$	$Q_{ab2}=50$	$B_{a2}=10$	$B_{b2}=2$	$B_{ab2}=11$

From J. H. Scott, Jr., "On the Theory of Conglomerate Mergers," *Journal of Finance,* September 1977, 1248.

Scott assumes further that the tax rate is 50% and that the price of the state-contingent claims for either state is .4. The computations under alternative assumptions are as follows:

With no merger:

If $R_a = Q_{a1} = 20$
If State 1 $Y_{a1} = (1-.5)(20)+.5(20)$ $20 \times .4 = 8$
If State 2 $Y_{a2} = (1-.5)(30)+.5(20)$ $25 \times .4 = \underline{10}$
$V_a^1 = 18$

If $R_a = Q_{a2} = 30$
If State 1 $Y_{a1} = \min(30, 20-4)$ $16 \times .4 = 6.4$
If State 2 $Y_{a2} = (1-.5)(30)+.5(30)$ $30 \times .4 = \underline{12.0}$
$V_a^2 = 18.4$

So $R_a^* = Q_{a2} = 30$.

    If $R_b = Q_{b1} = 25$

If State 1	$Y_{b1} = (1 - .5)(25) + .5(25)$	$25 \times .4 = 10.0$
If State 2	$Y_{b2} = \min[25,(20 - 2)]$	$18 \times .4 = \underline{7.2}$
		$V_b^1 = 17.2$

    If $R_b = Q_{b2} = 20$

If State 1	$Y_{b1} = (1 - .5)(25) + .5(20)$	$22.5 \times .4 = 9$
If State 2	$Y_{b2} = (1 - .5)(20) + .5(20)$	$20.0 \times .4 = \underline{8}$
		17

So $R_b^* = Q_{b1} = 25$.

With a merger:

    If $R_{ab} = 55$

If State 1	$Y_{ab1} = \min[55,(45 - 13)]$	$32 \times .4 = 12.8$
If State 2	$Y_{ab2} = \min[55,(50 - 11)]$	$39 \times .4 = \underline{15.6}$
		$V_{ab} = 28.4$

    If $R_{ab} = 45$

If State 1	$Y_{ab1} = (1 - .5)(45) + .5(45)$	$45.0 \times .4 = 18.0$
If State 2	$Y_{ab2} = (1 - .5)(50) + .5(45)$	$47.5 \times .4 = \underline{19.0}$
		$V_{ab}^1 = 37.0$

    If $R_{ab} = 50$

If State 1	$Y_{ab1} = \min[50,(45 - 13)]$	$32 \times .4 = 12.8$
If State 2	$Y_{ab2} = (1 - .5)(50) + .5(50)$	$50 \times .4 = \underline{20.0}$
		$V_{ab}^2 = 32.8$

So $R_{ab}^* = Q_{ab1} = 45$.

The numerical results above illustrate Scott's propositions. Like the Kraus and Litzenberger results they demonstrate that it is always profitable to increase the optimal level of debt, R^*, to equal one of the before-tax cash flows. This is because one can always increase the optimal debt level to the next highest cash flow, thereby decreasing the present value of future tax payments with no increase in the probability of incurring bankruptcy costs. To obtain the optimal capital structure we calculate the value of the firm when the debt level equals the pre-tax cash flow in state 1 and again when it equals the pre-tax cash flow in state 2. We then choose the debt level that results in the highest value of the firm. For the numerical example, the optimal debt level is set equal to the cash flow of the firm which is highest for a given state. However, after the merger the highest value of the firm is achieved with the state 1 cash flow of the merged firm which is lower than the assumed state 2 cash flow of the merged firm. If the merged firm were to maintain the capital structure of the unmerged firms at a level of 55, it would result in a value of the merged firm of 28.4. This is less than the value of the unmerged firms (18.4 + 17.2 = 35.6). Scott's example illustrates that optimal debt may be reduced, therefore, as a consequence of the pure conglomerate merger. Yet if the firm chooses an optimal level of debt after the merger, the value of the firm is increased to 37. This exceeds the sum of the components, which totaled 35.6.

These results are, of course, specific to the pattern of the numerical relationships chosen for Scott's example. They are general, however, to the extent that they are illustrative of the kind of possibilities that may conceivably occur. The general view is that conglomerate mergers may increase "debt capacity" (however defined) but may (or may not) increase firm value. Scott presents the possibility that the conglomerate merger may actually reduce the optimal level of debt. On the other hand, choosing an optimal level of debt after the merger may produce a value of the combined firm which is greater than the sum of the individual values of the components. Thus Scott concludes that the probability of bankruptcy is, in general, not an appropriate measure of the profitability of a conglomerate merger. He argues also that as a result of a conglomerate merger the resulting firm's optimal level of debt can either rise or fall.

These results illustrate a more general proposition about merger theory. Many possible motives for mergers can exist under various models and assumptions. Various types of complementarities may make mergers profitable. Alternative assumptions about tax rules can make mergers profitable or unprofitable under alternative assumptions. This makes modeling theories for testing mergers and approaching empirical data difficult to formulate.

6. The Option Pricing Model, Debt Capacity, and Mergers

Drawing on previous formulations by M. J. Brennan [1979] and by Cox, Ross, and Rubinstein [1979], R. C. Stapleton [1982] sets forth a framework for analyzing debt capacity without and with mergers utilizing the option pricing model under alternative assumptions. In his formulation, debt capacity is defined as the maximum amount of debt that can be raised at a given interest rate.

First the analysis is made under risk neutrality. The value of a loan or debt as derived by Stapleton is shown in Eq. (17.1).

$$(1 + r)D_j = \mu_j F^*(Y_j) - \sigma_j f^*(Y_j) + Y_j[1 - F^*(Y_j)], \qquad (17.1)$$

where

r = the risk-free interest rate,

Y_j = the debt obligation due at the end of the period,

X_j = cash flows at the end of the period (a one-period model is assumed), including the liquidation value of the assets,

μ_j = the mean of X_j,

σ_j = the standard deviation of X_j,

D_j = the market value of the promised debt obligations or equivalently the debt capacity,

$f^* =$ the standard normal density function,

$F^* =$ the cumulative standard normal distribution function.

With given values of the risk-free interest rate and the mean and standard deviation of X_j for a given level of debt obligations incurred, Y_j, Eq. (17.1) can be used with the additional constraint that $Y_j/D_j = (1 + i)$ to calculate debt capacity (i is equal to the effective yield to maturity on the debt).

To illustrate the calculation of debt capacity and some related relationships in the Stapleton formulation, let us use the following illustrative values:

$$\text{For Firm A} \qquad \mu_A = 100, \quad \sigma_A = 25, \quad r = 10\%, \quad Y_A = 68.$$

The solution by iteration for debt capacity utilizing Eq. (17.1) plus the constraint with $i = .12$ is $D_A^* = 60.7$. Hence $Y_A = D_A^*(1 + i) = (60.7)(1.12) = 68$. The left-hand side of Eq. (17.1) is 1.1 times D_A^* because the riskless rate is 10%. Thus the left-hand side of Eq. (17.1) is $1.1(60.7) = 66.77$.

The right-hand side of Eq. (17.1) is as follows:

$$
\begin{aligned}
\text{rhs} &= 100 \, F[(68 - 100)/25] - 25f\,[(68 - 100)/25] \\
&\quad + 68(1 - F[(68 - 100)/25]) \\
&= 100 \,(1 - F[(100 - 68)/25]) - 25f\,[(100 - 68)/25] \\
&\quad + 68(F[(100 - 68)/25]) \\
&= 100 \,(.1003) - 25(.1758) + 68(.8997) \\
&= 10.03 - 4.395 + 61.18 = 66.81.
\end{aligned}
$$

Therefore, the equality of rhs to lhs is verified. Finally, the probability that X will be less than Y is just $F(Y) = F(68)$, which is $.1003 = 10.03\%$.

In a like manner, Stapleton calculates debt capacity for different firms with the same expected cash flow but increasing standard deviations of cash flows. The calculation is also performed for different required yields. The results are summarized in Table 17.7.

The data in Table 17.7 indicate that at any given required yield the amount of debt obtainable declines at an increasing rate as the risk of the underlying cash flows increases. Debt capacity increases at a diminishing rate as the promised coupon increases.

The analysis is next extended to an application to pure conglomerate mergers in which no synergy is assumed. The only influence is the effect on the standard deviation of the combined firm in relation to the component firms. The results in Table 17.8 depend on the correlation between cash flows of the merging firms. This, in turn, produces the magnitude of the standard deviation of returns for the combined firm.

The new sigma in Table 17.8 is obtained using the expression in Eq. (17.2):

$$\sigma_{BD}^2 = \sigma_B^2 + \sigma_D^2 + 2\rho_{BD}\sigma_B\sigma_D. \tag{17.2}$$

The results in Table 17.8 follow directly from the application of Eq. (17.1) just as the computations were made for Table 17.7. For example, we simply verify that

Table 17.7 Debt Values: Risk Neutrality

Cash Flow	Firm A				Firm B				Firm C				Firm D			
Mean μ	100				100				100				100			
Standard deviation σ	25				30				35				40			
i percent	Y_A	D_A	$\frac{Y_A}{D_A}$	$P(X_A < Y_A)$	Y_B	D_B	$\frac{Y_B}{D_B}$	$P(X_B < Y_B)$	Y_C	D_C	$\frac{Y_C}{D_C}$	$P(X_C < Y_C)$	Y_D	D_D	$\frac{Y_D}{D_D}$	$P(X_D < Y_D)$
Debt level 1 — 12	68	60.7	1.12	.10	57	50.9	1.12	.08	42	38.4	1.12	.05	23	20.5	1.12	.03
Debt level 2 — 14	79	69.3	1.14	.20	70	61.4	1.14	.16	59	51.8	1.14	.12	45	39.5	1.14	.08
Debt level 3 — 16	86	74.1	1.16	.27	78	67.2	1.16	.23	70	60.3	1.16	.20	58	50.0	1.16	.15

From R. C. Stapleton, "Mergers, Debt Capacity and the Valuation of Corporate Loans," reprinted by permission of the publisher, from *Mergers and Acquisitions*, edited by Michael Keenan and Lawrence J. White. (Lexington, Mass.: Lexington Books, D.C. Heath & Co. Copyright © 1982, D.C. Heath & Co.)

Table 17.8 Debt Capacity and Merger: Risk Neutrality

	Firm B	Firm D		Firm BD $\rho = 0$	$\rho = 0.46$	$\rho = 1$
Mean μ	100	100		200	200	200
Standard deviation σ	30	40		50	60	70
i percent	Y_B	Y_D	$Y_B + Y_D$	Y_{BD}	Y_{BD}	Y_{BD}
Debt capacity[a] 12	57	23	80	136	114	84
14	70	45	115	158	140	118
16	78	58	136	172	156	140
Debt capacity[b] (α = .043)	48.6	31.4	80	114.3	97.2	80

[a] Debt capacity is defined as in Table 17.7.
[b] Debt capacity defined, as in Lewellen (1971), as the level of promised payments such that $P(X_j < Y_j) \leq \alpha$. Here, α is chosen so that the total debt of firms B and D is the same as that generated by a 12 percent interest-rate limit.

From R. C. Stapleton, "Mergers, Debt Capacity and the Valuation of Corporate Loans," reprinted by permission of the publisher, from *Mergers and Acquisitions*, edited by Michael Keenan and Lawrence J. White. (Lexington, Mass.: Lexington Books, D.C. Heath & Co., Copyright © 1982, D.C. Heath & Co.)

the left-hand side equals the right-hand side of Eq. (17.1) for the data in Table 17.8. At a yield of 12% the left-hand side is:

$$\text{lhs} = 1.1 \times 57/1.12 = 55.98.$$

The right-hand side is calculated as in Table 17.7. The standardized variable is:

$$(57 - 100)/30 = -1.43 \qquad F(-1.43) = 1 - .9236 = .0764.$$

Hence the right-hand side of the equation becomes:

$$(100 \times .0764) - (30 \times .1435) + (57 \times .9236) = 7.64 - 4.30 + 52.65 = 55.99.$$

Thus, again, it is demonstrated that the values shown in Table 17.8 satisfy Eq. (17.1). The other results in Table 17.8 are calculated in a similar manner. The spread of results in Table 17.8 seeks to illustrate that the effect of merger on debt capacity is dependent on the relative risks of the merging firms as well as on the correlation between the earnings of the firms. The sum of the individual debt capacities of firms B and D at a required yield of 12% is $80. Table 17.8 then shows the effect on debt capacity of merging firms, assuming that the cash flows of the firm are uncorrelated, correlated, and perfectly correlated. Even in a perfect correlation case debt capacity rises from $80 to $84. The specific numerical examples in Stapleton are special cases of the general propositions set forth by Shastri.

This contrasts with the results for Lewellen [1971] where debt capacity is defined as the level of promised payments such that the probability of X_j being less than Y_j is less than α. In the example in Table 17.8, α is chosen so that the total debt of firms B and D is the same as that generated by a 12% interest yield requirement. Thus for the Lewellen formulation we have the requirement, using the data of Table 17.8, that:

$$Pr(X_B < 48.6) = Pr(X_D < 31.4).$$

Now we can test the equality of the expression as follows:

$$\text{lhs} = 1 - F[(100 - 48.6)/30] = 1 - F(1.713) = 1 - .9564 = .0436,$$
$$\text{rhs} = 1 - F[(100 - 31.4)/40] = 1 - F(1.715).$$

Thus we have verified that lhs = rhs and that

$$Pr(X_B < 48.6) = Pr(X_D < 31.4) = .0436.$$

For the merged firm, when the correlation coefficient between the cash flows is zero, the standard deviation of the merged firm is 50. We then seek to verify that the debt capacity for the merged firm is 114.3. This is demonstrated by the following:

$$Pr(X_{BD} < 114.3) = 1 - F[(200 - 114.3)/50] = 1 - F(1.714) = .0436,$$

as above.

The results for the calculations for correlation coefficients of .46 and 1.0 are also shown in the table. The results illustrate that debt capacity is higher under the OPM formulation than under the limited formulation of Lewellen. Indeed, with perfect correlation between the cash flows in the Lewellen formulation, debt capacity is not increased. However, in the OPM model, debt capacity is increased as long as the sigmas of the merging firms are different, even when the correlation coefficient between the returns is 1.

Similar calculations of the effects of mergers on debt capacity are also developed by Stapleton for the risk averse case, using the results of Brennan [1979]. Here we don't have risk-neutral pricing, rather we have risk-averse pricing (greater covariances with the market lead to lower prices). Equation (17.1) is used again in Table 17.9; however, the location parameter for the distribution of cash flows (the mean return), has to be transformed to a certainty equivalent (rV). This can be calculated using the CAPM, since we assume exponential utility and a normal distribution. The determination of rV is given by Eq. (17.3):

$$rV = \mu_j - \lambda(\sigma_j \rho_{jm}) \qquad (17.3)$$

Thus, for a required yield of 12% and with $\lambda = \frac{1}{3}$ and a correlation coefficient with the market of 1 for firm B (whose $\sigma = 30$), the certainty equivalent $rV = 100 - [\frac{1}{3}(30 \times 1)] = 90$. This is substituted into Eq. (17.1) using rV instead of μ_j. Thus:

$$\text{lhs} = 1.1 \times (44/1.12) = 43.21.$$

For the right-hand side we first calculate the standardized variable which is:

$$(44 - 90)/30 = -1.53 \qquad F(-1.53) = 1 - F(1.53) = 1 - .9370 = .0630.$$

We can now evaluate Eq. (17.1):

$$90(.063) - 30(.1238) + 44(.9370) = 5.67 - 3.71 + 41.23 = 43.19.$$

Thus, lhs = rhs. The order debt capacity levels shown in Table 17.9 are calculated in a like manner.

The results in Table 17.9 illustrate that debt capacity declines as the correlation between the underlying cash flows in the market increase. If there is zero correlation between underlying cash flows in the market, debt capacities and debt values would be the same as they were under risk neutrality, since the underlying cash flows would

Table 17.9 Debt Capacity: Risk Aversion

Cash Flow			Firm B		Firm C	Firm D
Mean μ			100		100	100
Standard deviation σ			30		35	40
Correlation with market ρ_m		1	0.75	0	0.75	0.75
	i percent	Y_B	Y_B	Y_B	Y_C	Y_D
Debt level 1	12	44	47	57	28	0
Debt level 2	14	56	60	70	46	22
Debt level 3	16	63	68	78	56	41

From R. C. Stapleton, "Mergers, Debt Capacity and the Valuation of Corporate Loans," reprinted by permission of the publisher, from *Mergers and Acquisitions,* edited by Michael Keenan and Lawrence J. White. (Lexington, Mass.: Lexington Books, D.C. Heath & Co., Copyright © 1982, D.C. Heath & Co.)

be valued as if investors were risk neutral. In other words, the risk-adjustment factor in the CAPM drops out with the zero correlation term. Compared with the risk-neutral debt capacities of Table 17.7, the debt capacities under risk aversion in Table 17.9 are considerably lower.

Comparing Table 17.8 and Table 17.10 shows that under risk aversion the effect of mergers on debt capacity is much larger. Where the correlation coefficient, for example, is .46 the increase in debt capacity is larger in both absolute and relative terms, even though the initial debt capacities were smaller. This is a logical result because with risk aversion and the reduction in risk through merger, the impact on debt capacity is greater.

Thus the main results of the Stapleton formulation are quite strong. Using the OPM, the effects of merger on debt capacity are shown to be positive even when earnings of the component firms are perfectly correlated. By comparison, the Lewellen definition of debt capacity understates the effects of mergers.

Although debt capacity is increased, we should recall the results of Galai-Masulis and of Shastri. Their results suggest that in general the increase in debt capacity will benefit the creditors, but have a negative effect on the value of the common stock. However, if the increase in debt capacity is utilized after merger, the value of the common stock may be increased due to tax savings on interest payments.

7. Tests of the Performance of Conglomerate Firms

Empirical studies of conglomerate performance have been of two kinds. The first was a concern with their operating characteristics. In a study whose data ended in the early 1960s, Reid [1968] concluded that conglomerate mergers satisfied the desires of managers for larger firms, but did not increase earnings or market prices. For a later period, 1958–1968, Weston and Mansinghka [1971] found that conglomerates as a group raised the depressed premerger rates of return on total assets up to

Table 17.10 Debt Capacity and Merger: Risk Aversion

		Firm B	Firm D		Firm BD $\rho = 0.46$	Firm BD $\rho = 1$
Mean μ		100	100		200	200
Standard deviation σ		30	40		60	70
Correlation with market ρ_m		0.75	0.75		0.875	0.75
	i percent	Y_B	Y_D	$Y_B + Y_D$	Y_{BD}	Y_{BD}
Debt capacity	12	47	0	47	91	56
Debt capacity	14	60	22	82	116	92
Debt capacity	16	68	41	109	133	112

From R. C. Stapleton, "Mergers, Debt Capacity and the Valuation of Corporate Loans," reprinted by permission of the publisher, from *Mergers and Acquisitions,* edited by Michael Keenan and Lawrence J. White. (Lexington, Mass.: Lexington Books, D.C. Heath & Co., Copyright © 1982, D.C. Heath & Co.)

the average for all firms. In the Melicher and Rush study [1974] for 1960–1969, conglomerates acquired more profitable firms than nonconglomerate acquirers and increased the utilization of latent debt capacity.

A second type of empirical study focused on conglomerate performance within the context of the CAPM. Weston et al. [1972] compared conglomerates with mutual funds (using annual data for 1960–1969), finding that conglomerates provided higher ratios of return to systematic risk. Melicher and Rush [1973] analyzed conglomerates against a matched sample of nonconglomerates. Operating comparisons were based on annual data, while market comparisons utilized monthly data over the period 1965–1971. Conglomerates exhibited higher levels of systematic risk, but did not achieve significantly different rates of return or other performance measures. Joehnk and Nielsen [1974] compared levels of systematic risk and coefficients of determination for 21 conglomerates and 23 nonconglomerates (1962–1969). The market response for three years before and three years after each merger was not significantly different. Mason and Goudzwaard [1976] compared 22 conglomerates against randomly selected portfolios having similar asset structures for the years 1962–1967. They concluded that conglomerates performed statistically worse, on the basis of both return on assets and return on equity, compared to an unmanaged portfolio of similar industry investments.

In a later study, Smith and Weston [1977] retested their 1972 results, using monthly data and extending the coverage through 1973. Their research broadened the comparisons of Melicher and Rush [1973] by including mutual funds and closed-end investment companies as well as nonconglomerate firms. They studied a sample of 38 conglomerate firms. Conglomerates from their 1972 study were included for which complete data of monthly prices and dividends were available for the 10 years from 1964 through 1973. Similar data were available for 35 nonconglomerate firms that were part of a larger sample (matched by major industry) as developed by Melicher and Rush [1973]. Standard and Poor's Composite Stock Price Index was used as a surrogate for the overall stock market. For comparisons of managed portfolios, they compiled data for 104 mutual funds and also for 17 closed-end investment companies.

The risk-adjusted performance of conglomerates was found to be significantly better than that of the mutual funds. The higher-beta conglomerates performed better during the rising market, but less well during the flat market. However, on theoretical grounds, the risk-adjusted performance measure should not show better performance for higher-risk securities during an up-market or worse performance during a down-market situation. As discussed by Friend and Blume [1970] and Black et al. [1972], a possible reason for the early differentially better performance of conglomerates is that the CAPM from which the risk-adjusted performance measures are derived is misspecified. An alternative explanation is expectation errors coupled with institutional changes. The attitudes toward conglomerates changed considerably over time, exhibiting overoptimism about their potential during 1964–1968. During the second period, 1969–1973, some unfavorable institutional changes took place. Accounting rules were changed, adverse tax treatment was legislated, and antitrust suits were filed by the Department of Justice. Also the aerospace industry, which spawned many of the conglomerates as a form of defensive diversification, suffered from excess capacity and sharp product shifts with the escalation of the Vietnam war. Tests of operating effectiveness suggest an initial overoptimism about the potentials for management performance of conglomerates. Following 1969, conglomerates began to be viewed with considerable pessimism. These expectation changes are consistent with the risk-adjusted performance exhibited by the conglomerates.

As experience with conglomerates grew, investors were able to develop a more dependable basis for forming expectations with respect to their performance. We would expect conglomerates to continue to exhibit high betas because of the characteristics of the product-markets of conglomerate firms. Risk-adjusted measures of conglomerate performance are not likely to be significantly different from those of other firms and portfolios. Further tests of merger performance, using residual analysis, are covered in the following chapter.

SUMMARY

Most generally mergers form one economic unit from two or more previous ones. In recent years increased use has been made of tender offers in which the bidder makes an offer directly to the stockholders of the firm it is seeking to control (the target). After obtaining control the bidder may merge the companies.

Alternative theories of mergers have been formulated. Differential efficiency is a very general basis for mergers. It states that if the managers of firm A have superior ability, the assets of firm B may be more valuable under their control if the management of firm B is less efficient. A number of tax considerations may also be involved in mergers. One is the use of accumulated tax losses. Another is for owners of closely held firms to avoid paying taxes at personal income-tax rates on ordinary income that would be earned over a number of years in the future by selling their companies at the capitalized values of those future incomes. Thus a capital gains tax may be substituted for a tax on ordinary income. In addition, if stock is received in payment, realization of the capital gain can be deferred to a time period selected by the sellers.

The inefficient-management theory could have at least three formulations. One is inept management in some absolute sense—almost anyone could do better. In a second sense, inefficient management may not be performing up to its potential. In still a third sense we have the differential-efficiency theory discussed above. Still a fourth variation of the inefficient-management theory has been expressed in terms of agency theory. An agency problem arises when managers own only a fraction of the ownership shares of the firm. This may lead managers to work less efficiently or to consume more perquisites because the majority owners bear most of the cost. In large corporations the individual shareholder with small holdings does not have sufficient incentive or resources to monitor effectively the behavior of managers. The threat of a takeover by a firm is a monitoring device that will cause the managers to identify more closely with the interest of shareholders. The market for corporate control may effectively deal with inefficiency or agency problems. A variation of the agency theory is the managerialism theory of conglomerate mergers. The managerialism theory argues that mergers take place to increase the size of the firm for the sake of size alone or because the compensation of managers is based on the size of the firm.

Another theory states that mergers take place because the target company is undervalued. A company may be undervalued for a number of reasons. One is because management is not operating up to its potential or other aspects of the inefficient management theories. Another possibility is that bidders have special inside information. Another aspect of the undervaluation theory relates to the difference between the replacement value of a target firm's assets and their current market value. Thus if a bidding company wishes to add to capacity in a particular line of business, it may be able to acquire the additional capacity more cheaply by buying a company that produces the product rather than constructing the new capacity itself.

Another rationale set forth for mergers is synergy. The idea of synergy became almost a slogan during the conglomerate merger activity of the late 1960s. Most of the literature of financial economics has postulated the absence of synergy. If synergy is to have meaning, it represents the application of some economic concept. One possibility is economies of scale which may be expressed in a number of ways, including complementarity between two merging organizations. In connection with vertical integration the economies may come from the more efficient flow of information or the more effective methods of conducting transactions. Of course, the "2 + 2 = 5" effect may also come from improving efficiency or dealing with agency problems as well.

Another motive for mergers may be to increase a firm's market share, but it is not clear how this will increase the value of the combined firm. If the increased size of a firm relative to other firms implies a firm of larger absolute size, then we must be talking about economies of scale again. An alternative theory is that increased market share implies increased market power and some elements of monopoly control.

A final explanation of mergers has been developed in connection with the newer literature on long-range strategic planning. This approach emphasizes effective realignment of the firm to its changing environment. The emphasis here is that by external diversification the firm may more effectively acquire management skills for needed augmentation of its present capabilities.

Conglomerate mergers have been an area of particular study because they were the only type of merger permitted after the tightening of the legal rules in 1950. One potential source of synergy in conglomerate mergers was the application of the general management functions of planning and control to a wide range of companies, particularly those companies where these general functions had not been performed well. The pure financial theory of conglomerate mergers emphasized reduction in the probability of bankruptcy. If bankruptcy costs are large, debt capacity may be increased by conglomerate mergers. However, this simply transfers wealth from shareholders to debtholders in the firm.

Under alternative assumptions of the relative size of bankruptcy costs, the degree of interdependence or correlation between cash flows of the constituent companies, and different investor attitudes toward risk, a wide range of alternative models can be developed. These models predict the resulting effects on debt capacity.

In the option pricing model framework, the variance of the combined firm is decreased, which reduces the value of the combined stock and increases the value of the combined debt. Assuming that the value of the combined firm is still the sum of the individual constituents, the transfer from owners to creditors can be redressed by increasing the debt ratio. These effects are more complex than originally set forth because of variations in the relationships among the variances and leverage ratios of the individual firms as well as in the maturity patterns of their debt structures.

Another explanation for conglomerate mergers is that they represent an outgrowth of the computer age. Improved information systems have expanded the generic managerial capabilities of some firms, leading them to view conglomerate mergers as a natural extension of their existing capabilities. Studies of market relationships have found that the performance of conglomerate firms is not significantly different from the performance of other firms on average over extended periods of time.

PROBLEM SET

17.1 Discuss the assumptions and implications of the proposition that value is conserved (value additivity obtains) under the addition of income streams (mergers).

17.2 Summarize the sources of synergy or operating gains from mergers that have been presented in the literature. Evaluate the validity of the arguments for synergy.

17.3 Explain and illustrate how differential price-earnings ratios reflected in the terms of mergers result in increases or decreases in earnings per share of the merging firms. Do such effects on price-earnings ratios also have effects on the valuation of the firms resulting from mergers?

17.4 Explain and evaluate the managerialism theory of conglomerate mergers set forth by Mueller.

17.5 Explain the pure financial theories of conglomerate firms and evaluate their validity.

For Problems 17.6 and 17.7 assume the following:

i) We are dealing with a world where there are no taxes.
ii) The changes in the parameters affecting value are unanticipated; therefore redistribution effects are possible.
iii) Firms A and B initially have the following parameters:

$$\sigma_A = \sigma_B = .2 \qquad \text{Instantaneous standard deviation}$$
$$T_A = T_B = 4 \text{ years} \qquad \text{Maturity of debt}$$
$$V_A = V_B = \$2,000 \qquad \text{Value of the firm, } V = B + S$$
$$R_f = .06 \qquad \text{Risk-free rate}$$
$$D_A = D_B = \$1,000 \qquad \text{Face value of debt}$$

17.6 The correlation between the cash flows of firms A and B is .6. If they merge, the resultant firm will be worth $\$4,000 = V_A + V_B$, but its new instantaneous variance will be

$$\sigma_{AB}^2 = (\tfrac{1}{2})^2 \sigma_A^2 + 2(\tfrac{1}{2})(\tfrac{1}{2}) r_{AB} \sigma_A \sigma_B + (\tfrac{1}{2})^2 \sigma_B^2$$

$$= (.25)(.2)^2 + 2(.5)(.5)(.6)(.2)(.2) + (.25)(.2)^2$$

$$= .01 + .012 + .01 = .032$$

$$\sigma_{AB} = .179.$$

What will the market value of debt and equity in the merged firm be? If there were no other merger effects, would shareholders agree to the merger?

17.7 Given the results of Problem 17.6, suppose that the merged firm has 1,000 shares outstanding. Furthermore, suppose that the shareholders decide to issue $1,000 of new debt (which is not subordinate to outstanding debt), maturing in four years, and invest the proceeds in marketable securities, so that the new value of the merged firm is $5,000. What will be the new price per share? Assume the merged firm's instantaneous variance is unchanged by this investment.

17.8 You are given the following information:

	Firm A	Firm B
Value prior to merger	$1,000	$1,000
Face value of debt	$ 500	$ 500

In addition, the value of equity for firm A equals the value of equity for firm B, and the variance of returns for firm A and firm B are also equal. Using a risk-free rate of 8%, an appropriate time horizon of five years, and a variance for each firm of 10%, apply the OPM to calculate the value of equity of the two firms before the merger. Under the further assumption that the correlation between the percentage returns on firms A and B is zero, calculate the value of equity and the value of debt of the merged firm, using the OPM.

a) How does the new market value of equity and debt of the merged firm compare with the sum of the values of equity and debt of the constituent firms which combined in the merger?

b) How much additional debt would the merged firm have to issue to restore equity holders to their original position?

17.9 Empirical studies have established that the betas of conglomerate firms have been significantly above 1. What does this imply about diversification as a strong motive for conglomerate mergers?

17.10 Over a long period of time would you expect the risk-adjusted performance of conglomerate firms to be significantly different from the risk-adjusted performance of a broad market index? Explain.

17.11 Galai and Masulis argue that if two firms merge and thus decrease the probability of default on their debt along the lines of Lewellen's scenario, then the stockholders are actually hurt, since they have assumed some of the risk previously borne by the bondholders. Why might nonowner managers of a firm be motivated to transfer risk from bondholders to stockholders in this manner?

REFERENCES*

Alchian, A., and H. Demsetz, "Production, Information Costs, and Economic Organizations," *The American Economic Review,* December 1972, 777–795.

---

* Since Chapters 17 and 18 are closely related in subject matter, the reader is urged to consult the reference sections for both chapters.

Arrow, K. J., "Vertical Integration and Communication," *Bell Journal of Economics,* Spring 1975, 173–183.

Beckenstein, A. R., "Merger Activity and Merger Theories: An Empirical Investigation," *Antitrust Bulletin,* Spring 1979, 105–128.

Beman, L., "What We Learned from the Great Merger Frenzy," *Fortune,* April 1973, 70ff.

Black, F., M. Jensen, and M. Scholes, "The Capital Asset Pricing Model: Some Empirical Tests," in M. Jensen, ed., *Studies in the Theory of Capital Markets.* Praeger, New York, 1972.

Blume, M., "Portfolio Theory: A Step Toward Its Practical Application," *Journal of Business,* April 1970, 152–173.

Bock, B., *Statistical Games and the "200 Largest" Industrials: 1954 and 1968.* The Conference Board, Inc., New York, 1970.

Brennan, M., "The Pricing of Contingent Claims in Discrete Time Models," *Journal of Finance,* March 1979, 53–68.

Celler, E., *Investigation of Conglomerate Corporations Hearings* before the Antitrust Subcommittee of the Committee on the Judiciary, House of Representatives, 1969–1970, Parts 1–7. U.S. Government Printing Office, Washington, D.C., 1971.

Celler Committee Staff Report, *Investigation of Conglomerate Corporations.* U.S. Government Printing Office, Washington, D.C., June 1, 1971.

Chung, K. S., "Investment Opportunities, Synergies, and Conglomerate Mergers." Ph.D. dissertation, Graduate School of Management, University of California, Los Angeles, 1982.

———, and J. F. Weston, "Diversification and Mergers in a Strategic Long-Range-Planning Framework," Ch. 13 in M. Keenan and L. J. White, eds., *Mergers and Acquisitions.* D.C. Heath, Lexington, Mass., 1982.

Coase, R. H., "The Nature of the Firm," *Economica,* November 1937, 386–405.

Cox, J., S. Ross, and M. Rubinstein, "Option Pricing: A Simplified Approach," *Journal of Financial Economics,* September 1979, 229–263.

Dewing, A. S., "A Statistical Test of the Success of Consolidations," *Quarterly Journal of Economics,* November 1921, 84–101.

Fama, E., "Efficient Capital Markets: A Review of Theory and Empirical Work," *Journal of Finance,* May 1970, 383–417.

———, "Perfect Competition and Optimal Production Decisions Under Uncertainty," *Bell Journal of Economics,* Autumn 1972, 509–530.

———, "Agency Problems and the Theory of the Firm," *Journal of Political Economy,* April 1980, 288–307.

Friend, I., and M. Blume, "Measurement of Portfolio Performance under Uncertainty," *American Economic Review,* September 1970, 561–575.

Galai, D., and R. W. Masulis, "The Option Pricing Model and the Risk Factor of Stock," *Journal of Financial Economics,* January/March 1976, 53–82.

Gort, M., "An Economic Disturbance Theory of Mergers," *Quarterly Journal of Economics,* November 1969, 624–642.

Haugen, R. A., and J. G. Udell, "Rates of Return to Stockholders of Acquired Companies," *Journal of Financial and Quantitative Analysis,* January 1972, 1387–1398.

Higgins, R. C., "Discussion," *Journal of Finance,* May 1971, 543–545.

———, and L. D. Schall, "Corporate Bankruptcy and Conglomerate Merger," *Journal of Finance,* March 1975, 93–113.

Jensen, M., and J. Long, "Corporate Investment Under Uncertainty and Pareto Optimality in the Capital Markets," *Bell Journal of Economics,* Spring 1972, 151–174.

Jensen, M., and W. Meckling, "Theory of the Firm: Managerial Behavior, Agency Costs and Ownership Structure," *Journal of Financial Economics,* October 1976, 305–360.

Joehnk, M. D., and J. F. Nielsen, "The Effects of Conglomerate Merger Activity on Systematic Risk," *Journal of Financial and Quantitative Analysis,* March 1974, 215–225.

Keenan, M., and L. J. White, *Mergers and Acquisitions.* D.C. Heath, Lexington, Mass., 1982.

Kraus, A., and R. Litzenberger, "A State-Preference Model of Optimal Financial Leverage," *Journal of Finance,* September 1973, 911–922.

Levy, H., and M. Sarnat, "Diversification, Portfolio Analysis and the Uneasy Case for Conglomerate Mergers," *Journal of Finance,* September 1970, 795–802.

Lewellen, W. G., "A Pure Financial Rationale for the Conglomerate Merger," *Journal of Finance,* May 1971, 521–545.

———, and B. Huntsman, "Managerial Pay and Corporate Performance," *American Economic Review,* September 1970, 710–720.

Lintner, J., "Conglomerate and Vertical Responses to Market Imperfection: Expectations, Mergers and Equilibrium in Purely Competitive Markets," *American Economic Review,* May 1971, 101–111.

Livermore, S., "The Success of Industrial Mergers," *Quarterly Journal of Economics,* November 1935, 63–96.

Lynch, H. H., *Financial Performance of Conglomerates.* Harvard Graduate School of Business Administration, Boston, 1971.

Manne, H. G., "Mergers and the Market for Corporate Control," *Journal of Political Economy,* April 1965, 110–120.

Markham, J. W., "Market Structure and Decision-Making in the Large Diversified Firm," in J. F. Weston and S. I. Ornstein, eds., *The Impact of Large Firms on the U.S. Economy,* Chapter 14. D.C. Heath, Lexington, Mass., 1973.

———, *Conglomerate Enterprises and Public Policy.* Harvard Graduate School of Business Administration, Boston, 1973.

Mason, R. H., and M. B. Goudzwaard, "Performance of Conglomerate Firms: A Portfolio Approach," *Journal of Finance,* March 1976, 39–48.

Melicher, R. W., and T. H. Harter, "Stock Price Movements of Firms Engaged in Large Acquisition," *Journal of Financial and Quantitative Analysis,* March 1972, 1469–1475.

Melicher, R. W., and D. F. Rush, "The Performance of Conglomerate Firms: Recent Risk and Return Experience," *Journal of Finance,* May 1973, 381–388.

———, "Evidence on the Acquisition-Related Performance of Conglomerate Firms," *Journal of Finance,* March 1974, 141–149.

Merton, R., and M. Subrahmanyan, "The Optimality of a Competitive Stock Market," *Bell Journal of Economics,* Spring 1974, 145–170.

Modigliani, F., and M. H. Miller, "The Cost of Capital, Corporation Finance, and the Theory of Investment," *American Economic Review,* June 1958, 261–297.

Mossin, J., *Theory of Financial Markets*. Prentice-Hall, Englewood Cliffs, N.J., 1973.

Mueller, D. C., "A Theory of Conglomerate Mergers," *Quarterly Journal of Economics,* November 1969, 643–659. (See also comment by Dennis E. Logue and Philippe A. Naert, November 1970, 663–667; comment by David R. Kanerschen, 668–673, and reply by Dennis C. Mueller, 674–679.)

——, "The Effects of Conglomerate Mergers," *Journal of Banking and Finance,* 1977, 315–347.

Myers, S. C., "Procedures for Capital Budgeting under Uncertainty," *Industrial Management Review,* Spring 1968, 1–19.

Nielsen, N. C., *The Firm as an Intermediary between Consumers and Production Functions under Uncertainty.* Doctoral dissertation, Graduate School of Business, Stanford University, Palo Alto, Calif., 1974.

Reid, S. R., *Mergers, Managers and the Economy.* McGraw-Hill, New York, 1968.

Reinhardt, U. E., *Mergers and Consolidations: A Corporate Financial Approach.* General Learning Press, Morristown, New Jersey, 1972.

Schall, L. D., "Asset Valuation, Firm Investment, and Firm Diversification," *Journal of Business,* January 1972, 11–28.

Scott, J. H., Jr., "On the Theory of Conglomerate Mergers," *Journal of Finance,* September 1977, 1235–1250.

Shastri, K., "Valuing Corporate Securities: Some Effects of Mergers by Exchange Offers," University of Pittsburgh, WP-517, revised January 1982.

Shick, R. A., "The Analysis of Mergers and Acquisitions," *The Journal of Finance,* May 1972, 495–502.

Smith, K. V., and J. F. Weston, "Further Evaluation of Conglomerate Performance," *Journal of Business Research,* March 1977, 5–14.

Stapleton, R. C., "Mergers, Debt Capacity, and the Valuation of Corporate Loans," Ch. 2 in M. Keenan and L. J. White, eds., *Mergers and Acquisitions.* D.C. Heath, Lexington, Mass., 1982.

Summer, C., *Strategic Behavior in Business and Government.* Little, Brown and Company, Boston, 1980.

U.S. Federal Trade Commission, Staff Report: *Economic Report on Conglomerate Merger Performance.* U.S. Government Printing Office, Washington, D.C., November 1972.

——, Staff Report: *Economic Report on Corporate Mergers.* U.S. Government Printing Office, Washington, D.C., August 28, 1969.

——, *Statistical Report on Mergers and Acquisitions.* Bureau of Economics, November 1977.

Westerfield, R., "A Note on the Measurement of Conglomerate Diversification," *Journal of Finance,* September 1970, 909–914.

Weston, J. F., "The Determination of Share Exchange Ratios," in W. W. Alberts and J. E. Segal, eds., *The Corporate Merger,* pp. 117–138. University of Chicago Press, 1966.

——, "Discussion," *The American Economic Review,* May 1971, 125–127.

——, "ROI Planning and Control," *Business Horizons,* August 1972, 35–42.

——, *Mergers and Economic Efficiency,* Proceedings of a Workshop and Supplementary Papers, Vol. 1. U.S. Government Printing Office, Washington, D.C., November 1980.

————, *Mergers and Economic Efficiency,* Industrial Concentration, Mergers and Growth, Vol. 2. U.S. Government Printing Office, Washington D.C., June 1981.

————, and S. K. Mansinghka, "Tests of the Efficiency Performance of Conglomerate Firms," *Journal of Finance,* September 1971, 919–936.

Weston, J. F., and Edward M. Rice, "Discussion," *Journal of Finance,* May 1976, 743–747.

Weston, J. F., K. V. Smith, and R. E. Schrieves, "Conglomerate Performance Using the Capital Asset Pricing Model," *The Review of Economics and Statistics,* November 1972, pp. 357–363.

Williamson, O. E., *Corporate Control and Business Behavior.* Prentice-Hall, Englewood Cliffs, N.J., 1970.

————, "The Vertical Integration of Production: Market Failure Considerations," *The American Economic Review,* May 1971, 112–123.

Mergers and Tender Offers: Tests and Applications

We'll buy you out: Mergers and Acquisitions Come Back Into Style.

NEWSPAPER HEADLINE, 1978.

The preceding chapter dealt with theories of mergers and described some empirical tests of conglomerate merger performance. In the first part of the present chapter we review tests of merger theories by a consideration of studies in four areas: (A) tests of merger returns; (B) studies of tender offers; (C) studies of antitrust cases, and (D) corporate governance. We then draw (E) generalizations from the studies. In the second part of the chapter we discuss managerial aspects of mergers, covering (F) terms of mergers and (G) managerial policies in a valuation framework.

Recall that in Chapter 10, describing tests of the efficient market hypothesis, three basic types of empirical models were employed. These were Eqs. (7.32), (7.34), and (10.1).

$$R_{jt} = R_{ft} + [R_{mt} - R_{ft}]\beta_j + \epsilon_{jt}, \qquad (7.32)$$

595

$$R_{jt} = \hat{\gamma}_{0t} + \hat{\gamma}_{1t}\beta_{jt} + \epsilon_{jt}, \tag{7.34}$$

$$R_{jt} = a_j + b_j R_{mt} + \epsilon_{jt}. \tag{10.1}$$

Equation (7.32) uses the capital asset pricing theory. Equation (7.34) is the empirical market line derived from the CAPM. However, it does not require the intercept term to equal the risk-free rate. Equation (10.1) is the market model. Under appropriate definitions and assumptions, one can move from one model to another [Ellert, 1975, Appendix A]. However, as noted in Chapter 10, in empirical work the implications are different.

For example, the market model employs time series analysis, developing parameters for periods before and after a time interval influenced by the "event" under analysis. The meaning of the intercept term in the model is not defined and the nature of the event may influence its measurement. Thus if firms that have not been "performing up to their potential" are the ones that become target or acquired firms, the intercept term will be negative. If firms that have had excellent and improving performance in managing assets become acquiring firms, their intercept term will be positive. In the calculation of the residuals, the intercept for the control period is deducted and hence this form of selection bias will influence the results.

The CAPM form of the model involves the use of a risk-free return. Empirical tests have yielded estimates of the intercept term which are systematically greater than the return on a riskless asset.

Since the implicit empirical assumptions of the alternative models differ, the results of studies using different models require interpretation related to the characteristics of the model employed. In Chapter 10, the three models were used to test for market efficiency. In the present chapter, the models are used to test whether mergers or tender offers and other unique events produce temporary "abnormal" returns. Our discussion of the empirical studies of merger performance will take into account the implications of the particular statistical methodology employed.

A. TESTS OF MERGER RETURNS

1. Early Studies of Mergers[1]

Early empirical studies of mergers used comparative studies of merger performance to test for synergy from mergers. Progressive improvements in methodology were developed, leading to the use of asset pricing models and explicit recognition of the role of possible changes in risks resulting from the mergers.

Kelly [1967] was the first to study merger profitability by means of security market measures. Using a sample of 21 firms for which acquisitions yielded at least a 20% increase in sales, Kelly also compiled a second sample of 21 "nonmerging" firms (having no more than a 5% increase in sales due to merger) which, in all

---

[1] This section draws heavily on Krouse [1975].

other respects, matched the original 21 one for one. The period covered was from 1946 to 1960. Five measures of profitability (percentage change in price of common stock, in price-earnings ratio, in earnings per share, in net sales per common share, and in profit margin) were developed. The percentage change was computed from the average values of the respective parameters during the premerger period to the average of the postmerger period. (The premerger period was defined as the five years preceding the merger, the postmerger period as the five years following the merger.)

Nonmerging companies yielded insignificantly higher profit margin increases and gains in earnings per share; merging companies were somewhat better in comparisons based on price-earnings ratios and sales per share. In terms of capital gains (changes in stock prices), neither merging nor nonmerging companies were superior. In net, Kelly's conclusion was that mergers had little impact on the profitability (to shareholders) of acquiring companies and hence yielded little or no synergy.

While better than earlier studies, Kelly's work has shortcomings: in particular, his small sample and "matching technique" raise questions about the scope of his analysis and the adequacy of his comparison standard. Nonetheless, Kelly's work is important in that he measured changes in capital market values, and a standard of comparison, or control for other factors, is part of the test of merger gains.

Hogarty [1970] comes much closer in developing evidence on investment returns to test for merger synergy. For 43 firms, he develops an investment performance index based on changes in stock market values (adjusted for dividends). He then compares these indexes for acquiring firms with similarly constructed indexes for their respective industries. On an annual basis, the mean difference between the "investment performance" of acquiring firms in mergers and their industry average was a negative 5%—the "gain" of merging was 5% per year less (and significant at a 10% level). This result implies negative synergy. While Hogarty attempts to control for other factors affecting market-value changes by comparing each merging firm with the average performance of its industry, this method is open to a variety of obvious criticisms.

Lev and Mandelker [1972] employ an explicit paired-comparison experimental design which potentially could alleviate some of the objections one may make regarding the appropriateness of comparing the market-value performance of selected firms with their industry averages as a test of merger synergy. Measuring profitability by the annual rate of return of the market (with dividends reinvested and adjusting for stock splits), they calculated the difference between the postmerger five-year average and premerger five-year average for 69 firms. Subtracting the respective pre- and postmerger average of a matching firm from that of an acquiring firm, they tested differences in the mean residuals. (Measuring differences before and after the merger in this fashion corrects, or controls, for other factors which are presumed to identically affect the market value of the matching firm.) The market valuation of the acquiring firm increased an average of 5.6% more than that of the matching control firms, and this difference was significant at a 10% level. The practical problem of selecting a match to a merging firm which is adequately comparable both before and after the merger severely attenuates the results obtained by Lev and Mandelker.

In summary to this point, the evidence on capital market gains made by acquiring firms in mergers is conflicting, and is confounded by legitimate criticisms of the samples, methodologies, and control devices used to account for excluded variables. It is in this setting that the studies of Halpern [1973] and Mandelker [1974] appear. These two analyses begin the use of asset pricing models.

2. Halpern

Halpern attempts to directly measure buyer and seller premiums in mergers in a sample of approximately 75 acquisitions. Basically his method is to adjust the observed market prices of acquiring and acquired firms for general market variations during the period when merger information affects their share prices: the price change which remains unexplained by market variations is that attributable to the merger.

Two estimates are required to make the proposed share-price adjustments and measurements. First, Halpern needs a base period, the interval before the announcement date during which merger information is reflected in the stock prices. To determine this, he employs the "residual technique" developed by Fama, Fisher, Jensen, and Roll, and runs the following time-series regression:

$$_jR_{i,t} = \alpha_i + \beta_{1j}R_{m,t*} + \beta_{2j}R_{I,t*} + \epsilon_{i,t}, \qquad (18.1)$$

where $_jR_{i,t}$ is the *price relative* for company i in industry j during the month t, $_jR_{I,t*}$ is the industry price relative, and $_jR_{m,t*}$, the market price relative. The regression yields estimates of $\hat{\alpha}_i$, $\hat{\beta}_1$, and $\hat{\beta}_2$. Substituting these, he rewrites the regression equation in the form:

$$\epsilon_{i,t} = {_jR_{i,t}} - \hat{\beta}_{1j}R_{m,t*}R_{I,t*} - \hat{\beta}_{2j} - \alpha_i. \qquad (18.2)$$

Halpern then notes that if all of company i's price relative in month t could be explained by industry or market price relatives, the value of the merger, as measured by $\epsilon_{i,t}$, would be zero. Thus, a nonzero $\epsilon_{i,t}$ indicates that firm i's share price is not entirely accounted for by "normal" factors. Since mergers are unusual events, we would expect the estimated residuals to display unusual behavior during the merger adjustment period. A base date can then be chosen as that date before which "abnormal" residuals were observed. Because of extraneous influences, cross-sectional residuals (over merging firms) were calculated over time relative to the announcement date.

Halpern's analysis indicates that on the average, merger information is available for seven months before the *announcement* date. From the twenty-third until the eighth month prior to announcements, the cumulative average residuals are randomly increasing and decreasing. From the seventh month onward, they increase steadily. Average residual values are small and vary in size until the large positive value is encountered in the seventh month. Also, a large proportion of positive residuals in the seventh month seems to strengthen this result.

The second element of Halpern's analysis is calculating adjusted security prices. Excluding data from the 12 months prior to the merger, Halpern runs the following equation for each firm using five years of monthly observations:

$$R_{k,t}^b = \alpha_k^b + \beta_1^b R_{m,t}^b + B_2^b R_{I,t}^b + \epsilon. \qquad (18.3)$$

From the estimates $\hat{\alpha}_k^b$, $\hat{\beta}_1^b$, and $\hat{\beta}_2^b$ and the actual price relative in the market and industry for the adjustment interval, Halpern calculates the unbiased estimates of the expected price relative for each firm. Multiplying this relative by the base period price and adjusting for dividends paid during the adjustment period, he then obtains an unbiased estimate of the adjusted price. After calculating the gains to "buyers" and "sellers," the firms were classified as "larger" or "smaller" on the basis of their equity value at the base date. Halpern finds that the mean gain prior to dividend adjustment of larger firms exceeded those of smaller firms by a factor of 4. After the dividend adjustment, the gains were smaller for both firm types and approximately equal in absolute amount. Adjustments also had a tendency to make negative gains less negative and at times turned negative "gains" into positive ones.

Subsequently Halpern calculates price premiums, the gain relative to a base price, for both acquiring and acquired firms. While the premium accruing to smaller firms was significantly greater than zero (at 5%), the premium accruing to larger firms was not. His results suggest synergy or improvement in the performance of the smaller firms which is reflected in prices paid by acquirers.

3. Mandelker

Mandelker [1974] used the Fama and MacBeth [1973] methodology to examine the testable implications of what we have termed the "empirical market line,"

$$R_{it} = \hat{\gamma}_{ot} + \hat{\gamma}_{1t}\beta_{it} + \epsilon_{it}, \tag{7.34}$$

presented in Chapter 7.

First, Fama and MacBeth estimate betas with seven years of monthly data for individual securities using the regression analog of our Eq. (7.32):

$$R_{jt} - R_{ft} = (R_{mt} - R_{ft})\beta_j + \epsilon_{jt}, \tag{7.32}$$

which is the *ex post* form of the CAPM equation. The individual betas are ranked and placed in 20 portfolios with maximum dispersion of systematic risk in the attempt to minimize the measurement error in the beta estimates.

Second, they use the next five years to recalculate the betas and average them to obtain the portfolio betas. The betas for individual securities are updated every 10 months on the basis of the return data for the preceding five years.

Third, using monthly data for the next four years, they run cross-sectional regressions for each month across the 20 portfolios utilizing Eq. (7.34), the empirical market line. These provide estimates of γ_0 and γ_1, which have been used as measures of the empirical market line parameters in a number of other studies.

Mandelker used the Fama and MacBeth procedures, adding two additional steps for his study of mergers.

Fourth, he estimated the betas for individual firms involved in mergers, using the *ex post* form of the asset pricing relation, Eq. (7.32). The time period measured covered months prior to the merger as well as months following it.

Fifth, he calculated residuals for each month, using the gamma values from Eq. (7.34) and utilizing the values of returns and betas calculated in the fourth step.

Mandelker tested two hypotheses. One was that acquisitions took place in a market under conditions of perfect competition. The other was the hypothesis of efficient capital markets with respect to information on acquisitions. The stockholders of the acquired firms received cumulative average residuals that were positive, indicating that they earned abnormal gains from the mergers. This suggests that the acquired firms may have had unique resources whose values are realized to a greater degree by mergers. Alternatively, the acquired firms may have been operating at below their optimal levels of efficiency, and the mergers were seen as increasing the effectiveness of their operations. The possible benefits to be derived from the acquired firms are apparently perceived by a number of potential acquirers. The competition in the market for acquisitions results in competitive prices for the acquired firms. The acquiring firms appear to operate in a competitive market so that the prices they pay for the acquired firm's stock result in normal returns on the acquisitions. The acquiring firms earn a rate of return equal to other investment or production activities of similar risks. The average residuals for the acquiring firms are generally positive, but not statistically significant. This finding controverts the argument that acquiring firms overpay and lose from mergers.

With respect to the hypothesis of efficient capital markets, Mandelker's findings are consistent with the view that the stock market operates efficiently with respect to information on mergers. The price movements which take place at the time of the merger announcement and even before reflect all valuable information about the merger preceding the effective date of the transaction. The stock prices of the constituent firms at the date when the merger is consummated reflect the economic gains expected. The stock prices of the merged firms do not undergo postmerger adjustments. While significant changes in betas were observed, the rates of return adjusted efficiently to the changes in risk. Stockholders were not misled by accounting manipulations in mergers or by the artificial increase in earnings per share resulting from the differential price-earnings ratio game played by acquiring firms. The views that mergers reflect the desires of managers to control larger firms and their emphasis on growth maximization imply losses to the acquiring stockholders. But the finding of positive average residuals for the acquiring firms is inconsistent with the managerialism hypothesis.

4. Ellert

Ellert [1975, 1976] also employs the Fama-MacBeth methodology, updating their estimates of γ_{0t}. Ellert's studies, like the earlier findings of Halpern [1973] and Mandelker [1974], indicate that the impact on the market prices of merging firms takes place 7 to 12 months prior to the actual merger. The announcement necessarily precedes the merger, and there are leaks even before the public announcement. For acquiring firms, his evidence indicates that while the cumulative average residual (CAR) is generally positive during this period, it is either not significant or the magnitude of the change in CAR during this period is small. This evidence is inconsistent with the managerial theory and its related growth maximization prediction. It is also inconsistent with the monopolistic exploitation theory, at least in providing monopoly gains to acquiring firms.

Both Mandelker and Ellert find that very substantial increases in the CAR of acquiring firms take place during the period from 4 to 8 years prior to the merger activity. This is consistent with the hypothesis set forth by both Mandelker and Ellert that the differentially higher efficiency of acquiring firms prior to mergers leads to their subsequent expansion both externally and internally. With respect to acquired firms, both Mandelker and Ellert find that their CARs are significantly negative in the years and months running up to the period when information about their upcoming acquisition by others becomes available. In the subsequent 7 to 12 months through the actual merger date, the CARs turn strongly positive and are highly significant by statistical tests.

The finding of positive residuals for the acquired firms in the months preceding the merger is consistent with the theory of monopoly control with all the gains going to the acquired firms. However, the evidence of negative CARs in the period running up to the time information on the mergers becomes available is consistent with an alternative explanation. The inefficient utilization of economic resources by the management of the firms prior to the merger leads to their acquisition by firms with a record of above-average performance. Hence the evidence leans in the direction of efficiency and/or synergy as the explanation rather than the managerial or monopoly theories.

If differential efficiency between acquired and acquiring firms were the explanation for mergers, it is likely that there would be a number of acquiring firms bidding for an individual acquired firm. Competition among acquiring firms would, on the average, eliminate gains to the acquiring firm from the merger activity. This is consistent with the general findings of Mandelker and Ellert. If the acquiring firms had a unique synergistic relationship with an individual acquired firm, the gains from the merger would be attributable to both and could not be allocated individually. This is consistent with Halpern's finding that the absolute dollar amount of the gains is equally divided between acquiring and acquired firms. However, Halpern, Mandelker and Ellert find that while the absolute gains of acquired firms were statistically significant, neither the percentage premium returns nor CARs for the acquiring firms were statistically significant.

5. Langetieg

Langetieg [1978] reexamined 149 mergers using alternative performance indexes as well as a matched nonmerging control group of firms, and found that the results using alternative performance tests were generally consistent with the results of Mandelker. But the use of the control group changes the interpretation somewhat. For example, the acquired firms had a significantly negative cumulative average residual of 12.6% over the time interval $(-72, -19)$ months and a significantly positive stockholder gain of 10.6% over the time interval $(-6, -1)$. But the nonmerging control firms also exhibited negative excess returns in the time interval $(-72, -19)$. In two of the three paired difference tests, Langetieg concludes that some external influence affected both the merging firms and the control firms in a similar way over the similar time periods. For the shareholders of acquiring firms, if the starting point is viewed as 18 months before the merger, the net benefit is 6.1%, which is statistically significant. But the stockholder gain for acquiring companies is substantially less than that for acquired firms.

Langetieg also found that the postmerger performance of a consolidated firm over the period (1, 24) was a negative 12.9 percent. However, in the paired difference analysis, no significant cumulative difference existed. The postmerger performance of the consolidated companies reflected influences that affected similar nonmerging companies in the same way.

6. Dodd

Dodd [1980] is the first of a number of studies of mergers, tenders, and other aspects of corporate governance to employ the market model expressed in our Eq. (10.1). Like Halpern, he uses the announcement date rather than the completion of the merger as the "event." However, studies indicate that there is leakage of information even before the public announcement date. Since Dodd seeks to point up the importance of the role of the announcement date, he uses daily returns rather than monthly data employed in the previous merger studies.

Daily returns were studied for 151 merger proposals announced in the *Wall Street Journal* during 1971 to 1977. Of these, 71 were eventually completed, and 80 were canceled by either target or bidder management. The market reaction to the merger proposal over Day −1 and Day 0 was significantly positive for target firms (approximately 13%), and significantly negative (though smaller) for bidder firms (approximately − 1%).

Dodd concludes that the gains from mergers go to target firms and not to bidders. Bidder CARs for the period 10 days before the proposal to 10 days after approval are negative (−7.22%); the bidder CAR is also negative for canceled mergers regardless of which firm terminates negotiations.

Target shareholders earn large significant positive returns at the proposal announcement (13.43%). For completed mergers the CAR from 10 days before the proposal to 10 days after approval is 33.96%. For canceled mergers the CAR from 10 days before the proposal to 10 days after cancelation is 3.68% for the entire 80 cancelations. For target-initiated cancelations, the CAR is 10.95%. For bidder-cancelations, the target CAR over the same period is 0.18%; that is, returns revert to their pre-proposal level. Dodd observes that since the net effect of target-canceled mergers is positive, it cannot be concluded that managers are necessarily acting against the best interests of shareholders when they veto a proposed merger. Our further judgment would be that cancelations by targets are taken as a signal by the market that the bidder has uncovered a profitable opportunity, or that there is a possibility of a return bid from someone else. Bidder cancelations may be taken as a signal that the target does not represent a profitable investment opportunity.

7. Schipper and Thompson

Schipper and Thompson [1980] examine the market reaction to the announcement of a major acquisitions program. They propose that the stock price at the time of the announcement fully capitalizes the expected value of the program—the net benefits of anticipated mergers and the probability that they will occur.

Schipper and Thompson conclude that merger programs are capitalized as positive NPV projects. The positive premerger performance found in previous studies is viewed as a response to the merger program announcement. The small positive returns for acquirers at the merger event found in previous studies is consistent with the hypothesis that the initial capitalization of the acquisitions program is relatively accurate, with only a minor adjustment required at the actual merger, positive because of the resolution of uncertainty. Schipper and Thompson explain the negative postmerger performance found in some prior studies by the fact that many of the postmerger months in these studies fall in calendar time after the date of the regulatory changes.

8. Asquith and coauthors

Asquith [1980, 1982] also finds that most of the gains from a merger go to stockholders of target firms. He finds that the cumulative residual for unsuccessful bidding firms is significantly negative between the announcement date and the outcome date. He hypothesizes that poorly managed merger attempts reflect negatively on the bidding firm.

A study by Asquith, Bruner, and Mullins [1982] tests the Schipper and Thompson hypothesis discussed above. Their more refined tests find that while some of the positive effects of a merger program are capitalized, subsequent mergers also yield positive residuals for bidder firms. They further find that there appear to be positive effects from leakage of information before the announcement date. In addition, when the relative size of bidder and target firms is taken into account, they conclude that bidding firm stockholders gain from merger activity, consistent with value-maximizing behavior.

Asquith and Kim [1982] test whether the gain to shareholders from mergers is at the expense of bondholders by increasing the firm's risk through merger, which they refer to as an agency "incentive effect." An alternative hypothesis is a "diversification effect" which reduces default risk, resulting in wealth transfers from stockholders to bondholders. They conduct a number of careful tests, concluding that mergers have no discernible impact on bondholders. They conclude that mergers are not motivated by the agency "incentive effect." Nor do they find a "diversification effect," but this may be because of the finding from other studies that leverage is increased after mergers, which would be offsetting.

9. Keown and Pinkerton

While the Keown and Pinkerton [1981] study is treated by its authors as an analysis of insider trading, it also provides a test of the announcement impact. Keown and Pinkerton's sample of 194 firms appears to include both mergers and tender offers. Average residuals and CARs were calculated over the period from 126 days before the announcement to 30 days after. Substantial insider trading begins one month before the announcement and the activity is heightened in the 5–11 days preceding. For the entire sample, approximately $\frac{1}{2}$ of the total market reaction takes place prior to the announcement, with most of the remaining reaction taking place on the announcement day. There is also a significant increase in the trading volume in the three prior weeks. SEC records indicate that this increase is not caused by registered insiders; the implication is that trading is carried out through third parties. These results are consistent with other studies which also find evidence of leaks before the announcement date. But there is also support for semistrong form market efficiency in that the market reaction is complete by the day after the announcement.

10. Malatesta

Malatesta [1982] uses the *ex post* form of the CAPM model expressed in our Eq. (7.32). However, he does not constrain the intercept term of the model to be zero. Rather, "it enters as a component of predicted *normal* returns." [p. 21, emphasis in the original.] A distinctive variation in the Malatesta study is the calculation of the wealth effects of mergers by the abnormal dollar returns in addition to percentage returns. Malatesta also formulates a distinction between alternative definitions of "event" dates. He defines t_1 as the time when investors learn that the firm will invest resources in merger activity. A later time, t_2, is a resolution date at which a decision is made that the merger will take place or be abandoned. The announcement date is taken as a proxy for t_1, but Malatesta observes that for his sample in more than half the cases, the first public announcement was that a merger had essentially been agreed upon. For t_2 his proxy is "substantial board/management approval of the merger." [p. 20.] A problem here is that until stockholder approval takes place and the legal details completed, some risk remains that a merger will not actually take place. Some confounding of influences is involved for both reference dates.

Malatesta's findings based on percentage returns are generally consistent with those of previous studies. However, his results for dollar abnormal returns are different. Portfolios of firms experiencing an information event in the same month were formed both with equally weighted investments in each firm and with investments weighted in proportion to the market values of equity one month prior to the event. The dollar value cumulative excess return was calculated using the value-weighted portfolio forecast error and the total market value of equity of the firms in the portfolio at one month prior to the event. Monthly returns were studied over the period -24 to $+12$ months.

The first published reference to the merger in the *Wall Street Journal* was taken to be a proxy for t_1. For acquiring firms, percentage returns in the 24 months prior to t_1 were insignificantly different from zero, and post-announcement returns were significantly negative. For acquired firms, percentage returns in months -24 to -4 were negative, but only marginally significant; then, however, they began to rise. The market reaction to the announcement was significantly positive, and post-announcement returns were also positive.

The first published announcement of substantial board approval was taken as a proxy for t_2. Acquiring firms exhibited inferior performance following t_2 (the cumulative average forecast error dropped 8% over months $+2$ to $+12$). Acquired firms experienced significant share price appreciation at t_2. (All of the above results were essentially the same for both equally weighted and value-weighted portfolios.)

Dollar returns for acquiring firms (relative to the date of board approval) indicated cumulative excess negative returns of \$49.3 million per firm in the 24 months prior to t_2, but this figure was only barely significant. Acquired firms had significant positive abnormal returns of \$19.2 million in the four months prior to t_2. The effect of mergers seems to be a net reduction in shareholder wealth; the gain to acquired shareholders in the period -5 to t_2 is \$5 million less than the loss to acquiring shareholders.

When Malatesta recalculates the postmerger results with a risk adjustment, the negative postmerger performance of large acquirers is eliminated. The overall result becomes insignificantly positive.

The statistical methodology takes on even greater significance for the Malatesta study. As noted at the beginning of this chapter, the use of the CAPM as expressed in Eq. (7.32) in excess return form implies no intercept term. The intercept term in Malatesta's model is taken as a component of the normal return. It may reflect problems of measuring the risk-free return as well as the behavior of the intercept term calculated for the prior control period. One possibility is that the acquired firms had negative intercept terms while acquiring firms had positive intercept terms for periods in years before the merger "event." If so, the net present value of merger activity could well be positive rather than negative.

B. STUDIES OF TENDER OFFERS

A tender offer represents a cash or stock bid by one company (the bidder) for the ownership shares, often a control position, of another company (the target). A successful tender offer is followed by a formal merger in more than two-thirds of the cases. In a tender offer there is less likely to have been previous negotiations between the parties involved. Sometimes, however, the chief executive of the bidder company may make a courtesy call on his counterpart in the target company in hopes of achieving acquiescence and cooperation that would lead to a friendly relationship. In general there is likely to be a shorter period of time before the formal announcement during which information leaks take place. There is some plausibility also that synergy is more likely to be involved in mergers where previous discussions about fitting two companies together take place. In a tender offer the likelihood is greater that the bidder sees an opportunity for improving the management of the target firm or that its shares are undervalued for one of a number of possible reasons.

1. Dodd and Ruback

The study by Dodd and Ruback [1977] analyzes tender offers of New York Stock Exchange companies covering the period 1958 through 1976. The market model expressed in our Eq. (10.1) is employed. The control period uses data from month -73 through month -14, and from month $+14$ through month $+73$, where month zero is the month of the first public announcement of the tender offer. [Dodd and Ruback, p. 358.] Their study included unsuccessful as well as successful tender offers and included the following subsamples: (1) 172 bidding firms, of which 124 made successful tender offers and the remaining 48 made unsuccessful tender offers; (2)

172 target firms, of which 136 received successful tender offers and the remaining 36 received unsuccessful tender offers.

The highest t-values representing statistical significance pertained to the returns for the target firms in the month of the first public announcement of the tender offer. The favorable abnormal returns were about 21% for the successful offers and 19% for the unsuccessful offers. In addition, for the successful offers there was about a 9% positive residual for the period -12 to -1. For the bidding firms the residuals were a positive 12% for successful bids and about 8% for unsuccessful bids over the same period. There was a positive 3% cumulative average residual for successful bidders during the month of the first public announcement of the tender offer. The cumulative average residuals after the public announcement were not statistically significant for either bidding firms or target firms.

Dodd and Ruback [1977] were able to sharpen the empirical testing by analyzing a sample of unsuccessful tender offers. The period immediately following the time when the proposed merger or acquisition was supposed to have taken place, but for which the event does not occur in unsuccessful tenders, would carry a different set of predictions. The monopoly power theory implies that shareholders of both acquiring and acquired firms would lose because the monopoly gains from the merger that did not take place will now be lost. The managerialism theory argues that shareholders of both the acquired and acquiring firms would benefit if the merger did not take place. Hence the CARs for aborted mergers would become positive. The internal efficiency and the undervalued asset theories imply that the shareholders of both acquiring and acquired firms would be unaffected. The shareholders of acquired firms would be unaffected because the announcement of a tender offer provides new information about the firm. It has some potentials for improvement in efficiency or because of the undervaluation of assets that will probably be recognized by other firms. Under the internal efficiency or undervalued asset theory, other firms will recognize that the assets of the firm that would have been acquired can be improved in value and there will be new suitors. Hence the near-term performance for both acquired and acquiring firms under the internal-efficiency or undervalued-assets theory would be unaffected by the unsuccessful tender offer. If the acquiring firm had spent substantial sums of money in the negotiations, this might cause a decline in the CARs because such investments in the effort to acquire other firms would not come to fruition. The Dodd-Ruback data for unsuccessful tenders in the near term following the event date shows zero CARs for unsuccessful bidders as well as zero CARs for the target firms. This pattern is consistent with the internal-efficiency or undervalued-assets theory, but not with the other theories.

Dodd and Ruback point out that a very substantial proportion of unsuccessful target firms merge within five years of the aborted tender offer. [p. 370] This leads them to state that their conclusion that the results support the efficiency hypothesis is qualified by the possibility that the subsequent mergers may have been anticipated by the market. If so, the nondecline in the CAR after a tender is unsuccessful could be due to expectations of the future monopoly or synergistic gains from mergers. [Dodd and Ruback, p. 370.] However, since their sample period begins in 1958, and since most of the observations in their sample occur in the 1960s and 1970s, the monopoly explanation does not apply. The Celler-Kefauver Amendment, which greatly strengthened the Clayton Act of 1914, was enacted in 1950 and greatly reduced the relative number of horizontal and vertical mergers. [Stigler, 1966.] After the impact of the 1950 law, the largest proportion of mergers has been conglomerate where the issue has not been monopoly in individual markets. [See also FTC Staff Report, 1972.] Therefore, the Dodd and Ruback findings are consistent with the internal-efficiency or undervalued-asset theory as well as with the synergy theory, but not with the monopoly power or managerialism theories.

2. Kummer and Hoffmeister

Kummer and Hoffmeister [1978] studied 88 New York Stock Exchange firms for whom cash tender offers were made during the period 1956–1974. Their sample was divided into three groups: 44 passive-successful takeovers, where the management of the target firm expressed agreement, neutrality, or no public opinion about the proposed takeover; 15 resist-unsuccessful targets, representing cases in which tender offers were resisted by management, the tender offer failed, and no subsequent tender offers were announced within 10 months of the offer under study; and six resist-successful targets, representing firms that were taken over in spite of resistance by the incumbent management.

Of target firms in all categories, the cumulative abnormal residuals were negative for the period (−40, −4) months. These negative residuals were statistically significant for all categories except the passive-successful targets. The negative residuals were large, ranging from 10 to 20%. During the four months before the tender offer announcement for each category, the shareholders of target firms received gains of 6% that were statistically significant. During the month of the announcement of the tender offer, the average abnormal return ranged from 16 to 20% for the three categories of target firms. These returns were all highly significant from a statistical standpoint.

For bidder firms, the cumulative average residual rose to about 10% during the period (−28, −11). Another gain of 6 percentage points was achieved by shareholders of bidder firms during the period (−10, −1). An additional 5% abnormal gain was received during the month in which the tender offer was announced.

3. Firth

Firth's [1979] study of performance covers data for companies in the United Kingdom for the period 1972–1974. As in U.S. studies, the residuals for the acquired companies were slightly negative in the period (−36, −12) months. The residuals had no strong movement until one month before the takeover announcement. Halpern and Mandelker reported that generally seven months elapsed between the beginning of merger negotiations and the merger announcement. Tender offers, however, are less often associated with communications between the companies involved until very shortly before the public offer announcement.

The CARs in Firth's sample reached 38% for acquired firms within two months of the bid announcement. For the acquiring firms, the CARs were slightly positive before the announcement, but turned to a negative 4 to 5% within 24 months of the tender offer. In absolute amounts, the shareholders of acquired firms gained about 650 million British pounds, while the shareholders of acquiring firms lost about the same amount. This contrasts with the earlier Halpern study for the U.S. in which there was a total gain of about $28 million which was split almost equally among the acquired and acquiring firms. Firth comments that previous research for the United Kingdom showed that acquired firms on average had poor profitability records, but that the recovery potential was offset by the premiums paid by acquirers. He observes that the relative incidence of mergers in the United Kingdom has been higher than in the United States and suggests that acquired firms had the benefit of a stronger sellers' market for mergers. Also, Firth's data covered 1972–1974, whereas the U.S. studies covered longer periods starting in the 1950s. Analysis of mergers and tender offers in the United States for the years following 1970 might give results similar to those found by Firth for the United Kingdom.

4. Bradley

Bradley [1980] studied 258 cash tender offers that took place during the period July 1962 through December 1977. For calculating the residuals he uses the abnormal price indexes compiled by the Center for Research in Security Prices (CRSP) of the University of Chicago. Their procedure is to group securities into 10 equal control portfolios according to their estimated risk. Using the CAPM, an estimate of the daily excess return for an individual security is the difference between the realized return to the security less its control portfolio's return.

For the 161 successful tender offers the mean premium is 49%. The postexecution market price of a target share is 36% higher than its pre-announcement level. Hence there is a loss of 13% per target share to the acquirer and target shareholders realized a significant 36% capital gain on the shares not purchased in the offer. Bradley comments that these data do not support a corporate raiding interpretation of tender offers. Despite the significant premium paid, the acquiring stockholders realize an excess capital gain of 5% within 40 days of the offer with an excess capital gain of 4% taking place within five trading days of the offer. Bradley comments that these results are consistent with synergistic gains but cannot distinguish whether they come from market power or cost reductions.

In 33 unsuccessful tender offers the postexecution price level of a target share is 67% above the preannouncement level. This increase in the value of the target shares is higher than the rejected offer premium by 15%. The foregoing results hold for tender offers where all shares were bid for. For fractional tender offers the target shareholders realized a 36% capital gain relative to the preannouncement price. This mean price index is 19% above the rejected tender offer. For the unsuccessful bidders the market price of their shares on the 40th day after the offer is 4% below their preannouncement level. The negative returns for unsuccessful bidders are attributed by Bradley to the search and administrative costs of conducting a tender offer. Further analysis of unsuccessful takeovers in relation to single bid versus multiple bid situations would help sharpen the analysis. Our hypothesis is that positive returns are likely to be preserved with multiple bids, but to fall in the single-bid cases. The more fundamental question is to explain the reasons for single bids versus multiple bids.

Bradley also calculates the results in absolute dollar terms. Over the period from two months before the announcement to two months after the announcement the average acquirer's equity increased by $7.7 million, even though the average offer premium paid to tendering stockholders was also $7.7 million. Over the same period the value of the outstanding shares of target firms increased an average of $31 million. Thus, in contrast to Malatesta's findings on mergers, Bradley's results for tender offers represent substantial increase in value.

5. Jarrell and Bradley

Beginning with the Williams Act in 1968, increasing federal and state regulation of cash tender offers took place. The regulations provide for increased disclosure, a minimum tender period, and antifraud measures which facilitate defensive lawsuits by incumbent management.

Advocates of tender offer regulation support the view that shareholders need protection from undesirable takeovers, or corporate raiding, and that regulation provides more information and time for the shareholders' decision. Those opposed to regulation argue that it increases the information leakage in a takeover attempt, increasing competition for the target firm. The resulting higher premiums may benefit some target shareholders, but amount to a kind of tax against the acquiring firm, decreasing the incentive to engage in acquisitions activity; also, potential target shareholders in combinations foregone will be left worse off by regulation. If, as is argued, corporate takeovers result in more efficient management of target resources, then foregone desirable combinations also impose social costs. Regulation is seen as providing an advantage to incumbent (possibly inept) management and mitigating the disciplinary effect of the market for corporate control.

The authors set out a theory of corporate acquisitions based on the production of knowledge (k) through innovative activity by highly skilled management teams. This knowledge must be combined with some other resource (x) in order to produce gains. If there is no market for the exchange of k, the only way to generate returns from its production is to acquire x, often through corporate takeovers. If k is specific to its producer, information leakage will not be a problem. But if k is specific to the target firm (i.e., k may be knowledge of target-management inefficiency), information leakage may enable rival firms to appropriate the gains to k. At any rate, competition for the target will drive its price up. A sudden takeover reduces the leakage period, increasing returns to the producer of k; the delay and disclosure features of regulation increase leakage, reducing the returns to k and, thus, the incentive to produce it.

Jarrell and Bradley [1980] study the effects of such regulation. Their data included 161 tender offer targets between 1962 and 1977. Forty-seven of the takeovers were unregulated (pre-1968), 94 were subject to federal regulations alone, and 20 were subject to both state and federal regulations. Daily returns were calculated over the period from 40 days prior to the tender offer announcement to 80 days following.

The mean tender premium paid was increased from 32.4% (no regulations) to 52.8% (federal regulations only) to 73.1% (state and federal regulations). The percentage of target shares purchased was also increased by regulation from 42.1% to 71.8%. Cumulative abnormal returns to bidding firms were reduced by regulation.

Jarrell and Bradley conclude that the effect of regulation is to raise the purchase price of target firms, decrease returns to bidder firms, and to reduce the volume and profitability of takeovers. This problem is reduced to some degree by the decision of the U.S. Supreme Court announced June 24, 1982. By a vote of six to three the Court ruled invalid the Illinois Business Takeover Act which required a company to give state officials 20 days advance notice before offering to buy the shares of another firm. Illinois was one of 36 states that had passed laws regulating corporate acquisitions. The Supreme Court held that the Illinois law unconstitutionally interfered with interstate commerce.

C. STUDIES OF ANTITRUST CASES

Other studies which provide information on the role of mergers are those which analyze antitrust episodes. This was the major emphasis of the Ellert [1975, 1976] studies referred to above. Ellert analyzed the data for 205 defendants in antimerger complaints initiated by the Justice Department and Federal Trade Commission under Section 7 of the Clayton Act for the period 1950–1972. Of the complaints, 121 were issued by the Justice Department and 84 by the FTC. Ellert observes that the government had not lost a single Supreme Court merger case after the 1950 revision to the Clayton Act. In 60% of the cases studied, defendants canceled merger plans or were ordered to divest part or all of the assets previously acquired. The average duration of litigation measured by the interval between the filing of the complaint and the entry of the last judicial order was 34 months.

Ellert analyzes the behavior of the data for the 205 defendants and also the two groups broken into 123 defendants ordered to divest acquired assets and 82 defendants not required to divest assets. For both groups of defendants for a period preceding the filing of a merger complaint by four years, the residual performance was positive and statistically significant for both groups. The cumulative average residual was over 18% for defendants ordered to divest and about 13% for defendants not required to divest. For the 48 months prior to the filing of the merger complaint, defendants required to divest achieved a further positive residual that was statistically significant. For the same 48 months proximate to the filing of the merger complaint, defendants not required to divest had returns that were not statistically different from the average for the market. In the 12 months preceding the merger complaint, the residual performance was not statistically significant for either class of defendants.

On the filing of the merger complaint, the average portfolio residual declines by 1.86% for defendants ordered to divest and 1.79% for defendants not required to divest. While these percentages are small, they represent substantial absolute amounts when applied to the large dollar amount of assets involved. In the post-war period these percentages translate into an average dollar loss per respondent of about $7.5 million.

Following the filing of the merger complaint the behavior of the residuals is not statistically significant. This is true for the period between the filing of the merger complaint and the settlement of the litigation. Also, in the 48-month period following the settlement of the litigation, the behavior of the returns to the companies is not statistically different from the market as a whole. It is of interest to note also that final settlements which resolve future uncertainties are typically followed by statistically insignificant behavior of the residuals. On the other hand, settlements such as *nolo contendere,* which are more likely to be followed by private triple damage suits, result in a persistence of negative residuals that are statistically significant.

It is somewhat surprising that the magnitude of the negative movement in the residuals upon the filing of a complaint is relatively small. The $7–8 million involved is mainly accounted for by litigation costs. A possible explanation may be that there was no basis for bringing the complaint in the first place and that, therefore, nothing significant could be expected to be accomplished in the final action taken by the antitrust authorities. Ellert observes that these results "are also consistent with nonmonopolistic hypotheses of merger motivation. If merger is viewed as a means of expanding the operations of an efficient management group, a specific divestiture of assets would not be expected to constitute a large threat to stockholders, particularly if the firm may substitute internal expansion or external acquisitions in other markets in the future." [1976, p. 727.]

A similar explanation is related to case selection by the FTC and the Department of Justice. Ellert [1975, pp. 66–67] observed the following:

> *Observance of positive residuals in the pre-complaint stage is also consistent with a 'harassment' hypothesis. The argument here is that the administrative procedures of the Commission lead it to select firms which, from a variety of competitive pursuits, have experienced abnormally good stock price performance. Whereas the FTC bears the entire financial burden for prosecuting a case, most of its investigations are prompted by complaints from competing firms ... The Commission does not disclose the identity of a complaining party. These arrangements create an incentive to invoke the administrative process as a means to harass competitors. If the objective of harassment is to increase the production costs of a rival, it is likely that the prime targets would be among the innovative and most profitable of firms. By their performance, these firms constitute the greatest threat to the complainants within a dynamic competitive framework.*

Thus acquiring firms had a record of effective management of assets in the years preceding their merger activity. Ellert also observes that companies acquired were typically those whose premerger performance was consistent with ineffective management of assets. This is consistent with the role of mergers as performing a useful economic function in reallocating resources from less efficient to more efficient users.

Both Stillman [1980] and Eckbo [1981] analyze the residuals of the rivals to firms participating in mergers. They sought to distinguish between the possible efficiency vs. monopolization effects of mergers. The problem is somewhat complex because at the theoretical level alternative hypotheses can be formulated. The complexity is illustrated by Table 18.1.

In Table 18.1 three event dates are identified. They are announcement dates with respect to the merger, to its challenge by the antitrust authorities, and the announcement of a government decision. For firms participating in the merger, the

Table 18.1 Alternative Hypotheses of Merger Effects

Participating Firms	*Rival Firms*
I. Announcement of merger	
Collusion + Higher profits from colluding	+ Are part of the collusion
Efficiency + External investment with large positive NPV	+ Demonstrate how to achieve greater efficiency
	− Tougher competition
	0 Competition in marketplace unaffected by purchase of undervalued firm
II. Announcement of challenge	
Collusion − Collusion prevented	− Collusion prevented
Efficiency − Prevents a positive NPV investment, also litigation costs	+ Threat of more efficient rivals reduced
	− Also prevented from mergers for efficiency
0 Could do same thing internally	0 Can do internally
III. Announcement of decision	
Collusion − Collusion definitely prevented	− Collusion prevented
	+ Defendants prevented from being more efficient
0 (1) Negative impact already, at challenge date	0 (1) Negative impact already, at challenge date
(2) Leakage of likely judicial decision during trial	(2) Leakage of likely judicial decision during trial
(3) Underlying economics of the industry not affected	(3) Underlying economics of the industry not affected
Efficiency + Increased efficiency	+ Can now legally merge for efficiency
	− Tougher competition
	0 Could have accomplished the same thing internally

second column of Table 18.1 indicates that the predicted signs of the CARs are the same for the collusion vs. efficiency hypotheses at the times of the announcements of the merger and its challenge. It was for the purpose of sharpening the analysis that the residuals for rival firms were analyzed. But as the final column of Table 18.1 indicates, there is considerable overlap in the predicted signs for the alternative collusion and efficiency hypotheses. Nevertheless the pattern of these relationships is such that some judgments can be formulated.

Specifically, at the merger announcement date, if the sign of the effect on rivals is not positive, this is consistent with efficiency because efficiency can have a negative or zero sign. Similarly, at the date of the merger challenge, if the effect on the abnormal returns of rivals is not negative, this also is consistent with efficiency which can also take on a positive or zero sign. In general, when the effect on the CARs is the same for both participants and rivals, it is not possible to distinguish between collusion and efficiency. If the signs differ, then the two groups are affected differently, which tends to rule out the collusion hypothesis. However, at the decision date, the results are more difficult to interpret. This is because the effects on rivals can take any of the three possible signs for either outcome. In the light of the general framework presented, let us now look at the empirical results that have been compiled.

Stillman [1980] found that the effect of 30 major challenged horizontal mergers on the residuals of rivals was not statistically significant. The concentration-collusion theory argues that positive residuals should have been observed when the merger was in process and negative residuals when it was challenged. Lack of significance was observed both in relation to the original merger proposal and when it was challenged. Since the effect on rivals was not statistically significant, this casts doubt on the concentration-collusion theory that the mergers were in fact viewed as opportunities for increased possibilities of collusion among the firm's major rivals in the industry.

Eckbo [1981] extended the Stillman study, using a larger sample and a "control" sample of vertical mergers. Eckbo finds that on the announcement of the mergers, there are positive residuals both for the participants and their major rivals. This appears to be consistent with the monopoly theory. It is not unambiguous, though, because one could also argue that the announcement of the proposed merger conveys information to rivals of opportunities for increased efficiency by expanding scale. Eckbo further finds that at the announcement of the filing of a suit by the antitrust authorities, there is not much effect on the residuals of either the participants or their rivals; in fact, in cases brought by the Federal Trade Commission the effect on rivals is slightly positive. This is consistent with the explanation that the merger partners would have been more efficient and the rivals are protected from this increased efficiency by the Federal Trade Commission suit blocking the merger. Eckbo concludes that the positive performance of rivals of challenged mergers at the time of the original merger announcement reflects information conveyed by the proposed merger that efficiencies can be achieved by expanding scale either internally or externally.

The three studies appear to support the efficiency basis for mergers. Ellert emphasized that acquiring firms had positive residuals in prior years and acquired firms had negative residuals in prior years. Stillman's evidence was that rival firms did not benefit from the announcement of proposed mergers, which is inconsistent with the concentration-collusion hypothesis. Eckbo found positive residuals on the merger announcement, but no negative effects on rivals when it appeared that the merger would be blocked by the antitrust authorities. He interprets his pattern of relationships as indicating that the main effect of the merger is to signal the possibility for achieving economies for the merging firms, providing information to rivals that such economies may also be available to them.

D. CORPORATE GOVERNANCE

A number of other studies deal with corporate governance aspects of mergers and tender offer activity. In our judgment, the main significance of such studies is to emphasize the role of mergers and tender offers in dealing with agency problems. If the firm is not being managed in the best interests of shareholders, another group may see opportunities for increasing the value of the firm. The studies that will be treated next deal with this and related issues.

1. Grossman and Hart

Grossman and Hart [1980] deal with the problem that in a takeover bid, individual shareholders, anticipating a rise in the share price, may refuse to tender their shares, thus "free-riding" on the value added by the bidder activity. The reduction in returns to bidder activity may cause underinvestment in acquisition activity. Grossman and Hart analyze how to deal with the free-rider problem. They seek to formulate a set of rules of the game so that if some of the shareholders do not tender, there will be some risk that they will have something to lose. The rules, it is hoped, will result in an optimal amount of acquisition activity.

Grossman and Hart observe that it is possible to avoid the free-rider problem by providing for a contract written into the charter of the firm itself that permits the bidder to "expropriate" the shareholders remaining after the takeover to the extent of a dilution factor they call ϕ. This expropriation may be accomplished by selling assets or output of the firm to another firm owned by the new control group at prices below market value.

What Grossman and Hart are seeking to achieve is best understood in the light of socially desirable mergers, acquisitions, and takeovers. From a social standpoint, they should have a positive NPV. For value to be created, the bidding firm does something after the target firm is acquired. It changes the target firm in ways that will add value. Usually this involves the expenditure of resources by the bidding firm; at a minimum, it involves the expenditures required to research and to take over a company. The problem is that after the acquisition, all shareholders share proportionately in any gains that are created. Because the old shareholders participate proportionately in the gains, this reduces the incentive to bidder firms to make investments which create additional value. From a social viewpoint, this may lead to underinvestment in acquisition activity. The goal is to formulate rules of the game so that those who spend the resources are enabled to capture a portion of the gains commensurate with the resources they have committed and the risks they have incurred.

One of the implications of the Grossman and Hart model is the use of two-tier tender offers. A higher price and better terms, such as permitting a choice of cash or stock to fit the tax needs of the tendering shareholder, may be used on the first block of shares required for control. For the remaining shares the price is lower and the form of payment may be less attractive, such as the debt or preferred stock of the acquiring company. So shareholders have a strong incentive to tender in the first group rather than in the residual group. The first-tier offer is likely to be oversubscribed and, therefore, handled on a pro-rata basis by the acquiring company. The real price realized by tendering shareholders is an average of the first tier and second tier arrangements. Thus differential prices can be used to increase the probability of success of the tender offer. The possibility of such an arrangement permits the dilution factor ϕ that will be set in the original charter to be much lower than otherwise.

An illustration of this two-tier bidding is provided in the U.S. Steel tender for Marathon Oil which took place in early 1982. The first step was the bid by U.S. Steel on November 5, 1981, for 30 million Marathon common shares at a price of $125 per share. The second step was the provision that on the effective date of the merger each remaining shareholder of Marathon would be entitled to receive for each common share $100 principal amount of $12\frac{1}{2}$ percent guaranteed notes due 1994. Some dissatisfaction was expressed with the second step because the market value of the notes offered appeared to be in the $70 range. This offer represented an average value of $106 for Marathon shares. This was relatively close to Mobil's competing bid which was valued at $108. When the U.S. Steel bid was approved by shareholders on March 11, 1982, the value of the notes was $76, and the tender was valued at $101 per Marathon share.

However, it is more appropriate to view the two steps as the components of a single price. [Brudney and Chirelstein, 1978.] The two steps should be recognized as a useful social device for increasing the probability of success of tender offers. Thus it is a useful method of dealing with the managerial agency problem. Furthermore, competition among firms that make tender offers will push up the level of the average price in the two-part transaction. Grossman and Hart conclude that U.S. government policy on takeover bids from the Williams Act in 1968 to the present may have undesirable consequences. The disclosure provisions of the Williams Act require a bidder to make an announcement of intentions after buying 5% of the company. This encourages competition from other bidders but also aggravates the free-rider problem.

2. DeAngelo and Rice

Antitakeover amendments to corporate charters are studied by DeAngelo and Rice [1981]. Antitakeover amendments make the transfer of corporate control more difficult. DeAngelo and Rice analyzed a sample of 100 firms proposing amendments between 1974–1979. The main types of amendments found may be briefly described: (1) A staggered board typically requires that one-third of the board would be elected each year for a three-year term, delaying the point at which a new majority shareholder could gain board control. In the DeAngelo-Rice sample 53% had this provision. (2) A supermajority rule would require more than 50% approval for a merger, typically 67–80%. (3) What they call a fair merger price is essentially an antidiscriminatory treatment provision. A typical stipulation is that remaining shareholders receive compensation at least as large as the maximum share price paid to acquire majority control. Other provisions strengthen the position of the board of directors (usually management controlled), further limiting stockholders (particularly a new control group). Lockup provisions prevent circumvention of the antitakeover provisions and are typically adopted contemporaneously.

DeAngelo and Rice consider two hypotheses to explain antitakeover amendments. The managerial-entrenchment hypothesis states that incumbent management seeks job security at the expense of shareholders. It implies that the amendments increase the costs and weaken the disciplinary mechanisms in the stockholder/manager agency relationship. The managerial-entrenchment hypothesis predicts a negative share price reaction to proposed antitakeover amendments.

The stockholder-interests hypothesis holds that target shareholders may benefit from contractual mechanisms which enforce a cartelized response to an offer for control. The antitakeover amendments may place the target shareholders in a better bargaining position to obtain a higher price premium in a takeover. Subsidiary arguments might be that the provisions represent a type of long-term employment contract for managers, giving them incentives to pursue long-run maximization goals rather than short-term objectives.

In DeAngelo and Rice's empirical tests the mailing date of the proxy announcement is used as the best estimate of the date the amendments are compounded in the stock price. The analysis of daily returns indicates a weakly negative price impact, which is statistically insignificant. The methodology was varied in a number of ways without altering these results. DeAngelo and Rice observe that their tests may be biased against the managerial-entrenchment hypothesis because the proposal of antitakeover amendments may signal an increased probability that the firm will be approached with a merger or tender offer. Since stockholders in acquired firms typically earn positive abnormal returns, such a signal should impart an upward bias to the announcement return. The signaling hypothesis would imply positive returns; the management entrenchment hypothesis implies negative returns. The net effect of the two influences is uncertain. Their observance of nonsignificant negative returns implies that without the positive signaling influence the returns would be more strongly negative, consistent with the management entrenchment motive for antitakeover amendments.

3. Linn and McConnell

Linn and McConnell [1982] study a larger sample of 475 instances, proposed by 398 New York Stock Exchange corporations between January 1960 and December 1980. Most observations were clustered in the 1968–1970 and 1975–1978 years, with

97% appearing after January 1968. They investigated three alternative event dates: the date the amendments were ratified by the board of directors; the date of proxy mailing; and the date of the ratification vote at shareholder meetings. They also investigated intervals between these "events."

Linn and McConnell generally find positive but insignificant effects of the antitakeover amendment activity on stock prices. As a further check, they seek to measure the impact of the change in the Delaware corporation code in June 1969, which eliminated the supermajority approval requirement for mergers. The change in the Delaware law appeared to have a negative impact on stock prices. They also studied a small sample of antitakeover amendments that were rescinded. The results appeared to be negative, but probably not significant. On a very small (10 firms) sample of defeated antitakeover amendments, the results are insignificantly positive.

The evidence and alternative hypotheses on the effects of antitakeover amendments on stock prices are conflicting. DeAngelo and Rice find a negative, but not significant, influence. Linn and McConnell find a positive effect of antitakeover amendments on share prices, but predominantly insignificant. The conclusion suggested is that there is no effect of antitakeover amendments on share prices; but if there is no effect, why should a firm use resources to enact takeover amendments? One possible answer is that the absence of any effect of antitakeover amendments on stock prices is consistent with the operation of an efficient market for managerial services as well as for merger and takeover activity. But the results are also consistent with other hypotheses.

4. Dann and DeAngelo

Dann and DeAngelo [1981] analyze standstill agreements and negotiated premium buybacks. Standstill agreements limit a substantial shareholder's ownership to less than a controlling percentage for a specified number of years. Negotiated premium buybacks represent the repurchase of a substantial shareholder's block at a premium; the buyback may be a part of a standstill agreement. Like the antitakeover amendments, these mechanisms also reduce competition in the market for corporate control by reducing the threat of takeover by a substantial shareholder.

Two alternative hypotheses are considered. The management entrenchment hypothesis argues that standstills and buybacks are used to reduce a takeover threat, thereby increasing the job security of managers and reducing the ability of the market for corporate control to deal with the agency problem or managerial inefficiency. Small individual shareholders do not have the incentives or resources to monitor managers effectively. However, the large block shareholder will gain substantially from an increase in efficiency and typically has the resources to take action. The alternative stockholder-interests hypothesis would argue that the market for managerial labor disciplines managerial efficiency under the threat of reduced compensation for ineffective performance. If the market for managerial labor is effective, then the actions of a shareholder who accumulates a large block of shares simply represent a power struggle between competing groups for corporate control. If only a power struggle is involved, the attendant costs will simply cause a reduction in the value of the stockholders' wealth. By avoiding the costs of a power struggle, the stockholders will benefit.

In their empirical tests of the competing hypotheses, Dann and DeAngelo take the first public announcement in the *Wall Street Journal* as the date when the standstill or buyback is compounded in the stock price. The sample included 81 firms with 19 pure standstills, 51 pure repurchases, and 11 standstills with repurchase. The average standstill period was five years, and the average maximum ownership interest permitted was 20% (in agreements without repurchase), and 0% (in standstills with repurchase). The average stake repurchased was 9.8% of outstanding stock, larger than the average open market repurchase (5%), but smaller than most tender offer repurchases (14–15%). The average premium in premium repurchases was 16.4% over the preannouncement price; this is similar to the average premium in tender offer repurchases.

The results indicated a significantly negative stock price impact at day −1 and day 0 for standstill agreements. The negative reaction was stronger for standstills with repurchase than for pure standstills. This reaction is consistent with the managerial-entrenchment hypothesis.

The results for negotiated buybacks were also negative, but were not very significant. (Again, the negative reaction was reinforced if the buyback was accompanied by a standstill agreement.) This does not strongly support the managerial entrenchment hypothesis, but it definitely does not support the stockholder interests hypothesis which predicts a positive price reaction. Despite the similarities with tender offer repurchases (or open market repurchases), negotiated buybacks do not have the same positive wealth impact (up to 16%).

5. Bradley and Wakeman

Bradley and Wakeman [1982] add several variations to the Dann-DeAngelo study. On single block repurchases the effects on the repurchasing firm are negative, and significantly so. These effects are reinforced when the repurchase is associated with the termination of a prior takeover effort by the selling group. Bradley and Wakeman seek to separate the wealth transfer effect from information effects. For the nonmerger group (that is, where the repurchase is not associated with a takeover termination), the information effects appear to be insignificant. Thus the wealth transfer implied by the repurchase premium is the dominant effect; however, while these effects are negative they are not significant for the nonmerger group. For the merger group, the information impact is negative for both firms, suggesting that the repurchase premium causes a positive NPV project to be abandoned.

Bradley and Wakeman also study repurchases from corporate officers. Scholes [1972] had found a negative reaction to insider sales, indicating that insiders possessed adverse information about the company. Bradley and Wakeman find a slight wealth gain, which they suggest is consistent with portfolio rebalancing by the insider, and the company's willingness to purchase their shares may signal the absence of adverse information. They suggest that secondary distributions (studied by Scholes) may reflect a decision by the company not to make the repurchase, thereby confirming a signal of adverse information.

The third area covered by Bradley and Wakeman is the repurchase of small shareholdings. A rationale is to decrease shareholder servicing costs. They observe that the 1.25% gain is large in relation to estimates of savings, indicating that the repurchase also represents a positive information signal.

6. Dodd and Warner

Dodd and Warner [1981] study proxy contests, examining issues similar to those treated by Dann and DeAngelo in analyzing the role of block holders of shares. Dodd and Warner observe that for the sample analyzed in their study, only 16 (about 15%) of the dissident groups were led by another firm. They say that this indicates a weak relationship between proxy contests and other takeover activity. An alternative view is that proxy contests may also be viewed as competing with other forms of takeover activity at the margin. At any rate, similar issues are involved.

One hypothesis is that proxy contests are motivated to deal with the agency problem. Since boards of directors are generally dominated by management, to the extent that the board does not act in the best interests of shareholders, a proxy contest may be viewed as a form of managerial labor market discipline. If so, proxy contests should result in higher share prices. An alternative hypothesis is that a proxy contest is simply a power struggle for the control of the firm. If so, share prices should not be affected or should fall because of the expenditure of company resources in defending incumbents.

The Dodd-Warner sample covered 96 proxy contests between 1962 and 1978. 71 were control contests (the dissidents sought 50% or more of board seats); 25 were participation contests (the dissidents sought minority representation). Three events are pertinent: (1) The first announcement of the contest in the *Wall Street Journal;* (2) The stockholder meeting and election; and (3) The announcement of the election outcome.

Contrary to the improved-management hypothesis, there is little evidence of poor performance in the months and years preceding the contest. There is evidence of significant positive abnormal performance in the five months preceding the contest announcement. Daily returns show cumulative returns of +11.9 percent over the 60 days up to and including the announcement date. This is almost certainly related to the contest rather than to another simultaneous event: (1) The abnormal performance is concentrated in the days very close to the announcement; and (2) The *Wall Street Journal* announcement often comes relatively late in the proxy contest process, and preannouncement leakage is great. Positive performance persists in both control and participation contests (higher in control contests), and regardless of the eventual outcome (although it is higher for successful dissident groups).

Significant negative abnormal returns are observed in the period from the announcement through the election outcome; the mean cumulative residual is −4.3%. These returns are concentrated in control contests, but participation contests also exhibit insignificantly negative returns during this interim period. Again, these results persist in spite of outcome. Although these negative returns indicate that at least some of the preannouncement gains are not permanent, the net result over the entire period surrounding the contest remains positive for the entire sample.

Dodd and Warner conclude that proxy contests are associated with significant share price appreciation of an average magnitude of 5 to 10%, consistent with the improved management of corporate resources hypothesis. That the positive performance persists regardless of contest outcome indicates that it is the challenge per se that results in improved corporate performance. The erosion of early share price gains can be partly explained by the prior overvaluation caused by increased demand for the stock before the holder-of-record date.

E. GENERALIZATIONS FROM THE STUDIES

While the numerous studies reviewed are not always in complete agreement, some generalizations can be formulated on the basis of the dominant patterns observed. These generalizations relate to an evaluation of the role of mergers and related activities such as proxy contests on a number of important issues of corporate financial theory and policy.

For acquired firms, from the period just before the merger announcement date, the shareholders achieve significant positive gains. In an earlier period, the cumulative average residuals are negative, indicating that acquired firms had not been performing up to their potentials.

On average for the period just before the merger announcement date the shareholders of acquiring firms neither gained nor lost. But in tender offers where the negotiation period is shorter, gains for the shareholders of acquiring firms tend to be significantly positive. The conclusion indicated is that legislative enactments which have delayed the completion of tender offers have also reduced the gains for acquiring firms.

In earlier periods the CARs for acquiring firms are positive, indicating that acquiring firms have had a record of managing asset growth successfully. This leads to the further hypothesis that in pure conglomerate mergers the prospective depletion of internal investment opportunities leads acquiring firms to look to other industries where growth prospects are more attractive and to seek out firms that appear less capable of responding to these favorable prospects. [Chung, 1982.]

Some studies indicate that the CARs decline after the merger or tender offer. However, this appears to be accounted for by the nature of the industries in which the acquiring firms mainly operate. Netting out the industry effect, the CARs do not decline after the merger. These results contradict both the managerialism theory and the theory that mergers are not based on valid economic or business reasons.

Analysis of unsuccessful tender offers permits a further sharpening of the analysis among competing theories. The monopoly theory would hold that an unsuccessful tender offer should result in negative residuals for shareholders of both acquiring and acquired firms, since the gains from the monopoly rents will be lost. The managerialism theory predicts that shareholders of the acquiring firm would gain, since the proposed tender offer was uneconomic in the first place; aborting the combination therefore would be a blessing to shareholders of the acquiring firm. To the extent that these acquiring firms were ready to overpay the shareholders of the targets, the latter shareholders would lose if the tender offer does not succeed. An alternative theory would be that since the potentials for improving the management of the acquired firm or the possibilities of synergy between an acquiring and an acquired firm have been discovered and brought to light, no market reaction will occur when a particular tender offer is unsuccessful. The empirical results are that after unsuccessful tender offers there is no significant change in the CARs of the acquired firms. This is consistent with the new-information hypothesis. The effect on the bidding firms would be predicted to be negative because they have spent resources in search and costs of formulating the offer, and now these investments have no fruition. The data confirm that the residuals are negative, but they are not significant. [Dodd and Ruback, p. 368.] One reason why the negative residuals are not significant is that the market may view bidder firms as engaged in a series of tender offer attempts, because they have a track record of managing assets effectively. Hence the market reacts negatively if search costs for specific tender offers fall through. But taking a longer view [à la Schipper and Thompson], the market judges that this experience will be put to good use in other tender and merger activities.

The differences in results obtained may be explained in part by the signaling effect of the type of compensation used in an acquisition [H. and L. E. DeAngelo, 1982]. If a firm uses stock in the acquisition, this may imply that it considers its stock to be overvalued. If a firm uses cash, this may reflect the firm's judgment that its own stock is too valuable to use—it is undervalued. [Cf. Myers and Majluf, 1982 for a similar hypothesis with respect to internal investment decisions.] The empirical studies are consistent with this information hypothesis. The Bradley study is of cash tender offers, Dodd and Ruback study both cash and stock exchanges, and the Dodd study is on mergers with mainly stock swaps. Bradley found positive returns to acquiring firms, Dodd negative returns, and Dodd and Ruback no significant effects. When cash is used, this may signal that the stock of the acquiring firm is undervalued, and conversely when stock is used for the purchase. When both cash and stock are used, the two effects may be counterbalancing.

The studies of the effects of merger activity on rivals seek to distinguish between monopoly and efficiency motives for mergers. The concentration-collusion theory holds that there would be positive effects on rivals upon the announcement of major horizontal mergers. The evidence is somewhat conflicting on this point. The concentration-collusion theory also holds that when the government authorities make a final decision to prevent a merger the effects should be negative residuals for the rivals as well as for the participant firms. However, there appear to be no significant effects on any of the groups. This is inconsistent with the monopoly hypothesis. It may be that, regardless of the actions taken by the antitrust authorities, the underlying economic forces of the industry have now been identified. It would appear that opportunities for efficiencies will be effectuated internally if they are not permitted to take place externally. If there are no monopoly effects from the horizontal mergers, and if the economic results are ultimately the same, then the antitrust activities represent extra costs in the economic resource allocation process which delay the achievement of potential improvements in efficiency.

The corporate governance studies portray an important role for merger and take-over activity (including proxy contests) in utilizing the market for corporate control to deal with agency problems. The literature is not in agreement on whether the market for managerial labor and various forms of settling up in compensation contracts are sufficient to deal with the agency problem. However, it would be plausible that the market for corporate control, the threat of takeovers, and the market for managers all operate to deal with the agency problem. Grossman and Hart treat the free-rider problem in the functioning of the market for takeovers. Charter provisions for dilution after the completion of a merger or two-tier merger proposals are among the mechanisms for dealing with the free-rider problem.

Some studies indicate that antitakeover provisions, standstill agreements, and buyback provisions may have a negative, but not significant, influence on share prices. Other tests find a positive but not significant influence. Together the studies suggest no significant effect. This result could be consistent with an efficiently operating market for managers and a competitive market for corporate acquisitions. The Dodd-Warner study suggests that proxy contests represent an alternative at the margin for making the market for corporate control more effective. Their results are consistent with the hypothesis that proxy contests are not simply power struggles, but are associated with changes that result in the improvement of share price performance of the firm. These studies highlight the importance of the agency problem introduced into the literature by Jensen and Meckling [1976].

We view mergers and tender offers as a part of the general process of resource allocation in the economy. We would regard internal investments and external investments as alternatives that are not necessarily substitutable or mutually exclusive. Sometimes circumstances suggest the use of internal investments; other times, they suggest external investments. Particularly in long-range strategic planning it may appear that it will be less risky and hence more likely to produce a positive net present value if management capabilities are augmented by combining with an existing ongoing investment—another firm. On the other hand, internal investments made in areas in which management has had historical experience may involve less risk in that unexpected events or surprises may be less likely. Buying another firm may involve less than complete information and characteristics that may have been hidden from outsiders. Particularly when an acquiring firm sees investment opportunities unattractive in familiar areas and seeks to augment its capabilities by combining with firms in completely different types of operations, the risk of making investment mistakes is increased. Merger activity from a capability base to achieve expansion into concentrically related areas appears to offer prospects of the greatest success. [Rumelt, 1974.]

We would expect that soundly conceived internal investments as well as soundly conceived external investments will, on average, have positive net present values. We see no theoretical basis for arguing that either form of investment would be superior in the long run. Both internal and external investments have appropriate roles to perform in the resource allocation processes of the economy and in the efforts of individual organizations to maximize their value.

In the first part of this chapter we dealt with tests of alternative merger theories. In the second part we deal with managerial implications of the foregoing material. First, we consider terms of mergers; second, we consider merger analysis in a valuation framework.

F. TERMS OF MERGERS

Larson and Gonedes [1969] set forth a model of exchange-ratio determination. They reject the effect of mergers on earnings per share as a test and argue that the effects of mergers on market value would be an appropriate test. The market values of common stocks are used to determine the precombination wealth positions of the parties involved in a merger, and the result is compared with the postmerger wealth positions of the parties. Since the Larson-Gonedes decision horizon is the immediate postmerger market values, the postmerger price-earnings ratio of the merged firm receives their greatest emphasis. They observe that the earnings multiple of a combined firm will be a weighted average of the earnings multiples of the constituent firms if (1) the growth rate of the combined entity is a weighted average of its constituents' growth rates, and (2) the riskiness of earnings stream of the combined entity is a weighted average of the earnings streams (p. 722). The earnings multiple of a merged firm will exceed the average of its constituents' earnings multiples if the new growth rate exceeds the average of the constituents' growth rates. The earnings multiple of a combined entity will also be affected by its risk. The risk of the combined firm will be decreased, increased, or remain the same depending upon whether the covariance of the earnings stream with the market is decreased, increased, or remains the same.

The Larson-Gonedes model holds that the exchange ratio will be determined by each firm's assessment of the postmerger price-earnings multiple and postulates that each firm requires that its equivalent price per share be at least maintained as a result of the merger. Their model is summarized algebraically and graphically by Conn and Nielsen [1977], using the following symbols:

ER = exchange ratio,

P = price per share,

EPS = earnings per share,

PE = price-earnings multiple,

E = earnings,

S = number of common shares outstanding,

AER = actual exchange ratio.

In the formulations which follow, subscripts 1, 2, and 12 are used to refer to the acquiring, acquired, and combined firms, respectively.

An exchange ratio is determined depending upon postmerger advantages expected from the combined firm subject to the stockholder wealth constraint. This is expressed as follows:

$$P_{12} \geq P_1, \tag{18.4}$$

We use the equality relationship. The market price per share for the combined firm is defined in terms of earnings and the price-earnings ratio as

$$P_{12} \equiv (PE_{12})(EPS_{12}) \equiv P_1. \tag{18.5}$$

The expression for the earnings per share of the combined firm is then detailed as follows:

$$EPS_{12} = \frac{E_1 + E_2}{S_1 + S_2(ER_1)} . \tag{18.6}$$

In this equation, ER_1 represents the exchange ratio of shares of firm 2 for shares of firm 1 from the perspective of firm 1. In Eq. (18.7), Eq. (18.6) is used to restate Eq. (18.5):

$$P_1 = \frac{(PE_{12})(E_1 + E_2)}{S_1 + S_2(ER_1)} . \tag{18.7}$$

Equation (18.7) is then solved for ER_1 to yield Eq. (18.8a):

$$ER_1 = -\frac{S_1}{S_2} + \frac{(E_1 + E_2)}{P_1 S_2} PE_{12}. \tag{18.8a}$$

An example will illustrate the nature of Eq. (18.8a) and some subsequent relationships. Let us assume that firm 1 and firm 2 are contemplating a merger in which firm 1 will acquire firm 2. Table 18.2 contains the information gathered about the two firms.

Using the data from Table 18.2 in Eq. (18.8a), we obtain

$$ER_1 = -\tfrac{100}{100} + \tfrac{400}{2000} PE_{12}, \tag{18.8b}$$

which is expressed in simplified form as

$$ER_1 = -1 + \tfrac{1}{5} PE_{12}. \tag{18.8c}$$

Table 18.2

	Total Earnings, E	Number of Shares of Common Stock, S	Earnings Per Share, EPS	Price-Earnings Ratio, PE	Market Price Per Common Share, P
Firm 1	$200	100	$2.00	10	$20
Firm 2	$200	100	$2.00	20	$40

We then use some illustrative values of PE_{12} to indicate the required maximum exchange ratio that firm 1 may offer the shareholders of firm 2 if the wealth constraint for the shareholders of firm 1 is to be satisfied:

PE_{12}	0	7	10	11	12	15	20	30
Max. ER_1	−1	0.4	1	1.2	1.4	2.0	3.0	5.0

These data, of course, plot on a straight line as illustrated in Fig. 18.1. We have discussed the maximum ER_1. Let us now consider the minimum ER_2 that may be accepted by the shareholders of firm 2 if their wealth constraint is to be satisfied. Their basic requirement is

$$P_{12} \geq P_2/ER_2 \qquad (18.9)$$

Using the equality form of Eq. (18.9), we rewrite it utilizing the accounting determination of P_1. This is simply the price-earnings ratio times the earnings per share for the combined firm,

$$P_{12} = (PE_{12})(EPS_{12}) = \frac{P_2}{ER_2}, \qquad (18.10a)$$

and substituting for the earnings per share from Eq. (18.6),

$$P_{12} = \frac{P_2}{ER_2} = \frac{(PE_{12})(E_1 + E_2)}{S_1 + S_2(ER_2)} \qquad (18.10b)$$

We then solve for ER_2:

$$\frac{P_2 S_1 + P_2 S_2(ER_2)}{ER_2} = (PE_{12})(E_1 + E_2),$$

$$ER_2 = \frac{P_2 S_1}{(PE_{12})(E_1 + E_2) - P_2 S_2}. \qquad (18.11a)$$

Substituting the numerical values of our example, we obtain

$$ER_2 = \frac{4000}{400PE_{12} - 4000} = \frac{10}{PE_{12} - 10}. \qquad (18.11b)$$

Again, we show the nature of the relationship conveyed by Eq. (18.11b) by calculating values of ER_2 for a range of values of PE_{12}.

PE_{12}	11	12	15	20	30
Min. ER_2	10	5	2	1	0.5

The above data are plotted in Fig. 18.1; as indicated, ER_2 is in the form of a hyperbola. Two relationships of significance are portrayed in the figure. One is the intersection of the two ER-lines. The other is the four quadrants formed by the two lines. The two ER-lines intersect at a PE_{12} of 15, and $ER_1 = ER_2 = 2$. Thus, at an exchange ratio of 2 and a PE_{12} of 15, neither firm will have immediate gains or losses from the merger. The PE_{12} that brings about this result represents a weighted average of

Figure 18.1
Influence of AER and PE_{12} on merger gains and losses.

the two PE-ratios. The weighted average can be expressed in two forms as shown below:

$$PE_{12}^* = \frac{P_1 S_1 + P_2 S_2}{E_1 + E_2} = \frac{2000 + 4000}{400} = 15 \qquad (18.12a)$$

$$= \frac{(PE_1)S_1 + (PE_2)S_2}{S_1 + S_2} = \frac{1000 + 2000}{200} = 15. \qquad (18.12b)$$

By the shareholder wealth constraint formulated by Larson-Gonedes, the actual exchange ratio (AER) should be bounded by quadrant I, in which the shareholders of both firms gain from the merger. In the other three quadrants, the shareholders of one or both firms will suffer a wealth loss. The calculation of merger premiums and discounts can be illustrated using the data of our example both numerically as shown in Table 18.3 and graphically as in Fig. 18.1. Four cases are presented in the table illustrating results for each of the four quadrants. For various combinations of the actual exchange ratio and illustrative values of PE_{12}, the resulting equivalent prices for the shareholders of firm 1 and firm 2 are shown in the columns headed by P_{12} and P_2^*, respectively. In the following two columns, the premium or discount for the shareholder of each firm is calculated. The corresponding merger premium in graphic terms as measured in Fig. 18.1 is then shown in the final two columns of Table 18.3.

Conn and Nielsen calculated the premium or discount combinations for major mergers defined as involving an acquired firm with assets of at least $10 million prior to the merger. The period covered was 1960 through 1969 for a sample of 131 mergers. To avoid premerger announcement effects, the variables P_1 and P_2

Table 18.3   Calculation of Merger Premiums or Discounts

Case	AER	PE_{12}	P_{12}	P_2^*	$(P_{12}-P_1)/P_1$	$(P_2^*-P_2)/P_2$	1	2
					Premium or (discount)		*Merger Premium to*	
1	2.5	20	22.86	57.15	+14.3%	+42.9%	AB	BC
2	2.5	16	18.29	45.72	− 8.6%	+14.3%	−FG	FH
3	2.5	12	13.71	34.28	−31.4%	−14.3%	−KM	−JK
4	1.0	12	24.00	24.00	+20.0%	−40.0%	MN	−JN

$P_2^* =$ value of P_2 on the basis of the AER $= P_{12}AER$

$$P_{12} = (PE_{12})(EPS_{12}) = \frac{(PE_{12})(E_1 + E_2)}{S_1 + S_2(ER)}$$

$$Case\ 1: P_{12} = \frac{20(400)}{100 + 100(2.5)} = \frac{8000}{350} = \$22.86.$$

$$Case\ 2: P_{12} = \frac{16(400)}{350} = \frac{6400}{350} = \$18.29.$$

$$Case\ 3: P_{12} = \frac{12(400)}{350} = \frac{4800}{350} = \$13.71.$$

$$Case\ 4: P_{12} = \frac{12(400)}{100 + 100(1.0)} = \frac{4800}{200} = \$24.00.$$

were calculated using an average of monthly high and low share prices during the period three to five months prior to the month of merger announcement. The postmerger results were calculated for the month following the consummation of the merger.

Conn and Nielsen make the calculations with reference to announcement date, merger consummation date, and for the month following the consummation of the merger. The results are summarized in Table 18.4.

Two statistical tests were employed by Conn and Nielsen. A nonparametric chi-square test of the hypothesis of equal likelihood that a merger will fall in any one of the four quadrants is rejected at the 1% level. A first-difference test of the Larson-Gonedes model was also statistically significant. Conn and Nielsen observed that the statistical tests supported the Larson-Gonedes model, but they also noted and were concerned about the relatively large 40% of the mergers which did not fall into quadrant I. But rarely did the stockholders of the acquiring firm gain while the acquired stockholders lost. In any event, the pattern suggests a competitive market among acquiring firms in merger activity.

Conn and Nielsen noted that a large number of mergers fell into quadrant III; in these mergers, the postmerger market valuation of the combined entity was less than the sum of the valuations of the acquiring and acquired firms prior to the merger announcement. However, Conn and Nielsen acknowledged that leakages of merger information might occur even earlier than the three to five months lead time

Table 18.4 Number of Mergers by ex Post Quadrant and Changes in Quadrant Status From Month of Announcement to Month Following Merger Consummation

From Period of	To Period of											
	Announcement				Consummation				Month following consummation			
	I	II	III	IV*	I	II	III	IV	I	II	III	IV
Announcement												
I	78				66	8	3	1	60	14	3	1
II		36			4	25	7	0	5	23	8	0
III			12		0	3	8	1	1	3	5	3
IV				5	2	0	1	2	1	0	2	2
Consummation												
I					72				64	7	0	1
II						36			2	32	2	0
III							19		1	1	15	2
IV								4	0	0	1	3
Month following consummation												
I									67			
II										40		
III											18	
IV												6

* The roman numerals I, II, III, IV refer to the quadrants in which the *ex post* price-earnings ratios fall based on the prior decision rules.
Source: R. L. Conn and J. F. Nielsen, "An Empirical Test of the Larson-Gonedes Exchange Ratio Determination Model," *Journal of Finance*, June 1977, 754.

they used in their study. They also recognized that analyzing the effects of the merger only one month after the consummation date might be too restrictive. It would be of interest to analyze the results over longer periods of time subsequent to the merger. Finally, Conn and Nielsen did not provide any numerical measures of possible changes in risk resulting from the merger.

G. MANAGERIAL POLICIES IN A VALUATION FRAMEWORK

In the perspective of alternative merger theories and empirical tests, the foundation has been provided for guides to managerial policies toward merger and acquisition decisions. From an operational standpoint, mergers and acquisitions should be related

Table 18.5 Comparative Statistics for the Year Ended 1978

	Book Value Per Share	Price/ Earnings Ratio (P/E)	Number of Shares (millions)	Debt Ratio, % (B/S_A)	Beta for Existing Leverage	Internal Profit- ability Rate (r)	Invest- ment Rate (K)	Growth Rate (g)
Allison	$10.00	5.40	5	30	1.2	.04	0.1	.004
Connors	40.00	11.70	1	30	1.4	.12	1.5	.18
Dorden	40.00	9.88	1	30	1.6	.14	1.0	.14

to a firm's general planning framework. These requirements have been set forth in detail in other studies [Weston, 1970]. Here we focus on merger policies in a valuation framework. We make the concepts explicit by using an illustrative case example to convey the ideas.

The Allison Corporation is a manufacturer of materials handling equipment with heavy emphasis on forklift trucks. Because of a low internal profitability rate and lack of favorable investment opportunities in its existing line of business, Allison is considering a merger to achieve more favorable growth and profitability opportunities. It has made an extensive search of a large number of corporations and has narrowed the candidates to two firms, for a number of considerations. The Connors Corporation is a manufacturer of agricultural equipment and is strong in research and marketing. It has had high internal profitability and substantial investment opportunities. The Dorden Company is a manufacturer of plastic toys. It has a better profitability record than Connors.

Some relevant data on the three firms are summarized in Table 18.5.

Additional information on market parameters includes a risk-free rate, r_f, of 6% and an expected return on the market, $E(R_m)$, of 11%. Each firm pays a 10% interest rate on its debt. The tax rate, τ_c, of each is 50%. A period of 10 years is estimated for the duration of supernormal growth, T.

From the information provided we can first formulate the accounting balance sheets for the three firms (Table 18.6).

Dividing the internal profitability rate r by $(1 - \tau_c)$ and multiplying by total assets, we get the net operating income. From the net operating income we can obtain the market price per share and the total market value that would have to be paid for each of the three companies (Table 18.7).

Table 18.6 Accounting Balance Sheets (millions)

	Allison	Connors	Dorden
Debt	$15	$12	$12
Equity	50	40	40
Total assets	$65	$52	$52

Table 18.7   Market Price Per Share

	Allison	Connors	Dorden
1. Total assets (millions)	$65	$52	$52
2. Earning rate, $r \div (1 - \tau_c)$	.08	.24	.28
3. Net operating income (1) × (2) (millions)	$ 5.2	$12.48	$14.56
4. Interest on debt (millions)	1.5	1.20	1.20
5. Profit before tax (millions)	3.7	11.28	13.36
6. Taxes at 50% (millions)	1.85	5.64	6.68
7. Net income (millions)	1.85	5.64	6.68
8. Number of shares of common stock (millions)	5	1	1
9. Earnings per share of common stock, (7) ÷ (8)	$ .37	$ 5.64	$ 6.68
10. Price-earnings ratio (information provided)	5.4 ×	11.7 ×	9.88 ×
11. Market price per share, (9) × (10)	$ 2.00	$66.00	$66.00
12. Total market value of equity, (11) × (8) (millions)	$10	$66	$66

We now have earnings per share, market values per share, and total market values of equity for use in the subsequent analysis.

One popular criterion for evaluating desirability of making acquisitions from the standpoint of the acquiring company is to determine the effect on its earnings per share. Table 18.8 illustrates these effects based on the data in the present example.

Table 18.8

	Effects on Allison's Earnings per Share if it Merges:	
	With Connors	With Dorden
1. Number of new shares* (millions)	33	33
2. Existing shares (millions)	5	5
3. Total new shares (millions)	38	38
4. Earnings after taxes (millions of dollars)	5.64	6.68
5. Add Allison's after-tax earnings (millions of dollars)	1.85	1.85
6. Total new earnings (millions of dollars)	7.490	8.530
7. New earnings per share, (6) ÷ (3), $	.197	.224
8. Less Allison's old earnings per share, $	.370	.370
9. Net effect	(.173)	(.146)
10. Percent dilution [(9 ÷ 8)100]	47%	39%

* Each share of Connors and Dorden has a market value 33 times that of Allison. Hence 33 shares times the 1 million existing shares of Connors and Dorden is the total number of new Allison shares required.

It can be seen that the merger effects on Allison's earnings per share is a substantial decline. The percentage dilution in Allison's earnings per share would be 47% if Connors were acquired and 39% if Dorden were acquired. We believe that this widely used criterion is in error. It is the effect on market value that is relevant, not the effect on earnings per share.

In a valuation framework it is necessary to make a forecast of the key variables affecting value after the merger has taken place. This requires an in-depth business analysis of each proposed merger in terms of its impact on the key valuation factors. From the background provided, we observe that Allison is a manufacturer of materials handling equipment. Connors is a manufacturer of agricultural equipment with strength in research and marketing. Dorden is a manufacturer of plastic toys. While Dorden has a better profitability record than Connors, the toy industry is under the pressure of continuously creating new ideas and concepts if growth and profitability of a toy manufacturing firm are to continue. In addition, there seems to be less potential for favorable interaction of management capabilities in a merger between Allison and Dorden than there would be in a merger between Allison and Connors. Connors is known to have a strong research organization which may be able to develop new products in Allison's area of materials handling equipment. This merely sketches the kind of favorable carry-over of capabilities that may be achieved in a merger between Allison and Connors. Reflecting these qualitative considerations, the following estimates are made of the new financial parameters of the combined firms.

	NOI	*r*	*K*	*g*
Allison/Connors (AC)	18	.14	1.0	.14
Allison/Dorden (AD)	16	.13	1.0	.13

We can now proceed to evaluate the two alternative acquisition prospects, using a valuation analysis. First we calculate the new beta for the merged company under the two alternatives. We assume the beta for the combined companies is a market-value weighted average of the betas of the constituent companies. We use the new betas in the security market line equation to obtain the cost of equity capital for each of the two combined firms:

$$\beta_{AC} = 1.2 \left(\frac{10}{10+66} \right) + 1.4 \left(\frac{66}{10+66} \right)$$

$$= .1579 + 1.2158 = 1.374 = 1.37$$

$$k_e(AC) = R_f + [E(R_m) - R_f]\beta_{AC}$$

$$= .06 + [.05]1.37 = .1285 = 12.85\%$$

$$\beta_{AD} = 1.2 \left(\frac{10}{10+66} \right) + 1.6 \left(\frac{66}{10+66} \right)$$

$$= .1579 + 1.3895 = 1.547 = 1.55$$

$$k_e(AD) = .06 + .05(1.55),$$

$$= .1375 = 13.75\%$$

Given the debt cost of 10% and the cost of equity capital as calculated, we can then proceed to determine the weighted average cost of capital for the two combined firms.

	AC	AD
Debt, B	27	27
Equity, S	76	76
Value, V^L	103	103

We now continue our calculations:

$$\text{WACC} = k_0 = k_e(S/V) + k_d(1 - \tau_c)(B/V)$$

$$k_0(\text{AC}) = .1285(\tfrac{76}{103}) + .05(\tfrac{27}{103})$$

$$= .0948 + .0131 = .1079 = 10.8\%;$$

$$k_0(\text{AD}) = .1375(\tfrac{76}{103}) + .05(\tfrac{27}{103})$$

$$= .1015 + .0131 = .1146 = 11.5\%.$$

We now have all the information required to calculate the valuation of the two alternative combinations. We will use the Modigliani-Miller valuation model, Eq. (13.8), in the expressions below:

$$V^L = \frac{[E(\tilde{\text{NOI}})](1 - \tau_c)}{\rho} + \tau_c B + K[E(\tilde{\text{NOI}})](1 - \tau_c)\left[\frac{r - \text{WACC}}{\text{WACC}(1 + \text{WACC})}\right]T,$$

(13.8)

where

$K =$ the percent of earnings invested in new assets, $K \gtrless 1$,

$r =$ the tax-adjusted rate of return on new assets, $r > \text{WACC}$,

$T =$ the number of years during which $r > \text{WACC}$ (i.e., the number of years during which the firm experiences a rate of growth greater than the economy).

For ease of computation, we shall combine the first two terms in the equation. Equation (12.5) defined V^L as

$$V^L = \frac{E(\tilde{\text{NOI}})(1 - \tau_c)}{\rho} + \tau_c B.$$

(12.5)

In addition, Eq. (13.7) defined V^L as

$$V^L = \frac{E(\tilde{\text{NOI}})(1 - \tau_c)}{\text{WACC}} = \frac{E(\tilde{\text{NOI}})(1 - \tau_c)}{k_0}.$$

(13.7)

The two are equivalent formulations of V^L, so we can use the simpler, (13.7). We can now insert the numerical values to determine the value of the combined firm if Allison merges with Connors (AC) or alternatively with Dorden (AD). The results are shown below:

Merger AC:

$$V^L = \frac{18(.5)}{.108} + 1[18(.5)] \left[\frac{.14 - .108}{.108(1 + .108)} \right] 10$$

$$= 83.33 + 9 \left(\frac{.032}{.119664} \right) 10$$

$$= 83.33 + 90(.2674)$$

$$= 83.33 + 24.07$$

$$= 107.40 \approx 107.$$

Merger AD:

$$V^L = \frac{16(.5)}{.115} + 1[16(.5)] \left[\frac{.13 - .115}{.115(1 + .115)} \right] 10$$

$$= 69.57 + 8 \left(\frac{.015}{.128225} \right) 10$$

$$= 69.57 + 80(.1170)$$

$$= 69.57 + 9.36$$

$$= 78.93 \approx 79.$$

Using the results obtained, we make a summary comparison of the gains or losses from the two alternative mergers. The data are summarized in Table 18.9.

The data show that, based on estimates of the key parameters, a gain in value of $4 million would result from a merger between Allison and Connors. However, the merger between Allison and Dorden would result in a loss in valuation amounting to $24 million. We believe that comparing the effects on value represents the conceptually correct way of approaching merger analysis from a managerial standpoint. The results of this comparison permit some margin of error, yet clearly indicate that a

Table 18.9   Comparison of Two Mergers

	Allison/Connors (millions)	Allison/Dorden (millions)
Postmerger value, V	$107	$79
Less amount of debt, B	− 27	27
Value of equity, S	80	52
Less Allison's premerger market value	10	10
Gain in equity value	70	42
Cost if acquired at market price	66	66
Gain in value (loss)	4	(24)

merger between Allison and Connors is preferable to a merger between Allison and Dorden. Indeed, the gain in value of $4 million could be divided between the shareholders of Allison and those of Connors. Allison could pay a premium over the current market price of Connors and still achieve a gain in net value that would go to its shareholders.

The foregoing illustrative case example provides a general methodology for the management analysis of merger activity, which utilizes a number of principles: The acquiring firm is considering other firms as alternative merger candidates. To come up with a rational basis for analysis, prospective returns and risk from alternative merger combinations must be estimated. While historical data may be used as inputs, a forecast or estimate must be made of the returns and risk that may arise after alternative merger combinations have taken place.

Thus the forecast of the variables that measure prospective returns and risk for alternative postmerger combinations is critical to a sound evaluation of merger alternatives. The estimates of net operating earnings and of their potential growth may or may not reflect synergy between the combining firms depending on the nature and potential of the combined operations. Analysis in depth of the relevant product markets and the results of combining the organizations of the two firms is required. The resulting forecasts are subject to prediction errors which are sometimes of substantial magnitude.

We may obtain the measures of risk by market-value weighted averages of the betas (the systematic risk) of the combining firms. With the estimates of the new betas, along with a selection of market parameters, we can calculate the new relevant cost of capital for the merged firm, utilizing the security market line relationship. We must also estimate the effect of alternative merger combinations on the cost of debt. With estimates of the cost of equity capital and the cost of debt, we must formulate appropriate capital structure targets for the combined firm and use these to estimate a cost of capital.

Having obtained an estimate of the applicable cost of capital and the estimates of returns discussed earlier, we can apply valuation principles to formulate estimates of the value of alternative merger combinations. From these, we deduct the value of the acquiring firm in the absence of the merger to determine the total value remaining, which we next compare with the cost of acquiring the firm or firms with which a merger is being considered. If the value contributed by the merger exceeds the cost of the acquisition, the acquiring firm has a basis for making an offer that includes a premium to the shareholders of the acquired firm, yet still provides an increase in value for the shareholders of the acquiring firm.

Merger analysis thus involves the application of the same basic principles of cost of capital and valuation discussed in earlier chapters. However, the problems of application are more difficult. While merger analysis is fundamentally a form of capital budgeting analysis, the magnitudes of the alternative projects are usually quite large. Unlike standard capital budgeting projects in fields related to the firm's past experience, some mergers involve the analysis of industrial activities quite different from the firm's own experience. Prediction errors can therefore be sustantial. Our emphasis has been to avoid compounding large potential errors of forecasting with unsound valuation procedures. What we have done in the foregoing illustration has been to utilize the predictions of the relevant return and risk data and apply sound valuation procedures to the process of determining whether the costs of a prospective acquisition result in commensurate increases in prospective values.

SUMMARY

The first part of this chapter was summarized in Section E. Only the second part of the chapter will be covered here. Larson and Gonedes constructed a model specifying a region of mutually beneficial mergers. Conn and Nielsen used this model to measure market value changes in order to test the hypothesis that mergers were undertaken to increase values. They found some support for the hypothesis. They also observed that information about the intended merger appeared to be capitalized in the market well in advance of the actual merger announcement.

In the perspective of alternative merger theories and tests, we developed a framework for managerial analysis of prospective mergers. Basically, good forecasts of postmerger returns and risks are required as a starting point. Standard capital budgeting procedures, cost of capital analysis and valuation principles presented in the preceding chapters are then applied. The aim is to determine whether the value of the merged firm exceeds the value of the constituent firms. If it does, the merger has a valid social and private justification.

PROBLEM SET

18.1 Firm 1 and firm 2 are contemplating a merger in which firm 1 will acquire firm 2. The information in Table Q18.1 has been developed on the two firms. In the questions and answers related to this case, let subscripts 1 and 2 refer to the individual firms. Let ER_1 stand for the exchange ratio from the standpoint of firm 1 and ER_2 stand for the exchange ratio from the standpoint of firm 2. AER is the actual exchange ratio. PE_{12} will be the price-earnings ratio for the merged firm, after the merger.

a) The managements of the two firms are negotiating the terms of the merger, specifically the number of shares of firm 1 that will be exchanged for one share of common stock of firm 2. Three alternative criteria are under consideration:

Table Q18.1

	Total Earnings, E	Number of Shares of Common Stock, S	Earnings Per Share, EPS	Price-earnings Ratio, PE	Market Price Per Common Share, P
Firm 1	$400	100	$4.00	15	$60
Firm 2	$200	400	$0.50	30	$15

i) The effect on each firm's earnings per share after the merger.

ii) The expected market value of the merged firm's common stock per one original share immediately after the merger.

iii) The expected market value of the holdings per one original share after synergistic effects have been developed, for example, three years after the merger.

Of the three criteria, which would it be most rational for the management and shareholders of the firms to emphasize?

b) Using the estimates of the following range of post-merger PE_{12} values, determine which of ER_1 will equate P_1 to P_{12}.

Range of possible PE_{12} values: 12, 15, 20, 25, 30.

Make a graph on which ER_1 is plotted against PE_{12} and label the curve ER_1.

c) Calculate the ER_2 that will equate P_2 to P_{12} for the PE_{12} estimates given in part (b). Plot the curve ER_2 on the graph begun in part (b).

d) At what PE_{12} do the two curves intersect? What is the significance of this point of intersection?

e) For the following combinations, calculate and graph the premium or loss to each firm.

Actual exchange ratio (AER)	0.4	0.4	0.4	0.4	0.2	0.1
Post-merger price-earnings ratio (PE_{12})	30	26	22	18	16	18

18.2 The Jordan Corporation is a manufacturer of heavy-duty trucks. Because of a low internal profitability rate and lack of favorable investment opportunities in the existing line of business, Jordan is considering merger to achieve more favorable growth and profitability opportunities. It has made an extensive search of a large number of corporations and has narrowed the candidates to two firms. The Konrad Corporation is a manufacturer of materials handling equipment and is strong in research and marketing. It has had higher internal profitability than the other firm being considered, and has substantial investment opportunities.

The Loomis Company is a manufacturer of food and candies. It has a better profitability record than Konrad. Data on all three firms are given in Table Q18.2.

Additional information on market parameters includes a risk-free rate of 6% and an expected return on the market, $E(R_m)$, of 11%. Each firm pays a 10% interest rate on its debt. The tax rate, τ_c, of each is 40%. Ten years is estimated for the duration of supernormal growth.

a) Prepare the accounting balance sheets for the three firms.

b) If each company earns the before-tax r on total assets in the current year, what is the net operating income for each company?

Table Q18.2

	Book Value Per Share $	Price-earnings Ratio, PE	Number of Shares (millions)	Debt Ratio, B/S	β for Existing Leverage	Internal Profitability Rate, r	Investment Rate, K	Growth Rate, g
Jordan	20.00	6	4	1	1.4	.06	0.5	.03
Konrad	20.00	15	2	1	1.2	.12	1.5	.18
Loomis	20.00	12	2	1	1.5	.15	1.0	.15

c) Given the indicated price-earnings ratios, what is the market price of the common stock for each company?

d) What will be the immediate effects on the earnings per share of Jordan if it acquires Konrad or Loomis at their current market prices by the exchange of stock based on the current market prices of each of the companies?

e) Compare Jordan's new beta and required return on equity if it merges with Konrad with the same parameters that would result from its merger with Loomis.

f) Calculate the new required cost of capital for a Jordan-Konrad combination and for a Jordan-Loomis combination, respectively.

g) Compare the increase in value of Jordan as a result of a merger at market values with the cost of acquiring either Konrad or Loomis if the combined firms have the following financial parameters:

	NOI	r	WACC	K	g
Jordan/Konrad	32	.16	9.3%	1.0	.16
Jordan/Loomis	36	.13	10%	1.0	.13

18.3 Tables Q18.3 through Q18.5 provide financial information on three well-known conglomerate firms for which data adjusted for stock splits, etc., were readily available for 1962–1977. Data for the Dow-Jones Industrial Average are also presented for the same time period in Table Q18.6.

Table Q18.3   International Telephone & Telegraph Corporation

Year	Earnings Per Share, $	Dividends Per Share, $	Dividend Payout, %	Price Range	PE Ratio	Average Yield, %
1962	1.21	0.50	41	29– 16	19.0	2.2
1963	1.35	0.50	37	27– 20	18.0	2.1
1964	1.58	0.53	33	30– 26	18.0	1.8
1965	1.79	0.60	34	35– 24	16.6	2.0
1966	2.04	0.68	33	39– 29	16.9	2.0
1967	2.27	0.75	33	62– 36	21.6	1.5
1968	2.58	0.85	33	62– 44	20.8	1.6
1969	2.90	0.95	33	60– 45	18.4	1.8
1970	3.17	1.05	33	60– 30	14.3	2.3
1971	3.45	1.15	33	67– 45	16.4	2.0
1972	3.80	1.19	31	64– 48	14.8	2.1
1973	4.17	1.28	31	60– 25	10.2	3.0
1974	3.63	1.43	39	29– 12	5.7	6.9
1975	3.20	1.52	47	25– 14	6.2	7.7
1976	4.00	1.60	40	34– 22	7.0	5.7
1977	4.14	1.76	43	36– 28	7.9	5.4

Table Q18.4   Textron, Inc.

Year	Earnings Per Share, $	Dividend Per Share, $	Dividend Payout, %	Price Range	PE Ratio	Average Yield, %
1961	0.52	0.31	51	7– 5	12.4	4.9
1962	0.74	0.31	43	7– 5	9.1	4.6
1963	0.86	0.34	40	10– 7	10.3	3.9
1964	1.02	0.39	38	13– 9	11.4	3.3
1965	1.31	0.44	34	23–13	14.0	2.4
1966	1.77	0.53	30	26–19	13.1	2.3
1967	2.06	0.63	31	55–25	19.5	1.6
1968	2.26	0.73	32	57–40	21.7	1.5
1969	2.31	0.83	36	45–23	14.8	2.4
1970	1.99	0.90	45	26–15	10.5	4.3
1971	2.06	0.90	44	32–23	13.7	3.2
1972	2.32	0.92	40	36–30	14.4	2.7
1973	2.65	0.97	37	34–16	9.6	3.8
1974	2.83	1.08	38	22–11	6.1	6.3
1975	2.58	1.10	43	26–12	7.5	5.7
1976	3.23	1.15	36	31–20	8.0	4.4
1977	3.65	1.35	37	29–24	7.4	5.0

Table Q18.5   City Investing Company

Year	Earnings Per Share, $	Dividend Per Share, $	Dividend Payout, %	Price Range	PE Ratio	Average Yield, %
1961	0.20	0.10	50	8– 3	30.9	1.6
1962	0.21	0.10	48	7– 3	25.9	1.8
1963	0.17	0.10	59	5– 4	29.0	2.0
1964	0.17	0.11	65	5– 4	27.9	2.3
1965	0.19	0.11	58	7– 4	32.9	1.8
1966	0.59	0.12	20	12– 6	15.5	1.2
1967	1.07	0.12	11	28– 9	17.7	0.6
1968	1.97	0.14	7	39–18	14.6	0.5
1969	2.35	0.26	11	35–21	12.1	0.9
1970	1.44	0.45	31	27–10	13.3	2.4
1971	1.98	0.50	25	25–14	10.1	2.5
1972	1.98	0.52	26	22–13	9.1	2.9
1973	2.28	0.57	25	16– 8	5.3	4.7
1974	1.24	0.65	52	14– 4	7.4	7.1
1975	0.97	0.66	63	9– 4	6.2	9.4
1976	2.04	0.66	32	14– 7	5.2	6.2
1977	3.01	0.77	26	16–11	4.7	5.5

Table Q18.6   Dow-Jones Industrial Average (DJIA)

End of Calendar Year, Dec. 31	Price (end of year)	Earnings (for preceding 12 months)	PE
1962	652	36.43	17.9
1963	763	41.21	18.5
1964	874	46.43	18.8
1965	969	53.67	18.1
1966	786	57.66	13.6
1967	905	53.87	16.8
1968	944	57.89	16.3
1969	800	57.02	14.0
1970	839	51.02	16.4
1971	890	55.09	16.2
1972	1020	67.11	15.3
1973	851	86.17	9.9
1974	616	99.04	6.2
1975	852	75.66	11.3
1976	1005	96.72	10.4
1977	831	89.10	9.3

The year 1968 is generally regarded as the peak of the conglomerate merger movement. Subsequently changes in the tax laws treating mergers, in accounting rules, and in the antitrust climate took place.

a) Compare the growth rates in earnings for the three conglomerates and for the DJIA for the two time periods 1962–1968 vs. 1969–1977.

b) Compare the price-earnings ratios of the DJIA with price-earnings ratios of the three conglomerates for the years 1962, 1968, 1977.

c) Using the Gordon formula (Eq. 14.21a), establish some benchmarks for measuring the influence of expected growth on the price of stocks. Assume earnings (next year) of $1 per share, a required *cost of equity capital* of 10%, and a dividend payout of 40%. What is the indicated price and price-earnings ratio if the expected growth rate per annum in dividends per share is (i) 9%, (ii) 5%, and (iii) zero?

d) Given the same assumptions for the DJIA and the three conglomerates as in (c), except that $k_e = 15\%$ for the three firms, what growth rates are implied by the price-earnings ratios you obtained for the DJIA and the three firms in 1962, 1968, and 1977? How do these compare with the historical 1962–1968 growth rates measured in (a)?

e) To update the previous analysis, compare the growth rate in earnings per share of the DJIA with the three firms for the most recent five years. Also, compare the P/E ratio for the most recent year. (An illustrative answer to part (e) is for the five years ending in 1980 which was the latest data available when we went to press. Such data are readily available in *Moody's Handbook of Common Stocks* and *The Dow Jones Investor's Handbook.*)

REFERENCES

Asquith, P., "Mergers and the Market for Acquisitions." Unpublished manuscript, University of Chicago, January 1979.

————, "Merger Bids, Uncertainty, and Stockholder Returns." Manuscript, Harvard University, February 1982.

————, R. F. Bruner, and D. W. Mullins, Jr., "The Gains to Bidding Firms from Merger." Manuscript, Harvard University, October 1982.

Asquith, P., and E. H. Kim, "The Impact of Merger Bids on the Participating Firms' Security Holders." Manuscript, Harvard University, March 1982.

Bradley, M., "Interfirm Tender Offers and the Market for Corporate Control," *Journal of Business.* October 1980, 345–376.

Bradley, M., and L. M. Wakeman, "The Wealth Effects of Targeted Share Repurchases." Manuscript, University of Rochester, July 1982.

Brudney, V., and M. A. Chirelstein, "A Restatement of Corporate Freezeouts," *The Yale Law Journal.* 1978, 1354–1376.

Chung, K. S., "Investment Opportunities, Synergies, and Conglomerate Mergers." Ph.D. dissertation, Graduate School of Management, University of California, Los Angeles, 1982.

Conn, R. L., and J. F. Nielsen, "An Empirical Test of the Larson-Gonedes Exchange Ratio Determination Model," *Journal of Finance,* June 1977, 749–760.

Daems, H., *The Holding Company and Corporate Control.* H. E. Stenfert Kroese B.V., Leiden, The Netherlands, 1977.

Dann, L. Y., and H. DeAngelo, "Standstill Agreements, Privately Negotiated Stock Repurchases, and the Market for Corporate Control." Unpublished manuscript, The University of Pennsylvania, December 1981.

DeAngelo, H., L. DeAngelo, and E. M. Rice, "Going Private: Minority Freezeouts and Stockholder Wealth," working paper, University of Rochester, September 1982.

DeAngelo, H., and E. M. Rice, "Antitakeover Charter Amendments and Stockholder Wealth." Unpublished manuscript, The University of Pennsylvania, October 1981.

Dodd, P., "Merger Proposals, Management Discretion, and Stockholder Wealth," *Journal of Financial Economics.* June 1980, 105–137.

————, and R. Ruback, "Tender Offers and Stockholder Returns: An Empirical Analysis," *Journal of Financial Economics.* December 1977, 351–374.

Dodd, P., and J. B. Warner, "On Corporate Governance: A Study of Proxy Contests." Unpublished manuscript, University of Chicago, September 1981.

Easterbrook, F. H., and D. R. Fischel, "The Proper Role of a Target's Management in Responding to a Tender Offer," *Harvard Law Review.* April 1981, 1161–1204.

Eckbo, B. E., "Examining the Anti-Competitive Significance of Large Horizontal Mergers." Unpublished Ph.D. dissertation, University of Rochester, 1981.

Ellert, J. C., Antitrust Enforcement and the Behavior of Stock Prices. Doctoral dissertation, Graduate School of Business, University of Chicago, 1975.

————, "Mergers, Antitrust Law Enforcement, and Stockholder Returns," *Journal of Finance,* May 1976, 715–732.

Fama, E. F., L. Fisher, M. Jensen, and R. Roll, "The Adjustment of Stock Prices to New Information," *International Economic Review,* February 1969, 1–21.

Fama, E., and J. MacBeth, "Risk, Return and Equilibrium," *Journal of Political Economy,* May 1973, 607–636.

Federal Trade Commission, FTC Staff Report, 1972.

Firth, M., "The Profitability of Takeovers and Mergers," *The Economic Journal.* June 1979, 316–328.

Grossman, S., and O. Hart, "Takeover Bids, the Free-rider Problem, and the Theory of the Corporation," *The Bell Journal of Economics.* Spring 1980, 42–64.

————, "The Allocational Role of Takeover Bids in Situations of Asymmetric Information," *Journal of Finance.* May 1981, 253–270.

Halpern, P. J., "Empirical Estimates of the Amount and Distribution of Gains to Companies in Mergers," *Journal of Business,* October 1973, 554–575.

Hogarty, T., "The Profitability of Corporate Mergers," *Journal of Business,* July 1970, 317–327.

Jarrell, G., and M. Bradley, "The Economic Effects of Federal and State Regulations of Cash Tender Offers," *Journal of Law and Economics,* October 1980, 371–407.

Jensen, M. C., and W. H. Meckling, "Theory of the Firm: Managerial Behavior, Agency Costs and Ownership Structure," *Journal of Financial Economics.* October 1976, 305–360.

Kelly, E., "The Profitability of Growth Through Mergers," The Pennsylvania State University, University Park, 1967.

Keown, A. J., and J. M. Pinkerton, "Merger Announcements and Insider Trading Activity: An Empirical Investigation," *Journal of Finance.* September 1981, 855–869.

Krouse, C. G., "A Test of Competition in the Capital Market: The Case of Mergers." Manuscript of presentation to UCLA, AT&T Seminar, August 13, 1975.

Kummer, D. R., and J. R. Hoffmeister, "Valuation Consequences of Cash Tender Offers," *Journal of Finance,* May 1978, 505–516.

Langetieg, T. C., "An Application of a Three-Factor Performance Index to Measure Stockholder Gains from Merger," *Journal of Financial Economics.* December 1978, 365–383.

Larson, K. D., and N. J. Gonedes, "Business Combination: An Exchange Ratio Determination Model," *The Accounting Review,* October 1969, 720–728.

Lev, B., and G. Mandelker, "The Microeconomic Consequences of Corporate Mergers," *Journal of Business,* January 1972, 85–104.

Linn, S. C., and J. J. McConnell, "An Empirical Investigation of the Impact of 'Antitakeover' Amendments on Common Stock Prices," working paper, University of Iowa, January 1982.

Malatesta, P. H., "Corporate Mergers." Unpublished Ph.D. thesis, University of Rochester, 1981.

————, "The Wealth Effect of Merger Activity and the Objective Functions of Merging Firms." Unpublished manuscript, University of Rochester, March 1982.

Mandelker, G., "Risk and Return: The Case of Merging Firms," *Journal of Financial Economics,* December 1974, 303–335.

Manne, H. G., "Mergers and the Market for Corporate Control," *Journal of Political Economy.* April 1965, 110–120.

Myers, S. C., and N. S. Majluf, "Stock Issues and Investment Policy when Firms Have Information that Investors Do Not Have," working paper, Sloan School of Management, Massachusetts Institute of Technology, July 1982.

Rumelt, R. P., *Strategy, Structure, and Economic Performance,* Graduate School of Business Administration, Harvard University, Boston, Mass., 1974.

Schipper, K., and R. Thompson, "Evidence on the Capitalized Value of Merger Activity for Acquiring Firms," Carnegie-Mellon University Working Paper, 1980.

Scholes, M., "The Market for Securities: Substitution versus Price Pressure and the Effects of Information on Share Prices," *Journal of Business,* April 1972, 179–211.

Stigler, G. J., "The Economic Effects of the Antitrust Laws," *Journal of Law and Economics,* October 1966, 225–258.

Stillman, R. S., "Examining Antitrust Policy Towards Horizontal Mergers." Ph.D. dissertation, University of California, Los Angeles, 1980.

Weston, J. F., "Mergers and Acquisitions in Business Planning," *Rivista Internazionale di Scienze Economiche e Commerciali,* April 1970, 309–320.

Williamson, O. E., *Corporate Control and Business Behavior,* Prentice Hall, Englewood Cliffs, N.J., 1970.

Exchange Rate Systems and Parity Conditions

Like the traffic lights in a city, the international monetary system is taken for granted until it begins to malfunction and to disrupt people's daily lives.

ROBERT SOLOMON, *THE INTERNATIONAL MONETARY SYSTEM,* 1945–1976, *AN INSIDER'S VIEW,* NEW YORK, HARPER & ROW, 1977, P. 1.

A. INTRODUCTION

From a general economic standpoint the main issues in international finance relate to the volume of trade, the adjustment processes for achieving international equilibrium, and the issue of whether there are segmented international markets. Our emphasis in this book will be on the implications of adjustment processes for corporate financial policy. These in turn have implications for the activities of firms, such as sales, purchases, and investment policies.

The nature of risks in an international financial setting takes on new dimensions. We shall focus on corporate financial policies to manage these risks. In addition to

643

the pattern of cash inflows and cash outflows which the firm develops, we shall examine the changes in its balance sheet in terms of monetary versus nonmonetary net positions. We shall also examine the use of the forward market for dealing with foreign exchange fluctuations and analyze the use of money and capital markets for managing foreign exchange risks. Issues here are whether outlays to limit the risks of exchange rate fluctuations are worth the cost. These activities will also be examined for their influence on keeping the international financial markets performing as efficient markets.

Our presentation will emphasize some basic propositions in international finance which are the key to measuring returns and costs in international financial activities. These basic relations are best understood after background material on the adjustment processes in international finance have been developed first.

B. THE INTERNATIONAL FINANCIAL MECHANISM

The international financial markets as a part of a general system of financial intermedia-tion perform the functions of increasing efficiency in the production and exchange of goods and services. Money and prices convey information about economic alterna-tives and guide the choices among the alternatives. International finance, like financial intermediation in general, provides for shifting patterns of investments and savings that increase productivity and provide opportunities for saving surplus units to post-pone consumption and for deficit units to increase the output of real goods by utilizing these savings of (surplus) units willing to consume less now and more later.

1. The Economic Basis for International Transactions

The fundamental basis for international trade is the *principle of comparative advan-tage.* The law of comparative advantage states that trade will be mutually advantageous if one country is relatively more efficient in producing some products and other countries are relatively more efficient in producing other products. A classic illustration would be if you were a better typist than your secretary. Nevertheless, you hire your secretary to type your materials because your comparative advantage is your knowledge of international finance. To illustrate the opportunities for trade, consider the following example.

Let us postulate that opportunity costs in country A are reflected in prices of $3 for X and $1 for Y, while opportunity costs in country B result in prices of 12 marks for X and 6 marks for Y. The pattern is shown below:

	X	Y
Country A	$3	$1
Country B	M12	M6

At more than 6 marks per dollar, both goods X and Y would be cheaper in country B. Country B would export both X and Y and import neither. For example, at M8 = $1, B could sell X in A for $1.50 and Y in A for $.75. On the other hand, a rate of less than 4 marks per dollar would make both goods cheaper in country A. Country A would export both and import neither. For example, at M2 = $1, A could sell X in B for M6 and Y in B for M2. To achieve equilibrium between the two countries, the exchange rate would have to fall somewhere between 6 and 4 marks per dollar. Equilibrium would require that the exchange rate should be at the level at which each country's exports and imports are equal in total value measured in units of its own currency.

It can be seen from the example that the relative prices of X and Y are 3 to 1 in country A and 2 to 1 in country B. With a large number of products, the cheaper one country's currency is in relation to other currencies, the larger the range of that country's products that are underselling foreign products of the same type. As a result, the importing country will need greater amounts per unit of time of the exporting country's currency in order to buy the latter's relatively cheap goods. Differences in the patterns of relative prices result from differences among countries in resources, skills, and tastes, and in social and political aspects, which in turn lead to comparative advantages in different kinds of activities. As a consequence, there will be profit incentives for businessmen to engage in trade. These private benefits will, in turn, lead to social gains as the theory describes. Ideally, exchange rates will evolve to bring the trade between countries to levels on which the exports and imports of individual countries will be in balance in their own currency.

However, the ideal result is complicated by the existence of short- and long-term capital flows associated with borrowing and lending activities, shifts in the comparative rates of development of individual industries in different countries, differences in the domestic economic development programs among individual countries. What is required are some processes by which tendencies toward imbalances in international activities can be restored to relative equilibrium. We next examine the nature of these adjustment processes.

We propose to discuss the adjustment processes for international disequilibrium under two alternative exchange mechanisms: One is a gold standard with fixed exchange rates. The other postulates flexible exchange rates.

2. Gold Standard and Fixed Exchange Rates

The mechanism governing the relationship of prices to the flow of gold was first formulated in the mid-eighteenth century. Country A runs an export balance surplus, while country B runs a deficit. Hence gold flows into A while it flows out of B. Domestic prices in A rise, the prices in B fall. Country A is an attractive market in which to increase sales from other countries, and A's imports increase. Country A's goods are more expensive in other countries, so its export sales decrease. Thus A's export surplus will be reduced or reversed until equilibrium between relative price relationships of the countries is restored. The flow of gold operates through prices to function as an adjustment mechanism for international balances of trade and payments as well as to regulate the price-change relationships between countries.

In addition to price changes, income and employment effects may also enter into the adjustment process. If the surplus country was not functioning at full employment, the export surplus increases its income and employment. Income and employment decline in the deficit country. Also, in the adjustment process, employment may decline in *A* and increase in *B*. The above pattern for the surplus country *A* can be summarized as follows:

Payments surplus and gold inflow

lead to

Increasing money supply

which causes

Rising prices and increasing income

which lead to

Worsening trade balance

which causes

End to surplus and gold inflow.

The reverse process takes place for country *B*, the deficit area.

Under the gold standard, the exchange rates are said to remain "fixed" through this entire adjustment process, because of the inherent assumption that gold would flow to prevent exchange rates from moving beyond the "gold points." For example, let us suppose that the British pound contains four times as much gold as the U.S. dollar: the dollar contains .05 ounce of gold while the British pound contains .2 ounce of gold. A U.S. trade deficit vis-à-vis the United Kingdom would increase the demand for pounds to pay for the imports from the United Kingdom, and the dollar price of pounds would therefore rise, say to $4.10. We could take $1000 to the U.S. Treasury and get 50 ounces of gold since $1 contains .05 ounce of gold. Next we could transport the 50 ounces of gold to the United Kingdom, where we would get £250 in exchange: $50 \div .2 = 250$. With the rate of exchange of $4.10 to £1 less the cost of transporting the gold amounting to $.02 for insurance and interest loss, we would net $4.08 for each pound. Multiplying $4.08 times £250 yields $1020, or a profit of $20. Thus at any rate of exchange above $4.02 or below $3.98, by the actions of the gold arbitrageurs, the rate of exchange would be checked from falling outside the "gold points."

To the extent that a gold standard with fixed exchange rates worked, it was because maintaining two-way convertibility between a nation's monetary unit and a fixed amount of gold was a policy goal which received great emphasis and high priority. So long as it was recognized that convertibility was a major policy goal, speculative capital movements were likely to be stabilizing rather than destabilizing. In other words, the general expectation that the convertibility of the currency would be maintained was so strong that when a gold standard currency did weaken almost to its gold export points, one could reasonably assume that it would not drop much lower and indeed would probably rise. Speculators would then take the position that a rise in the value of the currency was imminent, and this would, of course, strengthen the currency.

During the post World War II period the international monetary system was not a gold standard, but rather a gold exchange standard. In addition to gold, nations held claims on the currency of other countries. Most countries simply related their exchange rates to one of the "key" or "reserve" currencies, holding part of their official reserves in that currency. Dollars and sterling were key currencies immediately after the end of World War II. Thus the monetary authorities outside the United States had the assurance of the U.S. Treasury that the two-way convertibility between dollars and gold would be maintained.

Because the growing volume of international trade required an increase in the supply of international reserves, the initial balance of payments deficits of the United States during the 1950s performed the role of augmenting the supply of key currencies. The rate at which new gold was being produced was far too low to meet the rate of growth in demand for official reserves to support the growing volume of international trade. Problems developed with the gold exchange standard in the early 1970s, giving rise to a substantial shift to the use of flexible exchange rates. In the next section, we describe the nature of the adjustment process under flexible exchange rates. This provides a foundation for the discussion of the broader issues of achieving international equilibrium under current conditions in the international economy.

3. The Adjustment Process under Flexible Exchange Rates

Under a regime of flexible exchange rates no attempt is made to tie the value of a currency to gold or to any one foreign currency. The exchanges of currencies that take place in the international financial markets are based on the forces of demand and supply for the currencies. Exchange rates are likely to be roughly related to the purchasing powers over goods and services of the respective currencies.

To illustrate the operation of the adjustment process let us assume an initial relationship of 1 dollar to 4 deutschemarks: $1 = DM 4.

Let us now assume that the volume of imports in the United States exceeds its exports in relationship to countries whose currency is the deutschemark. The demand for deutschemarks relative to dollars increases. The value of the dollar falls. For purposes of illustration, let us assume $1 = DM 2.

At the new exchange rate the prices of our imports and exports in dollars rise. For example, suppose that the Volkswagen sold in the United States for $2000 when the exchange rate was $1 to DM 4. A sale at $2000 provided the German exporter with DM 8000. At the new exchange rate the German exporter still seeks to receive DM 8000. But at the new exchange rates he must now ask $4000 for the VW.

Similarly, at the old exchange rate the price of wheat (a U.S. export good) was $4 per bushel. To obtain this price we needed to get DM 16. Now at the new exchange rates, in order to receive $4 per bushel, we need get only DM 8. Thus the prices of imports in dollars rise substantially at the new exchange rates. Conversely, the prices of exports in the foreign currency fall. The dollar price of exports could be increased and still represent substantially lower prices in the foreign currency.

In the United States at the new exchange rates, import purchases would have to be made at higher prices and export sales could be made under more favorable conditions than before. Conversely, foreign countries faced with lower prices in deutschemarks for both their imports and exports would be motivated to increase their purchases from us and reduce sales to us.

An argument for the use of flexible exchange rates is that the relations between the prices of domestic and foreign goods adjust through exchange rates. The prices of internationally traded goods carry most of the adjustment process. It is argued that under the gold standard with fixed exchange rates an incorrect exchange rate is adjusted not by changing exchange rates but by adjusting all other things. Under flexible exchange rates, when exchange rates are out of line, the correction takes place in the exchange rates themselves. Since domestic wages and prices are relatively inflexible, they cannot, in fact, make the necessary adjustments. However, exchange rates do not have the same built-in institutional barriers to upward and downward flexibility and hence they are much more flexible tools of adjustment.

4. Consistent Foreign Exchange Rates

Equilibrating transactions take place when exchange rates are not in proper relationships with one another. This is illustrated by some examples with (unrealistically) rounded numbers to make the arithmetic of the calculations simple. The analysis will point in the right direction if the reader remembers the general maxim that arbitrageurs will seek to "sell high and to buy low." First we discuss the consistency of spot rates. Let us suppose the dollar value of the pound sterling is $2 in New York City and $1.90 in London. The following adjustment actions would take place: In New York City, we sell £190 for $380. We sell the pounds in New York because this is where the pound value is high. In London, we sell $380 for £200. In London the dollar value is high in relation to the pound. Thus £190 sold in New York City for $380 can be used to buy £200 in London at a gain of £10. The sale of pounds in New York causes the value of the pound to decline, and the purchase of pounds in London causes their value to rise until no further arbitrage opportunities are left. Assuming minimal transportation costs, we postulate that the same foreign exchange prices obtain in all locations.

The relationship between the currencies of two individual localities can be generalized across all countries and is referred to as the *consistent cross rate*. It works in the following fashion: Assume that the equilibrium relation between the dollar and the pound is $2 to £1 and that that between the dollar and the franc is $.25 to fr. 1. Now, suppose that in New York City, £.10 = fr. 1. The following adjustment process will take place: We sell $200 for £100 and use these to obtain fr. 1000, which in turn will buy $250. We thus make a profit of $50 over our initial $200. In general, then, we sell dollars for pounds and pounds for francs since the pound is overvalued with respect to the dollar-to-pound and dollar-to-franc relationships. The dollar will fall in relation to the pound and the pound will fall in relation to the franc until consistent cross rates are reached. If the relation were fr. $1 = £.125$, the cross rates would be consistent. We check using the following relation:

$$\$1 = £.5, \qquad £1 = fr. 8, \qquad fr. 1 = \$.25.$$

The product of the right-hand sides of all three relationships must equal 1. *Check:* $.5 \times 8 \times .25 = 1$. We have thus established consistency between foreign exchange rates.

C. THE SHIFT FROM FIXED TO FLEXIBLE EXCHANGE RATES

We have described the adjustment processes under alternative types of mechanisms: fixed exchange rates and flexible exchange rates. Beginning in the 18th century and continuing through the early 1970s, the world adhered at least nominally to a gold exchange standard with fixed exchange rates. But recurrent international crises disturbed equilibrium and periodic devaluations took place. With the development of the Bretton Woods institutions after World War II, the International Monetary Fund and the World Bank, there was hope for improved stability. However, these expectations were not realized.

Particularly after the serious recession of the early 1930s, governments placed increased emphasis on full-employment policies and consequently were unwilling to accept the adjustment processes consistent with the gold standard or related systems of fixed exchange rates, which call for shrinkage in the domestic money supplies and incomes of countries with external deficits. This shrinkage occurs through contraction in the reserves of member (of the Federal Reserve System) banks which must make payments to foreigners in foreign currency when the home country imports more than it exports. The process is readily summarized by a series of journal entries that would take place. For an excess of imports into the United States from Japan the journal entries are as shown in Table 19.1.

Table 19.1

U.S. Commercial Bank	U.S. Central Bank (FED)
Dr. Yen	Dr. Yen
Cr. Reserves with FED (Central Bank)	Cr. Gold certificates
Dr. Deposits, Mr. Smith	Dr. Member bank deposits
Cr. Yen	Cr. Yen
Commercial Bank, Japan	Central Bank, Japan
Dr. Yen	Dr. Gold certificates
Cr. Deposits, Mr. Toyama	Cr. Yen
Dr. Reserves with Central Bank	Dr. Yen
Cr. Yen	Cr. Member bank deposits

On the assumption that credit balances are not expanded, the journal entries reflect the demand of the Japanese exporter (Mr. Toyama) to be paid. The U.S. commercial bank obtains yen from the U.S. central bank (FED) by reducing its reserves with the Federal Reserve Bank (FED). The FED had purchased the yen by paying with gold certificates. The yen received by Mr. Toyama in Japan became primary deposits in a commercial bank in Japan. The reserves of the commercial banks in Japan increase and so do the holdings of gold certificates by the central bank of Japan.

The net result of the journal entries is a decrease in the deposits of the U.S. importer at that individual's commercial bank accompanied by a reduction in the commercial bank's reserves with the FED. For the U.S. central bank, member bank deposits decrease as does its gold certificate account. The opposite net transactions take place in Japan.

For a normal volume of transactions, the exchange rate remains unchanged. However, there is a contraction in the effective money supply in the United States and an expansion in Japan. In utilizing its gold or other foreign-exchange reserves, the central bank is covering the country's balance of payments deficits. The shrinkage of domestic bank reserves would bring about a deflationary adjustment of the classic gold standard kind. The resulting multiple contraction in the domestic money supply would deflate incomes and prices, reduce spending on imports, and stimulate efforts to achieve exports.

However, to counteract the deflationary tendency, the governmental authorities of the deficit country may engage in offsetting transactions. The central bank in the deficit country could buy domestic securities to replenish the reserve positions of its commercial banks. It could also lower reserve requirements and reduce the discount rate. Alternatively, in its domestic fiscal policy, the deficit country could run internal deficits to offset the influences of its external deficits.

The reverse process may take place in a country with a balance of payment surplus. It could offset the expansion of the domestic reserves of its commercial banks by selling securities in the open market. Alternatively, it could run substantial governmental surpluses.

Counteracting governmental policies can neutralize the adjustment processes under any exchange system. The practice of neutralizing the international adjustment process was particularly pronounced after World War II when greater emphasis was given to full employment policies in individual national economies. The unwillingness to accept the automatic adjustment processes of an international financial system was also accompanied by efforts to intervene against freedom of trade and the free flow of capital between nations. A desire to control the adjustment process has led to tariff increases, the use of import quotas, and restrictions on lending and investing abroad.

Unwillingness to accept the international adjustment process resulted in increasing flows of international reserves away from deficit countries. In the case of the United States, the early balance of payments deficits were welcomed. They had the positive benefit of mitigating the dollar shortage and of increasing the rate of growth in international foreign exchange reserves. However, as the gold account of the United States shrank and as its balance of payments deficits increased rather than diminished, speculators began to become increasingly confident that the foreign exchange value of the dollar would not be maintained. Speculative sales of the dollar in favor of stronger currencies such as the German mark or Swiss franc further aggravated the drain on U.S. foreign exchange reserves. Finally these pressures built up to such a degree that the United States recognized the inevitable and in August 1971 suspended gold convertibility: *de facto* the dollar began to float in terms of its value in relation to other major currencies.

A new element was added to the international economic scene in 1974 when the Organization of Petroleum Exporting Countries (OPEC) quadrupled the price of oil. This step placed burdens on all oil-importing nations. The United States' response was unwillingness to permit the domestic price of oil and petroleum products to reflect the new world price levels of oil as set by the OPEC cartel. By imposing price controls on oil and petroleum products in the United States, the government discouraged domestic exploration and production while effectively subsidizing domestic consumption. As a result, the domestic consumption of oil in the United States was not greatly affected, and oil imports as a percentage of the total U.S. oil consumption increased in the years following 1974. Thus in 1977, for example, the United States imports of oil reached $46 billion, contributing importantly to the 1977 balance of trade deficit of approximately $27 billion. Under a regime of floating currencies, the value of the dollar in relation to the German mark, the Swiss franc, and the Japanese yen has fluctuated.

The previous analysis has used a balance of payments framework to appraise the need for international adjustment processes, including the devaluation or depreciation of the dollar. We next consider in somewhat more detail the role of a balance of payments analysis in defining the kinds of policies and adjustments that may have to be made in corporate financial policy in order to deal with changes in the international financial environment.

D. BALANCE OF PAYMENTS ANALYSIS

The balance of payments of a nation is a double-entry accounting statement of its transactions with the rest of the world during a specified time period, usually one quarter or one year. Inflows are recorded as a plus. (Sometimes the words "receipts" and "credits" are used but the terms "plus" and "minus" are preferred as being more neutral in their implications.) Outflows are a minus. (Sometimes called "debits" or "payments" but again "minus" is preferred.)

The basic entries in the balance of payments statement can be summarized into four categories of items as shown in Table 19.2. This summary indicates how the adjustment process can be complicated by a number of relationships going in different directions. Thus, if a given country runs a deficit by having an excess of imports over exports, instead of settling the balance by payments in the foreign currency, a number of other offsets may take place. As shown in Table 19.2, the offsets can take the form of increasing liabilities to foreigners, decreasing claims on foreigners,

Table 19.2 Effects on the Balance of Payments

Plus	Minus
Exports	Imports
Increase liabilities to foreigners	Decrease liabilities to foreigners
Decrease claims on foreigners	Increase claims on foreigners
Decrease investments; sell assets	Increase investments; buy assets

liquidating assets, or decreasing other foreign investments. Consequently, there will be a lag in the pressures that would result if payments in foreign currencies had to be made immediately. This lag will postpone the contraction in the money supply or incomes of the deficit country.

Similarly, a country that is increasing its investments abroad will improve its investment position, but it will be creating minus entries in its current balance of payments statement. The long-run outlook for a country which is making substantial foreign investments, however, may be favorable as a result of the future income that may be generated from those investments.

Until recently, the U.S. Department of Commerce followed the format for the balance of payment statement shown in Table 19.3. It has been modified to deemphasize individual balances for the reasons indicated below.

In the traditional balance of payments statement, line 11, the balance on goods and services, is considered significant as an indicator of the basic trade position of the United States. However, some people argue for greater emphasis on line 15, the balance on current account, in the belief that U.S. government grants are determined by diplomatic and military considerations which are not necessarily responsive to international economic conditions.

Still others suggest emphasis on line 26, the balance on current account and long-term capital, referring to it as the "basic balance." This balance is basic in the sense that it excludes the influence of more volatile items such as short-term capital movements. It places trade transactions and long-term capital movements "above the line." Short-term capital movements are placed "below the line" on the theory that they are accommodating or compensating transactions which have no real impact on the reserve position of the nation. However, short-term capital movements may represent transactions initiated because of expectations of changes in relative interest rates or foreign exchange rates. Thus, they may not represent simple accommodating entries. Furthermore, with more flexible exchange rates, long-term private capital movements became less important as adjustment flows to maintain fixed exchange rates; instead they are more responsive to prospects for returns from investments in different countries.

Line 33, the net liquidity balance, is a broader indicator of the magnitude of changes in liquidity claims or accommodations required to maintain fixed exchange rates. The net liquidity balance measures the amount of required private lending by the United States (if the balance is positive) or the required private lending by foreigners (if the balance is negative) before changes in foreign exchange reserves or official balances become necessary.

Table 19.3   Illustrative U.S. Balance of Payments

---

1. Merchandise balance
2.   Exports
3.   Imports
4. Military transactions
5. Transportation and travel
6. Investment income, net
9. Other services, net
11. Balance on goods and services
12. Remittances
13. Balance on goods, services, and remittances
14. U.S. government grants
15. Balance on current account
16. Long-term private investment

26. Balance on current account and long-term capital
    (basic balance)

   Nonliquid items
28. Claims
30. Liabilities
33. Net liquidity balance

   Liquid items
35. Claims
38. Liabilities

42. Official reserve transactions balance
43. Liquid liabilities to official agencies
46. U.S. reserve assets

Finally, line 42, official reserve transactions balance, measures what type and how much official action must be taken to accommodate or settle the effects of all other transactions. The use of this balance reflects the view that the key demarcation line in international transactions is between those of the official agencies and all other transactors.

Under flexible exchange rates, greater emphasis is placed on the fundamental transactions which determine the probable direction of changes in the foreign exchange value of the dollar. These include: balance on merchandise trade; balance on goods and services; balance on goods, services, and remittances; and current account balance. These balances successively indicate the effect of the basic transactions and of government loan and grant policies on the supply and demand for the currency of a country and, therefore, its probable exchange-rate movements. The short- or long-term private capital flows are not reflected since the prospects which give rise to their movements change within relatively short periods and hence do not have any fundamental, continuing effects on exchange rates.

The significance of alternative measures of "the balance of payments" depends on the circumstances of an individual country and the pattern of international economic developments taking place. To determine all contributing factors, one must analyze as many components of information as possible, including the more general economic developments taking place in individual countries. The balance of payments is one among a number of information sources that may be analyzed within a more general economic framework to develop judgments about adjustment processes taking place which will have implications for changes in foreign exchange rates as well. It is this kind of analysis which is required for formulating corporate financial policies of firms substantially affected by changes in foreign exchange rates. In Chapter 20, we analyze some of the fundamental relationships which reflect the broad economic adjustment forces reflected in balance of payments statements.

E. FUNDAMENTAL EXCHANGE RATE RELATIONSHIPS

As a foundation for subsequent analysis we summarize some fundamental exchange rate relationships.

1. The Fisher relation (FR)
2. The interest rate parity theorem (IRPT)
3. The purchasing power parity theorem (PPPT)
4. Forward parity theorem (FPT)
5. The measurement of real gains or losses

As general background for discussing each of these five relationships, we briefly present some institutional material. International business transactions are conducted in many different currencies. However, a U.S. exporter selling to a foreigner expects to be paid in dollars. Conversely, a foreign importer buying from an American exporter may prefer to pay in his own currency. The existence of the foreign exchange markets allows buyers and sellers to deal in the currencies of their preference. The foreign exchange markets consist of individual brokers, the large international money banks, and many commercial banks which facilitate transactions on behalf of their customers. Payments may be made in one currency by an importer and received in another by the exporter.

Exchange rates may be expressed in dollars per foreign unit or in foreign currency units per dollar. An exchange rate of \$.50 to FC 1 shows the value of 1 foreign currency unit in terms of the dollar. We shall use E_0 to indicate the spot rate, E_f to indicate the forward rate at the present time, and E_1 to indicate the actual future spot rate corresponding to E_f. An exchange rate of FC 2 to \$1 shows the value of the dollar in terms of the number of foreign currency units it will purchase. We will use the symbol X with corresponding subscripts to refer to the exchange rate expressed as the number of foreign currency units per dollar.

The fundamental exchange rate relationships are based on one or more of the following assumptions.

A1. Financial markets are perfect. (No taxes, no transactions costs, no controls)

A2. Goods markets are perfect. (No transportation costs or time, no barriers to trade)

A3. There is a single consumption good common to all.

A4. The future is known with certainty.

We shall first describe the relationships, then indicate how they are related to the above assumptions.

1. The Fisher Relation

The Fisher relation holds for the relationship between interest rates and the anticipated rate of inflation. While it can also be regarded as a purely domestic economic relationship, it is also used to develop some of the international relationships we shall present later. The Fisher relation states that nominal interest rates rise to reflect the anticipated rate of inflation. The Fisher relation can be stated in a number of forms, as shown below:

$$\frac{P_0}{P_1} = \frac{1+r}{1+R_n}, \tag{19.1a}$$

$$1 + r = (1 + R_n)\frac{P_0}{P_1}, \tag{19.1b}$$

$$r = \left[(1 + R_n)\frac{P_0}{P_1}\right] - 1, \tag{19.1c}$$

$$R_n = \left[(1 + r)\left(\frac{P_1}{P_0}\right)\right] - 1, \tag{19.1d}$$

where

P_0 = initial price level,

P_1 = subsequent price level,

P_1/P_0 = rate of inflation = T,

P_0/P_1 = relative purchasing power of the currency unit,

r = real rate of interest,

R_n = nominal rate of interest.

While the Fisher relation can be stated in a number of forms, its importance can be conveyed by a simple numerical example. Over a given period of time, if the price index is expected to rise 10% and the real rate of interest is 7%, then the current nominal rate of interest is

$$R_n = [(1.07)(1.10)] - 1 = 17.7\%.$$

Similarly, if the nominal rate of interest is 12% and the price index is expected to rise 10% over a given time period, the current real rate of interest is

$$r = [1.12(\tfrac{100}{110})] - 1 = 1.018 - 1 = .018 = 1.8\%.$$

An approximation of the relationship is

$$R_n \cong r + (T - 1).$$

For our data this would be

$$17.7\% \cong 7.0\% + 10\% \text{ for the first example.}$$

$$12.0\% \cong 1.8\% + 10\% \text{ for the second example.}$$

2. The Interest Rate Parity Theorem (IRPT)

The interest rate parity theorem holds that the ratio of the forward and spot exchange rates will equal the ratio of foreign and domestic nominal interest rates. The formal statement of the IRPT may be expressed as follows:

$$\frac{X_f}{X_0} = \frac{1 + R_{f0}}{1 + R_{d0}} = \frac{E_0}{E_f}, \tag{19.2}$$

where

X_f = current forward exchange rate expressed as FC units per $1,

E_f = current forward exchange rate expressed as dollars per FC 1,

X_0 = current spot exchange rate expressed as FC units per $1,

E_0 = current spot exchange rate expressed as dollars per FC 1,

R_{f0} = current foreign interest rate,

R_{d0} = current domestic interest rate.

Thus, if the foreign interest rate is 15% while the domestic interest rate is 10% and the spot exchange rate is $X_0 = 10$, the predicted current forward exchange rate will be

$$X_f = \frac{1 + R_{f0}}{1 + R_{d0}} (X_0)$$

$$= \frac{1.15}{1.10} (10) = 10.45;$$

that is, 10.45 units of foreign currency equal $1. Thus, viewed on an annual basis, the foreign forward rate is seen to be at a discount of 4.5%. If we assume the time period of a transaction to be 90 days, we must rework the problem accordingly. The first step is to prorate the interest rates on a quarterly basis: Thus for 90 days,

$$X_f = \frac{1.0375}{1.025} \quad (10)$$

$$= 10.122;$$

that is, the 90-day forward rate is 10.122, and it follows that on the quarterly basis the discount on the 90-day forward rate is 1.22%.

The approximation for IRPT is

$$R_{fi} - R_{di} \cong \frac{X_f - X_0}{X_0}.$$

The data for the annual example is used to illustrate the approximation.

$$.15 - .10 \cong \frac{10.45 - 10}{10},$$

$$0.05 \cong .045.$$

Alternatively, we can formulate the example to determine the effect on interest rates of expected changes in future foreign exchange rates. There is a dynamic relationship here that needs to be recognized. If the foreign exchange rate is expected to rise over a period of time, relative interest rates will reflect the rate of change in the expected foreign exchange rates, as illustrated in Fig. 19.1.

Figure 19.1 shows that as the value of the foreign currency falls (the exchange rate expressed in the number of foreign currency units per dollar rises), the ratio of foreign interest rates to domestic interest rates will rise. At the inflection point of the rise in the expected number of foreign currency units per dollar, the ratio of

Figure 19.1
Illustration of the interest rate parity theorem.

foreign interest rates to domestic interest rates will peak. When the expected ratio of the foreign currency to the domestic currency levels off, then the former ratio of nominal foreign interest rates to domestic interest rates will be reestablished.

We could also use the IRPT to express our results in terms of the interest rate parities required for given relationships between spot and future exchange rates. The transactions that result in interest rate parity are referred to as *covered interest arbitrage*. First, an arbitrage outflow situation will be described. The basic assumptions are as follows:

> U.S. interest rate 5%,
>
> German interest rate 7%,
>
> Spot exchange rate $1 = DM 4,
>
> Forward exchange rate discount 1% per annum.

The following arbitrage transaction will take place. In New York, we borrow $100,000 for 90 days (one quarter) at 5%. The loan repayment at the end of 90 days is

$$\$100,000[1 + (5\% \times \tfrac{1}{4})] = \$101,250.$$

At the spot exchange rate, we convert the $100,000 loan into DM 400,000. In Germany, we invest the DM 400,000 for 90 days at 7% and receive at the end of 90 days

$$\text{DM } 400,000[1 + (7\% \times \tfrac{1}{4})] = \text{DM } 407,000.$$

A covering transaction is also made. To insure against adverse changes in the spot rate during the 90-day investment period, we sell the investment proceeds forward. Since the forward exchange rate discount is 1%, then

$$4[1 + (1\% \times \tfrac{1}{4})] = \text{DM } 4.01$$

is required in exchange for $1 in 90 days (forward). We sell the investment proceeds forward, i.e., we contract to receive DM $407,000 \div 4.01 = \$101,496$. The result of the two transactions is shown below:

$$\text{Arbitrage profits} = \text{investment receipts} - \text{loan payments}$$

$$= \$101,496 - 101,250$$

$$= \$246.$$

The arbitrage transaction increases the *demand* for currency in New York and the *supply* of funds in Germany, which in turn raises the interest rate in New York and lowers it in Germany, thus narrowing the differential. The covering transaction increases the supply of German forward exchange while the arbitrage investment action increases the demand for spot funds. Both forces tend to increase the forward exchange discount. The interest rate differential decreases and the forward rate discount increases until both are equalized.

An arbitrage inflow takes place when the forward exchange rate discount exceeds the interest rate differential. The basic facts are now:

U.S. interest rate 5%,

German interest rate 6%,

Spot exchange rate DM 4 = $1,

Forward exchange rate discount 2% per annum.

The arbitrage transaction involves borrowing in the foreign country. In Germany, we borrow DM 400,000 for 90 days at 6%. The loan repayment at the end of 90 days is

$$DM\ 400,000[1 + (6\% \times \tfrac{1}{4})] = DM\ 406,000.$$

At the spot exchange rate, we convert the DM 400,000 loan into $100,000. In New York, we invest the $100,000 for 90 days at 5% and receive at the end of 90 days

$$\$100,000[1 + (5\% \times \tfrac{1}{4})] = \$101,250.$$

Again, we would make a covering transaction. To insure coverage for the loan repayment, we buy DM 406,000 forward. At a 2% forward exchange rate discount, it costs DM $4[1 + (2\% \times \tfrac{1}{4})] = $ DM 4.02 to buy $1 forward. Thus, repayment of principal plus interest requires

$$DM\ 406,000 \div 4.02 = \$100,995.$$

Thus we have

$$Arbitrage\ profits = investment\ receipts - loan\ repayments$$

$$= \$101,250 - \$100,995$$

$$= \$255.$$

The arbitrage transaction increases the *demand* for deutschemarks and increases the supply of dollars. The U.S. interest rate decreases and the German rate rises; thus the differential increases. Covering transactions increase the spot supply of deutschemarks, thus decreasing the premium on forward deutschemarks. The interest rate differential and the forward exchange rate discount decrease until both rates are equalized.

3. The Purchasing Power Parity Theorem (PPPT)

The purchasing power parity doctrine states that people will value currencies for what they will buy. If an American dollar buys the same basket of goods and services as five units of a foreign currency, we have an exchange rate of five foreign currency units to the dollar or 20 cents per foreign currency unit. An attempt to compare price indexes to computed purchasing power parity assumes that it is possible to compile comparable baskets of goods in different countries. As a practical matter, the parity rate is, in general, estimated from changes in the purchasing power of two currencies with reference to some past base period when the exchange rate was theoretically in equilibrium. Hence, in using the PPPT our emphasis is on formulating it as a statement that *changes* in exchange rates reflect *changes* in the relative prices between two countries. In formal terms, the PPPT may be stated as follows:

$$CX = \frac{X_1}{X_0} = \frac{P_{f1}/P_{f0}}{P_{d1}/P_{d0}} = RPC \qquad (19.3)$$

where

$\dfrac{X_1}{X_0} = \dfrac{E_0}{E_1}$, $\begin{aligned} X_0 &= \text{FC units per dollar now,} \\ X_1 &= \text{FC units per dollar one period later,} \end{aligned}$

$E_0 = \dfrac{1}{X_0} = $ dollars per FC unit now,

$E_1 = \dfrac{1}{X_1} = $ dollars per FC unit one period later,

$CX = \dfrac{X_1}{X_0} = $ change in exchange rate,

$RPC = \dfrac{P_{f1}/P_{f0}}{P_{d1}/P_{d0}} = $ change in relative prices = ratio of inflation rates,

$P_{f0} = $ initial price level in the foreign country,

$P_{f1} = $ foreign country price level one period later,

$T_f = $ foreign country inflation rate,

$P_{d0} = $ initial domestic price level,

$P_{d1} = $ domestic price level one period later,

$T_d = $ domestic inflation rate.

The nature of the relationships can vary. Some of the alternatives are suggested in Fig. 19.2. Line *a* implies that both the average and marginal relations are one to one. Line *b* implies that the marginal relation is one to one, but the average relation is not. Line *c* implies a relationship, but not a one-to-one relationship.

A few numerical examples will illustrate some of the implications of the purchasing power parity doctrine. Let us assume that for a given period, foreign price levels

Figure 19.2
Alternative parity relationships.

have risen by 32% while domestic price levels have risen by 20%. If the initial exchange rate is FC 10 to $1, the subsequent new exchange rate will be

$$\frac{1.32}{1.20} = \frac{X_1}{10}, \qquad X_1 = 1.1(10) = 11.$$

It will now take 10% more foreign currency units to equal $1, because the relative inflation rate has been higher in the foreign country. Alternatively, with an exchange rate of FC 10 to $1, let us assume that foreign prices have risen by 17% while domestic prices have risen by 30%. The expected new exchange rate would be

$$\frac{1.17}{1.30} = \frac{X_1}{10}, \qquad X_1 = .9(10) = 9.$$

In the present instance, the number of foreign currency units needed to buy $1 would drop by 10%. Thus the value of the foreign currency has increased by 10% due to the differential rates of inflation in domestic vs. foreign prices.

The approximation relationship is

$$T_f - T_d \cong \frac{X_1 - X_0}{X_0}.$$

Using the data from our above example we would have

$$.32 - .20 \cong \frac{11 - 10}{10},$$

$$.12 \cong .10.$$

Empirical studies indicate that while the purchasing power parity relationship does not hold perfectly, it tends to hold in the long run. More fundamentally, the doctrine predicts that an equilibrium rate between two currencies will reflect market forces and that random deviations from the central tendency will tend to be self-correcting; that is, it suggests the existence of some strong equilibrating forces. Furthermore, it argues that the relations between exchange rates will not be haphazard but will reflect underlying economic conditions and changes in these conditions. The relationships are not precise because of a number of factors. These include:

1. Differences in incomes or other endowments between the two countries.
2. Changes in government policies.
3. Transportation costs.
4. Lags in market responses.
5. Differences between the two countries in the price ratios of internationally traded goods to domestically traded goods.
6. The addition of a risk premium influence.

4. The Forward Parity Theorem (FPT)

The consistency among the previous three parity conditions—the Fisher effect, interest rate parity, and purchasing power parity—implies that the real rates of interest between the domestic and foreign country are equal. Then forward parity also holds. The theorem states that the forward exchange rate must be equal to the future (certain) spot exchange rate.

$$X_1 = X_f. \tag{19.4}$$

5. Measurement of Real Gains or Losses

The real gain or loss from holding foreign currency units or net assets denominated in foreign currency units can be calculated by utilizing a number of the relationships set forth thus far. We begin with the end-of-period value of a foreign investment expressed in foreign currency. This is

1) $$F_0(1 + R_{fo}),$$

where F_0 is the value of the foreign investment expressed in foreign currency. If we multiply this expression by the value of a foreign currency unit expressed in dollars and also by the ratio of domestic prices to obtain real values in dollars, we have

2) $$E_1(P_0/P_1)[F_0(1 + R_{fo})].$$

This represents the end-of-period value in deflated dollars of a position taken in foreign currency units. The initial investment in dollars is

3) $$E_0 F_0.$$

If this investment earns at the domestic real rate, its end-of-period value will be

4) $$E_0 F_0(1 + r_d).$$

One plus the real return is the ratio of the end-of-period value of the position in foreign currency units to the end-of-period value of the domestic investment.

5) $$1 + r_1 = \frac{E_1(P_0/P_1)[F_0(1 + R_{fo})]}{E_0 F_0(1 + r_d)}.$$

If the ratio on the right-hand side is equal to one, there is neither a benefit nor a loss from having a long position in foreign currency units as compared to having a long position in domestic currency units. We may next make use of the Fisher relation in the form

6) $$1 + r_d = (1 + R_{do})(P_0/P_1).$$

We then substitute the right-hand side of the above expression for $(1 + r_d)$ in Eq. (5) and obtain Eq. (7a). The F_0's cancel, and

7a) $$1 + r_1 = \frac{(E_1/E_0)(P_0/P_1)(1 + R_{fo})}{(1 + R_{do})(P_0/P_1)}.$$

The price ratios cancel to give us Eq. (7b):

7b) $$1 + r_1 = \frac{(E_1/E_0)(1 + R_{fo})}{1 + R_{do}}.$$

The interest rate parity relationship is written as Eq. (8):

8)
$$\frac{E_0}{E_f} = \frac{1 + R_{f0}}{1 + R_{d0}}.$$

The right-hand side of the equation is substituted in Eq. (7b) yielding Eq. (9).

9)
$$1 + r_1 = \frac{E_1}{E_0} \frac{E_0}{E_f}.$$

Next we cancel the E_0 and solve for r_1:

$$r_1 = (E_1/E_f) - 1. \tag{19.5}$$

Thus the real return (gain or loss) from a long or short position in a foreign currency or net assets denominated in foreign currency units can be determined by a relatively simple expression. It is the ratio of the actual value of the foreign currency's future spot rate in relation to the expected value of its future spot rate reflected in its current forward rate.[1] We can illustrate the measurement of real gains or losses by a number of simple examples. First let us assume that we are long in foreign currency units and that the relative devaluation of the foreign currency units is more than anticipated in the current spot rate (E_f):

$$E_1 = \$.20, \qquad E_f = \$.25.$$

The real gain or loss can therefore be calculated as follows:

$$r_1 = E_1/(E_f - 1) = (.20/.25) - 1 = -20\%.$$

Thus, if we are long in foreign currency units and the forward value of the foreign currency unit was $.25 but its actual spot value at the end of the period is $.20, there has been a loss of 20%. On the other hand, if the spot rate one period later is $.30, we can calculate the real gain as follows:

$$r_1 = (.30/.25) - 1 = +20\%.$$

If we have a short position in the foreign currency units, the signs of the above calculations will be reversed. Thus we have a powerful but simple measurement of gains or losses from long or short positions in foreign currency units or in assets denominated in foreign currency units. The practical implications are that a divergence between the current forward rate and the future spot rate will produce a real gain or loss. This means a violation of the forward parity theorem just discussed.

   An issue raised with regard to the effect of the shift from fixed exchange rates to flexible exchange rates concerns the possibility of an increase in uncertainty under flexible exchange rates which in turn could dampen the rate of growth in international trade. But if hedging can be used to limit risks from exchange rate fluctuations, increased fluctuations will be no problem unless the foreign exchange premium is

---

[1] The insight that the real return on an investment in foreign currency over the real domestic rate of interest can be calculated from the divergence between the anticipated and actual future spot rates of exchange is presented in A. Farber, R. Roll, and B. Solnik, "An Empirical Study of Risk over Fixed and Flexible Exchange," *Journal of Monetary Economics,* Supplementary Series, 1977, 235–265.

increased. Furthermore, if there were an increase in uncertainty and if it were accompanied by an increase in expected returns, the reward-risk ratio could remain unchanged. The simple expression for measuring real gains or losses could thus be used to measure the extent to which net returns from unhedged positions were increased or decreased.

A similar model was formulated by Grauer, Litzenberger, and Stehle [1976]. Their model can be expressed as follows:

$$X_{f0} = E_1(X_1) + L_1 \tag{19.6}$$

where

X_{f0} = the current forward exchange rate,

X_1 = the future spot exchange rate,

E_1 = the expected value operator at time 1,

L_1 = the premium or discount resulting from systematic risk.

Now we can employ our measure of the real return (gain or loss) from a long or short position in a foreign currency or net assets denominated in foreign currency units, as a measure of the premium or discount in the relationship between the current forward rate and the future spot rate. We repeat Eq. (19.5) expressed in dollars per foreign currency unit or foreign currency units per dollar:

$$r_1 = (E_1/E_f) - 1 = (X_f/X_1) - 1. \tag{19.5}$$

In terms of our previous examples, if we are long in foreign currency units and the current forward value of the foreign currency unit *was* \$.25 but its actual spot value at the end of the period *is* \$.20, the future spot rate is at a discount from the current forward rate. This implies that the purchasing power uncertainty reflected in exchange rates is negatively correlated with world wealth so that the risk premium represents a reduction rather than an addition to the real rate of return. Conversely, if the future spot rate is higher than the current forward rate, we obtain a real gain.

If we are in a short position in the foreign currency units, the determination of premiums or discounts will be reversed.

The Fisher relation requires assumptions A1, A3, and A4. The A3 assumption requires that relative prices remain unchanged. Even in a multigood world, IRPT and FPT which are financial arbitrage conditions will still hold. The effects of relaxing other assumptions will be discussed in the following chapter in connection with issues such as the nature of foreign exchange risk.

SUMMARY

International financial markets direct savings flows into countries which can best employ the funds. The law of comparative advantage states that trade will be mutually advantageous since different countries have different relative efficiencies in producing different goods. A comparative advantage means that even though one country could produce some good more efficiently in absolute terms, it has other opportunities which are so superior that it is preferable for some other country—less efficient and with lower opportunity cost—to produce the good.

With a gold standard, countries with surplus exports receive gold in exchange. Domestic prices in the country receiving gold rise, and this price increase in turn stimulates imports to restore the trade balance. Income and employment may also be affected by the adjustment process. Convertibility of currencies to gold at fixed rates forces exchange rates to be fixed. With fixed exchange rates, disequilibrium forces all adjustments to be on prices of individual goods or capital flows.

Floating exchange rates were introduced to allow currency value adjustments based on the relative price changes of each country. The primary advantage is that the exchange rate is a market rate and is more flexible than wages and prices in general. But countries may establish programs to avoid or retard the automatic exchange rate adjustment processes. These include tariffs, duties, quotas, and domestic price controls. Typically the impact is to force the adjustment into another direction, such as changes in real output.

In balance of payments accounting, inflows are recorded as pluses and outflows as minuses. A trade imbalance may trigger a number of offsetting transactions. The numerous subtotals of the balance of payments accounts provide much information about the short- and long-run developments for the economy of any country. Analysis of balance of payments trends can be useful for formulating corporate financial policy in managing exposure to exchange rate fluctuations and in the use of the international financial markets.

Foreign exchange markets enable buyers and sellers in different countries to deal in their own currencies. The foreign exchange rate is the price of one currency in terms of another and depends on the supply and demand relationships between the two currencies. There are strong forces linking spot, forward, future spot, and interest rates between countries. Arbitrage opportunities insure these relationships against breakdowns. The consistency of cross rates means that given any three countries, any one exchange rate will be determined by the other two exchange rates. If the relationship breaks down, an arbitrage opportunity will exist.

The Fisher relation holds that the nominal rate of interest is determined by the real rate of interest and the rate of inflation. The rate of inflation is also equal to the ratio of the expected future spot price to the current price. The current forward price is an estimate of what the future spot price will be.

The IRPT incorporates the Fisher relation by recognizing that between any two currencies the forward exchange rate should be the same as the spot exchange rate except for the anticipated effect of different rates of inflation. Since anticipated inflation rates are incorporated in the nominal interest rates of each country, there is a potential arbitrage possibility between current and forward exchange rates based on the relative interest rates of the countries. The process is known as covered interest arbitrage.

The purchasing power parity doctrine states that the change in exchange rates between countries depends on the relative changes in their prices for the same period. Thus the relative value of the currencies depend on what they will buy.

The forward parity theorem holds that the forward exchange rate will be equal to the future spot exchange rate. It particularly requires the certainty assumption. Implications of relaxing this assumption are developed in the following chapter.

The real return from holding an investment denominated in a foreign currency (over and above the domestic real return) is a simple relationship of the future spot to the forward exchange rate. This relationship directs the international flow of investible funds. The opportunity to make foreign investments broadens opportunities for portfolio diversification.

PROBLEM SET

19.1 You are given the prices of products in two countries as shown below:

	Product	
	X	Y
Country A	$3	$1
Country B	M12	M6

At an exchange rate of 5 marks per dollar, describe the pattern of exports and imports between countries A and B.

19.2 Country A and country B are each on a full gold standard with fixed exchange rates. Country A runs an export surplus while country B runs an export balance deficit. Describe the adjustment process that will restore balance to the flow of trade between the two countries.

19.3 Country A and country B are on the gold standard. The currency of country A contains .1 ounce of gold while the currency of country B contains .025 ounce of gold. What will be the par exchange rate between the two countries?

19.4 Consider two countries C and D operating in a world with complete flexible exchange rates. Country C runs a substantial export surplus to country D, which experiences a substantial trade deficit. Assuming no initial offsetting capital flows, explain the adjustment process to bring the trade between the two countries into balance.

19.5 Keep in mind Table Q19.5 listing the effects of individual transactions on the balance of payments.

Table Q19.5   Effects on the Balance of Payments, Country A

Plus (P)	Minus (M)
1. Exports	1. Imports
2. Increase liabilities to foreigners	2. Decrease liabilities to foreigners
3. Decrease claims on foreigners	3. Increase claims on foreigners
4. Decrease investments; sell assets	4. Increase investments; buy assets

Indicate the plus entry and the minus entry for the following transactions. For example, the country exports goods in the amount of $1000 paid for by the importer by a check on a foreign bank. The entry would be:

$$P1 \quad \$1000 \qquad M3 \quad \$1000$$

a) Country A exports \$10,000 of goods to country I paid for by the importer by a check on his account with a bank in country A.

b) Country A imports \$5000 worth of merchandise paid for by a check on a bank in country A.

c) Direct investment income of \$2000 was received by a firm in country A from a foreign subsidiary which paid by drawing a check on a bank in its own country F.

d) A multinational firm domiciled in country A made an investment of \$1 million on a direct basis to establish a foreign subsidiary in country G. Payment was made by drawing on its bank account in country A.

e) A citizen of country A made a gift of \$3000 to a friend in a foreign country who deposited the check drawn on a bank in country A in his own bank in country M.

f) A citizen in country A bought an airline ticket to Europe which he purchased from Lufthansa Airlines by a check for \$500 drawn on a bank in country A.

19.6 In January 1977 (when DM $3 = \$1$) it was expected that by the end of 1977 the price level in the U.S. would have risen by 10% and in West Germany by 5%. The real rate of interest in both countries is 4%.

a) Use the PPPT to project the expected DMs per \$1 at the end of 1977 (the expected future spot rate of DMs per \$1).

b) Use the Fisher relation to estimate the nominal interest rates in each country which make it possible for investments in each country to earn their real rate of interest.

c) Use the IRPT to estimate the current one-year forward rate of DMs per \$1.

d) Compare your estimate of the current forward rate in (c) with your estimate of the expected future spot rate in (a).

e) Prove analytically that the Fisher effect and the IRPT guarantee consistency with the PPPT relation when real interest rates in the different countries are equal. (Assume that all the fundamental relations hold.)

REFERENCES

Aliber, R. Z., *The International Money Game,* 3rd Ed. Basic Books, New York, 1979.

Caves, R. E., and R. W. Jones, *World Trade and Payments: An Introduction,* 2nd Ed. Little, Brown, Boston, 1977.

Chacholiades, M., *International Trade Theory and Policy,* 2nd Ed. McGraw-Hill, New York, 1978.

Cornell, B., and M. R. Reinganum, "Forward and Future Prices: Evidence from the Foreign Exchange Markets," *Journal of Finance,* December 1981, 1035–1045.

Dornbusch, R., *Open Economy Macro-Economics,* Basic Books, New York, 1980.

Feige, E. L., and K. J. Singleton, "Multinational Inflation Under Fixed Exchange Rates: Some Empirical Evidence from Latent Variable Models," *Review of Economics and Statistics,* February 1981, 11–19.

Grauer, F. L. A., R. H. Litzenberger, and R. E. Stehle, "Sharing Rules and Equilibrium in an International Capital Market Under Uncertainty," *Journal of Financial Economics*, June 1976, 233–256.

Grubel, H. G., *International Economics*. Richard D. Irwin, Homewood, Ill., 1977.

Huang, R. D., "The Monetary Approach to Exchange Rate in an Efficient Foreign Exchange Market: Tests Based on Volatility," *Journal of Finance*, March 1981, 31–41.

Johannes, J. M., "Testing the Exogeneity Specification Underlying the Monetary Approach to the Balance of Payments," *Review of Economics and Statistics*, February 1981, 29–34.

Kreinin, M. E., *International Economics: A Policy Approach*, 3rd Ed. Harcourt Brace Jovanovich, New York, 1979.

Lindert, P. H., and C. P. Kindleberger, *International Economics*, 7th Ed. Richard D. Irwin, Homewood, Ill., 1982.

Rolfe, S. E., and J. L. Burtle, *The Great Wheel: The World Monetary System*, Quadrangle/ The New York Times Book Company, New York, 1973.

Solnik, B. H., *European Capital Markets*. Lexington Books, Lexington, Mass., 1973.

Solomon, R., *The International Monetary System, 1945–1976, An Insider's View*. Harper & Row, New York, 1977.

Takayama, A., *International Trade*. Holt, Rinehart and Winston, New York, 1972.

Yeager, L. B., *International Monetary Mechanism*. Holt, Rinehart and Winston, New York, 1968.

———, *International Monetary Relations: Theory, History and Policy*, 2nd Ed. Harper & Row, New York, 1976.

International Financial Management: Tests and Implications

The exchanges between countries are at par only, whilst they have precisely that quantity of currency which in the actual situation of things, they should have to carry on the circulation of their commodities.

DAVID RICARDO, *PRINCIPLES OF POLITICAL ECONOMY AND TAXATION,* GONNER EDITION, LONDON, G. BELL AND SONS, LTD., 1927, PP. 213–214.

A fundamental dimension of international investment is the existence of exchange risk and mechanisms providing inducements to investors to carry that risk. Intertemporal equilibrium models of international capital markets which take into account exchange risk, the existence of different interest rates, and different tastes across the world will be treated in this chapter. It will be demonstrated that changes in relative prices of goods due to supply or demand shifts induce changes in exchange rates and deviations from purchasing power parity. Although there are some difficulties in testing international asset pricing models, empirical studies show that an international market structure of price behavior appears to exist. Finally, techniques to minimize foreign exchange exposure and methods of foreign currency translation will be discussed.

A. INTERNATIONAL DIVERSIFICATION

From the purely financial point of view, investors, whether they be firms or individuals, ought to consider the possibility of expanding their investments beyond the geographical limits of their own countries, if only because of the greater number and diversity of investment possibilities available. If the universe of assets available for investment is larger than just the assets in one country, even a country as large as the United States, our discussion in earlier chapters should suggest that investors may be able to reduce the risk of their investment portfolios by diversifying across countries. Solnik [1974b] has some empirical estimates for the risk of an internationally diversified portfolio compared to a diversified portfolio which is purely *domestic*. Using weekly data on stocks in eight major European countries and the United States, Solnik found that an internationally diversified portfolio would be $\frac{1}{10}$ as risky as a typical security, and $\frac{1}{2}$ as risky as a well-diversified portfolio of U.S. stocks alone. He used the variance of returns as a measure of risk. He also found that inter*industry* diversification is inferior to intercountry diversification.

In a related study, Jacquillat and Solnik [1978] compared the performance of multinational corporations with that of an internationally diversified portfolio. By the same risk measure as above, a portfolio of U.S. multinational firms has about 90% of the standard deviation of a purely domestic U.S. portfolio. Internationally diversified portfolios have only about 30% to 50% of the risk of the U.S. domestic portfolio. This is suggestive evidence that the international dimension has not yet been fully exploited by MNCs. A portfolio of MNC stocks is a poor substitute to the investor for a truly internationally diversified portfolio.

B. ASSET PRICING MODELS

Asset pricing models, similar in form and spirit to the CAPM, have been derived for international financial assets. In a manner analogous to the standard CAPM derivations in continuous time, Solnik develops an International Asset Pricing Model (IAPM), and tests it [1974a, 1974d]. A market portfolio, with properties similar to that in the CAPM, is specified by:

1. Market-value-weighted stocks,
2. A pure exchange-risk portfolio of risk-free assets of the various countries in the world. Relative weights in this portfolio depend on net foreign investment positions in each country and the relative risk aversions of citizens of each country.

A risk-pricing relationship similar in form to the standard CAPM is derived:

$$E(r_i) - R_i = \beta_i(E[r_m] - R_m),$$

where:

r_i = the return on a security i,

R_i = the riskless rate in the country of security i in terms of the currency of country i,

R_m = an average riskless rate, with weights as in the market portfolio,

r_m = the return on the world market portfolio,

β_i = the *international* systematic risk coefficient of security i.

In his empirical tests, Solnik [1974a, 1974d] used daily data on stocks of eight European countries and of the United States. The results are weakly consistent with his IAPM. Solnik [1974d] also used the Solnik IAPM to test whether assets are best regarded as being traded in national (segmented) or in international (integrated) markets. This test is a simple extension of his IAPM tests. He found some evidence that markets are integrated, in that the IAPM performs better than a purely national specification.

Grauer, Litzenberger, and Stehle [1976] (GLS) also derive an International Asset Pricing Model, but under the assumptions of identical tastes across countries. Stehle [1977], building on GLS, improved upon Solnik's specification of the integration hypothesis and corrected some econometric problems with Solnik's methodology. He also found weak evidence in support of integration.

1. Use of Consumption Opportunity Sets

A new development in the field of International Asset Pricing parallels an advance in the standard, domestic asset pricing theory. Breeden [1979] developed an asset pricing model which explicitly noted that individuals derive their utility from consumption. Maximizing lifetime utility from consumption, Breeden developed a more complete model for asset pricing, wherein pricing of an asset depended on covariances with aggregate consumption rather than any "market" index or portfolio. Such a model is more general than standard market models because, under certain conditions, a consumption-based model is equivalent to a multibeta model where an asset's pricing is allowed to depend on *many* state variables. In the field of International Finance, Stulz [1981] used Breeden's results to develop an asset pricing theory, much as Solnik [1974c] had followed Merton's [1973] lead.

Stulz extended Solnik's model essentially by allowing consumption opportunities to differ across countries, at least temporarily, until arbitrage through trade flows equalizes them. Stulz notes that Solnik's model requires the exchange rate to be perfectly correlated with the relative price of the two countries' imports (the terms of trade). The empirical evidence is that, although a correlation exists, it is not perfect [Isard (1978)]. Stulz allows the consumption opportunity set to differ across countries. By "consumption opportunity set" is meant the set of goods available for consumption, current prices, and the distribution of future prices of these goods. It is assumed that prices of commodities and the exchange rate itself, follow a stochastic Ito process. All assets are assumed to be traded, but all commodities are not. The law of one price (naive PPP) holds only for traded goods. A pricing relationship is derived, which states that

$$\mu - V_{aPm} = (T^W)^{-1}\{V_{aC} - V_{aP\alpha}C\} \quad \text{where} \quad T^W = T^F + T^D. \tag{26}$$

Stulz [1981, p. 396] comments on his equation (26) as follows:

> *Here μ is the vector of expected excess returns for domestic investors. The excess return of an asset for a domestic investor is defined as the return in the domestic country of a portfolio with a long holding of that asset financed by selling the nominal safe bond of the home-country of the asset. T^W is a measure of world risk-tolerance. V_{aC} is the vector of covariances between home-country returns of risky assets and changes in world consumption in domestic currency. V_{aPm} and $V_{aP\alpha}$ are the vectors of covariances of home-country returns with d ln Pm and d ln Pα. An increase in Pm means a decrease in the real value of a marginal dollar of consumption expenditures, whereas an increase in Pα means a fall in the real value of total consumption expenditures. Eq. (26) is the fundamental pricing equation of this paper.*

From his equation (26), a proposition is shown to follow: The expected excess real return of a risky asset is proportional to the covariance between the home currency rate of return of that asset and changes in world real consumption rate. Note that the return on an asset does not depend on unexpected changes in the exchange rate, so exchange rate risk is not rewarded.

As a further result, Stulz shows that the forward exchange rate is inversely proportional to the covariance between the changes in the exchange rate and changes in the real world consumption rate. This is the first full model to permit the forward rate to change through time, always remaining in equilibrium. Stulz finally notes that this more general model of asset pricing in international financial markets may explain why some previous models seemed to find the international financial markets to be segmented: If changes in the world consumption rate are not perfectly correlated with the market indices used by previous researchers, spurious results may flow from the misspecification of the tested models. The Breeden and Stulz models have not been systematically tested to date.

2. Difficulties of Testing IAPM

The IAPM is subject to the same sort of problem in empirical testing that Roll [1977] has noted with the conventional CAPM. Strongly influenced by Roll's critique, Solnik [1977] pointed out that testing the IAPM in a satisfactory manner is an essentially impossible task. All the problems in testing methodology observed by Roll continue to plague the testing of the IAPM—after all, merely a variant of the CAPM.

In addition, the IAPM has its own problems. Solnik makes two points:

1. It is well-documented that the covariance between national indices is quite low. In that case, even if markets were *completely* segmented and assets priced *entirely* in domestic markets, with no influence of the international financial markets, an "optimal" portfolio, artificially constructed by the researcher without regard to actual feasibility, will always end up being well-diversified internationally. Such

a portfolio will be mean-variance efficient, and an IAPM-type test will "succeed," using this "optimal" portfolio as a proxy for the "world market portfolio." This is a direct consequence of Roll's insight about the role of the index. So the success of the test tells us nothing about how assets are actually priced.

2. Even if there were no conceptual problem as above, there is a practical problem. In Solnik's derivation of the IAPM, the world market portfolio turns out to include a portfolio he calls a "pure exchange risk asset." Weights of the nominally riskless securities of different countries in this portfolio are shown to be dependent on the net foreign investment positions in the different countries, and the relative risk-aversions of citizens of the different countries. This specification would be difficult to implement in practice.

C. EXCHANGE RISK AND PURCHASING POWER PARITY

Fluctuating exchanges are often viewed as an additional source of risk facing the investor or trader importing and exporting goods. The prices of commodities, the yields on assets, are usually fixed in nominal terms, i.e., in fixed amounts of foreign currency at the time of transacting. An investor who buys a $100 pure discount bond, for example, knows only that he or she will receive $100 at the maturity of the bond. But if the investor happens to be German who needs marks for consumption, he or she does not know how many marks the dollars received will buy. That depends on the exchange rate between the $ and the mark. With the highly fluctuating exchange rates of recent years, this seems to be a new and substantial source of risk to the investor or trader.

Because the value of the investor's return at the end of the period is uncertain in terms of the investor's home currency, his or her consumption is uncertain. This is readily interpretable as the risk that the variations in exchange rates over a period will not exactly offset inflation differentials, which is another way of saying that PPP will not hold. Thus deviations from PPP acquire practical significance in terms of exchange risk.

The key to understanding departures from PPP, or equivalently, the phenomenon of exchange risk, is to recognize that there are many consumption goods. Further, people in different countries have different consumption baskets—they consume the goods in different proportions. For example, the Japanese consume more sake than wine and the French consume more wine than sake. Such differences may be caused by a variety of factors: social, cultural, historical—everything subsumed under the expression "different tastes."

The relative prices of goods can fluctuate over time because of shifts in supply or demand conditions. Demand conditions may change with changes in tastes due to shifts in the demographic composition of the population, for example. Supply conditions may change due to bad weather or because of technological innovation.

We now proceed to distinguish between two phenomena: fluctuations in inflation rates and fluctuations in relative prices. When we say "fluctuations in inflation rates," we assume that everyone has the same consumption basket of goods, and that relative prices are unchanged. This is an assumption for simplification. In reality, both the overall price level and the relative prices of goods are likely to fluctuate simultaneously.

1. Inflation Risk

Suppose that we are investors in the United States who have a security in England whose return is fixed in £ terms. Assuming that there is no inflation in the United States, but that the inflation rate in England is *uncertain,* the dollar value of our investment at the end of the period is uncertain and hence risky. Our position has "exchange risk." It is clear that this "exchange risk" is simply inflation risk. With no relative price fluctuations, arbitrage of physical goods will ensure that PPP holds, because now, in a sense, there is only one consumption good "composite" and PPP is the same as the law of one price, which always holds in perfect commodity markets. The change in exchange rate reflects exactly the change in inflation rates and nothing else.

However, the risk of our position is purely nominal. It can be eliminated by indexing all contracts, tying the quantity of £ from the investment to the price index in England, for instance, or contracting in "real" terms. To the extent this is not feasible or not done, it reflects information costs or transactions costs of doing so. In our present model of the world, it is perfectly feasible to eliminate nominal risk completely. In any case, the point is that it is a mistake to attribute the "risk" to the exchange rate. It is caused by uncertainty about the foreign price level, not so much by the phenomenon of fluctuating exchange rates. If all contracts were written in real terms, all profits, all returns on investments of all kinds, would be independent of the geographical location of the investor or the investment, and the exchange rate would have no real role to play beyond the arithmetic of conversions. Grauer, Litzenberger, and Stehle [1976] have shown that, in the case where all individuals in the world have the same tastes, if a real riskless asset exists, all individuals face the same investment and consumption opportunity set—and so which country the investor happens to be in is irrelevant. The exchange risk is then merely some sort of white noise that has no effect on anything real, though it gives apparent fluctuations in prices in nominal terms. Under the assumption of identical homothetic tastes (equivalent to one consumption good when relative prices are constant), for the exchange risk to be irrelevant is for goods arbitrage to be instantaneous and costless, so that the real price of a good will be the same everywhere in the world.

2. "Real" Exchange Risk

Thus far we have assumed, explicitly, that relative prices are constant. But for exchange risk to matter to the investor, it must not be purely nominal. Such "real" risk is caused, we shall now see, by relative price fluctuations. The assumption of one consumption good is now dropped.

Solnik [1974c] was the first to explore formally the implications to financial markets of a world where individuals in different countries consume different baskets of goods. We shall use Solnik's [1978] example of Japanese who consume more sake than wine and French who consume more wine than sake. (We shall follow his notation for ease of reference to the original.) Wine and sake are the only goods in the world. It is not necessary for this story that the French produce wine and only wine, or that the Japanese produce sake and only sake.

Suppose, to begin with, the price of sake equals the price of wine—i.e., the relative price is 1, in both countries. The relative price must be the same in both countries, else there will be goods arbitrage, since the transportation of goods is perfect, instantaneous, and costless by the assumptions of the model. Suppose also that the exchange rate, which we shall define to be the price of yen in francs, is also 1. Next postulate an exogenous shock, e.g., something damages the wine crop. Then the relative prices of the two goods will change at once to reflect the reduced supply of wine. Wine will become more expensive. Again, because of the possibility of goods arbitrage, the relative price between wine and sake must be the same in both countries. The question we seek to answer is: What will be the new exchange rate? Assume the following relationships:

Before the shock

	wine	sake
French consumption	9 units	1 unit
Japanese consumption	1 unit	9 units

Price of wine = Price of sake. The exchange rate $1:1$

After the shock

	wine	sake
French consumption	8 units	$1\frac{1}{2}$ units
Japanese consumption	$\frac{1}{3}$ unit	$9\frac{1}{2}$ units

The price of wine = 1.5 × price of sake (assumed also).

The exchange rate is to be determined.

Note that the consumptions have adjusted to the changed relative price. Now, we need to separate the effect of a relative price change from that of an inflationary change. We next assume that there is no general rise in the price level in either country. The governments in both countries do whatever they have to do to ensure that the price of the consumption baskets remain the same in terms of their respective local currencies: adjusting the money supply, etc.

Let the price of sake and wine in France be S_f^0 and W_f^0 and in Japan be S_j^0 and W_j^0 in francs and yen respectively before the shock. Let W_f^1, S_f^1; W_j^1, S_j^1 be the corresponding after-the-shock prices in nominal terms (i.e., in terms of the home currencies—francs in France and yen in Japan).

We know that

$$S_j^0 = W_j^0,$$

$$S_f^0 = W_f^0; \qquad \text{The relative price} = 1.$$

$$W_j^1 = 1.5 \ S_j^1,$$

$$W_f^1 = 1.5 \ S_f^1; \qquad \text{The new relative price} = 1.5.$$

In France: The consumption basket cost is $9 \ W_f^0 + 1 \ S_f^0 = 10 \ S_f^0$ francs before the shock. The consumption bundle after the shock costs $8 \ W_f^1 + 1.5 \ S_f^1 = 12 \ S_f^1 + 1.5 \ S_f^1 = 13.5 \ S_f^1$ francs. Because we are assuming no inflation, the price of the consumption basket in francs must be the same before and after the shock in nominal terms. Then $10 \ S_f^0 = 13.5 \ S_f^1$. So

$$S_f^1 = \tfrac{10}{13.5} S_f^0. \tag{20.1}$$

In Japan: The cost of the consumption bundle, in yen, is $9 \ S_j^0 + 1 \ W_j^0 = 10 \ S_j^0$ before the shock. After the shock, it is $9.5 \ S_j^1 + \tfrac{1}{3} \ W_j^1 = 9.5 \ S_j^1 + \tfrac{1}{3} \times 1.5 \ S_j^1 = 10 \ S_j^1$. By the no-inflation condition, $10 \ S_j^0 = 10 \ S_j^1$ or

$$S_j^1 = S_j^0 \tag{20.2}$$

Now we note that by the law of one price, the price of sake must be the same in both countries at a given time, after converting by the new exchange rate. Then after the shock, $\tfrac{10}{13.5} S_f^0$ francs must buy a unit of sake in both France and Japan, equation (20.1). Recall that $S_f^0 = S_j^0$ because the initial exchange rate was 1. By (20.2) we also have

$$S_f^0 = S_j^0 = S_j^1.$$

Hence we can substitute S_j^1 for S_f^0 in equation (20.1), to obtain

$$S_f^1 = \tfrac{10}{13.5} S_j^1.$$

This demonstrates that the new exchange rate will be .741 francs/yen. At the old exchange rate one yen was equal to 1 franc. At the new exchange rate one yen is now worth only .741 francs.

Cornell [1980] provides a verbal explanation of the algebraic development. Because the cost of wine has risen, less wine will be consumed in both France and Japan. Because the French government was holding the inflation in France to 0, the price of the French basket could not rise in terms of francs. Japan also offset the rise in cost of its own basket. But that basket rose less than did the French, so the offsetting also had to be less. Hence the cost of the *French* basket must rise in *yen*. It cannot rise in francs, as we have seen. Yet the law of one price (no goods arbitrage) requires that the French basket cost the same, after conversion for the exchange rate, in both France and Japan. The only way this can happen is if the price of yen falls relative to the price of francs, which is what happened. Stockman [1980] makes the same general point.

In the Solnik example, the exchange rate fluctuation is a "real" risk, because we cannot hedge it away merely by contracting in real terms. Those in France who have invested in Japan get only .741 of what they expected to get, in francs, and can only buy, in their own consumption baskets, .741 of what they had expected to buy if the shock had not occurred and the exchange rate had not changed.

In what sense is this an "exchange risk"? The "risk" was caused by a change in relative prices of goods. The risk did not come from the exchange rate directly. The exchange rate only reflected something more fundamental that changed. In fact, business firms always face the risk that there may be changes in the relative prices of their product relative to its substitutes, of the product relative to the inputs, etc. (So does any individual: a vegetarian, for example, always faces the risk that the price of his or her food will change relative to the price of meat.) The point is that it is important to recognize that "exchange risk" is essentially the same as "business" risk. The fact that the firm may be operating in two different countries causes it only to be *manifested,* partly, through the exchange rate. To ascribe the investor's risk to the phenomenon of exchange rate fluctuations, or to the fact of flexible exchange rates, is to mistake the symptom for the malady.

To return this discussion to PPP, recall that in the extended example of the wine and sake there was no inflation in either country. PPP would require that the exchange rate remain the same. But it did not. Hence PPP was violated. "Real exchange risk" is to be found wherever PPP is violated.

3. Roll's Study of PPP Violations

In an efficient market's perspective, we would expect PPP to hold on an expected-value basis, since the relative price fluctuations are random and not predictable, by their very nature. Observed violations of PPP should be uncorrelated over time.

Roll [1979] provided the first rigorous intertemporal specification of PPP and fused it with the notion of market efficiency. He set the *expected* return to intertemporal speculation conditional on information at the beginning of the period equal to zero. He found PPP to be valid in an average sense. However, the deviations from it attributable to relative price fluctuations dominated the effects of inflation on the exchange rates.

4. Empirical Investigation of Exchange Risk

We have established in theory that exchange risk, both nominal and real, may be substantial. Solnik [1974c] developed a model of exchange risk, as part of a larger theory of international asset pricing, which was empirically examined by Roll and Solnik [1977]. They used Solnik's formulation for exchange risk to test its magnitude and significance in asset pricing. Monthly data on six European countries, Canada, and the United States were used. The equilibrium relationship Solnik had derived showed that the difference between riskless nominal rates in two countries should be equal to the expected change in exchange rates plus a term depending on exchange rate covariances. Their findings indicate that exchange risk is substantial and significant.

D. MARKET EFFICIENCY

Having considered some fundamental ways in which the international financial markets may differ from domestic financial markets, we may now proceed to ask the sorts of questions we have been asking in our earlier studies of the domestic markets: To what degree are exchange markets efficient? What is the empirical magnitude and significance of exchange risk? Several possible approaches to the question of efficiency of the exchange markets are first examined.

1. Testing Arbitrage Relationships

The minimum requirement a market must satisfy if it is to be said to be efficient, is that no arbitrage possibilities must exist. Recall that the Interest Rate Parity Theorem (IRPT) is one such arbitrage relationship that must hold in international financial markets. Consistent and systematic deviations from IRPT outside the bounds of transactions costs, may be interpreted as evidence of inefficiency.

Frenkel and Levich [1977] study this question. They explicitly account for transactions costs and calculate a band around the interest rate parity line within which no arbitrage is profitable. Using weekly data for the period 1962–1975 and for three subperiods they found that a very high percentage of observations are within the neutral band (more than 90% in most cases.) They conclude that—after allowing for transaction costs and ensuring that the arbitraged assets are comparable—covered interest arbitrage does not seem to entail unexploited opportunities for profit.

2. Equilibrium Pricing Models

Another approach to testing the efficiency of international financial markets, but without confining the test to arbitrage relationships between assets of "equal risk," is to develop a model for the pricing of risky assets and test whether financial markets price assets accordingly. In our study of domestic financial markets, for instance, we saw that tests of the CAPM can be construed to be joint tests of market efficiency and of the model itself. But a rejection of the model in empirical testing would be a rejection of the notion of efficiency of the market in which the assets are traded.

3. Trading Rule Tests

Another approach is to examine the profitability of simple trading rules like filters. One such study is by Cornell and Dietrich [1978]. Using daily exchange rates for the period March 1973 to September 1975, for a sample of currencies of major industrialized nations, they set up some simple filter-rule based trading strategies, taking transaction costs into account.

In the moving average filter, when the exchange rate moves $X\%$ above the moving average for a prespecified interval, the rule calls for the investor to move into the foreign currency; when it falls $X\%$ below the moving average, the investor moves back into dollars. Moving averages of 10, 25, and 50 days were tried. None of these filter rules produced a profit of more than 4% per annum for the British pound, Canadian dollar, or Japanese yen. However, the situation was quite different with the German mark, the Dutch guilder, and Swiss franc. The 25-day moving average rule consistently produced profits of more than 15% per annum for all three currencies, with filters ranging from 0.2% to 2.0%. The simple filter did not do quite as well, because of the larger transactions costs accruing to the larger number of transactions it triggered. Still, it did produce profits of more than 10% for some filters.

The three currencies with the high trading-rule profits were also the three with the highest variance. Hence the "profit" observed may well be merely compensation for the greater risk of trading in these currencies. Since variance alone is not systematic risk, Cornell and Dietrich attempted to separate the systematic from the unsystematic portion of the total variation. Exchange rate variations were correlated with the S&P 500 index as the "market." The result was to eliminate almost entirely the risk of these currencies, casting doubt on the proposition that the "excess profit" was a "risk-premium."

As with all filter tests, the main problem in interpretation of the results seems to be that we do not know how to adjust for the different risks of the alternative strategies. Also, it does not appear that there is any way to determine, *ex ante,* the appropriate size of filter to test. They depend on historical relationships which are likely to be unstable over time.

4. Forward Speculation

A fourth approach to testing the efficiency of markets is to examine the returns to forward speculation. The basic assumption underlying the simpler versions of this class of efficiency tests is that the forward rate should be an unbiased forecaster of the future spot rate. But there may be good theoretical reasons for the forward rate to be systematically different from the expected (corresponding) future spot rate. For example, Stockman [1978] developed a simple model with only money supply uncertainty which shows that the forward rate may have a risk premium associated with it, which would lead it to be a biased estimator of the future spot rate. Another model that makes the same point is that of Grauer, Litzenberger, and Stehle [1976]. A forward bias can also come from the "real" exchange risk.

To turn to the empirical evidence itself, it appears that, on the whole, the forward rate is very close to the expected future spot rate. Stockman [1978], found that the risk premium is significant only for a couple of currencies (the British pound and the Swiss franc). He interpreted it to mean that the risk premium was not important. The risk premium, when significant, was not stable across subperiods. The question of exchange market efficiency was also studied by Cornell [1977]. Using monthly data on exchange rates for eight industrialized countries, Cornell finds:

1. There is some evidence of autocorrelation in the simple martingale model $E[X_t] = X_{t-1}$ where X is the spot exchange rate. Autoregressive models fit the data better.

2. He also tests the model $F_{t-1} = E_{t-1}[X_t] + L_t$ and $E_{t-1}[X_t] = X_t + u_t,$

where

X = the spot rate,

F = the forward rate,

L = a liquidity premium or risk-premium,

u = the error term.

Cornell explicitly allows for the fact that a bias may exist in the forward rate as a predictor of the future spot rate.

The results are that the liquidity premium is positive but generally insignificant. Furthermore, autocorrelations are found in the residuals of $F_{t-1} - X_t$, suggesting that the liquidity premium is not stationary. A test is constructed for determining whether the forward rate incorporates all information in the history of spot rates. Since L_t (the liquidity premium) is not identically zero, it is necessary to assume that it is uncorrelated with past spot rates (a reasonable assumption), in which case equations of the form: $F_{t-1} - X_t = a_0 + a_1 [X_{t-1} - X_{t-2}]$ can be estimated. The behavior of the coefficients in this and other autoregressive models is very similar to that of the corresponding coefficients in the autoregressive models for the exchange rate changes alone (with no forward rate). This leads Cornell to conclude that the market prices forward exchange contracts as if the exchange rates are generated by a stochastic process with a constant term and a random noise term, since the autocorrelations in exchange rates changes are apparently ignored by the forward pricing market. Cornell suggests that the autocorrelations in the data could be caused by data problems and the (efficient) market correctly ignores them. He also found that the martingale model slightly outperforms the forward rate as a predictor of future exchange rates.

5. Performance of Forecasting Services

A final way to test for the efficiency of the exchange market is to study whether forecasting services can "beat" the market. This is a test of efficiency in semistrong form. Levich [1979] analyzes the currency forecasts made by a forecasting service. He found that the particular service studied yielded profits consistently and significantly for some currencies. For other currencies, it lost. The results of such studies have been mixed and generally hard to interpret. On the whole, the picture that emerges from this literature on efficiency seems similar to the picture we have seen in earlier chapters of domestic financial markets. The evidence is consistent with weak-form and semistrong-form efficiency.

With the background of the general framework of Chapter 19 and the discussion of exchange risk, asset pricing models, and market efficiency in the present chapter, we next turn to the implications for management policy.

E. MANAGERIAL ASPECTS OF FOREIGN EXCHANGE RISKS

The exposure of a business firm to foreign exchange risks is defined by the pattern of its cash flow and asset stock positions which in turn depend upon the pattern of flow of future receipts and payments and the pattern of the firm's net monetary position. Monetary assets are those assets denominated in a fixed number of units of money such as cash, marketable securities, accounts receivable, tax refunds receivable, notes receivable, and prepaid insurance. Monetary liabilities are those liabilities expressed in fixed monetary terms, such as accounts payable, notes payable, tax liability reserves, bonds, and preferred stock.

The effects of a net monetary position exposure can be formulated as follows:

$$C_p = [(MA - ML)/X_0 - (MA - ML)/X_1](1 - t_{U.S.})$$
$$= (E_0 - E_1)(MA - ML)(1 - t_{U.S.})$$
$$= (E_0 - E_1)(NMP)(1 - t_{U.S.}),$$

where

C_p = cost of net monetary position (NMP) due to exchange-rate changes,

MA = monetary assets,

ML = monetary liabilities,

X_0 = exchange rate at the beginning = $1/E_0$,

X_1 = exchange rate a period later = $1/E_1$,

$t_{U.S.}$ = tax rate in the United States.

The effects of a decline in foreign currency value are:

a) Net monetary debtor gains.

b) Net monetary creditor loses.

Let us assume that

$$MA = FC\ 200,000; \qquad X_0 = 4, \qquad t_{U.S.} = .5;$$
$$ML = FC\ 100,000; \qquad X_1 = 5.$$

We calculate the net monetary position to which the effect of the exchange rate shift is applied.

1) $NMP = MA - ML = 200,000 - 100,000 = 100,000;$

$$C_p = NMP(E_0 - E_1)(1 - t_{U.S.}) = 100,000(.25 - .20)(.5)$$
$$= \$5000(.5) = \$2500.$$

Our calculations show a decrease in the dollar value of our asset position; that is, a loss of $2,500.

We now let ML = FC 300,000. Then

2) $NMP = MA - ML = 200,000 - 300,000 = -100,000;$

$$C_p = NMP(E_0 - E_1)(1 - t_{U.S.}) = -100,000(.25 - .20)(.5)$$
$$= -\$2500.$$

The net amount owed is decreased by $2500, representing a gain.

The effects of an increase in FC value are:

a) Net monetary debtor loses.

b) Net monetary creditor gains.

1) $\quad\quad$ MA = FC 10 million, $\quad$ $X_0 = 5$, $\quad$ $t_{\text{U.S.}} = 0$;

$\quad\quad\quad$ ML = FC 8 million, $\quad$ $X_1 = 4$,

$\quad\quad$ NMP = $10,000,000 - 8,000,000 = 2,000,000$,

$\quad\quad\quad$ C_p = NMP$(E_0 - E_1) = 2,000,000(.20 - .25) = -\$100,000$.

The cost is a negative \$100,000, representing a gain in the value of the net monetary position with revaluation upward in the FC currency.

2) $\quad\quad$ Let MA = FC 6 million. Then

$\quad\quad$ NMP = $6,000,000 - 8,000,000 = -2,000,000$,

$\quad\quad\quad$ C_p = NMP$(E_0 - E_1) = -2,000,000(.20 - .25) = +\$100,000$.

Both terms are negative, so their product is positive, indicating that revaluation upward results in a positive cost (or a *loss*) to a firm in a negative net monetary position (monetary liabilities exceed monetary assets). The FC values of its net obligations have increased.

The impact of an exposed position is similar if the exposure results from an excess of receipts over payments due to be paid in the foreign currency. A firm in this situation faces several combinations of patterns. We illustrate some of the alternatives:

1. The firm is exposed to a decline in the value of foreign currencies. Then:

a) Expected future receipts exceed expected future payments.

b) The net monetary position is positive—monetary assets exceed monetary liabilities.

A firm in such a position will lose from a devaluation (or decrease in value or depreciation in the value) of foreign currencies.

2. The firm is exposed to an increase in the value of foreign currencies. Then:

a) Expected future payments exceed expected future receipts.

b) The net monetary position is negative.

A firm in such a position is concerned about upward revaluation of foreign currencies.

We can state as a general proposition that unless the payments and receipts in relation to the future net monetary position of the firm exactly balance, the firm is exposed to a decline or increase in the value of foreign currencies. Ordinarily, the normal pattern of operations will put the firm in an exposed position which it can limit only by taking certain steps, all of which involve a cost. One strategy may be to rearrange the pattern of payments and the pattern of holdings of monetary assets and liabilities in foreign currencies to achieve perfect balance so that the net exposure is zero. But changes in the flow of receipts and payments or in the holdings of monetary assets and liabilities represent departures from the firm's normal operations. Such artificial changes from the firm's normal patterns will involve costs. To determine whether such adjustments are better than alternative methods of limiting exposure requires that management calculate the costs of altering the patterns of cash flows or of its net monetary position. This may be a rather complex undertaking for an individual firm, but is nonetheless necessary if the firm is to make a rational choice among alternatives.

The next broad strategic analysis of alternatives that a firm may make is to gather and evaluate information about expected future rates of exchange. The development of an information bank providing data which permit the formulation of expected future exchange rates involves costs. The firm could purchase a forecasting service instead of developing its own information, but this also requires costs as well as outlays and efforts to appraise the service's qualifications and reliability.

In one perspective, if the foreign exchange markets are efficient and the interest rate parity relationship always holds, then the future expected exchange rates will be reflected in the current forward rate of exchange. However, given the dynamic changes that take place in the world economic environment (uncertainty), it is likely that future spot rates will be different from the levels forecast for them by the current forward rates. In theory, random changes in the relationship could be eliminated by forming portfolios so that the relationships would be subject only to systematic changes. The true minimum cost of protection against exposure to foreign exchange risk would then be measured by the covariance of the performance of such portfolios with changes in a world (market) portfolio, appropriately defined and measured. Recall the previous discussions of the difficulties presented in the literature on international asset pricing models (IAPM). In addition, transaction costs occur in the formation of such portfolios.

The behavior of firms will inherently involve a comparison of three alternatives. One is to develop information about and formulate expectations of the relation between expected future exchange rates and the current forward rate. A second alternative is to seek to hedge by using the forward market. A third alternative is to hedge by utilizing the money and capital markets. A continuous comparison of these three alternatives will lead to arbitrage operations by the firms which will tend to produce efficiency in the foreign exchange markets. We next discuss a format for calculating the net receipts or costs of utilizing the three alternative approaches.

Initially we assume that it would be very expensive for the firm to rearrange the pattern of receipts and payments along with its position in monetary assets and monetary liabilities to achieve zero exposure. Let us then first consider the firm which, on balance, expects future receipts to exceed future payments and/or has a net monetary position that is positive. The risk exposure faced by the firm is a decline in the value of the foreign currency. Hence the firm fears depreciation in the value of the foreign currency and will take action to deal with this possibility. We now set forth the framework for analyzing the cost of the three alternative protective policies the firm may follow.

Let us initially assume that the current spot price of the foreign currency expressed in dollars is $.30 = E_0$. The exposure is FC 100,000. The forward rate, E_f, is equal to $.25$. The action taken by the firm depends on its expectation of the future spot rate and the degree of confidence in that expectation. If the firm judges that the future spot rate will be \$.23 and does not hedge, it will incur a loss of \$7000. However, if the firm expects the future spot rate to be \$.27, it will expect to incur a loss of only \$3000. The current forward rate is the market's best judgment of what the future spot rate will be. If E_1 will actually be \$.25, it is a matter of indifference whether the firm hedges its long position in foreign currency or whether it does not purchase protection. There is an important consideration, however. If the firm enters into the forward market, it knows the cost of its foreign exchange risk exposure. This cost can be taken into account in the supply price of the goods and services sold. Therefore obtaining protection against the foreign exchange risk exposure limits the expected loss and removes uncertainty due to fluctuations between the current forward rate and the actual future spot rate.

The firm seeking protection against the foreign exchange risk exposure may employ two alternative methods.[1] One is the use of the forward market. The other is the use of the money and capital markets. If the interest rate parity relationship holds, it is a matter of indifference as to which of these two methods is employed. However, because temporary differences may develop, it is the arbitrage behavior, seeking to benefit from these divergences, that brings the markets back to interest rate parity. Let us suppose that interest rates in the foreign market are 32% while interest rates in the domestic market are 10%. Then the expected ratio between the current spot rate and the current forward rate is 1.2. If the current spot rate is .3, the equilibrium forward rate is .25 $(1.32/1.10 = .30/E_f)$.

If parity obtains, the cost of hedging in the forward market or of borrowing in foreign currency and investing in the United States is the same. For example, if the amount of foreign currency involved is 100,000 FC units, then the cost of hedging in the foreign market, C_f, is

$$C_f = (E_0 - E_f)F_0$$
$$= (.30 - .25)100,000$$
$$= \$5,000.$$

In the money and capital markets the situation is different from the covered interest arbitrage operation because an exposure of FC 100,000 already exists. If FC 100,000 is borrowed in the foreign country to neutralize the foreign exchange risk exposure, the principal is covered by the future net receipts or net monetary assets position of the firm. Hence the cost of using the money and capital markets by borrowing foreign currency and investing in the United States is

$$C_{bf} = \text{Cost of borrowing in foreign country}$$
$$= \bar{E}_1 F_0 R_f - E_0 F_0 R_{\text{U.S.}} = (\bar{E}_1 R_f - E_0 R_{\text{U.S.}})F_0$$
$$= [.32\bar{E}_1 - .30(.10)]100,000.$$

---

[1] To simplify the discussion, we omit consideration of taxes here.

Now the cost of borrowing foreign currency depends on what the future spot rate will be, because interest on the foreign borrowing must be paid at the future spot rate. The firm can remove this uncertainty by buying the foreign currency in the amount of the required interest to be paid at the current forward rate. The cost of borrowing foreign now becomes

$$C_{bf} = \text{FC } 32,000E_f - \$3000.$$

Next, we evaluate at the current forward rate:

$$C_{bf} = 32,000(.25) - \$3000 = \$8000 - \$3000$$
$$= \$5000.$$

The cost of borrowing foreign will now be $5000, which is exactly the same as in the hedged case in which the foreign currency was sold in the forward exchange market. It should be emphasized that borrowing in the foreign market produces an interest obligation which will become due in the future. Hence to protect against this exposure, the action is to *buy* the foreign currency in the amount of the interest obligation in the forward market rather than *sell* it as in the hedging operation in the forward market. Because this strategy requires having foreign currency on hand in the future to pay the foreign interest, the effects on the position of the firm will be reversed if the firm does not cover its future interest payments to be made in foreign currency, but permits matters to depend upon the future spot foreign exchange rate. For example, if the future spot foreign exchange rate is higher than the current forward rate, the cost of borrowing foreign will be higher.

$$C_{bf} = (\bar{E}_1 R_f - E_0 R_{\text{U.S.}})100,000$$
$$= [.27(.32) - .30(.10)]100,000$$
$$= (.0864 - .03)100,000 = .0564(100,000)$$
$$= \$5640.$$

With the future expected spot rate being $.27 rather than $.25, costs of borrowing foreign are in excess of $5000. However, if the future spot rate falls below the current forward rate, the cost of borrowing foreign will be less than $5000. Hence, if the firm does not immediately cover its future interest payments to be made in foreign currency, it continues to be exposed to foreign exchange risk.

We next consider the position of the firm which is in a negative net monetary position or which will be required, at some time in the future, to make net payments in excess of future receipts. The situation is the reverse of the firm in a positive monetary position. Instead of facing the risk of devaluation of FC units, the firm faces the risk of appreciation in the value of FC units. Hence its protective action in the forward market is to buy the FC units. If it does not obtain this protection, it will face an uncertain cost if the future spot rate is higher than the current forward rate. If it uses the money and capital markets, it will borrow in the United States and invest in the FC units in which it will have to make future payments.

This analysis demonstrates that if a firm is in an exposed foreign exchange position, it will incur some costs to obtain protection against that exposed position. Even rearranging the firm's pattern of payments and receipts or monetary assets and liabilities will represent a departure from normal operations and therefore involve some costs. If the firm uses the forward market or borrows, it incurs some costs, but it will know the exact amount of these costs.

F. FOREIGN CURRENCY TRANSLATION

In December 1981, the Financial Accounting Standards Board (FASB) issued FASB No. 52, *Foreign Currency Translation,* superseding FASB No. 8 which had been issued in 1976. In general, translation gains or losses are carried directly to the equity account on the balance sheet and do not affect net income. Individual transactions gains or losses net of hedging costs and net of translation gains or losses do enter into the calculations which determine net income. Also, the method of translation is changed from the temporal method to the use of the current exchange rate for all balance sheet items and the use of the average exchange rate for the period for the income statement. However, the temporal method will continue to be applied to operations in highly inflationary economies, defined as those in which the price level doubles within a three-year period of time.

Since the temporal method of currency translation continues to be applied in the circumstances indicated, it will be useful to explain and illustrate both methods. The temporal method was essentially the monetary-nonmonetary method with one change. Under the monetary-nonmonetary method, the logic of defining exposure by the net monetary position was followed. Monetary assets and liabilities were translated at current exchange rates while nonmonetary assets and liabilities were translated at the applicable historical exchange rates. Under the monetary-nonmonetary method of translation, inventories were treated as real assets to which the applicable historical exchange rate was applied. The temporal method recognizes that alternative inventory valuation methods may be used. For example, FIFO charges the income statement for the historical costs of inventory flows, resulting in balance-sheet values that are closer to current values. The use of LIFO has the opposite effect. Thus if FIFO is used, the current exchange rate should be applied to the balance-sheet inventory account; with LIFO an applicable historical rate should be used. This was the distinction recognized by the temporal method. The two methods are now illustrated by a numerical example.[2]

In this example, the Canadian subsidiary of a U.S. company with a Canadian dollar functional currency started business and acquired fixed assets at the beginning of the year when the Canadian $/U.S. $ exchange rate was .95. The average exchange rate for the period was .90, the rate at the end of the period was .85, and the historical rate for inventory was .91. The LIFO inventory valuation method is employed.

---

[2] Taken from Peat, Marwick, Mitchell & Co., *Statement of Financial Accounting Standards No. 52, Foreign Currency Translation,* 1981.

The different methods are illustrated in Table 20.1. The temporal method used in FASB 8 and for inflationary economies in FASB 52 applies the current (end of period) rate to monetary assets and liabilities. It uses the applicable historical rates for the nonmonetary assets and liabilities. Since LIFO is used, the balance sheet inventory account reflects historical costs and the historical rate for inventories is used. In the income statement, the applicable average rates are applied to all items

Table 20.1 Translation of Canadian Subsidiary Financial Statements—19x1

		FASB 8		FASB 52	
Balance sheet	Canadian dollars	Rates used	U.S. dollars	Rates used	U.S. dollars
Cash and receivables, net	100	.85	$ 85	.85	$ 85
Inventory	300	.91	273	.85	255
Fixed assets, net	600	.95	570	.85	510
	1,000		$928		$850
Current liabilities	180	.85	$153	.85	$153
Long-term debt	700	.85	595	.85	595
Stockholders' equity:					
Common stock	100	.95	95	.95	95
Retained earnings	20		85		18
Equity adjustment from foreign currency translation	—		—		(11)
	1,000		$928		$850
Income statement					
Revenue	130	.90	$117	.90	$117
Cost of goods sold	(60)	.93*	(56)	.90	(54)
Depreciation	(20)	.95*	(19)	.90	(18)
Other expenses, net	(10)	.90	(9)	.90	(9)
Foreign exchange gain	—		70		—
Income before taxes	40		$103		$36
Income taxes	(20)	.90	(18)	.90	(18)
Net income	20		$ 85		$ 18
Ratios					
Net income to revenue	.15		.73		.15
Gross profit	.54		.52		.54
Debt to equity	5.83		3.31		5.83

* Historical rates for cost of goods sold and depreciation of fixed assets.

Peat, Marwick, Mitchell and Company, *Statement of Financial Accounting Standards, No. 52, Foreign Currency Translation,* December 1981, p. 52, reprinted with permission.

except cost of goods sold and depreciation. Depreciation expense in the income statement would employ the same rate as fixed assets on the balance sheet.

In contrast, FASB 52 applies the current rate to all balance sheet items except common stock to which the historical rate is applied. The average rate is applied to all income statement items. The net income figure that results is reflected in the translated retained earnings account. Total assets and claims are brought into balance by a translation adjustment account.

The use of the current method of FASB 52 results in financial ratios that are unchanged from their relationships in the foreign currency before translation. This is claimed to be an advantage of the new method. But if the underlying reality is a change in the ratios, preserving them is a distortion. The logic of the temporal method captures the underlying economic determinants of exposure as demonstrated in the previous discussion of the net monetary creditor or debtor position of the foreign subsidiary. It is difficult to discern the economic logic for the application of the current method prescribed by FASB 52.

SUMMARY

From the viewpoint of an individual or firm, investments in international portfolios offer greater diversification than purely domestic portfolios. Evidence establishes that internationally diversified portfolios are less risky (variance of returns is used as the measure of risk) than purely domestic portfolios and/or portfolios consisting of the securities of multinational companies.

Alternative forms of an international asset pricing model (IAPM) similar to the CAPM have been derived for international financial assets. The results of Solnik's tests are weakly consistent with his IAPM. In an extension of his IAPM, Solnik found that assets can be regarded as trading in international markets: that is, the IAPM performs better than a purely domestic specification. Stehle [1977] has also found evidence of integration.

Recently, Stulz [1981] has developed an international asset pricing model which has individuals maximizing utility from consumption. Stulz extends Solnik's IAPM by allowing consumption opportunities to differ across countries, at least until arbitrage through trade flows equalizes them. All assets are assumed to be traded but all commodities are not. Purchasing power parity holds *only* for those goods traded.

From his model Stulz derives the following proposition: The expected excess real return of a risky asset is proportional to the covariance between the home currency rate of return of that asset and changes in world real consumption. Since the return of an asset is not dependent on unexpected exchange rate changes, exchange rate risk is not rewarded. Also, if changes in world consumption rates are not perfectly correlated with market indices, tests of market integration will incorrectly accept the market segmentation hypothesis.

The IAPM is subject to the same criticisms in empirical tests as is the traditional CAPM. Solnik [1977] observed that the covariance between national stock-market indices is quite low. If assets are priced entirely in domestic markets, with no international influence, an "optimal" portfolio can be artificially constructed which is internationally diversified. This portfolio will be mean-variance efficient and an IAPM test will "succeed," using this proxy as the world market portfolio. This test, however, tells us nothing about the actual pricing of assets.

In Solnik's IAPM the world market portfolio contains a portfolio he calls a "pure exchange risk asset." The weights of the nominally riskless securities of different countries in this portfolio are shown to depend on net foreign investment positions in the different countries, and the relative risk aversions of citizens. This specification would be difficult to implement in practice.

To the individual agent dealing in goods or services in the international market, fluctuations in exchange rates appear to cause additional risk compared to purely domestic transactions. Most contracts are fixed in nominal terms in foreign currency units. Hence movements in exchange rates make consumption opportunities uncertain in terms of domestic currencies.

There are two types of phenomena to consider in the area of exchange risk: Inflation risk and relative price risk. The risk to an agent in a world of pure inflation risk is purely nominal. This risk *can be* eliminated by the appropriate indexation of contracts in real terms. As GLS show, if a real riskless rate exists, and agents have identical homothetic tastes, this nominal exchange risk is irrelevant to real magnitudes.

As long as individuals consume different baskets of goods, relative prices will vary. This relative price risk is due to changes in underlying preferences of individuals and/or changes in supply conditions in various countries. Exchange rate changes due to relative price movements represent real risks which can be hedged only at a cost. As we demonstrated, exchange rate risk is a form of business risk resulting from changes in relative prices which, in turn, reflect changes in demand and supply conditions.

In an efficient market we would expect PPP to hold on an expected value basis. Roll's [1979] study shows that PPP holds on average and that deviations from PPP are more attributable to relative price fluctuations than to inflation fluctuations. In examining other aspects of market efficiency, several different approaches have been used. We briefly describe the methods and results.

One requirement of market efficiency is that arbitrage profits are essentially zero. In the international literature this test has been applied to the interest rate parity theorem (IRPT). Frenkel and Levich [1977] test whether deviations of IRPT outside bands of transactions costs exist. They conclude that if the arbitraged assets are comparable, arbitrage opportunities do not exist.

Cornell and Dietrich [1978] set up simple trading rule tests for profitability. For some currencies (DM, Swiss franc), profits of more than 15% were observed. For other currencies, minimal profits were observed. *A priori,* however, there is little way to determine the size of the filter to test. Nor is it easy to evaluate the riskiness of alternative strategies.

Simple tests of market efficiency have implied that the forward rate should be an unbiased predictor of the spot rate. However, recent theoretical developments (e.g., Stockman [1978]) state that a bias should exist since a premium is associated with the risk agents take in forward exchange markets. Tests of measuring the extent of this "bias" have generally been unsuccessful. Stockman [1978] and Cornell [1977] have found evidence of a bias for only a few countries and, furthermore, the risk premium behaves erratically.

A final test of market efficiency which has been used is to see if forecasting services can "beat" the market. Levich [1979] found that forecasting services may yield profits consistently for some currencies. On the whole the literature on market efficiency seems to suggest that international markets are weak-form and semistrong-form efficient.

The exposure of a business firm to exchange risks is defined by its cash flow and asset stock positions. These in turn depend on expected future receipts and payments and the firm's net monetary position. Unless payments and receipts in relation to the future net monetary position of the firm exactly balance, the firm is exposed to a decline or increase in the value of foreign currencies. If the net monetary position of a firm is positive and expected receipts exceed expected payments, the firm will suffer from a devaluation. The opposite will hold with respect to an appreciation if the firm has a negative net monetary position and expected payments exceed expected receipts.

There are three methods of managing exchange risk. The firm will choose various combinations of these methods which will tend to produce efficiency in the foreign exchange markets. One alternative is to develop information about and formulate expectations between expected future exchange rates and the current forward rate. A second is to hedge by using the forward market. A third is to use the money and capital markets.

In comparing hedging versus money and capital markets it is important to note that IRPT will ensure agents are indifferent between the two. The benefit to the firm of using either the money and capital markets or hedging is that it knows what costs are involved.

PROBLEM SET

20.1 Agrimex, S.A., a Mexican corporation, borrowed $1,000,000 in dollars at a 15% interest rate when the exchange rate was 25 pesos per dollar. When the company repaid the loan plus interest one year later, the exchange rate was 40 pesos to the dollar?

a) What was the rate of interest on the loan based on the pesos received and paid back by Agrimex?

b) Use the Interest Rate Parity Theorem to illustrate this result.

20.2 An American manufacturing company has imported industrial machinery at a price of DM 4.6 million. The machinery will be delivered and paid for in six months. For planning purposes, the American company wants to establish what the payment (in dollars) will be in six months. It decides to use the forward market to accomplish its objective. The company contacts its New York bank which provides the quotations given in Table Q20.2. The bank states that it will charge a commission of $\frac{1}{4}$% on any transaction.

Table Q20.2

	DM	Swiss franc	$
Six-month Eurocurrency rates (% p.a.) denominated in the following currencies	8	7	9
Spot exchange rates (currency/Swiss franc)	1.1648		.56

a) Does the American company enter the forward market to go long or short of forward DM?

b) What is the number of DM/$? What is the dollar value of the deutschemark?

c) What is the equilibrium forward rate for the deutschemark expressed as DM/$?

d) Does the commission increase or decrease the number of DM/$ in the transaction?

e) What price in dollars can the American company establish by using the forward market in deutschemarks?

20.3 A West German company buys industrial machinery from a U.S. company at a price of $10 million. The machinery will be delivered and paid for in six months. The German company seeks to establish its cost in deutschemarks. It decides to use the forward market to accomplish its objective. The company contacts its Bonn bank which provides the quotations listed in Table Q20.3. The bank states that it will charge a commission of $\frac{1}{4}$% on any transaction.

a) Does the German company enter the forward market to go long or short of forward dollars?

b) What is the number of DM/$? What is the dollar value of the deutschemark?

c) What is the equilibrium forward rate for the deutschemark expressed as $/DM?

d) Does the commission increase or decrease the dollar value of the deutschemark?

e) What price in deutschemarks can the German company establish by using the forward market in dollars?

Table Q20.3

	DM	£	$
Six-month Eurocurrency rates (% p.a.) denominated in the following currencies	8	9.5	9
Spot exchange rates (currency/U.K. £)	3.878		$1.90

20.4 Globalcorp makes a sale of goods to a foreign firm and will receive FC 380,000 three months later. Globalcorp has incurred costs in dollars and wishes to make definite the amount of dollars it will receive in three months. It plans to approach a foreign bank to borrow an amount of local currency such that the principal plus interest will equal the amount Globalcorp expects to receive. The interest rate it must pay on its loan is 28%. With the borrowed funds, Globalcorp purchases dollars at the current spot rate which are invested in the United States at an interest rate of 8%. When Globalcorp receives the FC 380,000 at the end of three months, it uses the funds to liquidate the loan at the foreign bank. The effective tax rate in both countries is 40%.

a) What is the net amount that Globalcorp will receive if the current spot rate is FC 1.90 to the dollar?

b) How much less is this than the amount Globalcorp would have received if the remittance had been made immediately instead of three months later?

c) At what forward rate of exchange would the amount received by Globalcorp have been the same as that it would have obtained using the capital markets? Would Globalcorp have sold the FC forward short or long to hedge its position?

d) If a speculator took the opposite position from Globalcorp in the forward market for FC, would the speculator sell long or short? If the speculator received a risk premium for holding this position, would this place the current forward rate in FC above or below the expected future spot rate in FC per dollar?

20.5 Transcorp has made a purchase of goods from a foreign firm which will require the payment of FC 380,000 six months later. Transcorp wishes to make definite the amount of dollars it will need to pay the FC 380,000 on the due date. The foreign firm is domiciled in a country whose currency has been rising in relation to the dollar in recent years. The tax rate in both countries is 40%. Transcorp plans to borrow an amount in dollars from a U.S. bank to immediately exchange into FCs to buy securities in the foreign country which, with interest, will equal FC 380,000 six months later. The interest rate that will be paid in the United States is 12%, the interest rate that will be earned on the foreign securities is 8%. When at the end of six months, Transcorp is required to make the payment in FC, it will use the funds from the maturing foreign securities in FC to meet its obligation in FC. At the same time it will pay off the loan plus interest in the United States in dollars.

a) What is the net amount that Transcorp pays to meet the obligation of FC 380,000 in six months if the current spot rate is FC 2.00 to the dollar?

b) How much more is this than the amount Transcorp would have paid if payment had been made immediately instead of six months later?

c) At what forward rate of exchange would the amount paid by Transcorp have been the same as that it would have paid using the capital markets? Would Transcorp have taken the long position in the forward FC or have sold the FC forward short to hedge its position?

d) If a speculator took the opposite position from Transcorp in the forward market for FCs, would the speculator be long or short? If the speculator received a risk premium for holding this position, would this place the current forward rate in FC above or below the expected future spot rate in FC per dollar?

REFERENCES

Adler, M., "The Cost of Capital and Valuation of a Two-Country Firm," *Journal of Finance,* March 1974, 119–132.

———, and B. Dumas, "Optimal International Acquisitions," *Journal of Finance,* March 1975, 1–20.

Black, F., "International Capital Market Equilibrium with Investment Barriers," *Journal of Financial Economics,* December 1974, 337–352.

Bomberger, W. A., and W. J. Frazer, "Interest Rates, Uncertainty and the Livingston Data," *Journal of Finance,* June, 1981, 661–677.

Breeden, D. T., "An Intertemporal Asset Pricing Model with Stochastic Consumption and Investment Opportunities," *Journal of Financial Economics,* September 1979, 265–296.

Cohn, R. A., and J. J. Pringle, "Imperfections in International Financial Markets: Implications for Risk Premia and the Cost of Capital to Firms," *Journal of Finance,* March 1973, 59–66.

Cornell, B., "Spot Rates, Forward Rates, and Exchange Market Efficiency," *Journal of Financial Economics,* August 1977, 55–65.

Cornell, B., "Inflation, Relative Price Changes, and Exchange Risk," *Financial Management,* Autumn 1980, 30–34.

———, and K. Dietrich, "The Efficiency of the Market for Foreign Exchange Under Floating Exchange Rates," *Review of Economics and Statistics,* February 1978, 111–121.

Dumas, B., "Discussion," *Journal of Finance,* May 1977, 512–515.

Errunza, V. R., and L. W. Senbet, "The Effects of International Operations on the Market Value of the Firm: Theory and Evidence," *Journal of Finance,* May 1981, 401–419.

Fama, E. F., *Foundations of Finance.* Basic Books, New York, 1976.

———, and A. Farber, "Money Bonds and Foreign Exchange," *American Economic Review,* September 1979, 639–650.

Fieleke, N. S., "Foreign-Currency Positioning by U.S. Firms: Some New Evidence," *Review of Economics and Statistics,* February 1981, 35–42.

Frenkel, J., and R. Levich, "Covered Interest Arbitrage: Unexploited Profits?" *Journal of Political Economy,* April 1975, 325–338.

———, "Transactions Costs and Interest Arbitrage: Tranquil Versus Turbulent Periods," *Journal of Political Economy,* December 1977, 1209–1226.

Giddy, I. H., "Discussion," *Journal of Finance,* June 1978, 1030–1031.

Grauer, F. L. A., R. H. Litzenberger, and R. E. Stehle, "Sharing Rules and Equilibrium in an International Capital Market Under Uncertainty," *Journal of Financial Economics,* June 1976, 233–256.

Grubel, H. G., "Internationally Diversified Portfolios: Welfare Gains and Capital Flows," *American Economic Review,* December 1968, 1299–1314.

Hodgson, J. S., and P. Phelps, "The Distributed Impact of Price-Level Variation on Floating Exchange Rates," *Review of Economics and Statistics,* February 1975, 58–64.

Isard, P., "Exchange Rate Determination: A Survey of Popular Views and Recent Models." Princeton Studies in International Finance, No. 42, 1978.

Jacquillat, B., and B. Solnik, "Multinationals Are Poor Tools for Diversification," *Journal of Portfolio Management,* Winter 1978, 8–12.

Kravis, I. B., et al., *A System of International Comparisons of Gross Product and Purchasing Power.* Johns Hopkins University Press, Baltimore, 1975.

Lee, C., "A Stock Adjustment Analysis of Capital Movements: The U.S. Canadian Case," *Journal of Political Economy,* July 1969, 512–523.

Lee, W. Y., and K. S. Sachdeva, "The Role of the Multinational Firm in the Integration of Segmented Capital Markets," *Journal of Finance*, May 1977, 479–492.

Lessard, D. R., "International Portfolio Diversification: A Multivariate Analysis for a Group of Latin-American Countries," *Journal of Finance*, June 1973, 619–633.

———, ed., *International Financial Management: Theory and Application*. Warren, Gorham & Lamont, Boston, 1979.

Levich, R., "The Efficiency of the Market for Foreign Exchange: A Review and Extension," in D. Lessard, ed., *International Financial Management*. Warren, Gorham and Lamont, Boston, 1979, 243–277.

Levy, H., and M. Sarnat, "International Diversification of Investment Portfolios," *American Economic Review*, September 1970, 668–675.

———, "Devaluation Risk and the Portfolio Analysis of International Investment," in Elton and Gruber, eds., *International Capital Markets*, North Holland, 1975, 177–206.

Longworth, D., "Testing the Efficiency of the Canadian–U.S. Exchange Market Under the Assumption of No Risk Premium," *Journal of Finance*, March 1981, 43–51.

Merton, R. C., "An Intertemporal Capital Asset Pricing Model," *Econometrica*, September 1973, 867–887.

Robichek, A. A., and M. R. Eaker, "Foreign Exchange Hedging and the Capital Asset Pricing Model," *Journal of Finance*, June 1978, 1011–1018.

Rodriguez, R. M., "Corporate Exchange Risk Management: Theme and Aberrations," *Journal of Finance*, May 1981, 427–439.

Roll, R., "A Critique of the Asset Pricing Theory's Tests; Part I: On Past and Potential Testability of the Theory," *Journal of Financial Economics*, March 1977, 129–176.

———, "Violations of Purchasing Parity and their Implications for Efficient Markets," in M. Sarnat and G. Szego, eds., *International Finance and Trade*, Vol. 1, Cambridge, Mass., Ballinger, 1979, 133–176.

———, and B. Solnik, "A Pure Foreign Exchange Asset Pricing Model," *Journal of International Economics*, May 1977, 161–179.

Solnik, B., "The International Pricing of Risk: An Empirical Investigation of the World Capital Market Structure," *Journal of Finance*, May 1974a, 365–378.

———, "Why Not Diversify Internationally Rather than Domestically," *Financial Analysts Journal*, July/August 1974b, 48–54.

———, "An Equilibrium Model of the International Capital Market," *Journal of Economic Theory*, August 1974c, 500–525.

———, "An International Market Model of Security Price Behavior," *Journal of Financial and Quantitative Analysis*, September 1974d, 537–554.

———, "Testing International Asset Pricing: Some Pessimistic Views," *Journal of Finance*, May 1977, 503–512.

———, "International Parity Conditions and Exchange Risk," *Journal of Banking and Finance*, October 1978, 281–293.

Stehle, R., "An Empirical Test of the Alternate Hypotheses of National and International Pricing of Risky Assets," *Journal of Finance*, May 1977, 493–502.

Stockman, A., "Risk, Information, and Forward Exchange Rates," in J. A. Frenkel and

H. G. Johnson, eds., *The Economics of Exchange Rates.* Addison-Wesley, Reading, Mass., 1978, 159–179.

———, "A Theory of Exchange Rate Determination," *Journal of Political Economy,* August 1980, 673–699.

Stulz, R., "A Model of International Asset Pricing," *Journal of Financial Economics,* December 1981, 383–406.

———, "On the Effects of Barriers to International Investment," *Journal of Finance,* September 1981, 923–934.

Wallingford, B.A., "International Asset Pricing: A Comment," *Journal of Finance,* May 1974, 392–395.

Weston, J. F., and B. W. Sorge, *International Managerial Finance.* Richard D. Irwin, Homewood, Ill., 1972.

———, *Guide to International Financial Management.* McGraw-Hill, New York, 1977.

APPENDIXES

Discounting

A. INTRODUCTION

In any economy, capitalistic or socialistic, we find positive rates of interest. This reflects two underlying influences: the productivity of economic goods and time preference. Capital goods are goods used in the production of other goods and services. Some capital goods are specialized machinery and others are materials—such as iron, copper, or textiles—used in the production of machinery to produce other goods. More basically, our productive efforts may be used to produce goods that we consume immediately or to produce goods that will produce other goods and services for future use. One reason to use some of our productive efforts to have goods that will produce future goods is that the postponement of current consumption will enable us to have more wealth in the future than we would otherwise have. This is true whether we think of the use of actual goods or financial spending power used on current consumption vs. goods that will produce future goods. For example, we can consume grains now or plant them to harvest future crops that will represent larger quantities than the seeds with which

699

we started. Because of the productivity of goods they have a time value. A bushel of seeds today will become several bushels of grain in the future. So productivity is one basis for the time value of money and positive rates of interest.

A second basis is time preference. Would we rather have the use of an automobile now or wait five years? Clearly, it is more advantageous to have the use of goods now than to wait for them.

B. THE TIME VALUE OF MONEY: DISCRETE COMPOUNDING

1. Compound Future Sums

Because of productivity and time preference, a positive rate of interest is a universal phenomenon. It is a necessary guide to present vs. future uses of goods and to the allocation of goods among alternative uses when time is involved. Since a positive rate of interest is a general phenomenon, future sums will be greater than present values. For example, assume that if a company received funds immediately, it could earn a 10% return on those funds. We could then state the problem as follows: Let

$P =$ principal, or beginning amount $= \$1000$

$r =$ interest rate $= 10\% = .10$

$n =$ number of years $= 5$

$S_n =$ the value at the end of the year n

We can readily derive the applicable compound interest formula. The amount received at the end of the first year is $P(1 + r)$. This is again compounded to determine the amount received at the end of the second year and so on.

	End of Year 1	End of Year 2	End of Year 3	$\cdots$	End of Year n
Amount	$P(1 + r)$	$P(1 + r)(1 + r)$	$P(1 + r)(1 + r)(1 + r)$		
Received	$P(1 + r)$	$P(1 + r)^2$	$P(1 + r)^3$	$\cdots$	$P(1 + r)^n$

The result is the compound interest formula. In general terms it may be stated as follows:

$$S_n = P(1 + r)^n. \qquad (A.1)$$

We now have all the information needed to compute the value at the end of the fifth year, using a compound interest table* (Table A.1):

$$S_5 = \$1000(1.10)^5.$$

---

* All tables mentioned in Appendix A are located at the end of Appendix A.

We then look in the compound interest table to find that at 10% a dollar over a five-year period grows to $1.611. Since the amount we have is $1000, it is multiplied times the interest factor:

$$S_5 = \$1000(1.611) = \$1611.$$

Therefore, if the firm can earn 10% with the money, it is more worthwhile for it to receive the $1000 today rather than at the end of the fifth year.

2. Future Amounts and Their Present Values

A similar type of problem occurs when a company is offered an amount to be received in the future. It is desirable to compare that amount with the value of whatever amount could be received today. This requires the computation of the present value of the amount to be received in the future. The determination of present values involves the same formula except that it is solved for P, representing present value, instead of for S_n, which, in this situation, is known. By simple algebra the required formula would be:

$$P = \frac{S_n}{(1+r)^n} . \tag{A.2}$$

Using our previous example, we determined S_n to be $1611. Since the appropriate interest rate is 10% and the number of years is five, this is what is required to determine P. This can be done by using our previous information and making a division. We would be dividing $1611 by 1.611 to obtain the result $1000. But we can also use a present value interest table (Table A.2), which is the reciprocal of a compound interest table. In this case the formula is:

$$P = S_n(1+r)^{-n}. \tag{A.2a}$$

We can now insert the illustrative numbers:

$$P = \$1611(0.621)$$

$$= \$1000.$$

The results of compound interest and present value computations are just two different ways of looking at the same relationship.

3. Constant Payment Annuities

An annuity is a series of periodic payments made over a span of time. This is a frequently encountered type of compound interest situation. For example, a firm may sell some goods that will be paid for in installments. A basic question is, what is the present value of those installment payments? Or, the firm makes an investment from which it expects to receive a series of cash returns over a period of years. At an appropriate discount rate, what would the series of future income receipts be worth today? The firm needs this information in order to determine whether it is worthwhile to make the investment.

Some specific examples will further illustrate these ideas. The firm makes an investment. It is promised the payment of $1000 a year for 10 years with an interest rate of 10%. What is the present value of such a series of payments?

The basic formula involved is the present value of an annuity.

$$A_{n,r} = a \left[\frac{1 - (1 + r)^{-n}}{r} \right],$$ (A.3)

where

A = present value of an annuity,

a = amount of the periodic annuity payment,

r = interest factor,

n = number of annuity payments.

Equation (A.3) is derived by discounting the stream of payments, the first of which is made at the end of the first year. Mathematically, this is

$$A_{n,r} = \frac{a}{1 + r} + \frac{a}{(1 + r)^2} + \frac{a}{(1 + r)^3} + \cdots + \frac{a}{(1 + r)^n}$$

If we let $u = [1/(1 + r)]$ this becomes

$$A_{n,r} = au + au^2 + au^3 + \cdots + au^n.$$ (A.4)

Multiplying Eq. (A.4) by u and subtracting the result from Eq. (A.4) yields

$$A_{n,r} - uA_{n,r} = au - au^{n+1},$$

$$A_{n,r} = \frac{au(1 - u^n)}{1 - u}.$$

Substituting back the value of u we have:

$$A_{n,r} = \frac{a\left(\dfrac{1}{1+r}\right)\left[1 - \dfrac{1}{(1+r)^n}\right]}{\left(1 - \dfrac{1}{1+r}\right)}$$

$$= \frac{a[1 - (1 + r)^{-n}]}{(1 + r)\left(\dfrac{1 + r - 1}{1 + r}\right)}$$

$$= a \left[\frac{1 - (1 + r)^{-n}}{r} \right].$$ (A.3)

Note that if the number of payments is infinite, then the present value of the annuity becomes

$$\lim_{n \to \infty} A_{n,r} = \frac{a}{r},$$ (A.5)

since we know that when $r > 0$, then $\text{Lim}_{n \to \infty} (1 + r)^{-n} = 0$. An example of an annuity with an infinite number of constant payments is a *consol* bond. It pays a coupon at the end of each time period (usually a year) and never matures.

The expression in brackets in Eq. (A.3) is rather cumbersome. For convenience, then, instead of the cumbersome expression set out above, we shall use the symbol $P_{n,r}$, where $P_{n,r}$ = present value of an annuity factor for n years at r percent. Equation (A.3) above can, therefore, be rewritten as:

$$A_{n,r} = aP_{n,r}. \tag{A.3a}$$

Substituting actual numbers and using Table A.4 (the present value of an annuity interest table), we would have the following for 10 years at 10%:

$$\$6145 = \$1000(6.145).$$

In other words, applying an interest factor of 10% a series of payments of $1000 received for 10 years would be worth $6145 today. Hence, if the amount of investment we were required to make were $8000, for example, or any amount greater than $6145, we would be receiving a return of less than 10% on our investment. Conversely, if the investment necessary to earn annual payments of $1000 for 10 years at 10% were $5000 or any amount less than $6145, we would be earning a return greater than 10%.

A number of other questions can be answered using these same relationships. Suppose the decision facing the firm requires determining the rate of return on an investment. For example, suppose we would have $6145 to invest and that an investment opportunity promises an annual return of $1000 for 10 years. What is the indicated rate of return on our investment? Exactly the same relationship is involved, but we are now solving for the interest rate. We can, therefore, rewrite our equation as follows:

$$P_{10,10\%} = \frac{A_{10,10\%}}{a}.$$

We can now substitute the appropriate figures.

$$P_{10,10\%} = \frac{\$6145}{\$1000} = 6.145.$$

In Table A.4, which shows the present value of periodic payments received annually, we look across the row for year 10 until we find the interest rate that corresponds to the interest factor 6.145. This is 10%. We are earning a 10% return on our investment.

Let us consider another situation. Suppose that we are going to receive a return of $2000 per year for five years from an investment of $8424. What is the return on our investment? This is generally referred to as the internal rate of return on the investment, or it is also sometimes referred to as the DCF or discounted cash flow approach to valuing an investment.

We follow the same procedure as before.

$$P_{5,r} = \frac{\$8424}{\$2000}$$

$$= 4.212.$$

We look again in the present value of an annuity table (Table A.4) along the row for the year 5 to find the interest factor 4.212. We then look at the interest rate at the top of the column to find that it is 6%. Thus the return on that investment is 6%. If our required rate of return was 10% we would not find this investment attractive. On the other hand, if the required return on our investment were only 5% we would consider the investment attractive.

These relationships can be used in still another way. Taking the facts of the preceding illustration we may ask the following question: Given an investment that yields $2000 per year for five years, at an appropriate discount factor (or cost of capital) of 6%, what is that investment worth today? What is the present value of a series of future income flows? For example, if a firm were to make a sale of goods on an open account with a down payment of $1000 plus yearly payments of $2000 for five years, what would the present value of all of the payments be at a 6% interest rate? From our previous calculations we know that the series of payments of $2000 for five years at a 6% interest rate are worth $8424 today. When we add the $1000 down payment to this figure we would have a total of $9424.

4. Compound Sum of an Annuity

We may need to know the future value or future sum to which a series of payments will accumulate. The reason may be to determine the amount of funds required to repay an obligation in the future. The sum of an annuity can be determined from the following basic relationship:*

$$S_{n,r} = a \left[\frac{(1+r)^n - 1}{r} \right],$$
(A.6)

where

$S_{n,r}$ = the future sum to which an annuity will accumulate in n years at rate r,

a = the amount of the annuity payment.

Suppose the firm were to receive annual payments of $1000 a year for 10 years and is earning an interest rate of 10%. What will be the amount that the firm will have at the end of 10 years? We can solve this problem by consulting Table A.3. Utilizing our equation we would have:

$$S_{n,r} = \$1000 \, (15.937)$$

$$= \$15,937$$

---

* Note that the present value of an annuity can be obtained by discounting the expression back to the present:

$$A_{n,r} = a \left[\frac{(1+r)^n - 1}{r(1+r)^n} \right].$$

Now divide both terms in the numerator by $(1 + r)^n$. We have

$$A_{n,r} = a \left[\frac{1 - (1+r)^{-n}}{r} \right].$$

This is now in the form of Eq. (A.3), the present value of an annuity.

The 10 payments of $1000 with interest would amount to $15,937 by the end of the tenth year. Thus, if we had to make a payment of $15,937 in 10 years, we would be able to do it by annual payments of $1000 per year into a fund that earns interest at 10% per year.

5. Calculations for a Series of Unequal Receipts or Payments

In all of the previous illustrations we have assumed that the receipts flowing in or the payments to be made are of equal amounts. This simplifies the calculations. However, if unequal receipts or unequal payments are involved the principles are again the same, but the calculations must be somewhat extended. For example, suppose that the firm makes an investment from which it will receive the following amounts:

Year	Receipts	× Interest factor (15%)	= Present value
1	$100	.870	$ 87.00
2	200	.756	151.20
3	600	.658	394.80
4	300	.572	171.60
		PV of the investment =	$804.60

Using the present value interest table (Table A.2) at an interest rate of 15%, we obtain the amounts indicated above. The interest factor is multiplied by the receipts to provide the amounts in the present value column. The amounts for each year are then summed to provide the present value of the investment, which in this example is $804.60. What we are doing in this example is illustrating how an annuity of unequal payments which could not be computed directly from the present value of an annuity table (Table A.4) can be handled by breaking the problem into a series of one-year payments received at successively later time periods.

6. Annuities With Growing Payments

Previously we had assumed that annuity payments were constant through time. Now we consider the case where the payments are assumed to be growing at a constant rate, g. This is a more realistic assumption if, for example, we are modeling the growing dividends paid out by a firm. Let d_0 be the current dividend per share, and assume that it was paid just yesterday, so that it does not enter into the present value computations. The stream of growing dividends to be received starts with the first end-of-year dividend, $d_1 = d_0(1 + g)$. The dividend at the end of the second year is $d_2 = d_0(1 + g)^2$. The stream of payments is assumed to grow at a constant rate for n years, therefore its present value, PV, is

$$PV = \frac{d_1}{1 + r} + \frac{d_2}{(1 + r)^2} + \frac{d_3}{(1 + r)^3} + \cdots + \frac{d_n}{(1 + r)^n}$$

$$= \frac{d_0(1 + g)}{1 + r} + \frac{d_0(1 + g)^2}{(1 + r)^2} + \frac{d_0(1 + g)^3}{(1 + r)^3} + \cdots + \frac{d_0(1 + g)^n}{(1 + r)^n}$$

If we let $u = (1 + g)/(1 + r)$ this can be rewritten as

$$PV = d_0 u + d_0 u^2 + d_0 u^3 + \cdots + d_0 u^n$$
$$= u d_0 (1 + u + u^2 + \cdots + u^{n-1}). \tag{A.7}$$

By multiplying Eq. (A.7) by u and subtracting the result from Eq. (A.7), we obtain

$$PV - uPV = u d_0 (1 - u^n),$$

and solving for the present value of the growing annuity, we have

$$PV = \frac{u d_0 (1 - u^n)}{1 - u} .$$

Substituting back the value of u gives us

$$PV = \frac{\left(\dfrac{1+g}{1+r}\right) d_0 \left[1 - \left(\dfrac{1+g}{1+r}\right)^n\right]}{1 - \left(\dfrac{1+g}{1+r}\right)}$$

By rearranging terms and recalling that $d_0(1 + g) = d_1$, we obtain

$$PV = \frac{d_1 \left[1 - \left(\dfrac{1+g}{1+r}\right)^n\right]}{r - g} . \tag{A.8}$$

Equation (A.8) is the present value of n annuity payments which start at a level of d_0 and grow at a constant rate, g.

Note that if the number of payments is infinite, we can obtain a finite present value if we assume that the growth rate in dividends, g, is less than the time value of money, r. If $g < r$, then the fraction in the numerator of Eq. (A.8) goes to zero in the limit as n approaches infinity

$$\lim_{n \to \infty} \left(\frac{1+g}{1+r}\right)^n = 0, \quad \text{iff} \quad g < r.$$

Therefore, the present value of an infinite number of growing dividends is

$$\lim_{n \to \infty} PV = \frac{d_1}{r - g} . \tag{A.9}$$

Equation (A.9) is used frequently in the text, where it is called the *Gordon growth model*. It provides us with an estimate of the present value of a share of common stock where the stream of dividends received from it are assumed to grow at a constant rate which is assumed to be less than the discount rate (which in this case would be the cost of equity capital, k_e).

7. The Value Additivity Principle and the NPV Criterion

It is worth emphasizing that in calculating present value (PV) relationships we have been drawing on the value additivity principle. As the example from section

B.5 illustrates, the present value of amounts $(A + B + C + D)$ is equal to the present value of A plus the present value of B plus the present value of C plus the present value of D. In this earlier example, we had four cash flows $(F_1 + F_2 + F_3 + F_4)$. They came in different time periods. We can obtain the present value of cash flows that occur in different years by applying the appropriate discount factor and adding.

$$PV = \frac{F_1}{(1+r)} + \frac{F_2}{(1+r)^2} + \frac{F_3}{(1+r)^3} + \frac{F_4}{(1+r)^4}. \tag{A.10}$$

Using the actual numbers, we have:

$$PV = \frac{\$100}{(1.15)} + \frac{\$200}{(1.15)^2} + \frac{\$600}{(1.15)^3} + \frac{\$300}{(1.15)^4}.$$

This can also be written as:

$$PV = \$100(.870) + \$200(.756) + \$600(.658) + \$300(.572) = \$804.60.$$

In general, the present value calculations follow the principle of value additivity for any number of cash flows, simply involving addition of the individual flows. We can write:

$$PV = \frac{F_1}{(1+r_1)} + \frac{F_2}{(1+r_2)^2} + \cdots + \frac{F_n}{(1+r_n)^n}. \tag{A.11}$$

The value additivity relationship enables all types of computational operations to be performed. This makes possible the development of valuation relationships for a wide variety of cash flow patterns, as will be demonstrated in the subsequent materials.

Another general principle that flows from the preceding compound interest relationships is the net present value criterion. The net present value (NPV) is obtained by calculating the discounted value of the cash returns and subtracting the discounted value of the investments (or cash outflows) required to produce the positive cash flows. If a single investment is made, we add a single negative term to the present value calculations set forth above.

$$NPV = -I_0 + \frac{F_1}{(1+r)} + \frac{F_2}{(1+r)^2} + \cdots + \frac{F_n}{(1+r)^n}. \tag{A.12}$$

If investments over a period of years are required to produce the cash flows, their values are accumulated to the present:

$$NPV = -I_{-2}(1+r)^2 - I_{-1}(1+r) - I_0 + \frac{F_1}{(1+r)} + \frac{F_2}{(1+r)^2} + \cdots + \frac{F_n}{(1+r)^n}. \tag{A.13}$$

The net present value represents the addition to value created by an investment project. The applicable discount factor is the rate of interest or cost of capital appropriate to the characteristics of a project. Hence the NPV criterion is a general rule for allocating resources. By following the NPV rule, the financial markets produce the maximum amount of additions to the value of the economy. Individual investors can then buy and sell in the financial markets to obtain the use of funds for consumption in early years or to postpone consumption to later years. Nor do managers of individual firms need to consult the preferences of their shareholders or owners to determine whether they prefer investments that come to fruition in early years or later years. By following the NPV criterion, the maximum amount of additions to wealth will be achieved. The financial markets provide opportunities to the individual investors to arrange their consumption over time in years that they prefer. The NPV rule leads to the fundamental principles of valuation for flows of different kinds and different time patterns.

8. Compounding Periods Within One Year

In the illustrations set forth thus far the examples have been for returns that were received once a year or annually. If the interest rates are calculated for periods of time within one year a simple relationship can be followed, utilizing the principles already set forth. For compounding within one year, we simply divide the interest rate by the number of compoundings within a year and multiply the annual periods by the same factor. For example, in our first equation for compound interest we had the following:

$$S_n = P(1 + r)^n.$$

This was for annual compounding. For semiannual compounding we would follow the rule just set forth. The equation would become:

$$S_n = P\left(1 + \frac{r}{m}\right)^{nm}, \tag{A.14}$$

where m = the number of compoundings during a year.

We may apply this in a numerical illustration. Suppose the initial question is, "To how much would $1000 at a 6% interest rate accumulate over a five-year period?" The answer is $1338. Now we apply semiannual compounding. The equation would appear as follows:

$$S_{5/2} = \$1000\left(1 + \frac{.06}{2}\right)^{5(2)}.$$

Thus the new expression is equivalent to compounding the $1000 at 3% for 10 periods. The compound interest table (Table A.1) for 10 years shows that the interest factor would be 1.344. Our equation would, therefore, read:

$$S_{5/2} = \$1000(1 + .03)^{10},$$

$$= \$1344.$$

It will be noted that with semiannual compounding the future sum amounts to $1344 as compared with the $1338 we had before. Frequent compounding provides compound interest paid on compound interest, so the amount is higher. Thus we would expect that daily compounding, as some financial institutions advertise, or continuous compounding, as is employed under some assumptions, would give somewhat larger amounts than annual or semiannual compounding. But the basic ideas are unchanged.

The same logic is equally applicable to all of the categories of relationships we have described. For example, suppose a problem on the present value of an annuity was stated as the payment of $1000 a year for 10 years with an interest rate of 10% compounded annually. If the compounding is semiannual we would employ an interest rate of 5% and apply the compounding to a period of 20 years. When we compound semiannually we also have to divide the annual payment by the number of times the compounding takes place within the year. We would have the following expression:

$$A_{nm,r/m} = \$500(P_{nm,r/m})$$
$$= \$500[P_{10(2),10\%/2}]$$
$$= \$500(P_{20,5\%})$$
$$= \$500(12.462)$$
$$= \$6231.$$

It will be noted that with annual compounding the present value of the annuity was $6145. With semiannual compounding the present value is $6231. With more frequent compounding the resulting amounts will be somewhat higher because interest is compounded on interest more often.

C. THE TIME VALUE OF MONEY: CONTINUOUS COMPOUNDING

1. Compound Sums and Present Values

Continuous compounding simply extends the ideas involved in compounding periods within one year. Let us restate Eq. (A.14) in somewhat more general symbols:

$$V_t = P_0 \left(1 + \frac{k}{q}\right)^{qt}. \tag{A.14a}$$

Since we can multiply qt by k/k, we can set $qt = (q/k)(kt)$ and rewrite Eq. (A.14a) as

$$V_t = P_0 \left[\left(1 + \frac{k}{q}\right)^{(q/k)}\right]^{(kt)}. \tag{A.15}$$

Define $m = q/k$ and rewrite Eq. (A.15) as

$$V_t = P_0 \left[\left(1 + \frac{1}{m}\right)^m\right]^{kt}. \tag{A.15a}$$

As the number of compounding periods, q, increases, m also increases; this causes the term in brackets in Eq. (A.15a) to increase. At the limit, when q and m approach infinity (and compounding is instantaneous, or continuous), the term in brackets approaches the value 2.718 .... The value e is defined as this limiting case:

$$e = \lim_{m \to \infty} \left(1 + \frac{1}{m}\right)^m = 2.718 \ldots .$$

We may substitute e for the bracketed term.

$$V_t = P_0 e^{kt}. \tag{A.16}$$

Equation (A.16) is the expression for the case of continuous compounding (or continuous growth).

It is convenient to use natural logarithms to evaluate the formula for continuous compounding. We can rewrite Eq. (A.16) to express it as the relationship for $1 of initial principal. We obtain Eq. (A.17).

$$V_t = e^{kt}. \tag{A.17}$$

Next express Eq. (A.17) in log form, letting ln denote log to the base e.

$$\ln V_t = kt \ln e. \tag{A.18}$$

Since e is the base of the system of natural logarithms, ln e is equal to 1. Hence to use the table of natural logs, we have Eq. (A.19).

$$\ln V_t = kt. \tag{A.19}$$

For example, suppose our problem is to determine the future value of $1000 compounded continuously at 10% for eight years. Then $t = 8$ and $k = .10$, so $kt = .80$. We find .8 in the body of Table A.5 to be between .79751 and .80200. The first number corresponds to an interest factor of 2.22. We can then interpolate up to the .80000. This is the ratio .00249/.00449 which equals .555. Hence the interest factor is 2.22555. So the $1000 would compound to $2225.55 in eight years at 10%. This compares with $2144.00 with compounding on an annual basis.

Equation (A.16) can be transformed into Eq. (A.20) and used to determine present values under continuous compounding. Using k as the discount rate, we obtain

$$\text{PV} = \frac{V_t}{e^{kt}} = V_t e^{-kt}. \tag{A.20}$$

Thus, if $2225 is due in eight years and if the appropriate continuous discount rate k is 10%, the present value of this future payment is

$$\text{PV} = \frac{\$2225}{2.225} = \$1000.$$

2. Constant Payment Annuities

If we assume that an asset pays a constant amount per unit time then we can write that the payment at any point in time, a_t, is a constant, a_0.

$$a_t = a_0. \tag{A.21}$$

Using basic integral calculus (discussed in appendix D), we can express the present value of a constant payment stream as the discounted value of the payment function given in Eq. (A.21)

$$PV = \int_0^n a_t e^{-kt}\, dt. \tag{A.22}$$

Note that we have employed Eq. (A.20) to discount each payment. The stream of payments is assumed to start immediately ($t = 0$) and continue for n time periods. Hence the limits of integration in Eq. (A.22) are zero to n. Following the applicable rules of integral calculus to evaluate the definite integral, we obtain

$$
\begin{aligned}
PV &= a_0 \int_0^n e^{-kt}\, dt \\
&= a_0 \left[\frac{-e^{-kt}}{k} \right] \Big|_0^n \\
&= a_0 \left[\frac{-e^{-kn}}{k} - \frac{-e^0}{k} \right] \\
&= a_0 \left[\frac{1 - e^{-kn}}{k} \right].
\end{aligned}
\tag{A.23}
$$

Equation (A.23) is the continuous time analogue to Eq. (A.3) which was the discrete time version of the present value of an annuity of constant payments. Note that the continuous discount factor e^{-kn} in Eq. (A.23) is roughly equivalent to the discrete discount factor $(1 + r)^{-n}$ in Eq. (A.3) .

If we want the present value of an infinite stream of constant, continuously compounded payments we take the limit of Eq. (A.23) as n becomes infinite.

$$\lim_{n \to \infty} PV = \frac{a_0}{k}. \tag{A.24}$$

Equation (A.24) is exactly equal to Eq. (A.5).

3. Annuities with Growing Payments

For a stream of growing payments we can see from Eq. (A.17) that the payment function is

$$a_t = a_0 e^{gt}. \tag{A.25}$$

The present value of such a stream is

$$
\begin{aligned}
PV &= \int_0^n a_t e^{-kt}\, dt \\
&= a_0 \int_0^n e^{gt} e^{-kt}\, dt.
\end{aligned}
$$

Combining terms, we have

$$PV = a_0 \int_0^n e^{-(k-g)t}\, dt.$$

Using the rules of integral calculus, the solution to this integral is

$$PV = a_0 \left[\frac{-e^{-(k-g)t}}{k-g} \right]\Bigg|_0^n$$

$$= a_0 \left[\frac{-e^{-(k-g)n}}{k-g} - \left(\frac{-e^0}{k-g} \right) \right]$$

$$= a_0 \left[\frac{1 - e^{-(k-g)n}}{k-g} \right]. \tag{A.26}$$

Equation (A.26) is analogous to Eq. (A.8), the discrete compounding version of the present value of an annuity of growing payments which lasts for n years.

As before, the present value of an infinite stream of payments is obtained by taking the limit of Eq. (A.26) as n approaches infinity.

$$\lim_{n \to \infty} PV = \frac{a_0}{k-g}. \qquad \text{iff} \quad g < k. \tag{A.27}$$

D. SUMMARY

Consumption is allocated over time by "the" interest rate. Positive rates of interest induce people to postpone consumption and save part of their income. The pool of savings at any given time is used for investments which yield output in the form of goods that may be consumed at future dates.

The combined preferences of all members of society and the society's technology combine to determine the pattern of interest rates that will allocate consumption over time optimally. The structure of interest rates guides individuals into making investment decisions that are most desired by the society as a whole.

Present value or future value calculations at appropriately chosen interest rates, given the riskiness of the project, will tell an investor whether the future receipts are sufficient to justify the current investment. Since the pattern of interest rates is determined by the behavior of all members of society, a positive present value means not only that the project will yield a profit to the investor, but also that no member of the society has a superior use for the resources being invested. If many other investment opportunities were to appear that were superior to the one in question, the interest rate appropriate for the present value calculation would rise, and the present value of the project might then appear to be negative.

In order to evaluate projects with cash flows distributed over time it is necessary to express all flows in terms of their value at one specific point in time. Expressing them in terms of value today is discounting to net present value; expressing them at their value on some future date is compounding to future value. There is conceptually no difference between the two approaches.

Interest rates are traditionally expressed per annum, but cash flows may occur at discrete periods during the year, or may even be continuous. Again there is no conceptual difference between discrete and continuous formulations. However, the continuous form expressions are often more convenient for complex valuation problems. For example, some models of option pricing assume that stock price behavior is continuous, and consequently most option valuation expressions are in continuous form.

Table A.1 Compound Sum of $1 $S_n = P(1 + r)^n$

Year	1%	2%	3%	4%	5%	6%	7%	8%	9%	10%	11%	12%	13%	14%	15%	16%
1	1.010	1.020	1.030	1.040	1.050	1.060	1.070	1.080	1.090	1.100	1.110	1.120	1.130	1.140	1.150	1.160
2	1.020	1.040	1.061	1.082	1.102	1.124	1.145	1.166	1.188	1.210	1.232	1.254	1.277	1.300	1.322	1.346
3	1.030	1.061	1.093	1.125	1.158	1.191	1.225	1.260	1.295	1.331	1.368	1.405	1.443	1.482	1.521	1.561
4	1.041	1.082	1.126	1.170	1.216	1.262	1.311	1.360	1.412	1.464	1.518	1.574	1.631	1.689	1.749	1.811
5	1.051	1.104	1.159	1.217	1.276	1.338	1.403	1.469	1.539	1.611	1.685	1.762	1.842	1.925	2.011	2.100
6	1.062	1.126	1.194	1.265	1.340	1.419	1.501	1.587	1.677	1.772	1.870	1.974	2.082	2.195	2.313	2.436
7	1.072	1.149	1.230	1.316	1.407	1.504	1.606	1.714	1.828	1.949	2.076	2.211	2.353	2.502	2.660	2.826
8	1.083	1.172	1.267	1.369	1.477	1.594	1.718	1.851	1.993	2.144	2.305	2.476	2.658	2.853	3.059	3.278
9	1.094	1.195	1.305	1.423	1.551	1.689	1.838	1.999	2.172	2.358	2.558	2.773	3.004	3.252	3.518	3.803
10	1.105	1.219	1.344	1.480	1.629	1.791	1.967	2.159	2.367	2.594	2.839	3.106	3.395	3.707	4.046	4.411
11	1.116	1.243	1.384	1.539	1.710	1.898	2.105	2.332	2.580	2.853	3.152	3.479	3.836	4.226	4.652	5.117
12	1.127	1.268	1.426	1.601	1.796	2.012	2.252	2.518	2.813	3.138	3.499	3.896	4.335	4.818	5.350	5.936
13	1.138	1.294	1.469	1.665	1.886	2.133	2.410	2.720	3.066	3.452	3.883	4.363	4.898	5.492	6.153	6.886
14	1.149	1.319	1.513	1.732	1.980	2.261	2.579	2.937	3.342	3.797	4.310	4.887	5.535	6.261	7.076	7.988
15	1.161	1.346	1.558	1.801	2.079	2.397	2.759	3.172	3.642	4.177	4.785	5.474	6.254	7.138	8.137	9.266
16	1.173	1.373	1.605	1.873	2.183	2.540	2.952	3.426	3.970	4.595	5.311	6.130	7.067	8.137	9.358	10.748
17	1.184	1.400	1.653	1.948	2.292	2.693	3.159	3.700	4.328	5.054	5.895	6.866	7.986	9.276	10.761	12.468
18	1.196	1.428	1.702	2.026	2.407	2.854	3.380	3.996	4.717	5.560	6.544	7.690	9.024	10.575	12.375	14.463
19	1.208	1.457	1.754	2.107	2.527	3.026	3.617	4.316	5.142	6.116	7.263	8.613	10.197	12.056	14.232	16.777
20	1.220	1.486	1.806	2.191	2.653	3.207	3.870	4.661	5.604	6.728	8.062	9.646	11.523	13.743	16.367	19.461

Table A.2 Present Value of $1 $\qquad P = S_n(1 + r)^{-n}$

Years Hence	1%	2%	4%	6%	8%	10%	12%	14%	15%	16%	18%	20%	22%	24%	25%	26%	28%	30%	35%	40%	45%	50%
1	0.990	0.980	0.962	0.943	0.926	0.909	0.893	0.877	0.870	0.862	0.847	0.833	0.820	0.806	0.800	0.794	0.781	0.769	0.741	0.714	0.690	0.667
2	0.980	0.961	0.925	0.890	0.857	0.826	0.797	0.769	0.756	0.743	0.718	0.694	0.672	0.650	0.640	0.630	0.610	0.592	0.549	0.510	0.476	0.444
3	0.971	0.942	0.889	0.840	0.794	0.751	0.712	0.675	0.658	0.641	0.609	0.579	0.551	0.524	0.512	0.500	0.477	0.455	0.406	0.364	0.328	0.296
4	0.961	0.924	0.855	0.792	0.735	0.683	0.636	0.592	0.572	0.552	0.516	0.482	0.451	0.423	0.410	0.397	0.373	0.350	0.301	0.260	0.226	0.198
5	0.951	0.906	0.822	0.747	0.681	0.621	0.567	0.519	0.497	0.476	0.437	0.402	0.370	0.341	0.328	0.315	0.291	0.269	0.223	0.186	0.156	0.132
6	0.942	0.888	0.790	0.705	0.630	0.564	0.507	0.456	0.432	0.410	0.370	0.335	0.303	0.275	0.262	0.250	0.227	0.207	0.165	0.133	0.108	0.088
7	0.933	0.871	0.760	0.665	0.583	0.513	0.452	0.400	0.376	0.354	0.314	0.279	0.249	0.222	0.210	0.198	0.178	0.159	0.122	0.095	0.074	0.059
8	0.923	0.853	0.731	0.627	0.540	0.467	0.404	0.351	0.327	0.305	0.266	0.233	0.204	0.179	0.168	0.157	0.139	0.123	0.091	0.068	0.051	0.039
9	0.914	0.837	0.703	0.592	0.500	0.424	0.361	0.308	0.284	0.263	0.225	0.194	0.167	0.144	0.134	0.125	0.108	0.094	0.067	0.048	0.035	0.026
10	0.905	0.820	0.676	0.558	0.463	0.386	0.322	0.270	0.247	0.227	0.191	0.162	0.137	0.116	0.107	0.099	0.085	0.073	0.050	0.035	0.024	0.017
11	0.896	0.804	0.650	0.527	0.429	0.350	0.287	0.237	0.215	0.195	0.162	0.135	0.112	0.094	0.086	0.079	0.066	0.056	0.037	0.025	0.017	0.012
12	0.887	0.788	0.625	0.497	0.397	0.319	0.257	0.208	0.187	0.168	0.137	0.112	0.092	0.076	0.069	0.062	0.052	0.043	0.027	0.018	0.012	0.008
13	0.879	0.773	0.601	0.469	0.368	0.290	0.229	0.182	0.163	0.145	0.116	0.093	0.075	0.061	0.055	0.050	0.040	0.033	0.020	0.013	0.008	0.005
14	0.870	0.758	0.577	0.442	0.340	0.263	0.205	0.160	0.141	0.125	0.099	0.078	0.062	0.049	0.044	0.039	0.032	0.025	0.015	0.009	0.006	0.003
15	0.861	0.743	0.555	0.417	0.315	0.239	0.183	0.140	0.123	0.108	0.084	0.065	0.051	0.040	0.035	0.031	0.025	0.020	0.011	0.006	0.004	0.002
16	0.853	0.728	0.534	0.394	0.292	0.218	0.163	0.123	0.107	0.093	0.071	0.054	0.042	0.032	0.028	0.025	0.019	0.015	0.008	0.005	0.003	0.002
17	0.844	0.714	0.513	0.371	0.270	0.198	0.146	0.108	0.093	0.080	0.060	0.045	0.034	0.026	0.023	0.020	0.015	0.012	0.006	0.003	0.002	0.001
18	0.836	0.700	0.494	0.350	0.250	0.180	0.130	0.095	0.081	0.069	0.051	0.038	0.028	0.021	0.018	0.016	0.012	0.009	0.005	0.002	0.001	0.001
19	0.828	0.686	0.475	0.331	0.232	0.164	0.116	0.083	0.070	0.060	0.043	0.031	0.023	0.017	0.014	0.012	0.009	0.007	0.003	0.002	0.001	
20	0.820	0.673	0.456	0.312	0.215	0.149	0.104	0.073	0.061	0.051	0.037	0.026	0.019	0.014	0.012	0.010	0.007	0.005	0.002	0.001	0.001	
21	0.811	0.660	0.439	0.294	0.199	0.135	0.093	0.064	0.053	0.044	0.031	0.022	0.015	0.011	0.009	0.008	0.006	0.004	0.002	0.001		
22	0.803	0.647	0.422	0.278	0.184	0.123	0.083	0.056	0.046	0.038	0.026	0.018	0.013	0.009	0.007	0.006	0.004	0.003	0.001	0.001		
23	0.795	0.634	0.406	0.262	0.170	0.112	0.074	0.049	0.040	0.033	0.022	0.015	0.010	0.007	0.006	0.005	0.003	0.002	0.001			
24	0.788	0.622	0.390	0.247	0.158	0.102	0.066	0.043	0.035	0.028	0.019	0.013	0.008	0.006	0.005	0.004	0.003	0.001	0.001			
25	0.780	0.610	0.375	0.233	0.146	0.092	0.059	0.038	0.030	0.024	0.016	0.010	0.007	0.005	0.004	0.003	0.002	0.001	0.001			
26	0.772	0.598	0.361	0.220	0.135	0.084	0.053	0.033	0.026	0.021	0.014	0.009	0.006	0.004	0.003	0.002	0.002	0.001				
27	0.764	0.586	0.347	0.207	0.125	0.076	0.047	0.029	0.023	0.018	0.011	0.007	0.005	0.003	0.002	0.002	0.001	0.001				
28	0.757	0.574	0.333	0.196	0.116	0.069	0.042	0.026	0.020	0.016	0.010	0.006	0.004	0.002	0.002	0.002	0.001	0.001				
29	0.749	0.563	0.321	0.185	0.107	0.063	0.037	0.022	0.017	0.014	0.008	0.005	0.003	0.002	0.002	0.001	0.001	0.001				
30	0.742	0.552	0.308	0.174	0.099	0.057	0.033	0.020	0.015	0.012	0.007	0.004	0.003	0.002	0.001	0.001	0.001	0.001				
40	0.672	0.453	0.208	0.097	0.046	0.022	0.011	0.005	0.004	0.003	0.001	0.001										
50	0.608	0.372	0.141	0.054	0.021	0.009	0.003	0.001	0.001	0.001												

Table A.3 Sum of an Annuity for \$1 for *n* Years

$$S_{\overline{n}|r} = \$1 \left[\frac{(1+r)^n - 1}{r} \right] = \$1 C_{n,r}$$

Year	1%	2%	3%	4%	5%	6%	7%	8%	9%	10%	11%	12%	13%	14%	15%	16%
1	1.000	1.000	1.000	1.000	1.000	1.000	1.000	1.000	1.000	1.000	1.000	1.000	1.000	1.000	1.000	1.000
2	2.010	2.020	2.030	2.040	2.050	2.060	2.070	2.080	2.090	2.100	2.110	2.120	2.130	2.140	2.150	2.160
3	3.030	3.060	3.091	3.122	3.152	3.184	3.215	3.246	3.278	3.310	3.342	3.374	3.407	3.440	3.473	3.506
4	4.060	4.122	4.184	4.246	4.310	4.375	4.440	4.506	4.573	4.641	4.710	4.779	4.850	4.921	4.993	5.066
5	5.101	5.204	5.309	5.416	5.526	5.637	5.751	5.867	5.985	6.105	6.228	6.353	6.480	6.610	6.742	6.877
6	6.152	6.308	6.468	6.633	6.802	6.975	7.153	7.336	7.523	7.716	7.913	8.115	8.323	8.536	8.754	8.977
7	7.214	7.434	7.662	7.898	8.142	8.394	8.654	8.923	9.200	9.487	9.783	10.089	10.405	10.730	11.067	11.414
8	8.286	8.583	8.892	9.214	9.549	9.897	10.260	10.637	11.028	11.436	11.859	12.300	12.757	13.233	13.727	14.240
9	9.369	9.755	10.159	10.583	11.027	11.491	11.978	12.488	13.021	13.579	14.164	14.776	15.416	16.085	16.786	17.518
10	10.462	10.950	11.464	12.006	12.578	13.181	13.816	14.487	15.193	15.937	16.722	17.549	18.420	19.337	20.304	21.321
11	11.567	12.169	12.808	13.486	14.207	14.972	15.784	16.645	17.560	18.531	19.561	20.655	21.814	23.044	24.349	25.733
12	12.683	13.412	14.192	15.026	15.917	16.870	17.888	18.977	20.141	21.384	22.713	24.133	25.650	27.271	29.002	30.850
13	13.809	14.680	15.618	16.627	17.713	18.882	20.141	21.495	22.953	24.523	26.212	28.029	29.985	32.089	34.352	36.786
14	14.947	15.974	17.086	18.292	19.599	21.051	22.550	24.215	26.019	27.975	30.095	32.393	34.883	37.581	40.505	43.672
15	16.097	17.293	18.599	20.024	21.579	23.276	25.129	27.152	29.361	31.772	34.405	37.280	40.417	43.842	47.580	51.659

Table A.4 Present Value of $1 Received Annually

$$A_{\overline{n}|r} = \$1\left[\frac{1-(1+r)^{-n}}{r}\right] = \$1P_{n,r}$$

Years (n)	1%	2%	4%	6%	8%	10%	12%	14%	15%	16%	18%	20%	22%	24%	25%	26%	28%	30%	35%	40%	45%	50%
1	0.990	0.980	0.962	0.943	0.926	0.909	0.893	0.877	0.870	0.862	0.847	0.833	0.820	0.806	0.800	0.794	0.781	0.769	0.741	0.714	0.690	0.667
2	1.970	1.942	1.886	1.833	1.783	1.736	1.690	1.647	1.626	1.605	1.566	1.528	1.492	1.457	1.440	1.424	1.392	1.361	1.289	1.224	1.165	1.111
3	2.941	2.884	2.775	2.673	2.577	2.487	2.402	2.322	2.283	2.246	2.174	2.106	2.042	1.981	1.952	1.923	1.868	1.816	1.696	1.589	1.493	1.407
4	3.902	3.808	3.630	3.465	3.312	3.170	3.037	2.914	2.855	2.798	2.690	2.589	2.494	2.404	2.362	2.320	2.241	2.166	1.997	1.849	1.720	1.605
5	4.853	4.713	4.452	4.212	3.993	3.791	3.605	3.433	3.352	3.274	3.127	2.991	2.864	2.745	2.689	2.635	2.532	2.436	2.220	2.035	1.876	1.737
6	5.795	5.601	5.242	4.917	4.623	4.355	4.111	3.889	3.784	3.685	3.498	3.326	3.167	3.020	2.951	2.885	2.759	2.643	2.385	2.168	1.983	1.824
7	6.728	6.472	6.002	5.582	5.206	4.868	4.564	4.288	4.160	4.039	3.812	3.605	3.416	3.242	3.161	3.083	2.937	2.802	2.508	2.263	2.057	1.883
8	7.652	7.325	6.733	6.210	5.747	5.335	4.968	4.639	4.487	4.344	4.078	3.837	3.619	3.421	3.329	3.241	3.076	2.925	2.598	2.331	2.108	1.922
9	8.566	8.162	7.435	6.802	6.247	5.759	5.328	4.946	4.772	4.607	4.303	4.031	3.786	3.566	3.463	3.366	3.184	3.019	2.665	2.379	2.144	1.948
10	9.471	8.983	8.111	7.360	6.710	6.145	5.650	5.216	5.019	4.833	4.494	4.192	3.923	3.682	3.571	3.465	3.269	3.092	2.715	2.414	2.168	1.965
11	10.368	9.787	8.760	7.887	7.139	6.495	5.937	5.453	5.234	5.029	4.656	4.327	4.035	3.776	3.656	3.544	3.335	3.147	2.757	2.438	2.185	1.977
12	11.255	10.575	9.385	8.384	7.536	6.814	6.194	5.660	5.421	5.197	4.793	4.439	4.127	3.851	3.725	3.606	3.387	3.190	2.779	2.456	2.196	1.985
13	12.134	11.343	9.986	8.853	7.904	7.103	6.424	5.842	5.583	5.342	4.910	4.533	4.203	3.912	3.780	3.656	3.427	3.223	2.799	2.468	2.204	1.990
14	13.004	12.106	10.563	9.295	8.244	7.367	6.628	6.002	5.724	5.468	5.008	4.611	4.265	3.962	3.824	3.695	3.459	3.249	2.814	2.477	2.210	1.993
15	13.865	12.849	11.118	9.712	8.559	7.606	6.811	6.142	5.847	5.575	5.092	4.675	4.315	4.001	3.859	3.726	3.483	3.268	2.825	2.484	2.214	1.995
16	14.718	13.578	11.652	10.106	8.851	7.824	7.074	6.265	5.954	5.669	5.162	4.730	4.357	4.033	3.887	3.751	3.503	3.283	2.834	2.489	2.216	1.997
17	15.562	14.292	12.166	10.477	9.122	8.022	7.120	6.373	6.047	5.749	5.222	4.775	4.391	4.059	3.910	3.771	3.518	3.295	2.840	2.492	2.218	1.998
18	16.398	14.992	12.659	10.828	9.372	8.201	7.250	6.467	6.128	5.818	5.273	4.812	4.419	4.080	3.928	3.786	3.529	3.304	2.844	2.494	2.219	1.999
19	17.226	15.678	13.134	11.158	9.604	8.365	7.366	6.550	6.198	5.877	5.316	4.844	4.442	4.097	3.942	3.799	3.539	3.311	2.848	2.496	2.220	1.999
20	18.046	16.351	13.590	11.470	9.818	8.514	7.469	6.623	6.259	5.929	5.353	4.870	4.460	4.110	3.954	3.808	3.546	3.316	2.850	2.497	2.221	1.999
21	18.857	17.011	14.029	11.764	10.017	8.649	7.562	6.687	6.312	5.973	5.384	4.891	4.476	4.121	3.963	3.816	3.551	3.320	2.852	2.498	2.221	2.000
22	19.660	17.658	14.451	12.042	10.201	8.772	7.645	6.743	6.359	6.011	5.410	4.909	4.488	4.130	3.970	3.822	3.556	3.323	2.853	2.498	2.222	2.000
23	20.456	18.292	14.857	12.303	10.371	8.883	7.718	6.792	6.399	6.044	5.432	4.925	4.499	4.137	3.976	3.827	3.559	3.325	2.854	2.499	2.222	2.000
24	21.243	18.914	15.247	12.550	10.529	8.985	7.784	6.835	6.434	6.073	5.451	4.937	4.507	4.143	3.981	3.831	3.562	3.327	2.855	2.499	2.222	2.000
25	22.023	19.523	15.622	12.783	10.675	9.077	7.843	6.873	6.464	6.097	5.467	4.948	4.514	4.147	3.985	3.834	3.564	3.329	2.856	2.499	2.222	2.000
26	22.795	20.121	15.983	13.003	10.810	9.161	7.896	6.906	6.491	6.118	5.480	4.956	4.520	4.151	3.988	3.837	3.566	3.330	2.856	2.500	2.222	2.000
27	23.560	20.707	16.330	13.211	10.935	9.237	7.943	6.935	6.514	6.136	5.492	4.964	4.524	4.154	3.990	3.839	3.567	3.331	2.856	2.500	2.222	2.000
28	24.316	21.281	16.663	13.406	11.051	9.307	7.984	6.961	6.534	6.152	5.502	4.970	4.528	4.157	3.992	3.840	3.568	3.331	2.857	2.500	2.222	2.000
29	25.066	21.844	16.984	13.591	11.158	9.370	8.022	6.983	6.551	6.166	5.510	4.975	4.531	4.159	3.994	3.841	3.569	3.332	2.857	2.500	2.222	2.000
30	25.808	22.396	17.292	13.765	11.258	9.427	8.055	7.003	6.566	6.177	5.517	4.979	4.534	4.160	3.995	3.842	3.569	3.332	2.857	2.500	2.222	2.000
40	32.835	27.355	19.793	15.046	11.925	9.779	8.244	7.105	6.642	6.234	5.548	4.997	4.544	4.166	3.999	3.846	3.571	3.333	2.857	2.500	2.222	2.000
50	39.196	31.424	21.482	15.762	12.234	9.915	8.301	7.133	6.661	6.246	5.554	4.999	4.545	4.167	4.000	3.846	3.571	3.333	2.857	2.500	2.222	2.000

Table A.5   Natural Logarithms of Numbers Between 1.0 and 4.99

N	0	1	2	3	4	5	6	7	8	9
1.0	0.00000	.00995	.01980	.02956	.03922	.04879	.05827	.06766	.07696	.08618
.1	.09531	.10436	.11333	.12222	.13103	.13976	.14842	.15700	.16551	.17395
.2	.18232	.19062	.19885	.20701	.21511	.22314	.23111	.23902	.24686	.25464
.3	.26236	.27003	.27763	.28518	.29267	.30010	.30748	.31481	.32208	.32930
.4	.33647	.34359	.35066	.35767	.36464	.37156	.37844	.38526	.39204	.39878
.5	.40547	.41211	.41871	.42527	.43178	.43825	.44469	.45108	.45742	.46373
.6	.47000	.47623	.48243	.48858	.49470	.50078	.50682	.51282	.51879	.52473
.7	.53063	.53649	.54232	.54812	.55389	.55962	.56531	.57098	.57661	.58222
.8	.58779	.59333	.59884	.60432	.60977	.61519	.62058	.62594	.63127	.63658
.9	.64185	.64710	.65233	.65752	.66269	.66783	.67294	.67803	.68310	.68813
2.0	0.69315	.69813	.70310	.70804	.71295	.71784	.72271	.72755	.73237	.73716
.1	.74194	.74669	.75142	.75612	.76081	.76547	.77011	.77473	.77932	.78390
.2	.78846	.79299	.79751	.80200	.80648	.81093	.81536	.81978	.82418	.82855
.3	.83291	.83725	.84157	.84587	.85015	.85442	.85866	.86289	.86710	.87129
.4	.87547	.87963	.88377	.88789	.89200	.89609	.90016	.90422	.90826	.91228
.5	.91629	.92028	.92426	.92822	.93216	.93609	.94001	.94391	.94779	.95166
.6	.95551	.95935	.96317	.96698	.97078	.97456	.97833	.98208	.98582	.98954
.7	.99325	.99695	.00063[a]	.00430[a]	.00796[a]	.01160[a]	.01523[a]	.01885[a]	.02245[a]	.02604[a]
.8	1.02962	.03318	.03674	.04028	.04380	.04732	.05082	.05431	.05779	.06126
.9	.06471	.06815	.07158	.07500	.07841	.08181	.08519	.08856	.09192	.09527
3.0	1.09861	.10194	.10526	.10856	.11186	.11514	.11841	.12168	.12493	.12817
.1	.13140	.13462	.13783	.14103	.14422	.14740	.15057	.15373	.15688	.16002
.2	.16315	.16627	.16938	.17248	.17557	.17865	.18173	.18479	.18784	.19089
.3	.19392	.19695	.19996	.20297	.20597	.20896	.21194	.21491	.21788	.22083
.4	.22378	.22671	.22964	.23256	.23547	.23837	.24127	.24415	.24703	.24990
.5	.25276	.25562	.25846	.26130	.26413	.26695	.26976	.27257	.27536	.27815
.6	.28093	.28371	.28647	.28923	.29198	.29473	.29746	.30019	.30291	.30563
.7	.30833	.31103	.31372	.31641	.31909	.32176	.32442	.32708	.32972	.33237
.8	.33500	.33763	.34025	.34286	.34547	.34807	.35067	.35325	.35584	.35841
.9	.36098	.36354	.36609	.36864	.37118	.37372	.37624	.37877	.38128	.38379
4.0	1.38629	.38879	.39128	.39377	.39624	.39872	.40118	.40364	.40610	.40854
.1	.41099	.41342	.41585	.41828	.42070	.42311	.42552	.42792	.43031	.43270
.2	.43508	.43746	.43984	.44220	.44456	.44692	.44927	.45161	.45395	.45629
.3	.45862	.46094	.46326	.46557	.46787	.47018	.47247	.47476	.47705	.47933
.4	.48160	.48387	.48614	.48840	.49065	.49290	.49515	.49739	.49962	.50185
.5	.50408	.50630	.50851	.51072	.51293	.51513	.51732	.51951	.52170	.52388
.6	.52606	.52823	.53039	.53256	.53471	.53687	.53902	.54116	.54330	.54543
.7	.54756	.54969	.55181	.55393	.55604	.55814	.56025	.56235	.56444	.56653
.8	.56862	.57070	.57277	.57485	.57691	.57898	.58104	.58309	.58515	.58719
.9	.58924	.59127	.59331	.59534	.59737	.59939	.60141	.60342	.60543	.60744

[a]Add 1.0 to indicated figure.

Matrix Algebra

A. MATRICES AND VECTORS

A matrix is a rectangular array of numbers. The following are examples of matrices:

$$\underset{(3 \times 2)}{A} = \begin{pmatrix} 1 & 2 \\ 0 & 1 \\ -1 & 4 \end{pmatrix},$$

$$\underset{(3 \times 4)}{B} = \begin{pmatrix} 2 & 3 & 1.5 & 0 \\ -1 & 4 & -1 & -1 \\ 3 & 1.1 & 2 & -5 \end{pmatrix},$$

$$\underset{(2 \times 2)}{C} = \begin{pmatrix} 2 & 1 \\ 1 & -2 \end{pmatrix}.$$

The matrix A is a 3×2 matrix because it has three rows and two columns. The matrix B is a 3×4 matrix because it has three rows and four columns. The matrix C is a 2×2 square matrix because it has two rows and two columns.

Each number in a matrix is called an element. The element on the ith row and jth column of the matrix A is designated by a_{ij}. For example, in the matrix A above,

719

$a_{11} = 1$, $a_{12} = 2$, $a_{21} = 0$ and so on. Similarly, in the matrix B, $b_{12} = 3$, $b_{32} = 1.1$.

We say that two $m \times n$ matrices are equal if all their corresponding elements are identical. In other words, if both R and S are $m \times n$ matrices, then $R = S$ if and only if $r_{ij} = s_{ij}$ for all $i = 1, 2, \ldots, m$ and $j = 1, 2, \ldots, n$. For example,

$$\begin{pmatrix} 1 & 2 \\ -1 & 1 \end{pmatrix} = \begin{pmatrix} 1 & 2 \\ -1 & 1 \end{pmatrix} \quad \text{but} \quad \begin{pmatrix} 1 & 1 \\ 0 & 1 \end{pmatrix} \neq \begin{pmatrix} 1 & 0 \\ 1 & 1 \end{pmatrix}.$$

Vectors are matrices with only one row or one column. A $1 \times m$ matrix is called a row vector and a $m \times 1$ matrix is called a column vector. For example,

$$\underset{(1 \times 3)}{a} = (1 \quad -1 \quad 1), \qquad \underset{(1 \times 4)}{b} = (1 \quad 2 \quad 0 \quad 1)$$

are row vectors and

$$\underset{(2 \times 1)}{c} = \begin{pmatrix} 1 \\ -1 \end{pmatrix}, \qquad \underset{(3 \times 1)}{d} = \begin{pmatrix} 1 \\ 3 \\ 2 \end{pmatrix}$$

are column vectors. Each number in a vector is called a component of that vector. The ith component of the vector a is designated by a_i. So, $a_1 = 1$, $a_2 = -1$, $a_3 = 1$ in the vector a above.

Two $1 \times n$ row vectors or two $m \times 1$ column vectors are equal if all the corresponding components are the same. For example,

$$\begin{pmatrix} 1 \\ 2 \end{pmatrix} = \begin{pmatrix} 1 \\ 2 \end{pmatrix}, \qquad (3 \quad 1 \quad 2) = (3 \quad 1 \quad 2),$$

but

$$\begin{pmatrix} 1 \\ 2 \end{pmatrix} \neq (1 \quad 2), \qquad \begin{pmatrix} 1 \\ 2 \end{pmatrix} \neq \begin{pmatrix} 2 \\ 1 \end{pmatrix}, \qquad \begin{pmatrix} 1 \\ 2 \end{pmatrix} \neq \begin{pmatrix} 1 \\ 2 \\ 3 \end{pmatrix}.$$

B. THE OPERATIONS OF MATRICES

Addition and subtraction of two matrices A and B can be performed if A and B have the same dimension—that is, if the number of rows and the number of columns are the same. Addition and subtraction is carried out on each corresponding pair of elements. If $A + B = C$, then $a_{ij} + b_{ij} = c_{ij}$. For example,

$$\begin{pmatrix} 1 & 2 \\ 3 & 4 \end{pmatrix} + \begin{pmatrix} -1 & 1 \\ 2 & -1 \end{pmatrix} = \begin{pmatrix} 1-1 & 2+1 \\ 3+2 & 4-1 \end{pmatrix} = \begin{pmatrix} 0 & 3 \\ 5 & 3 \end{pmatrix},$$

$$\begin{pmatrix} 1 & 2 \\ 3 & 4 \end{pmatrix} - \begin{pmatrix} -1 & 1 \\ 2 & -1 \end{pmatrix} = \begin{pmatrix} 1-(-1) & 2-1 \\ 3-2 & 4-(-1) \end{pmatrix} = \begin{pmatrix} 2 & 1 \\ 1 & 5 \end{pmatrix},$$

$$\begin{pmatrix} 1 \\ 2 \end{pmatrix} - \begin{pmatrix} 1 \\ 1 \end{pmatrix} = \begin{pmatrix} 0 \\ 1 \end{pmatrix}, \qquad \begin{pmatrix} 1 \\ 2 \end{pmatrix} + \begin{pmatrix} 1 \\ 1 \end{pmatrix} + \begin{pmatrix} 2 \\ 3 \end{pmatrix}.$$

If we multiply a matrix A by a scalar, the resultant matrix is obtained by multiplying each element of A by that scalar. So if

$$A = \begin{pmatrix} 1 & 2 & 3 \\ -1 & 1 & 2 \end{pmatrix},$$

then

$$2A = \begin{pmatrix} 2 & 4 & 6 \\ -2 & 2 & 4 \end{pmatrix}, \quad -3A = \begin{pmatrix} -3 & -6 & -9 \\ 3 & -3 & -6 \end{pmatrix}.$$

We can also multiply two matrices together provided that the number of columns in the first matrix is equal to the number of rows in the second matrix. In order to form the product AB of the two matrices A and B, the number of columns of A must be equal to the number of rows of B. If we designate the result of the matrix multiplication AB by C, then C is again a matrix and C has the same number of rows as A and the same number of columns as B. To summarize: if A is an $m \times n$ matrix and B a $p \times q$ matrix, then the product AB can be formed only if $n = p$; further, if $C = AB$, then C is an $m \times q$ matrix.

To complete our definition of matrix multiplication, we have to describe how the elements of C are obtained. The following rule specifies c_{ij}, the element in the ith row and jth column of the resultant matrix C, in terms of elements in A and B:

$$c_{ij} = a_{i1}b_{1j} + a_{i2}b_{2j} + \cdots + a_{in}b_{nj} = \sum_{k=1}^{n} a_{ik}b_{kj}, \tag{B.1}$$

where n = number of columns of A = number of rows of B.

Equation (B.1) tells us that c_{ij} is a sum of products. Each product consists of an element from the ith row of A and an element from the jth column of B. We multiply the first element in the ith row of A with the first element in the jth column of B, the second element in the ith row of A with the second element in the jth column of B—and so on until the last element in the ith row of A is multiplied with the last element in the jth column of B—and then sum all the products. Another way to look at this is: to obtain c_{ij}, we "multiply" the ith row of A with the jth column of B.

An example further clarifies Eq. (B.1). Consider $C = AB$, where

$$A = \begin{pmatrix} 1 & 2 & 3 \\ 1 & 0 & 1 \end{pmatrix} \quad B = \begin{pmatrix} -1 & 3 & 0 & 0 \\ 2 & 1 & 1 & 0 \\ 1 & 0 & 0 & 1 \end{pmatrix}.$$

Since A is 2×3 and B is 3×4, the product AB can be formed and C would be 2×4. According to Eq. (B.1),

$$c_{11} = a_{11}b_{11} + a_{12}b_{21} + a_{13}b_{31} = 1 \times (-1) + 2 \times 2 + 3 \times 1 = 6,$$
$$c_{12} = a_{11}b_{12} + a_{12}b_{22} + a_{13}b_{32} = 1 \times 3 + 2 \times 1 + 3 \times 0 = 5,$$

and so on. The result $AB = C$ is

$$\begin{pmatrix} \boxed{1 \quad 2 \quad 3} \\ 1 \quad 0 \quad 1 \end{pmatrix} \begin{pmatrix} -1 & \boxed{3} & 0 & 0 \\ 2 & 1 & 1 & 0 \\ 1 & \boxed{0} & 0 & 1 \end{pmatrix} = \begin{pmatrix} 6 & \boxed{5} & 2 & 3 \\ 0 & 3 & 0 & 1 \end{pmatrix}$$

We should emphasize at this point that the product BA may not be defined even though AB is. We can take the above as an example. A is 2×3 and B is 3×4, so AB is defined, but BA is not, since $4 \neq 2$. In the event that BA is also defined, $BA \neq AB$ in general. For example, let

$$A = \begin{pmatrix} 1 & 1 \\ 0 & 1 \end{pmatrix}, \qquad B = \begin{pmatrix} 1 & 0 \\ 1 & 1 \end{pmatrix},$$

then

$$AB = \begin{pmatrix} 2 & 1 \\ 1 & 1 \end{pmatrix} \quad \text{but} \quad BA = \begin{pmatrix} 1 & 1 \\ 1 & 2 \end{pmatrix}.$$

C. LINEAR EQUATIONS IN MATRIX FORM

A system of linear equations can be expressed in matrix form. First, let us consider one simple linear equation, say $X_1 - 2X_2 + 2X_3 = 4$. Using matrix multiplication, the equation can be expressed as

$$(1 \quad -2 \quad 2) \begin{pmatrix} X_1 \\ X_2 \\ X_3 \end{pmatrix} = (1X_1 + (-2)X_2 + 2X_3) = 4.$$

Suppose we now have the following system of three equations:

$$X_1 \quad -2X_2 \quad +2X_3 = 4,$$
$$X_1 \quad + X_2 \quad + X_3 = 5,$$
$$-X_1 \quad +5X_2 \quad -3X_3 = 1,$$

using matrix multiplication, this is equivalent to

$$\underbrace{\begin{pmatrix} 1 & -2 & 2 \\ 1 & 1 & 1 \\ -1 & 5 & -3 \end{pmatrix}}_{3 \times 3} \underbrace{\begin{pmatrix} X_1 \\ X_2 \\ X_3 \end{pmatrix}}_{3 \times 1} = \begin{pmatrix} 1 \cdot X_1 - 2 \cdot X_2 + 2 \cdot X_3 \\ 1 \cdot X_1 + 1 \cdot X_2 + 1 \cdot X_3 \\ -1 \cdot X_1 + 5 \cdot X_2 - 3 \cdot X_3 \end{pmatrix} = \underbrace{\begin{pmatrix} 4 \\ 5 \\ 1 \end{pmatrix}}_{3 \times 1}.$$

And because of the equality definition of vectors, we must equate $(1 \cdot X_1 - 2 \cdot X_2 + 2 \cdot X_3)$ to 4 and $(1 \cdot X_1 + 1 \cdot X_2 + 1 \cdot X_3)$ to 5 and $(-1 \cdot X_1 + 5 \cdot X_2 - 3 \cdot X_3)$ to 1, which shows that the matrix formulation

$$\begin{pmatrix} 1 & -2 & 2 \\ 1 & 1 & 1 \\ -1 & 5 & -3 \end{pmatrix} \begin{pmatrix} X_1 \\ X_2 \\ X_3 \end{pmatrix} = \begin{pmatrix} 4 \\ 5 \\ 1 \end{pmatrix} \tag{B.2}$$

is equivalent to the system of linear equations. In general, Eq. (B.2) is written as $Ax = b$, where

$$A = \begin{pmatrix} 1 & -2 & 2 \\ 1 & 1 & 1 \\ -1 & 5 & -3 \end{pmatrix}, \qquad x = \begin{pmatrix} X_1 \\ X_2 \\ X_3 \end{pmatrix}, \qquad b = \begin{pmatrix} 4 \\ 5 \\ 1 \end{pmatrix}.$$

A is called the coefficient matrix, x is the vector of unknowns, and b is the vector of constants. Finding the solution to a system of linear equations is equivalent to solving for the unknown vector x in the matrix equation $Ax = b$. We will come back to solving $Ax = b$ in a later section.

D. SPECIAL MATRICES

There are several types of matrices that possess useful properties. Here we list some of the more important ones.

The zero (or null) matrix is a matrix with all elements (or components) being zero. For example,

$$\begin{pmatrix} 0 & 0 \\ 0 & 0 \end{pmatrix}, \qquad \begin{pmatrix} 0 & 0 & 0 & 0 \\ 0 & 0 & 0 & 0 \\ 0 & 0 & 0 & 0 \end{pmatrix}$$

are null matrices of dimensions 2×2 and 3×4. The zero matrix 0 possesses the property that

$$A + 0 = 0 + A = A$$

for any matrix A of the same dimension.

A diagonal matrix is a square matrix whose elements are all zeros except on the *main diagonal*, that is, D is a diagonal matrix if $d_{ij} = 0$ for $i \neq j$. For example,

$$\begin{pmatrix} 1 & 0 \\ 0 & 2 \end{pmatrix}, \qquad \begin{pmatrix} 1 & 0 & 0 \\ 0 & 3 & 0 \\ 0 & 0 & 4 \end{pmatrix}$$

are diagonal matrices. The elements $d_{11}, d_{22}, \ldots, d_{nn}$ are called elements on the main diagonal. Note that all diagonal matrices are square by definition.

The identity matrix, I, is a diagonal matrix which has ones on the main diagonal and zeros everywhere else. For example,

$$\begin{pmatrix} 1 & 0 \\ 0 & 1 \end{pmatrix}, \qquad \begin{pmatrix} 1 & 0 & 0 \\ 0 & 1 & 0 \\ 0 & 0 & 1 \end{pmatrix}, \qquad \begin{pmatrix} 1 & 0 & 0 & 0 \\ 0 & 1 & 0 & 0 \\ 0 & 0 & 1 & 0 \\ 0 & 0 & 0 & 1 \end{pmatrix}$$

are identity matrices of dimensions 2×2, 3×3, 4×4. The identity matrix has the useful property that

$$AI = A, \qquad IB = B$$

for all matrices A and B provided the matrix multiplication is defined; that is, A and B must be of appropriate dimensions.

E. MATRIX INVERSION DEFINED

Now, given a square matrix A, there may exist a matrix B, such that

$$AB = BA = I.$$

If such matrix B exists, then A is said to be nonsingular and the matrix B is called the multiplicative *inverse* of A. We usually write B as A^{-1} to denote inverse. A^{-1} plays a very significant role in solving the matrix equation $Ax = b$. If A^{-1} is known, we can premultiply both sides of the matrix equation by A^{-1} to get

$$A^{-1}Ax = A^{-1}b,$$

Since $A^{-1}A = I$, the equation becomes

$$Ix = A^{-1}b.$$

But $Ix = x$ where x is an $(m \times 1)$ matrix, therefore

$$x = A^{-1}b.$$

The system can now be solved for the unknown vector, x, by carrying out the matrix multiplication, $A^{-1}b$.

F. MATRIX TRANSPOSITION

Before we describe how to compute A^{-1} we must first define the transpose of a matrix. For a given matrix A, the transpose of A, denoted by A', is obtained from A by writing the columns of A as rows of A'. Formally, we have $a'_{ij} = a_{ji}$. For example, if

$$A = \begin{pmatrix} 1 & 2 & 3 \\ 3 & 2 & 1 \\ 4 & 3 & 2 \end{pmatrix}, \quad \text{then} \quad A' = \begin{pmatrix} 1 & 3 & 4 \\ 2 & 2 & 3 \\ 3 & 1 & 2 \end{pmatrix}.$$

Finally, if $A = A'$, then we say that A is a symmetric matrix. For example,

$$A = \begin{pmatrix} 1 & -1 & 4 \\ -1 & 2 & 5 \\ 4 & 5 & 3 \end{pmatrix}$$

is a symmetric matrix. Notice the entries of A are symmetric across the main diagonal, hence all diagonal matrices are symmetric.

The class of symmetric matrices is very important and arises very often in many real life problems. The covariance matrix in portfolio theory is a symmetric matrix. Furthermore, algebraic systems involving symmetric matrices are in general easier to solve.

G. DETERMINANTS

Given $x = A^{-1}b$, and A, the first step in finding A^{-1} is to first determine if A is nonsingular. To do that, we make use of the determinant function which is defined for all square matrices.

The determinant of a square matrix A, denoted by $|A|$, is a unique number associated with that matrix. For a 2×2 matrix

$$A = \begin{pmatrix} a_{11} & a_{12} \\ a_{21} & a_{22} \end{pmatrix}, \qquad |A| = a_{11}a_{22} - a_{12}a_{21}.$$

For example,

$$\begin{vmatrix} 2 & 1 \\ 3 & 4 \end{vmatrix} = (2 \times 4) - (1 \times 3) = 8 - 3 = 5.$$

So, the determinant of the matrix is 5.

The definition of a determinant of a 3×3 or higher order square matrix involves the notion of minors and cofactors of elements of the matrix. The minor of a_{ij}, denoted by $|M_{ij}|$, is the determinant of the *submatrix* of A obtained by deleting the ith row and jth column of A. Suppose

$$A = \begin{pmatrix} a_{11} & a_{12} & a_{13} \\ a_{21} & a_{22} & a_{23} \\ a_{31} & a_{32} & a_{33} \end{pmatrix},$$

then

$$|M_{11}| = \begin{vmatrix} a_{11} & a_{12} & a_{13} \\ a_{21} & a_{22} & a_{23} \\ a_{31} & a_{32} & a_{33} \end{vmatrix} = \begin{vmatrix} a_{22} & a_{23} \\ a_{32} & a_{33} \end{vmatrix} = a_{22}a_{33} - a_{23}a_{32},$$

$$|M_{21}| = \begin{vmatrix} a_{11} & a_{12} & a_{13} \\ a_{21} & a_{22} & a_{23} \\ a_{31} & a_{32} & a_{33} \end{vmatrix} = \begin{vmatrix} a_{12} & a_{13} \\ a_{32} & a_{33} \end{vmatrix} = a_{12}a_{33} - a_{13}a_{32},$$

and so on. The cofactor of a_{ij}, denoted by $|C_{ij}|$, is equal to $(-1)^{i+j}|M_{ij}|$. That is why sometimes cofactors are called signed minors. Whenever $i + j$ is even, $|C_{ij}| = |M_{ij}|$ and whenever $i + j$ is odd, $|C_{ij}| = -|M_{ij}|$. Take the 3×3 matrix, A,

$$A = \begin{pmatrix} 1 & 2 & 1 \\ 3 & 0 & 4 \\ 0 & 1 & 5 \end{pmatrix}, \qquad \text{then} \qquad |M_{11}| = \begin{vmatrix} 0 & 4 \\ 1 & 5 \end{vmatrix} = -4,$$

$$|M_{12}| = \begin{vmatrix} 3 & 4 \\ 0 & 5 \end{vmatrix} = 15, \qquad |M_{13}| = \begin{vmatrix} 3 & 0 \\ 0 & 1 \end{vmatrix} = 3.$$

The reader may check that $|M_{21}| = 9$, $|M_{22}| = 5$, $|M_{23}| = 1$, $|M_{31}| = 8$, $|M_{32}| = 1$, $|M_{33}| = -6$. Hence, $|C_{11}| = -4$, $|C_{12}| = -15$, $|C_{13}| = 3$, $|C_{21}| = -9$, $|C_{22}| = 5$, $|C_{23}| = -1$, $|C_{31}| = 8$, $|C_{32}| = -1$, $|C_{33}| = -6$.

The determinant of a general $n \times n$ matrix can now be defined in terms of minors, which are themselves determinants of $(n - 1) \times (n - 1)$ matrices. The rule is

$$|A| = a_{i1}(-1)^{i+1}|M_{i1}| + a_{i2}(-1)^{i+2}|M_{i2}| + \cdots + a_{in}(-1)^{i+n}|M_{in}| \qquad \text{(B.3a)}$$

$$= \sum_{j=1}^{n} a_{ij}(-1)^{i+j}|M_{ij}|.$$

The operation described is known as finding the determinant by expansion by the ith row of A. It is possible to expand by any row or column in A to find $|A|$, hence, expanding by the jth column, we have

$$|A| = a_{1j}(-1)^{1+j}|M_{ij}| + a_{2j}(-1)^{j+2}|M_{2j}| + \cdots + a_{nj}(-1)^{n+j}|M_{nj}| \qquad \text{(B.3b)}$$

$$= \sum_{i=1}^{n} a_{ij}(-1)^{i+j}|M_{ij}|.$$

Although Eq. (B.3a) and Eq. (B.3b) may look rather complicated at first glance, they are in fact quite simple. Each term of the sum in Eq. (B.3a) simply consists of an element in the ith row and its cofactor (signed minor). An example will clarify this further: Let

$$A = \begin{pmatrix} 1 & 2 & 1 \\ 3 & 0 & 4 \\ 0 & 1 & 5 \end{pmatrix}.$$

From Eq. (B.3a), taking $i = 1$, and expanding by the ith row,

$$|A| = a_{11}(-1)^{1+1}|M_{11}| + a_{12}(-1)^{1+2}|M_{12}| + a_{13}(-1)^{1+3}|M_{13}|$$

$$= 1 \cdot (-1)^2 \cdot \begin{vmatrix} 0 & 4 \\ 1 & 5 \end{vmatrix} + 2(-1)^3 \begin{vmatrix} 3 & 4 \\ 0 & 5 \end{vmatrix} + 1 \cdot (-1)^4 \begin{vmatrix} 3 & 0 \\ 0 & 1 \end{vmatrix}$$

$$= -4 + (-30) + 3 = -31.$$

In the above example $|A|$ was evaluated through expansion by the 1st row. According to Eq. (B.3b), we can also evaluate $|A|$ through expansion of the jth column. Let us take $j = 2$,

$$|A| = a_{12}(-1)^{1+2}|M_{12}| + a_{22}(-1)^{2+2}|M_{22}| + a_{32}(-1)^{3+2}|M_{32}|$$

$$= 2(-1)^3 \begin{vmatrix} 3 & 4 \\ 0 & 5 \end{vmatrix} + 0 \cdot (-1)^4 \begin{vmatrix} 1 & 1 \\ 0 & 5 \end{vmatrix} + 1(-1)^5 \begin{vmatrix} 1 & 1 \\ 3 & 4 \end{vmatrix}$$

$$= -30 + 0 + (-1) = -31,$$

which agrees with our previous result.

A key observation regarding the definition of the determinant of an $n \times n$ matrix is that we can express it in terms of determinants of $(n - 1) \times (n - 1)$ matrices (the minors). As in the above example, we reduce the determinant of a 3×3 matrix into a sum of terms involving determinants of 2×2 matrices. Since we know how to evaluate 2×2 determinants, the problem is solved. Now to evaluate a 4×4 determinant, we must first use Eq. (B.3a) or Eq. (B.3b) to reduce it in terms of 3×3 determinants, then use Eq. (B.3a) or Eq. (B.3b) again to reduce each 3×3 determinant to a sum of 2×2 determinants and then evaluate. So the reduction goes on, and we can now evaluate determinants of any size.

A well known theorem in matrix algebra states that a square matrix A is nonsingular if and only if $|A| \neq 0$. So the matrix in the previous example has a multiplicative inverse because $|A| = -31 \neq 0$.

H. THE INVERSE OF A SQUARE MATRIX

Given a nonsingular square matrix A, construct a new matrix B of the same dimension with $b_{ij} = |C_{ij}|$, the cofactor of a_{ij}. Then transpose B and call the resultant matrix the adjoint of A, "adj A." That is, adj $A = B'$. It can be shown that

$$(\text{adj } A)(A) = |A| \cdot I.$$

Since the nonsingularity of A implies $|A| \neq 0$, we can divide both sides by the scalar $|A|$:

$$\frac{1}{|A|} (\text{adj } A)(A) = I,$$

since $A^{-1}A = I$, it is immediately evident that $(1/|A|) (\text{adj } A) = A^{-1}$.

As an example take the 3×3 matrix A from the previous section. We have already computed the determinant as well as all the cofactors, so

$$B = \begin{pmatrix} C_{11} & C_{12} & C_{13} \\ C_{21} & C_{22} & C_{23} \\ C_{31} & C_{32} & C_{33} \end{pmatrix} = \begin{pmatrix} -4 & -15 & 3 \\ -9 & 5 & -1 \\ 8 & -1 & -6 \end{pmatrix},$$

$$\text{adj } A = B' = \begin{pmatrix} -4 & -9 & 8 \\ -15 & 5 & -1 \\ 3 & -1 & -6 \end{pmatrix}.$$

Since $|A| = -31$, the inverse of A is simply

$$A^{-1} = \frac{1}{|A|} \text{ adj } A = \begin{pmatrix} \dfrac{4}{31} & \dfrac{9}{31} & \dfrac{-8}{31} \\[2mm] \dfrac{15}{31} & \dfrac{-5}{31} & \dfrac{1}{31} \\[2mm] \dfrac{-3}{31} & \dfrac{1}{31} & \dfrac{6}{31} \end{pmatrix}.$$

The curious reader may verify that $A^{-1}A = I = AA^{-1}$, or

$$\begin{pmatrix} \dfrac{4}{31} & \dfrac{9}{31} & \dfrac{-8}{31} \\[2mm] \dfrac{15}{31} & \dfrac{-5}{31} & \dfrac{1}{31} \\[2mm] \dfrac{-3}{31} & \dfrac{1}{31} & \dfrac{6}{31} \end{pmatrix} \begin{pmatrix} 1 & 2 & 1 \\ 3 & 0 & 4 \\ 0 & 1 & 5 \end{pmatrix} = \begin{pmatrix} 1 & 0 & 0 \\ 0 & 1 & 0 \\ 0 & 0 & 1 \end{pmatrix} = \begin{pmatrix} 1 & 2 & 1 \\ 3 & 0 & 4 \\ 0 & 1 & 5 \end{pmatrix} \begin{pmatrix} \dfrac{4}{31} & \dfrac{9}{31} & \dfrac{-8}{31} \\[2mm] \dfrac{15}{31} & \dfrac{-5}{31} & \dfrac{1}{31} \\[2mm] \dfrac{-3}{31} & \dfrac{1}{31} & \dfrac{6}{31} \end{pmatrix}.$$

I. SOLVING LINEAR EQUATION SYSTEMS

Now suppose we have a system of linear equations:

$$X_1 + 2X_2 + X_3 = 1$$
$$3X_1 \qquad + 4X_3 = -1$$
$$X_2 + 5X_3 = 2$$

The matrix formulation would look like $Ax = b$, or

$$\begin{pmatrix} 1 & 2 & 1 \\ 3 & 0 & 4 \\ 0 & 1 & 5 \end{pmatrix} \begin{pmatrix} X_1 \\ X_2 \\ X_3 \end{pmatrix} = \begin{pmatrix} 1 \\ -1 \\ 2 \end{pmatrix}.$$

We know what A^{-1} is, and we know that the solution of the system is $x = A^{-1}b$, therefore

$$\begin{pmatrix} X_1 \\ X_2 \\ X_3 \end{pmatrix} = \underbrace{\begin{pmatrix} \dfrac{4}{31} & \dfrac{9}{31} & \dfrac{-8}{31} \\[2mm] \dfrac{15}{31} & \dfrac{-5}{31} & \dfrac{1}{31} \\[2mm] \dfrac{-3}{31} & \dfrac{1}{31} & \dfrac{6}{31} \end{pmatrix}}_{3 \times 3} \underbrace{\begin{pmatrix} 1 \\ -1 \\ 2 \end{pmatrix}}_{3 \times 1} = \underbrace{\begin{pmatrix} \dfrac{-21}{31} \\[2mm] \dfrac{22}{31} \\[2mm] \dfrac{8}{31} \end{pmatrix}}_{3 \times 1},$$

or

$$X_1 = \frac{-21}{31}, \qquad X_2 = \frac{22}{31}, \qquad X_3 = \frac{8}{31}.$$

As a check on the solution, we can insert the values into the original equation system.

$$\frac{-21}{31} + \frac{44}{31} + \frac{8}{31} = 1$$

$$\frac{-63}{31} + 0 + \frac{32}{31} = -1$$

$$0 + \frac{22}{31} + \frac{40}{31} = 2.$$

J. CRAMER'S RULE

A direct but not obvious corollary to our derivation of A^{-1} is Cramer's rule for the solution of a linear equation. The rule states that

$$X_i = \frac{|\hat{A}_i|}{|A|}$$

where $\hat{A}_i$ is the matrix obtained from A by replacing the ith column with the *constant vector*. Using the same example and applying Cramer's rule, we first substitute the constant vector for the first column in the numerator and then expand by the first row. Recall that the sign changes are the result of converting minors to cofactors.

$$X_1 = \frac{\begin{vmatrix} 1 & 2 & 1 \\ -1 & 0 & 4 \\ 2 & 1 & 5 \end{vmatrix}}{|A|} = \frac{1 \cdot \begin{vmatrix} 0 & 4 \\ 1 & 5 \end{vmatrix} - 2 \begin{vmatrix} -1 & 4 \\ 2 & 5 \end{vmatrix} + \begin{vmatrix} -1 & 0 \\ 2 & 1 \end{vmatrix}}{-31}$$

$$= \frac{-4 + 26 - 1}{-31} = -\frac{21}{31}.$$

Next we replace the second column of the original numerator by the constant vector, and again expand by the first row

$$X_2 = \frac{\begin{vmatrix} 1 & 1 & 1 \\ 3 & -1 & 4 \\ 0 & 2 & 5 \end{vmatrix}}{-31} = \frac{1 \cdot \begin{vmatrix} -1 & 4 \\ 2 & 5 \end{vmatrix} - 1 \begin{vmatrix} 3 & 4 \\ 0 & 5 \end{vmatrix} + 1 \cdot \begin{vmatrix} 3 & -1 \\ 0 & 2 \end{vmatrix}}{-31}$$

$$= \frac{-13 - 15 + 6}{-31} = \frac{22}{31},$$

and again for the third column,

$$X_3 = \frac{\begin{vmatrix} 1 & 2 & 1 \\ 3 & 0 & -1 \\ 0 & 1 & 2 \end{vmatrix}}{-31} = \frac{1 \cdot \begin{vmatrix} 0 & -1 \\ 1 & 2 \end{vmatrix} - 2 \begin{vmatrix} 3 & -1 \\ 0 & 2 \end{vmatrix} + 1 \cdot \begin{vmatrix} 3 & 0 \\ 0 & 1 \end{vmatrix}}{-31}$$

$$= \frac{1 - 12 + 3}{-31} = \frac{8}{31}.$$

This agrees with the previous result. All the determinants above were evaluated by expanding by the first row.

K. APPLICATIONS

In this section we present two applications of matrix algebra in the theory of finance.

1. Minimum Variance Portfolio

Suppose we are considering investing in three securities: X_1, X_2, and X_3, and we want to form the portfolio that minimizes the variance of return. Let σ_1^2, σ_2^2, σ_3^2 be individual variances of return, and x_1, x_2, x_3 be weights of investment in the portfolio of securities X_1, X_2, X_3 respectively. So $x_1 + x_2 + x_3 = 1$. Furthermore, let $\sigma_{12} = \sigma_{21}$ be the covariance of return between X_1 and X_2, $\sigma_{13} = \sigma_{31}$ the covariance of return between X_1 and X_3, $\sigma_{23} = \sigma_{32}$ the covariance of return between X_2 and X_3. Constructing the covariance matrix A we wish to solve for the weight vector X that will minimize the variance. Let

$$\underset{(3 \times 3)}{A} = \begin{pmatrix} \sigma_1^2 & \sigma_{12} & \sigma_{13} \\ \sigma_{21} & \sigma_2^2 & \sigma_{23} \\ \sigma_{31} & \sigma_{32} & \sigma_3^2 \end{pmatrix}, \qquad \underset{(3 \times 1)}{X} = \begin{pmatrix} x_1 \\ x_2 \\ x_3 \end{pmatrix}.$$

The variance of the portfolio with x_1 of X_1, x_2 of X_2, x_3 of X_3 can be expressed in matrix form as $\sigma_p^2 = X'AX$. To minimize the variance of the portfolio is equivalent to minimizing σ_p^2 subject to the weight constraint $x_1 + x_2 + x_3 = 1$. This constrained optimization problem can be solved by the method of the Lagrange multiplier.[1] Let

$$g(x_1, x_2, x_3, \lambda') = \sigma_p^2 + \lambda'(1 - x_1 - x_2 - x_3)$$
$$= X'AX + \lambda'(1 - x_1 - x_2 - x_3),$$

where $X'AX$ is the variance-covariance matrix of the portfolio and $(1 - x_1 - x_2 - x_3)$ is the implicit expression of the constraint which requires that the sum of the weights equal one. Then the first order conditions for an extremum are attained by setting all of the partial derivatives of g equal to zero:

$$\frac{\partial g}{\partial x_1} = 0 \tag{B.4a}$$

$$\frac{\partial g}{\partial x_2} = 0 \tag{B.4b}$$

$$\frac{\partial g}{\partial x_3} = 0 \tag{B.4c}$$

$$\frac{\partial g}{\partial \lambda'} = 0 \tag{B.4d}$$

The Eqs. (B.4a), (B.4b), and (B.4c) in matrix notation can be expressed as:

$$AX = \lambda e \quad \text{where} \quad e = \begin{pmatrix} 1 \\ 1 \\ 1 \end{pmatrix} \quad \text{and} \quad \lambda = \lambda'/2, \tag{B.5}$$

---

[1] Readers unfamiliar with the method of solving constrained optimization problems using Lagrange multipliers should consult Appendix D.

and (B.4d) is simply the reiteration of the constraint $x_1 + x_2 + x_3 = 1$. The solution to the matrix Eq. (B.5) will give us the answer in terms of λ, and the constraint condition will give us the value of λ, hence the complete solution.

As a numerical example, take

$$A = \begin{pmatrix} 2 & -1 & 0 \\ -1 & 2 & -1 \\ 0 & -1 & 2 \end{pmatrix}$$

as the covariance matrix for securities X_1, X_2, X_3. Then (B.5) becomes

$$\begin{pmatrix} 2 & -1 & 0 \\ -1 & 2 & -1 \\ 0 & -1 & 2 \end{pmatrix}\begin{pmatrix} X_1 \\ X_2 \\ X_3 \end{pmatrix} = \lambda \begin{pmatrix} 1 \\ 1 \\ 1 \end{pmatrix} = \begin{pmatrix} \lambda \\ \lambda \\ \lambda \end{pmatrix}.$$

Using Cramer's rule, substituting the λ vector for the first column, and expanding both numerator and denominator by the first column, we have

$$X_1 = \frac{\lambda \begin{vmatrix} 2 & -1 \\ -1 & 2 \end{vmatrix} - \lambda \begin{vmatrix} -1 & 0 \\ -1 & 2 \end{vmatrix} + \lambda \begin{vmatrix} -1 & 0 \\ 2 & -1 \end{vmatrix}}{2\begin{vmatrix} 2 & -1 \\ -1 & 2 \end{vmatrix} + 1\begin{vmatrix} -1 & 0 \\ -1 & 2 \end{vmatrix} + 0} = \frac{3\lambda + 2\lambda + \lambda}{6 - 2} = \frac{6\lambda}{4} = \frac{3}{2}\lambda.$$

Then substituting the vector λ in column 2 and expanding by column 1,

$$X_2 = \frac{2\begin{vmatrix} \lambda & -1 \\ \lambda & 2 \end{vmatrix} + 1\begin{vmatrix} \lambda & 0 \\ \lambda & 2 \end{vmatrix} + 0}{4} = \frac{6\lambda + 2\lambda}{4} = \frac{8\lambda}{4} = 2\lambda,$$

and finally substituting the vector λ in column 3,

$$X_3 = \frac{2\begin{vmatrix} 2 & \lambda \\ -1 & \lambda \end{vmatrix} + 1\begin{vmatrix} -1 & \lambda \\ -1 & \lambda \end{vmatrix} + 0}{4} = \frac{6\lambda + 0}{4} = \frac{6\lambda}{4} = \frac{3}{2}\lambda.$$

Since $1 = x_1 + x_2 + x_3 = \frac{3}{2}\lambda + 2\lambda + \frac{3}{2}\lambda = 5\lambda$, we have $\lambda = \frac{1}{5}$. Hence $x_1 = \frac{3}{10}$, $x_2 = \frac{2}{5}$, $x_3 = \frac{3}{10}$. In other words, if you have \$1,000 to invest, you should put \$300 in X_1, \$400 in X_2, and \$300 in X_3 to form the minimum variance portfolio. Note that we have not actually established that this is the minimum variance portfolio. We have merely determined an extreme point which may be either a maximum or a minimum. To guarantee that this is the minimum variance portfolio we would need to examine the second order conditions. (For a discussion, see Appendix D.)

2. Linear Regression

Very often, when we consider a security, we like to know how its return varies as the market fluctuates. Suppose we have the data in Table B.1:

Table B.1

	Return (in %)					
Security A	9	9.5	10.5	10.5	11	12
Market	8	9	10	11	12	13
STATE	1	2	3	4	5	6

Can we discern any pattern or simple relation between the return on security A and the market? First, we put the data on a graph:

We can see that an approximately linear pattern exists. The following question naturally arises: What is the equation of the straight line that "best" fits the data points? In mathematical terms, this is equivalent to finding the values of two constants a and b such that whenever the return on the market is given, then the expression $[a + b \times (\text{return on market})]$ will give the "best overall" predictive value of the return on security A. In symbols, let X_i, $i = 1, 2, 3, 4, 5, 6$, be the returns on the market given the various states of the world, let Y_i be the returns on security A, and let $\hat{Y}_i = a + bX_i$, the predicted return on security A using the best fitting straight line. We call $e_i = Y_i - \hat{Y}_i$, which is the difference between the observed value and the predicted value of return on security A, the error term. These error terms can be positive or negative. To find the best fitting straight line is equivalent to minimizing the magnitude of the error terms in a certain sense. The technique of minimizing the sum of the square of the error terms is called linear regression. In our example above with six different states, we have six error terms. Let

$$g(a, b) = \sum_{i=1}^{6} e_i^2 = \sum_{i=1}^{6} (Y_i - \hat{Y}_i)^2 = \sum_{i=1}^{6} (Y_i - a - bX_i)^2$$

be the sum of the squares of the error terms. The first order conditions for minimizing $g(a, b)$ are:

$$\frac{\partial g}{\partial a} = 0 \tag{B.6a}$$

$$\frac{\partial g}{\partial b} = 0 \tag{B.6b}$$

Equations (B.6a) and (B.6b) written in matrix form turn out to be:

$$\begin{pmatrix} 1 & 1 & 1 & 1 & 1 & 1 \\ X_1 & X_2 & X_3 & X_4 & X_5 & X_6 \end{pmatrix} \begin{pmatrix} 1 & X_1 \\ 1 & X_2 \\ 1 & X_3 \\ 1 & X_4 \\ 1 & X_5 \\ 1 & X_6 \end{pmatrix} \begin{pmatrix} a \\ b \end{pmatrix} = \begin{pmatrix} 1 & 1 & 1 & 1 & 1 & 1 \\ X_1 & X_2 & X_3 & X_4 & X_5 & X_6 \end{pmatrix} \begin{pmatrix} Y_1 \\ Y_2 \\ Y_3 \\ Y_4 \\ Y_5 \\ Y_6 \end{pmatrix}$$

Performing matrix multiplication, explained above, we get:

$$\begin{pmatrix} 6 & \sum_{i=1}^{6} X_i \\ \sum_{i=1}^{6} X_i & \sum_{i=1}^{6} X_i^2 \end{pmatrix} \begin{pmatrix} a \\ b \end{pmatrix} = \begin{pmatrix} \sum_{i=1}^{6} Y_i \\ \sum_{i=1}^{6} X_i Y_i \end{pmatrix},$$

This is equivalent to two equations and two unknowns (a and b). As a numerical example, let us take the data from Table B.1:

$$\sum_{i=1}^{6} X_i = 8 + 9 + 10 + 11 + 12 + 13 = 63,$$

$$\sum_{i=1}^{6} X_i^2 = 8^2 + 9^2 + 10^2 + 11^2 + 12^2 + 13^2 = 679,$$

$$\sum_{i=1}^{6} Y_i = 9 + 9.5 + 10.5 + 10.5 + 11 + 12 = 62.5,$$

$$\sum_{i=1}^{6} X_i Y_i = 8 \times 9 + 9 \times 9.5 + 10 \times 10.5 + 11 \times 10.5 + 12 \times 11 + 13 \times 12 = 666,$$

so

$$\begin{pmatrix} 6 & 63 \\ 63 & 679 \end{pmatrix} \begin{pmatrix} a \\ b \end{pmatrix} = \begin{pmatrix} 62.5 \\ 666 \end{pmatrix}.$$

By Cramer's rule, we have

$$a = \frac{\begin{vmatrix} 62.5 & 63 \\ 666 & 679 \end{vmatrix}}{\begin{vmatrix} 6 & 63 \\ 63 & 679 \end{vmatrix}} = \frac{479.5}{105} = 4.57$$

$$b = \frac{\begin{vmatrix} 6 & 62.5 \\ 63 & 666 \end{vmatrix}}{\begin{vmatrix} 6 & 63 \\ 63 & 679 \end{vmatrix}} = \frac{58.5}{105} = 0.56.$$

Therefore, the equation of the best fitting straight line is $Y = 4.57 + 0.56X$. Note that b is the slope of the straight line. Both the sign and the magnitude of b contain important information. If b is positive, we would expect that the return on security A moves with the market, while a negative b implies that returns on security A and the market generally move in opposite directions. The magnitude of b measures the degree of volatility of security A. The larger the magnitude of b, the more volatile the return on security A.

An Introduction to Multiple Regression

Business students are frequently confronted with journal articles that are riddled with econometrics. On the other hand, econometrics courses assume prior knowledge of matrix algebra and calculus and therefore present a formidable barrier to the curious. This appendix is written to provide an overview of multiple regression techniques which assumes only the rudimentary knowledge of calculus and matrix algebra provided in the other appendices. While not a substitute for a good econometrics course, this appendix enables the reader to understand and interpret the computer output from a typical multiple regression software package, and to have an introductory level of understanding of some of the typical errors made in econometric studies.

A. ORDINARY LEAST SQUARES LINEAR ESTIMATION

If we are trying to explain the distribution of sales revenue for the XYZ Company given a forecast of gross national product, we might choose a linear model like

$$\tilde{Y}_t = a + bX_t + \tilde{\epsilon}_t, \qquad \text{(C.1)}$$

735

where

$\tilde{Y}_t$ = sales revenue in year t,

X_t = forecast of gross national product for year t,

$\tilde{\epsilon}_t$ = error term (the difference between actual sales revenue and that predicted by the model).

Linear relationships have the virtue that they are simple and robust. Many natural phenomena are not linearly related, but linear approximations usually work very well within a limited range.

The object is to find the set of weights (a and b) in Eq. (C.1) which provide the best unbiased estimate of revenue given GNP. If GNP has any explanatory power the conditional distribution of revenues, $\tilde{Y}_t|X_t$, will be different from their unconditional distribution. This is illustrated in Fig. C.1. The mean and standard deviation of the unconditional distribution of Y_t are $196.9 and $60.1. The unconditional probability distribution of revenues is plotted along the y-axis. The conditional distribution of $Y_t|X_t$ is the distribution of error terms, ϵ_t. For example, given that $X_t = 1.26$ (its mean) then the estimated revenue is $196.9 (its mean) and the standard deviation of the estimate is $33.73. Notice that the conditional distribution has lower variance than the unconditional distribution. This is because knowledge of predicted GNP allows us to refine our estimate of sales revenue.

In order to obtain the best linear model to predict Y_t given X_t, we want to find the equation which minimizes the squared error terms. The error term is the difference between the actual revenue and the revenue predicted by the linear model. If we minimize the squared error terms, we are, in effect, minimizing the variance

Figure C.1
Revenues vs. forecasted GNP

of the conditional distribution. To see how this is accomplished rewrite Eq. (C.1) as follows:

$$\epsilon_t = Y_t - a - bX_t$$

The variance of the error terms is:[1]

$$\sigma_\epsilon^2 = E[(Y_t - a - bX_t) - (\bar{Y}_t - a - b\bar{X}_t)]^2, \tag{C.2}$$

$$\sigma_\epsilon^2 = E[(Y_t - \bar{Y}_t) - b(X_t - \bar{X}_t)]^2,$$

$$\sigma_\epsilon^2 = \sigma_Y^2 - 2b\,\mathrm{COV}(Y, X) + b^2\sigma_X^2.$$

We want to choose the slope, b, and the intercept, a, which minimize the squared error terms. To do this, take the derivative of σ_ϵ^2 with respect to b and set the result equal to zero:

$$\frac{\delta\sigma_\epsilon^2}{\delta b} = -2\,\mathrm{COV}(Y, X) + 2b\sigma_X^2 = 0.$$

Solving for $\hat{b}$, the estimated slope term, we have

$$\hat{b} = \frac{\mathrm{COV}(Y, X)}{\sigma_X^2}. \tag{C.3}$$

The intercept is determined by the fact that the line must pass through the mean values for both $\bar{Y}$ and $\bar{X}$. At that point, we have

$$\bar{Y} = \hat{a} + \hat{b}\bar{X}.$$

Therefore, solving for $\hat{a}$, we have

$$\hat{a} = \bar{Y} - \hat{b}\bar{X}.$$

The estimated slope and intercept terms are computed in Table C.1.

Having obtained estimates of the slope and intercept which minimize the squared error terms we now have the following linear equation

$$\hat{Y}_t = -23.42 + 174.84X_t.$$

It can be used to predict sales revenue when given a forecast of GNP. The difference between predicted revenue and actual revenue in any given year is the error of estimate, often called the residual.

$$\epsilon_t = Y_t - \hat{Y}_t.$$

Note that in Table C.1 the average error term $\bar{\epsilon}_t$ (except for rounding error in the calculations) is zero. This implies that the linear estimate is unbiased. In other words, on average, there is no error of estimate.

In linear regression, the residual errors indicate the extent of movement in the dependent variable (the variable on the left-hand side of the regression equation)

---

[1] This result follows from the properties of random variables discussed in Chapter 6.

Table C.1 Simple regression computations

t	Y	$Y - \bar{Y}$	$(Y - \bar{Y})^2$	X	$X - \bar{X}$	$(X - \bar{X})^2$	$(Y - \bar{Y})(X - \bar{X})$	$\epsilon = \hat{Y} - \bar{Y}$	ϵ^2
1969	125	−71.875	5,166.01	.86	−.40	.1600	28.750	−1.94	3.7636
1970	110	−86.875	7,547.27	.98	−.28	.0784	24.325	−37.92	1437.9264
1971	220	23.125	534.76	1.11	−.15	.0225	−3.469	49.35	2435.4225
1972	170	−26.875	722.27	1.18	−.08	.0064	2.150	−12.89	166.1521
1973	240	43.125	1,859.76	1.30	.04	.0016	1.725	36.13	1305.3769
1974	225	28.125	791.02	1.41	.15	.0225	4.219	1.90	3.6100
1975	195	−1.875	3.52	1.53	.27	.0729	−.506	−49.09	2409.8281
1976	290	93.125	8,672.27	1.71	.45	.2025	41.906	14.44	208.5136
Sum	1575		25,296.89	10.08		.5668	99.100	−.02≈0	7970.5932

$$\bar{Y} = \frac{\sum Y}{N} = \frac{1575}{8} = 196.875 \qquad \bar{X} = \frac{\sum X}{N} = \frac{10.08}{8} = 1.26$$

$$\sigma_Y^2 = \frac{\sum (Y - \bar{Y})^2}{N-1} = \frac{25,296.89}{7} = 3613.84 \qquad \sigma_X^2 = \frac{\sum (X - \bar{X})^2}{N-1} = \frac{.5668}{7} = .0809714$$

$$\sigma_Y = \sqrt{\sigma_Y^2} = \sqrt{3613.84} = 60.12 \qquad \sigma_X = \sqrt{\sigma_X^2} = .2846$$

$$\text{COV}(Y, X) = \frac{\sum (X - \bar{Y})(X - \bar{Y})}{N-1} = \frac{99.10}{7} = 14.16$$

$$b = \frac{\text{COV}(Y, X)}{\sigma_{\bar{x}}^2} = \frac{14.16}{.0809714} = 174.88$$

$$\hat{a} = \bar{Y} - b\bar{X} = 196.876 - 174.84(1.26) = -23.42$$

Symbol Definitions: $\bar{Y}, \bar{X}$ = The means of revenue and GNP respectively

                  N = The number of observations in the sample

                  σ_Y^2, σ_X^2 = The variances of revenue and GNP respectively

                  $\text{COV}(Y, X)$ = The covariance between revenue and GNP

                  $\hat{a}, b$ = The intercept and slope estimates

                  ϵ = The error term

which is not explained by the independent variable(s)—(the variable(s) on the right-hand side). If the residuals are small relative to the total movement in the dependent variable, then it follows that a major part of the movement has been explained. We define the summary statistic known as the squared multiple correlation coefficient, r^2, as the percentage of the total variation in the dependent variable which is explained by the regression equation. The square of the correlation coefficient is

$$r^2 = \frac{\text{variation explained by the regression equation}}{\text{total variation of the dependent variable}}$$

$$= \frac{\sum (Y - \bar{Y})^2 - \sum (\epsilon - \bar{\epsilon})^2}{\sum (Y - \bar{Y})^2}.$$

Note that $\sum (Y - \bar{Y})^2$ is the variance of the dependent variable, σ_Y^2, in our example. Note also that $\sum (\epsilon - \bar{\epsilon})^2$ is the variance of the residuals. Furthermore, the average error term, $\bar{\epsilon}$, is always zero, therefore, we can rewrite the squared correlation coefficient as[2]

$$r^2 = \frac{\sum (Y - \bar{Y})^2 - \sum \epsilon^2}{\sum (Y - \bar{Y})^2}. \tag{C.5}$$

---

[2] An important relationship, which is used in Chapter 6, is that

$$r = \frac{\text{COV}(Y, X)}{\sigma_Y \sigma_X}.$$

Proof follows from the definition of r^2, of σ_ϵ^2, and of b. First, rewrite r^2 and the definition of b

$$r^2 = \frac{\sigma_Y^2 - \sigma_\epsilon^2}{\sigma_Y^2}, \qquad b = \frac{\text{COV}(Y, X)}{\sigma_X^2}.$$

From Eq. (C.2), we have

$$\sigma_\epsilon^2 = \sigma_y^2 - 2b \, \text{COV}(Y, X) + b^2 \sigma_z^2.$$

Substituting in the value of b, we have

$$\sigma_\epsilon^2 = \sigma_y^2 - 2 \left(\frac{\text{COV}(Y, X)}{\sigma_z^2} \right) \text{COV}(Y, X)$$

$$+ \left(\frac{\text{COV}(Y, X)}{\sigma_z^2} \right)^2 \sigma_z^2$$

$$= \sigma_y^2 - \frac{[\text{COV}(Y, X)]^2}{\sigma_z^2}$$

Substituting this result into the definition of r^2 gives

$$r^2 = \frac{\sigma_y^2 - \sigma_y^2 + \dfrac{[\text{COV}(Y, X)]^2}{\sigma_z^2}}{\sigma_y^2}$$

$$= \frac{[\text{COV}(Y, X)]^2}{\sigma_z^2 \sigma_y^2}$$

Therefore, taking the square root

$$r = \frac{\text{COV}(Y, X)}{\sigma_x \sigma_y} \qquad \text{QED.}$$

Using the numbers from Table C.1,

$$r^2 = \frac{25{,}296.89 - 7970.5932}{25{,}296.89} = .6849.$$

This means that about 68.5% of the variance in the dependent variable, sales revenue, is explained by the independent variable, GNP. If all of the variance were explained, then the sum of the squared residuals, Σe^2, would be zero and we would have $r^2 = 1$. At the opposite extreme the equation would not reduce the variance of the dependent variable at all, in which case we would have $r^2 = 0$.

B. SIMPLE HYPOTHESIS TESTING OF THE LINEAR REGRESSION ESTIMATES

Now that we know how to estimate the slope and the intercept, the next logical question is whether or not we can reject the null hypothesis that they are equal to zero. In order to do this we can calculate t-statistics in order to test the significance of the slope and intercept terms.

The t-statistics are defined as the estimates of the intercept, $\hat{a}$, or the slope, $\hat{b}$, divided by their respective standard errors of estimate[3]

$$t_a = \frac{\hat{a}}{se(\hat{a})}, \qquad t_b = \frac{\hat{b}}{se(\hat{b})}. \tag{C.6}$$

We shall assume that the independent variable, X, can be treated as a constant in repeated samplings. In fact, this is where regression analysis derives its name. We say that Y is regressed on X. We also assume that the error terms are generated by random selection from a stationary statistical distribution with a mean of zero and a constant variance, σ_ϵ^2. Also, the error terms in successive samplings are independent. This specification of the error-generating process may be stated as

$$E(\epsilon) = 0 \tag{C.7}$$

$$\text{VAR}(\epsilon) = E[\epsilon - E(\epsilon)]^2 = E(\epsilon)^2 = \sigma_\epsilon^2 \tag{C.8}$$

$$\text{COV}(\epsilon_t, \epsilon_{t-1}) = 0. \tag{C.9}$$

In order to determine the standard error of estimate for $\hat{b}$, recall the definition given in Eq. (C.3).

$$\hat{b} = \frac{\text{COV}(Y, X)}{\sigma_X^2}. \tag{C.3}$$

We also know the observed values of Y are

$$Y = a + bX + \epsilon$$

---

[3] A good reference to the t-distribution is Hoel [1954], pp. 274–283.

Rewriting Eq. (C.3), using the definitions of $COV(Y, X)$ and σ_X^2, we have

$$b = \frac{\sum [(X - \bar{X})(Y - \bar{Y})]}{\sum [(X - \bar{X})(X - \bar{X})]}.$$

Substituting in Y yields

$$\hat{b} = \frac{\sum [(X - \bar{X})(a + bX + \epsilon - \bar{a} - \bar{b}X)]}{\sum [(X - \bar{X})(X - \bar{X})]}$$

$$= \frac{\sum [(X - \bar{X})(Y - \bar{Y}) + (X - \bar{X})\epsilon]}{\sum [(X - \bar{X})(X - \bar{X})]}$$

$$= \frac{\sum [(X - \bar{X})(Y - \bar{Y})]}{\sum [(X - \bar{X})(X - \bar{X})]} + \frac{\sum [(X - \bar{X})\epsilon]}{\sum [(X - \bar{X})(X - \bar{X})]}$$

$$= b + \frac{\sum [(X - \bar{X})\epsilon]}{\sum [(X - \bar{X})^2]}. \tag{C.10}$$

Equation (C.10) tells us that the estimated slope, $\hat{b}$, is equal to the true slope, b, plus a term which depends on the variance of X (in the denominator) and the error terms (in the numerator). The expected value of $\hat{b}$ is

$$E(\hat{b}) = b, \qquad \text{since} \qquad E(\epsilon) = 0. \tag{C.11}$$

Note that the expected value of the slope is equal to the true slope. Therefore we can say that the slope estimate is unbiased. The variance of b is

$$VAR(\hat{b}) = E[\hat{b} - E(\hat{b})]^2$$

$$= E\left[\bar{b} + \frac{\sum [(X_i - \bar{X})\epsilon_i]}{\sum (X_i - \bar{X})^2} - \bar{b} \right]^2$$

$$= E\left[\frac{\sum [(X_i - \bar{X})\epsilon_i]}{\sum (X_i - \bar{X})^2} \right]^2,$$

and since X is assumed to be a constant, we have

$$VAR(\hat{b}) = \left[\frac{1}{\sum (X_i - \bar{X})^2} \right]^2 E\left[\sum (X_i - \bar{X})\epsilon_i \right]^2.$$

Expanding the second term yields

$$E\left[\sum (X_i - \bar{X})\epsilon_i \right]^2 = E[(X_1 - \bar{X})^2 \epsilon_1^2 + (X_2 - \bar{X})^2 \epsilon_2^2 + \cdots$$

$$+ 2(X_1 - \bar{X})(X_2 - \bar{X})\epsilon_1 \epsilon_2 + \cdots]$$

$$= (X_1 - \bar{X})^2 E(\epsilon_1^2) + (X_2 - \bar{X})^2 E(\epsilon_2^2) + \cdots$$

$$+ 2(X_1 - \bar{X})(X_2 - \bar{X})E(\epsilon_1 \epsilon_2) + \cdots.$$

Using Eqs. (C.8) and (C.9), the above result can be reduced to

$$E\left[\sum (X_i - \bar{X})\epsilon_i\right]^2 = \left[\sum (X_i - \bar{X})^2\right]\sigma_\epsilon^2.$$

This means that the variance of the estimate of b can be written as

$$\text{VAR}(\hat{b}) = \frac{\sum (X - \bar{X})^2}{\left[\sum (X - \bar{X})^2\right]^2}\,\sigma_\epsilon^2$$

$$= \frac{\sigma_\epsilon^2}{\sum (X - \bar{X})^2}. \tag{C.12}$$

We now have the result that the slope estimate, $\hat{b}$, is distributed normally with a mean of b and a variance of $\sigma_\epsilon^2/\sigma_X^2$. The variance of the estimate of $\hat{b}$ provides a measure of the precision of the estimate. The larger the variance of the estimate, the more widespread the distribution and the smaller the precision of the estimate.

A similar derivation would show that the intercept estimate, $\hat{a}$, is also normally distributed with a mean of

$$E(\hat{a}) = a \tag{C.13}$$

and a variance of

$$\text{VAR}(\hat{a}) = \frac{\left(\sum X^2\right)\sigma_\epsilon^2}{N \sum (X - \bar{X})^2}, \qquad se(\hat{a}) = \sqrt{\text{VAR}(\hat{a})}, \tag{C.14}$$

where N is the number of observations in the sample.

Using Eqs. (C.12) and (C.14) for the sample problem of Table C.1, and given that the t-statistics defined in Eq. (C.6) have $N - m$ degrees of freedom (where $N = 8 =$ the number of observations and $m = 2 =$ the number of independent variables including the constant term), we can compute the appropriate significance tests for the slope and intercept. The standard error for the slope term is

$$se(\hat{b}) = \sqrt{\frac{\sigma_\epsilon^2}{\sum (X - \bar{X})^2}} = \sqrt{\frac{7970.5932/(8 - 2)}{.5668}} = 48.41$$

and the t-statistic for b is

$$t(\hat{b}) = \frac{\hat{b}}{se(\hat{b})} = \frac{174.84}{48.41} = 3.61.$$

We refer to the table of t-statistics (Table C.2) for $8 - 2 = 6$ degrees of freedom and a 95% confidence interval (in a two-tail t-test). That table shows that the t-statistic must be greater than 2.447 in order to reject the null hypothesis that the slope coefficient is not significantly different from zero. It is. Therefore, we can say that predicted GNP, the independent variable, is a significant explanatory variable for sales revenue given our sample data.

Table C.2   Student's t distribution

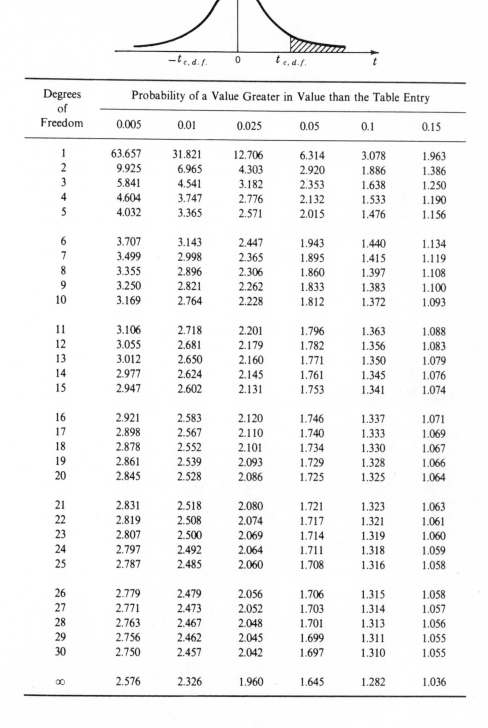

Degrees of Freedom	Probability of a Value Greater in Value than the Table Entry					
	0.005	0.01	0.025	0.05	0.1	0.15
1	63.657	31.821	12.706	6.314	3.078	1.963
2	9.925	6.965	4.303	2.920	1.886	1.386
3	5.841	4.541	3.182	2.353	1.638	1.250
4	4.604	3.747	2.776	2.132	1.533	1.190
5	4.032	3.365	2.571	2.015	1.476	1.156
6	3.707	3.143	2.447	1.943	1.440	1.134
7	3.499	2.998	2.365	1.895	1.415	1.119
8	3.355	2.896	2.306	1.860	1.397	1.108
9	3.250	2.821	2.262	1.833	1.383	1.100
10	3.169	2.764	2.228	1.812	1.372	1.093
11	3.106	2.718	2.201	1.796	1.363	1.088
12	3.055	2.681	2.179	1.782	1.356	1.083
13	3.012	2.650	2.160	1.771	1.350	1.079
14	2.977	2.624	2.145	1.761	1.345	1.076
15	2.947	2.602	2.131	1.753	1.341	1.074
16	2.921	2.583	2.120	1.746	1.337	1.071
17	2.898	2.567	2.110	1.740	1.333	1.069
18	2.878	2.552	2.101	1.734	1.330	1.067
19	2.861	2.539	2.093	1.729	1.328	1.066
20	2.845	2.528	2.086	1.725	1.325	1.064
21	2.831	2.518	2.080	1.721	1.323	1.063
22	2.819	2.508	2.074	1.717	1.321	1.061
23	2.807	2.500	2.069	1.714	1.319	1.060
24	2.797	2.492	2.064	1.711	1.318	1.059
25	2.787	2.485	2.060	1.708	1.316	1.058
26	2.779	2.479	2.056	1.706	1.315	1.058
27	2.771	2.473	2.052	1.703	1.314	1.057
28	2.763	2.467	2.048	1.701	1.313	1.056
29	2.756	2.462	2.045	1.699	1.311	1.055
30	2.750	2.457	2.042	1.697	1.310	1.055
∞	2.576	2.326	1.960	1.645	1.282	1.036

Next, compute the t-test to determine whether or not the intercept estimate, $\hat{a}$, is significantly different from zero. The standard error of $\hat{a}$ is

$$se(\hat{a}) = \left[\frac{\left(\sum X^2 \right) \sigma_\epsilon^2}{N \sum (X - \bar{X})^2} \right]^{1/2}$$

$$= \left[\frac{(13.2676)(7970.5932/6)}{8(.5668)} \right]^{1/2} = 62.35$$

and the t-statistic is

$$t(\hat{a}) = \frac{\hat{a}}{se(\hat{a})} = \frac{-23.42}{62.35} = -.375.$$

The t-statistic for $\hat{a}$ is less than 2.447, the required level for significance. Therefore, we cannot conclude that the intercept term is significantly different from zero.

Summarizing, up to this point we can write the results of the regression analysis as follows:

$$Y_t = -23.42 + 174.84X_t \qquad r^2 = .6849$$

$$(-.38) \qquad (3.61) \qquad df = 6$$

The numbers in parentheses are the appropriate t-statistics, and df designates the degrees of freedom.

C. BIAS AND EFFICIENCY

1. The Mean Square Error Criterion

The researcher is always interested in the bias and efficiency of the estimated regression equations. Unbiased estimates have the property that on average the sample statistic equals the true value of the underlying population parameter. The most efficient estimate is the one with the lowest possible variance of estimation. Frequently there is a tradeoff between bias and efficiency. One rule which weighs both of these aspects is the concept of "quadratic loss." The expected value of the distribution of quadratic loss is called the mean square error. It may be formally defined as

$$\text{MSE}(\hat{\theta}) = E(\hat{\theta} - \theta)^2, \qquad \text{(C.15)}$$

where θ is the population parameter and $\hat{\theta}$ is the estimate of that parameter.

The mean square error can be expressed in terms of the variance and the bias of the estimate by first adding then subtracting $E(\hat{\theta})$ in Eq. (C.15). The result is

$$\text{MSE}(\hat{\theta}) = E[\hat{\theta} - E(\hat{\theta}) + E(\hat{\theta}) - \theta]^2$$

$$= E[\hat{\theta} - E(\hat{\theta})]^2 + [E(\hat{\theta}) - \theta]^2$$

because the cross-product term has a zero expected value. Therefore, the mean square error can be written as

$$\text{MSE}(\hat{\theta}) = \text{Variance } (\hat{\theta}) + [\text{bias } (\hat{\theta})]^2. \tag{C.16}$$

Minimizing the MSE imposes an arbitrary judgment as to the relative importance of bias and variance. If it is thought that minimizing bias is of paramount importance then the MSE may be inappropriate.

2. Sources of Bias

A. LEFT-OUT VARIABLES   One of the most frequently encountered problems of regression analysis is that the empirical model is not founded on a sound theoretical footing. When this happens we say that the model is misspecified. If an important explanatory variable is left out of the regression equation, then the estimates of the coefficients for the variables included in the equations can be biased. This was one of the empirical difficulties in the early attempt to test for relationships between capital structure and value (see Chapter 13). The empirical work was done before a theoretical model of value had been derived. Therefore, relevant variables were often left out and the empirical results were biased.

Suppose that the true theoretical relationship is

$$Y_t = a + b_1 X_{1t} + b_2 X_{2t} + \epsilon_t, \tag{C.17}$$

but that the researcher mistakenly estimates the following regression equation

$$Y_t = a + \tilde{b}_1 X_{1t} + U_t. \tag{C.18}$$

From Eq. (C.3) the ordinary least squares estimate of $\tilde{b}_1$ is

$$\tilde{b}_1 = \frac{\sum (X_1 - \bar{X}_1)(Y - \bar{Y})}{\sum (X_1 - \bar{X}_1)(X_1 - \bar{X}_1)}. \tag{C.19}$$

By substituting the true relation (Eq. C.17) for Y into Eq. (C.19), we obtain

$$\tilde{b}_1 = \frac{\sum (X_1 - \bar{X}_1)(a + b_1 X_1 + b_2 X_2 + \epsilon - a - b_1 \bar{X}_1 - b_2 \bar{X}_2)}{\sum (X_1 - \bar{X}_1)(X_1 - \bar{X}_1)}$$

$$= \frac{\sum (X_1 - \bar{X}_1)(a + b_1 X_1 - a - b_1 \bar{X}_1)}{\sum (X_1 - \bar{X}_1)^2}$$

$$+ \frac{\sum (X_1 - \bar{X}_1)(b_2 X_2 - b_2 \bar{X}_2)}{\sum (X_1 - \bar{X}_1)^2} + \frac{\sum (X_1 - \bar{X}_1)\epsilon}{\sum (X_1 - \bar{X}_1)^2},$$

and because the error terms are assumed to follow Eqs. (C.7), (C.8), and (C.9), we have

$$\tilde{b}_1 = b_1 + b_2 \frac{\sum (X_1 - \bar{X}_1)(X_2 - \bar{X}_2)}{\sum (X_1 - \bar{X}_1)^2} \tag{C.20}$$

Equation (C.20) shows that when a relevant variable is left out of the equation specification the slope estimate, $\hat{b}$, is biased. The direction of the bias depends on the sign of b_2 (the relationship between Y and X_2) and on $\Sigma(X_1 - \bar{X}_1)(X_2 - \bar{X}_2)$, (the relationship between the independent variables, X_1 and X_2). If X_1, X_2, and Y are all positively related, then b will be biased upward. In general, the only way to eliminate misspecification bias is to be sure that the empirical test is appropriately founded on sound theory, rather than going on an ad hoc "fishing trip."

B. ERRORS IN VARIABLES There is almost always some measurement error involved when taking sample statistics. The degree of accuracy in estimating both independent and dependent variables can vary considerably, and unfortunately this problem also results in bias. For example, in Chapter 14, Friend and Puckett showed that measurement error is important when trying to estimate the relative effect of dividends and retained earnings on the price of common stock. The estimated equation was

$$P_{it} = a + bD_{it} + cR_{it} + \epsilon_{it},$$

where

$P_{it} =$ the price per share,

$D_{it} =$ the aggregate dividends paid out,

$R_{it} =$ the retained earnings of the firm,

$\epsilon_{it} =$ the error term.

Dividends can be measured without any error whatsoever, but retained earnings (the difference between accounting earnings and dividends paid) is only an estimate of true economic retained earnings on which value is based. Thus, retained earnings possesses a great deal of measurement error. Consequently, the estimate of the effect of retained earnings on the price per share was biased downward. This led earlier researchers to incorrectly conclude that dividends had a greater effect on price per share than retained earnings.

To demonstrate the effect of measurement error, suppose that both the independent and dependent variables have sampling error. This may be written as

$$X = x + w \qquad\qquad (C.21)$$

$$Y = y + v, \qquad\qquad (C.22)$$

where X and Y indicate the observations, x and y are the true values, and w and v are the measurement errors. Suppose, further, that the true variables have the following relationship:

$$y = a + bx. \qquad\qquad (C.23)$$

We would like to have unbiased estimates of a and b.

Substituting Eqs. (C.21) and (C.22) into Eq. (C.23) gives

$$Y = a + bX + z,$$

where

$$z = v - bw.$$

From Eq. (C.3), the estimate of b is

$$\hat{b} = \frac{\sum (X - \bar{X})(Y - \bar{Y})}{\sum (X - \bar{X})(X - \bar{X})}$$

$$= \frac{\sum (x + w - \bar{x} - \bar{w})(y + v - \bar{y} - \bar{v})}{\sum (x + w - \bar{x} - \bar{w})^2}$$

$$= \frac{\sum (x - \bar{x})(y - \bar{y}) + \sum (x - \bar{x})(v - \bar{v}) + \sum (y - \bar{y})(w - \bar{w}) + \sum (w - \bar{w})(v - \bar{v})}{\sum (x - \bar{x})^2 + 2 \sum (x - \bar{x})(w - \bar{w}) + \sum (w - \bar{w})^2}.$$

Given that the measurement errors, w and v, are distributed independently of each other and of the true parameters, then the last three terms in the numerator and the middle term in the denominator vanish as the sample size becomes large. Therefore, the limiting value of b is

$$\text{plim } \hat{b} = \frac{\sum (x - \bar{x})(y - \bar{y})}{\sum (x - \bar{x})^2 + \sum (w - \bar{w})^2}.$$

Dividing numerator and denominator by $\Sigma(x - \bar{x})^2$, we have,

$$\hat{b} = \frac{b}{\left(1 + \left[\sum (w - \bar{w})^2 / \sum (x - \bar{x})^2\right]\right)}. \tag{C.24}$$

Equation (C.24) shows that even if the errors of measurement are assumed to be mutually independent, independent of the true values, and have constant variance, the estimate, b, will be biased downward. The greater the measurement error, the greater the downward bias.

There are two generally accepted techniques for overcoming the problem of errors in variables: (1) grouping and (2) instrumental variables. Grouping procedures can reduce measurement error because when grouped the errors of individual observations tend to be canceled out by their mutual independence. Hence there is less measurement error in a group average than there would be if sample data were not grouped. An instrumental variable is one which is highly correlated with the independent variable but which is independent of the errors w and v (in Eqs. C.21 and C.22). This was the technique employed by Friend and Puckett in testing dividend policy. Instead of using the accounting measure of earnings, they used normalized earnings (a time series estimate of predicted earnings) to eliminate most of the measurement error bias.

3. Loss of Efficiency

A. MULTICOLLINEARITY   When two or more independent variables are highly correlated, it frequently becomes difficult to distinguish their separate effects on the dependent variable. In fact, if they are perfectly correlated it is impossible to distinguish. For example, consider the following equation:

$$S_t = a + b_1 R_t + b_2 L_t + b_3 O_t + \epsilon_t,$$

where S_t is the sales revenue of a ski shop, R_t and L_t are the sales of left and right downhill skis, and O_t is the sales of other items. The estimated coefficient b_1 is supposed to measure the impact of the sale of the right skis, holding all other variables constant. Of course this is nonsense, since right and left skis are sold simultaneously.

The usual multicollinearity problem occurs when two independent variables are highly, but not perfectly, correlated. And usually the effect is to reduce the efficiency of estimates of b_1 and b_2 by increasing the standard error of estimate. The best remedy for the problem is larger sample sizes.

B. SERIAL CORRELATION   One of the important assumptions for linear regression, Eq. (C.9), is that samplings are drawn *independently* from the same multivariate distribution. In other words, successive error terms should be independent. If this is not the case, we still obtain unbiased estimates of the slope and intercept terms, but there is a loss of efficiency because the sampling variances of these estimates may be unduly large. Consider the following two variable cases. Suppose that

$$Y_t = a + bX_t + \epsilon_t,$$

but that the error term follows a first order autoregressive scheme such as

$$\epsilon_t = K\epsilon_{t-1} + U_t$$

where $|K| < 1$ and U_t satisfies the assumptions

$$E(U_t) = 0,$$

$$E(U_t, U_{t-N}) = \begin{cases} \sigma_U^2 & \text{if } N = 0 \\ 0 & \text{if } N \neq 0 \end{cases}.$$

In general the tth error term can be written as

$$\begin{aligned} \epsilon_t &= K\epsilon_{t-1} + U_t \\ &= K(K\epsilon_{t-2} + U_{t-1}) + U_t \\ &= U_t + KU_{t-1} + K^2 U_{t-2} + \cdots + K^n U_{t-n} \\ &= \sum_{\tau=0}^{\infty} K^\tau U_{t-\tau}, \end{aligned}$$

$$E(\epsilon_t) = 0 \quad \text{since } E(U_t) = 0 \text{ for all } t.$$

The expected value of the squared error terms is

$$E(\epsilon_t^2) = E(U_t^2) + K^2 E(U_{t-1}^2) + K^4 E(U_{t-2}^2) + \cdots,$$

since the error terms, U_t, are serially independent. Consequently,

$$E(\epsilon_t^2) = (1 + K^2 + K^4 + \cdots)\sigma_U^2.$$

This is a geometric series which reduces to

$$E(\epsilon_t^2) = \sigma_\epsilon^2 = \frac{\sigma_U^2}{1 - K^2}. \qquad (C.25)$$

Equation (C.25) shows that the closer the relationship between ϵ_t and ϵ_{t-1}, the closer K is to unity and the greater will be the estimated error term and the loss of efficiency.

We can test for serial correlation by using the Durbin-Watson d statistic. If ϵ_t are the residuals from a fitted least squares equation, then d is defined as

$$d = \frac{\sum\limits_{t=2}^{n} (\epsilon_t - \epsilon_{t-1})^2}{\sum\limits_{t=1}^{n} \epsilon_t^2}.$$

Durbin and Watson have tabulated upper and lower bounds d_u and d_l for various numbers of observations, n, and numbers of independent variables, K.

When the error terms are serially independent, the d statistic has a theoretical distribution with a mean of 2, but sampling fluctuations may lead to a different estimate even when the errors are not autocorrelated. Table C.3 provides critical values for the d-statistic. If the computed d is smaller than the lower critical value, d_l, or above the critical value $(4 - d_l)$, then the null hypothesis of serial independence is rejected. When the statistic is larger than d_u but smaller than $(4 - d_u)$, then the null hypothesis is accepted. When neither of these two cases is true, then the test is inconclusive.

For the set of sample data in Table C.1, the estimated d statistic is computed below:

t	ϵ_t	$\epsilon_t - \epsilon_{t-1}$	ϵ_t^2	$(\epsilon_t - \epsilon_{t-1})^2$
1976	14.44	63.53	208.5136	4036.0609
1975	−49.09	−50.99	2409.8281	2599.9801
1974	1.90	−34.23	3.6100	1171.6929
1973	36.13	49.02	1305.3769	2402.9604
1972	−12.89	−62.24	166.1521	3873.8176
1971	49.35	87.27	2435.4225	7616.0529
1970	−37.92	−35.98	1437.9264	1294.5604
1969	− 1.94	—	3.7636	—
Sum			7970.5932	22995.1252

$$d = \frac{22{,}995.1252}{7{,}970.5932} = 2.88.$$

Table C.3 Critical Values for the Durbin-Watson Test: 5%
Significance Points of d_1 and d_u in Two-tailed Tests

n	$k' = 1$		$k' = 2$		$k' = 3$		$k' = 4$		$k' = 5$	
	d_l	d_u	d_l	d_u	d_l	d_u	d_l	d_u	d_l	d_u
15	0.95	1.23	0.83	1.40	0.71	1.61	0.59	1.84	0.48	2.09
16	0.98	1.24	0.86	1.40	0.75	1.59	0.64	1.80	0.53	2.03
17	1.01	1.25	0.90	1.40	0.79	1.58	0.68	1.77	0.57	1.98
18	1.03	1.26	0.93	1.40	0.82	1.56	0.72	1.74	0.62	1.93
19	1.06	1.28	0.96	1.41	0.86	1.55	0.76	1.72	0.66	1.90
20	1.08	1.28	0.99	1.41	0.89	1.55	0.79	1.70	0.70	1.87
21	1.10	1.30	1.01	1.41	0.92	1.54	0.83	1.69	0.73	1.84
22	1.12	1.31	1.04	1.42	0.95	1.54	0.86	1.68	0.77	1.82
23	1.14	1.32	1.06	1.42	0.97	1.54	0.89	1.67	0.80	1.80
24	1.16	1.33	1.08	1.43	1.00	1.54	0.91	1.66	0.83	1.79
25	1.18	1.34	1.10	1.43	1.02	1.54	0.94	1.65	0.86	1.77
26	1.19	1.35	1.12	1.44	1.04	1.54	0.96	1.65	0.88	1.76
27	1.21	1.36	1.13	1.44	1.06	1.54	0.99	1.64	0.91	1.75
28	1.22	1.37	1.15	1.45	1.08	1.54	1.01	1.64	0.93	1.74
29	1.24	1.38	1.17	1.45	1.10	1.54	1.03	1.63	0.96	1.73
30	1.25	1.38	1.18	1.46	1.12	1.54	1.05	1.63	0.98	1.73
31	1.26	1.39	1.20	1.47	1.13	1.55	1.07	1.63	1.00	1.72
32	1.27	1.40	1.21	1.47	1.15	1.55	1.08	1.63	1.02	1.71
33	1.28	1.41	1.22	1.48	1.16	1.55	1.10	1.63	1.04	1.71
34	1.29	1.41	1.24	1.48	1.17	1.55	1.12	1.63	1.06	1.70
35	1.30	1.42	1.25	1.48	1.19	1.55	1.13	1.63	1.07	1.70
36	1.31	1.43	1.26	1.49	1.20	1.56	1.15	1.63	1.09	1.70
37	1.32	1.43	1.27	1.49	1.21	1.56	1.16	1.62	1.10	1.70
38	1.33	1.44	1.28	1.50	1.23	1.56	1.17	1.62	1.12	1.70
39	1.34	1.44	1.29	1.50	1.24	1.56	1.19	1.63	1.13	1.69
40	1.35	1.45	1.30	1.51	1.25	1.57	1.20	1.63	1.15	1.69
45	1.39	1.48	1.34	1.53	1.30	1.58	1.25	1.63	1.21	1.69
50	1.42	1.50	1.38	1.54	1.34	1.59	1.30	1.64	1.26	1.69
55	1.45	1.52	1.41	1.56	1.37	1.60	1.33	1.64	1.30	1.69
60	1.47	1.54	1.44	1.57	1.40	1.61	1.37	1.65	1.33	1.69
65	1.49	1.55	1.46	1.59	1.43	1.62	1.40	1.66	1.36	1.69
70	1.51	1.57	1.48	1.60	1.45	1.63	1.42	1.66	1.39	1.70
75	1.53	1.58	1.50	1.61	1.47	1.64	1.45	1.67	1.42	1.70
80	1.54	1.59	1.52	1.62	1.49	1.65	1.47	1.67	1.44	1.70
85	1.56	1.60	1.53	1.63	1.51	1.65	1.49	1.68	1.46	1.71
90	1.57	1.61	1.55	1.64	1.53	1.66	1.50	1.69	1.48	1.71
95	1.58	1.62	1.56	1.65	1.54	1.67	1.52	1.69	1.50	1.71
100	1.59	1.63	1.57	1.65	1.55	1.67	1.53	1.70	1.51	1.72

From Table C.3 the critical values for the Durbin-Watson test are $d_l = .95$ and $d_u = 1.23$. Since our computed value is neither below $d_l = .95$ nor above the critical value of $(4 - d_l) = 3.05$, the null hypothesis of serial independence cannot be rejected. However, because $d = 2.88$ is greater than $d_u = 1.23$ but not smaller than $(4 - d_u) = 2.77$, we cannot accept the null hypothesis. Because serial correlation cannot be either accepted nor rejected, the test is inconclusive in this case.

D. SUMMARY

This has been an extremely brief overview of linear regression analysis. We have shown how to estimate the slope, the intercept, the standard errors of each, their t-statistics, and the correlation coefficient for a two variable case. Multivariate estimates of the same variables in a multiple regression equation have the same interpretations and are provided by many different computer software packages. The summary statistics for the example problem of Table C.1 would appear in a computer printout in something like the following form:

$$Y_t = -23.42 + 174.84X_t \qquad r^2 = .6849 \qquad d = 2.88.$$
$$(-.38) \qquad (3.61) \qquad df = 6$$

We can infer that sales revenue is significantly related to predicted GNP, with an intercept term insignificantly different from zero and a significant slope term. Because the Durbin-Watson test is inconclusive we cannot be sure whether or not serial correlation has reduced the efficiency of our estimates. Furthermore, additional testing would be necessary to determine whether or not left-out variables have caused a biased estimate of b_1.

The mean square error criterion is one way of trading off bias and loss of efficiency. It may be desirable, for example, to accept a small bias in order to gain much greater efficiency. Although we have not discussed all of the causes of bias or inefficiency, a few of the more important ones were covered. The interested reader should refer to an econometrics text for a more rigorous and detailed presentation.

REFERENCES

Christ, C. G., *Econometric Models and Methods*, Wiley, New York, 1966.

Dhrymes, P. J., *Econometrics: Statistical Foundations and Applications*, New York, Harper and Row, 1970.

Goldberger, A. S., *Econometric Theory*, Wiley, New York, 1964.

Hoel, P. G., *Introduction to Mathematical Statistics*, 3rd ed., Wiley, New York, 1954.

Johnston, J., *Econometric Methods*, McGraw-Hill, New York, 1963.

Rao, P., and L. Miller, *Applied Econometrics*, Wadsworth, Belmont, Calif., 1971.

Wonnacott, R. J., and T. H. Wonnacott, *Econometrics*, Wiley, New York, 1970.

Calculus and Optimization

Optimizing or maximizing are concepts basic to finance theory as well as to economics. In this brief review, we shall summarize the main concepts drawn on in the text. These include:

A. Functions

B. Differential Calculus

C. Optimization

D. Series

E. Integral Calculus

A. FUNCTIONS

A fundamental notion used in finance is the concept of a function. There are three ways to express functions: as (1) mathematical equations, (2) graphs, and (3) tables.

Example: Suppose a variable Y is related to a variable X by the following mathematical equation:

$$Y = 2X^2 - 3X + 6.$$

$Y = 2X^2 - 3X + 6$

X	Y
0	6
1	5
−1	11
2	8
−2	20

$Y = 2X^2 - 3X + 6$

Figure D.1

A shorthand way of expressing this relationship is to write $Y = f(X)$, which is read "Y is a function of the variable X" and where Y is the range and X is the domain of the function. X is also called the independent variable and Y the dependent variable, since Y's value $[f(X)]$ is *posited* to depend on X's value.

We can also express the function in a tabular and graphical manner. Thus the equation enables us to construct a range of Y values for a given table of X values. The data in the table can then be plotted in a graph as in Fig. D.1.

> *Definition:* The *dimension* of a function is determined by the number of independent variables in the domain of the function.

Example: $Y = f(X, Z)$ is a two-dimensional function

$Y = f(X_1, X_2, \ldots, X_n)$ is an n-dimensional function.

Example: From basic capital budgeting concepts (see Chapter 2), we know that the net present value (NPV) of an investment project is equal to

$$NPV = \sum_{t=1}^{N} \frac{NCF_t}{(1 + k)^t} - I_0,$$

where

NCF_t = net cash flow in time period t,

I_0 = the project's initial cash outlay,

k = the firm's cost of capital,

N = the number of years in the project.

We can express this relationship functionally as:

$$NPV = f(NCF_t, I_0, k, N) \qquad t = 1, \ldots, N.$$

Given values for the right-hand side independent variables we can determine the left-hand dependent variable, NPV. The functional relationship tells us that for every X which is in the domain of the function, a unique value of Y can be determined.

1. Inverse Functions

How about going the other way? Given Y, can we determine X? Yes, we can.

Definition: The function that expresses the variable X in terms of the variable Y is called the *inverse function* and is denoted $X = f^{-1}(Y)$.

Example:

$$Y = f(X) = 2X - 5$$

solving for X in terms of Y

$$X = \frac{Y+5}{2} = 2.5 + .5\,Y = f^{-1}(Y).$$

The inverse relationship can be seen more clearly if we graph the two functions (Fig. D.2). The inverse function, however, does not exist for all functions. But the inverse of a function always exists when we are dealing with one-to-one functions.

2. Linear Functions

An important type of function consists of *linear functions* of the form:

$$Y = a_1 X_1 + a_2 X_2 + \cdots + a_n X_n.$$

Figure D.2

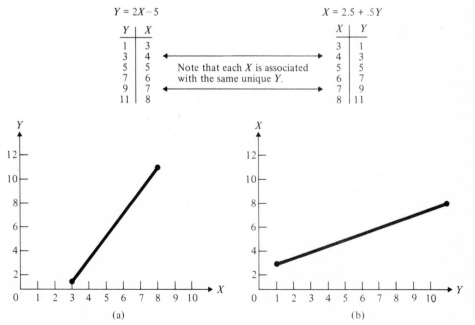

These functions are used in regression and in the CAPM. In two dimensions a linear function is a straight line, usually written as $Y = a + bX$ where a is the intercept on the Y axis and b is the *slope* of the line:

$$\text{slope} = \frac{Y_1 - Y_2}{X_1 - X_2} = \frac{\Delta Y}{\Delta X}$$

$$= \frac{\text{change in } Y}{\text{change in } X} = \frac{\text{rise}}{\text{run}}.$$

The CAPM is of the form $Y = a + bX$ where $E(R_j) = R_f + \lambda \beta_j$. This equation plots like the relationship in Fig. D.3a, as we see in Fig. D.3b.

The slope of the security market line in Fig. D.3b is $[E(R_m) - R_f]$, which is the market risk premium, λ.

The slope of a function is an important concept: it tells us the change in Y per unit change in X. The various types of slopes are pictured in Fig. D.4.

Example: Straightline depreciation is a simple linear function.

$$BV = c - \left(\frac{c}{N}\right) X,$$

where

BV = book value of the asset,

$\quad c$ = original cost of the asset,

$\quad N$ = estimated economic life of the asset,

$\quad X$ = number of years that have elapsed,

so that the book value after two years is $BV = c - (c/N)2$.

Figure D.3

(a)   (b)

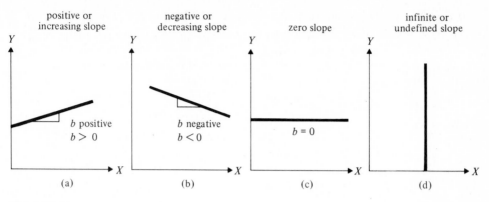

Figure D.4

3. Exponential Functions

As their names suggest, exponential functions are those in which the independent variable X appears as an exponent. They are useful for describing growth and compound interest. More formally:

Definition: The equation $Y = ma^X$ (a always > 0) is called an exponential function, and a is called the base.

Some properties of the exponential function are:

1. If $m > 0$, $a > 0$, then the function lies above the X axis.
2. If $m < 0$, $a > 0$, then the function lies below the X axis.
3. If $a > 1$, $m > 0$, then the curve rises to the right.
4. If $a < 1$, $m > 0$, then the curve rises to the left.

Example: An example of 3 and 4 above appears in Fig. D.5.

Figure D.5

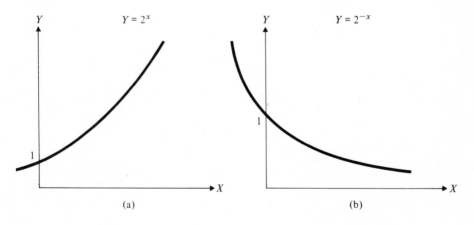

Example: Compound interest can be shown to be an exponential function. If you invest Z dollars in a bank that pays $r\%$ compound annual interest, then:

$Y_1 = Z + Zr = Z(1 + r) =$ cumulative amount of money by the end of the first year,

$Y_2 = Z(1 + r) + [Z(1 + r)]r = Z(1 + r)(1 + r)$

$\quad = Z(1 + r)^2 =$ cumulative amount of money by the end of the second year,

$$\vdots$$

$Y_n = Z(1 + r)^n =$ amount at the end of n years.

This last expression is simply an exponential function

$$Y_n = Z(1 + r)^n$$

$$Y = ma^x,$$ where the base is $(1 + r)$ and only n can vary.

Note that money grows exponentially (as in Fig. D.6a) when it is paid compound interest.

Example: Both compound value interest factors (CVIF) and present value interest factors (PVIF) are exponential functions. Consider the case of compounding and discounting $10 for five periods when the appropriate interest rate is 10%.

Figure D.6

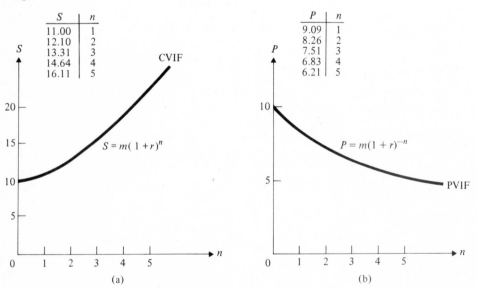

S	n
11.00	1
12.10	2
13.31	3
14.64	4
16.11	5

CVIF

$S = m(1 + r)^n$

P	n
9.09	1
8.26	2
7.51	3
6.83	4
6.21	5

$P = m(1 + r)^{-n}$

PVIF

(a)

(b)

Compound sum	Present value
$Y = ma^X$	$Y = ma^{-X}$
$S = m(1 + r)^n$	$P = m(1 + r)^{-n}$
$a = (1 + r) > 1$	$a = (1 + r)^{-1} < 1$
$n = 1, 2, \ldots, N$	$n = 1, 2, \ldots, N$
For $r = 10\%$	For $r = 10\%$
$\quad m = \$10$	$\quad m = \$10$
$\quad n = 1, 2, \ldots, 5$	$\quad n = 1, 2, \ldots, 5$
$S = 10 \cdot (1 + r)^n$ = compound value of \$10 at the end of the nth period	$P = 10 \cdot (1 + r)^{-n}$ = present value of \$10 at the end of the nth period

4. Logarithmic Functions

Definition: If $N = b^r$, where both $n > 0$, $b > 0$, then we define $r \equiv \log_b N$, which is read *"r is the log to the base b of N."*

In other words, $\log_b N$ is the number to which b has to be raised exponentially in order to equal N. So a log is simply an exponent.

Examples:

$$100 = 10^2$$

$$\text{so } \log_{10} 100 = 2$$

$$\tfrac{1}{2} = 2^{-1}$$

$$\text{so } \log_2 \tfrac{1}{2} = -1.$$

The two most widely used bases for logarithms are base 10 and base e, where e is an irrational number equal to $2.7182818\ldots$.

Definition: The logarithm to the base 10 of N is called the "common logarithm of N." It is usually designated log N.

Definition: The logarithm to the base e of N is called the *"natural logarithm of N."* To differentiate it from the common log, the natural log is usually designated ln N.

Definition: The function $Y = \log_b X$ is called a *logarithmic function.*

Since by definition $Y = \log_b X$ if and only if $X = b^Y$, we see that the exponential and logarithmic functions are inverse functions of each other:

$$X = 10^Y \Leftrightarrow Y = \log_{10} X$$

$$X = e^Y \Leftrightarrow Y = \ln X.$$

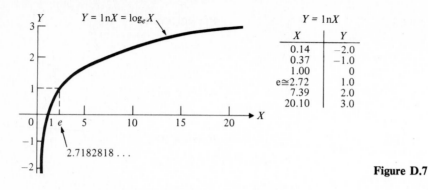

Figure D.7

The logarithmic function $Y = \ln X$ is graphed in Fig. D.7.

Some properties of the logarithmic function $Y = \log_b X$ are as follows:

1. The function equals zero when $X = 1$.
2. The function is an increasing function (i.e., it rises to the right) for all $b > 1$.
3. The function is a decreasing function (i.e., it falls to the right) for $0 < b < 1$. See Fig. D.8.
4. The function is negative when $0 < X < 1$ and $b > 1$.
5. The function is positive when $1 < X < \infty$.
6. The function is not defined when X is negative.

Example:

$$X = 2^{-Y} = \frac{1}{2^Y} = \left(\frac{1}{2}\right)^Y$$

so $Y = \log_{1/2} X$.

Since logarithms are simply exponents, the rules of logs simply mirror the rules of exponents:

Figure D.8

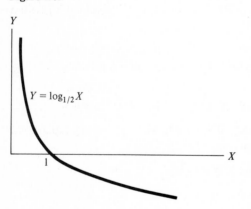

Exponents	Logarithms
$a^m \cdot a^n = a^{m+n}$	$\log_a (XY) = \log_a X + \log_a Y$
$\dfrac{a^m}{a^n} = a^{m-n}$ if $m > n$	$\log_a \dfrac{X}{Y} = \log_a X - \log_a Y$
$(a^m)^n = a^{mn}$	$\log_a (X^n) = n \log_a X$

B. DIFFERENTIAL CALCULUS

1. Limits

The central idea in calculus is the concept of the limit of a function. Often we want to know how the values of a function, $f(X)$, behave as the independent variable X approaches some particular point, a. If as $X \to a$ (read "X approaches a"), $f(X)$ approaches some number L, then we say that *the limit* of $f(X)$ as X approaches a is L. This is written more compactly as

$$\lim_{X \to a} f(X) = L.$$

Intuitively, the existence of a limit L means that the function of $f(X)$ will take on a value as close to L as one may desire, given that the independent variable takes a value that is sufficiently close to a.

Example: Many times we are interested in just what happens to a function as X increases without bound, that is when $X \to \infty$ (read "X approaches infinity"). For instance, what is lim. as $X \to \infty$ of $[(X + 1)/X]$? The way to evaluate this limit is to observe the behavior of $f(X)$ as X gets larger and larger. From the table and the graph in Fig. D.9 we see that $f(X)$ approaches 1 as $X \to \infty$, so we can write lim. as $X \to \infty$ of $[(X + 1)/X] = 1$.

Intuitively, as X gets very, very large, the fact that the numerator is greater by one than the denominator doesn't matter "much," so we have $X/X = 1$.

Figure D.9

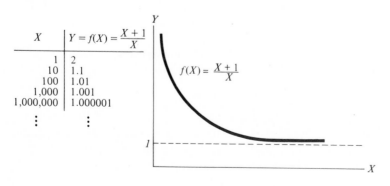

X	$Y = f(X) = \dfrac{X+1}{X}$
1	2
10	1.1
100	1.01
1,000	1.001
1,000,000	1.000001
⋮	⋮

$f(X) = \dfrac{X+1}{X}$

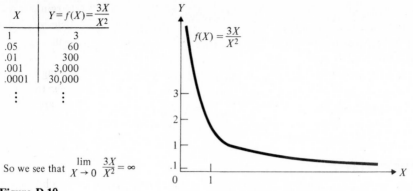

X	$Y=f(X)=\dfrac{3X}{X^2}$
1	3
.05	60
.01	300
.001	3,000
.0001	30,000
$\vdots$	$\vdots$

So we see that $\displaystyle\lim_{X\to 0}\frac{3X}{X^2}=\infty$

Figure D.10

Example: As we will see next, we are often interested to what happens to $f(X)$ as X gets very, very small—that is, when $X \to 0$. For instance, what is the lim. as $X \to 0$ of $(3X/X^2)$? Again, to evaluate this limit we see what happens to $f(X)$ as $X \to 0$ (Fig. D.10).

Example: Generally we assume that compounding and discounting occur discretely in annual periods. If the compounding is more than once a year the compound value interest factor is changed from $(1 + r)^n$ to $[(1 + r/m)]^{nm}$, where m is the number of times per year compounding occurs. We can now see with limits what is the relationship between the continuous compounding rate and the discrete compounding rate. Continuous compounding means

$$\lim_{m\to\infty}\left[\left(1+\frac{r}{m}\right)^{nm}\right]=e^{rn}\qquad\text{by definition of }e.$$

If r_c = the continuous compounding rate and r_d = the discrete compounding rate, then $e^{r_c n} = (1 + r_d)^n$. Taking natural logs:

$$\ln\,[e^{r_c n}] = \ln\,(1 + r_d)^n,$$

$$r_c n\,\ln e = n\,\ln\,(1 + r_d),$$

$$r_c n = n\,\ln\,(1 + r_d)\qquad\text{since }\ln e \equiv 1,$$

$$r_c = \ln\,(1 + r_d).$$

So, 5.25% continuously compounded is equal to 5.39% compounded annually. That is, if r_c = 5.25%, then using $\ln\,(1 + r_d)$ = 5.25%, r_d must be 5.39%.

2. Derivatives

The rate of change of a function (the change in Y per unit change in X) is an important concept in mathematics. It is referred to as the *derivative* of Y with respect to X. In finance and economics the rate of change is called "marginal." For example, the marginal cost of capital (MCC) is the rate of change of the total cost of capital per change in new capital raised. Analytically, the marginal quantities are simply the *slopes* of the total quantities.

The derivative is usually denoted as dY/dX, or $f'(X)$. The advantage of the $f'(X)$ notation is that it reminds us that *the derivative is itself a function:* the value of the derivative depends on where it is evaluated. Fortunately there are special rules of differentiation that can be used to guide calculations.

3. Rules of Differentiation

1. $f(X) = c$ (c is a constant), $f'(X) = 0$. This rule states that the slope of a horizontal line is zero, since by definition Y does not change when X changes.

2. $f(X) = X^n$, $f'(X) = nX^{n-1}$. In order to differentiate X^n, reduce the exponent by one and multiply by n.

3. $f(X) = g(X) \cdot h(X)$, $f'(X) = g'(X) \cdot h(X) + h'(X) \cdot g(X)$. The derivative of $g(X) \cdot h(X)$ equals $h(X)$ times the derivative of $g(X)$ plus $g(X)$ times the derivative of $h(X)$.

4. $f(X) = g(X)/h(X)$, $[h(X) \neq 0]$, $f'(X) = [g'(X)h(X) - g(X)h'(X)]/[h(X)]^2$.

5. $f(X) = c \cdot g(X)$, $[c$ constant], $f'(X) = c \cdot g'(X)$.

6. $f(X) = g(X) + h(X)$, $f'(X) = g'(X) + h'(X)$.

7. $f(X) = \ln X$, $f'(X) = 1/X$.

8. $f(X) = e^{g(X)}$, $f'(X) = g'(X)e^{g(X)}$.

9. $f(X) = X$, $f'(X) = 1$.

10. $f(X) = a^X$, $f'(X) = a^X \cdot \ln a$.

11. $f(X) = \log_b X$, $f'(X) = 1/(X \ln b)$.

12. $f(X) = \log [g(X)]$, $f'(X) = g'(X)/g(X)$.

Examples

1) $Y = 6X^3 - 3X^2 + 4X + 7$,

$$\frac{dY}{dX} = 6 \cdot \frac{d}{dX}(X^3) - 3 \cdot \frac{d}{dX}(X^2) + 4 \cdot \frac{d}{dX}(X) + \frac{d}{dX}(7)$$

$$= 6(3X^2) - 3(2X) + 4(1) + 0$$

$$= 18X^2 - 6X + 4.$$

2) $Y = X^2(X + 3)$

$$\frac{dY}{dX} = \left[\frac{d}{dX}(X^2)\right](X + 3) + \left[\frac{d}{dX}(X + 3)\right]X^2$$

$$= 2X(X + 3) + (1)X^2 = 3X^2 + 6X$$

3) $Y = X^{-4}$,

$$\frac{dY}{dX} = -4X^{-5} = \frac{-4}{X^5} \; .$$

4) $Y = \frac{(2X^2 + 6)}{X^3}$

$$\frac{dY}{dX} = \frac{4X(X^3) - (2X^2 + 6)(3X^2)}{(X^3)^2} = \frac{-2X^4 - 18X^2}{X^6}$$

5) $Y = \frac{2}{\sqrt{X}} = 2X^{-1/2}$,

$$\frac{dY}{dX} = 2 \cdot -\frac{1}{2} \cdot X^{-3/2} = -X^{-3/2} = \frac{-1}{X^{3/2}} = \frac{-1}{\sqrt{X^3}}$$

4. Chain Rule

An extremely useful and powerful tool in differential calculus is the chain rule, or the function of a function rule. Suppose Y is a function of a variable Z:

$$Y = f(Z),$$

but Z is in turn a function of another variable X:

$$Z = g(X)$$

Because Y depends on Z, and Z in turn depends on X, *Y is also a function of X.* We can express this fact by writing Y as a composite function (i.e., a function of a function) of X: $Y = f[g(X)]$.

In order to determine the change in Y from a change in X, the chain rule says:

$$\boxed{\frac{dY}{dX} = \frac{dY}{dZ}\frac{dZ}{dX} = f'(Z) \cdot g'(X) \qquad \text{Chain Rule}}$$

Intuitively the chain rule says, "Take the derivative of the outside (function) and multiply it by the derivative of the inside (function)." The reason behind the name "chain" rule is that there is a chain reaction relationship between X, Z, and Y:

$$\Delta X \xrightarrow{\text{via } g} \Delta Z \xrightarrow{\text{via } f} \Delta Y.$$

In words, a change in X has an ultimate impact on Y by causing a change in Z via function g, and this change in Z will in turn cause a change in Y by function f.

There is a temptation to look at the chain rule by canceling the intermediate dZ term:

$$\frac{dY}{dX} = \frac{dY}{dZ} \cdot \frac{dZ}{dX} = \frac{dY}{dX} \; .$$

This is incorrect! It is no more valid than canceling the 3s in:

$$3 = \frac{\cancel{3}9}{1\cancel{3}} \neq \frac{9}{1} \neq 9.$$

The usefulness of the chain rule can best be seen by considering some examples in which it is used.

Examples:

1) Suppose we wanted to differentiate

$$Y = (3 + 6X^2)^{10}.$$

We could, by a considerable amount of work, expand $(3 + 6X^2)^{10}$ and differentiate term by term. Instead we can use the chain rule. Note that if we wanted to simply differentiate $Z = (3 + 6X^2)$ that would pose no problem:

$$\frac{dZ}{dX} = \frac{d}{dX}(3) + \frac{d(6X^2)}{dX}$$

$$= 0 + 12X,$$

$$\frac{dZ}{dX} = 12X.$$

Likewise, if we let

$$Y = (Z)^{10},$$

then we can differentiate easily

$$\frac{dY}{dZ} = \frac{d(Z)^{10}}{dZ} = 10Z^{10-1} = 10 \cdot Z^9.$$

The chain rule says to simply multiply these two results together to get dY/dX:

$$\frac{dY}{dX} = \frac{dY}{dZ} \cdot \frac{dZ}{dX}$$

$$= [10 \cdot Z^9]12X$$

$$= [10 \cdot (3 + 6X^2)^9]12X$$

$$= 120X(3 + 6X^2)^9.$$

Intuitively, the chain rule says to take the derivative of the function outside the parentheses—in this case, $10 \cdot (\ )^9$—and multiply it by the derivative of what is inside the parentheses—that is, $12X$. So what seemed to be at first a rather forbidding problem turns out to be very easy to solve.

Two examples are given below:

$$\frac{d}{dX}(\sqrt[3]{5X+7}) = \frac{d}{dX}(5X+7)^{1/3}$$

$$= \tfrac{1}{3}(5X+7)^{-2/3} \cdot 5$$

$$= \frac{5}{3}\frac{1}{(\sqrt[3]{5X+7})^2}$$

$$= \frac{5}{3(5X+7)^{2/3}} \cdot$$

$$\frac{d}{dX}(e^{3X-4}) = e^{3X-4} \cdot 3$$

$$= 3e^{3X-4}.$$

5. Higher-Order Derivatives

In our development of derivatives we have emphasized that the derivative of a function is also a function. That is, the value of the derivative depends on the Point X at which it is being evaluated. Like $f(X)$, $f'(X)$ is also a function of X.

Example: Consider the function

$$f(X) = -10X^2 + 2,400X - 8,500, \qquad \text{then}$$

$$f'(X) = -20X + 2,400.$$

The value of this derivative depends on the point at which it is being evaluated:

$$f'(120) = -20(120) + 2,400 = 0,$$

$$f'(60) = -20(60) + 2,400 = 1,200.$$

Because it is also a function of X, we can take the derivative of $f'(X)$. This new function, $f''(X)$, is called the *second derivative* of the original function, $f(X)$. The *third derivative* is the derivative of the second derivative and is written $f'''(X)$. In principle we can go on forever and form derivatives of as high order as we like. Notationally these higher-order derivatives are symbolized in the same manner as the second derivative

$$f'''(X), f^{(4)}(X), f^{(5)}(X), \ldots, f^{(n)}(X)$$

$$\frac{d^3Y}{dX^3}, \frac{d^4Y}{dX^4}, \frac{d^5Y}{dX^5}, \ldots, \frac{d^nY}{dX^n} \cdot$$

Example:

$$Y = f(X) = X^3 - 7X^2 + 6X - 5,$$

$$f'(X) = 3X^2 - 14X + 6,$$

$$f''(X) = 6X - 14,$$

$$f'''(X) = 6,$$

$$f^{(4)}(X) = 0,$$

$$f^{(5)}(X) = 0,$$

$$\vdots$$

$$f^{(n)}(X) = 0.$$

As we shall see, higher-order derivatives play an important role in Taylor and MacLaurin series (see Section D of this appendix). The most important of the higher-order derivatives is the second derivative. Understanding the meaning of the second derivative is crucial. We know that the first derivative of a function, $f'(X)$, is the slope of a function or the rate of change of Y as a result of a change in X. The second derivative, $f''(X)$, is the rate of change of the slope of $f(X)$; that is, it is the rate of change of the rate of change of the original function, $f(X)$. Table D.1 and Fig. D.11 show various combinations of signs for $f'(X)$ and $f''(X)$ and the implied shape of the graph of $f(X)$.

Table D.1

	$f'(X)$	$f''(X)$	$f(X)$ is
a)	>0	>0	Increasing at an increasing rate
b)	>0	<0	Increasing at a decreasing rate
c)	<0	<0	Decreasing at an increasing rate
d)	<0	>0	Decreasing at a decreasing rate

Example: In developing the theory of investor choice under uncertainty, cardinal utility functions $[U(W)]$ are used. These utility functions should have the following property: $U'(W) > 0$, $U''(W) < 0$. That is, they should look like Fig. D.11b. Check to see if and when the following four functions have this property.

1) $U(W) = aw - bw^2$ (quadratic utility function),

   $U'(W) = a - 2bw > 0$ when $a > 2bw$,

   $U''(W) = -2b < 0$ when $b > 0$.

2) $U(W) = \ln W$ (logarithmic utility function),

   $U'(W) = \dfrac{1}{W} > 0$ W always > 0 by definition of log function.

   $U''(W) = \dfrac{-1}{W^2} < 0$

3) $U(W) = -e^{-aW}$ (exponential utility function),

$U'(W) = -(-a)e^{-aW} = ae^{-aW} > 0$ if $a > 0$,

$U''(W) = -a^2e^{-aW} < 0$.

4) $U(W) = W^a$ (power utility function),

$U'(W) = aW^{a-1} > 0$,

$U''(W) = a(a-1)W^{a-2} < 0$ when $a < 1$.

Example: Given the following linear demand function

$$p = 100 - 10q,$$

Figure D.11

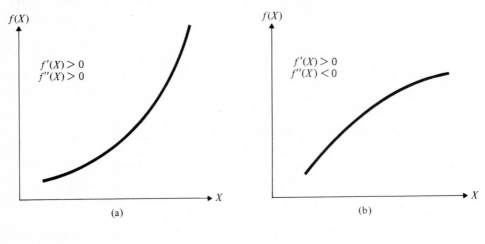

$f'(X) > 0$
$f''(X) > 0$

(a)

$f'(X) > 0$
$f''(X) < 0$

(b)

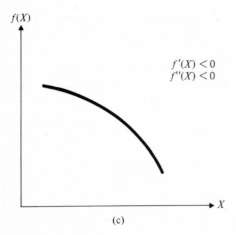

$f'(X) < 0$
$f''(X) < 0$

(c)

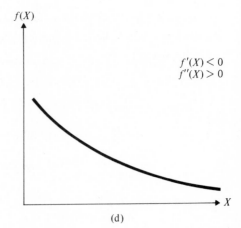

$f'(X) < 0$
$f''(X) > 0$

(d)

where

p = price per unit sold (i.e., average revenue),

q = quantity sold,

(note that p is the dependent variable here).

We can obtain the total revenue function by multiplying through by q:

$$TR \equiv pq = 100q - 10q^2, \quad \text{which is a quadratic equation.}$$

The first derivative of total revenue tells us how total revenue responds to changes in the quantity sold. Economists call this function the marginal revenue:

$$MR \equiv \frac{d(TR)}{dq} = 100 - 20q.$$

If we want to know by how much marginal revenue itself varies when quantity sold varies, we compute the slope of the marginal revenue. This is the second derivative of the total revenue function:

$$\frac{d(MR)}{dq} = \frac{d^2(TR)}{dq^2} = -20.$$

So marginal revenue declines at a constant rate of -20 per unit increase in quantity sold. Graphically the relationship between total, average, and marginal revenue is shown in Fig. D.12.

> *Definition:*   An important class of functions are those functions whose first derivative is positive for all values of the independent variable. Such functions are called *monotonically increasing* functions. Likewise, functions whose first derivative is negative for all values of the independent variable are *monotonically decreasing*.

6. Differentials

Let $Y = f(X)$, then the differential, dY, is defined as

$$dY = f'(X) \, dX.$$

If we regard $dX \equiv \Delta X$, a small increment in the independent variable X, then we can see that dY is an approximation to ΔY induced by ΔX because $f'(X) = \lim$. as $\Delta X \to 0$ of $(\Delta Y / \Delta X)$.

Example: Let $Y = 2X^2 + X + 2$, then $dY = (4X + 1) \, dX$. The concept of differentials is very useful when we consider integration later in Section E.

7. Partial Differentiation

So far we have only considered differentiation of functions of one independent variable. In practice, functions of two or more independent variables do arise quite

Figure D.12

frequently. Since each independent variable influences the function differently, when we consider the instantaneous rate of change of the function, we have to isolate the effect of each of the independent variables. Let $W = f(X, Y, Z)$. When we consider how W changes as X changes, we want to hold the variable Y and Z constant. This gives rise to the concept of partial differentiation. Note that only the variable X is changing, while both Y and Z remain constant. The rules for partial differentiation and ordinary differentiation are exactly the same except that when we are taking partial derivative of one independent variable, we regard *all other independent variables as constants.*

Examples:

1) $W = XY + YZ + XZ$,

$$\frac{\partial W}{\partial X} = Y + 0 + Z = Y + Z,$$

$$\frac{\partial W}{\partial Y} = X + Z + 0 = X + Z,$$

$$\frac{\partial W}{\partial Z} = 0 + Y + X = Y + X.$$

2) $W = X^2 YZ^3 + e^X + \ln YZ,$

$$\frac{\partial W}{\partial X} = 2XYZ^3 + e^X,$$

$$\frac{\partial W}{\partial Y} = X^2 Z^3 + \frac{1}{YZ} \cdot Z = X^2 Z^3 + \frac{1}{Y},$$

$$\frac{\partial W}{\partial Z} = 3X^2 YZ^2 + \frac{1}{YZ} \cdot Y = 3X^2 YZ^2 + \frac{1}{Z}.$$

C. OPTIMIZATION

A company seeks to maximize its profit. A production unit seeks to minimize its cost for a given level of output. An individual investor seeks to maximize his utility when choosing among investment alternatives. Indeed, we are all engaged in big and small optimization problems every day at work or at leisure. If we have a mathematical objective function, then we can solve our optimization problem using calculus. The procedure is divided into two steps:

1. Locate all *relative* maxima and minima of the objective function.
2. Compare the function value at the relative maxima and minima and at the boundary points (to be explained later) to pick the highest (lowest) value to be the *global* maximum (minimum).

To accomplish step 1, let us first consider the graph of a function $f(X)$ that appears in Fig. D.13. At the point $X = a$, the function $f(X)$ is said to have a relative maximum because $f(a) > f(Z)$ for all Z sufficiently close to a. Similarly, $f(X)$ has a relative maximum at $X = c$ and $f(X)$ has a relative minima at $X = b$ and $X = d$. One common characteristic those four points share is the slope of $f(X)$ at those points. If we draw tangent lines to $f(X)$ at $X = a, b, c, d,$ then all the tangent lines must be perfectly horizontal. In other words, the slopes $f'(a) = f'(b) = f'(c) = f'(d) = 0$. Thus we have the following theorem:

Theorem: If $f(X)$ has a relative maximum or minimum at $X = a$, then $f'(a) = 0$.

Note that the theorem does *not* say that if $f'(a) = 0$, then $X = a$ is a relative maximum or minimum. It says that if $f'(a) = 0$, then $X = a$ is a *candidate* for

Figure D.13

(a)   (b)

Figure D.14

relative maximum or minimum. There exist points for which the derivative of $f(X)$ is zero, but the points are neither relative maxima nor minima. Nevertheless, to locate all relative maxima and minima, we differentiate $f(X)$, set the result to zero and solve for X. That is, find all the solutions to the equation

$$f'(X) = 0.$$

The above equation is called the first order condition. The solutions are candidates for relative maxima and minima. To determine which of these solutions are indeed relative maxima or minima, we need the so-called second order conditions. Consider the relative maximum shown in Fig. D.14a. The slope, $f'(X)$, is zero at the top, positive to the left of the top, and negative to the right of the top. Therefore, as X increases from left to right, the slope, $f'(X)$, is decreasing from positive to zero to negative. We know from the previous section that if $f'(X)$ is decreasing, then the derivative of $f'(X)$, $f''(X)$, *is negative.* The condition $f''(X) < 0$ is called the second order condition for relative maxima. Similar reasoning would indicate that at a relative minimum, $f''(X) > 0$. We can now summarize step one: Find all the X such that $f'(X) = 0$; then for each of those X, if $f''(X) > 0$, it is a relative minimum, if $f''(X) < 0$, it is a relative maximum, if $f''(X) = 0$, we cannot tell (and have to use more sophisticated techniques).

Step two requires us to compare function value at the relative maxima and minima and the boundary points to determine the global optimum. Boundary points exist because we generally wish to optimize $f(X)$ in some interval, say $a \leq X \geq b$, then a and b are boundary points. Sometimes, the global maximum or minimum occurs at the boundary (see Fig. D.15). That is why we want to evaluate $f(X)$ at the boundary.

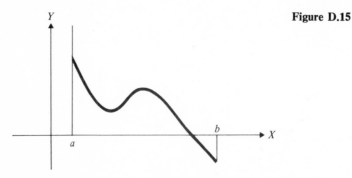

Figure D.15

Example: A monopolist faces a downward sloping demand curve given by $p(X) = 100 - 2X$, where X is the quantity and $p(X)$ is the price at that quantity. Suppose the fixed cost of production is 10 and variable cost is constant at 8 per unit. How many units should the monopolist produce to maximize profit?

$$\text{Profit} = \text{total revenue} - \text{total cost}$$

$$= \text{price} \times \text{quantity} - (\text{total variable cost} + \text{fixed cost}),$$

$$\pi(X) = (100 - 2X)X - (8X + 10)$$

$$= 100X - 2X^2 - 8X - 10$$

$$= 92X - 2X^2 - 10,$$

$$\pi'(X) = 92 - 4X = 0 \text{ (1st-order condition),}$$

so

$$92 = 4X \text{ or } X = 23,$$

$$\pi''(X) = -4,$$

hence

$$\pi''(23) < 0 \text{ (2nd-order condition).}$$

Therefore, $X = 23$ is a relative maximum. Implicit in this problem is the boundary $X \geq 0$. So, $X = 0$ is a boundary. Obviously $\pi(0) = 0$ because this is the decision of not getting into the business at all. $\pi(23) = 92 \times 23 - 2 \times (23)^2 - 10 = 1048 > \pi(0)$. The solution to this problem is therefore $X = 23$. The monopolist should produce 23 units. If we change the original problem by making the fixed cost 1060 instead of 10, then $X = 23$ is still the only relative maximum. But now $\pi(23) = -2 < \pi(0)$. So the monopolist is better off not getting into the business at all. Here the optimum point occurs at the boundary.

If our objective function has two independent variables, then we have to resort to partial derivatives. Suppose $Z = f(X, Y)$, let

$$f_x = \frac{\partial Z}{\partial X}, f_y = \frac{\partial Z}{\partial Y}, f_{xx} = \frac{\partial}{\partial X}\left(\frac{\partial Z}{\partial X}\right)$$

(taking partial derivative twice with respect to X),

$$f_{yy} = \frac{\partial}{\partial Y}\left(\frac{\partial Z}{\partial Y}\right), f_{xy} = f_{yx} = \frac{\partial}{\partial X}\left(\frac{\partial Z}{\partial Y}\right)$$

(taking partial derivative twice, first with respect to Y, then with respect to X). The conditions for relative maxima and minima are:

$$\left.\begin{array}{l} f_x = 0 \\ f_y = 0 \end{array}\right\} \text{ (1st-order conditions).}$$

In addition, if $f_{xx}f_{yy} > f_{xy}^2$, then the point is either a relative maximum or minimum.

To distinguish relative maximum and minimum, we have

$$f_{xx}, f_{yy} < 0 \quad \text{maximum}$$
$$f_{xx}, f_{yy} > 0 \quad \text{minimum} \Big\} \quad \text{(2nd-order conditions)}.$$

An example of using partial derivatives to find the optimum point is given in the application section of Appendix B.

1. Constrained Optimization

Very often, a business entity operates under certain constraints. They may be budgetary, technological or physical constraints. To solve this constrained optimization problem, we can use the method of Lagrange multipliers if the constraints are given as equations. For example, the production function of a firm may be $F(X, Y) = 2XY$, where X represents units of labor and Y represents units of capital. The budgetary constraint may look like

$$g(X, Y) = 100 - 2X - 10Y = 0,$$

where 100 represents the maximum amount of money to be spent on this production and 2 and 10 represent unit costs of labor and capital respectively. To use the method of Lagrange multipliers, we first construct a new function of three independent variables:

$$L(X, Y, \lambda) = f(X, Y) + \lambda g(X, Y)$$
$$= 2XY + \lambda(100 - 2X - 10Y),$$

where λ is a new variable which is called the Lagrange multiplier. The constrained optimum will appear as a solution to the first order condition:

$$\frac{\partial L}{\partial X} = L_x = 0$$

$$\frac{\partial L}{\partial Y} = L_y = 0 \quad \Big\} \quad \text{(1st-order conditions)}.$$

$$\frac{\partial L}{\partial \lambda} = L_\lambda = 0$$

Let

$$H = \begin{pmatrix} 0 & g_x & g_y \\ g_x & L_{xx} & L_{xy} \\ g_y & L_{yx} & L_{yy} \end{pmatrix} \text{ and } |H| = \text{determinant of } H \text{ (defined in Appendix B)},$$

then

$$|H| < 0 \quad \text{relative minimum} \Big\}$$
$$|H| > 0 \quad \text{relative maximum} \Big\} \quad \text{(2nd-order conditions)}.$$

Example: Take the production function and the budgetary constraint above and find the optimal combination of labor and capital.

$$L(X, Y, \lambda) = 2XY + \lambda(100 - 2X - 10Y)$$

$$
\left.
\begin{aligned}
L_x &= 2Y - 2\lambda = 0 \\
L_y &= 2X - 10\lambda = 0 \\
L_\lambda &= 100 - 2X - 10Y = 0
\end{aligned}
\right\} \quad \text{(1st-order conditions).}
$$

Solving these equations simultaneously gives us $X = 25$, $Y = 5$, $\lambda = 5$. (For a discussion of methods of solving system of linear equations, see Appendix B.) Therefore, under the budgetary constraint, the maximum output level is $f(25, 5) = 2 \times 25 \times 5 = 250$ when we employ 25 units of labor and 5 units of capital. We know that this must be the maximum point before computing the second order condition because a relative maximum is the only sensible solution. The interested reader may check that

$$|H| = \begin{vmatrix} 0 & -2 & -10 \\ -2 & 0 & 2 \\ -10 & 2 & 0 \end{vmatrix} = 80 > 0.$$

Another example of using the method of Lagrange multiplier can be found in the application section of Appendix B regarding the minimum variance portfolio.

The Meaning of λ

The solution of λ also has a meaning. The magnitude of λ measures how much the optimum changes as we relax the constraint. In the above example, the solution of λ is 5. That means if we relax the budgetary constraint one unit from 100 to 101, the optimal level of output would increase approximately 5 units to 255.

If the solution to λ is equal to zero, then the constraint is not binding. That means the constrained optimum is equal to the unconstrained optimum.

D. TAYLOR AND MACLAURIN SERIES

The Taylor and MacLaurin series are widely used in economics and finance. Their most important use is to help evaluate the value of a function around a certain point. Suppose we are interested in evaluating the function $Y = f(X)$ around a point a in its domain. Then we can make use of Taylor's theorem:

Taylor's Theorem. In the one-dimensional case we can evaluate the function $Y = f(X)$ around the point a in terms of its derivatives as follows:

$$f(X) = f(a) + f'(a)(X - a) + \frac{f''(a)(X - a)^2}{2!}$$

$$+ \frac{f'''(a)(X - a)^3}{3!} + \cdots + \frac{f^{(n)}(a)(X - a)^n}{n!}.$$

Alternatively, if we let $h = (X - a)$, then the Taylor series is:

$$f(a + h) = f(a) + f'(a)h + \frac{f''(a)h^2}{2!}$$

$$+ \frac{f'''(a)h^3}{3!} + \cdots + \frac{f^{(n)}(a)h^n}{n!}, \quad \text{[Pratt (1964) uses this.]}$$

where $f(a)$ = value of the function at point a. This is called a *Taylor series.*

Definition: If we evaluate the function around zero (i.e., if $a = 0$ above) then we have what is called a *MacLaurin series:*

$$f(X) = f(0) + f'(0) \cdot X + \frac{f''(0)}{2!} \cdot X^2 + \frac{f'''(0)}{3!} \cdot X^3 + \cdots + \frac{f^{(n)}(0)}{n!} \cdot X^n.$$

Definition: The sumbol $n!$ [read *"n factorial"*] represents the product of all positive integers from 1 to n (or vice versa). That is:

$$n! = n \cdot (n - 1) \cdot (n - 2) \cdot (n - 3) \cdot (n - 4) \cdots 4 \cdot 3 \cdot 2 \cdot 1.$$

Examples:

$$5! = 5 \cdot 4 \cdot 3 \cdot 2 \cdot 1 = 1 \cdot 2 \cdot 3 \cdot 4 \cdot 5 = 120,$$

$$10! = 10 \cdot 9 \cdot 8 \cdot 7 \cdot 6 \cdot 5 \cdot 4 \cdot 3 \cdot 2 \cdot 1 = 3,628,800,$$

$$(n - r)! = (n - r) \cdot (n - r - 1) \cdot (n - r - 2) \cdot (n - r - 3) \cdots 4 \cdot 3 \cdot 2 \cdot 1.$$

By definition $1! = 0! = 1$.

Intuitively, what the Taylor series is trying to do is to approximate the function $f(X)$ with the following polynomial:

1) $f(X) \approx T_0 + T_1(X - a) + T_2(X - a)^2 + T_3(X - a)^3 + \cdots$. The problem is to find the values of the coefficients (the Ts) of this polynomial. To find them, take the higher order derivatives of (1):

2) $f'(X) = T_1 + T_2 \cdot 2(X - a) + T_3 \cdot 3(X - a)^2 + T_4 \cdot 4(X - a)^3 + \cdots$

3) $f''(X) = 2T_2 + T_3 \cdot 2 \cdot 3(X - a) + T_4 \cdot 4 \cdot 3(X - a)^2 + \cdots$

4) $f'''(X) = 2 \cdot 3T_3 + T_4 \cdot 4 \cdot 3 \cdot 2(X - a) + T_5 \cdot 5 \cdot 4 \cdot 3(X - a)^2 + \cdots$

$$\vdots \qquad\qquad \vdots$$

If we evaluate (1) through (4) at $X = a$, then $(X - a) = 0$, so all terms involving $(X - a)$ will vanish:

1') $f(X) = T_0$

2') $f'(X) = T_1$

3') $f''(X) = 2 \cdot T_2$

4') $f'''(X) = 2 \cdot 3T_3$

Solving for the Ts

$$T_0 = f(X)$$

$$T_1 = f'(X)$$

$$T_2 = \frac{f''(X)}{2} = \frac{f''(X)}{2 \cdot 1} = \frac{f''(X)}{2!}$$

$$T_3 = \frac{f'''(X)}{3 \cdot 2} = \frac{f'''(X)}{3 \cdot 2 \cdot 1} = \frac{f'''(X)}{3!}$$

$$\vdots \qquad \vdots \qquad \vdots \qquad \vdots$$

Plugging these values of the Ts into (1) results in the Taylor series we stated earlier. The usefulness of Taylor series can best be seen with the help of a numerical example.

Example: Expand the function $f(X) = 1/X$ around 1, for $n = 0, 1, 2, 3$. Computing the derivatives:

$$f(X) = \frac{1}{X} \qquad \text{so} \qquad f(1) = \frac{1}{1} = 1,$$

$$f'(X) = \frac{-1}{X^2} \qquad \text{so} \qquad f'(1) = \frac{-1}{(1)^2} = -1,$$

$$f''(X) = \frac{2}{X^3} \qquad \text{so} \qquad f''(1) = \frac{2}{(1)^3} = 2,$$

$$f'''(X) = \frac{-6}{X^4} \qquad \text{so} \qquad f'''(1) = \frac{-6}{(1)^4} = -6.$$

a) The Taylor series approximation when $n = 0$ is:

$$T_0(X) = f(a), \qquad \text{since } a = 1 \quad \text{(we're expanding around 1)}$$
$$T_0(X) = f(1) = 1.$$

b) The Taylor approximation when $n = 1$ is:

$$T_1(X) = f(a) + f'(a)(X - a)$$
$$= f(1) + (-1)(X - 1)$$
$$= 1 - (X - 1).$$

c) The approximation when $n = 2$ is:

$$T_2(X) = f(a) + f'(a)(X - a) + \frac{f''(a)}{2!}(X - a)^2$$

$$= f(1) + (-1)(X - 1) + \frac{2}{2 \cdot 1}(X - 1)^2$$

$$= 1 - (X - 1) + (X - 1)^2.$$

d) The approximation when $n = 3$ is:

$$T_3(X) = f(a) + f'(a)(X - a) + \frac{f''(a)}{2!}(X - a)^2 + \frac{f'''(a)}{3!}(X - a)^3$$

$$= 1 - (X - 1) + (X - 1)^2 + \frac{-6}{3 \cdot 2 \cdot 1}(X - 1)^3$$

$$= 1 - (X - 1) + (X - 1)^2 - (X - 1)^3.$$

Expanding and rearranging the polynomials:

$T_0(X) = 1 \qquad$ (constant),

$T_1(X) = 1 - (X - 1) = -X + 2 \qquad$ (straight line),

$$T_2(X) = 1 - (X - 1) + (X - 1)^2 = X^2 - 3X + 3 \qquad \text{(parabola),}$$

$$T_3(X) = 1 - (X + 1) + (X - 1)^2 - (X - 1)^3 = -X^3 + 4X^2 - 6X + 4 \qquad \text{(cubic).}$$

Figure D.16 graphs the function $f(X) = 1/X$ and each of the approximating polynomials:

$$\frac{dT_2(X)}{dX} = 2X - 3 = 0, \qquad X = 1.5 = \text{min,}$$

$$\frac{dT_3(X)}{dX} = -3X^2 + 8X - 6 = 0$$

$$(-3X + 2)(X - 3) \qquad \text{inflection point} > 1.$$

From the graph we see that each successive Taylor series does a better job of approximating $f(X) = 1/X$ in the vicinity of 1; see Fig. D.17.

Example: Pratt (1964) uses Taylor series to derive a measure of absolute relative risk aversion. Let

$$X = \text{amount of wealth,}$$

$$U = \text{acceptable utility function,}$$

$$\pi = \text{risk premium, } \pi \text{ is a function, } \pi(X, \tilde{Z}),$$

$$\tilde{Z} = \text{a gamble (and a random variable),}$$

$$\tilde{Z} \sim E(\tilde{Z}) - \pi(X, \tilde{Z}).$$

1) $E\{U(X + \tilde{Z})\} = U[X + E(\tilde{Z}) - \pi(X, \tilde{Z})]$
   by choosing an actuarially neutral risk $E(\tilde{Z}) = 0$. So
1') $E\{U(X + \tilde{Z})\} = U[X - \pi(X, \tilde{Z})].$

Figure D.16

$T_2(X)$			$T_3(X)$			$f(X)$	
X^2-3X+3			$-X^3+4X^2-6X+4$			$Y=\dfrac{1}{X}$	
X	Y		X	Y		X	Y
0	3		0	4		0	∞
1	1		2	0		1	1
1.5	.75	−min	1	1		1.5	.666
.5	1.75		.5	1.875		2	.500
						.5	2

Figure D.17

Expand the right-hand side of (1′) using Taylor series:

$$U(X-\pi)=U(X)+\pi\cdot U'(X)-\frac{\pi^2}{2!}\,U''(X)-\cdots$$

> Pratt assumes second order and higher terms are insignificant.

Expand the left-hand side of (1′) using Taylor series:

$$E\{U(X)+\tilde{Z}\}=E\{U(X)+\tilde{Z}U'(X)+\frac{\tilde{Z}^2}{2!}\,U''(X)+\cdots \approx 0$$

$$=E\{U(X)\}+E\{\tilde{Z}\}U'(X)+\frac{E(\tilde{Z}^2)}{2!}\,U''(X).$$

But:

$$E\{U(X)\}=U(X) \qquad \text{not a random variable,}$$
$$E\{\tilde{Z}\}=0,$$
$$E\{\tilde{Z}^2\}=\sigma_Z^2 \qquad \text{since} \quad \sigma_Z^2=\sum p_i[Z_i-E(Z_i)]^2=\sum p_iZ_i^2=E(Z_i^2).$$

0

So

$$E\{U(X)+\tilde{Z}\}= U(X)+0+\frac{\sigma_{\tilde{Z}}^2}{2}\,U''(X).$$

Putting the left-hand and right-hand sides together:

$$U(X)+\frac{\sigma_{\tilde{Z}}^2}{2}\,U''(X)= U(X) - \pi\,U'(X).$$

Solving for π, the risk premium:

$$\pi = \tfrac{1}{2}\sigma_{\tilde{Z}}^2\left[-\frac{U''(X)}{U'(X)}\right]\}\qquad \text{a function of } \tilde{Z} \text{ and } X$$

always positive   a measure of absolute
by definition of   risk aversion
variance

E. INTEGRAL CALCULUS

1. Indefinite Integrals

Integration is the reverse process to differentiation. Given a function $f(X)$, the indefinite integral of $f(X)$, denoted by $\int f(X)\,dX$, is a function whose derivative is $f(X)$. In other words,

$$\int f(X)\,dX = F(X) \quad \text{if and only if} \quad F'(X)=f(X).$$

A peculiar feature regarding the indefinite integral of $f(X)$ is that it is not unique. Observe the following fact: if $F'(X) = f(X)$, so is $[F(X) + C]' = F'(X) + 0 = f(X)$ where C is an arbitrary constant. Therefore, both $F(X)$ and $F(X) + C$ can be an indefinite integral of $f(X)$. So, in general, we write

$$\int f(X)\,dX = F(X)+ C$$

to indicate that an arbitrary constant may be added to the answer.

As in differentiation, we have rules of integration which correspond very closely with those of differentiation.

2. Rules of Integration

1. $\displaystyle\int X^n\,dX =\frac{1}{n+1}\,X^{n+1}+ C. \qquad (n \neq -1)$

2. $\displaystyle\int \frac{1}{X}\,dX = \ln X + C. \qquad (X>0)$

3. $\int e^X \, dX = e^X + C.$

4. $\int c \cdot g(X) \, dX = c \cdot \int g(X) \, dX.$ $(c = \text{constant})$

5. $\int [g(X) + h(X)] \, dX = \int g(X) \, dX + \int h(X) \, dX.$

6. $\int a^X \, dX = \dfrac{1}{\ln a} a^X + C.$

7. Method of substitution (counterpart of chain rule in differentiation)

$$\int g(u) \frac{du}{dX} \, dX = \int g(u) \, du.$$

Example: $\int e^{2X} \, dX.$ To compute this integral, we first substitute $u = 2X$, then $du = 2 \cdot dX$ (recall $du = (du/dX) \cdot dX$, the differential), therefore $dX = (du/2)$. Hence $\int e^{2X} \, dX = \int e^u (du/2)$, by substituting u for $2X$ and $(du/2)$ for dX. But $\int e^u (du/2) = \frac{1}{2} \int e^u \, du$ (by rule 4) $= \frac{1}{2} e^u + C$ (by rule 3) $= \frac{1}{2} e^{2X} + C$ (by substituting back $2X$ for u). This example shows the essence of the method of substitution. When it is not obvious how to integrate directly, we substitute u for part of the expression, write everything in terms of u and du, and hopefully we come up with an expression in u that is easier to integrate (see also examples below).

Examples:

1) $\displaystyle \int 2X^2 + 3X + 1 \, dX = 2 \int X^2 \, dX + 3 \int X \, dX + \int 1 \, dX$

$$= 2 \cdot \frac{X^3}{3} + 3 \frac{X^2}{2} + X + C$$

$$= \tfrac{2}{3} X^3 + \tfrac{3}{2} X^2 + X + C.$$

2) $\displaystyle \int \frac{2X + 1}{X^2 + X} \, dX.$ Here we have to use the method of substitution again.

Let $u = X^2 + X$, then $du = (2X + 1) \, dX$,

$$\int \frac{2X + 1}{X^2 + X} \, dX = \int \frac{1}{u} \, du = \ln u + C = \ln (X^2 + X) + C.$$

3) $\displaystyle \int X\sqrt{X^2 + 1} \, dX.$ Let $u = X^2 + 1$, then $du = 2X \, dX$ or $dX = (du/2X)$.

$$\int X\sqrt{X^2 + 1} \, dX = \int X\sqrt{u} \, \frac{du}{2X} = \int \tfrac{1}{2}\sqrt{u} \, du$$

$$= \tfrac{1}{2} \int u^{1/2} \, du = \tfrac{1}{2} \cdot \frac{1}{3/2} u^{3/2} + C$$

$$= \tfrac{1}{3} (X^2 + 1)^{3/2} + C.$$

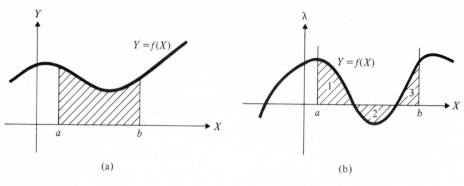

Figure D.18

3. Definite Integrals

A typical definite integral looks like $\int_a^b f(X)\ dX$ (read "integral of $f(X)$ from a to b"). Here, $f(X)$ is called the integrand, a is called the lower limit, and b is called the upper limit of integration. The main difference between an indefinite and a definite integral is that the result of indefinite integration is a function, while the result of definite integration is a number. The meaning of that number is as follows:

Let $\int_a^b f(X)\ dX = A$. If $f(X) \geq 0$, then A is simply the area under the curve $Y = f(X)$ from a to b, shown in Fig. D.18a. That area is equal to $\int_a^b f(X)\ dX$. Suppose now $f(X)$ is both positive and negative in the range of $a \leq X \leq b$, then A, the result of $\int_a^b f(X)\ dX$, is the *signed* area "under" $f(X)$ from a to b. By "signed area," we mean that the area above the X-axis is assigned a positive sign and the area below the X-axis is assigned a negative sign. Then A is the sum of all the positive and negative area (see Fig. D.18b). If the curve of $f(X)$ is the one in Fig. D.18b, then $\int_a^b f(X)\ dX = A =$ area 1 − area 2 + area 3.

The link between the definite integral and the indefinite integral is given by the next theorem, which is called the Fundamental Theorem of Calculus.

Theorem: Let $F(X)$ be an indefinite integral of $f(X)$, then

$$\int_a^b f(X)\ dX = F(b) - F(a).$$

The theorem shows us a way to evaluate the definite integral. We need only to find the indefinite integral of the integrand and then substitute the upper and lower limits and find the difference. Although the indefinite integral of a function is not unique, the theorem says that any one will do, as long as it is the same one in which you substitute the upper and lower limits.

Examples:

1) $\displaystyle\int_1^2 (X+2)\ dX = \left(\frac{X^2}{2} + 2X\right)\Big|_1^2 = \left[\frac{2^2}{2} + 2(2)\right] - \left[\frac{1^2}{2} + 2 \cdot 1\right]$

$= (2+4) - (\tfrac{1}{2} + 2) = 3\tfrac{1}{2},$

2) $\displaystyle\int_0^1 e^X \, dX = e^X \Big|_0^1 = [e^1] - [e^0] = e - 1.$

PROPERTIES OF DEFINITE INTEGRALS

1. $\displaystyle\int_a^a f(X) \, dX = 0.$

2. $\displaystyle\int_a^b f(X) \, dX = -\int_b^a f(X) \, dX.$

3. If $a < c < b$, then $\displaystyle\int_a^b f(X) \, dX = \int_a^c f(X) \, dX + \int_c^b f(X) \, dX.$

4. $\displaystyle\int_a^b cf(X) \, dX = c\int_a^b f(X) \, dX.$

5. $\displaystyle\int_a^b [f(X) + g(X)] \, dX = \int_a^b f(X) \, dX + \int_a^b g(X) \, dX.$

4. Applications

Example 1: Let the fixed cost of production be 100 and let marginal cost be $10/\sqrt{X}$ per unit. What is the total cost function for producing q units?

$$\text{Total cost} = \text{fixed cost} + \text{total variable cost}$$

$$= 100 + \int_0^q 10/\sqrt{X} \, dX$$

$$= 100 + \int_0^q 10X^{-1/2} \, dX$$

$$= 100 + 10\,\frac{1}{1/2} \cdot X^{1/2} \Big|_0^q$$

$$= 100 + [20\sqrt{q}] - [20\sqrt{0}]$$

$$= 100 + 20\sqrt{q}.$$

Example 2: Suppose an income stream of 10,000/yr. is coming in continuously for the next 10 years. How much is it worth today if the discount rate is 5%?

$$\text{Present value} = \int_0^{10} 10,000 e^{-0.5t} \, dt$$

$$= 10,000 \times \frac{-1}{.05} e^{-.05t} \Big|_0^{10}$$

$$= 10,000 \times \left(-\frac{1}{.05}\right) [e^{-.05 \times 10} - e^{-.05 \times 0}]$$

$$= -200,000[0.6065 - 1]$$

$$= 78,700.$$

Note that the formula for the present value of continuous discounting of a continuous flow is $\int_0^T (CF)e^{-rt} \, dt$, where CF = cash flow per time unit, T = time when cash flow ends, and r = discount rate.

5. Improper Integrals

Sometimes the limits of integration may be $-\infty$ or $+\infty$. Such a definite integral is called an improper integral. To evaluate an improper integral, we do not substitute $-\infty$ or $+\infty$ into the indefinite integral, but rather we substitute a variable b in place of $+\infty$ (or $-\infty$) and let $b \to \infty$ (or $-\infty$). In other words:

$$\int_a^\infty f(X) \, dX = \lim_{b \to \infty} \int_a^b f(X) \, dX,$$

$$\int_{-\infty}^a f(X) \, dX = \lim_{b \to -\infty} \int_b^a f(X) \, dX,$$

$$\int_{-\infty}^\infty f(X) \, dX = \lim_{\substack{a \to -\infty \\ b \to +\infty}} \int_b^a f(X) \, dX.$$

Example: Suppose the income stream in the previous example is perpetual, then the present value would be

$$PV = \int_0^\infty 10{,}000 e^{-.05\,t} \, dt$$

$$PV = \lim_{b \to \infty} \int_0^b 10{,}000 e^{-.05} \, dt$$

$$= \lim_{b \to \infty} 10{,}000 \left(-\frac{1}{.05}\right) [e^{-.05\,b} - e^{-.05 \times 0}]$$

$$= 10{,}000 \times (-20)[0 - 1], \quad \text{since } e^{-.05\,b} \to 0 \text{ as } b \to \infty.$$

$$PV = \$200{,}000.$$

Note that for a perpetual stream, we also have

$$PV = \frac{CF}{i} = \frac{10{,}000}{.05} = \$200{,}000 \qquad \text{where CF is the cost flow.}$$

This gives the same result as the integral calculus method.

REFERENCE

Pratt, J. W., "Risk Aversion in the Small and in the Large," *Econometrica*, January/April 1964, 122–136.

Indexes

AUTHOR INDEX

SUBJECT INDEX